Act defini
par R.

Referendum.

McGRAW-HILL SERIES IN POLITICAL SCIENCE

Joseph P. Harris, Consulting Editor

The American System of Government

McGRAW-HILL SERIES IN POLITICAL SCIENCE

Joseph P. Harris, Consulting Editor

The American System of Government

JOHN H. FERGUSON
Professor of Political Science, The Pennsylvania State University

DEAN E. McHENRY
Professor of Political Science, University of California, Los Angeles

1956 · FOURTH EDITION

McGRAW-HILL BOOK COMPANY, INC.
New York   Toronto   London

Endpaper photograph courtesy of Port of New York Authority.

Preface

Although national security and individual freedom continue to make rival claims, there are indications that the postwar crisis has eased. If the peak of fear and tension has passed, this is an appropriate time to review what has happened to our institutions during our preoccupation with long present dangers.

Take, for example, the impact of pressure for conformity in ideas and behavior. In his commentary *Democracy in America,* published in the 1830s, Alexis de Tocqueville described how democratic republics tended to curb freedom of expression through the "tyranny of the majority." The non-conformist, unwilling to choose between "we or they" alternatives, may lead a shunned and lonely existence.

During these crisis years we may have forgotten that democracy involves more than majority rule. Its proper functioning requires not only the formal protection of minority rights, but also a *respect* for the right of an individual or group to dissent. In our plural society, the individual's loyalties may be diffused widely among his nation, state, church, association, and other objects. Insistence upon absolute conformity to the will of the majority on all matters can be arbitrary totalitarianism.

This book is for those who care about the future of American institutions. The authors are aware of faults and blemishes, and they have considered it their duty to record them. Nevertheless, our years of close study of American governments have intensified our admiration of their enduring qualities. Although many criticisms are justified, the American system comes close to an optimum balance between stability and change, between order and progress.

If a new era of peace and security should come, as we hope it will, Americans will need more, not less, knowledge and understanding of their governmental institutions. And readiness to participate in the political process also is required. If popular government ever fails in the United States, we believe it will be due as much to citizen inertia and contempt for public affairs, as to external aggression or internal subversion. We appeal to all to accept the challenge to preserve and strengthen free institutions by participating in them.

This fourth edition records many changes that have taken place in the last three years. An armistice in Korea terminated the first experiment of the United Nations in attempting to stop aggression by armed force. The "cold war" reached a new peak of bitterness and now fluctuates between gestures of friendliness and toughness. While brandishing military might and strengthening alliances, both East and West continue with discouraging slowness to narrow the differences that stand in the way of disarmament and peaceful uses of atomic energy. Meanwhile, permanent solutions have still to be found for divided Germany, Korea, and Indo-China, for the dilemma arising out of rival claims made by Communist and Nationalist China, for peace and stability in the Middle East, and for the ignorance, poverty, and distress which plague so many people deserving of a happier fate. The United Nations, though crippled by East-West conflict, passed its tenth anniversary and carries on humane and conciliatory work around the world.

On the home front there has been a modest gain for various individual rights. Some restraints have been placed on congressional committees. The second Hoover Commission has filed a series of controversial reports on procedures and policies that will be on the agenda of executive and legislative branches for years to come. The Commission on Intergovernmental Relations has reappraised American federalism and has indicated ways to improvement and alteration. There has been another political shift, in the election of 1954, and the nation has experienced again the problems that arise from having the presidency in the hands of one party and the Congress of another.

Like its earlier editions, this work is organized along "conventional" lines in that it deals with national, state, and local governments in separate sections. We begin with historical background, general principles, and other essentials. The second part includes a discussion of Congress, the presidency, the courts, administrative organization, and the civil service. A third group of chapters is concerned with federal powers and functions of government. A final section contains a concise treatment of state and local governments. The latter section deliberately has been kept brief with the thought that instructors will want to supplement it with materials bearing upon the state in which they and their students are located. As an aid to this end the final chapter contains a list of references dealing with particular states.

For those who desire a general introduction to American government and full coverage of *national* institutions and functions without state and local, the first three parts are available in a separate volume entitled *The American Federal Government,* the fourth edition of which is published simultaneously with the present book.

To meet the demand for a briefer treatment of the whole compass of American government, the authors have prepared *Elements of Ameri-*

can Government. The scope of the *Elements* book is similar to that of the *American System,* but the former is considerably more compact and has been made simpler both through elimination of complicated materials and through substitution of less advanced terminology.

In these volumes the authors have striven for maximum clarity and simplicity of presentation. As a further aid, the publisher and authors have prepared a series of ten silent filmstrips to accompany these textbooks. A *Teacher's Manual* is available to instructors upon request. In the books themselves numerous charts, summaries, maps, and other illustrations have been included. As in the previous edition, four basic documents are included in the appendixes. The authors have also tried to sift the important from the mass of minutiae and thereby bring into focus major facts and problems of public policy. Many controversial subjects are introduced, but in doing so an attempt has been made to present fairly various points of view and to introduce readers to additional sources. The lists of references at the ends of chapters have been screened and brought up to date. A new feature is a list of review questions at the end of each chapter.

With the appearance of this edition the publisher and authors are pleased to announce the availability of a *Workbook in American Government* prepared and correlated with the three texts mentioned above by Professor W. V. Holloway and Emile B. Ader, of the University of Tulsa. The *Workbook* contains problems and questions that will greatly assist students in preparing and reviewing assignments.

Colleagues and librarians of The Pennsylvania State University and the University of California, Los Angeles, have aided us with criticisms, suggestions, and bibliography. For help in preparing the fourth edition, we thank Mrs. Eva Zimbler Huebscher for research assistance, and Mrs. Patricia MacRae for helping prepare the index.

John H. Ferguson
Dean E. McHenry

Contents

American Government

The following filmstrips correlated with *American Federal Government,*
American System of Government, and *Elements of American Government* are
available from the Text-Film Department, McGraw-Hill Book Company, Inc.

SET ONE (Filmstrips also available individually)

THE CONSTITUTION: Principles and Methods of Change

> Underlying philosophy and basic principles of the Constitution. Methods of change. Protec-
> tion of individual rights is included briefly. Correlated with Chapters 3 and 4 of *American*
> *Federal Government* and *American System of Government.* 37 fr.

FEDERAL SYSTEM, PART I: Theory and Federal-State Relations

> Federalism in theory and practice: distribution of powers between Federal government
> and the states; restrictions on the states and federal obligations to them. Correlated with
> Chapter 5 of *American System of Government* and *American Federal Government.* 27 fr.

FEDERAL SYSTEM, PART II: Interstate Relations and Centralization

> Relations between the states and problems of interstate competition and of centralization.
> Correlated with Chapter 6 of *American System of Government* and *American Federal*
> *Government.* 35 fr.

POLITICAL PARTIES AND ELECTIONS

> The role of the individual, political party, and public opinion in nominations and elections.
> The right to vote; various forms of the ballot. Correlated with Chapters 10 and 11 of
> *American Federal Government* and *American System of Government.* 39 fr.

CONGRESS: Organization and Procedure

> Organization and membership of Congress; party government and leadership. Detailed
> steps by which a bill becomes a law; consideration of suggestions for strengthening Con-
> gress. Correlated with Chapters 12 and 13 of *American Federal Government* and *American*
> *System of Government.* 44 fr.

ix

SET TWO (Filmstrips also available individually)

THE PRESIDENT: Office and Powers

> Structure and role of the Executive Branch. Selection of the President, and various individuals and agencies that help him in administering the government. Powers of the President examined in detail. Correlated with Chapters 14 and 15 of *American Federal Government* and *American System of Government.* 36 fr.

FEDERAL COURTS AND LAW ENFORCEMENT

> Structure of Federal judicial system—its powers, duties, and relationship to other branches of Government. Law-enforcement agencies considered. Correlated with Chapter 16 of *American Federal Government* and *American System of Government.* 40 fr.

PUBLIC ADMINISTRATION AND CIVIL SERVICE

> Structure and function of major governmental agencies with special emphasis on civil service. Correlated with Chapters 17 and 18 of *American Federal Government* and *American System of Government.* 44 fr.

FEDERAL FINANCE

> Taxation and monetary powers of the government. Financial administration and fiscal agencies. Analysis of governmental expenditures, revenues, and debts. Correlated with Chapters 19 and 20 of *American Federal Government* and *American System of Government.* 42 fr.

FOREIGN RELATIONS

> Principles and practices involved in foreign relations under federal system. Department of State and Foreign Service. Traditional foreign policies and recent developments. The United States and the UN. Correlated with Chapters 21 and 22 of *American Federal Government* and *American System of Government.* 43 fr.

ON THE FACING PAGE: Casting a ballot at a Vermont town meeting. (*Standard Oil Co.* (*N.J.*))

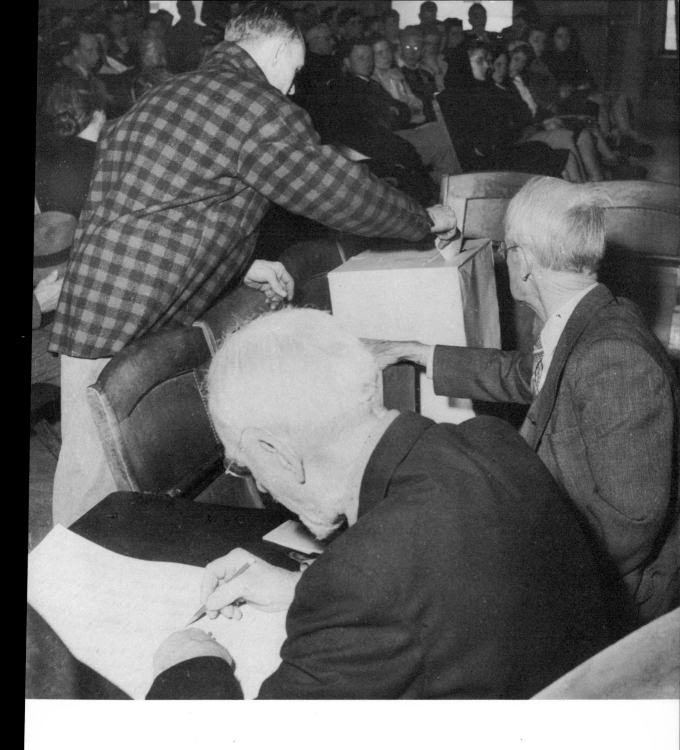

Essentials of American Government

From the American past. Historic scenes carry reminders of molding forces of our institutions. In Williamsburg, the Virginia House of Burgesses (chamber shown above) became a model for American legislative bodies. Independence Hall, Philadelphia (right), was a birthplace of independence. The shipload of immigrants at the turn of the century (below) symbolizes the growth of United States population.

National political conventions every four years (above) choose the presidential candidates and set the stage for weeks of vigorous political campaigning all over the country (below). Public-opinion polls (right) are used to test public sentiment and are followed with great interest during campaigns.

↓ *American Institute of Public Opinion*

Two of the many evidences of interstate and Federal-state cooperation are the Port of New York Authority, an agency governing tunnels, bridges, airports, and docks in the metropolitan area (above), and the nation-wide employment services, operated by the states in cooperation with the Federal government.

Political Institutions and Ideas

As I was born a citizen of a free State, and a member of the Sovereign, I feel that, howev feeble the influence my voice can have on public affairs, the right of voting on them mak it my duty to study them: and I am happy, when I reflect upon governments, to find inquiries always furnish me with new reasons for loving that of my own country. — J Jacques Rousseau [1]

No government demands so much from the citizen as Democracy and none gives so much. — James Bryce [2]

Arnold J. Toynbee, the eminent British historian, records twenty-one major civilizations in the history of mankind. To these must be added a larger, but unknown, number of primitive societies. Political institutions with authority to make and enforce laws—in other words governments—have been common to both civilized and primitive societies. Although forms and procedures have differed, evidence accumulated by social scientists indicates that some form of government is essential to successful group life.

Governments, like other social institutions, vary greatly; indeed it is not possible to find identical forms and procedures in the governments of any two societies. Differences are explained by such factors as geography, climate, history, customs, resources, and degree of enlightenment. Shaped by forces like these, distinctive governments have evolved in each coun-

try, and constitutional forms that are succe in one place might fail quite miserabl another.

Not only do political institutions vary they are constantly in the process of adapt and change. In Great Britain, for example, has passed from King to Parliament; the of Commons has taken predominance fro House of Lords; tight control of empir been replaced by a commonwealth relatic based on shared responsibility and consent.

Similar transformation has taken place United States. The nation now comman devotion formerly reserved for particular The negative individualism of old is be placed by a new attachment to positive ment. The electorate has expanded until sents almost universal adult suffrage. groups have become nationally organized and very powerful. Political parties have indispensable adjuncts of government. toral college is withering away. The pr has attained a commanding position.

[1] *The Social Contract* (Dutton, 1913), p. 3. First published in 1762.

[2] *Modern Democracies* (Macmillan, 1921), vol. 2, p. 608. Quoted by permission of the publisher.

National political conventions every four years (above) choose the presidential candidates and set the stage for weeks of vigorous political campaigning all over the country (below). Public-opinion polls (right) are used to test public sentiment and are followed with great interest during campaigns.

Two of the many evidences of interstate and Federal-state cooperation are the Port of New York Authority, an agency governing tunnels, bridges, airports, and docks in the metropolitan area (above), and the nation-wide employment services, operated by the states in cooperation with the Federal government.

CHAPTER 1

Political Institutions and Ideas

As I was born a citizen of a free State, and a member of the Sovereign, I feel that, however feeble the influence my voice can have on public affairs, the right of voting on them makes it my duty to study them: and I am happy, when I reflect upon governments, to find my inquiries always furnish me with new reasons for loving that of my own country. — Jean Jacques Rousseau [1]

No government demands so much from the citizen as Democracy and none gives back so much. — James Bryce [2]

Arnold J. Toynbee, the eminent British historian, records twenty-one major civilizations in the history of mankind. To these must be added a larger, but unknown, number of primitive societies. Political institutions with authority to make and enforce laws—in other words governments—have been common to both civilized and primitive societies. Although forms and procedures have differed, evidence accumulated by social scientists indicates that some form of government is essential to successful group life.

Governments, like other social institutions, vary greatly; indeed it is not possible to find identical forms and procedures in the governments of any two societies. Differences are explained by such factors as geography, climate, history, customs, resources, and degree of enlightenment. Shaped by forces like these, distinctive governments have evolved in each country, and constitutional forms that are successful in one place might fail quite miserably in another.

Not only do political institutions vary but they are constantly in the process of adaptation and change. In Great Britain, for example, power has passed from King to Parliament; the House of Commons has taken predominance from the House of Lords; tight control of empire has been replaced by a commonwealth relationship based on shared responsibility and mutual consent.

Similar transformation has taken place in the United States. The nation now commands the devotion formerly reserved for particular states. The negative individualism of old is being replaced by a new attachment to positive government. The electorate has expanded until it represents almost universal adult suffrage. Pressure groups have become nationally organized, vocal, and very powerful. Political parties have become indispensable adjuncts of government. The electoral college is withering away. The presidency has attained a commanding position. And, for

[1] *The Social Contract* (Dutton, 1913), p. 3. First published in 1762.

[2] *Modern Democracies* (Macmillan, 1921), vol. 2, p. 608. Quoted by permission of the publisher.

good or ill, more changes appear to be just around the corner.

POLITICAL DIVISIONS OF THE WORLD

The modern state is a product of the gradual evolution of political institutions over the centuries. The basic group of primitive man was the family or kinship group. As the family grew in size, clans and tribes were formed. Tribes were united by commerce, conquest, and alliance, and the early kingdoms made their appearance. Then the city-state emerged as the major political unit of the Mediterranean world. After a period dominated by the Roman Empire, Europe entered the feudal era, in which political authority was fragmented. Feudalism ended gradually with the merging of principalities and city-states into larger and larger kingdoms, until the modern national-state system became discernible during the latter part of the seventeenth century. Although the national state is today the dominant political unit, some attention must be given to lesser units, such as dominions, protectorates, trust territories, and colonies.

National States. Some seventy-five national states are at present in existence. From a legal point of view, they may be defined as permanent associations of people, politically organized upon a definite territory, and habitually obeying the same autonomous government.[3] For a state to exist, then, the following elements must be present: (1) population, (2) territory, (3) political organization or government, (4) sovereignty, and (5) unity sufficient to bind the community together for sustained collective action.

The state may have a large or small *population*. India has over 356,000,000 whereas Iceland has only about 144,000. Yet both are national states, with membership in the United Nations and diplomatic representation abroad.

Likewise, a state may have much or little *territory*. Luxembourg, with 999 square miles, is a member of the family of nations along with the Union of Soviet Socialist Republics, which has

[3] Amos S. Hershey, *The Essentials of International Law and Organization* (Macmillan, rev. ed., 1929), p. 158.

nearly 8,500,000 square miles within its territorial limits.

The *political organization* of a state may take any form, but it must be powerful and stable enough to command the obedience of the people and to fulfill the international obligations of statehood.

Sovereignty is the most provocative of the elements required of a state. The term means supreme temporal power, and all authorities agree that it must exist before a community can be treated as a national state. Where sovereignty shall rest and by whom it shall be exercised are among the most controversial of all political subjects. It may repose in an emperor or monarch, as in the days of Caesar or Henry VIII. Or it may rest in a church, feudal lords, the people (as in the United States), a parliament, a class, or the state itself conceived as an ideal person (as in Fascist Italy under Mussolini). There often is a difference between the theory regarding the location of supreme power and the actual situs, but for a community to be recognized as a state all agree that supreme authority must be located somewhere within its domain.

Unity is the most basic of all the elements essential to national statehood. Its absence, total or partial, explains many historical phenomena. Lack of a full measure of unity was one of several difficulties encountered in molding the original thirteen American colonies into an effective single nation. Lack of unity also helps to explain why the peoples of India, China, and parts of Africa have been slow about developing over-all political institutions. It accounts, in part, for the recent split between India and Pakistan. It also accounts for many of the difficulties encountered by those who would create a united states of Europe or a world federation or other forms of world government. Before these heroic goals can be achieved, a consciousness of identity and unity must exist with sufficient intensity to ensure cooperation by enough people to fulfill the purposes of community life.

States decide among themselves whether a given unit possesses the attributes of statehood. While unanimity is unnecessary, "recognition" by the more powerful states usually is indispens-

MAJOR POLITICAL UNITS OF THE WORLD

Status as of Jan. 1, 1956

NATIONAL STATES (By Population)

			China ("Communist")	UN	US		Afghanistan	UN	US	AS	Bolivia
UN	US	CN	India	UN	US	CN	Canada	UN	US	AS	Guatemala
UN	US		Russia (USSR)	UN	US	CN	U. of So. Africa	UN	US		Yemen
UN		AS	United States	UN	US	AS	Colombia	UN	US	AS	Ecuador
	US		Japan				Viet Nam (North)	UN	US	AS	Haiti
UN	US		Indonesia (USI)	UN	US		Netherlands	UN	US		Hungary
UN	US	CN	Pakistan		US		Viet Nam (South)	UN	US		Norway
UN	US	CN	United Kingdom				Korea (North)	UN	US		Syria
	US		Germany (West)	UN	US		Belgium	UN	US		Eire (Ireland)
UN	US	AS	Brazil	UN	US		Portugal	UN	US	AS	Uruguay
UN	US		Italy	UN	US	CN	Australia	UN	US	AS	Dominican Rep.
UN	US		France	UN	US		Greece	UN	US	AS	Salvador
UN	US		Spain	UN	US		China (Nationalist)	UN	US		Israel
UN	US		Poland	UN			Bulgaria	UN	US	CN	New Zealand
UN	US	AS	Mexico	UN	US	AS	Peru	UN	US		Liberia
UN	US		Philippines	UN	US	CN	Ceylon	UN	US	AS	Honduras
UN	US		Turkey	UN	US		Austria	UN	US	AS	Paraguay
UN	US		Egypt	UN	US		Sweden	UN	US	AS	Nicaragua
			Germany (East)	UN	US		Saudi Arabia	UN	US		Libya
	US		Korea (South)	UN	US	AS	Chile	UN	US		Lebanon
UN	US		Thailand (Siam)	UN	US	AS	Cuba	UN	US		Laos
UN	US		Iran (Persia)	UN	US		Nepal	UN			Albania
UN	US	AS	Argentina	UN	US		Iraq	UN	US	AS	Costa Rica
UN	US		Rumania		US		Switzerland	UN	US	AS	Panama
UN	US		Ethiopia	UN	US	AS	Venezuela	UN	US		Transjordan
UN	US		Yugoslavia	UN	US		Denmark	UN	US		Luxembourg
UN	US		Burma	UN	US		Finland	UN	US		Iceland
UN	US		Czechoslovakia	UN	US		Cambodia				

UN   member United Nations
US   recognized by United States
CN   member (British) Commonwealth of Nations
AS   member Organization of American States

UNITED NATIONS TRUST TERRITORIES (By Trustee)

United States:
Caroline Islands
Marianas
Marshall Islands

Italy:
Somaliland

France:
Cameroons
Togoland

Belgium:
Ruanda-Urundi

United Kingdom:
Tanganyika
Cameroons
Togoland

New Zealand:
Western Samoa

Australia:
New Guinea

Australia, New Zealand, and United Kingdom:
Nauru

MAJOR COLONIES AND PROTECTORATES (By Controlling Power)

United States:
*Puerto Rico

Belgium:
Belgian Congo

Netherlands:
Indies

France:
French West Africa
Algeria
Morocco
Madagascar
French Equatorial
Africa
Tunis

United Kingdom:
*Nigeria
Uganda
*Gold Coast
Kenya
Malaya
*Federation of
the Rhodesias
and Nyasaland

Sierra Leone
Jamaica
Basutoland
Aden
Somaliland
Trinidad

*Almost wholly self-governing territories.

3

able. Recognition is followed normally by exchange of diplomats, negotiation of treaties, and, perhaps, admission to the United Nations. Following recognition the newcomer is considered an international personality with all the rights, privileges, and immunities of international law.

Dominions. A dominion is a territory having autonomy in the conduct of its internal and external affairs, but maintaining a degree of affiliation with a mother country. The idea of dominion status grew out of British experience in granting larger and larger powers of self-government to Canada and other former colonies. Today the British dominions—Canada, Australia, New Zealand, Union of South Africa, India, Pakistan, and Ceylon—are independent national states that have chosen, for a variety of reasons, to remain associated with the United Kingdom and with each other through the Commonwealth of Nations. In 1952 the United States arranged commonwealth status with Puerto Rico, a former colony. Meanwhile, with old-fashioned colonialism under fire in and out of the United Nations, more dominion-type arrangements may be in the offing.

Protectorates. A protectorate is a territory that is controlled by another power, usually through military, economic, and financial ties, but which has not formally been annexed by the controlling power. Tunisia and Morocco are French protectorates in North Africa; Tonga in the Pacific, Uganda in Africa, and some of the Malay States in Asia are British protectorates. Although the United States acknowledges no formal protectorates, her influence over Haiti, Santo Domingo, Panama, and Cuba at times resembles that relationship.

Trust Territories. The mandate system was devised after the First World War as a means of administering territories taken from the defeated Central Powers by the victorious Allies. Under this arrangement, responsibility for control of such areas was given to the League of Nations, which in turn made some "advanced" state guardian of each area on behalf of the League.

The United Nations Charter created a new system of international supervision of dependent areas. Supervised by the Trusteeship Council, the new plan operates somewhat like the mandate system. The Charter placed no specific territories under trust, but left that to subsequent negotiations between the UN and the powers in possession of dependent areas. Australia, Belgium, France, New Zealand, and the United Kingdom received UN approval of trust agreements they submitted for territories formerly held by them under League mandate. The Union of South Africa refused to submit a trust plan for Southwest Africa, which it hoped to annex. The United States has been given trusteeship control over the former Japanese mandates of the North Pacific —the Caroline, Marianas, and Marshall Islands. After much disagreement the former Italian colonies in North Africa were speeded to independent nationhood; Italy was assigned a trusteeship over its former colony Somaliland with the understanding that complete independence would be granted in 1960. The trusteeship chapters of the Charter also laid down principles that should govern the administration of all colonial peoples, whether within the trust system or not.

Colonies. Colonies are territories in which sovereignty is exercised by a parent national state. Most colonies are geographically separated from the country administering sovereignty; European powers hold the greatest share of colonial possessions, which are located mainly on the continents of Africa and Asia and on islands. Actually, most colonies have been granted some degree of self-government, ranging from nearly complete internal autonomy to meager participation in local affairs. The United States has refrained from using the term "colony," and persists in calling its dependent areas "territories." Nevertheless, the status of the Virgin Islands and of Samoa is not unlike that of British colonies like Jamaica and the Bahamas, or French colonies like New Caledonia and Martinique.[4]

Nationalism. In order to understand the attitude of peoples toward their political units, their

[4] For a fuller discussion of territories of the United States, see Chap. 23.

behavior and aspirations, it is necessary to probe what Frederick L. Schuman calls "the cult of the nation-state." [5] The spirit of nationalism drives national states to glorify their own race, culture, institutions, ideals, and purposes. In its harmless form nationalism leads to commemoration of heroes and history in storybook, song, and dance. In its dangerous form it leads to jingoism, economic autarchy, violation of the rights of neighbors, and so to war. Persistence of extreme nationalist spirit constitutes a formidable barrier to international cooperation.

Nationalism operates also as a separatist influence within national states. In the 1930's, Sudeten German propaganda was a grave threat to Czechoslovakian unity. Between wars Yugoslavia was weakened by Croat nationalist aspirations for autonomy or a separate national state. The boundaries of a national state can rarely be drawn so perfectly as to include only persons of a common linguistic, cultural, ethnic, and religious background. The presence of any minority may lead to separatist agitation.

The nationalist spirit also motivates colonial peoples to revolt against their imperial masters. It drove Egyptian students to demonstrate against British "protection." It induced Indonesians to fight to the death against Netherlands forces. It whetted the will of the Annamese to expel their French overlords from Indo-China. It led the Irish to demand and receive independence, despite the economic and other advantages of the British connection. A rising nationalist spirit has played a large part in the achievement, during the postwar period, of national statehood by India, Pakistan, Burma, and Jordan.

One of the great tasks of the present age is to reconcile nationalist aspirations with the preeminent fact that this is an interdependent world. Nationalism can be tolerated, even encouraged, up to the point where its exercise invades the rights and security of other peoples. For China or India a new nationalism may serve to unite diverse elements and thereby promote social and economic progress. For the major

[5] See Frederick L. Schuman, *International Politics: The Destiny of the Western State System* (McGraw-Hill, 4th ed., 1948), pp. 422–510.

nations there is needed a new patriotism—a devotion to internationalism, a conviction that all peoples of the earth can live together in peace and security.

World Organization. While the nation-state has dominated the world scene for nearly three hundred years, and continues to do so, there has been in recent times a parallel development of international consciousness and institutions. The International Telecommunications Union, the Universal Postal Union, the Pan American Union, the League of Nations, and the United Nations are tangible evidences of this trend.

Of the dozens of private and public international organizations existing today, the United Nations is paramount. This is not the government of a new world state but merely an association of national states formed for consultation and cooperative action. Membership is not compulsory, and United Nations agencies must work through governments of national states. In joining, however, member states have limited their freedom of action and pledged their support to United Nations principles and decisions. In going this far, member states have admitted their limitations and confirmed their conviction that a new international community is required to meet the need of today's world.

FORMS OF GOVERNMENT

An observer of the governments of today is impressed with both their variety and similarity. If he were to classify them, the most meaningful terms would be unitary or federal, parliamentary or presidential, authoritarian or democratic. Or he might group them according to whether their constitutions are rigid or flexible.

Unitary or Federal. A government is *unitary* when the powers of government are concentrated in a single central government, with legal omnipotence over all territory within its boundaries. Local governments usually exist, but they are creatures of the central government and act as its administrative agents. Most of the national states of the world have governments of this type. Examples are Cuba, Belgium, France, Great Britain, Italy, and Japan. This form is also found within most of our forty-eight states and American territories like Alaska and Hawaii.

A government is *federal* if political authority is divided between self-governing parts and the central whole, each operating within its sphere of action as defined in the constitution. The geographic subdivisions and their governments are not mere creatures of the central government but share power and responsibility with it. Although the idea of federalism is old, the adoption of the federal system by the United States gave impetus to extensive adoptions of the plan by modern national states. Examples are Canada, Australia, Mexico, Brazil, and Switzerland.

A weak federation is often called a "confederation," which is a sort of association or league of sovereign states. Under this form, the central government has limited powers while the member states retain great autonomy and authority. Examples are the American states under the Articles of Confederation and the Confederate States of America during the Civil War. Some look upon the League of Nations and the United Nations as weak confederations.

Parliamentary or Presidential. In the *parliamentary* form, executive powers are exercised by a prime minister and his cabinet. They are usually members of the parliament and continue to hold ministerial office only so long as their policies are supported by a majority of parliament. Thus parliament is the supreme branch of government, with authority over the executive branch. Among the characteristics of this form is a weak titular executive like the British king or the French president. In recent years the parliamentary form has often been designated the "cabinet" form. The latter name properly emphasizes the fact that although parliament is the ultimate master, in Britain party discipline has grown so rigid that a cabinet rarely can be overthrown by vote of lack of confidence, so long as one party has a majority. The parliamentary form is also used in most of the countries of Europe and the British Commonwealth.

In the *presidential* form there is a separation of powers among the principal branches of government, usually executive, legislative, and judicial. The separation is almost invariably set forth in a written constitution. The chief executive generally is elected, and he continues in office to the expiration of his term, regardless of the support given him by the legislative branch. The legislature, executive, and the judiciary are coordinate branches, and each in its own field has its own constitutional authority. Although much criticized in recent years for its proclivity for stalemate, the presidential form has been continued in most of the countries that have adopted it. The form is found in the United States, the forty-eight states, most of the Latin-American republics, and a few other countries.

The *plural* executive, although less widely used, is attracting renewed interest. Known also as the "executive council" or "collegial" executive, it has long been used in Switzerland and was recently adopted in Uruguay. Selected either by parliament or popular election, executive councilors divide executive power among themselves, often on a bi- or multi-party basis. The commission plan of municipal and county government in the American states is somewhat similar.

Authoritarian or Democratic. An *authoritarian* or dictatorial form is one in which political authority is exercised by a single individual or a small group of people. This form is probably the oldest one known to man. Whether the social unit was the family, clan, tribe, city-state, or empire, power tended to gravitate to one or a few individuals who ruled with varying degrees of moderation. Even in so-called "democratic" Athens power was placed in the hands of citizens who made up only a comparatively small proportion of the population. Absolute monarchs, so common during the Middle Ages, still exist in some semifeudal states.

But the newest form of autocracy is the totalitarian national state. This concentrates power in one or a few men who organize the state for total and undeviating devotion to the public will as expressed through its leaders. Mass support is mobilized through propaganda, a single highly disciplined political party, the secret police, ruthless suppression of dissent, and a high level of state activity designed to promote economic and social welfare or enhance national power and prestige. Examples are Italy under Mussolini, Germany under Hitler, prewar Japan, the Soviet Union, Poland, and Hungary.

The *democratic* form is the one best known to Americans. Where this prevails government is based on the consent of the governed, as expressed through constitutions, elections, and public opinion. Precautions are taken to keep power responsible, or limited, dissent is tolerated and even encouraged, and individual rights are given special safeguards.

A distinction is made between *direct* or *pure* democracy and representative democracy. In the former, the body of citizens assemble periodically and perform the functions usually assigned to legislatures. Examples are found in ancient Greece and Rome, in the *Landesgemeinde* of some Swiss cantons, and in New England town meetings. Such direct democracy is practicable only in small units, where population is sparse and homogeneous, and where the issues are fairly simple. It has little applicability in modern national, state, and municipal governments, except in the form of the initiative and referendum and of other plebiscites and popular voting on propositions.

In a *representative* democracy, the voters wield influence through officials selected to express and enforce their will. This system appears to have originated in the medieval states of western Europe, was perfected in Britain, and is now widely practiced throughout the world.

In addition to describing a form of government the term "democratic" has other meanings. Some associate democracy with capitalism and argue that democratic forms of government cannot exist if government interferes much with private enterprise or goes into business itself. Others insist that there is more democracy, rather than less, where government expands services to equalize opportunities, surrounds profit-seeking business with greater controls, or undertakes to own and operate basic industries. Confusion is compounded when communists speak of their countries as "peoples' democratic republics," meaning by this that the proletariat has liquidated the exploiting classes and now operates the state by authoritarian measures for the welfare of the masses. Precise definition is obviously impossible where the term democracy is used to describe social and economic systems as well as political. But confining definition to political systems, the essentials of democratic government are apparent.

In the twentieth century, the rise of *communism* and *fascism* as prevailing "ideologies" in several countries has posed difficult problems of classification. Strictly speaking, they are not forms of government, but combinations of various social, economic, and political doctrines. Both vary widely between theory and practice. Both are authoritarian.

Modern communism, as practiced in the Soviet Union, is based on the writings of Marx, Lenin, and Stalin. Claiming that history teaches the inevitability of a class conflict whereby the propertied classes dominate and exploit the masses, communist leaders set out to establish in the Soviet Union a regime in which the proletariat would establish and maintain a socialist system. Ruthless measures and dictatorship, communists argue, were essential to achieve this result and ensure its success. Someday, however, the state will wither away, leaving a democratic and classless society. Many communists have given the impression that force and violence are essential to achieve their goals in other countries; other communists deny that these methods will be required, especially where change is possible through parliamentary methods.

To people outside the Soviet Union it became uncertain whether communism would be left free to compete for acceptance with other ideologies or whether it would be an instrument for extending the power and influence of the Soviet state. The latter impression gained ascendancy among many people, especially during the first decade after the Second World War, but there appears to be a growing disposition to believe in the possibility of "peaceful coexistence."

Fascism grew to great power in Italy and Germany between wars and has been a force in other sectors. This was a revolt of the conservative and nationalist elements against parliamentarians, radicals of the left, and internationalists. Liberal democracy gave way to dictatorship and ruthless suppression of dissidents. The nation became the supreme object of devotion and effort. Although private ownership of property and industry, trade unions, the church and other private associations were permitted, these were subordinated to the paramount interest of the state.

As with communism, outsiders were given the impression that fascism at home meant national aggrandizement abroad. Ensuing tension erupted in war, the aftermath of which continues to plague the world.

Constitutions: Rigid or Flexible. Governments are also classified according to the nature of their constitutions. Modern constitutionalism dates from the American and French revolutions. It involves the recognition of fundamental laws and practices under which governments conduct their affairs. Formerly constitutions often were classed as either *written* or *unwritten,* but this division has limited utility because few if any are wholly one or the other. The British constitution, classic example of the unwritten, consists of certain major statutes, court decisions, great settlements, and administrative ordinances, as well as customs. It is unwritten only in the sense that there is no single document which can be called the British constitution. The American Constitution, leading example of the written, includes customs and usages and interpretations that are not part of the formal document. One speaks with greater accuracy when one describes the British constitution as semi-documentary and noncomprehensive; the American as documentary and comprehensive.

The distinction between *rigid* and *flexible* constitutions is more meaningful and useful. It places emphasis on the amending process. A rigid constitution may be amended only in the manner prescribed in the document; ordinarily this requires a special constitutional convention, or a favorable vote by the legislative body by more than a simple majority. It may also require the affirmative vote of the people, or ratification by a prescribed number of the units of a federal state. The American Constitution must be classified as a rigid constitution, but a degree of flexibility is achieved through custom and usage and interpretations made by the courts, the Chief Executive, and the Congress.

FUNCTIONS OF GOVERNMENT

Although the role of government is highly controversial, there is general agreement over certain essential, or minimum, functions. All agree that only government should be permitted to enact laws and back them with sufficient force to compel acceptance and obedience. It is also generally agreed that governments should provide courts for the settlement of private controversies, protect life and property, defend the community from attack, conduct foreign relations, provide a medium of exchange and a postal system, and restrain individual, group, and commercial excesses. If government would confine itself to these, its role would be largely that of lawgiver, judge, policeman, and soldier. But few modern governments stop at this point. Instead, they have become gigantic regulatory and service institutions. This transition has been accompanied by diverse ideologies and vehement controversy.

Antistatism. *Anarchism* is a school of thought that seeks the complete elimination of the state, and its replacement by a free and spontaneous cooperation among individuals and groups. Anarchists regard the state as an instrument of domination and exploitation by the propertied classes. Most of them expect that the new society will come into being as a result of revolutionary action, but no new government or coercive system will replace the old. Anarchism has never become the gospel of the masses, but its proponents often touch a responsive chord in people concerned over the expanding authority of modern governments. Communists who expect the state to wither away and leave a democratic classless society operating through voluntary cooperation may also properly be called anarchists.

Syndicalism holds somewhat similar views concerning the role of the state. Using the general strike as a method of seizing power, the syndicalist would establish in place of the state a series of industries managed by the workers. These industries would be federated together on a functional basis; most syndicalists would permit this federation to exercise some coercive powers, particularly in the transitional period.

Individualism. The laissez-faire individualist regards the state as a necessary evil. He would have the state perform only the minimum or essential functions, leaving promotion and regulation of the economic order to private enterprise and to natural economic forces. That government is best, says a modern individualist, which governs least. To him government in recent years has constantly threatened individual freedom and private initiative. Economic *laissez faire,* once the creed of radicals, has become the doctrine of conservatism or even of reaction.

In order to be consistent, advocates of *laissez faire* must accept the withdrawal of nearly all forms of government support and paternalism. He who wants natural economic laws to govern production, distribution, and exchange must give up the protective tariff, governmental subsidy, marketing aids, and other services to business and agriculture. He must be prepared for the inequality that will result from unregulated operation of a "survival of the fittest" plan.

Individualism has a tremendous appeal to many Americans. It played a great part in the development of the country, in the early settlement of the East coast, in pushing back the frontiers to the West. It has been allied in many ways to opposition to state interference in individual opinions and conduct. Like many slogans, "free enterprise" is both appealing and vague, and its full implications are rarely examined.[6]

Progressivism. A middle way between individualist and collectivist views on governmental functions is advocated by a diverse group known by such designations as "progressives," "liberals," "new dealers," and proponents of the "welfare state." In one sense they seek to revive the utilitarian ideals of the greatest good to the greatest number. Supporters of this social-welfare point of view do not advocate socialism, although they are critical of the abuses of private enterprise and the profit motive. Seeking to correct and strengthen the existing economic order, they extend piecemeal the functions of government. In addition to the minimum functions, they would have government regulate, stimulate, coordinate, plan, and supervise the national economy; some utilities would come under public ownership and operation, and government would accept responsibility for providing full employment, social security, and housing. They also favor expanded public-health, education, and nutrition programs. As a means to achieving social justice, they often encourage nonbusiness groups, especially labor, farmers, and consumers. These will be recognized as the "New Deal" and "Fair Deal" programs that won wide acceptance in the United States during recent times.[7]

Collectivism. The state socialist advocates the public ownership of the principal means of production, exchange, and distribution. There are many varieties of socialist thought. Some derive their doctrine from the writings of Marx and Engels; some stem from other sources. Socialists condemn the capitalist system for concentrating wealth in the hands of the few and producing recurring economic crises. Having won power through the ballot box, most socialists anticipate a gradual transformation of the economic system from capitalist to socialist. Revolutionary socialists expect to win power only by violence, and hence predict a rapid transition to the new society.

Although socialist philosophy has made great headway in many countries of the world, it has never been adopted by a major political movement in the United States. The Labor parties of Great Britain, Australia, and New Zealand profess a mild socialist doctrine and have been able to place into force much of their programs. Social Democratic and Socialist parties of European countries have played a major part in continental politics for decades. The lack of headway made

---

[6] One of the ablest tracts for economic *laissez faire* is Friedrich A. Hayek, *The Road to Serfdom* (University of Chicago Press, 1944). The best answer to Hayek is Herman Finer, *Road to Reaction* (Little, Brown, 1946).

[7] For a study of the New Deal in action see Thomas P. Jenkin, *Reactions of Major Groups to Positive Government in the United States, 1930–1940* (University of California Press, 1945).

by the socialists in the United States may be explained in terms of the relatively high standard of living and the frequency with which the old parties borrow planks from socialist platforms in order to solve persistent problems.

Under a democratic state socialist scheme, as envisaged by socialists of British and Western

GRIN AND BEAR IT   By Lichty

"I wish political science was as advanced as medical science, Doc . . . you got more words that nobody knows the meaning of . . ."

Courtesy George Lichty and the *Chicago Sun-Times* Syndicate.

European countries, the government would nationalize credit and banking, transportation and communication, and the principal production industries. There would be central planning of the economic life of the country, and such private enterprise as was permitted to continue would be required to conform to the central plan.

In their practice to date, the Russian communists have behaved much like state socialists, except that they have been more revolutionary in methods and more total in application. Instead of withering away, the state has reached a new high in the functions performed and the obedience exacted.

Fascism as practiced in Italy and Germany

was clearly in the collectivist rather than the individualist tradition. While permitting private property and associations, the state demanded and received total control, loyalty, and obedience—hence the term "totalitarian." Generally the fascist dictators found it unnecessary to socialize industry, for their control was made complete and effective with private ownership.

THE ROLE OF POLITICAL SCIENCE

Quite naturally, something as old as government has attracted much thought and study. In consequence, a large body of theory and knowledge has accumulated which is of interest to all students of human society. But to the political scientist it is the nature of authority that inheres in all community life, the institutions by which authority is expressed, the methods by which control is achieved, and the aims and results of control that are his primary concern. While being aware that authority is expressed in many and diverse ways, the political scientist is chiefly concerned with its expression through what are commonly known as government and law.

Divisions of Political Science. The scope of political science is extremely broad, and for convenience is usually divided into the fields of political theory; public law; comparative government; governments of particular nations; public administration; international relations; political parties, elections, and public opinion. Beginning toward the end of the last century, colleges and universities in the United States have increasingly offered political science as a separate discipline. Closely related, however, are the disciplines of philosophy, history, anthropology, sociology, and economics. As a practical matter, the political scientist serves the aims of his profession as a scholar, teacher, or author, as a public official, a lawyer, an administrator, a consultant, or a researcher. Opportunities are numerous for the well qualified.

Expanding Frontiers. Public authority surrounds the modern American in ways undreamed of by his forefathers. Sometimes it appears in the form of a new restraint, sometimes it appears as a service, sometimes as a conscriptor of person and property. Whatever its form, authority as expressed through government makes itself felt upon Americans today from cradle to grave. To an American removed from pioneer days by only one or a very few generations, this growing authority over his life is greeted with mixed, and often hostile, emotions. But chafe as he will, the trend marches on.

Moreover, public authority accepts responsibility today for stimulating, planning, regulating, and coordinating the economy of the nation. From a nation devoted to laissez-faire principles Americans look increasingly to government for guidance and assistance in solving their economic problems. Read a recent political party platform and note the promises made to business, labor, farmers, homeowners, consumers, and the rest. Note also the pledges made to provide full employment, control prices, plan for careful use of natural resources, and sustain general prosperity. The day is gone when government will stand idly by and let the economy run its "natural" course from "boom to bust."

Similar trends are at work in the social realm. Next to military preparations, public-aided education is the largest consumer of the tax dollar and still demands are made for more. Social security, assistance to the needy, health programs, veterans' assistance, public housing, special programs for the mentally and physically handicapped, safe and efficient utility services—these and many more are demanded of today's governments.

As American society has grown more complex, the mere task of safeguarding life and property demands more and more public authority. Highway police were not needed to patrol dirt roads traveled by horsemen; only a rudimentary municipal police was needed when cities and villages were small; the FBI is of recent vintage; modern fire-fighting units have taken the place of volunteer bucket brigades; and thousands of large and diversified prisons and correctional institutions are required to supplement the ancient town lockup, county jail, and workhouse.

But it is in the fields of foreign affairs and national defense that authority manifests itself most conspicuously to twentieth-century Americans. The safety once enjoyed by isolation from Europe and Asia is a thing of the past. With its demise have come three wars since 1898 with major foreign powers and continuous fear of even bigger and more devastating conflicts. Huge military establishments and budgets, military intervention in nearly all phases of national life, unprecedented debt and taxation, and conscription have become commonplace. Unless feelings of national insecurity can be diminished, public authority is certain to grow and perhaps demand even greater sacrifice.

Role of the Citizen. The ordinary citizen, as well as the political scientist, is concerned over the extension of authority. If government is autocratic, the citizen is limited in what he can do, but under a democracy he has a decisive role to play. The citizen must first look to himself to make sure he is informed. This should be easier today than formerly because of the availability of radio, television, the press, and other mass media. But for most people it is harder to keep informed because of the increasing number and complexity of issues that must be understood.

The citizen must also learn to make wise choices. If he remains content to ratify by his votes the candidates proposed by political machines and vested interests, he must not expect honest government; if he votes for a demagogue, he will jeopardize his own rights as well as those of others; or if he votes blindly on referendum and initiative proposals, he must not be surprised if his government fails to meet some of his most urgent needs.

A citizen must also learn how and when to protest and give support. Well-organized protests at the right time can reform governments, change policies, and prevent abuse of power. But it is often easier to be against something and shout "Throw the rascals out" than it is to be for a cause. Programs designed to provide pure water supply, better schools, a competent civil service, effective business regulation, adequate mental hospitals, and other benefits require active and continuous support.

Moreover, the ordinary citizen needs to become a politician in the best sense of that term. Political parties starve for want of qualified and enthusiastic workers; pressure groups beg for aid and assistance; candidates and officials covet public interest and support; letters, telegrams, and interviews are needed and welcomed; qualified speechmakers are scarce; while more and better candidates are desperately needed. All this takes time, money, and interest, but democratic government flourishes or languishes in proportion to the number and quality of its lay politicians.

Political science has a special claim on college and university students. To them, more than others, the public will look for leadership and guidance. With government playing an increasingly vital part in the life of individuals and the community, the leaders of tomorrow must be able to understand, interpret, and direct forces that may improve or plague the lot of man. Effective citizenship is much more than a civic duty; it is also an opportunity for service richly rewarding in human satisfactions.

FOR FURTHER READING

Becker, Carl L.: *Modern Democracy* (Yale, 1941).

Bryce, James: *Modern Democracies* (Macmillan, 2 vols., 1921).

Coker, Francis W.: *Recent Political Thought* (Appleton-Century-Crofts, 1934).

De Grazia, Alfred: *The Elements of Political Science* (Knopf, 1952).

Ebenstein, William: *Today's Isms* (Prentice-Hall, 1954).

Field, G. Lowell: *Governments in Modern Society* (McGraw-Hill, 1951).

Finer, Herman: *The Theory and Practice of Modern Government* (Holt, 2d ed., 1949).

Gettell, Raymond G.: *Political Science* (Ginn, rev. ed., 1949).

Hall, H. Duncan: *Mandates, Dependencies and Trusteeships* (Carnegie Endowment, 1948).

Hallowell, John H.: *Main Currents in Modern Political Thought* (Holt, 1950).

Hayes, Carlton J. H.: *The Historical Evolution of Modern Nationalism* (Macmillan, 1948).

Jessup, Philip C.: *A Modern Law of Nations—An Introduction* (Macmillan, 1948).

Lindsay, A. D.: *The Modern Democratic State* (Oxford, 1947).

Lipson, Leslie: *The Great Issues of Politics* (Prentice-Hall, 1954).

MacIver, Robert M.: *The Web of Government* (Macmillan, 1947).

Peaslee, Amos J.: *Constitutions of Nations* (Rumford Press, 3 vols., 1950).

Pennock, J. Roland: *Liberal Democracy: Its Merits and its Prospects* (Rinehart, 1950).

Sait, Edward M.: *Political Institutions: A Preface* (Appleton-Century-Crofts, 1938).

Simon, Yves: *Philosophy of Democratic Government* (University of Chicago Press, 1951).

Tocqueville, Alexis de: *Democracy in America* (Knopf, 2 vols., 1945).

Wheare, Kenneth C.: *Federal Government* (Oxford, 3d ed., 1953).

——: *Modern Constitutions* (Oxford, 1951).

Wilson, Francis G.: *The American Political Mind: A Textbook in Political Theory* (McGraw-Hill, 1949).

REVIEW QUESTIONS

1. How does the national state differ from political units of other types in the modern world?

2. Distinguish between the terms "state" and "government."

3. What did Aristotle have in mind when he said that man is by nature a political animal?

4. What evidence is there that nationalism is a powerful force today? What evidence is there that nationalism is on the decline?

5. What factors are present in today's world that are forcing new political alignments and shaping new political institutions?

6. Compare the authority and function of the executive, legislative, and judicial branches under the presidential, parliamentary, and authoritarian forms of government.

7. Distinguish between the federal and unitary forms of government, and give examples of each.

8. Of the various forms of government, why has democracy been practiced in comparatively few places and for relatively short periods of time?

9. Distinguish between individualism, collectivism, and progressivism.

10. How can the drift from individualism to varying degrees of collectivism in the United States and elsewhere be explained?

11. How does political science differ from history, philosophy, anthropology, economics, and sociology?

12. The late Elihu Root said, "The principal ground for reproach against any American citizen should be that he is not a politician." What did he have in mind? Do you agree or disagree?

CHAPTER 2

Colonization, Independence, and Confederation

The basic institutions of American government and the prevailing philosophies of today were shaped in large measure during the Colonial period. . . . The English origin of the colonies has placed an indelible stamp upon the political habits of the United States. — Curtis P. Nettels [1]

The American revolution was in large measure a revolt against the centralized coercive power of Great Britain and the colonial aristocracy. The radicals had no intention of re-creating in America a form of government similar to that which they were fighting to overthrow. . . . The "nationalism" of the individual state is a factor too often overlooked. It was loyalty to one's country that moved men, whether radical or conservative, and one's country was the state in which one lived, not the thirteen more or less united states along the Atlantic Coast. — Merrill Jensen [2]

American institutions, like those of other nations, have their origin deeply embedded in the past. The development of political institutions divides itself naturally into four important periods: the Colonial, the Revolutionary, the Confederate, and the Constitutional. A brief historical review of government during the first three is essential to an understanding of the constitutional period which is the subject of succeeding chapters. Such a review ought not merely to engender respect for the past and an understanding of the present, but it should also contribute to the adventurous criticism and thinking so badly needed in modern times.

COLONIZATION

Basis of Britain's Title to America. Columbus discovered the West Indian Islands in 1492, but

[1] *The Roots of American Civilization* (Crofts, 1938), p. 162.

[2] *The Articles of Confederation* (University of Wisconsin Press, 1948), p. 163.

it remained for John Cabot, an Italian in the service of England, to explore what is now the eastern coastline of the United States. Although unwilling to assist Columbus, King Henry VII of England quickly realized the importance of his discovery and in 1496 commissioned Cabot to "seek out, discover and find whatsoever isles, countries, regions or provinces of the heathen and infidels whatsoever they be, and in what part of the world soever they be, which before this time have been unknown to all Christians" and "to set up our banners and ensigns in every village, town, castle, isle, or mainland of them newly found." Cabot made two voyages and by 1498 had discovered Newfoundland and St. Johns and sailed southward along the eastern coast of America to what is now the Maryland-Virginia border. England's title in the New World was thus based upon the law of discovery and conquest.

By a similar process, Spanish explorers established the title of their country to what is now

Florida, the Southwest, and western parts of America; French explorers planted the flag of France in the regions of Nova Scotia, the St. Lawrence River, the Great Lakes, and the Mississippi Valley to the Gulf of Mexico; while Dutchmen established claims in the valleys of the Hudson and Delaware Rivers.

Rights of the Indians. Wherever the early explorers traveled, they found Indians living in the tribal stage. Contrary to popular impression, the Indians were not nomadic but occupied well-defined areas. For example, tribes belonging to the Iroquois family inhabited the St. Lawrence and Great Lakes region, those belonging to the Muskhogean family lived in the southeastern section, while those belonging to the Sioux family occupied the north-central territory. European nations claimed the right of *dominion* over lands held by Indian tribes in consequence of discovery but accorded the Indians the right of *occupancy.*

This meant that European states claimed the right to colonize and manage external affairs, while the Indians retained ownership and possession of their lands with complete authority over internal tribal matters. This arrangement led the colonists to treat with the Indian tribes as "nations" and call their chiefs or sachems "kings." Although the Indians were brutally treated and ruthlessly exploited by the whites, land was seldom taken from them by conquest; rather, it appears that the colonists paid for most of the land taken, transfers being conveyed by solemn treaties.

Making North America British. Following the discovery of America, many attempts at colonization were made, but it was not until 1607 that the first permanent settlement was established at Jamestown, Va. The Pilgrim Fathers established the second settlement at Plymouth, Mass., in 1620. Then followed a series of settlements along the Atlantic seaboard until in 1732 the thirteenth colony, Georgia, was established.

The British, Dutch, Swedes, French, and Spaniards all played a part in colonizing America, but the British soon acquired a controlling influence. By 1664, in which year Holland's colonies (New Netherlands) were conquered, England had acquired dominion over all the Atlantic seaboard south of the Gulf of St. Lawrence to Florida. At the end of the French and Indian War, in 1763, England had eliminated Spanish control over Florida and French control over all her possessions in North America east of the Mississippi River. Thus, on the eve of the American Revolution, England had control over all the present United States east of the Mississippi River.

Three Types of Colonies. Before colonies could be established in America, it was necessary to have legal authorization to do so. This was granted by the king in charters, issued in some instances to trading companies, in others to individuals, and in still others to groups of colonists. The charters authorized three types of colonial governments; royal (often called "crown"), proprietary, and charter (sometimes called "corporate").

Royal Colonies. Royal colonies were the most numerous, including New Hampshire, New York, New Jersey, Virginia, North Carolina, South Carolina, Georgia, and Massachusetts (after 1691). The charters granted to persons establishing these colonies were subsequently canceled [3] or withdrawn, after which time the king exercised control directly through commissions and instructions issued to governors.

The commissions were very much alike. They appointed a governor as the king's representative or deputy who was to be governed by instructions. They also provided for a council composed of men appointed by the Crown or governor who would serve as an upper house of the legislature and assist the governor in discharging his duties. The governor was given power to suspend members of council from office, and in case of vacancies, to appoint others, subject, of course, to the Crown's approval. The commissions also authorized a general assembly of representatives to be chosen by the voters and a system of courts the judges of which were to be appointed by the governor with the advice of the council. Laws enacted by the legislature required the approval

[3] Massachusetts, however, restored her charter as an instrument of government in 1775.

of the Crown, and appeals could be taken from the highest colonial court to the King in Council. The royal colonies, mentioned above, were governed in this manner from shortly after their establishment until 1775.

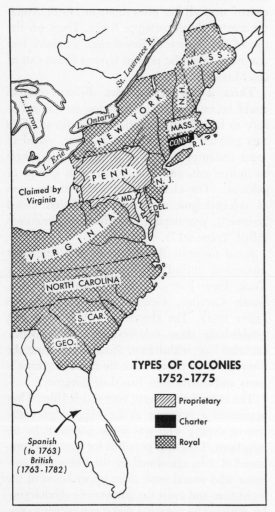

TYPES OF COLONIES
1752-1775

▨ Proprietary

■ Charter

▩ Royal

Of the thirteen colonies existing in the period immediately preceding the Revolution, eight were royal, three were proprietary, and two were charter.

Proprietary Colonies. At the time of the Revolution, there were three proprietary colonies: Maryland, Delaware, and Pennsylvania. Upon Lord Baltimore and William Penn, proprietors of these three colonies,[4] and their heirs was conferred absolute proprietorship of the territory. Their charters authorized them (the proprietors)

to appoint governors and other officers, establish legislatures, create courts and appoint judges thereto, create local governments, and exercise the usual prerogatives that in royal colonies belonged to the Crown.

In Delaware and Maryland, the legislature was bicameral, consisting of an upper house called a "council," whose members were appointed by the proprietor, and a lower house made up of representatives elected by freemen. In Pennsylvania the legislature was unicameral; a council existed but had no legislative powers and served merely as an advisory body to the governor. Laws were subject to veto by the Crown, except in Maryland, and appeals could be taken from the highest colonial court to the King in Council.

Charter Colonies. Charter colonies were Rhode Island and Connecticut. These differed in that charters were granted to the colonists as a group after they had already settled and there was no point at which the British government had authority to interfere with administration of the colonies. They were organized altogether upon popular and democratic principles: governors were elected annually by the freemen of the colony, and while they were supposed to be acceptable to the Crown, approval was seldom sought. Members of both branches of the legislature were likewise chosen annually by the freemen. Acts of the legislature were not subject to the governor's veto, nor was it necessary for them to be sent to England for approval. Judges and all other officers were appointed by the legislature, although appeals could be taken from the highest colonial courts to the King in Council.

Inhabitants of these colonies cherished the charters whose provisions left them almost complete autonomy and spared them many of the excesses of royal governors suffered by neighboring colonists. A story familiar to New Englanders illustrates the extent to which charters were treasured. In 1685, King James issued an order

[4] Penn was given title to Pennsylvania in 1681, and in 1682 he was given a supplemental deed by the Duke of York which included the area that became the state of Delaware in 1776.

for the repeal of the charter of Connecticut. The colony offered its submission, and in 1687 Sir Edward Andros went to Hartford and in the name of the Crown declared the government dissolved. The charter was not surrendered, however, but secreted in an oak tree which is still venerated and displayed to sight-seers. Immediately after the revolution of 1688, the people resumed the exercise of all its powers. Succeeding monarchs silently permitted them to retain it without any struggle or resistance. Unlike most of the colonies that adopted new constitutions after the Declaration of Independence, Connecticut retained her charter as a fundamental law until 1818 and Rhode Island hers until Dorr's Rebellion in 1842. Indeed it has been

Colonial Governments

Name	Founder	Date	Status in 1775	Government
Rhode Island.......	Roger Williams	1636	Charter (Self-governing)	*Charter* granted directly to colonists. *Governors* chosen by freemen for 1-year term. *Legislature* bicameral: both houses elected by freemen for 1-year terms. *Judges* appointed by governor in council. *Crown* could not veto laws, but cases could be appealed from highest colonial court to King in Council.
Connecticut........	Emigrants from Massachusetts	1636	Charter (Self-governing)	
Maryland..........	Lord Baltimore	1634	Proprietary	*Proprietor* owned colony but acknowledged sovereignty of King of England. *Governor* appointed by proprietor. *Legislature* bicameral (except in Pennsylvania). Upper house appointed by proprietor. Lower house elected by freemen. Laws (except those of Maryland) were subject to approval and veto by Crown. *Judges* appointed by governor and council. Appeals could be taken to King in Council.
Delaware..........	Swedes	1638	Proprietary	
Pennsylvania.......	William Penn	1681	Proprietary	
Virginia...........	London Company	1607	Royal	*Crown* controlled directly by commissions and instructions to colonial government. *Governor* appointed by Crown and acted as king's deputy. *Legislature* bicameral (except in Georgia). Upper house appointed by king, lower house elected by freemen. Upper house acted as governor's council. All laws subject to approval and veto by Crown. *Judges* appointed by governor. Appeals could be taken to King in Council.
Massachusetts......	Puritans of the Mass. Bay Colony	1628	Royal	
New Hampshire....	John Mason	1629	Royal	
North Carolina... ⎱	Eight nobles	1663	Royal	
South Carolina.... ⎰			Royal	
New York.........	Duke of York	1664	Royal	
New Jersey.........	Berkeley and Carteret	1664	Royal	
Georgia...........	James Oglethorpe	1732	Royal	

said that had all the colonies been allowed so much autonomy and independence, the Revolution would never have occurred.

New England Towns. In the New England colonies the principal unit of local government was the town (elsewhere called "township"). Counties existed but played a minor role, handling chiefly such matters as the administration of justice and the militia. The predominance of town government resulted from the fact that the first colonists came not as individuals but as church congregations or groups seeking religious freedom. Once here, the rugged soil, rigorous climate, the presence of hostile Indians and wild animals encouraged small-scale farming, manufacturing, trading, fishing, and residence in compact communities. The town was sometimes wholly rural, sometimes wholly urban, and sometimes partly rural and urban. The towns were incorporated and their boundaries defined by the colonial legislature. They were then left to govern themselves, provided, of course, they did nothing contrary to the laws of the colony.

Governmentally, the towns were pure or direct democracies. Town meetings, which were advertised meetings of voters, convened at least once a year (ordinarily in March) but many times oftener. In the early days nonattendance was punishable by fine. At these gatherings such laws were enacted and officials chosen as seemed necessary to manage local business. For the management of affairs between town meetings a board of selectmen consisting of from three to thirteen members was elected. Besides these, the principal officers were a town clerk and constable. Other officers were treasurer, assessor, surveyor of highways; the tithingman, a kind of Sunday constable who saw that people came to church and with foxtail wand kept them awake during sermons; the fence viewer, who supervised erection of boundary fences between adjoining properties; the hog reeve, who saw that rings were kept in noses of swine running at large; the field driver, who impounded stray cattle; the pound keeper, who caught and attended stray dogs; overseers of the poor, town criers, and many others. The town served as an electoral district for representation in the colonial legislature and representatives thereto were chosen by the town meeting.

Prominent individuals, usually wealthy landowners, often exercised disproportionate influence, town powers often were poorly defined, the right to vote was limited to property holders, town moderators often dominated proceedings, towns were often parochial in outlook, and petty issues often claimed excessive time and attention. Nevertheless, these gatherings of voters were social as well as political events and became deeply rooted in the affections of the people, resulting in a society as democratic as the world had seen. Today in the more rural parts of New England, the old machinery of town government functions much as it always did, but in more thickly populated sections, where the population is likely to be heterogeneous, many modifications have occurred.

Southern Counties. In the Southern colonies town government never took root; instead, the county was the primary unit of local government and administration. These colonies were settled more by individual entrepreneurs than by dissenting congregations; wild animals were scarce and there were comparatively few hostile Indians but, more important, the land and climate were suitable for large-scale agriculture, particularly the growing of tobacco, cotton, indigo, and rice. Instead of homogeneous, compact communities, the plantation system developed, necessitating a unit of local government larger than in the North. At first many local matters were attended to by the plantation owners. Later, parishes were established which served as both ecclesiastical and civil districts. These were governed by a vestry, consisting usually of several "selected men" chosen at first by the parishioners (though later the practice of cooptation became established), the minister, and churchwardens. A strong system of local government failed to develop, and before long the parish was overshadowed by the county.

Southern counties were less democratic than Northern towns. There was no popular assembly; rather the principal officers were usually lieutenant, sheriff, justices of the peace, and coroners. These officers were appointed by the governor of the colony commonly upon the recommendation of the justices of peace. The justices, ordinarily a self-perpetuating body of aristocratic planters, dominated county governments. Thus controlled, the county became the unit of representation in the colonial assembly, and the unit of military, judicial, highway, and fiscal administration.

Local Government in the Middle Colonies. In the middle colonies, both towns and counties exercised important functions. In New York and New Jersey the towns, resembling those of New England, played a larger role than the county, whereas in Pennsylvania and Delaware the county predominated. It was in these colonies that the practice of electing county officers, particularly governing boards, similar to those found in counties at the present time, originated.

Cities during the Colonial Period. Within themselves the colonies were unitary. Large cities did not exist; in fact, as late as the Revolution, only about 3 per cent of the population lived in boroughs (or cities), of which there were only twenty-four. These were established by charters issued by colonial governors and included New York, the oldest, Albany, Philadelphia, Annapolis, Norfolk, and smaller places mainly in Pennsylvania and New Jersey. In New England urban areas, such as Boston, the town-meeting system of rural areas proved sufficiently elastic for municipal purposes.

The principal governing authority in most of the boroughs was the common council composed of a mayor and recorder, both appointed by the governor, a small number of aldermen, and a somewhat larger number of councilmen elected by the voters. These acted as a single body, a quorum requiring the attendance of the mayor and a specified number of both aldermen and councilmen. The common council had control over all matters of administration, while the mayor and aldermen had certain judicial functions in addition to their duties as part of the common council. Three of the boroughs—Philadelphia, Annapolis, and Norfolk—were governed as "close corporations." There, the aldermen and councilmen held their positions for life, while the mayor and recorder were chosen by the common council from among the aldermen. When vacancies occurred among the aldermen, they were appointed by the common council, and vacancies for councilmen were filled by the mayor, recorder, and aldermen. These governing bodies were thus self-perpetuating and lacking in the democratic features obtaining in other colonial boroughs and present-day municipal governments.

Advantages and Disadvantages of Colonial Status. Certain advantages flowed from colonial status. There was, in general, a common tradition, culture, and language. Since most white inhabitants were British subjects, there was a common citizenship. Every colonist had a right to inhabit, if he pleased, any other colony; and he was capable of inheriting land in every other colony. The common law, with its invaluable guaranties of personal liberty, was the birthright and inheritance of all. Since appeals from local courts could be, and frequently were, taken to the King in Council, the law in the colonies was uniform as far as fundamental principles were concerned. England afforded protection from attacks by foreigners and pirates, handled foreign relations for the colonies, helped the colonists defend themselves against the Indians, counseled on questions of internal policy, and assisted with the administration of local laws. Moreover, England retained control over commerce among the colonies and with foreign nations, and while this was often irritating, it did prevent the erection of intercolonial trade barriers. Likewise, centralized control over monetary matters provided a uniform currency advantageous to all.

The most serious disadvantages arising from colonial status were that the colonies followed the fate of England in war or peace and were frequently embroiled in war whether they liked it or not;[5] the colonies were subject to the arbitrary whims and caprice of British kings and their agents; and, being distantly removed and without representation, there was always the danger that Parliament would enact legislation detrimental to the best interests of the colonists.

[5] For example, the war with France and her allies which lasted for over 50 years (1690–1748).

INDEPENDENCE

Disputes with Great Britain. Between the founding of Jamestown and the Declaration of Independence, 169 years elapsed. During this time, incessant disputes arose between the colonists and representatives of the British government, particularly the royal governors who were, for the most part, noblemen broken in fortune, frequently corrupt, and nearly always of weak character. Many of the disputes were local and personal, involving such matters as the taxation of proprietaries' lands, the extension of the franchise, the importation of convicts, the raising of troops, the issue of paper money, the organization of banks on insecure foundations, and the establishment of courts of law.

More serious quarrels arose when England enacted legislation monopolizing trade with the colonies, restricting the production and exportation of certain commodities (such as wool, wool products, and iron manufactures) in order to provide protection to manufacturers in England, and taxing colonists for the general support of colonial administration. In addition to outright disobedience to obnoxious laws and orders, the colonial legislatures frequently withheld appropriations for salaries for officials and soldiers until their demands were complied with, or addressed petitions to the home government. When, after the ascension of King George III to the throne in 1760, Britain decided to deal firmly with her high-spirited and recalcitrant

"Paying the Exciseman," a contemporary cartoon by a pro-American Englishman, shows Yankees forcing tea down the throat of a tarred and feathered Crown agent. It was a protest against both the Tea Act and the Stamp Act.

subjects in the American colonies, resentment was fanned to revolutionary fervor. All attempts at conciliation having failed by 1776, the colonists were faced with the alternatives of submission or rebellion, and, as we know, they chose the latter.

Committees of Correspondence. On the eve of the Revolution the colonists were faced with a determined government in England and governmental machinery in all the colonies, except Rhode Island and Connecticut, over which they could not hope to obtain control inasmuch as the governors, councils, and judges were, for the most part, loyalists beholden to the king and obliged to obey his commands. Revolutionary activity being treasonable and punishable by death, the only alternative was to persuade fellow colonists to form a "united front." This was done through a system of committees of correspondence.

The first of such committees was organized by Samuel Adams in Boston in 1772. Thereby was hatched what has been called by a bitter critic the "foulest, subtlest, and most venomous serpent ever issued from the egg of sedition." [6] Within a year almost every town in Massachusetts had formed similar committees and, encouraged by such events as the Boston Tea Party, they quickly spread to other colonies. By the end of 1773 a complete network of committees had been established, organized somewhat like modern political parties and performing many of the same functions. They not only exchanged ideas and information but took over the management of township, county, and colonial affairs. Later, they elected the Continental Congress and provided an agency through which the decisions of that body were enforced. Thus, although the regularly constituted British-controlled governmental machinery still remained, an extralegal system grew up beside it which sapped the old of its authority. A Tory later said that the work of the committees was "the

source of the rebellion" and a recent writer [7] has said:

The committees of correspondence that made the American Revolution possible were the town committees dominated by local "Sam Adamses" who were in close touch with Boston and other centers of radicalism. . . . Without their aid it is doubtful if the first Continental Congress would have been held in 1774 and the revolutionary movement in the colonies brought to its fruition in the Declaration of Independence. They made possible the domination of a great part of British America by cliques of radical patriots who looked to Sam Adams for leadership against the mother country. . . . After 1774, the colonies fairly bristled with hot-tempered Liberty Boys, who, instead of calling themselves Sons of Liberty [as those who had previously resisted the Stamp Act called themselves], were now known as the committees of correspondence. But under whatever name these patriots worked, their purpose remained the same: to defend colonial liberty with arms rather than submit to British "tyranny."

The First Continental Congress. Attempts on the part of Great Britain to punish the people of Massachusetts, who were more rebellious than others, united the colonies. On June 17, 1774, Massachusetts issued a call proposing that each of the colonies appoint delegates to attend a conference to consider relations with England. In response, delegates from every colony except Georgia met in Philadelphia on Sept. 5, 1774. The assemblage, which included the ablest men in the colonies, called itself the First Continental Congress. Whence came the delegates? Certainly they could not have been appointed by the regularly established colonial governments still under the domination of Britain. Rather, the delegations were appointed or elected by local committees, state conventions called by the local committees, or by state legislatures in which the revolutionary elements were dominant. The delegates styled themselves "the delegates appointed by the good people of these colonies."

[6] John E. Miller, *Sam Adams, Pioneer of Propaganda* (Little, Brown, 1936), p. 264. Quoted by permission of Little, Brown & Company and *Atlantic Monthly*.

[7] *Ibid.*, pp. 271–272. Quoted by permission of Little, Brown & Company and *Atlantic Monthly*.

The Congress adopted an impressive Declaration of Rights, called for repeal of obnoxious legislation passed since 1763, agreed to stop the importation and consumption of British goods, and established a continental association to oversee the enforcement of the boycott. The association was to consist of a system of committees elected in towns, cities, and counties throughout the country and supervised by colonial committees of correspondence, for the purpose of detecting and black-listing parties caught violating the boycott. Before adjourning on Oct. 26, it was agreed that Congress should convene again in May, 1775, unless their grievances had been redressed before that time.

The Second Continenal Congress. Britain was not in a mood to be conciliatory, but, rather, replied with more repressive measures. Massachusetts prepared for war, and before the time appointed for another congress to convene, blood had been shed at Concord and Lexington. The Second Continental Congress, which convened in Carpenters' Hall in Philadelphia on May 10, 1775, was a unicameral body comprised of practically the same men who had met earlier. Georgia, which had not sent delegates to the earlier congress, did so during the summer. As formerly, the delegates were chosen by popular conventions of the people of the various states or by the popular branch of the state legislatures, although after the Declaration of Independence and the establishment of new state governments the delegates were appointed by the legislatures of the states. Though "unique among the legislatures of history in that it had no authority to pass laws, no powers for enforcing the measures it did take, no means of raising money except printing, begging or borrowing," [8] the Second Continental Congress served as the official organ of government for the united colonies until March, 1781, when the Articles of Confederation became effective. It was, thus, America's first national government.

The Declaration of Independence. When the Congress met in May, 1775, there were few who desired or advocated independence. Washington, who had been appointed Commander in Chief of the colonial forces in July, 1775, said a year later: "When I took command of the army, I abhorred the idea of independence; now, I am convinced, nothing else will save us." Others had reached the same conclusion. Accordingly, Congress, on June 11, 1776, approved the appointment of a committee of five, with Thomas Jefferson as chairman, to draft a declaration of independence. A resolution to declare independence, introduced by Richard Henry Lee of Virginia, was approved by unanimous vote of Congress on July 2, and the entire declaration was approved two days later. It became the "birth certificate of the American nation." [9]

Creation by Declaration of a Nation with de Facto Status. Two important questions of constitutional law were raised by the declaration. The document declared "That these United Colonies are . . . absolved from all allegiance to the British Crown, and that all political connection between them and the state of Great Britain, is and ought to be totally dissolved. . . ." Did this destroy British sovereignty, as it announced, or did the colonies remain merely in a state of rebellion until the end of the war? The American view has been that the declaration made them independent and sovereign both internally and externally; hence all steps taken by Congress after that date had the sanction of law. This view was pointedly stated by Justice Story:

The Declaration of Independence has . . . always been treated as an act of paramount and sovereign authority, complete and perfect *per se,* and *ipso facto* working an entire dissolution of all political connection with, and allegiance to, Great Britain. And this, not merely as a practical fact, but in a legal and constitutional view of the matter by the courts of justice.[10]

From the standpoint of international law, however, the better view appears to be that since

[8] Lynn Montross, *The Reluctant Rebels: The Story of the Continental Congress, 1774–1789* (Harper, 1950), p. 8.

[9] The full text of the Declaration of Independence is given in Appendix I.

[10] Joseph Story, *Commentaries on the Constitution of the United States* (Little, Brown, 2 vols., 1873), vol. I, pp. 149–150.

foreign governments, with the exception of France and the Netherlands, refused to recognize the United Colonies and receive their ministers, they remained in a *de facto* status until 1783, after which their status became *de jure*. This meant that although Britain's sovereignty was doubtful, the United States was, nevertheless, not entitled to all the rights and privileges of nationhood until after the rebellion had terminated in its favor.

One Nation Created—Not Thirteen. The second question of constitutional law raised was whether one nation or thirteen of them were brought into existence by the declaration. If one, then only the central government had authority to levy war, send and receive ambassadors, ministers, and consuls, and make treaties. If thirteen, then all were competent to do these things. The words of the declaration are so ambiguous as to permit two interpretations. States' rights advocates called attention to these words: ". . . these United Colonies are, and of right ought to be *free and independent states . . .* and that as *free and independent states . . . they* have full power to levy war, conclude peace, and contract alliances, establish commerce, and do all other acts and things which independent states may of right do." On the other hand, nationalists stressed the statement that the declaration was made "in the name and by the authority of the good people of these colonies" by "the representatives of the United States of America, in general Congress assembled." To quote Justice Story, a stanch nationalist, again:

It [the Declaration of Independence] was not an act done by the State governments then organized, nor by persons chosen by them. It was emphatically the act of the whole *people* of the united colonies, by the instrumentality of their representatives, chosen for that among other purposes. . . . It was an act of original, inherent sovereignty by the people themselves, resulting from their right to change the form of government, and to institute a new one, whenever necessary for their safety and happiness. . . . It was, therefore, the achievement of the whole for the benefit of the whole.[11]

[11] *Ibid.,* p. 149.

Provincialism was strong; the newly created states were as jealous of each other as of Britain; the Congress was weak and at the mercy of the states; and many of the states proceeded as if they were sovereign. Nevertheless, in American law the theory has prevailed that a nation was created by the declaration and the states remained sovereign only in the sense that in matters of a local nature they were self-governing. Of this the Supreme Court said in a twentieth-century decision:

As a result of the separation from Great Britain by the colonies, acting as a unit, the powers of external sovereignty passed from the Crown not to the colonies severally, but to the colonies in their collective and corporate capacity as the United States of America. Even before the Declaration, the colonies were a unit in foreign affairs, acting through a common agency—namely, the Continental Congress, composed of delegates from the thirteen colonies. That agency exercised the powers of war and peace, raised an army, created a navy, and finally adopted the Declaration of Independence. Rulers come and go; governments end and forms of government change; but sovereignty survives. A political society cannot endure without a supreme will somewhere. Sovereignty is never held in suspense. When, therefore, the external sovereignty of Great Britain in respect of the colonies ceased, it immediately passed to the Union. . . .[12]

Converting Colonies into States. As events moved toward a showdown in 1775, crises developed in the internal affairs of the colonies, requiring them to reorganize their governments. The flight of most of the royal governors and other British officials left the people in the royal colonies without any official government, while in other instances, as in Massachusetts, resistance to British authorities made new arrangements necessary. Turning to Congress for advice, that body recommended that the states adopt "such governments as shall, in the opinion of the representatives of the people, best conduce to the happiness and safety of their constituents." Since no machinery existed with which

[12] United States *v.* Curtiss-Wright Export Corp., 299 U.S. 304 (1936).

to make the transition, Congress recommended that new governments be established by "assemblies or conventions" in the respective states. Most of the states did so in 1775 and 1776; Massachusetts slipped back to her charter of 1691 until a new constitution was adopted in 1780 which has remained in effect to the present; Rhode Island and Connecticut kept their colonial charters with only minor revisions. For the first time in the history of the world a large group of communities had begun the formation of their own governments under written constitutions. As they did so, they referred to themselves as "states" rather than "colonies" as theretofore.

Provisions of the New State Constitutions. The Revolution was a triumph for the radicals led by men like Samuel Adams and Thomas Paine. While hating England, the radicals had equally pronounced views on domestic matters. Basing their views on the natural rights of man, they abhorred strong government and pressed for political, economic, and social changes intended to weaken the power and influence of the aristocratic and well to do. The rebellion was, therefore, not merely one opposed to continued British rule; it was also a domestic political, economic, and social revolution. The cleavage between the radicals and conservatives was sharp and deep, and it had a profound effect upon the character of the new state constitutions, the Articles of Confederation, and later the Constitution.

The new state constitutions followed the main outlines of the Colonial governments and established the governmental framework of our present states. Seven of them contained bills of rights. All of them severely restricted the suffrage. All established three branches of government; each branch supposedly was independent of the other, but in practice the popularly elected lower house became supreme. Reflecting the colonies' dislike of governors, the new constitutions deprived executives of many powers held during the Colonial period. Executives were elected by the people in four states—by the legislature in the others—and customarily for terms of 1 year. Only in Massachusetts was the governor given the veto, and that could be overridden by two-

thirds of the legislature. In Pennsylvania and Georgia the legislature was unicameral, but in the other states the Colonial custom of having two houses was followed. The lower house, variously called "house of burgesses," "house of commons," or "house of representatives," was almost exactly like that of Colonial times; members were elected by the voters and served for 1-year terms. Lower houses retained the treasured prerogative of originating tax measures. The upper house, called "legislative council" in New Jersey and Delaware and "senate" or "council" elsewhere, was, as a rule, elected by the voters or the lower house for terms varying from 1 to 5 years. The senate was a smaller body than the house, its members were chosen for longer terms, and the qualifications of its members were more exacting. The senate came to be recognized as representing propertied interests, while the house represented the people of the state.

Even the judiciaries reflected the Revolutionary ideas. The selection of judges was changed from appointment by aristocratic Colonial governors to election by state legislatures or appointment by popularly controlled executives. Georgia went so far as to provide for popular election—the method now followed by all but a few states. Appointment was commonly for short terms, and judges were usually subject to removal by the legislatures. The court system and procedures, however, remained about as they had been. First, there were local peace magistrates and local inferior courts for the trial of petty civil cases and offenses. Above these stood a central court (analogous to our county or district courts of common pleas, quarter session, oyer and terminer, etc.) with civil and criminal jurisdiction over more serious cases. At the top stood a supreme court of review. Appeal to England was, of course, discontinued.

CONFEDERATION

Adoption of the Articles. Both the First and Second Continental Congresses met and functioned without constitutions. They were created to meet an emergency and were looked upon merely as temporary agencies. When war appeared imminent and independence desirable, steps were taken to place the central government on a firm and permanent basis. On June 12, 1776, the day after a committee was appointed to prepare a declaration of independence, Congress appointed another committee consisting of one member from each colony "to prepare and digest the form of a confederation to be entered into between these colonies." The committee reported a month later, and the plan was debated off and on until approved by Congress on Nov. 17, 1777. All but Delaware and Maryland ratified in 1778. Holding out for assurances over the proper distribution and control of the territories west of the Allegheny Mountains, Delaware ratified in 1779, while Maryland delayed until Mar. 1, 1781, on which date the Articles went into effect. They were the first constitution of the United States of America.[13]

Nature of the Confederation. It has been observed that, from a legal point of view, one nation, rather than thirteen, was created by the Declaration of Independence and suggested that in practice Congress was almost completely at the mercy of the states. The Articles removed all pretense about the nature of the new government. They demonstrated that the radicals were still in the saddle. The Articles were adopted by "delegates of the states," and Article III stated that the "states . . . severally enter into a firm league of friendship with each other." This was not, therefore, a union of all the people of the colonies considered as a whole, but a league of states. While binding themselves together "for their common defense, the security of their liberties, and their mutual general welfare," each retained "its sovereignty, freedom and independence, and every power, jurisdiction and right, which is [was] not expressly delegated to the United States, in Congress assembled." The Articles were, thus, another reflection of the radicals' abhorrence of strong government.

Government Established by the Articles. The governmental machinery authorized by the Articles was meager indeed. Congress was the sole organ of government. There was no executive branch, but Congress was authorized to ap-

[13] The text of the Articles is Appendix II.

point such committees and "civil officers" as its executive business might require, and these were to perform their duties under its direction. Nor was there a separate judicial branch such as exists today. Federal courts were authorized only "for the trial of piracies and felonies committed on the high seas," for "reviewing and determining finally appeals in all cases of captures," and for the settlement of disputes between the states.

The Congress was unicameral and comprised of not less than two or more than seven delegates from each state appointed annually by the state legislatures. No person could be a delegate for more than 3 years in any term of 6 years. The delegates were paid by the states, if at all; they voted by states, with each state having one vote, and delegates could be recalled at any time and replaced by others. Sessions were seldom attended by one-third the number of delegates the rules permitted, and as few as one-eighth of the entire body could negative resolutions.

Powers of Congress. In constructing the Articles, the central government was given many of the powers wielded by the British government during the Colonial period. No implied powers were granted; rather, Congress had only powers "expressly delegated." Specifically, some of those were: to declare war and conclude peace; conduct foreign relations, including the sending of ambassadors and making treaties; requisition revenue from the states in proportion to the value of land within each state; requisition soldiers in proportion to the number of white inhabitants in each state; borrow money, emit bills of credit, and coin money; build and equip a navy; settle disputes between the states; establish a postal system; regulate weights and measures; create courts for limited purposes; and appoint committees and officers. The most important of these, including the addition of amendments, could be exercised only with the concurrence of all the states, while the others required the approval of at least nine state delegations.

Obligations of States under the Articles. On their part, the states pledged themselves to observe their obligations and the orders of Congress; extend full rights to one another's citizens; give full faith and credit to the records, acts, and judicial proceedings of every other state; deliver up fugitives from justice to each other; submit their disputes to Congress for settlement, and allow open intercourse and commerce between the states. Retaining all powers not granted to Congress, the states were left with primary responsibility for protecting life and property and promoting the general welfare.

Weaknesses of the Confederation. Although adoption of the Articles had occasioned great jubilation, the weaknesses of the Confederation were soon apparent. The fundamental defect of the whole structure was the dependence of Congress upon the good will of the states. With a public debt of over 40 million dollars and current obligations to meet, Congress was powerless to lay and collect taxes but could only requisition

and urge the states to forward their quotas. Impoverished by war, harassed by social distress, and jealous of their prerogatives, the states either could not or would not pay their assessments. Of a total of $15,670,000 requisitioned between 1781 and 1786, only $2,419,000 was supplied, of which Georgia and North Carolina paid not a cent.

Congress was equally incapable of regulating interstate commerce, with the result that the states surrounded themselves with trade barriers, thereby hampering the free flow of commerce. Without power to regulate foreign commerce, Congress found itself incapable of competing with European rivals who discriminated against American trade. Possessing authority to coin money, Congress was prevented from doing so;

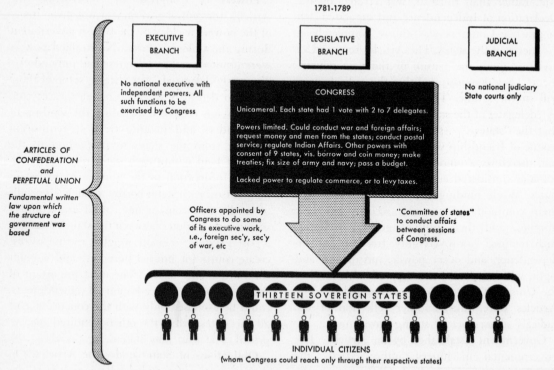

STRUCTURE OF GOVERNMENT UNDER THE ARTICLES OF CONFEDERATION
1781-1789

ARTICLES OF CONFEDERATION and PERPETUAL UNION

Fundamental written law upon which the structure of government was based

EXECUTIVE BRANCH

No national executive with independent powers. All such functions to be exercised by Congress

LEGISLATIVE BRANCH

CONGRESS

Unicameral. Each state had 1 vote with 2 to 7 delegates.

Powers limited. Could conduct war and foreign affairs; request money and men from the states; conduct postal service; regulate Indian Affairs. Other powers with consent of 9 states, vis. borrow and coin money; make treaties; fix size of army and navy; pass a budget.

Lacked power to regulate commerce, or to levy taxes.

JUDICIAL BRANCH

No national judiciary State courts only

Officers appointed by Congress to do some of its executive work, i.e., foreign sec'y, sec'y of war, etc

"Committee of states" to conduct affairs between sessions of Congress.

THIRTEEN SOVEREIGN STATES

INDIVIDUAL CITIZENS
(whom Congress could reach only through their respective states)

The government established by the Articles of Confederation was simple. The central government was weak and dependent upon the states. Adapted from Shephard L. Whitman, *Student Outline Series, Visual Outline of American Government* (Longmans, 1933). Used by permission of David McKay Company, Philadelphia.

hence a uniform system of currency was nonexistent. Meanwhile the states were flooded with paper money and currency of dubious value. Property holders and the commercial classes felt insecure because states could pass legislation impairing the obligation of contracts without external restraint.

As time went on, the states showed increasing disregard for the central government. Knowing that they were usurping powers of Congress, some of the states insisted on regulating relations with the Indians. Others sent agents abroad for the negotiation of agreements and treaties as if they were sovereign nations. Most states organized their own navy and army and some conducted war outside their jurisdiction without the consent of Congress. With lagging interest in union, and without sustained organizational support from the radicals who gave it birth, the Confederate Congress became increasingly helpless. Indeed, it was only by the determined and strenuous efforts of a few men that Congress was held together at all. Some members left in disgust.

Two amendments which would have authorized Congress to levy tariff duties on imports failed of ratification by only one state—Rhode Island on the first occasion, New York on the other. All other attempts to improve the Articles having failed, some of the states were on the verge of civil war by the end of 1786. How serious affairs were was illustrated by Shays' Rebellion (1786) during which a multitude of angry debtors attempted to prevent the collection of debts and taxes by preventing judges from holding court in several parts of Massachusetts. At one time it looked as if the state government might be overwhelmed. Although suppressed, the incident frightened the leaders and conservative elements within the population to the point that they were willing to take steps to improve the framework of government.

Achievements of the Confederation. Congress met annually in Philadelphia or other cities. Standing administrative committees were created to handle foreign, financial, military, and naval affairs, which proved to be the forerunners of our present departments of State, Treasury,

and Defense. Among other things, the Congress preserved the idea of union until our present constitution was adopted; it concluded the war with England and negotiated the peace; it established diplomatic and consular relations with foreign powers, sending, among others, such distinguished statesmen to represent the new republic abroad as Silas Deane, Benjamin Franklin, Thomas Jefferson, and John Adams; and it assisted with the formation and adoption of the present constitution. Its most brilliant achievement was the enactment of the Northwest Ordinance in 1787 by which the territory between the Alleghenies and the Mississippi, ceded to the United States by the states after the adoption of the Articles, was to be organized and governed. The colonial governments set up pursuant to the ordinance provided a model followed later in organizing territories and states west of the Mississippi as well as Alaska, Hawaii, the Philippines, Puerto Rico, and the Virgin Islands.

This review of achievements indicates that in spite of its weaknesses the Confederation had much to its credit. Indeed, some scholars who have recently studied the period contend that the picture given to us by conservatives and Federalists has overdrawn the difficulties of the time and the shortcomings of the Confederate Congress. Professor Merrill Jensen,[14] for example, contends that far from being a period of disillusionment and disintegration the period that followed the Revolution was one of "exuberant optimism" over newly found independence and the boundless opportunities that lay ahead. Instead of the general depression and distress pictured by the Federalists, Professor Jensen insists the period was one of social reform, economic progress, and cultural advancement. Trade barriers between the states, he says, "were the exception rather than the rule" and fewer than exist today.[15] National credit was "sound," national debt was "fantastically low" when compared with that of most countries today, money received by the Confederate government was

[14] *The New Nation: A History of the United States during the Confederation, 1781–1789* (Knopf, 1950).

[15] *Ibid.*, p. 340.

carefully spent, and many of the states were more successful in managing the creditor-debtor problem than has been generally believed.

Be this as it may, even the champions of confederation conceded the necessity for reform. The question was not whether the central government should or should not have greater powers but whether it should remain dependent on the states. The controversy was intense, as it is today over what powers should be given the United Nations, and we know that in the end the nationalists triumphed over the radicals who had precipitated the Revolution, dominated the state governments, and established and defended the Articles of Confederation. The movement for constitutional revision began to take tangible form in 1785.

The Conference at Alexandria. Ignoring Congress, Maryland and Virginia, who had had incessant disputes over tariffs and navigation on the Potomac and adjoining waters, agreed to confer about those problems. Both appointed commissioners who met first at Alexandria, Va., then at Washington's home at Mount Vernon, in March, 1785. The commissioners formed a plan which contemplated uniform import duties and regulation of commerce and currency in the two states. Realizing that other states might also be interested in these problems, they recommended that invitations be sent to them to meet at some future time.

The Annapolis Convention. Upon receipt of its commissioners' report, the Virginia legislature proposed that commissioners from all the states should meet at Annapolis for the purpose of considering the trade and commerce of the United States as a whole. Representatives of only five states appeared at the opening of the convention in September, 1786, but others had been appointed. When, after three weeks, the others did not appear, the delegates passed a resolution proposing that in 1787 another convention be called to meet in Philadelphia for the purpose of considering the state of the union. Congress was slow in approving the plan. Meanwhile, six states appointed delegates to the proposed Philadelphia convention. Finally, on Feb. 21, 1787, Congress recommended that the convention be held, in terms that ignored the Annapolis movement, but set the same place and date. Thereupon, all the other states, save Rhode Island, appointed delegates to attend the convention which formulated the present constitution.

FOR
FURTHER
READING

Adams, Randolph G.: *Political Ideas of the American Revolution* (New York: Facsimile Library, 1939).

Alden, John Richard: *The American Revolution, 1775–1783* (Harper, 1954).

Andrews, Charles M.: *The Colonial Background of the American Revolution* (Yale University Press, 1924).

Beard, Charles A., and Mary R. Beard: *The Rise of American Civilization* (Macmillan, rev. and enl. ed., 4 vols., 1927–1942).

Becker, Carl: *The Declaration of Independence* (Harcourt, Brace, 1922).

Bridenbaugh, Carl: *Cities in the Wilderness* (Ronald, 1938).

Burdick, Charles K.: *The Law of the American Constitution: Its Origin and Development* (Putnam, 1922).

Burnett, Edmund C.: *The Continental Congress* (Macmillan, 1941).

Channing, Edward: *Town and County Government in the English Colonies of North America* (Johns Hopkins Press, 1884).

Dickerson, Oliver M.: *American Colonial Governments* (Cleveland: Clark, 1912).

Dumbauld, Edward: *The Declaration of Independence and What It Means Today* (University of Oklahoma Press, 1950).

Jensen, Merrill: *The New Nation: A History of the United States during the Confederation, 1781–1789* (Knopf, 1950).

———: *The Articles of Confederation* (University of Wisconsin Press, 1940).

Kent, James (ed. by W. M. Lacy): *Commentaries on American Law* (Blakiston, 4 vols., 1889).

McIlwain, C. H.: *The American Revolution: A Constitutional Interpretation* (Macmillan, 1923).

Miller, John C.: *Triumph of Freedom, 1775–1783* (Little, Brown, 1948).

Montross, Lynn: *The Reluctant Rebels, The Story of the Continental Congress, 1774–1789* (Harper, 1950).

Nevins, Allan: *The American States during and after the Revolution* (Macmillan, 1924).

Osgood, Herbert L.: *The American Colonies in the 17th Century* (Columbia University Press, 1930).

——: *The American Colonies in the 18th Century* (Columbia University Press, 4 vols., 1924–1925).

Rossiter, Clinton: *Seedtime of the Republic* (Harcourt, Brace, 1952).

Saunders, Jennings B.: *Evolution of the Executive Departments of the Continental Congress, 1774–1789* (The University of North Carolina Press, 1935).

Smith, Joseph H.: *Appeals to the Privy Council from the American Plantations* (Columbia University Press, 1949).

Story, Joseph: *Commentaries on the Constitution of the United States* (Little, Brown, 4th ed., 2 vols., 1873).

Thorpe, Francis N.: *The Federal and State Constitutions, Colonial Charters, and Other Organic Laws of the States, Territories, and Colonies* . . . , H. Doc. 357, 59th Cong., 2d Sess. (7 vols., 1909).

Wissler, Clark: *Indians of the United States: Four Centuries of Their History and Culture* (Doubleday, 1940).

REVIEW QUESTIONS

1. What was the basis of Britain's title to American possessions in the New World? Can national states acquire titles today in the same manner? —

2. What rights were accorded to American Indians by colonizing powers during the early period of American history? What practical difference does it make today how American Indians were treated in earlier times?

3. Distinguish between the three types of colonies established by Britain in the New World. Why were three types established rather than one?

4. What were some of the important similarities and differences in colonial governments? In state governments established during the Revolutionary period?

5. What were the principal disputes with Britain that led to the Revolutionary War?

6. Trace the procedure by which the American Revolution was organized and consummated. How do you explain the fact that Britain found it impossible to restrain and subdue rebellion within her empire?

7. Compare the central government of the Revolutionary period with that established by the Articles of Confederation.

8. Did the Declaration of Independence create one nation or thirteen of them? What practical difference did it make whether one or thirteen nations were created?

9. What were the weaknesses and achievements under the Articles of Confederation?

10. Do you agree with Merrill Jensen's contention that the Articles of Confederation were more desirable and effective than has been generally believed?

11. Identify some of the significant features of American government which were inherited from Britain.

12. Trace the steps by which the Constitutional Convention of 1787 was called.

CHAPTER 3

Framing and Adopting the Constitution

But it is beginning to be realized that the Constitution of the United States, though possessing elements of novelty, is not, after all, the new creation that this idea would imply. It is not, properly speaking, the original composition of one body of men, nor the outcome of one definite epoch,—it is more and better than that. It does not stand in historical isolation, free from antecedents. It rests upon very old principles,—principles laboriously worked out by long ages of constitutional struggle. It looks back to the annals of the colonies and of the mother-land for its sources and explanation. And it was rendered possible, and made what it is, by the political development of many generations of men. — Charles E. Stevens [1]

With recommendations of the Annapolis Convention in hand, and with knowledge that several states had already appointed delegates, Congress adopted a resolution on Feb. 21, 1787, calling upon the states to send delegates to Philadelphia in order to meet on the second Monday in May.

. . . for the sole and express purpose of revising the Articles of Confederation and reporting to Congress and the several legislatures such alterations and provisions therein as shall when agreed to in Congress and confirmed by the states render the federal constitution adequate to the exigencies of Government & the preservation of the Union.

THE CONSTITUTIONAL CONVENTION

Delegates were promptly appointed in eleven of the states either by legislatures or by governors. New Hampshire was favorably disposed, but owing to local conditions failed to act before the convention was well under way. Rhode Island, where radicals who feared further centralization of power were in control, refused to send delegates. Credentials given the delegates authorized them to proceed to Philadelphia and there join with others in "devising, deliberating on, and discussing," to quote from credentials given the Pennsylvania delegation, "all such alterations and further Provisions, as may be necessary to render the federal Constitution fully adequate to the exigencies of the Union. . . ." [2]

Personnel of the Convention. In all, seventy-four delegates were appointed; fifty-five put in an appearance at some time or other; an average of thirty were present at the sessions; and, at the close, thirty-nine signed the completed document. Thomas Jefferson and John Adams were in Europe on diplomatic missions or they surely

[1] *Sources of the Constitution of the United States* (Macmillan, 1894), pp. viii–ix. Used by permission of the publishers.

[2] Copies of credentials furnished several delegations may be found in Charles C. Tansill (ed.), *Documents Illustrative of the Formation of the Union of the American States,* H. Doc. 398, 69th Cong., 1st Sess. (1927), pp. 55–84.

would have been appointed. Patrick Henry "smelt a rat"[3] and declined appointment. Richard Henry Lee, then attending the sessions of Congress in New York, also declined, explaining that because he was a member of Congress he ought not to participate in the convention. John Jay was asked to be a delegate but declined. Samuel Adams and John Hancock were not appointed, while Thomas Paine had gone to Europe. Otherwise, nearly all the important leaders of the country were designated to attend the convention.

The most distinguished figure was George Washington, who was still "first in the hearts of his countrymen." Others of prominence were James Madison, Edmund Randolph, and George Mason, of Virginia; Benjamin Franklin, Robert Morris, James Wilson, and Gouverneur Morris, of Pennsylvania; John Rutledge and Charles Pinckney, of South Carolina; Oliver Ellsworth, William Samuel Johnson, and John Sherman, of Connecticut; Rufus King, of Massachusetts; Alexander Hamilton, of New York; William Paterson, of New Jersey; and John Dickinson, of Delaware.

Qualifications of the Delegates. The delegates were, on the whole, young men. Franklin, the oldest, was eighty-one; Dayton (New Jersey), the youngest, was twenty-six; fourteen were fifty or over; twenty-one were less than forty. The average was forty-two.[4] Most of them came from the educated and professional classes. Twenty-five were college men and thirty-three were lawyers or had studied law.

Most outstanding of all was their wide experience in public affairs. Forty-six had served in the Colonial or state legislatures; ten had at-

tended state constitutional conventions; seven had been state governors. In national affairs, forty-two had been delegates to the Continental Congress; eight were signers of the Declaration of Independence; six were signers of the Articles of Confederation; seven had attended the Annapolis Convention; and three had been executive officers under the Continental Congress.[5]

From an economic point of view, the delegates belonged to the class described as "the rich, the well born, and the able." Charles A. Beard, after exhaustive research, has pointed out that:

1. All the delegates belonged to the professional and propertied classes—none represented in his personal economic interests the small-farming or mechanic class.

2. Most of the members came from towns on or near the coast, hence the hinterland with its small farmers, merchants, traders, and poorer classes generally was unrepresented.

3. Forty of the delegates had dealt extensively in public securities.

4. At least twenty-four delegates had engaged in lending money for interest.

5. Fourteen had invested in public lands for speculative purposes.

6. Eleven were personally interested in mercantile, manufacturing, and shipping enterprises.

7. At least fifteen were slaveholders.[6]

It is apparent, therefore, that the men who wrote the Constitution were practical men of affairs and that most of them had business and financial interests that stood to benefit by a revision of the Articles.

This is not to say that the men who wrote the Constitution were motivated solely, or even primarily, by personal and selfish considerations. Like all human beings, their thoughts were shaped by a multitude of factors. Fundamentally, it cannot be gainsaid, the Constitution reflects what in their judgment was necessary and ade-

---

[3] The "rat" apparently was a suspicion that the nationalists intended doing more than revise the Articles. More particularly, his opposition to the movement for revision was based upon a fear that Northern statesmen would carry out a project begun by John Jay whereby navigation rights on the Mississippi would be sacrificed to Spain to the detriment of the South. Moses C. Tyler, *Patrick Henry* (Houghton Mifflin, 1915), pp. 298–312.

[4] Sol Bloom (ed.), *History of the Formation of the Union under the Constitution* . . . (Government Printing Office, 1935), p. 16.

[5] *Ibid.;* Max Farrand, *The Framing of the Constitution of the United States* (Yale University Press, 1940 printing), pp. 38–39.

[6] *An Economic Interpretation of the Constitution of the United States* (Macmillan, 1939 ed.), pp. 149–151. Used by permission of The Macmillan Company, publishers.

quate to protect and promote the economic interests of the "upper" classes of which they were a part.[7]

If the document seems unduly cautious and conservative, one must remember that it provided for a more popular style of government than existed at that time in any other important country of the world. One must remember, also, that it contained provisions guaranteeing not only property rights but civil and political liberties as well. What is more significant, their handiwork has proved sufficiently flexible to permit control to pass from a small, wealthy, and conservative class to the masses without bloodshed or violence.

Estimates of the Delegates. Much praise has been heaped upon those who attended the convention and wrote the Constitution. Jefferson, writing from Paris, characterized them as "an assembly of demi-gods." A French chargé, writing to his government, said, ". . . if all the delegates named for this Philadelphia Convention are present, one will never have seen, even in Europe, an assembly more respectable for talents, knowledge, disinterestedness and patriotism than those who will compose it."[8] Charles A. Beard has written:

It was a truly remarkable assembly of men that gathered in Philadelphia on May 14, 1787, to undertake the work of reconstructing the American system of government. It is not merely patriotic pride that compels one to assert that never in the history of assemblies has there been a convention of men richer in political experience and in practical knowledge, or endowed with a profounder insight into the springs of human action and the intimate essence of government. It is indeed an astounding fact that at one time so many men skilled in statecraft could be found on the very frontiers of civilization among a population numbering about four million whites. It is no less a cause for admiration that their instrument of government should have survived the trials and crises of a century that saw the wreck of more than a score of paper constitutions.[9]

Perhaps Professor Farrand, a distinguished historian of the Constitution, is near the truth when he concludes:

Great men there were, it is true, but the convention as a whole was composed of men such as would be appointed to a similar gathering at the present time: professional men, business men and gentlemen of leisure; patriotic statesmen and clever, scheming politicians; some trained by experience and study for the task before them, and others utterly unfit. It was essentially a representative body, taking possibly a somewhat higher tone from the social conditions of the time, the seriousness of the crisis, and the character of the leaders.[10]

Organization of the Convention. The second Monday in May, 1787, fell on the fourteenth, and on that day delegates from several of the states gathered in Independence Hall in Philadelphia where Congress had sat and the Declaration of Independence had been adopted. Because representatives from a majority of states failed to appear, the delegates met daily only to adjourn, until finally, on May 25, a quorum was present.

The convention organized immediately. Their first act was to choose a president. Franklin was a logical choice because of his age and reputation and also because he was then president of the state in whose capital the convention was being held. He withdrew, however, whereupon the Pennsylvania delegation placed Washington's

---

[7] Beard concludes: "The members of the Philadelphia Convention which drafted the Constitution were, with a few exceptions, immediately, directly, and personally interested in, and derived economic advantages from, the establishment of the new system." Also, that "the Constitution was essentially an economic document based upon the concept that the fundamental private rights of property are anterior to government and morally beyond the reach of popular majorities." *Ibid.*, p. 324. Quoted by permission of The Macmillan Company, publishers. Cf. Charles Warren, *Congress, the Constitution and the Supreme Court* (Little, Brown, 1925), p. 78.

[8] Quoted in Homer C. Hockett, *The Constitutional History of the United States, 1776–1826* (Macmillan, 2 vols., 1939), vol. 1, p. 206.

[9] *The Supreme Court and the Constitution* (Macmillan, 1912), pp. 86–87. Quoted by permission of The Macmillan Company, publishers.

[10] Farrand, *op. cit.*, pp. 40–41.

name in nomination and he was promptly chosen by a unanimous vote. Major William Jackson, a former assistant secretary of war, who had actively sought the position, was chosen secretary and other minor officers were appointed. Steps were then taken to have rules formulated. Among others, those adopted provided that each state delegation should have one vote, that a majority of the states should constitute a quorum, and that the proceedings should be kept secret. To preserve secrecy, precautions were taken against "leaks." Sentries were placed at the doors to prevent eavesdropping, and according to the Beards, "they even had a discreet colleague accompany the aged Franklin to his convivial dinners with a view to checking that amiable gentleman whenever, in unguarded moments, he threatened to divulge secrets of state."[11] In spite of precautions the pledge to secrecy appears not to have been kept by all the members.[12]

Records of the Convention. Jackson's minutes consist of the formal journal of the convention, the journal of the Committee of the Whole House, and records of votes cast.[13] The minutes contain little more than a bare record of events and reveal little of what was said during the debates. Besides being meager, they were kept in an untidy manner and historians have found them frequently in error. Before the convention adjourned, the secretary was directed to leave his papers with Washington, who was instructed to keep them until further directed by Congress. Washington deposited them with the Department of State in 1796, where they remained untouched until 1818 when Congress ordered them to be printed.[14]

Fortunately for posterity, notes were kept by several of the delegates, the most complete and reliable of which were those kept by the indefatigable Madison. These were purchased by Congress after Madison's death in 1836 and published in 1840 under the title of *The Papers of James Madison.*[15] Immediately they became the most authoritative source of information about the convention. One should note that no official records of the convention were available to those who construed the Constitution for 30 years prior to 1819. One should also note that Madison's illuminating notes were unavailable for more than half a century.

The Virginia Plan. Preliminaries were over by May 29, whereupon the convention resolved itself into a committee of the whole for the purpose of hearing and giving searching consideration to various plans and proposals. The first and most important question presented to the committee was whether merely to revise the Articles or to construct a truly national government. The committee promptly decided in favor of a national government. Thereupon Governor Edmund Randolph of Virginia presented a plan prepared under the leadership of Madison. The Virginia plan, as it was called, represented the large-state group and those favoring a strong central government and contemplated a complete overhauling of the Articles. Details of this and other plans presented are suggested and compared in the chart on the following page.

Presented on May 29, the Virginia plan was discussed for 2 weeks during which time serious objections were raised. Critics contended that it contemplated too great a departure from the Articles and placed the small states in a position of inequality. Had the plan been adopted as proposed, Virginia, for example, would have had fifteen or sixteen representatives in Congress while Georgia, Delaware, or Rhode Island would each have had only two or three. Besides giving

[11] Charles A. Beard and Mary R. Beard, *The Rise of American Civilization* (Macmillan, 4 vols., 1927–1942), vol. I, p. 312. Quoted by permission of The Macmillan Company, publishers.

[12] Max Farrand (ed.), *The Records of the Federal Convention of 1787* (Yale University Press, 3 vols., 1911), vol. I, p. 15.

[13] The originals of most of these may be found at present in the National Archives, Washington, D.C.

[14] They may be consulted in many libraries under the title of *Journal, Acts and Proceedings of the Con-*

vention, . . . which formed the Constitution of the United States (Boston: T. B. Wait, 1819).

[15] The most pertinent documents, including Madison's notes, may be found in *Documents Illustrative of the Formation of the Union of the American States,* previously cited.

Plans before the Constitutional Convention *

Randolph, Virginia	Paterson, New Jersey	Pinckney, South Carolina	Hamilton, New York
Legislative			
Bicameral One house popularly elected; second chosen by first, from nominees of state legislatures	Unicameral Delegates to be chosen by state legislatures	Bicameral House of Delegates elected by people on basis of population (Negroes counting three-fifths); Senate elected by House of Delegates from four districts	Bicameral Assembly elected by people on basis of population; terms, 3 years; Senate elected for life terms by electors chosen by people
Voting based on money contributions or free population or both	Each state one vote	Each delegate and senator to have one vote	Congress to have power to pass all laws deemed necessary to common defense and general welfare of Union; Senate alone to declare war, approve treaties and appointments
Powers of Congress broad	Powers of Congress enlarged; states to collect taxes but Congress to act if states default	Powers of Congress broad	
Executive			
Single executive chosen by Congress for one term only	Plural executive chosen by Congress for one term only	President elected by Congress annually	President elected for life term by electors chosen by people within each state
Authority to execute laws and exercise executive rights vested in Confederate Congress	Authority to execute laws, appoint, direct military operations		Powers included: veto, execution of laws, war, treaties, appointments, pardons
Judicial			
Supreme and inferior courts; judges appointed by Congress for life; Council of Revision to exercise a suspensive veto over acts of the national and state legislatures	Supreme court only; judges appointed by plural executive for life	A federal court; admiralty courts might be established by Congress in each state; judges appointed for life	Supreme court appointed by President with consent of Senate for life terms; legislature given power to institute courts in each state
Federal-State Relations			
Federal government to admit new states and guarantee republican form of government; Federal government to negative state laws incompatible with the Union; also to use force against any state failing to fulfill its duty	Acts of Congress and treaties "Supreme law of the respective states"; conflicting state laws forbidden; Federal executive to use force against noncooperative states	Federal government to admit new states; states prohibited from keeping troops of war, entering into compacts, etc.; state laws to be approved by federal legislature before becoming effective	State laws contrary to Constitution are void; governors of states appointed by federal government and have veto over state legislation; a special court provided to hear controversies arising between United States and particular states over territories

* For texts of these plans, see Max Farrand (ed.), *The Records of the Federal Convention of 1787* (Yale University Press, 3 vols., 1911), vol. III, pp. 593–631.

the large states complete control over the legislature, adoption of the plan would have granted them full jurisdiction over the executive and judicial branches as well.

The New Jersey and Other Plans. Objections such as these led to counterproposals. Chief of these were the New Jersey, Pinckney, and Hamilton plans. Of these, the New Jersey plan, presented on June 15 by William Paterson, received most consideration. It contemplated a less radical departure from the Articles than the Virginia plan and won the support of confederationists and small-state delegations. After 4 days of debate the committee of the whole voted 7 to 3 to reject it in favor of something more akin to the proposals made by Governor Randolph of Virginia.

The Critical Period. After endorsing the Virginia plan, the convention reconstituted itself (on June 18) to hear and consider the report of the committee of the whole. The next 5 weeks (until July 26) was the crucial period. On several occasions the convention appeared ready to go on the rocks. Martin of Maryland reported, on June 28, that it was on the verge of dissolution, "scarce held together by the strength of a hair," and Franklin proposed that the convention henceforth open its sessions with prayers. To this suggestion Hamilton and others thought that to start at that late date would bring on "some disagreeable animadversions" and lead the public to believe that the convention was split with dissension. Another delegate observed that the true cause was that the convention had no funds with which to hire a preacher. Whatever the reason, the suggestion was not followed, but the delegates nevertheless found ways of compromising their differences.

The Connecticut Compromise. The Constitution has been referred to as a "bundle of compromises." This is true, although some of the compromises were of more importance than others. The crucial question was: How could a government strong enough to meet the exigencies of the hour be erected which would not "swallow up" the states nor place the small ones at the mercy of the larger?

The nationalists argued that since state sovereignty had been the fundamental weakness of the Articles, a new government to be strong must derive its authority directly from the people. Accordingly, they pleaded for representation proportionate in both houses to population or tax contribution or both. Small-state delegates, on the other hand, made it clear that they would never enter a union in which their identity and equality would be impaired. Said John Dickinson of Delaware, "We would sooner submit to a foreign power, than to submit to be deprived of an equality of suffrage, in both branches of the legislature, and thereby thrown under the dominion of the larger states." [16] The solution of this impasse was an absolute prerequisite to further progress.

Day after day the issue was debated until finally, as hope ebbed, Dr. Johnson of Connecticut renewed a suggestion previously made which led to a solution. Said he:

> The controversy must be endless whilst Gentlemen differ in the grounds of their arguments; Those on one side considering the States as districts of people composing one political Society; those on the other considering them as so many political societies. . . . On the whole . . . in some respects the States are to be considered in their political capacity, and in others as districts of individual citizens, the two ideas embraced on different sides, instead of being opposed to each other, ought to be combined; that in *one* branch the *people*, ought to be represented; in the *other*, the *States*.[17]

Several days later a committee of eleven, one from each state represented, was appointed to effect a compromise along the lines suggested by Dr. Johnson. They reported on July 5, and after 10 days more of bitter debate (on July 16) the convention agreed to representation in proportion to population in the House of Representatives and equal representation of the states in the Senate with the proviso that all revenue bills must originate in the most popular house. Before giving full assent, however, the small-

[16] Farrand, *The Records of the Federal Convention of 1787*, vol. I, p. 242.

[17] *Ibid.*, vol. I, pp. 461–462. This was Madison's rendition of Dr. Johnson's remarks.

state delegations insisted on receiving some guaranty that once the new government was established, their equality in the Senate would not be changed. Accordingly, a provision was inserted in the amendment article (Article V) stating that no amendment might ever be made to the Constitution which deprived any state of equal representation in the Senate without its consent. This became the only unamendable provision of the Constitution.

The Three-fifths Compromise. No less fundamental than the dispute between large and small states was one involving the economic interests of the sections. Underlying debate was a deep-seated conflict between the planting interests of the South, founded on slave labor, and the commercial and industrial interests of the North. Having leaped the hurdle of representation, the question arose of whether slaves should be counted in determining the number of representatives each state should have and for apportioning direct taxes.

There were six slave states, which for obvious reasons wanted the slaves counted for representation but not for determining their share of direct taxes. Northern delegates contended that it was unfair to include them for representation inasmuch as slaves were not in law and fact equal with freemen. Moreover, to count them equally would make it possible for Southern states to increase their representation by the mere expedient of importing more slaves. Naturally, Northern delegates wanted slaves counted when allocating quotas for direct taxes. In the end, Southern delegates agreed to a provision whereby three-fifths of all slaves would be counted in apportioning representatives provided they would be counted similarly when apportioning direct taxes.[18]

Commerce and Slave-trade Compromise. Sectionalism showed itself on still another question

of importance. Delegates from New England and the middle states where manufacturing, trade, and shipping interests were dominant came to the convention determined to see that the central government was given adequate powers to regulate interstate and foreign commerce. The planters of the South, however, were afraid that a government with those powers would prohibit the importation of slaves and enter into commercial agreements with foreign states which would adversely affect their interests.

Ultimately, Congress was given plenary power "to regulate commerce with foreign nations and among the several states," and the President was empowered to negotiate treaties. The South was placated by two provisions: one declaring that the slave trade could not be prohibited for 20 years; the other requiring that treaties receive the approval of two-thirds of the Senate before becoming effective. Although not a part of the compromise, insertion of the provision forbidding the taxation of exports helped to allay the fears of Southern delegates.

Concluding Sessions. By July 26, the larger issues had been agreed upon and the substance of the future Constitution formulated into twenty-six resolutions. On the date mentioned, these were referred to a Committee of Detail consisting of five men. After the appointment of this committee the convention recessed until Aug. 6, when it reassembled to receive the committee's report. For the next 5 weeks the convention labored for 5 or 6 hours daily, discussing article by article, section by section.

Finally, on Sept. 8, a Committee on Style was appointed to "revise the style of and arrange the articles which had been agreed to by the house." The committee arranged the document in its

---

[18] The Fourteenth Amendment, adopted after the Civil War (1868), modified this compromise provision by requiring that all persons, Negroes as well as white, should be counted when determining the number of representatives to which each state was entitled. While the Fourteenth Amendment said nothing about changing the basis for apportioning direct taxes, the three-

fifths ratio was rendered meaningless by the Thirteenth Amendment which abolished slavery.

There is reason to suspect that this compromise proved more advantageous to the North than to the South inasmuch as Southern states had their representation diminished by the provision for a period extending from 1789 to 1860, whereas direct taxes were levied only four times prior to the Civil War and on each occasion they remained in effect for only a short time.

present form (excepting the amendments) and on Sept. 13 reported its handiwork written in the handwriting of its chairman, Gouverneur Morris. The Constitution was formally adopted on the fifteenth and 2 days later the signatures of thirty-nine of the delegates present—all but Gerry, Mason, and Randolph [19]—were attached whereupon the convention adjourned.

Sources of the Constitution. For a long time there was a tendency in the United States to regard the Constitution as a new invention in political science. This impression was conveyed by the famous remark of the great English statesman William Gladstone when he observed that "as the British Constitution is the most subtle organism which has proceeded from progressive history, so the American Constitution is the most wonderful work ever struck off at a given time by the brain and purpose of man." Instead of having been "struck off at a given time," it had its roots deep in the past and, while containing some novel features, it is the embodiment of many antecedents.

In fact, there was little in the Constitution that was new. The men who wrote the document were familiar with the governments of antiquity, the English constitution, and the governments of western Europe. They were also familiar with the political writings of the period, the most outstanding of which were Blackstone's *Commentaries on the Laws of England,* John Locke's *Two Treatises on Government,* Montesquieu's *Spirit of Laws,* and Rousseau's *Social Contract.* The best read among them also knew the seventeenth-century works—Thomas Hobbes's *Leviathan* and James Harrington's *The Commonwealth of Oceana*—that influenced both colonial institutions and the ideas of later writers. Moreover, they were saturated with the revolutionary literature that some of their contemporaries, including some of those in attendance at the convention, helped to write and disseminate.

Of more immediate importance, however, were the records and experiences of the Continental Congress, the Articles of Confederation, the state constitutions adopted after 1775, and the colonial charters and governments. Indeed, words and phrases can be found in American colonial and revolutionary documents that are identical with or similar to virtually every provision of the Constitution. This is evident when a comparison is made of phrases from the Articles of Confederation and the constitution of Massachusetts with those from the Constitution, as shown on the following page.[20]

The Constitution was not, therefore, "solely the product" of the "creative wisdom" of the Founding Fathers. Rather, it is more accurate to say the Constitution was a digest of the most approved principles and provisions of the charters of government with which the authors of the Constitution were intimately acquainted.

THE CAMPAIGN FOR RATIFICATION

Overcoming of Weaknesses of Articles. Since the sole purpose for which the convention was called was for revising and improving the Articles, and the Constitution begins by referring to a "more perfect union," one might inquire as to how weaknesses of the Articles were overcome. The weaknesses and changes are made clearer by setting them forth in parallel columns as shown on page 39.

Ratification Procedure. The convention had been called to consider and suggest amendments to the Articles. Had the Articles been followed, it would have been necessary for Congress to consider and approve all the changes contained in the new Constitution and then refer them to the states to be approved by the legislature of *every* state before going into effect. Rather than follow this procedure the convention recommended one that was without legal sanction. It placed in the body of the Constitution itself (Article VII) a provision declaring that ratifications by conventions of the people of nine states should be sufficient for the establishment of the Constitution.

The document was then sent to the Confederate Congress with the advice that the Congress should approve it, then refer it to the state leg-

---

[19] These men were in agreement with most of the Constitution but believed provision should have been made for a second convention to discuss criticisms and suggestions made during the process of ratification.

[20] Cf. Warren, *op. cit.,* pp. 31–32.

Articles	*Constitution*
Congress shall have the power of "making rules for the government and regulation of the said land and naval forces. . . ."	Congress shall have power "to make rules for the government and regulation of the land and naval forces."
Congress shall have the power of "fixing the standard of weights and measures throughout the United States."	Congress shall have power to "fix the standard of weights and measures."
"Nor shall any person holding any office of profit or trust under the United States, or any of them, accept of any present, emolument, office or title of any kind whatsoever from any king, prince, or foreign state; nor shall the United States in Congress assembled, or any of them, grant any title of nobility."	"No title of nobility shall be granted by the United States; and no person holding any office of profit or trust under them shall, without the consent of the Congress, accept of any present, emolument, office, or title, of any kind whatever, from any king, prince, or foreign state."

Massachusetts	*Constitution*
"We . . . the people of Massachusetts . . . do . . . ordain and establish the following . . . as the Constitution of the Commonwealth of Massachusetts."	"We, the people of the United States . . . do ordain and establish this Constitution for the United States of America."
"Judgment shall not extend further than to removal from office and disqualification to hold or enjoy any place of honor, trust, or profit under this Commonwealth; but the party so convicted shall be, nevertheless, liable to indictment, trial, judgment and punishment, according to the laws of the land."	"Judgment . . . shall not extend further than to removal from office and disqualification to hold and enjoy any office of honor, trust or profit under the United States; but the party convicted shall, nevertheless, be liable and subject to indictment, trial, judgment and punishment according to law."
"All money bills shall originate in the House of Representatives; but the Senate may propose or concur with amendments as on other bills." [21]	"All bills for raising revenue shall originate in the House of Representatives; but the Senate may propose or concur with amendments as on other bills."

---

islatures which, in turn, should pass it along to conventions of the people in each state. It was also suggested that when nine conventions had approved, Congress should take steps to put the new government into operation and then go out of existence. Of this action on the part of the convention Professor Burgess wrote:

What they [the convention] actually did, stripped of all fiction and verbiage, was to assume constituent powers, ordain a Constitution of government and of liberty, and demand the *plébiscite*

thereon, over the heads of all existing legally organized powers. Had Julius or Napoleon committed these acts, they would have been pronounced *coups d'état.* Looked at from the side of the people exercising the *plébiscite,* we term the movement revolution.[22]

Several considerations prompted this presumptuousness on the part of the convention. The nationalists had triumphed at the convention and they wanted to eliminate as many obstacles to acceptance as possible. Their greatest

[21] The constitutions of seven other states contained the same statement. *Ibid.*

[22] John W. Burgess, *Political Science and Comparative Constitutional Law* (Ginn, 2 vols., 1902), vol. I, p. 105.

Weaknesses of the Articles	*How Overcome by Constitution*
1. States were sovereign.	1. People of the whole nation were made sovereign. A federal union was created from which secession was impossible and the Federal Constitution and laws were made the supreme law of the land.
2. No independent executive.	2. Article II provides for President chosen indirectly by the voters. President is given "the executive power"; he is made Commander in Chief of the Army and Navy, and he may take all steps necessary to see that laws are faithfully executed.
3. No federal courts. Federal laws enforced by state courts.	3. Separate system of federal courts provided by Article III with authority to enforce federal laws and annul state laws inconsistent with Federal Constitution or laws.
4. No power to collect taxes.	4. Article I, Section VIII, empowers Congress to "*lay* and *collect* taxes, duties, imposts and excises."
5. No power over interstate and foreign commerce.	5. Article I, Section VIII, gives Congress power to regulate commerce with foreign nations, among the several states and with Indian tribes.
6. Congress an assembly of *delegates* chosen by state legislatures who were expected to vote as instructed and could be recalled.	6. Congress composed of *representatives* who have definite tenure and can act in any manner they choose. House of Representatives chosen by direct vote of people, Senate by state legislatures (now direct popular vote).
7. Articles could be amended only by consent of all the states.	7. Can be amended with approval of three-fourths of states.
8. Congress had only specifically delegated powers.	8. Congress given implied powers as well as delegated.
9. Central government could not act directly upon people.	9. Central government exercises its powers directly upon the people and concurrently with state governments.

fear was that one or two state delegations in the discredited Congress would stymie action there or that one or two state legislatures would obstruct ratification. That this was a real danger is evident when it is recalled that Rhode Island had not been represented at the convention, most of the New York delegation had left the convention partly as a protest against its proceedings, and a number of delegates had spoken not only in opposition to the establishment of the Constitution but also to the proposed method of ratification.

Accordingly, the only chance of success was to hope that Congress would obediently refer the new Constitution to the states and that at least nine of them would provide for conventions. Besides improving the possibility of adoption, reference to conventions elected by the voters especially for the purpose of considering the Constitution would give greater validity to the words "We the people . . . do ordain and establish this Constitution." It would also serve to emphasize the outstanding difference between the Constitution and the Articles, *viz.,* that this was a union of the people and not of the states. The gravity of the emergency, they believed, justified circumvention of the Articles.

Federalists and Antifederalists. The contest over adoption of the Constitution reflected the long-standing differences between the conservatives and the radicals. The former, now called Federalists, had long favored strong central government and therefore supported ratification. The radicals, now called Antifederalists, still feared strong central government and the rise of aristocracy and therefore opposed ratification. The contest was intense and bitter. For the most part, the campaign for ratification was led by those who had attended the convention. Popular support came largely from the more populous sections along the seaboard and from groups interested in finance, manufacturing, trade, and shipping. The Federalists had talent, wealth, and professional abilities on their side and they spent freely to educate the public and influence convention delegates.[23]

Conspicuous among the leaders of the Antifederalists were some of the "Old Patriots" of the Revolution including Patrick Henry, Richard Henry Lee, Samuel Adams, George Mason, and Elbridge Gerry. Their followers were chiefly back-country pioneers and small farmers who distrusted the "upper" classes and had few resources with which to support a campaign. Generally speaking, Dr. Beard writes, they "could

[23] Beard, *An Economic Interpretation of the Constitution of the United States,* pp. 251–252.

[24] Beard, *The Supreme Court and the Constitution,* p. 102.

do nothing but gnash their teeth." [24] They were further weakened by property-holding and tax-paying qualifications for voting. Moreover, they labored under the difficulty of getting country voters out in late fall and winter to vote in town or county elections.

Criticisms of the Proposed Constitution. The Federalists dwelt upon the weaknesses of the Articles and labored to convince the people that the choice before them was the proposed Constitution or anarchy, chaos, and possibly civil war. Meanwhile, complaints were heard concerning almost every provision of the proposed document. The pious complained that the Constitution nowhere recognized the existence of God. Many who otherwise favored a stronger government strenuously objected to the fact that they were being asked to accept or reject the document with no opportunity of amending it prior to taking final action. Others opposed because the convention had exceeded its instructions and recommended adoption contrary to the method required by the Articles. Many contended that the President would become a monarch since he would serve for an indefinite number of terms.

Patriots like Patrick Henry, Richard Henry Lee, and others, noting that the document contained no bill of rights, dwelt upon dangers to liberty. The courts, it was feared, would usurp the powers and functions of state judiciaries. Paper money advocates feared the central government would upset the gains they had made through their state governments. Southerners were afraid the commercial interests of the North might dominate the Congress and use the treaty, tax, and commerce powers in a manner detrimental to their sectional interests. Northerners made a moral issue out of concessions made to the slave trade; while residents of larger states argued that too much had been conceded the small states. In general, the most persistent theme was that the states would be destroyed and the central government would become a tyrannical overlord. To offset these objections the Federalists yielded to the extent of promising the addition of a bill of rights as soon as the new government was organized. Without this concession the Constitution might never have been adopted.[25]

Ratification Completed. Immediately upon the adjournment of the convention on Sept. 15, the document was sent to Congress, which was then meeting in New York City. There it was received without enthusiasm. After all, it was expecting a great deal to ask Congress "to light its own funeral pyre," as Bancroft has said. Nevertheless, Congress obediently (on Sept. 28, 1787) adopted a resolution transmitting it to the state legislatures to be submitted by them to state conventions. One state after another then enacted legislation authorizing the election of delegates to attend the conventions.

Voters in most of the states went to the polls to choose delegates during the fall and winter of 1787–1788. The number of delegates attending the state conventions varied from about 30 in Delaware to about 355 in Massachusetts. Delaware, one of the small states that had been appeased by the Connecticut Compromise, was the first to ratify. Others ratified in the following order and by the division of votes mentioned:

1. Delaware, Dec. 7, 1787; unanimous.
2. Pennsylvania, Dec. 12, 1787; 46–23.
3. New Jersey, Dec. 19, 1787; unanimous.
4. Georgia, Jan. 2, 1788; unanimous.
5. Connecticut, Jan. 9, 1788; 128–40.
6. Massachusetts, Feb. 6, 1788; 187–168.
7. Maryland, Apr. 28, 1788; 63–11.
8. South Carolina, May 23, 1788; 149–73.
9. New Hampshire, June 21, 1788; 57–46.
10. Virginia, June 25, 1788; 89–79.
11. New York, July 26, 1788; 30–27.
12. North Carolina, Nov. 21, 1789; 184–77.
13. Rhode Island, May 29, 1790; 34–32.

The Campaign in Virginia and New York. Note that nine states, sufficient to make the Constitution effective, had ratified by the middle of June, 1788, but two of the largest states, Virginia and New York, were not among them. Everyone recognized the necessity of their adherence if the new union were to be successful; hence all eyes were upon the conventions in those states.

Virginia. The debate in the Virginia convention was one of the most celebrated in our history. Patrick Henry led the opposition, exclaiming and expostulating "in a turbulent stream of rhetoric." [26] He was supported in the convention by such celebrities as George Mason, William Grayson, and James Monroe; while outside, Richard Henry Lee worked sedulously against adoption. It was no easy task to engage such a brilliant orator as Patrick Henry in forensic combat, but Madison did so and once more distinguished himself. Of him during this contest Professor McLaughlin has written:

Madison was the active leader of the Federalist forces, and he led them well; his temper was never ruffled nor his reason clouded. A careful study of Henry's brilliant oratory leaves one in wonder that day after day his fervid exclamations were answered with imperturbable calmness and placid good sense. Madison had none of the graces of oratory; he was small and unimpressive; his manner seemed at times to betoken irresolution; when he rose to speak, his voice was low, and he stood hat in hand as if he had just come in to give a passing word of counsel. But he knew what he was talking about, he was prepared to speak, and he did not envelop his thought in ornamental rhetorical wrappings.[27]

Madison was ably supported by John Marshall, then a young man of thirty-two, and Edmund Randolph. Although the latter was one of the three who had refused to sign the Constitution, he had since been won over to the Federalist cause. Washington was not a delegate, but his influence was great. The Federalists prevailed by a majority of ten votes but not without promising the addition of a bill of rights.

---

[25] For further discussion of the Bill of Rights see Chap. 7. The most important source dealing with discussion of the proposed constitution is Jonathan Elliot, *Debates in the Several State Conventions on the Adoption of the Federal Constitution* (Washington, D.C.: printed by the editor, 2d ed., 5 vols., 1836–1845).

[26] Andrew C. McLaughlin, *The Confederation and the Constitution, 1783–1789* (Harper, 1905), p. 300.
[27] *Ibid.*

New York. Likewise, in New York the campaign was intense and bitter and the outcome doubtful. When the Constitution was published the opposition was at first overwhelming. To overcome this opposition Alexander Hamilton induced James Madison and John Jay to unite with him in publishing a series of anonymous

CALENDAR OF PRINCIPAL DATES LEADING UP TO THE MORE PERFECT UNION

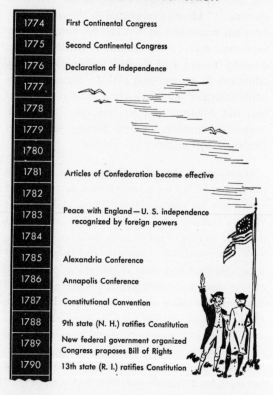

1774	First Continental Congress
1775	Second Continental Congress
1776	Declaration of Independence
1777	
1778	
1779	
1780	
1781	Articles of Confederation become effective
1782	
1783	Peace with England — U. S. independence recognized by foreign powers
1784	
1785	Alexandria Conference
1786	Annapolis Conference
1787	Constitutional Convention
1788	9th state (N. H.) ratifies Constitution
1789	New federal government organized Congress proposes Bill of Rights
1790	13th state (R. I.) ratifies Constitution

essays defending the new instrument and urging the necessity of its adoption. Gouverneur Morris was asked to join, but declined.

During the winter of 1787-1788—before the convention met in Albany—seventy-seven essays appeared in the New York press entitled "The Federalist" and signed first "a Citizen of New York," then "Publius." These, together with eight others (making a total of eighty-five), were later published in book form under the same title.[28] These essays did much to win support for the Constitution in New York and have since been considered the ablest exposition of the principles underlying the Constitution as

well as one of the world's greatest treatises on government. After 5 weeks of acrimonious debate, the New York Convention ratified the Constitution by the narrow margin of three votes, and then only upon condition that a bill of rights be added at the earliest possible moment.

Popular Participation in Adoption of the Constitution. The Constitution begins by saying "We, the people . . . do ordain and establish this Constitution . . ." and much has been said about popular sovereignty. While this is undoubtedly true in a juristic or legal sense, it is nevertheless an exaggeration of what actually occurred. Actually, comparatively few people participated directly in the adoption of the Constitution. The suggestion of calling a constitutional convention was not submitted to popular vote. Delegates to the Philadelphia Convention were not elected by the voters but, rather, appointed by the legislatures and governors. Finally, the Constitution was not submitted to the voters for popular approval. The only point at which the voters were allowed to participate directly was in choosing delegates to attend the state conventions which ratified the Constitution.

Even so, only a few people—estimated at 160,-000—participated in the choice of delegates. Of these probably not more than 100,000 favored adoption. Indeed, some historians are inclined to believe that the Constitution would have failed of adoption had it been submitted to popular referendum.[29]

THE "MORE PERFECT" UNION

Organization of National Government. The addition of Virginia and New York brought eleven states under the "new roof," whereupon the old Congress took steps looking toward the establishment of the new government. The informal organization of the old Congress was maintained until May 2, 1789, but for lack of a

[28] *The Federalist* has appeared in more than thirty editions. The best for present use are those by Henry C. Lodge (Putnam, 1888) and Paul L. Ford (Holt, 1898). A popular inexpensive edition was published by Random House, Inc., in the Modern Library Series, 1937.

[29] Beard, *An Economic Interpretation of the Constitution of the United States,* pp. 249–252.

quorum it transacted no official business after the preceding October. On Sept. 13, 1788, Congress chose New York as the capital city and designated the first Wednesday in January as the day for the choice of presidential electors by the states, the first Wednesday in February as the day upon which electors would meet in their respective states and vote for President, and the first Wednesday in March for the inauguration of the new government.

Electors were chosen and met accordingly; twenty-two senators and fifty-nine representatives were duly elected, and the first Congress assembled on Mar. 4, 1789, in Federal Hall on Wall Street. Because a quorum was lacking, no business was transacted until Apr. 6. Then the electoral votes were counted by the president of the Senate before a joint session of Congress. George Washington was found to have been elected President by unanimous vote and John Adams Vice-President by a substantial majority. After a historic trip from his home at Mount Vernon to the new capital, Washington was inaugurated on Apr. 30.

Immediately the new Congress proceeded to the task of creating and defining the powers, duties, and jurisdiction of the administrative and judicial branches of government, while the new president concerned himself with the selection of persons to fill the numerous offices. The promised bill of rights was proposed on Sept. 25, 1789. North Carolina ratified the Constitution in November, and Rhode Island did likewise in the following May after Congress had threatened to deprive her of the privilege of trading with the Union and secession had been threatened by several counties in which Federalist sentiment was strong.

FOR FURTHER READING

Beard, Charles A.: *An Economic Interpretation of the Constitution of the United States* (Macmillan, 1913).

——: *The Supreme Court and the Constitution* (Macmillan, 1912).

Brant, Irving: *James Madison, the Nationalist, 1780–1787* (Bobbs-Merrill, 1948).

Bryce, James: *The American Commonwealth* (Macmillan, new ed., compl. rev., 2 vols., 1922–1923).

Burgess, John W.: *Political Science and Comparative Constitutional Law* (Ginn, 2 vols., 1902).

Butzner, Jane: *Constitutional Chaff: Rejected Suggestions of the Constitutional Convention of 1787* (Columbia University Press, 1941).

Elliot, Jonathan (ed.): *Debates in the Several State Conventions on the Adoption of the Federal Constitution* (Washington, D.C.: printed by the editor, 2d ed., 5 vols., 1836–1845).

Farrand, Max: *The Framing of the Constitution of the United States* (Yale University Press, 1940 printing).

—— (ed.): *The Records of the Federal Convention of 1787* (Yale University Press, 3 vols., 1911).

Hamilton, Alexander, *et al.* (ed. by Paul L. Ford): *The Federalist* (Holt, 1898).

Harding, Samuel B.: *The Contest over the Ratification of the Federal Constitution in the State of Massachusetts* (Longmans 1896).

Holcombe, Arthur N.: *Our More Perfect Union* (Harvard University Press, 1950).

Long, Breckinridge: *Genesis of the Constitution of the United States of America* (Macmillan, 1926).

McLaughlin, Andrew C.: *The Confederation and the Constitution, 1783–1789* (Harper, 1905).

Miner, Clarence E.: *The Ratification of the Constitution by the State of New York* (Columbia University Press, 1921).

Padover, Saul K.: *The Living U.S. Constitution* (Frederick A. Praeger, 1953).

Prescott, Arthur T. (comp.): *Drafting the Federal Constitution* (Louisiana State University Press, 1941).

Rodick, Burleigh Cushing: *American Constitutional Custom: A Forgotten Factor in the Founding* (Philosophical Library, 1953).

Schuyler, Robert L.: *The Constitution of the United States: An Historical Survey of Its Formation* (Macmillan, 1923).

Stevens, Charles E.: *Sources of the Constitution of the United States* (Macmillan, 1894).

Stone, Frederick D., and John B. McMaster: *Pennsylvania and the Federal Constitution, 1787–1788* (Lancaster: Inquirer Printing and Publishing Co., for Historical Society of Pennsylvania, 1888).

Story, Joseph: *Commentaries on the Constitution of the United States* (Little, Brown, 4th ed., 2 vols., 1873).

Tansill, Charles C. (ed.): *Documents Illustrative of the Formation of the Union of the American States,* H. Doc. 398, 69th Cong., 1st Sess. (1927).

Umbreit, Kenneth B.: *Founding Fathers: Men Who Shaped Our Tradition* (Harper, 1941).

Van Doren, Carl: *The Great Rehearsal: The Story of the Making and Ratifying of the Constitution of the United States* (Viking, 1948).

White, Leonard D.: *The Jeffersonians* (Macmillan, 1951).

——: *The Federalists* (Macmillan, 1948).

**REVIEW
QUESTIONS**

1. Trace the steps by which the Constitution was drafted and ratified.

2. Characterize the delegates who attended the Constitutional Convention. What influence did these characteristics have upon convention proceedings and the Constitution?

3. What features of the Virginia plan were adopted by the Constitutional Convention? The New Jersey plan? Other plans?

4. What conflicts of interest manifested themselves at the Constitutional Convention? How were these reconciled? Who got the better of the compromises?

5. Upon what important sources of theory and experience did those who wrote the Constitution draw?

6. In what ways was the Constitution "more perfect" than the Articles of Confederation?

7. What were the basic differences of opinion and interest between those who favored the Constitution and those who opposed it?

8. Comment upon the role played by each of the following in framing and adopting the Constitution: *The Federalist Papers,* George Washington, James Madison, Gouverneur Morris, Benjamin Franklin, Samuel Adams, Patrick Henry, Thomas Jefferson, Alexander Hamilton.

9. How do you explain the fact that only a comparatively small number of people participated in the process of framing and adopting the Constitution?

10. Trace the steps by which the new national government was put into operation.

CHAPTER 4

Constitutional Principles and Methods of Change

Some men look at constitutions with sanctimonious reverence and deem them like the ark of the covenant, too sacred to be touched. . . . But the laws and institutions must go hand in hand with the progress of the human mind. . . . We might as well require a man to wear still the coat which fitted him when a boy as civilized society to remain ever under the regimen of their barbarous ancestors. . . . Each generation . . . has a right to choose for itself the form of government it believes most promotive of its own happiness. — Thomas Jefferson [1]

The Constitution was not a revolutionary document but was designed to establish what was regarded then as a strong central government. The document itself is brief and contains little detail as compared with state constitutions. Its provisions are built around several fundamental principles deemed of crucial importance to those responsible for its drafting and adoption. Although the principles remain, the Constitution has been by no means static. This chapter reviews fundamental features and methods by which the Constitution has been adapted to changing conditions.

PRINCIPLES

Popular Sovereignty. Sovereignty, or the authority and power to command and coerce all others, resides somewhere in every fully developed national state. During the Colonial period, the King and Parliament of England were sovereign; during the Revolution, Britain's sovereignty was suspended, the colonists claiming that

they themselves were supreme; under the Articles of Confederation, ultimate authority was reposed in each of the thirteen states. But adoption of the Constitution transferred sovereignty to the people of the country. The preamble declares that "We the People of the United States . . . do ordain and establish this Constitution for the United States of America," and the presumption of popular sovereignty runs throughout the document. Accordingly, when a sufficient number of qualified voters act in unison, there is no legal limit to their power. They reign in the American political world, said De Tocqueville, "as the Deity does in the Universe."

Sovereignty in the People of the Whole Nation. Although the principle itself is clear enough, several controversies have arisen over its application. The first and most troublesome arose between the advocates of States' rights and the nationalists. Admitting that the people were sovereign, the advocates of States' rights, of whom John C. Calhoun was the foremost and most capable spokesman, insisted that it was the people in each state who had ultimate legal authority. This meant, for example, that if the

[1] Quoted in Saul K. Padover, *Thomas Jefferson on Democracy* (New York: The New American Library of World Literature, Inc., 2d printing, 1949), p. 67.

people of a particular state wished to withdraw from the Union, they had the legal right to do so. The nationalists, on the other hand, claimed that it was the people of the whole nation irrespective of state lines who were sovereign. If this theory prevailed, the people of a particular state did not have final authority over their affairs; but, rather, their will was but a small segment of the whole and as such was subject to control by all the people of the nation. The Civil War settled the argument in favor of the na-

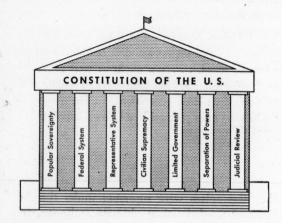

tionalists. In consequence, sovereignty rests in the people of the several states, taken collectively.

Sovereignty in Only Some of the People. Another controversy revolves around the nature of the franchise. The people are sovereign, yes. But which people, and how many of them? The courts have held that the word "people" as used in the preamble is synonymous with "citizens";[2] hence, aliens and nationals do not share sovereignty. But how many citizens exercise the rights of sovereignty? In practice, only those who vote or, at most, all those who are eligible to vote. But suppose that only a few are eligible to vote, as was the case during the formative years of the nation. Is the minority that holds political power obliged to extend the suffrage to the masses? The answer to this question is that at any given time sovereignty legally resides in

that body of qualified voters who are competent to participate in amending the Constitution; voting is a privilege to be extended at the discretion of those who presently exercise power; the unenfranchised have no legal right to vote. Thus, youths under twenty-one, Negroes before the Civil War, women before they were enfranchised, and millions of others who fail to qualify for voting are not among the "people" in whom sovereignty resides.[3]

Popular Sovereignty and the Right to Revolt. A third controversy, which is still heard, revolves around the question of whether the people have a legal right to revolt. Logically, if the voters are sovereign, it would seem that they can do anything they please whether by peaceful means or otherwise. Being reasonable and peace-loving people, they will normally use existing political machinery to express their will. But suppose only a few possess the franchise and will not enact legislation to enfranchise the masses. Or suppose that the administration in power acts dictatorially, suppressing liberties, and otherwise ignoring the Constitution. What then? Have the people, or groups of them, the right to revolt?

Opinion is sharply divided on this thorny question. During the early years of the republic, the right of revolution was stanchly defended, doubtless in justification of the revolt from England, but also because it accorded with the democratic theory that pervaded the political atmosphere of the time. Typical of the expressions were the words of the Declaration of Independence which ran:

We hold these truths to be self-evident. . . . That whenever any Form of Government becomes destructive of these ends, it is the Right of the People to alter or to abolish it, and to institute new Government, laying its foundation on such principles and organizing its powers in such form as to them shall seem most likely to effect their Safety and Happiness.

[2] Edward S. Corwin (ed.), *The Constitution of the United States of America*, S. Doc. 170, 82d Cong., 2d Sess. (1953), p. 59.

[3] Edward M. Sait, *Political Institutions: A Preface* (Appleton-Century-Crofts, 1938), p. 143; Thomas M. Cooley, *A Treatise on the Constitutional Limitations Which Rest upon the Legislative Power of the States of the American Union* (Little, Brown, 6th ed., 1890), pp. 39–40.

The thought was more colorfully stated by Thomas Jefferson in a letter prompted by Shays' Rebellion in Massachusetts: [4]

. . . God forbid that we should ever be 20 years without such a rebellion. The people cannot be all, & always, well informed. The part which is wrong will be discontented in proportion to the importance of the facts they misconceive. If they remain quiet under such misconceptions it is a lethargy, the forerunner of death to the public liberty. We have had 13. states independent 11. years. There has been one rebellion. That comes to one rebellion in a century & a half for each state. What country before ever existed a century & a half without a rebellion? & what country can preserve its liberties if their rulers are not warned from time to time that their people preserve the spirit of resistance? Let them take arms. The remedy is to set them right as to facts, pardon & pacify them. What signify a few lives lost in a century or two? The tree of liberty must be refreshed from time to time with the blood of patriots & tyrants. It is its natural manure. . . .

As memory of the Revolution dimmed, however, less emphasis came to be placed upon the right of revolution and more upon the right of existing governments to maintain law and order. In one of the few pronouncements upon the subject, the Supreme Court took the position that a state was justified in using as much military force as was necessary to put down an armed insurrection too strong to be controlled by the civil authority.[5] More recently, in upholding the conviction of eleven Communist leaders charged with conspiracy to teach and advocate overthrow of government by force and violence, a majority of the Supreme Court had this to say: [6]

[4] Letter to James Madison quoted in Dumas Malone, *Jefferson and the Rights of Man* (Little, Brown, 1951), pp. 165–166.

[5] Luther *v.* Borden, 7 How. 1 (U.S. 1849). This case grew out of Dorr's Rebellion in Rhode Island in 1842. The rebellion occurred as a result of the unwillingness of the established government to extend the suffrage to a greater number of people.

[6] Dennis *v.* United States, 341 U.S. 501 (1950).

That it is within the *power* of the Congress to protect the Government of the United States from armed rebellion is a proposition which requires little discussion. Whatever theoretical merit there may be to the argument that there is a "right" to rebellion against dictatorial governments is without force where the existing structure of the government provides for peaceful and orderly change. We reject any principle of governmental helplessness in the face of preparation for revolution, which principle, carried to its logical conclusion, must lead to anarchy. No one could conceive that it is not within the power of government to prohibit acts intended to overthrow the Government by force and violence.

This view, though at variance with utterances of some early American statesmen, is the one now acted upon by the Federal, state, and local governments if any of the people attempt to express their supposed right of revolution.

A Federal System. As noted on pages 5–6, a state may be organized on a unitary basis, or as a confederation, or as a federal union. The circumstances existing in 1787 precluded consideration of a unitary system; the only choice lay between continuing and strengthening the confederation or building a federal union. By heroic efforts, a plan was devised which retained the states as integral units while welding the entire population into a powerful unit for dealing with matters of national concern.

Though there was much doubt in the minds of people living at the time of the adoption of the Constitution about the practicability of a federal union, their fears were ill-founded. The American federal union, though severely strained by the Civil War, has stood the test of over a century and a half. It stands today as the oldest federal union in existence. So successful has it been that many other countries have followed the American model, and a number of people now visualize a world organized on a federal basis.

National Supremacy. In a federal system, jurisdictional conflicts are bound to arise between the central and regional governments. Experience demonstrates that when such conflicts arise federal law must be paramount or the interests of the people of the nation will be at the mercy of the inhabitants of individual states. Realizing this, the Founding Fathers never doubted the necessity of subordinating state laws to those of the Federal government if and when the two came into conflict. Accordingly, they stipulated that the Federal Constitution, acts of Congress, and treaties were the "supreme law of the land." When a conflict exists between federal and state law the matter is decided by Federal courts.

A Representative System. The Constitution established a representative democracy. Town meetings are still held in a few New England communities, and the referendum, initiative, and recall are used in a number of states. But, on the whole, American governmental institutions are run by representatives chosen directly or indirectly by the voters. This is especially true of the Federal government. As things stand, voters cannot initiate federal laws as they can in a number of states and cities. Nor can laws be enacted by referendums, although Congress can stipulate that referendums may be used to help determine when certain legislative provisions will become effective.[7] Nor are voters permitted to vote to recall federal officers as may be done in some of the states. Indeed, on only three occasions does the electorate participate directly in federal affairs: *viz.*, when voting for representatives, when choosing United States senators, and when voting for electors to choose the President and Vice-President. When these are chosen, all matters of government are left in their hands.

Three proposals have been made in recent years for allowing more direct participation in policy formation. One contemplates the direct

[7] This is provided in agricultural adjustment legislation wherein farmers must vote and approve by a two-thirds majority before marketing quotas become effective. See p. 572. This arrangement has been held by the Supreme Court not to be an illegal delegation of powers given to Congress. Currin *v.* Wallace, 306 U.S. 1 (1939); United States *v.* Rock Royal Cooperative, 307 U.S. 533 (1939). Advisory referendums are also apparently constitutional. Where these are used the legislature merely submits a proposal to the voters to determine public sentiment. After the referendums the legislature is free to use its discretion about passing or rejecting the proposals voted upon.

election of a President and Vice-President rather than election by the electoral college as at present. Another would require that constitutional amendments be submitted to popular referendum for ratification rather than to state legislatures or conventions as is now the case. The third proposes that the Constitution be amended to require a referendum vote before Congress can declare war except where the United States or a country in the Western Hemisphere is attacked. While there has been considerable sentiment in favor of each of these, none has been able to muster sufficient votes to pass the Congress. Whether the demand for more direct participation in the determination of governmental policies will become greater will, doubtless, depend upon the degree of confidence the public continues to have in those whom they elect.

Civilian Supremacy over the Military. It seemed clear to those who founded the American republic that large military establishments and tyranny went hand in hand. This view had been advanced in the writings of the leading political theorists of the period, like Locke, Rousseau, Montesquieu, Coke, and Blackstone, and the behavior of British troops in the colonies confirmed their impressions. It is not surprising, therefore, to find listed in the charges made against King George III by the Declaration of Independence: "He has kept among us, in times of peace, Standing Armies, without the Consent of our legislatures.—He has affected to render the Military independent of and superior to the Civil Power."

At the Constitutional Convention in 1787 broad military powers were given the President and Congress,[8] but safeguards were also provided. Only Congress could declare war; all revenue bills must originate in the most popular house of Congress; no money could be spent except as appropriated by Congress; no money could be appropriated for an army for longer than 2 years; a limitation was put upon suspension of the writ of habeas corpus; and the states were left with authority to officer and train their militias. During the debates over the ratification of the Constitution, its advocates

[8] These are discussed in Chaps. 14, 15, and 24.

agreed to support amendments which would go further and provide guaranties against quartering troops in any house without the consent of the owner and to assure people of the right to keep and bear arms. These guaranties were incorporated in the Second and Third Amendments.

Thoroughly entrenched by Constitution and long experience, the principle of civilian supremacy has not directly been challenged. But involvements in wars and international politics since 1898 have increased American military commitments; the defense establishment has grown to enormously large proportions; military personnel, active and retired, has integrated itself with all phases of economic, social, and political life; the military bureaucracy, with the aid of veterans' and other patriotic societies and supporting interests, has become a powerful pressure group; conscription has become an accepted accompaniment of war and is widely advocated as a desirable peacetime institution; and state militias have come increasingly under federal dominance. In consequence, many voices are raised in alarm lest the principle of civilian supremacy be lost.[9] That the principle still has vigor, however, was indicated by President Truman's dramatic dismissal of five-star General MacArthur in 1951 from his command in Japan and Korea. Vigor is also indicated by the zeal exercised by congressional committees in their investigation and review of military affairs.[10]

Limited Government. Government is admittedly a necessity, but it implies coercion and restraint. How to get enough governmental au-

[9] See especially U.S. Commission on Organization of the Executive Branch of the Government (hereafter cited as either First or Second Hoover Commission), *The National Security Organization* (1949), pp. 2–3; Harold D. Lasswell, *National Security and Individual Freedom* (McGraw-Hill, 1950), *passim;* Louis Smith, *American Democracy and Military Power* (University of Chicago Press, 1951), *passim;* and Burton M. Sapin and Richard C. Snyder, *The Role of the Military in American Foreign Policy* (Doubleday, 1954), *passim.*

[10] For a recent review of the tussle for funds, see Elias Huzar, *The Purse and the Sword: Control of the Army by Congress through Military Appropriations, 1933–1950* (Cornell University Press, 1950).

thority without creating an agency that will become abusive of liberty is a problem as old as human society. Those who wrote and ratified the Constitution thought they had found an answer to the paradoxical question: (1) They assumed that the people were sovereign. (2) The organization and powers of their governments were set forth in written documents in language as plain as could be commanded. (3) After carefully stating what powers they wished the Federal government to exercise, they left all residual powers to the states or to the people. (4) The three branches of government were separated and made to operate with elaborate checks and balances. (5) Both the Federal and state governments were specifically forbidden to perform certain acts. (6) The military was subordinated to civilian control. (7) Individual and personal rights were protected against invasion by either the Federal or state governments. (8) Powers could be exercised only by elected officers or those duly appointed by officials who had been chosen by the voters. And (9) it was provided that amendments could not be added to the Constitution unless desired by an overwhelming majority of the voters.

American governments, the states in particular, have frequently ignored injustices perpetrated by groups of citizens against races and minorities, and they themselves have occasionally been guilty of violating human liberties. On the whole, however, the record is a good one.

Recent years have witnessed a decline in emphasis upon keeping government limited in favor of sentiment for bigger and stronger governments. The industrial revolution, wars, depressions, and threats of communism and fascism have led many to fear their consequences more than they do strong government. To these people government has become the champion and protector of values and welfare. While professing respect for personal rights, many of the new schools look with impatience upon traditional restraints that impede prompt and vigorous governmental action. This poses the crucial question of whether American governments can continue to meet recurring crises, provide the manifold services expected of them, and still avoid becoming dictatorial. British and American experience suggests that this can be done, although even there emergencies tend to weaken the bulwarks of personal liberty and democratic control.

Separation of Powers. The three powers (or branches) of government may be united or separated. Where the parliamentary form exists, parliament is the central agency; the real executive, which is the prime minister and his cabinet, is selected by parliament from its own membership; and the courts are subordinate to the will of the legislature. Where dictatorships exist, powers are either united in the executive branch or, although technically separated, they are completely subordinate to the executive. Where powers are separated, each branch has its own powers and prerogatives the exercise of which serves to restrain the other branches, thus creating a check-and-balance system. The latter has been considered by many to be a safeguard against tyranny.

Origin of Doctrine. Colonial statesmen had read about the separation of powers in writings of the Englishman John Locke and the Frenchman Montesquieu, and their experience with autocratic British kings and colonial governors made them receptive to the theory. Consequently, this feature was incorporated into every one of the state constitutions adopted during the Revolution. A classic expression of the doctrine is found in the constitution of Massachusetts:

In the government of this commonwealth, the legislative department shall never exercise the executive and judicial powers, or either of them: the executive shall never exercise the legislative and judicial powers, or either of them: the judicial shall never exercise the legislative and executive powers, or either of them: to the end that it may be a government of laws, and not of men.

In view of the widespread distrust of political power generally and of a national government in particular, it was inevitable that powers should be separated in the new Constitution.

Constitutional Basis. Unlike the constitution of Massachusetts, quoted above, the Federal Constitution does not state categorically that the powers are and must remain separated. That they are separated is because of language used in creating the three branches: Article I begins by saying, *"All* legislative powers herein granted shall be vested in a Congress." Article II begins with the statement that *"The* executive power shall be vested in a President." And Article III states that *"The* judicial power . . . shall be vested in one Supreme Court, and in such inferior courts as Congress may from time to time ordain and establish." [11] This inclusive and exclusive language, coupled with the fact that the powers are set forth in three different articles, provides the constitutional basis for their separation.

Checks and Balances. Separation of powers is implemented by an elaborate system of checks and balances. To mention only a few: Congress is checked by the requirement that laws must receive the approval of both houses, by the President's veto, and by the power of judicial review of the courts. The President is checked by the fact that he cannot enact laws, that no money may be spent except in accordance with appropriations made by law, that Congress can override his veto, that he can be impeached, that treaties must be approved and appointments confirmed by the Senate, and by judicial review. The judicial branch is checked by the power retained by the people to amend the Constitution, by the power of the President with the advice and consent of the Senate to appoint judges, by the fact that judges can be impeached, and by the fact that Congress can determine the size of courts and limit the appellate jurisdiction of both the Supreme Court and inferior courts.

Criticisms of Separation of Powers. While the doctrine of separation of powers has many apologists, it also has its critics. Some think that in spite of their formal separation there are many ways whereby one or more of the branches acquires too much influence. Thus, the complaint is heard that the President by use of the radio, movie, press conference, patronage, and a widespread bureaucracy has acquired the ability to dominate Congress, to administer justice by the substitution of administrative adjudication, or by the exercise of undue influence over judicial

[11] Italics are the authors'.

decisions. Others complain because of legislative interference with administration. Still others think the courts have usurped authority which properly belongs to Congress and the President. Although there is some truth in each of these contentions, the fact is that it would be impossible to devise a workable system without a considerable number of interrelationships between the three branches. Moreover, existing checks and balances do tend to restrain, with the result that over a period of time each of the three branches manages to "hold its own" in relation to the others.

Another group of critics decries separation of powers because it leads to frustration of leadership and produces stalemates. They point to the British system where the three branches are united under Parliament with responsibility for leadership resting in the prime minister and cabinet who are at all times accountable to Parliament. The opposite is true under the American system, where the President may be of one political persuasion and Congress of another, with the result that little may be accomplished. Even when the presidential and congressional majorities are of the same party, leadership is difficult. Members of Congress are likely to be prejudiced against executive initiative because the President is not one of them. The President and his cabinet cannot defend their policies on floors of the House and Senate. The executive may outline a budgetary plan only to see it emasculated by Congress. The President may negotiate treaties but a minority of the Senate can prevent their ratification. The President is charged with responsibility for effective administration but Congress can intervene and obstruct by withholding appropriations, by attaching riders to bills, by failing to confirm presidential appointments, or by insisting upon rewarding the friends and districts of congressmen. At the same time, critics insist, the courts may construe the Constitution so narrowly as to frustrate both the President and Congress.

Unifying Devices. These possibilities do exist. At the same time there are factors that tend to unify powers. Most important is the political party. Another is the power of the President to initiate legislation, send messages to Congress, defend measures before committees, appeal and maneuver for public support, labor with individual congressmen, and threaten to withhold patronage. Meanwhile, if both the President and Congress persist, the courts can be brought to a more accommodating point of view, or if not, constitutional amendments can be sought.

In spite of these unifying devices, comparison with the British form leads to the conclusion that effective leadership is less likely to exist in the United States, except possibly during emergencies. In the past, however, Americans have not been conspicuously desirous of executive leadership. Various proposals have been made to ensure greater presidential leadership but early enactment of any of them seems unlikely. But if the emphasis upon a positive governmental program persists, the situation may change and bring with it modifications in the traditional patterns of checks and balances.

Judicial Review. The Constitution is silent on the important question of what would happen if the President, Congress, or the courts violated the Constitution. The President can, and often has, vetoed acts of Congress because he considered them in conflict with the Constitution. Likewise, Congress can retaliate in many ways against a President who violates the Constitution. Both the President and Congress have ways of reprimanding Federal courts whose conduct and decisions they consider contrary to the Constitution. These checks operate continuously, and usually without great publicity or discussion. But early in American history the courts undertook to declare acts of Congress unconstitutional and this has occasioned violent controversy. Acceptance of the principle of judicial review has made the Supreme Court the most powerful judicial agency in the world. Several other countries have emulated American practice, but in none of them have the courts come to play such an important role as in the United States.

Judicial Review Intended. Because the Constitution does not specifically grant the power of judicial review and the courts by their decisions have often irritated Congress, the President, and large sectors of the public, there has been much dispute over the courts' right to exercise the prerogative. The controversy has caused intensive historical research to discover the origin of the practice and the intent of those who wrote the Constitution. The evidence reveals that judicial review as we know it emerged with the adoption of written constitutions by the American states after their break with England in 1776.[12] The evidence also reveals that a majority of those who attended the Constitutional Convention favored judicial review.[13] Why, then, was specific provision not made for it? The answer seems to be that the framers of the Constitution believed the power to be clearly enough implied from language used.

Constitutional Basis for Judicial Review. One of the pertinent provisions is found in Article VI which reads, in part, "This *Constitution,* and the *Laws* of the United States *which shall be made in Pursuance thereof;* and all Treaties made, or which shall be made, under the Authority of the United States, shall be the supreme Law of the Land. . . ."[14] Another relevant provision is Article III, Section 2, which says, "The judicial Power shall extend to all Cases, in Law and Equity, arising under this Constitution, the Laws of the United States, and Treaties made, or which shall be made, under their Authority. . . ."

With these as background, the Supreme Court faced the issue for the first time in Marbury *v.* Madison.[15] Briefly, the facts were that Congress had provided in the Judiciary Act of 1789 that requests for writs of mandamus[16] might origi-

[12] Westel W. Willoughby, *The Constitutional Law of the United States* (New York: Baker, Voorhis, 2d ed., 3 vols., 1929), vol. I, p. 66; Charles G. Haines, *The American Doctrine of Judicial Supremacy* (University of California Press, 2d ed., 1932), Chaps. III, IV, and V.

[13] *Ibid.,* Chap. VIII; Charles A. Beard, *The Supreme Court and the Constitution* (Macmillan, 1912), *passim;* Arthur N. Holcombe, *Our More Perfect Union* (Harvard University Press, 1950), p. 42.

[14] Italics are the authors'.

[15] 1 Cranch 137 (U.S. 1803).

[16] Judicial orders commanding government officials to perform duties required by law.

nate in the Supreme Court. On the night of Mar. 3, 1801, Marbury had been appointed justice of peace for the District of Columbia by President Adams, whose term expired before the commission was delivered. The incoming President, Jefferson, and his Secretary of State, Madison, refused to deliver the commission to Marbury who immediately petitioned the Supreme Court for a writ of mandamus as he was permitted to do by the Judiciary Act of 1789. Chief Justice Marshall wrote the opinion for the Court. After first saying that he thought Marbury was entitled to the commission, he went on to declare that the Supreme Court was without authority to grant a writ compelling delivery. This was because the Judiciary Act of 1789 had enlarged the original jurisdiction of the Supreme Court as prescribed by the Constitution, hence was in violation of the Constitution and therefore null and void.

Chief Justice Marshall's justification is based upon the following assumptions: (1) that the Constitution is a written document that clearly defines and limits the powers of government; (2) that the Constitution is a fundamental law and superior to ordinary legislative enactments; (3) that an act of the legislature that is contrary to the fundamental law is void and therefore cannot bind the courts; (4) that the judicial power, together with oaths to uphold the Constitution that judges take, requires that the courts declare when they believe acts of Congress violative of the Constitution. Although Marshall's reasoning has had many critics and his facts may have been of doubtful accuracy,[17] the principle of judicial review was firmly embedded in the American system of government.

Experience with Judicial Review. To date there have been eighty or more cases in which federal statutes have been declared unconstitutional in whole or in part by the Supreme Court. After the Marbury decision, 54 years elapsed before another statute was invalidated by the famous Dred Scott Case.[18] In that instance, a divided court declared the Missouri Compromise of 1820 unconstitutional and by doing so

[17] Haines, *op. cit.,* pp. 193–203.

[18] Dred Scott *v.* Sandford, 19 How. 393 (U.S. 1857).

intensified the situation that later erupted in Civil War. The timetable of instances of judicial review is shown in the chart opposite.[19] Review of the cases discloses two that have led to adoption of constitutional amendments;[20] only a few involving large questions of public policy, like the one arising from the NIRA, where the Court was unanimous or nearly so; a few dealing with civil rights; several dealing with questions of a technical character; and a considerable number[21] of important, closely divided opinions many of which have been reversed by later courts.

Many who have reviewed American experience with judicial review contend that the Supreme Court has expanded its authority to such an extent that it has become a nonelective superlegislature. It is also insisted that the Court has shown undue partiality for property rights and excessive dependence upon legal formulas with the result that it has seriously retarded social progress. As evidence, critics offer the number of cases wherein the courts have declared welfare legislation unconstitutional only later to reverse their decisions in response to popular insistence.

While there is validity to these criticisms, there are few in the United States who advocate complete abandonment of judicial review. Various reforms have been suggested, but none has evoked popular enthusiasm. Experience in the United States and elsewhere suggests that while the courts may check political departments temporarily, they are likely to accommodate eventually if pressures are intense and persistent. Accordingly, whether important change is made

---

[19] A recent tabulation is found in Edward S. Corwin (ed.), *The Constitution of the United States of America*, S. Doc. 170, 82d Cong., 2d Sess. (1953), pp. 1241–1254. Information subsequent to Dr. Corwin's tabulation was obtained from the Administrative Office of the United States Courts and court decisions.

[20] The Dred Scott decision led to the Thirteenth and Fourteenth Amendments, while the decision in Pollock *v.* Farmers' Loan and Trust Co., 158 U.S. 601 (1895), led to the Sixteenth Amendment.

[21] Like those dealing with the questions of legal tender, child labor, minimum wages for women, federal taxation of state instrumentalities, and regulation of large-scale productive enterprises.

in the practice of judicial review is likely to depend upon the degree of judicial restraint and the intensity and duration of future crises.

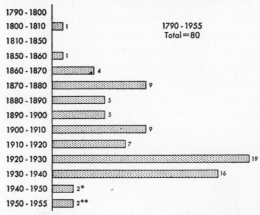

SUPREME COURT CASES DECLARING U. S. LAWS UNCONSTITUTIONAL

1790 - 1955
Total = 80

* Tot v. United States, 319 U. S. 463 (1943) and United States v. Lovett, 328 U. S. 303 (1946)
** United States v. Cardiff, 344 U. S. 174 (1952) and Toth v. Quarles, 350 U. S. 11 (1955)

Although judicial review of legislation is an important feature of American government, the number of statutes voided by the court is not, in most decades, large.

METHODS OF CHANGE

The American Constitution is the world's classic example of a written constitution. Nevertheless, it takes only cursory examination to discover that it has many unwritten features. Upon becoming acquainted with the document for the first time, one is likely to be astonished at finding that many of the most conspicuous features of the American system of government have no apparent constitutional foundation—features that have been added over the years by interpretation, custom, and usage.

Amendment. The most obvious manner by which the Constitution may be changed is by the addition of amendments. The method by which this is to be done is set forth in Article V, which reads:

The Congress, whenever two thirds of both Houses shall deem it necessary, shall propose Amendments to this Constitution, or, on the Application of the Legislatures of two thirds of the several States, shall call a Convention for proposing Amendments, which, in either Case, shall be valid to all Intents and Purposes, as Part of this Constitution, when ratified by the Legislatures of three fourths of the several States, or by Conventions in three fourths thereof, as the one or the other Mode of Ratification may be proposed by the Congress; Provided that no Amendment which may be made prior to the Year One thousand eight hundred and eight shall in any Manner affect the first and fourth Clauses in the Ninth Section of the first Article;

Proposal of Amendments. Article V provides two methods by which amendments may be proposed; *viz.,* by a two-thirds [23] vote of both houses of Congress, and by a constitutional convention called after receiving petitions from legislatures in two-thirds of the states. Thus far, out of thousands of resolutions introduced in Congress,[24] only twenty-seven have mustered the necessary two-thirds vote of both houses.[25] None has been proposed by the alternate method of constitutional convention.

Amendment Procedure

Method of Proposal	*Methods of Ratification*
(Either may be used.)	(States may select either method unless Congress specifies which should be followed.)
1. By two-thirds vote of both houses of Congress (method used to propose all 27 amendments)...	Legislatures in three-fourths (36) of the states (method used to ratify first 20 and the 22d amendments); or Conventions in three-fourths (36) of the states (method used to ratify 1 amendment—the 21st).
2. By constitutional convention called by Congress when petitioned to do so by two-thirds (32) of the states (method unused to date)............	Legislatures in three-fourths (36) of the states; or Conventions in three-fourths (36) of the states.

and that no State, without its Consent, shall be deprived of its equal Suffrage in the Senate.

Before proceeding to a discussion of the procedure set forth in this article, two observations of a general character may be made. One is that the proposal and ratification of amendments are solely legislative functions—the President need not sign proposed amendments before they are sent to the states, nor do the state governors need to sign instruments of ratification. The second observation is that, except for the provision that a state's equality of representation cannot be diminished without its consent, any provision whatsoever can be legally altered by amendment.[22]

[22] Observe, however, that prior to 1808 amendments could not be made to the first and fourth clauses in the ninth section of Article I, which clauses permitted the

If Congress is unwilling to submit amendments to the states, the legislatures thereof may force action by petitioning Congress to call a

slave trade for a period of 20 years after the adoption of the Constitution and stipulated that direct taxes must be apportioned among the states on the basis of population. These exceptions are no longer of importance.

[23] Two-thirds of the members present, assuming the presence of a quorum—not necessarily two-thirds of the total membership.

[24] For a compilation of these from 1789 to 1889, see Herman V. Ames, *The Proposed Amendments to the Constitution of the United States during the First Century of Its History* (American Historical Association, Annual Report, 1896, II, published as H. Doc. 353, pt. 2, 54th Cong., 2d Sess.). For those introduced between 1889 and 1928, see Michael A. Musmanno, *Proposed Amendments to the Constitution* . . . , H. Doc. 551, 70th Cong., 2d Sess. (1929).

[25] For those proposed but unratified, see p. 725.

constitutional convention for the purpose. Petitions have been addressed to Congress on many occasions. Some of these have been general in character, asking only that a convention be called. Others have urged calling a convention to consider specific matters such as the outlawing of polygamy, the direct election of the President and Vice-President, the control of trusts, and the direct election of senators. Petitions have never been received concerning any one subject from as many as two-thirds of the states, but enough were submitted urging the direct election of senators to play an important, if not decisive, role in forcing the submission of the Seventeenth Amendment. If two-thirds of the states were to petition, Congress would be under obligation to call a convention.

Ratification. Two methods of ratification are also provided by Article V; *viz.,* by legislatures in three-fourths of the states or by conventions in a similar number of the states. Congress may indicate which method of ratification is to be followed, as it did in proposing that the twenty-first be considered in conventions, but failure to express preference leaves the states free to choose either one. States must use either legislatures or conventions—something else cannot be substituted—and the decision to ratify is irrevocable.[26] A rejection, however, does not preclude reconsideration of the proposal either by the same legislature or convention or by subsequent ones. The usual procedure is for the governor of the state, upon receipt of copy of a joint resolution of Congress, to refer the matter to the state legislature. If the resolution calls for the use of conventions, the state legislature will usually enact the necessary authorization, stating where and when the convention will be held, the number of delegates, etc. If conventions are not called for, the legislature may consider the amendment at any time it wishes. Ratification is legally consummated the minute the requisite three-fourths of the states ratify.

Thus far, all but one of the twenty-two amendments have been approved by state legislatures. This method is simpler and less expensive inasmuch as legislatures are or will be in

session anyway. The convention method may be somewhat faster because those who attend do so for the single purpose of considering an amendment, whereas legislatures may be precariously divided along party lines and have many other matters to deal with. The convention method is also more likely to reflect clearly public opinion because the delegates are chosen after a campaign in which those who favor and those who oppose have done everything possible to elect a majority partial to their point of view. The principal reason that impelled Congress to require that the Twenty-first Amendment be ratified by conventions seems to have been the desire for speedy action at a time when public opinion, as expressed in the election of a Democratic President and Congress in 1932, was known to be sympathetic to repeal of prohibition.

Time Necessary for Completing Ratification. Ratification of an amendment may take place within a few minutes or many years after its proposal. Congress placed a time limit of 7 years in the Eighteenth, Twentieth, Twenty-first, and Twenty-second Amendments. When first taken, this action encouraged the belief that amendments "died of old age" unless a time limit were included or, as the Supreme Court said, unless ratification were completed "within some reasonable time after proposal." [27] But in 1939, the Supreme Court took a different view.[28] Holding that the child-labor amendment was still "alive" after 15 years, the Supreme Court said that the question as to whether there should be a time limit is a political one. Being such, Congress, and not the courts, must decide what is a reasonable period. If Congress wishes to limit the period for ratification to 7 or any other number of years, it may do so; otherwise, proposed amendments are before the states indefinitely. Apparently, then, a state could still ratify any of the five amendments that have been proposed and remain unratified by the requisite number of states. On one occasion Ohio ratified an amendment submitted 80 years earlier. Connecticut, Georgia, and Massachusetts, somewhat

---

[26] Hawke *v.* Smith, 253 U.S. 221, 231 (1920).

[27] Dillon *v.* Gloss, 256 U.S. 368 (1921).

[28] Coleman *et al. v.* Miller *et al.,* 307 U.S. 433 (1939).

embarrassed upon finding that they had never done so, ratified the first ten amendments as recently as 1939.[29] On the whole, the time required for ratification has been rather short, varying from 3 years and 11 months for the Twenty-second Amendment to only 7 months for the Twelfth. The average for the twenty-two amendments is about twenty-one months.[30]

The First Twelve Amendments. The first ten amendments, the famous Bill of Rights, were proposed by the first Congress in fulfillment of the pledge made by the Federalists in order to ensure the adoption of the Constitution. These, it should be noted, restrict the national government, not the states.[31] The Eleventh was added after the states had been incensed by a decision of the Supreme Court in which it held that Article III of the Constitution permitted states to be sued in Federal courts.[32] The amendment was intended to guarantee that a "sovereign" state would never again be summoned before the federal judiciary as Georgia had been in the case cited. The Twelfth Amendment grew out of the election of 1800 during which Jefferson and Burr defeated Adams and Pinckney. When the electoral college met to cast their ballots, they discovered that by voting for the President and Vice-President on the same ballot, as Article II required, Jefferson and Burr had exactly the same number of votes. Although everyone understood Jefferson to have been the candidate for President and Burr the candidate for Vice-President, a tie existed which necessitated putting the election up to the House of Representatives. To ensure that this would never happen again, the Twelfth Amendment was proposed and promptly ratified.

The Civil War Amendments. The next three amendments grew out of the Civil War. The Thirteenth prohibited slavery; the Fourteenth defined citizenship, forbade states to deprive persons of life, liberty, and property without due

process of law, forbade states to deny anyone equal protection of the law, and provided a method by which states were to be punished for denying the right to vote to adult male citizens. The Fifteenth went still further by specifically forbidding either the Federal government or the states to deny people the right to vote because of race, color, or previous condition of servitude. These three amendments were added only by resort to questionable methods. Approval of the Thirteenth was obtained with the help of West Virginia, whose secession from Virginia was of dubious legality, and with the aid of carpetbagger legislatures in several Southern states. Sufficient ratifications to the Fourteenth and Fifteenth were obtained only by making their approval a prerequisite for readmission of Southern states to full rights in the Union.

Although the Fourteenth provides that states shall be punished for denying adult males the right to vote by having their representation in Congress diminished, Congress has never enforced the provision and is not likely to do so. The late Senator Borah sponsored an amendment that would have repealed this unenforced section of the Fourteenth Amendment. Though stymied, there is still some sentiment for the proposal.

Sixteenth to Nineteenth Amendments. Forty-three years elapsed before additional amendments were added, during which time many people had become convinced that the Constitution could never again be changed by the amendment procedure. The next one overcame a decision of the Supreme Court wherein it was held that income taxes were direct taxes and as such must be apportioned among the states on the basis of population.[33] Since this precluded graduated income taxes based upon the capacity of people to pay, the Sixteenth Amendment was added.

The graduated income tax has become the Federal government's chief source of revenue. In recent years its rates and exactions have become so high that a movement has been started to repeal the amendment. Those favoring the

[29] Denys P. Myers, *The Process of Constitutional Amendment*, S. Doc. 314, 76th Cong., 3d Sess. (1940), pp. 10–20.

[30] *Ibid.*, p. 29.

[31] Barron *v.* Baltimore, 7 Pet. 243 (U.S. 1833).

[32] Chisholm *v.* Georgia, 2 Dall. 419 (U.S. 1793).

[33] Pollock *v.* Farmers' Loan and Trust Company, 158 U.S. 601 (1895).

repeal would add a substitute establishing a ceiling of 25 per cent on income, inheritance, and gift taxes levied by Congress. Since 1939, about half of the states have at one time or another acted favorably upon a resolution calling upon Congress to call a constitutional convention to consider and propose the substitute measure. Several states have since rescinded their approval, leaving about fifteen on record as favoring repeal and addition of the substitute.

The Seventeenth Amendment was added in 1913 in order to transfer the election of United States senators from the state legislatures to the voters themselves. The Eighteenth was proposed after America had entered the First World War and ratified 2 months after the armistice. Its primary purpose was to add federal power to that of the states for the purpose of more effectually eliminating the evils of the liquor traffic. The Nineteenth resulted from years of agitation on the part of feminist leaders and organizations who clamored for legal recognition of women's right to vote. Although many states had already granted women the privilege of voting, an amendment was necessary to ensure universal recognition of the privilege throughout the nation.

Recent Amendments. The *Twentieth Amendment* added three procedural changes. Formerly, Congress convened regularly on the first Monday in December and remained in session as long as it pleased, passing up the first Mar. 4 that came along. This was the "long session." But when it convened the following December, Congress could remain in session only until Mar. 4, at which time the 2-year term for which representatives were chosen and the term of one-third of the senators expired. This was the "short session."

Meanwhile, in the November that preceded the commencement of the short session, the entire membership of the House of Representatives and one-third of the Senate had stood for re-election. Although some were defeated in November, they nevertheless convened with the rest in December and continued to serve throughout the short session, *i.e.,* until the following Mar. 4. The fact that they could continue to serve for 4 months after having been defeated caused them to be dubbed "lame ducks." Meanwhile, the lame ducks served throughout the short session, and the new members chosen in the preceding November remained out of office. Since their terms began on Mar. 4, they could be called into special session at any time after that date, but if the President did not see fit to call a special session, they regularly convened in the following December—13 months after election.

The Twentieth Amendment changed this by ending all terms on Jan. 3 and providing that Congress would convene regularly on the same date. This means that both sessions of a Congress can be "long" and that only 2 months elapse between election and the commencement of duties. The second provision of the amendment moved the President's inauguration from Mar. 4 to Jan. 20. A third empowered Congress to provide for choosing a President and Vice-President in the event that something happened to prevent those elected in November of an election year from being inaugurated on the following Jan. 20. This was intended to overcome embarrassment such as occurred in the famous Hayes-Tilden contest of 1876, wherein controversy developed over which one was elected and the outcome remained uncertain until within a few hours of the date of inauguration.

The *Twenty-first Amendment* ended prohibition, which had imposed gigantic responsibilities upon the national, state, and local governments. Controversy had raged for more than two decades over the wisdom and desirability of attempting to interfere with personal liberty to the extent of forbidding the manufacture, transportation, and sale of intoxicating beverages. The depression which followed the stock-market crash of 1929 brought with it an economic and social revolution which, in turn, brought into positions of power and influence the critics of prohibition. The result was the Twenty-first Amendment, which repealed the Eighteenth and, significantly, gave the state long-coveted authority to control interstate shipments of intoxicating liquors.

The *Twenty-second Amendment* came as a political reaction to the breach made by Franklin D. Roosevelt in the two-term tradition. Proposed in March, 1947, by the required two-thirds of both houses of Congress, the amendment was ratified by the thirty-sixth state in February, 1951. With this change it became impossible for

CONSTITUTIONAL AMENDMENTS
A TIMELINE

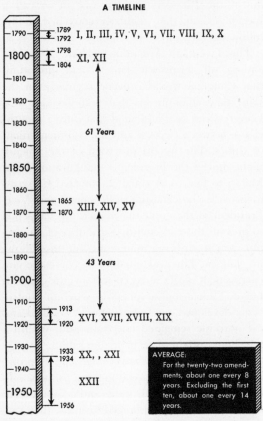

The most striking feature shown here is that Federal constitutional amendments come in groups, often with long intervals between.

any successor to President Harry S. Truman to be elected more than twice. In the event a Vice-President succeeds to the office of President during the first 2 years of a term, he may be elected to fill the presidency only once. If he succeeds during the last 2 years of a term, he may be elected twice. Thus, it is possible that someone might hold the office of President for a total of 10 years. It is too early to calculate the full effect of this amendment. Opposition to it was neither strong nor vocal, but thoughtful students point

out that the amendment is almost certain to reduce the President's ability to lead Congress and his party, especially during the last half of his second term. This, they contend, would be most unfortunate for a modern America that demands strong executive leadership.

Amendments Few and Hard to Obtain. Looking over the twenty-two amendments, one is impressed by the infrequency with which they have been added. Omitting the first ten, which were adopted within a short time after the Constitution became effective, an amendment has been adopted on an average of one about every 14 years. But this is too favorable a picture. The Thirteenth, Fourteenth, and Fifteenth were ratified under questionable circumstances. If these are omitted, the record is one amendment added approximately every 18 years. While amendments can be speedily proposed and ratified, as was illustrated by the Twelfth, opinion must be overwhelmingly in favor of a proposal before this can happen. Proponents must marshal a two-thirds vote in both houses, or a total of 290 votes in the lower house and 64 votes in the Senate if the total membership is present. Opponents, on the other hand, need muster but one-third of the membership in only *one* of the houses (145 votes in the House or 32 in the Senate) to block a proposal. The situation is, if anything, worse when it comes to ratification. Proponents must obtain affirmative action in both houses of state legislatures in thirty-six states,[34] or a total of seventy-two separate legislative bodies, while opponents need to induce only *one* house in thirteen different states, or thirteen separate legislative bodies, to block ratification. These facts suggest that a small minority, estimated by some to be as low as 5 per cent of the population, can permanently defeat an amendment desired by a considerable majority of the people. This is particularly true where the amendment is likely to affect adversely the economic interests of some geographic section of the country.

The magnitude of the effort involved has undoubtedly deterred more frequent use of the

[34] Except in the state of Nebraska, where the legislature is unicameral.

amending procedure. Where no structural or procedural change is sought, but merely a different interpretation of a general phrase, those interested in seeing the Constitution altered are likely to seek their objective by putting pressure upon the courts rather than by resort to the amendment procedure. This was conspicuously the case during the controversy over slavery, legal tender, child labor, and the program of the New Deal.

Proposals to Change Amendment Procedure. This situation has led many to advocate simplification of the amending procedure. The suggestions most frequently made are that the proposal of amendments be modified to require only a majority vote in both houses of Congress, and ratification be changed to require the approval of two-thirds (rather than three-fourths) of the states, a simple majority of states, or a majority of the people voting by referendum in a majority of the states. Thus far it has been impossible to evoke enthusiasm for any of the suggestions. In any case, a determined minority, anticipating certain amendments that would be sure to follow, would probably resist simplifying the amendment procedure as strenuously as it would oppose specific amendments themselves.

Other Suggested Amendments. Each year a number of resolutions proposing amendments are introduced in Congress where they are referred to the judiciary committees of the respective houses and seldom given serious consideration. Each year memorials are also adopted by one or more state legislatures calling upon Congress to call a convention for the consideration of suggested amendments. These, too, are referred to the judiciary committees and usually straightway forgotten. Something may come of them in the future if public opinion becomes sufficiently aroused. Among those currently active are suggestions for abolishing the electoral college; limiting presidential authority to make executive agreements and the scope of treaties (the proposed Bricker amendment); giving Congress power to outlaw child labor;[35] com-

[35] The proposal passed Congress in 1924 and has been ratified by twenty-eight state legislatures. See copy of text at the end of Appendix III.

pelling recognition of equal rights for women; giving Congress power to abolish the poll tax as a prerequisite for voting; giving Congress power to act when state officials fail to prevent lynchings; limiting the power of Congress to tax incomes, estates, and gifts to a maximum rate of 25 per cent; and fixing the number of justices on the Supreme Court and limiting congressional authority over the appellate jurisdiction of Federal courts.

Judicial Interpretation. As already intimated, a constitution also grows and changes by judicial interpretation. This is particularly true of the American Federal Constitution, because it is written in concise, general words and phrases which often admit of varying interpretations. Almost every clause of the Constitution has been before the courts, and it is chiefly from their decisions that an understanding of the document must be derived. Former Chief Justice Hughes epitomized the situation when he said, "We are under the Constitution, but the Constitution is what the judges say it is." A few illustrations make his meaning clear. The preamble, the courts have held, does not convey a grant of power; it is merely a declaration of purpose. A tax on incomes is a direct tax rather than an indirect one. Congress can create corporations, such as banks, to carry out its delegated powers. The Constitution does not follow the flag into newly acquired territories. The first ten amendments apply to the national government only. The courts have authority to declare acts of Congress unconstitutional. A federal petit jury must consist of twelve persons.

Ordinarily, in deciding cases that come before them, the courts follow the rule of *stare decisis; i.e.,* they decide as they did in previous cases unless there is some compelling reason for them not to do so. This practice permits the formation of a body of "judge-made law." But judges may depart from precedents, and these changes of opinion have the same effect, at least temporarily, as if formal amendments were enacted. American history is strewn with conspicuous instances of court reversals. In 1932 Justice Brandeis listed forty important instances wherein the Supreme Court had reversed itself or drastically modified its decisions.[36] Since his listing, more reversals have occurred than during any previous period of equal length.

Careful study reveals that since 1936 the Supreme Court has reversed or greatly modified its interpretations of at least four of the most controversial provisions of the Constitution—the tax power, the commerce power, the Fifth and the Fourteenth Amendments. Indeed, constitutional lawyers of two decades ago would scarcely recognize the Constitution of today. Then, Congress could not regulate manufacturing, mining, the generation of electric power, and agricultural production, because they had no direct effect upon interstate commerce. Now, these are admitted to have sufficient effect upon interstate commerce to permit federal control. Then, Congress could not tax state instrumentalities and their employees, nor could states tax federal employees. Now, most of these intergovernmental immunities are gone. Then, states deprived liberty without due process of law by fixing minimum wages for women. Today, they do not. Then, a primary was not an election; now it is. If one were forced to decide which has had the greater influence in shaping American institutions, the amendment article or judicial interpretation, a strong case could be made for the latter.

Legislative Elaboration. The Constitution is also what Congress says it is. Simple, general phrases may be elaborated by statutes in such a way as to give them unexpected meaning. Where this occurs, the effect is often as significant as if amendments were formally enacted. The principal basis for congressional elaboration has been the implied power that authorizes the enactment of all laws that are "necessary and proper" for carrying delegated powers into effect.

Illustrations of the use of this power are legion. Executive departments are anticipated by three casual references in the Constitution, but no direct authority to create them is given. Believing them necessary and proper for effective administration, Congress has not hesitated to

[36] Burnet *v.* Coronado Oil and Gas Company, 285 U.S. 393 (1932).

legislate them into existence. Nowhere does the Constitution prescribe the precise manner by which inferior officers of the government are to be selected. Article II, Section 2, merely states that their appointment may be vested in the President alone, in the courts of law, or in the heads of departments. Nevertheless, Congress many years ago enacted a civil service law which provided, among other things, for the creation of a Civil Service Commission and the recruitment of thousands of employees on the basis of ratings made in competitive examinations. The Constitution anticipates that the circumstance might arise when both the President and Vice-President might be removed from office and authorizes Congress to provide for the choice of a Chief Executive if such a contingency should arise. The provision was elaborated by the Presidential Succession Act of 1886 and more recently the Act of July 18, 1947, wherein it was provided that first the Speaker, then the President pro tempore of the Senate, then cabinet heads should become President in the order in which the departments were established.

By broadly interpreting its powers, Congress has established and implemented a huge defense establishment, created dozens of administrative boards and bureaus, annexed a far-flung empire, entered into the business of education, banking, insurance, construction, transportation, generating electric power, and found authority to regulate the economic and social life of a highly industrialized and complicated nation.

Executive Interpretation. The courts and Congress do not have a monopoly on the right to construe the Constitution. Over the years Presidents have insisted that the document meant what they said it did and their views have frequently prevailed. Jefferson, while admitting that his power to do so was doubtful, acquired Louisiana without prior authorization by Congress. Lincoln insisted that the Southern states had never been out of the Union. Johnson, Wilson, and Franklin D. Roosevelt contended that Congress could not restrict the removal of executive employees. Cleveland asserted the right to use federal troops within a state to enforce federal law or protect federal property. Theodore Roosevelt maintained that he could agree to supervise collection of Santo Domingo customs by executive agreement rather than by treaty as many in Congress preferred. Wilson asserted the right to arm merchantmen in spite of congressional opposition. Coolidge defended his refusal to send troops into a state to maintain order merely because a state legislature or governor asked him to do so.

Various presidents have insisted that they were justified in sending armed forces anywhere in the world to protect American lives and property without obtaining legislative approval. Franklin D. Roosevelt successfully contended that the Constitution was broad enough to justify a far-reaching program of recovery and reform. Illustrations could be multiplied, but enough have been given to suggest that the Chief Executive has played a significant role in modifying and expanding the Constitution.

Custom and Usage. Many of the unwritten provisions of the Constitution have been added simply by custom and usage. Political parties are not mentioned in the Constitution but long ago they became indispensable institutions. The electoral college, though looked upon as a brilliant invention by the framers of the Constitution, ceased functioning as originally intended as early as 1796. The President's cabinet is almost entirely the product of custom. Legislative com-

mittees are not authorized in the Constitution, but custom and usage have made them as permanent as if they were. Custom decrees that members of the House of Representatives should be residents of the districts from which they are chosen, etc.

The Constitution a Living Document. Originally only a skeletal framework of government, the Constitution became a "living" document. Though written and infrequently amended, it has kept pace with the American people, allowing them a maximum of freedom while providing machinery through which order might be maintained, domestic problems resolved with a minimum of violence, and national aspirations realized. Occasionally a voice is raised calling for a complete revision of the famous document.[37] Frequently, also, dissatisfied minorities clamor for drastic alterations. The latter may get their wish if revolutionary conditions prevail for a prolonged period of time. If such conditions can be avoided, total revision seems improbable. Amendments may be added occasionally but, as in the past, the Constitution is more likely to be adapted to changing needs and conditions by interpretation, custom, and usage.

[37] See especially William Y. Elliott, *The Need for Constitutional Reform* . . . (McGraw-Hill, 1935) and Henry Hazlitt, *A New Constitution Now* (McGraw-Hill, 1942).

FOR FURTHER READING

Ames, Herman V.: "The Proposed Amendments to the Constitution . . . during the First Century of Its History" in *Annual Report of the American Historical Association for the Year 1896* (Washington, D.C.: 1897), vol. II.

Beard, Charles A.: *The Supreme Court and the Constitution* (Macmillan, 1912).

Brown, Everett S.: *Ratification of the Twenty-first Amendment to the Constitution of the United States: State Convention Records and Laws* (University of Michigan Press, 1938).

Burdick, Charles K.: *The Law of the American Constitution: Its Origin and Development* (Putnam, 1922).

Carr, Robert K.: *The Supreme Court and Judicial Review* (Rinehart, 1942).

Cooley, Thomas M.: *A Treatise on Constitutional Limitations* . . . (Little, Brown, 6th ed., 1890).

Corwin, Edward S.: *Court over Constitution: A Study of Judicial Review as an Instrument of Popular Government* (Princeton University Press, 1938).

———: *The Twilight of the Supreme Court* (Yale University Press, 1934),

Crosskey, W. W.: *Politics and the Constitution in the History of the United States* (University of Chicago Press, 2 vols., 1953).

Haines, Charles G.: *The Role of the Supreme Court in American Government and Politics, 1789–1835* (University of California Press, 1944).

——: *The American Doctrine of Judicial Supremacy* (University of California Press, 2d ed., 1932).

Hazlitt, Henry: *A New Constitution Now* (McGraw-Hill, 1942).

Hehmeyer, Alexander: *Time for a Change: A Proposal for a Second Constitutional Convention* (Rinehart, 1943).

Heller, Francis H.: *The Sixth Amendment to the Constitution of the United States: A Study in Constitutional Development* (University of Kansas Press, 1951).

Horwill, Herbert W.: *Usages of the American Constitution* (Oxford, 1925).

McBain, Howard L.: *The Living Constitution: A Consideration of the Realities and Legends of Our Fundamental Law* (Macmillan, 1934).

Merriam, Charles E.: *The Written Constitution and the Unwritten Attitude* (Richard R. Smith, 1931).

Munro, William B.: *The Makers of the Unwritten Constitution* (Macmillan, 1930).

Musmanno, Michael A.: *Proposed Amendments to the Constitution . . .* , H. Doc. 551, 70th Cong., 2d Sess. (1929).

Myers, Denys P.: *The Process of Constitutional Amendment*, S. Doc. 314, 76th Cong., 3d Sess. (1941).

Orfield, Lester B.: *Amending the Federal Constitution* (Chicago: Callaghan, 1942).

Story, Joseph: *Commentaries on the Constitution of the United States* (Little, Brown, 4th ed., 2 vols., 1873).

Swisher, Carl B.: *The Growth of Constitutional Power in the United States* (University of Chicago Press, 1946).

——: *American Constitutional Development* (Houghton Mifflin, 1943).

Tansill, Charles C. (ed.): *Proposed Amendments to the Constitution Introduced in Congress, December 4, 1899–July 2, 1926*, S. Doc. 93, 69th Cong., 1st Sess. (1926).

Ten Broek, Jacobus: *The Antislavery Origins of the Fourteenth Amendment* (University of California Press, 1951).

Warren, Charles: *Congress, the Constitution, and the Supreme Court* (Little, Brown, 1925).

Wright, Benjamin F.: *The Growth of American Constitutional Law* (Reynal & Hitchcock, 1942).

REVIEW QUESTIONS

1. What is the constitutional basis for each of the principles discussed in this chapter?

2. Of what practical significance is the principle of popular sovereignty today?

3. What circumstances led the Founding Fathers to prefer a federal system to one that was unitary?

4. How does the representative system of government differ from a pure, or direct, democracy? What are the advantages and disadvantages of each?

5. Do you think our system of government has enough safeguards to ensure that the military can be kept permanently subordinated to civilian authority?

6. Defend and criticize the Supreme Court's decision in Marbury *v.* Madison.

7. How do you explain the comparatively large increase in the number of laws declared unconstitutional during the period 1920–1940? How do you explain the decrease since 1940?

8. Defend and criticize the doctrine of separation of powers.

9. On the whole, has judicial review been beneficial or harmful to the welfare of the American people?

10. Explain the procedure by which each of the amendments to the Constitution was added. Should any of the amendments which were proposed by Congress but which remain unratified by the required number of states be added to the Constitution?

11. Give examples of changes made in the American system of government by methods other than amendment.

12. Of the constitutional amendments now under consideration in and out of Congress, which should be added to the Constitution?

CHAPTER 5

The Federal System

Whether the Constitution, as it has divided the powers of Govt. between the States in their separate & in their united Capacities, tends to an oppressive aggrandizement of the Genl. Govt. or to an Anarchical Independence of the State Govts. is a problem which time alone can absolutely determine. — James Madison in 1821 [1]

The federal state is one in which authority is divided between self-governing parts and the central whole, each part operating in its sphere of action as defined in fundamental law. Among federal states of the modern world are the United States of America, Switzerland, Canada, and the Commonwealth of Australia. The unitary state concentrates power in a single central government, which has legal omnipotence over all territory within the state. Examples of unitary states in recent times include France, Great Britain, and most of the smaller nations of the world.

Under the federal scheme, matters that are considered of primary importance to the country as a whole are assigned to the national government. Usually these services include foreign relations, defense, foreign commerce, and monetary matters. Functions deemed principally of local interest are given to provincial (in United States, state) governments. Local affairs include such matters as regulation of local commerce, public education, roads and highways. In all federal systems a basic difficulty is the impossibility of distributing powers between central and local governments on a permanently satisfactory basis.

With changing conditions, alteration in distribution of powers is necessary; hence, there is a recurrence of constitutional crises in countries using the federal plan.

FEDERALISM IN THEORY AND PRACTICE

History of Federalism. Federalism has been practiced since ancient times. Greek city-states united into leagues for common worship and for the resistance of common enemies. In medieval times three notable confederations were established. The Lombard League was formed by northern Italian cities to resist the Hohenstaufens. In northern Germany the Hanseatic League achieved considerable commercial and political strength. The Netherlands Confederation bound the northern lowland provinces through the years of Spanish oppression.

Modern federations had a forerunner in the old Swiss Confederation, to which the authors of *The Federalist* allude frequently. It was, however, the launching of the United States that drew the attention of the modern world to the possibilities of federalism. The Founding Fathers found little in historical precedent that would guide them in building the first modern truly federal constitution and in solving the difficult problems of distribution of powers between national and state governments. It is remarkable,

[1] Letter to John G. Jackson in Gaillard Hunt (ed.), *The Writings of James Madison* (Putnam, 1910), vol. IX, pp. 71–72.

therefore, that they succeeded in framing a fundamental law that, with few amendments, has proved adaptable through a century and a half of revolutionary change.

Reasons for Adoption of Federalism. A careful examination of a world map reveals a striking geographic fact about nations with the federal form of government. Nearly all countries very large in area have adopted the federal principle. Among these far-flung nations utilizing federalism in one form or another may be listed the Soviet Union, United States, Canada, Australia, Argentina, Brazil, and Mexico. In addition, federal ideas have been embodied in the new governments of India and Pakistan, and have been proposed for the Western European Community.

In virtually all the modern federal systems, historical or ethnic factors have made the formation of a unitary government impossible. A federal union was the natural solution for the American states, which sought effective unity on common problems yet wished to preserve individuality in local affairs. Switzerland is a trilingual country, with strong traditions of cantonal self-government. The First Reich (1871–1918) and Second Reich (1918–1933) eras in Germany found federation an appropriate device in transition from individual principalities to the centralized, totalitarian state. Both Canada and Australia were made up of former colonies of Great Britain; in each the welding of these territories together under unitary form was ruled out because of both geographic extent and historical separation. In Canada the French problem made federation even more necessary. Although the Bolshevik program of reform required close coordination, the polyglot population and scattered lands and large area of Russia dictated federal form, if not spirit.

In two of the four Latin-American federations, Mexico and Venezuela, the adoption of federalism was due in large part to the desire to imitate the liberal institutions of the United States. Although strong reasons existed for the use of the federal plan in Argentina and Brazil, these countries in recent years have all but abandoned federalism through constant national

FEDERAL SYSTEMS OF THE WORLD

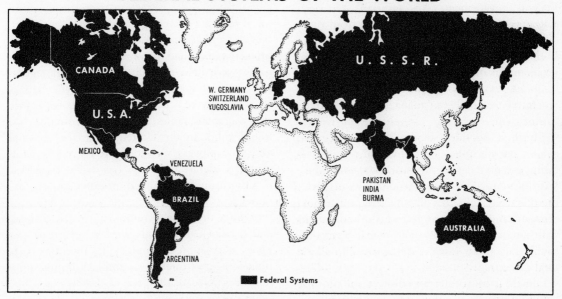

The fourteen nations named are deemed by the authors to be federal in form, although not invariably in spirit. Two nations that are sometimes listed as federations—Netherlands and Union of South Africa—we classify as unitary. For constitutional provisions, see Amos J. Peaslee, *Constitutions of Nations* (Rumford Press, 3 vols., 1950).

intervention in state affairs.[2] Following the Second World War the federal idea was found useful in the launching of new governments in India, Pakistan, Burma, Yugoslavia, Western Germany, and Indonesia, although the last mentioned subsequently became a unitary state.

Advantages of Federalism in the United States. In the United States federalism was adopted and is retained because it possesses certain merits. First, it secures the benefits of local self-government and civic training. Often the best judges of a public function are those close to it. Local needs vary, and services may be adapted to suit the community. Individuals are more apt to feel responsibility for and to participate in something that stems from city hall, county courthouse, or state capitol than something directed from a far-off national capital.

Second, it allows flexibility for experimentation and adaptation to areas with dissimilar interests and populations. If North Dakota wishes to try writing state hail insurance, it may gain valuable experience useful to other states and to the national government. State experiments in social insurance and in other fields may provide data on which might be built a sound policy for the Federal government. An agrarian American state meets problems vastly different from those of an industrialized state. A French-speaking Catholic province of Canada has on many social problems an outlook quite divergent from that of an English-speaking Protestant one. Under a federal system each can manage its local affairs to suit itself.

Third, it provides stability and a safeguard against encroachment on individual rights. Differing election dates and varied issues produce less drastic turnover of officeholders than under the unitary scheme. An all-powerful central government might sweep away rights of individuals and minorities, but division of authority between state and national governments provides a dual protection.

Fourth, it constitutes an effective compromise between fractionalization into many small nations and the centralization that destroys local

[2] Russell H. Fitzgibbon, "Constitutional Development in Latin America: A Synthesis," *American Political Science Review,* vol. 39 (June, 1945), pp. 511–522.

autonomy. Breaking up the American republic of today into forty-eight small nations is unthinkable. Certainly most Americans would reject also the centralization of all authority in Washington. The effectiveness of the compromise hinges upon either having static conditions (a natural impossibility) or possessing a fundamental law that is both sufficiently elastic to allow changes when persistently demanded by the public and rigid enough to resist momentary gusts of passion. Viewed over a long-time period, the American federal system has proved adaptable to the needs of a growing people and a dynamic society.

Shortcomings of American Federal System. No useful purpose is served, however, by heaping unstinted praise upon federalism and closing eyes to its several shortcomings. First, and most important, distribution of powers between two levels of government on a permanently satisfactory basis is impossible. Technological developments, economic conditions, wars, social changes—these alter the problems of government and may necessitate reallocation of responsibilities for particular public services. If the constitution in which powers are assigned is precise and inflexible, dissatisfaction over the resulting social lag may be very great.

At several critical periods in American history problems that had become clearly national in scope were held not subject to federal legislation. Three federal attempts to curb the evils of child labor were declared unconstitutional before the wages-and-hours law of 1938 finally was found valid. In the United States the national and state powers were defined in very general terms. Federal authority has been expanded mainly through liberalized interpretations of national powers by the Supreme Court.

Second, diffusion of authority leads to delay and deadlock in critical times. In war and economic depression the country has found its parts divided against themselves and lacking the unity necessary to solve the great issues at hand. The sense of corporate unity that has enveloped the nation during its major wars and the broad nature of the war powers have caused less embarrassment than have some domestic crises. During the depression of the early 1930's many cases of inactivity were the result of this disunity.

Third, confusion arises under the federal plan from the lack of uniformity in laws, and extra expense is incurred through the maintenance of two levels of government. While some progress has been made toward securing uniform state legislation in certain fields, the diversity of state law is enormous, to the great dismay of the individual and to the added expense of those doing business. Often it is said that two levels of government are more expensive than one; although the statement may be true, the scope of the problem makes the question speculative.

Although still one of the world's leading exponents of federalism, the United States has experienced profound changes in its own system,

WEIGHING FEDERALISM*

MERITS OF WELL-CONCEIVED LOCAL CONTROL

1. Promotes local unity, sense of neighborhood responsibility, spirit of self-reliance and capacity for group action.
2. Secures close adaptation of public services to local needs.
3. Promotes and safeguards freedom, democracy, and responsible government.
4. Promotes socially beneficial intercommunity competition.
5. Permits safe experimentation with new forms and methods of government, thus fostering a gradual improvement in government throughout the country.
6. Promotes political stability.
7. Promotes national unity and national security.
8. Relieves the national government of congestion of business.

MERITS OF WELL-CONCEIVED CENTRAL CONTROL

1. Unifies the nation.
2. Provides for the common or national needs of the population and for a coordinated development of the nation's resources.
3. Safeguards the nation's independence.
4. Safeguards the liberties of the people in a democratic country and provides for an equality of social, economic, and educational opportunities in the various sections of the country.
5. Responds quickly to changed national situations and takes care of national emergencies.
6. Is more efficient and economical in many respects than are local governments.
7. Gives common direction to local governments, impels them to maintain minimum standards of public service, and helps them to operate more efficiently.

SHORTCOMINGS OF EXCESSIVE DECENTRALIZATION

1. Results in an inefficient and an uneconomic management of local affairs.
2. Fosters local autocratic rule by petty officials and powerful minority groups.
3. Breeds narrow parochialism and produces national and regional disunity and disorganization.
4. Results in extreme inequality in the standards of public service and protection of civil rights throughout the country or the region.
5. Produces inertia and extreme rigidity in the organization and operation of the government.
6. Lessens national security.

DANGERS OF EXCESSIVE CENTRALIZATION OF GOVERNMENT

1. Promotes a rule of an irresponsible national bureaucracy and destroys democracy.
2. Results in a neglect of local needs.
3. Destroys local civic interest, initiative, and responsibility, individual freedom and self-reliance.
4. Results in the instability of governmental policies, and of the government itself.
5. Results in inefficiency and waste.
6. Produces a congestion of business, industry, arts, and culture in the capital and the economic and cultural decay of the rest of the country.
7. Weakens national unity and national security.

*Condensed from Paul Studenski and Paul R. Mort, *Centralized vs. Decentralized Government in Relation to Democracy* (Teachers College, Columbia University, 1941).

chiefly in the direction of expanding central authority at the expense of local autonomy.

Federalism Reconsidered. More than sixteen decades after the American federal system opened for business, the Congress created a body to study its operation. The Commission on Intergovernmental Relations was established in 1953 and given the task of examining the roles of the Federal government and the states. It was a large body, consisting of twenty-five members, of whom fifteen were appointed by the President, five by the president of the Senate, and five by the Speaker of the House.

After some initial difficulty in finding adequate leadership, the Commission settled down to work under the chairmanship of Mr. Meyer Kestnbaum. A series of study and advisory committees was established in each of the functional and fiscal areas principally involved in federal-state relations. Fifteen separate studies were published, in addition to the annual report.[3]

Although the report of the Commission reads at some points like a "states rights" tract, most of its recommendations are moderate and indicate a willingness to build upon the experience of the past. There is a careful review of how the federal system came into being, of the role of the states, of jurisdictional problems relating to federal and state functions, and of fiscal interrelationships such as the grant-in-aid. Specific recommendations are made in the latter part of the report, in which functions are described. Recommendations for major changes include increased state participation in soil and agricultural conservation, larger federal grants for highways (and reduced supervision), and a revised formula for old-age assistance payments to the states.

Among the controversial items, the Commission reported adversely on the proposed federal aid to elementary and secondary education. It stressed the difficulty posed by the fact that 12 per cent of the nation's children attend nonpublic schools. Another barrier was the choice of appropriate agencies for handling federal grants,

objections being raised to both direct dealing with school districts and to transmission through state governments.

In order to focus continuous attention on the problems of intergovernmental relations, the Commission suggested that a special assistant in the Executive Office of the President be given coordinating responsibilities. An "advisory board," appointed by the President, would meet from time to time and provide advice in the interlevel area. Much attention was given by the Commission to the fiscal aspects of federal-state relations, and several recommendations pointed to the need for careful review and coordination. In the natural resources field, the Commission supported a permanent "board of coordination and review" to advise the national government on policy and state cooperation.

The *Report* constitutes an important milestone in the evolution of American federalism. Its emphasis on the necessity of virile state governments may prove a valuable corrective to the centralist tendencies of the preceding quarter century. The numerous dissents indicate a lack of broad consensus. On one hand some commissioners, particularly the former governors, would have liked to see reversed the Supreme Court decisions that permitted the fuller exercise of federal powers.[4] Other commissioners, led by the "liberal" senators, felt that the Federal government must continue to extend efforts to serve the general welfare of the whole people.[5]

Unwieldy in size, the Commission was scarcely designed to make daring and imaginative proposals. Compared with its Canadian counterpart, the Royal Commission on Dominion-Provincial Relations, the American Commission appears to have been too large and excessively bound down with representatives of particular interests—congressional, state, partisan, and other—to achieve the desirable meeting of minds and agreement on ways and means of modernizing the federal system. Nevertheless

---

[3] U.S. Commission on Intergovernmental Relations, *Report . . .* (1955). The full list of publications appears on p. 295 of the report.

[4] *Ibid.,* pp. 59–60, footnotes 1 and 2. Six former governors were members of the Commission.

[5] *Ibid.,* pp. 277–279, for dissent of Senator Morse. On many of his separate statements and dissents on specific topics, he was joined by Senator Humphrey.

the several studies made by and under the Commission, plus surveys made in selected states, may serve as the facts-and-figures foundation on which sound policies and programs in federal-state relations can be constructed.

DISTRIBUTION OF POWERS

Delegated Powers of the National Government. The American national government possesses only those powers specifically delegated to it, or reasonably to be inferred from the Constitution. The Tenth Amendment declares: "The powers not delegated to the United States by the Constitution, nor prohibited by it to the States, are reserved to the States respectively, or to the people."

The major federal powers are enumerated as powers of Congress in Article I, Section 8. They are shown on the chart on page 71. Other federal powers are provided for in other parts of the Constitution.

That the national government today appears to possess powers not exercised in the years following 1789 does not disprove the fact that the United States has a central government of enumerated powers only. Some of the federal powers, especially tax and commerce, have grown tremendously in scope; the Constitution has shown great capacity for adaptation to changed conditions. Nevertheless, every activity of the national government must be justified under one or more of the specifically delegated powers. Congress lacks a general welfare power, under which it might do anything required by the public interest. Each act of Congress must be hung upon a constitutional "hook"—commerce, tax, monetary, or other. If no constitutional delegation can be found, or if one is improperly used, the legislation may be attacked as unconstitutional. The fact that Congress possesses only powers specifically delegated to it, or reasonably inferred, is one of the outstanding features of American government.

Implied Powers. After the list of powers of Congress given in Article I, Section 8, the Constitution grants Congress authority to "make all Laws which shall be necessary and proper for carrying into Execution the foregoing Powers, and all other Powers vested by this Constitution in the Government of the United States, or in any Department or Officer thereof." This "elastic" or "necessary and proper" clause has given rise to extended controversy over the breadth of national authority.

The "strict constructionalist" versus "broad constructionalist" conflict over this point has raged at several periods of national history. What unspecified powers reasonably might be implied from those specifically delegated? Hamilton and his followers claimed that Congress possessed authority to do many things in addition to the powers explicitly stated. Jefferson and his supporters insisted that federal powers should be interpreted by the letter of the Constitution and that no authority could be exercised unless specifically delegated.

Under John Marshall, Chief Justice from 1801 to 1835, the Supreme Court rendered many decisions that supported broad interpretation. The most celebrated case was McCulloch *v.* Maryland.[6] Maryland had levied a tax upon notes issued by the Baltimore branch of the second United States Bank. The cashier refused to pay the tax. Two principal questions were posed. First, may the United States charter such a bank? The Court answered that it might do so under the congressional power to coin money and to regulate the value thereof. Marshall argued:

We admit, as all must admit, that the powers of the government are limited, and that its limits are not to be transcended. But we think the sound construction of the Constitution must allow to the national legislature that discretion, with respect to the means by which the powers it confers are to be carried into execution, which will enable that body to perform the high duties assigned to it, in the manner most beneficial to the people. Let the end be legitimate, let it be within the scope of the Constitution, and all means which are appropriate, which are plainly adapted to that end, which are not prohibited, but consist with the letter and spirit of the Constitution, are constitutional. . . .

Another question involved the power of the state to tax the issue of the bank. The Court de-

[6] 4 Wheat. 316 (U.S. 1819).

nied to the state authority to tax a federal instrumentality on the ground that the "power to tax involves the power to destroy."

The ultimate decision regarding the validity of invoking implied power in a given instance is rendered by the Federal Supreme Court. In its decisions regarding the scope of national power the Court has been far from consistent. Very great latitude has been permitted by the Court in some lines and at certain periods. In other fields and at other times the Congress has been held to the letter of the fundamental law.

Over a century and a half the Court has built up lines of legal precedent on both sides of many such issues before the Court. Therefore, the judge who is predisposed for or against expansion of the scope of federal power may easily find important cases to support his decision. The judge wanting to interpret national power narrowly cites as authority cases from the Taney or Taft eras in the Court. The broad construction of federal authority is justified by citing from Marshall and Stone epochs.

Powers of the States. The state governments possess an indefinite grant of the remaining powers that are not given to the Federal government nor prohibited to the states. The sweeping nature of this authority is indicated in the language of the Tenth Amendment. This authority does not mean, however, that the states have unlimited power, for they specifically are forbidden to do many things, especially in Article I, Section 10. There the states are forbidden to make treaties, emit bills of credit, make other than gold and silver legal tender, pass a bill of attainder, pass an ex post facto law, impair the obligation of contracts, grant titles of nobility, tax imports or exports, lay tonnage taxes, keep troops or warships in peacetime, make compacts without congressional approval.

Being residual in nature, state powers are broader than those of the Federal government. States are assumed to have authority to do anything that is not prohibited in Federal or state constitutions. The principal state power, the police power, gives the state sanction to provide for the health, morals, safety, and welfare of its people.

All governmental power, however, cannot be classified exclusively into federal or state categories. Inevitably, some powers are shared by the two levels of government; these are usually called "concurrent powers." For example, both state and Federal governments set standards of weights and measures, tax and borrow, and enact bankruptcy laws.

The Supreme Law of the Land. The supremacy of the Federal Constitution, and of national law within its sphere, is assured by Article VI, Clause 2, which provides:

This Constitution, and the Laws of the United States which shall be made in Pursuance thereof; and all Treaties made, or which shall be made, under the Authority of the United States, shall be the supreme Law of the Land; and the Judges in every State shall be bound thereby, any Thing in the Constitution or Laws of any State to the Contrary notwithstanding.

Perhaps more than any other portion of the Constitution, this clause expresses the spirit of the Union. The Federal Constitution is paramount over all other forms of law, state or national. Federal law, if validly enacted under the Constitution, ranks above state law. State laws that conflict with valid federal laws or treaties may be adjudged unconstitutional on such grounds. The final verdict in a dispute between national and state jurisdiction or law is given by the federal judiciary.

In event of conflict between federal and state laws either an officer of the Federal government or a private citizen can institute a suit in Federal court. If the court finds the state law in conflict, the law is unenforceable. Failure of a state to respect the decision would justify the use of military force by the Federal government. The first occasion upon which a state law was declared unconstitutional by the United States Supreme Court was that of Fletcher *v.* Peck [7] wherein an act of Georgia was at issue. Since then nearly five hundred state laws have failed to meet the test of constitutionality. Fortunately, the Federal government has seldom found it necessary to resort to the use of force.

[7] 6 Cranch 87 (U.S. 1810).

Examples of the Distribution of Powers in the American Federal System

FEDERAL
Delegated

1. To tax.
2. To borrow and coin money.
3. To establish post offices and post roads.
4. To grant patents and copyrights.
5. To regulate interstate and foreign commerce.
6. To establish inferior courts.
7. To declare war, grant letters of marque and reprisal.
8. To raise and support an army.
9. To maintain a navy.
10. To provide for militia.
11. To govern territories and property.
12. To define and punish piracies and felonies on the high seas.
13. To fix standards of weights and measures.
14. To conduct foreign relations.
15. To make laws necessary and proper for carrying into execution the foregoing.

BOTH
Concurrent

1. Both Congress and states may tax.
2. Both may borrow money.
3. Both may charter banks and other corporations.
4. Both may establish and maintain courts.
5. Both may make and enforce laws.
6. Both may take property for public purposes.
7. Both may spend money to provide for general welfare.

STATE
Reserved to States

1. To regulate intrastate commerce.
2. To establish local governments.
3. To protect health, safety, and morals.
4. To protect life and property and maintain order.
5. To ratify amendments.
6. To conduct elections.
7. To change state constitutions and governments.

FORBIDDEN

Prohibitions upon Congress

1. No tax on exports.
2. Direct taxes must be proportionate to population of states.
3. Indirect taxes must be uniform.
4. Guaranties contained in Bill of Rights not to be abridged.
5. Preference may not be given to one state over another in matters of commerce.
6. State boundaries cannot be changed without consent of states involved.
7. Newly admitted states cannot be placed on plane of inequality with original states.
8. May not permit slavery.
9. May not grant titles of nobility.

Prohibitions on States

1. May not coin money, keep troops or ships of war in time of peace.
2. May not enter into treaties.
3. May not pass laws impairing obligation of contract.
4. May not deny persons equal protection of the laws.
5. May not violate Federal Constitution or obstruct federal laws.
6. May not prevent persons from voting because of race, color, or sex.
7. May not tax imports.
8. May not tax exports.
9. May not permit slavery.
10. May not grant titles of nobility.

UNITS OF AMERICAN GOVERNMENT

Number and Diversity of Units. One attribute of the American federal system that proves most confusing is the multiplicity of units of government and the diversity in their names, powers, and duties. Thus far only the two major levels of government, Federal and state, have been mentioned. Legally the state possesses all the power exercised by both state and local governments; in practice, however, it delegates both powers and functions to a multiplicity of political subdivisions. The full list of these local units is astonishing and causes the average citizen to despair of finding the precise government unit charged with the service concerning which he seeks information. Actually the total number of units of government declined nearly 25 per cent between 1942 and 1952, according to the Bureau of the Census, as shown in the accompanying table.

It has been pointed out elsewhere that the United States proper, without territories, contains more than 3 million square miles; the 1950 census recorded a population in that area of 150,-697,361.

The States. The states vary greatly in area, in population, and in wealth. Their equality in the Union is like the dictum that all men are created equal: politically it is so in one sense, but each individual is endowed differently in physique, in abilities, and in his share of the world's goods. In area the states vary from Rhode Island, with 1,214 square miles, to Texas, with 267,339 square miles. In population (1950 census) they ranged from Nevada, with 160,083, to New York, with 14,830,192. In wealth some far outstrip others in resources, access to markets, and industrial facilities. Pressure for federal aid often is most intense from the poorer states, and the use of federal grants helps to correct some of the inequalities between states.

Local Governments. Comments about units of local government are in place here. All but Rhode Island use counties (Louisiana parishes are similar), although the importance of the county varies considerably. In the South, West, and Middle Atlantic areas counties are the major units of local government; in New England they have a minimum of functions and exist largely for administrative convenience. The New Eng-

Total Government Units 1942 and 1952

Units of government	Number of units		Percentage change
	1942	*1952*	
United States government...	1	1	0.0
States....................	48	48	0.0
Counties..................	3,050	3,049	0.03
Municipalities.............	16,220	16,778	+3.4
Townships................	18,919	17,202	−9.1
School districts...........	108,579	67,346	−38.0
Special districts...........	8,299	12,319	+48.4
Total..................	155,116	116,743	−24.7

SOURCE: U.S. Department of Commerce, Bureau of the Census, *Governments in the United States in 1952*, State and Local Government Special Studies, no. 31 (1953), p. 1.

land town, embracing rural and urban territories, has broad governmental functions. The Middle Western township is a distant cousin but is primarily rural and is assigned less important powers and duties. School districts and other special districts usually have the power to tax and constitute an important category of governmental units.

ADMISSION OF STATES TO THE UNION

The thirteen states existing at the time of the federal Constitutional Convention were given an opportunity to be blanketed in as charter members of the Union. The new government was declared in operation after eleven states had ratified the Constitution. North Carolina and Rhode Island finally ratified in 1789 and 1790, respectively. The union of thirteen states lasted only 1 year, however, for the flow of new states continued with never a decade's interruption until the last contiguous continental territories, namely Arizona and New Mexico, became states in the year 1912.

Admission Procedure. Procedure for the admission of new states is well established. Congress, under Article IV, Section 3, has the sole power of admitting new states. The major restriction upon the authority of Congress is the requirement that territory of existing states may not be taken without their consent.

The admission process normally has involved five steps: (1) A territorial government is organized. (2) The territory applies to Congress for admission to the Union. (3) Congress enacts an "enabling act" outlining procedure for framing the constitution. (4) The territory frames a constitution. (5) Congress passes a resolution of admission.

Can Congress Impose Conditions for Admission? Congress can withhold, and has withheld, admission from would-be states until certain conditions are met. If, however, these conditions pertain to internal matters, they cannot be enforced after the admission of the state. Once admitted, the state achieves a condition of equality with all other states, and may not be bound by prior commitments.[8] On the other hand, conditions imposed regarding disposition of federal lands ceded to states and other matters under federal jurisdiction are fully enforceable in law.

The imposition of conditions on new states began in 1802 with the admission of Ohio. Although acts of admission usually described the

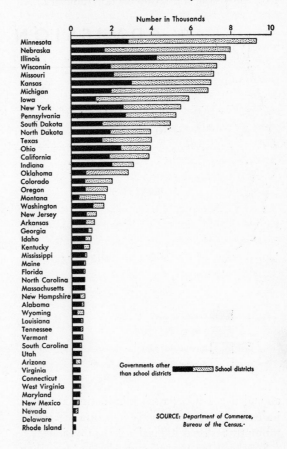

NUMBER OF GOVERNMENTS, by State 1952

Number in Thousands

SOURCE: Department of Commerce, Bureau of the Census.

status of each new state as "on an equal footing with the original states," Congress repeatedly placed detailed conditions on new members of the Union. Utah, on admission in 1896, was required to forbid polygamy and to assure nonsectarian public schools. Oklahoma, as a condition of admission in 1907, promised not to move its capital from Guthrie for a period of years. Four years later the state voted removal of the capital

[8] The leading case in this field is Coyle *v.* Smith, 221 U.S. 559 (1911).

to Oklahoma City. When the case was appealed to the United States Supreme Court, this restriction on the state was declared invalid on the ground that all states are politically equal and have full control over their internal affairs. The enabling act to admit Arizona was vetoed by President Taft in 1911 because of his objection to a provision for recall of the judiciary. An

RESTRICTIONS ON THE STATES

Some prohibitions against state action were necessary in order to protect the Federal government against state encroachments and to ensure national supremacy in national matters. Others were deemed necessary to assure individual rights against attack by the states. Powers denied to the states include those listed in Article I, Sec-

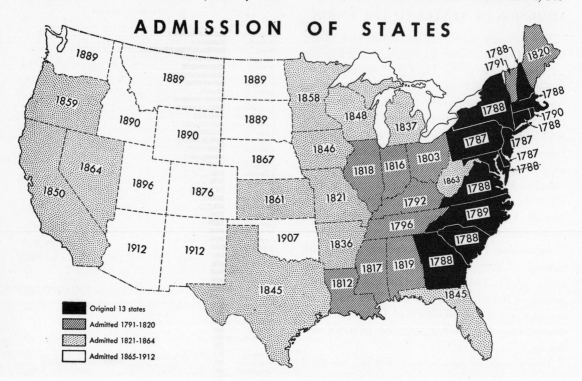

ADMISSION OF STATES

Original 13 states
Admitted 1791-1820
Admitted 1821-1864
Admitted 1865-1912

amended act was passed eliminating recall of judges; after admission in 1912, Arizona promptly restored judicial recall provisions.[9]

Statehood for Hawaii and Alaska. More than four decades after the last contiguous territories of continental United States became states, serious consideration is now being given to the admission of Hawaii and Alaska. Their important roles and loyalty during the Second World War have added much weight to their claims to statehood. The future of Puerto Rico is very much in doubt, for sentiment there appears to be divided sharply between those who wish independence and those who desire statehood.

[9] Frederick L. Bird and Frances M. Ryan, *The Recall of Public Officers* (Macmillan, 1930), p. 6.

tion 10. While the most sweeping prohibitions are contained in the Fourteenth Amendment, states are also restrained by the Fifteenth Amendment from withholding suffrage rights because of race, color, or previous condition of servitude, and by the Nineteenth Amendment because of sex.

Treaties and Compacts. Two provisions in Article I, Section 10, protect the Union by forbidding American states to enter into special arrangements with foreign nations, and by ensuring federal control over interstate agreements. No state may enter into a treaty, alliance, or confederation. This is an unconditional prohibition, and helps to make exclusive federal control over foreign relations. This clause was used frequently during and after the Civil War to sustain the Northern contention that states have no right to secede from the Union. It prevents New York from making a treaty with Canada with respect to the St. Lawrence waterway. It forbids Texas to join a league of nations or a Pan-American union. It makes impossible the adherence of the New England states to a new world union of the democracies.

The restriction against entering an agreement or compact with another state or foreign power is less drastic, for Congress may permit such action. Although informal "gentlemen's agreements" between state governors and foreign governments are not unknown, they are extremely rare. On the other hand, many interstate compacts have been negotiated and approved by Congress. A very lively interest in this device has developed during the last two decades. It will be evaluated in the next chapter.

Denial of Monetary Powers. No money may be coined by states, nothing but gold and silver coin made legal tender for payment of debts, and no bills of credit emitted. The courts have held that money means gold, silver, and copper coin and also that coinage involves molding a metallic substance of intrinsic value.[10] During the Revolution and Confederation the variety of moneys and the disparity of values were so great that stress was placed on the necessity of a uniform medium of exchange, with value controlled by the national government. States have been inclined not to interfere in this field; some discussion arose when states first began to issue sales-tax tokens, but it is now generally agreed that these do not constitute coin.

Since the Constitution forbids states to make other than gold and silver coin legal tender in payment of debts, state experimentation in monetary reform is curbed effectively. Notes issued by state banks have continued to circulate, but no state can force their acceptance. Congress alone retains the authority to establish other forms of legal tender. Thus a "United States note" may be inscribed "This note is legal tender at its face

[10] Griswold *v.* Hepburn, 63 Ky. 20 (1865). For a fuller discussion of federal fiscal power, see Chap. 19.

value for all debts, public and private" without any mention of gold or silver. But if a state government fell into the hands of monetary reformers who sought to issue "prosperity certificates," a state could not compel the acceptance of such scrip.

Indeed, the issuance of such scrip probably is forbidden by the constitutional provision that no state shall emit bills of credit. A bill of credit is a paper medium issued by a state and intended to circulate as money. State bank notes were not prohibited by this clause; they continued to circulate until taxed out of existence by the Federal government in the 1860's. The dated stamp scrip or warrants proposed under the "Retirement Life Payments" scheme which the California electorate defeated in 1938, 1939, and 1942 very likely would have been deemed bills of credit by the courts. The Canadian province of Alberta, under its "social credit" administration, in 1936 paid road workers with "prosperity certificates"; these might have been called a violation of the bills of credit prohibition if an American state had issued them. In placing this provision in the Constitution, its framers showed appreciation for the principle, known as Gresham's law, that a cheaper medium of exchange tends to displace the dearer when the two are permitted to circulate side by side.

Limitation of State War Powers. Three points among the list of restrictions touch upon the authority of the states in relation to war. States are forbidden to issue letters of marque and reprisal; Article I, Section 8, of the Constitution authorizes Congress to grant such documents. A letter of marque and reprisal empowers the holder to privateer and prey upon the commerce of another nation. Because such approval of privateering is likely to involve a country in war, the power wisely was reserved for the level of government with control over foreign relations.

States also are denied the right to keep troops or ships of war without the consent of Congress. This denial does not prevent the maintenance of a state militia that may be deemed necessary to put down armed insurrection too strong for civil authority to curb. Since the First World

War, the state militias have been organized as units of the National Guard, under joint federal-state auspices. The purpose of the restriction was to prevent the development of state armies and navies, and to ensure federal supremacy in the defense field. During the Second World War, Congress authorized states to form militia and guard units outside the National Guard organization.

The final restraint, forbidding a state to engage in war unless actually invaded, is of little practical importance today but may have constituted some deterrent on provocative incidents precipitated by state officers. Congress has the sole power to declare war, and it is fitting that the states should not compromise the position of the Federal government by rash actions on their international boundaries.

Limitations on State Tax Power. The authors of the Constitution were careful to forbid Congress to discriminate between states and ports in matters of regulation and taxation. It was fitting, therefore, that they should prohibit unfair uses of state tax powers. States were denied the right to tax imports or exports. Goods might be taxed by a state before shipment to another state or after arrival from another state. Long controversy has ensued over what constitutes arrival. The courts developed an "original-package" doctrine under which a commodity leaves the channel of trade only when the original box, bale, or carton in which it was shipped is opened. Only then is it taxable by the state. Reasonable state inspection fees on exported or imported goods may properly be collected. It is well established that states may not burden interstate commerce through taxation.

State tonnage duties on ships are prohibited except with the consent of Congress. This tax is charged on the basis of tonnage capacity of a vessel, for entering or leaving a port. It should be distinguished from a wharfage charge or fee, which validly may be collected from a ship for wharfage services.

The implied restriction, derived from the very nature of the federal system, that states cannot tax federal instrumentalities and the Federal government cannot tax states is of very great importance. It was stated in McCulloch *v.* Maryland (1819) in terms of "power to tax involves the power to destroy." The list of exemptions from state taxation expanded greatly through the years, including not only federal property, but also federal salaries, gasoline used by federal agencies, and income from federal bonds. Finally, in 1939 the Supreme Court began to narrow the field of reciprocal immunity.

The Fourteenth Amendment, Section 4, forbids states to assume or pay any debt or obligation incurred in aid of insurrection or rebellion against the United States. Such debts are declared illegal and void.

Protection of Personal and Property Rights. As is noted in Chap. 7, states are prevented from violating personal and property rights. They may not pass ex post facto laws, bills of attainder, or laws impairing the obligation of contract. Nor may they deny due process of law, deprive persons of equal protection under the law, or abridge the privileges and immunities of American citizens. When states violate liberties, a federal question arises that justifies resort to Federal courts. While this provides only a legal remedy, experience has demonstrated the wisdom of subjecting member units of the federal union to constitutional limitations enforceable by the central government.

Suffrage Restrictions. The Constitution in its original form gave to the states virtually the whole responsibility for determining who might vote in both federal and state elections. The electorate for federal officers was declared to be the same in each state as that for the most numerous branch of the state legislature. This situation was altered, however, by both the Fifteenth and Nineteenth Amendments; and Section 2 of the Fourteenth contained a penalty which might be invoked against states disfranchising a proportion of the male population.

The Fifteenth Amendment declares simply: "The right of citizens of the United States to vote shall not be denied or abridged by the United States or by any State on account of race, color, or previous condition of servitude." Congress is given authority to enforce this provision by appropriate legislation. The meaning is clear, and the amendment has been used to sweep away several attempts to restrain Negro participation in elections. A number of indirect ways have been developed, however, to bar colored people on grounds of illiteracy, nonpayment of poll taxes, and similar devices. Acts by private individuals and bodies are not included in this prohibition.

The Nineteenth Amendment banning discrimination on account of sex effectively ended all state denial of woman suffrage. As the amendment refers only to the right to vote, several states continued to ban women from jury duty.

The penalty contained in Amendment XIV, providing that a state's representation in the House of Representatives may be reduced in the proportion to which adult (twenty-one years) male citizens are denied the right to vote, has never been invoked by Congress.

FEDERAL OBLIGATIONS TO THE STATES

The number of federal guaranties to the states is not large, but taken together they are of considerable importance. The Federal government is bound to respect the territorial integrity of existing states in admitting new states; it must guarantee a republican form of government to the states; it is bound to protect states against domestic violence and foreign invasions; it is forbidden to alter the constitutional grant of two senators for each state; it cannot permit states to be sued by individuals in the Federal courts.

Territorial Integrity of the States. Under the terms of Article IV, Section 3, Clause 1:

New States may be admitted by the Congress into this Union; but no new State shall be formed or erected within the Jurisdiction of any other State; nor any State be formed by the Junction of two or more States, or Parts of States, without the Consent of the Legislatures of the States concerned as well as of the Congress.

The admission process, which has been explained earlier, is prescribed by Congress. Congress has great powers over admission, but it cannot impose conditions upon purely state matters, nor

can it carve up existing states without their consent. The territorial integrity of states was much discussed in the Constitutional Convention before the final language was agreed upon. It has been interpreted to mean that the territory of no state may be taken without its own consent. Actually several states, formed from parts of others, have been admitted. Kentucky, formerly a part of Virginia, secured that state's approval, and Congress admitted it as a separate state in 1792. Tennessee was formed in 1796 after North Carolina ceded the territory to the United States. Vermont was admitted to the Union in 1791, in spite of claims by New York to her territory. Massachusetts agreed to Maine's separation in advance of that state's admission in 1820. West Virginia's separation from Virginia was authorized by a "rump" or irregular legislature of Virginia during the Civil War.

Although continental territory of the United States (except that in the District of Columbia and Alaska) is fully organized into states, occasionally proposals are made for creating a new state out of a portion of one or two existing states. During 1941–1942 an amusing plan was advanced for the formation of a forty-ninth state called "Jefferson" out of the counties of southern Oregon and northern California. Frequently schemes for creating city-states of Chicago or New York are put forward. Before Congress could admit any such new state, however, the consent of the existing states concerned would have to be obtained.

A Republican Form of Government. "The United States shall guarantee to every State in this Union a Republican Form of Government. . . ." This statement appears in Article IV, Section 4. Various theories have been advanced to explain what the Founding Fathers meant by this provision. Some say it means representative government; others, the form used in 1789; still others declare it means democratic government with broad suffrage rights. The fact of the matter is that no one knows or is likely soon to secure a precise answer. The courts regard the question as political in nature and, therefore, decline to rule whether or not a given state government meets the requirements imposed by the

Constitution. Instead, the matter is left for the Congress and the President to determine as occasions for doing so arise.

The President may indicate his choice between two rival regimes by using troops to protect or restore order, as in Dorr's Rebellion of Rhode Island.[11] Congress may announce its acceptance or rejection of a particular state regime by seating or refusing to seat senators and representatives from the state concerned, as it often did in the reconstruction era. Several times during the era of Huey Long's predominance over Louisiana, efforts were made to persuade Congress to refuse seats to Louisiana legislators on the ground that they came from a state without republican form of government, but no action was taken.

Arguing that "republican form" meant representative government, a corporation operating in Oregon once sought to prove in the courts that the state government had lost its lawful authority through the adoption of the initiative and referendum. The Supreme Court indicated the political character of the question and declared that determination rested with the Congress through acceptance or rejection of senators and representatives.[12]

Defense against Invasion and Violence. The latter part of Article IV, Section 4, requires that the United States ". . . shall protect each of them against Invasion; and on Application of the Legislature, or of the Executive (when the Legislature cannot be convened) against domestic violence." This restatement of the federal obligation to protect against foreign enemies is the logical companion to the prohibition of state armies and navies and properly derives from the federal war power.

Much difficulty is encountered in determining when domestic violence reaches the point requiring federal intervention. The President makes this decision. Normally he sends in federal troops only after a request for help has come from the governor or legislature of the state concerned or when federal law or federal property is violated. President Cleveland broke the Chicago Pullman strike of 1894 with troops that he sent in over the protest of Governor J. P. Altgeld of Illinois. Cleveland used the grounds of protecting the mails and freeing interstate commerce of obstructions. President Roosevelt in 1941 used the Army to break up a strike in a California aircraft factory without any formal request from the governor.

Equal Representation in the Senate. No state may be denied equal representation in the United States Senate without its own consent. Since no state is likely to agree to reduction of Senate representation, the two-member-per-state basis is likely to remain indefinitely. The Constitution states that this portion of the fundamental law cannot be changed by amendment. It constitutes an "entrenched clause."

State Immunity from Suit. The original Constitution left the way open for the national judiciary to assume jurisdiction over suits between a state and citizens of another state. After the decision of the Supreme Court in Chisholm v. Georgia,[13] upholding a citizen's suit against the state, a great storm of disapproval arose. The Eleventh Amendment, outlawing such suits, was ratified finally in 1798. Under this amendment, a state may not be sued in Federal courts by an individual unless consent is given by law. Lacking such consent, the individual may seek remedy through legislative action on a "claim" bill.

STATE OBLIGATIONS TO THE UNION

Elections of Federal Officials. No separate federal election machinery is comprehended in the Constitution. Instead the states are obliged to conduct elections for federal officials. Presidential electors are chosen in each state in whatever manner the state legislature directs. All states now use the direct election method. Members of the House of Representatives are elected by the people, in most cases from single-member districts. Senators, under the Seventeenth Amendment, are elected at large in each state. For all three offices the suffrage requirements for voters are identical to those for the most

[11] Luther v. Borden, 7 How. 1 (U.S. 1849).

[12] Pacific States Telephone and Telegraph Co. v. Oregon, 223 U.S. 118 (1912).

[13] 2 Dall. 419 (U.S. 1793).

numerous branch of the state legislature. Each state decides for itself the method of nominating, if any, that shall be employed. Congress has used its power to set a common election date for federal officers, but Maine, which has an earlier date set in its constitution, is permitted to continue its own general election date.

Participation in Amending Process. States also are obliged to participate in the federal constitutional amending process. One of the methods of proposing amendments (federal constitutional convention) and both schemes of ratification (state legislatures and state conventions) require the participation of the several states.

FOR FURTHER READING

(See also works listed after next chapter.)

Anderson, William: *Federalism and Intergovernmental Relations* (Chicago: Public Administration Service, 1946).

——: *The Units of Government in the United States* (Chicago: Public Administration Service, 2d ed., 1942).

Bowie, Robert R., and C. J. Friedrich (eds.): *Studies in Federalism* (Little, Brown, 1954).

Bryce, James: *The American Commonwealth* (Macmillan, rev. ed., 2 vols., 1889).

Finer, Herman: *The Theory and Practice of Modern Government* (Holt, rev. ed., 1949).

Freeman, Edward A.: *A History of Federal Government in Greece and Italy* (London: Macmillan & Co., Ltd., 2d ed., 1893).

——: *A History of Federal Government from Foundation of the Achaian League to the Disruption of the United States* (London: Macmillan & Co., Ltd., 1863).

Graves, W. Brooke (ed.): "Intergovernmental Relations in the United States," *Annals of the American Academy of Political and Social Science,* vol. 207 (January, 1940).

Haines, Charles G.: "James Bryce and American Constitutional Federalism," in Robert C. Brooks (ed.), *Bryce's American Commonwealth, Fiftieth Anniversary* (Macmillan, 1939).

Karve, Dattatraya G.: *Federations: A Study in Comparative Politics* (Oxford, 1932).

MacMahon, Arthur W. (ed.): *Federalism Mature and Emergent* (Columbia University Press, 1955).

Maxwell, James A.: *The Fiscal Impact of Federalism in the United States* (Harvard University Press, 1946).

Mogi, Sobei: *The Problem of Federalism* (London: G. Allen, 2 vols., 1931).

Pound, Roscoe, and Others: *Federalism as a Democratic Process* (Rutgers University Press, 1942).

Powell, Alden L.: *National Taxation of State Instrumentalities* (University of Illinois Press, 1936).

Studenski, Paul, and Paul R. Mort: *Centralized and Decentralized Government in Relation to Democracy* (Teachers College, Columbia University, 1941).

Tocqueville, Alexis de: *Democracy in America* (Knopf, 2 vols., 1945).

U.S. Commission on Intergovernmental Relations: *Report* . . . (1955). In addition, 15 separate studies were issued.

Wheare, Kenneth C.: *Federal Government* (Oxford, 3d ed., 1953).

REVIEW QUESTIONS

1. What reasons can you give in support of Bryce's thesis that federalism is the "only possible form" for the United States? Why would a centralized system be "inexpedient" or "unworkable"?

2. The late Carl Becker described our federal system as "the most complicated, stable, toughly resistant and impregnable political structure ever devised by any people." Discuss.

3. Define federalism. Where and why is it used?

4. What powers has the national government? What powers have the states? What is the "necessary and proper" clause?

5. What is the "supreme law of the land" in the United States?

6. Critics often advocate reduction in the number of governmental units in the United States. How could the number of states be reduced? In your state, how can the number of counties, municipalities, districts, and other units be cut down? What change has taken place in the last decade?

7. If Congress decides to admit Hawaii and Alaska as states, what conditions validly can be imposed upon them?

8. What Federal constitutional restrictions limit the freedom of action of the several states?

9. List the federal obligations to the states and explain what they mean today.

10. What obligations do the states have to the Federal government?

11. What was the Commission on Intergovernmental Relations, and what did it accomplish?

CHAPTER 6

Interstate and Federal-State Relations

Leave to private initiative all the functions that citizens can perform privately; use the level of government closest to the community for all public functions it can handle; utilize cooperative intergovernmental arrangements where appropriate to attain economical performance and popular approval; reserve National action for residual participation where State and local governments are not fully adequate, and for the continuing responsibilities that only the National Government can undertake. — Commission on Intergovernmental Relations[1]

The proof of any political system is in its operation. How has our federalism worked? Have the states really honored their obligations to one another? Have they developed a capacity for cooperative endeavor among themselves? Most crucial of all, how has the federal-state relationship worked in practice? Is the obvious shift toward more centralized government going to stop short of leaving the states so weakened that they can no longer play the role of self-governing parts of a true federal union?

INTERSTATE RELATIONS

Constitutional Interstate Obligations. The Constitution imposes upon each state certain obligations to all other states. The principal interstate duties are enumerated in Article IV, which is devoted to states' relations. In each case the responsibility of the state is outlined in general form only, and it has remained for the courts to expound the meaning of the particular obligation in specific terms.

[1] U.S. Commission on Intergovernmental Relations, *Report . . .* (1955), p. 6.

Full Faith and Credit. The first among these interstate obligations is contained in Article IV, Section 1, which reads:

Full Faith and Credit shall be given in each State to the public Acts, Records, and judicial Proceedings of every other State. And the Congress may by general Laws prescribe the Manner in which such Acts, Records, and Proceedings shall be proved, and the Effect thereof.

In 1804 Congress extended coverage of this clause to acts, records, and proceedings of territories of the United States. The clause does not include foreign governmental acts and proceedings. Federal courts, also, are bound to give state court decisions full faith and credit.

In general, full faith and credit means that every state must accept another state's statutes, charters, deeds, vital records, judicial decisions, and court records. For example, an ordinary civil judgment of Iowa courts ordering Smith to pay Brown $1,000 will be enforced by Kansas courts without an examination of the case on its merits, but merely after a determination of the authenticity of the original judgment. A Massachusetts marriage license is accepted as proof of wedded status in Pennsylvania. A Texas birth certificate may be used in Oregon to establish date of birth. A will properly drawn in Idaho is binding in the courts of Wyoming.

Two notable exceptions to full faith and credit exist. First, the clause does not cover state proceedings under criminal law. A person convicted of a crime in Alabama is not punished for it in Kentucky. Such cases are handled through extradition, under which the state to which a fugitive from justice has fled delivers him up to the state where the crime was committed. Second, divorce decrees granted by courts of a state in which neither party has a bona fide residence sometimes are not accepted by the courts of other states. Mr. and Mrs. A, who have lived together in New York, separate. Mr. A proceeds to Nevada where, after a few weeks, he is granted a divorce, without summons to Mrs. A. Returning to New York, Mr. A remarries. The second Mrs. A bears two children. Ten years later Mr. A dies suddenly. The first Mrs. A demands and is granted the whole of Mr. A's estate on the ground that their marriage was never legally dissolved under the laws of New York. The late Mr. A is adjudged a bigamist, his children and their mother are left penniless, and the children have the stigma of illegitimacy. Divorces granted in the state in which a couple has been domiciled are valid; even those issued by a state in which one of the parties has actual residence generally are accepted, if proper procedure is followed.[2]

[2] The status of out-of-home-state divorces has been much controverted in recent years. In Williams *v*. North Carolina, 317 U.S. 287 (1942) the Supreme Court ruled that the full-faith-and-credit clause required the acceptance of two Nevada divorces obtained after 6 weeks of residence. The case was reheard by the Court in Williams *v*. North Carolina, 325 U.S. 226 (1945), and the Court held that North Carolina had power to determine the validity of domicile. The conviction of bigamy was upheld, and the state court sentence was sustained. The states with the shortest residence requirement before filing suit for divorce are: Idaho (6 weeks); Nevada (6 weeks), Wyoming (60 days), Arkansas (90 days), Florida (90 days), and Utah (90 days).

Privileges and Immunities. Further protection against interstate discrimination was secured through the provision that the citizens of each state are guaranteed the privileges and immunities of citizens of the several states. This clause, it will be seen, assures the citizen of one state the right to be protected, to travel, to reside, to secure habeas corpus, to sue in courts, to make contracts, to marry, to hold property, to enjoy tax equality, and to engage in trade or business in any other state.

Such guaranties are of great importance in making this one nation instead of many nations. The courts have ruled invalid several attempts by states to give their own citizens rights denied to citizens of other states. During the 1930's a number of proposals were made in states of the Pacific Southwest to curb the influx of migrants from drought and dust-bowl areas. It is quite valid for states to require of a citizen residence for a given period before achieving the right of suffrage, or securing eligibility to poor relief. No state, however, can directly forbid by law indigent migrants to enter. Local authorities plagued the migrants with vagrancy ordinances, and private individuals and groups conspired to frighten them away. California forbade by law the transportation of indigent persons into the state, but the statute was declared unconstitutional.[3]

The rights of resident citizens and of citizens of other states are not, however, precisely equal. States have been permitted three major exceptions and a number of minor ones to the application of the privileges-and-immunities clause.

First, corporations are not considered citizens under this clause, and, therefore, out-of-state concerns may be burdened with discriminatory legislation. States are subject to restraint in this field, nevertheless, under the due-process clause of the Fourteenth Amendment.

Second, the right to engage in certain professions or businesses may be restricted by state law to citizens who have resided in the state for a given number of months or years. By admis-

[3] Edwards *v*. California, 314 U.S. 160 (1941). The majority opinion rejected the law on grounds of obstruction of interstate commerce.

sion to the bar or to the practice of medicine in one state one does not thereby secure the right to practice in all states.[4]

Third, the privileges of sharing in the property or proprietary functions of a state may be denied to a nonresident, or offered to him on a very different basis. A state university may require payment of a tuition fee by a nonresident, although none is collected from residents. For example, the University of California charges $150 per semester tuition for out-of-state students and no tuition fee for Californians. States customarily charge much higher fees for fish and game licenses to nonresidents than to residents. It is valid for Idaho to charge local sportsmen $2 per season for a permit covering all fish and game, and to charge an out-of-state person $50 for the same privilege.

Extradition of Fugitives. The process of extradition is explained clearly in the second clause of Article IV, Section 2:

A person charged in any State with Treason, Felony, or other Crime, who shall flee from Justice, and be found in another State, shall on Demand of the executive Authority of the State from which he fled, be delivered up, to be removed to the State having Jurisdiction of the Crime.

It is similar to international extradition, but rendition between nations is carried out under treaty; among the American states no treaty is necessary, for the Constitution provides a direct and uniform rule. Any violation of state law, whether felony or misdemeanor, may be the basis for a request for rendition. Any person charged with a crime who leaves the state in which the alleged crime was committed may be extradited, whether he deliberately fled or not. Federal law extends extradition to territories.

Ordinarily the process works smoothly. Congress has directed by law that the governor of a state or territory has the duty of detaining the fugitive for whom extradition is asked. The governor of the state from which he fled is notified when the accused person is located. The formal

request for rendition then follows. Usually the governor delivers up the fugitive without question. Occasionally, however, governors examine the facts behind a requested extradition and refuse to hand over fugitives. This refusal may occur when an executive distrusts the system of justice used in the state making the request, as was the situation in *I Am a Fugitive from a Chain Gang.* Or it may be due to humanitarian considerations, such as a long record of reformed living. No court or officer has power to force a governor to render up a person if the governor refuses the request of extradition.

Interstate Cooperation. *Compacts.* The Constitution provides for interstate relations largely in negative, prohibitory terms. Even the provision for interstate compacts in Article I, Section 10, is in the form of a prohibition: "No State shall, without the Consent of Congress . . . enter into any Agreement or Compact with another state. . . ." Normally a compact is negotiated between representatives of state executives, ratified by the states concerned, and submitted to Congress for consent, which is given by law. Increasingly in recent years Congress has consented in advance to a compact or an idea for a compact; sometimes no compact or state ratification has followed. By 1955 nearly one hundred compacts had been authorized by Congress; about sixty of these became effective through state ratification. Most interstate compacts deal with relatively minor matters, especially with boundary lines, rivers, harbors, waterways, bridges, and the like. During the last 35 years several compacts have been made to deal with important economic and governmental problems.

Best known among interstate compacts, the New York Port Authority is scarcely typical. It was negotiated between New York and New Jersey in 1920 and approved by Congress in 1921. The original plan was to provide an agency for the coordinated development of the metropolitan port facilities of America's leading harbor. The authority was initially unable to make much progress in getting railroads, shipping lines, and others to cooperate in its comprehensive plan but soon scored a conspicuous success in building and maintaining bridge and tunnel

[4] For details see Council of State Governments, *Occupational Licensing Legislation in the States* (Chicago: The Council, 1952).

facilities across the Hudson River. It also operates airports, rail and truck freight terminals, and the world's largest bus terminal. The authority is directed by twelve commissioners, six from each state. The commissioners are unsalaried; they place responsibility for the operation of the vast enterprise on well-paid career officials. Authority power is not great. Each

PORT OF NEW YORK AUTHORITY

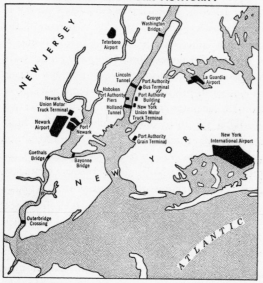

The principal physical facilities of the Port of New York Authority indicate the scope of that vast interstate enterprise.

major construction project requires the statutory approval of New York and New Jersey; and the governors of the two states have been given veto power over acts of the authority. In spite of these restrictions, the authority has made a remarkable record of success in operating a huge public enterprise.

The Interstate Oil Compact is an outstanding attempt to stabilize a chaotic industry by interstate action. It was negotiated by representatives of nine states in early 1935; the compact was ratified by Texas, Oklahoma, Kansas, New Mexico, Illinois, and Colorado; it was consented to by Congress later in 1935 and renewed biennially to 1943 and every 4 years since. More states came in subsequently. In 1954 there were twenty-five active and five associate members. The pur-

pose of the compact was declared to be prevention of oil and gas waste. The text of the compact does not mention control of production, the establishment and enforcement of quotas being left to the member states. The oil compact has suffered in effectiveness because of California's unwillingness to ratify. For an industry as competitive as petroleum it may be regarded as a modest success.[5]

Most widely accepted of all is the Crime Compact of 1934, for which blanket approval was given by Congress the same year. All forty-eight states by 1951 had ratified this agreement for interstate supervision of parolees and probationers. The reform of released convicts inevitably is complicated by the notoriety an ex-criminal achieves in his home community. Previously it has been difficult or impossible to provide proper parole facilities in other states. Now an ex-convict may have a chance to start anew under favorable circumstances and proper supervision in the state of his choice.

A new field for the compact is education. Forced by judicial decisions to equalize professional training for Negroes, several states formed the Southern Regional Educational Compact in 1948. By 1951 fourteen states had joined. The arrangement is simple. States having high-quality institutions for training in medicine, dentistry, law, veterinary medicine, and other professional fields agree to accept students (colored or white) from states with poorer facilities. Students pay no out-of-state fees; instead, the bill is paid by the state of their residence. This contract-for-service system makes available to each state, for thousands of dollars, services that would cost millions to duplicate. The Western Regional Education Compact, approved in 1953, had eight initial members: Arizona, Colorado, Idaho, Montana, New Mexico, Oregon, Utah, and Wyoming. The initial success of these ven-

[5] See Interstate Oil Compact Commission, *The Interstate Compact to Conserve Oil and Gas: A Summary of the Background, Organization, Purposes and Functions* (Oklahoma City: The Commission, 1954); and Wilfred D. Webb, "The Interstate Oil Compact—Theory and Practice," *Southwestern Social Science Quarterly*, vol. 21 (March, 1941), pp. 293–301.

tures suggests a wide range of new uses to which the interstate compact may be put.

Evaluation of the Compact Method. While the compact method is a useful device through which regional problems may be attacked, it is likely to succeed mainly in restricted areas and in noncontroversial fields. The compact is inflexible and difficult to amend. Commissions created by compacts are given little discretionary authority and rarely have any power of enforcement. If one state involved in the subject covered by the compact refuses to ratify, the whole project may fail because of limited adherence. Like a confederation requiring unanimous consent before acting, the compact scheme may be foredoomed to failure because the minority, however small, may veto the effectiveness of the majority will. Even when the necessary states do ratify, Congress may withhold consent, as it has from the New England flood-control compacts. If enforcement action is required, enforcement may be nonuniform in the participating states.

Granting these objections, however, it should be recognized that the compact still has a useful role in solving problems that fall between federal and single-state jurisdiction and competence. It is no cure-all, no panacea for all ills, but it may serve as a method through which states with common problems may work together on a modest cooperative basis. The status of the interstate compact was clarified by a ruling of the Supreme Court in 1951 that a state's obligations under a compact cannot be terminated by action of state courts.[6]

Many interstate agreements are made effective without any congressional action. Executive arrangements, more informal than compacts, often suffice to ensure parallel action between two or more states. Usually these are mere agreements to follow the principles of reciprocity, to give assurances that each will treat the other with fairness and equality.

Uniform State Laws. Uniform state action is another road to interstate cooperation. Founded in 1892, the National Conference of Commis-

sioners on Uniform State Laws is the leading organization promoting action in this field. Over the years conference subcommittees have drawn up with great care, and the general body has ratified, more than a hundred acts. In addition, several other national groups have prepared proposed laws that have had wide acceptance among the states. The conference is composed of representatives from each state, appointed by the governor; it is financed by the American Bar Association, state appropriations, and by other bodies.

Three laws—Negotiable Instruments, Warehouse Receipts, and Stock Transfer—have been adopted by all forty-eight states and by most territories, but the average act on the conference list has been adopted by few over 25 per cent of the states.[7] The advantages of uniform laws are obvious. Uniformity in state law simplifies greatly the task of doing business across state lines. Unfortunately, however, state legislatures do not always adopt proposed acts without amendment. A drastically amended uniform law is little more advantageous than one of homespun origin. Moreover, despite a clause declaring for uniform interpretation, the courts of the various states may give diverse interpretations to uniform laws. Prof. J. A. C. Grant has suggested that truer uniformity may be obtained from state adoption of federal laws. Where this happens statutes are uniform and a common system of interpretation may also prevail.[8]

The Council of State Governments. In view of the large number of interstate problems needing solution, it is surprising that the first general continuing interstate organization was established only in 1925. The parent organization was called the American Legislators' Association; in 1935, it fostered the establishment of the Coun-

[6] West Virginia *ex rel.* Dyer *v.* Sims, 341 U.S. 22 (1951).

[7] Rodney L. Mott, "Uniform Legislation in the United States," *Annals of the American Academy,* vol. 207 (January, 1940), pp. 79–92. Progress in this field may be followed in National Conference of Commissioners on Uniform State Laws, *Handbook of the . . . and Proceedings of the Annual Conference . . .* (annually).

[8] J. A. C. Grant, "The Search for Uniformity of Law," *American Political Science Review,* vol. 32 (December, 1938), pp. 1082–1098.

cil of State Governments, with broad functions.[9] The council provides the secretariat for the Governors' Conference, the American Legislators' Association, the Conference of Chief Justices, the National Association of Attorneys General, the National Association of Secretaries of State, and other bodies. It cooperates with the National Conference of Commissioners on Uniform State Laws and many other bodies of public officials. It publishes a monthly magazine, *State Government,* the only journal devoted exclusively to this field.

The council is governed by a board of managers, to which each state contributing to its support is entitled to appoint one member; associated groups also are represented. Every 2 years, the council holds a meeting of its general assembly, to which each participating state sends one senator, one representative, and one administrator. Here state and national problems of the broadest character may be considered. In recent years all forty-eight states have taken part in the work of the council. This participation is directed in each state by a state commission on interstate cooperation, established by state law and composed of members of the legislature and representatives of the executive branch.

These commissions on interstate cooperation keep the states in touch with the work of the council and with interstate problems generally; they provide a mechanism through which the states may be represented at national and regional conferences on particular interstate problems. The most important work in recent years has centered around the problem of state trade barriers. After national and regional conferences on trade walls, state representatives returned home and helped to repeal some existing barriers and to accomplish the defeat of proposed new ones. Much good work has been done in securing interstate action dealing with relief, crime, fisheries, water pollution, conservation of natural resources, and other problems. The Council of State Governments provides a much-needed agency through which the states may approach

the solution of common problems. In its first two decades of existence it secured participation of all of the states, focused national attention on the gravity of interstate problems, and provided machinery through which the solution of many problems could be sought.

Interstate Discrimination. *State Trade Barriers.* One of the primary motives in the formation of the Union was the elimination of state tariff barriers. It was recognized that the country could enjoy neither prosperity nor unity with walls built around each state. The Founding Fathers drew with great care the sections of the Constitution prohibiting state duties on imports and exports and assuring the Federal government of paramount power over interstate and foreign commerce. In spite of these constitutional provisions, the states over the years have managed to build up a large number of trade walls. The condition became particularly alarming during the 1930's, when discriminatory and counterdiscriminatory legislation reached state statute books with regularity.[10]

A state trade barrier may be defined as a statute, regulation, or practice that operates unfairly or tends to operate to the disadvantage of persons, products, or services coming from sister states and to the advantage of local residents. Examples are plentiful. Under the guise of protecting the health, morals, safety, and welfare of its people, a state law will require inspection and quarantine of plant and animal life. This requirement sounds legitimate, but it may be enforced in such a way that out-of-state nurserymen or stock raisers virtually are denied access to the state market. For example, New York state, seeking to curb Bang's disease, imposed a very rigid inspection on cattle being shipped into the state, even though it did little to clean up infected herds at home. If New York inspectors reject Louisiana cattle, then Louisiana's retaliatory quarantine embargo may be placed into effect, and movement of plant and

---

[9] For history and functions of the council, see the current issue of *The Book of the States,* published biennially in Chicago.

[10] The pioneer work in the trade-barrier field is F. Eugene Melder, *State and Local Barriers to Interstate Commerce* (University of Maine Press, 1937). The same author wrote *State Trade Walls* (New York: Public Affairs Committee, 1939).

The TRAILER to fit all State Laws

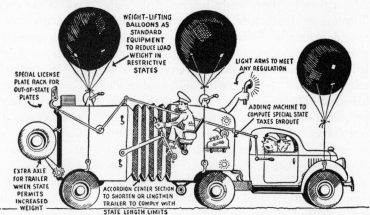

WEIGHT-LIFTING BALLOONS AS STANDARD EQUIPMENT TO REDUCE LOAD WEIGHT IN RESTRICTIVE STATES

SPECIAL LICENSE PLATE RACK FOR OUT-OF-STATE PLATES

LIGHT ARMS TO MEET ANY REGULATION

ADDING MACHINE TO COMPUTE SPECIAL STATE TAXES ENROUTE

EXTRA AXLE FOR TRAILER WHEN STATE PERMITS INCREASED WEIGHT

ACCORDION CENTER SECTION TO SHORTEN OR LENGTHEN TRAILER TO COMPLY WITH STATE LENGTH LIMITS

The interstate trucking industry is adversely affected by many state trade barriers. Courtesy of the Fruehauf Trailer Company.

animal life between New York and Louisiana be banned.

State laws governing motor vehicles, especially trucks, establish standards so diverse from those of other states that truckers of neighboring states cannot meet the requirements without excessive cost. State taxes and fees in other fields often are arranged so that out-of-state competition is stymied effectively. This practice is most common in the alcoholic-beverage field, over which

when the state seeks to purchase goods for its own use.

Removal of trade barriers requires action by the states themselves. The Federal government can assist in several ways. The Council of State Governments, a federal interdepartmental committee, and other bodies have worked hard to prevent new trade walls and to break down existing ones. Much progress has been made in this direction. After a careful analysis of the legal

HIGHWAY WRECKERS INC.

The body of a truck is stiff.
You cannot tell by looking* if
It's innocent, or overweight
And wrecking highways in your State.

*That's why we need lots of State Highway Patrol Weighing Stations.

FROM: The Highwaymen Come Riding, California Railroad Assn. (n. d.)

The railroads, faced with increasing competition from truckers, join the campaign for more stringent enforcement of highway load limits.

states have a special power stemming from the Twenty-first Amendment. Differentials to favor local manufacturers or products are established through high license fees for importation or for the privilege of selling in the state.[11] Discrimination against out-of-state wine is carried on by having two excise taxes: a high one for imported and a low one for native-produced beverage. In addition, most states have general laws giving resident producers and vendors an advantage

situation, the late Robert H. Jackson, who at that time was the Solicitor General, turned to the possibility of congressional action with these words:

We must not forget that while the commerce clause of itself will not keep open the channels of interstate trade, the Congress has a wide choice of means to use the grant of power effectively to achieve that end.[12]

[11] These data are drawn from Thomas S. Green, Jr., *Liquor Trade Barriers* (Chicago: Public Administration Service, 1939), pp. 12–19.

[12] Robert H. Jackson, "The Supreme Court and Interstate Barriers," *Annals of the American Academy*, vol. 207 (January, 1940), pp. 70–79, at p. 78.

He pointed out that while the more obvious discriminations by states might be curbed through litigation in the Federal courts, Congress must provide a statutory basis for a more general and positive attack. A careful study of federal legislation was made in 1940 to ascertain how it might be used to curb state and local trade barriers.[13] The most promising lines of action enumerated were: (1) cooperative action by federal agencies and the Council of State Governments in persuading states to defeat and repeal offensive legislation, (2) Federal court action against trade barriers through injunctions, antitrust prosecutions, and intervention as *amicus curiae* (friend of the court), (3) uniform state laws, drafted by federal agencies and enacted by the states, (4) standardization of name, quality, and containers for foods under the powers granted in the federal Food, Drug and Cosmetic Act, (5) pressure on states to relax barriers through federal grants-in-aid devices. The dangerous trend toward "Balkanization" of the country by the erection of trade barriers, which gained much support during the depression period, has been successfully halted and even reversed. Nevertheless, there still exists much state legislation of a restrictive character.

Tax Competition. Closely connected with the general trade-barrier problem are the tax discriminations used by some states against other states and out-of-state producers, and the tax factors by which residents and producers are aided. State laws often provide for tax exemption of businesses in order to induce them to move to or remain in the state. Florida once made a bid for rich and aged persons by providing in her constitution that no inheritance tax could be enacted.[14] Taxes that retaliate against other states by levies on insurance premiums, liquor, and other things are common. Conflicts often arise between states over the share of a large estate taxable by each. While the state in which the deceased person has been domiciled generally has the best claim, other states in which portions of the estate are located may claim the right to tax them.

The state sales tax has come into general use during the last decade. Many people make large purchases out of state in order to avoid payment of sales taxes. To plug this loophole, several states have levied "use" taxes, requiring payment of the equivalent of the sales tax before an article may be used in the state. If a citizen of California buys an automobile in Detroit, California requires that he pay either the California sales tax or use tax before it can be licensed in the state. Exceptionally heavy taxes may be charged against out-of-state corporations. Dairying states widely use taxes on oleomargarine to discourage consumption of vegetable fats and to promote the sale of butter fats. States also have engaged in open warfare through alcoholic-beverage taxes, which have favored home-produced liquors and applied heavy and retaliatory taxes on liquors from out of state.

FEDERAL-STATE RELATIONS

The term "centralization" refers to the relationship between different levels of government. The process of centralization involves assumption by the higher level of government of both activities and authority from the lower level.

Federal centralization is the tendency for the national government to assume influence or control over functions and fields formerly considered under state jurisdiction. State centralization is used to describe the process of state assumption of authority over former local activities.

It was inevitable that the relations between nation and state would not have remained static over 150 years. Changing social and economic conditions require the reallocation of responsibilities; virtually all these changes have strengthened the national government at the expense of the state. It is true, of course, that the states also have new and expanded functions, sometimes taken over from local governments. The over-all general tendency, however, has been in the direction of greater federal centralization. The

---

[13] U.S. Department of Commerce, Interdepartmental Committee on Interstate Trade Barriers, *A Summarized Report of the Legal Subcommittee* (December, 1940).

[14] Eventually Florida was induced to abandon this form of tax competition by a federal law setting up a credit for state taxation. See discussion of tax offset device, pp. 94-95.

purpose of this section is to examine some of the devices and avenues through which federal authority over the states and over former state functions has developed and to appraise some of the expedients to which the states have resorted to correct their own inadequacies.

Federal Grants-in-Aid. In a recent study by a committee of the Council of State Governments, federal grants-in-aid were defined as:

payments made by the national government to state and local governments, subject to certain conditions, for the support of activities administered by the states and their political subdivisions.[15]

The term includes both regular grants, which are "permanent" or recurring, and emergency grants, which are temporary and extraordinary. The term grants-in-aid does *not* include the following payments: (1) shared revenues, collected by the Federal government and paid in whole or in part to state or local governments; (2) payments in lieu of taxes, through which the nation reimburses the states and localities for services for which they cannot tax federal property; (3) payments for contractual services performed by the United States government; (4) payments of cash loans; (5) payments to individuals within states, as in the National Guard.

Nature of Subsidy System. Although the earliest grants to states were in land or money, without the imposition of conditions on their use, present-day grants are almost wholly *conditional*. This means that grants are made for specified purposes and subject to conditions stipulated by Congress or the administering agency. Other federal nations, such as Australia and Canada, make extensive use of "unconditional" grants to states or provinces; this type of grant is for general purposes and is accompanied by no detailed specifications as to use. The Commission on Intergovernmental Relations, reporting in 1955, rejected the idea of subventions for general state purposes. It feared that the net effect would be increased centralization.

The constitutional justification for federal grants is found both in the power of Congress to

dispose of territory and other property, and in its power to tax and spend.[16] The former no longer looms large on the grants front, now that most grants are in cash rather than in kind. In 1923 the Supreme Court had before it for the first time cases involving a modern conditional grant, the maternal and child health program. The act was challenged as invading state power and as burdening disproportionately the taxpayers of the several states. Although the Court did not provide direct answers to the issues, it did refuse to declare the aid program void, and it made virtually impossible the challenge by state or taxpayer of the validity of such an expenditure.[17] Subsequent cases have resulted in similar verdicts. The constitutionality of using the power to tax and spend for federal grants appears to be fully assured.

Today there are some twenty-five aided functions, and several proposals for new federal grants are pending. Arguments for and against grants-in-aid will be considered in a subsequent section of this chapter, but a general explanation of why the Federal government has made such extensive use of this device is in place here. Perhaps the greatest impetus comes from a desire to finance more and improved services by taxing on the broad base of the whole nation and spending in the areas of greatest need. The grant-in-aid offers a middle ground between direct federal assumption of certain state and local functions and their continuation under exclusive state and local financing, with haphazard coverage and diverse standards. It makes possible the achievement of national minimum standards, yet retains most of the benefits of administration close to the people.

Services Aided by Federal Grants. For the year 1952–1953 the largest regular federal grants-in-aid (excluding shared revenues, emergency grants, and payments to individuals within states) were for old-age assistance, highways, aid to dependent children, unemployment insurance and employment service, hospital con-

---

[15] Council of State Governments, *Federal Grants-in-Aid* (Chicago: The Council, 1949), p. 29.

[16] For fuller consideration of powers aspect, see p. 351.

[17] Massachusetts *v.* Mellon and Frothington *v.* Mellon, 262 U.S. 447 (1923).

struction, school-lunch program, and surplus agricultural commodities.[18] Lesser grants were made for agricultural experiment stations, agricultural extension work, cooperative projects in marketing, forestry cooperation, airport program, wildlife conservation, agricultural colleges, venereal-disease control, tuberculosis control, general health assistance, mental-health activities, heart-disease control, cancer control, maternal and child health, aid to crippled chil-

MAJOR FEDERAL GRANTS
BY PURPOSE, FISCAL YEAR, 1953

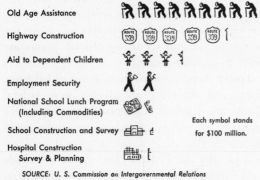

Each symbol stands for $100 million.

SOURCE: U. S. Commission on Intergovernmental Relations

Lesser grants were made for aid to the blind, schools, public health, and other services.

dren, child welfare, aid to the blind, vocational rehabilitation, housing, veterans' training, and some minor functions. There has been a tremendous increase in the use of grants-in-aid. In 1911–1912 the total federal grants scarcely exceeded $5,000,000; for 1952–1953 they were over $2,580,000,000 for regular, permanent functions. All forms of federal grants, including grants-in-aid, shared revenues, emergency grants, and payments to individuals within states, aggregated over $3,832,000,000 in 1952–1953.

Conditions Attached to Federal Grants. The basis of allocation, the state contribution, and the extent of federal control depend upon the nature of the service aided and the temper of Congress when the grant is authorized. Basis of allocation may be equal among the states, according to

[18] U.S. Secretary of the Treasury, *Annual Report . . . on the State of the Finances . . .* 1953 (1954), pp. 570–584.

need, number aided, rural population, total population, or some other formula or combination. Generally Congress requires that a state must match the federal contribution with a state contribution. The state appropriation often is required on a dollar-for-dollar basis, but sometimes it must be more or may be less; occasionally no matching is required.

Federal administrative controls vary greatly. Sweeping supervisory powers are exercised by federal road officials over the construction of federally aided state highways. The amount of control by federal authorities over educational services and agricultural experiment stations is almost nil.

It would be poor policy, indeed, for the Federal government to hand out money without some method of checking the stewardship of the states in its expenditure. On the other hand, petty and detailed checking is not likely to produce other than resentment. Constant federal pressure has done much to keep the spoils system out of state unemployment-insurance administration, and from state welfare agencies. Under the second Hatch Act, Congress attempted to keep state and local employees in federally aided functions out of politics. The law was so sweeping in its coverage, however, that it is regarded by many as invasive on civil rights.

Equalization through Variable Grants. All the grants that deviate from apportionment of equal amounts for each state and a standard matching formula might be considered variable. Such adjustments are made mainly to take into account need, both for financial aid and for the services being provided. When the results of existing apportionment and matching rules are studied, however, many programs are found deficient so far as equalizing tendencies are concerned. The hospital construction grants, for example, require $2 from the state for each $1 from the Federal government, although apportionment favors states with low per capita income. The "open end" method of allocating public assistance grants, under which there is no top limit of the amount of federal aid to each state and the Federal government is committed to pay a fixed proportion of the total state expenditures for this purpose, has led to far larger grants to the wealthier states. This fault has been only partially corrected by the rule under which the Federal government pays 80 per cent of the lowest monthly payments, and one-half of the payments above this amount, up to a fixed maxi-

ance is made for the highway and airport programs that favor the sparsely populated areas of the West, federal aid as at present constituted does not appear to aid the neediest states as much as its proponents desire. This condition arises in part from inability of states with the least re-

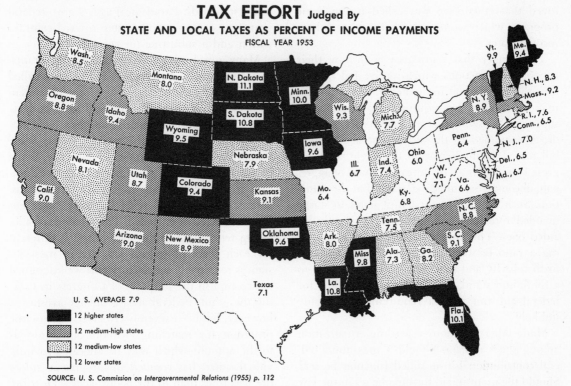

TAX EFFORT Judged By
STATE AND LOCAL TAXES AS PERCENT OF INCOME PAYMENTS
FISCAL YEAR 1953

Wash. 8.5
Montana 8.0
N. Dakota 11.1
Minn. 10.0
Vt. 9.9
Me. 9.4
Oregon 8.8
Idaho 9.4
S. Dakota 10.8
Wis. 9.3
Mich. 7.7
N. Y. 8.9
N. H., 8.3
Mass., 9.2
Wyoming 9.5
Iowa 9.6
Penn. 6.4
R. I., 7.6
Conn., 6.5
Nevada 8.1
Utah 8.7
Nebraska 7.9
Ohio 6.0
N. J., 7.0
Colorado 9.4
Ill. 6.7
Ind. 7.4
W. Va. 7.1
Del., 6.5
Calif. 9.0
Kansas 9.1
Mo. 6.4
Ky. 6.8
Va. 6.6
Md., 6.7
Arizona 9.0
New Mexico 8.9
Oklahoma 9.6
Ark. 8.0
Tenn. 7.5
N. C. 8.8
Miss 9.8
Ala. 7.3
Ga. 8.2
S. C. 9.1
Texas 7.1
La. 10.8
Fla. 10.1

U. S. AVERAGE 7.9

- 12 higher states
- 12 medium-high states
- 12 medium-low states
- 12 lower states

SOURCE: *U. S. Commission on Intergovernmental Relations (1955) p. 112*

Although there is no single accepted means to judge how hard a state is trying to finance its own services, one good criterion is the relation of state and local taxes to income payments. The states shaded black are making the greatest effort; those shown in white are making the least.

mum, after which the state pays all above the maximum.

When per capita grants are compared with per capita income, it is found that some of the richest states, such as Nevada, Montana, Wyoming, North Dakota, Colorado, California, and Washington, are among the largest recipients of federal subsidies in proportion to population. On the other hand, some of the states with lowest per capita income, such as Virginia, North Carolina, Kentucky, and Mississippi, are near the bottom in federal aid received.[19] Even when allow-

sources to raise matching funds. In their efforts to secure such funds, there is grave danger that states may neglect unaided functions.

Because of these considerations, much attention has been devoted to constructing variable grant formulas in education, health, and assistance fields. Of necessity, these formulas are complex, and no attempt will be made to describe them here. Among the problems encountered, according to the Council of State Governments' report, is that of measuring the states with reference to fiscal capacity and tax effort expended to raise their own funds. Perhaps the simplest and most acceptable of the ways to judge fiscal

[19] Council of State Governments, *op. cit.*, p. 85.

capacity is to use per capita income, with some adjustments for goods produced for home use and tax payments. Tax effort is harder to estimate, for there is considerable variation in state tax structures and rates. The Commission on Intergovernmental Relations rejected the idea of a general equalization formula but recognized that equalizing was called for in some programs which would not otherwise reach low-income states.

The danger that states may withdraw their support for functions which receive federal aid, thus shifting the cost to the Federal government, may be avoided by requiring maintenance of support at the same level reached in earlier years; or, as contained in the aid-to-general-education bill passed by the Senate in the Eightieth Congress, by specifying a definite percentage of aggregate income that must be spent for the function. Such controls might tempt states to starve unaided functions and spend extravagantly on aided ones. This might be curbed by establishing a ratio between state collections and state fiscal capacity and requiring a state to tax up to a minimum standard in order to be eligible for federal aid, but such a requirement is highly unlikely.

Many other questions regarding equalization among states remain. Should a maximum federal contribution for an aided function be set? Should the grant-in-aid formula be set in the law or left to the discretion of the administrator? These and other questions regarding variable grants require answers before the present haphazard grants-in-aid programs can achieve the goal of equalization.[20]

Appraisal of Federal Grants. Conditional grants-in-aid have both coercive and cooperative aspects. The bait of money is so attractive that rarely does a state resist the impulse to accept grants. Actually, however, the upper layer of government is only offering to provide something the lower might not be able to afford.

The clear alternative to federal grants, if services are to be standardized at a high level, is direct federal assumption of the many functions. The grant system postpones or renders unnecessary that more drastic step toward centralization. It implies that there is a virtue in local administration, but it insists upon uniform minimum standards. Paradoxical as it seems, federal grants to states are both a step toward centralization and a substitute for centralization.

Many unsolved problems concerning grants-in-aid remain. Prof. Joseph P. Harris once called attention to deficiencies in the present system of distributing grants.[21] State and local budgets have been distorted; unaided services have suffered, particularly in the poorer states; vocational education is expanded abnormally, while in the poorer states general elementary education is allowed to languish; old-age assistance booms, while general relief in many states has been neglected or curtailed. The methods of allocating federal aid to the states, though different for each form of federal aid, are in most instances reasonably satisfactory and well designed to accomplish the purposes of Congress in making the grant. Federal aid for old-age assistance, however, has been severely criticized because the provision for matching, without limitation as to the amount which may be allocated to individual states, has resulted in far greater aid to the wealthier than to the poorer states. Distribution is in proportion to wealth instead of need. Many proposals have been made to revise the formula to take into account the financial needs of the several states, and thus enable the poorer states to raise their standards.

The next great step in the federal-grant program probably will be toward aid for general education. In 1936 President Roosevelt appointed an Advisory Committee on Education to study federal aid to education. It issued a series of staff studies and made its own report in 1938 recommending federal aid as a means of equalizing opportunity in the several states. The proposal was revived after the war in the form

[20] For further reading, see especially Byron L. Johnson, *The Principle of Equalization Applied to the Allocation of Grants-in-Aid,* Bureau of Research and Statistics Memorandum No. 66 (Social Security Administration, 1947).

[21] Joseph P. Harris, "The Future of Grants-in-Aid," *Annals of the American Academy,* vol. 207 (January, 1940), pp. 14–26.

of a bill that would have provided 300 million dollars annually under a formula which would have given the poorer states the largest share.[22] The Commission on Intergovernmental Relations recommended against aid to general education. However, the White House Conference on Education, which met late in 1955, strongly endorsed federal aid, especially for school-building construction. Later President Eisenhower made a similar recommendation to Congress.

Senate, to milk for the benefit of these sections the larger and wealthier industrial states.[23]

In spite of such attacks, however, the grant system has grown and flourished. It has done much to raise the standards of essential services in the states and has provided an effective substitute for drastic centralization.

Other Forms of Federal Aid. In addition to grants-in-aid, there are several other varieties of

Balance Sheet on Federal Grants

Assets	*Liabilities*
1. Is useful device to join levels of government in common enterprise. 2. Provides way to finance key services beyond capacity of states and local governments. 3. Helps redistribute income and promotes progressive taxation. 4. Improves state and local standards of administration. 5. Provides substitute for direct national assumption of functions. 6. Induces state and local governments to enter neglected fields. 7. Involves two levels of government in checking upon extravagance. 8. Ensures a national minimum of services and performance level.	1. Permits Federal government to enter fields denied to it by Constitution. 2. Is spent for local, not national, purposes, thus leading to sectional jealousies and jockeying for benefits. 3. Places unfair tax burden on some states to support services in others. 4. Leads to extravagant spending both by Federal government and by states. 5. Distorts state budgets and tends to destroy budgetary control. 6. Violates doctrine that government which spends moneys should collect. 7. Brings federal control of local activities and builds bureaucracy. 8. Will lead to federal monopoly of tax power, destroy local independence.

SOURCE: Condensed from Council of State Governments, *Federal Grants-in-Aid* (Chicago: The Council, 1949), pp. 41–42.

The federal subsidy system is now so well established that it seems as though we are harking back to a far-off age in reading the attack written in 1932 by the late James M. Beck, former Solicitor General and ex-congressman:

. . . the great incentive and principal cause of these subsidies is the persistent desire of the smaller agricultural states of the South and West, with their wholly disproportionate representation in the

[22] Such a bill passed the Senate in both the Eightieth and Eighty-first Congresses.

federal aid to the states. These include shared revenues, in lieu payments, contractual arrangements, loans, payments to individuals within states, and a few others.

Most of the existing shared-revenue arrangements were made because the Federal government acknowledged an obligation to make a contribution to a state or local government. Federal revenues from national forests, mineral

[23] James M. Beck, *Our Wonderland of Bureaucracy* (Macmillan, 1932), p. 225. Used by permission of The Macmillan Company, publishers.

leases on the public domain, hunters of migratory birds, leases on flood-control lands, leases of federally owned power sites—all these are shared with state or local governments. Since most federal agencies do not pay state or local taxes, it is only fair that some contribution be made to compensate for the loss of revenue.

In some counties of Western states more than 90 per cent of the land area is owned by federal agencies; in 1950 the percentage of federally owned land areas was 84 of Nevada, 72 of Utah, 70 of Arizona, 65 of Idaho, 53 of Oregon, 52 of Wyoming, and 46 of California.[24] The laws permitting in lieu payments and shared revenues are so diverse that many cases of rank injustice can easily be found. The armed forces, for example, make no in lieu payments, so cities, counties, and states in which are located large military reservations may be called upon for expanded services at the very time when their tax bases are being reduced through federal land purchases.

Offshore Resources. In 1947 the Supreme Court's verdict in United States *v.* California[25] gave the Federal government control over lands lying under the marginal sea. Representatives of the states were alarmed lest Congress assert federal control not only over the coastal belt but over all submerged lands, previously submerged lands, and inland waterways as well. Such an interpretation would have affected every state in the Union and might have cast doubt upon the ownership of much land and many improvements.

California, Texas, and Louisiana took the lead in securing passage of legislation in Congress to "quitclaim" the disputed lands to the states. Fabulous petroleum resources of the marginal sea were at stake. The House passed such a bill in 1948, but Senate action was not obtained at that time. In 1952, after defeating a proposal to use revenues derived from federal control for aid to schools ("oil for the lamps of learning"), Congress enacted legislation giving the states control. President Truman vetoed the bill, branding it an "outright gift" of immensely valuable

resources to a few coastal states. The Eighty-third Congress enacted and President Eisenhower signed legislation returning the tidelands to the states.[26]

Contracts. Strictly speaking, a contractual arrangement under which a federal agency makes payments to a state agency for certain services is not federal aid. Examples are not hard to find. In 1946 Congress provided for remuneration of states for apprenticeship training furnished by state and local agencies. The GI Bill authorized veterans' unemployment allowances, administered under contract with state employment departments; the same legislation provides for educational benefits for veterans, which, if obtained in state colleges and universities, involve federal payments to states.

The National Guard is in a class by itself. Once grouped with federally aided state services, it now is so fully under federal control that at most it could be called a cooperative activity. Federal funds are paid out directly to individuals, not through the states. States have certain powers over their units of the National Guard and certain obligations to provide facilities.

Federal Credits for State Taxation. The Federal government can encourage states to take action along desired lines through still another use of the tax power, known as "tax offset," or federal credits for state taxation. This practice involves levying a federal tax but provides that the United States will yield and collect only a portion of the original rate if the state levies a similar tax for an approved purpose.

The device was employed first in the federal estate tax of 1924 which gave credit up to 80 per cent to taxpayers who paid a state inheritance tax. Its operation is best shown by example. Suppose Mr. A. M. Welloff died in Illinois, leaving to his daughter, Miss Welloff, a large estate on which the federal death duty was calculated to be $10,000. If Illinois collected as much as

---

[24] *Statistical Abstract, 1954* (1954), p. 179.

[25] 332 U.S. 19.

[26] For additional discussion of this problem, see Chap. 31. Good sources are: E. R. Bartley, *The Tidelands Oil Controversy* (University of Texas Press, 1953), and Robert J. Harris, "States' Rights and Vested Interests," *Journal of Politics*, vol. 15 (November, 1953), pp. 457–471.

$8,000 in state inheritance taxes, then the United States waived that amount and collected only $2,000 on the estate. Prior to the federal law, several states did not tax inheritances; Florida even advertised for the rich to retire there and escape the burden of estate taxation. Had Welloff died in Florida after 1924 and before Florida finally adopted an inheritance-tax law, the amount of tax paid on his estate would have been $10,000, but all would have gone to the Federal government. Naturally states hastened to enact laws to take advantage of this offset; now Nevada is the only taxless paradise where the rich can die without concern for state death duties.

The Unemployment Insurance Offset. Another decade passed before the tax offset was used again. During the prolonged discussions that preceded the enactment of the Social Security Act, the idea of utilizing the sanction of tax offset in order to ensure state cooperation was proposed. The plan was adopted with respect to unemployment insurance, the administration of which was left to the states but subjected to extensive federal controls through a grant-in-aid for administrative purposes.

The Social Security Act of 1935 levied a federal tax on the payrolls of employers of eight or more persons. This tax (which began at 1 per cent and ultimately increased to 3 per cent) is collected in full from employers doing business in states that have no "approved" system of unemployment compensation; in states with an insurance scheme approved by the Social Security Administration, the Federal government waives 90 per cent of its tax and collects only 10 per cent. For example, the Nuform Bustle Company of Des Moines would have to pay 3 per cent on its payroll to the United States Treasury if Iowa had no approved unemployment-insurance scheme, and the employees would receive no benefits if they became unemployed. Since Iowa adopted a proper unemployment-compensation plan, however, the company pays only ³⁄₁₀ of 1 per cent to the Federal government, plus whatever state payroll tax may be levied, and has the satisfaction of seeing its employees protected in lay-off seasons. Naturally, all states promptly enacted unemployment-compensation laws in order to

take advantage of the provisions of the federal law.

Evaluation of the Tax Offset. After the Supreme Court approved this exercise of the tax power,[27] renewed attention was directed toward the potentialities of this device. In the two instances it was employed, the tax offset proved so powerful that it virtually forced uniformity of action by the states. There were compelling reasons for the adoption of this coercive device in both cases. States with inheritance taxes were seriously threatened by the open bid of Florida for wealthy persons to establish residence there. Although unemployment-insurance laws could have been enacted by the states before 1935, actually interstate competition for business and industry was so keen that only Wisconsin enacted the necessary payroll tax and got its system under way. The federal law acted as an umbrella, permitting all states to enact unemployment-compensation laws without fear of driving industries to other states.

Congress is likely to use sparingly a weapon so powerful as the tax-credit device. Important as they are, federal grants-in-aid and other methods of inducing states to take desired action are less compelling, because the application of federal credits for state taxation has the sanction of forfeiture of tax revenues by a state that is unwilling to cooperate.

Federal Cooperation and Expansion. *Restricting Lanes of Interstate Commerce.* By the exercise of its power over commerce, Congress may help states to control some problems over which they otherwise could not make their control effective. The United States either refuses to allow passage, in or out of a state, of a certain commodity that the state seeks to prohibit or makes the commodity subject to the laws of the state immediately upon arrival.

The earliest experience with this form of cooperative effort was in the field of liquor. After the court ruled in 1890 that a state prohibition

[27] Steward Machine Co. *v.* Davis, 301 U.S. 548 (1937). The Court held the tax was an excise tax, the classification of employers was reasonable, and the state did not surrender any powers essential to sovereignty. See also p. 355.

law could not apply to liquor in interstate commerce,[28] Congress enacted the Wilson Act subjecting liquor shipments into states to state regulation from the time of their arrival. This act was upheld in the courts.[29] The method of "divestment" used in the Wilson Act was later used in subjecting to state regulation game birds and animals (1900), oleomargarine (1902), misbranded gold and silver (1906), plant life under quarantine (1926), convict-made goods (1929), and prize-fight films (1940).[30]

A stronger type of divestment occurs when the Federal government prohibits the movement of goods into a state in violation of state law. The Webb-Kenyon Act of 1913 forbade transportation of liquor into states forbidding its use. Dormant during nation-wide prohibition, the same principle was written into the Twenty-first Amendment, Section 2, which provides:

The transportation or importation into any State, Territory, or possession of the United States for delivery or use therein of intoxicating liquors, in violation of the laws thereof, is hereby prohibited.

The Webb-Kenyon method was also used in the Ashurst-Sumners Act of 1935, which banned the transportation of prison-made goods in violation of state law. After the Supreme Court held this law valid,[31] much hope was aroused that Congress might be able to ban the products of child labor from states prohibiting their sale. Instead, Congress chose to regulate child labor directly and uniformly through the Wages and Hours Law. In 1940 a second Ashurst-Sumners Act placed an absolute prohibition on all shipment of prison-made goods in interstate commerce.

A third type of federal restriction is imposed in order to prohibit the movement of goods and persons from a state in violation of that state's law. This variety of control has been extended

to automobile theft (1919), other stolen property (1934), kidnaped persons (1932), fugitive felons (1934).[32] After the oil-control features of the National Recovery Act of 1933 were declared unconstitutional,[33] Congress forbade shipments of petroleum in interstate commerce in excess of quotas set by state law.[34] This legislation assists oil-producing states in enforcing their laws relating to the production of petroleum and helps the states achieve the conservation goals anticipated in the Interstate Oil Compact.

Since 1949 the Federal government has helped state tax authorities locate evaders of state cigarette taxes by requiring sellers in interstate commerce to file monthly reports on sales to nondistributors.

The cooperative nature of this device has been demonstrated in the various examples of its use. In most cases it makes possible more effective state control, instead of displacing state with federal authority. As a consequence, the states have generally looked with favor upon this form of federal cooperation.

Cooperative and Reciprocal Arrangements. A number of other voluntary, cooperative arrangements have been made between state and Federal governments. Cooperation may be mere consultation between federal and state officials in order to exchange information and to plan together common or interrelated functions. State departments of agriculture usually act in close harmony with the United States Department of Agriculture. The federal Department of Labor holds an annual conference to which are invited state labor officials, who are encouraged to interchange ideas.

Relying upon its power to spend money, Congress has established many research and informational services which may induce states to undertake programs of action or raise standards of performance for existing activities. This is

---

[28] Leisy & Co. *v.* Hardin, 135 U.S. 100 (1890).

[29] *In re* Rahrer, 140 U.S. 545 (1891).

[30] Joseph E. Kallenbach, *Federal Cooperation with the States under the Commerce Clause* (University of Michigan Press, 1942), pp. 112–199.

[31] Kentucky Whip and Collar Co. *v.* Illinois Central, 299 U.S. 334 (1937).

[32] See Kallenbach, *op. cit.,* pp. 315–331.

[33] Panama Refining Co. *v.* Ryan, 293 U.S. 388 (1935). The grounds were excessive delegation of legislative authority to the President.

[34] The Connally Act of 1935, 49 Stat. 30, was renewed in 1937, 1939, and made permanent in 1942, 56 Stat. 381.

what Jane Perry Clark has called "informational inducement." [35]

Another little-noticed field of cooperation is reciprocal use of officials by Federal and state governments. Many state constitutions forbid state officers (to be distinguished from employees) from holding federal posts, but a considerable development has occurred in spite of this limitation. Federal use of state employees and agencies is the more extensive. During the First World War and the Second World War, conscription was federally supervised but locally administered by officials who were appointed by the states. State prohibition-enforcement agents, during the era of the Eighteenth Amendment, often were made part-time federal officers. Less direct state use of federal officials is found, although federal forest rangers may enforce state fish and game laws, and Federal Bureau of Investigation agents frequently apprehend violators of state criminal laws. The county agent or farm adviser performs functions for three levels of government—national, state, and county.

Federal-Local Relations. Previous to 1933 contacts between the Federal government, cities, and counties were largely informal. Federal marshals and district attorneys worked with sheriffs, police chiefs, and prosecutors; the Office of Education issued publications and otherwise served local school districts; cities and counties helped enforce federally fixed standards of weights and measures; but the relationship was seldom direct and formal.

Since 1933 the picture has changed. Contacts have increased manyfold and have become direct and formal. Recent legislation permits the use of federal aid in building highways within cities. The United States Housing Authority makes grants to municipal and county housing authorities for the construction of locally owned and managed housing projects. Indeed, federal-local contacts have become so numerous as seriously to disturb those who fear federal domination. [36]

Direct Federal Expansion of Activities. Perhaps more than all others combined, broadened interpretation of federal powers has been the avenue of federal encroachment on what were formerly state functions. An astounding expansion of federal governmental activities has taken place during the last 30 years. How this expansion has been accomplished and justified may best be studied in connection with the federal powers concerned. Classified by powers, the major expansion may be sketched in summary form.

The commerce power now extends federal control not only to every sort of transportation and communication, but also to manufacturing, mining, and other businesses that affect interstate commerce. In the decade from 1930 to 1940 alone, Congress validly employed the commerce power to regulate labor relations, control radio broadcasting, provide retirement system for railroad employees, fix minimum wages and maximum hours, regulate interstate bus and truck lines, control small streams even of doubtful navigability, regulate stock exchanges, forbid transportation of strikebreakers, punish extorters, kidnapers, and vehicle thieves. The most monumental of court decisions involving the commerce power were in the NLRB cases and in the Wages and Hours Case. [37]

Next in importance comes the tax power, and its implied companion, the spending power. Not only does the tax power justify the grant-in-aid, the tax offset, and expenditures for research and informational services, but it is used for regulatory purposes as well. Between the Civil War and the First World War, broad interpretation of the tax power permitted use of the power to tax state bank notes out of circulation, colored oleomargarine out of existence, phosphorus matches off the market, and to bring dealers of narcotics under federal control. Then the trend was reversed, and the court struck down as void several attempts to regulate through the tax power. This line of decisions was arrested in the Social

[35] Jane Perry Clark, *The Rise of a New Federalism* (Columbia University Press, 1938).

[36] See Wylie Kilpatrick, "Future Federal-State and Local Relations," *Municipal Finance,* vol. 26 (November, 1953), pp. 85–95.

[37] National Labor Relations Board *v.* Jones and Laughlin Steel Corporation, 301 U.S. 1 (1937), and United States *v.* Darby Lumber Co., 312 U.S. 100 (1941).

Security cases,[38] and the tax power now appears available for regulatory purposes.[39]

Through its monetary power, the Federal government validly has extended its activities into such diverse fields as incorporating credit unions, insuring bank deposits, chartering and regulating savings and loan associations, and participating in international stabilization funds. Congress has used the war power to justify in part the great regional-planning scheme of the Tennessee Valley Authority, to authorize the broad wartime controls covering production, transportation, distribution, conscription, and nearly every aspect of economic and social life in the country. Even the treaty power has been used as the basis of federal expansion of authority.

Now that many of the legal restraints on the use of federal power have been removed, our federalism must be sustained—as Livingston suggested recently [40]—by political forces. The need for an informed public opinion becomes even more acute.

Proposed Reform of the Federal System. *State Lines and Administrative Areas.* State boundaries of today are products of historical factors, early transportation limits, and other forces, many of which are no longer valid. Criminals and diseases, plagues of man, do not respect state lines. They may be dealt with effectively either through cooperative effort of two or more states, or they may be handled through federal action. Some students of federal problems feel that the answer to many interstate difficulties may be the drawing of state lines so that a smaller number of regional states might coincide with economic and physiographic lines. One form of regional action is secured through interstate compact or informal agreement of neighboring states, who agree to a common program for a common problem, as is the case with the Colorado River Compact or some of the recent river-pollution compacts.

The Federal government sets up various administrative areas to aid in the execution of national law; most of these groupings respect state lines but combine several states for administrative convenience. An independent federal agency like the Tennessee Valley Authority has broad planning powers over an area including portions of several states, and may be a forerunner of other regional projects under federal auspices. This practice is open to the objection, as in all federal plans, that the people of the area have no direct voice in the management of the scheme. If the Missouri Valley Authority were authorized, for example, the state officials in the areas fear that the states might lose power to decide for themselves many questions of great importance to their future. Some advantages might accrue from standardizing all federal administrative areas, but standardization would represent no particular contribution toward helping the states to settle interstate regional problems. The task of getting small states to consolidate with others appears virtually impossible, given the constitutional inviolability of the territory of a state without its own consent.

Alterations in the Federal System. Various proposals have been made for recasting the balance between nation and states. Some have urged that the Federal government be given full general police power—to provide for the health, morals, safety, and welfare of the people. This scheme would require a constitutional amendment, the ratification of which would be exceedingly difficult to secure. It should be recognized that assigning such a sweeping power to the Federal government would transform our system into a unitary one for all practical purposes.

A second school of thought, which prevailed throughout the New Deal era, argues that the language of the Constitution confers sufficient authority upon the Federal government to deal with national problems. It maintains that the courts were in error between 1933 and 1936 in narrowly construing federal powers, but that this

[38] Steward Machine Co. *v.* Davis, 301 U.S. 548 (1937), validated the unemployment insurance tax offset, and Helvering *v.* Davis, 301 U.S. 619 (1937), approved the old-age insurance scheme.

[39] See also p. 353.

[40] William S. Livingston, "The Legal and Political Determinants of American Federalism," *Southwestern Social Science Quarterly,* vol. 34 (June, 1953), pp. 40–56.

mistake has since been corrected through broad construction. Therefore, the constitutional crisis is over, for time and the new court personnel have combined to produce liberalized decisions. This policy comprehends no sudden changes in existing forms but calls for the remodeling of practices and rejuvenation within the old framework.

Finally, there are the vigilant States' righters, and the decentralists who see the virtues of local self-government slipping away in the face of growing state and federal centralization. The more rabid expend their energies shouting invectives at the federal octopus. The more thoughtful stress the desirability of improving state administration and legislation. They also urge greater use of the interstate organizations and arrangements discussed earlier in this chapter.

Amount of Centralization. Those who favor greater centralization raise many valid objections to the federal system as we have it. It does produce indefensible inequality in an essential public service like education. It provides an outlet for narrow sectional feelings, as evidenced by state trade barriers. It makes difficult the prompt solution of national problems on a national basis. The late Harold J. Laski once condemned our "obsolescent federalism" in these terms:

But a contracting capitalism cannot afford the luxury of federalism. It is insufficiently positive in character; it does not provide for sufficient rapidity of action; it inhibits the emergence of necessary standards of uniformity; it relies upon compacts and compromises which take insufficient account of the urgent category of time; it leaves the backward areas a restraint, at once parasitic and poisonous, on those which seek to move forward; not least, its psychological results, especially in an age of crisis, are depressing to a democracy that needs the drama of positive achievement to retain its faith.[41]

On the other hand, the dangers from excessive centralization appear worse. In a country huge both in area and population a distant national bureaucracy is not likely to understand local needs. Civic interest and participation in government may be reduced in proportion to the size of the political unit and the distance from the seat of power. Alexis de Tocqueville, the first foreign observer of this new republic, wrote more than a hundred years ago one of the strongest arguments for decentralization:

But I am of the opinion that a central administration is fit only to enervate the nations in which it exists, by incessantly diminishing their local spirit. Although such an administration can bring together, on a given point, all the disposable resources of a people, it injures the renewal of those resources. It may insure a victory in the hour of strife, but it gradually relaxes the sinews of strength. It may help admirably the transient greatness of a man, but not the durable prosperity of a nation.[42]

The answer for America probably lies in the middle ground. Federal centralization will continue to reduce the relative importance of the states, as national control over insurance, public utilities, agriculture, social services, and general business increases. Grants-in-aid may expand to general education and other fields, reemphasizing that although federal financing and control over policy are mounting, the state and its local subdivisions may still play an important role in administering functions close to the people served.

[41] Harold J. Laski, "The Obsolescence of Federalism," *New Republic,* vol. 98 (May 3, 1939), pp. 367–369.

[42] Alexis de Tocqueville, *Democracy in America* (Knopf, 2 vols., 1945), vol. I, p. 87.

FOR FURTHER READING

(See also works listed after preceding chapter.)

Anderson, William: *The Nation and the States, Rivals or Partners?* (University of Minnesota Press, 1955).

Ball, Vaughn C., and Others: "The Uniform Laws Movement: Symposium," *Ohio State Law Journal,* vol. 9 (Autumn, 1948), pp. 551–688.

Bard, Erwin W.: *The Port of New York Authority* (Columbia University Press, 1942).

Benson, George C. S.: *The New Centralization* (Rinehart, 1941).

Birch, A. H.: *Federalism, Finance, and Social Legislation in Canada, Australia, and the United States* (Oxford: Clarendon Press, 1955).

Bird, Frederick L.: *A Study of the Port of New York Authority: Its Purpose—Its Accomplishments—Its Plans for the Future* (New York: Dun & Bradstreet, 1949).

Bitterman, Henry J.: *State and Federal Grants-in-Aid* (Mentzer, 1938).

Clark, Jane Perry: *The Rise of a New Federalism* (Columbia University Press, 1938).

Council of State Governments: *Federal Grants-in-Aid, Report of the Committee on . . .* (Chicago: The Council, 1949).

——: *Trade Barriers among the States* (Chicago: The Council, 1939).

——: *The Book of the States* (Chicago: The Council, biennial).

——: *State Government* (Chicago: The Council, monthly).

Eisner, Mark, and Others: *Tax Barriers to Trade* (Philadelphia: Tax Institute, 1941).

Graves, W. Brooke: *Uniform State Action* (The University of North Carolina Press, 1934).

Green, Thomas S., Jr.: *Liquor Trade Barriers* (Chicago: Public Administration Service, 1940).

Heinberg, John G.: *Manual on Federal-State Relations . . .*, Missouri Constitutional Convention Report No. 3 (University of Missouri, 1943).

Johnson, Byron L.: *The Principle of Equalization Applied to the Allocation of Grants-in-Aid,* Bureau of Research and Statistics Memorandum 66 (Social Security Administration, 1947).

Kallenbach, Joseph E.: *Federal Cooperation with the States, under the Commerce Clause* (University of Michigan Press, 1942).

Key, Vladimir O.: *The Administration of Federal Grants to States* (Chicago: Public Administration Service, 1937).

MacDonald, Austin F.: *Federal Aid: A Study of the American Subsidy System* (Crowell, 1928).

Melder, F. Eugene: *State and Local Barriers to Interstate Commerce in the United States* (University of Maine Press, 1937).

Notz, Rebecca L.: *Acts of Congress Providing for Grants-in-Aid to States,* Public Affairs Bulletin 70 (Library of Congress, 1949).

Taylor, George R., and Others: *Barriers to Internal Trade in Farm Products* (Government Printing Office, 1939).

Thursby, Vincent V.: *Interstate Cooperation: A Study of the Interstate Compact* (Public Affairs Press, 1953).

U.S. Advisory Committee on Education: *Report of the Committee* (1938).

U.S. Department of Commerce, Marketing Laws Survey: *Bibliography of Barriers to Trade between States* (Bureau of Foreign and Domestic Commerce, 1942).

U.S. Department of Commerce: *A Summarized Report of the Legal Subcommittee of the Interdepartmental Committee on Interstate Trade Barriers* (1940).

U.S. National Resources Committee: *Regional Factors in National Planning and Development* (1935).

White, Leonard D.: *The States and the Nation* (Louisiana State University Press, 1953).

Zimmerman, Frederick L., and Mitchell Wendell: *The Interstate Compact since 1925* (Chicago: Council of State Governments, 1951).

REVIEW QUESTIONS

1. Explain the nature and scope of federal grants-in-aid. How has this device altered American federalism?

2. What is the "tax-offset device"? Does its use imply the loss of States' rights? How much use of it do you expect in the future?

3. How has Congress used its authority over commerce in order to cooperate with the states?

4. Define interstate compacts. Indicate the extent to which they have been used in the past and are likely to be used in the future.

5. What obligations are imposed by the Constitution upon states in their relations with one another?

6. What are state trade barriers? What can be done about them?

7. Discuss the trend toward centralization in this country. What is the outlook for state governments? What do you propose could be done to strengthen the states?

8. Discuss the following: payments in lieu of taxation, paramount interest in tidelands, equalization through variable grants.

9. Describe current proposals for federal aid to general education. What are some of the principal issues involved in extending subsidies to the states for elementary and secondary education?

10. If you were a member of a federal constitutional convention, called for the purpose of general modernization of the Constitution, what changes in our federal system would you support? Why?

CHAPTER 7

The Protection of Rights

> Heretics have been hateful from the beginning of recorded time; they have been ostracized, exiled, tortured, maimed and butchered; but it has generally proved impossible to smother them, and when it has not, the society that has succeeded has always declined. Façades of authority, however imposing, do not survive after it has appeared that they rest upon the sands of human conjecture and compromise. — Judge Learned Hand [1]

The problem of reconciling order and security with liberty is an old one compounded with difficulty today by the stresses of technology, war, economic depressions, unpopular ideologies, revolutionary conditions in many parts of the world, growing world interdependence, and the quest for national security in an atomic age. This chapter reviews the safeguards to individual rights and how they have been interpreted in the United States.

GENERAL CONSIDERATIONS

Rights Relative—Not Absolute. The Declaration of Independence speaks of "natural" or "unalienable" rights, and the language of the Constitution suggests that rights are absolute. If this were true, governments could under no circumstances legislate on matters proscribed. But this is not the case. Over the years many laws have been passed restricting vulgarity, profanity, slander, libel, and the like, even though in doing so freedom of speech was curtailed. The power to govern coexists with personal rights, and the two must be reconciled. Power cannot be exercised without regard to constitutionally protected rights and the latter cannot

be enjoyed without regard for other individuals and the community. This being the case, it becomes necessary to strike a balance, to draw boundary lines. This is done by legislatures, executives, and especially the courts, all of which are influenced by public opinion.

While admitting that rights are relative, there is danger, especially in periods of emergency or hysteria, that they may be emasculated. The Bill of Rights, it should be remembered, is as much a part of the Constitution as those sections delegating powers to Congress, including those granting the power to declare and prosecute war. "Our Constitution," wrote Justice Felix Frankfurter, "has no provision lifting restrictions upon governmental authority during periods of emergency. . . ." [2]

Curbs on Governments—Not Individuals. The rights clauses of the Constitution protect people from the actions of governments, not from one another. Sometimes the words are "Congress shall make no law . . . ," or "No state shall . . . ," but where such words are omitted they should be inferred. Thus, if a mayor suppresses free speech, the Constitution is violated. But if a gang of hoodlums breaks up a

---

[1] *The New York Times Magazine,* Feb. 6, 1955, p. 33.

[2] Dennis *v.* United States, 341 U.S. 494 (1950).

meeting, the action is probably illegal but does not violate the Bill of Rights.

The Constitution is violated if a state or the national government denies an accused person a fair trial, but a lynching mob can seize and destroy a suspect in complete disregard for his rights without violating the Constitution. If the state or the Federal government takes one's car for governmental use without paying for it, he is deprived of his property without due process of law, which is in violation of the Constitution; but if his car is stolen by another person, that is not in violation of the "due process" clause. This distinction is of great importance, because for every governmental offense there are dozens by private individuals and groups. Redress against the latter depends upon statutes or common law.

Both Federal Government and States Limited. The Bill of Rights limits the Federal government only.[3] Similar state restrictions are given elsewhere and are listed on page 107. Until recently Federal courts were inclined to interpret some of the restrictions on states narrowly. This was particularly true of that part of the Four-

[3] Barron *v.* Baltimore, 7 Pet. 243 (U.S. 1823); Twining *v.* New Jersey, 211 U.S. 78 (1908).

teenth Amendment which says that states may not violate the privileges and immunities of citizens of the United States, or take life, liberty, and property without due process of law, or deny to any persons under their jurisdiction equal protection of the law.

The courts still refuse to say that all rights guaranteed by the first ten amendments are among the privileges and immunities of citizenship. But the word "liberty" mentioned in the Fourteenth Amendment has been broadened to include at least freedom of the press, religion, speech, assembly, and petition. In other words, these rights have been "federalized." Neither the states nor local governments can breach them without running afoul of the Federal courts. This protection is of great value in view of opportunities and temptations that forty-eight states and thousands of cities and other local governments have to abridge liberties. Indeed, by far the most civil-rights cases reaching Federal courts challenge state and local action, not federal.

Rights of Aliens and Nationals Also Guaranteed. Rights are guaranteed to all "persons." This being the case, aliens, after admittance to

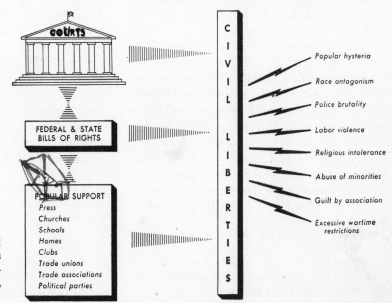

PROTECTIONS OF & DANGERS TO CIVIL LIBERTIES

Federal and state constitutional guarantees, enforced by the courts and backed by the popular support of groups and institutions, guard civil liberties.

the United States, and nationals are entitled to the same personal and property rights as citizens. They do not, however, enjoy certain "privileges and immunities" that are pledged to citizens only.

Privileges and Immunities of Citizens. In addition to guaranteeing certain "rights," the Constitution also mentions "privileges" or "immunities" that are derived from national citizenship. The actual words are: "No State shall make or enforce any law which shall abridge the privileges or immunities of citizens of the United States. . . ." The rights previously discussed in this chapter are guaranteed to *all persons,* but privileges or immunities are guaranteed only to *citizens* of the United States. The difference between rights and privileges or immunities is not altogether clear, nor has any complete list of the latter ever been made. The guaranty is important, however, inasmuch as states are expressly forbidden to violate it.

The Fourteenth Amendment made Negroes citizens, and the privilege-and-immunity clause was undoubtedly included to prevent the states from depriving the new citizens of rights guaranteed by the first eight amendments. Nevertheless, in early decisions [4] the Supreme Court narrowed the meaning of the words, saying that a right was to be distinguished from a privilege or immunity. The former included those mentioned in the Bill of Rights, but the latter included something additional.

While no complete list of privileges and immunities has been or can be made, experience suggests that they include freedom to pass from state to state and to engage in interstate commerce; governmental protection while on the high seas or in foreign countries; freedom to expatriate (except when the nation is at war); access to ports of the United States, to navigable waters, and agencies of the Federal government, including courts of law; freedom to vote for federal officers; [5] freedom to enjoy all rights and ad-

vantages secured by treaties; freedom to assemble peaceably, petition for redress of grievances, and for writ of habeas corpus; freedom to enter the country and to prove citizenship if questioned; and liberty to inform the Federal government of violations of its laws. [6] These the states may not violate. Aliens may enjoy some of them as a matter of grace, but they cannot demand them as a matter of right as citizens can. Neither are corporations protected by the privileges-and-immunities clause, inasmuch as they are not citizens within the meaning of the Fourteenth Amendment.

Limited Ability of Federal Government to Safeguard Rights. When Federal and state governments trespass upon civil liberties guaranteed by the Federal Constitution, the usual procedure is for the injured party to appeal to Federal courts. On occasions like these the courts play a negative role. Damage has already been done, and the victim may be unable to make protest or may have to wait years for adequate redress. Moreover, as indicated above, for offenses by private individuals and groups the Constitution provides no legal remedy. Much dissatisfaction has been expressed in recent years over these alleged inadequacies. The time has come, critics say, for the Federal government to play an affirmative role as well as a negative one. [7]

Among other things, critics argue, this requires legislation strengthening federal enforcement machinery and imposing penalties upon state and local officials and private parties who violate civil rights. In times past Congress has attempted to do just this. Soon after passage of the Thirteenth Amendment the worst forms of slavery were successfully outlawed. Passage of the Fourteenth Amendment was followed by a series of civil rights acts intended to outlaw the most serious forms of discrimination against Negroes.

---

[4] See especially Slaughter House Cases, 16 Wall. 36 (U.S. 1873).

[5] But not for state officers and offices. These are privileges of state citizenship rather than federal. Snowden *v.* Hughes, 321 U.S. 1 (1943).

[6] For a list of privileges that are not protected by the privileges-and-immunities clause see Edward S. Corwin (ed.), *The Constitution of the United States of America,* S. Doc. 170, 82d Cong., 2d Sess. (1953), pp. 969–970.

[7] See especially the excellent study by Robert K. Carr, *Federal Protection of Civil Rights: Quest for a Sword* (Cornell University Press, 1947).

One of the acts (that of 1875) went so far as to make it a federal crime to deny service on equal terms in hotels, public conveyances, theaters, and other places of amusement. Those responsible for these measures assumed that the Civil War amendments, each of which contained clauses saying Congress had power to take appropriate steps to see that its provisions were enforced, justified affirmative action.

These champions were, however, doomed to disappointment. In less than thirty years the program ended in failure. The Supreme Court led the way in a series of decisions that drastically narrowed the scope of federal authority.[8] Congress followed by repealing most of the statutes. After these events, administrative officers were reluctant to proceed at the risk of meeting further rebuffs. That this hesitation was justified is illustrated by the case of Screws *v.* United States.[9] Here the Department of Justice tried to enforce a remaining provision of the Civil Rights Act of 1866. Screws, a county sheriff in Georgia, was tried and convicted by federal officers of brutally beating and killing a Negro prisoner whom he held in custody. Although Screws was undoubtedly guilty, a majority of the Supreme Court interpreted the federal statute so technically and narrowly as to reverse the conviction and order a new trial, in which the defendant was acquitted.

To Secure These Rights. Recent years have witnessed a renewal of interest. One evidence of this was the appointment in 1946 of the President's Committee on Civil Rights, made up of distinguished citizens. The Committee's report, published under title of *To Secure These Rights*,[10] was widely read and proved to be highly controversial.

[8] See especially the Civil Rights Cases, 109 U.S. 3 (1883); the Slaughter House Cases, 16 Wall. 36 (U.S. 1873); and United States *v.* Cruikshank, 92 U.S. 542 (1876).

[9] 325 U.S. 91 (1945).

[10] U.S. President's Committee on Civil Rights: *To Secure These Rights* (1947). In addition to being published as a government document in 1947, the report was also published under the same title by Simon and Schuster.

Denials of Rights. The committee called attention to lynching and to the fact that the culprits are seldom discovered or punished. It discovered numerous instances of police brutality in various parts of the nation. Indeed, it quoted testimony given by J. Edgar Hoover, Director of the FBI, to the effect that at a particular jail "it was seldom that a Negro man or woman was incarcerated who was not given a severe beating, which started off with a pistol whipping and ended with a rubber hose."[11] The committee reported that Negroes, Mexicans, Indians, and other minorities often find it impossible to obtain justice, partly because of their poverty, partly because of the "complete absence of people of their own kind from jury lists," partly because of the fee system in many communities, which "sometimes stimulates arbitrary arrests and encourages unjust convictions," and partly because in certain states "the white population can threaten and do violence to the minority members with little or no fear of legal reprisals."

The committee also found some involuntary servitude among the poor, arising from state peonage laws imposing penalties for nonfulfillment of contracts to perform labor. It criticized the wartime treatment of Japanese-Americans along the West coast with resultant curtailment of liberty, forced removal to detention and relocation centers, and financial hardship. The committee discovered many instances of discrimination against aliens and even natives of American territories.

The committee also noted that because of restrictions on the right to vote in some states, particularly the poll tax requirement in several Southern states, comparatively few people went to the polls in these states. It found numerous violations of freedom of speech, press, religion, and assembly. It pointed out the dangers of "Red hunting" among civil servants by congressional committees and loyalty boards. It found an abundance of evidence indicating discrimination against Negroes in the armed forces, civil service, District of Columbia, American territories, by state and local governments, landlords, private employers, and in professional and service

[11] *Ibid.,* p. 26.

occupations. The committee was especially severe in its condemnation of racial segregation.

Proposed Remedies. After reviewing the American scene and finding conditions that were heartening as well as disappointing, the President's Committee on Civil Rights made numerous proposals. Most important of all, the committee said, it is necessary to have an informed and alert public that is both tolerant and aggressive in defense of rights for all, especially minorities and advocates of unpopular causes.

More specific suggestions included: (1) reorganization and strengthening of the Civil Rights Section of the Department of Justice; (2) creation by the states of divisions similar to the federal Civil Rights Section; (3) special training for federal and state police in the handling of cases involving civil rights; (4) establishment of federal and state permanent commissions on civil rights to maintain constant surveillance; (5) clarification and strengthening of federal statutes to make it unmistakably clear what conduct is and what is not a federal crime; (6) federal legislation outlawing police brutality, lynching, and all forms of peonage; (7) federal legislation outlawing the poll tax and other serious impediments to voting in primaries and elections; (8) self-government for the District of Columbia; (9) citizenship for the people of Guam and Samoa; (10) repeal of state laws discriminating against aliens; (11) federal and state action ending "Jim Crow" laws and other serious forms of racial segregation and discrimination; (12) withholding federal grants-in-aid from public and private agencies that practice discrimination and segregation.

Developments since the Report. Bitter controversy followed publication of the report, which had serious political repercussions in the presidential elections of 1948 and 1952. Nevertheless, the report led to much self-examination and some progress in the direction of recommendations made by the committee. The greatest change came from the Supreme Court when in 1954 it outlawed race segregation in the public schools.

Meanwhile, lynchings have virtually ceased; use of the poll tax has declined; additional states and municipalities have established fair employment practices commissions to help end discrimination in employment because of race, color, creed, or national origin; Congress has granted citizenship to the people of Guam; and the President, by executive order, has greatly reduced race segregation and discrimination in the armed forces, federally aided public housing, and the Federal civil service. Although rapid progress is being made in eliminating racial discrimination, Southerners in the Senate, armed with the filibuster, have prevented the passage of several important recommendations made by the President's committee, and inertia and apathy have slowed other reforms. Meanwhile, anxiety over communism and possible subversion has produced new threats to minority rights.

RIGHTS OF PERSONS AND PROPERTY

Life, Liberty, and Property. In general, all rights pertain either to life, liberty, or property. The term "life" includes not merely animal existence, but the retention of limbs and organs by which life is enjoyed. The word "liberty" embraces all our liberties—personal, civil, and political. This includes, among other things, freedom to move about, to think, to engage in some useful occupation, to make choices, to marry and establish a home, to participate in political activities, to speak, write, and worship. The word "property" includes the right to enter an occupation and engage in business, to acquire property, to hold and possess valuable objects, to enjoy the rewards of ownership, and to dispose of property by loan, lease, gift, or sale. These are the great liberties that the Constitution seeks to ensure "to ourselves and our posterity." In general, they can be regulated and restricted if due process of law is followed, although, as we shall see, there are certain practices that the Constitution proscribes altogether.

Due Process of Law. The Fifth Amendment forbids Congress to deprive any person of "life, liberty, or property, without due process of law," and the Fourteenth Amendment imposes the same limitation upon the states. This is one of the most important, as well as controversial, of all guaranties. The protection extends both to natural persons, *i.e.,* ordinary human beings, and to artificial persons such as corporations.

Procedural Due Process. Procedural due process means that in dealing with people governments must proceed according to "settled usages and modes of procedure." The standards are

fairly definite. The Constitution specifically mentions certain steps that must not be omitted, and others have crystallized from experience dating back to the days of Magna Charta. Among other things, proper procedure requires that (1) the government, or subordinate agency,

Rights Guaranteed by the Federal Constitution

To Citizens and Aliens against Encroachment by National Government

1. Writ of habeas corpus may not be suspended except during rebellion or invasion.
2. No bills of attainder.
3. No ex post facto criminal laws.
4. No class distinction to be created by grants of titles of nobility.
5. Treason is defined in Constitution; Congress may not enlarge number of treasonable offenses.
6. Heirs of persons convicted of treason may not be forbidden to inherit property.
7. No laws respecting religious institutions, and none that interferes with the free exercise of religion.
8. No laws abridging freedom of speech or press.
9. No interference with right to assemble peaceably and petition Congress.
10. No infringement of right of people to bear arms.
11. No soldiers to be quartered in private dwellings in time of peace without owner's consent.
12. No unreasonable searches and seizures and no warrants to be issued but upon probable cause.
13. No criminal prosecution except upon indictment or presentment by grand jury.
14. Cannot be tried twice for the same offense.
15. One accused of crime cannot be compelled to be a witness against himself.
16. Speedy, public, impartial trial by jury of 12 persons whose verdict of guilt must be unanimous.
17. Trial by jury in civil suits involving a sum of more than $20.

18. Those accused of crimes must be informed of charges and right to counsel, be present in courtroom when witnesses are called to testify against them, be given legal power to compel witnesses to testify in their favor.
19. No excessive bail or fines; no cruel or unusual punishment.
20. Slavery or involuntary servitude prohibited.
21. Life, liberty, and property may not be taken without due process of law.
22. Property may not be taken without just compensation.
23. Privilege of voting may not be abridged because of race, color, previous condition of servitude, or sex.

To Citizens and Aliens against Encroachment by State

1. Bills of attainder forbidden.
2. Ex post facto criminal laws may not be enacted.
3. No laws impairing obligation of contract.
4. Class distinction not to be created by grants of title of nobility.
5. Slavery or involuntary servitude prohibited.
6. Full faith and credit must be granted to acts, records, and judicial proceedings of other states or of the U.S.
7. Citizens of other states must be granted same privileges and immunities as are enjoyed by their own citizens.
8. Life, liberty, and property may not be taken without due process of law.*
9. Equal protection of the laws may not be denied.
10. Privileges of voting may not be denied because of race, color, previous condition of servitude, or sex.

---

* This has been interpreted to include guaranties of freedom of speech, press, religion, and assembly.

have jurisdiction over the person or object with which it seeks to interfere; (2) the legislation or order be properly enacted or prepared and published; (3) crimes must be clearly defined; (4) those accused must be properly apprehended and notified of the nature of the accusation and the time and place of the hearing; (5) opportunity must be given for the accused to prepare and present his defense; and (6) the tribunal before which the trial or hearing is to be conducted must be so constituted as to ensure an honest and impartial decision.

A recent case[12] illustrates procedural due process. Having information that a man named Rochin was selling narcotics, three California deputy sheriffs entered his home. Finding the outside door open, they entered and then forced open the door to Rochin's room. Inside they found him sitting on the side of the bed, upon which his wife was lying. On a night stand beside the bed were two capsules. When asked "Whose stuff is this?" Rochin seized the capsules and swallowed them. The police "jumped upon him," but the capsules were not forthcoming. They were later extracted at a hospital with a stomach pump and were found to contain morphine. Rochin was prosecuted and convicted of violating the narcotic laws of California. On appeal, the United States Supreme Court reversed the conviction, saying the police officers had violated the procedural guaranties of the Fourteenth Amendment. Said the Court:

This is conduct that shocks the conscience. Illegally breaking into the privacy of the petitioner, the struggle to open his mouth and remove what was there, the forcible extraction of his stomach's contents—this course of proceedings by agents of government to obtain evidence is bound to offend even hardened sensibilities. They are methods too close to the rack and the screw to permit of constitutional differentiation. It has long since ceased to be true that due process of law is heedless of the means by which otherwise relevant and creditable evidence is obtained.

Substantive Due Process. When it was added to the Constitution, the Fifth Amendment was

undoubtedly intended to guarantee the procedures known to common law, but beginning in the 1850's[13] state courts began to interpret the due-process clauses of state constitutions in such a manner as to require not only that the proper procedures be followed, but that the law itself should be reasonable. Cautiously at first, then boldly, the Federal courts accepted the doctrine, with the result that they claimed competence to scrutinize the *substance* or *content* of federal and state laws. Having the power of judicial review, this meant that the courts became a sort of superlegislature, or "third House," with authority to set aside any law which they deemed "unreasonable, arbitrary, or capricious." Accordingly, due process came to have both a procedural and substantive meaning. In other words, the courts came to concern themselves not only with *how* the government proceeds, but also with *what* it is attempting to do, or the substance of law.

Substituting their judgment of reasonableness for that of the political branches of government, the courts declared unconstitutional a few acts of Congress and many acts of state legislatures. Among the measures frowned upon were laws regulating wages and hours, requiring workmen's compensation, fixing prices, classifying businesses of certain types as public utilities for the purpose of stringent control, and making property valuations. Judicial restraints upon broad questions of public policy like these provoked great controversy, especially since opinion was often sharply divided within the Supreme Court itself.

Chief among the criticisms was that conservative courts were restraining popular legislation by the application of standards of reasonableness which at best were incapable of precise definition and which were established in cases decided in days gone by when conditions were different. In recent times, controversy has died down, partly because the social revolution of the 1930's led the courts to take a more generous view toward the exercise of public power. Current judicial attitudes may be sampled in the

---

[12] Rochin *v.* California, 342 U.S. 165 (1951).

[13] The first case appears to have been that of Wynehamer *v.* New York, 13 N.Y. 378 (1856).

cases upholding the fixing of prices for milk, upholding the fixing of minimum wages and maximum hours, and permitting the use of a more flexible formula in making utility valuations for purposes of rate making.

Equal Protection of the Laws. States are forbidden to "deny to any person within their jurisdiction the equal protection of the laws," but a similar restraint against the Federal government is unmentioned. Gross denial of equal protection by the Federal government would, however, undoubtedly be held to violate the due-process clause of the Fifth Amendment. Although the provision was inserted in the Fourteenth Amendment for the protection of Negroes, it stands also as a guaranty to others, including corporations.

The guaranty of equal protection does not require that persons be treated exactly alike: tariffs on uncut diamonds may be lower than on polished; minimum-wage laws may be enacted for women without also including men or children; maximum hours may be established for men in hazardous employments without also including nonhazardous industries; aliens may be forbidden to practice medicine, law, or other professions; taxes may be imposed upon retailers of certain products, like liquors, and not others; chain stores may be taxed more heavily than independents; the rich may be taxed at higher rates than the poor; etc. In cases like these, people, objects, or businesses are classified. The test is whether the classification is reasonable and appropriate. If it is, then everyone within each group must be treated alike.

On the other hand, equal protection would be denied if a law were so administered as to discriminate against Chinese launderers in favor of American;[14] if Negroes, women, or wage earners were systematically excluded from grand and petit juries;[15] if employers were denied the right to obtain injunctions while permitting them to employees;[16] if Negro barbers were forbidden to serve white children;[17] if resident alien Japanese were denied commercial licenses to fish in coastal waters;[18] or if state courts enforced restrictive covenants barring the sale or transfer of real estate to Negroes and other non-Aryans.[19]

The Problem of Racial Segregation. Although freed by the Civil War, Negroes were not everywhere given social equality. Many prewar restrictions were retained and others were promptly adopted compelling racial segregation. Ultimately these reached the Supreme Court for reconciliation with the equal-protection clause of the Fourteenth Amendment. In Plessy *v.* Ferguson [20] the now famous separate-but-equal doctrine was announced. At issue was a Louisiana law requiring railroads to provide separate coaches for white and colored passengers. The court upheld the law, saying it was within the scope of the police power to "provide equal but separate accommodations for the white and colored races" as one means of maintaining peace and order.

While this doctrine prevailed it was fiercely contested. The President's Committee on Civil Rights, discussed above, had this to say:

The separate-but-equal doctrine stands convicted on three grounds. It contravenes the equalitarian spirit of the American heritage. It has failed to operate, for history shows that inequality of service has been the omnipresent consequence of separation. It has institutionalized segregation and kept groups apart despite indisputable evidence that normal contacts among these groups tend to promote social harmony.[21]

As criticism mounted Federal courts began to yield. For many years they took a casual attitude in cases alleging that under segregation facilities were not in fact equal. On one occasion the Supreme Court thought a county school

---

[14] Yick Wo *v.* Hopkins, 118 U.S. 356 (1886).

[15] Norris *v.* Alabama, 294 U.S. 587 (1935); Smith *v.* Texas, 311 U.S. 128 (1940); Patton *v.* Missouri, 322 U.S. 443 (1947); Cassell *v.* Texas, 339 U.S. 282 (1949).

[16] Truax *v.* Corrigan, 257 U.S. 312 (1921).

[17] Chaires *v.* City of Atlanta, 164 Ga. 755, 139 S.E. 559 (1927).

[18] Takahashi *v.* Fish and Game Commission *et al.*, 334 U.S. 410 (1947).

[19] Shelley *v.* Kraemer, 334 U.S. 1 (1948).

[20] 163 U.S. 537 (1896).

[21] *To Secure These Rights,* p. 87.

board did not deny equal protection when it provided a high school for white children but none for colored ones.[22] But in the 1930's Federal courts began taking a more realistic view and in a series of cases [23] ruled segregation unconstitutional where evidence clearly indicated that accommodations and facilities were unequal. Finally, in 1954, in a momentous and historic decision,[24] the Supreme Court met the issue head on. The decision merits review.

The Desegregation Cases. The case gets its name from a Brown family whose Negro children were required by school authorities in Topeka, Kans., to attend segregated elementary schools. Similar cases had arisen in South Carolina, Virginia, and Delaware, and the four were joined by the Supreme Court for review and decision. In the Kansas case the United States District Court was of the opinion that segregation had a detrimental effect upon Negro children, but it denied relief on the ground that Negro and white schools were substantially equal with respect to buildings and facilities, transportation, curriculums, and educational qualifications for teachers.

In the other three cases the lower courts had found schools for Negroes and whites unequal and ordered either equalization or nonsegregation. None of the lower Federal courts had ruled against the validity of segregation itself. The Supreme Court had great difficulty with the issues involved. The cases were argued early in December, 1952; reargument was permitted just a year later; and decision was announced on May 17, 1954. Even though the decision was unanimous, orders for its implementation were postponed until further hearings were held.

Drawing upon the contributions of psychology and related disciplines, the Supreme Court struck at segregation, saying:

To separate them [children] from others of similar age and qualifications solely because of their race generates a feeling of inferiority as to their status in the community that may affect their hearts and minds in a way unlikely ever to be undone. . . . We conclude that in the field of public education the doctrine of "separate but equal" has no place. Separate educational facilities are inherently unequal. Therefore, we hold that the plaintiffs and others similarly situated for whom the actions have been brought are, by reason of the segregation complained of, deprived of the equal protection of the laws guaranteed by the Fourteenth Amendment.

Late in May, 1955, after extended hearings, the Supreme Court announced its order setting forth how compliance should proceed.[25] In essence, the order (1) reaffirmed and extended desegregation in education, saying: "All provisions of Federal, state or local law requiring or permitting such discrimination must yield to this principle;" (2) charged local school authorities with responsibility for integration under scrutiny of Federal district courts; and (3) instructed the courts to require "a prompt and reasonable start" but allow additional time if needed to solve administrative problems. Time will be required to comply with the order, and enforcement will be spotty, but the edict is clear and unmistakable. Meanwhile, the Court's reinterpretation of the equal-protection clause has brought into question legal segregation and discrimination of all types.

Prohibition of Slavery. The Thirteenth Amendment provides that "neither slavery nor involuntary servitude, except as a punishment for crime whereof the party shall have been duly convicted, shall exist within the United States or any place subject to their jurisdiction." The terms "slavery" and "involuntary servitude" are nearly synonymous, although the latter has a somewhat broader meaning. The obvious purpose of this language was to forbid all shades

[22] Cumming *v.* County Board of Education, 175 U.S. 528 (1899).

[23] See especially Missouri *ex rel.* Gaines *v.* Canada, 305 U.S. 337 (1938); Sipuel *v.* Board of Regents of the University of Oklahoma, 322 U.S. 631 (1948); Sweatt *v.* Painter, 339 U.S. 629 (1949); McLaurin *v.* Oklahoma State Regents for Higher Education *et al.,* 339 U.S. 637 (1949).

[24] Brown *et al. v.* Board of Education of Topeka *et al.,* 347 U.S. 483 (1954).

[25] Brown *v.* Board of Education of Topeka *et al.,* 348 U.S. 886 (1955).

and conditions of slavery. Though intended to free the Negro, the guaranty extends to people of other races as well.

Several interesting questions have arisen from the amendment. One of the first inquired whether the amendment applied to an uncivilized tribe of Alaskan Indians whose custom it had long been to practice slavery. The Supreme Court held that the amendment applied.[26] On another occasion, the question arose whether slavery was also outlawed within Indian tribes inasmuch as the Indians had long retained the right to govern their internal affairs. Again the amendment was held applicable.[27] It is now assumed that slavery cannot exist either within the forty-eight states or any American territory, either incorporated or unincorporated.

On various occasions the amendment has been held to forbid attempts on the part of shipping companies to force seamen to work on board vessels without having previously voluntarily contracted to do so,[28] the farming out of vagrants for hire, attempting to force people to work under threat of conviction for vagrancy, and state peonage laws that attempt to force laborers, renters, and sharecroppers to fulfill contracts that they may have made for labor.[29]

On the other hand, the amendment does not forbid certain acts of compulsion that require involuntary labor. On one occasion it was contended that a Florida law requiring all able-bodied men to perform work upon roads and bridges for 6 days each year or provide a substitute amounted to involuntary servitude. Distinguishing between a "duty" or "obligation" and a "servitude," the Supreme Court upheld the Florida statute, saying that the Thirteenth Amendment "certainly was not intended to interdict enforcement of those duties which individuals owe to the State, such as service in the

army, militia, on the jury, etc."[30] A similar decision was reached when it was contended that the military draft law of 1917 required involuntary servitude.[31] The courts have also permitted states and municipalities to compel criminals to work out their fines on the streets or public works. They have also upheld a state law compelling physicians to report contagious diseases without compensation. Also ruled invalid was a state law making it a misdemeanor for landlords intentionally to fail to furnish utility and other services promised in a lease.

THE FIRST AMENDMENT FREEDOMS

Religious Faith and Practice. As the Constitution came from the Constitutional Convention, it said nothing about the church or religious liberty, implying that the situation as it existed in the states would remain undisturbed. To confirm this understanding, the First Amendment provided that "Congress shall make no law respecting an establishment of religion, or prohibiting the free exercise thereof." Thus, so far as the Federal Constitution was concerned, states remained free to deal with the subject of religion as they saw fit, subject of course to limits in their own constitutions. This was the situation until recently. Present decisions of the Supreme Court construe the Fourteenth Amendment to include the same guaranties of religious liberty as those contained in the First Amendment. Accordingly, the Constitution now prohibits both Federal and state governments from interfering with the church or religious liberty.

Forbidding of a State Church. Note that the First Amendment proscribes laws respecting an *establishment* of religion. This means that Congress, and probably the states, cannot either directly or indirectly establish a state church or state religion nor show partiality for any religious sect, organization, or mode of worship. It does not mean that religious faith and practice may not be encouraged by law, nor that cognizance cannot be taken of religious principles of sects and individuals. Congress employs chap-

[26] *In re* Sah Quah (D.C. Alaska, 1886) 31 F. 327.

[27] United States *v.* Choctaw Nation, 38 Ct. Cl. 668, 566 (1903).

[28] If valid contracts have been entered into, however, performance probably could be enforced. See Robertson *v.* Baldwin, discussed on p. 452.

[29] Such persons may, of course, be sued for damage on grounds of fraud or breach of contract.

[30] Butler *v.* Perry, 240 U.S. 328, 333 (1916).

[31] Arver *v.* United States, 245 U.S. 366, 390 (1918).

lains to open its sessions with prayer, it supports chaplains in the Army and Navy, it has exempted ministers of religion and theological students from military draft, it has exempted religious institutions from payment of taxes and from provisions of the Social Security Act. During prohibition it made wine available for religious rites, and it has exempted conscientious objectors from strict military service. Such acts as these have been held not to violate the First Amendment.

Recently this provision has provoked considerable controversy, especially at the state level. Essence of the argument is whether the amendment was intended to erect a wall of separation between church and state or merely to prevent the showing of governmental preference toward particular faiths, churches, or sects. In a recent decision upholding a New Jersey law the Supreme Court had this to say:[32]

The "establishment of religion" clause of the First Amendment means at least this: Neither a state nor the Federal Government can set up a church. Neither can pass laws which aid one religion, aid all religions, or prefer one religion over another. Neither can force nor influence a person to go to or to remain away from church against his will or force him to profess a belief or disbelief in any religion. No person can be punished for entertaining or professing religious beliefs or disbeliefs, for church attendance or non-attendance. No tax in any amount, large or small, can be levied to support any religious activities or institutions, whatever they may be called, or whatever form they may adopt to teach or practice religion. Neither a state nor the Federal Government can, openly or secretly, participate in the affairs of any religious organizations or groups and vice versa. In the words of Jefferson, the clause against establishment of religion by law was intended to erect a "wall of separation between church and state."

Nevertheless, by a 5-to-4 vote, the Court upheld the law whereby patrons of Catholic schools were reimbursed with tax funds for bus fares

[32] Everson *v.* Board of Education, 330 U.S. 15–16 (1946).

paid going to and returning from school. School transportation, the court majority argued, was in the same category as police and fire protection and other public services. To withhold these, or any of them, from Catholics would discriminate against them and thereby interfere with their free exercise of religion.

Released-time Issue. A short time later the Supreme Court ruled on an arrangement whereby the public schools of Champaign, Ill., released time and classrooms to local religious groups for instruction. Only pupils whose parents gave written consent were required to attend religious classes. Protest was made by one of the parents who claimed that the Fourteenth Amendment was violated. The Supreme Court agreed,[33] saying the use of a tax-supported school system with its machinery for compulsory school attendance for religious instruction was unconstitutional support of an establishment of religion. This decision is difficult for the layman to reconcile with the Everson case mentioned above. It had widespread repercussions, affecting as it did similar arrangements in some 2,200 communities in forty-six states.[34]

Following the McCollum decision, many public schools turned to a plan whereby with parental consent children were released for religious instruction off school premises, usually in local churches. A New York City program like this came before the Supreme Court and was upheld in 1952 by vote of 6 to 3.[35] The court minority contended that the program employed the compulsory school law as a means of aiding churches and religious training. The majority denied the plan involved coercion, since parental consent was required and school officials were strictly neutral. Admitting that sepa-

[33] McCollum *v.* Board of Education, 333 U.S. 203 (1948).

[34] For critical analyses of the Everson and McCollum cases, see articles by Edward S. Corwin and Milton R. Konvitz in *Law and Contemporary Problems,* vol. 14 (Winter, 1949).

[35] Zorach *et al. v.* Clauson *et al.,* 343 U.S. 306 (1951). Justice Douglas wrote the majority opinion, Justices Black, Frankfurter, and Jackson dissenting.

ration of church and state is intended by the Constitution, the majority went on to say, "The First Amendment . . . does not say that in every and all respects there shall be a separation of church and state." Rather,

When the state encourages religious instruction or cooperates with religious authorities by adjusting the schedule of public events to sectarian needs, it follows our best traditions. . . . Government may not finance religious groups nor undertake religious instruction nor blend secular and sectarian education nor use secular institutions to force one or some religion on any person. . . . The Government must be neutral when it comes to competition between sects. It may not thrust any sect on any person. It may not make a religious observance compulsory. It may not coerce anyone to attend church, to observe a religious holiday, or to take religious instruction. . . . But it can close its doors or suspend its operations as to those who want to repair to their religious sanctuary for worship or instruction. No more than that is undertaken here.

While the "released time" issue appears to be settled, it remains unclear how far American governments may go toward encouraging churches and religious instruction. Some religious bodies, especially the Catholic Church, continue to press for federal and state financial aid for their schools. They are particularly desirous of aid for auxiliary services like transportation, school lunches, health services, books and supplies, scholarships, and perhaps buildings. The controversy engendered by demands like these is often heated. In Congress it has helped block federal aid to general public-school education. In some states, as in New Jersey, champions of aid to parochial schools have had a measure of success. But only future court decisions can tell how far in this direction governments can go.

Guaranty of Free Exercise of Religion. Also forbidden are laws prohibiting the *free exercise* of religion. Opinion differs so widely on the subject of what conduct is religiously motivated that distinctions are frequently close and hard to make. According to court decisions, the guaranty is not violated if Congress outlaws bigamous and polygamous marriages even though some Mormons thought these essential to their faith.[36] Nor is it violated if religious objectors are required to take military training as a condition for attendance at a state university.[37] Religious objectors may be drafted for military service,[38] and a state may deny them licenses to practice law.[39]

On the other hand, the free exercise of religion is abridged if children of religious sects like that of Jehovah's Witnesses are compelled to salute and pledge allegiance to the flag;[40] or if attendance at private religious schools is forbidden through the device of making attendance at public schools compulsory.[41] The free exercise of religion is also abridged if a municipal ordinance makes it illegal to distribute religious tracts without an official permit;[42] or if a state law requires those soliciting funds for religious purposes first to secure approval of a local public official.[43] The same is true if a municipal ordinance imposes a flat tax on those who make a livelihood by distributing religious tracts.[44]

Freedom of Speech and Press. The First Amendment also provides that "Congress shall make no law . . . abridging the freedom of

[36] Reynolds *v.* United States, 98 U.S. 145 (1878); Davis *v.* Beason, 133 U.S. 333 (1890).

[37] Hamilton *v.* Regents of the University of California, 293 U.S. 245 (1934).

[38] Arver *v.* United States, 245 U.S. 366 (1918). See also pp. 450–451.

[39] *In re* Summers, 325 U.S. 538 (1945). The court divided 5 to 4 in this decision.

[40] In Minersville School District *v.* Gobitis, 310 U.S. 586, decided in 1940, the Supreme Court ruled by an 8-to-1 verdict that a state law compelling school children to salute the flag was not an unconstitutional infringement of the free exercise of religion. Two years later three of the justices took occasion to say that they had changed their minds (Jones *v.* City of Opelika, 316 U.S. 584, 1942) and shortly thereafter the Gobitis decision was overruled by a 5-to-3 vote (West Virginia State Board of Education *v.* Barnette, 319 U.S. 324, 1942).

[41] Pierce *v.* Society of the Sisters, 268 U.S. 510 (1925).

[42] Coleman *v.* City of Griffin, 303 U.S. 404 (1938).

[43] Cantwell *v.* Connecticut, 310 U.S. 296 (1940).

[44] Follett *v.* McCormick, 321 U.S. 565 (1943).

speech, or of the press." Here, again, is a restriction that applied to Congress only until the courts' recent expansion of the Fourteenth Amendment. Now, the same restrictions apply to both Federal and state governments. In general, the intent of the provisions is to secure the unrestricted discussion of public affairs. Inasmuch as majorities need no special protection, the guaranties have meaning only insofar as they afford protection to minorities that propagate unpopular, even loathsome, ideas.

Since rights are not absolute, most people readily agree that the guaranties do not forbid laws holding people responsible for utterances that are libelous, slanderous, indecent, or obscene. The controversy begins when governmental officials attempt to censor or punish minorities for utterances about public affairs with which they disagree.

Wartime Interpretations. Looking over past experience,[45] one is likely to feel that guaranties of freedom of speech and press are meaningless, especially in time of war. In 1798 Congress passed the Alien and Sedition Acts providing severe punishment for anyone found publishing false, scandalous, and malicious criticism of the President or members of Congress.[46] During the Civil War opposition was suppressed by placing large zones under martial law, whether or not actual military operations were in progress within the area. Under the Espionage Act of 1917 and amendments of the following year, popularly known as the Sedition Act, dozens of pacifist, pro-German, Socialist, and radical publications were excluded from the mails,[47] while hundreds of people were imprisoned for alleged subversive criticism and agitation against the war policies of the government.[48] America's

entry into war in 1941 brought about a repetition of some of the experiences of the First World War. After 1945, and especially after fighting began in Korea, anticommunist sentiment and activity became far more pronounced.

In spite of this dark picture, the constitutional guaranties of free speech and press are not without significance. The notorious Minnesota "gag law," which empowered the courts to suppress publication of printed matter deemed to be scandalous, malicious, defamatory, or obscene,[49] was declared invalid. Later, a Louisiana statute imposing a tax upon large newspapers most of which were hostile to the late Huey Long was declared unconstitutional.[50] In a more recent case, the Supreme Court upheld the solicitation of members for the Communist Party if in doing so forceful resistance to or overthrow of the government was not advocated.[51] More recently, the Court upheld attendance and participation in Communist meetings where no unlawful conduct or utterances occurred.[52] The Court has also set aside state laws forbidding the display of banners and placards in aid of picketing in labor disputes;[53] it has declared a state law invalid that required labor organizers to register before soliciting members;[54] and the courts have reprimanded the Postmaster General for denying the magazine *Esquire* second-class mailing privileges because he thought its contents obscene.

"Bad Tendency" vs. "Clear and Present Danger" Tests. Since it is difficult to draw the line between permissible restraint and freedom, attempts have been made to find a satisfactory formula upon which to base decisions. In gen-

---

[45] By far the best discussion of this subject is found in Zechariah Chafee, Jr., *Free Speech in the United States* (Harvard University Press, 1941).

[46] Although these measures never reached the Supreme Court, they were generally approved by the lower courts. The acts expired in 1801. President Jefferson pardoned all who had been imprisoned, and many years later Congress refunded all fines collected.

[47] Including the now respectable *Nation* magazine.

[48] The most prominent of these was Eugene V. Debs,

Socialist leader and five times candidate for President. Debs started serving a 10-year sentence in April, 1919, and was pardoned by President Harding on Christmas Day, 1921. While in prison Debs polled nearly a million votes for President in the election of 1920.

[49] Near *v.* Minnesota, 283 U.S. 697 (1931).

[50] Grosjean *v.* American Press Company, 297 U.S. 233 (1936).

[51] Herndon *v.* Lowry, 301 U.S. 242 (1937).

[52] DeJonge *v.* Oregon, 299 U.S. 353 (1937).

[53] Thornhill *v.* Alabama, 310 U.S. 88 (1940); Carlson *v.* California, 310 U.S. (1940).

[54] Thomas *v.* Collins, 323 U.S. 516 (1944).

eral, it is agreed that there should not be *previous restraint.*[55] That is, people should not be required, under threat of penalty, to obtain censors' approval prior to publication. The general belief is that the law simply should hold people responsible for what is actually said or written.

Beyond this there is deep cleavage of opinion. One school contends that utterances are illegal if they have a "bad tendency," while the more tolerant school insists that the rule should be "clear and present danger." Under the former, it is sufficient that persons merely advocate revolutionary doctrines whether or not their remarks are taken seriously by anyone. Under the latter, one is judged guilty only if revolutionary doctrines are uttered under circumstances that are likely to lead clearly and immediately to an evil which government has power to prevent.

The bad-tendency rule prevailed until the 1930's; since then the more tolerant view has met with greater judicial favor. Even though the clear-and-present-danger rule has gained ascendancy, there are sharp differences of opinion over when the danger is sufficiently clear and dangerous to justify governmental restraint. Recently, the courts have shown an inclination to permit more restraint of individual freedom than they did in the period between 1937 and 1949. The practical differences between the two doctrines are illustrated by the following cases.

Gitlow Case. The bad-tendency test was applied in a case decided in 1925.[56] Benjamin Gitlow was indicted by New York State for the publication of a socialist manifesto pleading for organization of industrial workers, mass strikes, destruction of the bourgeois state, and substitution of a new regime dominated by the proletariat. The publication emphasized, however, that

It is not a problem of immediate revolution. It is a problem of immediate revolutionary struggle. The revolutionary epoch of the final struggle may last for years and tens of years. . . . The old order is in decay. Civilization is in collapse. The proletarian revolution and the communist reconstruction of

society—the struggle for these—is now indispensable.

Although no unlawful action had resulted from the appeal, and none was particularly imminent, a majority of the Supreme Court considered the publication a sufficient threat to justify restricting freedom of speech and press. Here the threat, rather than clear and present danger of illegal action, was the controlling consideration.

Terminiello Case. The clear-and-present-danger test is illustrated by a case decided in 1949.[57] Terminiello, a Catholic priest and follower of Gerald K. Smith, addressed a Chicago meeting. The hall was so heavily picketed that police escort was required to enter the building. Outside, the crowd yelled epithets, threw bricks and ice picks, broke windows, and generally attempted to force entry and break up the meeting. Inside, Terminiello fanatically lashed his critics, praised General Franco, and condemned Jews, Communists, Mrs. Roosevelt, Henry Wallace, and others with whom he disagreed.

At the close of the speech Terminiello was arrested for violating a Chicago ordinance declaring it illegal to make, aid, countenance, or assist in making any improper noise, riot, disturbance, breach of peace, or diversion tending to breach the peace. He was convicted and the verdict was upheld by the higher courts of Illinois. But the United States Supreme Court, by a 5-to-4 vote, supported Terminiello, saying:

. . . A function of free speech under our system of government is to invite dispute. It may indeed best serve its high purpose when it induces a condition of unrest, creates dissatisfaction with conditions as they are, or even stirs people to anger. Speech is often provocative and challenging. It may strike at prejudices and preconceptions and leave profound unsettling effects as it presses for acceptance of an idea.

Terminiello had not pleaded for violence, and there was no clear and present danger to the community great enough to justify restricting freedom of speech.

[55] Near *v.* Minnesota, 283 U.S. 697 (1931).
[56] Gitlow *v.* New York, 268 U.S. 652 (1924).

[57] Terminiello *v.* City of Chicago, 337 U.S. 1 (1949).

Anticommunist Affidavits. Two cases will illustrate the trend since 1949. One involved the constitutionality of the provision of the Taft-Hartley Act [58] requiring officers of labor unions to make an anticommunist affidavit. Failure to do so would deprive the union of its right of recourse to the National Labor Relations Board under the provisions of the Act. Among other things, the law requires labor leaders to swear that they do not believe in the overthrow of the United States by force or by any illegal or unconstitutional methods and that they are not members or supporters of organizations that believe in or teach the overthrow of the United States government by force. Leaders of the American Communications Association had not taken the oath when they filed a complaint with the National Labor Relations Board charging their employer with having committed an unfair labor practice. The Board dismissed the complaint, saying the union leaders should first have taken the anticommunist oath. Here, men and their unions were penalized not for anything they had done or were about to do but merely for beliefs or memberships they happened to hold. Nevertheless, the Supreme Court, in a divided opinion, upheld the legislation, saying Congress might impose penalties for beliefs and memberships as one way of protecting interstate and foreign commerce from possible political strikes.

Smith Act Prosecutions. Another case illustrating current trends involved eleven leaders of the Communist Party.[59] Proceeding under the Smith Act, passed in 1940, the government charged the Communist leaders with (1) willfully and knowingly conspiring to organize the Communist Party in order to teach and advocate the overthrow and destruction of the American government by force and violence; and (2) knowingly and willfully advocating and teaching the duty and necessity of overthrowing and destroying the American government by force and violence. As the trial developed, the men were not accused of committing overt acts of

any kind. Nor were they charged with writing or saying anything unlawful. Rather, they were accused of conspiring (*i.e.*, assembling, talking, and agreeing among themselves) to organize a political party for the purpose of teaching and advocating revolutionary change at some future time. After a protracted and sensational trial, a jury found the men guilty, and the Supreme Court upheld the conviction.[60]

The majority held that it was constitutional to restrict freedom of speech, press, and assembly in advance of any advocacy or overt acts where the intent and purpose of those engaged in the "conspiracy" was to "initiate a violent revolution whenever the propitious occasion appeared." Dissenting sharply, Justice Black said: "This is a virulent form of prior censorship of speech and press, which . . . the First Amendment forbids." Justice Douglas observed: "This record . . . contains no evidence whatsoever showing that the acts charged . . . have created any clear and present danger to the Nation." Whatever the merits of the argument may be, it is clear that the courts have responded to postwar world tensions by construing public powers broadly and narrowing freedom of speech and press accordingly.

Moving Pictures and Freedom of Speech and Press. Motion pictures did not exist, of course, when guaranties of freedom of speech and press were written into the Constitution. When they did appear the problem arose of whether they were to enjoy the same freedoms as other media of communication. The issue reached the Supreme Court in 1915.[61] Ohio had established a commission to approve for public showing only those films adjudged to be "of a moral, educational or amusing and harmless character." Had this sort of "previous restraint" been applied to the press, it would doubtless have been held unconstitutional. But the Supreme Court

---

[58] American Communications Association, C.I.O., *et al. v.* Douds, 339 U.S. 382 (1949).

[59] Dennis *v.* United States, 341 U.S. 494 (1950).

[60] Four justices—Vinson, Burton, Reed, and Minton —agreed with the majority view; two—Frankfurter and Jackson—concurred but set forth different reasons; two—Black and Douglas—dissented; while one justice —Clark—took no part in the decision.

[61] Mutual Film Corp. *v.* Industrial Commission, 236 U.S. 230 (1915).

upheld the Ohio law, saying that the exhibition of motion pictures was a "business pure and simple, originated and conducted for profit like other spectacles, not to be regarded, nor intended to be regarded by the Ohio Constitution, . . . as part of the press of the country or as organs of public opinion." Motion pictures being thus classed as spectacles, their censorship became common practice in most states.

This decision was followed until 1952 when it was reversed by the Supreme Court. In this case [62] the Court had before it a decision of the New York Board of Regents revoking a license issued for the showing of *The Miracle* because of complaints, coming chiefly from Catholics, that the film was sacrilegious. The Court met the issue squarely by declaring the "liberty of expression by means of motion pictures is guaranteed by the First and Fourteenth Amendments." After saying this the Court hastened to add that its decision did not give "absolute freedom to exhibit every motion picture of every kind at all times and all places." States can continue to exercise censorship over motion pictures as long as they do so in accordance with the basic principles of freedom of speech and press. What this decision means in concrete terms remains to be seen.

Freedom of Assembly and Petition. Where freedom of speech and press exists, it is essential that people be permitted to gather in groups to discuss mutual problems and, if they desire, make their opinions known to governmental authorities. These rights are guaranteed by the First and Fourteenth Amendments. These guaranties require, however, that the assembly be peaceful and that the petitioners ask only for objects that are lawful and not a menace to public safety. The right of petition carries with it no power to compel consideration. Thousands of memorials are received that are given no consideration whatever. When addressed to Congress or state legislatures, they are generally referred to committees where they are promptly pigeonholed and forgotten. When received in sufficient number on a particular subject, however, they are bound to impress individual legislators and sometimes the entire Congress. The right of petition has seldom been violated, but because the right of assembly is closely connected with speech and press it has been the subject of considerable litigation. One such case occurred when Mayor Hague, longtime boss of Jersey City, N.J., refused permission to persons whom he considered radicals to use public parks, halls, and streets as meeting places. His action was held to be a denial of the right of assembly as well as a denial of freedom of speech and press.

IN SEARCH OF SUBVERSIVES

Communist-control Measures. Communists have never been popular in the United States, partly because their views regarding social organization, religion, and economics collide with those which have been dominant in the United States; partly because many of them advocate change by revolutionary methods; and partly because the sympathy many of them hold toward the Soviet Union makes their loyalty and patriotism suspect. Whenever relations between the United States and the Soviet Union are strained, as they were during and following the First World War and again after the Second World War, antagonisms flare and express themselves in repressive measures. When this occurs the strain on American democracy is intense because of the deep-seated belief that punitive measures aimed at one unpopular minority are a threat to the freedom of all and a confession that the theory of toleration upon which the republic rests has failed.

In recent years the view has prevailed in the United States and in many other parts of the world that a distinction must be drawn between the brand of communism that is merely social theory and that which is organized as a militant "international conspiracy" with headquarters in Moscow for achieving world revolution and conquest. The former, it is argued, is tolerable; the latter can be justifiably suppressed. This analysis and dichotomy appears too simple to many and does violence to the concept of popular sovereignty, the democratic assumption that guilt is personal, the presumption of innocence,

[62] Burstyn *v.* Wilson, 343 U.S. 495 (1951).

and freedom of thought, association, speech, and press. The latter view has yielded stubbornly but surely, until by now the list of repressive measures has grown long. Some of them are as follows:

The Smith Act. Officially known as the Alien Registration Act of 1940, this measure became law at a time of alarm over pro-Nazis and

'HE BEEN CLEARED?'

The Chicago Sun-Times.

fascists of similar types. Among other provisions it outlawed speech and activities intended to create disloyalty among members of the armed forces, overthrow any American government by force or violence, assassinate public officials, or organize groups for these purposes. It was also declared illegal for one to become or be a member or affiliate of an organization if one knows its purposes to be among those proscribed. Violations are punishable by fines of not more than $10,000, 10 years' imprisonment, or both. Few fascists have been prosecuted under the act, but since the Second World War it has provided the basis for most federal prosecutions of Communists. Its constitutionality was

upheld in the case of Dennis *et al. v.* United States which is reviewed at some length below.

The McCarran Act. This measure, known officially as the Internal Security Act of 1950, is a long and involved one aimed at totalitarians in general and Communists in particular. Among many provisions, the law declares it illegal "for any person knowingly to combine, conspire, or agree with any other person to perform any act which would substantially contribute to the establishment within the United States of a totalitarian dictatorship" directed from abroad. It tightens laws against espionage. It bars Communists from federal employment and even from working "in any defense facility." Federal employees are forbidden to contribute money to Communist organizations. Contributions to Communist organizations are denied tax exemption. It is made illegal for Communists to obtain passports, or even to apply for them. Visas to visit or emigrate to the United States are denied to anyone who is or ever was a member of a totalitarian organization or who advocates "the economic, international, and governmental doctrines of world communism or the economic and governmental doctrines of any other form of totalitarianism. . . ." Naturalization laws were modified and deportations of subversives made easier. The law also outlawed picketing and sound trucks near court buildings where the intent is to influence court officials or proceedings. It also authorized the arrest and detention during national emergencies of those for whom "there is reasonable ground to believe that such person probably will engage in, or probably will conspire with others to engage in, acts of espionage or of sabotage. . . ."

To help with enforcement, the McCarran Act establishes a five-man Subversive Activities Control Board and empowers it to investigate and register all Communist-action and Communist-front organizations. Periodic reports are required from such organizations disclosing details of organization, finance, and lists of members with addresses. Before the lists are published, members must be notified that their names appear and be given an opportunity to contest the listing. Among other provisions, registered organizations can transmit their publications by mail or interstate and foreign commerce only if they are marked "Disseminated by ——, a Communist organization." Moreover, registered organizations may broadcast or televise only after announcing, "The following program is sponsored by ——, a Communist organization."

This is drastic legislation, the constitutionality of which remains to be determined. The measure has been denounced by many as unnecessary and dangerous to civil liberties. In his veto message, President Truman said the measure would help Communists more than it would hurt them, it would impose a staggering burden upon the Department of Justice and the Federal Bureau of Investigation (FBI), it would aid potential enemies by requiring the publication of complete lists of vital defense facilities, it would antagonize friendly governments, it would put the United States "in the thought control business," and it would "give government officials vast powers to harass all of our citizens in the exercise of their right of free speech." But two-thirds of both houses of Congress thought otherwise. Though this legislation was passed in September, 1950, no Communist organizations had registered as late as January, 1956. Meanwhile the law was being contested in the courts, and the Subversive Activities Control Board was engaged in tedious investigations and hearings that it hoped would provide the basis for compelling compliance with the registration provisions.

The Communist Control Act of 1954. Throughout the postwar period the most vocal anticommunists urged outlawry of the Communist Party. Some states did take this step, but doubts over constitutionality, fear of driving the Party underground, and theoretical implications caused hesitation elsewhere. Finally, on the eve of a congressional election and with the help of several "liberal" senators who were running for reelection and smarting under the charge of being "soft" toward Communists, an ambiguously worded measure passed Congress, intended to outlaw what was left of the Party.

The law purports to outlaw the Communist Party "or any successors of such party regardless of the assumed name" by declaring that it is not entitled to any of the rights, privileges, and immunities which other political parties enjoy under the laws of the United States or any political subdivision thereof. It then proceeds to strike at membership in the Party or other organizations advocating overthrow of the government by force or violence, but it stops short of making membership a criminal offense. Instead, it reverts to the McCarran Act provisions respecting membership in Communist-action organizations. These, it will be recalled, do not make membership a crime; they merely require that membership lists be filed and published. Meanwhile, prosecutions for membership in the Communist Party are proceeding under the Smith Act on the theory that joining and remaining identified with the Party is tantamount to conspiring to advocate the overthrow of government by force and violence. Lower courts have upheld several convictions, but the Supreme Court has yet to speak.

Other provisions of the Communist Control Act require Communist-infiltrated organizations to register with the Subversive Activities Control Board and withdraw benefits accorded by the National Labor Relations Act and Taft-Hartley Act from unions with Communist officers or employees, from employers who engage Communists to represent them in labor matters, and from Communist-infiltrated unions and employer organizations generally.

FAIR PLAY FOR THE ACCUSED

Definition of Treason. Treason is generally considered one of the highest crimes that can be committed in society, since its aim is an overthrow of the government. History is filled with instances where in times of excitement those in power have sought to destroy critics and enemies by arbitrarily declaring their conduct treasonable. Because of this experience, the Constitution includes a definition of treason; no acts other than those contained within the definition can be declared to constitute the offense. Congress can neither extend, nor restrict, nor define the crime. Its power is limited to prescribing the punishment. According to that definition, only two things are treasonable: (1) levying of war against the United States, and (2) adhering to enemies of the United States or giving them aid or comfort while the United States is at war. In so defining the term, the Constitution adopted the very words of the statute of treason enacted during the reign of Edward III. Thus, by implication, the Constitution recognizes the well-settled interpretation of these phrases which has prevailed for ages.[63]

Besides defining what constitutes treason, the Constitution declares that "no Person shall be convicted of Treason unless on the Testimony of two Witnesses to the same overt Act, or on Confession in open Court." This is to guarantee that no one can be convicted except for some overt act and then never upon the testimony of a single person, however high. It is also a guaranty that those in authority will not obtain confessions behind closed doors where the temptation to promise favor or use third-degree methods is always present. Instead, if there is to be a confession it must be made in open court.

Still further, the Constitution declares that while Congress may declare what punishment is to be meted out to those convicted of treason, "no Attainder of Treason shall work Corruption of Blood, or Forfeiture except during the Life of the Person attainted." This means that the children or heirs of traitors may not be forbidden, as part of the punishment, to inherit property. This is to ensure that innocent children will not suffer because of an offense of an ancestor.

What has been said above pertains to the Federal government only. Besides being a traitor under federal law, one can also commit treason against a state. Accordingly, most of the state constitutions in defining treason use language nearly identical with that contained in the Federal Constitution. Death is nearly always the penalty for treason under state law. The famous case of John Brown at Harpers Ferry, Va., is thought to be the only instance on record where the extreme penalty has been inflicted for treason against a state.

Habeas Corpus. The national Constitution forbids the Federal government, but not the states, to suspend the privilege of the writ of habeas corpus "unless when in cases of rebellion or invasion the public safety may require it." Such a writ is a command on the part of a judicial officer to have the body of someone being held in custody produced for the purpose of determining the legality of his detention. Without it, military and police officers could take people into custody, keeping them there indefinitely without hearing or trial. When the Bastille was stormed during the French Revolution, men were loosed who had been imprisoned for years without ever having been given trial. Under dictatorial regimes people are not infrequently spirited away by secret police to be put to death or confined in concentration camps without ever being heard of again. The privilege of the writ of habeas corpus is a protection against such restraints and it has been rightfully esteemed one of the great bulwarks of liberty.

When the writ is issued, the police must produce a prisoner and show adequate cause for his detention. If the judge is unconvinced, the prisoner must be set at liberty. The privilege of the writ can be suspended only in the event of rebellion or invasion, and then only when "the public safety may require it." [64] The only occasion since the Civil War when the writ has been suspended occurred in Hawaii during the Second World War. After its suspension, civilian laws were displaced by military orders, and civilians were tried by military tribunals without benefit of jury trial and other normal procedures. Although this system continued throughout most of the war, it was later declared illegal by the Supreme Court.[65] Congress had not intended, the Court said, the Hawaiian Organic Act to authorize such drastic subordination of civilian life to the military.

Bill of Attainder. A bill of attainder is a legislative act that inflicts punishment without

---

[63] For an able review of the constitutional provision as applied in recent cases, see J. H. Leek, "Treason and the Constitution," *Journal of Politics,* vol. 13, no. 4 (November, 1951), p. 604.

[64] For discussion of the wartime suspension of the writ, see p. 453.

[65] Duncan *v.* Kahanamoku, 327 U.S. 304 (1945).

judicial trial. In times of rebellion or political excitement it was not uncommon for Parliament to punish minorities by enacting special bills declaring them guilty of treason or felony. Punishment was often inflicted without allowing the accused party an opportunity to answer the charges, or even without the formality of proof. Indeed, in England it was not uncommon

penalty of exclusion from legal practice without judicial trial.

A more recent case involved three federal employees [66] accused by the Dies Committee of having associated with groups engaged in un-American activities. Because the men had been duly appointed and served meritoriously, the President refused to dismiss them, whereupon Con-

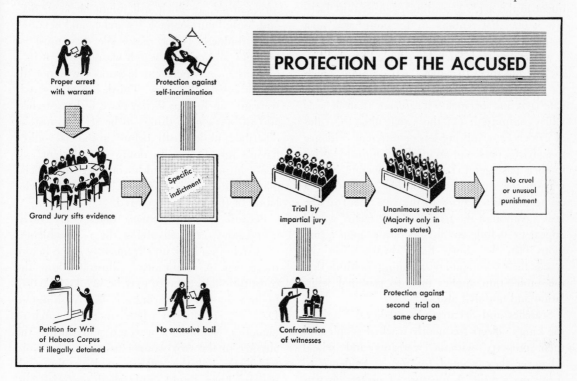

PROTECTION OF THE ACCUSED

Proper arrest with warrant

Protection against self-incrimination

Grand Jury sifts evidence

Specific indictment

Trial by impartial jury

Unanimous verdict (Majority only in some states)

No cruel or unusual punishment

Petition for Writ of Habeas Corpus if illegally detained

No excessive bail

Confrontation of witnesses

Protection against second trial on same charge

mon for Parliament to attaint a man after he was dead.

To guarantee that such things would not happen, the Constitution forbids both the Federal and state governments from enacting bills of attainder. Accordingly, legislatures enact laws defining crimes, but the courts must be the judge of innocence or guilt. A few attempts to violate the guaranty have occurred, the most notable being in 1865 when Congress passed the Test Oath Act. That law provided that no one might be admitted to practice before the Federal courts who could not swear that he had never voluntarily participated in rebellion against the United States. This, the Supreme Court said, was a bill of attainder since it imposed the

gress inserted a provision in a deficiency appropriation bill forbidding payment of their salaries and debarring them from future employment with the Federal government. This had the appearance of being legislative punishment without judicial trial.

The gentlemen in question continued in office for a brief time, then brought suit for salary, claiming that their constitutional rights had been violated. The Court of Claims, before which the case originated, refused to pass on the larger question of constitutionality but ruled that the men were entitled to unpaid salary. Three judges went further and expressed their

[66] Prof. Robert Morss Lovett, Goodwin B. Watson, and William E. Dodd, Jr.

belief that Congress had violated the constitutional provision forbidding bills of attainder, and with this view the Supreme Court later agreed by a unanimous decision.[67]

Ex Post Facto Legislation. Both the Federal and state governments are forbidden by the Federal Constitution to enact ex post facto legislation. Literally, ex post facto means "subsequent to the act." Accordingly, an ex post facto law is one that renders an act punishable in a manner in which it was not punishable when it was committed. Such laws have been held to include (1) those that make acts criminal which were innocent when done; (2) those that aggravate a crime or make it greater than it was when committed; (3) those that alter the rules of evidence, permitting less or different evidence to convict a person of an offense committed prior to their passage; (4) those that operate in any way to the disadvantage of one accused of a crime committed prior to the enactment of the law.[68] Although the term "ex post facto" would appear to include any act operating upon a previous fact, the courts have always given the words their common-law meaning, holding that the prohibition applies only to criminal legislation and not civil also.

Searches and Seizures. In medieval England the king's officers frequently seached people and their property without warrants and seized whatever they wanted for use as evidence to prove one's guilt. A measure of protection was found in the common-law maxim that a man's house is his castle and this guaranty was written into our Constitution. The Fourth Amendment states, "The right of the people to be secure in their persons, houses, papers, and effects, against unreasonable searches and seizures, shall not be violated, and no Warrants shall issue, but upon probable cause, supported by Oath or affirmation, and particularly describing the place to be searched, and the persons or things to be seized."

Several things should be noted about this provision. First, people are to be secure in their "persons, houses, papers, and effects." This includes outbuildings, including barn and garage, vehicle, office, shop, factory, or warehouse. It also restricts the tapping of telephone wires.[69] It also includes letters, books, accounts, and packages.[70] It does not include an open field, where, for example, an illicit still might be kept. Second, only "unreasonable" searches and seizures are forbidden. To be reasonable they must be made by authority of search warrant except in a few instances where circumstances will not allow or justify the delay. Third, before a search warrant can be issued, the place to be searched and the person or things to be seized must be described under oath before a judicial officer having jurisdiction. In doing so, sufficient evidence must be presented to convince the judicial officer that there is reason to believe that a violation of the law has occurred.

Because law-enforcement officers are often overzealous, cases involving the reasonableness of searches and seizures frequently come before the courts. A recent case[71] illustrates how the constitutional guaranty may be invoked. Acting upon a tip and proffering a bribe, Washington, D.C., officers entered a hotel room in search of narcotics. Without a warrant, and during the absence of the two women to whom the room had been let, the officers made a thorough search. They found contraband narcotics and seized them. Later the women were arrested, prosecuted, and found guilty of violating federal narcotic laws. On appeal, the Supreme Court released the women, saying the evidence used to convict them had been obtained by methods proscribed by the Fourth Amendment.

[67] United States *v.* Lovett, 328 U.S. 303 (1946).

[68] It should be noted, however, that laws that mitigate the character or punishment of a crime already committed may not violate the prohibition inasmuch as they are in favor of the accused party.

[69] Nardone *v.* United States, 302 U.S. 379 (1937). See, however, Olmstead *v.* United States, 277 U.S. 438 (1928).

[70] This provision explains why postal authorities cannot open letters and packages without warrants unless the sender gives them permission to do so by writing some such words as "this may be opened for postal inspection if necessary." *Ex parte* Jackson, 96 U.S. 727 (1877).

[71] United States *v.* Jeffers, 342 U.S. 48 (1951).

Search and Arrest. Especially difficult is the question of how far a search may extend and what may be seized while making a valid arrest. Two cases will illustrate this difficulty. In one,[72] two men named Harris and Moffett were suspected of violating the Mail Fraud Statute and the National Stolen Property Act. Warrants of arrest, but not of search, were obtained, and with these officers went to Harris's apartment in Oklahoma City, arrested him, and then proceeded to search the entire apartment looking for two stolen checks that were thought to have been used in effecting forgery. Over Harris's protest, and without a search warrant, the search continued for nearly 5 hours. The checks were not found, but Selective Service draft cards were. With these as evidence Harris was prosecuted and convicted for illegal possession of draft cards.

On appeal, the Supreme Court, in a 5-to-4 decision, upheld the conviction. The majority argued that because the arrest was made with a valid warrant the extensive search was incidental and justified. Moreover, evidence of another crime acquired in the process of making a lawful search could be used to convict. The minority opinions protested vigorously. Said Justice Frankfurter:

To find authority for ransacking a home merely from authority for the arrest of a person is to give a novel and ominous rendering to a momentous chapter in the history of Anglo-American freedom. An Englishman's home, though a hovel, is his castle, precisely because the law secures freedom from fear of intrusion by the police except under carefully safeguarded authorizations by a magistrate. . . . the Constitution protects both unauthorized arrest and unauthorized search. Authority to arrest does not dispense with the requirement of authority to search. But even if the search was reasonable, it does not follow that the seizure was lawful.

In the case just discussed, a simple arrest warrant was used to justify rummaging through an entire apartment. In another case[73] an arrest warrant was obtained for a man named Rabino-

witz who was suspected of forging postage stamps. With the warrant, officers went to the suspect's one-room office, where they not only made the arrest but also searched the desk, safe, and file cabinets for about an hour and a half. They found and seized 573 stamps, some of which had been forged, and these were used to convict. On appeal, the Supreme Court, by a 5-to-3 vote, upheld the conviction, saying that a valid arrest warrant justified the incidental search of Rabinowitz's office.

Indictment by Grand Jury. The Fifth Amendment provides, among other things, that no one, except persons employed in the armed forces, may be held "for a capital, or otherwise infamous crime, unless on a presentment or indictment of a Grand Jury." A "capital" crime is one punishable by death. An "infamous" one has never been clearly defined but is known to include offenses that are punishable by imprisonment, hard labor, or the loss of civil or political privileges.

If such a crime is committed, a grand jury composed of from sixteen to twenty-three persons[74] must (unless waived by the defendant) be assembled for the purpose of deciding whether there is sufficient evidence to proceed with trial. The accused cannot insist that he be permitted to appear before the grand jury, but permission to do so is sometimes given. If twelve or more grand jurors believe the evidence sufficiently incriminating to justify trial, a "true bill" is reported to the judge. If not, the accused must be promptly released until convincing evidence is produced. The form of the indictment is very important inasmuch as the accused can be tried only for offenses mentioned in it.

The grand jury has been the subject of much criticism on the ground that it is clumsy and ill suited to modern conditions, especially in cities. England, the country of its origin, has almost completely discarded the device and many of our states now permit trial upon "in-

[72] Harris *v.* United States, 331 U.S. 145 (1946).
[73] United States *v.* Rabinowitz, 339 U.S. 56 (1949).

[74] State grand juries may consist of any number. Indeed, Michigan has for years permitted the use of one-man grand juries, particularly in probes of alleged misconduct of public officials. See *In re* Oliver, 333 U.S. 257 (1947).

formation," *i.e.,* a simple affidavit by a prosecuting officer. The Federal courts, however, insist that the grand jury be used in capital and felonious cases.

Trial by Jury. Trial by jury in *criminal* cases is guaranteed both by provisions in the body of the Constitution [75] and by the Sixth Amendment. From these provisions and court decisions we find that (1) every person accused of a criminal offense against federal law is entitled to jury trial, except public officials who are subject to impeachment; (2) jury trial may be waived by the defendant with court approval; (3) federal juries must be composed of twelve persons,[76] either men or women, or both; (4) trials must be "speedy," *i.e.,* reasonably prompt; (5) trials must be "public" in order that friends of the accused may see that injustice is not done; (6) the jury must be "impartial" and to this end attorneys for both parties are permitted to question and challenge prospective jurors and cross-examine witnesses; (7) members of juries must be drawn from the district wherein the crime was committed and the district must have been defined prior to the trial; (8) the verdict must be unanimous; [77] (9) the trial must be in the presence of a judge having power to instruct the jury both as to law and facts; (10) the verdict of a jury is final unless upon appeal by the defendant a new trial is awarded because a mistake was made in law or the procedure followed.

Self-incrimination. Among provisions of the Fifth Amendment is one saying: "No person . . . shall be compelled in any criminal case to be a witness against himself." Similar provisions are included in almost all state constitutions. For centuries it was common practice in England and elsewhere to coerce suspected criminals into accusing themselves, often by torture. But in twelfth-century England protests were made which ultimately established the principle now

embedded in the common law and the American Constitution.

While the law on this subject is very technical, a few general rules may be noted. The words used in the Fifth Amendment suggest that the guaranty extends only to criminal cases, but the courts have long held that coerced self-accusations during investigations or in civil cases are also prohibited, since these might provide the basis for subsequent criminal prosecutions. The privilege is a personal one and may not be invoked on behalf of anyone else. It will not protect artificial persons, like corporations and associations, from the production of their books and records. One may not plead immunity in a federal case for fear of prosecution by a state or foreign country. The determination of when the privilege may be invoked rests with the courts. In general, comment may not be made to the jury about the defendant's refusal to testify. While states are required by federal law to provide a fair trial, the due-process clause of the Fourteenth Amendment does not require them to grant immunity against self-incrimination (most state constitutions, however, grant this).

Long taken for granted, this right has become recently the subject of heated controversy. Numerous witnesses have invoked the right in refusing to testify before congressional committees whether they were members of the Communist Party and to name others. Concerned over subversives in general and Communists in particular, a segment of the population applauded the use of questionable means by congressional committees and law-enforcement officers to force such witnesses to testify. Indeed, for a time, and in some quarters, it became popular to speak derisively of the Fifth Amendment. One United States Senator gained considerable popularity by dubbing those who pleaded their constitutional right before congressional committees "Fifth Amendment communists." While anticommunist sentiment was at its peak a number of persons lost their jobs because they exercised their privilege while under investigation.

Grants of Immunity. This constitutional guaranty unquestionably makes law enforcement

[75] Art. III, Sec. 2.

[76] State juries, however, may be abolished altogether or consist of fewer or more than twelve.

[77] Here, again, federal practice differs from that of some states. The latter may, if they wish, permit convictions by less than a unanimous vote.

more difficult than it would be if confessions could be forced by torture or otherwise. It is not surprising, therefore, that attempts are made to circumvent the right. This has been done by a number of states through the passage of laws providing "immunity baths" for those who confess in response to promises that they will not be prosecuted. Law-enforcement officers sometimes find it preferable to forego prosecuting a lawbreaker who is willing to confess in exchange for information about other crimes and criminals. These statutes have been held not to violate the Fourteenth Amendment, since the requirement there is one of due process and not specifically immunity from self-incrimination.[78]

Congress attempted something similar by passage of the Compulsory Testimony Act of 1954. This provides that on the application of the Attorney General or a congressional committee a United States district court may order a witness to testify after his claim of privilege. The Act further provides that one compelled to testify cannot be prosecuted for any matter covered by his answers. To many this appears to violate the spirit of the Fifth Amendment, if not its letter, but whether the Supreme Court will so hold remains to be seen.

Other Rights. Besides trial by jury, the Sixth Amendment also requires that one accused of a criminal offense shall be (1) informed of the charges for which he is to be tried; (2) present in the courtroom when witnesses are called to testify against him; (3) given legal power to compel witnesses to testify; and (4) assisted by legal counsel unless this right is waived.[79]

Bail and Punishment. The Eighth Amendment states, "Excessive bail shall not be required, nor excessive fines imposed, nor cruel and unusual punishments inflicted." Bail before trial is normally required to preserve the presumption of innocence which is fundamental to Anglo-American law. The Eighth Amendment assumes that offenders will be released on bail

and requires that the amount of money to be posted shall not be excessive. What is "excessive" has never been fixed by the courts; the amount must necessarily vary with circumstances and the gravity of the offense.

The provision that cruel or unusual punishments shall not be administered was directed mainly at the barbarity of early English law. It now prohibits punishments that are "so palpably excessive and disproportionate as to shock the sense of justice of all reasonable people."

A recent case is one of the very few that have arisen under this provision. It involved a young Negro, Willie Francis, sentenced to death in Louisiana. The electric chair accidentally failed to work when current was first applied, and a second attempt was threatened. The defendant appealed to the courts, contending in part that it was cruel and unusual punishment to force him to suffer the ordeal again. Rejecting his appeal by a 5-to-4 decision, the majority said: "The cruelty against which the Constitution protects a convicted man is cruelty inherent in the method of punishment, not the necessary suffering involved in any method employed to extinguish life humanely."[80]

Double Jeopardy. According to the Fifth Amendment, an accused person may not be "subject for the same offense to be twice put in jeopardy of life or limb." This was included to prevent persons from being tried over and over for the same offense. One is put in jeopardy "when he is put on trial, before a court of competent jurisdiction upon an indictment or information which is sufficient in form and substance to sustain a conviction and a jury has been charged with his deliverance."[81] One is not in jeopardy when the case is merely before a grand jury; hence the same evidence may be presented more than once for the purpose of obtaining an indictment. One may be tried a second time if the indictment was defective, if the jury cannot come to a decision, if the jury is discharged for some good reason such as illness of a juror, or if the term of court as fixed

---

[78] See, for example, Twining *v.* New Jersey, 211 U.S. 78 (1908); Adamson *v.* California, 332 U.S. 46 (1947).

[79] This right is thoroughly reviewed in a recent volume by William M. Beaney, *The Right to Counsel in American Courts* (University of Michigan Press, 1955).

[80] Louisiana *v.* Resweber, 329 U.S. 459 (1947).

[81] Thomas M. Cooley, *Constitutional Limitations* . . . (Little, Brown, 6th ed., 1890), p. 399.

by law comes to an end before the trial is finished. However, once a case is started, a prosecutor may not drop it in the hope of improving his chances of winning by discontinuing the case until a later time. Once trial has begun, the defendant is entitled to a verdict. When a decision has been reached, the prisoner is forever free from another trial for the same offense.

It is interesting to note that a person may by a single act violate both Federal and state law. If this happens, he may be tried in both Federal and state courts, acquitted in one, but found guilty in the other. Here, although there was but one act, two offenses were committed; hence the offender was not put in jeopardy twice for the *same* offense. A number of such instances have arisen, especially during prohibition when the Federal and state governments were concurrently responsible for the enforcement of liquor laws.

THE UNITED NATIONS AND HUMAN RIGHTS

Charter Provisions and Treaties. The United Nations Charter pledges the United States, along with other members, to promote and encourage "respect for, and observance of, human rights and fundamental freedoms for all without distinction as to race, sex, language, or religion." As a step toward fulfilling this pledge, the United Nations General Assembly, in December, 1948, adopted the Universal Declaration of Human Rights. This commits member states to promote, by teaching and education, respect for most of the rights guaranteed by American constitutions as well as some that are not mentioned in those documents. In addition, the United Nations has discussed a Draft Covenant on Human Rights and it has adopted a Convention on the Prevention and Punishment of the Crime of Genocide. The latter is aimed at stopping assaults upon masses, or groups, of people, as for example, Nazi persecution of the Jews. A Human Rights Commission was established to administer and promote the objectives of measures like these.

Constitutional Questions for the United States. The United States has signed the Charter and is, therefore, bound to promote and encourage respect for and observance of human rights and freedoms. It is also required by the Universal Declaration of Human Rights to promote respect for human rights through teaching and education. But to date the United States has not ratified the Genocide Convention, although enough nations have ratified to put it into effect, while the Covenant on Human Rights has still to be passed by the United Nations.

From a constitutional point of view, this question arises: What is the legal effect of treaties like those mentioned? Do they authorize the Federal government to restrain violations of civil rights? Until now it has been assumed that the Federal government can restrain state governments from violating rights guaranteed by the Constitution, but that it has only limited authority to prevent violations when perpetrated by private parties. The latter is chiefly a responsibility of the states. But if valid treaties are part of the supreme law of the land, cannot Congress implement the treaties and cannot the court restrain violations of the treaties with or without congressional authorization?

Only time and court decisions can give the answers to these difficult questions. Using Missouri *v.* Holland as a precedent, it might be held, as it has been by one or two minor courts, that the Charter of the United Nations is a part of the supreme law of the land and is effective now even without implementing statutes passed by Congress. Or the courts might take the position, as one or two have, that treaties like those under discussion are legally applicable in the United States only if implemented by statute. The first interpretation would permit Federal courts to grant relief immediately; the second one would permit relief only after Congress had enacted appropriate statutes. In either event, the Federal government would have a much clearer mandate for guarding civil rights, especially against violations by private individuals, than is generally assumed. Foreseeing this threat to States' rights, a coalition of senators rallied behind the proposed Bricker amendment, which would limit the President's authority to make treaties and executive agreements.

United Nations Activities Progress. While this controversy continues, the United Nations pursues its objective. Much educational work is done, and many charges of violations are aired before the Human Rights Commission and the General Assembly. All this helps create an awareness of the importance of the individual and his rights. The courts of some nations have taken judicial notice of Charter provisions and the Universal Declaration of Human Rights. Furthermore, several nations have incorporated portions of the Universal Declaration in newly adopted constitutions. The most concrete achievement was the approval of the Genocide Convention by enough nations to make it effective in many parts of the world.

FOR FURTHER READING

Baldwin, Roger N.: *Civil Liberties and Industrial Conflict* (Harvard University Press, 1938).

Barrett, Edward L., Jr.: *The Tenney Committee* (Cornell University Press, 1951).

Beaney, William M.: *The Right of Counsel in American Courts* (University of Michigan Press, 1955).

Becker, Carl L.: *Freedom and Responsibility in the American Way of Life* (Knopf, 1945).

——: *New Liberties for Old* (Yale University Press, 1941).

—— and Others: *Safeguarding Civil Liberty Today* (Cornell University Press, 1945).

Burdick, Charles K.: *The Law of the American Constitution: Its Origin and Development* (Putnam, 1922).

Carr, Robert K.: *The House Committee on Un-American Activities* (Cornell University Press, 1952).

——: *Federal Protection of Civil Rights: Quest for a Sword* (Cornell University Press, 1947).

Chafee, Zechariah, Jr.: *Government and Mass Communications* (University of Chicago Press, 2 vols., 1947), a report from the Commission on Freedom of the Press.

——: *Free Speech in the United States* (Harvard University Press, 1941).

Corwin, Edward S.: *Liberty against Government* (Louisiana State University Press, 1948).

Countryman, Vern: *Un-American Activities in the State of Washington* (Cornell University Press, 1951).

Dawson, Joseph M.: *Separation of Church and State Now* (Richard R. Smith, 1948).

De Haas, Elsa: *Antiquities of Bail: Origin and Historical Development in Criminal Cases to the Year 1275* (Columbia University Press, 1940).

Emerson, Thomas I., and David Haber: *Political and Civil Rights in the United States* (Dennis & Co., 1953).

Gellhorn, Walter: *Security, Loyalty and Science* (Cornell University Press, 1950).

Gellhorn, Walter (ed.): *The States and Subversion* (Cornell University Press, 1952).

Gerald, J. Edward: *The Press and the Constitution, 1931–47* (University of Minnesota Press, 1948).

Graves, W. Brooke: *Anti-discrimination Legislation in the American States,* Public Affairs Bulletin 65 (Library of Congress, 1948).

Griswold, Erwin N.: *The Fifth Amendment Today* (Harvard University Press, 1955).

Hocking, William E.: *Freedom of the Press: A Framework of Principle* (University of Chicago Press, 1947).

Holcombe, Arthur N.: *Human Rights in the Modern World* (New York University Press, 1948).

Johnson, Alvin W., and Frank H. Yost: *Separation of Church and State in the United States* (University of Minnesota Press, 1948).

Kesselman, Louis C.: *The Social Politics of the FEPC: A Study in Reform Pressure Movements* (The University of North Carolina Press, 1948).

Konvitz, Milton R.: *The Constitution and Civil Rights* (Columbia University Press, 1947).

Lasswell, Harold D.: *National Security and Individual Freedom* (McGraw-Hill, 1950).

Lauterbach, Albert T.: *Economic Security and Individual Freedom: Can We Have Both?* (Cornell University Press, 1948).

Lien, Arnold J.: *Privileges and Immunities of Citizens of the United States* (Columbia University Press, 1913).

Meiklejohn, Alexander: *Free Speech and Its Relation to Self-government* (Harper, 1948).

Mott, Rodney L.: *Due Process of Law* (Bobbs-Merrill, 1926).

Orfield, Lester B.: *Criminal Procedure from Arrest to Appeal* (New York University Press, 1947).

Pfeffer, Leo: *Church, State, and Freedom* (Beacon Press, 1953).

Prichett, C. Herman: *Civil Liberties and the Vinson Court* (University of Chicago Press, 1954).

Rankin, Robert S.: *When Civil Law Fails* (Duke University Press, 1939).

Ruchames, Louis: *Race, Jobs, and Politics: The Story of FEPC* (Columbia University Press, 1953).

Stouffer, Samuel A.: *Communism, Conformity, and Civil Liberties* (Doubleday, 1955).

Torpey, William G.: *Judicial Doctrines of Religious Rights in America* (The University of North Carolina Press, 1948).

United Nations: *Yearbook of Human Rights* (annual).

U.S. President's Committee on Civil Rights: *To Secure These Rights* (1947). (Also Simon and Schuster, 1947.)

U.S. Senate Committee on Education and Labor: *Violations of Free Speech and Rights of Labor; Hearings . . . ,* 75th Cong., 3d Sess., pursuant to S. Res. 266 (55 vols. bound in 14, 1936).

Weintraub, Ruth G.: *How Secure These Rights?* (Doubleday, 1949).

Wilcox, Clair (ed.): *Civil Rights under Attack* (University of Pennsylvania Press, 1952).

Wright, Benjamin: *The Contract Clause of the Constitution* (Harvard University Press, 1938).

**REVIEW
QUESTIONS**

1. What is meant when it is said that rights are relative—not absolute? Give illustrations.

2. What are the differences between privileges and immunities and rights?

3. What rights must the Federal government respect? The states? Both the Federal government and the states?

4. Defend and criticize the findings and recommendations of President Truman's Committee on Civil Rights.

5. Defend and criticize restrictions placed upon Communists in recent years by the Federal government.

6. Review the controversy that has been taking place over the "separate but equal" doctrine. Illustrate different points of view with appropriate Supreme Court decisions.

7. Compare the "substantive" concept of due process of law with the "procedural" concept, and illustrate both with appropriate Supreme Court decisions.

8. Illustrate with Supreme Court decisions differing interpretations of the constitutional guaranty of freedom of religion.

9. Distinguish between the "clear and present danger" doctrine and the "bad tendency" test. Illustrate both with appropriate Supreme Court decisions.

10. Explain to a person suspected of committing a crime the rights guaranteed him by the Constitution.

11. What has the United Nations done on behalf of human rights? What are some of the implications for the United States of UN action in this field?

12. What is meant when it is said that the price of liberty is eternal vigilance?

" Equal protection of law"

* Spazzacamino, Spazzacamino, ho freddo fame son poverino) in suo lago, dove son nato — Io la mia mamma, ritornerò. Egli deve adesso alla scuola — perchè algi piace questa occupazione.

questa classe è spazza i questa classe perchè Io devo andare Mi non piace questa multa. la spazza multa. alla casa mia / mi non discordai

CHAPTER 8

Population, Immigration, and Citizenship

A little of every race and every nation went into the melting-pot that poured me. . . . But I am an American because I have dreamt the dream of the founders of this democracy, and because I have a share in every act of faith that made their dream come true. Lincoln at Gettysburg spoke for me. Valley Forge was my Winter too. . . . Old Hickory talked my language. Ethan Allen thundered in my name. . . . The pioneers who climbed the hills and crossed the great valleys found a country broad enough for men of every race to live in self-respect and friendship with their neighbors. It is not race or creed or color that makes an American. It is a decent regard for the rights of a man and a healthy love of freedom. — *The New York Times* [1]

For it is safe to assert that nowhere in the world today is the right of citizenship of greater worth to an individual than it is in this country. It would be difficult to exaggerate its value and importance. By many it is regarded as the highest hope of civilized man. — Justice Frank Murphy [2]

The people of the United States are of diverse origin, race, and nationality; they are widely scattered on mainland, in territories, and abroad; they continue to grow in numbers by birth and immigration; they move about in search of opportunity and happiness; and the process of adjustment continues as it has since the republic was founded. Most are citizens, many are on the way to naturalization, some retain alien status. From these circumstances arise basic facts and problems of importance to those who would understand American political institutions and policies.

POPULATION

Population Growth. From the days of Colonial settlement to the time of the Civil War the population of the United States grew more rapidly than that of any other country of the world. This rapid growth is considered one of the outstanding phenomena of world history. From $2\frac{1}{2}$ million souls in 1776 the numbers increased by leaps and bounds until the First World War, since which time the rate of increase has been slower. In 1955 the population of continental United States was nearly 164 million. The population by decades and the decennial rates of increase are shown in chart on the following page.

It is apparent that while the growth has been continuous, the decennial rate of increase declined from 1860 until recently. This was due to a declining birth rate and diminishing immigration. Population experts predict that the population will continue to increase, possibly reaching 188 million by 1965, and over 300 million in the year 2000. In the first half of the 1950's, the popu-

[1] May 17, 1942.
[2] Schneiderman *v.* United States, 320 U.S. 118 (1942).

130

lation increase was 13.5 million, a figure greater than the total population of a number of national states.

Population Distribution. Of all the countries of the world only China, India, and Russia contain more people than the United States. Though large, the density of population is comparatively sparse, amounting to an average of only 50.7 per square mile as compared with 848 per square

Rural and Urban Population. Within the past hundred years the United States has changed from a nation whose chief occupation was agriculture to one of the most highly industrialized in the world. This metamorphosis has been accompanied by the growth of towns and cities and migration from rural to urban areas. Whereas in 1790, 95 per cent of all Americans lived in rural areas, nearly two-thirds now live

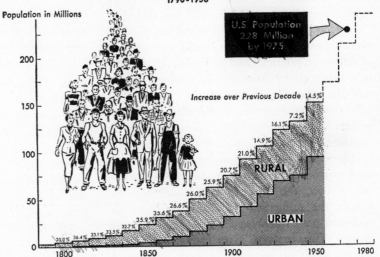

POPULATION OF THE UNITED STATES
1790-1950

Population in Millions

U.S. Population 228 Million by 1975

Increase over Previous Decade 14.5%

RURAL

URBAN

Only a decade or two ago, forecasters estimated that the United States population would reach 165 million by about 1990. That level will be reached in 1956, and new highs of 300 million by the year 2000 are now anticipated.

mile in the United Kingdom, 382 in the German Reich, 469 in Japan proper, and 197 in France. The most densely populated subdivision of the United States is the District of Columbia, while others in which there is greatest concentration of people are the Atlantic seaboard states of Rhode Island, New Jersey, Massachusetts, Connecticut, Maryland, and the agricultural-industrial states of New York, Pennsylvania, Ohio, and Illinois. The most sparsely poulated state is Nevada, with an average of only 1.5 inhabitants for each square mile. Wyoming, Montana, New Mexico, Arizona, Idaho, and Utah follow in the order named. The trend of migration within the United States has been predominantly from the Atlantic coast westward. The center of population continues to move westward, being located in 1950 at a point near Olney, Richland County, Ill.

in urban places. This trend is shown on the chart above.

The migration from rural to urban areas has had a profound effect upon American politics and governmental institutions. The most conspicuous result has been the diminution in importance of rural local government and the ascent of municipal government. Equally significant has been the gradual diminution of political influence in state and national politics of rural voters in favor of a new urban middle class of voters.[3] Because members of state legislatures and the Federal Congress are chosen from elec-

[3] For further development of this theme, see the writings of Arthur N. Holcombe. Note especially his *The New Party Politics* (Norton, 1933), *The Middle Classes in American Politics* (Harvard University Press, 1940), and *Our More Perfect Union* (Harvard University Press, 1950).

toral districts that follow arbitrary geographic lines, and not necessarily population concentration, rural elements continue to be overrepresented.

But when it comes to choosing candidates at large, as in the case of state governors and the President, urban elements can be dominant. As things now stand, so far as the President is concerned, neither party can hope to win without strong support among urban voters, and theoretically it is possible for a party to elect its presidential candidate without any support from rural voters. Professor Holcombe has said that "This dominating position of the urban population in presidential elections marks a revolution in American politics," and he predicts that "The new urban class politics will increasingly dominate the national political scene." [4]

A third consequence of the shift to urban centers has been the resulting encouragement of organized special interests. Where masses of people with widely varying interests live huddled together in the same old-fashioned legislative district, the candidates who are able to muster the numerical majorities necessary to win may poorly represent special interests and groups. This, in turn, gives encouragement to special group organization at local, state, and national levels to make certain that their interests are not overlooked.

A fourth consequence of the shift is that urbanization requires more governmental intervention in private affairs and also more services. As metropolitan dwellers sense their needs for better water, light, and sewage systems, better transportation and schools, better medical and recreational facilities, modern housing, employment offices and job insurance, attitudes favorable to the "welfare state" emerge. Thus, the urban trend must be listed as one of the most important causes of the shift from the individualistic to the positive state mentioned in Chap 1.

Racial Characteristics. Racially, the population of the United States is extremely heterogeneous, comprising people of all races and nationalities. The distribution according to the 1950 census was as follows:

[4] *The New Party Politics,* pp. 34–35.

Population, Continental United States, 1950

Race or nativity	Population	Per cent of total
All classes.........	150,697,000	100.0
White..............	135,215,000	89.7
Native white.....	125,068,000	83.0
Foreign white.....	10,147,000	6.7
Nonwhite..........	15,482,000	10.3
Negro............	14,894,000	9.9
Others...........	588,000	0.4

SOURCE: U.S. Bureau of the Census.

Each of these racial groups has made important contributions to American life. Besides helping with settlement, expansion, and the development of a high standard of living, each has also made distinctive contributions to the arts and sciences. Indeed, the greatness of America is due in large measure to its successful utilization and amalgamation of the genius inherent in the various racial streams which make up the population.

The ratio of whites to nonwhites (Negroes, Indians, Chinese, Japanese, and others) has remained nearly constant; hence no important political consequences have as yet become discernible. Of greater significance has been the continuous decline since 1900 of foreign white stock, *i.e.,* whites who have either immigrated to this country or who have been born here of foreign or mixed parentage.

In times past these groups tended to concentrate in certain areas where their political influence was great. The Irish, for example, have been especially influential in the larger cities of the Middle Atlantic and New England regions; people of Italian, Austrian, Russian, Polish, and Hungarian stock have wielded considerable influence in the Middle Atlantic region; folks of Scandinavian origin have been politically dominant in rural sections of the North Central region; while those of English stock have had considerable influence in the Middle Atlantic, East North Central, and New England areas. While their influence is still far from being negligible, it is certain to diminish if the present trend continues. At the same time there should be less need for Americanization programs such as there have been in the past, the number of naturalizations should diminish, and the population should become more homogeneous and "American."

IMMIGRATION

Colonial and State Control of Immigration. Except for Indians every person in the United

tition with each other for desirable immigrants and they lacked power to regulate foreign commerce.

State Regulation Unconstitutional. In order to strengthen their control, several states enacted laws requiring the bonding of captains of ships as a guaranty that immigrants would not become public charges and requiring the payment of a head tax for every immigrant. The laws of New York and Massachusetts came before the Supreme Court in the Passenger Cases and were

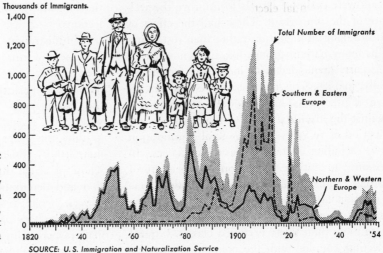

IMMIGRATION TO THE UNITED STATES
Years ended June 30, 1820–1954

Thousands of Immigrants.

Total Number of Immigrants

Southern & Eastern Europe

Northern & Western Europe

Wars, depressions, and quotas have greatly reduced immigration to the United States. Note the heavy Southern and Eastern European movement between 1900 and 1914, which was curbed after the First World War through the quota system.

SOURCE: U. S. Immigration and Naturalization Service

States is either an immigrant himself or the descendant of ancestors who immigrated to this country or who were brought here as slaves. Attempts to select immigrants date back to the Colonial period, when legislation was enacted to prevent the entrance of paupers, criminals, and certain religious sects like Catholics and Quakers. After the Revolution the states fell heir to the task, but in general few restrictions were added prior to 1830. After that date the arrival of increasingly large numbers gave rise to new social problems which led to a clamor for more stringent control. The states undertook the job and, except for a few federal laws enacted during the period, carried the brunt of the burden until 1882. State control was never entirely satisfactory inasmuch as the states were in compe-

declared unconstitutional on the ground that the states were taxing interstate commerce, thus interfering with powers granted exclusively to the Federal government.[5]

This decision left state inspection laws and programs aimed at paupers and diseased immigrants intact, but funds being necessary to execute the laws properly, New York made two attempts to modify her head-tax legislation to make it appear a legitimate exercise of the police power. Both attempts were declared unconstitutional.[6] The confusion that resulted from the incompetence of state governments to deal with

[5] How. 283 (U.S. 1849).

[6] Henderson *v.* Mayor of New York, 92 U.S. 259 (1875); People *v.* Compagnie Générale Transatlantique, 107 U.S. 59 (1883).

the subject made federal legislation imperative and it was soon forthcoming.

Federal Regulation. The first federal law dealing with the subject of immigration was enacted in 1819. This law, the first of a series of so-called "steerage legislation," limited the number of immigrants that could be brought over on one ship, prescribed minimum amounts of food and water to alleviate hardships en route, and required ship captains to file lists of passengers with certain information about each of them. Official immigration statistics date from this enactment.

Other federal laws enacted during the next 60 years were designed largely to improve the welfare of the immigrant. These had the effect of encouraging immigration rather than restricting it as many nativist groups like the Know-Nothing party demanded with increasing fervor. Finally, in 1882, Congress enacted its first restrictive legislation. This included a prohibition against the immigration of Chinese laborers for a period of 10 years and a general immigration law excluding certain undesirable classes. In response to antialien agitation on the part of nativist groups, organized labor, and others, one restriction after another was added after 1882 until by the time of the First World War there were more than thirty excluded classes. Careful selection, coupled with the policy of numerical restriction adopted in the 1920's, has greatly curtailed immigration. The trend of immigration is shown in the graph on the preceding page.

1952 Legislation. Immigration and naturalization have always aroused deep feelings, especially when social and political ferment abroad spurred groups to come to American shores who threatened competition in the economic sphere or whose race, religion, or national origin was distasteful to large segments of the population. Conditions that followed the Second World War were ripe for large-scale immigration and for a deep cleavage of point of view in the United States.

On the one hand were those who preferred a rather tolerant and generous policy; on the other were the more suspicious and fearful who wanted immigration kept to a minimum and large numbers excluded because of race, creed, religion, or national origin. Communists and other totalitarians were especially obnoxious. The controversy affected policy at many points, but especially as it was embodied in displaced-persons legislation, the McCarran Act of 1950, and the Immigration and Nationality Act of 1952, popularly known as the McCarran-Walter Act. The latter measure brings into one statute a number of laws enacted piecemeal over the years. It also makes important changes, some of which will be mentioned as the chapter proceeds. The new law was bitterly opposed by "liberals" and the President. The latter vetoed the bill, only to have it reenacted over his objections.

Administration. Responsibility for the enforcement of immigration laws rests chiefly with the Attorney General and the Secretary of State. The former performs most of his duties through the Immigration and Naturalization Service, which has a staff scattered over the nation. Within the Department of Justice is also a nonstatutory Board of Immigration Appeals, whose principal duty is one of reviewing exclusion and deportation decisions of immigration officers.

The Secretary of State is responsible for most matters pertaining to the issuance of passports and visas, including the determination of nationality of persons seeking entry into the United States. The Secretary's authority is carried out chiefly by the Bureau of Security and Consular Affairs at home and diplomatic and consular officers abroad. The Bureau houses the Passport Office and Visa Office. Consuls have great power in considering applications for visas; their denials may not be appealed to higher authority and complaints are numerous that this is arbitrary and unfair.

The Public Health Service is responsible for inspections and quarantines. Federal courts have limited authority to review decisions of immigration officials. Close liaison is supposed to be maintained among the Administrator of the Bureau of Security and Consular Affairs, the Commissioner of the Immigration and Naturalization Service, the FBI, and the Central Intelligence Agency. To study and check administration and other matters, the legislation of 1952 established a Joint Congressional Committee on Immigration and Nationality Policy, composed of five members from the House and a similar number from the Senate.

Selection of Immigrants and Nonimmigrants. Prior to 1924 the American government exercised no control over immigrants at the point of embarkation other than that exercised indirectly through shipping companies and their agents. This meant that thousands came to American ports only to be denied admission. The trials and tribulations encountered by countless numbers who arrived at Ellis Island and other ports of entry only to be sent back make up one of the most heart-rending chapters in American history. Much of this was changed by the Act of 1924, which charged American consuls stationed in foreign countries with primary responsibilities for the selection of immigrants.

People wishing to come to the United States are classified as either immigrants or nonimmigrants. If the former, they intend taking up permanent residence; if nonimmigrants, they wish only to pay a temporary visit, discuss official business, or travel across the United States en route somewhere else. Whether immigrant or nonimmigrant, a visa must be obtained from an American consul before embarkation. A passport and other documents must be submitted at the time application is made. After careful examination and inquiry, the consul determines whether an alien is admissible.

Either before or upon arrival at ports of entry, immigrants are inspected by representatives of the Public Health Service, travel documents are scrutinized by immigration officials, and travelers' possessions are evaluated by customs officials. If all is in order, aliens are admitted without further hindrance; if irregularities are discovered, they may be detained until the matter is satisfactorily adjusted or may be debarred from entrance.

Debarment and Deportation. The handling of immigrants arriving at ports of entry is a highly important task, involving as it does hopeful people who have journeyed far, who may not understand the language and customs, who are cut off from friends and relatives, who have no constitutional rights, and who may be short of funds. Equally delicate is the task of handling those who reach these shores but for one reason or another come under suspicion and may be deportable. Both debarment and deportation are handled by the Bureau of Immigration and Naturalization. Detention centers are maintained at numerous ports of entry, although many aliens are paroled pending final settlement of

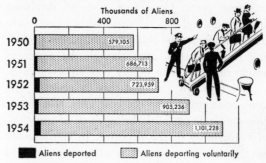

DEPORTATIONS & VOLUNTARY DEPARTURES

Thousands of Aliens

1950	579,105
1951	686,713
1952	723,959
1953	905,236
1954	1,101,228

■ Aliens deported ▨ Aliens departing voluntarily

SOURCE: U. S. Immigration and Naturalization Service

their cases. Mounting restrictions, involving long investigations into the background and views of thousands of people, have congested important detention centers and created heart-rending situations reminiscent of the days before 1924. Some improvement was made in 1954 when Ellis Island was closed to all but those whose freedom of movement was considered adverse to public safety and national security; other cases were transferred to detention centers in metropolitan New York.

In general, aliens may be debarred whenever they fail to meet requirements for admission, and they are deportable if subsequent to entry they are found to have entered the country illegally or to have since become members of excluded classes. Aliens whose offenses are comparatively minor may leave the country without expense to the United States, and many do. Deportation warrants are not executed for these, and they may reenter at some future time if their disqualifications are removed. Some aliens may, upon showing of convincing reasons for predicting good behavior in the future or severe hardship to close relatives, have deportation suspended by the Attorney General provided he reports to Congress and neither house registers disapproval. Other deportable aliens are arrested and ejected by warrant and may never reenter the country.

Of those deported by warrant, the principal offenses are usually entry without valid visa and violation of criminal statutes. By far the greatest number are normally returned to Mexico and Canada because of the fact that the long land frontiers make illegal entry easier than it is at maritime ports. Heretofore, costs of detaining immigrants and deportations within 5 years were assessed against the shipping companies providing transportation, even though the company might not have been in any way an accomplice.

The 1952 law changed this to provide that companies must bear the cost only when they knowingly or carelessly bring those of questionable eligibility or the deportee. In consequence of this change, expenses must usually be paid by the Federal government or the individuals concerned. Deportations are usually made to the country from which the alien last entered the United States, but it is sometimes impossible to find a nation willing to accept the deportee. In this event, he is either detained or placed on parole in the United States.

The "Wetback" Problem. The term "wetback" is commonly used to describe any illegal immigrant from Mexico to the United States; originally it was one who forded the Rio Grande into Texas. The magnitude of the problem is indicated by the numbers apprehended and deported annually: in 1949, 300,000; in 1952, 700,000; in 1953, 840,000; in 1954, 300,000. This is many times the total number of legal-quota and nonquota immigrants entering the country in any recent year.

The wetbacks are attracted to the United States by the higher rates of pay and the considerable demand for farm labor in the Southwest. Crossing the border is accomplished easily, frequently with the help of smugglers and "fixers" who supply cheap labor to cooperating employers. Once in the United States, the illegal entrant is difficult to distinguish from the Mexican-American who is domiciled here permanently, or from the Mexican national who is here legally. Serious complaints are made that the illegal entrant brings disease into the country, increases the crime rate, and undermines wage and working standards.

The United States has attempted to solve the problem by adding enforcement personnel, "cracking down" on smugglers and "fixers," establishing more ports of entry, enlisting the cooperation of the Mexican Government, employers, labor unions, states and communities most concerned. While some progress has been made, the problem remains a serious and difficult one.

Controversy over Fair Procedures. The courts have held that the power to regulate immigration, to debar and deport, is inherent in the fact that the United States is sovereign in foreign affairs.[7] The courts have also held that immigrants in the process of being admitted are without constitutional rights, while those who have been admitted for residence remain as a privilege rather than a right. Accordingly, the political branches—Congress and the President—have great latitude and discretion with which the courts are loath to interfere.[8] Without greater judicial safeguards, aliens are vulnerable to red tape and capriciousness.

The screening process is done administratively. For several years the Immigration and Naturalization Service insisted that it was exempt from provisions of the Administrative Procedures Act of 1946. This meant, among other things, that the Service could continue to permit its inquiry officers to make investigations and also render decisions, thus acting as both jury and judge. A respite came in December, 1949, when the Supreme Court overruled the Service, saying it came under the Administrative Procedures Act.[9] This ruling aroused the ire of enough congressmen bent on harassing aliens

[7] The leading case is Fong Yue Ting *v.* United States, 149 U.S. 698 (1893). See also p. 389.

[8] For a recent illustration, see Harisiades *v.* Shaughnessy, 342 U.S. 580 (1951).

[9] Wong Yang Sung *v.* McGrath, 339 U.S. 33 (1949).

to cause them to force through a rider permitting the Service to restore the old procedures.

The subject was dealt with again in the Immigration and Naturalization Act of 1952. While again exempting the Service from the Administrative Procedures Act, the new law did add some procedural safeguards. Chief among these was a provision that special inquiry officers shall not conduct proceedings in which they also perform investigative and prosecuting functions. Also recognized is the right to a hearing, to representation by counsel (at no expense to the government), to present witnesses, to cross-examine, and similar safeguards. Nevertheless, the administrative proceeding is the sole and exclusive one, and the decisions of the Attorney General are final. Court review is provided only when it is complained that the Attorney General is delaying unduly in holding deportation hearings or effectuating deportations.

Excluded Classes. The list of persons excluded has grown too long to be recited in full. Among others, it includes those who do not have proper travel documents; those ineligible to citizenship; those over sixteen who cannot read and understand some language or dialect; those who are not of good moral character; paupers, beggars, and vagrants; those likely to become a public charge; mental and physical defectives; contract laborers, unless exception is made by the Secretary of Labor, Secretary of State, and Attorney General; persons with loathsome or contagious diseases; drug addicts and chronic alcoholics; those who have committed crimes involving moral turpitude; polygamists; and many who hold obnoxious political views. For many years certain groups, mostly Orientals and inhabitants of the areas surrounding the East Indian Islands, were excluded because of race, but the Immigration and Nationality Act of 1952 repealed these provisions.

The ban because of political views is drastic and difficult to administer. Anarchists and others advocating revolution and violence have long been barred. The McCarran Act of 1950 went further, and its provisions were incorporated in the 1952 legislation. The intent is to bar those who are, or have been, voluntarily members or affiliates of the Communist Party or other totalitarian organizations. It also bars those who advocate, teach, or disseminate revolutionary or totalitarian doctrines. It even goes so far as to authorize consuls or the Attorney General to forbid admission to anyone who might possibly "engage in activities which would be prejudicial

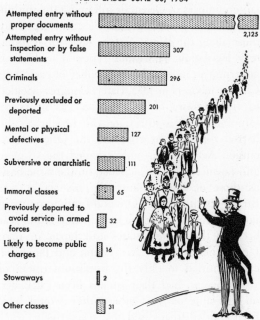

ALIENS EXCLUDED FROM THE UNITED STATES
YEAR ENDED JUNE 30, 1954

Attempted entry without proper documents	2,125
Attempted entry without inspection or by false statements	307
Criminals	296
Previously excluded or deported	201
Mental or physical defectives	127
Subversive or anarchistic	111
Immoral classes	65
Previously departed to avoid service in armed forces	32
Likely to become public charges	16
Stowaways	2
Other classes	31

Most of the aliens barred from entering the United States are persons without proper documents. Source: Immigration and Naturalization Service.

to the public interest, or endanger the welfare, safety, or security of the United States." Needless to say, probing the background and views of the thousands who apply for admission is a difficult and obnoxious task. Moreover, it invites capriciousness and reprisals by foreign governments. Critics see in legislation like this an "iron curtain" that is incompatible with democratic tradition and ideals.

Interestingly, the bars were lowered for a small group by the Central Intelligence Agency Act of 1949. This provided that as many as 100 aliens who might otherwise be barred might be admitted for permanent residence as a reward for disclosing secrets to American intelligence officers, provided the recommendation was concurred in by the Director of the Central Intelligence Agency, the Attorney General, and the Commissioner of Immigration. The legislation of 1952 granted another exception, to former Communists who had defected from the Party more than five years before applying for admission to the United States.

Repeal of Oriental Exclusion. The influx of large numbers of Orientals following the middle of last century led a number of states, especially those along the West coast, to enact discriminatory legislation of various types. The Federal government, in turn, began a policy of excluding Chinese laborers in 1882. Later, Congress yielded to the pressure of anti-Oriental elements by lumping most countries of the Orient in the barred zone and by adopting the Oriental Exclusion Act of 1924, which denied the Chinese and Japanese quotas calculated on the same basis as those of other countries. This action was deeply resented by all Orientals and accounts in no small measure for the tension that led to war between the United States and Japan in 1941. Under the Exclusion Act, China and Japan became entitled to only the minimum quota of 100, whereas, had their quotas been calculated on the same basis as others, they would have been entitled to 105 and 185, respectively.

When the Second World War found China and the United States allied, steps were taken to correct the long-standing insult to China, and in 1943 Congress placed Chinese immigration on the same basis as that of others, with the result that their quota was raised from 100 to 105. In 1946 the bars against Indians were lifted and they too were placed on the same quota basis as others. Filipinos, who had previously had a quota of 50, were also placed on the same basis as others following achievement of complete independence in 1946. For other Orientals, however, the law remained unchanged. Modifications were made, however, in the Immigration and Naturalization Act of 1952 which are discussed below.

The Quota System. Quota legislation adopted in 1924 and put into effect in 1929 was based on the national-origins principle. The percentage of each national group in the United States in 1920 to total population was found and applied to a maximum of 150,000 immigrants admissible each year to determine the quota for each nationality. The intent and effect of this procedure was to discriminate against immigrants from Southern and Eastern Europe. Orientals were, in general, barred. Resulting comparatively high quotas from Britain, Ireland, Scandinavia, and other countries of Northern Europe were seldom fully used, with the result that immigration was reduced to a trickle.

Discrimination of this sort offended large nationality groups in the United States, it was criticized on religious and moral grounds, it engendered ill will abroad, it complicated foreign relations, and it made it difficult to extend hospitality to many victims of totalitarian tyranny and war. Nevertheless, the policy has been stoutly defended. The ban on Orientals was moderated somewhat after the Second World War, but the same general pattern of discrimination was nevertheless incorporated in the 1952 legislation.

How Quotas Are Determined. The new legislation retains the national-origins principle as applied to the 1920 census. The world is divided into quota areas with each independent country, self-governing dominion, mandated territory, and territory under the international trusteeship system of the United Nations (other than territories for which the United States is trustee) being a quota area if so designated by the Secretary of State. An additional quota area is established for all other inhabited lands. No area has a quota of less than 100; the Chinese quota of 105 remains unchanged; and a quota of 100 is allotted to the "Asia-Pacific triangle," which region is part of a general quota area.

After making these exceptions, each quota area is given an annual quota equal to ⅙ of 1 per cent of the number of inhabitants from the area who lived in continental United States in 1920. Thus, the Italian quota should be ⅙ of 1 per cent of the number of people in the United States in 1920 of Italian origin; the French quota should be ⅙ of 1 per cent of the number of people in the United States in 1920 of French origin; and so on for each area.

The Factor of Ancestry. For most people, the area to which a quota is charged is determined by place of birth, but an exception is made for Orientals. For these, ancestry is also important, with the result that the small quotas allowed

most of the beneficial effects of this gesture are off-set by other provisions of the bill. The countries of Asia are told in one breath that they shall have quotas for their nationals, and in the next that the nationals of the other countries, if their ancestry is as much as 50 per cent Asian shall be charged to these quotas.

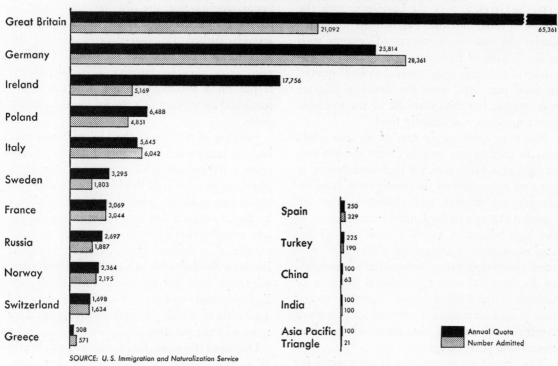

ANNUAL QUOTAS AND IMMIGRANTS ADMITTED IN 1954

	Annual Quota	Number Admitted
Great Britain	65,361	21,092
Germany	25,814	28,361
Ireland	17,756	5,169
Poland	6,488	4,851
Italy	5,645	6,042
Sweden	3,295	1,803
France	3,069	3,044
Russia	2,697	1,887
Norway	2,364	2,195
Switzerland	1,698	1,634
Greece	308	571
Spain	250	329
Turkey	225	190
China	100	63
India	100	100
Asia Pacific Triangle	100	21

SOURCE: U. S. Immigration and Naturalization Service

The annual quotas allowed under the 1952 act provide far more places for British and Irish immigrants than there are persons who wish to come. Quotas for several other countries, on the other hand, are far below the numbers of desirable applicants.

for the political units of the Asia-Pacific triangle will permit fewer native-born people from this region to emigrate to the United States. The rule is that any alien, regardless of place of birth, who attributes as much as one-half of his ancestry to peoples indigenous to the triangle is chargeable to area quotas for this region.

President Truman had some harsh words to say of this special treatment in his veto message:

The only consequential change in the 1924 quota system which the bill would make is to extend a small quota to each of the countries of Asia. But

It is only with respect to persons of Oriental ancestry that this invidious discrimination applies. All other persons are charged to the country of their birth. But persons with Asian ancestry are charged to the countries of Asia, wherever they may have been born, or however long their ancestors have made their homes outside the land of their origin. These provisions are without justification.[10]

Quota Lapse. Quotas are not cumulative; immigration visas not issued during a given year lapse. The ordinary qualified applicant of British

[10] *The New York Times*, June 26, 1952, p. 14.

or Irish birth can secure a quota number promptly; virtually all other nationalities have waiting periods of varying lengths. Quotas for particular countries are reduced by one for each individual involved in cases of suspension of deportation, of private bill enacted, and of displaced person allowed to convert status to that of permanent resident. As of Aug. 1, 1952, the Estonian quota was "mortgaged" until the year 2146, the Greek to 2014, the Latvian to 2274, the Polish to 2000, and the Yugoslavian to 2014.[11] Under the law "undersubscribed" quotas such as the British or Irish may not be used by nationals of countries with "oversubscribed" quotas. In fiscal year 1951, when the desire to migrate was intense, less than one-half of the available quota numbers was actually used.

Not more than 10 per cent of an area quota may be used in any month, except the last two months of a fiscal year. Of each area quota, 50 per cent is earmarked for immigrants (and accompanying spouses and children) who are "needed urgently in the United States because of the high education, technical training, specialized experience, or exceptional ability" and who show prospect of being "substantially beneficial" to the "national economy, cultural interests, or welfare of the United States." Another 30 per cent of each area quota is reserved for parents of American citizens if the latter are at least twenty-one years of age.

The remaining 20 per cent is earmarked for the children or spouses of aliens lawfully admitted for permanent residence. If quotas are not used by persons entitled to preference, they become available to others who can meet general requirements. Charging all displaced persons to area quotas should reduce immigration, while enlarging the numbers to whom preference is given makes American policy more selective than ever before.

Nonquota Immigrants. In addition to persons admitted under the quotas assigned by the national-origins system, a large number of persons are admitted outside of such quotas. The greatest

portion comes from Western Hemisphere countries; they accounted for 24 per cent of total immigration between 1930 and 1951. This exception from the quota system was made in the interest of good neighborliness. The 1952 act still does not require quotas for migrants from self-governing nations in North and South America, but it adds so many rigidities in the interest of health, economic solvency, and national security that the old free movement of people across the borders of the Americas is severely curbed. Colonial dependencies of the Americas are placed under subquotas of the administering powers; Jamaica, a British colony, is put on a subquota of 100, whereas it has furnished an average of 1,000 migrants in recent years.

Families of citizens of the United States may become nonquota immigrants. Fiancées of veterans were permitted to enter and, after their marriage, to remain in this country. Special provision was made for admission of skilled sheepherders. Certain aliens who enlist in the American armed forces overseas are entitled to enter outside of established quotas. Finally, Congress has been flooded with private bills to waive immigration laws for particular individuals; the Eighty-second Congress (1951–1952) received 3,302 bills, of which 732 were enacted, providing relief to 1,364 persons.

Displaced Persons. Since the Second World War the American government has been swamped by appeals to admit greater numbers of Europe's displaced people. Additional quotas were needed as well as financial assistance and liberalized rules. To the tune of bitter controversy, Congress accommodated in 1948, again in 1950, and most recently by passing the Refugee Relief Act of 1953.

This measure authorized special visas for 205,000 aliens, their spouses, and unmarried children under twenty-one. An additional 4,000 visas were allocated for orphans when adoptions could be arranged. Generous aspects of the law were offset by restrictive features requiring passports or other valid travel documents, security investigations and clearances, promises of jobs that would not displace American workmen,

---

[11] U.S. President's Commission on Immigration and Naturalization, *Whom We Shall Welcome, Report of the* . . . (1953), p. 104.

and funds enough to prevent applicants from becoming public charges.

These restrictions, coupled with conservative administration during the first 2 years, reduced entrance under the act to a trickle. A political explosion early in 1955, involving the protest resignation of Edward Corsi, special assistant for administering the act, served to focus public attention on the acute plight of refugees and escapees from countries behind the iron curtain.

ALIENS

Aliens, Nationals, and Citizens. The people now living within the jurisdiction of the United States may be divided into three classes—aliens, nationals, and citizens. An alien is one who though living in the United States owes permanent allegiance to a foreign country. Broadly construed, nationals include both citizens and noncitizens who owe permanent allegiance to the United States, although the word "national" is commonly used to refer only to noncitizens such as natives of Samoa. All nationals, whether citizens or not, are entitled to the protection of the American government wherever they may be. Citizens are nationals who enjoy a special status and upon whom rests the primary responsibility of organizing and controlling the nation.

The Number of Aliens. The first complete census of aliens in the United States resulted from compulsory registration required by the Alien Registration Act of 1940. About 5 million aliens registered. Practically all were located in fourteen states, with New York accounting for about 25 per cent. More recent and comparable figures are unavailable, but the total appears to have declined. A vigorous alien-address program begun in 1951 by the Immigration and Naturalization Service provides current data. Figures for 1954 and the distribution of aliens among the states are shown in the chart opposite.

The Status of Aliens. Generally speaking, aliens owe a temporary allegiance to the country in which they may be located and are, therefore, obliged to obey local laws. They must pay all taxes that are not discriminatory or confiscatory. They are generally exempt from military and jury services, although during times of domestic disorder the rules of international law permit them to be required to render police or militia service. They are, with a few exceptions, permitted to own property and engage in business, to sue and be sued in American courts, and to attend public schools and enjoy other public facilities. The civil rights guaranteed to citizens by the Constitution extend to them also and

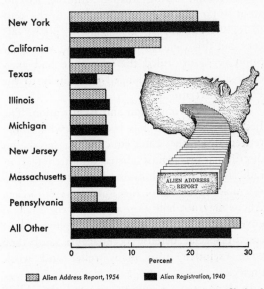

ALIEN POPULATION IN THE UNITED STATES
1940 AND 1954

New York
California
Texas
Illinois
Michigan
New Jersey
Massachusetts
Pennsylvania
All Other

Percent

▒ Alien Address Report, 1954   ■ Alien Registration, 1940

The total number of 2,365,811 alien residents filed address reports in 1954. Of these, 71 per cent lived in the eight states shown. Note heavy increases in Texas and California since 1940. Source: U.S. Immigration and Naturalization Service.

the equal-protection clause of the Fourteenth Amendment presumes to guarantee them from discriminatory treatment by the forty-eight states.

State and Local Discrimination. Nevertheless, aliens suffer discriminations of many sorts within the United States. They may not vote in any state, they are ineligible to hold many public offices, and most of the states require that only citizens may engage in certain occupations and professions. The Supreme Court has upheld a Pennsylvania law that forbids aliens to own rifles and shotguns;[12] an ordinance of an Ohio city

[12] Patsone *v.* Pennsylvania, 232 U.S. 139 (1914).

forbidding aliens to obtain licenses to operate pool halls;[13] and statutes of several Western states forbidding aliens to acquire title to real estate, although these now appear to be of questionable validity.[14] Aliens are frequently denied relief, pensions, workmen's compensation benefits, and employment on public works.[15]

Aliens have occasionally been the victims of race prejudice and even race riots leading to diplomatic intervention by their governments. Pennsylvania, fearing "fifth columnist" activity, went so far as to require aliens within the state to register and report periodically to public officers, but this came to an abrupt end when the Supreme Court ruled that the state had exercised a power that belonged exclusively to the Federal government.[16]

Federal Discrimination and Registration. The Federal government has been somewhat more reticent than the states in enacting legislation discriminating against aliens, although fear of radicals and fifth columnists has prompted considerable legislation of this kind in recent years. Aliens may not hold positions with the Federal government; they are forbidden employment in certain special defense occupations, and they were excluded from many relief and work projects.

In June, 1940, Congress enacted the Alien Registration Act charging the Department of Justice with the responsibility of registering and fingerprinting all aliens over fourteen years of age. Registration took place at post offices and other public places throughout continental America, Alaska, Hawaii, Puerto Rico, and the Virgin Islands. Henceforth aliens entering the country were to be registered and fingerprinted at American consulates before leaving for the United States. Moreover, Congress has length-

ened the list of deportable offenses and included within the McCarran Act drastic provisions for apprehending and detaining both citizens and aliens in the event of war, invasion, or insurrection.

What can happen to resident aliens is illustrated by three cases decided in 1952. The Alien Registration Act of 1940 authorized the deportation of a legally resident alien because of membership in the Communist Party, even though such membership had terminated before the law was passed. In one of the cases[17] a man named Harisiades, a Greek national, had come to the United States with his parents in 1916 and had resided here ever since. He had joined the Communist Party in 1925, and the party had discontinued his membership in 1939, as it had those of all aliens. Although he still believed in communist principles, he disclaimed personal belief in the use of force and violence. The Alien Registration Act, passed in 1940, was used as authority for ordering his deportation in 1946. The other two cases were similar. The defendants sought release by habeas corpus, and the cases ultimately reached the Supreme Court.

The defendants contended that the law passed in 1940 deprived them of liberty without due process of law, violated freedom of speech and assembly, and was ex post facto. But a 6-to-2 majority of the Supreme Court ruled against them. So far as due process of law was concerned, the Court said the power to deport aliens was inherent in every sovereign state and the policy toward aliens is so exclusively entrusted to the political branches of government as to be largely immune from judicial inquiry or interference. Freedom of speech and assembly were not violated because the facts indicated that the Communist Party did advocate the overthrow of government by force and violence which Congress had the power to prevent. On this point the Court relied upon the majority decision in Dennis v. United States, discussed elsewhere.[18]

As for the claim that the law was unconstitutional because it was ex post facto, the Court

---

[13] Ohio v. Deckebach, 274 U.S. 392 (1927).

[14] For the older view see Terrace v. Thompson, 263 U.S. 197 (1923); Porter v. Webb, 263 U.S. 255 (1923); Webb v. O'Brien, 263 U.S. 313 (1923); Frick v. Webb, 263 U.S. 326 (1923). The newer view is set forth in Oyama v. California, 332 U.S. 633 (1948).

[15] Heim v. McCall, 239 U.S. 175 (1915); Crane v. New York, 239 U.S. 195 (1915).

[16] Hines v. Davidowitz, 312 U.S. 52 (1941).

[17] Harisiades v. Shaughnessy, 342 U.S. 580 (1951).
[18] See p. 116.

said this constitutional provision prevented retroactive penalties in criminal cases, while "deportation, however severe its consequences, has been consistently classified as a civil rather than a criminal procedure." Justices Douglas and Black wrote a sharp dissent. As a result of this decision, resident aliens are peculiarly insecure. Even though they have been in the country for many years, they can never be certain that shifting public sentiment will not reflect itself in legislation making them liable for deportation with no assurance of judicial intervention.

Enemy Aliens. Nationals of states with whom a country is at war present a difficult problem. Prior to the First World War it was the general practice among nations to permit such aliens to remain during good behavior unless their expulsion was required by military considerations. But at the outbreak of the war most belligerent nations either ordered enemy aliens to leave or placed them in concentration camps. At the same time steps were taken by the belligerents to liquidate the commercial and property interests of enemy aliens found within their borders. In the United States resident enemy aliens are entitled to the right of protection of person and property as long as they conduct themselves properly, although the courts have held that the guaranties of the Fifth and Sixth Amendments are inapplicable to them.

During the First World War enemy aliens were not expelled, but several states enacted legislation requiring them to register, while the Federal government required registration, fixed zones within which they could not reside or enter, and otherwise drastically curtailed their utterances and activities. Although the property of resident enemy aliens was not itself confiscated, the financial and commercial interests of many were seriously injured by legislation creating an Alien Property Custodian with authority to seize properties that were owned or controlled by enemy countries or persons residing within those countries to prevent them from exercising any control over, or deriving any profit from, the use of property situated within the United States. Altogether, hundreds of millions of dollars' worth of property was sequestered,

which was subsequently held as a kind of pledge for the repayment by Germany of the war claims of American citizens. The settlement of these claims was a constant source of friction after the war, and as late as 1940 approximately 20 per cent of the property had not yet been returned or compensated. Although disapproved by accepted rules of international law, the Supreme Court has upheld the confiscation of private property believed to be enemy owned if adequate provision is made for return in case of mistake.

America's entrance into war in December, 1941, was followed by acts similar to those taken during the preceding World War. Enemy aliens over fourteen years of age were required to register and carry certificates of identification with them at all times. Travel was restricted, jobs could not be changed without advance notice, the possession of articles like firearms and cameras was forbidden, those with dubious records were arrested, given hearings, and then released, paroled, or interned. Alien Japanese and American citizens of Japanese descent living on the West coast were ordered to relocation camps where, after long delay, many of the loyal were separated and permitted to relocate in other parts of the country. Although upheld by the Supreme Court,[19] this treatment has been widely criticized as being both unnecessary and unjust. As during the First World War, billions of dollars' worth of enemy-owned property was sequestered for the duration and placed under the custody of the Alien Property Custodian.

CITIZENSHIP

General Rules for Determining Citizenship. Two general principles are employed by modern states for the determination of citizenship: *jus soli* and *jus sanguinis*. Where *jus soli* is followed, citizenship is determined by place of birth; where *jus sanguinis* is used it is the nationality of one's parents and ancestors that determines citizenship. There is frequently conflict between the two, in which case a person is

[19] Korematsu *v.* United States, 323 U.S. 214 (1944); *Ex parte* Endo, 323 U.S. 283 (1944). See also p. 453.

said to possess dual or multiple nationality. Thus, for example, one born in England of Italian parents is English by *jus soli* and Italian by *jus sanguinis*. Controversies arising out of conflicting claims are commonly settled by treaty, but in the absence of treaty the effective law is that of the country in which the person may be located. In practice, states seldom adhere strictly to one principle but employ both. Such is the case in the United States.

Citizenship Prior to 1868. All the colonial charters save that given to William Penn contained a provision stating that the inhabitants of the colonies and their children shall be deemed British subjects. English citizenship was terminated by the Declaration of Independence and passed immediately to the individual colonies. Since the states were admittedly sovereign under the Articles of Confederation, there was no national citizenship; rather, the inhabitants and their descendants were citizens of their state of residence with the same privileges and immunities as citizens in any of the other twelve states.

When the Constitution was adopted, persons recognized as citizens in the several states became also citizens of the United States. While recognizing a dual citizenship, the Constitution did not state whether state citizenship depended on United States citizenship or vice versa, but prior to 1868 the generally accepted view was that United States citizenship, except in cases of naturalization, was subordinate to and derived from state citizenship.

Citizenship Defined. In the famous Dred Scott Case, decided in 1857, the Supreme Court ruled that neither a state nor the Federal government could confer federal citizenship upon native-born Negroes, whether slave or free.[20] This, followed by the Civil War, led to the adoption of the Fourteenth Amendment which, among other things, defined citizenship, saying: "All persons born or naturalized in the United States, and subject to the jurisdiction thereof are citizens of the United States and of the State in which they reside."

Several things should be observed about the above definition: (1) It incorporated into the

[20] Dred Scott *v.* Sandford, 19 How. 393 (U.S. 1857).

Constitution as the basic rule to be followed in determining citizenship the principle of *jus soli* which had been followed since colonial days. (2) Two methods of acquiring citizenship were acknowledged: by birth and by naturalization. (3) Only those who are subject to the jurisdiction of the United States at the time of birth or naturalization are citizens. (4) Children born anywhere in the United States and subject to the jurisdiction of the Federal government are citizens regardless of the laws of any particular state. (5) American citizens are also citizens of the state in which they reside.

Rules Relating to Citizenship by Birth. Three things must be kept in mind throughout the discussion of rules that follows. One is that the courts have never decided under what circumstances one is a "natural-born" citizen. Another is that some people are citizens at birth because of the Fourteenth Amendment, while others are citizens at birth as a result of legislation enacted by Congress. A third is that in legislating upon the subject Congress has made some people citizens by birth *jus sanguinis*. From the Immigration and Nationality Act of 1952 and innumerable court decisions the following rules may be noted:

1. While artificial creatures like corporations are "persons" within the meaning of some provisions of the Constitution, they are not "persons" within the meaning of the citizenship clause of the Fourteenth Amendment. Hence, only human beings ("natural persons") are citizens and entitled to the privileges and immunities of citizens of the United States.

2. One is a citizen by birth if (*a*) born in the United States and subject to the jurisdiction thereof; (*b*) born in the United States of an Indian, Eskimo, Aleutian, or other aboriginal tribe; (*c*) found in the United States of unknown parentage while under five years of age, provided no one offers proof of birth outside the United States before the individual attains the age of twenty-one.

3. One is a citizen by birth if born in an American outlying possession of parents one of whom is a citizen who has been physically present in the United States or one of its possessions for a

continuous period of 1 year at any time prior to the birth of the child.

4. One is a citizen by birth if born outside the United States and its possessions of parents both of whom are citizens and one of whom has had a residence in the United States or one of its possessions prior to the birth of the child.

5. One is a citizen by birth if born outside the United States and its possessions of parents one of whom is a citizen who has been physically present in the United States or one of its possessions for a year prior to the birth of a child, and the other parent is a national but not a citizen.

6. One is a citizen by birth if born outside the United States and one of its possessions of parents one of whom is a citizen, the other an alien, if the citizen parent had been physically present in the United States or its possessions for 10 years prior to the birth of the child, at least 5 of which years were after attaining the age of fourteen, and provided the child comes to the United States and remains here continuously for 5 years between the ages of fourteen and twenty-eight.

7. One is a citizen by birth if born in Puerto Rico, Alaska, Hawaii, the Virgin Islands, Guam, the Canal Zone (if one's father, mother, or both are citizens), and the Republic of Panama (if one's father, mother, or both are citizens and employees of the government of the United States or one of its agencies).

8. The following are not American citizens by birth because though born within the United States they are not subject to the jurisdiction thereof: (*a*) children born of foreign sovereigns and diplomatic officers; [21] (*b*) children born on foreign public ships in American territorial waters; (*c*) children born of enemies in hostile occupation. Otherwise, children born within the United States of alien parents are American citizens. This is true even though the parents

[21] But children born of foreign consular officers in the United States are citizens, inasmuch as consuls are subject to the civil and criminal jurisdiction of the courts of the country in which they are stationed. See especially United States *v.* Wong Kim Ark, 169 U.S. 649, 678 (1898).

are traveling through or are within the country for a temporary stay only.

Citizenship of Women. Prior to Sept. 22, 1922, American women who married aliens expatriated themselves. On the other hand, alien women, if eligible for naturalization, acquired citizenship by marrying American citizens. Passage of the Cable Act on the date mentioned reversed these provisions and now American women do not lose citizenship by marriage nor do alien women acquire citizenship by marriage to Americans. Women who lost citizenship prior to 1922 and alien women who marry Americans may, if eligible for naturalization, be naturalized by a simplified procedure.

Naturalization. The term "naturalization" means the grant of a new nationality to a natural person after birth. Before the adoption of the Constitution most of the thirteen colonies had naturalization laws, but they varied widely. Since uniformity is obviously desirable, those who wrote the Constitution inserted a clause giving Congress power "to establish a uniform Rule of Naturalization . . . throughout the United States." [22] The power was first asserted in 1790, since which time naturalization has been controlled exclusively by the Federal government. Naturalization laws are administered by the Immigration and Naturalization Service in the Department of Justice, although certificates of naturalization are issued by the Federal district courts and state courts "having a seal, a clerk, and jurisdiction in actions of law or equity or law and equity, in which the amount in controversy is unlimited." Persons may be naturalized singly by their own action, or collectively by act of Congress.

Qualifications for Individual Naturalization. Until recently, race was an important qualification for naturalization, with Orientals bearing the brunt of discrimination. During and after the Second World War, restrictions were removed for Chinese, Filipinos, and the people of India, while in the Immigration and Nationality Act of 1952 all racial restrictions to naturalization were dropped. No longer will it be true, therefore, that many who are allowed to im-

[22] Art. I, Sec. 8.

migrate to American shores will be permanently barred from citizenship because of racial origin.

Many qualifications remain, however, and the list tends to grow longer. Petitioners must show lawful entry into the country; they must be of good moral character; they must be able to read, write, speak, and otherwise understand the English language; they must display a knowledge and understanding of the history, principles, and form of American government; they must take an oath declaring their attachment to the principles of American government and saying they are disposed to the good order and happiness of the United States; they must not have deserted the armed forces or evaded the draft while the nation was at war; they must not have applied for exemption from selective service because they were aliens; they may not be anarchists, communists, or totalitarians of other types—indeed, they are barred from naturalization if they ever were associated in any way with revolutionary or totalitarian organizations or the dissemination of their views. Titles of nobility must be renounced. Petitioners may not be citizens of countries with whom the United States is at war. Allegiance must be declared, and petitioners must state their attitude toward bearing arms.

Naturalization of Religious Pacifists. Until recently petitioners for naturalization were required to take an oath of allegiance which contained, among others, the following words: "I hereby declare . . . that I will support and defend the Constitution and the laws of the United States of America against all enemies, foreign and domestic. . . ." These words gave rise to the question of whether they required willingness to bear arms.

In 1929 the Supreme Court had before it a case involving Mme. Rosika Schwimmer, a Hungarian woman who testified that she had "no sense of nationalism, only a cosmic consciousness of belonging to the human family" and would for conscientious reasons be unable to take up arms in defense of the country if ordered to do so.[23] A second case concerned Douglas C.

Macintosh, a native of Canada who at the time was a professor of religion at the Divinity School of Yale University. In applying for citizenship he was willing to promise in advance to bear arms in defense only if he believed the war to be morally justified.[24] A third case involved Marie Bland, a First World War nurse of Canadian origin. She was willing to take the oath with the understanding that she would defend the United States so far as her conscience as a Christian would allow.[25] In all three instances the Supreme Court ruled that the words to "support and defend" implied the necessity of bearing arms.

The issue was reconsidered in 1946 in a case involving James L. Girouard, a member of the Seventh Day Adventist Church and a native of Canada. He was willing to perform noncombatant service in the Army but would not promise to bear arms. The Supreme Court split five to three in favor of Girouard, stating that the Court had not stated the "correct rule of law" in its previous decisions. According to the majority, Congress had never (not even in the Nationality Act of 1940) affirmatively indicated its intention of barring pacifists from naturalization.

In consequence of this reversal, pacifist aliens could naturalize if otherwise qualified, and a number did.

Congress clarified its intention in the McCarran Act of 1950 and more recently in the Immigration and Nationality Act of 1952. The latter gives the applicant three choices: (1) He may declare willingness to bear arms in the armed forces; (2) if an objector because of religious training and belief, he may indicate willingness to perform only noncombatant service in the armed forces; or (3) if an objector because of religious training and belief to bearing arms or performing noncombatant service, he may declare willingness to do work of national importance under civilian direction. This gives the naturalized citizen the same options open to citizens who are natural-born as provided in selective service and training legislation. While the law permits religious objectors to naturalize,

[23] United States *v*. Schwimmer, 279 U.S. 644 (1929).

[24] United States *v*. Macintosh, 283 U.S. 605 (1931).
[25] United States *v*. Bland, 283 U.S. 636 (1931).

those who are pacifists because of political, sociological, or philosophical reasons are excluded.

Procedure for Naturalizing Individual Aliens. Recent legislation modified procedures somewhat. A declaration of intention is no longer mandatory, but it may be filed by any alien over eighteen who has been lawfully admitted for permanent residence. The first mandatory step is filing a petition. This may be done by any alien eighteen years of age or over who has resided in the country for 5 continuous years and in the state where the petition is filed for 6 months. Then follows personal investigation, preliminary hearing, and final hearing in open court.

The investigation and preliminary hearing are conducted by employees of the Immigration and Naturalization Service, the final hearing by a Federal district court or a state court of record. The final hearing may be thorough, but usually it is perfunctory, the judge merely following the recommendations of the officers who conducted the preliminary proceedings. If the judge is satisfied that the petitioner is eligible for naturalization, the oath is administered, a certificate of naturalization is issued, and the erstwhile alien becomes a full-fledged citizen of the United States.

Collective Naturalization. At various times large groups of people have been made American citizens by a single legislative enactment. When the Constitution was adopted, all persons who were citizens of the original states became citizens of the United States. The treaties of acquisition conveyed citizenship to the inhabitants of the territories of Louisiana, Florida, New Mexico, and Alaska. In the joint resolution admitting Texas to the Union, American citizenship was substituted for Texan. By special acts Congress collectively naturalized the inhabitants of Hawaii in 1900, those of Puerto Rico in 1917, the Indian tribes in 1924, the inhabitants of the Virgin Islands in 1927, and those of Guam in 1950.

Distinctions between Natural-born and Naturalized Citizens. For the most part naturalized and natural-born citizens are entitled to the same rights and privileges. There are a few differences, however. Only a natural-born citizen may become President or Vice-President, although naturalized citizens may hold any other federal office. Natural-born citizens may live or travel abroad without impairing their status; naturalized citizens may lose citizenship if within 5 years they take up permanent residence abroad. Natural-born citizens who remain in the United States may have citizenship revoked for the commission of only a few very serious crimes; naturalized citizens are in greater jeopardy of loss of citizenship. Natural-born citizens are entitled to full protection by the American government wherever they may be, but because of claims arising out of dual citizenship the American government may, in the absence of treaty guaranties, find it inexpedient to afford full protection to those who return to their native land. With these exceptions, naturalized citizens are on a plane of equality with those who are natural-born.

Loss of Citizenship. Contrary to a general impression, federal and state laws do not deprive persons of citizenship for the commission of ordinary felonies. State laws frequently deny criminals certain privileges without depriving them of citizenship. Indeed, states could not take away federal citizenship if they wanted to. In federal law, nationality is forfeited upon conviction of treason, attempting by force to overthrow the American government, bearing arms against the United States, desertion from the armed and naval forces or draft dodging during war or national emergency, and conspiring to commit treason, rebellion, insurrection, or sedition.

Citizenship may be lost, however, for reasons other than the commission of crimes. It may be lost by (1) naturalization to a foreign state, taking an oath of allegiance to a foreign state, or formally renouncing American citizenship before an officer designated by the Attorney General or an American diplomatic or consular officer in a foreign state; (2) voluntary renunciation during wartime if approved by the Attorney General; (3) entering, or serving in, the armed forces of a foreign state if to do so causes one to acquire the nationality of that state; (4) accepting, or performing the duties of, any office, post, or employment under the government of a foreign state or political subdivision thereof for which only nationals of such state are eligible; (5) voting in a political election in a foreign state or participating in an election or plebiscite to determine the sovereignty over foreign territory; and (6) if a child, by the naturalization of a parent to a foreign state.

As already suggested, for naturalized citizens the list is longer. Their citizenship may be canceled if within 5 years after naturalization they take up permanent residence in their native land or elsewhere outside the United States. Citizenship is also lost if it is ever discovered that naturalization was achieved through concealment of a material fact, willful misrepresentation, fraud, or other illegal means. Conviction of contempt for refusing to testify before a congressional committee at any time within 10 years if accused of subversive activity is sufficient evidence of concealment and misrepresentation to justify cancellation of citizenship. Becoming a member or affiliate of revolutionary or totalitarian organizations within 5 years after naturalization is also grounds for revoking citizenship. Cancellation proceedings take place in Federal district courts. Revocation of citizenship may or may not be followed by deportation depending upon the nature of the offense.

Whom We Shall Welcome. President Truman's disapproval of the Immigration and Nationality Act of 1952 and passage by Congress over the veto highlighted the intense controversy that has surrounded immigration policy in recent years. Following the veto President Truman appointed a Commission on Immigration and Naturalization composed of distinguished citizens to explore the subject. The Commission's report, published in 1953 under the title of *Whom We Shall Welcome*, was generally critical of American policy.

The principal conclusion reached by the Commission was that the immigration and nationality law was unwise and injurious to the nation and should be "reconsidered and revised from beginning to end." More specifically the Com-

mission charged that the legislation (1) rested upon an attitude of hostility and distrust against all aliens; (2) discriminated on account of national origin, race, creed, and color; (3) ignored the needs of the nation in domestic affairs and foreign policies; (4) continued unnecessary and unreasonable restrictions and penalties; and (5) was badly drafted, confusing, and in some respects unworkable.

The recommendations made by the Commission were too numerous and detailed to recite here. A few of the more important were:

1. Abolish the national origins quota system and substitute a "unified quota system" which would allocate visas without regard to national origin, race, creed, or color.

2. Calculate the maximum annual quota at $\frac{1}{6}$ of 1 per cent of the latest census rather than the population of 1920, thus, with 1950 as a base, raising the annual quota from the present 154,657 to 251,162.

3. Place all immigration and nationality functions in a new independent Commission on Immigration and Naturalization, whose members would be appointed by the President and confirmed by the Senate.

4. Permit appeals from consular denials of visas, bring deportation procedures under the Administrative Procedures Act, and generally revise procedures to ensure greater fairness.

5. Bar deportation and denaturalization unless charges are brought within ten years.

6. Modify provisions that now bar or deter scholars, scientists, and other leaders from visiting the United States.

7. Continue excluding spies, saboteurs, active members of totalitarian organizations, and others who believe in or advocate totalitarian doctrines, but relax rules that ban people because of past or involuntary memberships or who have repudiated and now oppose totalitarian ideologies.

8. Give naturalized citizens the same status as the native-born and minimize restrictions on naturalization that create statelessness, disrupt family unity, or impose unreasonable conditions or procedures upon the acquisition or retention of citizenship.

In spite of the cogency and forcefulness of the Commission's conclusions and recommendations, and support for some of them from President Eisenhower, the Congress has been unwilling to undertake general revision of the legislation of 1952.

FOR FURTHER READING

Alexander, Norman: *The Rights of Aliens under the Federal Constitution* (Montpelier, Vt.: Capital City Press, 1931).

Beard, Annie E. S.: *Our Foreign-born Citizens: What They Have Done for America* (Crowell, rev. ed., 1939).

Bogue, Don J.: *The Structure of the Metropolitan Community* (University of Michigan Press, 1949).

Borchard, Edwin M.: *The Diplomatic Protection of Citizens Abroad* (New York: Banks Law Publishing Co., rev. ed., 1927).

Brinkman, Carl: *Recent Theories of Citizenship in Its Relation to Government* (Yale University Press, 1927).

Clark, Jane Perry: *The Deportation of Aliens from the United States to Europe* (Columbia University Press, 1931).

Davie, Maurice R.: *World Immigration* (Macmillan, rev. ed., 1936).

Fishel, Wesley R.: *The End of Extraterritoriality in China* (University of California Press, 1952).

Gettys, Cora Luella: *The Law of Citizenship in the United States* (University of Chicago Press, 1934).

Hansen, Marcus: *The Immigrant in American History* (Harvard University Press, 1940).

Hartman, Edward G.: *The Movement to Americanize the Immigrant* (Columbia University Press, 1948).

Holcombe, Arthur N.: *The More Perfect Union* (Harvard University Press, 1950).

——: *The Middle Class in American Politics* (Harvard University Press, 1940).

——: *The New Party Politics* (Norton, 1933).

Kansas, Sidney, *U.S. Immigration, Exclusion and Deportation, and Citizenship* (Albany: Bender, rev. ed., 1940).

Kohler, Max J.: *Immigration and Aliens in the United States* (New York: Bloch, 1936).

Konvitz, Milton R.: *Civil Rights in Immigration* (Cornell University Press, 1953).

——: *The Alien and the Asiatic in American Law* (Cornell University Press, 1946).

McKenzie, Roderick D.: *Oriental Exclusion* (University of Chicago Press, 1928).

Moore, John B.: *A Digest of International Law*, H. Doc. 551, 56th Cong., 2d Sess. (8 vols., 1906).

Myrdal, Gunnar: *Population: A Problem for Democracy* (Harvard University Press, 1940).

Seckler-Hudson, Catheryn: *Statelessness: With Special Reference to the United States* (Washington: Digest Press, 1934).

Silving, Helen: *Immigration Laws of the United States* (New York: Oceana Publishers, 1948).

Thompson, Warren S., and Pascal K. Whelpton: *Population Trends in the United States* (McGraw-Hill, 1933).

U.S. Department of Commerce, Bureau of the Census: *Forecasts of the Population of the United States, 1945–1975* (1947).

U.S. President's Commission on Immigration and Naturalization: *Whom We Shall Welcome, Report of the . . .* (1953).

U.S. President's Commission on Migratory Labor: *Migratory Labor in American Agriculture, Report of the . . .* (1951).

Wittke, Carl F.: *We Who Built America* (Western Reserve University Press, 1951).

REVIEW QUESTIONS

1. What are some of the political implications of population trends in the United States? Of racial trends?

2. What is the constitutional basis of federal regulation of immigration? What role may the states play in dealing with this subject?

3. Defend and criticize the restrictions which Congress has placed upon immigration.

4. How are immigration quotas determined for each nationality? How does the process differ since passage of the Immigration and Nationality Act of 1952?

5. What changes have been suggested for making fairer the procedures followed in admitting, debarring, and deporting aliens?

6. Defend and criticize provisions made in recent years for facilitating the emigration of displaced persons to the United States.

7. Compare the rights and privileges of resident aliens and citizens. Of naturalized and natural-born citizens.

8. Summarize recommendations made by President Truman's Committee on Immigration and reported in *Whom We Shall Welcome*.

9. Distinguish between the rule of *jus soli* and *jus sanguinis*. What is meant when it is said that a person has "dual nationality"?

10. Explain the rules which govern the determination of United States citizenship and illustrate each.

11. Explain to an alien the qualifications for naturalization and the steps he would have to take to become a citizen of the United States.

12. How, and for what reasons, may one forfeit citizenship or have it revoked?

CHAPTER 9

Public Opinion and Pressure Groups

The obvious weakness of government by opinion is the difficulty of ascertaining it. — James Bryce [1]

Americans of all ages, all conditions, and all dispositions constantly form associations. — Alexis de Tocqueville [2]

In its broadest sense the term "politics" means the relationship of the governor and the governed in every type of situation and institution involving people, not only in the state, but also in industry, a lodge, a club, a church, or a union.[3] For the student of government, however, the politics of the state is the major concern. He seeks data on how groups and individuals attempt to control offices and policies of government. He is only incidentally concerned with how the Reverend Brethren was selected moderator of the presbytery or with how John L. Lewis managed to rule the United Mine Workers so long. If the church starts a campaign to prohibit pinball games in taverns or if the union contributes $100,000 to a political fund, then the political scientist wants to know what they do and how they do it.

Even within the field of political science, the word "politics" has more than one meaning. Sometimes it is used to designate the entire art and science of government and is nearly synonymous with political science. More commonly, however, the term is used to indicate a subdivision of political science that includes public opinion, pressure groups, political parties, nominations and elections, legislation, and kindred matters. The other great division of political science comparable to politics is administration. Politics is policy formation; administration is policy execution. The loose and popular usage of "politics" to imply invidious manipulation and selfish spoils-seeking debases a word of lofty origin, a word that should be reserved for describing the citizen's role in the making of public policy.

As employed in the next three chapters, then, "politics" embraces all phases of the process of making public policy. Around the turn of the century, attention was directed toward the importance of political parties and their operation. In the 1920's came a fad of emphasizing the pressure group in the role of policy maker. Later, students of politics became intrigued with a new field called "public opinion," which in-

[1] *The American Commonwealth* (Macmillan, 2 vols., 1889), vol. 2, p. 345. Used by permission of the publishers.

[2] *Democracy in America* (Knopf, 2 vols., 1945), vol. 2, p. 106.

[3] Harold D. Lasswell, in his *Politics: Who Gets What, When, How* (McGraw-Hill, 1936), p. 1, declared: "The study of politics is the study of influence and the influential."

151

cludes some social psychology, propaganda and censorship, opinion measurement, and channels of communication. Each of these aspects will be dealt with in succeeding sections.

PUBLIC OPINION

The Democratic Political Process. The process of public policy making in free countries involves several distinct steps. In the first place, one must begin with individual opinion. Si

Groups also employ all the techniques of pressure commonly called "lobbying."

Third, there is the role of the political party. Parties make up their policy declarations, or platforms, from the opinions of individuals, often as crystallized by groups. In a two-party system party platforms are of necessity somewhat general in nature, for they represent compromises between diverse points of view. The American parties rarely place a plank in their platforms

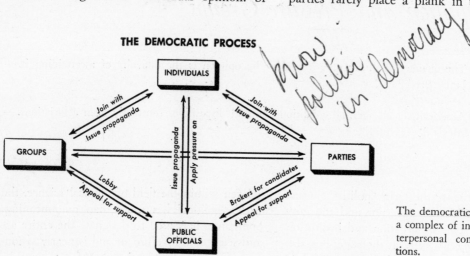

THE DEMOCRATIC PROCESS

The democratic process involves a complex of intergroup and interpersonal contacts and reactions.

Perkins's opinion on the tariff is determined by many factors, including emotions, environment, and reason. Emotions or impulses are classified variously by different psychologists, but lists of driving human forces normally include fear, sex, gregariousness, acquisitiveness, self-preservation, and others. Environment influences mightily the formation of the individual opinion; especially important are economic status, social standing, family situation, religious connections, and the like. The individual reasons within the framework of his impulses, his environment, and his mental abilities. Groups and persons with preconceived notions press the individual to accept their point of view on the subject.

Next, individuals of similar opinions unite to promote and to defend their interests. The groups they form—leagues, unions, associations, clubs, institutes, chambers—disseminate propaganda about their cause to influence individuals, other groups, political parties, and public officials.

until the policy represented by it is well worn and widely accepted. Parties act in the field of public policy formation as canalizers; taking the lesser streams of group opinion, they merge them into a mighty river. In that river as it flows to sea are the waters of thousands of tributaries, great and small. Naturally, much dilution of the original character of each contributing stream takes place.

Finally, public policy is formed by those who hold governmental power—executive, legislative, and judicial. Presidents and governors, legislatures and congresses, perhaps even courts, draw the policies they make public (through orders, laws, decisions) from the three major sources of opinion—individual, group, and party. A President who has wide public support may initiate "pet" projects conceived in his own mind or in those of influential advisers. Group pressure may result in congressional action for benefits regardless of party lines and party platforms. Where party discipline is strong, the party may play the major role in the declaration of public policy.

Meaning of Public Opinion. The term "public opinion" is a vague one. Like many other terms used in politics ("liberal," "reasonable," "sound," "efficient"), it means different things to different people. As popularly employed, public opinion

What of the inclusiveness of the word "public"? Does it mean the whole population? Does it mean only qualified voters? Rarely, if ever, could the whole population be considered as participating in public policy making. For practical purposes it means that sector of the population which can make a decision on the subject at hand on public questions.

WHAT IS THE AMERICAN PUBLIC?

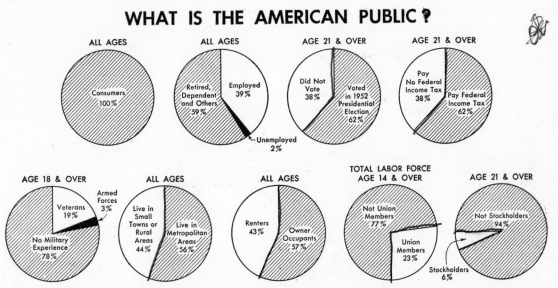

Various publics exist. Some of the groupings that affect attitudes on public questions are shown above. One of the most significant changes has been in the proportion of adults paying income tax. In 1940 only 12 per cent paid; in 1950 approximately 62 per cent paid. Courtesy of National Industrial Conference Board.

brings to mind an invisible force, mighty and mysterious, an unseen hand that guides democracies along the paths of righteousness. Used here, it means a belief, judgment or conclusion on a particular issue shared by a considerable section of the community, usually enough to influence policy. One of the pioneer public relations counselors has called it ". . . an ill-defined, mercurial and changeable group of individual judgments." [4] Public opinion is, then, an aggregate of individual beliefs.

[4] Edward L. Bernays, *Crystallizing Public Opinion* (New York: Boni & Liveright, 1923), p. 61. For recent comment of high quality, see Avery Leiserson, "Notes on the Theory of Political Opinion Formation," *American Political Science Review,* vol. XLVII (March, 1953), pp. 171–177.

Manifestations of Public Opinion. On hardly any issue can one say with finality that public opinion is "thus and so." There are several indexes of value, but no one is perfect, and each usually is capable of more than one interpretation. By a careful study of two or more, it may be possible for a student to draw valid conclusions regarding an issue.

First, *election returns* seldom show public sentiment on a single issue but rather on an aggregate of issues and candidates. A successful candidate will look upon his election as a mandate to follow a certain policy in respect to public problem No. 1, but his personality, stand on other issues, or party affiliation might have been quite as influential in determining election results. Rarely does one issue loom so large in a campaign that the verdict can be looked upon as a referendum on that question.

Second, *public referendums* and plebiscites may provide good evidence of the popular will on a given subject. Referendums are used in states permitting direct legislation and popular ratification of state constitutional amendments; they are also common in local governmental affairs. Their shortcomings arise from the fact that they are not very widely used and from the lack of intelligent participation by the voters. The latter weakness may be attributed to inertia or incapacity of the voters and to the complicated nature of many propositions.

Third, *lobbying and pressure* sometimes are mistaken for expressions of public opinion. All legislators and many administrators are under pressure by individuals and groups that pull and haul over every issue of importance. Of course, public officials take into consideration such pressure when deciding questions of policy. The pressure may, and often does, come from a very small minority. The legislator who determines his stand by counting the telegrams and letters he receives on a question and follows the advice of the greatest number often finds himself with the minority so far as real public opinion is concerned. With lobbying and pressure should be classed newspaper editorials and other types of private opinion, publicly expressed. No editor, however gifted or conceited, can claim unerringly to express the true voice of the people.

Fourth, *straw votes*, based on scientific sampling of a cross section of the population, have emerged as a reasonably accurate instrument of opinion measurement. Although perhaps too much has been claimed for the public-opinion polls, they do serve a useful purpose in indicating which way the winds of public sentiment are blowing.

Public-opinion Polls. The sampling of public opinion has been attempted for 50 years.[5] The earliest straw votes were conducted by newspapers. Because many polls involved the printing of ballots in the sponsoring journals or the

handing out of ballots on a very free basis, the results were likely to be highly inaccurate. Later other publications, notably the *Literary Digest,* undertook nation-wide polls of popular sentiment through mail ballots. Although this method proved more accurate than the ballot in the paper scheme, it was not possible to ensure a representative sample or cross section of the people.

During the 1930's "scientific" quota sampling was developed. This method requires a personal interview and great care to ensure the representativeness of the sample. In order to secure an accurate cross section of the population, the poll taker must obtain the proper proportion of persons from each state, sex, age group, income class, political party, and occupation. If a thoroughly representative sample is obtained, then the total number interviewed may be a very small fraction of the whole population. No matter how carefully controlled the quota sampling was, however, there was margin for error because of the natural tendency of the interviewer to approach the most available and articulate among the groups and categories assigned.

Over the years polling methods have changed gradually, from straight quota sampling toward probability sampling. The probability, or "pinpoint," method involves choosing barometer precincts or other small districts at random. The interviews are clustered in the adjoining houses, beginning with an assigned starting address. Interviewers call at every *n*th dwelling unit, and maintain age and sex ratios by a rotation plan. Both Gallup and Roper have moved toward probability sampling and have been well satisfied with results obtained. Among the advantages of the newer method for election forecasting are the more systematic selection of neighborhoods for interviewing, the availability of past election returns to judge the political representativeness of the sample, and the possibility of checking an interviewer's results against actual voting figures after the election.[6]

The two polls best known to the public are

[5] Claude E. Robinson, *Straw Votes: A Study in Political Prediction* (Columbia University Press, 1932), pp. 47–52.

[6] George Gallup, "The Future Direction of Election Polling," *Public Opinion Quarterly,* vol. 17 (September, 1953), pp. 202–207.

the American Institute of Public Opinion, headed by Dr. George Gallup, and the Roper Survey, conducted by Elmo Roper. Both were founded in 1935. The Gallup poll is conducted by a central staff in Princeton, N.J., and by several hundred part-time field workers throughout the country. Results are sold to subscribing newspapers. Gallup uses a somewhat larger sample than does Roper and is able to conduct

that of predicting election results. The *Literary Digest* poll flourished under the spell of its success in calling the elections of the 1920's and perished after its colossal failure in the 1936 election. Examination of the figures given below will indicate how badly the *Literary Digest* poll miscarried in 1936; its failure was due mainly to the reliance placed upon securing expressions of opinion by mail from automobile

---

330
1952 Pinpoint-I
9-22-52

THE GALLUP POLL

SPONSORED BY LEADING REPUBLICAN, DEMOCRATIC AND INDEPENDENT NEWSPAPERS

SUGGESTED INTRODUCTION: I'm taking a GALLUP POLL. I'd like YOUR opinion on a few leading topics of the day. This GALLUP POLL survey will be reported in (mention nearest *Institute newspaper*).

Here's the first question I want to ask you:

1. Do you think it would be a good idea, in planning the MAIN highways of the future, to have a separate lane for trucks?
   ¹☐ **Good Idea**   ²☐ **Fair**   ³☐ **Poor**   ⁴☐ **No Opinion**

2. How much thought have you given to the coming election for President—quite a lot, or only a little?
   ¹☐ **Lot**   ²☐ **Some**   ³☐ **Little**   ⁴☐ **None**

3. If the presidential election were being held TODAY, which political party would you like to see win—the Democratic party or the Republican party?
   ¹☐ **Democratic**   ²☐ **Republican**   ³☐ **Undecided**
   ⁴☐ **Other** ....   ⁵☐ **Refuses to Answer**

IF UNDECIDED IN 3, ASK:

4. As of today, do you lean a little more to the Democratic party or a little more to the Republican party?
   ⁶☐ **Dem.**   ⁷☐ **Rep.**   ⁸☐ **Other** ....   ⁹☐ **Undecided**

Now, I'd like to get your honest opinion on this next question. It doesn't make any difference to me how you vote . . . I only want to get YOUR views accurately:

12. If the presidential election were being held TODAY, which CANDIDATE would you vote for—Stevenson, the Democratic candidate, or Eisenhower, the Republican candidate?
   ¹☐ **Stevenson**   ²☐ **Eisenhower**   ³☐ **Undecided**
   ⁴☐ **Other** ....   ⁵☐ **Refuses to Answer**

IF UNDECIDED IN 12, ASK:

13. As of today, do you lean a little more to Stevenson or a little more to Eisenhower?
   ⁶☐ **Stevenson**   ⁷☐ **Eisenhower**   ⁸☐ **Undecided**

14a. Will you tell me who the head of the International Military Coordinating Commission is? ....
   ☐ **Don't know**

IF CHARLES FOSTER MENTIONED, ASK:

b. What is your opinion of Foster? ....,..
....
....

This is an extract from a Gallup questionnaire used in 1952. Information required for assuring the cross section was secured in part through questioning the respondent and in part by observation of the interviewer.

---

a poll on a given question in a shorter time. The Roper poll is conducted from a New York headquarters through a rather small number of field interviewers.

Two commercial polls that occasionally delve into election forecasting are the Crossley Poll and the United States Poll of the Princeton Research Service. Other polls, less well known to the public but doing important work on the frontiers of opinion research, are the Princeton Office of Public Opinion Research, directed by Hadley Cantril, and the National Opinion Research Center of the University of Chicago, headed by Clyde W. Hart.

Election Predictions. By far the most dramatic of the tests applied to public-opinion polls is

owners and telephone subscribers. A comparison of presidential election predictions and votes is shown in the table below.

Until 1948 Roper appeared to demonstrate an uncanny ability to predict popular votes in national elections, but in the 1948 presidential election he underestimated the Truman vote by well over 10 per cent. Gallup underrated the Democratic vote at four elections, actually missing by a wider margin in 1936 than in 1948.

Dozens of reasons have been offered to explain the 1948 debacle of the pollsters. Critics declare that the polls consistently have misjudged the opinions of lower-income groups, because such people are tense, insecure, and suspicious of college-trained interviewers. Most of

Year	Actual vote, per cent	Literary Digest, per cent	Gallup AIPO, per cent	Roper poll, per cent	Crossley poll, per cent	U.S. poll, per cent
1936	60.7	40.9	53.8	61.7	53.8	
1940	55.0	....	52.0	55.2		
1944	53.8	....	53.3	53.6	52.2	
1948	52.3	....	47.3	41.5	47.3	
1952	44.6	....	49.0	....	....	49.0

Democratic Percentage of Major-party Vote

NOTE: In 1952 only the new United States Poll predicted the election returns in precise terms; Gallup cautiously reported the figures with two modes of distributing the undecided: one giving Stevenson on a 2-to-1 ratio, and the other on a 3-to-1. The 2-to-1 distribution is used above. Actually, Eisenhower probably won a majority of the undecided group.

the polls completed their sampling weeks before the election and therefore could not take into account last-minute changes in opinions. After the 1948 election Gallup and Roper looked back over their records and found an unusually high proportion of their interviewees had answered "undecided." In 1952 the polls improved their techniques and interpreted results with great caution.

The significance of the opinion poll is still being debated hotly. Some enthusiasts predict that the poll has opened up a new era of democracy in which the masses become articulate and representatives hear the authentic voice of the people. Enemies of straw voting claim that polling in advance of an election has a band-wagon effect on voters who drop their own convictions and vote on what they believe to be the winning side. Critics have expressed fear that the polls might be rigged to show desired results but have been answered effectively with the argument that a successful business concern or journal will not risk its reputation lightly. Students of opinion measurement have been very active during recent years in working out new techniques and in rectifying errors. In general, they conclude that the modern opinion poll is a useful device of democracy, but is neither panacea nor taps for our institutions.

Propaganda. In a broad sense, propaganda is the "technique of influencing human action by manipulation of representations."[7] It is effort directed at securing public support for an opinion or a policy; it is special pleading or arguing for one's own convictions. Usage in English has added to the word an invidious connotation, narrowing the scope of its meaning. Now it means special pleading that is rigged in some respect, that conceals something or that states the case in overdrawn terms. In practice, Americans use propaganda to describe the arguments of opponents, but refer to their own pleadings as merely stating the case or as presenting the facts. Since few, if any, proponents of an idea ever present their arguments in a wholly impartial manner, it is well to adhere to a broad definition of the term. Therefore, the terms "propaganda," "special pleading," and "publicity" will be used as meaning much the same thing.

Over a 4-year period, 1937 through 1941, the endowed Institute for Propaganda Analysis issued regular bulletins reviewing various aspects of the propaganda question. A prerequisite of these studies was a classification of propaganda devices that appeared in one of the initial is-

[7] Harold D. Lasswell, "Propaganda," *Encyclopedia of the Social Sciences,* vol. 12, p. 521.

sues.[8] Seven common propaganda devices were isolated: (1) name calling, (2) glittering generalities, (3) transfer, (4) testimonial, (5) plain folks, (6) card stacking, and (7) band wagon.

Name calling is used as a substitute for arguing; bad names like red or fascist are assigned to opponents and the core of a controversy need never be reached. To employ glittering generalities or prove a point with a single instance, you devour an adversary with a sweeping generalization, such as: "John is a trade unionist and a socialist; therefore all unionists are socialists." Transfer means that an existing confidence in something is carried over to the propagandist's cause; thus every political movement calls itself 100 per cent American. The use of testimonials is common both in advertising and in politics; the opinion of a person is used to give prestige to a commodity or a candidate. Plain-folks appeal aims to win confidence by plain, homey doings; for example, the office seeker poses with his family or dons overalls and tries to act like a farmer. Card stacking includes any sort of fact juggling or falsification. A band-wagon appeal is an appeal to join the crowd, for "everyone's doing it."

The institute's classification is interesting and useful, but it is not complete, nor is each device mutually exclusive. It leaves out repetition, often called a leading weapon in word warfare. Hitler, in *Mein Kampf,* said:

The masses, however, with their inertia, always need a certain time before they are ready even to notice a thing and they will lend their memories only to the thousandfold repetition of the most simple ideas.[9]

The necessity for simplicity is stressed over and over in Hitler's writings; simple ideas must be repeated until the least intelligent can understand or will believe. The appeal, therefore, is mainly on the emotional plane. Other rules of propaganda include never admitting virtue on the other side, using the spectacular to attract attention, avoiding arguments.[10]

Censorship. Propaganda may be made more effective by the simultaneous use of censorship. Censorship is the suppression of facts or opinions that might undermine the existing order or authorities. In peacetime we have a mild form of censorship, in that lewd and immoral publications are denied transit and sale, and that some states make criminal the utterance of revolutionary sentiments advocating the overthrow of government by force.

In wartime censorship is more extensive; in general, it forbids the publication of any matter that may aid the enemy or handicap the nation's war effort. This is a very broad control, and specific regulation comes from agencies set up for the purpose. In the First World War both propaganda and censorship were handled by George Creel's Committee on Public Information.[11] In the Second World War, after some preliminary organizing and reorganizing, power over censorship was assigned to the office of Censorship, headed by Byron Price. The Office of War Information, directed by Elmer Davis, handled the affirmative publicity task.

Even in wartime, censorship in the United States has been largely of the so-called "voluntary" type. Newspapers and radio stations were given lists of what were regarded as matters best left unpublicized. If there was a question about whether or not a certain event should be hushed up, it might be referred to the appropriate governmental agency for a reply.

Censorship at the source is one of the most potent methods known. If the Army or Navy refuses to give out data on some military action of importance, newsmen have no alternative but to wait until a communiqué is issued. Many foreign governments close up sources of information and leave correspondents with no news to report. American reporters abroad have developed ingenious methods of evading censor-

[8] *Propaganda Analysis,* vol. 1, no. 2 (November, 1937).

[9] Adolf Hitler, *Mein Kampf* (Reynal & Hitchcock, 1940), p. 239.

[10] For further reading on general propaganda, see references listed at the end of this chapter.

[11] See James R. Mock, *Censorship—1917* (Princeton University Press, 1941).

ship imposed by foreign governments. Despite censorship at the source, they often manage to eke out information from reluctant officials. If one mode of communication is censored and another is not, then the free channel is used; in the 1930's stories were telephoned out of Germany with little restraint, while the same information was forbidden by telegraph and radio. American press and radio network correspondents frequently are withdrawn from censorship countries and assigned to free ones in order to write a series of articles on what goes on inside the censored country.

An intelligent student of public affairs can keep himself rather well informed regardless of censorship. In respect to news originating in this country, he must bear in mind that while libel laws deter the publication or broadcast of some stories, they eliminate chiefly those of doubtful validity or those concerning which there is no conclusive factual proof. Although the circulation of some books and magazines is interfered with occasionally by local authorities and by the Post Office Department, the cases of injustice are few. The reader or the listener must not forget to note the sources of his information and the nature of the channel through which he receives it. His suspicions should be aroused by a sensational story about one country date-lined from another country. The regular press services, especially Associated Press and United Press, have good reputations, and credence in their dispatches usually is justified, but some other services and "special correspondents" frequently slant the news to fit the prejudices of their owners and masters. Radio and television stations are licensed by the Federal Communications Commission and are restrained by the necessity of securing periodic renewal of licenses.

Channels of Communication. Public opinion is influenced actively through the dissemination of information—called "propaganda" or "education," depending on one's prejudices—and by a great number of other forces as well. The mediums through which opinion is influenced are varied. Nearly all social institutions, such as the family, the school, the church, and the club, in-

fluence the thinking of people on public questions. All of us acquire opinions from friends and associates, teachers, preachers, lecturers, debaters, novelists, and playwrights. The average person daily adopts points of view or information from newspapers, radio, television, motion pictures, magazines, pamphlets, and other instruments of distributing intelligence.

The Newspaper. The newspaper often is designated as the most potent molder of public opinion in the mass. Newspapers of some sort reach a majority of homes in the United States regularly. In 1954 there were 11,468 newspapers published in the United States. Of these, 1,875 were dailies, with an aggregate circulation of 54,048,953; Sunday circulation totaled 45,641,902.[12]

Since newspapers are widely read and, in some cases at least, highly influential, their ownership and policies are matters of vital public interest. Most newspapers are money-making enterprises, conducted mainly for the profit of their owners. To make a profit, a newspaper must build up a circulation, and, intimately connected with that, get advertising. Although the greater income derives from advertising, the newspaper must maintain its circulation at a high level in order to attract advertisers. With a few exceptions, the political policy of a newspaper is determined by the opinions of the owner or owners. It must be borne in mind, however, that a paper's policy may be influenced by the beliefs and sentiments of both readers and advertisers. The former, reader censorship, is often underestimated; newspaper buyers effectively modify policies by going on strike—refusing to buy or to resubscribe because of a disagreement with editorial policy. The latter, pressure by advertisers, frequently is overstressed; it is likely to be a subtle force operating as a restraining or accelerating force, but unlikely to manifest itself in the crude form of direct threats by advertisers.

Many of the evils of the newspaper world are blamed on the tendency toward concentrating ownership in fewer hands. News tends to be

[12] *Directory of Newspapers and Periodicals, 1954* (Ayer, 1954), p. 8.

standardized; the editorial prejudices of one man may be presented to millions daily; in a crisis extra power is concentrated in the hands of those who control chains of newspapers. The outstanding example of multiple newspaper control in America was found in the vast interests of the late William Randolph Hearst. Hearst at one time controlled twenty-nine daily newspapers in eighteen large cities; in three cities Hearst papers had more than one-half of all daily circulation; in three others his papers approached one-half.[13] In order to survive a severe financial crisis in 1938–1939, Hearst interests liquidated some less profitable holdings. By 1954 sixteen papers in twelve cities remained in the chain, but control was retained over news and feature services in others. In national influence the Hearst group is being pressed by the Scripps-Howard papers, which numbered nineteen in 1954.[14] The entrance and exit of Marshall Field as a champion of the liberal press has served to remind us how close to impossible it is to launch a new daily newspaper in a large metropolitan area even if great financial resources are available.

In general, the observing newspaper reader will find that a large proportion of the nonlocal dispatches in the average newspaper comes from one of the great wire services. Few newspapers can afford to keep a staff of reporters at the diverse spots in the world from which news is likely to originate. Therefore, nearly all dailies and many papers issued less frequently subscribe to one or more of the great news services. The Associated Press, designated AP, is a cooperative news-gathering agency owned by the newspapers it serves; it maintains bureaus in strategic points throughout the world but relies mainly on member newspapers for local news. The United Press is a private agency that sells its services on contract with newspapers, especially afternoon publications; its own staff collects news and wires it to subscribing newspapers. Both AP and UP present the news in an objective manner; a paper's local news may be colored and its editorial page may exhibit bias, but the reader desiring impartial treatment of the news may be reasonably certain of the accuracy of AP or UP news stories. The headlines, however, are composed in the newspaper office and may reflect the bias of the owner or staff; this factor is particularly important because many people scan newspapers superficially, scarcely reading beyond the heads.

Newspapers are not obliged to print all the news stories that the wire services send to them; obviously they could not, for space is limited and a great bulk of news stories is available. In choosing which dispatches are to be used and which are to be thrown away, the editor must exercise much discretion which may be highly effective in influencing public opinion. An editor, under orders from his owner-publisher, may throw away stories that place a certain political leader in a favorable or neutral light and print only those that show him unfavorably. Or, perhaps more deadly still, newspapers may decline to publish anything about a political enemy; many politicians feel that being ignored by the press is one of the worst things that can happen to them.

The Radio and Television. The broadcasting industry furnishes two very important modern mediums for influencing public opinion. Advertisers, politicians, and government recognize its importance as a means of conditioning the thinking of people. The number of receiving sets of all sorts was estimated in 1954 at 117 million.[15] This is enough for $2\frac{1}{2}$ sets to every family; it is believed that over 98 per cent of American homes have one or more receivers, a coverage considerably more complete than that of newspapers. In the same year there were the following major broadcasting authorizations: 2,697 AM (amplitude-modulation) standard-band stations, 569 FM (frequency-modulation) short-wave stations, and 573 television stations.

The early development of the broadcasting business was chaotic and haphazard. The Department of Commerce attempted to exercise some control under the authority of a weak act

[13] Oliver Carlson and Ernest S. Bates, *Hearst, Lord of San Simeon* (Viking, 1937), pp. 301–303.
[14] *Political Handbook of the World, 1954.*

[15] U.S. Federal Communications Commission, *Annual Report . . . 1954* (1955), pp. 105–109.

of 1912 governing ship-to-shore communications. The Federal Radio Act of 1927 and the Federal Communications Act of 1934 granted extensive powers over broadcasters to a regulatory commission. The system of control that the United States has evolved differs materially from that found in most other countries; here private initiative is given greater play, while abroad broadcasting is often a government monopoly in whole or in part, with radio advertising curtailed or forbidden.

The extent of governmental control bears upon the question of public opinion in several ways. Private owners cannot use radio or TV stations for the dissemination of their own particular ideas. They are, in addition, subject to the limitation imposed by law which requires that all candidates for public office shall have equal opportunities to rent time on the air. Moreover, the radio and TV audience is a fleeting thing; because listeners may tune out easily, the broadcaster's propaganda must be at once discreet and entertaining. The broadcaster must also bear in mind that he is engaged in a business vested with public interest, and if his record shows an overload of political propaganda on one side, he may be refused when he applies to the FCC for the renewal of his license to operate each 3 years.

Because radio and television time is sold for commercial advertising, political groups wishing broadcasting facilities for a desirable evening hour must pay large sums of money for the privilege or ask for "sustaining" (free) time. If a national audience is desired, then it is necessary to negotiate with one of the four great broadcasting systems—the National Broadcasting Company, the Columbia Broadcasting System, the Mutual Broadcasting System, or the American Broadcasting Company, or with some of the regional networks. These great chains own some stations and make contracts with others that are individually owned. The national networks exercise a fairly rigid supervision—called "editorial discretion" by them and "censorship" by their opponents—which operates to curtail what the broadcasting companies regard as "poor taste" or "propaganda." Until 1945 both NBC and

CBS followed the general rule of refusing to sell time for the discussion of public issues, except in the period between the national party conventions and the general election in November every 4 years. All networks give some time free of charge to opposing sides of important public questions.

News broadcasts constitute a second great means of influencing the public mind. The terse news reports over radio and television give a minimum of information on current events, and rarely give any suggestion of editorialization. Many of the news commentators, however, are clearly expressing opinions, and may have a considerable influence in determining public reactions to given situations.

It is now generally understood that the number of standard broadcast channels is limited by physical laws. The number available is also restricted by international agreement. The need for regulation is obvious to most people; the chaos of the 1926 period sufficed to convince even the most doubting that governmental assignment of frequencies was essential. As radio developed, it was inevitable that stations would unite to present common programs of regional and national interest. In 1948, over 1,100 AM stations were affiliated with one of the four national networks. After a 3-year study of chain broadcasting, the FCC in 1941 ordered stations not to make exclusive contracts with networks, to limit station contracts with networks to one year, and to cease affiliation with any chain owning more than one network. The latter provision forced NBC to dispose of its Blue Network, now the ABC. Both CBS and NBC protested vigorously against the FCC order and challenged its validity in the courts. Mutual favored the report. The courts upheld the FCC order and it is now in effect.[16]

It appears unlikely that American radio and television will follow the broadcasting systems of most other countries in establishing a publicly owned monopoly. For better or for worse, this country may be expected to continue with the existing plan of regulated private enterprise. The

[16] U.S. Federal Communications Commission, *Report on Chain Broadcasting* (1941).

principal controversy is likely to concern the extent of FCC control. Naturally, the established interests wish to retain their favorable position under a minimum of regulation, and the outsiders desire rules and orders that will permit them to enter the field. Serious questions of public policy emerge.

In 1946 the FCC issued a "blue book" entitled *Public Service Responsibility of Broadcast Licensees* which laid down the following standards that will be taken into account in granting or renewing licenses: (1) a reasonable number of sustaining programs, (2) some local "live" programs, (3) adequate time for discussion of public issues and balanced treatment of controversies, and (4) elimination of advertising excesses. The National Association of Broadcasters protested that these rules would mean censorship and loss of freedom of speech.

The ownership pattern in broadcasting also has been regulated by FCC rules, which now limit a single owner to seven stations in each category: AM, FM, and TV. The commission also has an order forbidding multiple ownership of AM stations in overlapping primary coverage areas. The regulatory body has sought in vain legislation which would permit it to control the transfer of station ownership. Stations are being sold for sums far in excess of their physical value. Since the number of standard-band frequencies available is strictly limited, the FCC grants what is in effect a monopolistic privilege. Other public utilities are forced to accept rate regulation, control of earnings, and checking on the quality of their service. Why should broadcast licensees be exempt? In 1949 the FCC further intervened in the program content field by banning "giveaway" programs; the networks fought the prohibition in court, and the Supreme Court invalidated the FCC regulation.[17]

Grave issues concerning the freedom of the air remain. The law requires a station permitting one candidate to speak to grant the same privilege to an opposing candidate. This has not assured true equality of access to the air to persons of diverse political and economic philosophies. Perhaps the greatest hope for fuller freedom of the air lies in the development of the FM field. Some authorities estimate that about 5,000 FM broadcasting stations may be possible in the United States. Such an expansion could open the air waves to nearly all opinion groups of the country. The development of FM, however, appears to have been stunted by the rapid rise of television. Instead of purchasing FM sets after the war, people in and near metropolitan areas turned to television. The video version of the radio medium is so attractive and absorbing that it has already cut heavily into AM listening and motion-picture attendance. The large investment required for a television station and the prospect for months or years of operating losses has tended to concentrate ownership in the hands of large economic interests. The FCC and the public have a great stake in seeing that maximum freedom is retained in television, which has so much potentiality for revolutionizing educational and entertainment practices.

The Motion Picture. The motion picture is also a powerful molder of opinions and attitudes. The statistics on the products of filmland are impressive. In 1954 between 50 million and 55 million Americans attended motion pictures weekly; the industry had a capital investment of nearly three billion dollars; the United States supplied most of the world films.[18] The ownership pattern of production, distribution, and exhibition facilities is similar to that of newspaper and broadcasting chains. Eight major corporations dominate the industry: Metro-Goldwyn-Mayer, Twentieth Century-Fox, Warner Brothers, Paramount, United Artists, Radio-Keith-Orpheum, Universal, and Columbia. Some producers of note are independent, but many have working agreements with one of the major studios.

Regular feature films are more likely to shape attitudes than opinion. There is a strong proclivity to glorify wealth, elaborate homes, and well-dressed people. Producers find it safer and more profitable to stress sex appeal rather than social

[17] Federal Communications Commission *v.* American Broadcasting Co., 347 U.S. 284 (1954).

[18] *Motion Picture and Television Almanac, 1955,* pp. ix and xvi.

problems. Crime is a favorite subject, but the Motion Picture Producers and Distributors of America (Johnston Office) requires that criminals be punished in the film.

Newsreels are second to the feature films in commercial importance. Generally about 10 minutes in length, they are almost invariably shown, even with double-feature programs. The five principal producers are Hearst Metrotone, Movietone, Universal, Paramount, and Warner Pathé. Each one does a fairly objective job of reporting.

A related field is that of educational and commercial films. They are made for and financed by organized groups, business concerns, and other bodies. Some second-grade movie houses will show advertising pictures if a fee is paid. Most of these pictures, however, are shown in schools, churches, clubs, and other groups.

Governments restrain the motion-picture industry comparatively little. A few states have established boards of censorship; occasionally a film is banned by some local authority. Most of the regulation of the industry either is self-imposed or comes from private associations.

Sporadically, proposals are made in Congress for legislation to break up the centralization of the production-distribution industry. Some are aimed at the device of "block-booking" and "blind-selling." These terms mean that an exhibitor buys a year's supply of films consisting largely of unknowns; if he declines to book blind, the distributor may refuse to supply him with any films, or may make the price impossibly high. Although no bill has yet been enacted by Congress, the companies, when threatened with antitrust prosecution, agreed to curb the worst abuses. Most of the companies have now reorganized in order to separate their producing and exhibiting functions.

PRESSURE GROUPS

Reason for Pressure Groups. Recognizing that "in unity there is strength," individuals with common interests and like points of view join together into a mass of associations, clubs, unions, and leagues. These groups, together with business companies, corporations, and partnerships, may have interests that they wish to promote or defend through governmental action or inaction. Increasingly organized groups and business interests are finding contacts with government essential to their welfare. Therefore, they set up headquarters in Washington and in the state capitals and bring pressure to bear upon both legislators and executives. This activity, popularly known as "lobbying," is usually quite a legitimate exercise of the right to petition for redress of grievances; normally it operates under the guaranties of freedom of speech and press.

The necessity for group representation arises in part from the impossibility of representing perfectly all the diverse elements of society through the regular elective and appointive officials. In this country nearly all legislatures are elected from single-member geographical districts, a situation that notoriously magnifies the strength of a majority or a plurality and minimizes the influence of minorities. Denied direct representation in legislative bodies, or achieving only a small measure of it, or frustrated in attempts to make parties take their policies, organizations have resorted to extralegal means of making their influence felt. Elective officials are constantly concerned that their actions harmonize with that phantom, public opinion. Pressure groups provide a real service in directing and stimulating expressions of opinion by their membership and other interested persons.

Special-interest groups are both numerous and varied. Several students have estimated that the number of significant pressure bodies operating on a national scale is about five hundred. Some of the groups have large numbers of dues-paying members, such as the great farm groups and labor unions; others lack a definite membership but are effective because they have money to spend and advocate a cause in which many people are vitally interested, like the public-utility companies. Lobbying organizations may also be classified according to their aims: most are interested in the welfare of a special sector of society; some, however, like the moral groups, have programs that are "uplift" in nature, designed to help the other fellow.

Farm Groups in Politics. The leading agrarian organizations on the national scene are the American Farm Bureau Federation and the National Grange; the Farmers' Union and groups set up on commodity lines, often producers' cooperatives, play a lesser but important role. The Farm Bureau is much younger than the Grange, but it has achieved a strength in Congress not enjoyed by its rival. It has a large dues-paying membership, a budget of commensurate size, and a staff of well-paid and qualified employees and officers. Nationally, the Farm Bureau has a reputation for being considerably to the left of the Grange; it has been a persistent advocate of farm relief, of "parity," of "McNary-Haugenism," of the AAA. The Farm Bureau was launched as a national organization in 1920. Its remarkable growth is due in no small part to the early connection between the bureau and the agricultural extension services, cosponsored by the state universities and the federal Department of Agriculture. The farm advisers or county agents sought means of reaching farmers in groups, and their connections with local Farm Bureau centers followed. Although there is no uniform pattern over the country, the county agent is the active promoter and organizer of the Farm Bureau in many states.[19] Before Congress, the Farm Bureau is vigorous, emphatic, and demanding. Geographically, the Farm Bureau is strongest in the Middle West.

The Grange has a rich historical background; after a modest beginning in the 1860's, it swept to great strength in the next two decades as the spearhead of agrarian revolt. While still retaining the trappings of old—the fraternal order form, the ritual, the glorification of farm life—the modern Grange has become the conservative among national farm groups. Its stand on present-day issues reflects the conservatism of the Northeastern farmers, who constitute the most influential section of membership. The Grange lobbies in Congress less actively than does its rival. It has been hostile to many New Deal proposals and unenthusiastic about others. The Farmers' Union is influential on the western side of the Mississippi Valley and is devoted to a program of cooperative endeavor. Representing less prosperous farmers, it takes a somewhat more liberal view on issues than does either the Grange or the Farm Bureau. Some of the organizations in particular commodity fields, such as dairymen, peanut growers, and others, exert very great influence upon legislation and administrative policy that concerns them.

Organized Labor. Leading the field of labor organizations in the United States is the newly unified American Federation of Labor—Congress of Industrial Organizations (AFL-CIO); unaffiliated but powerful in their own right are the railroad brotherhoods and other independent unions.

The AFL and the CIO merged in 1955 after 20 years of separate existence and recurring warfare. Conventions met in December to liquidate the two rival federations. Delegates from each then met together to adopt officially the constitution on which joint committees had been working for months. The former AFL officials took the lion's share of offices in the combined organization, as agreed in unity committee and justified by numbers of members.

Political action proved to be one of the most difficult areas in which to combine forces. Because political programs of the former AFL League for Political Education and the former CIO Political Action Committee were so different, the new AFL-CIO decided to approach integration slowly. The Committee on Political Education (COPE) will be the political front of the new federation. In view of the imminence of the 1956 election, the former AFL and CIO political chiefs were made co-chairmen for the time being. Following the election the chairmanship is expected to go to an AFL leader. The political tactics of the combined AFL-CIO are likely to represent an amalgam of those developed over the years by the political wings of the separate federations.

[19] The role of the county agent is traced thoroughly in Gladys Baker, *The County Agent* (University of Chicago Press, 1939). Two other books on farm organizations are Wesley McCune, *The Farm Bloc* (Doubleday, 1943), and Orville M. Kile, *The Farm Bureau through Three Decades* (Baltimore: Waverly Press, 1948).

The American Federation of Labor was organized in 1886, after previous experimentation with earlier adaptations of the British Trades Union Congress model. From the beginning the AFL engaged in both economic and political activities. Since the primary work on the economic front was done by the individual unions that belonged to the federation, the AFL and the state federations of labor tended to emphasize political activities. Samuel Gompers, founder of the AFL, opposed direct participation in politics and sponsored a policy of rewarding friends and defeating enemies. The AFL lobbies vigorously for its objectives in the political field but does not affiliate with any party. It prefers to support proved friends and to defeat opponents regardless of party label.

In the early thirties conflict within the AFL over organizing policies reached an acute stage. Some of the strongest member unions, which were set up on an industrial, as opposed to a craft, basis, sought to spur organization of the unorganized on an industrial basis. They formed a Committee for Industrial Organization in 1935; the next year the AFL council ordered these unions to quit the CIO or be suspended from the AFL. Conflicts of personalities over organizing zeal and other factors not directly connected with the industrial versus craft controversy were important in the split. Most of the unions originally connected with the CIO withdrew from the AFL.

In its new role of rival body, the CIO, led by John L. Lewis of the United Mine Workers, put organizers into the field in mass-production industries—steel, automobile, rubber, and others —and aroused a pitch of enthusiasm for unionism scarcely before known in the country. Soon the CIO unions claimed an aggregate membership above that of the AFL. Eventually the CIO was put on a more permanent basis and its name was changed to Congress of Industrial Organizations. On the political front, the CIO unions led in the formation of Labor's Nonpartisan League, which entered the campaigns of 1936 and 1938 with slashing aggressiveness but with only modest success.

The independent unions, especially the powerful railroad brotherhoods, maintain separate lobbyists in the national and state capitals, but in common matters they cooperate closely with AFL-CIO representatives. Although beset with family quarreling and jurisdictional disputes, American organized labor often is substantially united in its general legislative goals and methods. Lobbying of the direct and blunt type is employed widely. Through endorsements of candidates and campaign activities the unions seek to help friends and defeat enemies. Their success in recent decades in securing favorable legislation, like the National Labor Relations Act and the wages-and-hours law, is eloquent testimony as to the effectiveness of these methods. Many observers feel, however, that American labor someday will follow the lead of other labor movements in forming or joining a third party devoted to the interests of labor, perhaps attempting to serve farmers as well.[20]

In November, 1943, the CIO undertook political action on a scale and with a consistency previously unequaled in the American labor movement. The CIO Political Action Committee, headed by Sidney Hillman, was directed to conduct a broad campaign to mobilize organized labor for action on the progressive political front.[21] The CIOPAC collected its initial funds of more than $600,000 from the unions; it spent more than one-half this amount up to July 23 (the day Mr. Roosevelt was nominated), when it decided to freeze its funds from union sources and to raise money by individual contributions of $1. In mid-1944 it was decided to launch a companion organization, the National Citizens Political Action Committee, in order to include people not affiliated with CIO unions. Both committees continued in existence after the 1944 election. It is generally conceded that

[20] Valuable background material will be found in Mollie Ray Carroll, *Labor and Politics* (Houghton Mifflin, 1923); Lewis L. Lorwin, *The American Federation of Labor* (Brookings, 1933); Rowland H. Harvey, *Samuel Gompers, Champion of the Toiling Masses* (Stanford University Press, 1935).

[21] Joseph Gaer, *The First Round: The Story of the CIO Political Action Committee* (Duell, Sloan & Pearce, 1944), pp. 60–63.

the PAC was partly responsible for the heavy vote in the 1944 election and for the defeat of a number of alleged antilabor and reactionary members of the Senate and House.

In 1946 the labor groups relaxed, the vote was low, and labor-endorsed candidates were defeated in many areas. Enactment of the Taft-Hartley Act by the Eightieth Congress followed. Enraged, the unions plunged into political activity with renewed vigor. The AFL put money and effort into the work of its Labor's League for Political Education. The CIOPAC continued to serve as the political spearhead of the industrial unions. With some exceptions, the labor leadership supported Mr. Truman; his 1948 victory, and that of the Democrats in both House and Senate, may be attributed in part to labor's political activity.[22] Both sections of organized labor backed Stevenson in 1952.

Business Interests. Unlike farm and labor elements, business interests have no membership in the millions. Nor is there so much unity in the organization of business as exists among farmers and workers. Business, however, does have the power of money to a degree unmatched by the other two great elements in society. As America becomes more and more industrialized, commercial interests gain in relative importance. The Chamber of Commerce of the United States and the National Association of Manufacturers are the mightiest of business groups; behind them rank hundreds of trade associations in every conceivable industry.

The national Chamber of Commerce since 1912 has been the outstanding business group of this country. Its total affiliated membership has almost reached the one-million mark in good times, and it has connections with state and local bodies and branches. The Chamber of Commerce slogan "Less government in business and more business in government" was discredited considerably in the great depression, but that policy is still adhered to by many. Most proposals for social reform or protective labor legislation have received opposition. One feature

of Chamber of Commerce procedure differs from that of the average pressure group. The stand of Chamber lobbyists on pending national legislation sometimes is determined through a referendum, in which member organizations indicate their opinions by questionnaire answers. The Chamber of Commerce of the United States is reasonably representative of the various business interests of the country.

The National Association of Manufacturers was established in 1895. It is more vigorously antilabor and hostile toward social legislation than the Chamber. Besides lobbying in Congress, the NAM engages extensively in propaganda through motion pictures, radio, television, and press.

During and since the Second World War, forward-looking business interests have joined together to form the Committee for Economic Development, which has issued a number of basic economic studies.

Trade associations numbered approximately 8,000 in 1940, of which 2,000 were national in scope.[23] Each one exists for the purpose of defending or promoting interests of those who participate in the industry. Although they sometimes engage in price fixing and other practices of doubtful legality, it is quite proper for them to seek special representation for their industry or line. These groups, great and small, cover such diverse industries as brewing, tombstones, sugar refining, baking, and liquor distilling. While they are substantially united on labor and tax issues, they may fight each other over tariff schedules and other matters.

Other Groups. Through professional societies the physician, the attorney, the teacher, the dentist, the architect, achieve special representation for their professions. Women's groups of influence—the National League of Women Voters, the Federation of Women's Clubs, the Business and Professional Women's Clubs—are interested in a vast range of governmental matters, some affecting women and children, but some gen-

---

[22] For an account of 1948 and 1950 activities of CIOPAC, see Fay Calkins, *CIO and the Democratic Party* (University of Chicago Press, 1952).

[23] U.S. Congress, Temporary National Economic Committee, *Final Report of the Executive Secretary,* 77th Cong., 1st Sess., Senate Committee Print (1941), p. 85.

eral in nature. Efforts of a number of women's groups are coordinated through a Women's Joint Congressional Committee.

Reformers of all shades also secure a voice in Washington through organized groups, such as antiliquor, antivice, anti-spoils-system associations; religious groups often indulge in special pleading for reforms. Various veterans' organizations do battle with one another and with the peace groups, which are far from united on the issues. Public employees form organizations or unions to promote their interests; some are AFL, some CIO, but most are unaffiliated and independent.

Pressure-group Techniques. The men and women who represent organized groups before the legislative and executive branches of government are known as legislative agents, advocates, counsels, lobbyists, or executive secretaries. Popularly they are known as lobbyists. Many

come to this work after serving as members of Congress or as attachés or as holders of other public offices; a large proportion come from practicing law, which combines easily with the work of a legislative agent. Nearly all groups and their representatives are bipartisan in their approach, seeking support from all public officers, regardless of party affiliation.

Techniques of interest groups and lobbyists vary considerably, but most legislative pressure techniques can be classed under one of four headings: informational, social, propaganda, and campaign. Informational services may begin with the preparation of proposed legislation by attorneys for the interest group. After a legislator who will introduce the bill has been found, he is furnished with information about the matter. Group proponents present arguments for their side of the question when the bill is before committee, then present to all legislators

HOW THE PRESSURE GROUPS WORK

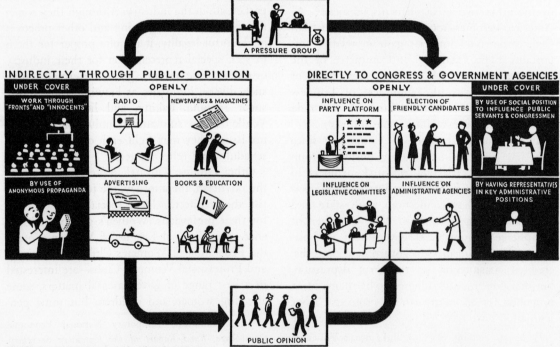

SOURCE: *Graphic Associates for Public Affairs Committee, Inc.*

Used by permission of Maxwell S. Stewart, Editor, Public Affairs Pamphlets.

literature and data in support of it. It must be borne in mind that special-interest groups oppose more measures than they support.

The social front is cared for by cultivating the personal acquaintance of as many legislators as possible, particularly of those strategically placed on the committees with which the lobbyist is most likely to deal. This cultivation may involve any sort of entertainment such as dinners, parties, and the like. Propaganda activities call for many kinds of publicity to influence public opinion, through mail appeals, radio talks, newspaper stories, and advertisements. The purpose often is to stimulate interested persons or group members to bring pressure to bear upon a legislator whose support is needed. The individual may be encouraged to telegraph, or write, or call upon the legislator, in an endeavor to win him over to the group's point of view.

Behind the other activities often lie a number of campaign activities. Groups in politics on other than a sporadic basis commonly find it advisable to survey the legislative field before the need of support becomes pressing. The legislator wants help at election time. The campaign period is the logical one in which to sound out the candidates and get them committed to a favorable point of view if possible. This sounding out may be done in writing, as in the answers to a questionnaire, or it may be done through a verbal promise, preferably given in a public meeting. If the candidate is favorable, the organization may endorse him openly, or it may prefer to send the word along to membership under cover. In any case, financial support of the candidate may reinforce the memory of the would-be official, and a campaign contribution from the group or from individuals connected with the group is valuable for this purpose. Some interests contribute to more than one candidate for an office, in order to ensure that they will have influence with the winner, whoever he may be.[24]

Although strict regulation of the lobby has

been demanded repeatedly, Congress imposed no general controls until the Congressional Reform Act of 1946, which requires lobbyists to register and file statements of expenditures made to influence legislation.[25] Registration laws are unlikely to be very effective, but they do, if enforced, bring pressure groups out into the open, a convenience to the legislators and the press. With campaign expenditures, however, the most effective restriction is an occasional legislative investigation.

Pressure Politics and Democracy. Pressure politics constitutes a very important element in American government. The power of pressure groups is demonstrated not only before Congress and state legislatures, but also in administrative agencies and in the several mediums of mass communication that have so much role in the formation of public opinion. On the whole, the activities of special-interest groups probably do more good than harm. Group representation provides a valuable supplement to the usual form of legislative representation and makes possible direct expression of points of view by those most fully affected by a proposed line of action.

On the other hand, serious abuses have developed. Some of these can be corrected by carefully drawn and enforced corrupt-practices legislation, but others pose such complex problems that only general solutions can be proposed. The most serious consequence of pressure-group preponderance is that general or national interests of the great masses of people are subordinated to the special interests of articulate and well-organized minorities. The consumer, for example, often has a completely inadequate voice

---

[24] In addition to the works on national groups (Herring, Odegard, Childs, Blaisdell, Schattschneider), techniques of lobbyists are dealt with in Belle Zeller, *Pressure Politics in New York* (Prentice-Hall, 1937), and

Dayton D. McKean, *Pressures on the Legislature of New Jersey* (Columbia University Press, 1938).

[25] For a study of the 1946 act and experience under it during the initial months of operation, see Belle Zeller, "The Federal Regulation of Lobbying Act," *American Political Science Review*, vol. 42 (April, 1948), pp. 239–271. Later developments may be traced in *Congressional Quarterly*. The largest spenders during 1953 were National Association of Electric Companies, Association of American Railroads, and National Milk Producers Federation.

in the determination of public policy because he has no powerful organization that can compete with farm, labor, and business groups. All Americans are consumers, but their interests as producers often outweigh consumer interests. An individual's own immediate selfish interests may appear to be served by a 50 per cent price increase in the product he is making, yet that price increase may be disadvantageous to users of that product all over the country. Since the consumers have no effective organization, their protests may not be heard at all.

General or national interests, as opposed to special-group interests, may receive support through (1) coalitions of groups, in opposition to the selfish demands of one group, (2) restoration of party responsibility and discipline in national affairs, and (3) development of a strong consumers' cooperative movement. The first method operates occasionally when labor and agriculture team up to forestall a tax policy demanded by business, or labor and business work together to defeat a farm subsidy plan, or business and agriculture jointly oppose wage demands by labor. The other methods will be discussed in subsequent chapters.

FOR FURTHER READING

PUBLIC OPINION, POLLS, PROPAGANDA, AND CENSORSHIP

Albig, William: *Public Opinion* (McGraw-Hill, 1939).

Barrett, E. W.: *Truth Is Our Weapon* (Funk & Wagnalls, 1953).

Bean, Louis H.: *How to Predict Elections* (Knopf, 1948).

Cantril, Hadley: *Gauging Public Opinion* (Princeton University Press, 1944).

Chase, Stuart, and M. Tyler: *Power of Words* (Harcourt, Brace, 1954).

Childs, Harwood L.: *An Introduction to Public Opinion* (Wiley, 1940).

Cole, W. S.: *America First: the Battle against Intervention, 1940–1941* (University of Wisconsin Press, 1953).

Doob, Leonard W.: *Public Opinion and Propaganda* (Holt, 1948).

——: *Propaganda—Its Psychology and Technique* (Holt, 1935).

Gallup, George: *A Guide to Public Opinion Polls* (Princeton University Press, 2d ed., 1948).

Koop, Theodore F.: *The Weapon of Silence* (University of Chicago Press, 1946).

Lasswell, Harold D.: *Democracy through Public Opinion* (Banta, 1941).

Lazarsfeld, Paul F., and Others: *The People's Choice: How the Voter Makes Up His Mind in a Presidential Campaign* (Columbia University Press, 2d ed., 1948).

Linebarger, Paul M. A.: *Psychological Warfare* (Infantry Journal, 1948).

Lippmann, Walter: *Public Opinion* (Macmillan, 1953).

MacDougall, Curtis D.: *Understanding Public Opinion* (Macmillan, 1952).

Mock, James R.: *Censorship, 1917* (Princeton University Press, 1941).

—— and Cedric Larson: *Words that Won the War* (Princeton University Press, 1939).

Public Opinion Quarterly. Issued by Princeton University Press since 1937.

Robinson, Claude E.: *Straw Votes: A Study in Political Prediction* (Columbia University Press, 1932).

Rogers, Lindsay: *The Pollsters* (Knopf, 1949).

CHANNELS OF COMMUNICATION

Allport, Gordon W., and Hadley Cantril: *Psychology of Radio* (Richard R. Smith, 2d ed., 1941).

Bryson, Lyman: *Time for Reason about Radio* (Stewart, 1948).

Chafee, J. Zechariah, Jr.: *Government and Mass Communications* (University of Chicago Press, 2 vols., 1947).

Charters, Werrett W. (chairman): *Motion Pictures and Youth: A Summary* (Macmillan, 1933). A summary of twelve Payne Fund studies on the influence of motion pictures on children.

Commission on Freedom of the Press: *A Free and Responsible Press: A General Report on Mass Communication* (University of Chicago Press, 1947).

Dale, Edgar: *How to Appreciate Motion Pictures* (Macmillan, 1933).

Field, Marshall: *Freedom Is More than a Word* (University of Chicago Press, 1945).

Frost, S. E., Jr.: *Is American Radio Democratic?* (University of Chicago Press, 1937).

Hettinger, Herman S. (ed.): "New Horizons in Radio," *Annals of the American Academy of Political and Social Science,* vol. 213 (January, 1941).

Huettig, Mae D.: *Economic Control of the Motion Picture Industry* (University of Pennsylvania Press, 1944).

Ickes, Harold L. (ed.): *Freedom of the Press Today* (Vanguard, 1941).

Inglis, Ruth A.: *Freedom of the Movies* (University of Chicago, 1947).

Lazarsfeld, Paul F.: *Radio and the Printed Page* (Duell, Sloan & Pearce, 1940).

Lee, Alfred M.: *The Daily Newspaper in America: The Evolution of a Social Instrument* (Macmillan, 1937).

Perlman, William J. (ed.): *The Movies on Trial* (Macmillan, 1936).

Robinson, Thomas P.: *Radio Networks and the Federal Government* (Columbia University Press, 1943).

Rose, Cornelia B., Jr.: *National Policy for Radio Broadcasting* (Harper, 1940).

Rosten, Leo C.: *Hollywood, the Movie Colony, the Movie Makers* (Harcourt, Brace, 1941).

Siepmann, Charles A.: *Radio's Second Chance* (Little, Brown, 1946).

Thorp, Margaret: *America at the Movies* (Yale University Press, 1939).

U.S. Federal Communications Commission: *An Economic Study of Standard Broadcasting* (1947).

——: *Public Service Responsibility of Broadcast Licensees* (1946).

——: *Report on Chain Broadcasting* (1941).

Waples, Douglas (ed.): *Print, Radio, and Film in a Democracy* (University of Chicago Press, 1942).

Watkins, Gordon S. (ed.): "The Motion Picture Industry," *Annals of the American Academy of Political and Social Science,* vol. 254 (November, 1947).

White, Llewellyn, and Robert D. Leigh: *Peoples Speaking to Peoples* (University of Chicago Press, 1946).

Willey, Malcolm, and Ralph D. Casey (eds.): "The Press in the Contemporary Scene," *Annals of the American Academy of Political and Social Science,* vol. 219 (January, 1942).

PRESSURE GROUPS

Blaisdell, Donald C.: *Economic Power and Political Pressures,* Temporary National Economic Committee, Monograph 26 (Government Printing Office, 1941).

Chase, Stuart: *Democracy under Pressure: Special Interests vs. the Public Welfare* (Twentieth Century Fund, 1945).

Childs, Harwood L.: *Labor and Capital in National Politics* (The Ohio State University Press, 1930).

Garceau, Oliver: *Political Life of the American Medical Association* (Harvard University Press, 1941).

Herring, E. Pendleton: *Group Representation before Congress* (Johns Hopkins Press, 1929).

Kile, Orville M.: *The Farm Bureau through Three Decades* (Baltimore: Waverly Press, 1948).

McCune, Wesley: *The Farm Bloc* (Doubleday, 1943).

McKean, Dayton D.: *Pressures on the Legislature of New Jersey* (Columbia University Press, 1938).

Odegard, Peter H.: *Pressure Politics: The Story of the Anti-saloon League* (Columbia University Press, 1928).

Rutherford, Mary L.: *The Influence of the American Bar Association on Public Opinion and Legislation* (Chicago: Foundation Press, 1937).

Schattschneider, Elmer E.: *Politics, Pressures and the Tariff* (Prentice-Hall, 1935).

Schriftgiesser, Karl: *The Lobbyists* (Little, Brown, 1951).

Zeller, Belle: *Pressure Politics in New York* (Prentice-Hall, 1937).

REVIEW QUESTIONS

1. A great foreign scholar (Gunnar Myrdal) says of the American masses: "They do not meet much. They do not organize. They do not speak for themselves: they are listeners in America." How can we have an informed public opinion if this is true?

2. Explain and discuss the concept of propaganda as used by the late Institute for Propaganda Analysis.

3. Explain in detail how the modern cross section or sampling survey of public opinion is made.

4. In what respect might the opinion poll constitute a danger to our usual governmental processes?

5. What are the most important influences molding our opinions? Discuss each, and assign an order of importance to your list of determinants.

6. What can a newspaper reader do to check up and get the most accurate possible picture of the news? Discuss the location of, and responsibility for, inaccuracies and bias.

7. An organization (American Civil Liberties Union) reported in 1936: "Of all means of communication radio today leads the field in affecting public opinion. Scores of programs are carried daily presenting news comment and, less often, political controversy. Each of these programs must face what is in effect a double censorship. . . ." Is radio the *chief* channel of communication now? What is this alleged censorship over radio?

8. "The potency of the motion picture in influencing the thought and opinions of large publics in the fields of politics and economics has not yet been thoroughly tested." (W. Albig.) Why has not the full power of the movies been utilized? What factors would condition and control the movies if they were so used?

9. Describe the policies and tactics of farm interests in national politics since the end of the Second World War.

10. How did the AFL and the CIO differ in their approach to politics prior to their amalgamation?

11. What are the principal political goals and methods of organized business in national politics?

12. Why do special-interest groups seek separate, extralegal representation in American government?

13. Can you propose a form of democratic, representative government under which special-group representation would be unnecessary?

CHAPTER 10

Political Parties

We proceed on the proposition that popular government in a nation of more than 150 million people requires political parties which provide the electorate with a proper range of choice between alternatives of action. The party system thus serves as the main device for bringing into continuing relationship those ideas about liberty, majority rule and leadership which Americans are taking for granted. — Committee on Political Parties, American Political Science Association [1]

Useful as they are in the democratic process, pressure groups cannot provide many of the services required to make big government operate in a responsible manner. Every large democratic jurisdiction in the modern state system utilizes political parties to crystallize opinion, to narrow both candidate and policy alternatives, and to provide responsibility.

GENERAL ASPECTS

Nature of the Political Party. A political party is usually defined as an organization of voters adhering to common principles and seeking power to control the government. In the United States, the Republican and Democratic parties frequently appear to support similar principles. Over much of American history the two major parties have resembled each other to an unusual extent, the resemblance forcing people to the conclusion that our parties were rival vote-catching arrangements manipulated by professional politicians seeking the spoils of office. Certainly under the two-party system parties have platforms and principles that are extremely general in nature, for an enormous amount of compromising must be done in framing them.

People encounter much difficulty in distinguishing between a political party and a pressure group. A vast organization like the Townsend movement of the 1930's appears at first blush to have all the characteristics of a political party. Indeed, a Townsend party appeared in several states, but the group proper has confined its political efforts to lobbying and to the support of, or opposition to, candidates of the regular parties. The primary difference between party and pressure groups is found in the essential aim: parties seek largely to capture offices; pressure groups aim mainly to influence policies.

Neither major American party has a definite membership. Persons may be considered members of a political party because they register as members, think themselves to be members, or pay their dues and hold a membership card. The first two are the most common forms of affiliation; the last is limited to small parties of the "left wing."

Factors in Party Allegiance. How is an individual's party affiliation determined, or how does one choose sides in the game of party politics?

[1] *Toward a More Responsible Two-party System* (Rinehart, 1950), p. 15.

Exact data on this subject are scarce, but some surveys that have been made shed light on certain of its aspects.

The first, and perhaps the most important, determinant is family tradition. Most voters take the party of their parents. This political ancestor worship is evidenced by the common expression, "My family is a Republican family," or "We have been Democrats for a hundred years." Because many other factors are influenced by family—economic status, religion, section of residence—this factor assumes an extraordinary importance.

Economic position ranks second in influence on party bias. No general rule applies to all periods, but recently there has been an increasing tendency for the well-to-do to vote Republican and for the less fortunate to vote Democratic. National origin plays a role too, for descendants of Northern Europeans tend to the Republican party, while those of Southern and Eastern Europeans prefer the Democratic party. This choice is probably connected with the economic role of each. Religious connections appear to play little part in pushing adherents into one party rather than the other, but it is an interesting fact that the Republican party is much more strongly Protestant than is the Democratic. Sectionalism, or geographic influence, is decisive in many cases and in certain parts of the country. In the South nearly everyone is Democratic; in Maine and Vermont the Republican majority is large.

The Two-party System. The two-party system exists in the United States, Great Britain, and some other democracies. Various explanations for it have been offered. First, some say that the peoples of the English-speaking countries are less doctrinaire and more inclined to compromise. Second, fewer problems of race, nationality, and religion factionalize the people than in the countries of continental Europe. Third, the early English two-party system was transplanted in the Colonial era and has been perpetuated. Fourth, the two-party plan is produced by the operation of the American voting systems, especially the electoral college and the single-member district plan of electing legislative representatives.

This fourth point requires elaboration. The importance of the presidency is now such that a third party secures adherents only with greatest difficulty, for "band-wagon" sentiment argues against "losing your vote" by supporting other than one of the two major parties. It is also true that the electoral-college method of electing the President would be very undemocratic if a strong third party should emerge. If no majority is won in the electoral college, the election of the Chief Executive is thrown to the House of Representatives, which must select from the highest three, each state casting one vote.

The single-member district scheme of electing legislative representatives also discourages the development of minor parties. It tends to magnify the strength of the leading party, yielding a proportion of legislative seats far above the proportion of popular votes received. For example, a party polling 52 per cent of the popular vote cast for representatives in Congress may receive 75 per cent of the seats, not only depriving the major opposition party of representation strictly proportionate to its voting strength, but usually eliminating minor parties almost completely.

The consequences of the two-party system are extremely important. First, it usually produces a situation in which one party actually has the power to govern. Under the parliamentary plan, the two-party scheme nearly always provides one party with a mandate from the electorate and a majority in the legislative body strong enough to carry out the mandate. Under the presidential plan, the separation of powers occasionally may lead to deadlock between executive and legislative branches, but normally it results in a situation in which the President has a congressional majority of his own party. In spite of the theoretical advantages of proportional representation (PR),[2] support has declined in the years of crisis, because of a new recognition that producing the power to govern through a roughly

[2] See p. 203.

democratic means is more important than representing all the elements in the body politic exactly in proportion to their strength in the electorate.

Second, major parties under the two-party system become moderate, compromising bodies, highly irritating to those who demand sharp definitions of party policy. Each party is faced with the task of attracting to the party standards an aggregation of interests strong enough to win power. Because each major party is at all times either the government or the opposition (alternative government), it is held close to realities and can ill afford to make irresponsible policy declarations.

Although there are some who would exchange the two-party plan for a multiparty scheme, the disadvantages of having many parties of strength would be very great under our form of government. The multiparty system produces instability, confuses the electorate with a multitude of alternatives, represents local groups and factions on a national scale, diffuses responsibility for action and inaction; it would make continued functioning of the electoral college virtually impossible.

Third Parties. Third parties have come and gone, but over a period of 165 years none except the Republican party has ever gained sufficient strength to displace an existing major party. Several times minor party candidates for the presidency have polled sufficient votes to hold the balance of power between the two majors, but they have been unable to keep their separate identity or strength for long. Since the Civil War third parties have made respectable showings on six occasions.[3] The Populists polled over one

[3] Leading sources on third parties are Nathan Fine, *Labor and Farmer Parties in the United States, 1828–1928* (New York: Rand School, 1928); Fred E. Haynes, *Third Party Movements since the Civil War* (Iowa City: State Historical Society of Iowa, 1916), and *Social Politics in the United States* (Houghton Mifflin, 1924); John D. Hicks, *The Populist Revolt* (University of Minnesota Press, 1931); William Hesseltine, *The Rise and Fall of Third Parties* . . . (Washington, D.C.: Public Affairs Press, 1948).

million votes in 1892; so did both Wallace, Progressive, and Thurmond, States' Rights, in 1948. Eugene Debs, Socialist candidate for the presidency, secured nearly a million votes both in 1912 and in 1920. With Theodore Roosevelt as a standard-bearer, the Progressives of 1912 polled over 4 million votes, exceeding the vote for President Taft, the official Republican candidate. The most recent great revolt came in 1924 when Robert M. La Follette, Progressive candidate, polled 4½ million votes for the presidency.

Third parties in American politics have played the role of innovators of policy, not of holders of office. The old parties have not hesitated to take plank after plank from Populists, Greenbackers, Socialists, and Progressives and install them in their own platforms. Much of what the left-wing parties advocated two or three decades ago may be found in the Democratic and Republican platforms of today. Those who participate in third-party movements may themselves never enjoy the fruits of office, but they may see the policies for which they worked become law of the land under old-party auspices.

Yet the similarity of the two old parties is so great that many persons argue that a recasting of the party system is needed. One party, they say, should become a genuine conservative party, and the other the party of progressive reform. During the 1920's it was thought that the Democratic party might die, and a farmer-labor or progressive party arise to replace it. Since the New Deal era, however, much attention has been given to the tendency for progressives to concentrate in the Democratic party, and for the Republican party to become the organ of conservatism. This division will be far from sharp, however, until the "solid South" is broken up and divides along natural party lines, and progressive elements of the Republican party are enticed or smoked out. At the moment there appears to be little evidence of either of these developments despite 1952 Republican gains in the South.

History of American Parties. The Democratic party is a venerable body, more than a century and a half old. It took form during Washington's administration, under the leadership of Jefferson, who was an exponent of strict construction. Known under various names, including Antifederalist, Republican, Democratic Republican, and Democratic, the party has shown enormous ability to survive under the most difficult of circumstances. Early in history it took a stand against high tariffs and enlisted the support of small farmers of the West and of urban workers of the East. After the extinction of the Federalist party around 1816, the party enjoyed a period of noncompetition in the political field. Substantial opposition was generated in the Jacksonian era, however, and the party, now labeled Democratic, soon faced a formidable Whig opponent. Although the Civil War made of the Democratic party a minority group for decades, the party rebounded with vigor in Congress and

captured the presidency twice with Cleveland, twice with Wilson, four times with Franklin D. Roosevelt, and once with Truman.

The Republican party of today is the successor of two earlier major parties. The Federalist party, led by Hamilton, emerged during Washington's administration as the champion of strong national government. It expired after making tactical errors during the War of 1812. When opposition crystallized against Jackson, it called itself National Republican, then Whig. In 1856 a new party, calling itself Republican, strode upon the scene, nominated John C. Frémont as presidential candidate, and took a strong stand on the slavery issue. Its victory in 1860 with Lincoln precipitated the Civil War, the results of which secured Republican predominance in national politics for the greater part of the period since then. Over the years it has

EVOLUTION OF AMERICAN PARTIES

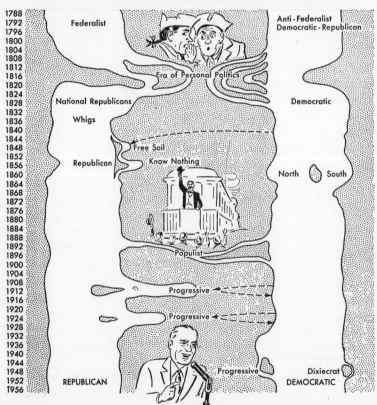

American parties, like two mighty rivers, have a distant origin and are fed by minor tributaries.

stood for high tariffs, strong national government, "hard" money, and conservatism; yet it has had room for trust busting and Theodore Roosevelt progressivism.

Functions of Parties. Parties perform certain necessary services in the governing process. Government without parties is possible; a number of states have made some offices nonpartisan by law and appear to conduct public affairs satisfactorily. In the great majority of cases, however, the political party is regarded as a necessity for free government.

The first function of a party is to canalize and crystallize opinion, to narrow the policy alternatives before the voters, to compromise diverse views of individuals, groups, and sections. This function, as shown in the previous chapter, is exceedingly important to the democratic political process. Individuals and pressure groups ordinarily cannot reduce the number of possibilities for action before federal or state public officers in such a way that there is general public understanding of the issues. A second service is similar; parties act as brokers of candidates for office. By selecting and promoting them, the parties narrow candidate alternatives before the electorate.

Parties also do much to educate and to interest voters in politics. They maintain elaborate publicity facilities. Great party leaders stimulate enthusiasm and interest in public affairs. Parties also do work in the field of naturalization of immigrants, once an important function of great urban party organizations.

Another group of services centers around party responsibility. If the control of government is achieved by a certain party, the electorate is entitled to hold that party accountable for its stewardship in office. This responsibility is very imperfectly realized in many states, but a rough measure of justice is done. The minority has no less responsibility than the majority, for the task is to expose the weaknesses of the majority, to furnish criticisms of the party in power.

Government in the United States is complicated both by the distribution of powers between the nation and the states, and by the separation of power into legislative, executive, and judicial. Parties correct this diffusion of governmental authority in part by providing somewhat compatible groups of officeholders.

Under the American system of government, parties also serve to make the electoral-college plan work. With only two parties, one candidate nearly always secures the necessary majority. Without parties, or even with the multiparty system, most elections would be thrown to the House of Representatives.

Finally, the political party often performs a social and humanitarian function. Parties and their auxiliaries hold bazaars, whists, dances, picnics; such events add to the enjoyment of the participants and to the political consciousness of a community. In areas where the political party is thoroughly organized, it plays an important role in humanizing big government. The party leader in the precinct or ward is an interpreter of the individual's needs and desires to public officials, and vice versa, the policies and structure of government are explained to the citizen by his local party leaders. Although such services sometimes extend into the field of special favors granted to the faithful and withheld from others, a great deal of legitimate aid may be rendered by a party.

PARTY ORGANIZATION

Party organization has two distinct parts, but interconnections are frequent and one is hard to describe without the other. The permanent organization includes the tiers of party committees that reach from bottom to top of the party hierarchy. The periodic organization consists of party primaries and conventions, meeting annually or less frequently and deciding highly important questions concerning party structure. The periodic organization will be dealt with in some detail in the next chapter. Primary emphasis here will be placed upon the permanent organization, formal and informal.

The National Committee. The national committee stands at the head of permanent party organization in the country. In the Democratic party it is composed of one man and one woman from each state and territory. The members most commonly are chosen by state delegations to national party conventions, but some states require that they be selected in state convention or committee, or elected in direct primary elections. The Republicans in 1952 decided to add, as ex officio members of the national committee, the state chairmen of the states carried by the party in the last election. This change was opposed by women and Southerners, whose representation will be diluted by the move. Nominally, the power of the national committee is great, but increasingly in recent years it has

PARTY ORGANIZATION, U.S.A.

National Chairman
EXECUTIVE COMMITTEE

NATIONAL COMMITTEE

Congressional Campaign Committee | Senatorial Campaign Committee

48 STATE CENTRAL COMMITTEES

3,000 County Central Committees

City Committees | Ward Committees

125,000 Precinct Committees

confined its work to ratifying the presidential nominee's choice for chairman, to electing other officers, and to planning the national convention. There is little significant difference between the Republican and Democratic practice in this regard.

By long usage the national chairman is selected by the presidential nominee and formally elected by the committee. He becomes party campaign manager and directs national headquarters. An executive committee, chosen by the chairman, is delegated most of the committee's authority for the 3 years between national campaign periods. Under the control of the national chairman, the central office is manned with workers doing research, advertising, publicity, money raising; others do "stratified electioneering," appealing to special groups of voters, such as women, veterans, Negroes, farmers, laborers, and foreign-born. Both parties keep some bureaus, especially publicity, open year in and year

out. The effective work of Charles Michelson, Democratic publicity chief, is credited with having played a decisive role in shaping public hostility toward the Hoover administration between 1930 and 1932.

In each state the national committeeman and committeewoman handle liaison work with the state organization and help to direct patronage matters when their party holds the presidency. In 1952 the Republicans created a new permanent advisory committee, to be appointed by the national chairman, from among Republican Senators, Representatives, governors, state chairmen, and members of the national committee. Its purpose is to help formulate party policies and campaign strategy.

Campaign Committees. The Senatorial Campaign Committee and the Congressional Campaign Committee are maintained by each party to direct campaign efforts in behalf of party aspirants for national legislative posts. Separate bodies were established to prevent campaigning from falling wholly into executive hands. The Republicans originated the plan, forming a joint body in 1866 during the struggle between President Johnson and the congressional leaders. Subsequently the body split into separate groups for Senate and House. The Republican Senatorial Campaign Committee of today is composed of seven members chosen for 2-year terms by the Republican caucus of the Senate. The Republican Congressional Campaign Committee is composed of one Representative from each state having a Republican in the House; selection is made by the state congressional delegation. The Democratic arrangements are nearly the same.

These committees function chiefly during campaigns. The task of each is to secure the reelection of old and the election of new party members to House and Senate. Each group attempts to maintain a small staff on a permanent basis. Since none has demonstrated much independent money-raising ability, each has relied for support mainly upon the party national committee. They compile the voting records of sitting members, analyze political possibilities in the various states and districts, and do other things to prepare for congressional elections.

State Central Committees. The state central committees oversee all party machinery in the state, direct campaigns for state offices, for United States senatorships, and for state efforts in behalf of the national party tickets. State committeemen are chosen in a variety of ways, by election or by appointment, and represent legislative districts, counties, or some other subdivision. Most of the state committees are not assigned significant powers, but a few may decide whether the party shall use the convention or primary nominating method. They range in number of members from a handful in some states to 678 in California. The large committees in practice delegate powers and duties to an executive group, which makes the effective decisions. Some state committees are given authority to fill vacancies that occur after convention or primary among the party nominees for offices. Occasionally the chairman of the state central committee is a political figure of importance; perhaps more commonly he is front for a stronger man or group in the background.

County Committees. County central committees coordinate the work of all lesser bodies, act on matters affecting county government, and deal in important matters with state central committees. There are over 3,000 counties in the country, and virtually all are organized by one or both parties.

District party organizations in considerable number stand between the state and local levels. They are set up in state senatorial, state representative, congressional, and state judicial districts. Naturally, their position in the party structure varies considerably from state to state and from urban to rural area.

Local Organization. The precinct, or polling district, is the basic unit in party organization. Its size depends upon population density and number of voters election officials can handle conveniently. Between 100 and 500 voters are included in the average precinct. Around 125,000 precincts exist in the United States; of these perhaps 100,000 have definite party organizations active in them. The chairman or executive of the party precinct unit is responsible for the party's direct contacts with voters in their home districts and provides the personal services in exchange for which people of the precinct may be willing to cast their ballots.

A ward committee is usually the next level of party organization in an urban community. A ward is a district from which city councilmen are elected. This party committee coordinates the work of precinct units and deals with local political problems, especially with municipal-council politics. A city committee oversees the ward and precinct levels and gives particular attention to municipal problems and offices. Township or village committees exist in rural areas to bring together precinct representatives and to plan party activities in relation to local governments.

Extralegal Party Groups. The informal organizations of parties often loom large in the political sky. This designation covers a wide range of clubs, associations, and other bodies on levels as diverse as neighborhood caucuses and great national campaign committees.

On the national scene, the most influential and the best-financed have been groups seeking the presidential nomination for a particular aspirant, like the National Citizens for Eisenhower and the National Volunteers for Stevenson. Such bodies have demonstrated a capacity for securing support and raising money among people who normally might shun direct party activity. After their first objective, securing the nomination, is achieved, they often continue in the general election campaign to appeal to the independent voters. Although their methods may differ from those of the regular party machines, such groups are likely to supplement national presidential campaigns.

On the state and local fronts, extralegal party organizations are assuming great importance. Official party bodies are closely regulated by state law, which sometimes denies them the discretion to mount a campaign effectively and often bars their participation in the primaries. Consequently informal groups have been set up to perform the functions from which formal party is precluded. An aggressive role in the nominating process is a common characteristic. Local clubs and organizations, federated on regional and state levels, search for candidates, narrow the field of aspirants in primaries, raise money and finance campaigns—both primary and general.[4]

Machines and Bosses. Although political parties appear essential to the proper functioning of democratic politics on a national scale, parties themselves are often controlled by a single autocrat or a group. Political parties in a big democracy are huge leviathans that must be manned and fed and directed. In parties and in areas where the civic spirit and interest are high, party affairs may be conducted on a democratic basis. The extent of intraparty democracy varies widely from party to party and from country to country. Commonly, however, party machinery in democratic countries falls under the control of a small group or an individual. A student of continental European politics has called this the "oligarchical tendency," in which control passes from the masses to professional leadership.[5]

The boss is a political leader who maintains power through corruption, spoils, and patronage. The machine is the organization through which the dominant group or individual rules. Political machines and bosses have flourished in American urban communities, utilizing legendary methods: bribery, patronage, special favors, rigged elections. During the past 20 years, however, the number of prominent bosses has declined to almost nil.

[4] For specific examples, see Frank J. Sorauf, "Extralegal Political Parties in Wisconsin," *American Political Science Review,* vol. XLVIII (September, 1954), pp. 692–704; Hugh A. Bone, "New Party Associations in the West," *ibid.,* vol. XLV (December, 1951), pp. 1115–1125; and Currin V. Shields, "A Note on Party Organization: The Democrats in California," *Western Political Quarterly,* vol. 7 (December, 1954), pp. 673–683.

[5] Robert Michels, *Political Parties: A Sociological Study of the Oligarchical Tendencies of Modern Democracy* (New York: Hearst's International Library Co., 1915), pp. 54ff.

Nonpartisanship. Shortly after the turn of the century, criticisms of political parties were so violent that one of the progressive reforms proposed in many states was the outright abolition of parties. It was argued that, especially in local government, the issues had little relation to national party alignment, and that there was no Republican or Democratic way to pave a street. This was answered with the assertion that the vital local problems are connected with state and national issues, and that the political party performs functions without which a big democracy cannot exist.

In practice, the elimination of parties from state and local affairs by legislation has produced disappointing results. In some instances the parties have continued to exist without recognition on the ballot, as in the Minnesota legislature. In most cases, however, parties cut out of local affairs have withered on what was left of the vine; they have been so weakened by the severance of roots from local politics that they have had to live from year to year on the plasma of national-election activity. Denied the leadership of his party, the urban voter in a nonpartisan election is often completely at sea and without knowledge on the stands of candidates on public issues. Politics degenerates into irresponsibility, with interests, groups, and individuals striving for power and influence.

Seeking to rid themselves of the evils of the party system, reformers abolished the system itself, expecting to see the evils expire too. Actually, however, spoils and corruption continued, and the voter no longer had a clear alternative to accepting the officeholders in control. Instead, he was forced to grope through the long ballot, searching, often in vain, for a clue on how to vote. Deploring the trend toward nonpartisanship in local government, the late Edward M. Sait declared:

Very soon there would be no parties anywhere in the United States, if they were left floating in the air without any local base. National organization depends ultimately upon precinct organization. The conduct of national campaigns depends upon continuous experience in fighting local campaigns. Democracy cannot live without parties and parties cannot live in the stratosphere.[6]

On the other hand, most authorities on local government favor nonpartisanship for municipal and county elections. Since most local jurisdictions that have abolished party designations are unlikely to return to partisanship, the party organization must be strengthened by other means. While the detailed steps toward restoring parties will vary from state to state, attention might be given to election of precinct leaders, to preprimary conferences, and to rigid party affiliation tests for candidates for state and congressional offices.

PARTY FINANCES

Campaigns Cost Money. Money is of key importance in American politics. An enormous amount must be spent to reach the largest par-

There are no really accurate figures on total campaign costs, for no adequate system of reporting expenditures has been devised. In 1936 the two national committees reported spending amounts that totaled more than 14 million dollars; of this over 5 million was Democratic and nearly 9 million Republican. This was the largest expenditure on record, but nearly as much was spent in 1928. The 1940 amendments to the Hatch Act of 1939 forbid any party committee to spend more than 3 million dollars in one campaign, but this law was evaded by assigning excess expenditures to state and auxiliary bodies.[7]

Official reports showed that both Republican and Democratic national committees spent between $2,000,000 and $2,800,000 in the 1940, 1944, and 1948 campaigns. After expenditures from other national and state groups and parties were added, the Republican 1940 total was nearly

WHAT CAMPAIGNS COST

At best the estimates of spending in campaigns are careful guesses. The advent of television has pushed election costs to new highs. Reprinted from *U.S. News & World Report,* an independent weekly news magazine published at Washington. Copyright, 1952, United States News Publishing Corporation. Issue of Oct. 3, 1952.

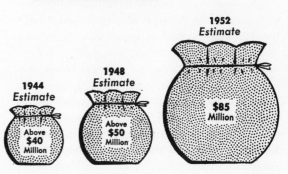

1944 Estimate Above $40 Million

1948 Estimate Above $50 Million

1952 Estimate $85 Million

ticipating democratic electorate in the world. Public inertia is high, and it takes much to break it down and secure political activity. The general use of the direct primary doubles the number of elections that must be fought. Elective offices are numerous. Terms of public officers are relatively short. It is necessary to buy the means of reaching voters; radio and television time, newspaper space, and literature printing cost much money.

[6] Edward M. Sait, *American Parties and Elections* (Appleton-Century-Crofts, 1942), p. 242. Copyrighted by the publishers; quoted by permission.

For a careful study of the effects of nonpartisanship, see Charles R. Adrian, "Some General Characteristics of Nonpartisan Elections," *American Political Science Review,* vol. 46 (September, 1952), pp. 766–776.

$15,000,000 and the Democratic was over $5,850,000. In 1944 the Republicans spent over $13,000,000 and Democrats nearly $7,500,000.

Figures for the Eisenhower-Stevenson campaign of 1952 showed the Republican national committee spending $2,937,549, the Democratic

[7] The matter of party funds is well handled by Prof. Louise Overacker in her *Money in Elections* (Macmillan, 1932). Later elections are covered in her articles, "Campaign Funds in the Presidential Election of 1936," *American Political Science Review,* vol. 31 (June, 1937), pp. 473–498; "Campaign Finance in the Presidential Election of 1940," *ibid.,* vol. 35 (August, 1941), pp. 701–727; "Presidential Campaign Funds, 1944," *ibid.,* vol. 39 (October, 1945), pp. 899–925. For 1948 and 1952 the most convenient source is *Congressional Quarterly* reports and *Almanac.*

$2,602,651. If expenditures of other national and state groups and parties were added, the total might have exceeded $75,000,000, of which around $6,000,000 was for radio and television.

Sources of Funds. Political funds come from various sources. Perhaps the most meaningful classification places on one side the contributions of well-wishers genuinely interested in the cause; on the other, the donations of those who want something in return. Neither major party has succeeded in getting more than a small proportion of its revenues through small donations (1 to 25 dollars) from individuals; the Democrats made real progress in this direction in 1940 and 1952. Revenues other than individual contributions have loomed larger in recent years. Losing out on big donations, the Democrats after 1932 secured much money through high-priced "Jackson Day" dinners, book sales, and trade-union contributions.

Since 1943 trade unions have been forbidden to contribute to political objectives and, under the Taft-Hartley Act, to spend union funds on them. These restrictions do not apply to contributions made from unions' political funds that are raised through voluntary contributions. In 1948 labor political organizations reported aggregate expenditures of $1,291,343; in 1950 of $1,618,623; in 1952 of $2,070,350; and in 1954 of $2,057,613. Much of this went to help Democratic candidates.

Officeholders are always a mainstay of financial support for the party in power. The Hatch Act and civil service rules prevent the taking of forced contributions from federal officers and from state and local employees who engage in federally aided work. Nevertheless many officeholders continue to make voluntary contributions; during 1950, for example, 1,162 persons from Washington, D.C., contributed $260,480 to the Democrats, while 23 gave $17,200 to the Republicans.

The individual contribution from the well-to-do person remains the mainstay of party finance. Corporations are forbidden by federal law and by the laws of thirty-six states to make campaign contributions. Therefore gifts from corporate sources are made by officers of the concerns, who may be compensated through bonuses or expense accounts. During 1954 fourteen DuPonts gave a total of $51,500 to Republican groups and candidates; 10 Rockefellers gave $66,000. The Hatch Act provision that no individual may contribute more than $5,000 to a political committee has not been a barrier to those who wish to contribute more; dozens evade this restriction each campaign year by making several contributions, none over $5,000, to several different committees. When a wealthy candidate is chosen for his ability to carry an important share of the financial burden of the campaign, he is called a "fat cat."

Legal Regulation. The principal federal law governing money in elections is the Corrupt Practices Act of 1925, as subsequently amended.[8] It contains three principal elements: financial reports are required; expenditures by candidates are limited; and contributions from certain sources are forbidden.

National political committees, defined as those attempting to influence the election of federal officers in two or more states, are required to report their financial transactions. Each must report quarterly on money received and spent; preliminary to general elections two reports are required; a cumulative statement is due at the end of each calendar year. Candidates must report twice, once before and once after the election. Individuals who contribute over $50 to other than political committees in two or more states are required to report. Committee reports must include a detailed and exact account of all contributions and expenditures, including the names and addresses of every person who contributed over $100, and a breakdown of expenditures over $10. A candidate's reports must show amounts and sources of all contributions received "with his knowledge or consent," and expenditures in certain categories, but unitemized totals suffice for others, and no reports at all are necessary for some.

[8] A convenient summary of federal and state laws governing money in elections is contained in U.S. Senate, Committee on Rules and Administration, *Election Law Guidebook, 1952,* Sen. Doc. 97, 82d Cong., 2d Sess. (1952).

The law sets an alternative limit on expenditures of either (1) a flat maximum of $10,000 by a candidate for Senator and $2,500 for Representative, or (2) 3 cents per vote cast, up to a $25,000 maximum for Senator and $5,000 for Representative.

The prohibitions on sources of contributions cover corporations and trade unions. Corpora-

Congress gave up control over political funds in the nominating process. Twenty years later, however, the Supreme Court reversed this decision and held that Congress could regulate primary elections of federal officers.[9]

Other legal regulations are found in the Hatch Act of 1939, as amended, which restricts public employees' participation in politics and

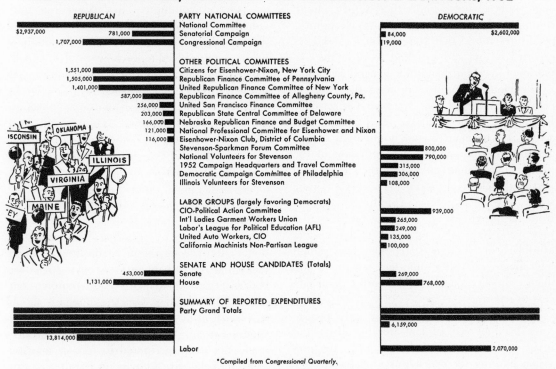

REPORTED EXPENDITURES, PRESIDENTIAL AND CONGRESSIONAL CAMPAIGNS, 1952*

REPUBLICAN		DEMOCRATIC
	PARTY NATIONAL COMMITTEES	
$2,937,000	National Committee	
781,000	Senatorial Campaign	84,000 $2,602,000
1,707,000	Congressional Campaign	19,000
	OTHER POLITICAL COMMITTEES	
1,551,000	Citizens for Eisenhower-Nixon, New York City	
1,505,000	Republican Finance Committee of Pennsylvania	
1,401,000	United Republican Finance Committee of New York	
587,000	Republican Finance Committee of Allegheny County, Pa.	
256,000	United San Francisco Finance Committee	
203,000	Republican State Central Committee of Delaware	
166,000	Nebraska Republican Finance and Budget Committee	
121,000	National Professional Committee for Eisenhower and Nixon	
116,000	Eisenhower-Nixon Club, District of Columbia	
	Stevenson-Sparkman Forum Committee	800,000
	National Volunteers for Stevenson	790,000
	1952 Campaign Headquarters and Travel Committee	315,000
	Democratic Campaign Committee of Philadelphia	306,000
	Illinois Volunteers for Stevenson	108,000
	LABOR GROUPS (largely favoring Democrats)	
	CIO-Political Action Committee	939,000
	Int'l Ladies Garment Workers Union	265,000
	Labor's League for Political Education (AFL)	249,000
	United Auto Workers, CIO	135,000
	California Machinists Non-Partisan League	100,000
	SENATE AND HOUSE CANDIDATES (Totals)	
453,000	Senate	269,000
1,131,000	House	768,000
	SUMMARY OF REPORTED EXPENDITURES Party Grand Totals	
		6,159,000
13,814,000		
	Labor	2,070,000

*Compiled from Congressional Quarterly.

The expenditure data shown above, as reported under the Federal Corrupt Practices Act, include only a small part of the total cost of the 1952 campaign.

tions, as noted above, are able to evade by making indirect contributions through corporate officers. Unions are permitted to collect and spend voluntary political funds. Both corporations and unions pay printing and other bills on behalf of candidates, carrying such expenditures on their books as "business expense," a practice that is doubly illegal in that it deprives the government of tax revenue as well as violates the corrupt-practices law.

After a court decision in 1921 indicating that Congress lacked power to regulate primaries,

limits expenditures by politial committees to 3 million dollars and contributions by individuals to $5,000. The Powers Act of 1944 forbids publication or circulation of political statements relating to candidates for federal office without containing the names of persons responsible; this legislation is interpreted by law-enforcement officers as applying to primaries as well as general

[9] The adverse decision was Newberry *v.* United States, 256 U.S. 232 (1921); the favorable one was United States *v.* Classic, 313 U.S. 299 (1941), reaffirmed in Smith *v.* Allwright, 321 U.S. 649 (1944).

elections. The Taft-Hartley Act of 1947 reiterates restrictions on trade-union spending for political purposes.

Failure of Controls. Many of the provisions of corrupt-practices laws, federal and state, are disregarded and evaded; on the whole they are archaic and ill suited to present-day conditions. The reporting provisions are badly drawn, and the resultant reports have such lack of uniformity that they defy careful analysis. Primaries ought to be included under the law; the House committee that investigated the 1950 election expenditures found that congressional candidates reported raising and spending more in the primaries of that year than in the general election.[10]

The House committee probing the 1952 expenditures reported that National Citizens for Eisenhower spent $1,200,000 in preconvention activities.[11] In many states, nomination is tantamount to election, and nonregulation of the primary means nonregulation of the most crucial part of the electoral process. The "two or more states" test of a political committee excludes from the provisions of the act committees that may spend huge sums on behalf of a senatorial candidate in a single state. The law should logically require all committees seeking to influence the election of one or more federal officers to report.

The maximum limits on campaign expenditures fixed by federal law are unrealistic and invite evasion. Consider, for example, the provision limiting the expenditures on behalf of a candidate for the United States Senate to $25,000. In a large state with over a million voters this would not pay for a postcard to mail to each voter, much less cover the cost of printing and addressing. The actual cost in hotly contested campaigns for the Senate in the larger states may even exceed a million dollars. The dodge which candidates use is to report only the ex-

penditures which they personally have made or know about, while committees carrying on the campaign spend vast sums of money which are not reported at all. If a political committee operates only in a single state it is not required to report its expenditures to federal authorities. The maximum limits set for campaign expenditures by candidates for the House are also ridiculously low.

The Hatch Act limitation of 3 million dollars on political committees and $5,000 on individual contributions has done much more harm than good. It has induced the proliferation of political committees, a development that actually has reduced the amount of responsibility in political spending.

Ceilings on expenditures or contributions are unworkable with present enforcement provisions. Perhaps the open and honest thing to do is to repeal, as did California recently, all limitations on amounts of money that can be expended.

Reform of Regulation. The main purpose of corrupt-practices laws should be to turn the light of publicity on spending. This cannot be done effectively without establishing a single depository for such reports and giving it power both to prescribe their form and to enforce compliance with the law. Greatest emphasis should be placed on getting full reports and fixing responsibility for spending. Political committees ought not to be permitted to receive contributions or make expenditures on behalf of a candidate without his consent.

Improvements in the law also are needed to eliminate inconsistencies in the categorization of expenditures. The present law requires detailed itemization of some expenditures, only totals for others, and no accounting at all for a few. Once the responsibility for spending is firmly fixed on the candidate or his authorized agents, it will be possible to invoke the powerful sanction of refusing to seat those who have not complied with the corrupt-practices law.

PARTY POLITICS IN FLUX

Present Party Alignment. At mid-century the country was beginning to feel the wind that

---

[10] U.S. House of Representatives, Special Committee to Investigate Campaign Expenditures, *Report . . . ,* H. Rept. 3252, 81st Cong., 2d Sess. (1951), p. 19. Data were obtained by questionnaire.

[11] U.S. House of Representatives, Special Committee to Investigate Campaign Expenditures, *Report . . . ,* H. Rept. 2517, 82d Cong., 2d Sess. (1953), p. 37.

changes the political weather. The impact of Franklin D. Roosevelt and the depression was fading; the war and postwar periods produced the problems that loomed large to a new generation. Whether the year 1952 marked the watershed and symbolized a long-run and deep-seated change cannot yet be stated with assurance. In any case, this is an appropriate time for stock taking. What was the difference, if any, between the Republican party and the Democratic party, at the half-century mark?

Adherents. First, consider the composition of the parties, or their patterns of support. After twenty years of intensive public-opinion polling and an even longer period of careful analysis of election returns, we have a fairly clear idea of the habitual voting behavior of various elements in the population.

The Republicans retained, even in the years of the New Deal and Fair Deal (1933–1953), a considerable backlog of support among professional and business-executive people. The G.O.P. remained the overwhelming choice of upper-income groups. The older elements of the population consistently veered toward the Republican side. Regionally, the party was strongest in the Northeastern and Middle Western sections. In terms of educational background, the Republicans won the majority of college people. Throughout the years of Democratic ascendency, their opponents maintained a bulwark of strength in small towns of most sections of the country.

The Democrats, for two decades after 1932, enjoyed the adherence of the majority of manual workers, skilled and unskilled, union and non-union. In virtually all sections of the country, the low-income groups voted (if they voted) the Democratic party line. The younger elements of the electorate showed pronounced preference for the party of Franklin D. Roosevelt. The South and border states supported the Democrats most consistently, but other states of the North and West were fairly faithful. Persons with only grade-school education tended to favor the Democratic party with their votes. The great cities went Democratic in election after election.

Independent Voters. In between the habitual supporters of the Republicans and of the Democrats are several elements that may be regarded as swinging in political preference. They are often identified as white collar by occupation, middle in income, and small-city and suburban in domicile. These groups have grown rapidly in size and political influence in the postwar period. As long as they divided somewhat evenly between the parties, their influence at the ballot box was not so plainly marked.

In 1952, however, independent voters found a champion in the form of Dwight Eisenhower, and a strong majority of these groups turned to him. Their support constituted an important element in his victorious coalition. They now retain the balance of power in a number of pivotal Northern industrial states. There is much evidence that they are internationalist on foreign affairs issues and moderate on domestic issues. An isolationist or ultraconservative Republican is unlikely to win their continued support for the party. Whether the Democrats can win back a considerable share in an economic recession remains to be seen. In the meantime their middle-class attitudes often are shaped by home ownership, acquisition of cars and appliances on credit, and identification with business interests, large or small.

Political Trends. The Democratic victory in the House and Senate elections of 1954 reemphasized the fact that the triumph of 1952 was that of Mr. Eisenhower, not of the Republican party. The presidential candidate ran about 5 million votes ahead of Republican congressional candidates, a margin of 16 per cent. The issue of the Korean War loomed much larger in the minds of the electorate in 1952 than was generally realized. Mr. Eisenhower was considered by many the ideal man to bring hostilities to a conclusion.

Looking ahead, emphasis must be placed on the importance of the major-party nominees for the presidency. An Eisenhower might easily sweep the nation again; a lesser Republican might have tough going against an attractive Democratic candidate. In the contest for Congress the Democrats have a number of advantages, having a larger proportion of safe seats in both House and Senate, and fewer borderline and pivotal seats to defend.

The various elements that constitute the basic coalitions of support for each party are likely to remain stable. The decisive factor is apt to be, as it was in 1952, the white-collar, middle-income, urban-suburban vote. Or, as in 1948, the farm vote of the Middle West.

Liberal vs. Conservative. One of the most persistent themes of critics of American parties is that a realignment should take place, making one party clearly left of center and the other right of center. Most assume that the Republican party could take on the conservative role by divesting itself of a few Northern and Western mavericks, and by adding reactionary Southern Democrats. Some think that the Democratic party could be transformed into a consistently progressive one, by shedding certain Southern elements and making a strong appeal to the economically underprivileged of the South and of other sections as well. Others argue that the Democratic party should be replaced by a new party with roots deep in the labor movement, and without the confusing and often contradictory traditions of the past.

Although it is possible to influence party alignment by changes in the electoral system, such as those proposed with respect to the presidency, parties win their adherents and take on their policy coloration less from deliberate planning and more from historical, emotional, and other factors. It appears likely that such changes as are made in the near future will be evolutionary rather than drastic and will take the form of gradual changes in the old parties rather than the launching of new. In point of fact the two major parties differ considerably, not only in the candidates they present for office, but on important domestic and international issues. So long as the system operates on the basis of shifting groups, with each party vying with the other for the support of the larger number, government will be by consensus, and government is apt to be conducted with due regard for the national interest.

Stronger and More Responsible Parties. Reform of the American political party system, discussed since the early years of the republic, took stage center in 1950 and the years following. Interest was focused on the problem by a competent and controversial report, *Toward a More Responsible Two-party System,*[12] made by a committee of the American Political Science Association.

Present Inadequacies. The committee appropriately put down criticisms of the existing party system, including the lack of discipline, the disparity between platforms and performance, and the weakness of leadership. The existing federal basis of party organization was criticized as productive of divergent approaches to party strategy and policy. Leadership was considered so diffused that no individual or body could deal authoritatively with major party problems. Membership remains a vague concept, scarcely more than a state of mind or a statement of preference.

Many organizational deficiencies were specified. The national convention was judged ". . . an unwieldy, unrepresentative and less than responsible body."[13] Neither the national committees nor the campaign committees of House and Senate were deemed adequate. Party platforms are vague to the point of being meaningless; the atmosphere in which they are written and adopted is far from deliberative; those who make the real decisions in Congress may be virtually unrepresented in the platform-framing process. Popular participation by party members in party affairs is at a low ebb.

Proposed Changes. The report called for stronger, better-integrated, and more responsible parties. National party bodies would be strengthened. The national convention should meet at 2-year intervals, and its size should be reduced.

[12] Supplement to *American Political Science Review,* vol. XLIV (September, 1950); also published separately (Rinehart, 1950). The chairman of the committee was E. E. Schattschneider, and its personnel included many of the leading students of politics.

[13] *Ibid.,* p. 3. Conventions are considered in the next chapter.

Composition of the national committee should be subject to national convention control, and the strength of the party in the sections of the country should be reflected in the apportionment of the committee. A new body, the "party Council," was proposed to govern the party between conventions and to coordinate the various party organizations.

Reliance would be placed on the party council, a body of fifty members, to prepare in advance drafts of the party platform, to interpret the adopted platform, and to resolve conflicts between national and state platforms.

Another series of recommendations concerned the conduct of party affairs in Congress. Frequent caucuses were suggested, with binding decisions used to carry out party policy pledges. Party leaders in Congress should be organized into an effective leadership committee, which would submit policy proposals to party membership, draw up slates for committee assignments, and generally plan party strategy in Congress.

In summarizing its case for action on reform proposals, the committee stressed the dangers of irresponsibility, of overextending the presidency, of disintegration of the two-party system, and of the emergence of extremism of left and right in the wake of frustration over inaction.

Criticisms of the Report. The report stimulated many dissents and critical replies.[14] Some denied the charge that American parties are irresponsible, stressing the different behavior of the two parties in office, especially in Congress. Others reject tight discipline for political parties representative of a plural society of immense diversity. The American system operates, it is argued, on a consensus basis, each party striving to win to its side enough groups and factions to tip the scales in its favor. Our individualism, coupled with the tradition that representatives serve local and sectional rather than national interests, militates against centralized and well-disciplined parties. Finally, the recommendations are criticized as being mainly mechanical, and that their application might lead to unexpected and undesired consequences.

[14] Among the many able commentaries on the report, are T. William Goodman, "How Much Political Party Centralization Do We Want?" *Journal of Politics,* vol. 13 (November, 1951), pp. 536–561; Julius Turner, "Responsible Parties: A Dissent from the Floor," *American Political Science Review,* vol. 45 (March, 1951), pp. 141–152; Austin Ranney, "Toward a More Responsible Two-party System: A Commentary," *ibid.* (June, 1951), pp. 488–499; Murray S. Stedman, Jr., and H. Sonthoff, "Party Responsibility—A Critical Inquiry," *Western Political Quarterly,* vol. 4 (September, 1951), pp. 454–468.

FOR FURTHER READING

Beard, Charles A.: *The American Party Battle* (Macmillan, 1928).

Bone, Hugh A.: *American Politics and the Party System* (McGraw-Hill, 2d ed., 1955).

Brooks, Robert C.: *Political Parties and Electoral Problems* (Harper, 3d ed., 1933).

Bruce, Harold R.: *American Parties and Politics* (Holt, 3d ed., 1936).

Calkins, Fay: *CIO and the Democratic Party* (University of Chicago Press, 1952).

David, Paul T., and Others: *Presidential Nominating Politics in 1952* (Johns Hopkins Press, 5 vols., 1954).

Donnelly, Thomas C. (ed.): *Rocky Mountain Politics* (University of New Mexico Press, 1940).

Douglas, Paul H.: *The Coming of a New Party* (McGraw-Hill, 1932).

Duverger, M.: *Political Parties: Their Organization and Activity in the Modern State* (Wiley, 1954).

Fine, Nathan: *Labor and Farmer Parties, 1828–1928* (New York: Rand School, 1928).

Fisher, Margaret J.: *Parties and Politics in the Local Community* (Washington, D.C.: National Council for the Social Studies, 1945).

Forthal, Sonya: *Cogwheels of Democracy: A Study of the Precinct Captain* (New York: William-Frederick Press, 1946).

Gosnell, Harold F.: *Grassroots Politics* (American Council on Public Affairs, 1942).

——: *Machine Politics: Chicago Model* (University of Chicago Press, 1937).

Harris, Louis: *Is There a Republican Majority?* (Harper, 1954).

Heard, Alexander: *A Two Party South?* (The University of North Carolina Press, 1952).

Herring, E. Pendleton: *The Politics of Democracy* (Norton, 1940).

Hesseltine, William B.: *The Rise and Fall of Third Parties . . .* (Washington, D.C.: Public Affairs Press, 1948).

Hicks, John D.: *The Populist Revolt* (University of Minnesota Press, 1931).

Holcombe, Arthur N.: *The Middle Classes in American Politics* (Harvard University Press, 1940).

Howe, Quincy, and A. M. Schlesinger, Jr.: *Guide to Politics* (Dial Press, 1954).

Kent, Frank R.: *The Democratic Party: A History* (Appleton-Century-Crofts, 1928).

Key, Vladimir O., Jr.: *Politics, Parties, and Pressure Groups* (Crowell, 3d ed., 1952).

Lubell, Samuel: *The Future of American Politics* (Harper, 1952).

McKean, Dayton D.: *Party and Pressure Politics* (Houghton Mifflin, 1949).

——: *The Boss: The Hague Machine in Action* (Houghton Mifflin, 1940).

Merriam, Charles E.: *Chicago: A More Intimate View of Urban Politics* (Macmillan, 1929).

—— and Harold F. Gosnell: *The American Party System* (Macmillan, 4th ed., 1949).

Minault, Sylvain S.: *Corrupt Practices Legislation in the 48 States* (Chicago: Council of State Governments, 1942).

Morse, Anson D.: *Parties and Party Leaders* (Boston: Marshall Jones, 1923).

Myers, William S.: *The Republican Party: A History* (Appleton-Century-Crofts, 2d ed., 1931).

Odegard, Peter H., and E. Allen Helms: *American Politics: A Study in Political Dynamics* (Harper, 2d ed., 1947).

Ostrogorski, M.: *Democracy and the Party System in the United States* (Macmillan, 1910).

Overacker, Louise: *Presidential Campaign Funds* (Boston University Press, 1946).

——: *Money in Elections* (Macmillan, 1932).

Peel, Roy V.: *The Political Clubs of New York City* (Putnam, 1935).

Pollock, James K.: *Party Campaign Funds* (Knopf, 1926).

Ranney, Austin: *The Doctrine of Responsible Party Government* (University of Illinois Press, 1954).

Reddig, William M.: *Tom's Town: Kansas City and the Pendergast Legend* (Lippincott, 1947).

Robinson, Edgar E.: *Evolution of American Political Parties* (Harcourt, Brace, 1924).

Rohlfing, Charles C., and James C. Charlesworth (eds.): "Parties and Politics: 1948," *Annals of the American Academy of Political and Social Science,* vol. 259 (September, 1948).

Sait, Edward M. (rev. by Howard R. Penniman): *American Parties and Elections* (Appleton-Century-Crofts, 5th ed., 1952).

Schattschneider, Elmer E.: *Party Government* (Rinehart, 1942).

Stromberg, Roland N.: *Republicanism Reappraised* (Washington, D.C.: Public Affairs Press, 1952).

Zink, Harold: *City Bosses in the United States* (Duke University Press, 1930).

REVIEW
QUESTIONS
1. What is a political party?

2. What are the principal determining factors of party allegiance?

3. Various writers (Ostrogorski, Larned, MacDonald, *et al.*) have complained that the two-party system falsifies and obscures the democratic political process. How serious are these defects? How would abandonment of the two-party system cure them?

4. The precinct leader has been called the "bone and sinew," "foundation," "real source of strength," and "backbone" of party organization. Why? Explain his methods.

5. Discuss the role of third parties in American politics. What part do they play in presidential elections? Congress? Party platforms?

6. Trace the history of the Democratic party from Jefferson to Stevenson.

7. Trace the history of the Republican party from Frémont to Eisenhower.

8. Describe the composition and functions of the following party committees: national, senatorial campaign, congressional campaign.

9. What are the principal provisions of federal law governing the expenditure of funds and the raising of money for national elections?

10. A generation ago most large cities of the United States had bosses or machines that were widely known for their power. How many can you name today? To what do you attribute the decline in number or notoriety?

CHAPTER 11

Suffrage, Nominations, and Elections

> Politics is the practical exercise of the art of self-government, and somebody must attend to it if we are to have self-government. . . . The principal ground for reproach against any American citizen should be that he is *not* a politician. — Elihu Root [1]

Some of the most crucial matters in the democratic state concern the terms under which the people participate in the political process. How is their consent obtained? What portion of the whole population should be entitled to vote? How should party affairs be conducted? The answers to these and similar questions can give a good index to the degree of democracy that prevails in a community, a state, or a nation.

THE RIGHT TO VOTE

Federal Requirements. Matters pertaining to suffrage are regulated chiefly by the states. Four federal requirements are set forth in the Constitution: (1) Those people permitted to vote for the most numerous branch of the state legislature are allowed in each state to participate also in elections of federal officers. (2) The Fourteenth Amendment establishes a penalty (reduction of congressional representation) that might be invoked by Congress against any state that disfranchised a proportion of its adult male population, but this penalty has never been applied. (3) The Fifteenth Amendment forbids states to deny or to abridge the right to vote on account of race, color, or previous condition of servitude. (4) The Nineteenth Amendment prohibits discrimination because of sex. By these

three amendments the amount of state discretion in suffrage matters has been reduced over the years, and the original reliance upon state definition of who might vote has been altered.

State Prerequisites for Voting. [2] 1. One universal requirement for voting is citizenship. All states now insist that a person must be a full-fledged citizen of the United States before exercising the franchise. Several states formerly permitted aliens to vote if they had declared their intention to become citizens.

2. A minimum voting age of twenty-one long prevailed in all states, but Georgia in 1944 and Kentucky in 1955 cut to eighteen. During the Second World War the paradox involved in drafting young men of eighteen to fight for their country, yet denying them the vote, inspired a campaign to reduce the voting age. Although only Georgia and Kentucky have made the change, the issue is being raised in other states. President Eisenhower has advocated a national constitutional amendment to set the voting age at eighteen. It has been argued that the eighteen to twenty-one group is as alert and as able to understand political issues as the age group seventy-five years and over, yet no one has suggested seriously that a maximum age for voting be established. If enfranchised in all states,

---

[1] From an address given in 1920. Quoted in an editorial in *The New York Times*, Nov. 11, 1951.

[2] Factual data are drawn from *The Book of the States*. See current issue for latest information.

the eighteen to twenty-one group would add approximately 8 million new voters to the American electorate.

3. Another qualification imposed in all states is a requisite period of residence. Most states indicate that a person must have lived in the state for 1 year, but several of the North and East demand only 6 months' residence, and a handful of states in the deep South insist upon 2 years. There are also requirements of residence in counties and in precincts; the median is about 90 days in the county and 30 days in the polling district.

4. Registration is almost uniformly demanded; only one state has no registration plan in operation, but several require only urban voters to sign up in advance. The purpose of registration is to prevent fraudulent voting.[3] It provides that voters be enrolled in advance of an election, and permits the inspection of the rolls by interested persons. A majority of the states have now adopted the permanent type of registration, under which a voter, once enrolled, remains on the rolls until he dies, moves, fails to vote in an important election, or otherwise disqualifies himself. A few states still retain the periodic system, which calls for a complete reregistration every year, 2 years, 4 years, or 6 years. Because periodic registration is more expensive and more trouble for the public, it is generally considered inferior to permanent registration.

5. The literacy test is employed in some form in seventeen states. In a few states this test of ability to read and write is carefully administered; it represents a defense against an uninformed electorate and a proper barrier against fraud, for the votes of illiterates might be bought and delivered in the presence of their assisters. On the other hand, it can be used unfairly to disfranchise political enemies or Negroes.

6. Many states disqualify various groups of persons from voting because of insanity, idiocy, feeble-mindedness, or conviction of a felony.

7. Evidence of tax payment is still required in several states. In the early days of the republic,

[3] Joseph P. Harris, *Registration of Voters in the United States* (Brookings, 1929), is the standard work on registration.

the right to vote was reserved carefully for those who held property. As the spirit of democracy spread, property qualifications were lessened and repealed. Today only a few vestigial property qualifications remain, usually as alternatives for other requirements. Five states, however, have retained poll taxes as prerequisites to voting. Because the poll tax has become one of the most controversial of questions concerning the right to vote, fuller examination is required.

Poll Taxes under Fire. Bitter controversy has been aroused by recent attempts to eliminate state poll taxes as prerequisites to voting in Alabama, Arkansas, Mississippi, Texas, and Virginia. They are head taxes of from one to two dollars on each adult (or each male) within specified age groups. In order to discourage poll-tax payment, usually no bills are sent out and little effort is made to collect; payments are often due far in advance of elections. Alabama has a cumulative tax; before a person can vote he must pay up delinquent taxes for each year missed between the ages of twenty-one and forty-five, a maximum of $36.

The effect of the poll tax has been to disfranchise poor people, both white and Negro, in the poll-tax states. Partly because of the poll tax, participation in elections is very low in the states using this device. In 1948 the seven states then having poll taxes accounted for less than 6 per cent of the major party vote for presidential electors, although they had more than 18 per cent of the nation's population in the 1940 census. Critics of the poll tax have stressed the corrupting influence of this requirement for voting. The participating electorate is so small that vested interests or political machines may control elections by buying poll-tax receipts for a few hundred persons. The basic argument against the poll tax is that voting is a right that should not be abridged through lack of capacity to pay.

Organizations seeking the elimination of the poll tax have concentrated their attack on three principal fronts. Initially, they sought congressional legislation to abolish the poll tax in federal elections. First introduced in the House of Representatives in 1940, the bill (under the power of Congress to control the "manner" of electing senators and representatives) would have outlawed poll taxes as fostering pernicious political activities. In various forms it was reintroduced in the next six Congresses and passed by the House of Representatives each time, but it was obstructed in the Senate through filibuster and threat of filibuster. Opponents of the legislation charge that the bill is unconstitutional and invasive of States' rights. Proponents cite eminent legal authorities who assert that the Federal government has adequate power to keep the states from denying the franchise to citizens on grounds of nonpayment of the poll tax, which is not a true "qualification." [4]

Second, Southern states are being urged to repeal their poll-tax laws. Six of them have removed the poll tax since the First World War: North Carolina in 1920, Louisiana in 1934, Florida in 1937, Georgia in 1945, South Carolina in 1950, and Tennessee in 1951. [5]

Third, court proceedings have been instituted to test the constitutionality of poll taxes in both state and Federal courts.

The White Primary. The most recent and effective device developed by the Southern states to disfranchise colored people is the white primary. Since the Democratic party usually enjoys supremacy in the states of the deep South, voting in the Democratic primary is far more important than voting in the general election. The earliest barriers to Negro participation in Democratic party affairs were erected by party rule. In 1923, however, the Texas legislature enacted a law forbidding Negro participation in Democratic primary elections. An El Paso Negro

physician, denied the right to vote in the 1924 Democratic primary, brought suit in the courts and secured a decision from the United States Supreme Court declaring the Texas law a violation of the equal-protection clause of the Fourteenth Amendment. [6] Then the Texas legislature repealed the voided statute and substituted a provision that the executive committee of each party might prescribe the qualifications for party membership. After the Democratic party banned Negro participation by party rule, the validity of the delegation of this authority was tested in the courts. The Supreme Court again ruled that equal protection had been denied. [7] Subsequently the state convention of the party limited the primary to white voters; since the party in Texas is a private association which conducts its own primaries, the Court held that it could exclude colored people without violation of equal protection. [8] Finally, this decision was reversed in 1944 when the Supreme Court declared invalid the same rules of the Texas Democratic party that forbade Negro voting, on the ground that the Classic case fused general and primary elections into a single instrumentality. [9] Also invalidated by the Supreme Court was a "preprimary primary," conducted by a Texas association consisting of all qualified white voters in a county. [10] South Carolina's attempt to retain the white primary by repealing all statutory references to primaries was declared void in the United States Circuit Court. Despite these rulings, it appears that widespread participation by Negroes in Southern primaries will not come for some time.

METHODS OF NOMINATING CANDIDATES

Early Presidential Nominations. No nominating methods were necessary in the first three presidential elections. Members of the electoral college considered themselves free agents but

---

[4] The question of constitutionality has been discussed at length in Senate hearings. See U.S. Senate, Committee on the Judiciary, *Hearings . . . on S. 1280,* 77th Cong., 2d Sess. (1942); and *Hearings . . . on H.R. 7,* 78th Cong., 1st Sess. (1943). The issues were reviewed in U.S. House of Representatives, House Administration Committee, *Anti-poll Tax Legislation, Hearings . . . ,* 80th Cong., 1st Sess. (1947), and Senate Committee on Rules and Administration, *Poll Tax, Hearings . . . ,* 80th Cong., 2d Sess. (1948).

[5] On the general problem see Henry N. Williams, "The Poll Tax and Constitutional Problems Involved in Its Repeal," *University of Chicago Law Review,* vol. 11 (February, 1944), pp. 177–183.

[6] Nixon *v.* Herndon, 273 U.S. 536 (1927).

[7] Nixon *v.* Condon, 286 U.S. 73 (1932).

[8] Grovey *v.* Townsend, 295 U.S. 45 (1935).

[9] Smith *v.* Allwright, 321 U.S. 649 (1944). The Classic case is explained on p. 191.

[10] Terry *v.* Adams, 345 U.S. 461 (1953).

managed to agree without difficulty upon Washington twice and Adams once. The emergence of political parties by 1800 brought with it the necessity of some machinery for making the party's choice.

The congressional caucus emerged quite naturally to fill the need. Composed of the party's senators and representatives in Congress, it was easy to convene and reasonably representative of party sentiment. The chief weakness of this scheme of nominating, however, was that it denied representation to states that had no congressmen of a particular party. In 1824, after the Federalist party had expired, the Democratic-Republicans in congressional caucus chose Crawford of Georgia; three other aspirants of the same party, Jackson, John Quincy Adams, and Clay, entered their candidacies. The election was thrown to the House of Representatives, which chose Adams, and the congressional caucus was badly discredited.

The national convention, composed of delegates from the various states, replaced the congressional caucus as a nominating body for the election of 1832. The Antimasonic party first employed the device in 1831; both the new National Republicans and Jackson's Democrats adopted this method which has been used since that time.

National Party Conventions. The national conventions have never been governed by federal law. For 20 years, between 1921 and 1941, the Supreme Court decision, Newberry *v.* United States, stood as a barrier to congressional attempts to regulate the nominating process.[11] A later decision, United States *v.* Classic, appears to mark a reversal of the Court's attitude.[12] No real attempt, however, has yet been made by Congress to utilize this renewed power. The only legal control is exercised by the states, which by law may establish methods of selecting delegates as well as rules governing their conduct.

When a convention will be held is determined largely by custom. Until recently Republicans

met in the second half of June or in early July, and Democrats about two weeks later. In 1952, however, both conventions were held in July; in 1956 both were scheduled in August. One reason for the later dates is the great expense, particularly of the television medium, involved in longer campaigns.

Where the convention will meet is decided by the national committee, but the decision rests upon several factors:

1. Financial inducement is offered by various cities; in recent years around $200,000 has been paid by business people of the successful city to secure a major party convention.

2. Strategic location of a city in a pivotal state or section is highly important, for each party hopes to arouse support in the region of the convention city.

3. Facilities and accessibility, including hotel, restaurant, and transportation services on an adequate scale and a mammoth meeting hall, are necessary.

Convention Representation and Delegates. The basis of representation in the national conventions of both parties until 1916 was each state two delegates for each senator and representative from the state in Congress.[13] In the Republican party this basis of representation was attacked on the ground that it gave the same voting strength to delegations from Southern states, where the party had little voting strength, as to Northern and Western states of the same population which regularly elected Republican members of Congress and cast their electoral votes for the Republican candidates. In most Southern states the Republican party was largely a paper organization controlled by

[11] 256 U.S. 232 (1921).
[12] 313 U.S. 299 (1941). The Classic case concerned prosecution for frauds perpetrated in a primary election.

[13] As used here, "delegate" means vote in convention. In order to honor party bigwigs, the state organizations often send huge delegations to national conventions, each individual casting only a fraction of one vote. In the Democratic convention of 1940, one district in Mississippi sent 54 delegates to cast its two votes; each delegate had $1/27$ of a vote. That same convention adopted a rule, effective in 1944, that no delegate may have less than one-half vote. Nevertheless, there were some one-third votes in the 1952 Democratic convention.

a few federal officeholders when the party was in power, and hence a Republican President could always control this sizable block of delegate votes in the national convention. Thus in 1912 President Taft had the solid support of the Republican delegations from the South, which enabled

PRESIDENTIAL PRIMARY SHORT BALLOT FOR DELEGATES INDICATING PREFERENCE: CALIFORNIA

SAMPLE BALLOT

(This number to be torn off by inspector)

MARK CROSSES (+) ON BALLOT ONLY WITH RUBBER STAMP; NEVER WITH PEN OR PENCIL

No 99391

(ABSENTEE BALLOTS MAY BE MARKED WITH PEN AND INK OR PENCIL)

(Fold ballot to this perforated line, leaving top margin exposed)

TUESDAY, JUNE 3, 1952

OFFICIAL PRESIDENTIAL PRIMARY ELECTION BALLOT
REPUBLICAN PARTY

To vote for the group of candidates preferring a person whose name appears on the ballot, stamp a cross (+) in the square in the column headed by the name of the person preferred.

For Delegates to National Convention. Vote for one group only.	
Candidates Preferring **THOMAS H. WERDEL**	Candidates Preferring **EARL WARREN**
☐	☐
A cross (+) stamped in this square shall be counted as a vote for all candidates preferring Thomas H. Werdel	A cross (+) stamped in this square shall be counted as a vote for all candidates preferring Earl Warren

California has long elected delegates to the national party convention on an at-large basis. Beginning with the 1944 presidential primary, the state eliminated from the ballot the names of individual candidates for delegate. The presidential primary short ballot used in 1952 is shown above.

him to defeat Theodore Roosevelt, who was favored by the majority of the delegates from the Republican states outside of the South. This bitter convention fight, leading temporarily to a division of the Republican party, forced the 1916 reforms which reduced the voting strength of the Southern states in the Republican national convention. Since then the basis of representation has been revised several times, each time reducing the vote accorded to states where the voting strength of the party is weak. The latest change was made in 1952 after the "regu-

lar" delegations from Texas, Louisiana, and Georgia, who supported Senator Robert A. Taft of Ohio for the nomination, were unseated and their seats given to contesting delegations favoring General Eisenhower.

The basis of state representation in the Republican national convention is as follows:

Delegates at Large

Four for each state.

Two for each representative elected at large.

Six additional if the state went Republican or elected a Republican governor or United States Senator at the last election.

District Delegates

One for each congressional district which cast 2,000 Republican votes at the last election.

One additional delegate for each congressional district which cast 10,000 Republican votes at the last election.

In 1952 the Republican convention had a total voting strength of 1,205 and in 1948, of 1,094.

In 1940 the Democrats yielded to Southern pressure and provided a modest bonus for states showing Democratic voting strength. Each state that went Democratic in a presidential election was given four extra votes at large in the national convention 4 years later. It yielded 1,176 in 1944 to 1,234 in 1948 and 1,230 in 1952. For 1956, an additional bonus of four votes was given to each state carried by a Democrat for President, governor, or Senator in the past four years. The new total was 1,372 votes.

In the conventions of both parties, several delegates are also accorded to Alaska, Hawaii, Puerto Rico, the Virgin Islands, and the District of Columbia, which, of course, have no electoral votes. This practice is designed to keep the parties alive in these areas.

Delegates are selected in two ways: (1) State and district conventions or party committees, in about two-thirds of the states, utilize state and congressional-district machinery to choose delegates and often to direct how they shall vote;

(2) presidential primaries, used in approximately one-third of the states, with choice directly by the electorate. The first method is favored by many party leaders, largely because it is flexible and provides maximum bargaining power for state interests. Three states use a combination of the two.

Presidential Primaries. Two main forms of the presidential primary are these: (1) election of delegates, who may be pledged or unpledged, and (2) popular expression of preference among presidential aspirants. A few states provide for both. The presidential primary is regaining favor. But even in its heyday (1924 with 24 states) it was not a decisive force. Leading candidates may remain out of the primaries (as did Stevenson in 1952) or fail utterly in them (as did Hoover in 1928), yet secure the nomination without difficulty. A strong tendency is noted for states using the presidential primary to select delegates pledged to a "favorite son," some man from the home state. Sometimes this

tactic is employed in a serious attempt to call the country's attention to his talents, but more often it is a subterfuge through which a state delegation is able to be in a better bargaining position and to throw its votes to a likely candidate who gives assurances that he will reward the state properly.

On the other hand, the 1952 preconvention campaigns stimulated a revival of public interest in the presidential primary. The sharp contest for delegates between Senator Robert A. Taft and General Dwight Eisenhower brought out Republican voters in record numbers. When aspirants for the nominations counted up, they discovered that 567 of the 1,205 Republican delegates and 576 of the 1,230 Democratic delegates were chosen via the primary method. People in states lacking the presidential primary complained about being deprived of a voice in choosing their presidential candidate. The Gallup poll reported that 53 per cent of those queried said that the people did not have enough to say

Mandatory Presidential Primaries of 1956	Date of primary	State	Delegates chosen	Delegates pledged?	Preference vote?	Delegates bound?
	March 13	New Hampshire	Elected	Can be	Yes	No
	20	Minnesota	Elected *	Must be	No	Yes
	April 3	Wisconsin	Elected	Must be	No	Can be
	10	Illinois	Elected *	No	Yes	No
	17	New Jersey	Elected	Can be	Yes	No
	24	Massachusetts	Elected	Can be	Yes	No
		Pennsylvania	Elected *	Can be	Yes	Can be
	May 7	Maryland	Party body	No	Yes	Yes
	8	Indiana	Party body	No	Yes	Yes
		Ohio	Elected	Must be	No	Yes
		West Virginia	Elected	No	Yes	No
	15	Nebraska	Elected	No	Yes	Yes
	18	Oregon	Elected	Can be	Yes	Can be
	June 5	California	Elected	Must be	Yes	Yes
		Montana	Party body	....	Yes	Yes
		New York	Elected *	No	No	No
		South Dakota	Elected	Can be	No	Can be

* At-large delegates chosen by state convention.

in choosing presidential candidates, and that 73 per cent favored a nation-wide primary election that would choose presidential candidates in place of the present national conventions. Another poll by Gallup in 1955 reported 58 per cent for presidential primaries.

PRESIDENTIAL PRIMARY LONG BALLOT FOR DELEGATES INDICATING PREFERENCE: OHIO

Ohio retains the long presidential primary ballot, listing the names of all candidates for delegate, together with the first and second choices for President of each.

National Convention Procedure. The order of business is much the same in both party gatherings. The national chairman calls the meeting to order. A temporary convention chairman is chosen and he gives the "keynote" address. Committees of the convention are set up with one delegate from every state and territory on each committee. The credentials committee determines which are the official delegates for the final roll call; occasionally there is a contest over the authenticity of a delegation's credentials, and control of this committee may affect the choice of candidate for the presidency. The committee on permanent organization brings in the slate of convention officers; its rejection may forecast a revolt against a leading presidential aspirant. A rules-and-order-of-business commit-

tee usually proposes rules of procedure identical with those of previous conventions. Finally, the platform-and-resolutions committee drafts the party declaration of principles and policies. The report on the platform is often hotly debated, but usually the majority report is adopted.

Choosing candidates for President and Vice-President comes as the final important action. The roll is called by states, and delegations place in nomination the favored aspirants; this place on the agenda is occasion for elaborate oratory by nominators and seconders and noisy floor demonstrations. When all contenders for the nomination are before the convention, the first polling begins by states in alphabetical order. Often, especially in Republican conventions, some candidate secures the requisite majority on the first ballot. Sometimes conventions deadlock and many votes are required; the Democrats took 103 ballots in 1924 before the warring Smith and McAdoo factions could agree on John W. Davis as a compromise candidate.

Voting is done by states, but delegations may be polled individually on demand of a single delegate. The Democrats have a unit rule under which a majority of a state delegation from a nonprimary state may cast the full vote of a state (unless forbidden by that state's law). In 1936 the Democrats abolished the companion two-thirds rule, though Southern Democrats clung to it as vital to the protection of the minority and as an assurance against party splits. Its repeal, and the retention of the unit rule, makes likely in future Democratic conventions quicker victories for aspirants with plurality support.

The vice-presidential contest may be decided by a number of considerations. The successful presidential aspirant may have traded support with another who receives the vice-presidential nomination (Garner in 1932). Or balance will be sought for the ticket by nominating one who contrasts with the presidential nominee in section, religion, personality, policy, or other attributes (Sparkman in 1952).

Reform of the National Convention. The national convention is one of our most criticized political institutions. To make the all-important choices of who shall be major party nominees for the presidency, we have two aggregations of a thousand or more delegates, chosen by miscellaneous means unlikely to produce majority choice, and meeting in an atmosphere of colossal clowning and high-pressure methods, wholly unregulated by federal law. Woodrow Wilson, in his first annual message to the Congress in 1913, urged the enactment of legislation to provide primary elections so that voters could select nominees for the presidency without the intervention of nominating conventions. He suggested that platforms be made by a new type of party convention composed of nominees for the Senate and House, national committeemen, and the presidential nominee.

Although the Congress took no action, the states moved rapidly to legislate regarding the selection of delegates and the expression of preferences by the electorate. After the Newberry decision it was assumed for 20 years that Congress lacked power to regulate the nominating process. During this interim, presidential primary enthusiasm waned, and the old-fashioned national convention with state and district convention-selected delegates returned to favor. Professor Overacker classifies proposals for a national presidential primary into three: (1) combine primary with existing conventions; (2) have existing conventions propose nominees but submit to primary for ratification; (3) eliminate the convention and provide for direct nation-

PRESIDENTIAL PRIMARY COMBINING ELECTION OF DELEGATES AND PREFERENCE VOTE: NEW HAMPSHIRE

New Hampshire combines the election of delegates and the pledging of the delegation through a preference vote. There is a chance that conflicting results may obtain, with one candidate securing the delegates and another the "popularity contest."

wide primary.[14] After examining the difficulties connected with each proposal, Overacker concludes that no plan is very promising.

More drastic proposals are likely to attract the attention necessary to secure reform on a national basis. Restoration of the congressional caucus (perhaps with nominees for Senate and House instead of sitting members) would help bring the legislative and executive branches closer together and assure greater deliberation and dignity. Two proposals to effect reform were before recent Congresses. One, the Douglas-Bennett bill, provided for a federal inducement for states to conduct presidential primaries. It would authorize the Federal government to enter into agreements with willing states for the conduct of such contests and would provide for compensating states up to 20 cents for each vote cast.

The other, a proposed constitutional amendment by Senator Smathers, would displace the convention with a uniform nation-wide primary for selecting presidential and vice-presidential candidates of the parties. The "nominating votes" (equivalent of electoral vote) of each state would be divided among presidential candidates in proportion to their popular votes. A majority would be required to nominate; if none were obtained in the first balloting by any candidate, then a second runoff primary would be held between the two receiving the highest number of votes in the first primary.

Neither proposal has been approved by Congress.

In view of widespread state opposition to both the national primary and the federal subsidy for state presidential primaries, attention to the improvement of state laws appears most likely to bear fruit. In 1955 the National Municipal League issued a draft of a "model state presidential primary law" as a basis for discussion. The proposed law would make the presidential primary mandatory for larger parties. Voters must register their party affiliations in advance in order to participate. June was proposed as

[14] Charles E. Merriam and Louise Overacker, *Primary Elections* (University of Chicago Press, 1928), p. 191.

the best month for voting. The state central committee of each party may certify a list of candidates for delegate. Presidential aspirants may file lists of proposed delegates. Voting would be by slate, all delegates being elected at large and the various slates winning places on the delegation in proportion to their popular showing. Presidential candidates could not bind their delegates after their support dropped below 10 per cent, or after they received support from only one state.

Nominations for Congressional and State Offices. The development of nominating methods may be indicated chronologically. Self-announcement and selection by informal caucus were used in the early days. This gave way in turn to the legislative caucus, which was composed of partisans in legislative bodies. Criticisms of the unrepresentative character of the legislative caucus led to a modification called the "mixed" (mongrel) caucus, composed of legislators and some outside representatives. Gradually this form was superseded by the delegate convention, set up especially to make nominations. The convention system later was denounced as unrepresentative and controlled by corrupt interests. It was replaced by the direct primary, in which party voters participate directly in the nominating process.

The Convention System. After 1910 the convention was replaced largely by the direct primary. Connecticut, in 1955, was the last state to adopt the primary, but it is in only partial or optional operation in several states. Important use is made of the convention plan of nominating for some state-wide congressional and state offices in Indiana and New York. It is optional with the parties in several Southern states. Subordinate employment is made of conventions for framing party platforms in many other states. The usual pattern of the delegate convention calls for the election of delegates by voters affiliated with the party, or by party groups and committees. The delegates meet in convention under a procedure not unlike that of a national convention.

The state and local convention method of nominating party candidates, discredited during the reform movement of the first two decades of the century, is being restored to favor in the thinking of many students of government. The direct primary has not brought all the improvements predicted by those who claimed it to be a panacea for many ills. The direct primary, particularly the open form, makes possible the sudden capture of a party's nomination by a maverick group or colorful individual with no previous responsibility in the party. Far from removing the control over the nominating process from bosses and machines, adoption of the primary in many states induced a sinister alliance of vested interests with newspapers. This combination succeeds in primaries because of public disinterest, disciplined machine vote, and blind following of newspaper endorsements. Restoration of the convention system for making

nominations of candidates for state-wide offices may produce abler and more responsible leadership. A major party in New York, for example, can offer a nomination to a leading citizen, whereas in some other states a party rarely can avoid a wide-open primary fight that drives men of reputation from consideration.

The Direct Primary. The direct primary is the most widely adopted of all nominating schemes. It is now mandatory or optional with the parties in forty-eight states. Connecticut, in 1955, was the last state to provide for this nominating method. Party voters indicate on a direct-primary ballot which aspirants they prefer to have as their party's nominees for public office. Usually this is done through a publicly conducted poll with all the safeguards of a general election. Most of the states use the "closed pri-

THE OPEN PRIMARY: WISCONSIN

OFFICIAL PRIMARY BALLOT
GENERAL ELECTION
REPUBLICAN PARTY

To vote for a person whose name is printed on the ballot, mark a cross (X) in the square at the RIGHT of the name of the person for whom you desire to vote. To vote for a person whose name is not printed on the ballot write his name in the blank space provided for that purpose.

STATE		COUNTY	
Governor — Vote for one		County Clerk — Vote for one	
WALTER J. KOHLER		MILDRED GUNDERSON	
Lieutenant Governor — Vote for one		County Treasurer — Vote for one	
GEORGE M. SMITH		WM. O. KELLY	
CONGRESSIONAL		Sheriff — Vote for one	
United States Senator — Vote for one		ELMER L. PAQUETTE	
PERRY J. STEARNS		Coroner — Vote for one	
EDWARD J. FINAN			
ANDREW G. JACOBSON		Clerk of the Circuit Court — Vote for one	
EDMUND KERWER		JOHN L. RITZINGER	
JOSEPH R. McCARTHY			
LEONARD F. SCHMITT		District Attorney — Vote for one	
Representative in Congress 9th District — Vote for one		VANCE L. SINCLAIR	
MERLIN HULL		ALVIN M. TANDBERG	

OFFICIAL PRIMARY BALLOT
GENERAL ELECTION
DEMOCRATIC PARTY

To vote for a person whose name is printed on the ballot, mark a cross (X) in the square at the RIGHT of the name of the person for whom you desire to vote. To vote for a person whose name is not printed on the ballot write his name in the blank space provided for that purpose.

STATE		COUNTY	
Governor — Vote for one		County Clerk — Vote for one	
WILLIAM PROXMIRE		County Treasurer — Vote for one	
Lieutenant Governor — Vote for one		Sheriff — Vote for one	
SVERRE ROANG			
Secretary of State — Vote for one		Coroner — Vote for one	
HERMAN F. JESSEN		Clerk of the Circuit Court — Vote for one	
CONGRESSIONAL		District Attorney — Vote for one	
United States Senator — Vote for one			
HENRY S. REUSS		Register of Deeds — Vote for one	
THOMAS E. FAIRCHILD			
		Surveyor — Vote for one	
Representative in Congress 9th District — Vote for one		Party Precinct Committeeman — Vote for one	
KENT L. PILLSBURY			

Under Wisconsin's open-primary scheme, each voter receives all ballots. In 1952 these two ballots were stapled together. The voter took both into the polling booth, marked the one of his choice, and deposited both used and unused ballots in the ballot boxes.

mary," which means that each voter may participate only in the nomination of candidates for the party with which he is registered or affiliated. The other type, the "open primary," is employed in eight states.[15] It allows the voter to decide in the voting booth in which party's primary he wishes to vote without having to register or otherwise publicly disclose his party affiliation.

Advocates of the "closed" primary system,

[15] The open primary is sometimes called the "Wisconsin type." It is used also in Idaho, Michigan, Minnesota, Montana, North Dakota, Utah, and Washington. North Dakota is considered by some to be a borderline open primary; voters are not registered by party and may vote whichever ballot they choose. *The Book of the States, 1954–1955,* p. 83, also lists Arkansas, Mississippi, Rhode Island, and South Carolina as states in whose primaries the voter receives both ballots.

usually strong party men, contend that only avowed members of the party, those who have registered as members of the party or who are willing to declare their party affiliation publicly, should be allowed to vote in its primary and thus participate in the selection of its candidates. On the other hand, those who favor the "open" primary maintain that a man's party affiliation is his own business and that it is an invasion of the secrecy of the ballot to require him to declare publicly with which party he is affiliated. Many voters strongly object to stating their party affiliation publicly. The requirement is particularly distasteful to persons who regard themselves as independents. Proponents of the "open" system maintain that no good purpose is served by requiring voters to register or state publicly their party affiliation, for they can be relied on to vote in the primary of the party of

THE CLOSED PRIMARY: ILLINOIS

Third District
Dorr Election Precinct

SPECIMEN REPUBLICAN PRIMARY BALLOT

For preference for President of the United States, for election of Delegates to National Nominating Convention and Committeemen, and for the Nomination of State, Congressional, Senatorial and County Officers, in the County of McHenry, in the State of Illinois. Election: April 8, 1952.

Raymond D. Woods
County Clerk

REPUBLICAN PRIMARY BALLOT

FOR PRESIDENT OF THE UNITED STATES:
(Vote for One)

☐ RILEY ALVIN BENDER

☐ ROBERT A. TAFT

☐ HAROLD E. STASSEN

FOR GOVERNOR:
(Vote for One)

☐ ANTHONY A. POLLEY

☐ RICHARD YATES ROWE

☐ WILLIAM G. STRATTON

☐ WILLIAM N. ERICKSON

☐ PARK LIVINGSTON

FOR LIEUTENANT GOVERNOR:
(Vote for One)

☐ JOHN WILLIAM CHAPMAN

FOR REPRESENTATIVE IN CONGRESS:
FOURTEENTH DISTRICT
(Vote for One)

☐ CHAUNCEY W. REED

☐ ROBERT L. FARNSWORTH

FOR DELEGATES TO NATIONAL
NOMINATING CONVENTION:
FOURTEENTH CONGRESSIONAL DISTRICT
(Vote for Two)

☐ CHARLES M. BURGESS

☐ LESTER B. CONVERSE

☐ CARL H. ZEISS

FOR ALTERNATE DELEGATES TO NATIONAL
NOMINATING CONVENTION:
FOURTEENTH CONGRESSIONAL DISTRICT
(Vote for Two)

☐ HENRY L. COWLIN

☐ VERNON W. KAYS

In Illinois, as in other closed-primary states, the voter is permitted to participate only in the primary of the party with which he is registered or affiliated.

their choice; the advocates of the "closed" system argue that the "open" system permits voters of one party to "raid" the opposite party and vote for the weak candidates. Studies of the subject indicate that there is actually little "raiding" carried on in "open" primary states, and that voters almost invariably vote for the candidate whom they wish to see elected.

Primary Procedures. In "closed" primary states the voter is given at the polls only the ballot of the party with which he has declared affiliation; in "open" primary states, however, he is given the ballots of all parties, and selects the one which he will vote in the secrecy of the polling booth. Having decided which party primary ballot he will use, the voter is permitted to vote only for the candidates of that party. He may be in favor of certain candidates of another party, but in the primary he must limit his votes to the candidates of one party.

In the State of Washington, however, the voter is given even greater choice. The names of the candidates of all parties are printed on the same "blanket" ballot under the office designation, and the voter is free to vote for the candidate of his choice, irrespective of parties. Thus a voter could vote for a candidate for the Republican nomination for governor and a candidate for the Democratic nomination for lieutenant governor. This system makes no effort to limit the party primaries to the avowed members of the party but is based on the theory that the primary election is an integral part of the election process and that the voter should be permitted to cast his ballot for the candidate of his choice. The system is anathema to advocates of the "closed" primary system, who contend that it will break down all semblance of party regularity and division, but it appears not to have had this effect in Washington. Both the major parties in the state are strong and healthy, and primary and final elections are vigorously contested.[16]

[16] For a good up-to-date consideration of the direct primary, see National Municipal League, *A Model Direct Primary Election System* (New York: The League, 1951), which was prepared by Joseph P. Harris and a committee of the League.

Those who seek party nominations usually are required to file petitions signed by a certain number or percentage of voters. Some states require the payment of a filing fee. In most states the individual obtaining the largest number of

BLANKET OR "WIDE OPEN" PRIMARY: WASHINGTON

PRIMARY ELECTION
Thurston County
TUESDAY, SEPTEMBER 14, 1954

To Vote for a Person Mark a CROSS in the Square at the Right of the Name of the Person for Whom You Desire to Vote

FEDERAL

REPRESENTATIVE IN CONGRESS

Congressman-at-Large		Vote for One
DON MAGNUSON	Democrat	☐
AL CANWELL	Republican	☐
W. O. "BILL" FRERICHS	Republican	☐
RICHARD B. CAMPBELL	Republican	☐
WILBUR R. PARKIN	Republican	☐
		☐

REPRESENTATIVE IN CONGRESS

Third Congressional District		Vote for One
RUSSELL V. MACK	Republican	☐
CLYDE V. TISDALE	Democrat	☐
WILLIAM E. VANCE	Democrat	☐
JIM CARTY	Democrat	☐
		☐

STATE

The voter in the state of Washington is permitted unusual freedom in the partisan primary. He receives a comprehensive primary ballot that includes all candidates of all parties. He may choose to vote in the Democratic primary for one office and in the Republican for another.

votes, even though not a majority, receives the nomination of his party for office. Eleven states, all Southern or border states, seek to ensure a majority choice by holding a subsequent "runoff" primary. If a candidate wins a majority in the first primary he receives the nomination; otherwise the two highest candidates run in the second or "runoff" primary. The Democratic nomination, it may be noted, is virtually equivalent to election in these states. A few states, notably California, permit an aspirant to enter the primaries of more than one party. This is called "cross filing." The highest objective of the cross filer is to win both party nominations and avoid a contest in the final election. In California practically all candidates enter the primaries of both major parties, but since 1952 the capturing of both nominations has been curbed by printing the party affiliation of each candidate after his name. A candidate, however, is not permitted to become the nominee of the opposite party unless he wins the nomination of his own party.

Variations. Combination schemes using both primary and convention plans have been adopted in several states. Five states—Colorado, Massachusetts, New Mexico, Utah, and Rhode Island—authorize party conventions or committees to propose candidates for nomination at primary elections. Other candidates may run in the primary without the endorsement of the party organization. Although the laws of the four states vary considerably, the purpose of the preprimary endorsement is the same in each case: to indicate to voters which candidates are regarded by the party officers as qualified and willing to accept the party's program.

In favor of having official party organizations propose candidates it is argued that better qualified candidates can be induced to run, more responsibility will be placed on party leaders, and a preliminary screening of candidates is needed prior to the primary election. Opponents of the plan say it, in effect, restores the old convention system, grants altogether too much power to party leaders, and places the independent candidate in a disadvantageous position. The National Municipal League committee on the direct primary came out in favor of preprimary endorsements by party bodies and recommended that the candidates proposed by them should be so designated on the ballot, but that independent candidates should be able to qualify by filing a petition and paying the required fee.[17]

In two states—Iowa and South Dakota—a postprimary convention is used to choose party

[17] *Ibid.,* pp. 20–34.

nominees in case no candidate polls 35 per cent of the vote in the primary election.

The nonpartisan primary, used for certain local and state offices in some states, is in reality a preliminary election rather than a primary in the usual sense. Under this plan, candidates enter their names for the nonpartisan office by filing petitions or paying fees or both. If any candidate for the office secures a majority in the first election, he is declared elected in some systems. Ordinarily, if there is no majority, the two highest candidates engage in a "runoff" contest at general election time. No party designations of any kind are permitted on the ballot. Mechanically the nonpartisan "primary" and election plan is usually superior to the partisan, for the chance of minority winners nearly always is eliminated.

CAMPAIGNS AND ELECTIONS

Methods of Campaigning. As a first step in a political campaign, regular party machinery is manned with full force. In a presidential contest the national chairman is in command; in a state-wide campaign, the state chairman or a comparable official is in charge. Headquarters agencies are placed on an active basis.

The strategy employed depends upon office sought, personality of the candidate, and circumstances. Candidates for the presidency increasingly take the "swing around the circle," making personal appearances in most sections. An incumbent President sometimes conducts a "front porch" campaign and makes few speeches; this is especially effective if the country is in a prosperous condition. Issues largely are determined by circumstances.

Voters are reached as individuals in a variety of ways: (1) Canvass by direct personal contact of party workers with voters. It may be a systematic house-to-house canvass, or an informal contact at a place where voters gather. (2) Appeals by mail are less effective than personal canvass but are often easier to make. Such approaches are expensive and require much care in the drafting but make possible stratified electioneering among individuals of different racial, occupational, or other groups.

Voters are reached in the mass through the

following: (1) Meetings of all kinds are held indoors and outdoors with single speakers and joint debates, sometimes impromptu and occasionally elaborately planned. (2) Radio and television appearances of candidates and other party speakers have grown of great importance in the last few campaigns. (3) Printed literature is prepared and distributed, including newspaper advertisements and articles, pamphlets, leaflets, posters, and others. (4) Motion pictures and recordings are used at meetings and have proved an effective campaign medium.

Authority over Elections. The states are required by the Constitution to provide for the election of members of both houses of Congress. "The Times, Places, and Manner of holding Elections for Senators and Representatives shall be prescribed in each State by the Legislature thereof; but the Congress may at any time by Law make or alter such Regulations. . . ." [18]

In 1872 Congress set as election day for federal officers the Tuesday after the first Monday of November in even-numbered years. Now all states except Maine, which has a constitutional provision requiring a September election, adhere to the congressional date. The manner of holding elections has been regulated by Congress in several respects: (1) In 1842 Congress enacted that Representatives be elected by districts composed of contiguous territory. (2) Thirty years later districts were required to be of equal population. (3) A 1901 act added the word "compact." (4) Congress has also ruled out oral voting in the election of representatives. Both items (2) and (3) were omitted in the 1929 act.

Otherwise, the states have wide authority over elections. As stated before, in providing who shall vote for the most numerous branch of the state legislature, states decide who shall vote for federal officers. But state voting requirements tend to uniformity, with citizenship, an age of twenty-one years, residence, and registration on the required list in virtually all states. Constitutional amendments restrict the authority of the state to discriminate because of race, color, previous condition of servitude, or sex.

[18] Art. I, Sec. 4.

Election Administration. In most states elections are supervised by a state election board or the secretary of state. Counties and cities place in charge of election administration either regular officials with other tasks (as county clerk) or create special officers (registrars or commissioners). Precincts are the essential cell units in elections. The number of officials in each de-

GENERAL ELECTION BALLOT FORMS PARTY COLUMN: INDIANA

This portion of the Indiana ballot of 1954 illustrates the straight-ticket party-column form. Twenty-five states use this form. Five additional states have party-column ballots, but do not permit straight-ticket voting.

pends upon the size of the precinct, the length of the ballot, the equipment, and the skill of the officers themselves.

The Australian ballot is in general use in this country; it is printed at public expense, secret, all-inclusive, available only on election day, and its use is protected by numerous safeguards. American ballots fall into two general types: (1) the office-block form (Massachusetts) on which candidates are listed by the office they seek, and (2) the party column type (Indiana) on which all candidates of a particular party are listed together. The voting machine is a mechanical adaptation of the Australian ballot. It has the obvious adavantages of speed, accuracy, and simplicity, but it is expensive, fragile, and sometimes discourages split voting.

The method of electing the President is examined in some detail in a subsequent chapter. It must be explained here, however, that the voter does not vote directly for his choice for the presidency, but for the electors who go through the formality of casting their ballots for the candidates to whom they have been pledged. Every state now elects presidential electors on a state-wide basis, with each voter able to vote for the whole number of electors to which his state is entitled. In recent years twenty-five states have adopted the "presidential short ballot," which eliminates the names of the individual electors from the ballot and permits the voter to mark his ballot for the whole slate of electors pledged to the presidential and vice-presidential candidates of his choice. Two other states in effect have the presidential short ballot through their general use of voting machines.

Absentee Voting. Absentee voting was originated for military personnel during the Civil War and expanded greatly during the Second World War. It was extended to civilians gradually during the past 40 years. All states now permit absentee voting by persons in the armed services. During the Second World War, especially just before the 1944 election, nearly every state extended its provisions for military voting, mainly in the direction of liberalizing registra-

tion rules and application forms and in extending the time for returning the ballots. The state absentee plans were supplemented by federal application forms and federal war ballots; the latter were honored by twenty states.

Absentee voting, as its name implies, permits a qualified person who is away from his legal residence or confined for some reason on election day to cast his ballot by mail or in advance of the election. Although state laws have a considerable variety of provisions, there are features common to most states.[19] (1) Application is made within the time limits set by law. (2) The ballot is mailed by election officials. (3) The absent voter fills out the ballot in the presence of a notary public or public official. (4) The ballot is returned to the election official by mail. (5) Absentee ballots are counted either in a central election office or sent to the precincts for counting. A few states permit a voter to cast his ballot in person a few days early in case he expects to be away on election day. Approximately one-half of the states provide for absentee registration, so that a person who is away at registration time can enter his name on the roll. This is of particular value to people who work

---

[19] A good source of information on absentee voting is George F. Miller, *Absentee Voters and Suffrage Laws* (Washington, D.C.: Daylion Co., 1949).

GENERAL ELECTION BALLOT FORMS
OFFICE BLOCK: MASSACHUSETTS

To vote for a Person, mark a Cross **X** in the Square at the right of the Party Name or Political Designation. **X**	To vote for a Person, mark a Cross **X** in the Square at the right of the Party Name or Political Designation. **X**
GOVERNOR Vote for ONE	**CONGRESSMAN** Ninth District Vote for ONE
HORACE T. CAHILL – of Braintree — Republican	CHARLES L. GIFFORD – of Barnstable — Republican
MAURICE J. TOBIN – of Boston — Democratic	WILLIAM McAULIFFE – of New Bedford — Democratic
HENNING A. BLOMEN – of Cambridge — Socialist Labor Party	
GUY S. WILLIAMS – of Worcester — Prohibition	
LIEUTENANT GOVERNOR Vote for ONE	**COUNCILLOR** First District Vote for ONE
ROBERT F. BRADFORD – of Cambridge — Republican	JOSEPH P. CLARK, Jr. – of Fall River — Democratic
JOHN B. CARR – of Somerville — Democratic	ROGER KEITH – of Brockton — Republican
ALFRED ERICKSON – of Quincy — Prohibition	
GEORGE LEO McGLYNN – of Springfield — Socialist Labor Party	
SECRETARY Vote for ONE	
FREDERIC W. COOK – of Somerville — Republican	**SENATOR** Third Bristol District Vote for ONE
MARGARET M. O'RIORDAN – of Boston — Democratic	JOSEPH F. FRANCIS – of Fairhaven — Republican
HORACE I. HILLIS – of Saugus — Socialist Labor Party	EDWARD C. PEIRCE – of New Bedford — Democratic

The Massachusetts or office-block type of ballot makes no provision for straight-ticket voting, but requires the voter to indicate which candidate he wishes for each office. Seventeen states use the office-block form. One additional state, Pennsylvania, has this type but permits straight-ticket voting.

in Washington, D.C., but maintain legal addresses in their home states and to those from states that require frequent reregistration.

Servicemen's Voting. During the Second World War, Congress and the country were beset with a great struggle over the right to vote of men and women in the armed forces. The necessities of war spread Americans by the millions over every continent and the seven seas. Servicemen experienced difficulty in voting because of (1) their inability to meet one or more of their states' qualifications, such as residence, age, poll tax, literacy, and the like; and (2) the impossibility of their returning to their home states to cast ballots or of their meeting absentee-balloting deadlines. Both in 1942 and in 1944 federal legislation was enacted to expedite service voting. In each case greatest encouragement was given for servicemen to utilize the absentee-voting procedure of their own states. The 1942 law, which permitted voting on a state "war ballot," was passed very late and used rather little. The 1944 act not only gave the serviceman a form on which to apply for a state ballot, but also provided him with an "official federal war ballot" which he could send to his state if the state absentee ballot did not reach him. Twenty states accepted federal ballots, totaling less than 85,000 ballots.

In 1952 there were an estimated 2½ million men and women of voting age in the armed services, of whom many were in the Korean combat zone. President Truman asked the American Political Science Association to study the problem of service voting. A committee was constituted and filed its report in March, 1952. It found that existing federal law provides that, during a *state of war,* absent servicemen have a right to vote for federal officers without registering and the poll tax is banned as a requirement for voting for federal officers. Applicable both in war and peace are several recommendations to states that they liberalize and standardize procedures for service voting, and a list of federal responsibilities, including provision of postcard application forms and free air mail for all balloting materials.

The Selective Service Act of 1948 also bans the poll tax as a requirement for voting for President, Vice-President, and members of Congress *by inductees;* this applies both in war and peace, but not to volunteers!

The committee recommended that the "in time of war" limitation on the basic right to vote and poll-tax ban be removed and these provisions be made applicable at all times. The Secretary of Defense ought, the committee thought, to press the states for compliance with the principles in the federal law and to report each 2 years on servicemen's voting. It also urged that states enact laws giving full absentee voting privileges to spouses and dependents of service personnel and to civilian personnel and their dependents stationed overseas.

Although considerable doubt exists with reference to the constitutionality of applying a federal ballot to presidential elections, a majority of the committee favored authorizing a federal ballot for congressional elections (and perhaps for the presidential) in the 1952 election only.[20] The Eighty-second Congress ended without action on these recommendations.

Proportional Representation. Proportional representation (PR) is a system of voting that yields to each party or group the approximate strength to which its vote entitles it. PR is applied to the selection of legislative bodies and is designed to correct the absurd disproportion produced by the single-member district plurality plan. Several methods of PR are in use in different parts of the world, but the Hare plan of single transferable vote is the most common in the United States. Under the Hare system, several representatives are elected from a single district. The voter indicates his choice of candidates by writing numbers—1, 2, 3, 4, etc.— opposite the candidates of his choice. The ballots are collected and counted centrally.

The first step in counting PR ballots is to establish the "quota." This is done by dividing the number of valid ballots by the number of candidates to be elected plus one. If nine seats in a city council are to be filled, and the number of votes cast is 100,000, then the quota is 10,001. It is figured:

$$9 \text{ councilors} + 1 = 10 / \overline{100,000} \quad \frac{10,000 + 1 = 10,001 \text{ quota}}{}$$

The ballots are sorted by first choices, and all candidates with more than the quota are declared elected. Their surplus beyond the quota is distributed to second choices on the ballots concerned. Finally, candidates with the lowest number of votes are eliminated and their ballots distributed by second choices until all seats are filled.

Proposed only occasionally for use in selecting members of Congress and of state legislatures, PR has been used successfully in several cities including New York and Cincinnati. Proponents maintain that it (1) ensures minority representation, (2) reduces power of small organized machines, (3) makes legislative bodies truly representative.[21] The case against PR, once the preserve of bosses and others inconvenienced by it, recently has been argued forcefully by competent students of government. The disadvantages are that it (1) increases the number of groups and parties; (2) reduces the chances of one group securing the power to govern; (3) is too complicated for the voter to understand.[22]

After observing the instability of governments in continental European countries under the multiparty system, Americans have become increasingly cautious over PR lest adoption of the reform would eliminate the likelihood of a clear majority in legislative bodies. PR is unlikely to be adopted by the Federal government in the United States. It will be proposed seriously as a panacea for some of the ills of state legislatures and might conceivably prove a good remedy.

In local affairs, where fewer great policy decisions are made and the work of government is mainly administration, PR provides a fair method of representation. Even in municipal government, however, PR has been losing ground and its prospects for the future appear dim.[23]

Initiative, Referendum, Recall. Although not employed in federal politics in the United States, the initiative, referendum, and recall play an important part in the government of many states and their subdivisions.

The initiative is an electoral device through which an individual or group may propose statutory legislation or constitutional amendments by securing the signatures of the requisite number of voters and may place the measure before the electorate for adoption or rejection. The drafting of such measures normally is done by interested groups or their attorneys. The number or proportion of signatures required is set by law or constitution. Some states require that initiative propositions be submitted to the legislature before they are placed before the people, but if the legislature takes adverse or no action, then the matter is taken up by the electorate. If a majority of the voters favor an initiative measure or a part of the constitution, it goes into effect; frequently statutes thus adopted have a privileged status and may not be repealed by the legislature.

The referendum is a scheme through which voters may, by petition, force submission to the whole electorate of a bill passed by the legislature. The number or proportion of voters' signatures required usually is less than that of the initiative. Emergency measures commonly are excluded from referendum action. If the voters disapprove of the act as passed by the legislature, it becomes null and void. The referendum is used by more states than is the initiative, and it has been proposed seriously for inclusion in the Federal Constitution in connection with a con-

[21] See George H. Hallett, Jr., *Proportional Representation—The Key to Democracy* (Washington, D.C.: The National Home Library Foundation, 1937), pp. 58–74.

[22] Ferdinand A. Hermens, *Democracy or Anarchy? A Study of Proportional Representation* (Review of Politics, University of Notre Dame, 1941); and *P.R.: Democracy and Good Government* (Review of Politics, University of Notre Dame, 1943).

[23] Its demise in New York is traced in Belle Zeller and Hugh A. Bone, "The Repeal of P.R. in New York City—Ten Years in Retrospect," *American Political Science Review*, vol. 42 (December, 1948), pp. 1127–1148.

gressional declaration of war. The most common reasons given for adopting the initiative and referendum are that they (1) provide a check on corrupt and inert legislatures; and (2) provide a useful device for the education of voters. Those who oppose direct legislation often argue that these devices (1) place an additional burden on an already overburdened electorate, and (2) modify representative government by destroying legislative responsibility.

The recall is an instrument through which voters may, by signing petitions, require a special election to determine whether or not an official shall be superseded before his term expires. The number or proportion of signatures required varies considerably. If the majority of votes are for the recall of an official, the office is then declared vacant. A successor may be chosen on the same ballot, elected at a subsequent election, or appointed by some official or body. Various restrictions are placed upon the use of the recall to prevent attempts to remove just after election to office, or repeated attempts. The recall has been adopted in some form in eleven states and a thousand municipalities. Despite the lack of constitutional authority, two states have attempted to inaugurate the recall of federal officials. Arizona and North Dakota sought to apply their recall to federal judges, senators, and representatives. Candidates for Congress were requested to state in advance their willingness to abide by a recall vote on their removal; federal judges serving in the state would be asked to resign in case of an adverse vote in a recall election. The indirect or advisory recall never functioned and it obviously lacked any real sanction.[24]

The case for the recall is that it (1) provides a continuous control by the electorate over public officials, and (2) removes single officials from the shelter of a ticket and forces them to stand on their own merits. Against the recall are the arguments that it (1) gives a powerful weapon to minorities and factions which may be used for petty personal and partisan purposes,

[24] Frederick L. Bird and Frances M. Ryan, *The Recall of Public Officers* (Macmillan, 1930), pp. 16–17. This is the best general source on the recall.

and (2) weakens official courage and independence by rendering the officer vulnerable to momentary fits of public indignation.

The Overburdened Voter. Even a casual examination of American ballots and election returns gives ample evidence of the impression that the voter is assigned more work than he can or will perform satisfactorily. In simple and small communities a large amount of direct democracy may be successful. The town meeting of New England and the *Landesgemeinde*

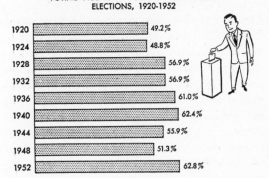

NATIONAL VOTING RECORD
ESTIMATED PERCENT OF AMERICAN CITIZENS OF VOTING AGE THAT VOTED IN PRESIDENTIAL ELECTIONS, 1920-1952

Year	Percent
1920	49.2%
1924	48.8%
1928	56.9%
1932	56.9%
1936	61.0%
1940	62.4%
1944	55.9%
1948	51.3%
1952	62.8%

retained in a few Swiss cantons are examples of government that functions very close to the people. Of course direct democracy can have only very limited application in modern America, where the communities are too large and the problems of government too technical for use of the mass-meeting technique. The other possibility is representative government, in which voters choose representatives who devote such time as is necessary to public affairs. A hundred years and more ago there arose a mistaken idea that the more offices made elective, the more democratic a government was. The mania for popular election swept through the states and local governments and dozens of minor officials were given their own pedestals and made elective by the people. Although a few states and local governments have experienced reorganizations that reduced the number of elective offices, most of them today elect too many officials. Not only does this seriously diffuse executive power, but it places a burden of impossible proportions on the voter. Unable to secure easily information concerning the stewardship in office of a particular obscure incumbent, he relies either on the recommendation of a newspaper or the party label or some other unreliable index.

The Short Ballot. A generation ago critics of the long ballot were well organized and articulate. They sought:

1. That only those offices should be elective which are important enough to attract (and deserve) public examination.

2. That very few offices should be filled by election at any one time, so as to permit adequate and unconfused public examination of the candidates.[25]

The short-ballot movement made some headway, but its work remained only partially done when the reform tide had ebbed. The Federal government has few elective officers and a rather short ballot—including candidates only for presidential elector, senator, and representative. With the presidential short ballot, eliminating candidates for elector from the ballot, the remaining federal elective offices certainly qualify as important enough to attract public attention. Most states, counties, and municipalities, however, continue to burden the voter with the task of selecting officers—ranging from tax commissioner to dogcatcher—who should be appointed by a chief executive. Several states have general-election ballots that include the names of candidates for thirty or more offices plus complicated initiative-and-referendum propositions numbering twenty and over.

The number of elections in the United States is staggering. In the 1940's an average of more than 100,000 separate elections were held in the United States annually. In 1944, on 151 days out of 364, elections were held somewhere in the country. It appears that the second short-ballot principle had been more honored than the first, in that elective offices are filled at scattered times. These minor elections for school and special districts and for local governments often fail to attract any considerable proportion of the eli-

[25] Richard S. Childs, *Short Ballot Principles* (Houghton Mifflin, 1911), p. vii.

gible voters. In the average Northern and Western state, 50 to 80 per cent participation in state and federal elections is common, while local elections often attract less than 25 per cent of the eligibles.

Getting Out the Vote. It is easy to say that the American voter must be made more alert to his civic responsibilities, but it is difficult to make him so. Certainly all efforts to stimulate interest in and discussion of public affairs are to be encouraged. Compulsory voting has been suggested as a remedy for nonvoting. It has been used with some success in Australia, Belgium, Czechoslovakia, Holland, and other countries. The usual form is to impose a fine upon those who fail to participate in elections; in some cases the nonvoter is disfranchised as well. Proposed repeatedly in the United States, compulsory voting has not been applied by any state.

Cannot the task of the voter be made easier? It can by reducing the number of elective offices and the number of elections. Contrary to uninformed opinion, neither of these steps reduces the measure of democracy; actually moderate reform along these lines will make more, not less, democracy. If the elective offices are reduced to a reasonable number, the remaining officers can be given the responsibility over a larger sphere of activity and can be empowered to appoint the necessary subordinates to carry out the work. In the end, the governor or mayor assigned additional authority following the abolition of executive offices, such as comptroller and commissioner of works, is likely to be more truly responsible to the public than those officers were when on an elective basis. The electorate can judge the general conduct of a mayor or governor but is unable even to name the incumbents of other elective executive offices, much less judge the quality of their work. Although there are some good arguments against mixing national and local affairs, the multiplicity of elections has been carried too far. Not only is the expense of conducting elections greater than necessary, but the participation in local elections is so small that consolidation of elections is urgently needed.

FOR
FURTHER
READING

Albright, Spencer D.: *The American Ballot* (American Council on Public Affairs, 1942).

Bean, Louis H.: *Ballot Behavior* (American Council on Public Affairs, 1940).

Berelson, Bernard R., and Others: *Voting: A Study of Opinion Formation in a Presidential Campaign* (University of Chicago Press, 1954).

Bontecou, Eleanor: *The Poll Tax* (Washington: American Association of University Women, 1942).

Burnham, W. Dean: *Presidential Ballots, 1836–1892* (Johns Hopkins Press, 1955).

Campbell, Angus, and Others: *The Voter Decides* (University of Michigan Press, 1954).

—— and Robert L. Kahn: *The People Elect a President* (University of Michigan Press, 1952).

Council of State Governments: *Book of the States* (Chicago: The Council, biennial).

David, Paul T., and Others: *Presidential Nominating Politics in 1952* (Johns Hopkins Press, 5 vols., 1954).

Hallett, George H., Jr.: *Proportional Representation: The Key to Democracy* (Washington, D.C.: National Home Library Foundation, 1937).

Harris, Joseph P.: *Election Administration in the United States* (Brookings, 1934).

——: *Registration of Voters in the United States* (Brookings, 1929).

Heard, Alexander, and D. S. Strong: *Southern Primaries and Elections* (University of Alabama Press, 1950).

Hermens, Ferdinand A.: *Democracy or Anarchy? A Study of Proportional Representation* (Review of Politics, University of Notre Dame, 1941).

Johnson, John B., and J. J. Lewis: *Registration for Voting in the United States* (Council of State Governments, 1946).

Key, V. O.: *Southern Politics in State and Nation* (Knopf, 1949).

McGovney, D. O.: *The American Suffrage Medley* (University of Chicago Press, 1949).

Merriam, Charles E., and Louise Overacker: *Primary Elections* (University of Chicago Press, 1928).

Miller, George F.: *Absentee Voters and Suffrage Laws* (Washington: Daylion Co., 1949).

National Municipal League: *A Model Direct Primary Election System* (New York: The League, 1951).

Peel, Roy V., and Thomas C. Donnelly: *The 1932 Campaign* (Farrar, Straus, 1935).

Porter, Kirk H.: *A History of Suffrage in the United States* (University of Chicago Press, 1918).

Proceedings of the National Convention (the major parties, quadrennial).

Robinson, Edgar E.: *They Voted for Roosevelt: The Presidential Vote, 1932–1944* (Stanford University Press, 1947).

——: *The Presidential Vote, 1896–1932* (Stanford University Press, 1934).

Titus, Charles H.: *Voting Behavior in the United States: A Statistical Study* (University of California Press, 1935).

REVIEW
QUESTIONS

1. What constitutional authority does the Federal government have over the right to vote?

2. Name the most common prerequisites for voting required by the several states.

3. Describe the current status of poll taxes. What federal and state action has been under active consideration?

4. Trace the historical development of presidential nominating methods.

5. To what legal controls are national party conventions subjected?

6. What factors influence the choice of dates and places for national conventions?

7. Explain the difference between Republican and Democratic methods of computing state representation in national conventions.

8. What is the presidential primary? Describe the various forms used. How extensively is it used today?

9. Describe the procedure and politics of national party conventions, with special reference to those of 1952 and 1956.

10. Trace the evolution of nominating methods for state and congressional offices. What are the several variations of convention and primary in use today?

11. Explain some of the factors that determine the strategy of a candidate campaigning for office.

12. Describe the process of absentee voting. What are the principal issues and problems posed by armed-services-personnel voting?

13. What is proportional representation? How extensively has it been adopted in the United States?

14. Describe the three "instrumentalities of popular control": initiative, referendum, and recall.

15. Do you think the American voter is overburdened? If so, what can be done to relieve him?

ON THE FACING PAGE: United States Supreme Court building. (*Library of Congress photo*)

Federal Institutions

Of the President's many functions, three of the most important are his annual message to Congress (above), his signing of bills into law (at left, former President Truman signs the Atomic Control Bill), and his frequent cabinet meetings (below).

Two opposite sides of the work of Congress are represented by a well-publicized Senate hearing, such as the stock-market hearing pictured below, and the ever-continuing paper work involved in daily proceedings. The three pictures here show a bill being assigned a number by the bill clerk (right), a committee-approved bill being assigned to a House calendar (below, left), and a bill being checked by a clerk after its final printing on parchment.

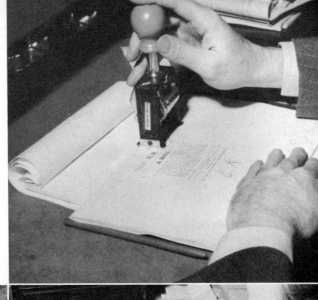

Top 3 photos, Black Star, bottom, Harris & Ewing

At the top of the judicial branch of the national government is the Supreme Court (above). In the operation of federal prisons today there is much evidence of overcrowding, as shown at the left. At the bottom, agents of the Border Patrol, Department of Justice, supervise the loading of Mexican nationals into a plane for transportation to temporary work in the United States.

CHAPTER 12

Congress: Organization and Politics

Instead of the function of governing, for which it is radically unfit, the proper office of a representative assembly is to watch and control the government: to throw the light of publicity on its acts: to compel a full exposition and justification of all of them which any one considers objectionable; to censure them if found condemnable, and, if the men who compose the government abuse their trust, or fulfil it in a manner which conflicts with the deliberate sense of the nation, to expel them from office, and expressly or virtually appoint their successors. — John Stuart Mill [1]

As a rule competition in the electoral market works like Gresham's law: the soft money drives the hard money out of circulation. The competitive odds are heavily against the candidate who, like Burke with the electors of Bristol, promises to be true to his own best reason and judgment. The odds are all in favor of the candidate who offers himself as the agent, the delegate, the spokesman, the errand boy of blocs of voters. — Walter Lippmann [2]

Congress is the first of the three branches of government to be considered. The Founding Fathers chose to assign the Article I position to the legislative department. All three of the branches are king-size in importance. But the state of Congress is perhaps our best index to the prospects for effective popular government.

STRUCTURE AND HISTORY

The first article of the Federal Constitution provides for the legislative branch of government, the "Congress of the United States." Although but recently separated from England, the new country took from the mother country the general outline of its legislative institutions. Several other examples and forerunners, together with the necessity of compromising large and small state demands, played a part in the molding of Congress, 1787 model.

The English Parliament. The Parliament of the mother country, directly and indirectly, was the most influential factor affecting the thinking of the Founding Fathers in respect to the legislature. English parliamentary institutions had developed from the Witenagemot of the Saxon kings, through the despotic rule of the Normans.[3] The "model parliament" of 1295 had representation of clergy, barons, and commoners. The lords spiritual and lords temporal came to meet together, while the commoners met apart;

[1] "Representative Government" in *Utilitarianism, Liberty and Representative Government* (Dutton, 1910), p. 239. First ed., 1861.

[2] *The Public Philosophy* (Little, Brown, 1955), p. 48.

[3] See Sir Courtenay Ilbert, *Parliament, Its History, Constitution and Practice* (Holt, 1911), pp. 7–31.

from this flows the two-house tradition. Gradually, although with notable interruptions, Parliament gained power to legislate by bill, to levy taxes, to choose and depose kings. Both tradition and form were transplanted from the British Parliament to the American colonies. Parliamentary supremacy was becoming well established by the time of the American Revolution. The House of Lords, spiritual and temporal, and the House of Commons were separately organized to represent distinct elements in society. The American constitutional convention delegates, of course, had not the advantage of British experience with broadened franchise, gained in the Reform Acts of 1832 and 1867, or with the operation of "classical" parliamentary government, as developed in the Disraeli-Gladstone era.

American Legislatures. American colonial legislatures, as shown in a previous chapter, followed a pattern that had general rather than detailed similarity. Each colony had a legislative assembly, usually a two-house organization. The upper chamber, or "governor's council," often had legislative, executive, and judicial powers. In the royal colonies, as is commonly the case in the British crown colonies of today, members of the council were appointed by the Crown on recommendation of the governor. In proprietary colonies, appointment came from the proprietor. The two charter colonies, Connecticut and Rhode Island, elected the councilors. Pennsylvania had no governor's council and was thereby the only colony which had a single-house legislature.

Intended as a popular body, the lower house was elected by the colonial subjects who could meet the property qualifications required for voting. The members—called "burgesses," "representatives," or "commoners"—represented the people who lived in the districts from which they were selected.

Revolutionary Assemblies. After an initial period of chaotic rule by "rump" legislatures, eleven of the newly independent states reformed their legislatures in the new constitutions adopted between 1775 and 1780; only Rhode Island and Connecticut kept their old constitutions. In all thirteen states the state legislatures were given broad powers. Eleven of the states continued with bicameral legislatures. Pennsylvania retained its single-house plan until 1790; Georgia experimented with unicameralism from 1777 to 1789. The two-house states kept the lower house much as before the Revolution. The upper house, soon to be termed "senate" generally, was made elective by districts, but its members were assigned longer terms than were lower-house members.

Early National Legislatures. The First Continental Congress, assembled in Philadelphia in 1774, was more like a convention than a national legislature but must be regarded as a stone-age ancestor of the Congress of today. The Second Continental Congress, which provided such national government as the country had during the Revolutionary War, may be compared with a modern European constituent assembly, for it both governed the emerging nation and framed the Articles of Confederation. This was a unicameral body, to which each state sent its delegates.

Under the Articles of Confederation, the country was governed principally by the Congress. It was a one-house body with a rather fluid membership of delegates from the states. Each state had one vote, which might be cast by the two to seven delegates from that state. States could appoint and recall delegates as they saw fit.

Other Considerations. More telling as determinant of congressional structure in the Constitution than the precedents cited above, however, was the necessity of compromising the differences between large and small states. Under the terms of the "great compromise," each state was represented equally in the Senate. The seats in the House of Representatives were to be apportioned among the states according to their populations.

Little serious consideration is given today to departure from the two-house plan for Congress. The national utilization of the bicameral plan, however, has led states to imitate. Both Pennsylvania and Georgia promptly abandoned the single-chamber plan after Congress was made a two-house body. Vermont, admitted in 1791, used unicameralism until 1836. The bicameral stereotype prevailed in all states for a hundred years, until Nebraska adopted her single-house plan in 1934 and put it into effect in 1937.

THE POWERS OF CONGRESS: GENERAL ASPECTS

Legislative Powers of Congress. Legislative powers may be classified into six groups: (1) delegated, (2) implied, (3) inherent, (4) concurrent, (5) prohibited, and (6) reserved. Since these have been commented upon earlier [4] they will be dealt with briefly here.

Delegated powers are those specifically enumerated in the Constitution, most of them in Article I, Section 8. These have been given by the sovereign people to the central government at Washington.

Implied powers are those that may reasonably be deduced from delegated powers, or, to use the language of the Constitution, those that are "necessary and proper" for carrying delegated powers into execution. The fact that the Federal government has implied powers does not mean that anything can be done that may seem necessary and proper. If that were true, the system would be unitary rather than federal. Instead, implications can be made only from some specifically delegated power.

Inherent powers arise from the fact that the United States is a sovereign state and in its international relations may exercise those powers generally exercised by other national states.

Reserved powers are those that have not been delegated to the Federal government. Some are retained by the states. Certain ones that states have been prohibited from exercising have been reserved to the people.

Concurrent powers are those exercised by both national and state governments. The term also refers to powers, like bankruptcy, which may be exercised by the states until such time as Congress decides to assert its authority.

Prohibited powers are denied either to both Federal and state governments, or to Federal only, or to the states only.

[4] See p. 69.

Restrictions on Congressional Power. Although the powers of Congress, as exercised and construed, are great, the national legislature is subject to several limitations, both explicit and implied.

No Emergency Powers. It cannot be emphasized too often that in dealing with domestic affairs the Federal government has only such powers as are granted to it by the Constitution. In periods of stress it has been claimed, sometimes by Congress but oftener by the President, that the national government is endowed with powers that are neither delegated nor implied but that arise from the fact that the government speaks for a sovereign nation. This is true only in the field of international relations. President Roosevelt urged Congress to enact sweeping legislation beginning in 1933, arguing as partial justification for its constitutionality that emergency conditions demanded the steps taken. The Supreme Court acknowledged that extraordinary conditions might afford a reason for an *extraordinary use* of existing powers but insisted that critical circumstances could not enlarge the scope of constitutional authority. "Emergency does not create power. Emergency does not increase granted power or diminish the restrictions imposed upon power granted or reserved," said the Court in 1934.[5] A year later a unanimous Court voided the NIRA, saying, among other things, "extraordinary conditions do not create or enlarge constitutional powers."[6] Thus, in emergencies Congress must rely upon some delegated power. If none can be found, the Constitution requires that the matter be left to the states or that an amendment be sought.

No Specific "Police Power." Unitary governments ordinarily have authority to take whatever steps are necessary to protect and preserve the health, safety, morals, and convenience of the people. This is commonly referred to as the "police power." In the United States this power is one reserved to the states; it is not possessed by the national government, except within the

[5] Home Building and Loan Association *v.* Blaisdell, 290 U.S. 398 (1934).

[6] Schechter *v.* United States, 295 U.S. 495 (1935).

District of Columbia and other territories. State and local governments undertake to regulate physicians and contagious diseases, to dispose of garbage and sewage, to provide hospitals and schools, to ensure pure food and water supply, and to do a host of other things simply because the welfare of the population demands them. The Federal government, however, may do such things only to the extent that they are reasonably required to regulate interstate and foreign commerce properly, conduct a postal system, raise and support an army and navy, or exercise some other power delegated by the Constitution.

Specific Denials. As noted above, the Constitution mentions certain things that Congress is forbidden to do. The delegated powers may not, therefore, be exercised in such a manner as to do things expressly forbidden. Congress may not, for example, tax exports, pass ex post facto laws, grant titles of nobility, nor impair the liberties guaranteed by the Bill of Rights.

Clearly Granted. As noted above, Congress has implied power, but it is frequently difficult to decide what is and what is not a "necessary and proper" use of a delegated power. Although permitting a liberal construction of the phrase, the courts insist that there must be some clear and direct relationship between a delegated power and the object sought by its exercise. The power to coin money and regulate its value justifies the creation of national banks; the power to coin money justifies the printing of paper notes; the power to regulate interstate commerce justifies the fixing of passenger and freight rates for interstate carriers, and also the regulation of intrastate commerce that directly affects interstate commerce; the power to tax to promote the general welfare justifies the establishment of land-grant colleges, a retirement system for aged employees, and the subsidization of farmers. In these instances the courts have found a clear and direct relationship between some delegated power and the object or purpose of the enactments. But when Congress required railroads to establish a retirement system for superannuated employees, the Court construed the act to be "an

attempt for social ends" which had nothing to do with interstate commerce.[7] A revised measure based upon the taxing and spending powers was passed later and has been generally thought to be constitutional. Likewise, in the NIRA decision, the Supreme Court considered the burden upon interstate commerce caused by depressed local businesses so indirect as to be beyond the scope of the commerce power.[8]

No Delegation of Legislative Powers to Executive. One of the fundamental principles of the Constitution is that the legislative, executive, and judicial branches are separate and independent of each other. Many laws are passed embodying general principles and authorizing administrative officers to fill in details, but too much cannot be left to the administrators. Congress must clearly declare its will and establish primary standards. If this is not done but left to the executive, the courts will hold that Congress has illegally delegated powers granted solely to itself. The first case in which it was held that legislative powers had been delegated arose from a section of the NIRA.[9] In that case the Supreme Court ruled that in authorizing the President to make regulations governing interstate shipments of "hot oil"[10] too much discretion had been allowed. Later, major portions of the NIRA were declared unconstitutional chiefly because Congress had allowed too much discretion to the President and code authorities.

No Delegation to States. Likewise, powers granted to Congress cannot be delegated to the states. This means that Congress cannot authorize states to regulate interstate commerce, coin money, declare war, or exercise any other power conferred exclusively upon it by the Constitution. When in 1918 Congress passed legislation providing that longshoremen injured during the course of employment were entitled to the rights and remedies of the state wherein the injury

[7] Railroad Retirement Board *v.* Alton R. Co., 295 U.S. 330 (1935).

[8] Schechter *v.* United States, 295 U.S. 495 (1935).

[9] Panama Refining Company *v.* Ryan, 293 U.S. 388 (1935).

[10] That is, oil produced in excess of quotas established by state law.

occurred, the Supreme Court held that Congress had transferred its authority to the states.[11] Thereupon, Congress reenacted the measure providing a uniform system of federally administered insurance for maritime workers injured on board vessels.[12] Sometimes there is overlapping between state and federal jurisdiction, in which case a state might act under a reserved power on a matter which Congress is also competent to deal with under a delegated power. This often happens. When it does, and the matter does not require uniform treatment throughout the country, the state law is allowed to stand until Congress acts, after which the state law must yield.

No Delegation to People. Many states have provisions that permit the use of the initiative and referendum. The initiative is a device whereby a law may be proposed by a petition circulated and signed by a predetermined number of qualified voters. The referendum permits laws to become effective upon the favorable vote of a certain number of voters. There is no provision in the Federal Constitution for the use of these devices. All federal laws must originate in and be approved by Congress, otherwise there would be an illegal delegation of powers.

No Usurping of State Powers. Just as the states may not invade the domain of Congress, so may Congress not usurp powers reserved to the states. Finding the demarcation line is extremely difficult, with the result that political and judicial opinion shifts from time to time. Thus, prior to 1937 the Supreme Court was inclined to halt federal power in favor of state. While this temper lasted, federal laws were declared unconstitutional which taxed the salaries of state judges and state instrumentalities, regulated the employment of children, induced farmers to contract to curtail production, regulated manufacturing, mining, and local businesses, and permitted local governments to reorganize their indebtedness under federal laws. More recently, however, most of these decisions have been reversed. Even so, it is clear that there

are still areas where the Federal government may not trespass. State powers would be usurped if Congress were to regulate commerce that is very local and isolated, or to tax with intent to burden or destroy state and local governments and their activities.

No Usurping from Other Branches. Just as all legislative powers belong to Congress, the executive power is given solely to the President and the judicial power entirely to the courts. Congress is precluded, therefore, from usurping executive and judicial powers. In 1876 Congress provided that postmasters could be removed by the President only with the concurrence of the Senate. Forty years later President Wilson resisted the statute, contending that the power of removal belonged to the executive. The Supreme Court agreed with the President, saying that the statute was an unwarranted infringement of the executive power.[13] Neither can Congress invade the province of the judiciary. In 1792 Congress directed federal circuit judges to investigate claims and report their findings to the War Department for final action. The courts objected and in Hayburn's Case [14] ruled that the legislature had imposed a nonjudicial duty upon them inasmuch as executive officials were permitted to review and possibly modify or reverse decisions made by the judges.

Nonlegislative Powers. In addition to making laws, Congress performs several other important tasks. A distinction is made, therefore, between legislative powers upon which general laws are based, and nonlegislative powers from which Congress gets authority for its other functions. Nonlegislative powers may be classified as (1) constituent, (2) electoral, (3) executive, (4) directory and supervisory, (5) inquisitorial, and (6) judicial.

Constituent are those that relate to changing the Constitution, including authority to propose amendments either by the concurrence of two-thirds of both houses, or by calling a convention for the purpose when petitioned to do so by two-thirds of the states. Herein is also included

[11] Knickerbocker Ice Co. *v.* Stewart, 253 U.S. 149 (1920).

[12] See p. 555.

[13] Myers *v.* United States, 272 U.S. 52 (1926). See also p. 275.

[14] 2 Dall. 409 (U.S. 1792).

authority to decide what method of ratification shall be followed by the states and whether a time limit shall accompany the amendment.

Electoral are those relating to the election of President and Vice-President. The electoral votes must be counted in the presence of both houses, and in the event of a tie or lack of a majority, election of the President devolves upon the House and that of the Vice-President upon the Senate. Moreover, Congress must provide for settling disputes if certain electoral votes are contested and also provide a method of choosing the President and Vice-President upon the death or disqualification of both of these officers either before or after their inauguration.

Executive powers are those used when performing functions that are essentially executive in character. The appointment of officers is generally an executive prerogative; thus, when the House and Senate appoint their own officers and committees it may properly be said that they are exercising executive powers. The same is true when the Senate confirms presidential appointees and gives advice and consent to the ratification of treaties.

Directory and supervisory powers are closely related. Although the President is usually thought to be the chief administrator, Congress exercises considerable control and supervision over the administrative branch. It is Congress that decides whether there is to be a department, commission, board, or other agency. After creating them, Congress may expand the agencies, consolidate them, or abolish them altogether. Congress defines their powers and duties, appropriates all funds without which they cannot operate, authorizes the employment of personnel, and subjects them to periodic investigation and review. Indeed, work of this kind absorbs far more of the energy and time of Congress than any other.

Direction and review go on constantly. They may result from complaints received by congressmen from constituents back home, from newspaper articles and editorials, from a congressman's own experience and thinking, or from mere rumor. Inquiry takes a variety of forms. Almost all agencies are required to make annual reports to Congress. Irregularities may be discovered and disclosed by the Bureau of the Budget or General Accounting Office. Congressmen often write to administrators for information and explanations or they may call upon them personally. Agencies may be excoriated in congressional debate, or special investigations may be undertaken by congressional committees. Senatorial confirmation of an appointment or approval of a treaty may occasion widespread inquiry. Normally, the most thorough review occurs when representatives of the various agencies appear before committees to defend budgetary estimates for the following year.

Inquisitorial is a term used to describe congressional authority to conduct investigations.[15] These may be conducted by the House and Senate as a body or, as is commonly the case, by standing or special committees. The Senate, because it is smaller in size and its members have longer terms, has conducted some of the best-known investigations. The power to make investigations may be, and frequently is, delegated to permanent departments, commissions, and legislative courts, or to commissions composed of individuals who have no official connection with the government. Congress itself, or its instrumentalities, may issue subpoenas to summon witnesses and compel the production of books and papers. Warrants of arrest may also be issued. Failure to obey congressional writs and orders may be punished by Congress itself. In practice, however, Congress now leaves trial and punishment to the courts. Witnesses occasionally refuse to appear and give testimony before congressional committees.

Judicial powers are those that enable Congress to pass judgment upon certain parties. Each house of Congress is the sole judge of the qualifications of its own members and each house can expel its members provided two-thirds of

[15] For an excellent review of the subject of congressional investigation see M. Nelson McGeary, *The Development of Congressional Investigative Power* (Columbia University Press, 1940).

them agree. Impeachment and contempt proceedings are also judicial in nature.[16]

BASIS OF REPRESENTATION

The House of Representatives was intended as the popular branch of Congress and therefore was made larger and more responsible to the public will than was the upper chamber. The Senate, the deliberative house of Congress, was made a smaller body and removed from popular passions and pressures.

Constitutional Provisions. As provided in the Constitution, seats in the United States House of Representatives are apportioned among the states according to population, determined by the census each 10 years. Members are elected by the people, and the electorate is the same as that for the most numerous branch of the state legislature. The Fifteenth Amendment forbids states to deny the vote to any person because of

[16] The impeachment process is fully explained on p. 242.

race, color, or previous condition of servitude. The Nineteenth prohibits discrimination on account of sex. Although the Fourteenth Amendment provides for penalty against states that deny the vote to adult male citizens, by reducing proportionately representation in the House, the penalty has never been invoked and may be regarded as a dead letter.

In its original form the Senate was composed of two senators from each state, chosen by the state legislature. The rising tide of democracy swept aside the old method of selection and imposed the new, as contained in the Seventeenth Amendment. It provided that the people of each state should elect Senators directly. The electorate is the same as that for the House.

Methods of Apportionment. The apportioning of House seats among the states has given rise to periodic controversies. The original sixty-five members of the House were allocated in the Constitution. Thereafter assignments were made by Congress after each census, ranging from the

CHANGES IN ELECTORAL VOTE AND HOUSE REPRESENTATION

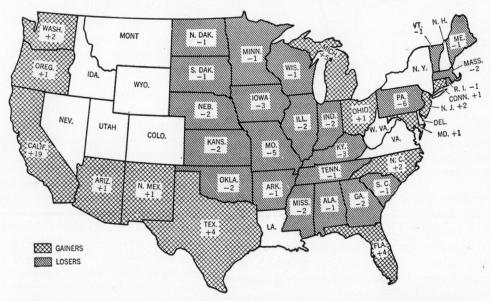

The shift of national political power as a result of population changes in forty years, 1912–1952, is shown on the map above. Adapted from David G. Farrelly and Ivan Hinderaker, "Congressional Reapportionment and National Political Power," *Law and Contemporary Problems*, vol 17 (Spring, 1952), p. 362.

basis of 1 representative for each 30,000 (1792) to 1 for 345,000 (1951). Only after the 1920 census did Congress deadlock and fail to carry out the constitutional mandate to reapportion each 10 years. The Reapportionment Act of 1929 set the "permanent" number of House

CONGRESSIONAL DISTRICTS IN ILLINOIS
(25 Districts)

1 to 13—304,229 to	462,419
14—355,643	
15—324,129	
16—353,631	
17—344,573	
18—314,715	
19—325,903	
20—281,468	
21—345,287	
22—336,693	
23—318,549	
24—388,302	
25—335,394	

In most respects, the Illinois redistricting of 1951 conformed to standards of equality, compactness, and contiguousness. But in Cook County, the 4th and 13th exceed 400,000, although the 20th is under 200,000. The 21st, not compact and barely contiguous, has some of the earmarks of a "gerrymander." Map adapted from one by Illinois Legislative Council.

members at 435 and provided for automatic reapportionment in case Congress fails to act. The law provided that after each census the President shall report to Congress the population and the number of representatives to which each state shall be entitled according to two complex mathematical formulas: (1) equal proportions and (2) major fractions. Should Congress fail to act within 60 days, the reapportionment goes into effect automatically, utilizing the formula employed in the last reapportionment.

In 1931 Congress took no action, and the presidential plan based on major fractions was deemed in force. In 1941, however, after the 60-day period had elapsed, the 1929 act was amended to require that the equal-proportions method be used beginning with the Seventy-eighth Congress (1943–1944).[17] The present rule, therefore, requires the President to figure apportionment of House seats only by equal proportions.

Apportionment within States. No provision requiring election of representatives by district appears in the Constitution. It was imposed by law in 1842, however, and has prevailed ever since that time. The original law required that each district should elect one representative and that the district must be composed of contiguous territory. In 1872 another rule was added requiring districts of substantially equal population. In 1901 the feature of compactness was added. Thus the requirement from 1901 until 1929 was for single-member districts of compact and contiguous territory, as nearly equal in population as practicable.

Requirements of compactness, contiguity, and equality were not included in the law of 1929 and are not now in effect.[18] Gerrymandering, or arranging a district for personal or partisan advantage, was curbed somewhat by these limitations while they existed. The matter now rests primarily with the states. Many have constitu-

[17] 55 Stat. 762, adopted Nov. 15, 1941. In 1931 the allocation of seats was identical under both formulas, so Congress permitted the major-fractions plan, used in 1911, to prevail. In 1941 the two methods showed only one difference: under major fractions Arkansas lost one seat and Michigan gained one; under equal proportions Arkansas kept its seat and Michigan gained none. Democratic elements pushed through a bill to substitute equal proportions for major fractions. In 1951 the two methods produced only one difference: major fractions would have taken one seat from Kansas and have added it to California's total; equal proportions let Kansas keep its seat and held California's gain to seven. In 1951 the President submitted the census figures and the proposed reapportionment based on 435 members and the method of equal proportions. Congress took no action, and the states were notified of their entitlement to House seats.

[18] Wood *v.* Broom, 287 U.S. 1 (1932).

tional restrictions against gerrymandering and other districting abuses.[19]

In practice many of the states tend to frustrate the goal of representation in the House of all people on the basis of equality. Often this occurs through failure to reapportion congressional districts. In recent years the most serious problems have arisen in Illinois and Ohio, where lack of redistricting has yielded great discrepancies between the districts in each state. The 1940 census showed one Illinois district over eight times as large as another; in Ohio one was more than four times another.

Court rulings have clarified to some extent the question of what can and cannot be done in the reapportionment procedure. It is well established that a state legislature may not redistrict except by law; two-house resolutions without gubernatorial signature have been ruled inadequate.[20] If a state is allocated new seats in the House and does not redistrict, the new members are elected at large.[21]

Reapportionment Problems. Some controversy continues over the number of House seats and the mode of allocating them among the states. Several Representatives have expressed discontent over the large number of constituents each member must serve when the total membership is held down to 435, yet few would enlarge the House except to provide representation for Alaska and Hawaii. Some competent students of Congress even advocate gradual reduction of House size to about 300 for maximum efficiency.

The mathematical formulas by which House seats are allocated to the states are still being

disputed actively by statisticians. The Congress and the public are inclined to judge the rival methods by their results. In general, "major fractions" is slightly more favorable to large states, and "equal proportions" to small states. Two more extreme methods are sometimes dis-

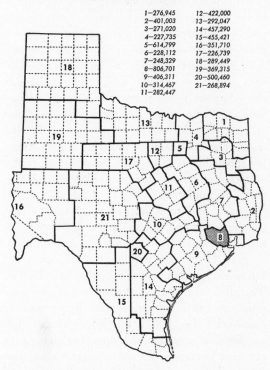

CONGRESSIONAL DISTRICTS IN TEXAS
(21 Districts & 1 At-Large)

1—276,945	12—422,000
2—401,003	13—292,047
3—271,020	14—457,290
4—227,735	15—455,421
5—614,799	16—351,710
6—228,112	17—226,739
7—248,329	18—289,449
8—806,701	19—369,315
9—406,311	20—500,460
10—314,467	21—268,894
11—282,447	

The last congressional redistricting of Texas was in 1933. Having gained one seat in 1951, Texas elected the new member on an at-large basis. The 8th district appears to be the most populous in the nation. Courtesy of Texas Legislative Reference Librarian.

cussed: "rejected fractions," which was used for 50 years and which is by far the most favorable to the larger states, and the proposed "included fractions," which gives the small states the most generous treatment.[22]

---

[19] The most thorough study of apportionment problems is Laurence F. Schmeckebier, *Congressional Apportionment* (Brookings, 1941).

[20] Smiley *v.* Holm, 285 U.S. 361 (1932), involved Minnesota, and Koenig *v.* Flynn, 285 U.S. 379 (1932), involved New York.

[21] In 1941 Congress provided by law for the contingency that a state might not redistrict after a national reapportionment. It followed the same rules established by the courts. A state gaining seats in the House may elect the new members at large. A state losing seats and not redistricting must elect all members at large. 55 Stat. 761.

[22] The various plans are discussed in "Legislative Reapportionment," *Law and Contemporary Problems*, vol. 17 (Spring, 1952), pp. 253–469. Equal proportions is favored by Laurence F. Schmeckebier, "The Method of Equal Proportions," pp. 302–313; included fractions is advocated by Walter F. Wilcox, "Last Words on the Apportionment Problems," pp. 290–301.

The long-standing (1842–1929) law requiring representatives to be elected by districts was often violated by states that resorted to the device of representative at large. This departure from the normal pattern, when resulting from gain or loss of House seats through reapportionment, received the sanction of the courts in 1932 and of statute law in 1941. During 1951 the practice was criticized severely by a committee of the American Political Science Association [23] and by President Truman in a message to Congress. Five states with more than one representative now elect members at large: North Dakota and New Mexico, which have two each elected by the whole state, and Texas, Washington, and Connecticut, each of which elects one at large in addition to others elected by districts. The complaint is that the device makes for inequality both of work load and of representation and offers the possibility of majority-party manipulation.

Finally, and most important, there is a case for the restoration to federal law of the requirements of equality, compactness, and contiguousness. Legislation without some kind of enforcement procedure is unlikely to be effective. Therefore, the leading proposals include sanctions as well as principles. Representative Emanuel Celler had a bill before recent congresses that would allow no more than a 15 per cent deviation, for each congressional district within a state, from the number obtained by dividing the total population of the state by the number of Representatives allocated to the state.[24] Representatives elected from districts that do not conform to the requirements would be denied their seats. The American Political Science Association committee proposed a de-

tailed time schedule for redistricting, with the ultimate sanction that Congress itself might draw the lines in a state that refused to abide by the rules. This is more realistic as an enforcement procedure than relying on the courts, which have refused to intervene to bring about more equitable apportionment.[25]

Senate Apportionment. Equal representation of the states in the Senate has produced very disproportionate representation by population. The greatest extreme, of course, is shown by New York, which has nearly a hundred times the population of Nevada, yet each state has two senators. The Constitution provides, however, that no state may be deprived of equal representation in the Senate without its own consent. As a practical matter, changing the basis of representation in the Senate appears out of the question, short of a great upheaval or general alteration of our federal system. The disproportionate influence of small states is especially noticeable in treaty and constitutional amendment proceedings, in which, because a two-thirds majority is required, a minority representing a minute fraction of the nation's population can frustrate the will of the majority.

CONGRESSIONAL PERSONNEL

Qualifications. The House of Representatives has a short term (2 years) and a low age requirement (twenty-five). Each Representative must be a resident of the state from which he is elected, and he must have been a citizen of the United States for at least 7 years. Custom decrees that a Representative must reside in the district that he represents, but there have been exceptions. The Constitution provides that each house is judge of "the elections, returns, and qualifications" of its own members. Under such authority, the House has barred regularly elected members for their beliefs, faith, and practices. The House has refused admission to a polygamist and to a socialist who had been convicted

[23] "The Reapportionment of Congress," *American Political Science Review*, vol. 45 (March, 1951), pp. 153–157.

[24] H. R. 2648, 82d Cong., p. 3. After the 1951 legislatures finished redistricting, there were at least 115 House districts with over 15 per cent variation in population. James E. Todd, "The Apportionment Problem Faced by the States," *Law and Contemporary Problems*, vol. 17 (Spring, 1952), p. 337.

[25] "The remedy for unfairness in districting is to secure a state legislature that will apportion properly, or to invoke the ample powers of congress." Colegrove v. Green, 328 U.S. 549 (1946).

of sedition. Denial of the right to take a seat requires only a simple majority vote. Expulsion of a sitting member of the House requires a two-thirds vote. Vacancies in the House normally are filled by special election called by the executive authority of the state concerned.

United States Senators serve long terms (6 years) and have a higher age requirement (thirty years). Like the Representative, a Senator must be a resident of the state he represents. Nine years of citizenship are required in the upper house. Power to judge its own membership extends to the Senate, too, and is employed even more vigorously than in the House. The Senate refused to admit two duly elected members (Frank L. Smith of Illinois and William S. Vare of Pennsylvania) because of huge expenditures in primary elections of 1926. Thus, although since the Newberry decision Congress has not attempted to regulate money in primaries, the Senate may bar offenders from the seats they win. Since the adoption of the Seventeenth Amendment, Senate vacancies may be filled by appointment of a governor if state law authorizes it.

Representatives would like very much to have terms of 4 years, and there is much to be said for the change. Besides relieving members of the House from the insistent pressure of repairing political fences for reelection, the 4-year term would reduce considerably the possibility of a deadlock with a President of one party and the House majority of another. The 4-year term for House would introduce problems in connection with the Senate term, for the present scheme used in the Senate requires election of one-third of the membership each 2 years. Extending the Senate term to 8 years with one-half of the senators elected each 4 years is one possibility, but it might lead to deadlock between President and Senate majority. The Senate term might be reduced to 4 years; although this would virtually eliminate the possibility of deadlock, with all Representatives and Senators and the President elected at the same time, it is not likely to prove popular with the Senate, two-thirds of which must vote affirmatively in order

to submit the necessary constitutional amendment.

Previous Experience of Congressmen. It is well known that nearly 60 per cent of the members of the two houses are attorneys. The second largest occupational group is composed of persons in the various branches of business enterprise. Farmers, teachers, and newspapermen follow next in order. Getting a start in American politics commonly requires either wealth or an occupation that can combine with the erratic periods of service involved. Once successfully established in a safe seat, the representative or senator may abandon his normal occupational pursuits and live on his congressional salary. Certainly membership in Congress constitutes a full-time job, and the salary has been made somewhat commensurate with it. For the lawyer the field of state and local politics has more than the usual glamour; he receives a form of advertising which usually helps his law practice, and he may work himself into line for a judicial post. Or he may win a seat in Congress.

A review of the personnel of the Congress in 1955 revealed that the average age of Senators was fifty-seven, while that of Representatives was fifty-one. Nearly all had previous public experience before election to congressional office. A large majority of them had attended college or professional schools.[26]

Privileges. Privileges of Senators and Representatives include certain immunity from arrest and extraordinary freedom of speech. The constitutional provision that national legislators are immune from arrest except for treason, felony, and breach of peace has been interpreted by the courts to prohibit only arrests in civil suits. In criminal cases members are as liable to arrest as any other citizens. The same clause declares that "for any speech or debate in either house, they shall not be questioned in any other place." This means that Senators and Representatives may speak and act freely without fear of criminal prosecutions or civil suits. Of course, the

[26] For further information see George B. Galloway, *The Legislative Process in Congress* (Crowell, 1953), pp. 370–375.

House and Senate have full power to determine their own rules, to discipline members for excesses, and, in extreme cases, to expel a member. For mild offenses and indiscretions a member is called to order. Occasionally a house will censure a member; the leading recent example is the Senate censure of Joseph McCarthy in 1954.

Although the desirability of granting a large measure of privilege to legislators is widely recognized, it is apparent that immunity may be abused. From the floor of the House or Senate, or in a committee, persons can be defamed, yet left without practical means of fighting back. In the long run, perhaps rules of fair conduct by congressional committees can correct some of the worst abuses. Real progress has been achieved under the House committee "ground rules" adopted in 1955. Acquisition of self-restraint by *all* Senators and Representatives is highly unlikely.

Since the Congress traditionally deals lightly with misconduct on the part of its own members, some other means are needed to protect individuals against false accusations. One proposal is to permit victims of attacks made under congressional immunity to clear their names and secure redress by suing the United States for damages. Additional protection could be provided by making "informing witnesses" subject to civil suits for damages by those against whom they make libelous accusations.

Principles of Conduct for Members of Congress

As a member of the Congress of the United States I do solemnly subscribe to the following code and do pledge my strength and honor to its fulfillment:

I. In the same sense in which a judge debars himself from decisions in which he has a direct personal financial stake, so I shall debar myself from legislative decisions, or if I take action or choose to vote, I shall fully disclose the nature of my interest.

II. I shall never use my office to exert extra-legal pressures over the decisions of executive or administrative agencies.

III. I shall treat witnesses who testify before committees on which I sit with courtesy and fairness, following self-imposed limitations which for centuries have been the hallmark of the judicial process.

IV. I shall not abuse my privilege of Congressional immunity; I shall not say things on the floor of Congress that I am not prepared to say outside, nor shall I betray the official confidence of the Congress or of any committee thereof.

V. I shall not indulge in personal vilification of any kind, but I shall not hesitate to criticize public figures and public policies with determination and courage whenever facts of a public nature justify such criticism.

VI. I shall not vote on any issue without an attempt to consider the voiceless interest of the unorganized in our society.

VII. I shall strive constantly to interpret the interests of my constituents in the perspective of the total national interest.

VIII. I shall try to be loyal to the promises of my political party, and thus strengthen party teamwork and party responsibility in the Congress.

IX. I shall not waste my own or my colleagues' time with irrelevant and inconsequential talk in committee or on the floor.

X. Whether as a member of the majority or the minority, I shall attempt in all my actions and words to educate and clarify, never to obscure or confuse.

SOURCE: William Benton, "A Decalogue for Members of Congress," *The New York Times Magazine,* Aug. 12, 1951. Proposed by the former Senator from Connecticut but not adopted.

Compensation. Congressional perquisites of office include salary, mileage, stationery, clerk hire, and the postal frank. The salary of Senators and Representatives is now $22,500 per year, all of which is subject to income taxation, but members may claim "business expense" deductions for the extra cost of maintaining a second residence. The Speaker of the House and the president of the Senate receive $35,000 each per year. These salaries are determined and may be altered by law. Each member is allowed 20 cents per mile traveling expense to and from Washington once each session. An allowance for clerk hire is made for each member; this sometimes is used to employ members of his family or political supporters. Official mail may be sent under postal frank free of charge to the sender. This privilege is often used for the dissemination of political and partisan speeches and "extensions of remarks" from the *Congressional Record*. There is a contributory retirement plan.

The public reacts unfavorably to proposals for increases in congressional compensation. In 1873 there was a great storm over a "salary grab." In early 1942 there was a controversy over the adoption of congressional pensions, and the legislators were attacked viciously for enacting the new perquisites of office. The law was repealed promptly. The Seventy-eighth Congress voted an expense account of $2,500 per year for Representatives, but the Senators declined to include themselves.

The Legislative Reorganization Act of 1946 [27] relieved members of Congress of some concern over making ends meet in their personal budgets. The Joint Committee on the Organization of Congress had recommended a salary of $15,000, taxable on the same basis as that of a businessman who must divide his time between two places of business. Congress amended the bill, however, to set the salary at $12,500 and to pro-

vide a tax-free expense allowance of $2,500. The latter was widely criticized as a special privilege. In 1952 a successful move was made to subject the whole compensation of $15,000 to taxes just

WHAT IT COSTS TO RUN CONGRESS

A SENATOR GETS THIS:

Salary—$22,500 a year

Expenses—$64,500 a year, average, for staff pay

Office help—Staff of about 10 people

Office space—A three or four-room suite in Washington, plus an office in his home State

EXTRAS—Free postage • Allowance for long-distance calls • Travel allowance • Allowance for telegrams • $1,200 yearly stationery allowance • Low-cost pension and life insurance

A MEMBER OF THE HOUSE GETS THIS:

Salary—$22,500 a year

Expenses—$26,200 a year, average, for staff pay

Office help—Staff of about 3 people

Office space—A two-room suite in Washington, plus an office in his home district

EXTRAS—Free postage • Allowance for long-distance calls • Allowance for telegrams • Travel allowance • $1,200 yearly stationery allowance • Low-cost pensions and life insurance

---
Cost of Congress, including upkeep of buildings and grounds, comes to 75 million dollars a year

Per member of the House and Senate, $140,000 a year

Reprinted from *U.S. News & World Report*, an independent weekly news magazine published in Washington. Copyright, 1955, United States News Publishing Corporation. Issue of May 20, 1955.

as the committee had recommended in 1946. This involved stating in the law that members of the Congress were entitled to business-expense deductions for living expenses in Washington.

Evidence was soon available indicating that the $15,000 salary was not adequate. A survey

[27] 60 Stat. 831. The chief documents of the committee were U.S. Congress, Joint Committee on the Organization of Congress, *Hearings,* parts 1–4 (1945), and *Organization of the Congress, Report* . . . , S. Rept. 1011, 79th Cong., 2d Sess. (1946). For a fuller coverage of the committee's work, see Chap. 13.

by a leading newspaper revealed that the typical Senator and Representative required an outside income in order to balance his personal budget.[28] The extraordinary demands on the national legislator include the necessity of maintaining two homes, social entertainment, campaign and political costs, and travel between Washington and home. The salary most frequently suggested as adequate was $25,000 per year.

In 1955, having received the report of a commission on judicial and congressional salaries, Congress proceeded to pass, and the President to sign, a bill providing both Senators and Representatives with the sum of $22,500 per year.

Retirement. The retirement plan included in the 1946 act, though quite generous, aroused surprisingly little opposition, in view of the "bundles for Congressmen" campaign that ridiculed an earlier proposal. Although the retirement provisions for members of Congress were incorporated in the civil service retirement system, the provisions are entirely different from those applicable to civil service employees. Members are free to elect whether they will come under the system, and upon doing so are required to pay into the fund 6 per cent of their salaries, which entitles them to receive a retirement allowance, after the age of sixty-two and a minimum of 6 years of service, of 2½ per cent of their annual salary multiplied by their years of service. The maximum for congressmen who have served for 30 years was set at $7,500 annually and raised to fit the new salary scale. When the plan was first instituted, members with past service were permitted to qualify upon payment of only about $2,500 in lump sum. In contrast to ordinary retirement plans, members are not required to retire when they reach the retirement age, but may continue to serve in Congress as long as they are able to be reelected. The effect of the plan has not been to induce overage members to retire; rather, it has provided a needed degree of security for members who have served long in Congress and face the prospect of defeat or retirement without provision for their old age.

[28] Cabell Phillips, "The High Cost of Our Low-paid Congress," *The New York Times Magazine,* Feb. 24, 1952, pp. 7, 41–42, 44.

Sessions and Congresses. A Congress has a life of 2 years, coinciding with the term of office of Representatives. Each Congress since the first (1789–1790) has been numbered consecutively; the Congress elected in 1954 and serving 1955–1956 is the Eighty-fourth; that elected in 1956 and serving 1957–1958 will be the Eighty-fifth.

A regular session occurs once each year. Since the Twentieth Amendment was adopted, each regular session begins on Jan. 3, unless another date is provided by law. Under the 1946 act, the regular session adjourns July 31 unless otherwise provided by Congress. In even-numbered years during normal times adjournment comes in early summer in order to leave time for campaigning. In odd years Congress holds forth until middle or late summer. The President has power to call special sessions. Within each 2-year Congress, sessions are numbered consecutively, whether regular or special, beginning with "first" for each Congress.

The original constitutional provision regarding sessions called for the assembling of Congress on the first Monday of December of each year. The first regular session met 13 months after election. The second regular session convened in December after a new Congress had been elected but with the old personnel. This became known as the "lame-duck" session; for many defeated members of Congress continued to function for 3 months after their rejection by the electorate. The Twentieth Amendment, fathered by Senator Norris and adopted in 1933, abolished the lame-duck session and provided that a new Congress, fresh from the elections of November, begins active legislative work early in January.

PARTY GOVERNMENT

Party lines are rather loosely drawn in the House and Senate. Like the houses of the British Parliament, organization and procedure are linked to partisanship. There is not, however, in the American Congress the strict discipline imposed in the House of Commons. Groups, sectional and economic, often claim a greater share of a congressman's loyalty than does his party. On the other hand, the parties in Congress play a far larger role than do the parties in many state legislatures, especially in the Western states.

The Caucus or Conference. In the House members elected as Democrats affiliate with the Democratic caucus, while the Republicans join the Republican conference. These are the partisan groups from which partisan officers in the House draw their authority, and in the name of which the majority and minority perform their important functions in the House. In tangible form, the caucus or conference is a meeting of all Representatives elected to the House under the label of a particular party. Meeting on the eve of a new Congress, the party group elects its own officers and nominates its candidates for the House offices. Each group has its chairman and secretary.

Only rarely does caucus or conference bind members to vote on the House floor according to the caucus decision. Both parties, upon occasion, attempt to bind their members, but there is often much insurgency. The Democratic rule permits the caucus to set the party "line" if two-

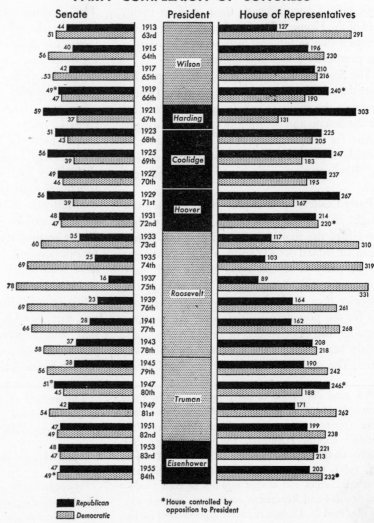

PARTY COMPLEXION OF CONGRESS

Senate	President	House of Representatives
44 / 51	1913 63rd	127 / 291
40 / 56	1915 64th	196 / 230
42 / 53	1917 65th — Wilson	210 / 216
49* / 47	1919 66th	240* / 190
59 / 37	1921 67th — Harding	303 / 131
51 / 43	1923 68th	225 / 205
56 / 39	1925 69th — Coolidge	247 / 183
49 / 46	1927 70th	237 / 195
56 / 39	1929 71st — Hoover	267 / 167
48 / 47	1931 72nd	214 / 220*
35 / 60	1933 73rd	117 / 310
25 / 69	1935 74th	103 / 319
16 / 78	1937 75th — Roosevelt	89 / 331
23 / 69	1939 76th	164 / 261
28 / 66	1941 77th	162 / 268
37 / 58	1943 78th	208 / 218
38 / 56	1945 79th	190 / 242
51* / 45	1947 80th — Truman	246* / 188
42 / 54	1949 81st	171 / 262
47 / 49	1951 82nd	199 / 238
48 / 47	1953 83rd	221 / 213
47 / 49*	1955 84th — Eisenhower	203 / 232*

Since 1913 the President's party has usually commanded both houses of Congress but there are notable exceptions.

■ Republican
▨ Democratic

*House controlled by opposition to President

SOURCE: *Historical Statistics of the United States and Congressional Directory*

thirds of those voting approve. No member is bound, however, on questions of constitutional construction, or on matters on which he has made contrary pledges to his constituents. The Republicans get along without formal rules in their conference but take such actions as are deemed necessary by majority vote. A Democratic caucus rule provides that violators of group regulations automatically cease to be members of the caucus. Since the fall of Cannon in 1910 the Republicans have generally been tolerant of independence, but in 1925 thirteen Republicans who supported Senator La Follette for President were not invited to the conference and were read out of the party. Both parties limit caucus attendance to their partisan members of the House.[29] During the last twenty years caucus action in binding members on legislation has practically fallen into disuse.

The Senate party caucuses play less important roles than do the House groups. As in the House, however, the majority caucus nominates officers for the Senate and determines committee assignments for the majority. The minority caucus provides a list of committee posts for the minority. Binding caucus decisions are exceedingly rare.

Party Leadership. The post in the House most sought after is the speakership, and it is within the gift of the majority party. Intraparty differences are ironed out in caucus, and the candidate of the party is agreed upon before each new Congress opens. Second most desirable is the majority floor leadership. Often a greater contest for this post develops than over the speakership, for the floor leader in recent years commonly has inherited the speakership when vacated. The majority floor leader is chief spokes-

man and strategist of his party on the floor. The minority caucus goes through the motions of nominating a candidate for the speakership, too. After he is defeated for election on the floor of the House, he becomes minority floor leader, generalissimo of the opposition forces. Both majority and minority floor leaders keep in touch with members on the floor through whips, who canvass party membership in the House and inform Representatives of forthcoming business and of the position of the party on it.

Party organization on the Senate side follows much the same pattern. Assigned a constitutional presiding officer, the Senate selects its next highest officer, the president pro tempore. The nominee of the majority-party caucus is formally elected on the floor of the Senate. Majority and minority floor leaders are chosen by the respective caucuses. The Democratic party in the Senate has a steering committee.

Strengthening Leadership. The La Follette committee report recommended the establishment of majority and minority policy committees in both the House and the Senate. These bodies were to formulate legislative policy for the parties and to expedite consideration and passage of matters on which the party had made commitments to the people. The act failed to include provisions for policy committees, but the Senate secured its policy groups through an appropriation bill in 1947. No such committees have been established in the House, which has continued with its informal steering committees.

Senate majority and minority policy committees meet weekly during sessions. Each has a staff and a substantial budget.[30] Democratic policy committeemen are appointed by the floor leader; Republican ones are elected by the conference for two-year terms.

The record of the Senate policy committees in the first three Congresses after their establishment is generally regarded as disappointing.[31]

[29] A good description of party government in Congress is in Floyd M. Riddick, *The United States Congress, Organization and Procedures* (Manassas, Va.: National Capitol Publishers, 1949), pp. 42–57. See also his *Congressional Procedure* (Chapman & Grimes, Inc., 1941), pp. 29–40. To the latter he appends the Democratic rules and sample minutes of both Democratic caucus and Republican conference, pp. 352–365. See also Paul D. Hasbrouck, *Party Government in the House of Representatives* (Macmillan, 1927).

[30] $45,715 each per annum in the Eighty-first Congress.

[31] George B. Galloway, "The Operation of the Legislative Reorganization Act of 1946," *American Political Science Review,* vol. 45 (March, 1951), pp. 41–68, at pp. 51–52.

POLITICAL COMPOSITION
OF EIGHTY-FOURTH CONGRESS BY STATES

THE SENATE

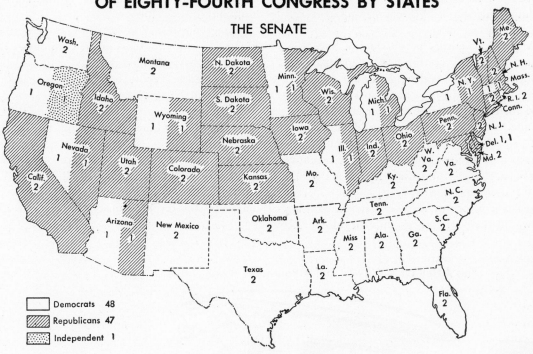

Democrats 48
Republicans 47
Independent 1

THE HOUSE OF REPRESENTATIVES

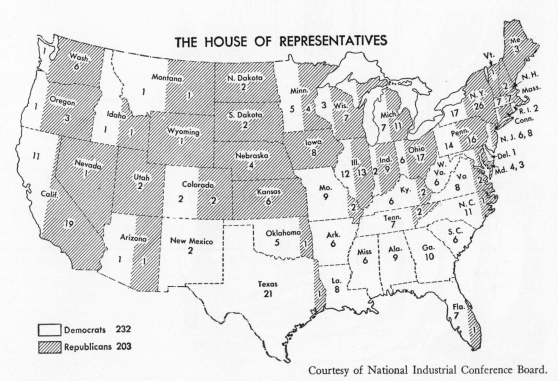

Democrats 232
Republicans 203

Courtesy of National Industrial Conference Board.

They have done some useful work, but they have not done the job that needed doing in providing leadership and strengthening party responsibility.

Meanwhile, parties in the House have continued with their steering bodies, which the La Follette committee said "seldom meet and never steer." They are party rather than House bodies, and therefore have no budget or staff from the House. Actually they are considerably more active than the above quotation indicates. The Democratic steering committee is an executive committee of the caucus and makes many day-to-day decisions on party strategy with respect to legislation before the House. The Republicans now call their steering group "the House Re-publican policy committee." It is used as an advisory or consultative agency by the Republican leadership in the House.

Neither the formal policy committees of the Senate nor the informal steering committees of the House have fulfilled the need expressed by the La Follette report for "some mechanism which could bring about more party accountability for policies and pledges announced and made in the national platforms of the major political parties." [32]

Party Role in Committees. Until 1911 the Speaker of the House appointed all committees of that body. The principal reform that followed the successful revolt against arbitrary rule by

[32] *Organization of the Congress,* p. 12.

"It's A Hell Of A Way To Run A Railroad"

Nov 48

The seniority system is firmly entrenched and helps explain the great power of congressional committees.

Speaker Cannon in March, 1910, was the election of standing committees by the House. Each party receives representation on each standing committee of the House somewhat in proportion to its strength in the whole House. For example, if the Republicans hold two-thirds of the House seats, they would take about two-thirds of the places on each committee. Actually each major party chooses its own representatives for standing committee assignments. In practice the parties exercise little discretion in individual committee assignments of old members, who receive reassignment, as a matter of course, to committees on which they previously served. For newly elected members, however, the process described below is fraught with importance. Minor parties secure committee posts through one of the major parties.

The Republican conference uses a Committee on Committees for selection of committee personnel. This committee is composed of one representative from each state having Republican members of the House. Members are selected by the Republican state delegations and ratified by the conference. The Committee on Committees meets and draws up a slate of Republican members for the standing committees of the House; it also recommends personnel for the party steering committee. In voting within the Republican Committee on Committees, members cast the number of votes their state has in Republican representatives in Congress.

The Democratic caucus first elects its members of the House Ways and Means Committee; these then determine, sometimes in consultation with the party steering committee, standing-committee assignments for Democratic representatives. After approval by the party caucus, party slates are reported on the floor of the House and are accepted quickly and without difficulty.

Senate selection of committee personnel is similar to that of the House. Standing committees are elected, but the nominating process within the parties is the crucial matter. The Republicans use the Committee on Committees device. The Democrats in the Senate employ their steering committee as a Committee on Committees. In the Republican party, appointment to the committee-selecting body is made by the caucus chairman; in the Democratic, appointment is by the floor leader. Considerations of seniority are influential in both. The slates of the two parties are accepted almost automatically on the floor of the Senate.

Campaign Committees. Not satisfied that the proper attention would be given by national party organizations to the campaigns of congressional candidates, a joint congressional campaign committee was organized by the Republicans for the campaign of 1866. The Democrats followed suit. In 1916 the senatorial element split off the Republican committee, and formed a separate group. The Democrats did likewise in 1918. Today there are four such campaign committees: Republican congressional campaign committee, Democratic congressional campaign committee, Republican senatorial campaign committee, and the Democratic senatorial campaign committee. In recent years they have been quite active. Each party's House campaign group is composed of one representative from each state having representation in the House. The membership of both Republican and Democratic senatorial campaign committees is appointed by the appropriate caucus chairman.

ORGANIZATION AND LEADERSHIP

Speaker of the House. The House of Representatives chooses its own Speaker. The nominee of the majority party invariably is elected by the House. This election takes place at the beginning of each new Congress. The Constitution does not require it, but every Speaker has been at the time of his selection a member of the House. Seniority is an important consideration in choosing a Speaker, but personal popularity and political backing are also prerequisites. The tradition is now well established that Speakers are reelected in subsequent Congresses if their party maintains a majority.

Unlike the impartial and judicious Speaker of the British House of Commons, the American House presiding officer acts as a party leader and uses the powers of his office to promote his party's program. Like the presidency, the speakership can be an office of great magnitude or one of only modest influence. It depends upon the incumbent and the circumstances in his party, in Congress, and in the country. The most powerful Speakers, like Reed, Cannon, and Longworth, built up the authority and prestige of the office to a high level. Others have been content to deal with the House as merely its presiding officer.

Nominal powers of the Speaker include appointment of select and conference committees, signature of documents in behalf of the House, reference of bills to committees, and general conduct of parliamentary business, which includes recognition of members who wish to have the floor. Since the loss in 1911 of the power to appoint standing committees, the greater authority of the Speaker has flowed from his work in presiding. Speaker Reed established that members present but refusing to answer to their names could be counted for purposes of securing a quorum. He also refused to put motions that were dilatory or intended to obstruct the business of the House.

The power over recognition, as developed by Speaker Gillette and others, permits the presiding officer to use his discretion as to who is entitled to the floor. The Speaker may ignore entirely the attempt of a member to claim the floor, unless he has explained his purpose in an interview. More bluntly, the Speaker may turn to one who seeks the floor and ask: "For what purpose does the gentleman rise?" If the purpose is not regarded as proper, the Speaker may reply: "The Chair cannot recognize the gentleman for that purpose." The Speaker rules on all points of order, and his decisions rarely are overruled on appeal to the House. It is possible for the Speaker to vote if he chooses; he may speak to a question if he wishes.[33]

House Floor Leaders. The majority and minority floor leaders, selected by their respective

[33] The best sources of information on the development of the speakership include Mary P. Follett, *The Speaker of the House of Representatives* (Longmans, 1896); Chang-wei Chiu, *The Speaker of the House of Representatives since 1896* (Columbia University Press, 1928).

party caucuses, fill posts that have developed into their present form since the turn of the century. The majority leader, when of the same party as the President, often is the administration spokesman. Each floor leader is manager of his party's program on the floor and has effective control, through cooperation with the Speaker, over important aspects of procedure.

House Rules Committee. Over a period of more than a century the House Rules Committee has built up authority over the procedure of the House until now it has virtual life-and-death power over legislation in the lower house. Each Congress is deluged with such a mass of proposed legislation (10,000 to 15,000 bills introduced each 2 years) that full consideration cannot be given to all. Most of these fall by the wayside in the committees to which they are referred and are never reported out. But the committees approve and report to the House itself more bills than can be adequately considered and some bills which are opposed by the leadership of the House. Consequently there is need for a sifting device to select those bills which are of greater importance to the nation and which are likely to win the approval of the House. For many years this function has been performed by the Rules Committee, which formerly was headed by the Speaker.

The traffic jam of bills awaiting action by the House is usually so great that only those which receive the blessing of the Rules Committee through a special rule which enables them to be taken up out of order are considered by the House. Bills on certain subjects, like taxation and appropriations, however, are highly privileged and may be called up without a special rule. Moreover, on certain days, private bills and minor bills which are noncontroversial are taken up and passed, normally by unanimous consent. But important legislative measures ordinarily are taken up only as a result of a special rule proposed by the Rules Committee.

This situation does give the Rules Committee great power. While it cannot initiate legislation, it can block that recommended by other committees, virtually exercising a veto power. On occasion it has held hearings on the merits of legislation already considered by other committees and has refused to bring in a special rule unless proposed bills were altered to suit its wishes. If the Rules Committee is controlled by party leaders who are friendly to the administration, it can block legislation which might be embarrassing to the administration and keep the track clear for the President's legislative program.

If a majority of its members are unsympathetic to the President's legislative program, however, its influence is just the opposite. During President Truman's administration the latter condition generally prevailed. A majority of the members of the Rules Committee of both parties was opposed to the President's legislative program on labor and other economic issues and managed to prevent these measures from coming before the House. The membership of the Committee was largely conservative, consisting of members of both parties who came from safe districts, and as a result blocked many social reform measures.

In 1949, after the Democratic victory of the previous year, the House trimmed the powers of the Rules Committee, providing that after the Rules Committee had held a bill for 21 days without any action, the chairman of the committee which recommended it could move on a specified day to take the bill up in the House without a special rule, and if a majority so voted, the bill would be made the order of business. In order to make the motion, however, recognition by the Speaker was necessary, which, in effect, gave the Speaker the decision whether he would permit the issue to be raised.

In 1951 the old rule was restored by a conservative combination, including most of the Republican members and many Southern Democrats, and at present the Rules Committee is again the most powerful single committee in the House. This power is exercised without any effective means to make the members individually responsible to the nation, to the Congress, or to their party for the decisions which they make. While a committee with such powers is required to screen out unimportant and undesirable legislation, means are needed to make its members

subject more fully to the control of the party leadership and the House itself.

Senate Leaders. The Vice-President of the United States, as president of the Senate, conducts himself as a rather impartial presiding officer. He votes only in case of a tie. His appointive power is slight. A president pro tempore is elected by the Senate after nomination by the majority-party caucus. He presides over the upper house in the absence of its president, and succeeds to the presidency of the United States in the event of the death or disability of the President, Vice-President, and Speaker of the House.

COMMITTEE SYSTEMS

Role of Standing Committees. Seventy years ago Woodrow Wilson in his doctoral dissertation characterized American government as "government by the Standing Committees of Congress." [34] As the two houses have grown larger in membership and the problems with which they deal have increased in number and complexity, they have delegated more and more important decision making to committees. Standing committees, indeed even their chairmen acting unilaterally, may relegate to the pigeonhole bills desired by the majority of Congress or the people. They are "little ministries" with enormous power. A member of the British House of Commons serving on a committee to consider a bill declares: "I swear that my constituents have no local interest in the bill and I have no personal interest in it." A member of a House or Senate committee, far from disclaiming such interests, often flaunts his bias and proceeds to champion the case of his district or state or favorite pressure group. [35]

[34] *Congressional Government* (Houghton Mifflin, 1885), p. 56. Dr. George B. Galloway recently declared: "The real locus of the legislative power is not in the House or Senate as such; it is in their standing committees." Galloway, *The Legislative Process in Congress,* p. 649.

[35] For a valuable study of legislative behavior, see Ralph K. Huitt, "The Congressional Committee: A Case Study," *American Political Science Review,* vol. XLVIII (June, 1954), pp. 340–365.

House Standing Committees. The methods of the party groups in selecting standing-committee personnel have been described already. Standing committees are by far the most important class of committees, for they constitute the screen through which the great mass of proposed legislation is sifted. After the party groups have completed their slates of committee assignments, they are put together in resolution form and adopted by the House. Few new members are given committee posts of great importance. The majority committeeman who is senior in point of service generally is made chairman. When the Democrats are in the majority, this means that the principal chairmanships are held by Southerners. In the Eighty-fourth Congress, for example, nine standing committees (out of nineteen) were headed by Representatives from the deep South and five more from the border states, while the speakership was held by Sam Rayburn of Texas.

The rule of seniority produces an experienced corps of committee heads, who averaged at the beginning of the Eighty-fourth Congress 19.89 years in the House. But a heavy price is paid in vesting leadership in a group that averages 62.27 years of age. Nearly one-half of the chairmen were past the age at which retirement is compulsory in most public enterprises and private companies.

The nineteen House standing committees range in number of members from nine to fifty, averaging over twenty-seven. With a few exceptions, members are now limited to a single standing-committee assignment. Before the enactment of the Legislative Reorganization Act of 1946 there were many more committees. In the Seventy-ninth Congress, the number of regular House committees was forty-seven, and members were permitted to serve on two or more of all but the most important committees.

Public bills are referred to committees by the Speaker, who sometimes exercises considerable discretion but is ultimately subject to the will of the House. Once assigned, it is difficult to secure rereference of a bill. Traditionally, standing-committee chairmen wield great power over the

meeting, procedure, and action of their committees.

Committees of the House hold their meetings and conduct hearings during the morning hours. About one-half have regular meetings days; the remainder meet on call of the chairman. Most committee meetings are open to the public, but some are closed. On important bills extended hearings may be held by committees or subcommittees, with witnesses from various parts of the country testifying. When consideration of a bill is completed by a committee, it may vote to report the bill out to the House with a favorable recommendation, or it may defeat the bill and "pigeonhole" it. The most influential of the House committees, after Rules, are Ways and Means, Appropriations, Commerce, Banking and Currency, Agriculture, Armed Services, and Foreign Affairs.

Other House Committees. House select committees are established for various purposes. Their personnel is appointed by the Speaker. They are created by simple resolution. Usually a select committee is given the task of studying some problem for a definite period of time. The best known select committees are investigating committees. Such committees generally are given power to meet, even after Congress has adjourned, to administer oaths, to subpoena persons and records, and the like.[36]

Senate Committees. Senate standing committees are "elected" by the Senate, but this process is more properly described as ratification of the slates selected by the two major party groups. The majority party receives all chairmanships. The rule of seniority is highly important in the Senate also, but the longer term and the greater tendency to reelect Senators make overwhelming sectional domination less likely. In the Eighty-

[36] Four works of importance deal with congressional investigating committees: Marshall E. Dimock, *Congressional Investigating Committees* (Johns Hopkins Press, 1929); Ernest J. Eberling, *Congressional Investigations* (Columbia University Press, 1928); McGeary, *op. cit.;* and Telford Taylor, *Grand Inquest: The Story of Congressional Investigations* (Simon and Schuster, 1955).

fourth Congress, however, eight of the fifteen standing committees were headed by Senators from the deep South. Some of the most important committees are led by men of advanced age—in their seventies and eighties; the average age of chairmen in 1955 was 66.73 years, and the average length of service in Congress was 21.73 years. Senate committees varied in size from nine members on the smallest to twenty-three on the largest, which was Appropriations. Each Senator is limited to two committees, but when the two parties are rather evenly divided, third committee assignments are authorized. Before the 1946 reform law, the number of Senate committees had ranged from thirty-three to seventy-three in recent Congresses.

At the time of introduction, bills are referred by the presiding officer to the committee which is to consider the proposed measure. The committee may consider the bill, hold hearings if it chooses, and report or not report back to the Senate. The Appropriations Committee alone meets on call of the chairman; all others have regular meetings.

Investigating committees of the Senate are even better known than those of the House. The power of the Senate to conduct investigations between sessions was fully assured in McGrain *v.* Daugherty,[37] and the Senate has used its power with vigor. Among well-known Senate inquiries were Teapot Dome, munitions, the Truman committee investigating war expenditures, and the Kefauver committee on organized crime. Members of Senate select committees are appointed by the president of the Senate.

Joint Committees. Frequently the House and Senate have business in common which requires the forming of joint committees for its solution. Some of these are set up to plan memorials, monuments, or commemoration celebrations. Some deal with common facilities like capital buildings and grounds, printing, library, and other problems.

More important are the joint investigating

committees occasionally established by two-house resolution or by statute. A recent example is the Joint Committee on the Organization of Congress. The Temporary National Economic Committee, which reported in 1941, contained members of both houses and representatives of several federal executive agencies.

The most common joint committees are conference committees. These bodies are established on a temporary basis to compromise the differences between Senate and House versions of the same bill. House conferees are appointed by the Speaker and those of the Senate by the Vice-President of the United States. Most important pieces of legislation are amended in some form or other in the second house. Then the amended bill is sent back to the first house for acceptance. If the first house declines to accept the amendments, this house may ask the second to recede from the amendments. If it will not, then a conference is arranged. Normally three representatives and three senators constitute such a committee, though many are larger. If the conferees can agree on a compromise, then the results are reported to each house. Should the House and Senate both agree to accept the conference committee recommendation, then the bill is deemed passed in the form the conference committee has proposed. If, on the other hand, one or both houses refuse to accept, then the bill dies or another conference must be arranged.

Committee Changes. Reform of the committee system was a prime objective of the 1946 act and "the keystone in the arch of congressional reform." [38] Senate standing committees were reduced in number from thirty-three to fifteen; in the House the reduction was from forty-seven to nineteen. Jurisdiction was defined with some care. Senators were limited to two standing-committee assignments with some exceptions permitted. Although House members were not limited by statute, in practice they are not assigned to more than one major standing committee; select and joint committees are in addition.

[37] 273 U.S. 135 (1927).

[38] Galloway, "The Operation of the Legislative Reorganization Act of 1946," p. 41.

Special committees were not forbidden by the act, but the report of the La Follette committee urged their abolition. In actual practice rather few have been authorized: at the outset of the second session of the Eighty-fourth Congress, the Senate had one (exclusive of the two policy committees) and the House had two. One of the strong deterrents to the creation of special investigating committees is the fact that nearly every proposal for one cuts into the jurisdiction of one or more of the standing committees. The trend is for standing committees and their subcommittees to conduct most of the investigations.

The number of subcommittees is large. In the House, in the first session of the Eighty-fourth Congress, eight standing committees had subcommittees, ranging in numbers from three for Interstate and Foreign Commerce to seventeen for Agriculture. In the Senate, in 1955, eleven standing committees had created subcommittees, from two for Government Operations to fourteen for Judiciary. Some of the leading investigations of the era, including the Army-McCarthy hearings of 1954 and the Kefauver probe of juvenile delinquency, were conducted by subcommittees.

There has also been a significant move toward more joint standing committees. Ten of these bodies were in existence when the Eighty-fourth Congress opened in 1955.

About half of the House standing committees abide by the law that requires regular meeting days; the Senate committees, with one exception, have established meeting times. Committees have experienced difficulty in meeting the requirement that a majority must be present to report a measure or recommendation. The statutory provision that committees should have witnesses file in advance written statements of proposed testimony is perhaps more often ignored than observed.

Largely through standing committees and their subcommittees, Congress since reorganization has conducted a record number of investigations.[39] Relatively few were special committees.

The House conducted more investigations than did the Senate, but the upper house was more generous with funds. Such inquiries make valuable contributions to the understanding of governmental problems by the public and by the Congress.

On the other hand, committees and subcommittees of Congress frequently conduct hearings and other proceedings in such a way that individual rights are violated or fair play does not prevail. Sensational accusations are made by irresponsible witnesses, with the result that the victim suffers from loss of reputation and of earning power even though he can prove the charges ill-founded and false. Persons before congressional inquiries have been deprived of such fundamental privileges as the right to counsel, the right to confront and cross-examine accusers, and the right to be heard. Under the cloak of immunity, both Senators and Representatives have made charges they could not substantiate, yet those attacked have no remedy and no way to secure compensation.

The action of the House of Representatives in adopting in 1955 a set of rules on the conduct of committees may prove a turning point.[40] It requires that no fewer than two members constitute a quorum for taking of testimony and receiving evidence. The subject of investigation must be announced at the outset by the chairman. Committee rules must be made available to witnesses. Witnesses may be accompanied by counsel. If testimony tending to defame a person is anticipated, it must be received in executive session, the person concerned afforded an opportunity to testify, and the person given the right to request additional witnesses. Material secured in executive sessions cannot be released without the consent of the committee. Witnesses may submit "brief and pertinent" sworn statements for the record, subject to the discretion of the committee. A witness may obtain a transcript of his testimony on payment of the cost.

Many proposed reforms are not included in

[39] *Congressional Quarterly* reported that the committees of the Eighty-third Congress had available for investigations the sum of $8,172,894. A total of 117 separate investigations were conducted after the first session.

[40] H. Res. 151, 84th Cong., 1st Sess., by Rep. Clyde Doyle of California.

this list, but when considered with the Speaker's ban on televised and broadcast committee hearings, they place the House far ahead of the Senate in the safeguards afforded to individuals against maltreatment before congressional committees.

FOR FURTHER READING

(See also works listed after next chapter.)

Alexander, De Alva S.: *History and Procedure of the House of Representatives* (Houghton Mifflin, 1916).

Bailey, Stephen K., and Howard D. Samuel: *Congress at Work* (Holt, 1952).

Barth, Alan: *Government by Investigation* (Viking, 1955).

Brown, George R.: *The Leadership of Congress* (Bobbs-Merrill, 1922).

Chamberlain, Joseph P.: *Legislative Processes: National and State* (Appleton-Century-Crofts, 1936).

Chiu, Chang-wei: *The Speaker of the House of Representatives since 1896* (Columbia University Press, 1928).

Dennison, Eleanor E.: *The Senate Foreign Relations Committee* (Stanford University Press, 1942).

Dimock, Marshall E.: *Congressional Investigating Committees* (Johns Hopkins Press, 1929).

Eberling, Ernest J.: *Congressional Investigations* (Columbia University Press, 1928).

Erwin, Spencer: *Henry Ford vs. Truman H. Newberry: A Study in American Politics, Legislation and Justice* (Richard R. Smith, 1935).

Ewing, Cortez A.: *Congressional Elections, 1896–1944* (University of Oklahoma Press, 1947).

Follett, Mary P.: *The Speaker of the House of Representatives* (Longmans, 1896).

Galloway, George B.: *The Legislative Process in Congress* (Crowell, 1953).

Griffith, Ernest S.: *Congress: Its Contemporary Role* (New York University Press, 1951).

Gross, Bertram M.: *The Legislative Struggle: A Study in Social Combat* (McGraw-Hill, 1953).

Hasbrouck, Paul D.: *Party Government in the House of Representatives* (Macmillan, 1927).

Haynes, George H.: *The Senate of the United States: Its History and Practice* (Houghton Mifflin, 2 vols., 1938).

Kalijarvi, Thorsten V., and C. E. Merrow: "Congress and Foreign Relations," *Annals of the American Academy of Political and Social Science,* vol. 289 (September, 1953).

Luce, Robert: *Legislative Principles* (Houghton Mifflin, 1930).

——: *Congress—An Explanation* (Harvard University Press, 1926).

——: *Legislative Assemblies* (Houghton Mifflin, 1924).

McGeary, M. Nelson: *The Development of Congressional Investigative Power* (Columbia University Press, 1940).

Riddick, Floyd M.: *The United States Congress: Organization and Procedure* (Manassas, Va.: National Capitol Publishers, 1949).

——: *Congressional Procedure* (Chapman & Grimes, 1941).

Rogers, Lindsay: *The American Senate* (Knopf, 1926).

Schmeckebier, Laurence F.: *Congressional Apportionment* (Brookings, 1941).

Steiner, Gilbert Y.: *The Congressional Conference Committee* (University of Illinois Press, 1951).

Taylor, Telford: *Grand Inquest: The Story of Congressional Investigations* (Simon and Schuster, 1955).

Torrey, Volta: *You and Your Congress* (Morrow, 1944).

Westphal, Albert C. F.: *The House Committee on Foreign Affairs* (Columbia University Press, 1942).

Wilson, Woodrow: *Congressional Government* (Houghton Mifflin, 1885).

Wooddy, Carroll H.: *The Case of Frank L. Smith: A Study in Representative Government* (University of Chicago Press, 1931).

Young, Roland: *This Is Congress* (Knopf, 1943).

REVIEW QUESTIONS

1. How did the bicameral principle originate? Is there justification for it in Congress today?

2. Compare the House of Representatives and the Senate in respect to qualifications and selection of members.

3. What powers have the Senate and the House to expel or refuse to seat regularly elected members?

4. What are the powers and duties of the Speaker of the House? How does he rank in prestige with other high officials?

5. Describe the committee systems of the United States Senate and House.

6. What is the role of the political party in the legislative process?

7. Name and discuss the American forerunners of the Congress of the United States.

8. What were the principal provisions of the Reapportionment Act of 1929?

9. What is the present status of the traditional principles of apportionment: equality, compactness, and contiguousness?

10. To what privileges and compensation are members of the House and Senate entitled under present law?

11. Explain the following terms: "session," "a Congress," "lame duck," "gerrymander," "equal proportions," "franking privilege."

12. How do the Republicans select House committee members? How do the Democrats?

13. How do the Republicans select Senate committee members? How do the Democrats?

14. Describe the operation of House and Senate standing committees, with special reference to the powers of chairmen.

15. Why are there joint committees of the two Houses? Give some examples of joint committees and tell how they operate.

CHAPTER 13

Congressional Procedure and Reform

I have begun a sketch, which those who come after me will successively correct and fill up, till a code of rules shall be formed . . . the effects of which may be accuracy in business, economy of time, order, uniformity and impartiality. — Thomas Jefferson [1]

Because Congress is without leadership and its organization is disintegrated, the gulf between its promise and its performance on legislation takes on the proportions, but not the grandeur, of the Grand Canyon. Without a center of responsibility, there can be no strong leadership and no coordinated legislative program. National interests are subordinated to sectional and special interests, and Congress fails to perform adequately its tremendously important function of holding the executive branch accountable. — National Committee for Strengthening the Congress [2]

In order to carry on its legislative and nonlegislative business, Congress must have rules of procedure and an organization of considerable size and complexity. If parliamentary practices appear to the reader to place too much importance on being ancient, it may be well to recall that standards and ways of doing things have been hammered out over the years on the anvil of controversy. The compromises reached often set precedents to which reference could be made when similar situations arose another time. The House of Representatives, in particular, has a special problem imposed by its large size and heavy work load, and often is the object of ill-informed criticism. During the past ten years there has been much healthy, informed criticism

of congressional practices, and substantial improvements have been made.

PROCEDURE IN THE HOUSE

Introduction of Bills. A bill is introduced in the House of Representatives merely by sending it to the clerk's desk. A member must appear as its sponsor. Before formal introduction, however, a great deal of planning and drafting must be done. Actually the two main sources of bills are executive agencies and private pressure groups, not the legislators themselves. An idea for legislation may be taken to private attorneys for drafting, or it may be whipped into the form of a bill or resolution by the staff of the Legislative Counsel.

Simple bills are designated "HR" or "S" depending upon the house of origin and are numbered consecutively during a Congress. Joint resolutions, marked "H.J. Res." and "S.J. Res.," differ from ordinary bills only in that they are

[1] Preface to his *Manual*, quoted in Alice F. Sturgis, *Sturgis Standard Code of Parliamentary Procedure* (McGraw-Hill, 1950), p. xi.

[2] Letter to members of Congress from Robert Heller, chairman, Jan. 7, 1952.

intended for temporary situations. Neither concurrent resolutions, which deal with matters pertaining to the legislative branch, nor simple resolutions, which concern internal matter in one house only, are submitted to the President for signature.

No limit is imposed on the number of bills a member may introduce. Each Congress in the last 20 years has faced an average of about 14,000 bills introduced; slightly less than 1,000 were enacted in an average Congress. All bills not enacted are wiped off the records at the close of a Congress. In order to secure consideration in the next 2-year period, it is necessary to reintroduce the proposed legislation.[3]

[3] Procedure is covered most adequately in Floyd M. Riddick, *Congressional Procedure* (Chapman & Grimes, 1941), and *The United States Congress: Organization and Procedure* (Manassas, Va.: National Capitol

Committee Stage. Reference to committee is the next step in the legislative process. In committee, bills are given a preliminary examination. Most of them are buried as meriting no further consideration. The more important pieces of legislation are studied in detail, public hearings are held, and the testimony of interested persons is heard. The committee arrives at its verdict. If it is favorable, the proposed legislation, often in amended form, is forwarded to the floor of the House. On important matters the committee report may be extensive and exhaustive; on minor matters it may convey little more than a simple affirmative. In general, bills that secure favorable committee action are in a strong position to secure passage in the House; conversely, committee rejection of a measure makes passage extremely unlikely.

Although committee action is often taken in executive (closed) session, the vote of individual committeemen usually is available to the public. Hearings of the major committees on important legislation are published, some in the "documents" series of Congress. Minority reports also may be filed.

Calendars. Each bill reported out of committee to the floor of the House is placed on one of three principal calendars. Bills raising revenue, appropriating money or property, directly or indirectly, are placed on the "Union" Calendar. All other public bills, not fiscal in nature, go to the "House" Calendar. All bills of a private character are assigned to the "Private" Calendar. Noncontroversial bills may be transferred from either Union or House Calendar to the Consent Calendar, provided request is filed. Bills withdrawn from committee by petition are placed before the House on the Discharge Calendar. Members keep track of bills mainly through the daily issue of *Calendars of the United States*

Publishers, 1949). Current developments in congressional procedure were covered in the reviews of each session of Congress, contained in the *American Political Science Review*. For two decades they were written by E. Pendleton Herring, by Orman R. Altman, and by Floyd M. Riddick. Beginning with the Eighty-first Congress, Riddick's reviews were transferred to the *Western Political Quarterly*.

House of Representatives and History of Legislation. Listed in this publication are the special orders of the day, unfinished business, bills in conference, the four calendars mentioned, with all bills on them, a history of active bills, and a summary table on status of fifteen or twenty major bills.

A rule of the House requires that bills be taken up in their calendar order, but numerous exceptions are made in order that action may be secured on the more important measures.

Selection for Consideration. Several devices are used to select bills for consideration out of calendar order: (1) A motion may be made to suspend the rules (on first and third Mondays and during last six days of session) and must receive a two-thirds vote. (2) Some committees may bring up privileged matters (especially revenue and appropriation bills). (3) Special orders or rules are highly privileged and may be brought in at any time by the Rules Committee and adopted by a majority vote. (4) Bills may be brought by unanimous consent from the Consent Calendar (on first and third Mondays) for immediate consideration. (5) Committees may call up for passage some of their own bills, otherwise unprivileged, from House or Union Calendars (on Wednesdays except during the last two weeks of a session). (6) Members may secure unanimous consent for immediate consideration of a measure.[4]

The special rules recommended by the Rules Committee and adopted by the House almost invariably call for immediate consideration of a particular bill. In the Eighty-third Congress, 154 special rules were adopted; of the total about one-half were "open" rules that merely set the

[4] A seventh device was created by the Eighty-first Congress (1949–1950) but abolished at the opening of the Eighty-second. It permitted chairmen of committees to move for immediate consideration of bills on two specified days of the month when the Rules Committee refused, after 21 days, to report a special rule. See Glendon A. Schubert, "The Twenty-one Day Rule," *Political Science* (New Zealand), vol. 5 (March, 1953), pp. 16–29.

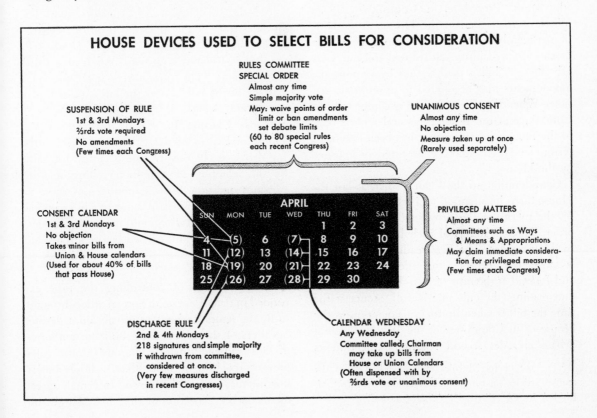

HOUSE DEVICES USED TO SELECT BILLS FOR CONSIDERATION

RULES COMMITTEE
SPECIAL ORDER
Almost any time
Simple majority vote
May: waive points of order
        limit or ban amendments
        set debate limits
(60 to 80 special rules
        each recent Congress)

SUSPENSION OF RULE
1st & 3rd Mondays
⅔rds vote required
No amendments
(Few times each Congress)

UNANIMOUS CONSENT
Almost any time
No objection
Measure taken up at once
(Rarely used separately)

CONSENT CALENDAR
1st & 3rd Mondays
No objection
Takes minor bills from
Union & House calendars
(Used for about 40% of bills
that pass House)

PRIVILEGED MATTERS
Almost any time
Committees such as Ways
        & Means & Appropriations
May claim immediate considera-
        tion for privileged measure
(Few times each Congress)

DISCHARGE RULE
2nd & 4th Mondays
218 signatures and simple majority
If withdrawn from committee,
        considered at once.
(Very few measures discharged
in recent Congresses)

CALENDAR WEDNESDAY
Any Wednesday
Committee called; Chairman
        may take up bills from
        House or Union Calendars
(Often dispensed with by
⅔rds vote or unanimous consent)

APRIL

SUN	MON	TUE	WED	THU	FRI	SAT
				1	2	3
4	(5)	6	(7)	8	9	10
11	(12)	13	(14)	15	16	17
18	(19)	20	(21)	22	23	24
25	(26)	27	(28)	29	30	

stage for preferential consideration; the other one-half were "closed" rules that "gagged" the House to a considerable extent. Nearly all the closed rules specify that points of order may not be raised against the bill as proposed by a standing committee; many restrict amendments either absolutely or allow only the committee to propose amendments. Both open and closed rules usually set maximum time limits on debate and in other ways provide for expeditious handling of House measures.[5]

Committee of the Whole. The House, sitting in a more informal capacity, handles all Union Calendar bills as the "Committee of the Whole House on the State of the Union." Private Calendar bills are discussed as in "Committee of the Whole." The House resolves itself into such a status on passage of a motion directing this action. The Speaker appoints a member to act as chairman, and himself retires. Sometimes the length of debate on a particular bill is set in the motion to resolve; usually time is divided into one-half for those opposing, one-half for those supporting. Procedure in Committee of the Whole is freer than in the House. Attendance of 100 members suffices for a quorum, in place of the usual majority. No record roll-call votes are taken. A bill is read section by section, and amendments may be offered to appropriate sections. When the work at hand is completed, the Committee of the Whole rises and reports back to the House the action that has been taken. Its recommendations may be accepted or rejected by the House.

Consideration on the Floor. When at last the House turns its attention to a certain bill, debate on the merits of the proposed legislation is in order. Three readings of each bill are required by House rules. The first reading requirement is satisfied by printing the title in the *Record* and *Journal* at the time of introduction. The second reading, the only one in full, occurs at the time the bill is taken up for consideration in the House or in Committee of the Whole. General debate precedes second reading. Amendments

may be offered as the appropriate sections are read. Some amendments are general, "considered" amendments, seriously intended as alterations in the bill at hand. Others are *pro forma,* involving the striking out of the last word or two of a section; in the short debate that may ensue a member may make some point he otherwise could not have made.

In the conduct of debate on a particular bill, management of the pro side is in the hands of the chairman or other ranking members of the committee that recommended the measure. Ranking minority members of the same committee may be recognized as in charge of the cons. Time for debate generally is predetermined in the House, and the time is divided equally between sponsors and opponents. The members in control grant time to those who wish to speak. It is very common for members to ask the one who has the floor if he will yield. If the member who holds recognition wishes to step aside for a moment, a question or brief statement may be interposed.

At the conclusion of consideration, the Speaker states: "The question is on the engrossment and third reading of the bill." If adopted, the bill is ordered engrossed and read a third time. Then: "The question is upon the final passage of the bill." After the bill is passed, it is sent to the Senate.

House Closure. In a body the size of the House of Representatives, the necessity of curbing debate is obvious. Debate is cut off formally by the adoption of a motion calling for the previous question. Such a motion may serve to close debate upon either passage of a bill or upon amendments to a bill. Should the previous question be called for and carried before any debate takes place, each side is given 20 minutes to present its case.

Other methods of controlling the time expended in debate are used. Special orders brought in by the Rules Committee usually limit debate. Speakers of the House have built up authority to refuse to put dilatory motions. House rules prevent speeches of more than 1 hour, unless unanimous consent be given. Informal agreements on the allocation of time increasingly are

[5] The use of special rules may be followed in the annual articles on congressional sessions by Floyd M. Riddick in *The Western Political Quarterly.*

made between majority and minority leaders and have proved highly satisfactory in curbing excessive verbosity.

Voting in the House. Four methods of voting are used by the House: (1) Usually the first attempted is viva voce, or voice vote. If this is indecisive, or one-fifth of a quorum requests, another method may be used. (2) Division means standing vote, counted by the Speaker. (3) Voting with tellers involves the members' filing past a given point to be counted for or against a bill. (4) Yeas and nays voting requires a call of the roll by the clerk, each member's vote being recorded. The first three methods are rapid, but provide no record roll call through which a citizen may examine the voting record of his representative. The fourth method takes a great amount of House time, for the names of 435 members must be called orally, and those who

did not respond the first time are called again. This process often takes a half hour or more.

On one spectacular occasion, in 1935, the Scripps-Howard newspapers recorded the votes of Representatives participating in a teller vote. The vote was upon the so-called "death sentence" on utility holding companies. The press gallery was filled with staff members who knew congressional personnel; they simply put down the names of the members of the House who filed by with the "aye" group, and those who appeared with the "no" group. Ordinarily, however, the public is left in the dark concerning the votes of individual congresssmen, unless the yeas and nays are recorded by full roll call.

Several state legislative bodies have solved the problem of making record roll-call votes in brief time by installing an electric recording device. The names of the legislators appear on an illumi-

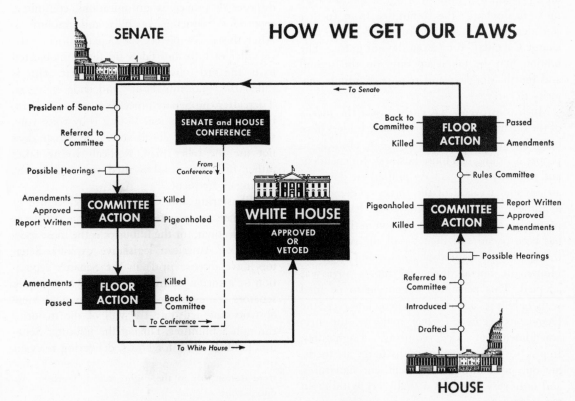

A simplified diagram of congressional procedure. The several steps through which a House bill passes are indicated. Adapted from *Under the Dome: How Our Congress Works* (Chamber of Commerce of the United States, 1953).

nated board on the front wall of the chamber. Each legislator's desk is fitted with a panel containing "yes" and "no" buttons. When buttons are pushed, the great scoreboard shows how each legislator votes. Vast amounts of time have been saved in the states where used, but Congress has not seen fit to adopt such a scheme.

Laymen often are confused by the pairing of House members for record votes. Pairs are personal contracts between two members; usually they are of opposite points of view and different parties. If one is absent, the other does not vote; the pairing is announced after a roll call.

Discharge Rule. Withdrawal of a bill on which a House committee refuses to report may be obtained under the discharge rule. The rule was first adopted in 1910 and, in several different forms, has persisted since that time. The present rule, adopted in 1935, provides that when signatures of 218 members of the House are obtained on a petition to withdraw a bill, a sponsor may move to discharge the committee from further consideration. The matter is placed on a "Discharge Calendar" for "seven days of grace." The motion may be taken up only on the second and fourth Mondays and requires a simple majority to carry.

Much controversy has ensued over the merits of the discharge rule. Majority party leaders have been inclined to debunk it as an obstacle to proper handling of House business. Independent and minority elements have praised the device as an essential weapon of the forces of democracy in the struggle against domination. Each major party, depending upon its situation in the House, has been friend and then foe of the rule. After the Democrats secured a slight majority in the House, the liberal discharge rule of 1931 was adopted. This permitted a petition to be filed with only 145 signatures. When, however, the Democrats secured a great majority, the 1935 amendment was added, requiring 218 signatures. In practice many attempts to discharge are made, but only a handful receive sufficient signatures, and only very few bills actually are withdrawn from committee.[6]

[6] In the Seventy-eighth Congress twenty-one discharge motions were filed, and three bills actually

SENATE PROCEDURE

General Aspects. Introduction of a Senate bill is accomplished by the announcement by a senator that he introduces it. The title of the bill is read, constituting first reading. Second reading is considered completed if there is no objection, and the bill is sent to the committee requested by the author. The Senate committee system already has been described; it does not differ in important respects from that of the House. After a standing committee reports favorably on a bill, it is placed on the Senate calendar for at least one day before being taken up. A rather simple calendar is sufficient to serve the needs of the Senate, and the smaller size of the upper house makes unnecessary the elaborate, selective and restrictive devices employed in the House of Representatives.

The Senate normally meets at high noon. During the first hour or more of the day the Senate disposes of prayer, communications, committee reports, introduction of bills and resolutions. After this is completed, the Senate turns to the calendar of bills and takes up those unobjected to in the order listed on the calendar. This is called the "morning hour" and ends at 2 P.M. Thereafter the Senate proceeds to the consideration of other legislation. Voting is by voice vote, standing vote, or roll-call vote. The Senate does not use the teller plan. Roll-call voting takes rather little time and is used very commonly. Pairing is frequent.[7]

Filibustering and Closure. The reluctance of the Senate to impose restrictions on debate is widely known, for the filibuster is the most spectacular of American legislative exploits. Senators have intense pride in the Senate's reputation as a forum of free discussion. Occasionally senators representing a minority point of view obstruct and frustrate the will of the majority through a filibuster. During the filibuster Senators hold the floor for hours, delivering relevant

were discharged; in the Eighty-second, fourteen produced none.

[7] The procedure of the Senate is dealt with exhaustively in George H. Haynes, *The Senate of the United States* (Houghton Mifflin, 2 vols., 1938).

and irrelevant remarks, aimed primarily at obstruction until some concessions are obtained. The longest filibuster on record is that of Wayne Morse who in 1953 spoke for over 22 hours on a tidelands-oil bill.

The closure rule of the Senate, adopted in 1917, requires a petition to end debate signed by one-sixth (sixteen) of the Senators. On the second day after this is filed, the Senate must vote by a two-thirds majority to bring debate to a close. After adoption of a closure motion, no Senator may speak more than one hour to the question, and other delaying parliamentary tactics are greatly restricted. Closure has been invoked in the Senate only four times between 1917 and 1955, but threat of its use has been sufficient to head off or terminate several filibusters. A mild form of closure, capable of stopping spur-of-the-moment filibusters, is found in the unanimous consent agreements by which the debate on particular measures is limited in advance.[8]

In 1949, after a filibuster on civil rights legislation, the Senate adopted a revised closure rule by which any matter under Senate proceedings (except change of rules) is subject to closure. A two-thirds vote of the total membership of the Senate (64 members) is necessary to carry closure, rather than the old requirement of two-thirds of those present. The net result of these changes is to make closure more difficult to use, but to extend the possibility of its use to procedural matters.

Amendments and Riders. Senate rules governing amendments to bills traditionally have not been so strict as those in the House. This was especially true in respect to the requirement that an amendment be "germane," which means pertinent or in close relationship. Except to general appropriation bills, the Senate was free to add unrelated amendments to bills. Sometimes a whole bill of subsidiary interest would be amended onto an appropriation bill.

This is called a "rider." The government of Cuba was provided for under the "Platt Amendment," a rider to an Army appropriation bill in 1901; this continued on the statute books, highly offensive to Cuban pride, until the inauguration of the "good-neighbor policy" after 1933. Presidential authority to reduce the gold content of the dollar was granted in a Senate rider to the Agricultural Adjustment Act of 1933. The President has no item veto, and therefore must sign or veto the whole bill presented to him. The Reorganization Act of 1946 placed new restrictions on amendments to appropriation bills, and the worst abuses appear to be curbed.

Appointments and Treaties. By the Constitution the Senate is given special powers over appointments and treaties. The President nominates and the Senate confirms officers of the United States by simple majority. The fundamental law speaks of "advice and consent" by the upper house.[9] The development of "senatorial courtesy" and the political contacts of President and Senators will be treated subsequently. The procedure of the Senate on appointments is to receive the nominations of the President and to refer them to appropriate committees. After these committees report, action on the confirmation takes place on the floor.

Treaty ratification requires a two-thirds vote on the floor. A treaty is received from the President and referred to the Committee on Foreign Relations. Upon its report the Senate usually resolves itself into the "Committee of the Whole" for deliberation on the treaty. This is the only remaining use of the Committee of the Whole in the upper house. The Committee considers and reports its recommendation back to the Senate.

MATTERS OF JOINT CONCERN

Conference Committees. If both houses pass identical versions of the same bill, it is enrolled, signed, and sent to the President. In case different versions of the same bill have been passed and neither house will recede, then the bill is

[8] Franklin L. Burdette, *Filibustering in the Senate* (Princeton University Press, 1940), tells the interesting story of Senate filibuster and closure. Lindsay Rogers, *The American Senate* (Knopf, 1926), presents a convincing case for the freedom of debate of the Senate.

[9] On the confirmation of appointments, see Joseph P. Harris, *The Advice and Consent of the Senate* (University of California Press, 1953).

sent to a conference committee. These committees, usually consisting of three or more members from each house, meet to thrash out their differences. Each house may choose to instruct its conferees, but normally they are left free to negotiate for themselves. After agreement is reached, each set of conferees reports back to its house. The report may be accepted, or rejected and further negotiation ordered. Conference committees, as the late Senator Norris frequently pointed out, have become a sort of third house of our legislative bodies. They are often criticized because proceedings are secret, bills may be rewritten arbitrarily, and their reports seldom are considered carefully.[10]

The Legislative Reorganization Act of 1946 confines the reports of conference committees to legislative controversies submitted and stipulates that where the rule is violated the conference report shall be subject to a point of order. In practice, however, such points of order are not sustained.

Records and Laws. Records of debates and proceedings in the Senate and House are printed in the *Congressional Record,* which has been the public and official record since 1873. The *Record* is substantially a stenographic report of the debates and proceedings. It is well known that a great many speeches that appear in the *Record* were not delivered orally but are "extensions of remarks" included by unanimous consent. In addition to the *Record,* each house keeps a journal of its proceedings and acts. The journal of the previous day is read, usually in part only, at the opening of the session each day. Once enacted and signed by the President, measures become laws and may be found in the *Statutes at Large of the United States* for the particular session. From time to time statutes are codified in *The Code of the Laws of the United States of a General and Permanent Character . . .* , commonly called "U.S. Code."

[10] An early work on this subject is Ada C. McCown, *The Congressional Conference Committee* (Columbia University Press, 1927); a more recent one is Gilbert Y. Steiner, *The Congressional Conference Committee* (University of Illinois Press, 1951).

Impeachment. Constitutional authority to impeach is vested solely in the House; power to try impeachment cases rests with the Senate alone. The House usually refers a motion proposing impeachment of an officer to the appropriate standing committee or to a specially created investigating committee. If an impeachment motion is adopted by the House, a committee may be set up to draft articles of impeachment. After their adoption, managers are chosen in whatever manner the House directs. The Senate, upon being informed of House action, sets up a committee to prepare for the trial.

The House managers appear in the Senate at the appointed time and commence their prosecution of the case. If the President is impeached, the Chief Justice of the Supreme Court presides over the Senate trial. The accused officer has a right to appear and to testify in his own behalf. A two-thirds vote of the Senate is necessary for conviction. The Senate has sat as a court of impeachment on only twelve occasions in the country's history. Nine cases involved judges, of whom four were convicted and removed, four were acquitted, and one resigned under fire. The first officer ever impeached was a Senator in 1798, but the Senate dismissed that case for want of jurisdiction. Two reconstruction-era cases were the only ones involving executive officers: President Andrew Johnson was acquitted in 1868; Grant's Secretary of War was acquitted in 1876.

Selection of President and Vice-President. It has been more than one hundred years since the House of Representatives was called upon to elect a President. The Constitution provides that if no candidate for President secures a majority of the electoral votes, the House shall choose from among the three highest. In selecting a President, the House votes by states, each state having one vote. The successful candidate must secure the votes of a majority of the states. The House elected Thomas Jefferson President, following the indecisive election of 1800, and John Quincy Adams after that of 1824.

Should no candidate secure a majority of the electoral votes for Vice-President, the Twelfth

Amendment provides that the Senate shall choose from among the two highest candidates. A majority of the total membership of the Senate is necessary to elect. The electoral vote was inconclusive only in 1836; in that case the Senate chose Richard M. Johnson as Vice-President during the Van Buren administration.

Staff Services. One of the significant developments of recent years is the provision of professional staff services for the legislative branch. Of course Congress from its earliest days had clerks, messengers, and page boys, but the "clerk hire" moneys appropriated rarely were used to employ persons whose expertness in techniques, such as bill drafting, or in subject-matter fields, such as money and banking, qualified them as high-level assistants or advisers. As Congress faced problems of greater and greater complexity, the need was felt for more than the meager services that could be provided by the clerks previously employed by members and standing committees. In order to meet the executive branch on a basis of equality, the legislative branch found it advisable to provide itself with a professional staff capable of analyzing executive proposals and formulating and drafting counterproposals.

The office of the Legislative Counsel was established in 1919 to provide bill-drafting services to the Congress. Following the Reorganization Act of 1946, appropriations were increased, and the staff expanded in size and in immunity from politics.

The Legislative Reference Service of the Library of Congress provides aid both to individual legislators and to committees of Congress. In the first 5 years after reorganization, its staff more than doubled and appropriations increased fourfold.

Members' offices still employ a large proportion of congressional staff. The 1946 act provided each Senator with funds for a top assistant; clerk-hire allowances have been increased for members of both houses.

Committees have received some of the greatest expansion in terms of both quantity and quality of personnel. The reorganization law authorized each standing committee to appoint up to ten employees, including four professional staff members, who should be "permanent," appointed "without regard to political affiliations," and "on the basis of fitness." In 1955 the professional salaries ranged up to a maximum of $13,600. While most of the professional personnel has survived three changes of congressional majorities (1949, 1953, and 1955) the experience is "spotty," and the full realization of the ideal of an impartial committee staff, equally able to serve Democrats and Republicans, is still some distance away.[11]

Congress has not seen fit to appoint a personnel director to supervise staff hiring. The result has been that some who have been employed in new positions have not possessed the highest qualifications, and other staff members who are well qualified have found their abilities utilized to less than the fullest extent.[12]

CONGRESSIONAL PROBLEMS

Among national legislatures and parliaments of the world, the American Congress stands out as one of the most successful. For over a century and a half it has proved reasonably representative of the national will. The Senate is unquestionably the outstanding second chamber among national parliamentary bodies. The Congress provides one of the few remaining examples of the two-house plan operating on a substantially coordinate basis. Although its time and energy have often been frittered away upon unimportant issues chosen because of excessive localism, narrow partisanship, and desire for meddling, when great national issues have emerged upon the scene, the Congress has rarely, if ever, failed to serve the country loyally. Nevertheless, the Congress is ill organized to meet many of the most insistent challenges

[11] For a good discussion of this problem see Max M. Kampelman, "The Legislative Bureaucracy: Its Response to Political Change, 1953," *Journal of Politics,* vol. 16 (August, 1954), pp. 539–550.

[12] Gladys M. Kammerer, "The Record of Congress in Committee Staffing," *American Political Science Review,* vol. 45 (December, 1951), pp. 1126–1136.

of today. What progress has been made in re-tooling Congress? What problems remain unsolved?

The Reorganization of Congress. The reform of Congress, long discussed sporadically in academic and congressional circles, became a major item on the agenda of American democracy in 1945 and 1946. Improvements in organization and procedure had been urged for several years by the Committee on Congress of the American Political Science Association and by many individual critics. The Seventy-ninth Congress accordingly established a joint committee to study its own organization. After extended hearings, the committee filed its report on Mar. 4, 1946.[13] The committee, headed by Senator Robert M. La Follette, Jr., managed to reach agreement on many of the acute organizational problems facing Congress. The report called for the creation of majority and minority policy committees in each house, a joint legislative-executive council composed of congressional and executive leaders, a fairly drastic reorganization of committee systems of the Senate and House, increases in aids to Congress, reduction of petty duties that take congressional time, and more adequate compensation of members. The committee was unable to reach agreement on reform of the seniority system or of House Rules Committee powers. It considered the proposal of a question hour and of Senate filibusters as outside of the scope of its powers. As shown in the table on the following page, the act [14] fell short of the committee recommendations in several particulars.

Relations with the Executive. The over-all leadership of Congress is most likely, under modern conditions, to come from the executive. The President is representative of the whole nation, the generalissimo of the administration, the people's choice. The nation, and its Congress, quite properly look to him for guidance.

[13] U.S. Congress, Joint Committee on the Organization of Congress, *Hearings,* parts 1–4 (1945), and *Organization of the Congress,* Report of the . . . pursuant to H. Con. Res. 18, S. Rept. 1011, 79th Cong., 2d Sess. (1946).

[14] 60 Stat. 831.

But the Congress should not abdicate its functions to the executive. Experience has shown that the American system works best with the President accepting and actively playing the role of chief legislator, but the Congress should examine critically every recommendation and check constantly his performance. Even if that role is granted, however, improvements are required in the mechanism of legislative-executive liaison.

All the three leading plans for the reform of Congress called for an improved and formalized congressional body to consult with the President and other representatives of the executive branch. The act failed to make such provision. Four main aspects of the problem will be dealt with under separate headings.

Consultation with President. Although the proposed forms varied considerably, all had in common the idea of a formal council representing Congress to meet regularly with the President and to formulate and carry out national policy. This was dropped out of the reorganization bill when the policy committees for each house were stricken out. Until the House officially creates policy committees it would appear impossible to carry out the original plan of having the two majority policy committees constitute the congressional side of a joint legislative-executive council.

Informal weekly conferences take place at the White House between the President and his party's congressional leaders. These occasions provide an opportunity for the executive and the legislative leaders to discuss program and strategy and to keep informed. Many of the proposals for an executive-legislative council simply involved the formalization and extension of what already existed.

Question Period. Executive-legislative relations might be improved and made more direct if the two houses would amend their rules to permit cabinet members to be questioned in person on the floor of the House or Senate. This proposal is generally known as the "Kefauver Plan" after its chief sponsor, the Senator from Tennessee. The La Follette committee felt that it had no jurisdiction over the matter, and

Three Plans for Congressional Reform and the Reorganization Act

Features	National Planning Association *	American Political Science Association †	Joint Committee of Congress ‡	Legislative Reorganization Act §
Leadership	Majority and minority policy committees, each house	Legislative council to plan majority program in Congress	Majority and minority policy committees, each house	No provision; Senate policy groups added later
Relations with President	Majority policy committees consult with President	Legislative council to promote liaison and cooperation	Joint council of executive and policy committees	No provision
Question period	Experiment with department heads	No recommendation	No jurisdiction	No provision
Liaison with departments	....	Committees parallel departments and work with them	Committees review agencies within their jurisdiction	No provision
Control over administration	Broader appropriation bills; control through Accounting Office	House committee on appropriations oversees administrative performance	Service audits by Comptroller General; no more indefinite appropriations	Service audits; definite appropriations
Members' offices	Adequate personal staffs	Substantial clerk hire increase	An administrative assistant for each	No provision; Senate got assistants later
Library of Congress	Expansion of reference service	More funds and better facilities	Increased funds and services	Increased funds and services
Legislative counsel	....	More appropriations and services	Expanded funds and personnel	Expanded funds and personnel
Number of committees	15 each house	Eliminate inactive	Senate 16; House 18	Senate 15; House 19
Committee jurisdiction	Equivalent in Senate and House	Parallel committees in the two houses	Clearly defined jurisdiction	Clearly defined jurisdiction
Committee staffs	Adequate staffs	Independent qualified experts	Four added experts per committee	Four added experts per committee
Committee chairmen	Find substitute for seniority	Six-year tenure *or* party group choose; curb chairman's power	No agreement	No provision
Retirement	Annuity at 55	Contributory plan like civil service	Contributory plan	Contributory plan
Salaries	$25,000	$15,000	$15,000, taxable as businessman's	$12,500 plus $2,500 expenses
Reduction of work load	Reduce or reallocate	Home rule for D.C.; delegate claims; cut private bills	Home rule for D.C.; delegate claims; digest bills	Delegate small claims; allows suits v. U.S.
Lobbyist control	No provision	Groups register; reveal membership and finances	Groups register; list expenditures	Groups register; list expenditures

* Robert Heller, *Strengthening the Congress* (Washington, D.C.: National Planning Association, 1945).
† George B. Galloway and Others, *The Reorganization of Congress* (Washington, D.C.: Public Affairs Press, 1945).
‡ *Report of the Joint Committee on the Organization of Congress* (1946).
§ 60 Stat. 831.

the 1946 act contained nothing that authorizes the practice.

Obviously this proposal would introduce into the Congress something like the question hour used in British legislative bodies. The device has proved effective, in British countries and elsewhere, in producing immediate accountability of an executive officer to parliamentary and public opinion. Applied to the United States, it could narrow the widening gap between executive and legislative branches by giving each an opportunity to speak to the other officially and frequently. Much misunderstanding arises from the lack of communication. As Kefauver proposed it, the question period would be limited to 2 hours per week total, the executive officials could decline to appear, and care would be exercised to see that only pertinent and reasonable questions were asked. It is difficult to understand why the House and Senate have not long since amended their rules to permit, at least on an exploratory basis, the questioning of executives on the floor of the legislative bodies. It should be noted, however, that executive officers are frequently called upon to testify before committees of both houses, which, in a sense, constitutes a "question period."

Liaison with Departments. One of the most promising levels for legislative-executive collaboration is that of standing committee and administrative department or agency. Two of the reform plans referred to this area, but the act of 1946 did little to help, with the exception of simplifying the committee system and clarifying jurisdiction. The way is open, nevertheless, and all that is required is willingness on the part of the committee and agency involved. One such scheme of collaboration was commended to the La Follette committee as a model. During the Second World War the House Committee on Public Buildings and Grounds consulted monthly with the National Housing Administrator and other executive agency heads.

Oversight of Administration. The 1946 act directed standing committees to exercise continuous watchfulness over administrative agencies in their sphere. The report advised against the practice of creating special committees to investigate particular problems. Standing committees can follow the affairs of the agencies through administrative reports to Congress, through its own inquiry into the execution of law, and through conferences like those described in the section above.

Great difficulty is encountered when Congress undertakes oversight of the administration. The line between presidential and congressional authority should be drawn between detailed action and broad policy, but nonprecise definition leaves a vast "gray area" that often becomes a battleground. Committees, acting under the instructions given in the 1946 act, use their powers of investigation to dig and delve into administrative minutia in such a way (as in the McCarthy probe of the Army) that demoralization results. On the other hand, most committees perform their "watchdog" functions without undue poaching on presidential prerogative. Senatorial confirmation of appointments offers another formal opportunity to review the record of the administration and to criticize it. Control of spending, considered under another section, is one of the most potent weapons in the congressional arsenal, yet its use often has been for venting petty and individual spites rather than criticism of broad, general policies.

Fiscal Controls. One of the most needed reforms, and one of the greatest failures of the Reorganization Act, was in the field of fiscal control. The House and Senate Appropriations Committees and the House Ways and Means and Senate Finance Committees operate with little coordination. Appropriation bills are passed without any over-all limitation being placed upon total appropriations and without precise reference to expected revenues. In short, the Congress adopts no general fiscal policy. The power of the purse, one of the greatest that might be used by Congress to assure accountability of the executive, is dissipated in a maze of numerous appropriation bills, considered at different times, by different committees and subcommittees, amid an atmosphere of pressure and hurry.

The report sought to correct some of these evils by (1) the adoption of annual federal budget totals; (2) strengthening of the Appropriations Committees; (3) service audits by the Comptroller General; (4) discontinuance of indefinite appropriations, and (5) elimination of legislation from appropriation bills.

The act set up the procedure to be followed in determining budget totals or the "legislative budget." The four fiscal committees were directed to meet together to determine over-all receipts and expenditures and to set a ceiling on expenditures. This they have failed to do. In 1950 a consolidated appropriations bill embracing eleven supply bills was used, but in 1951 Congress went back to ten separate ones, each considered by itself.[15] Interest in the legislative budget continues, but real progress will probably have to await formation of a small joint budget committee, employment of more staff, and greater determination to resist pressures for spending.

Staffing changes have been made. The House Appropriations Committee has increased its clerical staff but has relied heavily upon administrative agencies for investigative staff.[16] The Senate did relatively more in staffing, but neither has adequate personnel to review the huge expenditures requested.

Other aspects of fiscal controls will be considered in the chapter on public finance.

Work Load. The work load of Congress has not been lightened under the Reorganization Act, but it has been redistributed. The aids and the committee changes mentioned above have had a part in shifting work or in permitting the members to do a better job than previously. Members sit on fewer committees now, but each committee has many more bills.

Title IV of the 1946 act was the "Federal Tort Claims Act" which delegated authority to settle claims of $1,000 or less against the United States to administrative officers. Twelve exceptions were listed, however, and the Congress has been flooded with private claims bills under these exceptions. Private immigration bills also have been introduced in great numbers, for no restriction on them exists.

Home rule for the District of Columbia was recommended by the committee as a means of freeing Congress from the burden of serving as a municipal council for Washington. The Senate in 1949 passed home-rule legislation, but the House has been unable to agree.

Further reform is needed in order to divest Congress of additional time-consuming detail. A program for additional progress along this line would include reduction of exceptions under the tort claims act, self-government for the District of Columbia, delegation of immigration and deportation cases to an agency or tribunal, and various other means already suggested.

Petty Matters. Even a cursory observer of Congress is impressed with the amount of legislative time wasted on relatively minor issues, and the hasty fashion (especially in the House) in which matters of great importance are dealt with. A large proportion of the bills on the calendars of the two houses concern petty matters that might more properly be handled by delegating rule-making authority to administrative agencies. An extreme proposal along this line is one made with reference to the British Parliament. Some years ago Sir Stafford Cripps urged that the "mother of parliaments" confine its lawmaking solely to one omnibus appropriation and planning bill per session. The American Congress certainly would not be willing to abdicate to this extent, but it might well provide for the settlement of private claims through courts or administrative tribunals, and for reduction in the number of minor public bills by the delegation of legislative authority (with appropriate standards) to the executive. Some progress has already been made through the flexible tariff, executive trade agreements, blanket appropriation measures, and the like. In time of war Congress appropriates billions of dollars to the military establishments with a minimum of restrictions on where or how the money shall be spent. In peacetime, the small-

---

[15] Paul H. Douglas, *Economy in the National Government* (University of Chicago Press, 1952), pp. 56–57.

[16] George B. Galloway, "The Operation of the Legislative Reorganization Act of 1946," p. 64. In fiscal 1950 the House had less than one Appropriations staff member for each billion dollars.

town post office, a veterans' hospital, a port dredging job, all must be authorized according to the political formula worked out in detail by Congress.

The congressman also is expected to serve his constituents as an "errand boy," in varied fields quite divorced from legislation. One represent-ative estimated that three-fourths of a mem-ber's time is taken up by contacting executive agencies, dealing with District of Columbia mat-ters, handling claims against the government, finding jobs for constituents, and other petty functions. Such work is so time-consuming that few members find it possible to study legisla-tion adequately.

Control of Lobbying. Title III of the 1946 act was the "Regulation of Lobbying Act." It put into law the requirement that organized groups reveal their expenditures in influencing legisla-tion, their membership, and their contributions. The act does not curb or regulate lobbying ac-tivity but merely requires reports on receipts and expenditures. In the Eighty-first Congress, a House select committee worked at interpreting the meaning of the vaguely drafted act.[17] It declared as covered by the act the following types of activity: pamphleteering; legislative functions of multipurpose organizations; legis-lative activities of business firms; part- and full-time legislative agents, including attorneys and public relations counselors; and research insti-tutes and foundations that seek to influence legislation. Not included, according to the com-mittee, are publishers of newspapers, maga-zines, and books that are distributed through the ordinary channels of commerce.

From the beginning of operation under the act, it was apparent that the statute was loosely

[17] U.S. House of Representatives, Select Committee on Lobbying Activities, *General Interim Report,* House Report 1085 (1950), and *Report and Recommendations on Federal Lobbying Act,* House Report 3239 (1951). See also Belle Zeller, "The Federal Regulation of Lob-bying Act," *American Political Science Review,* vol. XLII (April, 1948), 239–271; W. Brooke Graves, *Administration of the Lobby Registration Provisions of the Legislative Reorganization Act of 1946* (Library of Congress, 1950).

drawn. Its coverage was not really clear, and many other imperfections have been noted after a few years of operation. The select committee recommended that the title of the act drop "lob-bying" and use "Legislative Interests Reports Act," that radio and television be excluded from coverage, that persons convicted of violation not be banned from lobbying, that detail in reports be reduced, that contingent fees be prohibited, and that groups and persons with less than $1,000 per year be exempted from reporting.

The Lobbying Act has been subjected to much litigation in the Federal courts. The lower courts held some portions constitutional and some un-constitutional. In 1953 and 1954 the Supreme Court spoke. In United States *v.* Rumeley [18] the court held that the term "lobbying activities" meant direct representation before Congress, not indirect attempts to exert influence through the community. In United States *v.* Harriss [19] the constitutionality of the act was upheld. Reject-ing contentions of violation of due process, free-dom of speech and press, and freedom of peti-tion, Chief Justice Warren, speaking for the court, said:

Present-day legislative complexities are such that individual members of Congress cannot be ex-pected to explore the myriad pressures to which they are regularly subjected. Yet full realization of the American ideal of government by elected rep-resentatives depends to no small extent on their ability to properly evaluate such pressures. Other-wise the voice of the people may all too easily be drowned out by the voice of special interest groups seeking favored treatment while masquerading as proponents of the public weal. This is the evil which the Lobbying Act was designed to help prevent.

All Congress wants to know, the Chief Justice declared, is "who is being hired, who is putting up the money, and how much."

Congress and the Public. That Congress has done a poor job in public relations is generally agreed. The executive branch has great advan-tages of prestige and concentrated responsibil-

[18] 345 U.S. 41 (1953).
[19] 347 U.S. 612 (1954).

ity. The Congress is large and unwieldy, fettered by tradition and handicapped by the lack of leadership from within. A number of proposals have been made for improving public understanding of Congress and its problems. First, the House and Senate might reduce the amount of time spent in session, concentrating into one or two days a week the important legislative business that must be conducted on the floor. Second, these sessions could be transmitted directly over radio and television to the whole country and ought to command more attention from the newspapers. Third, public interest should be focused on committee proceedings, where detailed work is done on legislation; this would be made easier by regularizing the meeting times of committees and making provision for public attendance at committee hearings. Fourth, recesses should be taken at appropriate intervals, so that legislators could return to their districts and report in person to their constituents.

Instead of representing the national interest, most members of Congress look first to local and sectional interests. Senators and Representatives commonly regard themselves as "ambassadors of locality," rather than delegates of the whole nation. This is demonstrated many times over in every session, but especially in the scramble over the "pork barrel" of rivers and harbors appropriations, and in the "logrolling" over economic issues like the tariff and farm relief. The electorate of a district or state then is informed of the glorious service of its legislator, often through an extension of remarks from the *Record* such as: "What Blanton's Twelve Counties, Seventeenth District (Texas), Have Received from Government since 1933." Yet, in another sense, the representative should serve his district; for he is elected by it and is to some extent at least expected to represent its views on public questions.

Local interests gain exaggerated importance in this country through the tradition that a representative must live in his district. The custom is so well established that it would be very difficult to change. The advantages of the British system, under which the member of Parliament need not be, and usually is not, a resident of his district, should not be overlooked.

The interests of the country as a whole occasionally may be served through the alliances and counteralliances made by various economic, sectional, and partisan groups. A few congressmen, and especially senators, enjoy such prestige in their home states that on most issues they are left free to serve the country with detachment and distinction. In the past, Senators Borah of Idaho, Norris of Nebraska, Cutting of New Mexico, and others enjoyed such popularity in their states that they were able to devote themselves largely to national interests as they saw these, without the diversion and distortion of localism.

Congressional Investigations. The congressional investigating committee, used and abused so much in recent years in both the legislative-executive struggle and the loyalty-subversion exposé, has become one of the great problems of Congress. Inherited from the House of Commons through the colonial and state legislatures, the power to investigate has been narrowed or broadened according to its exercise by Congress and its interpretation by the courts. The first Congress, in 1792, appointed a select committee to inquire into a military disaster suffered in an Indian attack in the Northwest Territory.[20] The Eighty-fourth Congress, in 1955–1956, conducted over one hundred investigations, mainly through subcommittees of its standing committees.

The early probes were thought justifiable under the legislative power, but the executive from the beginning asserted its power to withhold secret documents. As early as 1798 the power to administer oaths was given by statute to congressional leaders and punishment for perjury prescribed. Unfriendly witnesses were incarcerated directly on orders of House or Senate. In 1857 provision was made by law for 1-year imprisonment on conviction of refusal to testify. In Kilbourne *v.* Thompson, decided in 1881, the Supreme Court sustained a suit for

[20] Telford Taylor, *Grand Inquest: The Story of Congressional Investigations* (Simon and Schuster, 1955), p. 22.

damages against the sergeant at arms of the House, who had jailed for contempt a witness who refused to testify.[21] The resolution directing the inquiry contained no suggestion of remedial legislation; the Court held that it invaded the proper functions of the judiciary. Not until 1897 did the Court specifically hold the act of 1857 constitutional; the conviction of a witness who refused to answer questions of a Senate committee was sustained. The leading recent case is McGrain *v.* Daugherty (1927), in which the Senate's authority to probe the official conduct of a former Attorney General was upheld, but the court did indicate that a witness might refuse to answer if the bounds of power are exceeded by a committee or if the questions are not pertinent to the matter under inquiry.[22]

Lacking a full-scale Supreme Court review of the scope of congressional committee power since the beginning of the loyalty-subversion type of probe, one can forecast the pattern of constitutionality only by putting together the scattered rules derived from earlier decisions. It appears that a congressional investigation is valid if it (1) falls within the federal legislative power (not invading judicial, executive, or state spheres), and (2) does not violate constitutional guaranties, including self-incrimination. A skillful draftsman can design a resolution in such a way that the chances of its being voided for usurpation of the judicial function are minimized; a careful chairman or counsel should be able to avoid the States' rights hazard. But the possibilities of conflict with the executive are manifold and constitute an abundant source of dispute.

Probes vs. Rights. The case of congressional investigations versus individual rights is still more perplexing. Two events of 1953 have an important bearing on the subject. In United States *v.* Rumeley, the Supreme Court overruled the conviction of the executive secretary of the Committee on Constitutional Government, who refused to answer a House committee's questions regarding purchasers of alleged propaganda books.[23] The majority opinion relied on a narrow construction of congressional intent in authorizing the particular investigation, but the concurring opinion invoked the freedom of the press as the ground for freeing Mr. Rumeley. The other event of 1953 was the enactment of a law granting immunity to witnesses testifying before congressional committees.[24] The grant was confined to probes of threats to national security or defense, and subject in each case to approval by the Federal district court. Obviously, the greater the extension of "immunity baths," the less the possibility of witnesses claiming the privilege against self-incrimination. The possibility that testimony to a congressional committee under a grant of immunity might lead to state prosecution was eliminated by a Supreme Court decision in 1954.[25]

While awaiting further definition by the courts of the scope of investigative power, Congress itself has moved to correct some of the most flagrant abuses of individual rights by its committees. The 1955 "ground rules" adopted by the House were a promising beginning; the Speaker's ban on televised House hearings eliminated some of the temptation to sensational exposure. If the Senate does as much, the worst of the era of "trial by ordeal" may be over. A Supreme Court decision clarifying the line of demarcation between committee powers and individual liberties is needed as a basis for orderly conduct of future investigations.

[21] 103 U.S. 168 (1881).
[22] 273 U.S. 135 (1927).

[23] 345 U.S. 41 (1953).
[24] 68 Stat. 745.
[25] Adams *v.* Maryland, 347 U.S. 179 (1954).

FOR FURTHER READING   (See also works listed after preceding chapter.)

Burdette, Franklin L.: *Filibustering in the Senate* (Princeton University Press, 1940).
Burns, James M.: *Congress on Trial: The Politics of Modern Lawmaking* (Harper, 1949).
Colegrove, Kenneth: *The American Senate and World Peace* (Vanguard, 1944).

Dangerfield, Royden J.: *In Defense of the Senate: A Study in Treaty-making* (University of Oklahoma Press, 1933).

Finletter, Thomas K.: *Can Representative Government Do the Job?* (Reynal & Hitch-cock, 1945).

Fleming, Denna F.: *The Treaty Veto of the American Senate* (Putnam, 1930).

Galloway, George: *Limitation of Debate in the United States Senate,* Public Affairs Bulletin 64 (Library of Congress, 1948).

——: *Congress at the Crossroads* (Crowell, 1946).

—— and Others: *The Reorganization of Congress* (Washington, D.C.: Public Affairs Press, 1945). A report of the Committee on Congress of the American Political Science Association.

Graves, W. Brooke: *Administration of the Lobby Registration Provisions of the Legislative Reorganization Act of 1946* (Library of Congress, 1950).

Heller, Robert: *Strengthening the Congress* (Washington, D.C.: National Planning Association, 1945).

Kammerer, Gladys M.: *The Staffing of the Committees of Congress* (University of Kentucky, 1949).

Kefauver, Estes, and Jack Levin: *A Twentieth Century Congress* (Duell, Sloan & Pearce, 1947).

Luce, Robert: *Legislative Problems* (Houghton Mifflin, 1935).

——: *Legislative Procedure* (Houghton Mifflin, 1922).

McCown, Ada C.: *The Congressional Conference Committee* (Columbia University Press, 1927).

Rogers, Lindsay: *The American Senate* (Knopf, 1926).

U.S. Congress: *Official Congressional Directory.* Issued for each session of each Congress.

——: *Congressional Record.* Issued daily when House or Senate meets. Bound volumes available after close of each session.

U.S. Congress Joint Committee on the Organization of Congress: *Report of the Joint Committee on the Organization of Congress* . . . pursuant to H. Con. Res. 18, S. Rept. 1011 (1946).

——: *Hearings,* parts 1–4, 79th Cong., 1st Sess. (1945).

U.S. House of Representatives: *Cannon's Procedure in the House of Representatives,* H. Doc. 731, 80th Cong. (1948).

Walker, Harvey: *The Legislative Process* (Ronald, 1948).

REVIEW QUESTIONS

1. Trace the progress of a bill from introduction in the House to signature by the President.

2. What is the discharge rule? How has it been used in recent years?

3. What is filibustering? Trace efforts to secure an effective closure rule.

4. Describe Senate appointment-confirmation proceedings. Describe Senate treaty-ratification proceedings.

5. Describe the roles of House and Senate in impeachment proceedings.

6. Explain the role of the House in selecting a President in case no candidate secures a majority of electoral votes.

7. Explain the Senate's role in choosing a Vice-President if there is no electoral majority.

8. To what extent are charges of external control of Congress justified?

9. Do you believe that local and sectional influences loom too powerful in Congress?

10. What did the 1946 Legislative Reorganization Act do to improve relations between executive and legislative? What remains to be done?

11. What committee changes were effected by the 1946 act? What additional ones would you propose?

12. How did the 1946 act regulate lobbying? How has the lobbying section of the act worked out in practice?

13. What did the 1946 act provide in the way of additional personnel for committees and congressional services?

14. Propose and defend additional reforms of Congress beyond those provided in the 1946 act.

15. What rules of procedure ensure fair treatment of witnesses and others named before Senate and House committees? What further reforms would you deem desirable?

CHAPTER 14

President: The Office

If Congress, from its composition and the mode of its selection, tends to reflect the "local spirit" predicted by Madison, the prime organ of a compensating "national spirit" is, of course, the President—both as Chief Executive and as the leader of his party. Without the unifying power of the highest office, derived from the fixed tenure gained by his election and the sense that the President speaks for and represents the full national constituency, it would be difficult to develop the centripetal momentum so essential to the total federal scheme. — Herbert Wechsler [1]

When the Constitutional Convention of 1787 came to discuss the execution of laws, it was necessary to justify the establishment of a separate executive branch. Under the Articles of Confederation no separate executive existed; Congress exercised all executive authority through committees and special agents, but in general this plan had worked rather badly. The office of governor, found in all the states, was also a possible model. Although authority, terms, and modes of election varied, all were separately organized and all were single executives. The separation of authority between Crown and Parliament, then undergoing change in Britain, was cited by those who desired an independent executive. Those who wanted no separate executive argued that the tyranny of George III gave ample support to their view. Montesquieu and Locke were quoted on their advocacy of the separation of powers by proponents of the separate executive. In the Convention of 1787, however, little controversy arose

over the necessity of national executive. Madison's notes contain no record of a delegate having spoken against an executive branch, although some delegates wanted an executive "absolutely dependent" on the legislative branch.[2]

STRUCTURE AND ROLE

Form of the Executive. If a separate executive were to be established, should it be single or plural? Some proposed vesting the executive authority in a group or council, like the two consuls of Rome. This plural type of executive has the obvious disadvantage of dividing authority, which can so easily lead to irresponsibility The convention's decision for a single executive was made by a vote of seven states to two.[3] Even after the single executive was agreed upon,

[1] "The Political Safeguards of Federalism: The Role of the States in the Composition and Selection of the National Government," *Columbia Law Review*, vol. 54 (April, 1954), p. 552.

[2] Charles C. Tansill (ed.), *Documents Illustrative of the Formation of the Union of the American States*, H. Doc. 398, 69th Cong., 1st Sess. (1927), pp. 131–134. Hereafter cited as *Documents*.

[3] *Documents*, p. 146. The vote was taken on June 4, 1787. It was phrased: "Shall the blank for the number of the executive be filled with a single person?" *Ibid.*, p. 145.

many argued for making executive actions subject to a council of advisers, a device already used to curb the powers of many governors. Diffusion of authority was charged against this plan, too, and eventually the convention was won over to a single chief magistrate, styled "President," with no advisory council.

The desire to make the President subject to some advisory body did lead to giving the Senate power to advise and consent to appointments and treaties proposed by the executive. On the whole, however, the President was left free to set up his own advisory services. The cabinet, without a constitutional or statutory status and completely under executive control, is the leading formal agency for consultation. Each chief executive may choose in addition such other advisers as he deems fit.

Scope of Executive Authority. The question of powers of the separate, single executive was most perplexing and most crucial. The heritage of colonial and revolutionary days directed that a weak executive, if any, be established. Years of struggle with royal and proprietary governors taught American colonists to distrust executive power. The aversion of the people to monarchy, particularly to George III, strengthened the position of those who desired a weak executive.

On the other hand, the breakdown of central government under the Articles of Confederation led some to demand an energetic executive. It was argued that if the separation of powers were desirable, it was logical to have three coordinate branches, with no one predominant over the others. The convention finally decided to vest in the President most, but not all, of the executive power. Power to confirm appointments and to ratify treaties was reserved for the Senate. The President was given important legislative and some judicial authority. Sections 2 and 3 of Article II of the Constitution were devoted to an enumeration of presidential powers. The President was made Commander in Chief of the Army and Navy, was given power to appoint, to make treaties, to receive ambassadors and ministers, to grant reprieves and pardons, to enforce laws, and to perform certain duties in connection with the

Congress. The legislative, executive, and judicial functions of the President will be examined in the next chapter.

Much of the President's authority accrues to him by virtue of factors beyond the formal powers. His prestige as chief representative of the American people, and as leader of his political party, plays a large part in making him a strong leader if he chooses the role and has the personal qualities to fill it.

THE SELECTION PROCESS

Constitutional Provisions. Direct election of the President was considered a practical impossibility by most of the framers of the Constitution, even though direct election of the governor had been successful in New York and Massachusetts.[4] Selection by Congress was most widely supported in the convention; this selection method was included in both Virginia and New Jersey plans, and was adopted unanimously at one point in the convention's proceedings.

The electoral-college mode of selection eventually chosen was a compromise, combining, its craftsmen felt, the virtues of independence from the legislative branch with indirect popular participation. Each state chooses, in any way its legislature specifies, electors equal in number to the Representatives and Senators from that state. All states now use popular election on a state-wide basis. The electors meet in their own states and cast ballots for presidential and vice-presidential candidates. The results in each state are sent to the national capital and opened in the presence of Congress. Under the original plan each elector voted for two persons; the candidate receiving a majority of electoral votes became President, and the second highest became Vice-President.

This scheme caused a tie between Jefferson and Burr in 1800. Although the electors clearly intended that Jefferson should be President and

[4] James Wilson of Pennsylvania favored direct election. Madison records Wilson as saying that while apprehensive that he might be regarded as visionary, ". . . in theory he was for an election by the people." *Ibid.,* p. 134.

Burr Vice-President, under the terms of the Constitution each had exactly seventy-three votes, and election was thrown to the House of Representatives. In the House some Federalists supported Burr, but eventually Jefferson was elected. It was clear that the mode of election was defective and must be amended. The Twelfth Amendment corrected this by providing for separate voting for President and Vice-President. If no presidential candidate secures a majority of electoral votes, the House of Representatives chooses from the three highest, with each state casting one vote. Only two presidential elections have been thrown to the House: the 1800 Jefferson-Burr mix-up and the 1824 contest among Clay, John Quincy Adams,

Jackson, and Crawford. If no vice-presidential candidate secures a majority, the Senate chooses from the two highest.

Great confusion can arise over the counting of electoral votes. In 1876 Samuel J. Tilden led Rutherford B. Hayes by 184 to 165 electoral votes, but Congress, with Democratic House and Republican Senate, disagreed over the acceptance of conflicting returns from certain states. Eventually, in 1877 Congress created by statute an Electoral Commission composed of five members of the House, five Senators, and five Supreme Court justices. The verdict of the commission, rendered on a strictly partisan basis, awarded the twenty disputed votes to Hayes, which gave the presidency to him. A law of

"Don't Expect Me To Get This Real Accurate, Bub"

Although the electoral college is antiquated, critics are unable to unite on proposals for reform.

1887 declares that each state shall determine the authenticity of its selection of electors.

Procedure in the States. Within this constitutional framework, a standardized state procedure has developed, under which electors are elected popularly on a general-ticket basis. With few exceptions, this scheme has been followed throughout the country for over a hundred years. Since each state has a number of electoral votes equal to its total of United States Senators and Representatives, each voter casts his ballot for a considerable group. This ranges from forty-five in New York, thirty-two in California and Pennsylvania, twenty-seven in Illinois to three in Nevada, Delaware, Wyoming, and Vermont. The list of electors is made up by the official party organization in each state.

The threat, in 1944 and 1948, of some Southern electors elected under the Democratic label to bolt their party and vote for a third-party presidential candidate has served to focus extraordinary interest on the law and tradition governing the selection and pledging of electors. Professor Silva found twenty-seven states in which electors were nominated by state party conventions; ten, by other party bodies; seven, in party primaries; three, in optional primary or convention; in Pennsylvania alone the presidential nominee selects his party's candidates for elector.[5]

Although most state laws concerning electors appear to be based on the assumption that electors will vote automatically for their party's nominees, only California and Oregon require it directly. States have power, if they choose to exercise it, to require pledges of candidates for elector, or to direct electors concerning their conduct in case their party's presidential or vice-presidential candidate dies before the meetings of the electoral college.

At one time the states followed a uniform practice of printing the names of all would-be electors on the ballots, but this was expensive in the large states and virtually impossible when

a voting machine was used. Consequently, by 1952 twenty-seven states, including most of the larger ones, had adopted the "presidential short ballot," on which the names of individual electors do not appear, but a phrase such as "Twenty-five Electors pledged to vote for Dwight D. Eisenhower for President and Richard Nixon for Vice-President."[6] The electors selected then assemble in the state capital and go through the formality of casting their ballots; a 1934 federal law requires that the electors meet on the first Monday after the second Wednesday in December.[7] No general official meeting of all electors in the country is held, though in recent years attempts have been made to assemble as many as possible in Washington for unofficial celebrations.

Under the terms of the Twentieth Amendment, the two houses of Congress meet in joint session on Jan. 6 following a presidential election. The electoral votes are counted and the results are announced. Inauguration takes place on Jan. 20.

Electoral-college Shortcomings. It is not difficult to find fault with the electoral-college system of choosing the President. Under the original plan it was expected that the leading citizens chosen as electors would be free agents and would select as President the outstanding American who met the formal requirements. After the emergence of the party system, electors were more and more bound to vote for the candidates adopted by their party.

The principal methods of selecting presidential electors that emerged in the early years were: (1) choice by state legislatures, (2) elec-

[6] The states using the presidential short ballot are California, Colorado, Connecticut, Delaware, Florida, Illinois, Indiana, Iowa, Kentucky, Maryland, Maine, Massachusetts, Michigan, Missouri, Nebraska, Nevada, New Hampshire, North Carolina, Ohio, Pennsylvania, Texas, Utah, Washington, and Wisconsin. In addition New Jersey, New York, and Rhode Island have, in effect, adopted the short ballot through general use of the voting machine.

[7] For a careful statement of how the college meets and does its work, see Robert G. Dixon, "Electoral College Procedure," *Western Political Quarterly,* vol. 3 (June, 1950), pp. 214–224.

[5] Ruth C. Silva, "State Law on the Nomination, Election, and Instruction of Presidential Electors," *American Political Science Review,* vol. 42 (June, 1948), pp. 523–524.

tion by the people through districts, and (3) popular election by state-wide general tickets. Selection by legislatures was the most widely used method in the first eight elections, 1788 through 1816. As sentiment for popular election rose, the district and general ticket plans grew in importance. Although the district system pro-

Election by general ticket, at large, serious distorts the presidential vote in each state. In 1948, for example, Mr. Truman won California by a margin of 17,865 over Mr. Dewey, and Ohio by 7,107; in these two states Mr. Truman won 50 electoral votes with 3,365,925 popular votes, and Mr. Dewey received no electoral

NUMBER OF STATES USING SEVERAL METHODS OF CHOOSING PRESIDENTIAL ELECTORS, 1788-1836

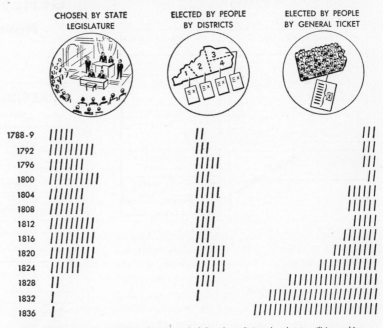

	CHOSEN BY STATE LEGISLATURE	ELECTED BY PEOPLE BY DISTRICTS	ELECTED BY PEOPLE BY GENERAL TICKET
1788-9	IIIII	II	III
1792	IIIIIIIII	III	III
1796	IIIIIIII	IIIII	III
1800	IIIIIIIIII	III	II
1804	IIIIIIII	IIIIII	IIIIII
1808	IIIIIII	IIIII	IIIIII
1812	IIIIIIIII	IIIII	IIIII
1816	IIIIIIIII	III	IIIIIII
1820	IIIIIIIII	IIIIII	IIIIIIIII
1824	IIIIII	IIIIII	IIIIIIIIIII
1828	II	IIII	IIIIIIIIIIIIIIII
1832	I	I	IIIIIIIIIIIIIIIIIII
1836	I		IIIIIIIIIIIIIIIIIIIIIIII

The legislative caucus has been displaced by popular election as a means of choosing presidential electors.

In order to simplify presentation, the minor methods have been eliminated, and states utilizing combination methods have been grouped in category indicating final choice.

SOURCE: Figures Compiled from Historical Statistics of the United States, 1789-1945 (1949), p. 288.

duced an electoral vote more proportionate to popular vote, states found they could increase their relative influence in presidential elections by shifting to the general-ticket "winner-take-all" plan. After the 1824 election the general-ticket plan rapidly displaced both selection by legislatures and election by districts.[8]

[8] Thomas Jefferson wrote James Monroe in 1800: "All agree that an election by districts would be best if it could be general; but while 10 states chuse either by their legislature or by a general ticket, it is folly & worse than folly for the other 6. not to do it." Paul L. Ford (ed.), *The Writings of Thomas Jefferson* (Knickerbocker Press, 1896), vol. VII, p. 401.

votes for his 3,340,953. If approximately 12,500 voters had shifted from Truman to Dewey, Mr. Dewey could have won all 50 electoral votes, and the election would have been thrown to the House of Representatives, despite Truman's popular lead of over 2,000,000 in the nation.

It is a sort of "unit rule," under which the winner of a plurality in each state takes all, and the national total of popular votes counts for nothing officially. This distortion within each state would not be a serious matter if the result were fair and equitable nationally. Of course, it is not. Good luck has produced a majority winner in nearly every presidential campaign, ut a streak of bad luck may bring repeated minority winners. The charts that follow show how the popular and electoral votes were related in past elections. In three crucial contests, of Truman-Dewey in 1948, of Wilson-Taft-Roosevelt in 1912, of Lincoln-Breckenridge-Bell-Douglas in 1860, an electoral majority was secured without a popular majority, but in each

PRESIDENTIAL ELECTIONS: THE SHORT BALLOT

PRESIDENTIAL ELECTORS		UNITED STATES SENATOR	
Vote for One Party		Vote for One	
Dwight D. Eisenhower......For President Richard M. Nixon......For Vice-President	} Republican	Edward Martin	Republican
Adlai E. Stevenson......For President John J. Sparkman......For Vice-President	} Democratic	Guy Kurtz Bard	Democratic
Stuart Hamblen.........For President Enoch A. Holtwick......For Vice-President	} Prohibition	Ira S. Sassaman	Prohibition
Vincent Hallinan........For President Charlotta Bass......For Vice-President	} Progressive	William J. Van Essen	Socialist
Darlington Hoopes......For President Samuel H. Friedman....For Vice-President	} Socialist	Frank Knotek	Industrial Government
Eric Hass..........For President Stephen Emery......For Vice-President	} Industrial Government	Anna Chester	Militant Workers
Farrell Dobbs..........For President Myra Tanner Weiss.....For Vice-President	} Militant Workers		

The voter may insert in blank spaces below names of candidates of different parties for Presidential Elector, or names of persons not nominated by any party	JUDGE OF THE SUPREME COURT
Vote for Thirty-Two	Vote for One
	John C. Arnold — Republican
	Harry M. Montgomery — Democratic

Twenty-seven states in 1952 utilized the presidential short ballot. As shown on this Pennsylvania ballot, the names of candidates for electors are eliminated and the voter sees on the ballot only the names of presidential and vice-presidential candidates.

case there was a popular plurality. Hayes in 1876 and Harrison in 1888 were elected with a majority of electoral votes, but with a minority of popular votes.

Reform of Presidential Selection. Four principal proposals have been made for altering the present method of choosing the President.

Popular Election. This is simple and direct; it is in keeping with democratic tradition; it assures a majority or plurality choice. Objections to direct election come from the smaller states and from the South. The smaller states would lose their advantage of a certain minimum of three electoral votes and its consequent multiplication of their influence in presidential elections. The Southern states would suffer for their virtual exclusion of the Negro from elec-

tions. Since Southern participation in voting is low, influence in presidential elections would drop accordingly. Opposition from these two

THE LONG BALLOT

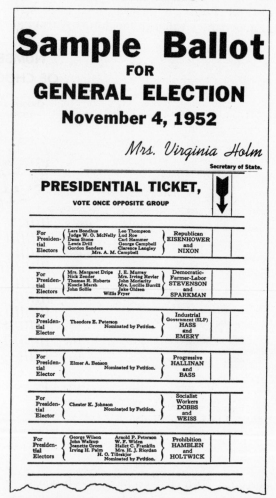

The presidential long ballot, which includes names of electors, no longer serves a useful purpose. It is retained in states like Minnesota where the number of electors does not crowd the ballot.

sources makes proposal of the necessary constitutional amendment by a two-thirds vote in each house of Congress a practical impossibility. Ratification by three-fourths of the states also could not be expected under present conditions.

Abolition of Electors. Although the abolition of electors is an incidental feature of other proposals for reform, it is the sole end sought by one school of electoral-college critics. They would retain the device of electoral votes on the present basis. All states would have, in effect, the presidential short ballot; no meeting of electors would take place; the electoral vote would be assigned automatically according to the popular-vote returns. In May, 1934, Senator Norris of Nebraska secured much Senate support for a proposed constitutional amendment embodying this plan, but he failed by a narrow margin to muster the necessary two-thirds vote. While the proposal is mild, indeed, its adoption would meet the threat made in both 1948 and 1952—of individual electors violating their pledges and voting for the presidential candidate of another party. No great enthusiasm has been generated behind this proposal, possibly because it is such a small matter to take through the many formalities of constitutional amendment, and also because it might divert attention from more fundamental reform.

Election by Districts. A strong case can be made for reverting to this popular method, which was most favored in the early days of the republic. The plan would divide electors among the parties in at least rough proportion to that now prevailing in Senate and House. One elector would be elected by each congressional district; additional electors would be chosen at large in each state for each Senator (and Representative-at-large, if any). The typical situation would have the voter casting ballots for one district elector and two at-large electors. While each state's at-large electors probably would come from a single party, the other party might capture some of the district electors.

The district plan could be reestablished by state action, without Federal constitutional amendment. Its constitutionality appears assured under a decision of the Supreme Court; in 1891 the legislature of Michigan changed to the district system, and its validity was upheld.[9] Adop-

tion of the district plan by a single state or a few states would put them at a disadvantage for reasons stated by Jefferson a century and a half before. Therefore increasing interest has been shown in the possibility of imposing the district plan by Federal constitutional amendment. In recent Congresses this has been known as the "Coudert plan," after its sponsor, a member of the House from New York. As this is written, Congress has not yet subjected the proposal to thorough study. One can reason, however, that adoption would incite state legislatures to gerrymander congressional districts even more than in the past. Because of the general pattern of rural control of legislatures, the Republicans would probably gain some advantage on this front. The district plan might enable the Republicans to win without carrying the great metropolitan areas. If so, the influence of minorities concentrated in urban centers would be reduced. It seems likely that presidential elections, under the district system, would be neck-and-neck affairs, occasionally with minority winners, in view of the close margin between the two parties in the House in recent Congresses. Objections to this plan can be expected from the majority party in states where the existing winner-take-all scheme works repeatedly to its advantage. Political activists in the pivotal states will be reluctant to see the decisive importance of their states diminish, as it will under any plan that allows the parties to share electoral votes of a state.

Proportionate Division of Electoral Vote. This plan, best known as the "Lodge-Gossett" proposal, would abolish electors and the general-ticket system, and substitute a scheme of sharing the electoral vote of each state between presidential candidates in proportion to their popular vote. The calculations within each state would be carried out to three decimal places; in 1948 the formula would have produced a nation-wide electoral-vote distribution of approximately 261.2 for Truman and 222.5 for Dewey, instead of 303 to 189 under the present system.

[9] McPherson *v.* Blacker, 146 U.S. 1 (1892). The law, enacted by a temporary Democratic majority that sought a chance to win some presidential electors, was speedily repealed by the Republicans after the 1892 election.

In the form adopted by the Senate in 1950, the plan permitted election by a plurality, if 40 per cent or more. Should no candidate receive as much as 40 per cent, the election of President would be thrown to the House and Senate, sitting in joint session. The choice would be between the two highest in electoral vote, each legislator voting as an individual.

The Lodge-Gossett proposal received surprisingly strong support from the Senate in 1950, when it passed by a substantial majority. Previously the plan, originated by former Representative Lea of California, had secured favorable House committee action on more than one occasion. In 1950, however, the House decisively rejected Lodge-Gossett, and it has not again reached the congressional high point achieved at that time.

In retrospect, the coalitions supporting and opposing the proposal were indeed strange: There were Republicans and Democrats on both sides; some liberals and some conservatives allied to support, others to oppose; large-state and small-state legislators were found in both camps. To some extent this odd alignment arose from the lack of information and understanding, particularly during Senate consideration; in part it stemmed from careful analysis (or misanalysis) of the possible impact of the proposal on national politics.

Among valid arguments of proponents are that Lodge-Gossett would (1) strengthen minority parties in "one-party" states; (2) encourage presidential campaigning in all states instead of the present concentration on large and pivotal states; (3) lessen the strategic leverage of organized minorities—ethnic and ideological—in states with large metropolitan areas; (4) reduce the unfairness inherent in the general-ticket plan that gives all of a state's electoral votes to the winner of a popular plurality, even by the narrowest of margins; (5) eliminate from the Constitution the manifestly unfair arrangement of having the President chosen by the House, each state voting as a unit, if no electoral majority is secured.

Opponents counter with the contention that the proposal would (1) give the Democrats a considerable advantage in presidential elections; (2) increase greatly the influence of Southern elements in the Democratic party; (3) produce more minority winners, through abolition of the requirement for a majority of electoral votes and substitution of a 40 per cent plurality; (4) upset the existing balance under which urban influence is preponderant in presidential elections and rural power in congressional politics; (5) endanger the two-party system by fostering the growth of "splinter" parties that would build up fractional electoral votes.

The answer to the question about the impact of Lodge-Gossett centers around the political future of the "solid South." If the Republicans succeeded, as former Senator Lodge predicted, in making inroads in the Southern states, a two-party system might emerge in the region. But until or unless that occurred, the South would have its influence augmented in the Democratic party and in national politics. And in the meantime the Democrats would enjoy, under Lodge-Gossett, an advantage that the Republicans could overcome only by mustering in the North popular majorities possibly running into the millions of votes.[10]

PREREQUISITES AND PERQUISITES

Presidential Term of Office. In the Constitutional Convention sharp controversy arose over the length of a presidential term. Alexander Hamilton once expressed himself as favoring a life term for the executive. The two alternatives considered most carefully, however, were (1) 6 or 7 years without reeligibility, or (2) 4 years with the possibility of reelection.[11]

[10] For further information see Ruth C. Silva, "The Lodge-Gossett Resolution: a Critical Analysis," *American Political Science Review*, vol. 44 (March, 1950), pp. 86–99; and "Reform of the Electoral System," *The Review of Politics*, vol. 14 (July, 1952), pp. 394–407.

[11] The 7-year term was adopted first (*Documents*, p. 135). Then a 6-year term was substituted (*ibid.*, p. 415). Finally the 4-year plan was agreed upon (*ibid.*, p. 676).

Arguments for the longer term have been given in most effective form by William H. Taft, between his single term in the presidency and his chief-justiceship. A 7-year term without re-eligibility, Taft once declared, would give the President "courage and independence" and relieve the federal employee from the "absorbing and diverting" interest in securing his reelection.[12] Against the long term, perhaps the strongest point is that during 6 or 7 years the popular will may change greatly and the views of the executive may become quite out of harmony with public sentiment.

The Federalist numbers 71 and 72, probably written by Hamilton, are devoted to the defense of the 4-year term with reeligibility. This plan was adopted, he asserted, because it offers inducement for a President to do well, it gives the public the value of an executive's experience, and it secures a stability of policy. A 2-year term would be too short to obtain the "desired firmness and independence."

After Washington declined to serve a third term, there grew up a tradition that the limit of two terms should apply to all who served as President. When Grant was proposed for a third term, a storm of disapproval arose. Theodore Roosevelt, who reached the office through the vice-presidency and served only one full term, was sharply criticized for seeking election in 1912. Although the Republican forces made anti-third term a major issue in the 1940 campaign, the tradition was broken with the reelection of Franklin D. Roosevelt. Those who oppose the third term on principle fear that a man who serves so long in the presidency may build up a machine that will dominate the government and control the people. This is the consideration that prompted several states and some of the Latin-American republics to forbid even a second term to their governors and presidents. Proponents of the third term argue that a President should serve as long as he is willing and able and the people wish to reelect him. They maintain that popular controls through elections,

legislative controls through Congress, and judicial controls through the courts are adequate to prevent the rise of dictatorship in the country.

The Eightieth Congress submitted to the state legislatures a proposed constitutional amendment which declared: "No person shall be elected . . . more than twice . . ." or more than once if he succeeded to the presidency and served more than two years of the term of another.[13] This proposal became the Twenty-second Amendment on Feb. 26, 1951, when the legislatures of Utah and Nevada voted for ratification. Since its adoption claims have been made that House action in submitting the amendment to the states was invalid because the required quorum was not present.[14]

Qualifications and Compensation. The Constitution restricts eligiblity to the presidency to natural-born citizens who are at least thirty-five years of age, and who have been resident in the United States for 14 years. Few controversies have arisen over these requirements. In order to provide for those who were born before the United States existed, persons who were citizens at the time of the adoption of the Constitution were made eligible. It is possible that a person born abroad of American parents might be regarded as "natural-born." Few complaints have been voiced over the age requirement. Theodore Roosevelt reached the presidency at forty-two; only five others reached it in their forties. The question of residence in the United States was

[12] William H. Taft, *The Presidency* (Scribner, 1916), p. 4.

[13] A similar proposal was the subject of extended hearings in 1940: U.S. Senate, Committee on the Judiciary, *Third Term for President of the United States, Hearings . . . ,* 76th Cong., 3d Sess. (1940). See also Charles W. Stein, *The Third Term Tradition* (Columbia University Press, 1942). The full text of the Amendment is given in Appendix III.

[14] Various objections to the amendment are considered carefully in Joseph E. Kallenbach, "Constitutional Limitations on Reeligibility of National and State Chief Executives," *American Political Science Review,* vol. 46 (June, 1952), pp. 438-454. Congressional consideration is treated in Paul G. Willis and George L. Willis, "The Politics of the Twenty-second Amendment," *Western Political Quarterly,* vol. 5 (September, 1952), pp. 469-482.

SIX PRESIDENTIAL ELECTIONS, 1932—1952
Popular & Electoral Votes

Democrat   Republican   Other

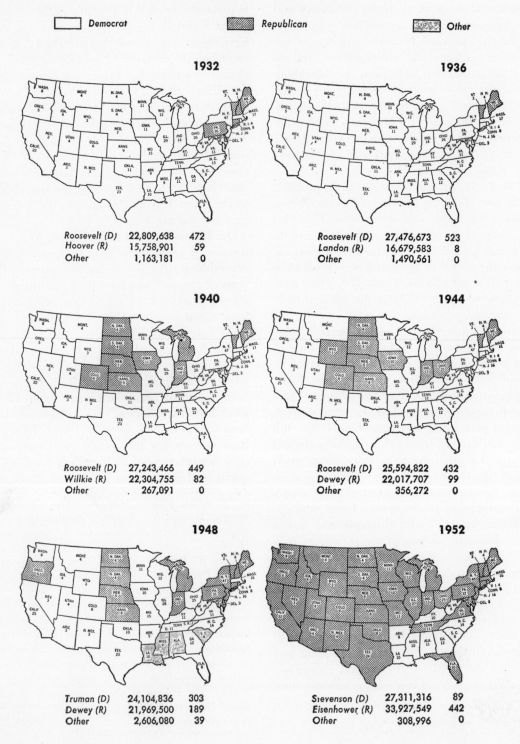

1932

Roosevelt (D)	22,809,638	472
Hoover (R)	15,758,901	59
Other	1,163,181	0

1936

Roosevelt (D)	27,476,673	523
Landon (R)	16,679,583	8
Other	1,490,561	0

1940

Roosevelt (D)	27,243,466	449
Willkie (R)	22,304,755	82
Other	267,091	0

1944

Roosevelt (D)	25,594,822	432
Dewey (R)	22,017,707	99
Other	356,272	0

1948

Truman (D)	24,104,836	303
Dewey (R)	21,969,500	189
Other	2,606,080	39

1952

Stevenson (D)	27,311,316	89
Eisenhower (R)	33,927,549	442
Other	308,996	0

raised in connection with Herbert Hoover, who had lived abroad for many years, but interpretation of this clause as requiring residence of 14 years continuously and immediately preceding election appears unwarranted.

The compensation of the President is fixed by statutory law,[15] but it may not be diminished or increased during his term of office. From 1909 to 1949 it was $75,000 per year; in January, 1949, it was raised to $100,000 and an additional $50,000 tax-free expense allowance was provided. Beginning in 1953 the salary and allowance were both made taxable. Travel, official entertaining, and White House are supported out of separate budget items. Even when all presidential perquisites are considered, however, the chief executive receives less compensation than hundreds of people in business and entertainment.

Succession. According to the Constitution, if the President vacates his office, the Vice-President succeeds; if both offices fall vacant, Congress determines by law ". . . what officer shall then act as President. . . ." [16] In a statute enacted in 1886, Congress provided that the heads of the executive departments should succeed in the following order: State, Treasury, War, Justice, Post Office, Navy, and Interior.[17] The Twentieth Amendment provides that if no President is chosen by the beginning of the next term, the Vice-President-elect shall serve as President until such time as a President qualifies. If neither President-elect nor Vice-President-elect has qualified, Congress may declare who shall act as President.

Prior to the time Harry S. Truman was sworn in following the death of Franklin D. Roosevelt in April, 1945, six Vice-Presidents had succeeded to the presidency, all because of the deaths of the Presidents. William H. Harrison died in April, 1841, one month after his inauguration, and was succeeded by Tyler. General Zachary Taylor, who died in 1850, was followed by Fillmore. The assassination of Lincoln in 1865 left the presidency for Andrew Johnson. President James A. Garfield, who died from an assassin's bullet in 1881, was followed by Chester A. Arthur. McKinley's assassination in 1901 opened the way for the brilliant career of Theodore Roosevelt. Warren G. Harding's death in 1923 left the presidency to Calvin Coolidge. Only Roosevelt, Coolidge, and Truman managed to secure election for another term in the presidency. No provision is made in the law or Constitution for succession in case the President becomes disabled. Garfield, Wilson, and Eisenhower had substantial periods of incapacity but no method of removing the executive exists unless it be impeachment.

The death of Franklin D. Roosevelt in April, 1945, just at the end of the war in Europe and on the eve of the San Francisco Conference, focused the attention of the country on presidential succession law. President Truman soon recommended to Congress that a new succession law be enacted, replacing the heads of the executive departments with the Speaker of the House and the president pro tempore of the Senate. At the time, President Truman's sentiments were believed to be motivated largely by the fact that Secretary of State Edward R. Stettinius, Jr., was almost wholly lacking in political experience. The President repeated his recommendation in his State of the Union message of January, 1946.

In 1947 a new act was passed, providing that should both the President and Vice-President become unable to discharge the powers and duties of the presidency, the succession should be: Speaker of the House, president pro tempore of the Senate, and heads of the executive departments in order of the 1886 act except that the posts of Agriculture, Commerce, and Labor were added to the end.[18] The new act has been criticized severely for its failure to define "disability"

---

[15] Benjamin Franklin argued in the constitutional convention against any salary for the President. Madison recorded concerning this suggestion: "It was treated with great respect, but rather for the author of it, than from any apparent conviction of its expediency or practicability." *Documents,* p. 141.

[16] Art. II, Sec. 1, cl. 5.

[17] 24 Stat. 7. The other cabinet posts did not then exist.

[18] 61 Stat. 380. Subsequently, under the National Security Act of 1947, the Secretary of Defense displaced the Secretary of War, and the Secretary of the Navy was eliminated.

and for the possible unconstitutionality both of classifying the Speaker and the president pro tempore as "officers of the United States," as the Constitution requires for succession, and of declaring that he who succeeds becomes President and is entitled to serve out the remainder of the full term.[19]

It is difficult to see how the Speaker of the House and the president pro tempore of the Senate would be better material for the presidency than the heads of the executive departments. While the speakership normally is filled by a person of long experience in legislative matters, proved executive ability is rare in that office. The president pro tempore of the Senate seldom is a man of distinction and sometimes is a party wheel horse of indifferent qualification except that of long seniority. On the other hand, the Secretary of State and the Secretary of the Treasury are often experienced in both administration and politics.

THE PRESIDENT AND HIS COLLEAGUES

The Cabinet. After the proposal for a council of advisers was eliminated by the Constitutional Convention, many assumed that the Senate would attempt to fill this role. But the first Senate was reluctant to advise directly with President Washington. Therefore, formal preconsultation, even on appointments and treaties, was dropped, never to be revived.

President Washington began to call department heads into consultation, and these early meetings were soon known as "cabinet" meetings. The cabinet has remained as it began, an informal group without legal sanction, its personnel determined by custom and by the will of the President. The cabinet meets only at the request of the President, it exercises only such

authority as he chooses to vest in it, and it may be dissolved if the executive wishes. In practice, the cabinet plays an important part in the determination of executive policy and in coordinating administrative work. Reemphasis must be given to the fact that the cabinet is the creature of the President. No votes are taken, unless the President asks for one; as Lincoln once said, the only vote that counts is the President's own.

Traditionally the cabinet has been composed of the heads of executive departments. Sometimes the Vice-President is included as a member. In cabinet personnel, as in other cabinet matters, the President is the master.

During the Eisenhower Administration the cabinet was composed of the President, the Vice-President, and ten heads of departments. Seven others, in early 1955, sat at the cabinet table and participated in discussion: the Ambassador to the United Nations, the Director of the Bureau of the Budget, the Special Assistant (Disarmament), the Administrator of Defense Mobilization, the Chairman of the Civil Service Commission, the Assistant to the President, and the Deputy Assistant to the President. The cabinet met rather regularly on Fridays; on at least one occasion a cabinet meeting was televised.

Mr. Vice-President. Vice-Presidents often have become the forgotten men in American history. The office is one of importance, and yet it is the butt of endless jokes. Almost the only Vice-Presidents remembered from one generation to another are those who succeeded to the presidency. The Vice-President presides over the Senate, and he becomes President when that office falls vacant. These duties alone should make the office one of the most coveted in the gift of the people. In practice, however, it is looked upon as a political graveyard to be avoided by politicians of promise.

The reasons for the discrepancy between the potentialities of the office and its reputation are to be found principally in the method of nominating for the office. Each party, as seen earlier, uses the vice-presidency to balance the ticket, or to appease or reward some element. Thus the proper running mate for Alfred E. Smith, Catholic and Eastern, was Joseph T. Robinson,

[19] See Ruth C. Silva, *Presidential Succession* (University of Michigan Press, 1951); also her "The Presidential Succession Act of 1947," *Michigan Law Review*, vol. 47 (February, 1949), pp. 451–476; Everett S. Brown and Ruth C. Silva, "Presidential Succession and Inability," *Journal of Politics*, vol. 11 (February, 1949), pp. 236–256; Joseph E. Kallenbach, "The New Presidential Succession Act," *American Political Science Review*, vol. 41 (October, 1947), pp. 931–941.

Protestant and Southern; for Wendell Willkie, a novice in politics and identified with Eastern corporate interests, Charles McNary, veteran Senator and champion of farm and progressive interests. While in both these cases the vice-presidential candidates were able men, the method often produces candidates of questionable qualifications.

Second, the constitutional responsibilities of office are not great. The Senate is a body with customs and traditions that the presiding officer must respect and accept. As president of the Senate, he fills a correct and impartial role, voting only in case of a tie. Vice-President Dawes, who tried to modernize the Senate, found the upper chamber unwilling to accept his proposals, or even to listen patiently. A vigorous man gets restive under such conditions; his frustration is noticed and the prestige of the office degenerates accordingly.

The considerable possibilities of the office have been demonstrated by recent Vice-Presidents, as diverse as Henry A. Wallace and Richard M. Nixon. Both Mr. Roosevelt in 1940 and Mr. Eisenhower in 1952 were strong enough in their respective parties to choose running mates without the usual trading of votes and appeasing of factions. Roosevelt gave Wallace an important role in the war effort. Eisenhower assigned Nixon a variety of congressional, diplomatic and executive tasks, including the honor of presiding over the cabinet in the absence of the President.[20] In 1955 the salary of the office was set at $35,000 per year.

HEADQUARTERS STAFF

The Chief Administrator. The Constitution vests in the President the "executive power" of the United States. In fact, however, the President has less sweeping authority over administration than might be assumed from the language of the fundamental law. Congress frequently determines the structure and authority of administrative agencies; it decides what func-

tions require new agencies or remodeled ones, determines powers and duties, and controls in many other ways the framework within which administration operates. Many bureaus, however, have been established by executive order rather than an act of Congress and consequently may be reorganized or even abolished and their functions assigned elsewhere by similar executive act. Presidential authority over the Administration has been weakened during the last half century by several developments, but the factors operating to strengthen the hand of the President have outweighed them.

Since the turn of the century, especially during the administrations of Theodore Roosevelt, Woodrow Wilson, and Franklin Roosevelt, presidential authority over administration has increased markedly. The power to appoint and remove executive officers gives the President a commanding position in the field of personnel. Increasingly complex international situations have dictated more executive discretion in foreign affairs, trade, and defense matters. Economic depression intensified the tendency to delegate more authority in the fields of relief and business regulation.

The emergency nature of many governmental responsibilities is especially important in explaining augmented presidential power over administration. Whereas Congress once was able to stipulate in great detail the precise form, duties, and procedure of administrative agencies, now such variable factors as business conditions, foreign tariff rates, and droughts in farm regions require flexibility and loose construction of statutes. The trend is toward a situation under which Congress lays down broad principles and standards in legislation, leaving to the President and other executive officers the responsibility for details. Such details often include the whole structure and personnel of administrative agencies and the allocation of funds for specific purposes.

The Presidential Secretariat. Viewed from the standpoint of the President, the first essential in fulfilling his responsibilities as chief administrator is an able corps of attachés to aid him in keeping abreast of administrative work. For the

[20] Irving G. Williams, *The American Vice-Presidency: New Look* (Doubleday, 1954), p. 69. The Vice-President was made a member of the National Security Council in 1949. 63 Stat. 579.

early Presidents this was no great task, requiring only a small secretariat. To keep informed concerning the administrative leviathan of today requires most careful organization and planning. The administrative picture may be visualized with the President in the center, surrounded by concentric circles. Within the first are the President's secretaries and the White House staff that functions under them, a total of over 250 employees in the White House Office. President Eisenhower employed a "chief of staff" concept and placed direction of the presidential offices in the hands of his "Assistant to the President," Mr. Sherman Adams. In 1954 he established a cabinet secretariat as a part of his executive staff, headed by an officer with the title of "Secretary to the Cabinet." This secretariat prepares the agenda for cabinet meetings, keeps the official records of what was decided, and follows through to see that the executive departments carry out the cabinet decisions. This development indicates the increased role assigned to the cabinet by President Eisenhower.

President Hoover introduced the pattern of three principal executive secretaries. The number and duties vary from President to President and from time to time. Usually, one is assigned to public relations and the control of information going out of the White House; a second handles visitors of the President, sifting the important from the unimportant and keeping the executive appointment calendar; the third may be given miscellaneous duties. In addition, each President has personal secretaries and clerks.

A later development was the authorization of "administrative assistants" to the President, in addition to the executive secretaries. The President's Committee on Administrative Management urged that the lack of staff assistance to the President be remedied by the appointment of six administrative assistants who ". . . should be possessed of high competence, great physical vigor, and a passion for anonymity." [21] The Administrative Reorganization Act of 1939 authorized their appointment. In 1955 five were serv-

ing with this title. The incumbents of the office have followed the plan outlined by the President's committee: they have carried out the assignments of the President unobtrusively, collecting data, conferring with public officials, American and foreign, multiplying the eyes and ears of the President in effective fashion.

In addition to the executive secretaries and assistants, the President's staff in 1955 included five special assistants, a special counsel, a secretary to the cabinet, and a staff secretary. Their assistants and the Army, Navy, and Air Force aides complete the principal officers of the White House staff.

One student of presidential staffing criticized the White House office organization for permitting too many high-ranking aides direct access to the President.[22] This alleged fault may have been corrected by President Eisenhower's use of Governor Adams as "chief of staff."

Other Executive Office Agencies. Beyond the White House staff, the Executive Office of the President includes the Bureau of the Budget, the National Security Council, the Council of Economic Advisers, and the Office of Defense Mobilization.

An early concept was that grouping "staff" services in the presidential office gave the executive another form of control over "line," or operating, administrative agencies. "Staff" types of agencies, housekeeping in nature, might include personnel, budgeting, planning, purchasing, reporting, and other central services provided for operating agencies engaged in such "line" functions as public health, welfare, conservation, defense, and regulation of business. The objective of well-developed staff agencies, working in close cooperation with the President, and thereby giving him a strategic position in the cockpit of control, could not be achieved fully in 1939 when the Executive Office of the President was created. The Reorganization Act of that year forbade transfer of Civil Service Commission and General Accounting Office.

In the war and postwar periods the magnitude

[21] U.S. President's Committee on Administrative Management, *Report . . . with Studies . . .* (1937), p. 5.

[22] Bradley D. Nash, *Staffing the Presidency,* National Planning Association Pamphlet 80 (December, 1952), p. 16.

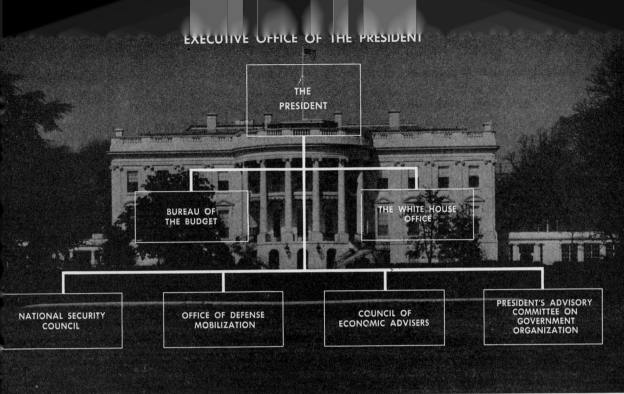

THE
PRESIDENT

BUREAU OF
THE BUDGET

THE WHITE HOUSE
OFFICE

NATIONAL SECURITY
COUNCIL

OFFICE OF DEFENSE
MOBILIZATION

COUNCIL OF
ECONOMIC ADVISERS

PRESIDENT'S ADVISORY
COMMITTEE ON
GOVERNMENT
ORGANIZATION

Photograph by McPhearson from Monkmeyer

of the executive branch has led to some rethinking about staff services. The present tendency appears to be one of allowing the Executive Office to perform a coordinating role with emphasis on program and policy development, leaving routine staff services to the operating departments. The new General Services Administration, created in 1949 to provide central purchasing, property maintenance, transportation, and other services, was made a separate agency outside of the Executive Office of the President. Several agencies that were in the presidential office have been abolished.

Since each of the four agencies remaining in the Executive Office is discussed in subsequent chapters, only their general roles will be described here. In its legislative reference work, the Bureau of the Budget provides central clearance to ensure that the legislative proposals of executive agencies conform with the policies of the President.[23] The Bureau also has extensive

duties in developing budget policies and estimates, recommending management improvements, coordinating statistical services, and the like.

The Employment Act of 1946 created the Council of Economic Advisers.[24] The three economists who constitute the Council help the President prepare his annual economic report to Congress, study economic trends, and recommend to the President appropriate policies. Perhaps anticipating something like the public disagreement that developed late in the Truman Administration among Council members, the Hoover Commission recommended that the body be displaced by a single-headed Office of Economic Adviser. President Eisenhower transferred administrative authority to the chairman.

The two defense agencies in the Executive Office of the President are the National Security Council and the Office of Defense Mobilization. The National Security Council was created by the National Security Act of 1947 [25] and assigned the weighty task of advising the President on policies relating to national security. The Cen-

[23] For an excellent analysis of legislative clearance, see Richard E. Neustadt, "Presidency and Legislation: the Growth of Central Clearance," *American Political Science Review,* vol. 48 (September, 1954), pp. 641–671.

[24] 60 Stat. 24.
[25] 61 Stat. 497.

tral Intelligence Agency operates under the direction of the Council. The Office of Defense Mobilization was established by executive order in 1953 and charged with directing and coordinating all mobilization activities.

Calling attention to the useful work of special advisory commissions and of individual consultants appointed by the President, the first Hoover Commission recommended that the chief executive be given adequate funds to operate freely in this sphere. The Hoover group also felt strongly that the President should have power to organize and reorganize his own office without the approval of Congress and to appoint his own staff (except the Civil Service Commission) without confirmation by the Senate.

LINE ORGANIZATION

The Executive Departments. Most important among the line functions are the regular executive departments of the Federal government, now ten in number. According to custom, the heads of the departments are considered members of the President's cabinet by virtue of their offices. These departments were established by Congress in the following order:

State (originally Foreign Affairs), 1789
War, 1789 (lost cabinet status, 1947)
Treasury, 1789
Navy, 1798 (lost cabinet status, 1947)
Interior (originally Home), 1849
Agriculture, 1862 (elevated to full membership status, 1889)
Justice (Attorney General, 1789), 1870
Post Office (Postmaster General, 1789), 1872
Commerce (originally Commerce and Labor), 1903
Labor, 1913
Defense (originally National Defense Establishment), 1947
Health, Education, and Welfare (1953)

The theory underlying the organization of departments is that similar functions should be grouped for convenience and efficiency into a relatively small number of departments, the heads of which should coordinate the endeavors of the operating services and be responsible to the Chief Executive. While this is the theory, several federal departments possess functions that are not related to their major functions. Interior, for example, has served as a catchall for miscellaneous agencies that failed to fit elsewhere. At the same time, several activities—like public health, transportation, public works, and conservation—are divided among half a dozen departments.

Each executive department is headed by a secretary, appointed by the President with the advice and consent of the Senate. The department head usually is chosen for political qualifications: political prominence, campaign support, factional affiliation, sectional considerations. It is not surprising, therefore, that his main contribution often proves to be his conduct of departmental external relationships—with President, with Congress, with press, and with public. Usually he is not prepared to manage the detailed operation of his department; that is better left to the permanent career officials, operating under the supervision of the secretary and his political aides. He has important duties in determining departmental policy, appointing and removing officers, and settling disputes and appeals.

The Reorganization Act of 1939 banned new departments but gave the President considerable power to reshuffle bureaus and agencies. President Roosevelt promptly created three new "agencies" which are much like departments in fact but not in name. The "administrator" of each was invited to sit with the President's cabinet. In the beginning these agencies were the Federal Security Agency, Federal Works Agency, and Federal Loan Agency. Reorganized many times during and after the war, by the time the Hoover Commission reported in 1949 the first two still existed under their original names. The Housing and Home Finance Agency, created in 1947, contained some of the activities originally vested in the Loan Agency, which was abolished.

The first Hoover Commission recommended that a new department be created in the welfare-education field. Several existing functions of the Federal Security Agency, notably the Public Health Service, Food and Drug Administration, and Bureau of Employment Security, would be transferred to other departments. The new Department for Social Security and Education would embrace the remaining social security services, education, vocational rehabilitation, Indian affairs, and certain lesser activities that are related.[26] President Truman, in his 1949 reorganization plan 1, proposed instead to transform the present Federal Security Agency into a Department of Welfare, headed by a Secretary of Welfare, and continuing to perform all of the services of the existing Agency except employment and unemployment compensation, which were sent to the Department of Labor. Of all the seven plans submitted to Congress in June, 1949, the one providing for a Department of Welfare alone was nullified by adverse congressional action.

In 1953 President Eisenhower's reorganization plan 1 was allowed to go into effect, and the Department of Health, Education, and Welfare took its place among the executive departments. Most, but not all, federal activities in the welfare field are now under the new department.

The Hoover Commission favored the retention and strengthening of the new Housing and Home Finance Agency but suggested the breakup of the Federal Works Agency. President Truman took the first step toward reassignment of the works function in his reorganization plan 7, which went into effect in August, 1949, transferring the Public Roads Administration to the Department of Commerce. In the meantime and before the plan went into effect, Congress enacted a statute creating the General Services Administration, of which Public Roads was one agency. Finally the plan went into effect, taking Public Roads from General Services and giving it to Commerce.

Independent Establishments. After the ten great executive departments come some forty-five bodies which are not part of any department yet each of which, by itself, is insufficient in size or importance to justify the status of a department. The reasons for their separate establishment are as numerous as the agencies themselves, but a few major arguments are common

[26] Hoover Commission, *Social Security and Education; Indian Affairs* (1949), pp. 3–12.

to many. First, the work of the agency may be so unique that it does not fit into any existing department. Second, the service provided must be fully protected from partisan politics. Third, special interests find it easier to watch and bring pressure on separate agencies than on departmentalized ones. Fourth, possession of quasi-legislative and quasi-judicial powers requires independence from the President.

The more important of existing independent establishments, together with the years in which they were created, are the following:

Civil Service Commission, 1883
Interstate Commerce Commission, 1887
Federal Trade Commission, 1914
Tariff Commission, 1916
Federal Power Commission, 1920
General Accounting Office, 1921
Veterans' Administration, 1930
Tennessee Valley Authority, 1933
Securities and Exchange Commission, 1934
Federal Communications Commission, 1935
National Labor Relations Board, 1935
Maritime Commission, 1936 (changed to Federal Maritime Board, 1950)
Civil Aeronautics Board, 1940
Atomic Energy Commission, 1946

Nearly one-half of those listed are regulatory commissions with varying responsibilities for supervising commercial activities.

Congress has seen fit to assign much responsibility for the execution of laws to such independent bodies. To some extent this represents a diffusion of the executive power, which the Constitution vests in the President both directly and by its charge that he take care that the laws be executed faithfully. In virtually every case, the independent agency is governed by a board or commission, appointed by the President for terms sufficiently long for a President to be unable to secure control in one term. This has the advantage of insulating a board or commission from the political whim of the executive, but the disadvantage of continuing in office those whose policies long since have been repudiated at the polls. When a change of administration involves a transformation in policy, as in 1953, the disparity between presidential and commission views on public questions may be a very critical matter. It is now settled that Congress may in the law creating agencies regulate and limit the power of the President to remove members of regulatory commissions.

"Fourth Branch?" The status of independent agencies has brought condemnation upon them as "a headless fourth branch of government," "miniature independent governments," and "irresponsible commissions." Under President Roosevelt's reorganization orders of 1939 some progress was made in incorporating independent agencies into the departmental system, but a large number of the establishments were exempted from any change. The 1939 act withheld from the President the power to alter the status of most of the regulatory commissions. One proposal insistently urged by the President's Committee on Administrative Management was that the administrative functions of regulatory commissions should be separated from judicial functions. Administrative work would be coordinated into an appropriate regular department; semilegislative and semijudicial work would continue independent of presidential control.[27]

[27] Robert E. Cushman, "The Problem of the Independent Regulatory Commission," in U.S. President's Committee on Administrative Management, *op. cit.*, pp. 207–243. See also the same author's book entitled *The Independent Regulatory Commissions* (Oxford, 1941).

The first Hoover Commission suggested that some commissions be divested of their administrative duties but that the remaining ones should transfer all administrative responsibility to their chairmen.[28] President Truman took the first steps toward the latter end in his initial plans under the Reorganization Act of 1949, which fixed administrative authority on the chairmen of the Civil Service Commission and the Maritime Board, and in 1950 on the chairmen of the Federal Trade Commission, the Federal Power Commission, the Securities and Exchange Commission, and the Civil Aeronautics Board. Plans proposing the same type of reform for the Interstate Commerce Commission, the Federal Communications Commission, and the National Labor Relations Board were rejected by the Senate.

The problem of effective supervision of agencies outside the regular Departments remains unsolved. A former Treasury official has suggested that presidential control might be aided by creating two new cabinet posts "at large." These "ministers without portfolio" would have their assignments fixed by the President, and might achieve a measure of coordination in an area previously known for its uncoordination.[29]

[28] First Hoover Commission, *The Independent Regulatory Commissions* (1949), pp. 5–6.

[29] Daniel W. Bell in Nash, *op. cit.*, p. 12.

FOR FURTHER READING
(See also works listed after next chapter.)

Agar, Herbert: *The People's Choice* (Houghton Mifflin, 1933).

Bean, Louis H.: *Ballot Behavior: A Study of Presidential Elections* (American Council on Public Affairs, 1940).

Brownlow, Louis: *The American Presidency* (University of Chicago Press, 1949).

Burnham, W. Dean: *Presidential Ballots, 1836–1892* (Johns Hopkins Press, 1955).

Corwin, Edward S.: *The President: Office and Powers* (New York University Press, rev. ed., 1948).

Ewing, Cortez A. M.: *Presidential Elections, from Abraham Lincoln to Franklin D. Roosevelt* (University of Oklahoma Press, 1940).

Hart, James: *The American Presidency in Action 1789* (Macmillan, 1948).

Hatch, Louis C.: *A History of the Vice-Presidency of the United States* (New York: American Historical Society, 1934).

Hobbs, Edward H.: *Behind the President: A Study of Executive Office Agencies* (Washington: Public Affairs Press, 1954).

Hyman, Sidney: *The American Presidency* (Harper, 1954).

Laski, Harold J.: *The American Presidency* (Harper, 1940).

Learned, Henry B.: *The President's Cabinet* (Yale University Press, 1912).

Levin, Peter: *Seven by Chance: The Accidental Presidents* (Farrar, Straus, 1948).

MacBride, R. L.: *The American Electoral College* (Caldwell, Idaho: Caxton, 1953).

Macmahon, Arthur W., and John D. Millett: *Federal Administrators: A Biographical Approach to the Problem of Departmental Management* (Columbia University Press, 1939).

Marcy, Carl: *Presidential Commissions* (Columbia University Press, 1945).

Meriam, Lewis, and Laurence F. Schmeckebier: *Reorganization of the National Government: What Does It Involve?* (Brookings, 1939).

Nash, B. D.: *Staffing the Presidency* (Washington: National Planning Association, 1952).

Patterson, Caleb P.: *Presidential Government in the United States* (The University of North Carolina Press, 1947).

Pollard, James E.: *The Presidents and the Press* (Macmillan, 1947).

Reynolds, Mary T.: *Interdepartmental Committees in the National Administration* (Columbia University Press, 1939).

Short, Lloyd M.: *Development of National Administrative Organization in the United States* (Johns Hopkins Press, 1923).

Silva, Ruth C.: *Presidential Succession* (University of Michigan Press, 1951).

Stanwood, Edward: *A History of the Presidency* (Houghton Mifflin, 2 vols., 1916). Vol. 1 covers 1788–1897, and vol. 2, 1897–1916.

Stein, Charles W.: *The Third Term Tradition* (Columbia University Press, 1942).

Stoddard, Henry L.: *Presidential Sweepstakes: The Story of Political Conventions and Campaigns* (Putnam, 1948).

Taft, William H.: *The Presidency* (Scribner, 1916).

Thach, Charles C.: *The Creation of the Presidency: A Study in Constitutional History* (Johns Hopkins Press, 1922).

U.S. Commission on Organization of the Executive Branch of the Government (second Hoover Commission): *Report . . .* (20 vols., 1955). In addition 13 task-force reports were published.

U.S. Commission on Organization of the Executive Branch of the Government (first Hoover Commission): *Report . . .* (19 vols., 1949). In addition, 19 task-force reports and 6 subcommittee reports were published.

U.S. House of Representatives: *Amend the Constitution with Respect to Election of President and Vice-President . . . Hearings. . . .* 81st Cong., 1st Sess. (1949). Briefer hearings were held by the same committee in 1947.

——: *Documents Illustrative of the Formation of the Union of the American States,* H. Doc. 398, 69th Cong., 1st Sess. (1927).

U.S. National Archives Establishment: *United States Government Organization Manual* (issued annually).

U.S. President's Committee on Administrative Management: *Report . . . with Studies of Administrative Management in the Federal Government* (1937).

U.S. Senate: *The Electoral College,* S. Doc. 243, 78th Cong., 2d Sess. (1944).

U.S. Senate: *Presidential Succession . . . Hearings. . . .* 80th Cong., 1st Sess. (1947).

Wallace, Schuyler C.: *Federal Departmentalization: a Critique of Theories of Organization* (Columbia University Press, 1941).

Williams, Irving G.: *The American Vice-Presidency: New Look* (Doubleday, 1954).

REVIEW
QUESTIONS

1. What previous experience and knowledge weighed heavily in determining the form and scope of the chief executive office by the Constitutional Convention of 1787?

2. What would the American presidency be like today if the convention had persisted in its early inclination for selection by Congress?

3. What defect in the electoral-college scheme was corrected by the Twelfth Amendment?

4. Would the following be valid actions under the Federal Constitution? Why? (*a*) State A provides its presidential electors be chosen by the state legislature. (*b*) State B requires that all but two of its electors be elected by voters in congressional districts rather than at large.

5. Describe at least three proposed reforms in the mode of electing a President, and outline the main arguments for and against each one.

6. What are the principal arguments pro and con on limiting a President to two 4-year terms?

7. Explain the difference in provisions concerning presidential succession before and after the 1947 law on the subject.

8. What are the general responsibilities of the President as "chief administrator"?

9. What are "staff services"? Which have been brought into the Office of the President?

10. Name the regular executive departments of the Federal government, and explain the theory of departmentalizing.

11. How did the cabinet originate? What are its functions today?

12. What are the "independent establishments"? Should they be grouped into regular departments?

13. Enumerate and discuss the principal recommendations of the two Hoover Commissions regarding organization of the executive branch.

CHAPTER 15

Powers of the President

> The Presidency has become a powerful and amorphous office. Its influence extends, with varying degrees of authority, over the whole political order. It encompasses, in fact, a domain far broader than appears on paper. Congress can pass a statute; the Executive must convert it into the law-in-action. Congress can decree a new agency; the Executive must endow it with the breath of life. Congress alone has power to declare war; the President may so conduct foreign affairs that it has no alternative. — Walton Hamilton [1]

The "wide discretion" and "great power" that former president William Howard Taft declared the Constitution gave to the presidency have been subjected to new scrutiny and acid tests. Within a 2-year period some questioned President Truman's authority to order troops to Europe and others challenged his power to seize and operate the steel mills—both without congressional authorization. Although Truman appears to have been vindicated in the first case and restrained in the second, the scope of presidential authority remains like an uncharted sea. We know the rocks upon which the S.S. *White House* has been buffeted, but the ocean remains to be sounded fully and the peripheral shore is dimly seen. Nevertheless we recognize in the presidency one of the most powerful offices ever created by a democratic nation.

APPOINTMENT AND REMOVAL

Scope of the Appointing Power. The power to appoint is one of the most far-reaching in the list of presidential powers. Through it the

[1] "The Ever-growing Power of the Presidency," *The New York Times Magazine*, Aug. 29, 1943, p. 6.

President commands the allegiance of a great number of federal officers and secures the support of many national legislators for his program.

In Article II, Section 2, the President is given power to "nominate, and by and with the advice and consent of the Senate, shall appoint Ambassadors, other public Ministers and Consuls, judges of the Supreme Court, and all other officers of the United States which shall be established by law; . . ." The article goes on to provide that Congress may vest appointment of "inferior officers" in the President alone, in the courts, or in department heads. Thus, appointments to the federal services fall into two general groups: those that require senatorial confirmation, called "officers," and those that do not, called "inferior officers." There is no logical line of demarcation between the two. Included in the "officers" category are diplomats, judges, department heads, regulatory commissioners, marshals, and collectors of customs. Often Congress seeks to enlarge this group in order to broaden the possibilities of patronage. Some bureau chiefs and virtually all subordinate employees fall within the "inferior officers" group.

Senatorial Confirmation. The Senate has interpreted "advice and consent" as justification for withholding confirmation from proposed officers on grounds that sometimes appear petty or personal. It rarely interferes with the President's selection of his own cabinet; a notable exception was Charles B. Warren, nominated by President Coolidge as Attorney General and rejected in 1925 by the Senate. Appointments to the diplomatic corps normally secure the Senate's approval without difficulty, but the Senate's rejection of Martin Van Buren as Minister to Britain will be remembered from the Jackson administration. Supreme Court justiceships may be filled by the President without much interference, yet the Senate refused to consent to President Hoover's appointment of Circuit Judge John J. Parker in 1930 largely because of Negro and labor opposition.

Other appointments, especially those of a local nature, are subject to a custom called "senatorial courtesy." This is an unwritten rule which requires the President to confer with and secure the consent of the Senator or Senators of his party from a state before making a nomination to an office in that state. The effect of the rule is virtually to transfer the nominating power for such offices from the President to the individual Senators of his party. Almost invariably the Senate will reject a presidential appointment if a personal objection is raised by a Senator of the President's party from the state involved.

Senatorial Courtesy in Practice. A recent example of the operation of senatorial courtesy arose from President Truman's choice of two candidates to fill district court judgeships in Illinois. In August, 1951, Senator Paul H. Douglas of Illinois went before the Senate Judiciary Committee and opposed the President's nominees on the grounds that he was not consulted concerning them and that his own choices were better qualified. The Senator produced results of a poll of the Chicago Bar Association in support of the latter contention. When the nominations reached the floor with an adverse committee recommendation in October, Senator Douglas stated:

I do not want to label the nominees themselves as being personally obnoxious to me. I regard them as estimable men and fine citizens. But I should like to point out that they were nominated without consultation with me, without any indication of the reasons for their selection, and contrary to the recommendations of the much more highly qualified men whose names I had forwarded and who were supported by the heavy preponderance of informed opinion in Illinois.[2]

The Senate rejected both nominees without a roll-call vote.[3]

Sometimes when Senators who are unpopular with their colleagues attempt to obstruct confirmation of an appointment, the Senate will approve in spite of their protests. Only a few rejections occur during each session of Congress; these may be attributed mainly to the fact that the President fails to accept suggestions from Senators and appoints those whom they do not recommend.

Reconsideration. After the Senate has confirmed an appointment of the President, can it subsequently call the matter back for reconsideration? In a case arising from the desire of the Senate to reconsider confirmation of several appointees of President Hoover to the Federal Power Commission,[4] the Supreme Court declared that it could not. Shortly after taking office, these appointees had reversed the policies of the commission and dismissed several employees. Under the rules of the Senate, the matter might be brought up for reconsideration, but the Court ruled that once the consent was given and the officers had been fully installed, it was not possible for the Senate to withdraw confirmation.

Presidents may fill vacancies that occur during recess of the Senate, but such commissions expire at the end of the next session. Existing law prohibits the payment of a salary to an officer appointed to fill a vacancy that existed when the Senate was in session. Usually a Pres-

[2] *Congressional Record,* 82d Cong., 1st Sess., Oct. 9, 1951, p. 1310.

[3] For a careful review of this and other instances, see Joseph P. Harris, *The Advice and Consent of the Senate* (University of California Press, 1953).

[4] United States *v.* Smith, 186 U.S. 6 (1932).

ident will not give a recess appointment to a person previously rejected by the Senate.

Power to Remove. Although it takes the President and the Senate to appoint officers, the first Congress declared by law that the President alone might remove all officers appointed by him except judges. In the reconstruction controversies between President Johnson and Congress, the executive was forbidden by law to remove officers without the consent of the Senate. This was repealed about 20 years later. In the meantime, however, an act of 1876 provided that first-, second-, and third-class postmasters might be removed only with the consent of the Senate. In spite of the act, President Wilson removed one Myers from his office of postmaster of Portland, Ore. A legal suit arose over Myers's claim for back salary, and he alleged that his removal was illegal under the 1876 law. The statute was declared unconstitutional by the Supreme Court; the power to remove, said the Court, was implied not only from the power to appoint, but also from the general authority of the executive to see that the laws are executed faithfully.[5]

After the Myers verdict, the President's removal power appeared limited only in respect to judges. Then, in the early stages of the New Deal came a decision that modified this conception. Humphrey, a Federal Trade Commissioner, was removed by President Roosevelt because the Commissioner's philosophy of business regulation differed widely from Mr. Roosevelt's. Under the law the President was empowered to remove for "inefficiency, neglect of duty, or malfeasance in office," but he gave no such reason. The Court took notice that a regulatory commission's powers are quasi-legislative and quasi-judicial in nature and ruled that the President's removal authority could be limited in respect to officers exercising such powers.[6] Apparently the present rule is that the President may remove executive officers at will, but that regulatory commissioners with part judicial and part legislative powers may be protected by statutory limitations on the removal power.

[5] Myers *v.* United States, 272 U.S. 52, 164 (1926).
[6] Humphrey's Executor (Rathbun) *v.* United States, 295 U.S. 602 (1935).

WAR AND DIPLOMATIC POWERS

The War Powers. As Commander in Chief of the armed forces, the President has extensive authority over both military and foreign policy of the country. The executive shares power over the military establishments with Congress, which may make rules, appropriate money, and declare war; the Senate confirms appointments of military officers. Presidential control of the militia is limited to periods when it is called into the service of the United States. By his actions, nevertheless, the President virtually may force Congress to appropriate money, as when Theodore Roosevelt ordered the fleet around the world despite congressional disapproval. Likewise, a President by belligerent use of the armed forces may involve the country in a state of war, leaving Congress with no alternative but to declare it. Without consulting Congress, Presidents have often ordered marines to land in Central American and Caribbean countries to protect American property and lives.

In time of war the powers of the President as Commander in Chief are even greater. He directs the armed forces on land and sea. He governs conquered territory until Congress provides by law for its civil government. Without much statutory authority Lincoln suppressed civil rights, seized enemy property. Wilson exercised vast powers, largely conferred upon him by act of Congress.

In the Second World War, President Franklin Roosevelt could rely upon a great mass of specific legislation, granting to the executive additional emergency and war powers. His control of radio was assured under the Federal Communications Act of 1934. Congress provided for calling the National Guard into federal service more than a year before it declared war. Discretion was given the executive in the execution of the selective service law of 1940. A series of laws, beginning not long after war broke out in Europe, step by step gave the President very great authority over the industrial facilities of the country, over matters of production, priorities, conditions, and contracts. After war was declared, power over foreign communications, war functions and agencies, alien property, and a host of other matters was added by congressional action.[7]

Recent Problems. The hostilities that commenced in Korea in June, 1950, have focused much attention on the length and breadth of presidential power in time of emergency, but without a formal declaration of war. President Truman's prompt action in ordering American armed forces to aid the South Koreans was challenged then and subsequently as exceeding his authority as Commander in Chief. He ought, critics in Congress and out argued, to have consulted Congress and sought congressional approval. After the entry into battle by Chinese Communist troops, the Korean war broadened far beyond the police action originally anticipated. Even then, a substantial body of opinion supported the President's action as a valid exercise of his power to dispose and assign the armed forces. The issue also was raised in 1951 and 1952 over presidential authority to send troops to European duty. In view of the speed with which the nation is likely to become involved in international crises, the President's plenary authority over the armed forces no doubt will prevail. Thoughtful citizens, however, will continue to fear future misuse of such near-absolute power. The most effective check of Congress appears to be the power of the purse, but rigid controls through appropriations are not very likely under crisis conditions.

On Dec. 16, 1950, the President proclaimed the existence of a national emergency. This action made available a large number of powers which had been terminated by joint resolution in 1947.[8] These were authorized by statutes enacted as

[7] A convenient compilation of war powers previous to the Second World War is contained in the appendix of E. Pendleton Herring, *Presidential Leadership: the Political Relations of Congress and the Chief Executive* (Farrar, Straus, 1940). For powers during the Second World War, see Margaret Fennell, *Acts of Congress Applicable in Time of Emergency,* Public Affairs Bulletin 35 (Library of Congress, 1945). For powers existing at the outset of the Korean hostilities, see Margaret Fennell, *Provisions of Federal Law Enacted for War and Emergency Periods,* Public Affairs Bulletin 88 (Library of Congress, 1950).

[8] 161 Stat. 449.

early as 1901, and included: calling of personnel of Army, Navy, Marines, and Coast Guard; credit control by Federal Reserve Board; suspension of 8-hour day in government employment and contracts; issuance of war-risk insurance; and many others.

In the Formosa Strait crisis of 1955, President Eisenhower secured from Congress, in advance, "authorization" through a joint resolution to employ the armed forces in protecting Formosa and the Pescadores against attack.

Foreign Affairs. As in military affairs, the President dominates the field of foreign affairs. The Constitution gives him authority to make treaties (with the consent of two-thirds of the Senate), to appoint diplomats and consuls (subject to ratification by a Senate majority), and to receive foreign diplomatic and consular representatives.

Treaties. Most treaties are negotiated through the usual diplomatic channels, utilizing the regular diplomatic agents of the countries involved. A projected treaty to govern international extradition between the United States and Brazil would be negotiated by the State Department and the Brazilian ambassador in Washington, or by the Brazilian foreign ministry and the American ambassador in Rio de Janeiro. For a convention or treaty of extraordinary importance or of a multilateral nature, the Secretary of State or some special agent or commission may negotiate it. President Wilson himself went to Europe to participate in framing the Treaty of Versailles. When negotiation is completed, the Chief Executive sends the treaty to the Senate for its approval. Individual Senators are consulted frequently in advance of and during negotiation stages. The Senate Foreign Relations Committee plays the key role in the ratification process. It holds hearings, at which State Department officials may be called to testify. A two-thirds majority on the floor of the Senate is required to approve a treaty.

The scope of the treaty-making power is not known precisely. Apparently the power may not be used to accomplish something specifically forbidden to the Federal government by the Constitution. But the treaty power has been used to achieve federal control in spheres where no other authority existed. In 1916, after adverse lower-court decisions voided attempts under the commerce clause to regulate and protect migratory birds, a treaty was negotiated and ratified with Great Britain, acting for Canada, providing that each country should protect such wild fowl. After the treaty came into force, Congress implemented it by enacting a law providing for the protection of migratory birds. The treaty and act were found constitutional in Missouri v. Holland.[9] As a result of this case, the power of Congress to enact laws in support of treaties obviously becomes broader than its ordinary statute-making authority, but the precise limits of such power are as yet unsettled.

Executive Agreements. The President may also make international arrangements without senatorial participation. "Executive agreements" are pledges of certain action by executives of two countries. For example, the President will exchange letters with the prime minister of Canada, in which each agrees to permit citizens of the other country to travel without passports. A famous example from history is the "gentlemen's agreement" between President Theodore Roosevelt and the Emperor of Japan, under which Roosevelt agreed to try to persuade Congress to kill exclusion legislation and the Japanese agreed to forbid the emigration of coolies.

During the last 20 years the "trade agreement" has come into prominence. It is neither treaty nor executive agreement but deserves a special category created by the Trade Agreements Act of 1934 and the subsequent renewals. Recognizing its inability to reduce tariff rates due to the pressure of affected groups, Congress vested in the President authority to adjust tariff barriers by negotiation and allowed him to proclaim in effect special trade agreements with individual foreign countries. These reciprocal trade agreements are not submitted to the Senate for confirmation but are fully enforceable in the courts.

Recognition. Another highly important power of the President in foreign affairs is his authority to recognize countries and governments.

[9] 252 U.S. 416 (1920). See also pp. 391–396.

This is done simply by receiving diplomatic representatives of the nation or regime, or it may be accomplished by altering the assignments or instructions of our agents abroad. For example, after the Italians completed the conquest of Ethiopia in 1936, the American legation in Addis Ababa was reduced to a consulate. Likewise the President may indicate dissatisfaction with a nation's representative by dismissing or

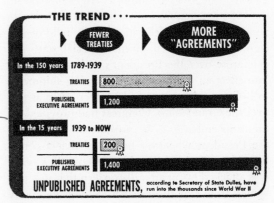

The increased use of executive agreements in recent years is one of the reasons proponents give for the Bricker Amendment. Reprinted from *U.S. News & World Report,* an independent weekly news magazine published at Washington Copyright, 1954, United States News Publishing Corporation. Issue of Feb. 5, 1954.

asking the recall of a diplomat or consul to the United States. A more extreme form of indicating displeasure with a country involves closing its consulates, as were those of Germany in 1940.

Recognition may be used as an instrument in foreign policy, for it has often been withheld to show disapproval of a government. From the time of the Bolshevik revolution of 1917 until 1933, this country indicated distaste for the Communist regime by maintaining no official contact with the Soviet government. When President Roosevelt decided to open diplomatic relations, he cabled directly to the President of the Council of Soviets. The Russian government sent M. Litvinov, its foreign commissar, to discuss Soviet-American problems. After the talks had concluded, the two nations exchanged ambassadors. The extinction of the independence of a nation is recognized by the United States through the closing of a legation or embassy. Recognition by the United States often is a most crucial matter for a new regime in a Latin-American republic; by withholding recognition, as from the Grau San Martin government in Cuba in 1933, this country may cause the downfall of one and the rise of another regime.

Delegation. Although the question of the delegation of legislative authority by Congress to the President requires more detailed attention in another place, this delegation in the field of foreign affairs has been given a special status. A case arose over the President's action in putting into effect an arms embargo, banning shipments to Bolivia and Paraguay which were then at war over the Gran Chaco. Congress had provided for the arms embargo to be proclaimed in force by the President whenever he found that a condition of war existed. President Roosevelt's order was attacked by an aircraft concern that was prevented from exporting planes to the belligerents. The Supreme Court upheld the constitutionality of the legislation and the proclamation on the ground that the President had a very special responsibility over foreign affairs.[10] The neutrality laws of the late 1930's employed the arms embargo as a prominent feature, and their constitutionality was regarded as certain after the Curtiss-Wright case.

Occasionally treaties and laws conflict, and the courts are faced with the question of which to enforce. They have equal standing; so the courts enforce the latest expression of policy, whether law or treaty.

The Bricker Amendment. Contending that the presidential power over foreign affairs has expanded so much that a curb is required, a bipartisan congressional bloc led by Senator Bricker of Ohio has proposed a remedial constitutional amendment. Its sponsors contend that

[10] United States *v.* Curtiss-Wright Export Corporation, 299 U.S. 304 (1936). For a good discussion of the foreign affairs power, see Foster H. Sherwood, "Foreign Relations and the Constitution," *Western Political Quarterly,* vol. 1 (December, 1948), pp. 386–399.

there is a real danger that internal law may be altered by international agreement without legislation, that actions or proposals of the United Nations and its agencies may threaten our constitutional rights.

In its original form the three substantive sections of the proposed amendment were as follows:

Sec. 1. A provision of a treaty which conflicts with this Constitution shall not be of any force or effect.

Sec. 2. A treaty shall become effective as internal law in the United States only through legislation which would be valid in the absence of treaty.

Sec. 3. Congress shall have power to regulate all executive and other agreements with any foreign power or international organization. All such agreements shall be subject to the limitations imposed on treaties by this article.[11]

Proponents argue that the amendment will make it unmistakable that treaties cannot enlarge or violate the Constitution. Treaties affecting internal law must be implemented through legislation which (this is the "which clause") could have been passed without a treaty. Section 3 would bring executive agreements under congressional control and would subject them to the "which clause."

Opponents of the Bricker amendment maintain that it would seriously weaken this country in international relations, that there is no valid basis for fear of the abuse of the foreign affairs power by the President and the Senate under the present provisions of the Constitution, that adequate checks are in the hands of Congress and the courts. The procedure for treaty making and ratifying would be so cumbersome and involved that the necessary flexibility for an age of crisis would be lost. In 1954 the Senate joint resolution containing the Bricker amendment secured favorable Senate committee ac-

[11] S. J. Res. 1, 83d Cong., 1st Sess. This is the text given in John W. Bricker, "Making Treaties and Other International Agreements," *Annals of the American Academy,* vol. 289 (September, 1953), pp. 136–137. The wording was altered in the 84th Congress.

tion. But it failed, by a margin of only one vote, to muster the necessary two-thirds majority of the whole Senate. Resubmitted in recast form to the Eighty-fourth Congress, the amendment promises to come up again and again despite vigorous opposition from the Eisenhower Administration.

JUDICIAL AND ADMINISTRATIVE POWERS

Pardons and Reprieves. The President's power to grant pardons and reprieves is judicial in nature, and it is exclusive. A pardon is a release from liability for punishment. If the pardon is absolute, it wipes out all charges and restores the condition that existed before the alleged crime was committed. If it is conditional, it may leave certain disabilities or obligations on the offender. A reprieve, also issued by the executive, postpones the execution of a penalty; its use may be dictated by humanitarian considerations, or by the expectation of new evidence. An amnesty is a group pardon, issued by the President to a class of offenders. A good example of amnesty is Jefferson's freeing of all convicted under the Sedition Act of 1798.

In general, Congress cannot restrict the President in the exercise of his pardoning power. A congressional attempt to avoid by statute the full effect of President Johnson's proclamation of amnesty for Confederates convicted of treason was declared unconstitutional on the ground that it interfered with the pardoning power.[12] A nice problem in the separation of powers is raised with the question of whether the President may pardon a person found guilty of contempt of a Federal court or one of the houses of Congress. It appears that the President may pardon any offender except those convicted by impeachment. President Roosevelt issued a last-minute pardon to Dr. Francis E. Townsend, old-age-pension advocate, who was held in contempt of a House of Representatives investigating committee; no contest arose, however, for the leading sponsor of the pardon was the chairman of the House com-

mittee. Even earlier a presidential pardon for contempt of court was upheld in the Supreme Court.[13]

Execution of the Laws. The constitutional provision that the President ". . . shall take Care that the Laws be faithfully executed . . ." and that section requiring his oath to preserve, protect, and defend the Constitution give the executive very broad responsibilities. In practice, Congress confers upon subordinate officials and upon independent agencies law-enforcement duties. The President's role is to oversee execution of the laws. This general responsibility is carried out through the various powers of the President—appointment, war, foreign affairs, legislative—and through an indefinite authority that flows from his oath and the execution of the laws clause.

A striking illustration of this extra authority is found in one of the most dramatic cases in American constitutional law, *in re* Neagle.[14] Because of an adverse court decision, David S. Terry and his adventuress wife threatened bodily harm to Mr. Justice Field of the Supreme Court. Acting under no specific law, a deputy marshal was assigned to protect Field while riding circuit in California. Meeting Field in a railroad-station restaurant, Terry attacked him, and the marshal shot and killed Terry. The marshal, Neagle, was charged in the state court with murder. The Federal court issued a writ of habeas corpus directing his release, and it was upheld in the Supreme Court. The highest tribunal declared that the executive possessed authority implied by the nature of government under the Constitution. It follows, therefore, that the President may use as much force as necessary or expedient to execute the laws and protect federal property and agents.

In enforcing the law the President has very great discretion. First he must interpret the law, a process that touches upon both legislative

---

[12] *Ex parte* Garland, 4 Wall. 333 (U.S. 1867).

[13] *Ex parte* Grossman, 267 U.S. 87, 122 (1925).

[14] 135 U.S. 1 (1890). The background of the case is described in interesting fashion by Carl B. Swisher, *Stephen J. Field, Craftsman of the Law* (Brookings, 1930), pp. 321–361.

and judicial sides. After interpretation, the President decides which laws to enforce vigorously, slightly, or not at all. The laws on the statute books are so extensive that the President and his subordinates must pick and choose those that are to be singled out for particular attention.

Inherent Power Limited. A highly significant controversy over the powers of the President arose during the Korean conflict over the government's seizure of the steel industry in 1952. The United Steelworkers of America voted to strike on Jan. 1 if negotiations failed to produce a satisfactory new contract when the old one expired. The strike was deferred in order to allow time for the Wage Stabilization Board [15] to consider the issues. In March the WSB recommended a pay boost, union shop, and fringe benefits. This settlement was accepted by the union but rejected by the steel industry. On Apr. 8, on the eve of the new strike deadline, President Truman seized the steel industry and directed the Secretary of Commerce to operate it. A district court judge ruled the seizure invalid in late April, and the appeal was hurried into the Supreme Court.

Mill owners' counsel argued that the presidential order constituted lawmaking, a function expressly confined to the Congress. The government attorneys based their case not on any specific powers granted to the President by statutes, but on the aggregate of his "inherent" powers exercised to avert a national catastrophe. No specific statute was cited as justification for the action. The Court ruled that the President lacked the authority to order the seizure, possessing the power neither as Commander in Chief, nor as custodian of executive power, nor as executor of the laws, nor as Chief Executive acting under the aggregate of his powers.[16] The

minority opinion stressed the paramount responsibility of the President faithfully to execute the laws.

LEGISLATIVE POWERS

The Veto Power. The Founding Fathers also departed from strict separation of powers by giving the President power to recommend and to veto legislation. Bills passed by both houses of Congress must be submitted to the President before becoming law. If he approves, he signs a measure. If he disapproves, he returns it to the house of origin with his objections. The proposed legislation is then dead unless each house votes by a two-thirds majority to pass it over his veto, in which case it becomes law without presidential approval. If the President does not return the bill within 10 days, excluding Sundays, it becomes law without his signature. But if Congress adjourns before the 10 days have elapsed, the President may kill the bill simply by failing to act upon it; this is a "pocket veto," [17] and it is absolute. The President may approve legislation within the 10-day limit even when Congress has finally adjourned.[18]

All bills and joint resolutions except constitutional amendments are sent to the President for approval. Concurrent resolutions, in which both houses join in a declaration of principles or opinion, and simple resolutions, which deal with internal affairs of one house, need not be sent to the President because neither has the effect of law.[19]

[15] Created in 1950 to administer the wage-stabilization functions of the Defense Production Act of 1950, and the labor dispute functions defined in Executive Order 10233. The agency was abolished following the Korean armistice.

[16] Youngstown Sheet and Tube Co. *v.* Sawyer, 343 U.S. 579 (1951). The majority opinion was written by Mr. Justice Black. The dissenting opinion came from Chief Justice Vinson. The vote was 6 to 3.

[17] Okanogan Indians *v.* United States, 279 U.S. 655 (1929). An attack on the pocket veto was made in the 79th Congress through H. Res. 98, which would change the rules of the House to make delivery to the clerk delivery to the House during interim periods between sessions of the same Congress.

[18] Edwards *v.* United States, 286 U.S. 482 (1932).

[19] In recent years Congress has been encroaching on the President's veto power by using the concurrent resolution to nullify executive acts and terminate delegated powers. Both the Reorganization Act of 1939 and the Lend-Lease Act of 1941 contained provisions for nullification or termination by concurrent resolution. The problem is discussed in Howard White, "The Concurrent Resolution in Congress," *American Political Science Review*, vol. 35 (October, 1941), pp. 886–889;

Governors in thirty-eight states are empowered to exercise the "item veto" in respect to appropriation bills, but the President does not possess this power. The item veto gives the executive power to strike out specific sections or parts yet sign the remaining portion of the bill. During the decade of the thirties, after Congress showed an inability to resist group pressure for higher and higher appropriations, a proposal to give the President an item veto arose. A general item-veto power could not be conferred without a constitutional amendment, and dozens have been proposed in the House and Senate. Although a considerable amount of support for this scheme has been evident at times, no action has yet been taken. Interest then shifted to the possibility of inserting a clause into each appropriation bill, bestowing on the President the power to strike out items. Competent attorneys have maintained that this power may be given by Congress without constitutional amendment. In favor of giving the President an item veto are the arguments that it will help reduce extravagance, eliminate pork-barrel legislation, and assure executive responsibility for fiscal affairs. Contrariwise, it is argued that legislative responsibility will be weakened and presidential power increased to an unwarranted extent.[20]

Power to Recommend Legislation. Presidential authority to recommend legislation and call special sessions of Congress is found in Article II, Section 3:

He shall from time to time give to the Congress Information of the State of the Union, and recommend to their Consideration such Measures as he shall judge necessary and expedient; he may, on extraordinary Occasions, convene both Houses, or

and John D. Millett and Lindsay Rogers, "The Legislative Veto and the Reorganization Act of 1939," *Public Administration Review,* vol. 1 (Winter, 1941), pp. 176–189. The Administrative Reorganization Act of 1949 provided that either house could nullify a reorganization plan proposed by the President.

[20] See Bryant Putney, "Extension of the Veto Power," *Editorial Research Reports,* vol. 2, no. 24 (Dec. 28, 1937). A Gallup poll released Nov. 16, 1945, showed strong public support for giving the item veto to the President by constitutional amendment.

either of them, and in Case of Disagreement, between them, with Respect to the Time of Adjournment, he may adjourn them to such Time as he shall think proper; . . .

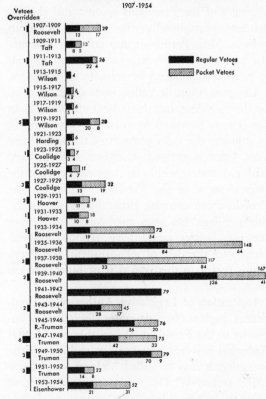

PRESIDENTIAL VETOES
1907-1954

The use of the veto varies widely from President to President and from period to period. Note that the largest number of vetoes overridden (Wilson, 1919–1921, and Truman, 1947–1948) occurred when a President of one party faced a Congress of another.

The President's major annual message, roughly comparable to the Speech from the Throne in British countries, is called the State of the Union message. Both Washington and Adams delivered their important messages in person and orally. Jefferson declined to appear before Congress, preferring to send written messages. Wilson revived the practice of appearing personally, and it has been continued since that time. Lesser messages may be sent in considerable number; they are read by a clerk, often inaudibly, and printed in the *Congressional Record*.

The personal appearance of a President before a joint session calls public and congressional attention to his message, which now invariably is heard by tens of millions over the radio and heard and seen by additional millions through television and newsreel. The annual and special messages of the Presidents recommend the enactment of certain bills or the adoption of certain policies. Most Presidents also attempt to secure the passage of their proposals through appeals to public opinion and by pressure on Congress.

Congress may be called into special session by the President, but the federal executive lacks the power, possessed by many state governors, to stipulate the exact purpose of the special session. Once assembled, Congress may proceed with any matter within its competence, even the impeachment of the President. Although the President can convene either house separately, this privilege has been used very little. Since the two houses rarely have serious disagreement over the date of adjournment, the President's power in this regard is of little practical importance.

Delegation of Legislative Authority to President. Congress often delegates discretionary authority to the President. When this presidential discretion involves actual policy making by the executive, it may be called "delegation of legislative authority." On two occasions in recent years the courts ruled that Congress made unconstitutional delegations of legislative authority to the executive. Both of these cases arose out of the National Recovery Act of 1933. The first concerned a provision in the law giving the President discretion to bar from interstate commerce oil produced in excess of state quotas. Here the Court ruled that Congress failed to establish sufficient standards or policy to guide the executive.[21] The second case arose over the general NRA code-making authority which the Court found delegated lawmaking to an even greater extent and was therefore even more unconstitutional.[22]

Other instances of delegation have received approval in the courts, or have not been tested. The flexible tariff, under which the President may alter duties on imports as much as 50 per cent, was found constitutional.[23] The special responsibility of the President for foreign affairs has been treated already; congressional delegation of power to proclaim when a state of war exists between other countries was declared valid in the Curtiss-Wright case. No one has successfully challenged the validity of vesting in the executive the authority to alter the gold content of the dollar.

It is difficult to draw the line between invalid delegation and valid delegation. The general rule is that Congress must fix primary standards. After these are fixed, power to fill in details may be conferred upon the executive. The Court has not, however, been consistent, and the line of demarcation between proper and improper delegation can only be guessed, after careful reading of the cases cited and judging the contemporary temper of the Court.

Emergency Powers. Congress has conferred upon the President by law many powers that the executive may exercise only during an "emergency." The existence of such powers was brought forcibly to the attention of the nation when the newly inaugurated President, Franklin Roosevelt, proclaimed a bank holiday and prohibited gold and silver exports and foreign exchange transactions. This action was taken under the "Trading with the Enemy Act" of 1917; doubt whether the act was still in force existed, but the President's proclamation was validated three days later by the Emergency Banking Act, and the President was given control over gold during a "national emergency."

After this beginning followed a decade of controversy over emergency powers. Congress repeatedly added to this category of presidential

[21] Panama Refining Co. *v.* Ryan, 293 U.S. 388 (1935). For a fuller discussion, see p. 96.

[22] Schechter Poultry Corp. *v.* United States, 295 U.S. 495 (1935). See also p. 473.

[23] Hampton & Co. *v.* United States, 276 U.S. 394 (1928). The constitutionality of reciprocal trade agreements appears assured from an earlier decision on the 1890 law giving the President power to suspend the free list on articles of any country discriminating against the United States. See Marshall Field & Co. *v.* Clark, 143 U.S. 649 (1892).

authority, although not without strong opposition. In point of fact, however, much of the heat was over delegation of discretionary authority to the President without limitation as to emergency periods. The definition of an emergency is left to the President, but it is clear that either periods of foreign danger or economic depression or both are implied in the various statutes.

THE CHIEF MAGISTRATE

The People's Choice. James Bryce, one of the greatest foreign students of American institutions, entitled a short chapter in his *American Commonwealth* "Why Great Men Are Not Chosen Presidents." [24] He gave three reasons: (1) A small proportion of first-rate Americans enter politics; (2) American politics offers few opportunities for individual distinction; and (3) prominent men make more enemies than "safe" men. Bryce was impressed with the excess of party loyalty and the power of party organization; he blamed party managers for choosing undistinguished candidates rather than risking loss of an election with a prominent one. Looking back over American history, one may see that Bryce was troubled especially by the fact that between Jackson and Lincoln a number of inconspicuous politicians and soldiers served as Presidents, and that Clay, Calhoun, and Webster, the leading men of the time, never reached the chief executive office. If Bryce could have reviewed 150 years of the American presidency, instead of two-thirds of that, he certainly would have been impressed with men who came later. There is evidence in his own subsequent writings that he modified the views previously expressed.[25]

The nominating method affects the quality of presidential timber greatly. The candidate must be reasonably prominent in the country. Some record in public office is almost indispensable— usually as a governor or a federal department head, seldom as a Senator or Representative. His own policy convictions and beliefs are important in relation to conditions in the country

and sentiment in the party. Personal factors, like religion and personality, are taken into consideration. The aspirant for the presidency normally must have some solid political support, especially in his own state. Presidential hopefuls are most likely to be successful in getting a major party nomination if they reside in a large and pivotal state. A state ranking below twelfth or fifteenth in population is quite unlikely to produce a serious candidate. Moreover, if the state is sure to go for one party, neither party, under normal conditions, will choose a candidate from that state. The party naturally takes for granted a state that it wins regularly; the party with a hopeless position in a given state will gain nothing from seeking a candidate there.

The successful candidate for the presidency may be the active leader of his party if he has the personal qualities and can command the backing. Theodore Roosevelt, Woodrow Wilson, and Franklin D. Roosevelt all made vigorous party leaders. William H. Taft, Warren Harding, and Calvin Coolidge made no real effort to dominate party affairs. Under favorable political conditions and with the requisite personal qualities, the President can be a strong executive. He is elected by the whole people; he can take swift, decisive action.

Able men increasingly are elected President. When the two parties are evenly balanced, the candidates put forward by each tend to be outstanding. When one party enjoys a considerable majority over the other, the minority party appears to find the stronger candidates, as with Cleveland, Wilson, and Franklin D. Roosevelt by the Democrats.

Future of Executive Power. Although sentiment against additional authority for the President had reached a high pitch by the end of the Second World War, it was obvious that any halt in the expansion of executive powers was likely to be temporary rather than permanent. Under the American system of government, leadership must come, if there is to be any, from the President. Even if the Congress should reorganize itself by concentrating authority in the hands of its own leaders, this action would be unlikely

[24] (Macmillan, 2 vols., 1889), vol. 1, pp. 71–80.
[25] See especially James Bryce, *Modern Democracies* (Macmillan, 2 vols., 1921), vol. II, pp. 66–76.

to upset the trend toward placing more and more responsibility on the Chief Executive. Strengthening the Congress is essential. The House and Senate should do more of their own thinking and planning and drafting. The Union will still look to the President, however, for broad national leadership, and Congress will continue to get most of its proposed bills from the executive agencies that are doing the day-to-day job of administering existing law.

Actually, further expansion of executive power may be expected. The conditions of the modern world are so critical, both in war and in peace, that speedy and positive action is necessary. The President alone can provide this kind of leadership. Congress can investigate, criticize, revise, and do certain other things well, but the legislative branch is unable to act swiftly enough to beat an aggressor to the punch some Sunday morning at 8 A.M. E.S.T. Therefore, contingents of United States armed forces might be ordered to meet an invasion of Norway without a declaration of war by Congress. Congress has found itself unable to resist pressure groups sufficiently to reduce tariffs or to reorganize administrative agencies. Finally, the job is delegated to the President. Many Americans demand strong executive leadership; others decry the trend, fearing for the future of democracy with so much power in a single executive.

FOR FURTHER READING

(See also works listed at end of preceding chapter.)

Berdahl, Clarence A.: *The War Powers of the Executive in the United States* (University of Illinois Press, 1921).

Binkley, Wilfred E.: *President and Congress* (Knopf, 1947).

——: *The Powers of the President* (Doubleday, 1937).

Chamberlain, Lawrence H.: *The President, Congress, and Legislation* (Columbia University Press, 1946).

Corwin, Edward S.: *The President's Control of Foreign Relations* (Princeton University Press, 1917).

Harris, Joseph P.: *Advice and Consent of the Senate* (University of California Press, 1953).

Hart, James: *Tenure of Office under the Constitution* (Johns Hopkins Press, 1930).

——: *The Ordinance-making Powers of the President of the United States* (Johns Hopkins Press, 1925).

Herring, E. Pendleton: *Presidential Leadership: the Political Relations of Congress and the Chief Executive* (Farrar, Straus, 1940).

Holt, William S.: *Treaties Defeated by the Senate: A Study of the Struggle between President and Senate over the Conduct of Foreign Relations* (Johns Hopkins Press, 1933).

Humbert, William H.: *The Pardoning Power of the President* (American Council on Public Affairs, 1941).

Larkin, John D.: *The President's Control over the Tariff* (Harvard University Press, 1936).

McClure, Wallace M.: *International Executive Agreements: Democratic Procedure under the Constitution of the United States* (Columbia University Press, 1941).

Milton, George F.: *The Use of Presidential Power, 1789–1943* (Little, Brown, 1944).

Morganston, C. E.: *The Appointing and Removal Power of the President of the United States,* S. Doc. 172, 70th Cong., 2d Sess. (1929).

Rich, Bennett M.: *The Presidents and Civil Disorder* (Brookings, 1941).

Small, Norman J.: *Some Presidential Interpretations of the Presidency* (Johns Hopkins Press, 1932).

Taft, William H.: *Our Chief Magistrate and His Powers* (Columbia University Press, 1916).

U.S. Senate, Committee on the Judiciary: *Treaties and Executive Agreements: Hearing before a Subcommittee. . . .* 83d Cong., 1st Sess. (1953).

REVIEW QUESTIONS

1. What is the scope of the President's power to appoint and remove?

2. Describe senatorial courtesy and indicate how it operates in practice.

3. What are the war powers of the President? To what extent could Congress constitutionally restrict his authority to assign the armed forces where and when he sees fit?

4. Indicate the length and breadth of the treaty power. To what extent have the rights of citizens under the Constitution and the Bill of Rights been abridged under it?

5. Define "pardon," "reprieve," and "amnesty."

6. Describe the "seizure" of the steel industry in 1952, and explain the Supreme Court's verdict on its constitutionality.

7. To what extent is the title "chief legislator" properly applied to the President of the United States?

8. What options has the President when he receives a bill passed by both houses of Congress? Explain each.

9. Explain the following: "pocket veto," "item veto," "regular veto."

10. What additional authority accrues to the President by virtue of his role as party leader and "the people's choice"?

CHAPTER 16

Federal Courts and Law Enforcement

> [The American] . . . is probably the most complex legal system in the world; a system where constitutionally independent courts of the Nation operate side by side—and often in identical matters—with the separate court systems of each of the sovereign forty-eight states; where federal courts administer state law and state courts administer federal law; where the very essence of federalism, the areas where federal and state law touch and overlap, is made integral in the national judicial structure to a degree greater than in any other federated government. — Leland L. Tolman [1]

While courts are essential in all organized societies, their organization and role vary with the form of government, political theories, social and economic relationships, traditions, and customs. Thus, British courts differ in organization and function from those of the United States in spite of their common origin. The courts of France, Switzerland, and the Soviet Union differ even more. American courts have changed little in form over the years, but the role they perform has been far from static. Modernizing and adapting them to our changing society is a task calling for the wisest statesmanship.

THE ROLE OF THE COURTS

Settling Disputes. One of the oldest functions of courts is that of deciding who is "right" in a dispute. It may be that two or more private individuals are engaged in controversy. If so, this is a *civil* case. Rather than permit the contestants to resort to violence, courts exist to hear the claims and make a decision. Or it may be that a government, or government official, is

involved in controversy with private citizens over a matter involving monetary damages. This is also a civil case even though the government is one of the parties.

Or it may be that the government is accusing someone of violating a law and is seeking to inflict punishment upon the accused. When this is taken to court it becomes a *criminal* case. Or it may be that a dispute arises which cannot be settled by criminal prosecution or ordinary civil suit. This may be a case in *equity*. In cases like these the courts provide "substantial justice" when a remedy "at law" is not readily available. Thus, if one believes an act of Congress unconstitutional, the only way relief can be obtained, since the government cannot be prosecuted or sued without its consent, is by asking a Federal court for an injunction to prevent further enforcement of the objectionable statute. This would be a case in equity. To illustrate further, a Federal court might mistakenly have sentenced a man to 10 years' imprisonment when the maximum allowed by the law was 5 years. A request for correction would be a case in equity.

Settling disputes involves several different

[1] *Columbia Law Review,* vol. 54 (April, 1954), p. 650.

286

functions. One of the most important is that of fact finding. Doing this thoroughly, expeditiously, and fairly is essential but by no means easy. It may be done in ordinary civil and criminal cases with the help of grand and petit juries or, where the law permits, by judicial officers themselves. In cases requiring the review of administrative orders and decisions of regulatory bodies, like the Federal Trade Commission, facts as found by the government agency are usually accepted by the courts if supported by sufficient evidence. Dispute settlement also requires proper conduct of the trial, interpretation of the law, application of the law to the particular case, review by appellate tribunals, rule making, and judicial administration.

Interpreting the Law. Courts have also to interpret the law. The types of law applicable in the United States are constitutional, statutory, administrative, international, and common. *Constitutional law* is, as the name suggests, the fundamental law, which in the United States is embedded in written constitutions. *Statutory law* stems from acts of legislative bodies. *Administrative law* arises from the orders and decisions of executives, administrators, and so-called "independent establishments." *International law* arises from treaties, agreements, and customs followed by national states in their dealings with one another and with citizens of other states. *Common law* is a body of legal precepts founded on reason as applied in past judicial decisions. It obtains in all American states except Louisiana, but there is no federal common law. Federal courts are guided by common-law principles, but the fact that the national government is based on delegated powers precludes judicial application of the common law itself.

Whatever the law involved, the meaning of words and phrases may be obscure when an attempt is made to relate them to concrete situations. So far as the Constitution is concerned, the part played by the courts in expanding its meaning has been discussed in Chap. 4. The judicial role is equally significant where other types of law are concerned. When, for example, a statute or executive order uses the word "may," does this mean "shall"? Does the word "acquire" give authority to take by condemnation? Does a nineteenth-century statute governing "vehicles" today govern motorcars and airplanes? Does the term "innkeeper" refer to one who operates an overnight tourist motel? How undressed must one be to be legally "nude"? When does a tramp become a "vagrant"? How fast is "forthwith"? The law abounds with such words as "due," "reasonable," "fair," "equitable," and "proper." Construing words like these is one of the important tasks of courts.

In performing this task, the courts follow the rule of *stare decisis; i.e.,* they follow precedent established in previous cases unless there is some compelling reason for not doing so. But following precedents may mean that social concepts, cruelties, and injustices from the past are projected into modern times. Moreover, in making decisions judges often reflect personal predilections and establish new rules, or "judge-made law."

Lawmaking by the judiciary became so pronounced in the United States, especially after the Civil War, that it evoked much controversy and serious thought.[2] Among the questions raised was the one of whether it was consistent with democratic theory and practice to permit the judicial branch, which by its nature and organization is the most insulated from the popular will, to play such an important part in formulating public policies. Why should judges appointed for life terms, critics ask, be permitted to decide whether or not there is to be racial segregation in the states when this is a subject of vast social and political import? Why should judges be permitted to prevent Congress from enacting child-labor legislation for more than 20 years? Why should judges be permitted to prevent the states from enacting minimum wage laws for women for nearly a quarter of a cen-

[2] For excellent recent studies of the subject see: Fred V. Cahill, Jr., *Judicial Legislation: A Study in American Legal Theory* (Ronald, 1952); Jerome Frank, *Courts on Trial* (Princeton University Press, 1949); and Milton R. Konvitz (ed.), *Law and Social Action: Selected Essays of Alexander H. Pekelis* (Cornell University Press, 1950).

tury? Why should judges make it so difficult for Federal and state governments to regulate business corporations?

While critics raised questions like these, the general public acquiesced until revolt broke into the open in 1937. Since this date the controversy has lessened, except where civil rights are concerned, but the issue is by no means resolved. Regardless of whether one favors more or less judicial intervention in public affairs, it is obvious that as interpreters of law the courts are less aloof from the political process than is suggested by formal robes, ancient ritual, and somber courtrooms.

Checking and Balancing. In Chap. 4 it was pointed out that judicial review was a fundamental principle of the American system of government. Accordingly, restraining the executive and legislative branches is an important function of the courts. While fear of judicial annulment serves constantly as a restraint, comparatively few acts of the President and Congress have actually been declared unconstitutional.[3]

With the three branches of government separated, disputes will inevitably arise between them. Those between the executive and Congress are likely to be short-lived inasmuch as frequent elections permit differences to be resolved by the voters. The situation is different, however, in the event of controversy between the political branches and the courts. Judges are appointed for life, and their interpretations of the Constitution may mean that no legislation is possible for long periods of time until the Constitution can be amended. Though judicial review is generally accepted, it is also widely recognized that the courts must exercise self-restraint if they are not to negate powers granted to the other branches of government.

The 1937 Controversy. Usually when acts of Congress are declared unconstitutional there is a short flurry of criticism which soon subsides, but this is not what happened during the early days of the New Deal.

Between 1933 and 1937 the Supreme Court

[3] For acts of Congress declared unconstitutional, see p. 53.

consisted of nine justices, all of whom had been appointed prior to 1933 and all but two of whom (McReynolds and Brandeis) had been appointed by Republican presidents. Their average age was seventy-two (in 1937), the highest in Supreme Court history, and it so happened that four (McReynolds, Sutherland, Butler, and Van Devanter) of the six who were over seventy were "conservatives," while the fifth (Chief Justice Hughes) was a "middle-of-the-roader" and only the sixth (Brandeis) a "liberal."

In 3 years this court declared New Deal statutes, or provisions thereof, unconstitutional in twelve instances, five of them during the court term beginning in October, 1935. On most of the measures the Court was sharply divided into "conservative" and "liberal" blocs, as is shown in the table opposite. It is apparent that Justices Hughes and Roberts held the balance of power. This meant that in 5-to-4 decisions, of which there were ten during the 4-year period, either Hughes or Roberts cast the deciding vote, and in all probability it was the latter oftener than the Chief Justice.

The situation as it existed during President Roosevelt's first term was unprecedented in several ways. First, the economic crisis was of major proportions, an emergency psychology was present, and the President was one of such character as to act boldly—even rashly, as many insist. Second, the justices were older than at any other period. Third, no vacancies occurred during the 4-year period. Fourth, seldom, if ever, had the Supreme Court been so rigidly and evenly divided into blocs. Fifth, never had the courts been called upon to pass judgment upon so many measures involving extremely controversial points of constitutional law in such a short period of time, and in no similar period had they declared so many statutes unconstitutional.

Flushed with victory in the election of November, 1936,[4] the President decided upon a showdown with the courts. Less than 3 weeks

[4] Nothing was said, however, in the platform of the Democratic party or by the President during the campaign which foreshadowed the drastic proposals that the President later submitted.

Affiliation of Supreme Court Justices with Majority and Minority Groups * (On basis of 27 important cases decided between 1933 and 1937)	Justice	By whom appointed and when	Age, 1937	Voted for constitutionality (No. of cases)	Voted against constitutionality (No. of cases)	Per cent favorable to New Deal	
	Brandeis......	Wilson '16	81	19	8	0.704	"Liberals"
	Stone.........	Coolidge '25	65	20	7	0.741	
	Cardozo......	Hoover '32	67	20	7	0.741	
	Roberts.......	Hoover '32	62	15	12	0.555	Held balance of power
	Hughes........	Hoover '30	75	17	10	0.626	
	Van Devanter.	Taft '10	78	6	21	0.222	"Conservatives"
	Sutherland....	Harding '22	75	6	21	0.222	
	Butler........	Harding '22	71	5	22	0.185	
	McReynolds...	Wilson '14	75	4	23	0.148	

* For a similar chart based upon a smaller sampling of cases, see H. Arthur Steiner, *Significant Supreme Court Decisions, 1934–1937* (Wiley, 2d ed., 1937), p. 6. See also Charles Herman Prichett, *The Roosevelt Court: A Study in Judicial Politics and Values, 1937–1947* (Macmillan, 1948).

after inauguration, on Feb. 4, he sent a message to Congress which prompted one of the most exciting debates in American history.

Court Enlargement Plan. The immediate target of the President's proposals was the aged justices on the Supreme and lower courts.[5] Age undoubtedly has its effect upon judicial decisions and there have been many, including the then Chief Justice,[6] who have advocated retirement at seventy-five or earlier. To compel retirement, however, required a constitutional amendment, and the President was unwilling to brook the delays and difficulties which this would certainly encounter.

[5] Besides the six on the Supreme Court, a total of twenty-four judges who were seventy or over sitting on lower courts were affected by the President's bill. *Adverse Report on Reorganization of the Federal Judiciary,* S. Rept. 711, 75th Cong., 1st Sess. (1937), p. 33.

[6] Charles E. Hughes, *The Supreme Court of the United States* (Columbia University Press, 1928), pp. 73–77.

Accordingly, he proposed to "rejuvenate" the courts by making it possible to appoint a new judge for every federal judge who had served 10 years and who remained on the bench after reaching the age of seventy, provided the Supreme Court should never exceed fifteen and not more than fifty new judges should be added to the lower courts. This would tend to embarrass older judges into retiring or resigning, but if they chose to remain it was with knowledge that younger judges might be appointed to "assist" and perhaps counterbalance their conservatism. Since there were at the time six justices on the Supreme Court over seventy, had they not retired the President might have appointed six additional judges, raising the membership of the Court to the maximum of fifteen. As things then stood, the addition of six "liberals" to the three already on the Court would have ensured more favorable consideration of "New Deal" legislation.

Improving Court Management. Three additional proposals were less controversial. One was that the Chief Justice be empowered to assign circuit and district judges to serve temporarily in districts other than their own. Another, that the Supreme Court be authorized to appoint a "proctor" who would be a business manager for the judicial system with the expectation that delays and inefficiencies might be eliminated. The third was that when the constitutionality of a federal law was challenged in a private suit before a lower court, the Attorney General should be notified and given opportunity of defending the law.

Moreover, it was suggested that such cases should be decided only by courts consisting of three judges. Furthermore, if the lower court should declare the law unconstitutional, either the Attorney General or one of the private parties might take an appeal directly to the Supreme Court. This, it was hoped, would eliminate the situation where private parties could rush to district courts and obtain injunctions from a single judge which would render the enforcement of an act of Congress impossible for several months or years while the measure was running the gamut of legal procedures en route to the Supreme Court where final judgment would be rendered.

The proposal that new justices be authorized for those who failed to retire or resign was defeated in its entirety. Out of it, however, came a measure permitting Supreme Court justices with 10 years of service to retire at seventy with full pay. Otherwise, all the President's recommendations were adopted at the time or have been since, either in whole or in part. By an act dated Aug. 24, 1937, district judges may be transferred from one district to another within the same judicial circuit by the senior circuit judge, or from within one circuit to another by the Chief Justice. By the same act, the Attorney General must be given notice of proceedings involving the constitutionality of federal statutes. Moreover, all such proceedings must be conducted before courts consisting of three judges, one of whom must be a circuit judge.[7]

[7] Temporary restraining orders may still be issued by a single judge when delay would cause irreparable damage.

Still further, if the decision is against the constitutionality of a statute, the case may be appealed by either party directly to the Supreme Court where the matter must be heard "at the earliest possible time and shall take precedence over all other matters not of a like character." The proposal to create a business manager for the courts was defeated at the time but adopted 2 years later with the establishment of the Administrative Office of the United States Courts.

Court Changes without "Packing." Although failure to enact the principal feature of his program was a serious political defeat, it has been said that the President "lost his battle but won his war." There is truth in the statement. Shortly after the controversy, vacancies occurred by resignation, retirement, or death, permitting the appointment of younger men. By the fall of 1937 the "liberals" were clearly in the majority and by September, 1942, only two of the men who constituted the Supreme Court during the President's first term (Stone and Roberts) remained, while the President had appointed 38 out of the 55 sitting on the Courts of Appeals and 138 of the 230 judges sitting on district and other United States courts. It is safe to say that all of these appointees held views acceptable to the President at the time of appointment.

Even before any changes were made in the personnel of the Supreme Court, the Court manifested a change of mind by (1) reversing its previous attitude toward state minimum-wage laws for women; (2) redefining the commerce clause to include manufacturing; (3) upholding the tax provisions of the Social Security Act; and (4) upholding the Railway Labor Act. Although still not without reverberations, the President's reelection for a third term in 1940 and the outbreak of war in 1941 silenced criticism. Meanwhile, the country adjusted itself to an interpretation of the Constitution that greatly broadened the powers of both the Federal government and the states.

The 1952 Controversy over Inherent Powers. The checking and balancing function was again illustrated in 1952. Then, it will be recalled, President Truman seized the steel mills and kept them operating pending settlement of a dispute between labor and management. The President argued that his constitutional authority to take care that the laws are faithfully executed and to be Commander in Chief of the Army and Navy justified his action even though Congress had passed no legislation stipulating when and how seizure was to be made. First the district court held the President's action unconstitutional and the steel mills reverted to their owners; then the Court of Appeals stayed the lower court's order pending review by the Supreme Court and the mills opened again under government management; finally, in almost record-breaking time (less than 2 months after the mills had been seized), the highest court ruled against the President. The mills once more reverted to private owners while the strike recommenced and continued for several weeks afterward. The Supreme Court decision was 6 to 3, and the economic and military consequences were serious, but there was remarkably little indignation registered over the verdict. Once more the American public had witnessed its system of separation of powers and judicial review in full cycle.

Checks on the Courts. Because of the great authority of the courts, a number of proposals have been made to restrict judicial power. Among these are [8] a constitutional amendment forbidding judicial review; setting up a special body to deal with social and economic legislation; the recall of judges, as is provided in the Constitution of Arizona; the recall of judicial decisions, as proposed in the Bull Moose Platform of 1912; permitting Congress by two-thirds vote to override judicial decisions, as proposed by former Senator La Follette; and requiring an extraordinary majority vote by the Supreme Court before invalidating legislation, as now is done in some of the states.

Suggestions like these are heard less often today than formerly. Even without them there are numerous checks on the courts. Judges are human and sensitive to criticism and therefore are not likely to resist the persistent pressure of public opinion. If they grossly misbehave, judges

[8] Cahill, *op. cit.*, pp. 61–62.

can be impeached. Their decisions can be overridden by constitutional amendment, although this is a slow process. Of course, judges die, retire, and resign, providing opportunities for the appointment of younger men. As a last resort, Congress could refuse to appropriate money for judicial salaries and expenses, or amend the jurisdiction of the courts to prevent certain types of cases from ever reaching either the lower courts or the Supreme Court. Indeed, in many respects the judiciary is the weakest of the three branches. It possesses neither the power of purse nor that of sword.

Judicial Administration. The courts must also perform many tasks of an administrative character. In the first place, they have some appointments to make that require the examination and selection of applicants. These include clerks, commissioners, messengers, stenographers, and other aides. Second, each court must superintend civil and criminal procedure. This involves such duties as the issuance of writs and warrants, taking of bail, the appointment of grand and petit juries, the admission of attorneys to practice, the assessment and collection of fees, the admission of evidence, and court procedures in general. Third, the courts handle noncontentious cases, *i.e.,* those in which parties are not in dispute. These include administering estates, appointing receivers in bankruptcy, issuing licenses, performing marriages, and naturalizing aliens. Fourth, the courts must enforce their orders. This is usually done through the issuance of writs by the courts.[9] Disrespect for these

[9] The most common are *warrants,* which are commands for appearance, arrest, search or seizure; *summonses,* which direct plaintiffs in civil suits to appear and make answer to complaints; *subpoenas,* which compel the appearance of witnesses or the production of evidence; *writs of execution,* which direct defendants to satisfy judgments awarded in civil suits; *writs of ejectment,* which eject defendants from real estate held by them which the court has found belongs to plaintiffs; *injunctions,* which restrain from threatened damage to property; *mandamuses,* which order public officials to perform some act required by law; and *certiorari,* which order public officials, especially inferior judicial tribunals, to send up records for review.

may be declared contempt of court and punished by fine or jail.[10]

Until recently, administration was divided between the Department of Justice and the courts. Criticism of the inefficient manner in which the judiciary operated led, in 1922, to the establishment of an annual conference of senior circuit judges under the chairmanship of the Chief Justice. Although many beneficial reforms resulted, responsibility for administration still remained divided. Attention was focused upon the question in 1937 when the President proposed the creation of a "proctor" under the supervision of the Supreme Court with responsibility for administrative matters pertaining to the judicial system; but the proposal was lost sight of in the heat of controversy over the President's alleged attempt to "pack" the courts. Two years later, however, Congress established the Administrative Office of the United States Courts. The office is subordinate to the annual conference of senior circuit judges and the Supreme Court. It is conducted by a director and assistant director appointed by the Supreme Court for as long as their services are satisfactory.

Administrative Office. By the creation of the Administrative Office, a clear distinction was made between judicial administration and law enforcement. The Department of Justice still retains full responsibility for the latter, while the task of over-all administration of the judicial system was centralized in the hands of the Administrative Office. The office is divided into four main divisions. One, called the Division of Business Administration, provides the courts with quarters, supplies, and clerical and administrative service, including the payment of salaries and expenses. The second, called the Division of Procedural Studies and Statistics, is designed to furnish information about the state of judicial business throughout the country and to make recommendations whereby justice may be given with greater dispatch and economy.

[10] Persons may be fined or imprisoned for contempt of court. Trial is usually without jury if the contempt is committed in the presence of the court but otherwise with jury if the defendant insists.

The third, the Probation Division, exercises a general supervision over the federal probation system, which was previously conducted by the Bureau of Prisons in the Department of Justice. The fourth, the Bankruptcy Division, keeps in touch with bankruptcy proceedings pending before Federal courts. One interesting result of the work of the office has been the inauguration of periodic conferences in the various circuits, attended by both federal and state judges and attorneys.

CONSTITUTIONAL COURTS

Where a federal form of government exists, either the Federal government may enforce all law, state as well as national; or the states may enforce all law; or each may assume responsibility for enforcing its own. Under the Articles of Confederation, the states undertook the enforcement of enactments of Congress but this proved so unsatisfactory that the Constitution authorized the Federal government to enforce its own laws, leaving the states to do likewise.

Accordingly, the President, acting through various administrative agencies, is charged with the responsibility of detecting and prosecuting violations of federal laws while a federal judiciary is responsible for the trial of cases involving federal matters. At the same time, each state has a law-enforcement and judicial system of its own. Care must be taken not to confuse the two.

Types of Federal Courts. There are two general types of Federal courts: *constitutional* and *legislative*. Constitutional are those established by authority of Article III to exercise "the judicial power of the United States." They consist of the Supreme Court, circuit courts of appeals, district courts, and the Court of Claims. Legislative courts do not exercise the judicial power but are special courts created to aid with the administration of laws enacted pursuant to powers delegated to Congress.

The difference is not in method of procedure; nor is one created by the Constitution and the other by the legislature. Both are authorized by the Constitution and both are created and organized by Congress. The difference lies in the source of their authority and the nature of the cases over which they have jurisdiction. Article III mentions the types of cases and controversies to which the judicial power extends, and these must all come before constitutional courts. But legislative courts are created as necessary and proper instruments to carry into execution such powers as those of regulating interstate commerce, spending public funds, laying and collecting import duties, and governing the territories. Legislative courts are described later in this chapter.

troversies between citizens of different states (diverse citizenship), (5) controversies between citizens of the same state claiming lands under grants of different states, and (6) controversies between a state, or its citizens, and a foreign state, or its citizens or subjects.

This last has been qualified by the Eleventh Amendment, Congress, and the courts in accordance with the precept that a sovereign cannot be sued without his consent. Accordingly, states now may be sued in Federal courts without their

FEDERAL COURT SYSTEM

Constitutional courts derive their power from Article III, legislative from the powers of Congress. The Court of Claims recently was transferred from legislative to constitutional category. District of Columbia courts are both constitutional and legislative.

CONSTITUTIONAL COURTS

| Supreme Court |
| Courts of Appeals |
| District Courts |
| Court of Claims |

District of Columbia Courts

LEGISLATIVE COURTS

| Customs Court |
| Court of Customs & Patent Appeals |
| Territorial Courts |
| Tax Court of the U.S. |
| Court of Military Appeals |

Jurisdiction. Article III of the Constitution extends "the judicial power of the United States" to nine classes of "cases" and "controversies" [11] depending upon the nature of the subject matter and the character or citizenship of parties in dispute. Those that may be brought because some *federal question* is involved are (1) cases arising under the Constitution, (2) cases arising under federal laws and treaties, and (3) admiralty and maritime cases. Those that may be brought because of the *character or citizenship of the parties* involved include (1) cases affecting ambassadors, other public ministers, and foreign consuls, (2) controversies to which the United States is a party, (3) controversies between two or more states, (4) con-

[11] Because the judicial power extends only to "cases" and "controversies," the Supreme Court has long taken the position that it cannot give advisory opinions (*i.e.,* opinions for the benefit of the President or Congress on the probable constitutionality of contemplated measures) but must wait until real cases arise. The supreme courts of many states issue advisory opinions and many feel that the United States Supreme Court could do likewise without seriously distorting the Constitution.

consent only by another state in the Union or the Federal government itself. If an alien, citizen of another state, or citizen of the same state wishes to sue a state, he can do so only with the consent of the latter, and then only in state courts. States may, however, initiate suits in Federal courts against aliens, citizens of other states, and foreign governments, although it is customary for disputes with the latter to be settled by diplomatic negotiation. Nothing has happened to prevent citizens of a state from suing or being sued by citizens of another state in Federal courts.

Jurisdiction Not Exclusive. Although the cases mentioned above may come before Federal courts, the Constitution does not insist that they be brought there. Congress is free to distribute jurisdiction over them as it pleases. Indeed, Congress may completely divest Federal courts of jurisdiction in certain instances. As matters stand, Federal courts are given *exclusive* jurisdiction over some of them, *concurrent* jurisdiction over others, and totally *denied* consideration of still others. The division of responsibility is as follows:

Exclusively Federal	Concurrent	Denied Federal
1. Civil actions in which states are parties (subject to exceptions noted above)	1. Civil case involving amounts of $3,000 or more	1. Civil suits involving citizens of different states where the amount at issue is less than $3,000
2. All suits and proceedings brought against (but not necessarily those initiated by) ambassadors, others possessing diplomatic immunity, and foreign consuls		
3. All cases involving federal criminal laws		
4. All admiralty, maritime, patent-right, copyright, and bankruptcy cases		
5. All civil cases against the Federal government where consent to sue has been granted		

Supreme Court. Article III states that "The judicial power of the United States shall be vested in one Supreme Court, and in such inferior Courts as Congress may from time to time ordain and establish." Only a Supreme Court is specifically mentioned, its creation being mandatory. Others are "inferior courts" which may be created or abolished by Congress at will.

The Supreme Court was created by the Judiciary Act of 1789. The Court held its first two terms on Wall Street in New York City, but in neither term were there any cases. Its next two terms were held in Philadelphia, thereafter it met in Washington. As first constituted it consisted of a Chief Justice and five associate justices. Its membership was reduced to five in 1801; increased to seven in 1807; increased to nine in 1837 and ten in 1863; reduced to seven in 1866; and in 1869 it was fixed at nine where it has remained ever since.

Justices are appointed by the President by and with the advice and consent of the Senate. No qualifications are stated in the Constitution; hence the President is free to appoint anyone for whom senatorial confirmation can be obtained.

Terms of federal judges are for good behavior and they are removable by impeachment only.[12] After reaching the age of seventy judges may resign and receive full salary as long as they live, provided they have served as federal judges for 10 years or more. Or they may retire at seventy with 10 years of experience, or sixty-five with 15 years of service, and receive full pay for life. If they retire (but not if they resign), they are still federal judges and eligible for service upon assignment in the lower courts. The Chief Justice's salary is $35,500, the associate justices' $35,000. These are fixed by Congress and while they can be raised at any time, they cannot be diminished during the tenure of any particular judge.

[12] To date (1956) nine judges of constitutional courts have been impeached. Of these only four were convicted. Samuel Chase, who was acquitted in 1805, was the only member of the Supreme Court in this group. The number would undoubtedly have been greater had not other judges of minor Federal courts resigned when threatened with impeachment. On the removal of judges, see William S. Carpenter, *Judicial Tenure in the United States* (Yale University Press, 1918).

Characteristics of the Justices. Although the Constitution does not require it, every chief and associate justice has been a lawyer. All have been men. As lawyers, many of them have had large corporations or men of wealth for their clients, others have been professors of law, while still others have spent most of their years in politics or as consultants to administrative agencies. Some have been men of wealth, but most have been moderately well-to-do. Their average age at the time of appointment has been well over fifty, while the average age of those sitting at particular times has varied from about forty-nine to seventy-two years, the latter being as recently as 1937.[13] Most of the judges have been prominent members of the same political party as the President who appointed them. Most of them have had previous political or judicial experience, a number having served on state supreme courts and in Congress. Practically all have come from the Eastern part of the nation, Massachusetts and New York accounting for nearly one-fourth of the total. Most of the justices have been college trained, more having attended Harvard, Yale, and Princeton than any other particular college or university.[14] Some of the justices have been brilliant, more have been of average ability, and a few have been decidedly mediocre. In spite of their robes, justices are human and influenced by the same considerations as other members of the human race.[15]

Jurisdiction. The Supreme Court has original and appellate jurisdiction. Its original jurisdiction extends to two types of cases: (1) those affecting ambassadors, other public ministers, and consuls; and (2) those in which states are

parties. Congress cannot increase the number of cases that may originate before the Supreme Court.[16] In all cases other than those involving states and representatives of foreign governments, the Supreme Court has appellate jurisdiction, both as to law and facts "with such exceptions, and under such regulations as Congress shall make." In accordance with this provision, Congress has defined in detail the appellate jurisdiction of the Court.

Comparatively few cases commence in the Supreme Court and, although juries may be used, they seldom are. The great majority of cases that reach the Supreme Court are started elsewhere. At present, cases come to it from state courts, circuit courts of appeals, and, in a few instances, Federal district courts. Cases reach the Court either by appeal or by writ of certiorari.[17] The expectation is that only questions involving constitutionality and those of great national importance will reach the highest court in the land.

Sessions and Conferences. The Supreme Court begins its term annually on the first Monday in October and usually ends early in the following June. Special sessions may be called by the Chief Justice when the Court is adjourned, but the occasion must be of unusual importance and urgency.[18] All sessions are held in the Court's

---

[13] Justice Story, appointed at the age of thirty-two by President Madison, was the youngest ever to sit on the Court. For data concerning the ages of Supreme Court justices, see U.S. Senate Committee on the Judiciary, *Hearings on S. 1392, a Bill to Reorganize the Judicial Branch of the Government,* 75th Cong., 1st Sess. (6 parts, 1937), part 1. Also see Morris L. Ernst, *The Ultimate Power* (Doubleday, 1937), Chap. XXV.

[14] Ernst, *op. cit.,* p. 296.

[15] For an interesting account of the lives of the Chief Justices up to and including Chief Justice Charles E. Hughes, see Kenneth B. Umbreit, *Our Eleven Chief Justices* (Harper, 1938).

[16] Marbury *v.* Madison, 1 Cranch 137 (U.S. 1803).

[17] On appeal, cases are removed to a superior court for the purpose of subjecting the entire cause—the facts as well as the law—to review and revisal. A *writ of certiorari* is a command issued by a superior court directing an inferior court (state or Federal) to send up the record and proceedings in a cause before verdict, with its certificate to the correctness and completeness of the record, for review or retrial. Formerly many cases reached the Supreme Court by *writ of error.* This was a common-law writ by which the record was removed after final judgment to a superior court for the purpose of obtaining a review of the law (not the facts also) to ascertain whether errors of law were made by a lower court. Congress abolished the writ in 1928, substituting appeal as a method of obtaining relief.

[18] In 1942 the Court held its only special session since 1920 when the justices were called to meet on July 29 to consider a petition for writ of habeas corpus which would have transferred the trial of seven Ger-

beautiful and spacious white marble building located across from the capitol building in Washington.

The Chief Justice is the executive officer of the Court; he presides at all sessions and conferences, and announces its orders. Legally, however, his decisions have no greater weight than those of other justices. The associate justices have precedence according to the date of appointment, or, if two happen to have been appointed at the same time, then according to their age. In the absence of the Chief Justice, the associate justice first in precedence performs his duties. The Court divides its time about equally between the hearing of cases and intervening recesses. That is, the Court holds sessions daily, except Saturday and Sunday, for about 2 weeks and then recesses for 2 weeks during which time the justices study and write opinions.

By the time oral argument is finished the justices have usually made up their minds.[19] Following an examination of records and briefs, the justices compare their views and register their votes at a Saturday's conference. The Chief Justice usually states his opinion first but votes last. After a decision has been reached, the Chief Justice either assigns the opinion to be written to one of those who voted as he did or agrees to write the opinion himself. If he voted with the minority, the senior associate justice in the majority assigns the case to one with whom he agreed. Every judge goes to conference with the knowledge that he may have the responsibility of writing the opinion that will accord with his vote. This means that every justice must be keenly attentive to every case. It also means that every justice must organize his own thoughts inasmuch as he is required to vote before listening to plausible and convincing opinions written by his colleagues. If a majority cannot reach an agreement, the case may be reargued one or more times.

Decisions and Opinions. Several hundred cases reach the Supreme Court each year. A large number of appeals and petitions for writs of certiorari are disposed of without serious consideration for want of jurisdiction or merit. Many petitions for certiorari are merely granted or denied upon comparatively short briefs without oral argument. Others involving rather well settled points of law about which the Court can come to a decision without oral hearings are disposed of in *per curiam* decisions. The remainder are cases of considerable importance and are disposed of only after oral hearing and then in written opinions.

A decision may be unanimous or divided. If divided, both a majority and dissenting opinion are usually written. Again, one or more justices might agree with the conclusion reached in the majority or dissenting opinions but for different reasons. In that event, concurring opinions may be written. Thus, in a case involving complicated and controversial issues, there may be as many as four written opinions: the majority opinion, one dissenting, one concurring with the majority, and another concurring with the minority. Six justices constitute a quorum and at least a majority must concur before a decision is made. If a majority cannot agree, even though the case may be reargued, the decision of the lower court is allowed to stand. Opinions, as well as information about the disposition of other cases, are published and may be found in many libraries in volumes known, since 1882, as *United States Reports.*[20]

---

man saboteurs from the special military tribunal, before which they were then being tried, to the regular courts. The motion was promptly dismissed, the military tribunal resumed its proceedings and shortly thereafter found the defendants guilty. Five were promptly put to death while the other two were sentenced to life imprisonment at hard labor.

[19] These remarks are based upon the account given in Hughes, *op. cit.,* pp. 56–65, an account written by the former Chief Justice after he had been an associate justice but retired to become the Republican presidential candidate in 1916 and before he reentered the Court in 1929.

[20] Prior to 1882 these volumes were published under the name of the court reporter who prepared them for publication. Their titles, the number of volumes, and dates of issue are Dallas, 4 vols., 1790–1800; Cranch, 9 vols., 1801–1815; Wheaton, 12 vols., 1816–1827; Peters, 16 vols., 1828–1842; Howard, 24 vols.,

FEDERAL JUDICIAL CIRCUITS AND DISTRICT COURT AREAS

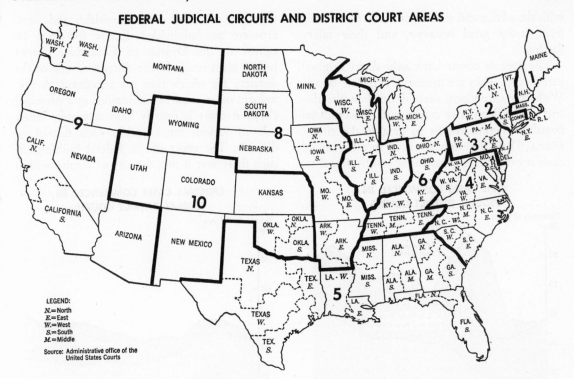

LEGEND:
N.=North
E.=East
W.=West
S.=South
M.=Middle

Source: Administrative office of the
United States Courts

Courts of Appeals. Immediately below the Supreme Court stand the Courts of Appeals, created in 1891 to facilitate the disposition of cases and ease the burden upon the Supreme Court. The courts operate in the District of Columbia and ten circuits, or regions, into which the country and its territories have been divided. Each court comprises from three to nine appeals judges. Each court of appeals usually hears cases in divisions consisting of three judges, but all judges may sit on cases under review. The justices of the Supreme Court may also sit as judges, each within a circuit to which he has been assigned.[21] Time, however, prevents justices of the high court from "riding circuit" as they did in the early days of the republic. District judges may also be assigned to serve on the

1843–1860; Black, 2 vols., 1861–1862; Wallace, 23 vols., 1863–1874; and Otto, 17 vols., 1875–1882.

[21] Since there are ten circuits and only nine Supreme Court justices, one justice is assigned two circuits. In 1955 Justice Clark was assigned to both the eighth and tenth circuits, while the Chief Justice presided over the court of appeals for the District of Columbia as well as the fourth circuit.

appeals courts, although in no case may they sit in judgment of cases in which they may have participated as district judges. In some circuits, court is always held in the same city; in others, it may be held in two or more designated cities. The courts sit at regular intervals in buildings owned or leased by the Federal government. Appeals judges are appointed by the President

CASES COMMENCED IN
FEDERAL COURTS OF APPEALS

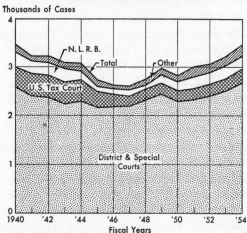

Thousands of Cases

N. L. R. B.
Total
Other
U.S. Tax Court

District & Special Courts

1940   '42   '44   '46   '48   '50   '52   '54
Fiscal Years

with the advice and consent of the Senate. Their term is for good behavior, and their salary $25,500.

The appeals courts have only slight original jurisdiction. They are primarily appellate courts. With few exceptions, cases decided in the district courts, legislative courts, and quasi-judicial boards and commissions go next to the circuit courts. Their decisions are final in all criminal cases not involving questions of constitutionality.

the three districts—eastern, middle, and western—are not subdivided. Except for those assigned to the District of Columbia, district judges must reside in the district, or one of the districts, for which they are appointed. A permanent office must be maintained at a principal city, but court is usually held at regular intervals in various cities within each district or division. The court sits in federal buildings if such there are; if not, the city or county within

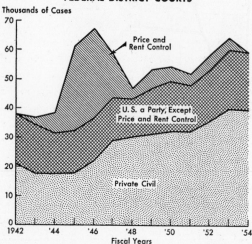

CIVIL CASES COMMENCED IN FEDERAL DISTRICT COURTS

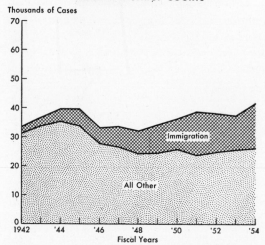

CRIMINAL CASES COMMENCED IN FEDERAL DISTRICT COURTS

Their decisions may be reviewed only by the Supreme Court.

District Courts. Beneath the appeals courts are the United States district courts, of which there are eighty-four in the forty-eight states. From one to as many as eighteen judges serve in each district, although in a few instances one judge serves two or more districts. The judges are appointed by the President with Senate approval. Their term is for good behavior and their salary $22,500. A small state may constitute a district in itself; otherwise, the districts are arranged with respect to population, distance, and volume of business. Some of the districts are subdivided into divisions. California, for example, is comprised of two districts—northern and southern—but each district is subdivided into a northern and southern division. In Nebraska there is only one district but eight divisions. In Pennsylvania, on the other hand,

which court is held provides the building, together with light and heat, without expense to the Federal government.

Excepting the few that originate in the Supreme Court and those of a special nature that commence in the legislative courts, most other cases and controversies start before district courts. Theirs is chiefly original jurisdiction; no cases come to them on appeal, although cases begun in state courts are occasionally transferred to them. It is here that nearly all accused of committing federal crimes are tried and that the grand and petit juries are used if at all. Ordinarily, cases are tried with only one judge presiding, but three judges must sit in certain types of cases.[22]

[22] Since 1937 this has been required in most cases involving the constitutionality of federal statutes. Appeal may be taken in such cases directly to the Supreme Court. This, it will be recognized, was part of

Court of Claims. Since governments cannot be sued without their consent, there are two methods by which one might obtain satisfaction for injury done. One is for the legislature to enact general or special legislation whenever necessary, and this was the practice until 1855 and still remains so in special instances. The other is for the government to consent to be sued. The former results in the introduction of a multitude of bills which are time-consuming and frequently petty in nature. To avoid this the Court of Claims was established in 1855 with authority to adjudicate all claims arising out of the Constitution, acts of Congress, regulations of the executive departments, or out of contracts entered into by the Federal government or its agents. Claims are forever barred, however, unless brought within 6 years.

The court consists of a chief justice and four associate justices who are appointed by the President with Senate approval for terms of good behavior. The court sits in Washington, beginning on the first Monday in December each year. In 1953 Congress amended the law to provide that this court "is hereby declared to be a court established under Article III of the Constitution of the United States," thus removing it from legislative court status.

Court Officers; United States Commissioners. Attached to each district court are the usual clerks, a reporter (since 1945), stenographers, bailiffs, and other attendants. These are all appointed by the court and responsible to it. Referees in bankruptcy and probation officers are also appointed by the courts. In addition, each court appoints one or more commissioners who serve for terms of 4 years.

These are usually part-time quasi-judicial officers who perform about the same functions as do justices of peace in the states. Unlike the justices of peace, they do not try petty cases; but they do hold preliminary hearings in criminal cases, issue search and arrest warrants, bind persons over for the grand jury, release them on bail, or discharge them for lack of evidence. They are paid from fees.

the outcome of President Roosevelt's proposal to reorganize the Federal courts.

LEGISLATIVE COURTS

The present legislative courts are the Customs Court, Court of Customs and Patent Appeals, Territorial Courts, courts for the District of Columbia, Tax Court, and Court of Military Appeals.[23] Since legislative courts do not come within the scope of the judicial article (Article III), their judges need not serve for terms of life or good behavior and they may be removed by methods other than impeachment. Moreover, they have only such jurisdiction as Congress wishes to give them.[24]

United States Customs Court. When goods enter the country, they are met by customs officers who place valuations upon them and collect tariff duties. Controversies inevitably arise, and to adjudicate these the Customs Court was established. It is composed of nine judges appointed by the President with Senate approval for good behavior. Not more than five may be from the same political party. The office of the court is located in New York City and most of its business is conducted there, although sessions are held in other cities, including San Juan, Puerto Rico.

United States Court of Customs and Patent Appeals. Created in 1910, this court is composed of five members appointed for terms of good behavior. The court is in continuous session, and although it usually sits in Washington, it may

[23] In addition to the legislative courts mentioned, there was until recently the United States Court for China which had jurisdiction over cases involving American citizens in China. It was abolished on May 20, 1943, when the United States entered into treaty abandoning extraterritorial rights in the Chinese republic. For an excellent discussion of this subject, see Wesley R. Fishel, *The End of Extraterritoriality in China* (University of California Press, 1952). There was also an Emergency Court of Appeals established in 1942 to handle appeals bearing upon price and rent controls. Its three or more judges were designated by the Chief Justice of the Supreme Court from among circuit and district judges. With the repeal of wartime controls need for this court gradually disappeared.

[24] For an excellent discussion and description of legislative courts, see Robert J. Harris, *The Judicial Power of the United States* (Louisiana State University Press, 1940), Chap. IV.

convene in any judicial circuit at any time. The court hears appeals from the decisions of the Customs Court and the United States Patent Office, and its judgments and decrees are final with the exception that they may be reviewed upon certiorari by the Supreme Court.

Territorial Courts. These are courts set up pursuant to the power given to Congress to make all needful rules and regulations respecting American territories. The most important are located in Hawaii, Alaska, Puerto Rico, the Virgin Islands, and the Panama Canal Zone. These differ from district courts in that they have jurisdiction over all matters, local as well as federal, which Congress may assign directly or indirectly through the territorial government.

Within each territory there is usually a court resembling a district court with general jurisdiction over the entire area and, in addition, a system of local courts similar to those found in the American states. Unlike their counterparts in the states, judges with general jurisdiction serve for a specified number of years. In Hawaii the term is 6 years; in the Virgin Islands, Canal Zone, and Puerto Rico, 8 years; in Alaska, 4 years.

District of Columbia Courts. Although similar, the Supreme Court draws a distinction between territorial courts and courts of the District of Columbia. Because the District of Columbia is permanent, and not transitory like other territories, the "judicial power" of the United States as defined in Article III operates within it. Accordingly, its courts are constitutional and parallel with other "inferior courts."

Nevertheless, the same courts are legislative inasmuch as Congress is given full authority to govern the district which constitutes the seat of government. Within the District there exists a United States district court, a United States Court of Appeals, a municipal court, and a municipal court of appeals. The first two deal with federal cases; the others mentioned handle local controversies.

Other Legislative Courts. The Tax Court is a sixteen-member body established in 1942 as a successor to the abolished Board of Tax Appeals. As the title suggests, it hears disputes arising from decisions of the federal tax-collection agencies. In the postwar period a considerable number of cases coming before the court involved excess profits on war contracts.

The Court of Military Appeals, established in 1950, is a newcomer. While located in the Department of Defense for administrative purposes, it consists of three civilian judges appointed by the President with Senate approval. More details are given later in this chapter.

CRIMINAL LAW ENFORCEMENT

The Department of Justice. In the Federal government, as in many of the states, law enforcement is not centralized in a single agency but rather is widely dispersed. The Department of Justice, however, is the focal point of much of the responsibility and activity. The office of Attorney General was among the first established in 1789, and although a member of the President's cabinet, the Attorney General was not made head of a department until 1870. Among its many and expanding duties, this department supervises and directs the work of district attorneys and marshals; it operates federal penal and correctional institutions; it conducts all suits in the Supreme Court in which the United States is a party; it investigates violations of many types; it furnishes legal counsel in federal cases; and it renders legal advice, upon request, to the President and his principal advisers.

Federal Police. No single unified federal police force exists. Rather, the detection and apprehension of lawbreakers is the responsibility of units within several departments. Probably every agency makes investigations of some sort or another, but police work is a major duty of several of them and only an auxiliary function of others. Those having a major responsibility include:

1. Internal Revenue Service (Treasury)
2. Bureau of Narcotics (Treasury)
3. Secret Service (Treasury)
4. Coast Guard (Treasury)
5. Bureau of Customs (Treasury)
6. Federal Bureau of Investigation (Justice)
7. Immigration and Naturalization Service (Justice)

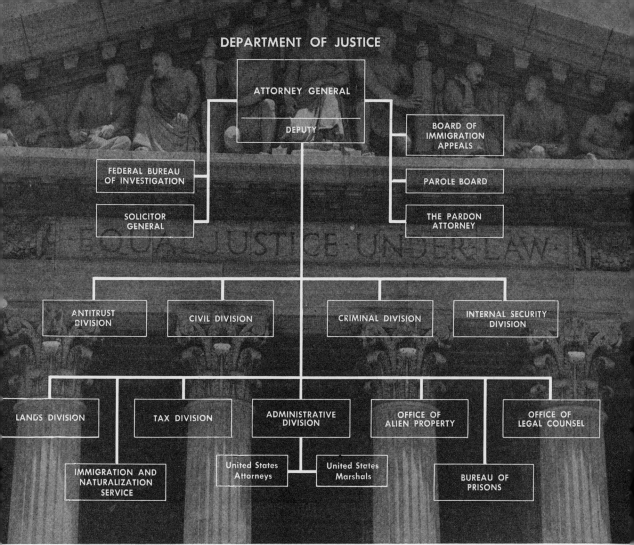

DEPARTMENT OF JUSTICE

United Press Photograph

8. Bureau of the Chief Post Office Inspector (Post Office)
9. Food and Drug Administration (Health, Education, and Welfare)
10. Plant Pest Control Branch; Plant Quarantine Branch; Animal Disease Eradication Branch; Animal Inspection and Quarantine Branch; and Meat Inspection Branch (Agriculture)

Agencies for which police functions are auxiliary are too numerous to mention here but will be dealt with at appropriate points in pages that follow. Although the number of police agencies is imposing, the number of people involved is comparatively small. In 1949 a careful student [25]

[25] Bruce Smith, *Police Systems in the United States* (Harper, rev. ed., 1949), p. 193.

estimated that fewer than twenty thousand persons made up the entire federal police establishment.

Dispersed as the police agencies are, many problems arise. Most of the agencies grew slowly over the years and are now so firmly entrenched as to defy change. Respective jurisdictions are often vaguely defined, leaving doubt over which agency is responsible for particular types of offenses. Functions overlap and duplicate. There is much bureaucratic rivalry, distrust, and intrigue. Personnel is far from being of uniform caliber and training. Each agency must work out its own relationship not only with other federal organizations but also with a multitude of state and local officers. Careful students of the problem advocate better coordination of police functions or perhaps consolidation of agencies.[26]

The Federal Bureau of Investigation. Of all federal police agencies, the FBI is best known. Problems of the First World War and later of prohibition gave rise to the conviction that a permanent body of trained agents was required to help with law enforcement. The conviction also grew that, in order to ensure the closest cooperation with district attorneys, marshals, and the courts, these should be under the Department of Justice. Aided by a wave of kidnaping, racketeering, and gangsterism which swept over the country, the FBI was organized in 1934. Under the direction of J. Edgar Hoover, several thousand agents, popularly known as "G men," have been specially recruited and trained, and almost every device known to modern science has been adopted for use in detecting violators.

The FBI investigates threats to the security of the United States, including the loyalty of its employees and applicants for positions, and it investigates all criminal matters not specifically assigned to other agencies. The Bureau is primarily a fact-finding agency; it does not draw conclusions itself from the facts discovered, but rather it leaves that task to the administrative agency most concerned or the courts.

The Bureau does not assume responsibility for violations of state and local laws, but it offers assistance. Its fingerprint files, laboratory, and advisory services are available, and the Bureau operates a National Academy for giving specialized training to state and local law-enforcement officers. To date, however, because of distrust of federal police, coupled with local pride and lack of interest, Bureau services to state and local governments have been limited.

Secret Service. Older than the FBI, the Secret Service has more limited jurisdiction but certainly ranks high in quality and breadth of services. Originally created in 1860 to suppress counterfeiting, the Secret Service was given additional duties of protecting the President and his family, detecting forgery of government checks, and otherwise safeguarding the fiscal and credit functions of the United States. Its "T men" rival the men of the FBI in thoroughness of training and devotion to duty.

Common Federal Criminal Offenses. Within recent years the number of federal violations has increased by leaps and bounds in step with the rapid expansion of federal activities. Thousands are apprehended and prosecuted each year. Although the various offenses cannot be detailed here, some idea of their character is shown by the following list:

Counterfeiting and forgery
Customs Act violations
Embezzlement and fraud
Escape, flight, mutiny, etc.
Extortion and racketeering
Immigration Act violations
Internal Revenue Act violations
Interstate Commerce Act violations
Juvenile delinquency
Kidnaping
Larceny and theft
Liquor-law violations
Narcotic Drug Act violations
National Bank and Federal Reserve Act violations
National bank robbery
National Bankruptcy Act violations
National Firearms violations
Postal-law violations
Selective Service Act violations
White Slave Traffic Act violations

Machinery of Prosecution. Many violations of federal laws are dealt with by executive and administrative procedures, but a larger number must be dealt with before Federal courts. The Department of Justice, upon receipt of evidence from one of the police agencies, turns the matter over to one of the United States district attorneys who prepares the case, with the assistance of specialists when necessary. There is always one attorney in each judicial district and

[26] For further discussion see *ibid.,* pp. 190–203; Arthur C. Millspaugh, *Crime Control by the National Government* (Brookings, 1937), *passim;* Brookings Institution, *Report on the Organization of Federal Law Enforcement Activities,* prepared for the Select Committee (Senate) to Investigate the Executive Agencies of the Government, 75th Cong., 1st Sess. (1937).

usually several assistants. They are appointed by the President with Senate approval, which means that partisan considerations affect the selection. Their terms are for 4 years. Upon them falls the primary responsibility of proving guilt in the courts.

Within each judicial district there is also a United States marshal and perhaps several deputies. These have traditionally been partisan appointments for 4-year terms. The first Hoover Commission recommended that they be brought under the merit system, which President Truman attempted to accomplish by reorganization plan 4 of 1952, but the Senate disapproved the plan. Marshals are to the Federal courts what sheriffs are to states and counties. It is their duty to make arrests, take charge of prisoners, and execute court orders. They have authority to command all necessary assistance and on occasion have appointed deputies—otherwise known as *posse comitatus*—by tens, hundreds, or thousands. Marshals are, to quote a former Attorney General, "the first line of federal defense on occasions of domestic disturbance." [27]

Criminal Procedure. In the background of criminal procedures are the constitutional guarantees of individual rights discussed in Chap. 7. The precise rules that must be followed are prescribed by the Supreme Court acting under the authority of acts of Congress.[28] Their purpose is the "just determination" of every criminal proceeding.

Complaint and Examination. A federal criminal case begins with the making of a complaint, under oath and before a commissioner or other officer, against a person charged with an offense against the United States. If the complaint indicates that an offense probably has been committed, a warrant for arrest or a summons to appear is issued.

When he appears before a commissioner, the defendant is informed of the complaint against him and of his rights both to have counsel and to have preliminary examination. If he waives examination, he is held to answer in the district court. If examination is held, evidence is heard by the commissioner, the defendant having the right to cross-examine witnesses against him and introduce evidence for himself. The commissioner then decides whether to discharge or hold for trial.

Indictments and Informations. The next stage is formal accusation of a crime either by indictment or information. Indictment is by grand jury, which consists of from 16 to 23 members, of whom 12 must vote affirmatively in order to effect an indictment. A grand jury remains in existence until discharged by the court, or until its maximum tenure of 18 months is exhausted. In practice the more populous districts often have several grand juries in existence simultaneously; they do routine criminal indictments or may conduct special investigations into particular law-enforcement problems.

Indictment is used in all cases in which the death penalty may be involved. The Fifth Amendment guaranty of a grand-jury indictment extends to all infamous crimes; the rules draw the line between offenses punishable by 1 year or more of imprisonment, which require indictment unless waived, and lesser offenses, which may be prosecuted on the basis of information. Of all criminal proceedings commenced in Federal district courts in recent years, there are approximately two cases by grand-jury indictment to one by information of the prosecuting attorney.

The accused is then arraigned. Arraignment consists of reading (or summarizing) the indictment or information to the defendant in open court and calling upon him to plead. He may plead guilty, not guilty, or—with the consent of the court—*nolo contendere,* a halfway house which is neither an admission of guilt nor a full denial. Surprising as it may seem, the great majority of the criminals accused before Federal courts plead guilty; in the postwar period about 85 per cent have so pleaded. Only 5 to 7 per cent actually are tried.

[27] Homer Cummings and Carl McFarland, *Federal Justice* (Macmillan, 1937), p. 544.

[28] The basic authorizing act was 54 Stat. 688 (1940). The Supreme Court appointed an advisory committee, which prepared various drafts. The new rules were adopted by the Supreme Court and went into effect on Mar. 21, 1946.

Trial by Jury and Court. Trial by petit jury is a right that extends, under Article III and the Sixth Amendment, to most federal criminal proceedings, except when waived by the accused. Only petty offenses are excluded. Juries must consist of 12 members except when the parties agree to a smaller number.

The rules of evidence, unless otherwise provided by Congress, are governed by the principles of the common law. In jury trials, any

Detention and Probation. After sentence those convicted of violating federal laws must be assigned to the type of care appropriate to their case. Violators of federal statutes include men and women, boys and girls, normal people, and persons with various physical and mental ailments. Punishment should not only "fit the crime," as Gilbert and Sullivan had their Mikado declare, but it should fit the individual concerned.

FEDERAL PRISONERS RECEIVED FROM THE COURTS
FISCAL YEARS ENDED JUNE 30, 1946-1954

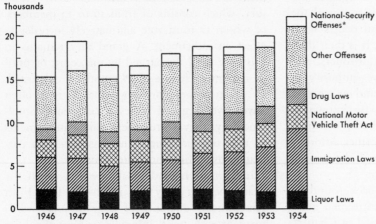

*Court martial cases; violations of Selective Service Acts and other war-related or National-Security Laws

The major groups of prisoners, by offense, received by federal correctional institutions. Source: *Federal Prisons.*

party may request that the court instruct the jury on particulars of the law, and the judge is required to inform counsel on proposed instructions before their arguments to the jury. The jury verdict must be unanimous to convict.

Sentence. Before imposing sentence, the judge gives the defendant an opportunity to make a statement in his own behalf or in mitigation. The judgment of conviction sets forth the plea, verdict or findings, and the sentence. In imposing sentence, the court has before it a report from its probation service on the defendant's record, characteristics, and other information that might prove helpful in imposing appropriate treatment or sentence. Appeal may follow in an appropriate court.[29]

[29] For further consideration of federal criminal procedure, see recent standard works on the subject, including those of Clark and Marshall, Clements, and Yankwich.

Recently the Federal government has made real strides toward improving the treatment of first offenders and minors. The 1946 rules require that, unless the judge specifies otherwise, a probation report on a defendant be available to the court before sentence is pronounced. The Juvenile Delinquency Act of 1948 and the Federal Youth Correction Act of 1950 make possible special handling of youthful offenders. Considerably more federal offenders are on probation or on parole than are incarcerated in the United States prison system.

The federal probation system is under the supervision of the Administrative Office of the United States Courts, but primary control is by the district courts. A Parole Board of five members appointed by the Attorney General grants and revokes paroles of federal prisoners.

There are no federal "jails," only "prisons" and other correctional institutions. The Bureau of Prisons of the Justice Department is in charge of most of them. Many federal offenders must be kept in state and local jails. These are inspected by the Bureau of Prisons and often found wanting. In 1953, for example, federal officers inspected 474 jails in 39 states, and of these 11 were rated good, 287 fair, 143 poor, and 33

Although civilians ordinarily are not subject to military law, military personnel can be hailed before civilian courts for offenses against civilians or for acts committed outside military territory. Persons discharged from the Armed Forces cannot be brought to trial before military courts even for crimes committed before release.[31]

UNITED STATES PRISON SYSTEM

🏠 Institutions for Juveniles 　 🏰 Penitentiaries

🚩 Prison Camps 　 🏛 Reformatories

🏛 Detention Headquarters 　 🏰 Medical Center

🏛 Public Health Service Hospitals 　 🏛 Correctional Institutions

bad. The federal correctional institutions, which now have a capacity of about 20,000, are shown on the map above.

MILITARY JUSTICE

Military Laws. Under its authority to "make rules for the government and regulation of the land and naval forces," Congress has enacted a considerable body of military law. Disciplinary rules for all the services were standardized with the adoption of the Uniform Code of Military Justice in 1950.[30] The operation of the new system of military justice is described below.

[30] 64 Stat. 107. The Code replaces the Articles of War (Army), the Articles for the Government of the Navy, and the Disciplinary Laws of the Coast Guard.

The largest system of criminal justice in the United States during most of the war and postwar years has been the military courts-martial system. At the peak of mobilization for the Second World War, military justice handled about one-third of all criminal cases tried in the nation.[32]

Justice in Uniform. Military personnel traditionally has been subject to a different system of justice than have civilians. The British acquired the basis of their system from the Romans. The

[31] Toth *v.* Quarles 350 U.S. 11 (1955).

[32] Delmar Karlen and Louis H. Pepper, "The Scope of Military Justice," *Journal of Criminal Law, Criminology and Police Science,* vol. 43 (September–October, 1952), pp. 285–298.

Second Continental Congress adopted the English court-martial. It has been retained, with some revisions, to the present. The basic pattern is trial of an accused person by a board especially appointed for the purpose.

During the Second World War, military justice was frequently under attack. Severe penalties were imposed occasionally and were publicized widely. The rival interests of command for discipline and of the accused for a fair trial often were resolved in favor of the former. Throughout the services there was a shortage of law officers who were sufficiently skilled to conduct, prosecute, or defend serious cases. Considerable diversity existed, not only in procedures but in verdicts, among the several services. In 1948 a rider on the Selective Service Act of that year made extensive changes in Army courts-martial, particularly affecting appeals of serious cases.

Court of Military Appeals. When Congress enacted in 1950 the Uniform Code of Military Justice, it created the United States Court of Military Appeals, which is sometimes called the "GI supreme court." The court consists of three judges appointed by the President from civilian life and for terms of 15 years. The court sits in Washington, D.C.

The Court of Military Appeals has no original jurisdiction and has three types of appellate jurisdiction. It has *mandatory* jurisdiction over all cases in which the death sentence has been given or in which generals or admirals are involved. It also is required to review cases *certified* to it by the judge advocate general of one of the three services. The bulk of cases, however, come from *petitions* for review from defendants who have received adverse verdicts lower down on the military-justice ladder. In choosing which of the many petitions for review it will grant, the court has full discretion. During 1951–1953 the court granted about 15 per cent of petitions received. The court does not review cases that involve sentences of less than 1 year or the equivalent.

Cases come to the court from the boards of review of the service departments. These boards are somewhat comparable to courts of appeal in the civilian court system. They review automatically the most serious cases decided by courts-martial within their services.

Pretrial Procedure. Below the Court of Military Appeals and the boards of review there is an extensive courts-martial system. The military-justice process begins with the commission of an alleged offense. Charges are brought by a person in the armed services who has personal knowledge of the violation. A preliminary informal inquiry is conducted. If the facts appear to merit further action, an officer is assigned to conduct a pretrial investigation in order to determine the truth or falsity of the charges. The accused has the right to counsel, to call defense witnesses, to be informed of the charges, to know who is the accuser and who are the witnesses against him, to cross-examine, to refuse to testify against himself. The officer in charge of the investigation recommends a course of action.

Lesser offenses may be handled through nonjudicial punishment. Maximum penalties for an enlisted man may not exceed 2 weeks of withheld privileges, of restriction to limits, or of imposition of additional duty. On board a naval vessel confinement up to 7 days is permitted. A man so disciplined is guaranteed the right to appeal to superior authority.

Courts-martial. Crimes of greater gravity go to courts-martial: moderate offenses to "summary"; other noncapital to "special"; and the most serious to "general." The *summary court-martial* consists of a single officer, who may try enlisted and noncommissioned-officer personnel, and mete out less severe punishment. Both trial and defense counsel are appointed by the commanding officer who convened the court, but the accused may request the services of any officer as his defense counsel, or may employ civilian counsel at his own expense.

Special courts-martial consist of three or more members, who are empowered to punish offenders with bad-conduct discharges, reduction in rank, two-thirds pay deduction for up to 6 months, or 6 months at hard labor. Procedure is rigidly specified to provide maximum protection for the accused. A special court may be convened only by a commanding general or officer of equivalent rank.

General courts-martial consist of five or more members, and if the accused requests it, must have at least one-third enlisted personnel. This court may adjudge sentences of death, dishonorable discharge, and similar heavy penalties. It may be convened only by very high authority, such as the President, the Secretary of the Department of Defense, or a top commanding officer designated by the Secretary.

Review and Appeal. Convening authorities and supervisory authorities have review powers. The service departments also have intermediate boards of review that survey the decisions of courts-martial. Final appeal is to the Court of Military Appeals. Although no provision is made for appeal to the Supreme Court from the Court of Military Appeals, such an appeal doubtless may be made if the highest tribunal accepts it.

From experience gained since the Uniform Code went into effect in 1951, it would appear that the revised system of military justice is working well. The objective of providing for the accused the guaranties to a fair trial that prevail in the civil courts seems to be achieved. Indeed, in some particulars, the accused in uniform enjoys rights and prerogatives (such as free counsel regardless of economic need) denied to his civilian counterpart. The influence of command in courts-martial effectively has been reduced. The Court of Military Appeals, with an initial complement of able judges, has taken long strides toward the desirable goals of standardization and equalization.[33]

[33] For further information consult U.S. Department of Defense, *Annual Report of the United States Court of Military Appeals and the Judge Advocates General of the Armed Forces* (annual); Department of the Army, *Manual for Courts-Martial* (1951); Department of the Navy, *Index and Legislative History, Uniform Code of Military Justice* (1950); "A Symposium of Military Justice," *Vanderbilt Law Review,* vol. 6 (February, 1953).

FOR FURTHER READING

Aumann, Francis R.: *The Changing American Legal System* (Ohio State University Press, 1940).

Boudin, Louis B.: *Government by Judiciary* (New York: Godwin, 1932).

Brookings Institution: *Report on the Organization of Federal Law Enforcement Activities,* prepared for the Select Committee (Senate) to Investigate the Executive Agencies of Government, 75th Cong., 1st Sess. (1937).

Cahn, Edmund: *Supreme Court and Supreme Law* (Indiana University Press, 1954).

Callender, Clarence N.: *American Courts: Their Organization and Procedure* (McGraw-Hill, 1927).

Carpenter, William S.: *Judicial Tenure in the United States* (Yale University Press, 1918).

Carr, Robert K.: *Federal Protection of Civil Rights: Quest for a Sword* (Cornell University Press, 1947).

——: *The Supreme Court and Judicial Review* (Farrar, Straus, 1942).

——: *Democracy and the Supreme Court* (University of Oklahoma Press, 1936).

Collins, Frederick L.: *FBI in Peace and War* (Putnam, 1943).

Corwin, Edward S.: *Court over Constitution* (Princeton University Press, 1938).

Cummings, Homer, and Carl McFarland: *Federal Justice* (Macmillan, 1937).

Curtis, Charles P.: *Lions under the Throne: A Study of the Supreme Court of the United States* (Houghton Mifflin, 1947).

Cushman, Robert E. (ed.): "Ten Years of the Supreme Court: 1937–1947," *American Political Science Review,* vol. 42 (February, 1948), pp. 32–67.

Dodge, Arthur J.: *Origin and Development of the Office of Attorney-General,* H. Doc. 510, 70th Cong., 2d Sess.

Ewing, Cortez: *The Judges of the Supreme Court, 1789–1937* (University of Minnesota Press, 1938).

Field, Oliver P.: *The Effect of an Unconstitutional Statute* (University of Minnesota Press, 1935).

Floherty, John J.: *Inside the FBI* (Lippincott, 1943).

Frank, Jerome: *Courts on Trial* (Princeton University Press, 1949).

Gilbert, Wilfred C.: *Provisions of Federal Law Held Unconstitutional by the Supreme Court of the United States* (Government Printing Office, 1936).

Haines, Charles G.: *The Role of the Supreme Court in American Government and Politics, 1789–1835* (University of California Press, 1944).

——: *The American Doctrine of Judicial Supremacy* (University of California Press, 2d ed., 1932).

Harris, Robert J.: *The Judicial Power of the United States* (Louisiana State University Press, 1940).

Hart, Henry M., and Herbert Wechsler (eds.): *The Federal Courts and the Federal System* (Foundation Press, 1953).

Hughes, Charles E.: *The Supreme Court of the United States* (Columbia University Press, 1928).

Langeluttig, Albert G.: *The Department of Justice of the United States* (Johns Hopkins Press, 1927).

Mayer, Lewis: *The American Legal System* (Harper, 1955).

Military Jurisprudence: Cases and Materials (Lawyers Cooperative Publishing Co., 1951).

Millspaugh, Arthur C.: *Crime Control by the National Government* (Brookings, 1937).

Philos, Conrad D.: *Handbook of Court-martial Law* (Chicago: Callaghan, rev. ed., 1951).

Pound, Roscoe: *Organization of Courts* (Little, Brown, 1940).

Prichett, Charles Herman: *Civil Liberties and the Vinson Court* (University of Chicago Press, 1954).

——: *The Roosevelt Court: A Study in Judicial Politics and Values, 1937–1947* (Macmillan, 1948).

Roberts, Owen J.: *The Court and the Constitution* (Harvard University Press, 1951).

Schiller, A. Arthur: *Military Law: Statutes, Regulations and Opinions of the Judge Advocates General* (West Publishing Co., 1952).

Shartel, Burke: *Our Legal System and How It Operates* (University of Michigan Law School, 1951).

Smith, Bruce: *Police Systems in the United States* (Harper, rev. ed., 1949).

Sunderland, Edson R.: *Judicial Administration* (Chicago: Callaghan, 2d ed., 1948).

Talbott, Forrest: *Intergovernmental Relations and the Courts* (University of Minnesota Press, 1950).

Umbreit, Kenneth B.: *Our Eleven Chief Justices: A History of the Supreme Court in Terms of Their Personalities* (Harper, 1938).

U.S. Bureau of Prisons: *Federal Prisons* (Leavenworth, Kans.: Federal Prisons Industries, Inc., Press, published annually).

——: *Handbook of Correctional Institution Design and Construction* (1949).

U.S. Director of the Administrative Office of the Courts: *Annual Report.*

U.S. Senate, Committee on the Judiciary: *Adverse Report on Reorganization of the Federal Judiciary,* S. Rept. 711, 75th Cong., 1st Sess. (1937).

——: *Hearings on S. 1392: A Bill to Reorganize the Judicial Branch of the Government,* 75th Cong., 1st Sess. (6 parts, 1937).

Warren, Charles: *The Supreme Court in United States History* (Little, Brown, 3 vols., 1922).

Wendell, Mitchell: *The Relations between Federal and State Courts* (Columbia University Press, 1949).

Williams, Charlotte: *Hugo L. Black: A Study of the Judicial Process* (Johns Hopkins Press, 1950).

Willoughby, William F.: *Principles of Judicial Administration* (Brookings, 1929).

Yankwich, Leon R.: *The New Federal Rules of Criminal Procedure* (Los Angeles: Parker & Co., 1946).

REVIEW QUESTIONS

1. Why was a dual system of courts decided upon by the Constitutional Convention of 1787? Would it have been better for them to have provided for a single system of Federal courts? A single system of state courts?

2. What do courts do besides settle disputes?

3. What were some of the results or consequences of the controversy of 1937 between President Franklin D. Roosevelt and the Congress over suggested changes in court organization and practice?

4. Distinguish between "constitutional" and "legislative" courts and give illustrations of each.

5. Give illustrations of cases over which the Federal courts have exclusive and concurrent jurisdiction. Illustrate also the cases which may not be taken to the Federal courts.

6. Compare each of the Federal courts as to jurisdiction, organizational detail, and functions.

7. What are the principal "police" agencies of the Federal government? Would it be better to have a single unified federal police system?

8. Describe how the Department of Justice is organized and the functions it performs.

9. Describe the federal penal system. How does this compare with the system found in one of the states?

10. What functions are performed by the Administrative Office of the United States Courts? United States commissioners? District attorneys?

11. What steps are customarily taken in a criminal prosecution by the Federal government?

12. Compare the law and procedures which apply under military and civil law.

CHAPTER 17

Administrative Organization and Procedure

Organization is the arrangement of personnel for facilitating the accomplishment of some agreed purpose through the allocation of functions and responsibilities. It is the relating of efforts and capacities of individuals and groups engaged upon a common task in such a way as to secure the desired objective with the least friction and the most satisfaction to those for whom the task is done and those engaged in the enterprise. — John M. Gaus [1]

There is no more forlorn spectacle in the administrative world than an agency and a program possessed of statutory life, armed with executive orders, sustained in the courts, yet stricken with paralysis and deprived of power. An object of contempt to its enemies and of despair to its friends.

The lifeblood of administration is power. — Norton E. Long [2]

After policy has been formed, by the processes described in the first part of this book, it must be executed. The administrative process involves both policy interpretation and implementation. The initial consideration of public administration is to secure an effective machinery for carrying out the will of the policy makers—legislators, executives, judges, electorate. Certain general aspects of this question have been dealt with already in previous chapters on the executive branch. The task here is to inquire more deeply into the subject, seeking a fuller explanation of organizational theory and practice.

ORGANIZATION: THEORY AND PRACTICE

Administrative organization is not an end in itself, but a means to an end. [3] It exists to put into force, to administer the policies determined by policy formers. A well-organized and well-managed administrative unit will produce the

results desired by policy makers, legislative and executive, with efficiency and speed, and with due respect for the rights of the affected parties. Under the most simple circumstances—as in a village with a population of 100—elaborate departmental organization is unnecessary, and responsibilities may be subdivided with ease among part-time officials. A great nation, on the other hand, requires a mighty administrative leviathan with hundreds of thousands of civil servants and vast, complex administrative organization.

Staff and Line. The great functions that government provides are usually assigned to operating departments and are called "line" functions.

[1] *The Frontiers of Public Administration* (University of Chicago Press, 1936), pp. 66–67.

[2] "Power and Administration," *Public Administration Review*, vol. 9 (Autumn, 1949), p. 257.

[3] Herman Finer, "Organization, Administrative," *Encyclopedia of the Social Sciences* (Macmillan, 1930), vol. 11, p. 480.

They provide the basic services and regulation that government is established to perform. Similar functions are usually grouped together and placed in a common department. In a small city, for example, fire and police services might be included in a department called "public safety," and all health and charitable work grouped in a "public-welfare" department. In a national state, the armed forces could be directed by a department of "national defense," and all services to business placed in a department of "trade and commerce."

In order to control and to provide specialized services for these departments, "staff" agencies are created to furnish personnel, planning, finances, or other services needed by the operating or "line" agencies. Through "staff" agencies, the administrative head can keep informed of "line" developments and may exert direction and control. The Bureau of the Budget, located in the Executive Office of the President, is an example of a staff agency.

A case often is made for the independence from direct executive or legislative control of a particular staff or line agency. It is argued that a business or entrepreneurial public function ought to be free of the usual governmental restrictions on finance and personnel which were designed to fit ordinary functions. Crusaders for the merit system usually demand independent status for a personnel agency in order to keep it away from the taint of spoils. Making regulatory bodies independent of regular departments is common on the ground that such agencies possess quasi-legislative and quasi-judicial powers and must therefore not be subject to external control under the separation of powers principle.

Constitutional and Statutory Provisions. The Federal Constitution is notably silent regarding administrative structure. In Article II, Section 2, it states that the President can require an opinion in writing of the principal officer in each of the executive departments on any subject relating to the duties of his office. In the same section, Congress is given authority to vest by law the appointment of inferior officers in the President alone, in the courts, or in the heads of departments. One may infer from these provisions that the framers of the Constitution anticipated executive departments headed by individuals responsible to the President. Certainly the presumption that Congress should establish such departments, functions, and organization as necessary is justified.

Congress acted promptly, and in its first sessions (1789) created the departments of Foreign Affairs,[4] War, and Treasury. Each department was to be headed by a "secretary," appointed by the President. The first Congress also created the offices of Postmaster General and Attorney General, without the status of executive departments. For the next hundred years nearly all federal functions, as they were created, were grouped into existing or new departments.

The independent agency, responsible to no department, is largely a product of the last 60 years. Its persistence has been due primarily to the conviction that regulatory commissions must be free. The immunity from external control of the Interstate Commerce Commission, for example, is considered of high importance by the common carriers.

Administrative Reorganization. During the last quarter century, great impetus has been given to putting the house of the executive branch of the Federal government in better order. Reorganization efforts have centered around three important surveys: the President's Committee on Administrative Management, the Commission on Organization of the Executive Branch of the Government (1949), and the second Commission of the same name (1955).

The President's Committee was set up in 1936. Personnel consisted of Louis Brownlow, chairman, Charles E. Merriam, and Luther Gulick. The Committee concentrated on problems of management, considered mainly from the presidential point of view. Its report was issued in January, 1937, and was followed by nine special studies. In general, it can be said to have been influential, but Congress failed to adopt many of its recommendations.

[4] Subsequently changed to State. See Lloyd M. Short, *The Development of National Administrative Organization in the United States* (Johns Hopkins Press, 1923).

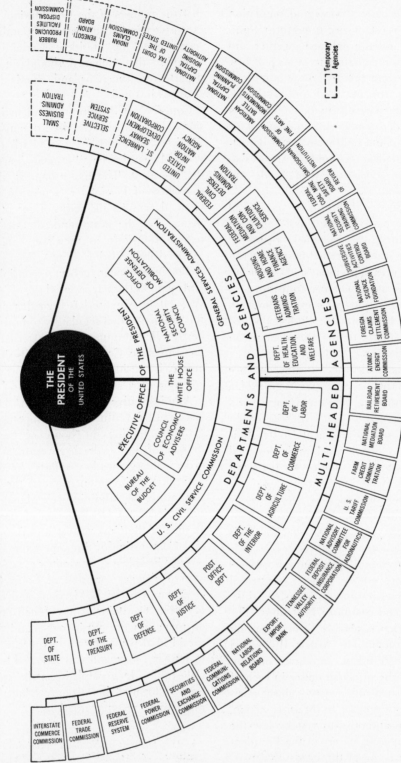

The organizational expanse of the executive branch in 1955. Minor agencies have been excluded from this diagram. The goal of the first Hoover Commission of reducing to thirty the number of agencies reporting to the President is far from being realized. Source: Bureau of the Budget.

The first Hoover Commission was established by Congress in 1947. It consisted of twelve members, of whom four were appointed by the President, four by the Speaker of the House, and four by the president pro tempore of the Senate. The two parties were represented equally. Task forces were put to work in specialized fields. The Commission's nineteen reports and twenty-four task-force reports recommended many changes. By 1955, 72 per cent of the first Hoover Commission recommendations were reported adopted.

The second Hoover Commission was set up by Congress in 1953. Its composition was similar to that of its predecessor, except that bipartisanship was not required. Seven Republicans and five Democrats were appointed to the Commission. Its powers were greater than the first Hoover group, in that the new body could recommend the elimination of functions deemed competitive with private industry. As this is written, reports of the Commission and of its task forces have been published; some of them have stirred up much controversy. It is too early to assess their impact.

Mr. Herbert Hoover, while Secretary of Commerce, in 1925 reported on the confusion of functions then existing. He found that nine departments and independent agencies were engaged in public works, five in conservation, six in aiding the Merchant Marine, four providing veterans' aid, three governing territories, three aiding education, and every one purchasing its own supplies.

New Departments. Two principal solutions are proposed for this problem. One is that new departments should be created. The other is that bureaus and agencies might be reshuffled within existing departments. Most of the reports and studies of reorganization have included both features.

The Department of Health, Education, and Welfare (HEW), finally created under President Eisenhower's reorganization plan 1 of 1953, had been recommended repeatedly by various survey groups over a period of 30 years. For a variety of reasons, Congress held out against the establishment of a new department, despite the urging of Presidents, committees, and the second Hoover Commission. At the time its functions were transferred to the new department, the Federal Security Agency had more employees than three of the executive departments.

Another common recommendation for a new Department is to handle the public works function. Both the Brookings Institution report in the 1920's and the President's Committee on Administrative Management report in the 1930's favored a department of public works. Although one of its task forces proposed the transformation of the Department of the Interior into a "Department of Works," the majority of the first Hoover Commission recommended a strengthened Interior Department.

A third proposal is for a "Department of Natural Resources," either as a reorganization of Interior or as a new and separate department. A strong minority of the first Hoover Commission supported such a proposal.

Transfer of Bureaus. The other solution is to reorganize bureaus and services within departments through transfers so that like functions will be brought together and duplication and overlapping of activities minimized. This process is sometimes derisively called "reshuffling" the bureaus. During the last twenty years this type of administrative reorganization increasingly has been carried out by delegation of authority from Congress to the President. President Hoover asked for power to reorganize at least three times during his administration, but he was granted it only belatedly in 1932 through an amendment to an appropriation bill. The Committee on Administrative Management advocated "continuing executive responsibility for efficient organization." [5] There is a need for organizational flexibility to meet changing situations. Again and again it has been shown that Congress is subjected to such great pressure from employees and groups that it rarely is able to pass reorganization legislation. Consequently, Congress has been delegating this task to the Chief Executive, subject to congressional veto

[5] U.S. President's Committee on Administrative Management, *Report with Special Studies* (1937), pp. 36–38.

through a concurrent or a single-house resolution. The main outlines of the various laws permitting reorganization by executive order are shown in the following table. It will be seen that these delegations usually are for limited periods, that many restrictions are placed on the use of the powers granted, and that the Congress normally retains the power to nullify.

passage of a concurrent resolution by both houses within the prescribed time. The Eighty-first Congress enacted the necessary legislation in June, 1949, granting the President sweeping power to reorganize.[7]

The new act authorizes presidential reorganization plans affecting nearly every agency of the executive branch, except that they cannot abolish

Executive Powers over Administrative Reorganization, Delegated by Congress, 1932–1957

Years	Administration	Statute	Exemptions	Nullification	Use
1932–1933	Hoover	Approp. Act, 47 Stat. 413	No abolition of functions	Within 60 days by action of either house	11 Hoover plans killed in House
1933–1935	Roosevelt	Approp. Act, 47 Stat. 1517		No provision; in effect after 60 days	Extensive abolitions and shuffles
1939–1941	Roosevelt	Reorg. Act of 1939	17 exempt agencies; no new depts.	Within 60 days; both houses, concurrent res.	3 great "agencies" created, etc.
1941–1945	Roosevelt	First War Powers Act	Accounting Office; no new depts.	No provision	Several shifts and shuffles
1945–1948	Truman	Reorg. Act of 1945	6 agencies wholly; no new depts.	Within 60 days; both houses	Several orders, 1946–1947
1949–1957	Truman and Eisenhower	Reorg. Act of 1949 (as extended)	Cannot extend life of agency; no abolition of depts.	Within 60 days; either house	42 plans into force 1949–1954

The first Hoover Commission recommended strongly that Congress enact legislation giving the President even more authority over reorganization than was granted in earlier acts.[6] Indeed, the Commission declared that many of its most important proposals probably could not be put into effect unless presidential power to reorganize were revived and extended. It called for a forthright delegation, without exceptions, but subject to congressional nullification through the

a department, increase a term of office, or extend the life of an expiring agency. The courts of the District of Columbia are exempt, as are the Comptroller General and the General Accounting Office. Reorganization plans lie before Congress for 60 days; if either house disapproves within that period, the plan is dead. Thus the act is stronger than that of 1945 in that there are

[6] First Hoover Commission, *General Management of the Executive Branch* (1949), pp. ix–xii.

[7] 63 Stat. 203. A good analysis of the act is Ferrel Heady, "The Reorganization Act of 1949," *Public Administration Review,* vol. 9 (Summer, 1949), pp. 165–174.

fewer exemptions, but weaker in that either house can nullify, instead of action by both being required as under the earlier act.

INTERNAL DEPARTMENTAL ORGANIZATION

Departmental Management. Federal executive departments are directed by single heads, although this is not always true of other levels of American government. It is fortunate that the first Congress established the initial departments with single heads; for that type of overhead management has advantages over the plural, or board-commission, form, in that it concentrates responsibility for action and makes for greater speed and flexibility.

Within the department, policy is directed by the secretary, who is responsible to the President, but who must, in turn, rely on various aides to keep in touch with a great department employing up to 500,000 persons. He is assisted by undersecretaries and assistant secretaries, who are usually appointed for political reasons, and by administrative assistants, but there is a strong tendency to develop in most departments a group of "career" men among the top assistants who constitute the management staff. The undersecretaries and assistant secretaries may supervise a group of bureaus, or a certain type of service or function running through several bureaus in the department.[8] Professor Macmahon favors the functional type of assignment for assistants as distinguished from the subject-matter type but recognizes the difficulty of defining responsibilities in precise terms. Department heads convene principal staff aides and bureau chiefs for "departmental cabinet" meetings, at which policy questions may be ironed out, efforts coordinated, and progress reported.

The latest thorough study of departmental management was made by the first Hoover Commission.[9] First, it stressed the necessity of grouping the numerous agencies of government into

[8] Arthur W. Macmahon, "Departmental Management," in U.S. President's Committee on Administrative Management, *op. cit.,* pp. 249–270.

[9] First Hoover Commission, *General Management of the Executive Branch* (1949), pp. 29–45.

departments ". . . by major purposes in order to give a coherent mission to each Department." Within each department, subsidiary bureaus and agencies should also be grouped according to major purposes. The commission further recommended that each department head should have power to organize his department as he thought best. For the typical department, the department head might have an undersecretary and the necessary number of assistant secretaries to cover

The remarkable success in securing the adoption of first Hoover Commission recommendations is pictured here by the Citizens Committee for the Hoover Report.

the department's functions. Since all these officers would be of policy rank, the commission proposed that they should be appointed by the President with Senate confirmation.

Another type of administrative unit found within a department or an independent agency is the staff office, which performs subsidiary services for the operating agencies. These staff services are generally located near the department head. They include offices charged with providing personnel, legal, financial, research, informational, and other services. As the President keeps in touch with and controls federal line functions through his staff agencies, so the department head, within his department, contacts and manages his operating bureaus through personnel, financial, and other staff officers. The first Hoover Commission urged that all major executive agencies be equipped with adequate staff assistants for legal counsel, finances, personnel, supply, management research, information, and congressional liaison.

Bureaus and Other Units. Within each department the major subfunctions and line services are divided into "bureaus," but these major units may also be called "services" or "offices" or "administrations." The internal organization is de-

Below the bureau level, terminology and organizational practice are even more variable. The title "division" is used most commonly to indicate a subdivision of a bureau, but "unit," "branch," and "section" are employed also. The lower in the administrative ladder, the less chance that form is bound by statute, and the

TYPICAL ORGANIZATION OF A FEDERAL AGENCY

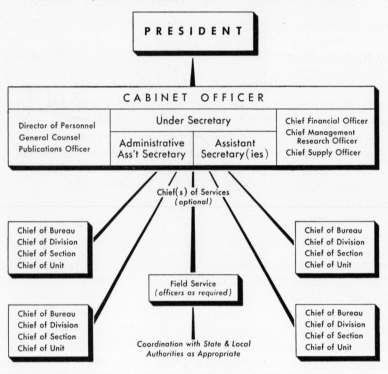

The first Hoover Commission suggested some standardization in internal organization of departments and major agencies, including grouping bureaus by major purposes, strong staff offices, standard nomenclature, and—above all —giving the department head power to reorganize his own administrative setup. Adapted from first Hoover Commission, *General Management of the Executive Branch*, pp. 30–42.

termined by both statutes and executive orders. Many of the bureaus in the federal structure have a statutory basis, a fact that renders reorganization difficult unless the President is delegated authority to transfer units. Bureau heads generally are called "director," "commissioner," or "chief." Civil service status of the bureau head varies, but an increasingly large proportion of them are found within the classified service, and many others are appointed within the spirit of the merit system.[10]

more chance that reorganization can be achieved by executive action.

The first Hoover Commission proposed a standard nomenclature for agencies within a department: service, bureau, division, branch, section, and unit. The bureau would be the principal operating agency, but when several bureaus with closely related functions were operating in the same department, they would be grouped into a common "service." Bureaus would be divided further into smaller agencies as required,

[10] Arthur W. Macmahon and John D. Millett, *Federal Administrators* (Columbia University Press,

1939). See also Schuyler C. Wallace, *Federal Departmentalization* (Columbia University Press, 1941).

utilizing the names "division," "branch," "section," and "unit."

ADMINISTRATIVE PROBLEMS

Administrative Areas. In national administration most functions are provided largely by field officers operating from offices spread over the country. About 90 per cent of federal civil employees are found in field services, and 10 per cent in Washington, D.C. Obviously, if the Department of Agriculture operated solely in the nation's capital, it would contact directly few agrarian problems and serve few farmers. It must reach out into every section and state. This spread over a wide geographic area raises grave problems of organization. Into what administrative areas shall the nation be subdivided? Shall each bureau of each department maintain branch offices in every area, reporting to the bureau in Washington? Or shall all field offices of a department clear through a central field office? Should the field services of the various federal agencies in a given locality be coordinated, or should each operate independently of the other?

The Federal government employs a bewildering variety of administrative areas. Americans were once reasonably familiar with the old nine corps areas of the Army Department (now "Army Areas"), but few realized that the country was divided on several different bases by particular services and corps of the Army. For general administrative purposes the Navy uses seventeen naval districts, but it uses other areas for procurement, recruiting, and other purposes. Most of the federal administrative areas follow state lines. For each area there is designated a headquarters city, and federal offices tend to congregate in San Francisco, New York, Chicago, Boston, New Orleans, Denver, and Atlanta.[11]

It is sometimes proposed that federal administrative areas be standardized; this might result in simplification for the public, in some saving in office rent, and in improved coordination of the various field services. Against it may be argued that the regional needs of federal agencies vary, and that placing them in a strait jacket would decrease their effectiveness.[12]

Federal Field Services. The problem of relationship between headquarters and field service is a knotty one. The typical organization has a direct line of authority from bureau in Washington to regional or field offices throughout the country. For example, a field employee of the Department of the Interior works out of the Denver regional office of the Geological Survey, which in turn reports to the Survey office in Washington. A newer form of organization is found in the Social Security Administration, where regional offices supervise the work of several bureaus of the Administration dealing with old-age insurance, unemployment insurance, and public assistance. The regional director coordinates operations in his region and sends along data to the appropriate bureau of the Administration in Washington. It appears that the latter form would be most difficult to apply to a vast executive department.

How, then, can regional or area coordination be obtained? During the decade of the 1920's "federal business associations" were organized to acquaint field workers with the work of other departments and services in their district. Professor Fesler, who studied this problem for the Committee on Administrative Management, recommended the revitalization of these business associations.[13] They should be, according to this authority, supervised by a regional coordinator of staff (personnel, purchasing, and like) agencies. Local post offices were urged as local clearinghouses for information on federal functions. President Roosevelt, however, established field offices of the Office of Government Reports

---

[11] U.S. National Resources Committee, *Regional Factors in National Planning* (1935), pp. 71–73.

[12] See James W. Fesler, "Standardization of Federal Administrative Regions," *Social Forces,* vol. 15 (October, 1936), pp. 12–21; "Federal Administrative Regions," *American Political Science Review,* vol. 30 (April, 1936), pp. 257–268; and *Area and Administration* (University of Alabama Press, 1949).

[13] "Executive Management and the Federal Field Service," in U.S. President's Committee on Administrative Management, *op. cit.,* pp. 275–294.

in nearly every state and charged them with furnishing information to the public, with liaison work with state agencies, and with reporting to Washington public sentiment on the work of federal agencies.

The two Hoover Commissions gave less attention to field-service problems than did the President's Committee, but the first one did make some pertinent criticisms and a few general suggestions. It found too many separately organized field offices representing departments, bureaus, and even divisions of bureaus. Much of the ineffectiveness of field offices, it reported, is attributable to failure to delegate authority. Lines of direction and supervision between specialized headquarters units and the field often are confused. Inadequate reporting and inspection leave central officials in the dark about field performance. Various federal field offices lack coordination of effort. Cooperation with state and local governments and with private organizations is far from adequate.[14]

Recommendations of the first Hoover Commission included greater standardization of regional boundaries and headquarters, utilization of pooled administrative services (supply, motor transport, space, and other), strengthened reporting and inspection practices, and uniformity of relationships with officials of state and local governments.

Boards and Commissions. Although the plural form of executive has been rejected for federal departments, this is common for independent agencies. Boards and commissions have important uses under a number of circumstances. When quasi-legislative and quasi-judicial powers are assigned to an agency, the plural headship is thought to be advantageous, because independence and continuity are important to policy making and adjudication. Teachers, social workers, and others maintain that the board form is desirable for managing educational, welfare, and some other activities, because a "meeting of minds" is valuable and protection from politics is essential. In instances where the board-commission type has been employed for

administrative work, confusion of responsibility and "buck passing" often have resulted.

As previously pointed out, the solution of the President's Committee on Administrative Management for the federal board-commission problems was to place substantially all of them in the executive departments. The work of regulatory commissions was to be divided, the administrative portion being handled through the appropriate department, and the legislative-administrative aspects remaining with the commission, a relatively autonomous body within the same department. Congress did not accept this solution, preferring to leave the regulatory commissions with their independent status. It is still possible, therefore, for the Federal Trade Commission to follow a policy in regard to business regulation that is out of harmony with that of the Department of Commerce.

The first Hoover Commission found many faults with the independent regulatory commissions, but its proposals for change were less drastic than those of its predecessor. It recommended that all administrative responsibility of a commission be vested in its chairman. The Hoover group suggested several transfers of administrative duties from regulatory commissions to the Departments of Commerce and Interior, but rejected the proposal of its task force that a consolidated transportation commission be established. Some critics of the independent commissions regard as a backward step the Hoover recommendation that all regulatory commissioners be protected against removal by law and that the bipartisanship requirement be extended to all commissions.[15] Some of President Truman's first plans under the Reorganization Act of 1949 made the chairmen of plural bodies the executive officers and administrative chiefs, leaving with the full commissions rule-making and adjudicative authority. These were the Civil Service Commission, the Maritime Commission, the Federal Trade Commission, the Federal Power Commission, the Securities and Exchange Commission, and the Civil Aeronautics Board. The Senate nullified plans which similarly

[14] First Hoover Commission, *General Management of the Executive Branch* (1949), pp. 42–45.

[15] First Hoover Commission, *The Independent Regulatory Commission* (1949), pp. 5–16.

would have transferred administrative authority into the hands of chairmen of, respectively, the Interstate Commerce Commission, the Federal Communications Commission, and the National Labor Relations Board.

In summary, federal boards and commissions are used for several reasons. First, the plural-headed body is established to ensure independence in the exercise of quasi-judicial and quasi-legislative powers. Examples of this are found in the Interstate Commerce Commission, the Federal Communications Commission, and other regulatory bodies. Second, the board may be used to secure interest-group representation, as on the War Production Board or the War Labor Board. Third, this form may be employed when wide discretionary or policy-forming authority is vested in an agency, as with the Civil Service Commission and the National Labor Relations Board. Finally, it is utilized, coupled with over-lapping terms of office, simply to maintain continuity and prevent abrupt changes when Presidents change; this is important in justifying Tariff Commission independence. The part-time advisory board or commission, much used in state and local affairs to enlist the volunteer services of public-spirited citizens, is employed increasingly in national affairs. According to Prof. David S. Brown several hundred federal advisory bodies now exist.[16]

Government Corporations. The corporate form of organization, so common in private business enterprise, has been adapted for use in publicly owned or controlled businesses. Most governmental activities are carried on through the departmental-bureau type of organization. A few have independent status and are not directly responsible to an administrative chief, as are the regulatory boards and commissions, but are subjected to indirect control through appointments and fiscal checks of the Chief Executive. Even less common are the government corporations, incorporated under state or federal law, to carry out some federal function.

Several types of government corporations are

possible. First, there are fifteen wholly government-owned corporations, such as some twenty-four farm credit banks and corporations.[17] Second, there are twenty-four "mixed enterprises" owned in part by the government and in part by others; the Banks for Cooperatives and the Home Loan Banks fall in this category. Third, the corporation may be owned by private shareholders but wholly controlled by the government; this type of "public-utility trust" is used extensively in Great Britain but not in the United States.

The reasons for the adoption of the government corporation form are several. Independence in management is secured, freedom from dependence on annual appropriations and other fiscal controls is attained, and continuity of policy is achieved. Originally some of the federally owned corporations were incorporated under the laws of a particular state, but the advantages of federal incorporation appear greater. Government corporations have boards of directors, sometimes composed wholly or in part of public officials acting ex officio, that determine the policies of the agencies. The directors employ a general manager, who performs functions like those of a manager in private enterprise. Employees generally do not have civil service status, for this might interfere with businesslike conduct of corporation affairs. Financial independence is considerable, with some corporations enjoying the power to borrow money on their own credit and most having authority to reinvest their own earnings. Government corporations may sue and be sued in the courts,

[16] "The Public Advisory Board as an Instrument of Government," *Public Administration Review*, vol. 15 (Summer, 1955), pp. 196–204.

[17] Harold Seidman, "The Theory of the Autonomous Government Corporation: A Critical Appraisal," *Public Administration Review*, vol. 12 (Spring, 1952), pp. 89–96. An extensive literature is available. See Harold A. Van Dorn, *Government Owned Corporations* (Knopf, 1926); Marshall E. Dimock, *Government Operated Enterprises in the Panama Canal Zone* (University of Chicago Press, 1934), and *Developing America's Waterways* (University of Chicago Press, 1935); John McDiarmid, *Government Corporations and Federal Funds* (University of Chicago Press, 1938); John Thurston, *Government Proprietary Corporations in the English Speaking Countries* (Harvard University Press, 1937).

sovereign immunity from suit being dropped under the corporate form.

Under the Government Corporation Control Act of 1945 some standard rules and practices were established.[18] No new government corporations can be created unless authorized by law; all with state incorporation were required to reincorporate under federal law by June 30, 1948. Controls over finances were set up, requiring a "business-type" budget, annual audit, and fuller fiscal reports.

, The first Hoover Commission made a number of recommendations designed further to increase uniformity and to curb the financial independence of government corporations.[19] Among the changes proposed were that major capital additions should require congressional approval, that boards should have advisory powers only, and that standardization should prevail in regard to borrowing powers, federal liability for corporation obligations, and budgetary presentation. The Hoover group also proposed that federal corporations should surrender to the Treasury government securities held by them and should receive in return non-interest-bearing credit.

The more important examples of federal government corporations are the Panama Railway, Tennessee Valley Authority, Federal Deposit Insurance Corporation, Export-Import Bank, and more than 5,000 units of the Farm Credit Administration.

The Separation of Powers. One of the cardinal principles of the American constitutional system is the separation-of-powers doctrine. The principal powers of government, according to this formula, are divided into three parts—legislative, executive, and judicial. So long as governmental problems and functions remained simple, it was possible to have the legislative branch declare public policy by law, and to confine the executive and judicial branches to interpretation and enforcement of such law. This process is found today in many activities of the various levels of American government. For example,

Congress adopts and the President signs a bill forbidding counterfeiting of coins of the realm and providing for 10 years' imprisonment of all convicted of the crime. The law comes into force and is published in the *Statutes-at-large*. Secret service agents of the Treasury apprehend one Joe Luger in the act of molding lead 50-cent pieces. He is arrested, jailed, and tried in the courts. The prosecutor is the United States District Attorney for the area. On conviction Luger is sentenced to serve 10 years in Atlanta penitentiary. In this instance, the conventional methods of policy formation and law enforcement are followed, and the separation-of-powers doctrine proves suitable.

Under modern conditions, however, the problems of government have become so complex and kaleidoscopic that more flexible administration is required in many cases. When, for example, Congress decided that railroad services and rates must be regulated, it created a regulatory commission for the purpose and gave to that body extensive powers to make rules and regulations and to render decisions in cases of conflict. The alternative to this action would have been to establish rates and standards of service in the law and to make them enforceable through the judicial process. The latter scheme would have proved impossible to operate fairly, for it would have produced uneven returns for operating concerns, ranging from unreasonably large profits to severe losses. Therefore the regulatory commission was established, with powers not only to enforce law (administration), but to make rules (legislation), and to settle disputes over law and fact (adjudication).

For a time the courts stood in the way of this development, declaring it violative of the separation-of-powers doctrine.[20] Eventually it was accepted on the ground that the powers granted to administrative agencies were "quasi-legislative" and "quasi-judicial." While the power of Congress to delegate "rule-making" authority to the President has been restricted in two recent

[18] 59 Stat. 557.
[19] First Hoover Commission, *Reorganization of Federal Business Enterprises* (1949), pp. 5–12.

[20] See Charles G. Haines, "The Adaptation of Administrative Law and Procedure to Constitutional Theories and Principles," *American Political Science Review,* vol. 34 (February, 1940), p. 6.

decisions, delegation of authority to regulatory bodies to legislate and to adjudicate appears well established.[21]

ADMINISTRATIVE LEGISLATION AND LICENSING

Need for Quasi-legislation. As governmental problems have grown more complex, numerous, and changeable, Congress and the state legislatures increasingly have entrusted to administrative officers and bodies the responsibility for making detailed rules and regulations. Legislative bodies have delegated this authority for good reasons. First, the administrative officials are more expert in the technical problems to be dealt with. Second, the legislature saves time that may be used for larger problems of public policy. Third, flexibility is secured, so that rules may be adapted to changed conditions and experience.[22]

In 1937 Prof. James Hart found 115 federal agencies empowered to issue rules and regulations that affect the public.[23] Most of these authorizations have been made in the last half century; they have been exercised vigorously during war and crisis, especially in the Wilson and Franklin D. Roosevelt administrations. Administrative rule-making agencies include the President, most of the executive departments, many independent boards and commissions, and other bodies. A rule or regulation that is validly made is enforceable in the courts as law.

Rules for Rule Makers. While the necessity for administrative legislation has been established, several safeguards are required to avoid abuses of authority. Proper notice of proposed action is required. Opportunity to testify at a public hearing usually is made a prerequisite. After a rule or regulation has been made, it is published in

usable form and circulated widely. Some over-all regulation of administrative legislation appears desirable in order to reduce inconsistencies of content and form.

President Roosevelt by executive order implemented the Federal Register Act of 1935 with details on form for proclamations and orders. The Division of the Federal Register is located in the National Archives and Records Service, which is a part of the General Services Administration. The *Federal Register,* issued five times a week, contains presidential proclamations and executive orders and other documents of general applicability and legal effect. While regularization at the departmental level and the prenatal procedural safeguards have not been fully assured, the other proposals—postnatal publicity, coordination, and uniformity—have had some measure of acceptance.

A thorough study of these problems was made by the Attorney General's Committee on Administrative Procedure. Its report,[24] filed in January, 1941, and the thirteen supporting monographs,[25] constitute the chief source of data in this field. In 1946 Congress enacted and the President signed the Administrative Procedure Act. In addition to its general provisions requiring agencies to inform the public regarding organization, procedure, rules, policies, and interpretations, there are some specific requirements about rule making. (1) Notice must be published in the *Federal Register* stating the time, place, nature, and authority for the proposed rules. (2) Interested persons may participate by submitting views, data, and arguments. (3) Rules must be published at least 30 days before the effective date. (4) The right to petition for issuance, change, or repeal of a rule is guaranteed.[26]

---

[21] Compare the Panama Refining case and the Schechter case rulings with the delegation to regulatory bodies described on p. 322.

[22] See Frederick F. Blachly and Miriam E. Oatman, *Administrative Legislation and Adjudication* (Brookings, 1934), pp. 43–53; James Hart, "The Exercise of the Rule-making Power," in U.S. President's Committee on Administrative Management, *op. cit.,* pp. 314–352.

[23] Hart, *op. cit.,* p. 319.

[24] U.S. Attorney General's Committee on Administrative Procedure, *Administrative Procedure in Government Agencies, Report of the . . . ,* S. Doc. 8, 77th Cong., 1st Sess. (1941).

[25] S. Doc. 186, 76th Cong., 3d Sess. (1940). There were also twenty-seven mimeographed monographs.

[26] See Foster H. Sherwood, "The Federal Administrative Procedure Act," *American Political Science Review,* vol. 41 (April, 1947), pp. 271–281.

Licensing Powers. Another form of delegating authority to administrative officials is involved in licensing. Licensing laws customarily prohibit the practice of a profession or the operation of a business unless a permit or license has been secured in advance. The discretionary authority possessed by a licensing officer or body sometimes is very great.

Licenses of importance usually are subject to suspension or revocation for cause. A radio station that violates the conditions under which its license was granted may face revocation, suspension, or failure to renew by action of the Federal Communications Commission.

State and local governments utilize licensing more than does the Federal government. The principal federal uses of licensing are authorized in the following statutes:[27]

1916 Warehouses Act
1920 Water Power Act
1921 Packers and Stockyards Act
1922 Grain Futures Act
1927 Radio Commission Act (now Federal Communications Act of 1934)
1934 Securities and Exchange Act

To these were added licensing of armament manufacturing in 1935 and of atomic materials in 1946.

A rather simple example of federal licensing is found in the live-poultry amendment added to the Packers and Stockyards Act of 1935.[28] Enacted to curb fraudulent practices that restrain interstate commerce at large centers of population, the act authorizes the secretary to designate which markets require regulation. All poultry handlers within a designated market must secure a license from the secretary in order to continue in business. Licenses may be denied because of a record of unfair practices

within the past 2 years or inability to meet financial obligations. In administering the act, the department proceeds informally and provides much aid to applicants in filling out forms and preparing the necessary financial statement.

The second Hoover Commission recommended that Congress should be explicit in its delegation of licensing powers to administrative agencies, especially with reference to revocation and suspension.[29] In revocation proceedings, a licensee should be given an opportunity to answer to and rectify alleged violations of the license. In renewal proceedings, administrative action should be taken before expiration date, assuming the application was filed on time and no violation has occurred.

ADMINISTRATIVE ADJUDICATION

Adjudicative Agencies. Administrative adjudication has been defined by Blachly and Oatman as ". . . investigation and settling of a dispute on the basis of fact and law, by an administrative agency which may or may not be organized to act solely as an administrative court."[30] So long as the administrative process remains clear of conflict, adjudication is unnecessary. When a dispute arises, however, its settlement requires adjudication. In instances where the decision is rendered by an administrative officer or body, the adjudication is called "administrative." Thereafter litigation continues in the courts and is called "judicial review of administrative action." Court review will be dealt with in the next subsection.

Why should administrative tribunals exist and administrative bodies be assigned quasi-judicial powers? First, because expertness is required in many technical fields of administration. Second, informal proceedings save time and expense and make possible adaptability to changed conditions. Third, decisions are rendered by officers acquainted with the social and economic philosophy underlying the function. Fourth, when government enters a new field of activity, the administrative process provides

---

[27] Charles V. Koons, "Growth of Federal Licensing," *Georgetown Law Review,* vol. 24 (January, 1936), pp. 293–344.

[28] U.S. Attorney General's Committee on Administrative Procedure, *Monograph of the . . . , Part 11, Administration of the Packers and Stockyards Act, Department of Agriculture,* S. Doc. 186, 76th Cong., 3d Sess. (1940), pp. 3–4, 10–13.

[29] Second Hoover Commission, *Legal Services and Procedure* (1955), pp. 58–59.

[30] Blachly and Oatman, *op. cit.,* p. 91.

the necessary flexibility for experimentation by trial and error. The Attorney General's Committee on Administrative Procedure pointed out that the "great bulk of administrative decisions are made informally and by mutual consent." [31] This means that potential disputes are ironed out by investigation, consultation, and adjustment before formal procedure is resorted to.

When formal adjudication is required, greatest care must be given to how the tribunal is constituted and what its procedure is like. Blachly and Oatman classify these adjudicative authorities into several groups, of which three are of great importance.[32] First, a few courts are largely concerned with administrative matters. Examples are the Tax Court, the Court of Claims, the Customs Court, and the Court of Customs and Patent Appeals. These tribunals operate like courts of law and are presided over by "judges." Second, several administrative tribunals are found within executive departments, as the Civil Aeronautics Board, the Patent Office, and the like. The members are specialized—but less detached than those judges of the first group. Third, the great regulatory commissions with administrative quasi-judicial and quasi-legislative powers. These include the Interstate Commerce Commission, Federal Trade Commission, Federal Communications Commission, Federal Power Commission, Securities and Exchange Commission, and others. In addition, there are executive department heads, as the Secretary of Agriculture, endowed with adjudicative powers. Also there are various licensing authorities, and the Comptroller General.

Methods of Adjudication. The first step in formal administrative adjudication involves the filing of a complaint or a request for hearing by an interested party; the dispute may arise between conflicting private interests, or between the public agency and a private interest. Second, a "hearing officer" takes testimony and evidence upon which a fair decision may be based; in some cases the officer has power to render an initial decision in the case. Third, the

board or commission or head, advised by legal staff, renders the ultimate decision in the case, subject to the court review prescribed by law.

The hearing-examiner problem has claimed much attention in the several studies of the administrative process. In 1954 there were fewer than three hundred such officers, most of whom worked regularly in Washington, D.C. Under the terms of the Administrative Procedure Act, the Civil Service Commission was assigned the task of selecting and promoting hearing officers. The Commission set up a board of examiners, which gave examinations to both incumbents and new applicants. About one-third of the incumbents were found disqualified, but the Commission—faced with a barrage of appeals and protests—retained all incumbents. In 1954 the Commission tightened up on transactions involving hearing examiners. But the agencies continue to have a good deal of power over their examiners.

Reforms Proposed. The second Hoover Commission was concerned over administrative intrusion into judicial functions and made a number of recommendations that tended in the direction of further separation of the function of prosecuting from the function of deciding.

The most sweeping departure was contained in the proposal for an "Administrative Court of the United States" with three sections: (1) a Tax Section, with jurisdiction of the existing Tax Court; (2) a Trade Section, which would have the adjudicatory authority now vested in the Federal Trade Commission, the Interstate Commerce Commission, the Federal Communications Commission, the Civil Aeronautics Board, the Federal Reserve Board, the United States Tariff Commission, the Federal Power Commission, and the Interior and Agriculture Departments; (3) a Labor Section, which would take over the unfair labor practice cases from the National Labor Relations Board.[33] The Hoover group suggested that Congress study and determine whether the trade and labor sections should have original or appellate jurisdiction.

[31] *Administrative Procedure in Government Agencies,* p. 35.

[32] Blachly and Oatman, *op. cit.,* pp. 120–162.

[33] Second Hoover Commission, *Legal Services and Procedure* (1955), pp. 87–88.

The thinking of the Departments and agencies was reflected in the report of the Conference on Administrative Procedure convened by President Eisenhower in 1953. Each of the fifty-seven with rule-making and adjudicatory functions was invited to send a delegate. After careful committee work and four plenary sessions spread over six months, the Conference produced a number of recommendations, including:

1. An "office of administrative procedure should be established in the Department of Justice and given the duty of studying procedures in the agencies and developing uniform rules of practice"

2. The filing of "abbreviated records" with the Courts of Appeals should be authorized in the review of federal agency orders

3. A "bureau of hearing examiner administration" should be set up in the Civil Service Commission

The second Hoover Commission agreed on the desirability of a coordinating agency. It proposed for the Department of Justice an "office of legal services and procedure" to work on simplification, clarification, and uniformity. Like the earlier Attorney General's Committee, the Hoover group proposed that a corps of "hearing commissioners" be created and given fixed terms and independent status. Control and direction would come from the proposed "Administrative Court," a judicial agency.

CONTROL OVER ADMINISTRATIVE ACTION

Judicial Review of Administrative Action. The right to appeal decisions, rules, and orders by administrative bodies to the courts of law is widely regarded as necessary and proper. Although the great majority of instances of administrative action are accepted without formal dispute, as noted before, the volume of cases before administrative bodies nevertheless is large. Only a very small proportion of these cases is appealed to the ordinary courts, but such cases constitute an important share of the total litigation before the Federal courts.

Judicial review has as its objective, according to the Attorney General's Committee on Administrative Procedure, ". . . to serve as a check on the administrative branch of government—a check against excess of power and abusive exercise of power in derogation of private right." [34] That committee stressed that the courts can review to ensure the fairness of administrative action, but that they cannot assure the correctness of such action. The volume of administrative action is too great to permit extensive review, and the court cannot match the administrative bodies in specialization and expertness. The appropriate role of the court in reviewing administrative action would appear to include examination of the propriety of the interpretation of the law, and assurance that the proceedings have not been unreasonable.

In practice these principles have been followed generally by the Federal courts in reviewing administrative action. The Federal courts, faced with a case involving a request for review of administrative action, first see that the Constitution has been followed, especially that there has been no deprivation of liberty or property without due process of law, either procedural or substantive. Next, the court may look to the federal law under which the administrative body was created or the right of appeal was established; considerable variation exists in the right of appeal, the methods of appeal, and the degree of administrative finality. Even in cases where the Constitution is not violated and statutory requirements are met, the remedies of an aggrieved person are not exhausted. He may sue an official for damages, or seek an injunction to forbid certain acts by an administrative agency. In general the courts have required due notice and a full and fair hearing on the procedural side.

Congress has provided for appeal of administrative decisions to various court levels. Appeals from several of the regulatory commissions go directly to the United States Courts of Appeals. Action of other bodies is reviewable in the district courts, or before a three-judge panel in the

[34] *Administrative Procedure in Government Agencies,* p. 76.

district courts. Customs and patent appeals go to the Court of Customs and Patent Appeals.

In considering court reviewability of administrative action, one of the most important aspects concerns control over findings of fact. If the court finds that there are no facts to support the action, it holds due process lacking.[35] Beginning with the Interstate Commerce Commission, fact finding by the agency was declared in the statute to be prima facie evidence. Fact finding by several other agencies is conclusive if supported by the weight of evidence. While the courts at times have inclined to let stand administrative findings of fact unless proved insubstantial, occasionally they have intervened to the extent of reviewing the facts fully and anew.

Questions of law, however, fall under the full purview of the courts. The court may set aside administrative action because of errors of law. In many cases, of course, questions of fact and law are intermingled, and the court has all necessary discretion to rule as it sees fit. Commenting on the lack of sharp distinction between questions of law and fact, John Dickinson concluded: "The knife of policy alone effects an artificial cleavage at the point where the court chooses to draw the line between public interest and private right."[36]

Reform of Court Review. Complaints over judicial review of administrative action may be divided into two groups. One set is voiced by those who fear administrative finality and who allege that an aggrieved person has insufficient remedies. The other is presented by defenders of the administrative process, who feel the courts have interfered excessively in substituting their own findings of fact and judgment for those of the administrative body. Both sides in the controversy have agreed to the proposition that improvements in the judicial review of administrative action are possible; that procedures lack

uniformity, clarity, and other attributes of a desirable appellate system.

The Logan-Walter bill became the center of this controversy in 1939.[37] Backed by the American Bar Association, the bill passed both houses during 1940 but was vetoed by President Roosevelt. This legislation would have given the Court of Appeals for the District of Columbia jurisdiction to hear and determine, within 30 days of issuance, whether an administrative rule conflicted with law or Constitution. Decisions and orders of administrative agencies could be reviewed in the Court of Appeals within 30 days, and set aside on grounds that fact findings were erroneous, due notice or fair hearing was denied, or law or Constitution violated. Appellate court decisions were to be final except where the Supreme Court called them up for review through writ of certiorari or certificate. The judicial review features of the bill were attacked vigorously as likely to lead to endless court litigation, and to render impossible proper functioning of administrative agencies.

A portion of the report of the Attorney General's Committee on Administrative Procedure was devoted to court review. This report found that in general the existing diversity governing court review of administrative action is not troublesome. The committee proposed no innovations so far as judicial review is concerned but concentrated instead on adjusting procedure to minimize the necessity for appeals.[38] The Administrative Procedure Act of 1946 simply provided for judicial review to remedy every "legal wrong." Judicial review is authorized except when precluded by law. The law occupies a middle ground between the Logan-Walter school, which wanted every administrative act subjected to judicial review, and some defenders of the agencies, who wished to minimize court appeals. Actually, the law slightly broadened court review, but the extent has been controlled by the courts themselves through their interpretations. The second Hoover Commission reem-

---

[35] See analysis of Frederick F. Blachly and Miriam E. Oatman, *Federal Regulatory Action and Control* (Brookings, 1940), pp. 119–124.

[36] John Dickinson, *Administrative Justice and the Supremacy of the Law* (Harvard University Press, 1927), p. 55.

[37] It was H.R. 6324 and S. 915 in the 76th Cong. Secs. 3 and 5 related to judicial review.

[38] *Administrative Procedure in Government Agencies,* pp. 75–95 and pp. 115–120.

phasized the virtues of "plain, simple, and prompt" judicial review "for every legal wrong resulting from agency action or inaction." [39]

Legislative Control. Administrative action is also subject to external control by legislative bodies. (1) Congress determines the statutory framework (structure, powers, duties) within which the federal administrative agencies operate. Although in recent years this control is less rigid, due to the tendency to draft legislation in general terms, supremacy of the legislature in matters of policy has been retained. (2) Congressional and state legislative control over appropriations provides a second avenue of checking administrative responsibility. The stewardship of a particular agency is reviewed regularly in budget hearings, and the purse strings may be tightened to indicate legislative displeasure with administrative conduct. (3) Congress and nearly all state legislatures possess power to investigate as ancillary to the power to legislate. A large proportion of the investigating committees that are established concern themselves wholly or partially with inquiring

about administrative conduct. The possibility that an investigation will be made is itself an effective deterrent on administrative excesses.

The task of securing the correct amount and quality of legislative control over administration is at once intricate and colossal. Lack of vigilance by a legislative body may lead to administrative highhandedness. Over-intervention in the detail of the administrative process and personnel can bring irresponsible conduct and spoils politics. The legislative branch properly determines general policy and structure and makes inquiries into administrative practices to see that legislative intent is being carried out. It should not attempt to administer, directly or indirectly, nor interfere in administration in such a manner that initiative will be curbed, flexibility made impossible, and able personnel driven from public service.[40]

[39] Second Hoover Commission, *Legal Services and Procedure* (1955), p. 75.

[40] For able discussions of these problems, see Frank C. Newman and H. J. Keaton, "Congress and the Faithful Execution of Laws: Should Legislators Supervise Administrators?" *California Law Review,* vol. 41 (Winter, 1953–1954), pp. 565–595; and Leonard D. White, "Congressional Control of the Public Service," *American Political Science Review,* vol. 39 (February, 1945), pp. 1–11.

FOR FURTHER READING

(See also works at end of Chap. 14.)

American Society for Public Administration: *Public Administration Review* (quarterly).

Appleby, Paul H.: *Policy and Administration* (University of Alabama Press, 1949).

Blachly, Frederick F., and Miriam Oatman: *Federal Regulatory Action and Control* (Brookings, 1940).

——: *Administrative Legislation and Adjudication* (Brookings, 1934).

Caldwell, Lynton K.: *The Administrative Theories of Hamilton and Jefferson: Their Contributions to Thought on Public Administration* (University of Chicago Press, 1944).

Committee on Public Administration of the Social Science Research Council: *Case Reports in Public Administration* (Chicago: Public Administration Service, 1940 and thereafter). Looseleaf, 100 reports.

Cushman, Robert E.: *The Independent Regulatory Commissions* (Oxford, 1941).

Davis, John A.: *Regional Organization of the Social Security Administration: A Case Study* (Columbia University Press, 1950).

Dickinson, John: *Administrative Justice and the Supremacy of the Law* (Harvard University Press, 1927).

Dimock, Marshall E., and Gladys Dimock: *Public Administration* (Rinehart, 1953).

Doyle, Wilson K.: *Independent Commissions in the Federal Government* (The University of North Carolina Press, 1939).

Emmerich, Herbert: *Essays on Federal Reorganization* (University of Alabama Press, 1950).

Fesler, James W.: *Area and Administration* (University of Alabama Press, 1949).

Freund, Ernst: *Administrative Powers over Persons and Property* (University of Chicago Press, 1928).

Gaus, John M.: *Reflections on Public Administration* (University of Alabama Press, 1947).

———, Leonard D. White, and Marshall E. Dimock: *Frontiers of Public Administration* (University of Chicago Press, 1936).

——— and L. O. Wolcott: *Public Administration and the United States Department of Agriculture* (Chicago: Public Administration Service, 1940).

Gellhorn, Walter: *Federal Administrative Proceedings* (Johns Hopkins Press, 1941).

———: *Administrative Law: Cases and Comments* (Chicago: Foundation Press, 3d ed., 1954).

Glaser, Comstock: *Administrative Procedure: A Practical Handbook for the Administrative Analyst* (American Council on Public Affairs, 1941).

Goldberg, Sidney D., and Harold Seidman: *The Government Corporation: Elements of a Model Charter* (Chicago: Public Administration Service, 1953).

Graham, George, and Henry Reining, Jr. (eds.): *Regulatory Administration* (Wiley, 1943).

Graves, W. Brooke: *Public Administration* (Heath, 1950).

———: *Basic Information on the Reorganization of the Executive Branch, 1912–1948,* Public Affairs Bulletin No. 66 (Library of Congress, 1949).

Gulick, Luther: *Administrative Reflections from World War II* (University of Alabama Press, 1948).

——— and Lyndall Urwick (eds.): *Papers on the Science of Administration* (New York: Institute of Public Administration, 1937).

Hart, James: *An Introduction to Administrative Law, with Selected Cases* (Appleton-Century-Crofts, 1940).

———: *The Ordinance-making Power of the President of the United States* (Johns Hopkins Press, 1925).

Landis, James M.: *The Administrative Process* (Yale University Press, 1938).

Latham, Earl, and Others: *The Federal Field Service: An Analysis with Suggestions for Research* (Chicago: Public Administration Service, 1947).

Leiserson, Avery: *Administrative Regulation: A Study of Representation of Interests* (University of Chicago Press, 1942).

Lepawsky, Albert: *Administration: The Art and Science of Organization and Management* (Knopf, 1949).

McDiarmid, John: *Government Corporations and Federal Funds* (University of Chicago Press, 1938).

Macmahon, Arthur W., and John D. Millett: *Federal Administrators: A Biographical Approach to the Problem of Departmental Management* (Columbia University Press, 1939).

Meriam, Lewis, and Laurence F. Schmeckebier: *Reorganization of the National Government: What Does It Involve?* (Brookings, 1939).

Millett, John D.: *Management in the Public Service* (McGraw-Hill, 1954).

Millspaugh, Arthur C.: *Toward Efficient Democracy: The Question of Governmental Organization* (Brookings, 1949).

Pennock, J. Roland: *Administration and the Rule of Law* (Rinehart, 1941).

Pfiffner, John M., and Vance Presthus: *Public Administration* (Ronald, 3d ed., 1953).

Pritchett, C. Herman: *The Tennessee Valley Authority: A Study in Public Administration* (The University of North Carolina Press, 1943).

Redford, Emmette S.: *Administration of National Economic Control* (Macmillan, 1952).

Sanders, Jennings B.: *Evolution of Executive Departments of the Continental Congress, 1774–1789* (The University of North Carolina Press, 1935).

Seckler-Hudson, Catheryn (ed.): *Processes of Organization and Management* (Washington, D.C.: Public Affairs Press, 1948).

Short, Lloyd M.: *Development of National Administrative Organization in the United States* (Johns Hopkins Press, 1923).

Simon, Herbert A.: *Administrative Behavior: A Study of Decision-making in Administrative Organization* (Macmillan, 1947).

Truman, David B.: *Administrative Decentralization* (University of Chicago Press, 1940).

U.S. Attorney General's Committee on Administrative Procedure: *Administrative Procedure in Government Agencies, Report* . . . S. Doc. 8, 77th Cong., 1st Sess. (1941).

U.S. Commission on Organization of the Executive Branch of the Government (second Hoover Commission): *Report* . . . (19 vols., 1955). In addition, 18 task-force reports were published.

U.S. Commission on Organization of the Executive Branch of the Government (first Hoover Commission): *Report* . . . (19 vols., 1949). In addition, 19 task-force reports were published.

U.S. President's Committee on Administrative Management: *Report . . . with Studies of Administrative Management in the Federal Government* (1937).

Urwick, Lyndall: *The Elements of Administration* (Harper, 1944).

Waldo, Dwight: *The Administrative State: A Study of the Political Theory of American Public Administration* (Ronald, 1948).

Wallace, Schuyler: *Federal Departmentalization: A Critique of Theories of Organization* (Columbia University Press, 1941).

Warren, George (ed.): *The Federal Administrative Procedure Act and the Administrative Agencies* (New York University School of Law, 1947).

White, Leonard D.: *The Jeffersonians* (Macmillan, 1951).

——: *The Federalists: A Study in Administrative History* (Macmillan, 1948).

——: *Introduction to the Study of Public Administration* (Macmillan, 3d ed., 1948).

Willoughby, William F.: *Principles of Public Administration* (Johns Hopkins Press, 1927).

REVIEW QUESTIONS

1. What is the constitutional relationship between the President and the administrative structure? Between Congress and the administrative structure?

2. How can you explain the reluctance of Congress to establish new departments? Trace the recent history of efforts toward this end.

3. To what extent has Congress been willing to entrust power to reorganize agencies to recent Presidents (Hoover to Eisenhower)? What provisions for nullification were made?

4. Explain some of the problems involved in defining proper administrative areas and in organizing effective field services.

5. Under what circumstances would the board-commission form of organization be appropriate for an administrative agency headship? Discuss.

6. Describe the recent experience of the Federal government in providing for judicial review of administrative action.

7. What safeguards have been erected to prevent abuses of authority in administrative rule making?

8. Under what circumstances is the government corporation a proper form to organize a federal undertaking? Discuss some of the problems connected with public corporations.

9. To what extraordinary stresses and strains is the separation-of-powers doctrine subjected under modern conditions when a single agency of government may not only administer a law but also make rules and regulations and render decisions in case of conflicts?

CHAPTER 18

The Civil Service

We must have government to live, to work, to advance, to enjoy the fruits of our labor. The success or failure of that government, and the kind of service which it renders, will rest in the last analysis upon the capacity and character of the men and women who constitute it. We must therefore maintain a governmental system under which the government attracts to the public service its share of the capacity and character of the man power of the nation. — Commission of Inquiry on Public Service Personnel [1]

After administrative organization and powers, the next important prerequisite to effective administration is manpower. In the days when the republic was young, few employees were necessary, and the task of hiring and firing was not unlike that of a small business concern. Today, however, the administrative leviathan of the Federal government has reached enormous size, requiring careful management of every phase of personnel work. Machinery has been devised to cope with this great problem. Personnel agencies of Federal, state, and municipal governments have done a fairly good job and have received much public support.

No government exists for the purpose of employing people; it is to accomplish the goals of fostering agriculture, regulating commerce, protecting life and property, that public employees are needed. If the personnel system can find and recruit the person most qualified for the job to be filled and can maintain his morale at a high level, the public interest obviously will be better served than if an ill-equipped person is given the job or if the incumbent is dissatis-

[1] *Better Government Personnel* (McGraw-Hill, 1935), p. 15.

fied with the work. This places great emphasis on the importance of personnel work in modern governments.

DEVELOPMENT OF AMERICAN MERIT SYSTEMS

Early Personnel Policies. The Constitution charges the President with appointing and the Senate with confirming "officers" of the United States. Authority to appoint "inferior officers" may be vested by law in the President alone, in the heads of executive departments, or in the courts. President Washington established the tradition of appointing for competency. Adams showed preference for those of his own political leanings. Jefferson sought to replace Federalists with his own partisans; this turnover has been computed as involving about 25 per cent of employees under presidential control.[2] The political complexion of Madison and Monroe was Jeffersonian, minimizing the incentive to change; John Quincy Adams failed to alter the

[2] Carl R. Fish, "Removal of Officials by the Presidents of the United States," *Annual Report of the American Historical Association for the Year 1899* (Government Printing Office, 1900), vol. I, p. 70.

general policy of long continuance in office. This era, from 1789 to 1829, has been termed the "period of relative administrative efficiency."[3]

The Spoils System. When Andrew Jackson took office on Mar. 4, 1829, he found many federal offices occupied by political opponents. In December of that year he gave his first annual message to Congress, in which he recommended limiting appointments to 4 years:

There are, perhaps, a few men who can for any great length of time enjoy office and power without being more or less under the influence of feelings unfavorable to the faithful discharge of their public duties. Their integrity may be proof against improper considerations immediately addressed to themselves, but they are apt to acquire a habit of looking with indifference upon the public interests and of tolerating conduct from which an unpracticed man would revolt. . . . The duties of all public officers are, or at least admit of being made, so plain and simple that men of intelligence may readily qualify themselves for their performance; and I can not but believe that more is lost by the long continuance of men in office than is generally to be gained by their experience.[4]

The case for rotation in office was strong in Jackson's time. Governmental work was still relatively simple. Jackson's regime, representing a definite break with the past, would not be frustrated by bureaucrats held over from the John Quincy Adams administration.

Between 1829 and the close of the Civil War the spoils system flourished. To job spoils were added other types of spoils—contracts, graft, and the like. In this period of national expansion opportunities for corruption were plentiful. While the spoils system has not been wholly eliminated even today, important reforms were proposed and adopted in the two decades after the Civil War.

Civil Service Reform. Even before the Civil War steps were taken to bring some order out of the chaos then prevailing in the personnel field. Acts of 1853 and 1855 established four classes of clerks in Washington departmental offices and set up a scale of salaries.[5] "Pass" examinations were introduced in each Department, providing that an appointee must pass some departmental test before taking office. In 1871, during Grant's administration, an appropriation-bill rider authorized the President to set up regulations on appointments and to ascertain fitness of candidates for positions. Accordingly, President Grant created an Advisory Board of the Civil Service, and the first competitive examinations were given in 1872. Lacking appropriations for the purpose, Grant abandoned the experiment in 1875. Progress was made in the Hayes administration, especially in relation to federal employees in New York City.

In July, 1881, President James A. Garfield was fatally wounded by a disappointed office seeker. Public indignation over the spoils system reached a high pitch and provided an impetus for the enactment of the Pendleton Act in January, 1883. The law established a Civil Service Commission of three members and provided for open competitive examinations. Discrimination for political reasons was forbidden. Appointment continued to be a function of the President or department head, but his choice was limited to those who ranked in the top four on the eligible list prepared by the Commission. The act left to the President and Congress the extension of the "classified service," those employees coming under the protection of the formal merit system.

State and Local Adoptions. The American states followed the Federal government in adopting civil-service systems, but fewer than one-half of the states have seen fit to embrace

---

[3] William E. Mosher, J. Donald Kingsley, and O. Glenn Stahl, *Public Personnel Administration* (Harper, 3d ed., 1950), pp. 17–18.

[4] James D. Richardson (ed.), *Messages and Papers of the Presidents* (New York: Bureau of National Literature, 20 vols., 1897–1916), vol. 3, pp. 1011–1012. Fish, *op. cit.*, p. 74, reports that Jackson removed 279 out of a total of about 610 officers.

[5] The growth of reform sentiment is interestingly described in U.S. Civil Service Commission, *History of the Federal Civil Service, 1789 to the Present* (1941), pp. 32–52.

this reform fully. New York and Massachusetts pioneered with their legislation of 1883 and 1885. Other states that now have state-wide merit systems are Wisconsin, Illinois, Colorado, New Jersey, Ohio, California, Connecticut, Kansas, Maryland, Michigan, Tennessee, Maine, Alabama, Rhode Island, Minnesota, Virginia, Oregon, and North Carolina. It will be noted that all the populous states, excepting Pennsylvania and Texas, are included in the list of those with state-wide civil-service systems. All states, in order to be eligible for social security grants, have established merit systems for employees in aided functions.

A number of counties have adopted civil service plans. Some have remarkably good records in the personnel field, but perhaps the majority are in the hands of spoilsmen. Less progress has been made on the county level than in any other strata of government. Most of the large cities and a great many smaller municipalities have some sort of civil-service systems. Policemen and firemen often are protected even where other employees are not.

Townships and special districts rarely utilize civil service systems, but school districts commonly have either formal or informal merit systems. Teacher-tenure plans represent only minor variations from the general pattern of a protected personnel.

PERSONNEL AGENCIES

United States Civil Service Commission. Because it was established first and because national institutions serve as models for the states, the United States Civil Service Commission deserves initial consideration. Established under the Pendleton Act, signed by President Arthur on Jan. 16, 1883, the Commission consists of three members appointed by the President, with Senate confirmation. No more than two might be members of the same political party. Commissioners serve for no fixed term, but at the pleasure of the President. From an original negative conception of eliminating politics in appointments, the Commission has come to play the leading role in a positive and broad per-

sonnel-improvement program. The personnel study of the President's Committee on Administrative Management computed the average length of service by commissioners at 4.7 years.[6]

The Commission is charged by the act with advising the President on civil service rules. Evidently the relationship of Commission and President rarely has been intimate. The body files an annual report, reviewing its work and making recommendations for extension of the classified service. The administrative work of the Commission under a reorganization plan of 1949 is the responsibility of the chairman alone. Acting through an executive director appointed by him, the chairman oversees and supervises the work of the several bureaus, divisions, offices, and boards.

Geographically the country is divided into fourteen civil service regions, each with a regional office at a central city. These offices publicize and conduct examinations and serve the personnel needs of the field services of the various federal agencies.

Other Federal Personnel Agencies. While the Civil Service Commission is the principal federal personnel agency, other agencies play important parts in the field. The Commission is not, except for its own employees, the appointing agency; appointment is made by the department or agency in which the appointee will serve. The federal executive departments and other large agencies have directors of personnel. Such officers are placed in charge of selecting from civil service eligible lists the individuals most likely to prove suitable for particular positions, and they also take over many routine personnel duties of heads of Departments and other agencies.

The personnel offices in the operating departments and agencies have emerged, since 1938, with key roles in appointing, rating, promoting, and otherwise serving federal employees. The decentralization program proposed by the

[6] Floyd W. Reeves and Paul T. David, "Personnel Administration in the Federal Service," in U.S. President's Committee on Administrative Management, *Report . . . with Studies . . .* (1937), p. 74.

first Hoover Commission placed even more stress on the importance of personnel offices in operating units. For some 2 million federal civil workers, there are about 25,000 employees of personnel offices. The Hoover group criticized overstaffing in the offices of some of the agencies; in some instances it found one personnel worker for as few as thirty-eight employees. Under the reforms proposed, recruiting, examining, and selecting of employees would be conducted largely by the operating agencies, subject to the uniform employment standards and regulations determined and supervised by the Civil Service Commission. Much of this has been achieved.

Reform of Personnel Organization. The Federal government has tried two types of overhead organization for its central personnel agency.

From the beginning of the formal civil service in 1883 until 1949, the *commission* was the dominant force in Federal personnel matters. It possessed administrative, rule-making, and adjudicative powers. The form had the advantage of providing a "council of minds" when policy was being determined or judicial-type decisions were being rendered; it also served to insulate the agency to some extent against partisan political pressures. Over the years, however, a number of disadvantages were pointed up: responsibility for administration was diffused, expertness often was lacking among lay commissioners, and independent status deprived the chief executive of what could have been a principal managerial "arm."

The net effect of putting into force some of the first Hoover Commission recommendations has been to establish a hybrid *commission-administrator* plan. In a reorganization plan of 1949 the chairman of the Civil Service Commission was vested with all administrative authority, including the functions of appointing, supervising, and directing personnel and internal organization. In practice, much of the administrative work is delegated by the chairman to the "executive director," who is appointed by the chairman. The Commission as a body retains power to make rules and regulations,

hear appeals, investigate, and recommend improvements. The office of personnel, which the first Hoover Commission recommended be established in the Executive Office of the President, has not been created; the need for it may have been met by the practice of President Eisenhower in including the Chairman of the Commission among those who attend and participate in cabinet meetings.

Many students of public personnel problems feel that the next step is to transfer management of the function to a *single administrator*. This was the core of the President's Committee on Administrative Management personnel recommendation. The first Hoover report contained a statement of additional views by James K. Pollock, who made a strong case for going the whole distance toward a "modern concept" by vesting management under a single personnel commissioner.

Negative vs. Positive Approach. Even more important than the overhead organization of personnel management is the attitude and approach of the managers. American civil service, in its early and formative years, was developed to the theme of "fighting the spoilsmen." The Commission took over the job of personnel administration from the Departments and performed it for them. Between 1938, when personnel offices were authorized in the Departments and agencies by executive order, and 1949, when the first Hoover Commission underscored the need for decentralization, much conflict ensued. The Commission held somewhat tenaciously to its negative, policing approach. The Departments and agencies sought to get the best person for the job, a task requiring initiative and aggressiveness in a period of relatively full employment.

After 1949 the shift of emphasis and function changed. The Hoover recommendation that primary responsibility for recruiting and examining be placed on Departments and agencies was put into force. The Commission reluctantly shifted toward a role of setting standards for the personnel offices of operating agencies, and away from the extreme centralization under

which it handled most detailed personnel transactions.

EXTENT OF THE CLASSIFIED SERVICE

Federal employment at the end of December, 1954, totaled 2,381,321, of whom approximately 86 per cent were under the classified
civil service. Of the total, 154,465 were on duty

of 1940,[7] the President was authorized to include in the classified service, with few exceptions, all non-policy-forming positions. Nevertheless, when President Truman in 1952 issued
a reorganization order to bring postmasters, customs officials, and marshals into the classified
category, the Senate disapproved and nullified
the action.

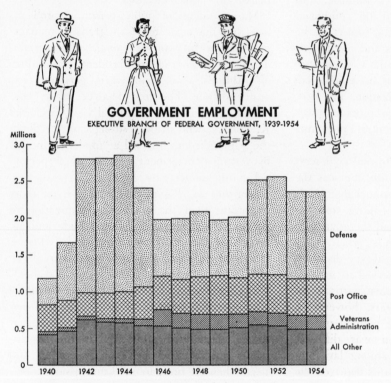

GOVERNMENT EMPLOYMENT
EXECUTIVE BRANCH OF FEDERAL GOVERNMENT, 1939-1954

The trend of federal employment.
Before large-scale reduction of
civilian employees can be made,
the Department of Defense—
which employs about one-half of
the total—will have to be cut.
Data from U.S. Civil Service
Commission.

in foreign countries, and 72,526 in territories
and possessions of the United States. Their distribution among the several Departments and
agencies may be seen on the chart above.

Expansion of Coverage. The Pendleton Act
provided that the "classified service" should be
extended by presidential order or by act of Congress. Only 13,900 positions, or 10.5 per cent of
executive employees, were included in the
classified group in 1883. Each President who
has served since then has increased the number
of positions included; at times the motivation
appears to have been the improvement of the
public service; at others, the "blanketing-in" of
political appointees. Under the Ramspeck Act

Who Should Be Exempt? The Federal civil
employees outside the formal classified civil
service are in two principal groups: those in
exempt positions and temporary employees. The
task force of the first Hoover Commission
identified three exempt categories: (1) positions of a policy-forming character; (2) positions of a confidential nature; and (3) positions for which competitive examinations are
impractical.[8]

Some agencies have employees exempt from
the classified service under specific statutory

[7] 54 Stat. 1211.
[8] First Hoover Commission, *Task Force Report on
Federal Personnel* (1949), p. 19.

provision; examples are the **Tennessee Valley Authority** and the Foreign Service. Other agencies by tradition have their own merit systems separate and apart from the regular civil service; examples are the Federal Bureau of Investigation, the Public Health Service, and the Forest Service. In addition there are positions for which it has been deemed impracticable to recruit through the competitive system; some of these require a "pass examination," noncompetitive, to assure minimum standards; others have no examinations.

Policy-determining Positions. Not long after a new Administration took office in 1953, one of the great personnel issues that emerged was: How high should civil service go? [9] What is the proper line of demarcation between the permanent career service and political executives? A few years ago some reformers were inclined to impress even bureau chiefs and assistant secretaries into the classified service; now it seems necessary to reexamine the possibility of a constructive administrative role for the political supporter of the President.

President Roosevelt, from 1933 onwards, brought into Federal employment a large number of able and dynamic administrators. The conditions were favorable: The service was expanding rapidly, and private employment conditions were adverse. President Eisenhower, however, beginning in 1953, faced almost opposite conditions: The service was being reduced, and nearly full employment prevailed in the private sector of the economy. Moreover, many executives recruited during the Roosevelt-Truman eras were now entrenched as career administrators with classified civil-service protection.

To open up these positions, the President issued an executive order [10] that created "Schedule C" and transferred to it all positions of a

[9] For an able discussion of the issue, see Herman M. Somers, "The President, the Congress, and the Federal Government Service," in *The Federal Government Service: Its Character, Prestige, and Problems* (Columbia University, The American Assembly, 1954), pp. 52–80, at p. 69.

[10] Executive Order 10440, Mar. 31, 1953.

"confidential or policy-determining character." By October, 1954, 1,127 positions had been placed in the category; [11] but about one-half of

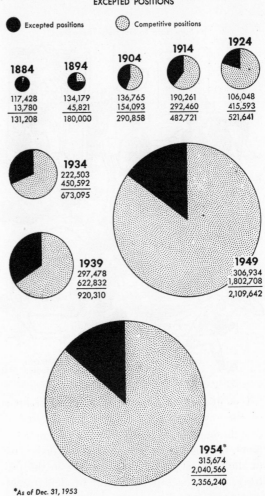

GROWTH OF THE FEDERAL GOVERNMENT SERVICE
SHOWING THE DIVISION BETWEEN COMPETITIVE AND EXCEPTED POSITIONS

● Excepted positions   ○ Competitive positions

1884
117,428
13,780
131,208

1894
134,179
45,821
180,000

1904
136,765
154,093
290,858

1914
190,261
292,460
482,721

1924
106,048
415,593
521,641

1934
222,503
450,592
673,095

1939
297,478
622,832
920,310

1949
306,934
1,802,708
2,109,642

1954*
315,674
2,040,566
2,356,240

*As of Dec. 31, 1953

Courtesy of The American Assembly, *The Federal Government Service: Its Character, Prestige, and Problems*, p. 41.

incumbents were retained and a further 20 per cent of new posts filled from the existing service. The able task force of the second Hoover Commission was alarmed over Schedule C mainly because it opened the way to a clean

[11] Second Hoover Commission, *Task Force Report on Personnel and Civil Service* (1955), pp. 36–37.

sweep of existing personnel in a future change of Administration. Omitting the "confidential" employees, such as private secretaries and chauffeurs, the task force estimated that 755 positions might be considered in the "political executive" category.

"It's Sure Hard To Get Help These Days"

HERBLOCK
The Washington Post

Uses of Political Executives. A substantial part of the 1955 task force report was devoted to examining ways of strengthening top management through political executives. Correct use of the political executive, according to the task force, is in the top command of departments and agencies, not—as some of the Schedule C posts were—on bureau, divisional, and field-office levels. The positions reserved for political executives are in three groups: (1) heads of agencies and their deputies; (2) assistant agency heads; and (3) aides, assistants, heads of policy offices, etc.

The second Hoover Commission endorsed these recommendations, and urged that non-career executives relieve career administrators of responsibility for advocating or defending policies. Political executives are required at the

departmental level. A new Schedule D was proposed for policy-determining positions that should be filled by political executives; [12] Schedule C would be reserved solely for confidential positions.

The Higher Civil Service. The second Hoover Commission and its task force then turned to strengthening top management. They proposed the establishment of a "senior" civil-service group of top career administrators carefully selected from all parts of the civil service. Like earlier critics of the Federal personnel system, they noted the deficiency in career administrators. Senior civil servants would be given appointments as individuals—as in the military service with appropriate status, rank, and salary—yet assigned to positions (billets) on a flexible basis. An initial goal of 1,500 senior civil servants was set; ultimately perhaps 3,000 would be required. Each would be politically neutral, and each would be obligated to serve where needed most. A "Senior Civil Service Board" would select, review performance, and set rules and standards.

Employees Outside the Classified Civil Service. Positions exempted from the classified service include those so provided by (1) statute; (2) Schedule A, for which no examinations are required; (3) Schedule B, for which a noncompetitive examination must be taken to prove minimum qualifications; and (4) Schedule C, which are policy-determining or confidential in character.

Leaving aside the employees under merit systems such as those of the TVA, the FBI, the Atomic Energy Commission, the Foreign Service, and the Veterans' Administration (professional), the task force of the second Hoover Commission estimated that there were 220,000 employees exempted under Schedules A, B, and C. Well over one-half of these positions are overseas. According to the Hoover report, either these positions should be brought into the competitive civil service or a special merit system should be established to fit their needs. Independent merit systems should be certified by the President. Provision should be made for trans-

[12] Second Hoover Commission, *Personnel and Civil Service* (1955), pp. 31–33.

ferability of employees in the smaller federal merit systems into the general competitive ranks, and vice versa.

The second Hoover Commission also took note of the continued political clearance of appointees to rural letter carrier positions, and urged that these posts be taken out of politics. Likewise it asked for transfer to the competitive category the positions of marshals, customs officials, and mint employees. The Hoover group did not, however, follow its task force in urging inclusion of attorneys in the competitive service, or in freeing the appointment of postmasters from political clearance.

Merit-system Groups. The expansion and improvement of the merit system has been made possible in large part through the interest and support of citizens and groups. Two national organizations deserve special mention in this regard. The Civil Service Assembly of the United States and Canada grew out of a conference held in Washington in 1906 on the invitation of President Theodore Roosevelt and the United States Civil Service Commission. It is the organization of civil-service commissioners and personnel engaged in public personnel administration. It is not an aggressive promotional group but works mainly in the research and technical fields. Through annual conferences and periodicals—monthly *Newsletter* and quarterly *Public Personnel Review*—the assembly provides mediums for the interchange of views and the discussion of problems by personnel administrators and students.

The National Civil Service League, launched in 1881, is the crusading organization in this field. It has conducted campaigns for the extension of the merit-system idea and for the expansion of the classified service after systems have been adopted.[13]

In the states there are many citizens' groups operating wholly or partially in the field of merit-system reform and defense. The League of Women Voters—national, state, and local—

has been one of the most vigilant and informed of these groups.

THE SELECTION PROCESS

Recruitment. The first task in a personnel program is to interest potential personnel in applying for positions. On the whole this work has been done poorly by American public personnel agencies. Those who knock at the gates asking for admission to the federal service often are largely self-informed about the prospects of public employment. As a result of their passiveness, personnel agencies commonly have failed to cultivate the most promising sources of able recruits. They have contented themselves with publishing a formal announcement of forthcoming examinations and having it posted in public places. Recently there has been some improvement in recruiting practices.

The field from which recruiting is done is limited by the prerequisites stipulated for the position under consideration. Age limits are used, but ordinarily American personnel agencies are very liberal and permit a great age range for most jobs. Outside pressure is exerted to keep open maximum opportunities for public employment to persons of middle age or after. Authorities in the personnel field favor induction of persons into the public service while they are young, making possible a long and specialized career in the government service.

Closely related to age of recruiting is the question of education. In many instances the idea of giving everyone a chance has been used to justify low educational requirements or none at all. For professional posts, of course, a license to practice or a professional degree is required, but strenuous opposition develops to allegedly "undemocratic" barriers in the form of educational prerequisites. Untrained persons may be eliminated later through examinations, but the cost of giving tests to unqualified persons represents waste of public funds. Another important question in regard to education concerns the desirable type of training. Since American civil service examinations have been largely practical in nature, persons with specialized training have been favored. The experience of the Brit-

[13] For further information, see Frank M. Stewart, *The National Civil Service Reform League: History, Activities and Problems* (University of Texas Press, 1929).

ish and other great civil service systems has favored the recruiting of those with general education, with specialization to follow induction.

Experience is another qualification commonly required. This varies widely with the position. Personnel agencies often stress experience to the exclusion of education, thus favoring the older applicant over the younger. Citizenship and residence almost invariably are required, al-

application form. The blank should call for data necessary to establish the applicant's eligibility for the post to be filled. Spaces are provided for name, address, age, education, experience, references, and a variety of other matters. A photograph of the applicant usually is required. If the application is approved, the candidate for the job may take the examination. The application may be rejected if the appli-

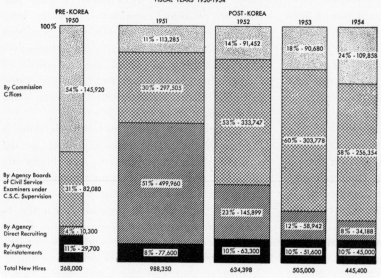

NEW HIRES IN THE FEDERAL CIVIL SERVICE
FISCAL YEARS 1950-1954

	PRE-KOREA 1950	1951	POST-KOREA 1952	1953	1954
By Commission Offices	54% - 145,920	11% - 113,285 / 30% - 297,505	14% - 91,452 / 53% - 333,747	18% - 90,680 / 60% - 303,778	24% - 109,858 / 58% - 256,354
By Agency Boards of Civil Service Examiners under C.S.C. Supervision	31% - 82,080	51% - 499,960	23% - 145,899	12% - 58,942	8% - 34,188
By Agency Direct Recruiting	4% - 10,300				
By Agency Reinstatements	11% - 29,700	8% - 77,600	10% - 63,300	10% - 51,600	10% - 45,000
Total New Hires	268,000	988,350	634,398	505,000	445,400

The recruitment picture over recent years. Note expansion of agency-board hiring and extensive use of direct agency method in early Korean crisis. Courtesy of The American Assembly, *The Federal Government Service: Its Character, Prestige, and Problems,* p. 118.

though a waiver of the residence requirement is made occasionally for positions for which qualifications are rare. Sex usually is specified in a recruiting announcement; far more and better paid jobs are available for men than for women.

The public is informed of opportunities in government employment through the common formal printed announcement, inquiries in schools, use of mailing lists, newspaper advertisements and stories, and radio programs.

Both Hoover Commissions pointed the way to the improvement of recruiting, through wider distribution of announcements, better information programs, and expansion of college recruiting.

Application. After he has been interested in the available position, the recruit fills out an

cant lacks some stipulated requirement, or if he has something in his record that disqualifies him.

Private industries place emphasis on the application, and work over the completed form with much care. Since a formal examination is to follow directly, public personnel agencies have neglected to check up on statements entered. In cases where no formal test is to be administered, the application form is far more extensive, for it and the references offered may provide the whole basis for judgment of the applicant.

Examination. Today most of the positions under the federal, state, and local merit systems are filled from eligible lists made up of persons who have passed a formal written examination. From the beginning federal tests were practical in nature, related to the duties of the office sought. Practical examinations are characteristically American and are rather well suited for selecting clerical and manipulative workers. General examinations are typically British and have proved superior for the selection of persons capable of filling the higher administrative posts. Each of these two types of examinations has proved its value, and each appears to have its place in an adequate testing program. It is not enough to test technical abilities alone and leave out of consideration capacity for growth, as may be done under "practical" American tests. The general British examination would be misapplied if used as the sole test for mail sorters in the post office. The obvious conclusion is that both achievement and capacity are needed in varying degrees by public employees, and the case is rarely found where one is needed to the complete exclusion of the other.

Examinations accordingly are designed to test for these different qualities. Aptitude tests are used to measure general, social, and mechanical intelligence and capacity. Abstract or general intelligence is reported in terms of intelligence quotient (IQ), as revealed by the Army alpha test and its modern successors. Persons who fall below the level of IQ judged necessary for the occupation concerned may be eliminated from consideration. Social intelligence may be tested through several standardized examinations, the purpose of which is to disclose adjustments and reactions to altered circumstances and different people. Mechanical intelligence tests have been experimented with recently; they are intended to test potential mechanical capacity rather than achievement.

Achievement tests measure informational and technical training—such as speed of typing, accuracy of arithmetic, knowledge of tools. These fall distinctly in the category of practical tests specified in so many American civil service laws.

Forms of Examinations. In form, the usual examination is written rather than oral, and objective rather than essay. The oral examination has been used very satisfactorily in some places, but it is both slow and open to abuses. The interview held by the appointing officer after certification may prove sufficient for ascertaining personality, particularly when he may choose between the three highest. The short answer or objective type of examination has displaced almost entirely for the civil service the traditional essay form. The essay examination is slow to read and difficult to grade fairly, especially when a very large number of papers are involved; the essay also places a premium on literary ability and penmanship. The objective examination, on the other hand, has the assets of speedy grading and definite and standardized answers. The latest development in this field is the machine-scored test, which can be fed to a counting machine for accurate grading and lightning results. The objective tests take the usual forms—completion, true-false, multiple choice, and matching.

Formerly the United States Civil Service Commission administered virtually all the examinations for the competitive civil service. The first Hoover Commission led the way in recommending that primary responsibility be placed on Departments and agencies, subject to Commission supervision. By fiscal year 1954, 58 per cent of "new hires" were by agency boards of examiners, compared with 24 per cent by Commission offices; the remainder were divided between agency direct recruiting and reinstatements. The second Hoover Commission favored more open continuous examinations, available at any time, more use of interviews, with improved techniques, and fuller validation of tests and employment standards.

Preparation of Eligible List. Applicants who receive a passing grade in the examination have their names listed on a register in the order of their scores, except that veterans are given preference. This eligible list for a particular position (as stenographer, patrolman, senior attorney) is made available to appointing officers. When the eligible list becomes exhausted or obsolete, another examination is held to renew it. Eligible lists are based upon the classification system employed by the jurisdiction. If this classification provides for thousands of minute categories, flexibility is lost; for a bookkeeper post in one agency may not be filled by a person on the eligible list for bookkeeper in another agency. The question of classification is taken up in a subsequent section of this chapter.

Veterans' Preference. Veterans' preference constitutes one of the most hotly controversial questions in the public personnel field. The first preference law was enacted by Congress at the close of the Civil War; in 1919 preference was extended on a generous scale.

As the Second World War drew to a close, Congress enacted the Veterans' Preference Act of 1944, which virtually closes the greater part of the federal service to male nonveterans for a long time to come. The act[14] provides that preference shall be given to (1) ex-service men and women with service-connected disabilities, (2) wives of disabled servicemen who are themselves unable to work, (3) unmarried widows of deceased servicemen, and (4) any ex-service person. Those in categories 1, 2, and 3 are entitled to have ten points added to examination scores; moreover, certain types of jobs, such as guards, elevator operators, messengers, and custodians, are reserved exclusively for these groups. Veterans in the fourth category receive five extra points. Persons of all categories receive generous credit for military and other experience, some waivers of age, height, weight, physical and educational requirements, and special privileges when appointments are being made.

Those who favor veterans' preference maintain that this is a proper way for a government to show its appreciation to those who risked their lives in its behalf. Opponents of preference grant the obligation of government to veterans but wish to meet it in ways that will not lower the efficiency of the public service.

The first Hoover Commission sought to put veterans' preference on a defensible basis by grouping all applicants as "outstanding," "well qualified," "qualified," and "unqualified"; within each quality category, veterans would be considered ahead of nonveterans. This proposal should eliminate the appointment of veterans incapable of doing a job, yet give qualified veterans absolute advantage over nonveterans in the same quality group.

[14] 58 Stat. 387.

Appointment. When the appointing officer wishes to fill a vacancy, he sends to the personnel agency for the eligible list. If he is a federal official, this process is handled by the director of personnel of his department or establishment. The request for eligibles is called a "requisition" and generally must state the title, duties, salary, and qualifications required. Federal law prescribes that the three names ranking highest on the eligible list shall be certified to the appointing officer. In the various other jurisdictions the number certified ranges from one to seven. The appointing officer is permitted to choose from among those certified to him. The arguments for allowing some latitude are strong, for personality and other factors not adequately assessed in written examinations may be judged from oral interview by the appointing officer.

Certification of eligibles by a civil service commission may be made out of regular order owing to two factors. First, veterans' preference in some jurisdictions (including the Federal government under the Preference Act of 1944) requires the disabled veteran to be certified ahead of others on the eligible list. Second, appointments to the federal positions in Washington are required to be apportioned among the states in proportion to their population. Although the latter has not been rigidly applied, it does favor those eligibles from some states and places at a disadvantage those from states the quotas of which are filled.

The usual procedure is for the appointing officer to review such information as the personnel agency has on the eligible persons. Then the one adjudged the most promising candidate is called for interview. If personal qualities and appearance are found to be satisfactory, appointment follows; if unsatisfactory, the second choice may be interviewed and appointed. Sometimes all certified persons are interviewed before a selection is made.

The first Hoover Commission and its personnel task force used strong words to condemn the excessive centralization that was a barrier to getting the right person promptly into the correct job. It proved impossible to break the bottleneck so long as a closed central register of eligibles must be maintained for the whole country. An active register containing thousands of names is drawn upon constantly by appointing agencies. The letter of the law appears to require that the top three names must be certified, but in practice dozens of names may be out to different agencies simultaneously.

The appointing officer is in a difficult spot. From the "grab bag" of the active register he has certified the names of three people whose places near the top of the register may have resulted from a high score on a written examination, from veterans' preference, or from the fact that others ahead on the register had already been certified or appointed, or had declined. From personal interviews, the appointing officer may conclude that none of the eligibles has the personality or ability to do the job at hand. Under existing procedures he usually must either appoint one of the eligibles or allow the position to remain vacant and hope for a better list next time.

To correct the existing defects, both Hoover Commissions recommended not only decentralization of recruiting and examining but also giving appointing officers more leeway than the "rule of three" allows.

Several abuses may be present at the appointing level. In order to appoint some person who is qualified mainly by political services, provisional appointments sometimes are made when no eligible list is available. It is possible later that provisional appointees may be blanketed into the permanent service after noncompetitive examinations. In some jurisdictions appointing officers may conspire to appoint political friends by securing "waivers" from persons higher on the eligible list by threats or promises.

Appointed at last, the new civil servant is not yet fully secure. Normally he must serve out satisfactorily a period of probation, up to 6 months in length. Within this period, or at the close of it, the probationer may be dropped from the service if he has been found unsuitable. Few civil-service agencies have adequate systems for efficiency rating; the reluctance of a superior officer to dismiss except for serious deficiency is general. As a result, the probationary test period is much less meaningful than might be expected.

Career-conditional Appointments. One of the most difficult problems of the federal service is that of emergency expansion of government employment due to the extraordinary demands made by economic depression or war. During the Korean War a rider to an appropriation bill, the Whitten amendment, virtually froze the permanent civil service at September, 1950, levels. For more than 4 years nearly all appointments to the service were made on an indefinite basis.

In January, 1955, a new system of filling positions went into effect, under which employees to the competitive service will serve 3 years in conditional status before achieving full career standing. Competitive examinations and eligible lists will continue to be used, except that the first year of appointment is probationary and is considered a part of the examination.

The immediate task in 1955 was to analyze the records on an estimated 673,000 indefinite employees. Approximately one-third were eligible for full career status; another one-third qualified for career-conditional; the remaining one-third must remain as indefinite unless qualified through future examination.

The keynote of the career-conditional plan is flexibility. In future expansions or contractions of the federal service, the career employees will enjoy protection, yet the total force can be adjusted to needs without unduly inflating or deflating the permanent ranks. The order also facilitated the transfer of employees from other federal merit systems, such as the Foreign Service, into the general competitive service.

CLASSIFICATION AND COMPENSATION

Duties Classification. The term "classification" is used in the personnel field in two separate ways. It is employed in a jurisdictional sense to indicate whether or not positions are within or without the "classified" or merit service. The more common use is in an occupational sense, classifying jobs on the basis of duties performed. A duties or occupational classification is necessary in order to simplify the task of personnel management and to render possible the elemental justice of equal pay, prestige, and title for equal work.

Occupational classification is accomplished through a process of job analysis. This may be

class is the basic unit; it is composed of a number of similar positions, as, for example, typists or clerks. Every position is then placed in a class; within each class the qualifications and scale of compensation for each position are nearly the same.

CLASSIFICATION AND COMPENSATION
under the
CLASSIFICATION ACT OF 1949
AS AMENDED
with Minimum Salary for Each Grade
and Number of Steps in Parenthesis ( )

Grade	Salary	Steps
GS 18	$14,800	(none)
GS 17	13,975	(4)
GS 16	12,900	(5)
GS 15	11,610	(5)
GS 14	10,320	(6)
GS 13	8,990	(6)
GS 12	7,570	(6)
GS 11	6,390	(6)
GS 10	5,915	(7)
GS 9	5,440	(7)
GS 8	4,970	(7)
GS 7	4,525	(7)
GS 6	4,080	(7)
GS 5	3,670	(7)
GS 4	3,415	(7)
GS 3	3,175	(7)
GS 2	2,960	(7)
GS 1	2,690	(7)

GS 18 — Bureau Chief, National program head or top consultant

CPC 10 — Direct & supervise mechanics, janitors

CPC 1 — Run errands, check parcels, light manual work

GS 1 — Simplest routine work or elementary technique

GS = General Schedule

Grade	Salary	Steps
CPC 10	$4,905	(7)
CPC 9	4,460	(7)
CPC 8	4,020	(7)
CPC 7	3,695	(7)
CPC 6	3,440	(7)
CPC 5	3,200	(7)
CPC 4	2,955	(7)
CPC 3	2,745	(7)
CPC 2	2,600	(7)
CPC 1	1,945	(7)

CPC = Crafts, Protective and Custodial

The pattern of advancement in the federal classified service. The salaries shown were set in 1955. The CPC schedule will be eliminated eventually, under the terms of a 1954 act.

done by the personnel agency or by an outside body or concern. In order to find out what work and responsibility a particular job involves, questionnaires are filled out and interviews held. When this is completed, individual positions are arranged into classes, groups, and services. Each class is assigned specifications—including title, duties, and qualifications. The plan is put into force by law or by executive order. The

Under the Classification Act of 1949 [15] the policy of equal pay for equal work is supported by varying rates of compensation in proportion

[15] 63 Stat. 782. The Classification Act of 1923 arranged classes into great services which were, at the time the 1949 act went into effect, (1) professional and scientific, (2) subprofessional, (3) clerical, administrative, and fiscal, (4) custodial, and (5) clerical-mechanical.

to the difficulty, responsibility, and qualifications involved. The act covers about one million positions in the federal service. A "position" consists of the work, duties, and responsibilities assignable to an officer or employee. A "class" includes those positions sufficiently similar in kind of work, level of difficulty or responsibility, and qualification requirements to warrant similar treatment. A "grade" embraces all classes sufficiently equal as to responsibility and qualifications to justify placing them within one range of rates of compensation. Each position is placed in the appropriate class and grade. The act established two schedules of grades and salary ranges: a "General Schedule" (GS) of eighteen grades and a "Crafts, Protective, and Custodial Schedule" (CPC) of ten grades. A law passed in 1954 means the ultimate abolition of CPC by transfer of some positions to GS and others to area wage boards. The Civil Service Commission administers the classification scheme.

The Postal Pay Act of 1945 provides the classification for about 500,000 federal employees; it contains ninety-two pay schedules. Most of the other federal employees are subject to classification-compensation grades established through some sort of wage-board procedure.

The second Hoover Commission and its task force in 1955 complained that the Classification Act had too many grades, was devoid of flexibility in setting pay rates, and provided insufficient difference between top and bottom pay rates. To correct these faults, it recommended that grades GS 1–6 be combined into three grades, and GS 7–11 be combined into three. The higher grades would be left as is, except that GS 15 and up would be absorbed into the senior civil service. The postal workers classification plan was criticized, and eventual transfer to the general scheme was forecast.

Compensation. Once the job of classification is done, the next great task is that of fixing compensation schedules. Although it appears only elemental justice that like pay should be fixed for like work, a great range of compensation for comparable work is found in jurisdictions without adequate classification and salary standardization systems. With the installation of proper classification plans, however, the basis for salary uniformity for work of a given class and grade has been established.

The public wage scale ought to be kept in some degree of harmony with that of private employment. Wages must be high enough to attract and hold good public employees, but not so high as to make government work overly attractive. In practice, public personnel agencies constantly base salaries upon studies of comparable positions in private employment. If the usual starting wage for a file clerk is $200 per month in private New York offices, a public agency in the same city will have to approximate that for a beginner in the same line.

Another aspect of the same problem is to provide justly for differences of education or experience required for the various posts within a public service. The occupant of a job requiring a long and expensive professional education, as a physician or attorney, will demand higher compensation than a public-relations officer, who may have no educational requirement. Deference to such considerations is difficult to allow, however, and the main reliance must be placed upon competition; if naval architects are hard to find, the compensation must be raised until one is attracted.

Within each class of positions several rates of compensation will be provided, ranging from a minimum, through some intermediate categories, to a maximum. Thus a typist might enter at $2,690 per year, and advance, with some five intermediate salaries, to a maximum of $3,200. Ordinarily a new employee starts at the minimum rate; his aspiration to move on to the next salary rank constitutes an important incentive to do well.

Increments. Sentiment is strong among public employees to make salary increases within a given position automatic, an annual or biennial increment. Such a plan produces overemphasis on time serving and seniority and fails to take into account value of services performed, as decided by superior officers, with or without formal efficiency ratings.

Standard compensation schedules may be departed from through differentials justified by some special circumstances. A construction worker on a remote Pacific island or on the Panama Canal might reasonably be paid a bonus for working under adverse climatic conditions. While adding to the difficulties of administration, some differentials would appear justified when working and living conditions vary greatly.

If public salaries are to be based upon rates for comparable private employment, consideration must be given to the fluctuations in business conditions. While public pay may not be so flexible as compensation for private employment, substantial justice may be achieved by the fact that the public salary dips less to the depths in depression periods and fails to rise as much in prosperity. The civil servant therefore may be envied in bad times and pitied in good times. If a depression is long, the public employee is likely to have a flat percentage salary cut; if cost of living increases sharply, he may lobby through an increase. A few jurisdictions have attempted to adjust salaries to a cost-of-living index formula.

EFFICIENCY AND MORALE

Service Ratings. How can the efficiency of public employees be tested? Civil-service agencies have experimented with various systems to rate performance. The simplest and surest method of rating is one based upon quantity and quality of production at some routine task. Like piecework in industry, this can apply only to a limited number of jobs—as typist, machine operator, or other work capable of unit measurement. It is possible also to rate employees by examinations or tests given at regular intervals, but this method has had little development.

The formal rating schemes have had broader application. They require that the superior officer indicate on a form of some kind his evaluation of each employee under his direction. One common method is to rate by traits or level of performance, utilizing a "graphic rating scale" on which the supervisor checks the description appropriate to the employee's qualities and work. Another method, called "man-to-man comparison," requires the superior officer to rank his subordinates in terms of best, average, and poorest.

In recent years most attention has been given to the Probst system of service rating, developed by Mr. J. B. Probst of the St. Paul Civil Service Bureau.[16] It causes the rating officer to assess the qualities of an employee in great detail, covering principally personality traits and characteristics. The Probst system has been used in several jurisdictions and is generally looked upon more favorably than have been the graphic rating and man-to-man methods.

The basic difficulty with efficiency rating schemes lies in securing unprejudiced and frank evaluations by superior officers. In the judgment of authorities on personnel, service ratings are still in a rudimentary stage. However imperfect, they are nevertheless improving and represent an advance over the uncoordinated efforts of individual supervisors to judge performance. Certainly at the present stage of development service ratings should not be the only criteria employed in deciding on promotion but may properly be used as one of the factors to be considered.

In place of the then existing federal rating system, the first Hoover Commission proposed an "ability and service record" rating under which the supervisor would (1) evaluate ability, past performance, progress, and potential usefulness on specific factors, and (2) discuss with the employee his strengths and weaknesses. The Hoover group urged that the rating not be used as a basis for determining salary increases, lay-offs, or dismissals.

The Eighty-first Congress proceeded to enact, however, the Performance Rating Act of 1950. The second Hoover Commission reported in 1955 on the failure of the rating system: approximately 98 per cent of those rated were deemed "satisfactory," while the "outstanding" and "unsatisfactory" categories went practically

[16] See John B. Probst, *Service Ratings* (Chicago: Bureau of Public Personnel Administration and Civil Service Assembly, 1931).

unused because of onerous restrictions attached to each. Abolition of the system was recommended; an annual report from supervisors on exceptional and unsatisfactory employees was suggested in its place.

Disciplinary Action. It is obvious that civil servants should not be immune from disciplinary action, including removal. They are obliged to perform their duties faithfully, to obey the law, and to avoid conduct unbecoming in a public employee. Sometimes these obligations are set forth in specific detail in an administrative code; most American governments have failed to prescribe employee rights and duties with clarity. The rules for the conduct of federal employees are found in laws such as the Hatch Act, and in the rules of Civil Service Commission and operating agencies. The administrative employee of the United States may not participate in partisan political activities.[17]

An employee of the classified service may be removed only for such cause "as will promote the efficiency of said service" and he must be notified in writing of the charges and given a public hearing.[18] The Civil Service Commission rules give the Commission a restricted power to investigate, but the real authority over removals is in the hands of the appointing officer. Responsibility for discipline and removal in the federal service rests almost completely with the head of the department or agency.

Many forms of disciplinary action exist. A minor infraction may be dealt with by reprimand or warning. Intermediate offenses may be handled by demerits in service ratings, loss of seniority, or transfer to an undesirable location of work. Serious violations may lead to suspension, demotion, or dismissal. In the federal service, except in loyalty cases, no appeal is possible from disciplinary action approved by a department head. Proposals have been made to authorize the Civil Service Commission to review disciplinary cases, or to establish a special court to hear appeals from disciplinary action. Some civil-service jurisdictions follow the existing federal scheme of permitting broad discretion on the part of the appointing officer. Others vest important disciplinary authority in the personnel commission. Still others allow appeals to the courts on a liberal basis.

Two principal laws govern the separation of federal employees from the service. Under the Lloyd–La Follette Act of 1912, nonveterans are subject to what the second Hoover Commission called a "simple and just method consonant with the requirements of an efficient public service."[19] Under the Veterans' Preference Act of 1944, veterans may be dismissed only if elaborate requirements are followed. Each group, nonveteran and veteran, constitutes about 50 per cent of the service.

Morale and Prestige. Morale is defined as a state of mind, with reference to confidence. Prestige is related to morale, but is different. It means the respect for achievement or standing of an individual or group. Both high morale and high prestige are important to the effective functioning of a public body.

Among the commonly recognized prerequisites to high morale in the public service are such factors as security from spoils politics, fairness in wages and working conditions, recognition of good work, and adequacy of retirement system. Group morale or *esprit de corps* may be heightened by an agency through attention to its employees' social life, living conditions, credit facilities, unions, and associations.

Many of the same factors that produce high morale also contribute to the prestige of an agency or of public employment generally. A worker wishes to be well thought of, to enjoy the admiration of people. The American public service has not enjoyed the prestige value of the British civil service. This low esteem may be traced to several factors, notably to spoils politics, low wages, and insecurity of tenure. Recently advances have been made on these fronts, and prestige has improved. Plenty of room for further improvement remains, however, and the

---

[17] The Hatch Act of 1939 covered this aspect most fully. See 53 Stat. 1147.

[18] 37 Stat. 539.

[19] Second Hoover Commission, *Personnel and Civil Service* (1955), pp. 69–70.

nation may well aspire to making employment in its service as attractive as that in any private concern.[20]

Reductions in Force. The fairness or unfairness with which government carries out reductions in force greatly affects morale. In the layoffs of 1953–1954, following the change of administration and the end of the Korean War, existing law and the practices followed undermined the confidence of many civil servants. Here again the Veterans' Preference Act was the controlling factor. For reduction in force purposes, employees are initially divided into three groups: (1) career, (2) career-conditional, and (3) indefinite. Permanent employees in the competitive classified service (group 1) may not be laid off before lower-tenure groups (2 and 3) are.

Within each group, however, veterans have preference over nonveterans. Seniority is only a minor factor. The very few employees with "outstanding" performance ratings receive some additional credits.

From this complicated set of rules comes the practice of "bumping": A career employee who cannot be retained in his present post because of reductions may accept a lesser position in the same agency, dislodging an employee of a lower group, preference, or seniority. The "bumped" employee may, in turn, displace someone below him, and the process continues like a chain reaction. Thus one case of "bumping" high up in an agency may result in demotions in considerable number all along the line. Moreover, efficiency or even seniority has little to do with this process; typically a veteran with relatively short service may displace a career nonveteran with much longer service and experience.

The second Hoover Commission called for modification of the Veterans' Preference Act to give more credit to years of service, performance, and usefulness.

Turnover. Evidence of widespread employee dissatisfaction may be found in the high turnover rate that plagues the federal service. Between 1951 and 1954, from 445,000 to 988,000 persons had to be recruited each year in order to maintain a work force that ranged from 2,330,000 to 2,603,000; no less than one out of each four positions fell vacant each year.

The task force that surveyed the personnel field for the first Hoover Commission secured the views of nearly 3,500 college seniors toward the public service as a career. Government employment was rated below private industry in salary, opportunities for promotion, incentives to improve efficiency, prestige and recognition, and other categories. Public service was more attractive than private only in security of job, opportunities for service, and leave, retirement, and health benefits.

The second Hoover task force summarized in 1955 the factors affecting morale in the public service as management-employee relations, material rewards, working conditions, and prestige. Prestige, it reported, is most affected by general attitudes of Congress, the public, and the press; behavior of federal employees and officials; and specific problems such as security and politics in the merit system.

The task force proposed a program to raise morale and prestige by (1) maintaining high standards of personal conduct by federal employees; (2) defending the public service against sweeping, unsupported charges and taking action on accurate, specific charges; (3) protecting public servants against unfair attacks—a task in which the political executive should take the lead.[21]

Loyalty Program. Near the beginning of the "cold war" President Truman in March, 1947, set up a loyalty program for the federal service; later in the same year a Loyalty Review Board was created by the Civil Service Commission to handle cases arising from it. The Board was abolished by President Eisenhower in April, 1953, and final responsibility for dismissing em-

---

[20] For further reading, see Leonard D. White, *The Prestige Value of Public Employment* (University of Chicago Press, 1929); and *Further Contributions to the*

Prestige Value of Public Employment (University of Chicago Press, 1932).

[21] This outstanding report was prepared under the chairmanship of President Harold W. Dodds of Princeton University; George A. Graham was director of the task-force staff.

ployees as security risks was placed in the hands of Department and agency heads.[22] An Investigations Division was set up in the Civil Service Commission to direct background security investigative activities; the Security Appraisal Office of the Commission coordinates agency operations in the employee security field and maintains security-hearing-board rosters for the agencies. Over one-third of the Commission expenditures for fiscal year 1954 were for security investigations.

The loyalty programs have been criticized both on the grounds that they have undermined employee morale and because employees in loyalty proceedings have been denied several basic rights, including presumption of innocence until guilt is proved, nonadmissibility of association evidence, right to be informed of charges, right to confront and cross-examine accusers, and immunity from double jeopardy.[23] In 1955 a loyalty case involving a professor of medicine, Yale University, was reviewed by the Supreme Court. Instead of deciding the constitutional issue of due process, the court invalidated his dismissal because of faulty procedure by the Loyalty Review Board.

In March 1955 President Eisenhower approved seven revisions in procedure governing security-risk cases: (1) The statement of charges against an employee should be drawn specifically, and should be given to the employee at the time of his suspension. (2) The employee should be interviewed prior to suspension, and the final decision to suspend should be made by an Assistant Secretary or above. (3) A legal officer should be present at hearings to advise both the Security Board and the employee, if he is not represented by counsel. (4) Agency heads should review periodically the personnel of Security Boards to ensure high caliber. (5) Before an agency makes an adverse security evaluation of an employee who has previously been cleared by another agency, its head should consult with the head of the other agency to ensure that all relevant information has been considered. (6) Every effort should be made to produce witnesses so that they can be confronted and cross-examined by the employee, so long as such production "would not jeopardize the national security." (7) All violations of law disclosed in security investigations should be reported to the Department of Justice.

Although these new rules should improve loyalty proceedings, critics continue to point out alleged deficiencies. Department and agency heads still possess final authority to fire in security cases; a number of congressional leaders would prefer a new independent agency to take appeals from department and agency heads. Other complaints center around the nonmandatory language of the new procedural "rules"; each one is stated in terms of "should be," not "must." In 1954 the annual conference of the American Assembly held at Arden House, Columbia University, urged that the loyalty-security program be taken out of partisan politics, and to this end that a commission of outstanding citizens be appointed by the President to review it. Acting on this recommendation, Congress created a commission to be appointed jointly by the President, the Vice-President, and the Speaker for this purpose. Although the controversy is likely to continue so long as the danger of internal subversion remains, it is to be hoped that the program will be corrected of features which have led to serious criticisms, and be removed from partisan politics.

Retirement and Welfare. The national government first adopted a retirement plan for its employees in 1920. Most of the permanent civil service receives retirement, disability, and survivor protection under the Civil Service Retirement Act of 1920. An employee contributes 6 per cent of salary to the retirement fund; the balance of money required comes from appropriations. Employees may retire as early as fifty-five, after 30 years of service, but the normal retiring age is sixty-two for a full annuity. Although the average annuity being paid is low ($1,504 in 1954), there does not appear to be great dissatisfaction with the scheme.

---

[22] Executive Order 10450.

[23] The operation of the program was reviewed critically by a former Attorney General in Francis Biddle, *The Fear of Freedom* (Doubleday, 1952), pp. 197–245.

The federal system is based on actuarial reserves, which by adding contribution, appropriation, and compounded interest, produce an appropriate benefit at retirement age. Employee contributions, plus interest, are refundable on separation from the service before qualifying for an annuity.

Additional "fringe" benefits are available during an employee's working years. Sick leave, rest periods, overtime, vacations with pay, group life and accident insurance are among the services commonly provided. Workmen's compensation for federal employees is administered by the Bureau of Employees' Compensation, Department of Labor. A system of cash incentive awards was established in 1954; employees who perform outstanding services or make important inventions can be rewarded by heads of departments or by the President. Most of all the prestige of the service needs bolstering.

FOR FURTHER READING

Boutecou, E.: *Federal Loyalty Security Program* (Cornell University Press, 1953).

Brooks, Earl: *In-service Training of Federal Employees* (Chicago: Civil Service Assembly, 1938).

Carpenter, William S.: *The Unfinished Business of Civil Service Reform* (Princeton University Press, 1952).

Case, Harry L.: *Personnel Policy in a Public Agency* (Harper, 1955).

Charlesworth, James C. (ed.): "Bureaucracy and Democratic Government," *Annals of the American Academy,* vol. 292 (March, 1954).

Civil Service Assembly of the United States and Canada: *Public Personnel Agencies in the United States: A 1949 Census* (Chicago: The Assembly, 1949).

——: *Placement and Probation in the Public Service* (Chicago: The Assembly, 1946).

——: *Oral Tests in Public Personnel Selection* (Chicago: The Assembly, 1943).

——: *Employee Relations in the Public Service* (Chicago: The Assembly, 1942).

——: *Recruiting Applicants for the Public Service* (Chicago: The Assembly, 1942).

——: *Employee Training in the Public Service* (Chicago: The Assembly, 1941).

——: *Position-classification in the Public Service* (Chicago: The Assembly, 1941).

——: *Public Relations of Public Personnel Agencies* (Chicago: The Assembly, 1941).

——: *Public Personnel Review* (quarterly, began publication 1940).

——: *A Digest of State Civil Service Laws* (Chicago: The Assembly, 1939).

——: *Newsletter* (monthly, began publication 1930).

Commission of Inquiry on Public Service Personnel: *Better Government Personnel* (McGraw-Hill, 1935). Twelve monographs were published in 5 volumes, including those by Greer and Wilmerding listed below.

Corson, John J.: *Executives for the Federal Service* (Columbia University Press, 1952).

Feldman, Herman: *A Personnel Program for the Federal Civil Service,* H. Doc. 773, 71st Cong., 3d Sess. (1931).

Field, Oliver P.: *Civil Service Law* (University of Minnesota Press, 1939).

Graham, George A.: *Education for Public Administration* (Chicago: Public Administration Service, 1941).

Greer, Sarah A.: *Bibliography of Civil Service and Personnel Administration* (McGraw-Hill, 1935).

Gulick, Luther (ed.): "Improved Personnel in Government Service," *Annals of the American Academy of Political and Social Science,* vol. 189 (January, 1937).

McLean, Joseph E. (ed.): *The Public Service and University Education* (Princeton University Press, 1949).

Marvick, Dwaine: *Career Perspectives in a Bureaucratic Setting* (University of Michigan Press, 1954).

Meriam, Lewis: *Public Personnel Problems from the Standpoint of the Operating Office* (Brookings, 1938).

——: *Personnel Administration in the Federal Government* (Brookings, 1937).

——: *Public Service and Special Training* (University of Chicago Press, 1936).

——: *Principles Guiding the Retirement of Public Employees* (Appleton-Century-Crofts, 1918).

Mosher, William E., and Others: *Public Personnel Administration* (Harper, 3d ed., 1950).

Probst, John B.: *Service Ratings* (Chicago: Bureau of Public Personnel Administration and the Civil Service Assembly, 1931).

Sageser, L. B.: *First Two Decades of the Pendleton Act: A Study of Civil Service Reform* (University of Nebraska, 1935).

Smith, Darrell H.: *The United States Civil Service Commission: Its History, Activities and Organization* (Johns Hopkins Press, 1928).

Spero, Sterling D.: *Government as Employer* (New York: Remsen Press, 1949).

——: *The Labor Movement in a Government Industry* (Doubleday, 1924).

Stewart, Frank M.: *The National Civil Service Reform League: History, Activities and Problems* (University of Texas Press, 1929).

Torpey, W. G.: *Public Personnel Management* (Van Nostrand, 1953).

U.S. Civil Service Commission: *Annual Report* (yearly).

——: *Federal Employment under the Merit System* (1941).

——: *History of the Federal Service, 1789 to the Present* (1941).

U.S. Commission on Organization of the Executive Branch of the Government (second Hoover Commission): *Personnel and Civil Service* (1955).

——: *Task Force Report on Personnel and Civil Service* (1955).

U.S. Commission on Organization of the Executive Branch of the Government (first Hoover Commission): *Personnel Management* (1949).

——: *Task Force Report on Federal Personnel* (1949).

U.S. Department of Agriculture, Personnel Office: *Personnel Administration: Development in the Department of Agriculture, First Fifty Years* (1947).

U.S. President's Committee on Administrative Management: *Report . . . with Studies . . .* (1937). Study 1 is "Personnel Administration in the Federal Service," by Floyd W. Reeves and Paul T. David.

U.S. President's Committee on Civil Service Improvement: *Documents and Reports to Accompany Report on Civil Service Improvement* (3 vols., 1942).

——: *Report of . . . ,* H. Doc. 118, 77th Cong., 1st Sess. (1941).

White, Leonard D.: *Further Contributions to the Prestige Value of Public Employment* (University of Chicago Press, 1932).

——: *The Prestige Value of Public Employment* (University of Chicago Press, 1929).

Wilmerding, Lucius, Jr.: *Government by Merit* (McGraw-Hill, 1935).

Ziskind, David: *One Thousand Strikes of Government Employees* (Columbia University Press, 1940).

REVIEW QUESTIONS

1. Sketch the high points in the history of the American civil service and indicate the role of the Pendleton Act of 1883.

2. Indicate the approximate size of the present federal service, the geographic distribution, and the principal departments affiliated with it.

3. Describe the common forms of personnel agencies, and indicate the advantages and disadvantages of each.

4. What are some of the problems involved in duties classification and salary standardization?

5. What limitations, if any, should be placed upon the right of public employees to organize unions and bargain collectively?

6. Discuss factors which may play a part in building high morale in the public service.

7. To what extent should the higher positions in the public service be exempt from the classified civil service and filled by partisans of the President and congressional majority?

8. What progress have we made toward establishing an attractive career in governmental service?

9. What did the first and second Hoover Commissions recommend regarding the civil service? To what extent has it been carried out?

10. Describe the loyalty and security programs through which the Federal government has sought to protect the public service from subversive influences.

ON THE FACING PAGE: TVA's Norris Dam. (*TVA photo*)

Federal Powers and Functions

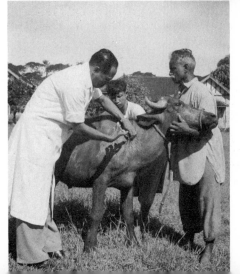

An important part of United States external affairs is participation in the United Nations, whose experts are at work in many parts of the world. Liberia's first rice mill (above, left) was set up by an American expert sent by the Food and Agriculture Organization of the UN. At bottom, left, another FAO expert, in Burma, inoculates a buffalo against rinderpest in the UN program for controlling animal disease. Above, the Security Council is shown in session in the UN world headquarters in New York City.

↑ Standard Oil Co. (N.J.)

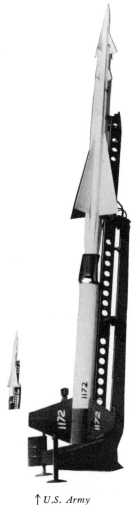

↑ U.S. Army

United Press ↓

The nation's defense program is the largest item in the budget. It includes not only maintenance of the Armed Forces but wide-ranging research programs as well. The guided missile Nike, shown above, was developed in the Army research program. In laboratories throughout the country, scientists are engaged in research on radioactive materials for the government (above, right). As a member of the North Atlantic Treaty Organization, the United States participates in combined maneuvers with other nations. In Exercise Mainbrace (right), a NATO exercise, ships and men of eight nations took part.

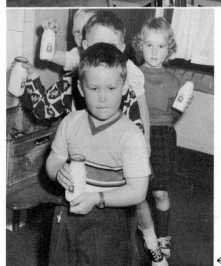

These three scenes indicate the national government's wide range of services. Above is a post office crew at work sorting the day's mail. At the left, kindergarten children are getting milk under the School Milk Program. Below, a federal meat inspector gives his seal of approval.

CHAPTER 19

The Tax Power and Revenues

Every government always has a fiscal policy whether it realizes it or not. The real issue is whether this shall be a constructive one or an unconscious, bumbling one. — Paul A. Samuelson [1]

Let the end be legitimate, let it be within the scope of the Constitution, and all means which are appropriate, which are plainly adapted to that end, which are not prohibited, but consist with the letter and spirit of the Constitution, are constitutional. — Chief Justice John Marshall [2]

The power to tax, Marshall reasoned in McCulloch *v.* Maryland, involves the power to destroy. Even more important, however, is its use in providing the fuel necessary to make the mechanism of government operate and in creating the authority through which a fiscal policy can be carried out. Above and beyond the use of the tax power to produce revenue are its utilization to regulate social and economic conditions and its use to level the peaks and valleys of the business cycle.

THE POWER TO TAX

The Tax Clause. The most serious weakness of the Articles of Confederation was that Congress could assess the states but lacked authority to lay and collect taxes directly from the people. In view of this, it is not surprising that authority to tax stands first on the list of powers delegated to Congress by the Constitution. The first paragraph of Article I, Section 8, provides:

The Congress shall have Power to Lay and collect Taxes, Duties, Imposts and Excises, to pay the Debts and provide for the common Defence and general Welfare of the United States; but all Duties, Imposts and Excises shall be uniform throughout the United States.

This brief clause, pregnant with meaning itself, but more so when read with the knowledge that Congress has power to do whatever is necessary and proper to carry it into effect, is authority for nearly all federal taxation.

Four Types of Levies. Note that Congress may lay and collect levies of four types: (1) taxes, (2) duties, (3) imposts, and (4) excises. A tax is an exaction for the support of government. The word "taxes," as used in the tax clause, refers to direct taxes and was probably intended to include only property and capitation (poll) taxes, although in 1895 the Supreme Court ruled that a tax on income from property was also a direct tax.[3] Direct taxes (other than income) have been levied only five times since 1789, the last to

[1] *Economics: An Introductory Analysis* (McGraw-Hill, 2d ed., 1951), p. 395.

[2] McCulloch *v.* Maryland, 4 Wheat. 316 (U.S. 1819).

[3] See also p. 352.

help finance the Civil War. If income taxes are excluded, no federal revenues are today collected from direct taxes. "Duties," "imposts," and "excises" include all indirect taxes. "Duties" and "imposts" are nearly synonymous terms referring to tariffs. An "excise" is an internal tax generally imposed upon manufactures but sometimes upon consumption and retail sales. In 1954, income taxes accounted for the largest amount of federal revenue, then followed excises, taxes, and tariffs (duties and imposts), in the order mentioned.[4]

Controversy over Income Taxes. As noted elsewhere,[5] the Constitution requires that all direct taxes be apportioned among the states on the basis of population. Toward the end of the last century the question arose as to whether a tax upon incomes was a direct or indirect tax. If direct, then income taxes must be apportioned among the states on the basis of population; if indirect, the Constitution would be satisfied if taxes were graduated but uniform within all classifications throughout the country. The controversy arose from a graduated federal income-tax law enacted in 1894 that did not provide for apportionment among the states. One Pollock, a stockholder in the Farmers' Loan and Trust Company of New York, brought suit to enjoin his company from paying the tax upon its income derived from real-estate, state, and local government bonds. The Supreme Court had considerable difficulty in reaching a decision. A similar law, enacted in 1861 but which had expired in 1872, had been upheld by a unanimous court,[6] but in the cases at hand[7] the Supreme Court ruled that taxes upon incomes were direct, hence unconstitutional, because they were not apportioned among the states.

These decisions precluded the enactment of future income-tax legislation inasmuch as administration would be difficult if apportionment were undertaken and, what was worse, it would be impossible to devise a tax schedule that would

fall upon people in proportion to their ability to pay. Though from an economic point of view the Court was undoubtedly correct in saying that a tax on income was a direct tax,[8] there could be no doubt that their decision was a clear reversal of previous precedents. The Court's decisions were the subject of much controversy and have been roundly condemned by many.[9] The decisions stood, nevertheless, until rendered insignificant by adoption of the Sixteenth Amendment.

The Income-tax Amendment. Years of agitation, particularly in the West and South, led to the adoption of the Sixteenth Amendment in 1913. It reads:

The Congress shall have power to lay and collect taxes on incomes, from whatever source derived, without apportionment among the several States, and without regard to any census or enumeration.

Note that the amendment does not settle the argument of whether a tax upon incomes is direct or indirect. It merely obviates the necessity of apportionment.

Shortly after the adoption of the income-tax amendment a dispute arose over what the words "from whatever source derived" were intended to mean. Some argued that the phrase was not intended to enlarge the list of what might be taxed but merely to reverse the Pollock decisions

[8] Economists generally agree that a tax upon incomes is a direct tax in the sense that it cannot readily be passed on to someone other than the person from whom collection is made. But the courts had previously held that not only income taxes but certain others which economists agree are direct were indirect within the meaning of the Constitution. For example, the Supreme Court had held federal taxes on carriages, on corporations' earnings, and inheritances to be indirect, although most economists would classify them as direct. Edwin R. A. Seligman, *The Income Tax* (Macmillan, 1911), pp. 533–534.

[9] See especially Edward S. Corwin, *Court over Constitution* (Princeton University Press, 1938), pp. 194–201; Charles E. Hughes, *The Supreme Court of the United States* (Columbia University Press, 1928), p. 54; Charles Warren, *The Supreme Court in United States History* (Little, Brown, 3 vols., 1923), vol. III, pp. 421–422; and Seligman, *op. cit.*

[4] For the amounts, see p. 360.

[5] P. 56.

[6] Springer *v.* United States, 102 U.S. 586 (1881).

[7] Pollock *v.* Farmers' Loan and Trust Co., 157 U.S. 429 (1895), 158 U.S. 601 (1895).

rendering it unnecessary to apportion income taxes. Others interpreted the phrase literally saying "from whatever source derived" meant just that. If this opinion prevailed, there would be no doubt but that Congress could tax incomes of state employees, or income derived from federal, state, and local bonds. The argument was temporarily settled in 1916 when the Supreme Court restricted the amendment to its narrowest construction.[10] The decision was reaffirmed in 1928 when the Court held that Congress was forbidden to tax interest on state and local government bonds even in an indirect way.[11] However, in 1938, the Supreme Court endorsed federal taxation of income paid employees by state governments and by doing so created the distinct impression of favoring the broader, more literal interpretation of the Sixteenth Amendment. If this impression is correct, legal obstacles to federal taxation of income from state and local government securities have probably been removed.

Purposes for Which Congress Might Tax. The tax clause suggests that there are three purposes for which Congress may lay and collect taxes: to pay the debts, to provide for the common defense, and to provide for the general welfare. These phrases are so general that endless controversy has arisen over their meaning.

For Revenue or Regulation? The primary assumption underlying the tax clause is that taxes are levied to obtain revenue, but Congress often has legislated with mixed motives. Tariff laws, in addition to raising money, have also sought to protect American industry, and their constitutionality has never seriously been contested. In 1866 Congress levied a tax of 10 per cent on notes issued by state banks, for the purpose of driving them out of existence, and the measure was upheld.[12] In 1882 Congress imposed a head tax upon immigrants, the proceeds being earmarked for temporary care of the immigrants and not for the general support of government, and the Supreme Court sustained the

legislation.[13] In 1902 Congress imposed a tax of 10 cents a pound on colored oleomargarine in order to discourage its consumption in favor of butter, and the law was upheld.[14] In 1912 a tax of 2 cents a hundred was laid upon matches made with poisonous phosphorus, for the purpose of protecting workmen from the horrid occupational disease known as "phossie jaw." Although the law destroyed the white phosphorus industry, it was never challenged. Again, in 1914 and 1919 Congress required dealers in narcotics to pay a tax and submit to regulation, and the legislation was upheld.[15]

In all the above cases which reached the Supreme Court, the Court refused to look behind the face of tax legislation into the motives that prompted its enactment.

Court Halts Use. A halt was called, however, in 1922. In two cases coming before it in that year, the Court distinguished between a "true" tax intended to raise revenue and tax measures intended to penalize or regulate matters reserved for state control. In the first case, the Supreme Court had before it the child labor law of 1919.[16] That measure levied a tax of 10 per cent upon the net profits of all establishments employing children in violation of standards set up in the act. The Drexel Furniture Company, doing business in North Carolina, permitted a boy under the age of fourteen years to work in its factory during the taxable year 1919. Whereupon Bailey, the United States collector of internal revenue, notified the company that it was obliged to pay 10 per cent of its net profits for the year. Upon appeal to the Supreme Court, the law was declared unconstitutional. The tax, the Court said, was not a true one but a penalty intended to regulate business, a matter reserved to the states. The second case[17] involved a federal law enacted in 1921 intended to abolish dealings in futures upon the grain markets by imposing a tax of 20 cents a bushel upon all contracts for future de-

[10] Brushaber *v.* Union P. R. Co., 240 U.S. 1 (1916).

[11] National Life Insurance Co. *v.* United States, 277 U.S. 508 (1928).

[12] Veazie Bank *v.* Fenno, 8 Wall. 533 (U.S. 1869).

[13] Head Money Cases, 112 U.S. 580 (1884).

[14] McCray *v.* United States, 195 U.S. 27 (1904).

[15] United States *v.* Doremus, 249 U.S. 86 (1919).

[16] Bailey *v.* Drexel Furniture Company, 259 U.S. 20 (1922). See also p. 542.

[17] Hill *v.* Wallace, 259 U.S. 44 (1922).

livery and subjecting boards of trade to detailed regulations. Hill, representing the Board of Trade of the City of Chicago, brought suit against Wallace, the Secretary of Agriculture, seeking to enjoin collection of the tax and enforcement of the law. The Court declared the law unconstitutional, saying the tax was a penalty enacted to regulate a subject reserved to the states.

The same reasoning was followed later (at least until 1937), and may be illustrated by several decisions. The Revenue Act of 1926 imposed a special excise tax of $1,000 upon retail liquor dealers who carried on business within a state contrary to state and local laws. Tested in 1935, the Supreme Court held the exaction to be not a tax but a penalty for the violation of state laws, the effect of which was to usurp the police powers of the states.[18] A case arose in the following year from the first Guffey Coal Act wherein the bituminous coal industry was brought under federal control. The act levied a tax of 15 per cent upon all bituminous coal producers, 90 per cent of which was rebated to those who agreed to comply with a code established for the industry. This tax, the Court ruled, was not a true tax but a penalty designed to accomplish results beyond the reach of federal powers.[19]

Suppressing Weapons. A case decided in 1937[20] raised some doubt about what the attitude of the Court might be in the future. The Court had before it the National Firearms Act of 1934, which, in addition to requiring dealers in firearms to obtain an annual license of $200, required the payment of a tax of $200 on each transfer of sawed-off shotguns, other firearms capable of being concealed (except revolvers and pistols), machine guns, and mufflers or silencers for any firearms. Although expected to produce some revenue, the principal purpose of the legislation was probably the suppression of traffic in such weapons. Mr. Justice Stone stated:

Every tax is in some measure regulatory. To some extent it interposes an economic impediment to the activity taxed as compared with others not taxed. But a tax is not any the less a tax because it has a regulatory effect . . . and it has long been established that an Act of Congress which on its face purports to be an exercise of the taxing power is not any the less so because the tax is burdensome or tends to restrict or suppress the thing taxed.

In other words, a tax may be a penalty and the courts are incompetent to inquire into the motives that led to its enactment. This comes close to returning to the position adhered to prior to 1922. What regulation the Court might consider "offensive" and what levy might not operate as a tax must await future decisions.

The AAA. The controversy took a slightly different turn when the Agricultural Adjustment Act was placed on the statutes in 1933. This set up a far-reaching plan for controlling farm production. The Department of Agriculture entered into contracts with farmers agreeing to pay them for cooperating in a nation-wide effort to bring farm production in line with market needs as one means of raising farm income and contributing to national recovery from the depression. Funds for the program were obtained from a processing tax collected from the first domestic processor of the farm product brought under control. This was an excise tax collected from the miller, the packing company, the cotton ginner, the tobacco manufacturer, and other processors and passed on to consumers in the form of higher prices. The excise met the constitutional requirement of uniformity since it was collected at the same rate from all producers of particular products regardless of their geographic location. Here, then, was a uniform excise tax levied by Congress for the purpose of raising revenue to spend among farmers as a means of regulating production and thereby helping the nation recover.

The constitutionality of the act was challenged, and the case reached the Supreme Court in 1936.[21] The Court majority of six held the measure unconstitutional, chiefly on the ground that the processing taxes were being used to co-

[18] United States *v.* Constantine, 296 U.S. 287 (1935).
[19] Carter *v.* Carter Coal Co., 298 U.S. 238 (1936).
[20] Sonzinsky *v.* United States, 300 U.S. 506.

[21] United States *v.* Butler, 297 U.S. 1 (1936).

erce farmers as a means of regulating farm production—something reserved to the states by the Tenth Amendment. A strong dissent written by Justice Stone contended that the tax was a uniform excise; that it was used to raise money to be spent to provide for the general welfare; that production control was a necessary and proper incident to the primary purpose of helping the nation recover; and that, this being the case, state powers were not usurped by the Federal government. The decision temporarily halted the farm program, but new devices were discovered for achieving the same end. Because of this decision, subsequent farm legislation has been based primarily on the commerce power, the theory being that production control is incidental to the regulation of the flow of goods to national markets.

The Social Security Act. The issue rose again from passage of the Social Security Act in 1935, but with a different result. One feature of this measure imposed a payroll tax on employers and employees to be used for creating an old-age and survivors' insurance plan. This was immediately challenged but was upheld by the Supreme Court.[22] The majority of seven insisted that the tax was a uniform excise and income tax, even though a number of employments were exempt. The majority also contended that the revenues were being spent to provide for the general welfare and therefore powers reserved to the states were not being invaded. The minority countered by contending the tax was not uniform, since many employments were exempted, that the funds were not being spent for the general welfare but for only a portion of the population, and that powers reserved to the states were being usurped.

Another feature of the act levied taxes on employers of eight or more workers for the establishment of the unemployment-insurance program now so widely accepted. The law stipulated that employers would be given a 90 per cent credit on the federal tax if states enacted compensation plans conforming with federal standards. When this reached the Supreme

Court it was upheld by a 5-to-4 vote.[23] Again the majority reasoned that the tax was uniform, that it was spent to provide for the general welfare, and that state powers were not violated. The tax-offset device did not unduly coerce the states merely because the law had made it attractive for them to cooperate. The minority insisted the tax was not uniform because of its many exemptions, the funds were used for the benefit of special groups rather than for the general welfare, the states were improperly coerced and their powers invaded. It is difficult to reconcile this and the other social security tax case discussed above with the Butler case holding the AAA unconstitutional. In consequence of the broader interpretation, Congress may now use the tax power for almost any nation-wide welfare program.

Gambling Tax. In 1953 the Supreme Court upheld the validity of an occupational tax on persons in the business of accepting wagers, and a percentage tax on all bets except one type licensed by states.[24] The majority ruled that the tax was not invalid merely because it burdened or discouraged a particular business. Although the tax was accompanied by a registration requirement, the Court held that self-incrimination was not violated. Mr. Justice Black, dissenting, declared that the statute required a man to register and confess he was engaged in gambling; thus "it creates a squeezing device contrived to put a man in federal prison if he refuses to confess himself into a state prison as a violator of state gambling laws."

Limitations on the Taxing Power. Even though the taxing power has been broadly interpreted, it is not without limits. Some of these are expressly stated in the Constitution; others are implied.

No Taxes upon Exports. A search of the Constitution discloses only one type of tax that Congress is expressly forbidden to lay. The single prohibition is that Congress may not place any tax or duty on articles "exported from any state." This provision was added upon the insistence

[22] Helvering *v.* Davis, 310 U.S. 619 (1937).

[23] Steward Machine Co. *v.* Davis, 301 U.S. 548 (1937).

[24] United States *v.* Kahriger, 345 U.S. 22 (1953).

of Southern states who feared that their exports, particularly of cotton, might be discriminated against. "Exports" refer to goods shipped from any state to a foreign country and not to articles shipped from one state to another. A tax upon the production of articles even though applied to that portion which is intended for export is not considered an export tax. The provision would be violated, however, if a tax were laid on articles in the process of exportation, or if bills of lading and insurance policies for articles being exported were taxed.

Direct Taxes to Be Apportioned. The first restriction is that direct taxes (other than income) must be laid in proportion to the population of each state. In levying direct taxes, Congress must first decide exactly how much money it wishes to raise and then allot to each state that proportion of this sum which the population of the state bears to the total population of the country. This provision makes administration clumsy and results in taxation that bears no relation to people's ability to pay. Hence, the infrequent resort to direct taxes throughout our history.

Indirect Taxes to Be Uniform. A second restriction is that indirect taxes must be "uniform throughout the United States." This does not mean that they must be the same for everything and everybody; it is geographic uniformity that is required. Congress is free to make classifications for the purpose of taxation, but once having done so, the tax cannot be more nor less for objects within the same class at any point within the United States. The tariff on men's shoes, for example, may be higher than the tariff on women's, but the rate on men's cannot be less at the port of New Orleans than at New York. Employers of fewer than eight persons are exempt from paying a payroll tax to the Federal government from which to pay unemployed workmen, but all employers of eight or more must be taxed at the same rate whether they live in Maine or California. Large corporations may be required to pay at higher rates than smaller ones, but all of the same class and size must pay at the same rate whether they operate in

Kansas or Ohio. Since only incorporated territories—Hawaii and Alaska—are integral parts of the "United States" the uniformity clause also applies to them. It does not apply, however, to unincorporated territories. Therefore, people or objects in such territories as Puerto Rico and Samoa might be taxed at rates either higher or lower than those charged within the forty-eight states, Hawaii, and Alaska.

Taxes Not to Discriminate between Ports. The third restriction is that Congress may not levy any tax that gives preference "to the ports of one state over those of another." While federal levies must be uniform at all ports, Congress is not required to treat all ports alike in *every* respect. Congress has, for example, established ports of entry, erected lighthouses, improved rivers and harbors at some ports without doing the same for all.

Implied Restrictions upon the Taxing Power. In addition to the general limitations, expressed and implied, mentioned above, several others pertaining particularly to the use of the taxing power should be noticed.

State and Federal Governments Not to Burden One Another. In a federal system, especially where the power to tax is shared concurrently by the national government and states, one government is likely to tax the other either deliberately or otherwise. This happened early in our history when Maryland and several other states imposed taxes upon bank paper issued by the National Bank for the purpose of impeding the operations of the bank. This action led to the famous case of McCulloch *v.* Maryland [25] wherein the Supreme Court held that the Federal government, its agents and instrumentalities could not be taxed by the states, saying that "the power to tax involves the power to destroy." While observing that a federal tax upon the states would be more justifiable than a state tax upon the Federal government, the Court nevertheless pointed out that federal taxes that burdened the states would not be permitted.

Following this doctrine of intergovernmental immunity, the Supreme Court held federal sal-

[25] 4 Wheat. 316 (U.S. 1819).

aries immune from state taxation [26] and state salaries free from federal taxation.[27] Likewise, federal securities were declared free from state taxation,[28] and the securities of state and local governments, and the interest on them, immune from federal taxation.[29] Later the immunity was extended to cover sales of goods to the government. Thus, a state tax on the sale of gasoline to the Federal government was held invalid,[30] while a federal tax on the sale of motorcycles to a municipal police department was held void.[31] So the web of reciprocal immunity was spun.

The doctrine of intergovernmental immunity has always had its critics, but not until 1902 were modifications made. In that year the Court distinguished between functions that were strictly governmental and others that were commercial or proprietary in nature. The former were still immune from taxation but the latter were not. This meant that the national government might tax liquor monopolies,[32] the salaries of persons employed in the management of municipally owned railways and other utilities,[33] or the proceeds from the sale of athletic tickets by state universities.[34] Whether the reverse would be true, *i.e.,* that states might tax federal instrumentalities engaged in proprietary operations, has never been judicially determined. In the case of the TVA the states have not attempted to tax its operations, but the Federal government has expressly authorized the Authority to pay the

states in which its projects are located an amount equivalent to the taxes that would be collected from a similar private enterprise.

Within recent years the courts have gone even further in breaking down the doctrine of intergovernmental immunities. The first significant break with the past occurred in 1938 when it was held that the salaries of officers of the New York Port Authority were subject to federal taxation.[35] The Supreme Court went still further a year later, holding that the states might tax the salaries of federal employees and the Federal government might tax the incomes of employees of state and local governments.[36] A tax on income, said the Court, is neither economically nor legally a tax upon the source. Hence, there is no basis for the assumption that a tax upon the salary of employees by one government is tantamount to an interference by one government with the other in the performance of its functions.

As far as the Federal government is concerned, the test in the future is to be, apparently, whether its taxation imposes a burden so direct as to impede the operations of a state or local agency engaged in a strictly governmental function. The same is probably true for the states, although the Court made it clear that the states would not be permitted to tax federal employees or instrumentalities if Congress declares its intention that they should be immune. Since these recent decisions, all state and local government employees have become subject to federal taxation while at least forty states have imposed taxes upon the incomes of federal employees living within their jurisdiction.

Taxation of Judges' Salaries. To ensure judicial independence, the Constitution provides that federal judges [37] shall be paid compensation which "shall not be diminished during their continuance in office." From this provision controversy has arisen over whether judges might

[26] Dobbins *v.* Commissioners of Erie County, 16 Pet. 345 (U.S. 1842).

[27] Collector *v.* Day, 11 Wall. 113 (U.S. 1871).

[28] Weston *v.* Charleston, 2 Pet. 449 (U.S. 1829).

[29] Mercantile Bank *v.* New York, 121 U.S. 138 (1887); Pollock *v.* Farmers' Loan and Trust Company, 158 U.S. 601 (1895).

[30] Panhandle Oil Co. *v.* Mississippi, 277 U.S. 218 (1928).

[31] Indian Motocycle Co. *v.* United States, 283 U.S. 570 (1931).

[32] South Carolina *v.* United States, 199 U.S. 437 (1905).

[33] Metcalf and Eddy *v.* Mitchell, 269 U.S. 514 (1926); Helvering *v.* Power, 239 U.S. 214 (1934).

[34] Allen *v.* Regents of University of Georgia, 304 U.S. 439 (1938).

[35] Helvering *v.* Gearhardt, 304 U.S. 405 (1938).

[36] Graves *v. ex rel.* O'Keefe, 306 U.S. 466 (1939).

[37] And, incidentally, the President. What is said here about federal judges would probably apply to the President as well.

be required to pay taxes upon that portion of their income received from salaries. The issue of immunity from taxation first arose when Congress abolished fees charged by justices of peace in the District of Columbia. This was declared unconstitutional insofar as it applied to incumbent justices.[38] Later, during the Civil War, Congress taxed salaries of federal judges and, although never judicially tested, the legislation was generally thought to be unconstitutional and the money was later refunded. In 1919 Congress enacted a revenue law which did not exempt judges' salaries but when tested it was declared unconstitutional.[39] A later law imposed a tax upon the salaries of only those judges appointed subsequent to enactment of the legislation, but this, too, proved unacceptable.[40] In this instance the Supreme Court said that the Constitution imposed upon Congress the duty "definitely to declare what sum shall be received by each judge out of the public funds." Less than this amounted to an unconstitutional threat to judicial independence.

This doctrine prevailed until 1938 when it was overruled.[41] The case grew out of the revenue acts of 1932 and 1936, which taxed the salaries of judges appointed subsequently. A circuit judge named Woodrough, appointed in 1933, paid under protest a tax of more than $600 and then brought suit to recover the amount and prevent future collections. The district court, following precedents mentioned above, held the acts of Congress violative of the Constitution; but the Supreme Court by vote of 7 to 1 upheld the tax measures. The majority concluded that judicial independence was not threatened by subjecting judicial salaries to a general, nondiscriminatory tax. Rather, said the Court, "To subject them [judges] to a general tax is merely to recognize that judges are also citizens, and that their particular function in government does not generate an immunity from sharing with their fellow citizens the material burden of the

government whose Constitution and laws they are charged with administering." Although the measures here in question applied only to judges appointed after passage of the tax laws, Congress later (in 1939) extended the law to those appointed prior to 1932.

State Powers Not to Be Invaded. The review of cases above has already suggested that the line of demarcation is hard to draw where the federal tax power leaves off and state powers begin. Because the power to tax is concurrent, Congress can tax almost anything and so can the states. Some of the limits to which the courts will allow Congress to go in using the taxing power for regulatory purposes have been indicated, but more needs to be said about possible limits on the so-called "spending power."

Congress may tax to raise money to spend to provide for the "general welfare." The word "general" refers to that which is designed to benefit a considerable number of people as contrasted with something which is local or private. But may Congress spend money for any and all general purposes? One school, led by James Madison, which interprets the Constitution narrowly, insists that Congress can spend money only to carry out the delegated powers mentioned in the Constitution. Others, led by Alexander Hamilton and Joseph Story, insist that the taxing-and-spending clause is complete in itself and not limited to the fulfillment of other enumerated powers. The latter interpretation would authorize Congress to tax and spend for *any* purpose as long as it provides for the *general* welfare.

The Supreme Court had never met the issue squarely until reviewing the AAA in the Butler case discussed above. Then, while applying the taxing-and-spending clause narrowly enough to invalidate the AAA, it endorsed the broad interpretation of the power. Today, this interpretation provides the constitutional basis for expenditures for public relief, public works, old-age and survivors' insurance, unemployment compensation, soil conservation, most federal education programs, and many other activities. If an expenditure is for a "general" purpose it

[38] United States *v.* More, 3 Cr. 159 (U.S. 1805).

[39] Evans *v.* Gore, 253 U.S. 245 (1920).

[40] Miles *v.* Graham, 268 U.S. 501 (1925).

[41] O'Malley *v.* Woodrough, 307 U.S. 277 (1938).

would probably not be disallowed for constitutional reasons.

This is not to say, however, that Congress possesses a broad, plenary authority to do whatever it thinks necessary to provide for the general welfare. Recall the tax clause which says that "Congress shall have power to lay and collect taxes, duties, imposts and excises, to pay the debts, provide for the common defense and the general welfare of the United States." Some historians [42] contend that a semicolon, rather than a comma, should appear between the word "excises" and the phrase "to pay the debts." With a semicolon, the sentence would be divided into two parallel parts giving Congress not only the power to lay and collect taxes, but also the power to proceed to do whatever it deemed necessary to pay the debts, provide for the common defense and the general welfare. Thus, Congress would possess a general police power. With a comma, the sentence means that taxes may be levied *in order to* pay the debts, provide for the common defense and the general welfare. So far as the history of the clause is concerned, the draft of the Constitution reported by the Committee on Style did contain a semicolon, but the semicolon was displaced by a comma in the final draft. Some contend that the copyist took unwarranted liberty with the document. Be that as it may, the courts have always held that Congress does not have a general-welfare power. As matters stand, Congress has no separate power to provide for the general welfare but may spend money to obtain such ends. This accounts for the resort to taxation, subsidies to the state and local governments, and federal spending rather than to more direct methods of providing for the public welfare.

The spending power is subject to two specific restrictions in addition to the general limitations discussed earlier in this chapter. An appropria-

[42] See especially, Charles A. Beard, *Public Policy and the General Welfare* (Farrar, Straus, 1941), Chaps. 6 and 7; and Edward S. Corwin, *The Twilight of the Supreme Court* (Yale University Press, 1934), pp. 152–154. See also Charles Warren, *The Making of the Constitution* (Little, Brown, 1937), pp. 464–479.

tion may not be made for "armies" for a period of longer than 2 years; [43] and no money may be spent unless appropriated by Congress.

GOVERNMENTAL REVENUES

Income Taxes, Personal and Corporate. Personal and corporate income taxes yield a larger revenue than any other single type of federal tax.

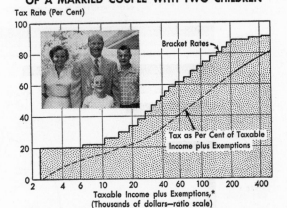

**INDIVIDUAL INCOME TAX RATES
EFFECTIVE ON 1954 INCOME
OF A MARRIED COUPLE WITH TWO CHILDREN**

Tax Rate (Per Cent)

Bracket Rates

Tax as Per Cent of Taxable Income plus Exemptions

Taxable Income plus Exemptions,*
(Thousands of dollars—ratio scale)

* Deductions must be added to this quantity to get adjusted gross income.

The personal income tax and how it affects a family of four. Adapted from Committee on Economic Development, *Federal Tax Issues in 1955*, p. 6.

In 1953–1954 the personal income tax brought in 32.4 billion dollars, and the corporate income tax 21.4 billion dollars. These sums constituted 50.2 and 33.3 per cent of the year's total federal tax receipts, exclusive of social security transactions.

The personal income tax is "progressive" in that rates are higher for those with the highest incomes. In 1955 the tax began at 20 per cent on the first $2,000 of net income, after deductions, and rose to 91 per cent on net income exceeding $200,000. A flat deduction of $600 was allowed to the taxpayer and to each of his dependents.

The corporate income tax has a much-less-

[43] Art. I, Sec. 8, cl. 12. Appropriations may, however, be made for the Navy and other branches of the government for longer than 2 years.

marked progressive feature. In 1955 the normal tax rate on corporate income was a flat 25 per cent, plus a surtax of 22 per cent for net income over $25,000.[44]

Death and Gift Taxes. Like the income tax, the inheritance tax received its first important application during the Civil War, when every possible source of revenue had to be explored,

inheritance tax applies to that part of a deceased person's estate passing to a particular heir or beneficiary. In order to guard against evasion by making gifts before death, the Federal government taxes such gifts. Over the years some of the other methods of evasion have been plugged by making subject to death taxes property in joint estates (like joint bank accounts),

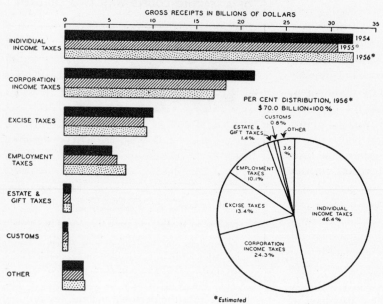

FEDERAL BUDGET REVENUES
FISCAL YEARS, 1954 - 1956

GROSS RECEIPTS IN BILLIONS OF DOLLARS

INDIVIDUAL INCOME TAXES — 1954, 1955*, 1956*

CORPORATION INCOME TAXES

EXCISE TAXES

EMPLOYMENT TAXES

ESTATE & GIFT TAXES

CUSTOMS

OTHER

PER CENT DISTRIBUTION, 1956*
$70.0 BILLION=100%

CUSTOMS 0.8%
ESTATE & GIFT TAXES 1.4%
OTHER
3.6%
EMPLOYMENT TAXES 10.1%
EXCISE TAXES 13.4%
INDIVIDUAL INCOME TAXES 46.4%
CORPORATION INCOME TAXES 24.3%

*Estimated

Courtesy of National Industrial Conference Board.

but it was repealed within a decade. After two intervening attempts, both meeting adverse court decisions, a death tax was enacted in 1916 and has been retained since that time. In recent prewar years federal revenue from death and gift taxes totaled between 300 million and 375 million dollars per year, which represented roughly 6 per cent of federal tax revenues; in 1953–1954 the two taxes yielded about 928 million dollars, but this was only about 1.4 per cent of total federal tax revenues.

The term "death taxes" includes two different forms: (1) An estate tax is levied on the total estate left by a deceased person; and (2) an

[44] Unless otherwise noted, figures on revenues and expenditures are drawn from Treasury Department data.

community property (jointly held by husband and wife under the laws of certain states), and certain trusts.

Federal death taxes are progressive, allowing an estate of $60,000 to pass tax free, then rising from 3 per cent on an estate above that figure to a maximum of 77 per cent. In 1924, as described previously, a federal tax offset or credit for state taxation was provided. Since 1926 states have been permitted to take as much as 80 per cent of the original or basic federal tax, but the offset feature does not apply to subsequent federal levies on estates.

Excise and Sales Taxes. The Constitution mentions excise taxes as part of the federal taxing power, and such levies soon were made upon liquor and several other commodities and transactions. Reduced, repealed, and restored excise taxes have had a very shifting history, increasing during war and depression, declining in peace and prosperity. Viewed from the standpoint of revenue, the present excise taxes of greatest importance are on liquor and tobacco, the former yielding more than 2,780 million dollars in 1952–1953 and the latter 1,654 million dollars. After these come manufacturers' excise taxes on selective luxury and quasi-luxury items: playing cards, amusement admissions, radios, musical instruments, sporting goods, toilet preparations, and the like. Wartime taxes were added to travel and communication services: rail tickets, telephone calls, telegraph messages, and others. Some taxes, as stated earlier in this chapter, are for purposes of regulation, not revenue; these include such diverse commodities as narcotics, oleomargarine, and machine guns.

Selective sales or excise taxes, such as the Federal government employs, are not subject to the principal criticism that applies to general sales or manufacturers' taxes, as used by the states. The burden of the general sales tax falls most heavily upon the individual or family with the least capacity to pay. A family with an annual income of $3,600 must spend a large portion of it for food, clothing, and other items taxable under the general sales tax; the family with $36,000 per year in income spends a much smaller proportion on taxable commodities and therefore pays out a smaller proportion of its income in sales tax. Proposals for a general federal sales tax have often been made, but the progressive forces in Congress have been able to secure their defeat.

Customs Duties. Throughout much of American history customs duties constituted the largest source of federal revenue. Indeed, the national treasury often was filled to the overflowing point by customs revenue. After the Civil War customs duties declined in relative importance as a source of revenue, and after the First World War tariff revenue was far outranked in size by income taxes. For the fiscal year 1954 customs receipts were just over 562 million dollars, an amount less than that re-turned by the corporate income tax, personal income tax, death taxes, liquor excise, tobacco excise, manufacturers' excises, and payroll or employment taxes.

The tariff has been a controversial topic in American politics because of its protective aspect, not its revenue features. Young industries sought the fostering care of government while they entered fields of production previously commanded by foreign producers. Later these "infant industries" argued that differences in the cost of production as between the United States and foreign nations should be equalized through tariff duties. Since the enactment of the Trade Agreements Act of 1934, significant steps were taken toward reducing tariff barriers through reciprocal trade agreements. Revenue from customs duties has continued modest since that time. As an important source of revenue customs duties are of doubtful validity; for they add to the prices consumers must pay, providing an erratic and irresponsible subsidy system for home producers.

Payroll Taxes. A newcomer of imposing size, payroll taxes entered the federal revenue picture only with the enactment of the Social Security Act of 1935. Since these revenues are earmarked for particular purposes, they do not affect significantly the general federal fiscal picture. The tax for old-age insurance is collected both from employee and employer; the rate started at 1 per cent on each and is now 2 per cent, but will rise gradually to 4 per cent by 1975. The federal tax for unemployment insurance was fixed at 3 per cent of each employer's total payroll, but 90 per cent of this is waived if the state in which the employer operates has an unemployment-insurance system approved by the Social Security Administration. A few states require employee contributions to unemployment insurance, but most finance from employer contributions alone. Revenues derived from the small federal payroll tax for unemployment insurance ($\frac{1}{10}$ of 3 per cent) are allocated to the states for administrative expense incurred in their unemployment-compensation programs. During the fiscal year of 1954 federal payroll taxes yielded a total of nearly 6 billion dollars.

Nontax Revenues. A great variety of nontax revenues accrue to the Federal government. Federal enterprises of a business nature—the Post Office, the Panama Canal and Panama Railroad, the Maritime Administration—return revenues to the Treasury, but little if any net profit is found after deducting operating expenses. Some relatively small amounts are obtained by the sale of public lands and by the rental of lands income. Revenue from federal grants-in-aid and from state proprietary enterprises, especially liquor stores, constitutes the greatest part of nontax state revenue.

Local governments are supported mainly by the traditional general property tax, which in 1953 yielded 87 per cent of all local tax revenue. Sales taxes now occupy second place. Licenses and permits are third. State grants to local gov-

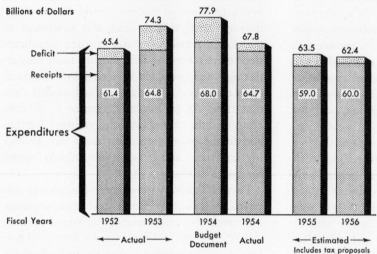

BUDGET TOTALS

Billions of Dollars

SOURCE: *Bureau of the Budget*

Expenditures have exceeded receipts causing an unbalanced budget for the year shown.

or of privileges (such as grazing or mineral extraction) on the public domain. Another source of nontax revenue is federal profit obtained through minting money. This profit represents the margin between the value of the metals used in minting (plus minting cost) and the face value of coins minted; it was over 73 million dollars in 1953–1954. Other forms of nontax federal revenues are found in fines and penalties exacted for crimes, gifts, interest on loans, and fees.

State and Local Revenues. The largest source of state tax revenues is state sales taxes, including general, motor-vehicle fuel, liquor, and tobacco taxes; sales taxes produced 58.8 per cent of the aggregate tax revenues of American states in 1953. Individual and corporate income taxes, license and privilege taxation, property taxes, and death and gift taxes return significant state

ernments and income from municipal utility undertakings (water and electricity) occupy an important place in local nontax revenues. State enterprises are not leading revenue producers.

Duplicating Taxation. The traditional sources of federal revenue were customs duties and excise taxes, especially on liquor and tobacco. Adoption of the Sixteenth Amendment and the coming of the First World War brought a transformation and a diversification of the federal revenue pattern. State governments, no longer able to subsist on the revenue obtainable from the general property tax, even earlier had turned to other forms of taxation. During the last 40 years federal and state taxes have been increasingly duplicative. This duplication may not be serious in some fields; for example, the federal tax on gasoline may be justified in view of the large federal grant-in-aid for state highways. In other fields, however, duplication is costly, awkward, and sometimes unfair; double taxation of incomes has resulted in an erratic pattern and in tax competition between the states. Federal-state duplication is found also in liquor and tobacco.

One solution for the problems arising from duplication is for the Federal government to allow *credits for state taxation*. The tax-offset device, as illustrated by federal death taxes, permits sharing of a source of revenue and encourages a measure of uniformity in the states. Only Nevada has no inheritance tax in order to take advantage of the federal credit for state taxation. A similar plan might be suitable for sharing the income tax. Thirty-one states had personal income taxes in 1954. Since the maximum state tax rate ranges from 2 to 11 per cent, and especially because the other states do not tax individual incomes as such, much competition exists between states seeking to serve as the residence of wealthy persons. A tax offset, permitting credit for state taxation up to about 25 per cent of the federal tax, would regularize personal income taxation in the country and prevent unfair competition.

Another proposal is that the different levels of government should agree on a *separation of sources*. Usually the plan is that the states should enjoy exclusively the field of general sales taxation, while the Federal government would have wholly the taxation of personal income. Such plans can work effectively to separate state and local tax sources, for state legislative action alone often suffices to make the separation. Dividing sources between Federal and state governments, however, would require unanimous consent of all forty-nine legislative bodies concerned or make a federal constitutional amendment necessary.

A more effective plan would be to enact a tax that would be *federally collected*, but *shared with the states*. This alternative would have some advantages over the tax-offset plan, for it would eliminate the expense and trouble of two returns on separate forms. A federally collected state-shared tax would not eliminate the possibility of duplication if any state persisted in its determination to tax the commodity or income item concerned.

Tax coordination between Federal and state governments is also found in mutual *deductibility,* particularly in the income-tax field. The Federal law permits a taxpayer to deduct state individual and corporate income taxes paid; some states reciprocate by allowing a similar deduction on federal taxes paid.

Federal-state cooperation in assessment and collection is achieved through the *exchange of information*. Since 1950, audit information has been exchanged for federal and state tax authorities. The tendency toward *uniformity of tax bases* and methods of tax computation helps open the way toward further cooperation. Utah has led the way in offering taxpayers the option of paying a fixed percentage of their federal income-tax payment in lieu of paying on state rates. Among proposals that have been made for additional cooperation is one for federal withholding of state income taxes from federal employees living in states with such taxes.[45]

Reciprocal Tax Immunity. The constitutional doctrine of reciprocal tax immunity has been traced earlier in this chapter. The idea of blanket immunity of all federal transactions and instrumentalities from state taxation, and those of the state from federal taxation, went far beyond the extent necessary to protect one level of government from undue burden by the other. At its height it banned state taxes on salaries of federal officials, on income from federal bonds, on sales to federal agencies; while the states enjoyed similar immunity from federal taxation. Beginning in 1938 the Supreme Court reduced considerably the scope of this immunity. The federal personal income tax is now collected from state and local government employees, and most of the states having an income tax apply it to federal employees as to anyone else. The greatest controversy arose over a Treasury proposal to eliminate tax exemption on government securities. Until recently standard practice has been that

[45] For a full discussion of these problems, see U.S. House of Representatives, Committee on Ways and Means, *Coordination of Federal, State, and Local Taxes,* H. Rept. 2519, 82d Cong., 2d Sess. (1953).

the Federal government make income from its own bond issues exempt from federal taxation, and most state governments have exempted their securities issues from their own taxes. This led to very complete immunity from taxation of most public securities issued in the country. In 1939 the Treasury Department started a campaign to secure the elimination of tax-exempt bonds. Extended hearings were held.[46] The principal opposition to the proposal came from representatives of state and local governments, who recognized that removal of tax immunity would require them to offer higher interest rates. This point was granted, but the more important question was whether or not the added interest rates might be offset by the revenue that would be derived from taxing income from public bonds. The greatest beneficiary from the old system of immunity is the person of very large income who invests heavily in tax-exempt state and local securities. Once his income reaches a point where he must pay one-half or more of the additional amount in federal income tax, the wealthy person will buy up exempt bonds, the income from which is untaxable.

Abolition of tax exemption is not an easy process. First, the Federal government has taken the lead, beginning in 1941, by making its own new bond issues subject to federal income taxation. The states might well be encouraged to take similar action in respect to their own issues. Next, the Federal government might commence taxing income from state and local government securities. This step has been delayed by the vehemence of state and local opposition but may be expected eventually. Finally, the states could follow the federal example and apply their taxation to federal bonds. These changes probably would apply only to future issues of securities; under the contract clause of the Federal Constitution it might be difficult to make them applicable to existing issues on which tax exemption

has been assured. If only future issues are covered, however, it will take a long time to correct the evils of the existing situation.

An Intergovernmental Fiscal Program. During the Second World War a thorough study of intergovernmental fiscal relations was completed by a committee of experts appointed by the Secretary of the Treasury.[47] Stressing the cooperative approach, the committee proposed the establishment of a federal-state fiscal authority, which would promote joint administration of selected overlapping taxes, facilitate interstate cooperation, conduct research, and perform other services of mutual interest to Federal and state governments. This authority would be composed of three members, of which one would be appointed by the President, one by delegates of the states, and a third by the first two.

According to the committee, a number of specific taxes may be coordinated to the advantage of both Federal and state governments. For the income tax, cooperation in administration is recommended, involving joint returns, joint audits, and joint use of personnel. Death taxes need overhauling, with the Federal government extending the offset to all its levies including the gift tax, and the states improving their administration. Tobacco taxes, now levied by both levels of government, ought to be put on a federally collected, state-shared basis. To simplify payment, it was proposed that the unemployment-insurance tax offset be increased to 100 per cent, so that the taxpayer would pay solely to the state.

Tackling next the problems of tax immunities, the committee urged establishment of a standard policy for federal payments in lieu of taxes to state and local governments. To break the log jam over tax-exempt securities, the committee suggested consideration of both a federal bank for loans to states and municipalities, and a direct federal subsidy of $\frac{1}{2}$ of 1 per cent on the bond issues of state and local governments.

[46] U.S. House of Representatives, Special Committee on Taxation of Governmental Securities and Salaries, *Hearings,* 76th Cong., 1st Sess. (1939). See also U.S. House of Representatives, Committee on Ways and Means, *Hearings on Taxation of Governmental Securities,* 76th Cong., 1st Sess. (1939).

[47] U.S. Treasury Department, Committee on Intergovernmental Fiscal Relations, *Federal, State, and Local Government Fiscal Relations . . . a Report . . . ,* S. Doc. 69, 78th Cong., 1st Sess. (1943). Members of the committee were Harold M. Groves, Luther Gulick, and Mabel Newcomber.

The committee examined the results of federal grants-in-aid in the states. In many of them aided functions get the lion's share of state resources, due to the matching requirement. The need for a national minimum standard, especially in elementary education, was urged. The committee commended for use in grants-in-aid the "graduated bracket system of distribution," a sliding scale like that now in use on several of the Social Security grants to the states.

FOR FURTHER READING

THE TAX POWER

Bruton, P. W. (ed.): *Cases and Materials on Federal Taxation* (West, 1953).

Burdick, Charles K.: *The Law of the Constitution: Its Origin and Development* (Putnam, 1922).

Corwin, Edward S.: *Court over Constitution* (Princeton University Press, 1934).

Larkin, John D.: *The President's Control over the Tariff* (Harvard University Press, 1936).

Powell, Alden L.: *National Taxation of State Instrumentalities* (University of Illinois Press, 1936).

Seligman, Edwin R. A.: *The Income Tax* (Macmillan, 1911).

Story, Joseph: *Commentaries on the Constitution of the United States* (Little, Brown, 2 vols., 4th ed., 1873).

Warren, Charles: *The Supreme Court in United States History* (Little, Brown, 3 vols., 1923).

——: *The Making of the Constitution* (Little, Brown, 1923).

TAXATION AND REVENUES

Altman, George C.: *Introduction to Federal Taxation* (New York: Commerce Clearing House, rev. ed., 1938).

Blakey, Roy G., and Gladys C. Blakey: *Sales Taxes and Other Excises* (Chicago: Public Administration Service, 1945).

——: *The Federal Income Tax* (Longmans, 1940).

Blough, Roy: *The Federal Taxing Process* (Prentice-Hall, 1952).

Groves, Harold M.: *Postwar Taxation and Economic Progress* (McGraw-Hill, 1946).

——: *Financing Government* (Holt, 4th ed., 1954).

Lutz, Harley L.: *Public Finance* (Appleton-Century-Crofts, rev. ed., 1947).

Manning, Raymond E.: *Federal Excise Taxes,* Public Affairs Bulletin 59 (Library of Congress, 1947).

Paul, Randolph: *Taxation in the United States* (Little, Brown, 1954).

Shoup, Carl, and Others: *Facing the Tax Problem* (Twentieth Century Fund, 1947).

Shultz, W. J.: *American Public Finance* (Prentice-Hall, 6th ed., 1954).

Tax Institute (formerly Tax Policy League, Philadelphia): *Tax Barriers to Trade* (Princeton, N.J.: The Institute, 1941).

——: *Federal-State-Local Tax Coordination* (The Institute, 1954).

——: *Tax Policy* (The Institute, monthly).

Tax Research Foundation: *Tax Systems* (Chicago: Commerce Clearing House, 9th ed., 1942). Issued at irregular intervals, annual supplements.

Taylor, P. E.: *Economics of Public Finance* (Macmillan, rev. ed., 1953).

U.S. Treasury Department, Tax Division, Analysis Staff: *Overlapping Taxes in the United States* (Jan. 1, 1954).

U.S. Treasury Department, Committee on Intergovernmental Fiscal Relations: *Federal, State and Local Government Fiscal Relations . . . a Report . . .*, S. Doc. 69, 78th Cong., 1st Sess. (1943).

REVIEW   1. To what extent has the federal tax power been used to regulate rather than raise
QUESTIONS   revenue?

2. What considerations led to the adoption of the Sixteenth Amendment? How serious are threats of its repeal?

3. As used in the Constitution, what is the meaning of the terms "taxes," "duties," "imposts," and "excises"?

4. What were the main issues raised in the social security tax case? How were they decided?

5. Enumerate and discuss specific limitations on the taxing power.

6. Name and discuss implied restrictions on the taxing power.

7. Explain existing personal and corporate income taxes and their importance in the federal revenue picture.

8. Is it fair to require employers to collect, at their own expense, income taxes and social security taxes from employee payrolls?

9. Compare the main sources of federal and state-local tax revenues.

10. Discuss the problem of duplicating taxation between Federal and state governments, and suggest possible corrective steps.

11. What is the constitutional basis of reciprocal tax immunity? Discuss some of the problems posed by it.

12. What are the prospects that a comprehensive intergovernmental fiscal program might be placed in operation? Discuss.

CHAPTER 20

Fiscal Administration, Money, and Banking

The relationship between the legislative and the executive branches largely determines the success or failure of democratic government. Hence, the budget, because it is at the same time the most important instrument of legislative control and of executive management, is at the very core of democratic government. — Harold D. Smith [1]

Although governments are not created for the purpose of collecting and spending money, considerations of revenues and expenditures underlie virtually every governmental problem. Governmental services cost money. By managing the purse strings, executives and legislatures are able to exert both detailed and general controls over the various governmental activities. For the executive, finance is a control over administration ranking with that of personnel. For the legislative body, finance looms much more important than personnel or any other form of control. The scope of the federal taxing power having been dealt with in the previous chapter, this chapter is devoted to a description and criticism of financial administration, with incidental attention to state and local practices.

FINANCIAL ADMINISTRATION

Constitutional Provisions. The Constitution places the primary responsibility for finances upon Congress. Appropriations are made by law, but the President's participation through the veto has not been particularly forceful because the executive normally is preoccupied with the ne-

cessity of securing succor for the agencies under his control. Moreover, he possesses no power to veto items or to reduce portions of appropriation bills. The President has used his constitutional power to recommend appropriations to the Congress, but his most effective sanction over congressional action came from his role as leader of the majority party. When his party was in control of both houses and when he was accepted as its leader, his influence often was great over fiscal and other matters. The idea of legislative supremacy in the financial field was established in Britain after centuries of controversy between King and Parliament. After the victory of Parliament, however, responsible government developed in Britain, and the Parliament gave to the real executive, now under its own control, vast powers over money matters. In Britain today only the government (*i.e.*, the executive) may introduce legislation involving the appropriation of money.

Early Federal Organization. As American Federal government developed after 1789, the financial responsibilities of Congress multiplied. The various committees of the two houses, and individual members as well, introduced and pressed for the adoption of fiscal measures raising and expending moneys. It proved difficult

[1] "The Budget as an Instrument of Legislative Control and Executive Management," *Public Administration Review,* vol. 4 (Summer, 1944), p. 181.

to fix specific responsibility for action; the trading of votes for appropriations (logrolling) and the distribution of favors among state and congressional districts (pork barrel) led to immense waste of public funds. The fidelity of financial

port of which was sent to Congress with presidential approval on June 27, 1912.[2] The commission recommended that the President should submit to each session of Congress a budget, containing a budgetary message, financial state-

I'm On My Side of the Fence, Ain't I?

transactions was inadequately checked, opening opportunities for corruption. Although the Secretary of the Treasury was required to provide Congress with compilations of requests for appropriations, he was given no real authority over these estimates.

The Budget and Accounting Act of 1921. The need for reform in federal financial practices was first stated prominently by President Taft's Commission on Economy and Efficiency, the re-

ments, and estimates prepared through the Secretary of the Treasury.

The important task of preparing the national budget, under the direction of the President, was assigned by the 1921 act to the Bureau of the

[2] It was entitled "The Need for a National Budget" and was H. Doc. 854, 62d Cong., 2d Sess. This era is well covered in Frederick A. Cleveland and Arthur E. Buck, *The Budget and Responsible Government* (Macmillan, 1920).

Budget, which was created for this purpose. Originally a portion of the Treasury Department, the Bureau was transferred to the Executive Office of the President by executive order in 1939. Under the terms of the law, the Bureau of the Budget has power "to assemble, correlate, revise, reduce, or increase the estimates of the several departments or establishments." President Roosevelt strengthened the Bureau notably on several occasions after 1933, adding power to apportion appropriations, to require departments to set up reserves, responsibility for statistical services, and duties of research, planning, and investigation.

The Bureau of the Budget Now. The functions of the Bureau of the Budget were enumerated in an executive order in 1939 and now are as follows: [3]

1. To assist the President in budget and fiscal control preparation
2. To supervise and control budget administration
3. To conduct research on administration and to advise departments and agencies on improved organization and practices
4. To aid the President in bringing about more efficient and economical conduct of government service
5. To assist the President by coordinating departmental advice on proposed legislation
6. To assist with proposed executive orders and proclamations
7. To plan the improvement of statistical services
8. To keep the President informed on the work of the government

To accomplish these ends, the Bureau is organized, under a director and his assistants, into appropriate offices and divisions. The offices, each headed by an assistant director, are: budget review, legislative reference, management and organization, and statistical standards. The divisions, each concerned with a broad phase of executive functions, are: commerce and finance, international, labor and welfare, military, and resources and civil works. About 450 persons are now employed.

Reforms instituted in the last few years have brought the personnel and powers of the Bureau near to the level urged for it by Arthur E. Buck in his able analysis made for the President's Committee on Administrative Management. Each department and larger independent establishment has its own budget officer, who prepares and edits estimates and works with the Bureau of the Budget in the budget conferences and hearings that are necessary before a budget document can be submitted to Congress.

Much of the legislative reference work is nonfiscal, but it constitutes one of the great tasks of the Bureau. The Hoover Commission noted that the Bureau, during the Eightieth Congress, advised the President or executive Departments on 5,992 bills and gave the President information on 1,438 bills passed by Congress.[4] After an initial period of getting acquainted, the Eisenhower Administration appeared to rely heavily upon the Budget Bureau's facilities for the central clearance of legislation.[5]

The statistical services of the Bureau include the approval of forms and questionnaires used by federal agencies, in order to secure simplification and to avoid overlapping. The administrative management division, concerned with aiding departments to secure efficiency and economy, makes studies of particular agencies or problems and reports to the appropriate authorities. Its contribution, also nonfiscal in nature, is to improve the machinery of administration.

Department of the Treasury. Several tasks of the Treasury Department fall within the field of fiscal management. Taxes are collected mainly through the Internal Revenue Service. Customs duties are collected by the Bureau of Customs.

Even more directly related to the matter of

[3] Executive Order 8248, Sept. 8, 1939. One of the best studies of the bureau is Fritz Morstein Marx, "The Bureau of the Budget: Its Evolution and Present Role," *American Political Science Review,* vol. 39 (August and October, 1945), pp. 653–684, 869–898.

[4] First Hoover Commission, *Budgeting and Accounting* (1949), pp. 24–25.

[5] Richard E. Neustadt, "Presidency and Legislation: The Growth of Central Clearance," *American Political Science Review,* vol. XLVIII (September, 1954), pp. 641–671.

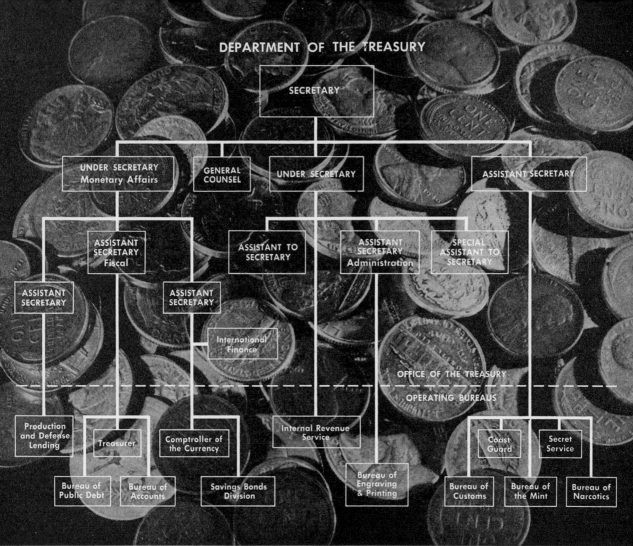

DEPARTMENT OF THE TREASURY

SECRETARY

UNDER SECRETARY
Monetary Affairs

GENERAL
COUNSEL

UNDER SECRETARY

ASSISTANT SECRETARY

ASSISTANT
SECRETARY
Fiscal

ASSISTANT TO
SECRETARY

ASSISTANT
SECRETARY
Administration

SPECIAL
ASSISTANT TO
SECRETARY

ASSISTANT
SECRETARY

ASSISTANT
SECRETARY

International
Finance

OFFICE OF THE TREASURY

OPERATING BUREAUS

Production
and Defense
Lending

Treasurer

Comptroller of
the Currency

Internal Revenue
Service

Coast
Guard

Secret
Service

Bureau of
Public Debt

Bureau of
Accounts

Savings Bonds
Division

Bureau of
Engraving
& Printing

Bureau of
Customs

Bureau of
the Mint

Bureau of
Narcotics

Crane photograph from Black Star

over-all financial administration, however, is the function of the Fiscal Service of the Treasury Department. Headed by a Fiscal Assistant Secretary, the Service was created by executive order in 1940 and charged with accounting, debt, and custodial functions. The Fiscal Assistant Secretary keeps in touch with the financial operations of the various departments and agencies and informs the Secretary of the Treasury. Responsible to him is the Commissioner of Accounts, who heads the Bureau of Accounts and who has the duty of supervising the accounting of the Treasury Department and of keeping the central accounts of the entire government. In addition, the Bureau of Accounts issues all Treasury warrants, makes disbursements for most of the federal agencies, and designates depositories

with which government money may be placed.

Also in the Fiscal Service is the Bureau of the Public Debt, headed by the Commissioner of the Public Debt. Federal borrowing is handled by this agency. Special staffs may be created from time to time to promote bond selling, but the actual issuance and control stem from the Bureau of the Public Debt.

Another agency of importance in the Fiscal Service is the Office of Treasurer of the United States. The Treasurer receives and disburses public funds and is the custodian of public money. After Congress has appropriated funds, he credits them to the proper disbursing officer, following receipt of a warrant signed by the Secretary of the Treasury and countersigned by the Comptroller General.

The Comptroller General. The General Accounting Office (GAO), of which the Comptroller General is head, was created by the Budget and Accounting Act of 1921. It is an agency of the legislative branch of the government. The Comptroller General was given wide powers over accounting, audit, and investigation.

The Comptroller General is appointed by the President, with Senate confirmation, for a term of 15 years. His GAO staff of about ten thousand employees works in the several offices and divisions, including audits, investigations, claims, accounting systems, transportation, personnel, administrative services, and general counsel.

Under the Budget and Accounting Procedures Act of 1950, the Comptroller General:

1. Prescribes principles and standards of accounting for all executives agencies

2. Cooperates with the agencies and the Treasury in developing accounting systems

3. Approves agency accounting systems that he deems adequate

4. Reviews accounting systems of the agencies

5. Audits financial transactions of all legislative, executive, and judicial agencies [6]

The 1921 Act has often been criticized because it grants to the Comptroller General accounting as well as auditing functions, and it is contrary to accepted principles of financial administration for the auditor to be also the chief accounting officer and through the power of settling accounts to control the acts of administrative officers. During the first term of the Franklin D. Roosevelt Administration there were many conflicts between the heads of executive agencies and the Comptroller General, particularly when he used his powers of disallowance to block public policies which he disapproved. Since then, however, after the first Comptroller General retired, relations between this officer and executive departments and agencies have greatly improved. The first Hoover Commission proposed a new "accountant general" under the Secretary of Treasury, who would set up methods and pro-

cedures, subject to the approval of the Comptroller General. It also recommended that the GAO cease bringing carloads of vouchers to Washington for audit, and do sample audit in the field. The latter change was made following 1949. The second Hoover Commission commended the improvements made in both auditing and accounting fields by the GAO. It urged careful study of internal auditing within the agencies.

THE BUDGETARY PROCESS

Following the confusion and irresponsibility that characterized early Federal financial administration, a new era opened with the enactment of the Budget and Accounting Act of 1921. State reforms came both before and after the national, spreading over a period of the last 40 years. The following analysis of the budgeting process is based primarily upon federal practice, except where otherwise noted.

Definition of a Budget. A budget is a comprehensive financial plan, the central instrument of financial administration. The budgetary process, according to A. E. Buck, involves three elements: (1) the financial plan, (2) the procedure for formulating, authorizing, executing, and controlling the plan, and (3) some governmental authority responsible for each stage of the procedure.[7]

The budget document is the blueprint in which a government forecasts its expenditures and estimates its revenues. It is for a given fiscal period, usually for one year but sometimes (especially in state governments) for a biennium. The fiscal year of the Federal government is from July 1 to June 30. Some state and local governments use the calendar year as the fiscal year.

The second of these elements names the four stages in the budgeting process. The first is formulation, involving assembling of estimates from operating agencies and their inclusion in the financial plan. The second is authorization of the budget, through legislation adoption. The third, budget execution, consists of controlling the expenditures authorized. The fourth stage is

[6] Second Hoover Commission, *Budget and Accounting* (1955), p. 58.

[7] Arthur E. Buck, *The Budget in Governments of Today* (Macmillan, 1934), p. 46.

entered when accounts are checked and transactions audited.

Responsibility for the steps in budgetary procedure is fixed upon various officers and agencies in each level of government. Increasingly, authority to prepare the budget is given to the Chief Executive or to some officer or bureau re-

an independent officer or agency, or one responsible to the legislative branch.

Budget Formulation. Under the Budget and Accounting Act of 1921, the responsibility for budget formulation was placed upon the President, who was provided with the assistance of the Bureau of the Budget. Originally a part of

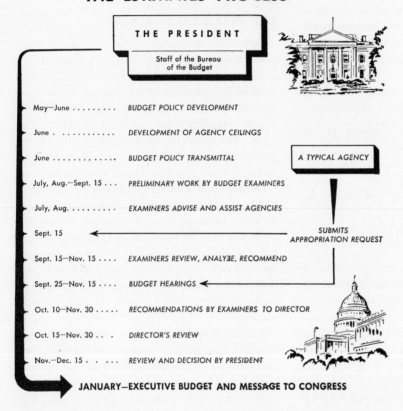

THE ESTIMATES PROCESS

THE PRESIDENT

Staff of the Bureau of the Budget

May–June	BUDGET POLICY DEVELOPMENT
June	DEVELOPMENT OF AGENCY CEILINGS
June	BUDGET POLICY TRANSMITTAL
July, Aug.–Sept. 15 . . .	PRELIMINARY WORK BY BUDGET EXAMINERS
July, Aug.	EXAMINERS ADVISE AND ASSIST AGENCIES
Sept. 15	
Sept. 15–Nov. 15	EXAMINERS REVIEW, ANALYZE, RECOMMEND
Sept. 25–Nov. 15	BUDGET HEARINGS
Oct. 10–Nov. 30	RECOMMENDATIONS BY EXAMINERS TO DIRECTOR
Oct. 15–Nov. 30 . . .	DIRECTOR'S REVIEW
Nov.–Dec. 15	REVIEW AND DECISION BY PRESIDENT

A TYPICAL AGENCY

SUBMITS APPROPRIATION REQUEST

JANUARY—EXECUTIVE BUDGET AND MESSAGE TO CONGRESS

Since Federal budgets are prepared and submitted annually to Congress the budgetary process is a continuous one.

sponsible to him. The executive needs budgeting power to strengthen his position over the administration, and, in turn, he is the official with greatest authority to enforce compliance of spending officers. Universally budgets are authorized by legislative bodies, but there is some variation in the procedure on budget bills. Execution is the responsibility of several officers and agents, including the budget preparer, accounting officer, head of operating agency, purchasing agent, personnel agency. Accountability is enforced through a postaudit, conducted by either

the Department of the Treasury, in 1939 it was moved to the Executive Office of the President. The President determines general fiscal policy, and then delegates to his budget director power to proceed with budget formulation.

The Estimates. The various operating departments and agencies are called upon by the Budget Bureau to submit their estimates of expenditures for the forthcoming fiscal period. These preliminary estimates are analyzed by the budget agency. The Chief Executive is consulted on matters of policy and settles serious disagreements between budget director and operating agency. The revised estimates are then put into final form and printed. Normally the operating departments and agencies request more than they expect to receive but wish to have a safe margin that may be lost in estimate cuts.

The form and contents of budgets vary considerably. A good budget will contain several essential features. First, the executive's budget message reviews the general financial picture—anticipated revenues, business conditions, estimated expenditures, and the like. Second, financial statements compare the fiscal present with the past and with estimated future operations. Then the body of the budget contains the appropriation estimates—the executive's recommendations. The usual practice is to organize the estimates according to Departments and agencies. The better budgets often have a parallel column with amounts appropriated for the last one or two fiscal periods.

In practice, the process of budget formulation involves much negotiation between budget agency and operating Department, and between budget agency and Chief Executive. Under the federal law, the Bureau of the Budget is given power "to assemble, correlate, revise, reduce, or increase the estimates of the several departments and establishments." These estimates are subject to preliminary editing and adjustment within the operating agency by either Department head or departmental budget officer. There is a natural tendency to overestimate one's needs in order to be on the safe side. Much "padding" of estimates may be eliminated by officers within a particular department and before estimates go to the budgeting agency. Sometimes the Chief Executive sets in advance a maximum amount allowable for each department. When this is done, the departmental adjustments of estimates loom of much greater relative importance, for the main controversies will then tend to be intradepartmental.

Budgeting Agency. Next, departmental estimates are transmitted to the budgeting agency. Normally the Budget Bureau is saddled with the task of bringing down the expenditure estimates of operating agencies to a level stipulated by the Chief Executive or indicated by estimated revenues. This requires budget hearings, in which departmental officers present their cases to budget officers. The budget officer must decide, and often this decision involves a substitution of his judgment for that of the departmental officer. When a layman decides between the bomber and the carrier in defense estimates, or for or against experimentation with polio vaccine in those of the Public Health Service, the necessity for maturity on the part of the budgeteer is painfully obvious. Appeals to budget director or Chief Executive are possible, but not often politic.

Budget Authorization. Budget or appropriation bills are drawn either by the executive budget officer or by a legislative committee. It is now recognized as proper practice for the Chief Executive to submit the budget and to be responsible for what is contained in it. In the Federal and in most state and local governments the legislature can decrease or increase the executive's recommendations. The existence of this power diminishes the full measure of responsibility possessed by the executive in Great Britain, where only the ministers can introduce appropriation bills and Parliament is denied the authority to increase any item.

Appropriation Bill. Congress and other American legislative bodies have well-established procedures for dealing with appropriation measures. The budget bill is introduced in the manner used for other bills. In Congress and in many state legislatures revenue bills must originate in the lower house; although this restriction does not apply to appropriation measures, custom decrees that introduction in the House of Representatives is necessary. The budget goes to the legislature with the executive's budget message, detailing the fiscal picture of past, present, and future. The printed budget document shows many details not found in the appropriation bill that accompanies it. The bill may be written with considerable detail, or it may include only the principal totals and subtotals. The former is called the "segregated-item" type of appropriation measure; the latter is known as the "lump-sum" variety. The segregated-item bill is unduly restrictive and allows little administrative discretion; the lump-sum plan liberates the executive from detailed limits and permits flexibility for adjustment and economy. Federal appropriation bills are a great mixture, with some items providing for millions of dollars and some for only a few dollars.

After introduction, the budget bill is referred to the proper committee. In both the United States Senate and House of Representatives the "appropriations" committees have subcommittees for each executive department and independent agency.[8] These bodies conduct hearings and call in and question heads of operating agencies. Usually these officers are not permitted to advocate other than the estimate submitted by the Chief Executive. In some badly managed jurisdictions, officers violate the spirit and sometimes the letter of budget law by lobbying for the restoration of their own unrevised estimates. After hearings are completed, the committee makes its recommendation, and the house debates and acts. The same procedure or a similar one is followed in the second house.

Executive Action. Having been enacted by both houses, and having compromised any possible differences, the appropriation bill is sent to the executive for signature. The President is forced to approve or to reject the measure as a whole; naturally he approves almost invariably, for the agencies cannot long operate without money. Many state governors and some local executives have an item veto power, permitting them to strike out or to reduce any portion of an appropriation measure. As shown earlier, such a power in the hands of the President would strengthen materially his position in the budgetary process.

Widespread abuses still persist in the authorization of budgets by legislative bodies. Few appropriations committees have adequate staffs for

dealing with the intricate problems involved in budget bills. Decisions often, perhaps inevitably, are made with considerations of "logrolling" and the "pork barrel" predominating. Most suggestions for improvement involve expansion of the role of the executive in authorization, as well as in other phases of budgeting.

Some features peculiar to federal budgetary procedure should be noted here. The President includes in his budget the appropriations requested by judicial and legislative branches of government, but he has no power to alter these estimates. In some of the best state and local jurisdictions, one single omnibus budget bill is used to cover all the appropriation items proposed by the executive. In Congress, however, a separate bill is introduced for some departments, other departments are grouped together for the purpose, and at least one bill each year is devoted to the independent establishments.

In 1950 Congress combined all appropriations into a single omnibus bill, but the experiment has not been repeated. The chairmen of the appropriations subcommittees of each house have charge of the bills on the floor of each house. Since the budget estimates are made up considerably in advance of the fiscal period, it is inevitable that unusual needs will arise and will require added appropriations for some purpose. These demands are handled through "deficiency" appropriation estimates and bills.

Budget Execution. The principal agencies of financial administration of the American national government have been described already. Those with roles in budget execution include the Treasury Department, the Bureau of the Budget, the General Accounting Office, and its head, the Comptroller General. Custody of funds is in the hands of the Treasury. Under current federal practice, the Treasury notifies the operating departments and agencies of the amount of money they may expend during the fiscal year. The agencies may then incur obligations. Bills are paid through disbursing officers located in various parts of the country. Most disbursing officers are in the Treasury Department, but the armed forces and Post Office still have their own

[8] The U.S. Senate Appropriations Committee brings in three members of certain committees with jurisdiction over the subject matter of the budget items under consideration. These three members sit with Appropriations while the budget of their special interest is being considered.

disbursing agencies. Advances of funds are made available to disbursing officers through local depositaries.

Claim Settlement. The great majority of claims against the United States are settled promptly by the disbursing officers, in accordance with rules and regulations. Doubtful claims are referred to the Comptroller General for settlement, over which he has final jurisdiction.[9]

The Director of the Bureau of the Budget since 1933 has been empowered to apportion appropriations for each agency by periods of the fiscal year. This is one of the most important of fiscal powers, for it enables the executive to keep a quarter-by-quarter check of financial transactions of the operating establishments. Under this scheme spending agencies are given only a certain proportion of their total appropriation to spend in any given period; one common limit in state and local governments is no more than one-tenth in any one month.

Accounts are kept by the operating departments and establishments. The departmental accounting officers report monthly expenditures to the Bureau of the Budget. The Treasury also maintains a set of accounts, showing general transactions. The Fiscal Service of the Treasury, created by executive order in 1940, was directed "to establish and maintain a complete system of central accounts for the entire Government," and to prescribe standards and forms for departmental financial reports.[10] Nevertheless, the Comptroller General still possesses the power to prescribe forms, systems, and procedure for accounting to the departments and establishments. Some diffusion of responsibility for accounting persists.

After the financial transaction is complete, auditing is in order. It involves the examination of the records to check on the validity of accounts and payments. In governmental circles the theory is current that a postaudit should be conducted by an officer or body independent of the executive or spending agencies. The task of checking to see whether or not expenditures have been made in accordance with law is assigned either to an independent auditor or to one responsible to the legislative branch. The Comptroller General, with 15-year term and removal only by Congress, was intended to be such an officer, but only recently has the work been performed effectively.

Budget Reform. Both the first and second Hoover Commissions gave much attention to budgeting and accounting. The recommendations of the former that were put into effect included statutory provision in 1949 for performance budgeting in the Department of Defense, improved accounting procedures under an act of 1950, authorization of the President to prescribe form and contents of the budget, and administrative reorganization of the Bureau of the Budget in 1952.

Despite these changes, however, the second Hoover group found much more that needed doing. The budgeting process stretches over as long as 18 months. The budget document exceeds 1,200 pages and weighs more than 5 pounds. Huge unexpended appropriations are being carried forward from year to year; in the mid-1950's the "carry-over" was from 50 billion to 75 billion dollars per year. The Commission quoted with approval the conclusions of its task force, adding: ". . . under present procedures there is no effective control over expenditures either by the Congress or the Executive Branch." [11]

Both Hoover groups praised the performance or program budget and recommended its adoption or extension of its use. The idea is not a new one, for it has long been used in state and local governments with progressive budgeting processes. Emphasis is placed on the work or service to be performed, not merely the salaries, supplies, and equipment required by a particular agency.

Using the Naval Medical Center at Bethesda, Md., as an example, the first Hoover Commission reported that the hospital received allotments from twelve different Navy appropria-

---

[9] His decisions are available in *Decisions of the Comptroller General of the United States.*

[10] Executive Order 8512, Aug. 13, 1940.

[11] Second Hoover Commission, *op. cit.,* p. 17.

tion titles; at no place in the budget was the cost of operating the Bethesda facility totaled or the work of the hospital set forth clearly. The performance budget, on the other hand, describes the significance and scope of the work, gives reasons for increases and decreases, outlines current and future programs, presents per bed and per patient costs for each hospital, and summarizes the complete cost of Navy medical care.

budget executor. For the armed services, the comptrollers would be responsible only to the civilian Secretary, not to the military Chief of Staff.

Expanded Budget Bureau. Perhaps the outstanding feature of the second Hoover Commission's report in this area was the proposal to expand Bureau general managerial functions, including the stationing of its representatives

BUDGET AUTHORIZATIONS,
Related to Expenditures

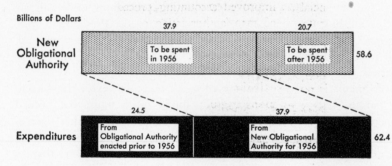

FISCAL YEAR 1956, ESTIMATED

Billions of Dollars

This diagram, prepared by the Bureau of the Budget, shows how money appropriated for one year may be spent in another. The second Hoover Commission recommended that budgeting be shifted from an obligation to a cost basis.

Statutory changes of 1949 and 1950 made performance budgeting mandatory. The budget of fiscal 1951 was the first government-wide program budget.

Cost Basis. Most federal budgets, the second Hoover Commission pointed out, are based on estimated obligations to be incurred in the budget year. Into the obligations figure go contracts to be awarded, orders to be placed, and other commitments involving future charges against the government. Large sums carried over from previous years are not taken into account when the obligation basis is used. The Commission recommended that budgets be formulated and administered on a cost basis. To help restore congressional control of the purse, appropriations should be based on anticipated charges for goods and services to be received during the fiscal year.

Agency Comptrollers. The head of each federal agency should have, according to the second Hoover group, an agency comptroller as fiscal adviser, supervisor of accounting, and

in the agencies, as well as more funds and additional personnel.

PUBLIC EXPENDITURES

Increasing Cost of Government. It is commonplace to observe that the cost of governments is increasing, both absolutely and per capita. The accepted figures show that all levels of American government—national, state, and local—in 1913 expended 2,919 million dollars. The same levels in 1938 spent 16,312 million dollars, and in 1953 they spent 110,600 million dollars. Over the period of 25 years, 1913–1938, the cost of Federal government increased almost exactly ten times. The cost of state government grew almost proportionately. Local governments tripled in expenditures in the quarter century. While population did increase significantly over this period, cost of government per capita quadrupled.

Comparison of governmental costs with national income is perhaps most significant. In 1913 the national income was estimated at 35,400 million dollars; governmental expenditures amounted to 8.2 per cent of this amount. In 1938 national income was figured at 68 billion dollars; the cost of government was 24 per cent of the total. In 1942, when national income was 122 billion dollars, public expenses were more than

defense, 45.7 per cent; education, 9.2; interest on debt, 6.4; highways, 4.6; natural resources, 3.4.

Federal expenditures, excluding business enterprises, in 1953 were for the following principal functions, listed in order of amount: national

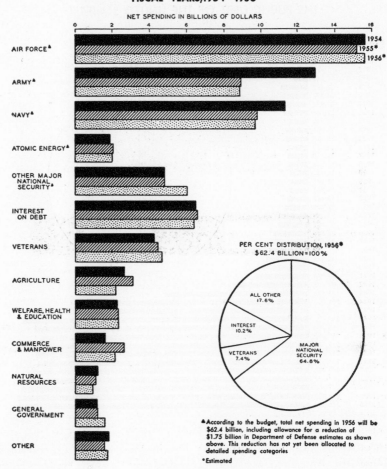

FEDERAL BUDGET EXPENDITURES
FISCAL YEARS, 1954 - 1956

Courtesy of National Industrial Conference Board.

38 per cent. In 1953 national income was estimated at 305 billion dollars, and aggregate governmental expenditures were about 36 per cent of that total.

Expenditures by Functions. Compilations are available to show what the various functions of government cost. A breakdown of the total (110.6 billion dollars) for all governments—national, state, and local—in 1953 indicates that the largest expenditures were as follows: national

defense; interest on debt; old-age and survivors' insurance; veterans' services; international assistance; and foreign affairs.

On the same basis, state expenditures in 1953 were for the following, in order of amount: highways, education, public welfare, health and hospitals, unemployment compensation, natural resources, and general control.

Similarly, local government expenditures were for the following, in order of the amount of expenditure: education, highways, public welfare, hospitals and health, police, sanitation, and general control.

THE PUBLIC DEBT

The Debt Problem. Failure to keep the revenues of government in balance with the expendi-

During the First World War the country was saddled with a national debt of $25,500,000,000. This was reduced to $16,185,000,000 by 1930. Then depression spending intervened, and the federal debt passed the 40-billion-dollar mark during 1939. Once in war, budgets were pushed up to undreamed-of heights; for fiscal year

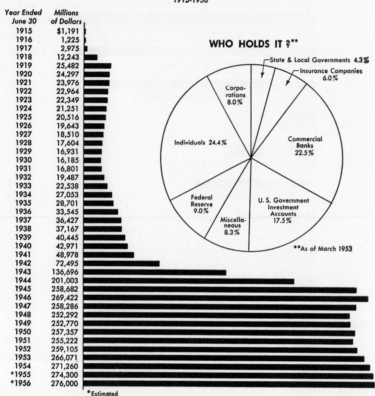

THE PUBLIC DEBT OF THE UNITED STATES
1915-1956

Year Ended June 30	Millions of Dollars
1915	$1,191
1916	1,225
1917	2,975
1918	12,243
1919	25,482
1920	24,297
1921	23,976
1922	22,964
1923	22,349
1924	21,251
1925	20,516
1926	19,643
1927	18,510
1928	17,604
1929	16,931
1930	16,185
1931	16,801
1932	19,487
1933	22,538
1934	27,053
1935	28,701
1936	33,545
1937	36,427
1938	37,167
1939	40,445
1940	42,971
1941	48,978
1942	72,495
1943	136,696
1944	201,003
1945	258,682
1946	269,422
1947	258,286
1948	252,292
1949	252,770
1950	257,357
1951	255,222
1952	259,105
1953	266,071
1954	271,260
*1955	274,300
*1956	276,000

*Estimated

WHO HOLDS IT ?**

State & Local Governments 4.3%
Insurance Companies 6.0%
Corporations 8.0%
Individuals 24.4%
Commercial Banks 22.5%
Federal Reserve 9.0%
Miscellaneous 8.3%
U. S. Government Investment Accounts 17.5%

**As of March 1953

Deficit financing has been the rule since the First World War. Individuals and Commercial banks are the largest holders of Federal securities.

tures results more often in deficits than in surpluses. In depression, war, and expansion governments borrow. The resulting debt burden is enormous, both in interest charges and in repayments. Virtually every governmental unit has some power to borrow. Local governments, and some states, are restricted within certain limits. The nation and other states may borrow as much and so long as the public will approve, and lenders will lend. It appears quite reasonable that governments should spend more in times of emergency and repay this in times of peace and prosperity.

1945, expenditures of over 100 billion dollars were made; receipts for the same period accounted for over 46½ billion dollars, leaving a deficit of about 54 billion dollars. The debt limit has been raised again and again. At the moment of writing the gross debt is about 275 billion dollars.

From governmental borrowing practices we can learn lessons that apply to an individual's conduct too. First, do not borrow for a longer period than an improvement will last. Frequently governments will borrow for improvements but leave repayment of the loan until long after the improvement has outlived its utility. Second, do not pay ordinary operating expenses out of borrowed money. Loans sometimes are sought for ordinary operating expenses during normal times, because public bodies prefer not to levy the taxes necessary to finance them. Third, spread repayment over a period of time. Loans often are obtained for fixed periods and the whole amount falls due at a particular time, but the government makes no provision for accumulating enough funds to repay. The last abuse is corrected through issuing term bonds and setting up sinking funds to redeem them when due. Another satisfactory solution is to issue serial bonds, with redemption periods staggered over the years.

Several states have gone to considerable lengths to limit debts of local governments. Often this limitation is based upon assessed valuation. Restrictions may be avoided by increasing assessed valuation, or by forming special districts to perform certain services that require a considerable outlay, such as a water district. Debt-limitation laws have not proved very successful. The states have established central agencies to oversee local budgets and debts with varying degrees of success.

Debt Policy and Pay as You Go. Most of us are indoctrinated with the idea that debt is unfortunate, and that a well-run family or government is one that keeps its expenditures as low as its income. The other side of the picture, however, is that few families would ever enjoy home ownership and few business ventures would ever be launched were it not for borrowed money. No sweeping verdict against all types of borrowing is in order. During war and depression, people come to accept the necessity of governmental spending beyond the possible limit of current income. In the fiscal year 1945, the Federal government alone cost about 53 per cent of the total national income. The impossibility of taking all in taxes is obvious. Therefore, we have accepted a theory that national debt incurred in war and depression should be paid off during peace and prosperity. State and local governments may borrow for improvements, but, like businesses that expand with capital outlay, these

obligations are to be paid off as quickly as possible.

In recent years, however, a new theory of national debt has developed. The public debt, primarily national, will be used as a device for controlling economic life. This national debt rose to nearly 270 billion dollars in 1945–1946. The gross federal debt outstanding as of June 30, 1955, was nearly 275 billion dollars. Instead of paying off this debt as rapidly as possible, it might even be permitted to increase. Government would use the proceeds obtained by borrowing to prime the pump of private enterprise. Proponents of the permanent debt argue that private investment cannot take up individual savings and that government must assume this role.

MONETARY POWERS

The Borrowing Power. If tax revenues are insufficient to meet current expenditures, governments, like individuals, may borrow to meet their obligations. Article I, Section 8, Clause 2 gives Congress authority "To borrow Money on the credit of the United States." Congress may authorize the borrowing of money from any source, foreign or domestic, and up to any amount. The only collateral required, at least so far as the Constitution is concerned, is "the credit of the United States." The power to borrow, together with the power to coin and regulate the value of money, implies authority to issue paper money and compel its acceptance as legal tender. The power also justifies the creation of national banks to buy and sell government bonds. The Federal government may exempt its securities and the income derived from them from future federal taxes, although since 1939 it has not done so. States and local governments, as noted above, may not tax federal securities nor the income derived from them unless Congress gives its consent at the time securities are issued. When Congress borrows money, it pledges repayment in currency the value of which Congress itself has power to determine. In this lies the danger that future circumstances might lead to debt repudiation through the expedient of changing the value of the dollar, in which case it would be difficult to find any legal remedy except for injured parties to plead that property had been taken without due process of law.

The Power to Coin Money. In order to provide money with a fixed and uniform standard of value throughout the country, Congress was authorized "To Coin money, regulate the Value thereof, and of foreign coin. . . ." [12] Congress authorized the first mint and laid the foundation of our monetary system in 1792. The monetary power was essential to the new nation.

The words of the Constitution authorize Congress to "coin money" and during our early history this was thought to include authority to make either metallic coins or print paper notes. Proceeding upon this assumption, Congress authorized the First and Second National Banks (created in 1791 and 1816, respectively) to issue paper notes and their constitutionality was never questioned. During the Civil War, however, when Congress issued 450 million dollars' worth of treasury notes ("greenbacks") and made them legal tender, the courts were called to pass upon their constitutionality. The decision was awaited with considerable anxiety inasmuch as it was bound to have a tremendous effect not only upon the credit of the national government but upon the banking and credit system of the country as well.

The Court announced its decision in the famous case of Hepburn v. Griswold.[13] "Money" was defined to mean gold, copper, and silver coins; while coinage was defined as "the conversion of metal into money by governmental direction and authority . . . to mold into form a metallic substance of intrinsic value and stamp on it its legal value." Accordingly, said the Court, only metallic coins could be manufactured by the Federal government and made legal tender in payment of debts between private parties created before enactment of the law. The law was, therefore, unconstitutional; it exceeded the powers delegated to Congress, violated the spirit of the Constitution, and deprived creditors of property without due process of law.

The decision in Hepburn v. Griswold was

[12] Art. I, Sec. 8.
[13] 8 Wall. 603 (U.S. 1870).

reached by a 4-to-3 vote, there being two vacancies. On the day on which the decision was announced, President Grant sent to the Senate the names of two men to fill the vacancies existing on the Court. Four days later, by a 5-to-4 vote, with the two new justices joining the three who had dissented in the previous case to make the majority, the Court voted to reconsider the issues involved.[14] Less than 15 months after the first decision, the Court reversed itself,[15] this time saying that the power to issue paper notes in wartime and make it legal tender was implied from the power to coin money and fight a war. Authority to make paper money legal tender in time of peace was upheld 13 years later.[16]

The Power to Regulate the Value of Money. Closely related to the coinage power is the authorization to regulate the value of domestic and foreign money in the United States. This enables Congress to establish and maintain a uniform monetary standard throughout the country and to raise or lower the value of money whenever it sees fit. Since money is the lifeblood of the economic system of the nation, the use of this power is certain to have a tremendous effect, for good or for ill, not only upon domestic affairs but international as well.

The authorization enables Congress to determine whether the monetary system shall be based on a standard of gold, silver, or something else. It enables Congress to prescribe the relationship that shall exist between precious metals, as, for example, 15 grains of gold to 1 of silver,

[14] President Grant was accused of "packing" the Court, but the evidence seems to suggest that no understanding was reached between the President and the two new jurists to the effect that they would act as they subsequently did. The incident was unfortunate, nevertheless, and greatly diminished the prestige of the Court. See Robert E. Cushman, *Leading Constitutional Decisions* (Appleton-Century-Crofts, 7th ed., 1940), pp. 222–223; Charles E. Hughes, *The Supreme Court of the United States* (Columbia University Press, 1928), pp. 51–53; Charles Warren, *The Supreme Court in United States History* (Little, Brown, 3 vols., 1923), vol. III, pp. 220–254.
[15] Legal Tender Cases, 12 Wall. 457 (U.S. 1871).
[16] Julliard v. Greenman, 110 U.S. 421 (1884).

or as William J. Bryan advocated, 16 to 1. The authorization also permits Congress to compel the surrender of money of a particular type, as it did gold and gold certificates in 1933. Moreover, Congress may abrogate gold clauses in private contracts [17] although it may not abrogate promises to pay in gold or its equivalent contained in contracts between the national government and other parties.[18] Finally, this power, along with the borrowing, taxing, and spending powers, is authority for the establishment and regulation of the banking and credit system of the nation.

The Power to Punish Counterfeiting. Article I, Section 8, also empowers Congress "To provide for the Punishment of counterfeiting the Securities and current Coin of the United States." The inclusion of this clause was probably unnecessary, since had it not been expressly granted it would have been implied from the power to coin money. The power is a concurrent one—the states as well as the national government may punish for counterfeiting, although most states leave detection and punishment to the Federal government.

States Denied Authority over Money. Besides granting Congress authority to coin money and regulate its value, the Constitution expressly forbids the states to "coin Money; emit Bills of Credit; [and] make any Thing but gold and silver Coin a Tender in Payment of Debts. . . ."[19] Since states are forbidden to "coin money," there are no state mints where coins are made. Several states have recently enacted sales taxes authorizing the issuance and circulation of tokens of various sorts with which to pay taxes when purchases are made. These, it was contended, were "money" "coined" by the states. The Supreme Court upheld their use, however, inasmuch as the tokens were not to pass currently as coins but were to be used only as evidence that tax was paid.[20]

The states are also forbidden to "emit" bills of credit. These refer to paper money issued on the credit of a state government with the intention that it will circulate as a common medium of exchange. Although state governments cannot themselves issue paper money, they may authorize state-incorporated banks to do so. In this event the notes are issued on the credit of the banks and not on that of the state; hence, according to definition, they are not legally "bills of credit." Prior to the Civil War state banks issued bank notes in large amounts. Issued only upon the credit of the banks, their value was ofttimes uncertain; moreover, since the states lacked authority to make them legal tender, many people objected to their use for that reason. In consequence, shortly after the Civil War Congress undertook to force them out of existence by imposing a tax of 10 per cent upon them at the time of issuance. When challenged in the courts, the measure was upheld as a constitutional exercise of the power to tax, coin money, and regulate the value thereof.[21] The tax accomplished its purpose, with the result that state bank notes have been nonexistent for many years.

The states are also forbidden to "make anything but gold and silver coin a tender in payment of debts." When something is made legal tender, it must be accepted by creditors when offered in payment of debt. Since the only thing that the states can make legal tender is gold and silver coin, which must all be manufactured by the United States, the practical result is that Congress is solely responsible for the determination of what shall be legal tender.

MONEY, BANKING, AND CREDIT

The Monetary System. Acting under the terms of its constitutional power to coin money and regulate its value, Congress has exercised far-reaching influence over the economic life of the country. The Constitution did not specify

---

[17] Norman *v.* Baltimore and Ohio R.R., 294 U.S. 240 (1935).

[18] Perry *v.* United States, 294 U.S. 330 (1935). Although in this case it was said that Congress had exceeded its powers by abrogating gold clauses in its own obligation, the Court added that one must show actual loss or damage before being entitled to recovery.

[19] Art. I, Sec. 10.

[20] Morrow *v.* Henneford, 182 Wash. 625 (1935).

[21] Veazie Bank *v.* Fenno, 8 Wall. 533, 552 (U.S. 1889). See p. 353.

what monetary unit should be used. In 1792 Congress, on the recommendation of Secretary of the Treasury Alexander Hamilton, established the decimal system based on the dollar, which is now perhaps the most widely accepted monetary unit in the world. In departing from the traditional British pound, shilling, and pence scheme, this country liberated itself from a cumbersome plan that makes the figuring of interest or tax rates a nightmare of confusion. If an early Congress had been equally farsighted in adopting the metric system of weights and measures, the convenience of posterity would also have been served.

Manufacture of metal coins is carried out in federal mints located in Philadelphia, Denver, and, until its closing in 1955, San Francisco. During the Second World War these mints also produced large quantities of coin for friendly and allied foreign nations. In recent years the mints have produced mainly 1-cent, 5-cent, 10-cent, 25-cent, and 50-cent coins. Gold coin was called in during the crisis of 1933, and production has not resumed. Silver dollars are still in circulation but are rare items in many sections of the country. Since 1950 there has been more than 1½ billion dollars in coin in circulation.

Paper money has circulated in some form or other throughout American history. Although states were forbidden by the Constitution to issue paper money, state-chartered banks continued to issue until their notes were taxed out of existence during the Civil War. After 1863 banks chartered by the national government issued paper money freely. While there are many types of paper currency in circulation today, most of it consists of Federal Reserve notes, backed by commercial paper, silver certificates, backed by Treasury silver bullion, and United States notes, issued and backed by the Treasury.

At many periods of American history there has been sharp controversy over monetary standards. Gold has always been a major factor in the monetary system; over much of the period silver has also played an important role. William Jennings Bryan's great crusade of 1896 resulted in part from the demonetization of silver in 1873. Support for coinage of silver at that time was motivated largely by debtor aspirations for a cheaper money. In the last quarter century the silver bloc in Congress has been interested principally in assuring a ready market and high price for silver mined in the United States. Since 1933 the United States has been legally off the gold standard but has continued to buy gold and silver at prices above the world market. The store of gold in the vaults of the federal treasury has reached over 20 billion dollars. Monetary theorists disagree over the utility of this gold, most of it stored at Fort Knox, Ky.

The Federal Reserve Plan. The Federal Reserve System was established in 1913, replacing the national banking system created during the Civil War. The power of the Congress to charter banks had been exercised in respect to the first Bank of the United States (1791–1811) and the second Bank (1816–1836) and its constitutionality assured in McCulloch *v.* Maryland.[22] The national banking system of 1863–1864 was designed to stabilize the medium of exchange and to assist the sale of government bonds. After the paper money of state banks was taxed out of existence, the banks chartered by the national government enjoyed a monopoly over the issue of currency.

In successive depressions and panics the national banking scheme was proved inadequate. Senator Carter Glass, author of the 1913 legislation, declared of the old plan: "The Siamese twins of disorder were an inelastic currency and a fictitious reserve system."[23] Inelasticity arose from the requirement that note currency might be issued by national banks only to the extent to which they were holders of government bonds. As national indebtedness was reduced, the volume of currency was reduced. The fictitiousness of the old reserve system, according to Glass, was produced by the tendency of local banks to send their surplus funds to the money centers of the great cities. There funds would be loaned for speculation, the end result of which would be panic and depression.

The Federal Reserve System of today is super-

[22] See p. 69.

[23] Carter Glass, *An Adventure in Constructive Finance* (Doubleday, 1927), p. 60.

vised by the Board of Governors, composed of seven members appointed by the President for 14-year terms. From its Washington headquarters, the Board determines general monetary and credit policies and oversees the twelve district Federal Reserve Banks and member private banks. The influence of the Board over credit conditions in the country is exerted mainly ernors. Reserve Banks hold on deposit reserve balances of member banks, extend credit facilities to them and other business concerns, and issue Federal Reserve notes which account for most of the money now in circulation. These notes may be backed by commercial paper, thus avoiding the inelasticity of the old national banking system, because the issue of currency can be

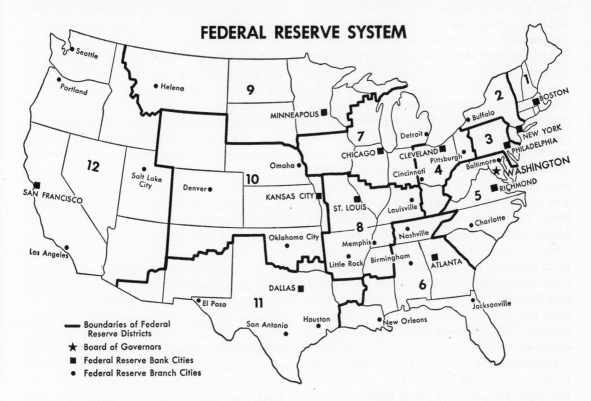

FEDERAL RESERVE SYSTEM

- Boundaries of Federal Reserve Districts
★ Board of Governors
■ Federal Reserve Bank Cities
● Federal Reserve Branch Cities

through its powers to alter the requirements for reserves against deposits in member banks and to change the rediscount rate, which is the rate at which Federal Reserve Banks lend money to private banks.

Actually the twelve Federal Reserve Banks are privately owned, for their stock is held by the member banks. All national banks are required to subscribe to the capital stock of their districts. State banks may become members; if they do, a similar obligation to purchase stock is required. The Federal Reserve Banks are governed by regional boards of directors. Each board has nine members, of which six are selected by member banks and three by the national Board of Gov-

great when demand for loans is great and less when borrowing is little.

The general utility of the Federal Reserve System has been conceded rather widely. There is still disagreement, however, over the success of the plan in decentralizing and regionalizing banking operations.

Nationally Chartered Banks and Savings Institutions. The Office of the Comptroller of the Currency oversees the national banking system, including the chartering, operation, and liquidation of banks. Bank examiners review the books of national banks twice a year. Violators of the law may lose their charters through suits filed by the Comptroller. Although there are more state-chartered banks than national, the national banks do a larger volume of business.

Federal deposit insurance began in 1933, when there was a banking crisis and many "runs" on banks. The Federal Deposit Insurance Corporation (FDIC) was organized and given the task of assuring the safety of all bank deposits up to $5,000, increased to $10,000 in 1950. Insured banks pay a premium to the FDIC, which builds up a fund out of which depositors are compensated if a member bank fails. Over a hundred million depositors now enjoy insured accounts. Members of the Federal Reserve System are required to belong; most state banks find it to their advantage to join, if they can meet the standards of FDIC. The existence of the insurance scheme stands guard against future panics.

Since 1933 savings and loan associations also have been chartered under national authority. The chartering and examining agency is the Home Loan Bank Board of the Housing and Home Finance Agency. A deposit insurance scheme is handled by the Federal Savings and Loan Insurance Corporation. All federally chartered associations are required to participate; state-chartered and certain other credit institutions may apply and, if approved, be insured. Like the FDIC, deposits up to $10,000 are protected.

Business Credit. A complete list of federal aids to business through provision of credit facilities would include the Federal Reserve System and FDIC, already mentioned in this chapter; the Export-Import Bank of Washington, discussed in Chap. 25; and certain lending and guaranty activities of the General Services Administration and of the Small Business Administration, which are to be covered here.

The General Services Administration has some modest responsibilities for loans to establish productive facilities, stockpile critical materials, and procure tools and materials for defense.

The Small Business Administration, created in 1953, inherited the small-business-loan portion of the Reconstruction Finance Corporation activity. Such activities are justified by their proponents as necessary in order to prevent excessive concentration of economic power in the hands of a few giant corporations. They take the form of loans and guaranties, contracts with Federal agencies which are subcontracted to small businesses, advice to small concerns on new products, and disaster loans. Loans are limited to $150,000, and may be made only when financing is not otherwise available at reasonable terms. The second Hoover Commission expressed some doubts about various aspects of the agency's work, but recommended another two years of life, but with an audit such as government corporations have, and an interest rate high enough to earn operating expenses and a fair interest rate on its borrowings from the Treasury.[24]

Although liquidated by act of Congress in 1953, the Reconstruction Finance Corporation requires mention because of its vast size and the great role assigned to it in the depression of the 1930's, the war of the 1940's, and in the period of postwar readjustment. This gigantic institution was set up during the Hoover Administration in 1932. In order to afford flexibility of action, it was given the corporate form of organization. In the early 1950's criticisms of RFC management and policies reached a climax with disclosures of irregularities and favoritism. In 1954 its functions were distributed among other agencies.

During the depression the RFC came to the aid of many businessmen and many state and local governments. As the war approached, RFC funds were used to finance expansion of war industries, and later its resources were devoted almost entirely to this purpose. After the war it helped finance reconversion. During the war period the RFC went into business itself on a large scale. Indeed, as of January, 1945, it and its subsidiaries were operating 125 plants, among them steel mills, aircraft factories, munitions plants, and the like. The RFC also helped finance some of the other federal agencies, including the Federal Deposit Insurance Corporation, the Export-Import Bank, and the Federal Home Loan Banks.

[24] Second Hoover Commission, *Lending Agencies* (1955), p. 91.

FOR FURTHER READING

FINANCIAL ADMINISTRATION AND BUDGETS

Bartelt, Edward F.: *Accounting Procedures of the United States Government* (Chicago: Public Administration Service, 1940).

Benson, George C. S.: *Financial Control and Integration—with Special Reference to the Comptroller General* (Harper, 1934).

Buck, Arthur E.: *The Budget in Governments of Today* (Macmillan, 1934).

——: *Public Budgeting* (Harper, 1929).

Cleveland, Frederick A., and Arthur E. Buck: *The Budget and Responsible Government* (Macmillan, 1920).

Dawes, Charles G.: *The First Year of the Budget of the United States* (Harper, 1923).

Dewey, Davis R.: *Financial History of the United States* (Longmans, rev. ed., 1934).

Douglas, Paul H.: *Economy in the National Government* (University of Chicago Press, 1952).

Faust, Martin L.: *The Custody of State Funds* (New York: National Institute of Public Administration, 1925).

Mansfield, Harvey C.: *The Comptroller General: A Study in the Law and Practice of Financial Administration* (Yale University Press, 1939).

Mosher, Frederick C.: *Program Budgeting: Theory and Practice with Particular Reference to the U.S. Department of the Army* (Public Administration Service, 1954).

Morey, Lloyd: *Introduction to Governmental Accounting* (Wiley, 1927).

Naylor, Estill E.: *The Federal Budget System in Operation* (Washington, D.C.: Haworth Co., 1941).

Oakey, Francis: *Principles of Government Accounting and Reporting* (Appleton-Century-Crofts, 1921).

Powell, Fred W. (comp.): *Control of Federal Expenditures: A Documentary History, 1775–1894* (Brookings, 1939).

Selko, Daniel T.: *The Federal Financial System* (Brookings, 1940).

——: *The Administration of Federal Finances* (Brookings, 1937), Pamphlet Series no. 18.

Smith, Darrell H.: *The General Accounting Office: Its History, Activities, and Organization* (Johns Hopkins Press, 1927).

Studenski, Paul, and H. E. Krooss: *Financial History of the United States* (McGraw-Hill, 1952).

Smithies, Arthur: *The Budgetary Process in the United States* (McGraw-Hill, 1955).

U.S. Bureau of the Budget: *The Budget of the United States Government* (annual). Also summarized in *The Federal Budget in Brief* (annual).

U.S. Commission on Organization of the Executive Branch of the Government (second Hoover Commission): *Budget and Accounting* (1955).

——: *Task Force Report on Budget and Accounting* (1955).

U.S. Commission on Organization of the Executive Branch of the Government (first Hoover Commission): *Budgeting and Accounting* (1949).

——: *Task Force Report on Fiscal, Budgeting, and Accounting Activities* (1949).

U.S. Comptroller General: *Annual Report.*

U.S. President's Committee on Administrative Management: *Report . . . with Studies of Administration Management in the Federal Government* (1937). Study No. 2 is "Fiscal Management in the National Government" and contains studies by Arthur E. Buck and Harvey C. Mansfield.

U.S. Senate, Select Committee to Investigate the Executive Agencies of the Government: *Financial Administration of the Federal Government,* Sen. Doc. 5, 75th Cong., 1st Sess. (1937).

Willoughby, William F.: *Financial Conditions and Operations of the National Government, 1921–1930* (1931).

——: *The National Budget System with Suggestions for Its Improvement* (Johns Hopkins Press, 1927).

Wilmerding, Lucius, Jr.: *The Spending Power: A History of the Efforts of Congress to Control Expenditures* (Yale University Press, 1943).

EXPENDITURES AND DEBT

Abbott, Charles C.: *Federal Debt: Structure and Impact* (Twentieth Century Fund, 1953).

Committee on Public Debt Policy: *Our National Debt: Its History and Its Meaning Today* (Harcourt, Brace, 1949).

Haig, Robert M., and Others: *The Sales Tax in the American States* (Columbia University Press, 1934).

Harris, Seymour E.: *The National Debt and the New Economics* (McGraw-Hill, 1947).

Stewart, Paul W., and Rufus S. Tucker: *The National Debt and Government Credit* (Twentieth Century Fund, 1937).

Studenski, Paul: *Chapters on Public Finance* (Richard R. Smith, 1935).

Van Sant, Edward R.: *The Floating Debt of the Federal Government* (Johns Hopkins Press, 1937).

MONETARY POWERS, MONEY, AND BANKING

Bach, George L.: *Federal Reserve Policy-making* (Knopf, 1950).

Beyen, Johan W.: *Money in a Maelstrom* (Macmillan, 1949).

Burdick, Charles K.: *The Law of the Constitution; Its Origin and Development* (Putnam, 1922).

Corwin, Edward S.: *Court over Constitution* (Princeton University Press, 1938).

——: *The Twilight of the Supreme Court* (Yale University Press, 1934).

Crawford, Arthur W.: *Monetary Management under the New Deal* (American Council on Public Affairs, 1940).

Federal Reserve System: *The Federal Reserve System: Its Purposes and Functions* (Federal Reserve System, 2d ed., 1947).

Fellner, William J.: *Monetary Policies and Full Employment* (University of California Press, 2d ed., 1947).

Glass, Carter: *An Adventure in Constructive Finance* (Doubleday, 1927).

Goldenweiser, E. A.: *American Monetary Policy* (McGraw-Hill, 1951).

Hansen, Alvin H.: *Monetary Theory and Fiscal Policy* (McGraw-Hill, 1949).

Kemmerer, Edwin W., and Donald L. Kemmerer: *The ABC of the Federal Reserve System* (Princeton University Press, rev. ed., 1950).

Moulton, Harold G.: *Controlling Factors in Economic Development* (Brookings, 1949).

Story, Joseph: *Commentaries on the Constitution of the United States* (Little, Brown, 4th ed., 2 vols., 1873).

U.S. Senate: *The Constitution of the United States of America* (annotated), S. Doc. 232, 74th Cong., 2d Sess. (1938).

——: *Monetary, Credit, and Fiscal Policies,* S. Doc. 129, 81st Cong., 2d Sess. (1950).

Warburg, Paul M.: *The Federal Reserve System: Its Origin and Growth* (Macmillan, 1930).

Warren, Charles: *The Supreme Court in United States History* (Little, Brown, 3 vols., 1923).

Weissman, Rudolph L.: *The New Federal Reserve System* (Harper, 1936).

Weyforth, William O.: *The Federal Reserve Board: A Study of Federal Reserve Structure and Credit Control* (Johns Hopkins Press, 1933).

Willoughby, Westel W.: *The Constitutional Law of the United States* (Baker, Voorhis, 2d ed., 3 vols., 1929).

Wright, Benjamin F.: *Contract Clause of the Constitution* (Harvard University Press, 1938).

REVIEW QUESTIONS

1. Describe the process of budget formulation in the Federal government.

2. Explain the various steps in budget authorization.

3. Which United States agencies have roles in budget execution, and what are these roles?

4. What aspects of federal budget procedure were criticized by the two Hoover Commissions? Why?

5. What justification is there for the argument that automatic budget balancing is unnecessary and may be unwise from the point of view of securing a sound economy?

6. Describe the Federal Reserve System and how it operates today.

7. Trace the growth of the public debt, and discuss the various theories concerning it.

8. Explain the functions of the Comptroller General, Bureau of the Budget, Fiscal Service of the Treasury.

9. Describe Federal regulation of private banking and credit. Under what power of the national government is such supervision justified?

10. How does the Federal government insure deposits in banks and savings and loan associations?

CHAPTER 21

Foreign Relations: Powers and Conduct

What, then, has democracy failed to accomplish? It has brought no nearer friendly feeling and the sense of human brotherhood among the peoples of the world toward one another. Freedom has not been a reconciler. — James Bryce [1]

The resiliency of the American Constitution is nowhere better illustrated than in the field of foreign affairs. The constitutional phrases granting powers in this field are amazingly brief to provide the basis for large undertakings and serious commitments in all parts of the world.

Some provisions, like the two-thirds rule for ratifying treaties, have proved embarrassing at times; others, like the ambiguous words stating the authority and scope of treaties, have become highly controversial. Still the powers have proved flexible enough to permit the nation to become one of the foremost of the world. This chapter reviews these powers, controversies which surround them, and the way in which foreign relations are handled from day to day.

CONSTITUTIONAL POWERS

Delegated Powers. In no other field does the Federal government have such great powers as in international relations. Some powers over international relations are given to the President, others to the Senate, and others to Congress. The President is authorized to "make treaties," to "nominate . . . and appoint Ambassadors, other public ministers and consuls," and to "re-

ceive Ambassadors and other public ministers." From these brief provisions the President has become the sole instrument of communication with foreign governments; he takes the initiative in formulating foreign policies; he negotiates treaties and agreements; he decides which governments will be recognized; when diplomatic and consular relations with foreign governments will begin and terminate; and he chooses, directs, transfers, and recalls diplomats and consuls who represent the nation abroad.

The Senate approves treaties and confirms ambassadors, other public ministers, and consuls nominated by the President. To both houses of Congress is given authority to declare war, regulate foreign commerce, to lay and collect tariffs, to define and punish piracies and felonies on the high seas, to make rules concerning captures on land and water, and to define and punish violations of international law. Moreover, both houses of Congress influence the conduct of foreign relations by control of the purse, investigations and hearings, their ability to debate and enact general legislation governing the Department of State, the diplomatic service, the Army and Navy, and international affairs generally.

Inherent Powers for Dealing with Foreign Affairs. When dealing with domestic matters the Federal government is limited to the use of dele-

[1] *Modern Democracies* (Macmillan, new ed., 2 vols., 1924), vol. II, p. 533. Quoted by permission of the publishers.

gated powers, but in the international sphere it has others that are said to be inherent. That is to say, it derives others from the fact that the United States is a sovereign nation in a world of national states that are recognized by international law as being fully competent to deal with matters pertaining to their respective interests. While some have been inclined to deny the existence of inherent powers, all doubt about the matter has been removed by recent decisions of the Supreme Court.[2]

Commenting in the Curtiss-Wright case upon the differences between federal powers for dealing with domestic or internal affairs and those for handling foreign affairs, the Court said, "That there are differences between them, and that these differences are fundamental, may not be doubted." The Court continued by saying:

It results that the investment of the Federal government with the powers of external sovereignty did not depend upon the affirmative grants of the Constitution. The powers to declare and wage war, to conclude peace, to make treaties, to maintain diplomatic relations with other sovereignties, if they had never been mentioned in the Constitution, would have vested in the Federal government as necessary concomitants of nationality. . . . As a member of the family of nations, the right and power of the United States in that field are equal to the right and power of the other members of the international family. Otherwise, the United States is not completely sovereign.

Federal Powers Exclusive. Moreover, federal powers in this field are not shared concurrently with the states but are exclusive. The states are not recognized in international law and the Constitution forbids them to enter into "any treaty, alliance or confederation," or, without the consent of Congress, to enter into any agreement or compact with a foreign power. These prohibitions give the Federal government an unquestioned monopoly over international relations.

[2] United States *v.* Curtiss-Wright Export Corporation, 299 U.S. 304 (1936); Harisiades *v.* Shaughnessy, 342 U.S. 580 (1951); Galvan *v.* Press, 347 U.S. 522 (1953).

The President vs. Congress. The President's foreign-relations powers are discussed in Chap. 15; hence only a few of their implications will be touched upon here.[3]

While it is nothing new for the President and Congress to clash over foreign affairs, they have done so oftener and with greater intensity in recent years, partly because of the new position of the United States in relation to the rest of the world. As long as powers remain separated, a certain amount of tension must be accepted as inevitable, although wise and able Presidents and congressional leaders will from time to time devise ways of keeping the friction to a minimum. The President may negotiate with foreign powers, but if he wishes to make commitments he must remember that Congress has constitutional authority to check, restrain, or even repudiate. Conversely, the Congress must remember that the President also has great powers. How to reconcile differences arising from these grants of power is the problem, and for the most part it must be solved in the political arena rather than in the courts. Bipartisanship may diminish the conflict, but this depends upon a transitory will to cooperate. It may be, as some suggest, that the plan of having powers separated is outmoded in the twentieth-century era of push-button warfare. Insofar as this is true, adaptations will occur, and indeed they are occurring, although this may seem to be a painfully slow process to those who are in a hurry.

Current controversy centers around two questions: the President's authority to commit and use troops in peacetime without congressional consent, and the scope of the power to make treaties and executive agreements.

The Commitment of Troops. Congress has been given the power to raise and support an army and navy, to lay the taxes and make necessary appropriations, and to declare war. To the Senate is given authority to approve appointments and treaties. All this is admitted by every-

[3] For an excellent recent review of the issues, see Daniel S. Cheever and H. Field Haviland, Jr., *American Foreign Policy and the Separation of Powers* (Harvard University Press, 1952).

one. But as the President executes the laws, performs as Commander in Chief, negotiates treaties, and formulates foreign policy he may find it desirable, or necessary, to make promises in advance to foreign governments, dispatch troops to various parts of the world, or even order them into action that may amount to war. Where shall the line be drawn?

When Congress declares war or otherwise authorizes the use of troops abroad, no constitutional problem arises. But in 1950–1951 President Truman wanted to send more troops to central Europe than Congress had authorized. Moreover, in 1950 he ordered American forces to undertake "police action" in Korea without any specific mandate from Congress. Indeed, over the years Presidents have dispatched troops abroad on many occasions without congressional authorization, as when President McKinley ordered troops to Peking during the Boxer Rebellion in 1900, or when President Wilson ordered troops into Mexico in 1913 to avenge attacks upon Americans.

What is the justification? The answer seems to be that situations arise that cause a President to conclude that as Commander in Chief he must take whatever risks are involved in committing troops to troubled areas. If the action is more or less routine, or localized and limited, the President is usually not widely criticized. But when the issues are large, costly, and highly controversial, and when the President lacks overwhelming political support in and out of Congress, his exercise of this authority is likely to be contested. In other words, the limits are political rather than legal.

Problem Posed by UN Charter. The issue came to a head in discussions over American adherence to the United Nations Charter. This document contemplates the use of contingents of armed forces furnished by member nations for the purpose of stopping future aggression. Adherence to the Charter raised the question of how far the President would be allowed to go in committing the forces furnished by the United States to participate in conflicts undertaken by the United Nations. Only Congress can declare war. But if the President is henceforth to be permitted to send American troops into action in cooperation with others, has the power to declare war not been taken from Congress and given to the President? Does the Constitution not require that congressional approval be first obtained in every instance before American forces are ordered into combat?

After much discussion, Congress passed the United Nations Participation Act in 1945, saying, among many things, that it was giving advance approval to the President to take action through the United Nations short of the use of armed forces but that the President might use armed forces only in accordance with agreements between the Security Council and the United States to which congressional consent would be required. In other words, Congress did not give advance blanket approval of the use of armed forces through the Security Council but indicated that it might do so if and when special agreements were submitted to Congress for approval. The special agreements have not yet been concluded.

The Korean War. Nevertheless, shortly after fighting started in Korea, in June, 1950, the President ordered American troops to provide "cover and support" to South Korean forces. This order was given before the Security Council voted to apply sanctions. Congressional authorization was not asked for either before or after. When the Security Council did vote to apply sanctions, as it could because of the absence of the Soviet representative, it only recommended (not ordered) that other nations do as the United States had already done. In other words, the President committed the nation to what proved to be serious, bloody, and prolonged military action on his own responsibility and later continued the effort upon recommendation of the Security Council.

How could this be done under the Constitution? The answer is, because Congress acquiesced—indeed, it later supported the action enthusiastically with appropriations, etc.—and the effort met with sufficient popular support or indifference to avoid a serious contest. This suggests that with or without permissive legislation, a strong-willed President can assert what he deems to be his prerogative, thus committing the nation to a course leading to war, and leaving the legal correctness of his action to be settled later in the political arena or by historians.

Many decry this situation and suggest that presidential action in Korea and elsewhere has not been justified by results. Others insist that in an atomic age the security of the nation, and peace of the world, demands that the President be able to act quickly alone or in concert with other nations. Feeling runs high over this issue and is reflected somewhat in the campaign for the Bricker amendment discussed below.

Issue in North Atlantic Treaty. The question came dramatically to the fore again in 1949, during discussions of the North Atlantic Pact. After considerable advance discussion with Senate leaders, the President proposed a treaty with Article V reading:

The Parties agree that an armed attack against one or more of them in Europe or North America shall be considered an attack against them all; and consequently they agree that, if such an armed attack occurs, each of them, in the exercise of the right of individual or collective self-defense recognized by Article 51 of the Charter of the United Nations, will assist the Party or Parties so attacked *by taking forthwith,* individually and in concert with the other Parties, such action as it deems necessary, *including the use of armed force,* to restore and maintain the security of the North Atlantic Area.[4]

Critics contended that the italicized words could be construed by the President to justify automatic use of force and thereby impair the prerogative of Congress to declare war. Ultimately, Senate approval was given but only after spokesmen for the President and Senate supporters gave repeated assurances that Article V was not to be construed as enlarging executive power or diminishing that of Congress to declare war. In spite of these assurances, a strong President might at some future time act boldly and take his chances on obtaining congressional approval of his "executive war."

[4] Italics supplied.

Eisenhower Obtains Advance Approval. President Eisenhower recognized this when he tried an unprecedented approach early in 1955. Communist China was threatening to invade offshore islands—Formosa and the Pescadores—held by nationalist Chinese forces with United States support. The President's own political party was sharply split over the proper course to follow in the Far East, and the Democrats controlled both houses of Congress. A misstep by the President would have provoked a political storm and might also have precipitated a third world war. Under these circumstances the President asked Congress in advance for approval of the use of force, if necessary. Congress promptly, and with overwhelming majorities in both houses, approved the request. So far as constitutional law is concerned the request made by the President was probably unnecessary; that it was made attests the restraining role of Congress, especially where political factors are delicately balanced.

The Treaty Power. The President makes treaties by and with the advice and consent of two-thirds of the Senate.[5] When properly made, treaties, like statutes, become part of the "Supreme Law of the Land."

The treaty power has been used to deal with a wide range of subjects. Some treaties have terminated wars. Others have acquired land, such as the Louisiana Territory from France, the Southwest Territory from Mexico, Alaska from Russia, and the Virgin Islands from Denmark. Others have secured protection, even special rights on certain occasions, for American citizens and nationals abroad. Others have provided for the exchange of consuls, extradition of fugitives, immigration, tariffs, military, naval, and air bases, rights upon the high seas and territorial waters, and a host of other matters. In general, treaties may deal with any subject of mutual concern to one or more nations. When concluded, some treaties, like those terminating a war or the recognition of certain

[5] That is, two-thirds of those present, assuming the presence of a quorum—not two-thirds of the entire membership of the Senate.

rights, become effective without implemental legislation. Others, like those calling for appropriations and special administrative agencies, can have no practical effect until implemented by congressional statute. The implied-power clause gives Congress all authority necessary for making treaties effective.

Limits to the Treaty Power. Treaties, like statutes, are subject to interpretation by the courts and can be declared unconstitutional, although to date none has been. In decisions involving treaties the Supreme Court has intimated that the treaty power extends to "all proper subjects of negotiation between this Government and those of other nations."[6] What would not be a "proper subject" has never been decided but can be imagined. A treaty, for example, by which the Federal government guaranteed all aliens the right to vote for state and local officers when state laws excluded them from exercising the franchise would doubtless deal with an improper subject, because the Constitution leaves the determination of voting qualifications to the states.

The Supreme Court has also intimated that provisions of treaties must be "consistent with our institutions" and "the distribution of powers between the General and State Governments."[7] Here, again, one can only guess at what the Court meant. Apparently, using these criteria, a treaty would be invalid if its effect were to alter any of the fundamental features of our political system—popular sovereignty, representative government, separation of powers, judicial review, etc.—discussed in Chap. 4, or if powers reserved to the states were subverted.

The Supreme Court has also said the treaty power could not be used "to authorize what the Constitution forbids."[8] Apparently, then, a treaty could not diminish the equality of representation of a state in the Senate without the consent of the state concerned. Nor could it provide for imposition of tariffs on exports because these are expressly forbidden. Nor could a treaty subvert provisions of the Bill of Rights.

[6] Holmes *v.* Jennison, 14 Pet. 540, 569 (U.S. 1840).
[7] *Ibid.*
[8] Geofroy *v.* Riggs, 133 U.S. 258 (1890).

Proponents of the Bricker amendment, discussed below, charge that the limitation suggested here has been invalidated, especially by Missouri *v.* Holland, but opponents insist that it is still true that the national government cannot under the guise of a treaty do any of the things expressly forbidden by the Constitution.

Finally, treaties must be made "under the Authority of the United States," which means that they must be made by the President with the advice and consent of the Senate and not by anyone else.

Treaty Power Is Broader than Delegated Legislative Powers. Article VI contains the statement that "This Constitution, and the Laws of the United States which shall be made in Pursuance thereof; and all Treaties made, or which shall be made, under the Authority of the United States, shall be the supreme Law of the Land. . . ." Note that laws, that is, acts of Congress, must be made *in pursuance of the Constitution* in order to be part of the supreme law; but treaties need be made only *under the Authority of the United States.* This raises the question of whether something might be held unconstitutional if done under a delegated power but constitutional if done by treaty. Fortunately, for purposes of illustration, this very question has been considered by the courts.

Missouri v. Holland. In 1913 Congress enacted a law, basing it upon the commerce power, which forbade the killing of migratory birds except under strict regulation. The legislation was declared unconstitutional by the lower courts on the ground that migratory birds were property of the state, hence not interstate commerce. Thereupon, in 1916, a treaty was entered into with Great Britain whereby both countries agreed to protect migratory birds. Two years later Congress passed a law forbidding the killing, capturing, or selling of birds protected by the treaty except in accordance with regulations set by the Secretary of Agriculture. Missouri brought suit against Holland,[9] a federal game warden, to restrain him from enforcing the law, contending that the measure was an unwarranted invasion of powers reserved to the states.

[9] Missouri *v.* Holland, 252 U.S. 416 (1920).

Missouri lost. The treaty dealt with a proper subject, it was made under the authority of the United States, and the statute in question was a necessary and proper means of making the treaty effective. Accordingly, the Federal government may regulate some domestic matter in fulfillment of a treaty which it would be prevented from doing by a statute based upon an enumerated legislative power.

Can Treaty Power Be Used to Regulate Local Affairs? Following this decision, many urged that the Federal government make treaties pledging the abolition of child labor. This could be done, it was contended, by stipulating that the contracting parties would prevent the exportation or importation of each other's goods except where they were produced or handled by businesses that did not employ children. This, it was urged, was an appropriate subject for negotiation with other nations, the treaty would be enacted under authority of the United States, and it would violate no expressed prohibition in the Constitution. Though the argument is plausible, the step was never taken. That it was seriously proposed, however, illustrates the potential scope of the treaty power. The doctrine, if carried to its logical conclusion, could be used to justify federal regulation of nearly all domestic matters. Indeed, if Congress could get other governments to cooperate to the extent of making a treaty, the distinction between delegated and reserved powers could be almost entirely obliterated.

UN Charter as a Treaty. This question has assumed new importance since the United States has joined the United Nations. Article I, Section 3, of the UN Charter, for example, pledges the United States, along with other members, to promote and encourage ". . . respect for human rights, and fundamental freedoms for all without distinction as to race, sex, language, or religion. . . ." Until now it has been supposed that Congress lacked delegated power to impose penalties upon private parties who show disrespect for human rights and fundamental freedoms.

But since Congress has ratified the Charter, does not the logic of the Missouri *v.* Holland decision suggest that Congress can now implement it with legislation that otherwise would be considered beyond the scope of federal power? If Congress should enact a law implementing the Charter and the courts should follow the Missouri *v.* Holland precedent, it would be necessary to examine the other criteria mentioned above. Are human rights and freedoms "proper subjects" for treaty making? Are the treaty provisions "consistent with our institutions" and "the distribution of powers between the General and State Governments"? Do treaty provisions transgress expressly forbidden provisions of the Constitution? Of course, no one can foretell what the Supreme Court might say, but the decision would probably hinge on whether a majority of judges thought state-reserved powers had been impaired.

In California courts the problem has been adjudicated recently, and the result may be instructive. A lower court held the state alien land law unconstitutional on grounds of conflict with the United Nations Charter, which it held to be self-executing. The state Supreme Court on appeal, however, held the statute invalid on the ground that it conflicted with the equal-protection clause of the Fourteenth Amendment. All judges agreed that the United Nations Charter was not a self-executing treaty.[10]

Apprehension over the probable attitude of the Court accounts in part for reluctance on the part of some Senators to approve American adherence to such international commitments as the Genocide Convention and the Covenant on Human Rights. It also explains sentiment that exists for the proposed Bricker amendment, which is discussed below.

Treaties Not Superior to Statutes. Treaties and statutes sometimes conflict, in which case the question arises as to which is to be enforced. The question was considered by the Supreme Court in the Head Money Cases, decided in 1884.[11] There Congress had imposed on vessel owners a tax of 50 cents for each alien passenger brought into the United States from foreign ports. Since this conflicted with certain

[10] Fujii *v.* California, 242 P. 2d 617 (1952).
[11] 112 U.S. 580.

treaties previously entered into, the courts were urged to declare the statute ineffective. The Supreme Court refused to do so, however, with the result that treaties are not superior to statutes; but if they conflict, the one last enacted will be enforced. This, it will be recognized, places power in the hands of Congress to repudiate a solemn treaty whenever sufficient votes can be mustered. This has, in fact, happened on a few occasions with embarrassing results.

NUMBER OF TREATIES AND EXECUTIVE AGREEMENTS COMPARED

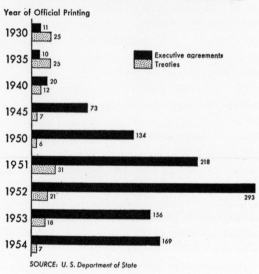

Year of Official Printing

SOURCE: U. S. Department of State

International Executive Agreements. Arrangements with other nations are often made by executive agreements rather than by treaties. Indeed, since 1900 executive agreements have been used more frequently than treaties. They differ from treaties only in that they do not require senatorial approval. The Constitution contains no express recognition of the President's power to make international agreements without the consent of the Senate; his authority to do so must either be granted or implied from acts of Congress or previous treaties, or implied from powers clearly delegated to the President.

Most executive agreements have been made by authority of congressional statutes or treaties. Among these are innumerable postal conven-

tions entered into by authority of legislation dating back to 1792; embargoes upon shipments of munitions to warring South American countries; the much-publicized reciprocal tariff agreements entered into by authority of the Trade Agreements Act of 1934; and agreements entered into with allies under the Lend-Lease Act of 1941.

Others have been implied from constitutional provisions conferring upon the President diplomatic powers, making him Commander in Chief of the Army and Navy and requiring that the laws be faithfully executed. Theodore Roosevelt's *modus vivendi* of 1907 whereby the American government undertook to collect customs for Santo Domingo to ensure payment of obligations owed to foreign bankers is a conspicuous illustration. The armistice of 1918, the resumption of diplomatic relations with Russia in 1933, the agreement to occupy and defend Iceland in 1941, the Atlantic Charter Agreement of 1941, the Potsdam Agreement of 1945, are other examples. These are part of the supreme law of the land whether or not later implemented by statute or treaty. Their frequent use, sometimes under circumstances that suggest that the President is deliberately flouting the will of Congress, has given rise to some alarm lest Congress, especially the Senate, be stripped of one of its most cherished prerogatives. Nevertheless, that the President has constitutional authority to make such agreements appears incontestable. He is limited, however, by the realization that as a practical matter public sentiment must approve his conduct, that he cannot bind his successors to fulfillment of the agreements, and that most agreements of this type cannot be carried out without subsequent congressional approval embodied either in statutes or treaties.

The Proposed Bricker Amendment. During the troubled postwar period critics of the President and the vague, ill-defined limits of his authority over foreign affairs rallied around the Bricker amendment. This was a proposal to amend the Constitution sponsored originally by Senator John Bricker, of Ohio. When brought to a vote in the Senate in February, 1954, the proposal as amended mustered 50 favorable votes to 42 negative but failed of passage because of the requirement that constitutional amendments must be approved by two-thirds of those present and voting. On the following day a substitute amendment sponsored by Senator Walter George, of Georgia, also failed to obtain a two-thirds majority but by the narrow margin of one vote. The closeness of this outcome reflected the intensity of feeling engendered by the issues involved and long acrimonious debate.

Provisions of the two proposals voted upon were as follows:

they considered unnecessary; in their opinion this is the way the Constitution now reads. The second and third proposals they thought would weaken the President's hands in dealing with foreign nations, while the "which clause" would enable the states to nullify federal power. The fourth item was opposed as vague and unnecessary. There was no special objection to the fifth item, since its desirability was obviously dependent upon the other provisions.

The President and his supporters gave way to the extent of agreeing to accept if necessary a proposal similar to the first item mentioned

Bricker Proposal *	*George Substitute*
A provision of a treaty which conflicts with the Constitution shall not be of any force or effect.	The same.
A treaty shall become effective as internal law in the United States only through legislation *which would be valid in the absence of treaty.*†	Nothing similar.
Congress shall have power to regulate all executive agreements with any foreign power or international organization. All such agreements shall be subject to the limitations imposed on treaties by this Article.	An international agreement other than a treaty shall become effective as internal law in the United States only by an act of Congress.
Congress shall have power to enforce this Article by appropriate legislation.	Nothing similar.
This Article shall be inoperative unless ratified by legislatures of three-fourths of the states within 7 years.	The same.

* As approved by the Senate Judiciary Committee.
† This is the famous "which clause" prompted by the doctrine announced in Missouri *v.* Holland.

These proposals appealed to four principal schools of opinion: (1) partisan critics of Presidents Roosevelt and Truman; (2) isolationists and extreme nationalists; (3) champions of States' rights; and (4) those who are internationalists but who nevertheless believe the limits of presidential authority should be clarified and subjected to more effective checks and balances.

Presidential Objections. The President and his supporters opposed any change at all. The first item in both the Bricker and George proposals

above. To further soothe senatorial critics, executive leaders agreed not to ask for ratification of the Genocide Convention, which outlaws mass extinction of a people, and the Covenant of Human Rights, a United Nations declaration of civil liberties. While both the Bricker and George proposals were defeated the controversy has had significant political effects, one of which has been to make the President more cautious in dealing with foreign affairs, at least temporarily. The issues are far from dead, and critics of presidential authority can be expected to continue their efforts on behalf of the Bricker amendment or something similar.

'But I Don't Want a SNAFU Car'

BRICKER PROPOSAL

PRESIDENT

Snafu

FOREIGN POLICY DUAL CONTROL

Courtesy of John Stampone and *Air Force Daily.*

GENERAL ASPECTS OF DIPLOMATIC AND CONSULAR PRACTICE

Diplomacy is steeped in formality and etiquette, much of which dates back to antiquity. The most important custom has to do with the ranking of diplomatic officers.

Classification of Diplomats. All nations, except Russia, follow the classification of diplomats agreed upon by the Congress of Vienna in 1816 and supplemented from time to time. At present there are five classes: the first includes ambassadors, legates (envoys of the pope chosen from the cardinals for special assignments), and nuncios (envoys of the pope assigned to permanent posts and chosen from outside the rank of cardinals); the second, envoys extraordinary, ministers plenipotentiary, and apostolic inter-nuncios (envoys of the pope next in rank to nuncios); the third, ministers resident; the fourth, chargés d'affaires; and the fifth, a group known as diplomatic agents. Envoys rank within each class according to the date of arrival at their post, the one in the highest rank with the most seniority at a given post being known as the *doyen,* or dean of the diplomatic corps.

Envoys of the various classes perform practically the same functions and enjoy the same rights and privileges, the chief difference being a matter of prestige. Those of the first class are supposed to be the personal representatives of the sovereign, while those of the other are merely the representatives of their governments, although in modern times this has little practical significance. Those of the first class occupy embassies; those of the remaining classes, legations. Those of the first three classes are accredited to heads of states, while those of the fourth and fifth classes are accredited to ministers of foreign affairs. There is a tendency to consider chargés d'affaires as temporary officers, while diplomatic agents are as a rule assigned only to states that are not fully sovereign, such as Tunisia and Morocco.

Classification of Consuls. Diplomats represent their country in its political relations with other governments; consuls are commissioned to act as agents for the purpose of assisting with the administration of American laws in foreign ports, assisting American tourists, affording protection to Americans and their interests, and promoting trade. The classification of consuls in all states is almost the same, though there is much less fussing about the matter than with diplomats. Those of the United States are divided into four classes: consuls general, consuls, vice-consuls, and consular agents. Which is appointed to a particular post depends to a large extent upon the commercial and financial importance of the place so far as American interests are concerned. Some of the consuls general are given supervisory jurisdiction over all consular offices of lesser rank within a given area. Thus, the one at London has supervisory jurisdiction over all consular offices in the British

Isles, except Ireland; and the one at Antwerp has supervisory authority over all Belgium and Luxembourg.

Appointment and Reception of Diplomats. Diplomats are invariably appointed by heads of states. In the United States chiefs of important missions are appointed by the President with senatorial confirmation. Before sending the name of a diplomat to the Senate for confirmation, the President, acting through the Department of State, usually ascertains whether the person is acceptable to the government to which he is to be accredited. The act of determining whether the envoy is *persona grata* is called *agréation* and the approval *agrément*. When confirmed by the Senate, the diplomat is given a "letter of credence," which is an official commission to be presented to the sovereign upon arrival at his post. The reverse of this procedure is followed when diplomats are sent to the United States. The President receives diplomats of higher rank, while those of lesser rank are received by the Secretary of State. Congress has nothing to do with the matter. The receptions that take place at the White House are formal and stiff, with meticulous regard for ceremony and protocol. Receptions consume considerable time, inasmuch as the largest diplomatic body in the world—over 500 members—is now stationed in Washington.

Appointment and Reception of Consuls. As in the case of diplomats, consuls must be *persona grata,* although *agrément* is not usually obtained in advance. They are usually appointed by heads of states or by ministers of foreign affairs. In the United States those above the rank of consular agent are appointed by the President from among career Foreign Service officers, while consular agents are appointed by the Secretary of State usually upon the recommendation of a superior officer located within the country or region in which the officer will serve.

Upon appointment they are given by their own government what is known as a "consular commission," which is presented to the secretary of foreign affairs upon arrival at the point of service. Though as a rule they are not re-

ceived by sovereigns or heads of states, they may be, particularly if their government is without diplomatic representation in that country. The receiving government issues an "exequatur" which entitles the consul to the rights and duties pertaining to his office. The reverse of this procedure is followed when foreign consuls are sent to the United States. That reception of consuls is a large task is illustrated by the fact that more than a thousand foreign consular officers are stationed within the forty-eight states and in American territories.

Privileges and Immunities of Diplomats. International law and treaties accord diplomats a number of privileges not enjoyed by ordinary persons. Among others, they are entitled to safe conduct through neutral and friendly states while their own nation is at war; they are exempt from the payment of customs duties and taxes; they may worship as they please in embassies or legations even though their particular mode of worship would otherwise be illegal, as formerly was true in Mohammedan countries; they have certain ceremonial privileges such as displaying their national flag and insignia; they are entitled to certain marks of respect, such as being addressed by appropriate title and being seated according to rank at public functions; and they are entitled to perform certain civil functions, such as notarial services.

Diplomats also enjoy certain immunities. Their person, residence, place of doing business, archives, and mails are inviolable. They cannot be arrested, though their guilt be obvious; nor can they be tried by the courts of the country in which they are stationed for crimes committed while there. Neither can they be sued nor compelled to give testimony in court. These immunities extend also to members of a diplomat's family and official personnel. If diplomats misbehave, they may become *persona non grata,* whereupon their recall may be requested or they may be dismissed by the government to which they are accredited. If an offense is serious, they probably will be prosecuted in the courts of their home states.

Privileges and Immunities of Consuls. The privileges and immunities of consuls are less absolute than those of diplomatic agents inasmuch as they are based almost entirely upon treaty provisions. The treaties of most countries accord them privileges similar to those enjoyed by diplomats. Though their persons are not absolutely inviolable, they are entitled to protection and the government that fails to provide it is expected to make reparation. Their archives are inviolate, but immunity does not extend to their private papers or personal effects; nor, in the absence of treaty provisions, is the consulate free from visit and search. They are generally liable for civil suit and may be prosecuted on criminal charges unless exempted by treaty provisions.

The Removal of Diplomats and Consuls. As noted above, diplomats and consuls must be *persona grata* at all times to the governments receiving them. Frequently when it is discovered that a foreign representative has lost favor, his own government learns of it in time to effect a transfer, or asks him to resign, before an issue arises. Where an agent can no longer be tolerated, he may be peremptorily dismissed, although the usual course is to intimate to his government that his recall is desired. Normally, before departing, diplomats and consuls pay a brief formal call to the chief of state or minister of foreign affairs, although where feeling has run high this is sometimes omitted.

THE DEPARTMENT OF STATE

Origin. Before the Revolution, several American colonies sent agents to England (but not to other countries) to represent their individual interests, but these were not of diplomatic or consular rank. Rather, Britain managed foreign affairs for the colonies until the breach in 1776. Thereupon, the control of external affairs passed to the Continental Congress which presumed to represent the "united colonies." Its agents were nowhere received, however, except by France, who seized upon the opportunity presented to encourage dissension within the empire of her ancient enemy. Successful conclusion of the war led other states to recognize the new republic. The Netherlands was first, in 1782, then followed Spain, Portugal, and others, including

Britain herself after final settlement was made in the Treaty of Paris.

The Department of State antedates the Constitution itself. It may be traced to the Committee on Secret Correspondence appointed by the Continental Congress in 1775 "for the sole purpose of corresponding with our friends in Great Britain, Ireland and other parts of the world." This committee has been aptly called "the embryo of an American foreign office." Its name was changed to that of Committee of Foreign Affairs in 1777, but its function remained the same. Composed of a shifting membership which met intermittently, the committee proved to be a poor vehicle.

Accordingly, it was superseded in January, 1781, less than 3 months before the adoption of the Articles of Confederation, by a Department of Foreign Affairs, directed by a secretary and small staff. Robert Livingston was appointed the first secretary, serving until 1784. He was succeeded by John Jay, who held the post until the Constitution went into effect.[12] Upon organizing the new government, the first executive department to be established was a Department of Foreign Affairs, created in July, 1789. Shortly thereafter, when assigned a number of duties relating to "home affairs," its name was changed to that of Department of State, by which it has since been known.

The Secretary of State. The Secretary of State is the chief of both the department and the Foreign Service. Next to the President himself, the Secretary is the highest ranking executive officer[13] in the Federal government. He is always the personal choice of the President, and he continues to serve as long as the President desires or until impeached. In ceremonial matters the Secretary ranks first among cabinet members, always sitting immediately to the President's right at cabinet meetings. He is the only department head who is not required to make an annual report to Congress, and when asked to fur-

[12] Actually, a little longer. He continued unofficially to superintend the office until Jefferson entered upon his duties in March, 1790.

[13] The Vice-President, it will be recalled, is a *legislative* officer until he becomes acting President.

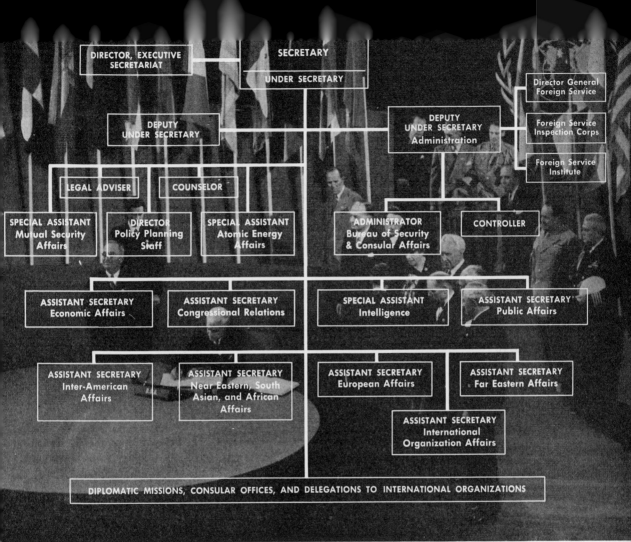

nish Congress with information affecting foreign policy, he may refuse to do so if he thinks the public interest would suffer thereby. The Secretary frequently acts as spokesman for the President, and upon the death, resignation, or removal of the President, Vice-President, Speaker, and president pro tempore of the Senate, he becomes acting president.[14]

The Secretary is nearly always one of the most prominent men in the President's party. Of the

[14] This is due to presidential succession acts rather than to any constitutional provision. It can, therefore, be changed at will by Congress. Thus far, no Secretary of State has ascended to the presidency in the manner provided for by Congress.

men who have held the post, all but a very few have been lawyers. Only two (Bryan and Kellogg, from Nebraska and Minnesota, respectively) have come from west of the Mississippi, and to date none has been selected from the West coast area. Easterners have, therefore, dominated the office. Only comparatively few of the Secretaries had extensive previous diplomatic experience, John Hay (1898–1905) being the only one since the Civil War. Many, one may guess, neither spoke nor understood any foreign language well.

Though mostly politicians, and though lacking in certain qualifications, their caliber has, on the whole, been high. Thomas Jefferson, the first Secretary, is without a peer among American patriots, philosophers, and statesmen. An extended list of the most meritorious would doubtless include John Marshall, James Madison, James Monroe, John Quincy Adams, Henry Clay, John C. Calhoun, Daniel Webster, William H. Seward, James G. Blaine, John Hay, Elihu Root, William Jennings Bryan, Charles E. Hughes, and Cordell Hull. While some have been weak, mediocrity has been the exception

reau of Inter-American Affairs, Bureau of European Affairs, Bureau of Far Eastern Affairs, and the Bureau of Near Eastern, South Asian and African Affairs. Each is headed by an Assistant Secretary who makes all decisions for his area except those requiring the approval of the Secretary, Undersecretary, or the President. These are the primary offices through which matters pertaining to the respective regions are channeled. It is to them that the Foreign Serv-

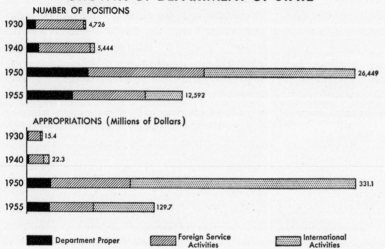

GROWTH OF DEPARTMENT OF STATE

NUMBER OF POSITIONS

1930   4,726
1940   5,444
1950   26,449
1955   12,592

APPROPRIATIONS (Millions of Dollars)

1930   15.4
1940   22.3
1950   331.1
1955   129.7

Department Proper   Foreign Service Activities   International Activities

Departmental growth reflects turbulence on the international front and increased awareness of the need for American participation in world affairs. Source: Department of State.

rather than the rule. Indeed, as one scans the list, one is impressed by the large number whose names are indelibly associated with major events in American history.[15]

Departmental Organization. Internal organization has fluctuated considerably in recent years. Both the Department itself and the Hoover Commissions made intensive study of the best way to streamline the Department to meet its new responsibilities. In response to these recommendations Congress has authorized the staff and structure shown in the chart on page 399.

Special attention should be called to the four regional bureaus. These are known as the Bu-

[15] Brief but reliable discussions of each of the secretaries and the major events of their administrations may be found in Samuel F. Bemis (ed.), *American Secretaries of State and Their Diplomacy* (Knopf, 10 vols., 1927–1929).

ice officers scattered throughout the world address their messages and reports, and it is through them that the Department communicates with officers in the field. On most matters the regional bureaus also maintain and supervise relationships with foreign embassies and legations in the United States. One should note that a similar bureau exists for handling relationships with the United Nations.

Other Agencies Handling Foreign Affairs. Foreign relations involves many more agencies of the Federal government than the Department of State. Indeed, the first Hoover Commission reported in 1949 that it had found "some forty-five other units" of the Federal government participating. To illustrate: the Departments of Agriculture, Commerce, and Labor are concerned with foreign trade and related matters; the Treasury Department regulates and taxes imports and is involved in many sorts of financial dealings abroad; the Department of Justice administers immigration and naturalization; the Department of Interior administers American overseas territories and international programs designed to protect fish and wildlife; the Post Office Department handles mail to and from all parts of the world through treaties and agreements with other nations; the Department of Defense has commitments in all parts of the world; practically every major agency is involved with one or more programs of the United Nations. This dispersal of responsibility was a major concern of the first Hoover Commission, whose recommendations are mentioned below.

In spite of these recommendations proliferation continues. In 1953 Congress ordered the establishment of two independent agencies and the transfer to them of functions previously performed by the Department of State. One of these, the Foreign Operations Administration (FOA), was given the task of handling mutual security programs and technical assistance; the other, the United States Information Agency (USIA), was assigned responsibility for "selling" the United States and its policies to people in all parts of the world. FOA was abolished in 1955 and its functions returned to State where they are performed by the International Cooperation Administration, but this should not be interpreted as being an indication that the disposition to proliferate has ended. For a new office was established under title of Special Assistant to the President on Disarmament. Popularly known as the "Secretary of Peace," this officer is based in the White House Office and expected to make studies and recommendations that may help to bring disarmament about.

Hoover Commission Criticisms and Proposals. The growing importance of foreign affairs presents the question of how the various activities can best be coordinated, directed, and controlled. Numerous official inquiries have been made to ascertain the answer. The first Hoover Commission paid special attention to the subject. Among its recommendations were the following: (1) Congress should refrain from granting foreign-affairs powers of an executive nature to any officer or agency except the President or an established executive department or agency; (2) Congress should not establish by legislation the precise functions and membership of coordinating and advisory bodies within the executive branch but, rather, should leave these flexible; (3) Congress should discontinue making specific grants of foreign-affairs powers and supporting funds to subordinate divisions and officers within departments and agencies; (4) the President should make more use of cabinet-level committees where the issues transcend the responsibility of any single department; (5) a presidential staff secretary should keep the President advised on policy issues being considered by the cabinet-level committees and help head off overlapping assignments or conflicts that might appear; cabinet-level committees and other interdepartmental committees should be given sufficient staff and secretarial aids to facilitate work of the committees and help narrow the issues for presidential consideration and decision.

So far as the State Department itself is concerned, some of the Commission's recommendations were: (1) the Department should concentrate on defining the objectives of foreign policy, on formulating proposed policies, and on recommending the choice and timing of the various instruments available for carrying out foreign policy; as a means to this end, the Department should not be given responsibility for operating specific programs overseas or at home, as, for example, the administration of occupied areas and the Voice of America; (2) the Department should continue to discharge its traditional tasks of representation, reporting, and negotiation; (3) the Secretary of State should be given a clear and unmistakable line of authority down through all departmental agencies, including the Foreign Service; (4) within action units responsibility for decisions should be clearly defined with adequate machinery by which the decision maker can consult but never be required to obtain the concurrence of staff advisory units or other action units; (5) the personnel of the State Department and the Foreign Service should be merged.

These recommendations, and others not mentioned, were directed to three parties: Congress, the President, and the Department of State. Congress has followed the recommendations in some respects, but not all, while many of the proposals have been put into effect by executive action.

THE FOREIGN SERVICE

The Department of State may be likened to the trunk of a tree whose limbs and branches extend in all directions. The division through which foreign policies are administered is known as the Foreign Service of the United States.

Creation of the Foreign Service. Throughout most of the history of the nation, diplomatic and consular officers were divided into two separate services. For many years appointments to both were on a political basis, and positions within the two services were not interchangeable. The spoils system had baneful effects, while morale and efficiency suffered because experienced and competent persons in one service had no way of transferring to the other except by resigning and once more obtaining appointment by the President with senatorial confirmation.

Starting under Cleveland in 1895, the consular service was gradually placed upon a merit basis, while slight improvement came to be made in the diplomatic service. Long agitation culminated in passage of the Rogers Act in 1924 which, among other things, combined the two services, provided for recruitment and promotion of permanent officers on the basis of merit, established the Foreign Service Officers' Training School, classified positions, raised salaries, and provided a retirement system. This, together with amendments added since, particularly by the Moses-Linthicum Act of 1931 and the Foreign Service Act of 1946, is the basic law today.

Administration of the Foreign Service. By the act of 1946 as amended in 1949, the Secretary is made the unquestioned chief of the Service. Responsible to him is a Director General appointed by the Secretary from among high-ranking Foreign Service officers. The Foreign Service is placed under the general superintendence of a Board of the Foreign Service composed of representatives of the Departments of State, Agriculture, Commerce, and Labor. A Board of Examiners is given the task of prescribing and supervising examinations required of candidates for appointment.

Foreign Service personnel is divided into six groups: (1) chiefs of missions; (2) Foreign Service officers; (3) Foreign Service Reserve officers; (4) Foreign Service staff officers and employees; (5) alien clerks and employees; and (6) consular agents. Of these, only persons in the first four categories must be American citizens. Positions are carefully classified, a salary range is stated for each class, and assignments are to be made to a class and grade rather than to some particular post. Thus, the diplomatic and consular service remain united, with transfers between them frequent, as under the Rogers Act.

The law of 1946 made many other changes designed to improve the quality of those who serve the nation abroad. One of the most glaring defects of the Foreign Service had been the fact that political appointees usually held the most important diplomatic posts. While this is still possible, the new law goes far toward encouraging more frequent use of career men. Among other things, the law requires the Foreign Service Board to recommend to the President annually a list of the most meritorious senior Foreign Service officers for consideration when vacancies arise. The law also creates the position of career minister, to be held only by top Foreign Service officers. These may be appointed chiefs of missions, with senatorial approval, without jeopardizing their career status as was the case under the Rogers Act. The new law further encourages the use of career men by stipulating that the President may, without obtaining senatorial consent, assign Foreign Service officers to head missions the chiefs of which are minister resident, chargé d'affaires, commissioner, or diplomatic agent.

Other important changes affecting personnel were made by the 1946 law, only a few of which can be noted. Salaries were raised, more generous provision was made for travel, post, and cost-of-living allowances, officers were to be aided in returning to the United States for more frequent and extended stays in order to retain closer identification with American life, the retirement system was broadened and a disability benefit plan added, the Foreign Service Institute was created with authority to extend and improve the training of recruits and those already in service, and improvements were made in recruitment, promotion, and removal methods.

Chiefs of Missions. Chiefs of missions [16] include the ambassadors, ministers, and other diplomats who head American embassies and legations abroad. As noted above, ambassadors, ministers, and career ministers are appointed by the President by and with the advice and consent of the Senate to serve at the pleasure of the President, but the President alone may assign Foreign Service officers to head missions of lesser rank. While it may be hoped that more important posts will be filled by career men, the fact remains that some of the incumbents have been appointed because of personal friendship, political expediency, financial or other contributions to the President's party, and a number of future appointments will doubtless be made for the same reasons.

Foreign Service Officers. Next to the chiefs in rank are the Foreign Service officers who constitute a permanent corps of especially recruited and trained people. To be eligible for appointment, one must be between twenty and thirty years of age, a citizen for 10 years, and if one is married his wife must also be a citizen of the United States. Officers are divided into six numerical classes and a seventh known as the class of "career minister." Entrance is by examination. Appointment of beginners is usually to class six; experienced employees of the Department of State may, if able to pass the examinations, transfer in. Promotion from the

[16] A list of incumbent chiefs of missions and other Foreign Service personnel is published quarterly by the Department of State under the title *Foreign Service List*.

lowest grade upward is based upon merit ratings. Retirement is normally at the age of sixty for all except career ministers, who serve until sixty-five. Those who reach class two or three and fail to be promoted within a reasonable period of time are retired on the principle of "promotion up or selection out" of the service.

Examinations are given as often as necessary to obtain needed personnel. They are prepared by the Board of Examiners mentioned above and given in cooperation with the Civil Service Commission. The examinations are both written and oral. The former usually requires one day and is conducted by the Civil Service Commission in principal cities throughout the nation. The examinations are designed to test English expression, general ability, general background, and competence in one modern language. Candidates obtaining a weighted grade of seventy in the written examination take the oral one sometime later in Washington or other designated cities. Those making a combined grade of eighty must also pass a rigid physical examination and security investigation, after which they are placed on a register from which they are chosen when needed. After a period of orientation the officer is usually assigned to some consular post with the rank of vice-consul or to an embassy or legation as third secretary. During his early years he may expect to be shifted from post to post about every 3 years, serving in either diplomatic or consular establishments or both.

Foreign Service Reserve. The increase in business occasioned by the recent war led to establishment, in 1941, of an Auxiliary Foreign Service. This included presidential appointees to serve during the emergency only. Recognition of their value led to inclusion of provisions in the act of 1946 establishing the Foreign Service Reserve. This is made up of six classes corresponding to those for regular Foreign Service officers. Only citizens of 5 years' standing are eligible for appointment. The Secretary of State makes appointments on behalf of the President. Reserve officers may come from other governmental agencies, with the approval of the department head concerned, or from those not employed by the Federal government. Appointments may be made for as long as 4 consecutive years, but when their term has expired they cannot be reappointed until expiration of a period of time equal to the preceding tour of duty. The class to which a reserve officer is appointed depends upon his age, qualification, and experience. While on active duty he is entitled to the same salary and allowances as Foreign Service officers of like class and grade. Creation of this reserve makes possible the employment of qualified specialists for temporary periods without disturbing the independence and integrity of the Foreign Service officers' corps itself.

Foreign Service Staff Officers and Employees. It takes a large number of staff officers, technicians, clerks, and office personnel in addition to the chiefs of missions and Foreign Service officers to handle foreign affairs. Their recruitment, classification, salary, promotion, removal, and retirement are, therefore, matters of great importance. The act of 1946 attempts to systematize and improve all such matters pertaining to this group. Selection is on the basis of merit. Personnel is divided into twenty-one classes with graduated salaries.

The Foreign Service Institute. Mention has already been made of the Foreign Service Institute authorized by the act of 1946. This took over the functions of the old Officers' Training School, created by the Rogers Act, but its broadened authority is worthy of note. The Institute is headed by a director, appointed by the Secretary of State, who is usually a scholar and educator. The Institute has its own quarters and full- or part-time staff composed either of those already employed by the government or of private scholars and specialists. The Institute is not, however, another university or college to which any qualified student might go. Rather, it is limited to government employees concerned with foreign affairs. In addition to operations in Washington, the Secretary of State may make grants of money or other gratuitous assistance to nonprofit institutions cooperating with any of the programs conducted by the Institute. The Institute may also pay the tuition and expenses of enrolled officers and employees whom it assigns to take special training and instruction at or with public or private nonprofit institutions, trade, labor, agricultural, or scientific associations or commercial firms. The Institute is trying to do for the benefit of the Foreign Service what the Army and Navy have long been permitted to do for the training of officers.

Integration Program. During 1955 and 1956 the merging of Foreign Service and Department of State civil-service personnel constituted a difficult problem. The integrated service was intended to correct a division that the first Hoover Commission called "a source of serious friction and increasing inefficiency." Although it was obvious the Foreign Service officers might lose the "feel" of their own country after long and continuous duty abroad, there were too few places in the Department of State to give them regular and extended home assignments. Likewise Department of State officials who had never known a foreign mission from the inside were less able to understand the problems of the overseas posts.

The United States became the last of the great powers to merge its foreign-affairs personnel. The enlargement of the Foreign Service Officer Corps was carried out in two ways: First, lateral entry of eligible Department staff was permitted. Second, a vigorous program of recruiting young men and women as junior officers in the Foreign Service was instituted.

By mid-1955, about 600 civil servants had qualified for the Foreign Service and received senatorial confirmation; of these about 100 received overseas assignments. The recruitment campaign of spring, 1955, netted 4,400 applications to take the examination in June. The plan is to appoint 250 junior officers, at class six (base grade) level of the Foreign Service Officer Corps.

Expansion of the Foreign Service officer group by integration is being carried out under the plan drawn up by a committee headed by President Henry M. Wriston, of Brown University. It will add 2,300 positions to the Foreign Service, and will enable Foreign Service officers to spend 2 out of each 6 years in the United States.

SELECTED FUNCTIONS OF THE DEPARTMENT OF STATE AND FOREIGN SERVICE

The primary function of the Department of State is one of providing the President with the facts and advice necessary for determining foreign policy. Next in importance is the Department's duty of executing foreign policy, of administering far-flung offices and personnel, and of enforcing laws of the United States relating to external affairs. Basic foreign policies are discussed in the next chapter; here will be mentioned only a few routine functions in order to illustrate the work done by the Department and Foreign Service.

Conducting Communications. The work of the Department of State requires endless communication not only with people in the United States, but with Americans and foreigners scattered in all parts of the globe. All mail, written, telegraphic, and even telephonic, reaching or leaving the Department is channeled through the Office of Communications and Records. All communications must be routed to the proper persons and filed for quick reference.

Of primary importance are communications with American diplomats and consuls in the field and representatives of foreign governments stationed in Washington. Letters to American representatives usually take the form of "instructions" while letters from the field are called "despatches." These are ordinarily forwarded in diplomatic pouches which enjoy special immunities. There is much communication by cable, and in the last few years by air-grams (brief messages dispatched by air mail and specially delivered upon arrival), and in emergencies by direct telephonic conversations. Telegrams are nearly always sent in code which must be deciphered by groups of experts in the Department.[17]

The Department also broadcasts news reports weekly to officers in the field and keeps them up to date on international events by sending them a monthly political digest containing materials gleaned from political reports reaching the Department from all parts of the world. Communications to and from the Department and foreign representatives in this country usually take the form of "notes." The originals of all communications dating back to the days of the Committee of Secret Correspondence have been preserved in the Department's archives. These constitute an invaluable storehouse of knowledge and one of the priceless assets of the nation. All except those of recent years may be consulted for research purposes by qualified scholars.[18]

Making Treaties. The President "makes" treaties by and with the advice and consent of two-thirds of the Senate. During the century and a half ending Apr. 30, 1939, about 800 treaties had been put into effect.[19] Some of these were bilateral, that is, between the United States and one other country; while others were multilateral, that is, between the United States and more than one other government.

Negotiation. Usually one government or another indicates through its ambassador or minister a desire to negotiate a treaty covering certain matters. When this is done, it is customary for the government proposing the agreement to submit to the other a complete draft of its proposal. Thereafter discussions may take place in either the capital city of one of the interested nations or in any other convenient place. Those conducted in this country usually take place within the Department of State. Throughout the negotiations, representatives keep in touch with their governments and proceed according to instructions. The negotiations may be concluded

[17] For an intriguing description of the decoding work done during and immediately following the First World War, see Herbert O. Yardley, *The American Black Chamber* (Bobbs-Merrill, 1931). Though this particular institution was discontinued by Secretary Kellogg, similar work has since been done on an even larger scale.

[18] A large part of this diplomatic correspondence is being published in documents known as *Papers Relating to the Foreign Relations of the United States.*

[19] Wallace McClure, *International Executive Agreements* (Columbia University Press, 1941), p. 8. In addition to the 800 treaties that were put into effect, 200 more intended treaties were approved by the Senate but for various reasons were never put into operation.

within a short time or extended over months or even years, depending upon how complex, urgent, or controversial the subject matter is.

Signing the Treaty. When the text finally suits the chief executives of both countries, a time and place are fixed for the signing of the treaty. Meanwhile, the duplicate originals of the treaty will have been prepared in what is referred to as the *alternat*—that is, with parallel columns containing the two languages side by side, the language of one of the countries being in the left-hand column of the original it is to keep but in the right-hand column of the original to be kept by the foreign government. At the appointed hour, the duly authorized plenipotentiaries appear, sign, and place their seal upon the document.

Obtaining Senatorial Approval. The original kept by the American government is usually next sent to the Senate where it is given a first reading and sent to the Committee on Foreign Relations. The Senate committee considers the matter, sometimes after public or secret hearings, then reports to the Senate. After debate, the matter is put to a vote in the Senate. If two-thirds of those present (assuming the presence of a quorum) approve, the President may proceed; if not, and the signatories still wish to see it adopted, it may be submitted to the Senate again when the President thinks its chances of obtaining approval are more favorable.

Much has been written and said for and against the requirement of senatorial approval. The intention behind the provision was to provide the President with advice and counsel and to give the states an effective voice in the conclusion of treaties. The first intention has rarely been fulfilled, but the second has been frequently. Out of more than 1,000 treaties submitted to the Senate more than 100 have either been rejected or were never acted upon at all. While the proportion unfavorably acted upon is small, many of the treaties were of outstanding importance, as, for example, the one defeated in 1920 which would have enrolled the United States as a member of the League of Nations.

That the rule requiring senatorial approval of treaties permits minority control is admitted.

That the provision also restrains the President may also be conceded. The point in controversy is whether these results are salutary or otherwise. Feeling runs high on the issue. Generally speaking, the rule is criticized by those who think the United States should have played a larger role in world affairs, while defenders include those who believe the contrary and distrust presidential leadership. Critics offer as a substitute approval by a simple majority in both houses of Congress; but since this requires a constitutional amendment, the proposal of which can also be prevented by a minority of the Senate, there appears little likelihood of early success.

Meanwhile, the President tends to circumvent the Senate by use of executive agreements, or tries to assure himself of senatorial support by widespread public discussion and by tactfully inviting members of the Senate to participate in negotiations leading up to ratification. That the latter method can be successful was demonstrated by the overwhelming approval which was given by the Senate to the treaty of adherence to the United Nations and some of the regional security pacts. There is consolation for critics in the fact that the very difficulty of obtaining senatorial approval may lead to intense interest and discussion which, if followed by overwhelming popular support, is likely to ensure continuation and success of a policy after initial ratification is obtained.

Ratification and Proclamation. Note that the Senate does not ratify; it merely gives advice and consent to ratification. When the Senate has been heard from, the President notifies the other party, whereupon ratifications are exchanged by plenipotentiaries meeting at an appointed time and place. The treaty is then published and proclaimed, at which time it becomes legally enforceable.[20] The original is kept in the Archives

[20] Treaties are published in pamphlet form at the time of their proclamation in Department of State, *Treaty Series*. Those concluded prior to 1937 have been compiled and edited by William M. Malloy, *Treaties, Conventions, International Acts, Protocols and Agreements between the United States of America and Other Powers, 1776–1909* (1910–1939). Another edition is now in preparation. See Hunter Miller, *Treaties and Other*

of the Department of State. After proclamation, the State Department must study and report on its operation and answer thousands of inquiries from people in all walks of life concerning its application.

Issuing Passports. Another important function of the State Department is that of issuing passports. The work of issuing them is headed by the Passport Office in Washington. Passports should be distinguished from visas. The former are permits granted by the American government to its citizens to *leave* the country or another country, while visas are permits to *enter* another country and must be obtained from officials of the country one is about to enter.

The American government will issue passports only to those who owe it allegiance—never to aliens. Within the forty-eight states passports are issued only by the Passport Office itself; within most of the territories they are issued by the chief executives; abroad they are granted by the higher-ranking consuls and in a few instances by officers attached to diplomatic posts.

Those in the United States wishing to obtain passports must make application either at the Passport Office itself, or at passport agencies located at a few principal cities, or before the clerk of any Federal or state court having authority to naturalize aliens. If outside the forty-eight states but in one of the territories, application is made to the chief executives. If abroad, application is made to American consuls.

Until recently the State Department had nearly unlimited discretion in granting or denying passports. Hearings were not held and explanations were seldom given to those denied passports. When challenged recently by persons denied travel permits because of pro-communist sympathies, lower Federal courts declared State Department procedures arbitrary. In consequence, modifications have been made but it is too early to tell whether these will be fair to all concerned.

Issuing Visas. Most aliens wishing to enter the United States must obtain visas, which are usually nothing more than the word "visa" en-
International Acts of the United States (Government Printing Office, 1931–).

sconced in seal and signature on one of the blank pages of the passport. Applications must be made to American consuls. As noted in Chap. 8, the large numbers seeking entrance into the United States, plus the fact that immigration laws and regulations have become so numerous and complex, places a difficult and time-consuming burden upon consular officers. Their rejections of applications, it will be recalled, are final, but their approvals may be reviewed by superior officers where applicants are suspected of being dangerous to national security and welfare. Entrance visas are good for 6 months and are ordinarily renewable for a second period of similar length.

Promotion of Cultural Relations, Interpretation, and Propaganda. Although the United States has long engaged in activities looking toward the interchange of culture with foreign nations, it was not until recently that it deliberately embarked upon a large-scale program. During the early 1930's the program was directed largely toward Latin America as part of the "good-neighbor policy." As the Second World War loomed on the horizon, the program was accelerated by realization of the commercial and strategic importance of Latin America in the event of a war in which the United States might become involved. Since the war less attention has been paid to this region and more to parts of the world where communism appeared to be a greater threat to American interests.

The division of responsibility for the program is something like this: the Assistant Secretary of State for Public Affairs is primarily concerned with the exchange program; the United States Information Agency concentrates on interpreting American objectives abroad; while the Foreign Cooperation Administration (formerly Foreign Operations Administration) concerns itself primarily with strengthening the economies and armed forces of friendly nations through loans, grants, and technical assistance.

The Exchange Program. Of special interest is the exchange of personnel for educational purposes between the United States and other countries. Most of the participants fall within one of three categories: trainees in government, visiting professors and leaders, and graduate students.

Trainees are usually employees of governments who exchange to study and observe how things are done. Some of those coming to the United States study agricultural economics, soil conservation, rural electrification, and related subjects under the Department of Agriculture;

leaders of farm and labor groups. These people usually stay only for short periods of time.

Students (postgraduate only) desiring to participate in the program submit applications to the Institute of International Education, where a selection committee makes choices without regard to financial standing but on the basis of ability. Cooperating governments help finance

EDUCATIONAL AND PROPAGANDA DIRECT OBLIGATIONS OF THE U.S. INFORMATION AGENCY

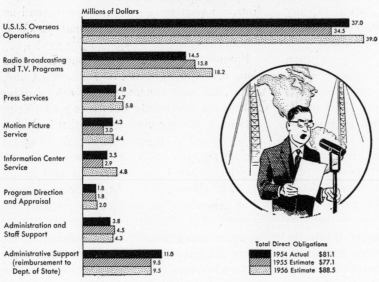

Millions of Dollars

Category	1954	1955	1956
U.S.I.S. Overseas Operations	37.0	34.5	39.0
Radio Broadcasting and T.V. Programs	14.5	15.8	18.2
Press Services	4.8	4.7	5.8
Motion Picture Service	4.3	3.0	4.4
Information Center Service	3.5	2.9	4.8
Program Direction and Appraisal	1.8	1.8	2.0
Administration and Staff Support	3.8	4.5	4.3
Administrative Support (reimbursement to Dept. of State)	11.0	9.5	9.5

Total Direct Obligations
1954 Actual $81.1
1955 Estimate $77.1
1956 Estimate $88.5

SOURCE: U. S. House of Representatives Subcommittee of the Committee on Appropriations, *Hearings on the Dept. of State Appropriations for 1956* . . . (U. S. Information Agency) p. 7

During the years 1954 to 1956 expenditures for the purposes shown fluctuated only slightly.

others study matters related to health under the Public Health Service; others study public administration under the Bureau of the Budget; others study civil aviation under the Civil Aeronautics Administration; and so on. In turn, trainees may be sent abroad for similar study. The program is financed by a three-way participation of the Federal government, the foreign government concerned, and the trainee.

In the case of professors and distinguished visitors, cooperating governments usually pay whatever expense is necessary. The visitors include educators (other than professors), newspapermen, doctors, scientists, directors of radio stations, officials of publishing houses, and persons who have a wide popular influence such as

travel and maintenance while various universities and foundations provide scholarships.

Interpretation and Propaganda. Interpreting American institutions and policies has become another important task. American diplomats and consuls have always attempted to create a favorable impression of their country, but in the modern world of conflicting ideologies this has become a major function. Every conceivable device is employed in the process. Governmental employees are indoctrinated and expected to "tell the truth" about their country. Libraries and information centers operate in many countries to present American aims and purposes in a favorable light. A steady stream of favorable releases is fed to the press and radio. Pamphlets, books, and magazines are published especially for this purpose and distributed by the thousands. Radio scripts and broadcasts are produced in great numbers and beamed around the world. Motion pictures and other visual materials are produced and widely disseminated. Fairs, exhibits and conferences are held in various regions of the world to explain and justify the American point of view. Business, professional, and labor groups

This "Campaign of Truth," as it is called, has grown to be big business. The zeal and costs entailed are often the subject of criticism. Spokesmen for the programs are nearly always given a "rough time" when they appear before congressional committees to defend expenditures. Congressmen insist on asking the embarrassing question: What are the taxpayers getting for their money?

THE *VOICE OF AMERICA'S* GLOBAL BROADCASTING NETWORK

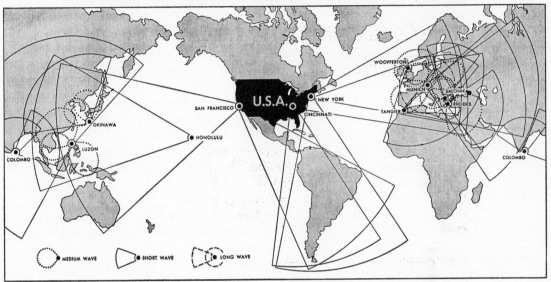

The Voice of America facilities map, as of April, 1954.

are briefed and urged to do their part. The exchange of persons is counted on to help. The various programs of economic and military assistance are expected to win friends and influence people. Refugees and others who have special reasons for disliking communism and unfriendly nations are aided and encouraged to assist.

Not all propaganda is directed toward foreign shores. The department also interprets foreign policy constantly to the American public. This is done by press conferences, press and radio releases, publications, speeches, liaison officers who keep in contact with Congress and private groups,[21] and conferences for leaders of public opinion.

Propaganda directed at foreign listeners is not intended to be objective and impartial; it is frankly pro-American and pro-free-enterprise. Measuring its value is difficult if not impossible. Those responsible for the program claim great to modest success, even behind the "iron curtain." Critics, on the other hand, insist that the propaganda is "loaded" in favor of the administration point of view, that it gives a distorted view of American life, that listeners recognize it as propaganda and discount it accordingly, that it reaches only a few behind the iron curtain and probably does more to solidify opinion behind

[21] The influence of private groups on foreign policy is ably discussed by Franklin L. Burdette in "Influ-

ences of Non-congressional Pressures on Foreign Policy," *The Annals of American Academy of Political and Social Science,* vol. 289 (September, 1953), p. 92.

communist regimes than it does to gain sympathizers for the American point of view, and that deeds not words must win the hearts and minds of men.

The Department of State and other agencies concerned justify these efforts in the domestic field not only by reference to the imperative importance of foreign affairs but also by the fact that they do not have an organized constituency to support such interests as the Department of Defense has in veterans' groups, the Department of Labor has in unions, and the Department of Agriculture has in farm groups scattered over the nation.

FOR FURTHER READING

American Foreign Service Association: *American Foreign Service Journal* (monthly).

Bailey, Thomas A.: *A Diplomatic History of the American People* (Appleton-Century-Crofts, 2d ed., 1942).

Beard, Charles A.: *President Roosevelt and the Coming of the War, 1941: A Study in Appearances and Realities* (Yale University Press, 1948).

——: *American Foreign Policy in the Making, 1932–1940: A Study in Responsibilities* (Yale University Press, 1946).

Bemis, Samuel F. (ed.): *A Diplomatic History of the United States* (Holt, rev. ed., 1942).

——:*American Secretaries of State and Their Diplomacy* (Knopf, 10 vols., 1927–1929).

Binkley, Wilfred E.: *The Powers of the President* (Doubleday, 1937).

Briggs, Herbert: *The Law of Nations* (Appleton-Century-Crofts, 1952).

Cheever, Daniel S., and H. Field Haviland: *Foreign Policy and the Separation of Powers* (Harvard University Press, 1952).

Childs, James R.: *American Foreign Service* (Holt, 1948).

Colegrove, Kenneth W.: *The American Senate and World Peace* (Vanguard, 1944).

Corwin, Edward S.: *The President, Office and Powers* (New York University Press, rev. ed., 1948).

——: *Constitution and World Organization* (Princeton University Press, 1944).

——: *The President's Control of Foreign Relations* (Princeton University Press, 1917).

Dahl, Robert A.: *Congress and Foreign Policy* (Harcourt, Brace, 1950).

Dennison, Elinore E.: *The Senate Foreign Relations Committee* (Stanford University Press, 1942).

Ferguson, John H.: *American Diplomacy and the Boer War* (University of Pennsylvania Press, 1939).

Graham, Malbone W.: *American Diplomacy in the International Community* (Johns Hopkins Press, 1948).

Hackworth, Green H.: *Digest of International Law* (8 vols., 1940–1944).

Hershey, Amos S.: *Diplomatic Agents and Immunities* (Government Printing Office, 1919).

Holt, William S.: *Treaties Defeated by the Senate* (Johns Hopkins Press, 1933).

Hulen, Bertrand D.: *Inside the Department of State* (McGraw-Hill, 1939).

Hull, Cordell: *The Memoirs of Cordell Hull* (Macmillan, 2 vols., 1948).

Kennan, George F.: *American Diplomacy, 1900–1950* (University of Chicago Press, 1951).

Lay, Tracy H.: *The Foreign Service of the United States* (Prentice-Hall, 1925).

McCamy, James L.: *The Administration of American Foreign Affairs* (Knopf, 1950).

McClure, Wallace: *International Executive Agreements* (Columbia University Press, 1941).

Macmahon, Arthur W.: *Administration in Foreign Affairs* (University of Alabama Press, 1953).

Markel, Lester, and Others: *Public Opinion and Foreign Policy* (Harper, 1949).

Mathews, John M.: *American Foreign Relations, Conduct and Policies* (Appleton-Century-Crofts, rev. and enl. ed., 1938).

Moore, John B.: *A Digest of International Law* (Government Printing Office, 8 vols., 1906).

Morgenthau, Hans J.: *Politics among Nations: The Struggle for Power and Peace* (Knopf, 1948).

Parks, Wallace Judson: *United States Administration of Its International Economic Affairs* (Johns Hopkins Press, 1951).

Rossiter, Clinton: *The Supreme Court and the Commander-in-Chief* (Cornell University Press, 1951).

Schuman, Frederick L.: *International Politics* (McGraw-Hill, 5th ed., 1953).

Stuart, Graham H.: *American Diplomatic and Consular Practice* (Macmillan, 3d ed., 1952).

Thomson, Charles A. H.: *Overseas Information Service of the United States Government* (Brookings, 1949).

U.S. Commission on Organization of the Executive Branch of the Government (first Hoover Commission): *Foreign Affairs* (1949).

——: *Task Force Report on Foreign Affairs* (1949).

Westphal, Albert C. F.: *The House Committee on Foreign Affairs* (Columbia University Press, 1942).

Whittington, William V.: *The Making of Treaties and International Agreements and the Work of the Treaty Division of the Department of State* (Government Printing Office, 1938).

Yardley, Herbert O.: *The American Black Chamber* (Bobbs-Merrill, 1931).

REVIEW QUESTIONS

1. Explain the powers given by the Constitution to the President and Congress for dealing with foreign affairs. What limits are there to each of these powers?

2. How does an executive agreement differ from a treaty? How do you explain the extensive use of the former, especially in recent years?

3. Defend and criticize the proposed Bricker amendment.

4. What are the various classes of diplomats? Of consuls? How are these officials appointed, and what privileges and immunities do they enjoy?

5. Describe the organization and functions of the Department of State. What suggestions for change were made by the first Hoover Commission?

6. Explain to a prospective candidate for the Foreign Service the essential features of the Service. Point out the advantages and disadvantages of entering the Service.

7. What improvements can you suggest in the Foreign Service?

8. What federal agencies in addition to the Department of State are deeply involved in overseas programs?

9. Explain how a treaty is negotiated and put into effect.

10. Defend and criticize the two-thirds rule for ratifying treaties.

11. Distinguish between a passport and a visa. What rules govern the issuance of these?

12. Defend and criticize the educational and propaganda efforts made by the United States to influence public opinion abroad.

CHAPTER 22

Foreign Policies and the United Nations

Today we are faced with the pre-eminent fact that, if civilization is to survive, we must cultivate the science of human relationships—the ability of all peoples, of all kinds, to live together and work together, in the same world, at peace. — Franklin D. Roosevelt [1]

No lesson has been taught more emphatically by two world wars than that of interdependence of peoples and nations. It has now become obvious to all that the political units and the people within their respective jurisdictions must learn to get along together. For years the American public has been sharply divided over the wisest course in the face of changed circumstances. To many the path of aloofness from Old World entanglements and neutrality appeared to offer the greatest hope of security and peace; but in consequence of the Second World War and the discovery of even more terrible weapons, most Americans have come to the conclusion that the new world interdependence demands collective action to maintain the peace.

TRADITIONAL FOREIGN POLICY

Isolation. The American Revolution was won by the revolting colonies in alliance with France. Made in 1778, the alliance was soundly based on the self-interests of the two participants. The contracting parties agreed that they would fight until the independence of the United States was recognized. This alliance, the only formal one entered by the United States until the ratification of the North Atlantic Pact in 1949, was finally

ended in 1800. From then until more than a century later the basic foreign policy of the United States was one of aloofness from involvement in the political affairs of Europe. Washington set the pace in his Farewell Address, delivered in 1796, when he said that the "detached and distant situation" of the United States made possible aloofness from Europe's controversies, and asked: "Why quit our own and stand on foreign ground?"

As ties increased with the outside world there were few advocates of absolute isolation, but many of limited participation in world affairs. The contemporary "isolationist" would continue United States collaboration in international work along social, cultural, and technical lines, but opposes membership in a general security organization that may use American economic or military power to keep the peace.

Neutrality. To political aloofness was coupled the belief that the best policy in time of war was to remain neutral. Indeed, during the nineteenth century the United States stood as the foremost apostle of neutrality and did much to establish and reinforce a body of rules for the protection of those who chose to remain at peace while others fought. By following the policy the United States remained free of military involvement in all wars between foreign

[1] Undelivered Jefferson Day Address, April, 1945.

states for a century and a quarter, except for the unfortunate conflict with Britain in 1812 which grew out of the Napoleonic Wars. More recently, the policy delayed American entrance into the First World War for 2½ years; and kept the United States out of the Sino-Japanese War, which began in 1931, for 10 years; out of the Ethiopian War altogether; and out of the Second World War for more than 2 years.

Because to many this policy appeared to offer the best guaranty of noninvolvement in foreign wars, it has been stoutly defended. After 1920, studies of the factors that led the United States to become involved in the First World War, disillusionment with results of that war, and the frightful prospects of involvement in another conflict led to enactment of "neutrality" legislation in 1935 and 1937 designed to prevent a repetition of what happened between 1914 and 1917. Chief among the provisions were those authorizing the President to impose an embargo upon the sale of arms to warring powers, to restrict the travel of citizens and ships in war zones, and to require that purchasers pay cash for war materials and carry them in non-American vessels. Application of most of the provisions was not mandatory, with the result that the President applied them or not as he saw fit. In the end sentiment favoring intervention in the war against the Axis became so strong as to lead to their repeal.

The Monroe Doctrine. An equally basic foreign policy has been the Monroe Doctrine enunciated in 1823 by President Monroe as a warning to European powers who, it was feared, were intent upon restoring Spain's authority over recently revolted Latin-American republics. The announcement first declared that "In the wars of the European Powers in matters relating to themselves we have never taken any part, nor does it comport with our policy so to do." It then went on to say:

We owe it, therefore, to candor and to the amicable relations existing between the United States and those powers to declare that we should consider any attempt on their part to extend their system to any portion of this hemisphere as dangerous to our peace and safety. With the existing colonies and dependencies of any European power we have not interfered and shall not interfere. But with the Governments who have declared their independence and maintained it, and whose independence we have, on great consideration and on just principles, acknowledged, we could not view any interposition for the purpose of oppressing them, or controlling in any other manner their destiny, by any European power in any other light than as the manifestation of an unfriendly disposition toward the United States.

The audacity of this statement is emphasized when it is recalled that the population of the United States had just reached 10 million. That it was possible to proclaim and enforce it was due in large measure to British assistance given because it was also to her interest to ban further European colonization in this hemisphere.

The "America for the Americans" policy of the United States has remained as it began, a proclamation of policy by the Chief Executive. It has no standing in law, yet it has been supported by Congresses and Presidents for a century and a quarter. One should note that as originally pronounced it said nothing about interrelationships between American states. As one authority put it, "The Doctrine states a case of United States *vs.* Europe, not United States *vs.* Latin America." [2]

Nevertheless, in times past, especially during the administration of Theodore Roosevelt, the doctrine served to justify a paternalistic "big stick" policy on the part of the United States. Said President Theodore Roosevelt:

If a nation shows that it knows how to act with reasonable efficiency and decency in social and political matters; if it keeps order and pays its obligations, it need fear no interference from the United States. [But] chronic wrongdoing, or an impotence which results in a general loosening of the ties of civilized society . . . may force the United States, however reluctantly, in flagrant cases

[2] J. Reuben Clark, *Memorandum on the Monroe Doctrine* (Government Printing Office, 1930), p. 19.

of such wrongdoing or impotence, to the exercise of an international police power.[3]

Acting under assumptions such as these, the United States intervened with force on numer-

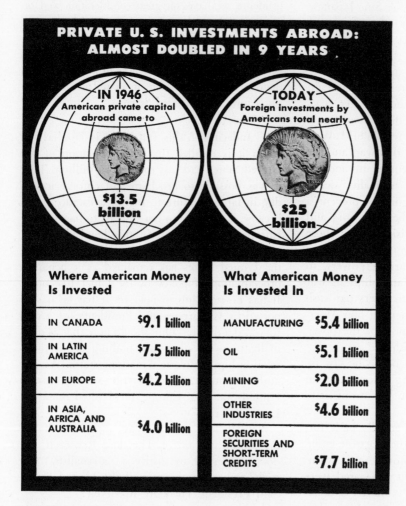

PRIVATE U. S. INVESTMENTS ABROAD: ALMOST DOUBLED IN 9 YEARS

IN 1946
American private capital abroad came to
$13.5 billion

TODAY
Foreign investments by Americans total nearly
$25 billion

Where American Money Is Invested	
IN CANADA	**$9.1** billion
IN LATIN AMERICA	**$7.5** billion
IN EUROPE	**$4.2** billion
IN ASIA, AFRICA AND AUSTRALIA	**$4.0** billion

What American Money Is Invested In	
MANUFACTURING	**$5.4** billion
OIL	**$5.1** billion
MINING	**$2.0** billion
OTHER INDUSTRIES	**$4.6** billion
FOREIGN SECURITIES AND SHORT-TERM CREDITS	**$7.7** billion

Expanding investments abroad lead inevitably to greater involvement in foreign affairs by the American government. Reprinted from *U.S. News & World Report,* an independent news magazine published at Washington. Copyright, 1955, United States News Publishing Corporation. Issue of April 1, 1955.

ous occasions, to the violent displeasure of most American republics. Happily, forcible intervention has not occurred since the withdrawal of troops from Nicaragua in 1933. Meanwhile, the "good-neighbor" policy announced in 1933 has produced a friendlier relationship.

Expansion. As noted elsewhere[4] American

history is characterized by constant expansion —south to Panama, Puerto Rico, and the Virgin Islands, southwest to Mexico and later to Samoa, northwest to Alaska and the western tip of the Aleutians, west to the Pacific, then to Hawaii, Guam, and the Philippines. Expansion led to friction with Britain over the Canadian boundary and rival claims in the Caribbean, with Mexico over Texas and the Southwest, with Spain over Florida, the Southeast, Cuba, and South America, with China and Japan in the Far East, and with Latin-American republics.

Taking a broad view, American diplomacy has eliminated all potentially hostile competitors in the Western Hemisphere, secured title to a vast domain, and established defense bastions in the

[3] Message to Congress, December, 1904, *Foreign Relations of the United States, 1904* (Government Printing Office, 1905), p. 41.

[4] Chap. 23.

Atlantic, the Caribbean, and the Pacific. Americans prefer to call it expansion in accordance with "manifest destiny"; others call it imperialism. Be that as it may, the expansionist urge has been a constant stimulus as well as the occasion for many difficulties and considerable suspicion and ill will. From the viewpoint of the American nationalist, however, the achievement is by no means a small one.

Foreign Investments and Trade. Before the Second World War, American citizens had more than 13 billion dollars invested in foreign countries. These funds were invested in enterprises of various sorts: railroads; mines; government securities; ocean shipping; oil lands, wells, and refineries; rubber, sugar, coffee, and banana plantations; churches and mission schools, etc. Needless to say, what happens in countries where citizens' investments are large becomes of immediate concern to the investors themselves and also to their government to which they turn for protection.

Closely related to investments is foreign trade, which normally accounts for between 7 and 10 per cent of all commerce. While this appears small in proportion to the fuss that is made over it, the volume is significant, particularly for certain industries like manufacturing of textiles, processed food products, rubber and silk products, and machinery. Whether justified or not, a tremendous amount of treasure and effort has been poured into opening foreign markets and expanding foreign trade.

While foreign investors and traders are normally expected to look after themselves, to abide by the laws of the countries in which they are doing business, and to obtain protection by recourse to local authorities, the American government is constantly alert to promote their interests and to protest against what it considers unfair and unjust treatment. This has frequently turned into "dollar diplomacy," a term used to refer to the use of governmental power and influence with a view to obtaining special privileges for its citizens, coupled perhaps with important economic, political, and strategic advantages for the nation itself.

Protection and promotion are usually pro-vided through diplomats and consuls, but unfortunately many occasions have arisen when the American government has intervened with force, either alone or in concert with other nations. Illustrations from the past readily come

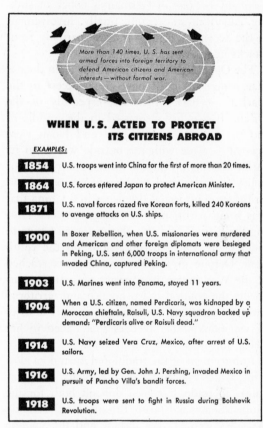

More than 140 times, U. S. has sent armed forces into foreign territory to defend American citizens and American interests—without formal war.

WHEN U.S. ACTED TO PROTECT ITS CITIZENS ABROAD

EXAMPLES:

1854 U.S. troops went into China for the first of more than 20 times.

1864 U.S. forces entered Japan to protect American Minister.

1871 U.S. naval forces razed five Korean forts, killed 240 Koreans to avenge attacks on U.S. ships.

1900 In Boxer Rebellion, when U.S. missionaries were murdered and American and other foreign diplomats were besieged in Peking, U.S. sent 6,000 troops in international army that invaded China, captured Peking.

1903 U.S. Marines went into Panama, stayed 11 years.

1904 When a U.S. citizen, named Perdicaris, was kidnaped by a Moroccan chieftain, Raisuli, U.S. Navy squadron backed up demand: "Perdicaris alive or Raisuli dead."

1914 U.S. Navy seized Vera Cruz, Mexico, after arrest of U.S. sailors.

1916 U.S. Army, led by Gen. John J. Pershing, invaded Mexico in pursuit of Pancho Villa's bandit forces.

1918 U.S. troops were sent to fight in Russia during Bolshevik Revolution.

Reprinted from *U.S. News & World Report,* an independent weekly news magazine published at Washington. Copyright, 1954, United States News Publishing Corporation. Issue of Dec. 17, 1954.

to mind: During the Boxer Rebellion in 1900 the United States, in cooperation with European powers and Japan, sent troops to China to protect lives and property; American intervention in Latin America between 1898 and 1934 occurred a number of times for the same reason; war with the Barbary States grew out of the fact that tribute had been levied on American commerce entering the Mediterranean; the war with England in 1812 arose over impressment of seamen and other interferences with commerce; in 1853 Commodore Perry threatened to bombard Japanese ports unless they were promptly opened to American commerce; after much difficulty with both the allied and central powers during the early part of the First World War the United States later entered the war against Germany because of Germany's policy of sinking American ships; and, finally, involvement in the Second World War arose partially from attacks upon American ships.

The Open Door. The idea of the open door is that Americans must have equal access to the markets of backward areas, especially of the Orient. It was first expressed in the middle of the last century, when China and Japan were opened to trade with the outside world. In its early twentieth century form, the open-door policy was designed to assure Americans and Britishers commercial privileges in a China that was being partitioned by foreign powers. During the First World War Japan forced China to yield many valuable concessions on the continent. Despite great power agreements reached at the Washington Conference of 1921–1922 assuring the political independence and territorial integrity of China, Japan began in 1931 a series of violations of her pledges that ended in her defeat in the Second World War.

Enforcement of the traditional open-door doctrine, which concentrated on equality of opportunity to trade, has been difficult both for the United States and Great Britain. Until recently Asia has seemed very distant and the volume of trade with the Far East has been very small. When Japan undertook her aggressive steps in China, the American people were unprepared to run the risks involved in requiring the Japanese to respect treaties and promises. So long as Japan remained the only great power in east Asia equipped with a powerful navy and a large army, it proved impossible to curb her designs to control the greater part of the Orient both politically and economically. In the new situation brought about by the defeat of Japan and the emergence of Red China and Russia as strong Asiatic land powers and of the United States as the greatest sea power, the open-door policy will probably pass finally into obsolescence. The question of security has emerged so

important that what was primarily a commercial doctrine will unquestionably be subordinated.

NEW AMERICAN POLICY

Collective Security. Having been drawn into two world wars in spite of a high resolve to remain neutral, the traditional American policy of isolation has been abandoned. It is now assumed that this ought to be one world; that no nation is likely long to enjoy peace and prosperity while others are afflicted by war and want; that in a day of atomic and hydrogen bombs, rockets, and long-range planes, neutrality by a major power is virtually impossible.

Modifying the isolationism of the past, the United States has embarked on a new policy of collective security. The change did not come suddenly, for over the years the United States had steadily increased its participation in international legislation and organization. While it did not join the League of Nations and the World Court, a large sector of the American public favored doing so and the American government did cooperate with many League activities. Moreover, as Professor Henry Reiff [5] pointed out, in the late 1930's the United States had joined about forty international administrative unions and had perfected more than eighty general agreements with other nations dealing with humanitarian, economic, and cultural matters.

The Second World War reinforced those who had insisted that growing world interdependence demanded positive and continuous cooperation with other nations. Accordingly, in the midst of the war the foreign ministers of the major allied powers agreed at Moscow that a general international organization would be launched at the earliest practicable time. A proposed charter was drafted at Dumbarton Oaks in the fall of 1944 by representatives of United States, Great Britain, Soviet Union, and China. The Charter of the United Nations was the product of the San Francisco Conference of April–June, 1945. Ratification of that Charter

[5] "The United States and International Administrative Unions: Some Historical Aspects," *International Conciliation*, no. 332 (September, 1937).

by the United States Senate in August of the same year completed and formalized the abandonment of isolation and the adoption of collective security.

As provided for in the United Nations Charter, collective security means that the member nations unite their resources to remove the causes of war, to settle disputes peacefully, and if necessary to resist aggression by armed might. Primary responsibility for enforcing peace is placed on the Security Council, which is given authority to settle disputes by various means, including the use of economic and armed force.

Regional Security. The United Nations Charter assumed that in the postwar era the five big powers would cooperate. The Charter, nevertheless, recognized the need for regional-security arrangements subordinate to the United Nations and consistent with its purposes. Soon after the Second World War, the victorious Allies became divided into blocs that resorted to "cold war" against one another. On one side were the United States, Britain, France, and most of the countries of the Western world. On the other was the Soviet Union, her satellites of Eastern Europe and the Balkans, and a China with communist leadership rapidly gaining power. As time passed, neutralist sentiment increased and other blocs, notably the League of Arab States, appeared.

Although several new factors are present, this alignment of blocs clearly represents the re-emergence of the balance-of-power relationship which has been present in nearly every state system. In this situation mutual fear and suspicion prevented the disarmament anticipated by the Charter and otherwise led to the deterioration of international affairs. The outbreak of fighting in Korea in 1950 brought already critical affairs to the verge of a third world war.

Faced with what it considered a threat to the "free world," the American government began a vast program in 1947 designed to "contain" communist expansion. When British forces withdrew from Greece in 1947 the "Truman Doctrine" was announced which promised American support to parts of the world threatened by communism. Then followed the "Marshall Plan" for economic recovery in distressed nations, the Economic Cooperation Act, the Mutual Defense Assistance Act, the North Atlantic Pact, and more recently the Mutual Security Program and variations thereof. Early programs emphasized financial and technical assistance directed particularly toward Western Europe; emphasis then shifted to building the armed strength of friendly powers; still more recently technical assistance has been stressed and special attention paid to Asiatic countries. The Soviet bloc repudiated the program from the start, calling it "Anglo-American imperialism."

The North Atlantic Treaty. Ratification of the North Atlantic Pact in 1949 was one of the most momentous events in the history of American foreign affairs. For the first time in a century and a half the United States had bound itself by a peacetime alliance that would almost certainly lead to war if one of the contracting parties were attacked. The pact is based upon the assumptions that American security is tied to that of Western Europe and that its strategic frontier runs from Norwegian Lapland to the Adriatic Sea. The key provision of the pact is Article V, which reads: "The parties agree that an armed attack against one or more of them in Europe or North America shall be considered an attack against them all. . . ." Participating nations are the United States, Britain, Canada, France, Belgium, Netherlands, Luxembourg, Norway, Denmark, Iceland, Portugal, Italy, Greece, Turkey, and (since 1955) Western Germany. The constitutional question, discussed in the previous chapter, of congressional delegation of power to declare war was avoided simply by not specifying what aid would be furnished to a victim of attack.

Since the Pact became effective, a North Atlantic Treaty Organization (NATO) has been created to effectuate the purposes of the treaty. A governing North Atlantic Council, composed of the foreign ministers of participating states, has come into existence along with a permanent Council of Deputies and a number of committees and boards. Headquarters are at Rocquencourt, France. Planning for united and coordinated action in the event of war is their principal function. An international army, popularized by its first Supreme Commander, General Dwight Eisenhower, has evolved slowly.

Critics of the Pact declare that, like alliances of old, this one will not prevent war but actually

that the rearmament of Europe retards economic recovery and thus encourages communism.

Supporters of the Pact claim that, since the United Nations security machinery has not been activated, member nations are justified under

NORTH ATLANTIC TREATY ORGANIZATION (NATO)
JULY 1954

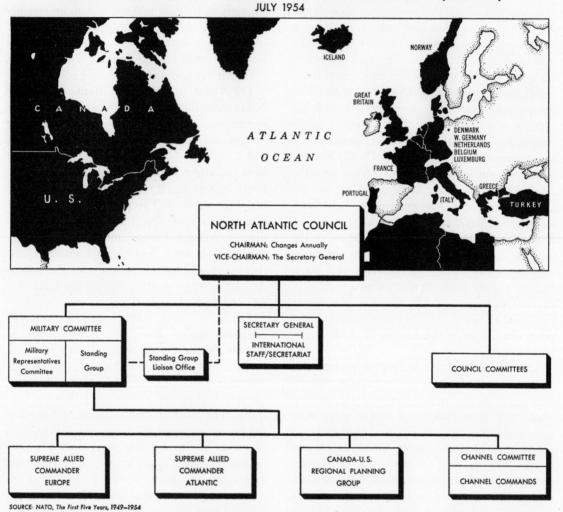

SOURCE: NATO, *The First Five Years, 1949–1954*

will encourage it, that the Pact violates both the letter and spirit of the United Nations Charter, that the Pact aggravates and even institutionalizes the East-West rift, that American aid must of necessity be "too little and too late" to allies that can easily be overrun by invading land forces or obliterated by atom bombs, and

the Charter in invoking their right of individual and collective self-defense, that any intending aggressor will be deterred by the power of the combination, that economic recovery will be accelerated once security from invasion is assured, that peace is the objective, and that the chances for peace are greater if the United States declares clearly and in advance what it will do if aggression comes.

Whatever the merits of the argument, there can be no doubt but that the Pact signalized the abandonment, at least temporarily, of universal collective security for a system of collective regional defense.

The Pacific Pacts. Similar insecurity in the western Pacific area has led to American entry other nations: Britain, France, Australia, New Zealand, Pakistan, the Philippines, and Thailand. The pact also provides protection for free Viet Nam, Laos, and Cambodia, although they are not members. In addition, the United States has concluded a trilateral treaty for similar purposes with Australia and New Zealand (ANZUS in 1951), and bilateral pacts with the Philippines (1951), Japan (1951), South Korea (1953), and

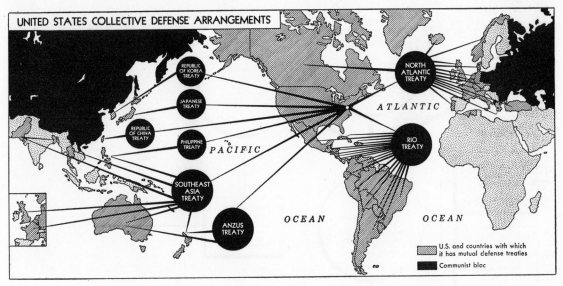

UNITED STATES COLLECTIVE DEFENSE ARRANGEMENTS

REPUBLIC OF KOREA TREATY

JAPANESE TREATY

REPUBLIC OF CHINA TREATY

PHILIPPINE TREATY

SOUTHEAST ASIA TREATY

ANZUS TREATY

NORTH ATLANTIC TREATY

RIO TREATY

ATLANTIC

PACIFIC

OCEAN   *OCEAN*

U.S. and countries with which it has mutual defense treaties

Communist bloc

Existing security pacts bind the United States to nearly half of the countries of the world. Source: Department of State.

into a series of security arrangements with friendly nations. Although several of the pacts mention the possibility of a future general security organization for the Pacific region, the political situation in Asia is not conducive to a comprehensive pact. The several pacts vary considerably, but most of them require consultation in case of threat or actual armed attack on the territory or forces of a member power in the Pacific area.

The broadest of these, in terms of membership, is the Manila Pact, which formed the South East Asia Treaty Organization (SEATO) following the 1954 armistice in the Indochina War. The United States—seeking to resist aggression, check subversion, and aid with social and economic development—joined with seven the Republic of China (Nationalist, based on Formosa, in 1954).

In spite of these many treaties and the outpouring of much financial, technical, and military aid, American efforts in the Far East have been only partially successful. Outright opposition by the Soviet Union and Communist China, aided by strong feelings of nationalism and anticolonialism, has inclined large sectors of this region toward a neutral position.

Inter-American Unity. Meanwhile, in the Western Hemisphere the "big stick," "manifest destiny," and "dollar diplomacy" have given way to "Pan-Americanism" and the "good-neighbor policy."

United States participation in the Pan American movement dates from 1889. Through numerous conferences held since that date, the American republics have been collaborating in technical, humanitarian, economic, and finally political and strategic matters. Once known as the International Bureau of American Repub-

the United States has opposed Union consideration of political questions; on the other hand, the Latin Americans have been reluctant to vest much power in the Union because it was dominated by the United States.

ORGANIZATION OF AMERICAN STATES

THE INTER-AMERICAN CONFERENCE

Supreme Organ of the Organization Decides general action and policy (Meets every 5 years)

THE MEETING OF CONSULTATION OF MINISTERS OF FOREIGN AFFAIRS

Considers urgent problems and acts as the Organ of Consultation

SPECIALIZED CONFERENCES

Meet periodically to consider technical matters

INTER-AMERICAN PEACE COMMITTEE

Washington, D. C.

ADVISORY DEFENSE COMMITTEE

INTER-AMERICAN DEFENSE BOARD Washington, D. C.

THE COUNCIL OF THE ORGANIZATION

Permanent Executive Body and Provisional Organ of Consultation Washington, D. C.

SPECIALIZED ORGANIZATIONS

Permanent agencies performing specialized technical functions

INTER AMERICAN STATISTICAL INSTITUTE 1941   Washington, D. C.

INTER-AMERICAN ECONOMIC AND SOCIAL COUNCIL

Washington, D. C.

INTER-AMERICAN CULTURAL COUNCIL

COMMITTEE FOR CULTURAL ACTION

Mexico, D. F

INTER-AMERICAN COUNCIL OF JURISTS

INTER-AMERICAN JURIDICAL COMMITTEE

Rio de Janeiro

THE PAN AMERICAN UNION

Washington, D. C.

General Secretariat of the Organization

DEPARTMENT OF INTERNATIONAL LAW

DEPARTMENT OF CULTURAL AFFAIRS

DEPARTMENT OF ECONOMIC AND SOCIAL AFFAIRS

DEPARTMENT OF ADMINISTRATIVE SERVICES

INTER-AMERICAN INSTITUTE OF AGRICULTURAL SCIENCES 1944   Turrialba, Costa Rica

PAN AMERICAN SANITARY BUREAU 1902   Washington, D. C.

AMERICAN INTERNATIONAL INSTITUTE FOR THE PROTECTION OF CHILDHOOD 1927   Montevideo

INTER-AMERICAN COMMISSION OF WOMEN 1928   Washington, D. C.

PAN AMERICAN INSTITUTE OF GEOGRAPHY AND HISTORY 1929   Mexico, D. F.

INTER-AMERICAN INDIAN INSTITUTE 1940   Mexico, D. F.

• *The Directors of these Departments are the Executive Secretaries of the respective Councils*

▸ *The Director of this Department is also the Treasurer of the Organization*

lics, the common organization was named Pan American Union in 1910. The governing board of the Union has long been composed of the ambassadors to Washington of the several Latin-American nations, with the United States Secretary of State serving as chairman. Until recently

A new spirit entered United States relations with Latin America in the late 1920's. Known during the Franklin D. Roosevelt administration (1933–1945) as the "good-neighbor policy," the new plan involved a cooperative and friendly approach by the United States. Applying something like the golden rule to its relations with the other American republics, this country ceased military intervention, terminated dollar diplomacy, and ended many unequal treaties. By the time war broke out in Europe, inter-American solidarity had been proclaimed, and the nations were able to take a united stand on various issues of the crisis years. At the Mexico City Conference in 1945 a regional security arrangement was agreed upon, an economic charter adopted, and reform of the composition and powers of the Pan American Union proposed. Eventually every one of the American nations declared war on the Axis countries, and all (Argentina belatedly) took part in the San Francisco Conference and joined the United Nations.

At Bogotá, Colombia, in early 1948 the American republics agreed to the charter of a broader system known as "The Organization of the American States." The Pan American Union continues as the central organ and secretariat of OAS. The other organs are the Inter-American Conference, which meets each four years or so; meetings of consultation among the foreign ministers; and the Council, which is composed of one representative with rank of ambassador from each member republic. In addition there are specialized conferences and organizations, and various subsidiary councils.

The regional security arrangement outlined at Mexico City in 1945 was completed in Brazil during 1947. Known as the Treaty of Rio de Janeiro, it is a pact of mutual defense. In case of armed attack on any American state in the Western Hemisphere, all other signatories are bound to aid the victim Nineteen nations signed the treaty and nearly all, including the United States, ratified during 1948.

Economic and Social Cooperation. Hitherto the United States has been chiefly concerned with its own expansion, investments, commerce, and social and cultural welfare. This has resulted in high tariffs and other trade restrictions, rivalries for concessions and markets, monopolies and cartels, and other measures designed to create self-sufficiency, the cumulative effect of which has been lowered standards of living and war.

Since adoption of the reciprocal tariff program in 1934 the United States has been committed to a freer movement of trade between countries. More recently, at San Francisco and other wartime conferences the United Nations gave proper recognition to the long-run importance of economic and social matters in producing conditions conducive to lasting peace. One of the major agencies of the United Nations is the Economic and Social Council. Under its general direction are currency stabilization, international loan, relief and rehabilitation, food and agriculture, educational, and other functions.

While the spirit of dollar diplomacy dies hard and the United States has doubtless acted from mixed motives, the various assistance programs mentioned above reflect a growing awareness of the economic and social needs of others. It is not too much to say that never before has a country helped others so much in the economic and technical sphere. Beginning with the $3,750,000,000 loan to Britain in 1946, the United States has poured out vast sums in grants and loans to help revive the economies of a third of the countries of the world. Most of this has been handled outside the United Nations, but the world organization has not been entirely bypassed.

One of the current programs is known popularly as "Point Four." The name came from the fact that President Truman listed the item as fourth in a plan for the nation proposed to Congress in his inaugural address of January, 1949. The President suggested a "bold new program" designed to help raise the living standards of two-thirds of the peoples of the world who live in economically underdeveloped areas. Some of the funds are spent through the United Nations, in which case they are used chiefly to provide economic and technical assistance to underdeveloped areas on the basis of need and willingness to cooperate. Money spent directly by the United States has the same general objectives, but because it is often impossible to disassociate them from the policy of containing communism a number of needy areas have been skeptical about accepting aid. While expenditures have been pitifully small in proportion to the need, they have helped to improve living standards, reduce disease, decrease mortality, and enhance opportunity. The program is administered by the International Cooperation Administration of the Department of State.

The United States also participates in the Colombo Plan, a program of economic and technical assistance launched in 1950 by a group

subsequently admitted by vote of the General Assembly upon recommendation of the Security Council. The Charter stipulated that it should go into effect when ratified by the United States, the Soviet Union, Great Britain, France, China, and a majority of the other signatories. Amendments were authorized, and even general Charter review, the latter to occur 10 years later unless a conference should be convened for the purpose before this date.

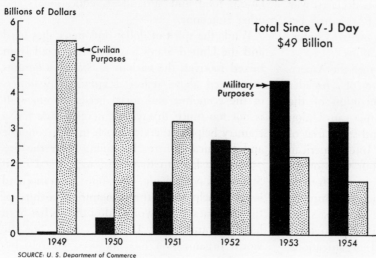

FOREIGN GRANTS AND CREDITS

Billions of Dollars

Total Since V-J Day
$49 Billion

Civilian Purposes

Military Purposes

SOURCE: U. S. Department of Commerce

Assistance for economic purposes has declined while aid for military objectives has risen.

of British Commonwealth nations. Colombo projects are concentrated mainly in the crucial areas of southern Asia and South East Asia. The program is characterized by the large degree of mutual participation by the cooperating nations.

THE UNITED NATIONS

The Charter. The Charter opens with an inspiring preamble beginning "We the peoples of the United Nations. . . ." After this appears a statement of purposes and principles to which members pledged themselves. Then follow nine chapters and 111 articles.[6]

Membership was open to all fifty nations participating in the San Francisco Conference and such other "peace-loving" nations as should be

[6] Text of the Charter is Appendix IV.

The United States was the first to ratify when the Senate gave its approval in early August, 1945, by vote of 89 to 2.[7] The Charter came into force on Oct. 24, 1945, upon receipt of notice

[7] In addition to ratification of the Charter, Congress also provided for United States membership by enacting the United Nations Participation Act, 59 Stat. 619, which became law on Dec. 20, 1945. It provides for appointment of a chief delegate by the President, with Senate approval. This representative has the status of an ambassador and is United States representative on the Security Council. Other representatives were authorized. The President was empowered to provide for United States participation in economic and communications sanctions. He was also given power to negotiate with the Security Council, subject to approval of Congress by act or joint resolution, concerning the military forces and facilities that the United States will furnish.

of ratification by the Soviet Union, the twenty-ninth state to approve and the last of the Big Five.

The General Assembly. The General Assembly consists of delegates from all the member nations; each nation has not more than five delegates but only one vote. Decisions on important questions like elections, suspensions, expulsions, budgets, and trusteeship must be made by two-thirds vote, but decisions on matters of less importance are made by ordinary majority.

over the Economic and Social Council and the Trusteeship Council. The Assembly's power to elect is considerable, extending to the nonpermanent seats on the Security Council, the judgeships on the International Court of Justice, the Economic and Social Council, and part of the Trusteeship Council. Funds for the UN are se-

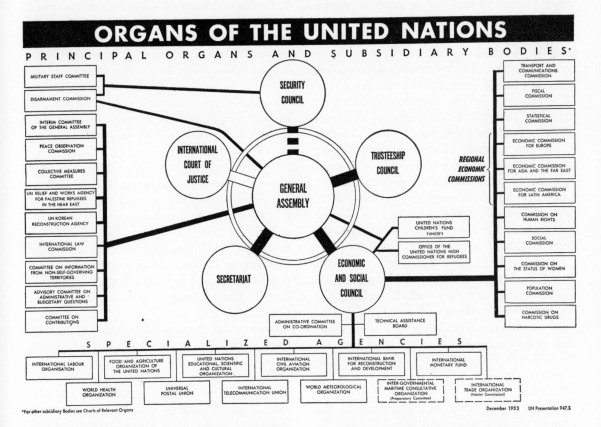

ORGANS OF THE UNITED NATIONS

PRINCIPAL ORGANS AND SUBSIDIARY BODIES*

*For other subsidiary Bodies see Charts of Relevant Organs

December 1953   UN Presentation 947.1

The functions of the Assembly are to deliberate, to administer, to elect, to approve budgets, to initiate amendments. The late Senator Vandenberg called it a "town meeting of the world." It has general authority to discuss any matter within the scope of the Charter and may make recommendations except on disputes being considered by the Security Council. The Assembly oversees the work of all organs of the United Nations and is assigned special responsibilities

cured by the Assembly through the apportionment of expenses among member nations.

Frustrations arising from the cold war led to two developments in the Assembly which the Soviet bloc opposed as unwarranted by terms of the Charter. One of these was the establishment in 1947 of an Interim Committee, popularly known as the "Little Assembly." Each nation was entitled to one representative, and this "committee of the whole" was to function between sessions of the parent body. Its primary task was defined as being one of preparing recommendations for the General Assembly, although it was permitted to exercise a limited amount of delegated authority. While temporary at first, the Interim Committee has continued, although its usefulness has been impaired by the refusal of the Soviet bloc to participate.

A second development came in 1950 when the Assembly approved the "Uniting for Peace" resolution. Inspired by the inability of the Security Council to function on matters pertaining to fighting in Korea following the return of the Soviet representative, this resolution permits the Assembly to *recommend* that collective measures be taken by member states against aggressors in the event that the Security Council is prevented by the veto from fulfilling its function. That this was an attempt to bypass the Security Council seems quite clear. Whether it conforms with the Charter is debatable, and whether it will prove to be feasible is doubted by many. Nevertheless, under the circumstances, a majority thought it worth trying. Meanwhile, extensive studies are in progress seeking to place the General Assembly in greater readiness in the event it is called upon to act.

Obviously the General Assembly is not a full-blown "parliament of mankind." Its powers are modest indeed, and they include nothing like the lawmaking authority of a national parliament or congress. But when the nations and their peoples are ready for a more perfect union, the General Assembly may be the key instrument through which this goal may be achieved.

Security Council. Those who drafted the Charter thought peace and security could be maintained only if an international agency were in existence with authority and power to apply collective measures against an aggressor nation. The Security Council was born of this conviction. It is composed of eleven member nations, of which five—the United States, the Soviet Union, Great Britain, China, and France—hold permanent seats and six are elected to nonpermanent seats for 2-year terms by the General Assembly. The Charter mentions as standards in election to nonpermanent seats the ability to contribute to maintenance of peace and security and equitable geographic representation.

For settling disputes the Council is given powers ranging from negotiation, conciliation, arbitration, and judicial decision to interruption of communications, severance of diplomatic relations, economic sanctions, and military action. Plans for the employment of armed forces were to be made by a military staff committee under the Security Council, but the committee has been so deadlocked from the beginning that no progress has been made. Should agreement be reached, member nations have pledged themselves to assign contingents of armed forces for United Nations use. Under the voting formula agreed to at the Yalta Conference, a decision to use force requires the concurrence of all permanent members of the Security Council, thus making certain that military sanctions could not be used against one of the Big Five.

The Security Council is also given power to oversee regional arrangements, which are permitted provided they are consistent with the UN Charter. The Council also has a major responsibility for the achievement of disarmament. To fulfill this function a Disarmament Commission has been established which is composed of all eleven members of the Council plus Canada. Disarmament proposals are reviewed in Chap. 24.

Great-power Predominance. Much of the criticism of the UN stems from the predominant position assigned to the major nations in the Security Council. But as long as the spirit of nationalism remains what it has been, it is difficult, if not impossible, to devise an acceptable alternative to the veto. The United States was as eager for inclusion of the veto in the Charter as was the Soviet Union, and has shown no enthusiasm for modifying its position. The "Little Assembly" proposed that the veto be abolished where the admission of new members and peaceful settlements are involved, but it went no further. Champions of stronger world government would subordinate national sovereignty to majority will, but how this can be made acceptable in the near future is far from clear.

Other critics question the whole concept of an international police force with authority to impose sanctions upon national states, especially as long as these remain heavily armed. In spite of the problems it creates, retention of the veto on at least the application of sanctions appears to be a prerequisite to having any international organization with universal membership. This being the case, the Security Council's usefulness will be limited, as intended, to those areas where the five permanent members find themselves able to agree.

Looking back over the first decade of the Security Council, one must exert himself to find achievements to balance the disappointments. The basic cause of the meager record in security matters has been the deep East-West split. The extent of this cleavage was not anticipated by the founding fathers at San Francisco, who counted on continuance of the kind of cooperation that characterized joint efforts in wartime. Obviously the UN, based on a one-world principle, cannot fulfill the expectations of its founders so long as the nations of the world are grouped into two hostile armed camps.

Despite the "iron curtain" and the suspicions entertained by those on both sides of it, substantial progress has been made in peaceful settlement of international disputes. Nearly all the major postwar problems among nations have been brought before the UN. Although handicapped by the frequent use of the veto power by Russia, the Security Council has been able to act effectively in some cases. The greatest achievements are the settlements in Palestine, Indonesia, and Kashmir, where fighting wars were stopped through UN mediation and intervention. Armed only with the moral power of the world organization, UN representatives negotiated truces and peaceful settlements. In spite of the veto, the Security Council provided facilities for the airing of all sides, for investigation, and for mediation. Each settlement tends to contribute to the formulation of patterns of good conduct.

Economic and Social Council. To get at some of the basic causes of war through improved standards of living, social and economic progress, the United Nations created the Economic and Social Council and its cooperating agencies. The council is composed of eighteen members, elected by the Assembly for 3-year terms.

While the field of operation of the Economic and Social Council is broad, its actual coercive powers are meager. It can study, report, recommend, prepare agreements, and call conferences. Although the Charter does not provide specifically for their subordination to the council, several United Nations agencies are supervised by the council.

The oldest of these is the *International Labor Organization* (ILO), the only major agency of the League of Nations to which the United States belonged. The principal problems that have concerned the ILO are labor standards, migration of workers, full employment, public works, workers' health, and welfare of colonial peoples. The ILO functions through its conference, which meets at least once a year and is composed of delegates representing government, labor, and employers of each member country. An executive body, called the "governing body," manages the affairs of the ILO between conferences. The secretariat, headed by the director, is termed the International Labor Office. After the outbreak of war in Europe, the ILO transferred its headquarters from Geneva, Switzerland, to Montreal, Canada. In the past the ILO has operated mainly through the framing of international conventions regarding the conditions of labor.

The *Food and Agriculture Organization* (FAO) was launched in interim form at the close of the conference held at Hot Springs, Va., in May and June, 1943. It has been called the "first permanent United Nations agency." The FAO hopes to stimulate increased food production and improved nutrition. Its methods are mainly research and informational—the collection of statistics, the exchange of expert personnel, the dissemination of information.

The *International Monetary Fund* was one of two agencies established under the Bretton Woods agreements of July, 1944. Its purpose is to encourage world trade and prosperity through stabilizing the value of currencies of participating nations.

The *International Bank for Reconstruction and Development* is the second of the Bretton Woods agencies. This organization tries to guarantee or make direct loans to countries in need of capital for rebuilding areas devastated by the Second World War or for developing new productive facilities.

The *United Nations Educational, Scientific, and Cultural Organization* (UNESCO) was born in London in November, 1945. UNESCO is designed to be the agency through which member nations are encouraged to exchange information and ideas through all the diverse mediums of communication.

The *International Civil Aviation Organization* (ICAO) developed from the Chicago Conference of November–December, 1944. Although it was established as an interim organization limited to 3 years, subsequent agreements are expected to make the body permanent. Its powers are largely technical and advisory, but ICAO may later become a highly important regulatory body for world civil aeronautics.

Trusteeship Council. The San Francisco Conference had to start from scratch in preparing sections of the Charter on dependent areas. The Dumbarton Oaks Conference had not touched this important field, and the great powers had been unable to meet together before the San Francisco convening date. The Charter, in three chapters on trusteeship, establishes general policy to govern all dependent areas, sets forth the rules governing territories placed under United Nations "trust," and establishes the Trusteeship Council to supervise the system.

In the Atlantic Charter, signed by President Roosevelt and Prime Minister Churchill at sea in August, 1941, Great Britain and the United States declared that they sought no territorial aggrandizement. At San Francisco many compromises were necessary. First, the American State Department view had to be reconciled with that of the Army and Navy. Then, the United States and British drafts had to be brought into agreement. Finally, there ensued a spectacular fight over whether the goal of colonial peoples should be self-government or independence.

As finally adopted, the general provisions regarding trusteeship admonish nations with dependent areas to ensure their political, economic,

social, and educational advancement, to develop self-government, to report on progress in their colonies to the UN, and to adopt an attitude of good-neighborliness.

The international trusteeship system had no specific territories assigned to it by the Charter. Trust territories were to come later from the following sources: (1) old League mandates, (2) conquered Axis colonies, and (3) other colonies voluntarily placed under the trusteeship plan. All the mandates except Southwest Africa, which may be annexed by the Union of South Africa, promptly were transferred to the trusteeship system by action of the mandatory powers. The United States accepted trusteeship over the former Japanese mandates of the Pacific—the Marshalls, the Carolines, and the Marianas. Former Italian colonies in North Africa were placed under temporary UN administration, then launched as the Kingdom of Libya, while Italy was given a trusteeship over Italian Somaliland. No important colonial power has yet indicated willingness to place its colonies under trust.

The Trusteeship Council was made a principal organ of the UN. It consists of member nations administering trust territories, other members of the Big Five, and enough other nations to make an equal number of states administering and not administering trust territories. The council has modest powers of accepting petitions, considering reports, and visiting trust areas. It supervises all ordinary trust territories. Trust areas of strategic importance are supervised by the Security Council and, as the United States Army and Navy demanded, the trust power has a free hand to maintain bases. Although the new system does not contain striking new departures, it does obligate all nations with colonies to treat them decently and to report on their stewardship to the UN.

International Court of Justice. In early April, 1945, just on the eve of the San Francisco Conference, a committee of jurists representing many nations met in Washington to consider the form and organization of the judicial organ of the United Nations. Like the question of dependent areas, judicial matters were little considered at

Dumbarton Oaks. The work of the committee of jurists was put before the conference at San Francisco. The principal controversy over judicial organization at the conference was over the continuation of the old Permanent Court of International Justice. The statute of the League court was reasonably satisfactory, and forty-five nations had accepted the principle of compulsory jurisdiction over disputes arising from treaties. On the other hand, several nations that were not members of the United Nations adhered to the World Court. It finally proved advisable to adopt a new statute creating a new International Court of Justice. Charter provisions regarding the court are very brief; the statute of the court is annexed to the Charter.

The court consists of fifteen judges, no two of whom may be nationals of the same state. The term of office is 9 years. The court sits at The Hague. Judges are elected by the General Assembly and the Security Council, each proceeding independently to elect from a list of nominees proposed by national groups. Membership in the court is automatic for all members of the UN. The statute made the new court successor to existing treaty provisions which named the old court as arbiter in disputes.

In view of the great tension of the era, it is not surprising that the International Court of Justice has heard few cases. Most of the serious disputes between nations have been of a "political" nature and have not been submitted to adjudication. The court has, however, decided a few cases and rendered several advisory opinions.

THE UNITED STATES IN ONE WORLD

Can UN Keep the Peace? Only a fool or a seer would attempt a final answer to this all-important question. A start has been made toward building world organization, but national sovereignty dies hard. The UN machinery appears to be fairly well suited for the achievement of the humanitarian objectives of the Charter, it has had modest success in settling legal disputes and codifying international law, it has provided a medium for airing grievances and molding public opinion, and it has had consid-

erable success in mediating disputes between minor powers.

But, judging from the experience with the Military Staff Committee, the operation of the Security Council in the Korean dispute, the failure to achieve disarmament, and the constant imminence of new conflicts, the organization seems poorly devised for applying forceful collective measures. Its success in preventing war or repelling aggression depends upon the cooperation of the big powers, and until that is achieved the United Nations will continue to fall short of its major objective. Although sharp disagreements have marked all sessions, some consolation may be derived from the thought that differences were openly discussed and world opinion could make itself felt. It is far better for national spokesmen to argue, even in public, than for their nations to fight another war of devastation and exhaustion.

It is too soon to judge how the police action taken by the UN during 1950–1953 against North Korea and Red China will go down in history. UN action was possible only because at the time North Korea invaded below the 38th parallel the delegate of the Soviet Union was absent from the Security Council and hence unable to veto. Under United States leadership UN forces bolstered South Korean troops and eventually expelled the enemy. It was a costly and devastating operation for both sides; it severely strained the UN; and the end was a stalemate, not a clear military victory. Only future events can indicate whether the results obtained were worth the effort and sacrifice: if the police action serves to deter peacebreakers in the future, the UN may have landed a bargain; if other breaches of the peace occur again soon, the price may have been paid in vain.

Many proposals have been made to revise the Charter in order to strengthen the UN and make it a more effective instrument for maintaining the peace, particularly to modify or repeal the veto, which the Soviets have used frequently to block action. Article 109 of the Charter provides that two-thirds of the members of the General Assembly and seven members of the Security Council may call a general conference at any time to consider revisions of the Charter, but so far no such proposal has been presented. At the tenth-anniversary session of the General Assembly held at San Francisco in June, 1955, all the member states pledged their continued support of the UN, but none proposed a Charter-revision conference. It is generally believed that the strengthening of the Charter will have to be delayed until the East-West tensions have been eased, and any earlier attempt might result in weakening rather than strengthening the present organization.

Toward World Government? Strong criticism of the UN is voiced by two principal schools of thought in the United States. Some people, despite the great changes in the world that render their position less and less tenable, persist in isolationist leanings. A considerable number of people, without much knowledge of other countries and lacking clearly formulated views on these matters, are thrown into the isolationist-imperialist camp by their despair over the bad news of international rivalries that so often comes from UN sessions.

On the other extreme, sometimes equally lacking in faith in the UN, are the advocates of world federation or world government. The disagreement of this group with supporters of the UN is mainly over tactics, not policy. Many UN backers hope ultimately for its development into a stronger union, but they stress the necessity of taking one step at a time, as was done in early American history in the transition from Continental Congress to Articles of Confederation to Constitution.

The world federalist, however, argues that the way to start is to form a federation of those nations willing or fit to join, and to allow other nations to enter after they are converted. Critics question whether this approach would not leave Russia and her neighbors out and lead to a situation in which the world would be continuously divided into two armed camps, with war between them always a possibility. Federalists reply, however, that as a practical matter the world is now divided into two armed camps and it would be better for willing nations to federate than to depend upon their uncertain and loose-jointed devices for achieving united action. Moreover, federalists contend, for the rest of the world to federate would convince or force the Soviet bloc either to join or to cooperate.

Logical though this may appear to many, at the moment the mirage of world federal government—or even a federation of democracies, which ought to be nearer the realm of possibility—seems unlikely of realization. Most people are still devoted to their nation-states. They may be willing to cooperate in limited world government, but Americans will remember that it was only a short time ago that their government was unwilling to associate itself with the League of Nations.

The solution appears to be one of holding the gains embodied in a universal organization like the United Nations until enough people and statesmen are convinced that the nation-state system must be more drastically modified if the interests of civilization are to be served. Perhaps the San Francisco Charter is to the United Nations what the Articles of Confederation were to the United States, a device for preserving unity of diverse states until the necessity for more perfect union was clear to all.

FOR FURTHER READING

American Association for the United Nations: *Changing World* (monthly).

Bailey, Thomas A.: *The Man in the Street: The Impact of American Public Opinion on Foreign Policy* (Macmillan, 1948).

——: *A Diplomatic History of the American People* (Appleton-Century-Crofts, 3d ed., 1946).

Bemis, Samuel F.: *The Latin American Policy of the United States* (Harcourt, Brace, 1943).

Besterman, Theodore: *Unesco: Peace in the Minds of Men* (New York: Frederick A. Praeger, 1951).

Brinton, Crane: *From Many, One: The Process of Political Integration: The Problem of World Government* (Harvard University Press, 1948).

Brown, William A., and R. Opie: *American Foreign Assistance* (Brookings, 1953).

Brookings Institution: *Major Problems of United States Foreign Policy, 1954: A Study Guide* (Brookings, 1954). Similar volumes have been issued annually since 1947.

Chamberlain, Lawrence H., and Richard C. Snyder (eds.): *American Foreign Policy* (Rinehart, 1948).

Chase, Eugene P.: *The United Nations in Action* (McGraw-Hill, 1950).

Clark, Grenville: *A Plan for Peace* (Harper, 1950).

Cook, Thomas I., and M. C. Moos: *Power through Purpose* (Johns Hopkins Press, 1954).

Council on Foreign Relations: *The United States in World Affairs, 1950* (Harper, 1951). Similar volumes have been published for other years.

Culbertson, Ely: *Total Peace: What Makes Wars and How to Organize Peace* (Doubleday, 1943).

Dean, Vera Micheles: *Foreign Policy without Fear* (McGraw-Hill, 1953).

———: *The United States and Russia* (Harvard University Press, 1948).

Dulles, John F.: *War or Peace* (Macmillan, 1953).

Eichelberger, Clark M.: *UN: The First Ten Years* (Harper, 1955).

Feller, A. H.: *United Nations and World Community* (Little, Brown, 1952).

Fox, William T. R.: *The Super-powers: The United States, Britain and the Soviet Union— Their Responsibility for Peace* (Harcourt, Brace, 1944).

Goodrich, Leland M., and Edvard Hambro: *The Charter of the United Nations, Commentary and Documents* (Boston: World Peace Foundation, 1946).

Graham, Malbone W.: *American Diplomacy in the International Community* (Johns Hopkins Press, 1948).

Griswold, A. Whitney: *The Far Eastern Policy of the United States* (Harcourt, Brace, 1938).

Harley, J. Eugene: *Documentary Textbook on the United Nations* (Los Angeles: Center for International Understanding, 2d ed., 1950).

Haviland, H. Field: *The Political Role of the General Assembly,* United Nations Study No. 7 (Carnegie Endowment, 1951).

Hoskins, Halford L.: *The Atlantic Pact,* Public Affairs Bulletin 69 (Library of Congress, Legislative Reference Service, 1949).

Ismay, Lord: *NATO, The First Five Years, 1949–1954* (NATO, 1954).

Kennan, George F.: *American Diplomacy, 1900–1950* (University of Chicago Press, 1951).

Leonard, L. Larry: *International Organization* (McGraw-Hill, 1951).

Lie, Trygve H.: *In the Cause of Peace* (Macmillan, 1954).

Lissitzyn, Oliver J.: *The International Court of Justice* (Carnegie Endowment, 1951).

Maclaurin, John: *The United Nations and Power Politics* (Harper, 1951).

McCloy, John J.: *Challenge to American Foreign Policy* (Harvard University Press, 1953).

Numelin, Ragnar: *The Beginnings of Diplomacy: A Sociological Study of Intertribal and International Relations* (Philosophical Library, 1951).

Pan American Union: *Annals of the Organization of American States* (quarterly, commenced 1949).

Perkins, Dexter: *The Evolution of American Foreign Policy* (Oxford, 1948).

Ross, Alf: *Constitution of the United Nations: Analysis of Structure and Function* (Rinehart, 1950).

Randall, Clarence B.: *Foreign Economic Policy for the United States* (University of Chicago Press, 1954).

Schiffer, Walter: *Legal Community of Mankind* (Columbia University Press, 1954).

Schuman, Frederick L.: *International Politics* (McGraw-Hill, 5th ed., 1953).

——: *The Commonwealth of Man* (Knopf, 1952).

Sprout, Harold and Margaret: *Foundations of National Power* (Van Nostrand, 2d ed., 1951).

Streit, Clarence: *Union Now* (Washington: Federal Union, Inc., 1943).

Stuart, Graham H.: *Latin America and the United States* (Appleton-Century-Crofts, 3d ed., 1949).

United Nations: *United Nations Bulletin* (monthly).

——: *Yearbook* (annual).

United Nations Conference on International Organization: *Documents of the . . .* (New York: UN Information Organizations, 15 vols., 1945).

U.S. Department of State: *Papers Relating to the Foreign Relations of the United States* (1861–19—).

——: *Peace and War: United States Foreign Policy, 1931–1941* (1942).

U.S. Senate Committee on Foreign Relations: *A Decade of American Foreign Policy, Basic Documents, 1941–1949,* 81st Cong., 1st Sess., Sen. Doc. 123 (1950).

Van Alstyne, Richard W.: *American Crisis Diplomacy* (Stanford University Press, 1951).

Vandenbosch, Amry, and Willard N. Hogan: *The United Nations: Background, Organization, Functions, Activities* (McGraw-Hill, 1952).

Vinacke, Harold M.: *The United States and the Far East* (Stanford University Press, 1952).

Walters, F. P.: *A History of the League of Nations* (Oxford, 2 vols., 1951).

Whitaker, Arthur P.: *The Western Hemisphere Idea, Its Rise and Decline* (Cornell University Press, 1954).

Wright, Quincy (ed.): *A Foreign Policy for the United States* (University of Chicago Press, 1947).

——: *A Study of War* (University of Chicago Press, 2 vols., 1942).

REVIEW QUESTIONS

1. Compare what in this chapter is called "traditional" with "new" foreign policy.

2. How do you explain the shift in American foreign policy in recent times?

3. What provisions are common to the regional security arrangements which the United States has entered into in recent years?

4. Defend and criticize regional security arrangements entered into by the United States and the Soviet Union.

5. What basic principles underlie the United Nations?

6. Explain the organization and functions of the principal organs of the United Nations.

7. How is the United Nations supposed to proceed when a dispute arises which threatens the peace?

8. What have been some of the successes and shortcomings of the United Nations?

9. What are some of the proposals made for improving the organization, powers, and procedures of the United Nations?

10. What procedures are required for making changes in the United Nations Charter?

CHAPTER 23

American Territories

An ambition to win the mastery of the Pacific and control its rich commerce runs persistently through the entire history of the United States. It was a powerful motivating force in every acquisition of territory on the Pacific from Oregon and California to Hawaii and the Philippines. — Foster H. Dulles [1]

In 1790 the territory of the United States consisted of a comparatively small strip of land commencing with Maine on the north, ending with Georgia on the south, and extending beyond the Appalachians to poorly defined limits. By 1850 the southern boundary had been extended to the Florida Keys, the northwest to the 49th parallel, the west to the Pacific Ocean, and the southwest to the Rio Grande. The next three-quarters of a century witnessed the building of an overseas empire.

From a land area of 888,811 square miles in 1790 the United States had more than quadrupled its domain by 1940 to include a total of 3,735,209 square miles. It is a portentous fact, perhaps ominous so far as other nations are concerned, that during the same period no other nation successfully extended and maintained its sovereignty over an area of equal size. More recently, the fortunes of the Second World War left a legacy of additional territory and responsibility.

POWER TO ACQUIRE AND GOVERN

Authority to acquire territory from foreign states is implied from the war and treaty powers; authority to acquire unclaimed territory by discovery is inherent in the fact that the United States is a sovereign nation; while authority to acquire territory within existing territorial limits of the United States is both implied from the spending power and the two provisions noted below conferring power to govern territories. The Constitution assumes that where territory is acquired within the forty-eight states it will either be ceded by the states or purchased from the states or private parties.

Authority to Govern. Authority to govern territories is expressly conferred in two sections of the Constitution. The first says Congress shall have power

to exercise exclusive Legislation in all Cases whatso-ever, over such District (not exceeding ten miles square) as may, by Cession of particular States, and the Acceptance of Congress, become the Seat of the Government of the United States, and to exercise like Authority over all Places purchased by the Consent of the Legislature of the State in which the Same shall be, for the Erection of Forts, Magazines, Arsenals, dock-Yards, and other needful Buildings. . . .

The second provision, previously quoted, says that "Congress shall have power to dispose of

[1] *America in the Pacific: A Century of Expansion* (Houghton Mifflin, 1932), p. 1.

431

and make all needful rules and regulations respecting the Territory . . . belonging to the United States."

Scope of Federal Power. Congress has exclusive jurisdiction over territories outside the forty-eight states, as in Alaska, Hawaii, and Puerto Rico. The same is true for the District of

shall have power "to exercise like [*i.e.,* exclusive] authority over *all places purchased by the consent of the legislature of the state in which the same shall be,* for the erection of forts, magazines, arsenals, dock-yards, and other needful buildings. . . ." In other words, federal jurisdiction is exclusive only over places purchased

THE AMERICAN EMPIRE

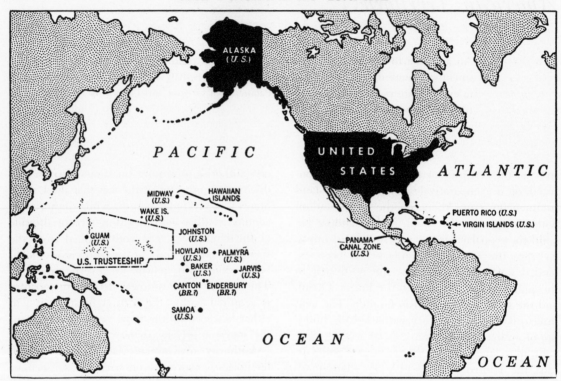

Columbia inasmuch as the state that formerly owned the area ceded it to the United States. But the extent of federal authority over places owned *within* the states is not so clear. The question is of considerable importance when one realizes that the Federal government owns hundreds of places such as prison camps, old soldiers' homes, army camps, shipyards, arsenals, post offices, and public lands. In every instance it becomes necessary to determine whether federal or state law applies.

The only thing said about the subject in the Constitution is contained in the provision, quoted in full above, which says that Congress

with the consent of the legislature of the state in which they are situated.

If purchase is made without state approval, as is often the case, state law continues to control, although, since the property is owned by the Federal government, it cannot be discriminated against or unreasonably burdened. The Federal government ordinarily requests state approval and the states grant it in some such language as this: "The United States, or such person or persons as may be by them authorized, shall have the right and authority to purchase the fee simple of a sufficient quantity of land in the city of Columbia on which to erect a post office and a court house; provided, that the said purchase does not exceed four acres." This would automatically convey exclusive jurisdiction over the four acres to the Federal government.

This arrangement has had some interesting results. The courts have held that one who committed robbery on a road through the West Point Military Reservation could not be convicted in a state court. On the other hand, many have been tried and convicted by the Federal government for crimes committed on federal land acquired with state consent. On another occasion the courts ruled that inmates of a federally owned asylum for disabled volunteer soldiers ceased to be citizens and residents of the state, hence ineligible to vote, because the state had consented to federal purchase. On still another occasion the courts held that a resident on a federal reservation, purchased with the consent of the state, was not a resident of the state, hence not entitled to sue for divorce in the state court even though the Federal government had made no provision for such cases. Other illustrations similar to these can easily be imagined.

Methods Used to Acquire Territory. Looking over the American territories and possessions, five methods of acquisition can be observed. A minor proportion was acquired by discovery and occupation. Another negligible proportion has been obtained by lease. A somewhat larger proportion was obtained by voluntary cession and annexation. A considerably larger amount was acquired by conquest or directly in consequence thereof. The largest proportion was acquired by purchase. How particular territories were acquired, together with other pertinent information, is shown on the chart given on page 436.

Types of Territories. When territory is acquired, sovereignty changes, with the result that the new sovereign must provide some method whereby its will is recognized and executed. Sometimes a territory is left "unorganized," again it is "organized." In the latter event a local legislature is created with considerable authority over matters of local concern.

A distinction is also made between an "unincorporated" and an "incorporated" territory. If Congress expressly declares that a territory is incorporated into the United States, or by a long series of acts clearly implies this intention, the territory becomes known as an "incorporated territory." Otherwise, it is known simply as an "unincorporated territory." This distinction is of considerable practical importance.

Distinctions between Incorporated and Unincorporated Territories. Over the years the following distinctions have emerged between a territory that is incorporated and one that is not. First, an incorporated territory is considered to be *a part of* the "United States" whereas others merely *belong to* the United States as a piece of property.[2]

To illustrate, this means that wherever the geographical domain of the United States is referred to in the Constitution or statutes, incorporated territories are included, but not others. Thus, when the Fourteenth Amendment says that "All persons born or naturalized *in the United States,* and subject to the jurisdiction thereof, are citizens of the United States and of the State wherein they reside," this makes persons born within incorporated territories citizens by birth, but not those born within unincorporated territories. Or again, when the Constitution says that all indirect taxes must be "uniform throughout *the United States,*" this means such taxes must be levied at the same rate within incorporated territories as within the forty-eight states; but federal taxes would not need to be uniform within unincorporated territories.

A second distinction is that all the guaranties of personal liberties contained in the Constitution—both "fundamental" and "formal"—follow the flag into incorporated territories,[3] but only guaranties of "fundamental" rights follow the flag into those that are unincorporated. While no complete list of fundamental and formal rights has ever been made, the former would include the right to life, liberty, and property,

[2] De Lima *v.* Bidwell, 182 U.S. 1 (1901); Downes *v.* Bidwell, 182 U.S. 244 (1901); Dorr *v.* United States, 195 U.S. 138 (1904).

[3] Hawaii *v.* Mankichi, 190 U.S. 197 (1903); Rassmussen *v.* United States, 197 U.S. 516 (1905); Balzac *v.* Puerto Rico, 258 U.S. 298 (1922).

while the latter refers only to procedural rights such as trial by jury, indictment by grand jury, and the right of counsel. Thus, the people of Hawaii and Alaska enjoy the same personal rights as persons within the forty-eight states, but those in an unincorporated territory like Puerto Rico cannot claim trial by jury, indictment by grand jury, etc., as rights guaranteed by the Constitution.

A third distinction is that incorporated territories are understood to be in a stage preparatory to statehood, whereas others are not. Speaking of this in 1953 a Senate committee said, "Under all American traditions and precedents, historic and legal, statehood has invaryingly been the destiny of all incorporated territories."[4] Though this is the understanding, Congress is the sole judge as to when the territory should be admitted as a state.

Territorial Governments Subordinate to the National Government. Congress has complete dominion over every aspect of territorial affairs. This means that it may legislate not only concerning external affairs of the territory but also concerning every subject upon which the legislature of one of the forty-eight states might legislate. Thus, Congress possesses not only all its delegated powers, but also reserved powers for use within territories whenever it thinks necessary. To state it otherwise, the relationship between the government at Washington and its territories is like that within a unitary state rather than a federal state.

Though Congress may legislate directly with respect to such local matters as schools, roads, garbage collection, sewage disposal, and water supply, it usually transfers its responsibility to a territorial government. After doing so, the territorial government, like cities within a state, has only such powers as are granted to it. Congress may authorize the President to oversee administration within the territories or veto Colonial legislation; Congress itself may amend or abrogate the acts of Colonial legislatures; and the United States courts may declare void

[4] U.S. Senate Committee on Insular Affairs, S. Rept. 1271, 83d Cong., 2d Sess., to accompany S. Rept. 3378 (1953).

any action of a territorial government that is not in harmony with acts of Congress or the Constitution.

Administrative Supervision of Territories. For years administrative responsibility for American territories has been divided among three departments—War, Navy, and Interior. This is still the case, but to a lesser extent than previously. As a consequence of executive orders beginning in 1934, the Army has been divested of all except the Panama Canal Zone and the Navy of all islands with native populations. As a result, the Office of Territories in the Department of Interior is the principal administrative unit. Transfer to a civilian agency, many hoped, would lead to greater democracy within the territories and more solicitude on the part of the American people for the welfare of the natives.

Besides the departments mentioned, there are others directly or indirectly interested in territorial problems. In Alaska alone there were fifty-two different federal agencies at work in 1939. The Soil Conservation Service, Post Office Department, Rural Electrification Administration, Census Bureau, Civil Aeronautics Authority, FBI, Immigration and Naturalization Service, Housing Agency, Social Security Administration, Army, and Navy were only a few of the agencies. For the most part today, each goes its own way, as in the forty-eight states, without clearing through either any central agency in Washington or the governor's office in the territories. This has led to considerable criticism, particularly on the part of some of the territorial governments. A partial solution has been found in Puerto Rico and the Virgin Islands, where all federal agencies at work in the islands, except the District Court and Department of Justice, are required to make reports to the Secretary of the Interior. The latter is authorized to recommend measures designed to eliminate unessential and overlapping services.

The first Hoover Commission studied and criticized management of territorial affairs. Its only recommendation, however, was that Congress should undertake a comprehensive study of the problem. One alternative suggested was to take all territorial and occupational duties from the armed forces and assign them to a special secretary who would report directly to the Secretary of Defense. Another alternative, and one looked upon by the Commission with more favor, was to create a separate Administration of Overseas Affairs and give it jurisdiction over all territorial and occupational activities abroad except State Department diplomatic and consular services. The assignment to Interior of supervisory responsibility over all populated American territories but the Canal Zone is a step in the direction indicated, but it falls far short of the goal sketched by some members of the Hoover Commission.

Democratic Trends. American acquisition and control of territories and their peoples has always been seriously criticized at home as well as abroad. To many critics it appears contradictory for a democracy to hold and control subject people. While American policy has been paternalistic and usually humane, it has been slow to encourage self-government and self-determination. Recent years have witnessed some shift in policy. Independence for the Philippines was the most dramatic step, even though it be conceded that American motives were not entirely altruistic. More recently, Hawaii and Alaska have been encouraged by high official sources to expect statehood; the District of Columbia has moved closer to self-rule; Puerto Ricans were permitted to choose their governor and later commonwealth status; the Virgin Islands were given a new organic act with provisions for more democratic and efficient government; naval governors have been displaced by civilian ones in the Pacific islands; supervisory authority has been shifted from military departments to Interior; citizenship has been granted to most people in the territories; territories have been encouraged to study their needs and express their desires; studies have been made seeking ways of more clearly delimiting federal and local authority; and attempts have been made to achieve more efficient administration. Meanwhile, large-scale public-welfare and public-works programs have been authorized and aided in most of the territories. Moreover, the United Nations has given non-self-governing people everywhere a medium through which world opinion can be brought to bear upon their status and problems.

ALASKA AND HAWAII

Alaska. Separated from the state of Washington by a 400-mile corridor belonging to Canada, Alaska was the first noncontiguous territory added to the American empire. Its vast sprawling territory encompasses 586,400 square miles —an area more than twice as large as Texas, thirteen times as large as Pennsylvania, and three and one-half times as large as California.

Shortly after its purchase from Russia in 1867, Alaska was made an incorporated territory, but it remained unorganized until 1884. Since it is incorporated, both fundamental and formal rights are protected by the Constitution. At the same time, all general laws of Congress apply unless they specifically state otherwise. The residents have no vote in presidential elections, while their only Representative in Congress is a delegate elected every 2 years, who has a seat without vote in the House of Representatives.

The treaty with Russia provided that those inhabitants who wished to retain their allegiance to Russia should depart within 3 years. All others, except "uncivilized" native tribes, were collectively naturalized, while their children subsequently born within the territory became citizens by birth. Members of the "uncivilized" tribes are considered wards of the Federal government, although they were collectively naturalized in 1924 along with tribal Indians in the states. Accordingly, nearly everyone now born within the territory is an American citizen.

Hawaii. Twenty-four hundred miles south and west from San Francisco lie the Hawaiian Islands, "Uncle Sam's capital of the American Pacific." Though twenty in number, there are eight principal islands. Beginning with Hawaii at the southeastern end of the series, these extend 390 miles in a northwesterly direction in the following order: Hawaii, Kahoolawe, Maui, Lanai, Molokai, Oahu, Kauai, and Niihau. The total area, including the small outlying islands, is about twice the combined size of Delaware and Rhode Island.

Before annexation in 1898, Hawaii was an independent republic with a long tradition of monarchical rule. Like Alaska, it is now an incorporated territory, becoming so by the Organic Act of 1900. Though citizens, the people have no vote in presidential elections, and their only Representative in Congress is a delegate chosen by the voters every 2 years who has a nonvoting seat in the House of Representatives. General laws of Congress apply to the territory unless exception is expressly made. Residents enjoy the guaranties of both fundamental and formal rights contained in the Constitution.

The act of 1900 collectively naturalized all within the territory who previously owed allegiance to the Hawaiian government. Since then, those born within the territory have become American citizens by birth. Many aliens in the territory at the time of annexation and many immigrants who have since arrived have become naturalized, but because American laws have barred Chinese, Japanese, Filipinos, and other Orientals from becoming American citizens, a substantial number remain aliens.

In addition to the many aliens, there are a considerable number who possess dual nationality. This arises from the fact that children born there are citizens by the rule of *jus soli* and yet because of the former allegiance of their parents they are also considered citizens by another state that follows the rule of *jus sanguinis*. Though the vast majority of the children are undoubtedly loyal Americans, their dual citizenship has tended to make them suspect. This is especially true of many Japanese who have never taken steps permitted by Japanese law to expatriate themselves and in consequence owe allegiance to both the United States and Japan. The situation could and should be remedied by treaty, as it has been with a number of other countries, as soon as circumstances permit.

Governments. Alaska and Hawaii have governments that are similar, except that the latter has been given greater autonomy. Both have for chief executives governors appointed by the President with the consent of the Senate for 4-year terms. Hawaii has been the only American

Principal American Territories	Territory	Date acquired	Status before acquisition	How acquired
	District of Columbia	1790	Part of Maryland	Donated by Maryland
	Alaska	1867	Possession of Russia	Purchase by treaty
	Hawaii	1898	Independent republic	Mutual agreement
	Puerto Rico	1898	Spanish colony	War and treaty with Spain
	Guam	1898	Spanish colony	War and treaty with Spain
	Panama Canal Zone	1904	Territory of Panama	Perpetual lease and annual payment
	Samoan Islands	1904	Independent	Treaty with native chiefs
	Virgin Islands	1917	Danish colony	Purchase by treaty
	Trust territory of the Pacific islands	1947	Japanese mandates	War

territory where the governor is chosen from among local residents, but the custom was instituted for Puerto Rico in 1946 for the first time. Except for a secretary who is appointed by the President to assist with administration, other executive and administrative officers are appointed by the governors.

The legislatures of both territories are bicameral and elected by the voters. They resemble American state legislatures both in organization and by the way they proceed. With a few exceptions, the legislatures have authority to deal with all matters of local concern. Their enactments must be sent to Washington where Congress may disapprove them, but this rarely happens.

The judicial systems of the two territories are somewhat different. In Alaska there are no local territorial courts. Instead, a United States district court is divided into four divisions to enforce and interpret both federal and territorial laws. Judges are appointed by the President to serve for terms of good behavior. Summary cases are handled by United States commissioners ap-

pointed by the judge of each judicial district. The commissioners are at once justice of peace, probate judge, coroner, town clerk, recorder, jailer, and guardian of minors and the insane. Their formal education may be sketchy and they may know little law. Indeed, it is reported that commissioners have been known to issue a divorce decree by the simple expedient of tearing up the marriage license and refunding the fee.[5]

In Hawaii there is a dual system of courts: Federal and territorial. The Federal consists of a district court, manned by judges who are appointed by the President from among citizens and residents of Hawaii for terms of 6 years. Territorial courts consist of a supreme court, five circuit courts which resemble county courts in the states, and district courts corresponding to those of justices of peace. Territorial courts have jurisdiction over all nonfederal cases arising within the territory. Decisions of the terri-

[5] Merle E. Colby, *A Guide to Alaska, Last American Frontier,* American Guide Series (Macmillan, 1939), p. 54.

Incorporated or unincorporated	Citizenship of natives	Legislature	Executive
Incorporated	U.S. citizens	U.S. Congress	3 commissioners appointed by President for 3-year terms
Incorporated	U.S. citizens	Senate elected for 4-year terms House elected for 2-year terms	Governor appointed by U.S. President for 4-year term
Incorporated	U.S. citizens	Senate elected for 4-year terms House elected for 2-year terms	Governor appointed by U.S. President for 4-year term
Unincorporated	U.S. citizens by collective naturalization, 1917	Senate elected for 4-year terms House elected for 4-year terms	Governor elected by voters for 4-year term
Unincorporated	U.S. citizens by collective naturalization, 1950	Unicameral legislature elected for 2-year terms	Governor appointed by U.S. President for 4-year term
Unincorporated	Not U.S. citizens	None	Governor appointed by U.S. President for 4-year term
Unincorporated	Not U.S. citizens	None	Governor appointed by U.S. President for 4-year term
Unincorporated	U.S. citizens by collective naturalization, 1927	Unicameral legislature elected for 2-year terms	Governor appointed by U.S. President for an indefinite term
Unincorporated	Not U.S. citizens	None	High Commissioner appointed by U.S. President for indefinite term

torial supreme court are final but may be reviewed by the United States Supreme Court when the matter concerns an act of Congress or provisions of the Constitution. Decisions of the Federal district court in both Alaska and Hawaii may be appealed to the Ninth Circuit Court of Appeals with headquarters in San Francisco.

Local governments exist in both territories. In Alaska there are a few incorporated towns and a large number of unincorporated towns and villages. There are no counties. Local governments in Hawaii consist of five counties, two cities (Honolulu and Hilo), and a number of unincorporated towns and villages.

Campaigns for Statehood. Agitation for admission to statehood has been incessant in Hawaii and Alaska. Plebiscites and hearings have amply demonstrated that the people of these territories want statehood. It is argued that historically territories have been admitted after a period of tutelage; that as American citizens they are entitled to equal rights and participation in government; that continued territorial status is contrary to the ideal of democracy over which Americans have been so effusive; that they are discriminated against by acts of Congress, particularly those appropriating funds for public improvements; that they are controlled by a Congress in which they have no vote, by a President whom they may not help elect, and by a Constitution that they may not help to amend; that they pay the same federal taxes as do citizens on the mainland; that their sons are conscripted; and that they are qualified by character, education, and experience to assume the full obligations that would arise from statehood.

The chief objections of those who voice opinions are that the process of Americanization has not gone far enough, especially in Hawaii where there are many of oriental ancestry, and that it is unfair to give newly admitted territories equality of voting power in the Senate with existing large states; in times past, the Army and Navy have objected because they thought statehood would subject their handling of bases and installations to more civilian controls.

Statehood for both territories has been strongly urged by recent Presidents, Secretaries of In-

terior, Republican and Democratic party platforms, and the Annual Conference of State Governors. Bills to admit both territories have been pushed vigorously in recent Congresses, were passed by the House early in 1950, but were blocked by the Senate. Two new factors have helped prevent favorable action: one is fear on the part of Southern Senators that statehood would increase the voting strength of those favoring the enactment of federal civil-rights legislation; the second is a partisan split which leads Republicans to favor statehood for Hawaii but not for Alaska while the Democrats prefer just the opposite.

PUERTO RICO AND THE VIRGIN ISLANDS

Puerto Rico. Puerto Rico, where Columbus first set foot in the New World, lies in almost a direct line southeast from Florida through Cuba, then Haiti, and then Santo Domingo. Situated between the Greater and Lesser Antilles, the island guards the approaches to central and northern South America—hence its name "Key to the Caribbean." The island itself is 95 miles long from east to west and 35 miles wide. Its land area, including adjacent islands, is 3,435 square miles; its population is about 2,211,000.

Acquired from Spain in 1898, Puerto Rico became an organized territory by the Foraker Act of 1900. Later, in 1917, on the eve of the entry of America into the First World War, in what looked like a bid for greater loyalty, the Jones Act reorganized the government of the island, giving it greater autonomy. The same measure made Puerto Ricans citizens of the United States. From this it was contended that the territory had been incorporated, but the Supreme Court held otherwise.[6]

Toward Greater Independence. In response to continuing demands for greater home rule, the government of Puerto Rico has been in transition for the past several years. Until recently its government was much like those of Alaska and Hawaii. In 1946 the President appointed the first native governor; a year later Congress

---

[6] Balzac *v.* Puerto Rico, 258 U.S. 298 (1922).

passed legislation permitting the voters to elect their chief executive with the understanding that he would appoint heads of executive departments while the President would retain authority to appoint members of the supreme court and the auditor. In 1950 Congress passed the Puerto Rican Federal Relations Act which authorized the people of the island to formulate their own constitution. A constitution was drafted and the voters, by overwhelming majority, approved the document. The President and Congress approved shortly thereafter, and the "Commonwealth of Puerto Rico" was proclaimed on July 25, 1952.

Commonwealth Status. The precise meaning of the term "Commonwealth" as applied to Puerto Rico is unclear; [7] but it is certain that something unique and new has been added to American constitutional experience. The people of the island are declared to be politically sovereign; they formed and adopted their own constitution; their laws no longer are subject to congressional approval; and they may add amendments to their constitution without congressional approval.

Nevertheless, they are neither fully independent nor a state of the American Union; certain limits are implied by the Federal Relations Act, and the debates which occurred in Congress at the time the constitution was approved; general laws of the United States are applicable in the island; and the people remain United States citizens. All this suggests a station halfway between complete independence and the previous territorial arrangement.

In 1953 the United States was excused by the United Nations from making annual reports for its "non-self-governing territory" on the plea that Puerto Rico was now fully self-governing.

In defending this position the American delegate made the remarkable statement that he was authorized to state on behalf of the President of the United States that if, at any time, the legislative assembly of Puerto Rico adopts a resolution in favor of more complete or even absolute independence, he would immediately recommend to the Congress that such independence be granted.[8] While this is not a promise of independence by the American government, it suggests a readiness to keep step with other Western colonial powers in showing greater solicitude for the interests and political aspirations of dependent peoples.

Commonwealth Government. The new constitution of Puerto Rico resembles American state constitutions. The governor is elected every four years. The bicameral legislature consists of a twenty-seven-member senate and a fifty-one-member house of representatives. Eleven members of each house are chosen at large, the remainder by districts. The constitution includes a curious feature for guaranteeing minimum representation to minority parties. The judiciary consists of a five-member supreme court and inferior courts to be established by the legislature. As a guaranty of judicial independence, members of the supreme court are appointed for life (or good behavior), the court cannot be enlarged except at its own request, and the chief justice is made the administrator of the entire judiciary.

A bill of rights adds some interesting features: wiretapping is expressly forbidden, the death penalty shall not exist, the military shall always be subordinate to civil authority, and the employment of children under fourteen is forbidden in occupations prejudicial to health. Still more exceptional was the inclusion in the draft constitution submitted to the United States Senate of certain "human rights" inspired, apparently, by the United Nations Declaration of Human Rights.

These provided that everyone was entitled to a free public education, a job, a standard of living adequate for the health and well-being of

---

[7] The subject is fully explored in "Puerto Rico: A Study in Democratic Development," *The Annals of the American Academy of Political and Social Science,* vol. 285 (January, 1953). See also Gordon K. Lewis, "Puerto Rico: A New Constitution in American Government," *The Journal of Politics,* vol. 15 (February, 1953), p. 42; and Henry Wells, "Ideology and Leadership in Puerto Rican Politics," *The American Political Science Review,* vol. 49 (March, 1955), p. 1.

[8] *Yearbook of the United Nations* (1953), p. 538.

himself and his family, social protection in the event of unemployment, sickness, old age, or disability. Strong objections were raised in the American Congress to these provisions on the ground that they were legally unenforceable, socialistic, and communistic, with the result that they were finally omitted.

Puerto Rico is represented in Washington by a resident commissioner elected by the voters every 4 years. He is accredited to the executive branch and has a nonvoting seat in the House of Representatives.

The Virgin Islands. These scenic islands lie 40 miles east of Puerto Rico and 1,400 miles southeast of New York. They consist of fifty islands and cays, only three of which are inhabited or of any considerable size. Nearest to Puerto Rico is Saint Thomas, 14 miles long and 2 miles wide. Three miles to the east lies another island of about the same size called Saint John. Forty miles southward lies Saint Croix, largest of the three. The total area of these three is only 140 square miles, Saint Croix having nearly two-thirds of it all. Total population is about 27,000. Although of little economic importance, the islands have much of historic and scientific interest, while their strategic location and the excellent harbor at Charlotte Amalie (Saint Thomas) makes them of prime value to any power wishing to control the Caribbean and the approaches to North and South America.

The islands have been an organized territory since shortly after their purchase from Denmark in 1917. Legislation enacted in 1927 made all natives citizens who lived in the islands on Jan. 17, 1917, while an act of June 28, 1932, extended citizenship to all inhabitants regardless of their place of residence in 1917.

Government Old Style. By the Organic Act of 1936 two municipalities were created: one for Saint Croix and the other for Saint Thomas and Saint John. These were not municipalities in the American sense but, rather, miniature states, almost completely independent of each other for purposes of local government and yet tied together for the purpose of handling matters of mutual concern.

Each municipality had a single-house legisla-

ture called a "municipal council," which was elected by the voters. Sitting separately, the councils dealt with local matters within their respective jurisdictions, but once a year or oftener at the call of the governor, the two met jointly in Saint Thomas to constitute the "Legislative Assembly of the Virgin Islands." The governor was appointed by the President, with Senate consent, and both Federal and territorial courts were in operation.

Government New Style. Dissatisfaction with existing arrangements led to a plebiscite in April, 1953, on the following questions and with the results indicated:

	Yes	No
1. Do you favor the creation of a single legislature for the Virgin Islands?	1,190	543
2. Do you favor the creation of a single treasury for the Virgin Islands?	1,142	578
3. Do you favor the election of the governor by the people of the Virgin Islands?	966	767
4. Do you favor a resident commissioner for the Virgin Islands in the Congress of the United States?	1,392	370

With this mandate before it Congress revised the Organic Act in 1954.

Under the new arrangement the two separate municipalities were abolished and their functions transferred to the central government. The territorial legislature became an eleven-member unicameral body of senators with authority to meet annually in the capital city of Charlotte Amalie, Saint Thomas. Legislative terms are for two years. Six senators are chosen at large, while the remaining five are chosen by districts.

The governor continues to be appointed by the President, with Senate approval, but he was given greater authority over appointments, administration, and legislation. His term remains the same: at the pleasure of the President or until a successor is appointed and qualified. The President also appoints a government secretary and an attorney general, while the Secretary of the Interior appoints a comptroller and holds him responsible for making audits and reports on financial matters. The judicial power is vested in a district court, with jurisdiction similar to that of its counterpart on the continent, and inferior courts established by the local legislature.

In spite of the preference shown by the electorate in the plebiscite, Congress refused to authorize a resident commissioner with nonvoting status in the House of Representatives. Smallness of the population was the principal reason given for this denial.

SAMOA AND GUAM

American Samoa. Samoa lies south of the equator, 4,160 miles south of San Francisco and 2,263 miles beyond Hawaii. The Samoan archipelago stretches almost directly east and west and comprises innumerable islands, most of which are very small and uninhabited. The two largest, Savai'i and Upolu, together with a few smaller islands are known as Western Samoa. These belonged to Germany until seized by New Zealand during the First World War and afterward made a mandate under supervision of New Zealand. Eastern, or American, Samoa is made up of the island of Tutuila, a small outlier called Aunuu, and a group of three small islands known collectively as Manua, Rose, and Swains. Altogether, the American islands comprise only 76 square miles. The chief interest of the United States in the islands is its naval base at the Tutuilian harbor of Pago Pago, one of the finest in the South Seas.

Germany, England, and the United States each had claims upon the islands until 1899 when a tripartite arrangement left Eastern Samoa to the Americans. A year later the native chiefs ceded Tutuila and Aunuu to the United States and 4 years later ceded the Manuan and Rose Islands. In 1925 Swains, which had long belonged to American citizens, was annexed. Though an executive order promptly placed the newly acquired islands under command of the Navy, Congress steadfastly refused to accept the islands formally until 1929. The islands must now be classified as an unorganized and unincorporated territory.

Guam. Guam is the largest and southernmost of the Marianas Islands. It lies 4,000 miles west of Hawaii and only 1,300 miles directly south of Japan among fourteen other tiny islands to which the Japanese fell heir for their participation in the First World War. The island is 30 miles long by 4 to 8½ miles wide, comprising a total of 225 square miles.

Guam was a trophy of the war with Spain. Immediately after its cession to the United States, the whole island was declared a naval station and such it has remained except for the brief interlude when conquered and occupied by the Japanese. Guam may now be classified as an organized but unincorporated territory. Most of its people were made citizens of the United States by act of Congress in 1950.

Governments. Until recently, both Samoa and Guam were ruled by naval officers about as they governed battleships. The commandant had absolute power, subject to the rules and regulations of the Navy Department and the acts of Congress. Natives often held minor posts, and in Guam a locally elected legislature had been permitted for the purpose of advising the commandant. Long, and sometimes violent, agitation followed by numerous congressional inquiries was the result. This, plus the growing awareness of security risks inherent in malcontented islanders and the fact that non-self-governing peoples had a vehicle in the Trusteeship Council of the United Nations for focusing world opinion upon their grievances, led to change.

In 1950 Guam was organized with a civilian or retired naval officer for governor appointed by the President with the consent of the Senate, a unicameral legislature of not more than twenty-one members, a Federal district court, and minor local courts. The new organic act contains a bill of rights, and the civilian regime has undertaken programs designed to improve the welfare and living standards of the Guamanians.

Samoa remains unorganized, but in 1951 its first civilian governor was appointed and the Department of Interior displaced Navy. Pending organization along lines followed in Guam, the new governor has been instructed to employ more natives in the civil service and otherwise prepare the islanders for the greater home rule many of them want.

THE PANAMA CANAL ZONE

The Panama Canal Zone is a strip of territory leased in perpetuity from the Republic of Panama in 1904. For it the United States agreed to pay an original sum of 10 million dollars and an annual rental of 250 thousand dollars (after 1936, $430,000). The Zone extends 5 miles on each side of the historic canal and includes certain other territory, including islands in the Bay of Panama on the Pacific side. All economic activity centers around the canal, defense establishments, and auxiliary services.

Every resident in the Zone must be an employee of one of the government agencies. Virtually all the inhabitants are white officials and their families from the States, Negroes, or those who are part Negro from the Caribbean region. The population is concentrated at both ends of the canal; however, more (roughly three-fifths) live in the Balboa district nearest the Pacific Ocean than in the Cristobal district nearest the Caribbean.

The Canal Zone is a government reservation. When thought of as a territory it must be classed as one that is unorganized and unincorporated. People born there are nationals but not citizens by the rule of *jus soli*. However, if born of American parents who have previously lived in the United States the requisite period of time, children are citizens. Residents vote for no officer of the United States, unless they do so by mail or return home, and no delegate is sent to Washington.

Government. Prior to 1951, two government-owned corporations—the Panama Railroad Company and the Panama Canal—managed affairs in the Canal Zone. The former had its own board of directors and was subject to only indirect control from Washington. The Panama Canal was the responsibility of the President, who operated through the Secretary of Army and the governor of the Zone. In addition to running the canal and many auxiliary enterprises, the Panama Canal also provided civil government for the region. The first Hoover Commission had much to say about these relationships, and the President followed its advice in many respects in 1950.

As things stand since the change, the two corporations have been merged into the Panama Canal Company. In addition, the Canal Zone government was created. The Company, of which the United States is the sole stockholder, manages the historic canal, the railroad that parallels it, and the multifarious business enterprises in the Zone. Canal Zone government is separate, except for the fact that the governor is also a director and president of the board of the Company. It is headed by a civil governor appointed by the President with Senate approval for a term of 4 years. There is no local legislature.

The principal court in the Canal Zone is a United States district court divided into two divisions: one for the Balboa district, the other for the Cristobal district. One judge, appointed by the President for a term of 8 years, heads the court and serves both divisions. Minor civil and criminal cases are handled by magistrate courts existing in each town and whose officers are appointed by the governor. Appeals may be taken from the district court to the Fifth Circuit Court of Appeals with headquarters at New Orleans, thence to the Supreme Court.

Local subdivisions, called towns, and rural divisions have been created for administrative purposes. They differ from those usually found in the United States in that they have no local legislature nor executive but only administrators and judicial officers appointed by the governor to perform under supervision of one of the central administrative departments.

GUANO ISLANDS

Before Chile became a large-scale producer of nitrates, the small islands in the Pacific Ocean were important sources of guano, the accumulated excrement of sea birds. Being of considerable commercial value, shipping companies of various countries engaged in extensive explorations for possession of guano islands around 1841. Their activities led the United States to enact the

Guano Island Act of 1856, which provided that whenever an American citizen discovered and occupied an island with guano deposits that did not belong to another country, the President might consider the island as belonging to the United States. The discoverer, meantime, was to be allowed the exclusive right to exploit the guano deposits under the protection of American naval vessels. By authority of this legislation, the United States now lays claim to a number of Pacific islands, but in several instances its claims are disputed by other powers, especially Great Britain and Colombia.

Though title to some of the islands remains in doubt, the United States has fairly clear title to seven—Midway, Wake, Kingman Reef, Johnston, Howland, Baker, and Jarvis. A *status quo* arrangement was entered into in 1928 with Colombia respecting several tiny atolls useful as lighthouse stations, while an agreement was entered into with Great Britain in 1937 whereby both parties agreed to joint use of Canton and Enderbury, leaving the determination of sovereignty until a future date.

Four of the islands just mentioned—Midway, Wake, Kingman Reef, and Johnston—are naval reservations governed by the Navy. These are all uninhabited except for naval personnel who are stationed ashore. The others—Jarvis, Baker, Howland, Canton, and Enderbury—are under the jurisdiction of the Division of Territories and Island Possessions in the Department of the Interior. Actual contact is made by a field representative, located in Honolulu. Though normally uninhabited, groups of four Hawaiians were settled on Jarvis, Baker, and Howland in 1935, while a number of officers and employees of the national government and transpacific air transportation companies are now stationed on Canton and Enderbury. Justice for those not under the Navy is administered by the United States district court in Hawaii, all trials taking place in Honolulu.

TRUST TERRITORY OF THE PACIFIC ISLANDS

The mandate system established by the League of Nations ended when the United Nations came into being in 1945. At the close of the First World War the United States refused to accept responsibility for mandated territory, but a quarter of a century later sentiment had changed. The Marshall, Caroline, and Marianas Islands had been mandated to Japan as a reward

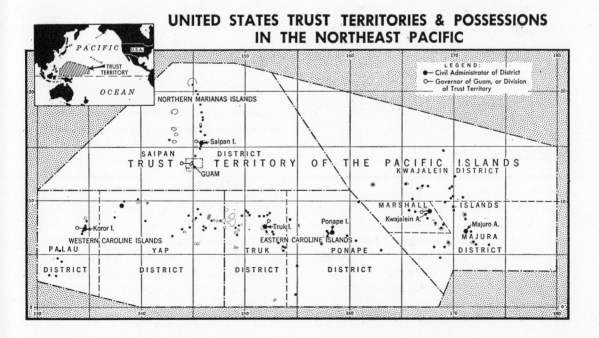

UNITED STATES TRUST TERRITORIES & POSSESSIONS IN THE NORTHEAST PACIFIC

for her contribution during the First World War. Wresting them from the Japanese in the recent conflict proved to be a costly and bloody ordeal. Having done so the United States had the option of annexing and governing the islands as ordinary territories or of accepting trusteeship under the United Nations. Decision did not need to await a peace treaty with Japan, because technically ownership lay with the League of Nations and its successor. The strategic value of the islands could not be gainsaid. A battle royal developed between those in the defense departments who wanted to retain exclusive jurisdiction and those in the Department of State and elsewhere who thought the United States should abstain from what appeared to be territorial aggrandizement. The fact that trust territories might be either strategic or nonstrategic provided a solution. By November, 1946, the decision was reached in favor of strategic trusteeship, and this arrangement was subsequently approved by the United Nations.

The territory includes ninety-eight islands and atolls, with a total land mass of 687 square miles and a total population of 55,000 native inhabitants. Under the present arrangement the islands are referred to as "trust territory" with the United States designated administering authority. Congress legislates for the islands; the Department of the Interior governs through a High Commissioner in collaboration with native leaders and institutions. Reports must be made to the United Nations; visits, petitions, and questionnaires must be permitted. The United States pledges itself to use the islands to further international peace and security. It also agrees to promote the welfare of the people. It obliges itself to

promote the development of the inhabitants of the trust territory toward self-government, or independence as may be appropriate to the particular circumstances of the trust territory and its peoples and the freely expressed wishes of the people concerned.[9]

[9] Trusteeship Agreement for the Japanese Mandated Islands, Art. 6.

The islands may be fortified. Basic freedoms are guaranteed "subject only to the requirements of public order and security." Citizenship status may be decided by Congress. Members of the United Nations must not be discriminated against. Changes in the trust agreement cannot be "altered, amended or terminated without the consent of the administering authority."[10]

THE DISTRICT OF COLUMBIA

The national capital remained in New York until 1790, except for a brief sojourn in Trenton to escape an epidemic of scarlet fever. Philadelphia would doubtless have been chosen the permanent capital had the Southern planters found the Quakers' views on slavery congenial. Instead, the Residence Bill, enacted in 1790 after an historic compromise in which the North agreed to a southerly location and the South to federal assumption of state debts, provided that Philadelphia should become the temporary capital while search was made for a suitable plot "10 miles square" somewhere on the banks of the Potomac. Accordingly, Philadelphia became the seat of government until 1800, then Washington.

The District of Columbia and the City of Washington. An area "10 miles square" was ceded by Maryland and Virginia for the establishment of the national capital. The latter's cession was retroceded in 1846. In view of the congestion that now exists in Washington and environs, it is interesting to read from the act of retrocession which says:

Whereas no more territory ought to be held under the exclusive legislation given to Congress over the District which is the seat of the General Government than may be necessary and proper for the purposes of such a seat; and whereas experience hath shown that the portion of the District of Columbia ceded to the United States by the State of Virginia has not been, nor is ever likely to be, necessary for that purpose . . . Therefore,

Be it enacted . . . That . . . all that portion of the District of Columbia, ceded to the United

[10] *Ibid.*, Art. 15.

States by the State of Virginia be ceded . . . and forever relinquished to the State of Virginia.[11]

In consequence of this act, the District now consists of the 70 square miles ceded by Maryland. The District is a corporate entity somewhat analogous to a county, while within the same territory a municipal corporation known as the City of Washington exists. Hence the name: Washington, District of Columbia. Though the two exist in coterminous boundaries, they are controlled by a single government.

Government of the District. In view of the constitutional provision which says that *Congress* shall have power to exercise exclusive legislation over the District, Congress is the lawmaking body for the area. A committee has been established by the House and another by the Senate for the purpose of studying District problems and recommending legislation. Laws enacted for the District are administered by a three-member Board of Commissioners, two of whom are civilians appointed by the President by and with the advice and consent of the Senate. The third is an officer of the Corps of Engineers of the Army detailed by the President for an indefinite term, lasting usually about four years. The two civilians must be residents of the District; their term is for 3 years, or until replaced. Until recently there existed an astonishing number of boards, commissions, and offices, many of which were almost completely autonomous. In May, 1952, President Truman pointed to no less than eighty and observed this to be one-third more than all the Departments and agencies in the huge executive branch of the Federal government! Because this condition made the Board of Commissioners incapable of providing responsible and efficient government, President Truman issued, and Congress allowed to become effective, reorganization plan 5 for 1952, giving the commissioners authority to streamline District government.

The judiciary, as was noted in Chap. 16, consists of a Court of Appeals, a district

[11] *District of Columbia Code* (1940 ed.), vol. I, p. XLVI.

court, a municipal court of appeals, and a municipal court. Judges are all appointed by the President by and with the advice and consent of the Senate. District government is financed in part by an annual lump-sum appropriation made by Congress, and in part from taxes levied by Congress, usually upon the recommendation of the Board of Commissioners.

Disfranchisement of the Residents of the District. Until 1871 the District was governed by a mayor and legislative council chosen by the people, and between the year mentioned and 1874 the District was represented in the House of Representatives by a delegate chosen by the voters. In spite of having the appearance of being democratic, the locally elected officials were without effective power because of the constitutional provision which says that Congress shall have power to exercise exclusive legislation over the District. After considerable experimentation, the present form of government was created in 1874, whereby residents of the District elect none of the officials who run the government under which they live.

Neither are residents of the District permitted to vote for presidential and vice-presidential electors, or members of Congress. This is because the Constitution requires that "states" appoint electors, that Representatives be apportioned among the "states" on the basis of population, and that "states" shall be represented in the Senate. Since the District is not a state, it could obtain representation only by the adoption of a constitutional amendment. A Citizens' Joint Committee on National Representation for the District of Columbia, with affiliated organizations throughout the United States, has worked strenuously to arouse sentiment in favor of a constitutional amendment, but outside a few circles, the American public has shown little interest in the matter.

Meanwhile, residents of the District have worked strenuously for at least the right to choose local officials. This requires no constitutional amendment but merely an act of Congress. Not only does this request appear reasonable, fair, and consistent with democratic theory and practice, but it would also help to relieve a sorely pressed and overburdened Congress. The La Follette–Monroney report of 1946 on the reorganization of Congress proposed self-government as a means of lightening the burden on Congress, but the suggestion was omitted in the act which finally passed. Since then the issue has been before Congress constantly. An important factor blocking success is fear on the part of race-conscious citizens and congressmen that a new democratic arrangement would bring changes in the segregation pattern that has prevailed in the District.

Though residents have no vote in the District, a large percentage are able to maintain voting residences in their home states, and both major political parties have influential local organizations in the District which send delegates to the national party conventions. In addition, it should be said that local residents are capable of obtaining a measure of personal representation by having constant access to congressmen from their home states or districts and, of course, the House and Senate committees hold frequent sessions at which interested residents and organizations may appear.

FOR FURTHER READING [12]

GENERAL WORKS

Austin, Oscar P.: *Steps in the Expansion of Our Territory* (Appleton-Century-Crofts, 1903).

Blanchard, Paul: *Democracy and Empire in the Caribbean: A Contemporary Review* (Macmillan, 1947).

Dulles, Foster H.: *America in the Pacific: A Century of Expansion* (Houghton Mifflin, 1932).

Farrand, Max: *The Legislation of Congress for the Government of the Organized Territories of the United States, 1789–1895* (Newark: Baker, 1896).

Haas, William (ed.): *The American Empire* (University of Chicago Press, 1940).

Hall, H. Duncan: *Mandates, Dependencies, and Trusteeships* (Carnegie Endowment, 1949).

Latham, Edward (ed.): *Statehood for Hawaii and Alaska* (H. W. Wilson, 1953).

Oliver, Douglas L.: *The Pacific Islands* (Harvard University Press, 1951).

Pratt, Julius W.: *America's Colonial Experiment* (Prentice-Hall, 1950).

Reid, Charles F.: *Overseas America: Our Territorial Outposts* (New York: Foreign Policy Association, 1942).

Remington, Woodbern E.: *Cross Winds of Empire* (John Day, 1941).

Snead, Mabelle C., *Territorial Possessions of the United States* (Vantage, 1954).

U.S. Commission on Organization of the Executive Branch of the Government (first Hoover Commission): *Overseas Administration, Federal-State Relations, Federal Research* (1949).

U.S. Department of Commerce, Bureau of the Census: *Fifteenth Census of the United States—1930—Outlying Territories and Possessions* (1932).

U.S. Department of Interior: Annual reports of governors of the respective territories.

——: General information regarding each of the territories.

Weinberg, Albert K.: *Manifest Destiny: A Study of Nationalist Expansionism in American History* (Johns Hopkins Press, 1935).

ALASKA

Alaska Planning Council: *Alaska Development Plan* (Juneau, Alaska: The Council, January, 1941).

——: *General Information Regarding Alaska* (Juneau, Alaska: The Council, 1941).

[12] Consult also innumerable government documents pertaining to particular areas.

Anderson, H. Dewey, and Walter C. Eells: *Alaska Natives: A Survey of Their Sociological and Educational Status* (Stanford University Press, 1935).

Colby, Merle E. (American Guide Series): *A Guide to Alaska, Last American Frontier* (Macmillan, 1939).

Hilscher, Robert H.: *Alaska Now* (Little, Brown, 1948).

Pilgrim, Marietta S.: *Alaska, Its History, Resources, Geography, and Government* (Caxton Printers, Ltd., 1939).

Spicer, George W.: *The Constitutional Status and Government of Alaska* (Johns Hopkins Press, 1927).

U.S. National Resources Committee: *Regional Planning—Alaska, Its Resources and Development* (1937).

HAWAII

Barber, Joseph, Jr.: *Hawaii: Restless Rampart* (Bobbs-Merrill, 1941).

Chambers, Henry: *Constitutional History of Hawaii* (Johns Hopkins Press, 1896).

Clark, Thomas B.: *Hawaii, the Forty-ninth State* (Doubleday, 1947).

Fergusson, Erna: *Our Hawaii* (Knopf, 1942).

Pratt, Julius W.: *Expansionists of 1898: The Acquisition of Hawaii and the Spanish Islands* (Johns Hopkins Press, 1936).

PUERTO RICO

Diffie, Bailey W., and Justine W. Diffie: *Puerto Rico: A Broken Pledge* (Vanguard, 1931).

Federal Writers' Project (American Guide Series): *Puerto Rico: A Guide to the Island of Boriquen* (New York: The University Society, Inc., 1940).

Pagan, Bolivar: *Puerto Rico: The Next State* (Washington, D.C.: privately printed, 1942).

Petrullo, Vincenzo: *Puerto Rican Paradox* (University of Pennsylvania Press, 1947).

Tugwell, Rexford G.: *The Stricken Land: The Story of Puerto Rico* (Doubleday, 1947).

Van Deusen, Richard J., and Elizabeth K. Van Deusen: *Puerto Rico: A Caribbean Isle* (Holt, 1931).

THE VIRGIN ISLANDS

Tansill, Charles C.: *The Purchase of the Danish West Indies* (Johns Hopkins Press, 1932).

THE PANAMA CANAL ZONE

Dimock, Marshall E.: *Government-operated Enterprises in the Panama Canal Zone* (University of Chicago Press, 1934).

Padelford, Norman J.: *The Panama Canal in Peace and War* (Macmillan, 1942).

Smith, Darrell H.: *The Panama Canal: Its History, Activities, and Organization* (Johns Hopkins Press, 1927).

SAMOA, GUAM, AND OTHER PACIFIC ISLES

Keesing, Felix M.: *The South Seas in the Modern World* (John Day, 1941).

——: *Modern Samoa* (Stanford University Press, 1934).

Leff, David N.: *Uncle Sam's Pacific Islets* (Stanford University Press, 1940).

Ryden, George H.: *The Foreign Policy of the United States in Relation to Samoa* (Yale University Press, 1933).

Thompson, Laura: *Guam and Its People: A Study of Cultural Change and Colonial Education* (San Francisco: American Council, Institute of Pacific Relations, 1941).

United States Navy: *Handbook on the Trust Territory of the Pacific Isles* (1948).

———: *Trust Territory of the Pacific Islands* (1948).

WASHINGTON, D.C.

Caemmerer, Hans P.: *A Manual on the Origin and Development of Washington* (Government Printing Office, 1939).

———: *Washington: The National Capital* (Government Printing Office, 1932).

Federal Writers' Project (American Guide Series): *Washington: City and Capital* (Government Printing Office, 1937).

REVIEW
QUESTIONS

1. What constitutional power or powers were used to acquire each of the territories which belong to the United States?

2. What circumstances led to the acquisition of each of the territories?

3. Distinguish between a territory that is incorporated and one that is not, and give examples of each. What practical difference does it make whether a territory is incorporated or unincorporated?

4. Describe the form of government found in each of the territories.

5. What "democratic trends" are apparent in American territories?

6. What difference would it make to the people of Hawaii and Alaska if they were given statehood?

7. What changes do you think ought to be made in the status and government of each of the territories?

8. What precisely does the term "Commonwealth" mean as it is applied to Puerto Rico?

9. Could "home rule" be granted to the District of Columbia without amending the Constitution? Would statehood for the District require a constitutional amendment?

10. Defend and criticize: (*a*) statehood for Hawaii and Alaska; (*b*) "home rule" for the District of Columbia; (*c*) citizenship for all peoples in American territories; (*d*) complete independence for Puerto Rico.

11. What agencies of the American government are responsible for the administration of territorial affairs? What changes would improve administration?

CHAPTER 24

War Powers and National Defense

The war power is the most dangerous one to a free government in the whole catalogue of powers. It usually is invoked in haste and excitement when calm legislative consideration of constitutional limitations is difficult. It is executed in a time of patriotic fervor that makes moderation unpopular, and is interpreted by judges under the influence of the same passions and prejudices. — Justice Robert H. Jackson [1]

What, then, is the source of our strength? That source is our ethical and moral standards and precepts, and our democratic faith in man. This faith is the chief armament of our democracy. It is the most potent weapon ever devised. Compared with it, the atomic bomb is a firecracker. — David E. Lilienthal [2]

WAR POWERS

Powers Granted to Federal Government. Foreseeing the possibility that the nation might become embroiled in war, the Constitution gave the national government powers adequate for the occasion. The clear presumption of that document is that the President is to act as Commander in Chief but that Congress should enact the basic legislation necessary for successful defense and prosecution of wars. Accordingly, more delegated powers contained in Article I, Section 8, relate to national defense and war than to any other single subject. First, Congress is given power to tax and spend money "to provide for the common Defense." Second, Congress is authorized "To declare War, grant Letters of Marque and Reprisal, and make Rules concerning Captures on Land and Water." Third, Congress is empowered "To raise and

support Armies" and "To provide and maintain a Navy." After these are created, Congress may "make Rules for the Government and Regulation of the land and naval Forces." Fourth, Congress may "provide for organizing, arming, and disciplining the Militia, and for governing such Part of them as may be employed in the Service of the United States." These are supplemented by the implied-power clause authorizing whatever is necessary and proper for carrying them into execution. Moreover, there is strong judicial support for believing that the war powers are inherent ones like those pertaining to foreign affairs.[3]

Disarming of States. While granting broad powers to the central government, the states were forbidden to "keep Troops, or Ships of War in time of Peace" without the consent of Congress, or to "engage in War, unless actually invaded, or in such imminent Danger as will

---

[1] Woods *v.* Cloyd W. Miller Co., 333 U.S. 138 (1947).
[2] *The New York Times Magazine,* Mar. 6, 1949, p. 11.

[3] See especially United States *v.* Curtiss-Wright Export Corporation, 229 U.S. 304 (1936).

not admit of delay." This left the states with power only to maintain a militia for the purpose of preserving order and, under remote circumstances, repelling invasion. But even their control over the militia was rendered tenuous by the provision that Congress might provide for its organization, arms, discipline, and use by the Federal government.

Declaration of War. Only Congress can "declare" war. A declaration is a formal announcement made, usually, by a joint resolution adopted by at least a majority of both houses and signed by the President. The President may, if he wishes, veto the declaration and, in turn, Congress could pass it over the veto, although these circumstances have never occurred. Typical of declarations is the one adopted after the attack on Pearl Harbor:

Public Law 328—77th Congress

Joint Resolution

Declaring that a state of war exists between the Imperial Government of Japan and the Government of the people of the United States and making provisions to prosecute the same.

Whereas the Imperial Government of Japan has committed unprovoked acts of war against the Government and the people of the United States of America: Therefore be it

Resolved by the Senate and House of Representatives of the United States of America in Congress assembled, That the state of war between the United States and the Imperial Government of Japan which has thus been thrust upon the United States is hereby formally declared; and the President is hereby authorized and directed to employ the entire naval and military forces of the United States and the resources of the Government to carry on war against the Imperial Government of Japan; and, to bring the conflict to a successful termination, all of the resources of the country are hereby pledged by the Congress of the United States.

Approved, Dec. 8, 1941, 4:10 P.M.

Congress may declare war at any time and against anybody—other than a member state in the Union [4]—although Congress usually waits for a request from the President.

"Executive Wars." Though only Congress can declare war, *hostilities* may be started by order of the President acting as Commander in Chief without prior congressional approval. Indeed, as was suggested on page 390, this has happened on many occasions. If the engagement is of a large and serious nature, the President usually asks Congress to declare war immediately before or after the start of hostilities; but if it is of a limited or local nature, no declaration may be asked for.

Indeed, an "executive war," if of small proportions, can be fought from beginning to end without formal declaration by Congress. Even though the President asks Congress to make declaration, circumstances have usually reached such a critical state as to leave Congress with no alternative but to comply. Not until Congress acts, however, do domestic rules and laws of war go into effect. This means that until Congress makes a formal declaration a conflict, however serious, is not legally "war" so far as our laws are concerned.

Conscription of Manpower. As noted above, Congress has the power to "raise and support armies" and "provide and maintain a navy." The Constitution also contemplates that the states will recruit and train militias according to a discipline prescribed by Congress. Nowhere does the Constitution state how manpower is to be obtained, but Congress is given authority to do what is necessary and proper in order to "raise" and "provide" personnel. Obviously no constitutional difficulty arises as long as the Federal government relies upon volunteers, but serious questions emerge when it resorts to compulsory recruitment. The problem divides itself into conscription during a war or on the eve thereof and conscription for peacetime training and service.

Wartime Conscription. Historically, conscription has been looked upon as alien to American

---

[4] The Prize Cases, 2 Black 635 (1863). The declaration may be made against a foreign state only. Conflict with member states is treated as insurrection if on a small scale and rebellion if on a large scale.

ideals and institutions. It was first used during the Civil War but without too great success. It was resorted to again in 1917, after war had been declared; and it was adopted in September, 1940, more than a year before entrance into war. The principal objection on legal grounds has been that forcible enrollment amounted to involuntary servitude and thus violated the Thirteenth Amendment. Upon first glance this contention seems plausible, because under conscription one is compelled against one's wishes to absent oneself from home and render what may be an obnoxious service. There can be no doubt that it is "involuntary," but is it a "servitude"? In a series of cases that arose during the First World War the Supreme Court distinguished between a "servitude" and a "duty" or "fundamental obligation" and upheld the draft.[5] Although questioned several times since, there has been no serious doubt that conscription is constitutional at least during wartime or when the country faces grave danger of war.

Peacetime Conscription. Although willing to resort to compulsion in the face of war, the thought of permanent conscription, to escape which many people who are now Americans fled from Europe, has been unpalatable. It was adopted more than a year before Pearl Harbor only after strenuous resistance and then only by narrow margins in both houses. When advocated as a permanent policy during and after the Second World War, it met with unyielding opposition and its fate remains uncertain.

The principal legal question involved in peacetime is not whether the citizen's rights are violated, but whether the plans envisaged do not amount to federal usurpation of prerogatives reserved to the states. Most plans contemplate a federal draft of all men between the ages of eighteen and twenty-one for a year's training under federal military auspices. But, it is argued, the adult manhood of the nation constitutes the militia whose training is reserved to the states.[6] A strong case is made showing that

it was the intent of those who wrote the Constitution that federal forces should be comprised of a small volunteer standing army and navy in peacetime with a citizens' militia under state control and training which could be called into federal service as occasion demanded.

Assuming this to be true, the question remains whether the courts would be bound by original intention in the face of modern conditions. In any event, the power to raise and provide an army and navy, when coupled with the implied power, establishes a strong presumption in favor of the constitutionality of peacetime conscription as long as the system adopted does not dispossess the states of coordinate authority to officer and train militias. Recent peacetime conscription acts have not been seriously contested on constitutional grounds.

Conscription of Labor. Admitting that Congress may draft manpower to serve in the Army or work for the government, can a law be enacted compelling civilian workmen to perform labor for private parties who may profit from the labor expended? Does this not amount to involuntary servitude in violation of the Thirteenth Amendment? A general labor draft failed of enactment during the Second World War, but severe strictures were placed upon the mobility of labor, the penalties being inability to get other jobs or the threat of reclassification and draft into military service. The War Labor Disputes Act did not make it a crime to discontinue working even in plants that had been seized by the government. Had measures been adopted making it a crime to refuse to work for government or private employers, cases challenging their constitutionality would doubtless have reached the Supreme Court, without which a definitive conclusion is impossible.

There is ample judicial precedent for legislation compelling service on behalf of government, but little in support of legislation com-

[5] Selective Draft Law Cases, 245 U.S. 366 (1918).

[6] The pertinent constitutional provision (Art. I, Sec. 8) is: "Congress shall have power . . . To provide for organizing, arming, and disciplining, the Militia, and for governing such Part of them as may be employed in the Service of the United States, reserving to the States respectively, *the Appointment of the Officers, and the Authority of training the Militia* according to the discipline prescribed by Congress." Italics supplied.

pelling workmen to serve private employers. The nearest precedent is found in the case of Robertson *v.* Baldwin.[7] There two seamen who had contracted with a private shipper deserted before completion of the trip. They were apprehended by authority of a federal law dating back to 1790, detained in prison until time for the departure of the ship, and then put back on the ship and compelled to render service until their contract had been fulfilled. The seamen challenged the federal statute, saying they had been compelled to render involuntary servitude in violation of the Thirteenth Amendment. The Supreme Court dismissed the idea that the amendment created a distinction between involuntary servitude for private persons and servitude for governmental agencies. It went on to uphold the statute, however, saying that the amendment was not meant to apply to seamen's contracts because since time immemorial these had been treated as exceptional and had always involved the surrender of a certain amount of personal liberty during the life of the contracts.

According to this decision, whether workmen were forced to labor for the government or for private parties would make no difference. The test would be whether the amendment was intended to apply to the particular employments in which labor was forced. If it could not be shown that historically employment contracts in war industries had been treated as so exceptional as to permit the surrender of a certain amount of personal liberty during the course of the contracts, then a labor draft would be unconstitutional, or the precedent reviewed above would need to be reversed, or the courts would need to evolve some new basis of justification.

Conscription of Property. If manpower can be commandeered, what of property? Here the question is whether private property is taken for public use without just compensation or without due process of law. War measures adopted during the last two major wars authorized seizure of war plants and equipment under certain circumstances, always with the understanding that owners would be recompensed.

The power to do so has been upheld and reaffirmed recently in the following words:

The Constitution grants to Congress power "to raise and support Armies," "to provide and maintain a Navy," and to make all laws necessary and proper to carry these powers into execution. Under this authority Congress can draft men for battle service. . . . Its powers to draft business organizations to support the fighting men who risk their lives can be no less.[8]

Curfews. In February, 1942, shortly after commencement of war with Japan, the President created certain military areas and zones and authorized commanding military officers to control conduct in and passage to and from the regions. Shortly thereafter the entire West coast was declared such a zone and an order was issued requiring every alien German, Italian, and Japanese, and all persons of Japanese ancestry (even though natural-born American citizens) to be in their residences between the hours of 8 P.M. and 6 A.M.

Congress subsequently approved these orders and provided criminal penalties for their violation. Martial law was not declared; hence civil courts remained open and available for the trial of offenses. Hirabayashi, a natural-born American citizen of Japanese ancestry, was arrested for violating the curfew and the case ultimately reached the Supreme Court.[9] The Court took note of the defendant's citizenship and the obviously discriminatory character of the legislation but proceeded to sustain his conviction on the ground that the war emergency and the large number of persons of Japanese ancestry upon the West coast were sufficient cause to justify the curfew. This sets the stage for curfews applied to all citizens in future emergencies occasioned by war.

Internment of Japanese-Americans. More drastic still were orders issued early in 1942 evacuating all persons of Japanese ancestry, whether aliens or citizens, from their homes along the West coast. Without making any test

[7] 165 U.S. 275 (1896).

[8] United States *v.* Bethlehem Steel Corp., 315 U.S. 289 (1941).

[9] Hirabayashi *v.* United States, 320 U.S. 81 (1942).

of loyalty or possible menace to national safety, all Japanese in the area (approximately 120,000) were compelled to leave, report to control stations, and thereafter live in internment camps administered by the War Relocation Authority, a civilian agency. Evacuation occasioned severe hardship, and life in the camps was anything but congenial, especially for parents accustomed to family life and children.

Once in the camps, those whose loyalty was beyond question were permitted to leave as long as they did not return to the West coast area and could find employment or other means of support or educational opportunities in other parts of the country. To its victims the order made the rights of citizenship appear meaningless and called forth severe criticism from large segments of the population.

The drastic action taken during the war was never fully approved by many citizens. Remorse deepened, especially when it appeared that there was no evidence of disloyalty on the part of Japanese-Americans but, rather, countless instances of heroic patriotism. Finally, Congress, in 1948, authorized payment of reparations. The Attorney General was authorized to adjudicate and pay claims amounting to $2,500 or less, while claims for larger amounts were to be settled by the Court of Claims.

The Hirabayashi case upheld the curfew without expressly passing upon the constitutionality of evacuation and detention in internment camps. In 1944 a case was brought before the Supreme Court by Korematsu, concededly a loyal American citizen, in which the evacuation program was upheld as justified at the time it was undertaken.[10]

About the same time another loyal citizen challenged her detention by writ of habeas corpus.[11] She had been detained for 2 years, first at Tule Lake Relocation Center in California and then at Central Utah Relocation Center. Her citizenship and loyalty were conceded. Without altering approval given to the curfew and evacuation program given in cases previously decided, and without deciding what power the Reloca-

tion Authority might have to detain other classes of citizens, the Court ruled that it had no authority to detain loyal citizens like this for a longer period of time. This decision suggests that evacuation and detention, though justified by the war powers during periods of grave national emergency, cannot be prolonged beyond a reasonable time required for separating the loyal from probable saboteurs.

Rules for the Armed Forces. As noted above, Congress is given authority to "make rules for the government and regulation of the land and naval forces." Prevailing rules are found in the Uniform Code of Military Justice adopted in 1950 and discussed in Chap. 16. So far as the power is concerned, two things should be noted: (1) military courts have nearly exclusive jurisdiction over cases involving violations of military law; Federal civilian courts may intervene only to make certain that military tribunals are operating within their jurisdiction and proceeding according to law; (2) provisions of the Fifth and Sixth Amendments respecting grand and petit juries do not apply to cases arising in the land and naval forces, and other procedural guaranties contained in these amendments are of limited applicability.

Martial Law and Its Declaration. Martial law is the law of necessity. It is sometimes resorted to during grave emergencies when civil authorities fail to maintain law and order. The Constitution nowhere mentions the term. Authority for its use is implied from the power to declare war; to provide for calling forth the militia to execute the laws of the Union, suppress insurrections, and repel invasions; from the President's powers to serve as Commander in Chief, and to see that the laws of the Union are faithfully executed; and from the obligation imposed upon the Federal government to guarantee to every state protection against domestic violence. Nor does the Constitution expressly state whether the President or Congress is to declare martial law. As matters stand, Congress has delegated broad powers to the President, authorizing him to use such force as he deems necessary to enforce the laws and preserve order. The President is to judge, therefore, when

[10] Korematsu *v.* United States, 323 U.S. 214 (1944).
[11] *Ex parte* Endo, 323 U.S. 283 (1944).

circumstances necessitate resort to this drastic remedy.

Distinction between Martial Law and Mere Use of Troops. Martial law must be distinguished from the mere use of troops to patrol or to assist the police in maintaining order. Under martial law, a military officer is placed in complete command of a given area, the civil courts of law are closed, and military law and procedure (*i.e.,* trial by courts-martial, etc.) are substituted. But when troops are sent into conflict areas during minor and isolated disturbances, they are usually sent there to aid the civil authorities. In this event they act a role similar to that of deputy sheriffs, doing nothing on their own responsibility; and violators are apprehended in the usual manner and prosecuted before civil courts. "Military law," the Supreme Court said on one occasion,[12] "can never exist where the courts are open, and in the proper unobstructed exercise of their jurisdiction."

Instances of Declaration of Martial Law. Throughout the history of the nation, martial law has never been declared during peacetime, although qualified martial law was twice declared in the period immediately following the First World War,[13] and on innumerable occasions federal troops have been used to maintain order. The most conspicuous instances where martial law has been resorted to by federal authorities occurred in 1814 when, during an attack by the British, General Andrew Jackson placed New Orleans and vicinity under military rule; and again, when President Lincoln placed the Southern and border states under martial law during the Civil War. Martial law was not declared anywhere within the Union during the Mexican, Spanish-American, and First World Wars. During the Second World War, Hawaii was placed under martial law after the attack on Pearl Harbor and remained in that condition during most of the war period. This was drastic action which many thought precipitous and unwarranted, and which the Supreme Court later declared illegal.[14]

Suspension of Writ of Habeas Corpus. A declaration of martial law is usually accompanied by suspension of the writ of habeas corpus. Authority for doing so is contained in the words, "The Privilege of the Writ of Habeas Corpus shall not be suspended, unless when in Cases of Rebellion or Invasion the public Safety may require it." But who is to determine when the public safety requires the suspension of the writ? The Constitution does not say. Early decisions of the Supreme Court took it for granted that the power of suspension lay with Congress, but during the Civil War Lincoln, upon the advice of his Attorney General, declared that the power lay with him and issued proclamations authorizing the suspension of the writ in places both within and without the area of active hostilities. Lincoln's action was declared illegal by Chief Justice Taney sitting as a circuit judge[15] on the ground that Congress alone possessed the power of suspending the operation of the writ. A short time thereafter, Congress enacted legislation authorizing suspension of the writ and proclamations issued pursuant to this legislation by President Lincoln were subsequently upheld by the Supreme Court.[16]

Thus, the question of whether the President might suspend the writ in the absence of congressional authorization was not definitely settled, nor has it been since. Writers still dispute the point, but the weight of judicial precedent appears to support the contention that the President cannot suspend the writ by virtue of his own authority but must wait for congressional authorization to do so.[17]

Whether the writ may be suspended outside zones of actual military operations is also greatly

[12] *Ex parte* Milligan, 4 Wall. 2 (U.S. 1866).

[13] During a race riot that occurred in Omaha, Neb., in 1919, and during a steel strike at Gary, Ind., in the same year. For a review of these and other instances where federal troops have been used to quell disturbances, see Bennett M. Rich, *The Presidents and Civil Disorder* (Brookings, 1941). See also Robert S. Rankin, *When Civil Law Fails* (Duke University Press, 1939).

[14] Duncan *v.* Kahanamoku, 327 U.S. 304 (1945).

[15] *Ex parte* Merryman, 17 Fed. Cas. No. 9487 (1861).

[16] *Ex parte* Milligan, 4 Wall. 2 (U.S. 1866).

[17] Cf. Rankin, *op. cit.,* especially pp. 185–191.

disputed, but the weight of opinion appears to dictate that the writ should be suspended only in zones of military operations and then only when the civil courts fail to function properly and successfully. Except for the instance that occurred during the Civil War and in Hawaii during the recent war, the writ has never been suspended by the Federal government.

Federal Government and State Militias. The Constitution contemplates a cooperative, joint control and use of state militias. The obvious theory is that Congress shall prescribe such general rules as are necessary to ensure a militia system with uniform arms and discipline, yet leaving to the states the details of organization, the appointment of officers, and training. Once in existence, Congress is then authorized to provide for calling the militias of the respective states into federal service when occasion demands. When called into federal service, the states lose all jurisdiction. Although Congress provides for calling militias into federal service, the principle is well established that the President alone is the judge of when the call shall be made.

The Constitution states that Congress may call the militia into federal service for three purposes: (1) to execute the laws of the union; (2) to suppress insurrections; and (3) to repel invasions. There has been considerable controversy over whether "to repel invasions" authorizes use outside American territory. Although the language used appears to forbid use beyond American borders, the issue is academic, because under present legislation the militia is also the National Guard which becomes a part of the Regular Army when called into federal service. And, of course, the Regular Army can be sent anywhere.

Limitation on the War Powers. Only one restriction on the war powers is explicitly stated, but others are implied. The expressed limitation is that no appropriation of money "to raise and support armies" shall be for longer than 2 years. This was copied from the British law at the time, which, however, limited appropriations to 1 year. Note that the restriction applies to "armies" and is not repeated in the following phrase which authorizes creation of a navy. The restriction prevents the appropriation of permanent funds for the Army and gives every congressman, particularly every member of the House of Representatives whose term, it will be recalled, is for 2 years, an opportunity of scrutinizing the organization and policies of the military. By this means, the Constitution expects that the Army will be kept in complete subordination to the civil branches of government.

Implied Limitations. From a legal point of view, implied limitations for the war powers are the same as for other powers granted by the Constitution. "No doctrine," said former Justice Davis, "involving more pernicious consequences, was ever invented by the writ of man than that any of its [the Constitution's] provisions can be suspended during any of the great exigencies of government. Such a doctrine leads directly to anarchy or despotism. . . ."[18] Nevertheless, as Professor Clinton L. Rossiter has clearly pointed out,[19] there is during modern wars a strong tendency for Congress, the courts, and public opinion to abdicate responsibility in favor of executive action, accepting possible abuse of power as one of the inevitable concomitants of war.

THE PROBLEM OF SECURITY

The Pros and Cons of Preparedness. Where issues as important as national security are involved, it is natural that opinions differ sharply. Some insist that human nature is so cussed as to make war inevitable. To them the fact that there have always been wars is positive proof that they will recur in the future. Those of this opinion are usually skeptical of peace programs but advocate instead a program of unilateral national preparedness as the method most likely to minimize the possibility of war and ensure victory if it should come. To them preparedness

[18] *Ex parte* Milligan, 4 Wall. 2 (U.S. 1866).
[19] *Constitutional Dictatorship: Crisis Government in the Modern Democracies* (Princeton University Press, 1948), and *The Supreme Court and the Commander in Chief* (Cornell University Press, 1951).

is a form of national insurance against inevitable wars.

Others insist that man is naturally a cooperative, social creature, capable of evolving a social system in which wars are minimized or entirely eliminated. This group is generally skeptical of obtaining security through a program of national preparedness. They deny the appropriateness of calling preparedness insurance. The latter provides security against such things as accidents, fires, floods, sickness, and death, whereas national defenses are directed at other people or communities. Insurance does not create in others fear and suspicion leading to counter defensive plans, but national armaments do. Thus, this group believes that instead of contributing to peace and security, armaments actually sow the seeds of war. Accordingly, those of this persuasion urge reduction of armaments, the broadening of understanding among races, the gradual transfer of loyalty from national states to larger legal and political units, and the erection of international machinery through which disputes among nations can be settled by amicable or legal procedures rather than by recourse to international violence.

Meaning of "Adequate" Defense. Almost every speaker on the subject pledges support for "adequate" defense. But what is adequate? The term is obviously relative. No defenses at all are adequate along the 3,000-mile Canadian border. Virtually no navy and a small army were adequate before 1900. What might be adequate for the defense of continental United States would be insufficient to carry the attack to another continent. What might be adequate for a small agrarian nation might not be for a large imperialist power. What would be adequate with allies would not be without them. What was adequate before the atom bomb is less so now. Obviously, the concept of adequacy is variable. It depends upon geography, the amount of good will that exists, the strength of allies and potential enemies, technological developments, and foreign and domestic policies followed by various countries of the world. All this suggests that national defense programs cannot be static but must be adapted to changing conditions. It also suggests that in the long run the best defense is a program designed to minimize world tensions.

DEPARTMENTAL UNIFICATION

Toward Merger. With postwar expenditures for national defense reaching staggering sums and accounting for a third or more of all federal expenditures, attention was naturally drawn to ways and means of ensuring maximum returns. Until 1947 the War and Navy Departments were organically separate, and each had its own nearly autonomous air force. Coordination was obtained through liaison officers, joint meetings of chiefs of staff, committees, boards, cabinet officers, and conferences with the President.

Over the years many complained of this separation, alleging that it prevented integrated planning, that it led to rivalries for public and congressional favor, that it encouraged competition in recruitment and procurement, and that it led to duplication, inefficiency, and confusion. The experience of both world wars indicated the necessity for a unified command, which was achieved only after expensive delays, while the disaster at Pearl Harbor was attributed in large measure to the division of responsibility between the Army and the Navy. Unification, with a single supreme command over both departments, resting in one person directly responsible to the President, was urged.[20]

Opponents resisted, saying that a single chief would inevitably show preference for one branch or another; that a single head would become so powerful as to dominate other branches of the government; and that greater efficiency, economy, and striking power would not result. They pointed with pride to the long record of achievements under separate departments.

Those favoring unification launched a vigorous campaign shortly after the war closed. President Truman, the Army, and their partisans favored change; the Navy and its friends opposed. Extensive hearings were held, and various proposals were widely debated both in and

[20] Early stages of unification are ably discussed in Robert H. Connery, "Unification of the Armed Forces: The First Year," *The American Political Science Review,* vol. 53 (February, 1949), p. 38.

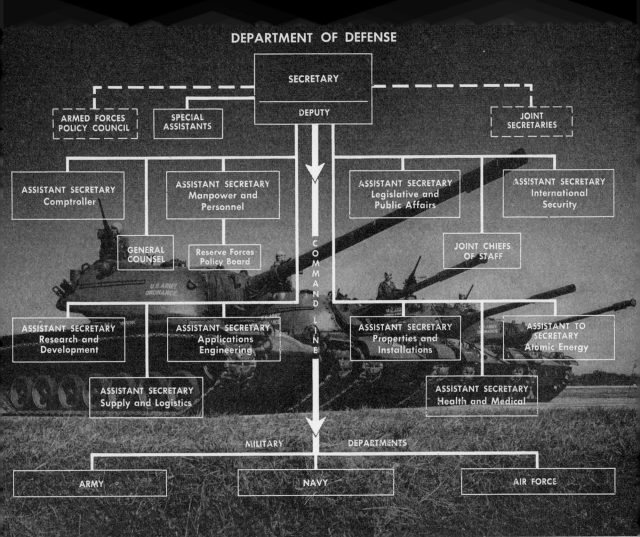

DEPARTMENT OF DEFENSE

SECRETARY / DEPUTY

- ARMED FORCES POLICY COUNCIL
- SPECIAL ASSISTANTS
- JOINT SECRETARIES

- ASSISTANT SECRETARY — Comptroller
- ASSISTANT SECRETARY — Manpower and Personnel
- ASSISTANT SECRETARY — Legislative and Public Affairs
- ASSISTANT SECRETARY — International Security

- GENERAL COUNSEL
- Reserve Forces Policy Board
- JOINT CHIEFS OF STAFF

- ASSISTANT SECRETARY — Research and Development
- ASSISTANT SECRETARY — Applications Engineering
- ASSISTANT SECRETARY — Properties and Installations
- ASSISTANT TO SECRETARY — Atomic Energy

- ASSISTANT SECRETARY — Supply and Logistics
- ASSISTANT SECRETARY — Health and Medical

COMMAND LINE

MILITARY DEPARTMENTS

- ARMY
- NAVY
- AIR FORCE

out of Congress. Washington has seldom, if ever, witnessed a more bitter and intransigent struggle. The National Security Act of 1947 was the result. This, as amended in 1949 and since, provides the basis for present defense organization.

Present Defense Organization. In the Executive Office of the President are two primary interdepartmental agencies: the National Security Council and the Office of Defense Mobilization. The former consists of the President, Vice-President, Secretaries of State and Defense, and the Director of the Office of Defense Mobilization. This body advises the President on security matters. Under the Council's direction is the Central Intelligence Agency, which operates with great secrecy and digests information bearing upon security obtained from every possible source. Also under the Council is an Operations Coordinating Board, which seeks maximum cooperation of all government agencies in carrying out national defense policies. The Office of Defense Mobilization, operating under the guidance of an interdepartmental board and advisory bodies, makes detailed plans for mobilizing and controlling the nation's economic and human resources in the event of war.

While the agencies just mentioned advise and plan, the Department of Defense administers and executes most policies related to national security. The Department is headed by a civilian Secretary. Advising him is a chief of staff who is the nation's top military officer. Within the Defense Department are three subordinate Departments (Army, Navy, and Air Force) each of which is headed by a civilian Secretary. Advising each of these is a chief of staff (called Chief of Naval Operations by the Navy) who is the top military officer in his particular department. The three chiefs of staff combine, under the nonvoting chairmanship of the chief of staff to the Defense Secretary, to form the Joint Chiefs of Staff.[21] The top officials of the Department

COMPOSITION OF THE MILITARY FORCES

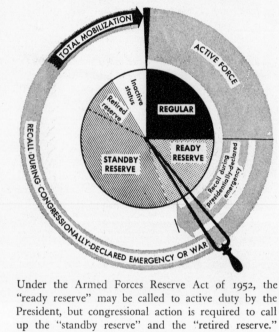

Under the Armed Forces Reserve Act of 1952, the "ready reserve" may be called to active duty by the President, but congressional action is required to call up the "standby reserve" and the "retired reserve." Source: Department of Defense.

constitute an Armed Forces Policy Council to advise on broad questions of policy. These are assisted by a body of experts drawn from all three services and known as the Joint Staff. Of course, a host of boards, bureaus, staff and line officers and employees, drawn from both military and civil life, surround this skeleton organization.

Unified Commands. One outcome of the National Security Act of 1947 was the establishment

---

[21] Under 1952 legislation the Commandant of the Marine Corps sits with the Joint Chiefs and has co-equal status when matters affecting marines are under consideration.

of unified commands. Under this arrangement, areas of the world in which the United States has stationed armed forces are divided into five unified command areas: Alaskan, Pacific, Far East, Caribbean, and European. Each area is under a commander in chief who is attached to one of the three military departments but who reports to the Secretary of Defense. Typically the Alaskan area is commanded by an officer of the Air Force; the Pacific by an officer of the Navy; the Far East, Caribbean, and European by officers of the Army.

Reserves. Since the Second World War much effort has gone into enlarging and strengthening reserve forces. Present policies and programs are based upon the Universal Military Training and Service legislation, discussed below, and the Armed Forces Reserve Act of 1952, as amended in 1955.

Essential features of the present system are the "ready reserve," "standby reserve," and "retired reserve." The ready, whose ceiling is presently 2,900,000 men, can be called into active duty during an emergency declared by the President. The standby can be called only in time of war or emergency declared by Congress, unless the ready reserve cannot fulfill requirements of a partial mobilization. The retired group can be tapped in case of grave need.

Legislation enacted in 1955 requires a member of the ready reserve (other than National Guardsmen who are under a separate code) to participate in forty-eight scheduled drills and not more than seventeen days active duty annually, or in lieu thereof, a maximum of thirty days of active duty for training. Noncompliance with this requirement extends the annual active duty to forty-five days and may lead to discipline under the Uniform Code of Military Justice.

Persons entering the Armed Forces incur a military obligation of eight years if over twenty-six years of age and six years if younger. Transfer to the ready reserve follows termination of active duty. Combat veterans remain in the ready reserve only until screened and transferred to the standby reserve.

THE MILITARY DEPARTMENTS

Army Department. Military tasks are numerous, the more so because of the charged atmosphere of the past decade. Among others, they include helping formulate national policies on matters relating to security; collaboration with the United Nations on security measures; operating or assisting government in occupied areas; providing assistance to special overseas missions like those in Greece, Turkey, Iran, and certain Latin-American countries; recruiting, training, disciplining, and equipping the armed forces; fostering research on a wide range of matters; planning military strategy and tactics; operating and maintaining military posts, vessels, and establishments; keeping informed about military plans and resources of other nations; collaborating with National Guard units; and helping maintain order when ordered to do so by the President.

Civilian Functions. In addition to military functions, the Army Department has been given numerous duties of a civil nature. It governs the Panama Canal and business operations within the Zone. The Corps of Engineers helps the Federal Power Commission investigate water-power sites; it develops and executes plans for improvement of harbors and rivers, flood control, and the generation of hydroelectric power and irrigation. The department makes surveys of the Great Lakes and international water boundaries. It constructs national monuments and memorials; assists communities stricken with disaster; preserves the American Niagara Falls; establishes harbor lines; approves plans and issues permits for bridges and other construction on navigable waters; removes wrecks from, and regulates the use of, navigable waters. Imposing as this list appears, the major proportion of the funds and personnel of the department are devoted to military matters.

Service Areas. Headquarters for the Army are, of course, in Washington. But numerous matters are handled by area offices. Within continental limits six areas plus the Military District of Washington, D.C., exist, each with a headquarters and commanding officer. Principal American territories are also areas, while abroad functions are performed by the unified commands mentioned above.

Components of the Army. The Army of the United States consists of the Regular Army, the Army National Guard, the Women's Army Corps, Organized Reserve Corps, and the Reserve Officers' Training Corps. The Regular Army is a permanent, professional force made up of officers and soldiers who have chosen the Army as a career or who may have been drafted. The Army National Guard consists of two parts: one, for the District of Columbia and territories like Hawaii and Alaska, is under the exclusive control of the Regular Army; the other is, during normal times, a state organization.

Although largely financed by the Federal government and trained in accordance with discipline prescribed by the Regular Army, state Guard units are officered and trained by state appointees. This duality of responsibility helps explain the constant undertone of hostility and friction that exists between officers of the Regular Army and those of the state Guards. The officers and men of the Guard are volunteers who take regular training at armories near home or at special encampments. During wartime or national emergencies the Guard may be called into federal service, during which it loses its state character and becomes an indistinguishable part of the federal army.

The Women's Army Corps (WAC) was authorized in 1948 and has since been thoroughly integrated into all but the combat phases of the Army. It carries out vital work in communications, medical service, personnel administration, and intelligence. The Organized Reserve is made up of volunteer officers, men and women. This is a federal reserve entirely unrelated to the National Guard. Older members are generally those who have served in previous wars; younger ones usually receive their training in college Reserve Officer Training Corps (ROTC) units or in special Citizens' Military Training Camps. Members generally remain on an inactive status without pay, although they may be occasionally ordered to spend short periods in active duty.

During wartime or national emergencies they may, of course, be called into active service. ROTC units exist in a number of high schools and colleges for giving basic and advanced training.

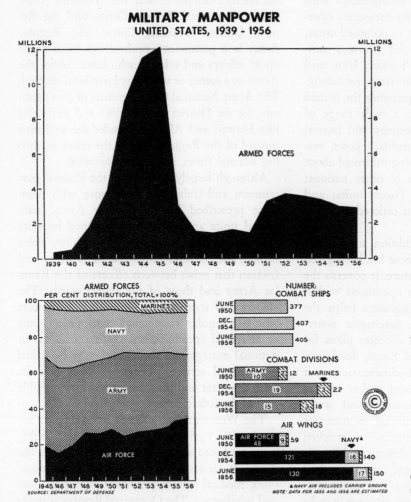

MILITARY MANPOWER
UNITED STATES, 1939 - 1956

Courtesy of National Industrial Conference Board.

cruits, trains, and disciplines personnel. It aids the development and building of bases, ports, and harbor facilities at home and at many places abroad. It operates a number of naval hospitals and a home in Philadelphia for aged servicemen.

Navy Department. *Functions.* The duties of the Navy Department are numerous, varied, and far-flung. Its staff also helps formulate national policies and plans for war. It helps promote research designed to improve naval operations. It designs ships, operates a number of yards for shipbuilding, and oversees construction by private companies. It maintains and deploys the fleet. It governs several Pacific islands and supports American forces in occupied areas. It re-

It operates a radio system for communication with vessels. It sends officers to advise friendly foreign governments, and it frequently dispatches ships to strategic areas to support foreign policy. It handles leases of enormous oil reserves in Alaska and western United States. It manufactures numerous supplies and equipment needed for naval operation and maintenance.

Components of the Navy. The Navy consists of the Regular Navy, Marine Corps, Coast

Guard, Naval Reserve, Naval Air Reserve, Naval Reserve Officers' Training Corps (NROTC), and Marine Corps Reserve. The Regular Navy is a permanent professional force of male and female officers and enlisted personnel. The Marine Corps comprises the Navy's personnel who are especially trained and equipped for landing operations, land fighting, and occupation. The Coast Guard is a part of the Navy at all times, although it operates under the Treasury Department in peacetime. It serves as the seaboard police for the nation and as an auxiliary to the Navy and Merchant Marine. The various reserves exist to provide a force of qualified officers and enlisted men available for immediate mobilization.

The Fleet. The fleet consists of all fighting ships and auxiliary vessels assigned to the Navy Department. It is divided into "capital" ships, meaning battleships, which are huge, heavily armed carriers of destruction; cruisers, which are smaller, faster, and more lightly armed; aircraft carriers; destroyers, which are especially designed and armed for pursuit and convoy duty; submarines; and auxiliary craft. Before the Korean conflict about a third of the total fleet was in active duty; the remainder was in "moth balls" at "berthing areas" along the American coast. After June, 1950, the Navy expanded rapidly but more recently it has again contracted.

Most naval vessels in active service are divided about equally between two major fleets, the Atlantic and Pacific. For operational purposes the two major fleets are organized into task fleets and forces and subdivisions thereof.

Air Force Department. Air power first demonstrated its military importance during the First World War. Ever since, there have been sharp differences of opinion over the future potential of air power and the best methods of development and use. Before 1947 the War and Navy Departments each had an air force of its own. This was justified on the ground that forces could best be developed and directed by the departments whose land or naval operations they were intended to assist. Thus, the Navy could best train and direct pilots and planes used to supply and support naval operations; the Army could best train and direct pilots and planes used to supply and support land operations. When cooperation was desired it was assumed this could be achieved through joint conferences, committees, and the President.

Although it was obvious to all that the separate air forces played an important role in the Second World War, many thought a better job could have been done if responsibility had not been as divided as it was. Many also believed that if left under the Army and Navy the air force would be neglected by departmental officers whose chief interests lay with other phases of defense. Foreseeing future wars when air power would be even more decisive, champions insisted upon an autonomous air force equipped with sufficient money and manpower to keep abreast of the rapid technological changes that lay ahead. Passage of the National Security Act of 1947 authorized a separate Department of Air Force with rank equal to those of the Army and Navy. Today, the Army and Navy have relatively few aircraft, and these are used chiefly for local supporting operations.

Air Force Department Functions. Being new, the Air Force Department has not been saddled with functions unrelated to its major objectives. Like the other military departments, one of its primary duties is that of helping formulate national policies on matters related to security. The department must collaborate intimately with other agencies, particularly those concerned chiefly with defense, in order to secure maximum coordination and economy.

In no field is scientific research more decisive; accordingly, a large part of the department's attention is devoted to such matters. The department also keeps informed about the air power of other nations. For this purpose, it maintains attachés in other nations and collaborates with United States intelligence agencies. It also supports government in occupied areas and special missions to friendly countries. Recruiting, training, and disciplining personnel are primary tasks, for which the draft laws have not been used. Planning home defenses is an important assignment, made more so by the omnipresent threat of "push-button" warfare with rockets, disease germs, and atomic weapons. Procuring equipment and supplies and planning for industrial mobilization are also important tasks.

Components of the Air Force. The Air Force consists of a body of professional officers and enlisted personnel. Since 1948 women may enlist and become officers. Civilians may enroll in the Air National Guard, the Air Force Reserve, the Air Reserve Officer Training Corps (Air ROTC), Civil Air Patrol, or Air Scouts. The first three are similar to their counterparts in other branches of the service. The Air Patrol is a legal auxiliary of a semimilitary character. Its purpose is to enroll, train, and equip air-minded citizens to meet local and national emergencies and to generally promote the advancement of aviation. Air Scouts are given nonmilitary training in aeronautics, communications, and navigation. A limited number of Senior Scouts attend summer encampments, and a few are taken for short flights as passengers.

Training Schools. Officers are trained for all branches of the service in existing civilian institutions and those especially provided for the purpose. For the Army, the United States Military Academy located at West Point, on the Hudson River north of New York City, is the principal training center for officers. The United States Naval Academy located at Annapolis, Md., a short distance east of Washington, D.C., plays a similar role for the Navy. An Air Force Academy was authorized in 1954 and Colorado Springs, Colo., has been chosen as its site. The Coast Guard maintains an academy at New London, Conn.

For postgraduate or in-service officers' training, three schools are held jointly by the military departments. The National War College stresses the broad aspects of national policy with emphasis upon foreign policy, international relations and law, and logistics. The Industrial College of the Armed Forces stresses the economic problems of mobilization and war. The Armed Forces Staff College deals especially with problems of administration. In addition, selected officers are assigned for special study to civilian educational institutions, and a number of specialized schools are conducted by each of the three military departments. Interestingly, the Air Force Department has what it calls the Air University consisting of the Air Tactical School, the Air Command and Staff School, and the Air War College.

VOLUNTEERS OR CONSCRIPTS?

Past Use of Conscription. Throughout most of our history military and naval personnel have been obtained by volunteer enlistment, the exceptions occurring during the Civil War, First World War, the Second World War, and since. Although conscription worked badly during the Civil War, it worked smoothly during the First World War, and the same pattern has been followed since.

The first instance of peacetime conscription occurred with the adoption of the Selective Training and Service Act in September, 1940—more than a year before Pearl Harbor but at a time when it was obvious that the United States was becoming increasingly involved in the war. Conscription was continued throughout the war and for several months after V-J Day. When the act expired in May, 1946, it was first extended for only 6 weeks and then renewed on a much restricted basis until the following Mar. 31. More than a year later, in June, 1948, another conscription law was enacted that has remained on the statutes, with amendments, ever since.

As the legislation stands, administration is the responsibility of the Selective Service System with headquarters in Washington and state capitals. Regional boards are set up to handle appeals, while local draft boards of three or more civilians handle details. The law sets the maximum authorized strength for the Army, Navy, Marine Corps, and Air Force, then permits as many to be drafted as necessary to meet these quotas.

The first step in the draft process is registration. This is required of all men between eighteen and twenty-six. Men may not be drafted until eighteen and a half, and then not until those from nineteen to twenty-six have been called. After registration, questionnaires are sent by which additional information is secured.

Then follow classification, physical examination, and perhaps induction. Listed below are the classes in which men are placed:

I-A and I-A-O. Examined and acceptable

I-A and I-A-O. Not examined

I-A and I-A-O. Induction postponed

I-S. Statutory deferment—high school

I-S. Statutory deferment—college

I-O. Conscientious objector, examined and acceptable

I-O. Conscientious objector, not examined

I-C. Inducted

I-C. Enlisted or commissioned

I-C. Discharged

I-C. Reserve

I-W. At work

I-W. Released

I-D. Member of reserve component

II-A. Occupational deferment, except for agriculture

II-A. Apprentice

II-C. Agricultural deferment

II-S. Occupational deferment-student

III-A. Dependency deferment

IV-A. Completed service—sole surviving son

IV-B. Officials

IV-C. Aliens

IV-D. Ministers, divinity students

IV-F. Unfit for service

V-A. Over age of liability

Only those in Class I are liable for draft, but those placed in other classes may later be shifted to Class I and thereby become eligible. Men are not chosen by national lottery, as during the war, but rather by birthday sequence. Men in the twenty-five-year-old bracket are taken first, then others from the older to younger. Deferments may be granted by local boards to permit high school students to continue their courses, if their record is satisfactory, until graduation or age twenty-one, whichever is first. College students may be deferred until the end of the academic year. Appeals from local boards may be made to appeal boards, thence to state and national headquarters. The period of service for men eighteen and a half through twenty-five is 24 months, plus 6 years in a reserve after discharge.

Campaign for Universal Military Training (UMT). Ever since the First World War there has been agitation for the adoption of a permanent program of military training for all young men. An intense campaign was launched about a year before the end of the Second World War to achieve this result before the nation returned to peacetime habits. Although the proposal was defeated then, the campaign has continued ever since. The effort met with partial success in June, 1951, when Congress approved the principle of universal training and established a National Security Training Commission with instructions to prepare and report concrete plans.

The plan proposed in 1951 called for drafting all young men at age eighteen for 6 months' training in a National Security Training Corps. This would mean that about 400,000 youths would be in training continuously and require the employment of one trainer or administrator for every two trainees (or a total of about 200,000 overhead personnel), an estimated initial cost of over 4 billion dollars and annually thereafter over 2 billion dollars. Trainees would receive modest pay, perhaps a dollar a day; they would not be members of the armed forces but would wear distinctive uniforms and comply with a special disciplinary code; they would be required to remain in the reserves for a number of years after the period of training. After a sensational parliamentary battle in the House of Representatives a bill embodying provisions similar to these was defeated in 1952.

1955 Version. Another plan sponsored in 1955 called for imposing an eight-year military obligation on men over eighteen and one-half years of age. Men who did not volunteer would be drafted for two years and spend six years following active duty in the ready reserve.

A greatly modified version ultimately passed Congress. This provides that a young man ordered to report for induction may do one of three things: (1) enlist in the reserves for six years and spend two of these years in active service; (2) enlist in the reserves for eight years, undergo six months' training, and be deferred from induction for the remainder of the period by participating in the reserves; (3) enlist in the Army National Guard or Air National Guard until age twenty-eight and avoid induction into active service altogether.

These alternatives became available in 1955 but the number of young men responding was disappointing to sponsors of the legislation. Most young men, apparently, preferred either to volunteer for the usual tour of duty or take their chances of being drafted under older provisions of the Selective Service legislation.

Arguments for and against UMT. Spearheading the campaign for UMT were Presidents Truman and Eisenhower, their defense advisers, major veterans' groups, some important newspapers and periodicals (notably *The New York Times* and the Hearst press), and scattered individual educators. Opposed to the proposals were virtually all important religious, educational, liberal, farm, and labor organizations.

Those who favor UMT argue that there is nothing in the present situation to justify the expectation that there will not be another war; hence the United States must remain "fully prepared." A choice must be made between a large standing army with a small trained reserve, or a small standing army and a huge citizen reserve comprised largely of those who have had at least one year of training. The latter is preferred because a large standing army is contrary to American tradition, all citizens need to be trained to fight a total war which may come unexpectedly and quickly, and it would prove cheaper in the long run. Adoption of this plan, it is argued, would not arouse fear and suspicion in other nations but rather would serve notice of intention to back up commitments made under the United Nations Charter. It is further suggested that this show of determination and force would increase national bargaining strength at the conference table, especially with Russia. Finally, it is urged that the training would improve the patriotism, health, morals, religion, skills, and minds of those who take the training.

Opponents insist that such a plan is alien to American life; countries that have had conscription often have been dictatorial and warlike; countries like France, that have long had conscription in peacetime, were not necessarily better prepared when war came because of it; it will lead to military domination of civilian life; the training of all youths will be wasteful because most of them will never see combat or if war does come they will need to be retrained, especially since the character of warfare is rapidly changing; the billions of dollars spent on a program of this type could be better spent on scientific research, public health, and education; if adopted it would encourage other nations to do likewise, when diminution of militarism is called for; its adoption would be an evidence of lack of faith in world cooperation and collective security; and that patriotism, health, religion, morals, knowledge, and skills can be better taught as traditionally by civilians in homes, schools, and churches.

PLANNING MOBILIZATION

Rigid or Fluid Plans? Advance planning for contingencies of all sorts is one of the important functions of the defense agencies. Some experts think master plans should be formalized and embodied in legislation well in advance of crises in order to ensure readiness. Others believe it is better to keep plans fluid until near war and then call upon Congress for the desired action. Those of this persuasion argue that formalized plans are likely to be outdated when an emergency arrives, that too much attention to detailed planning now may lead to regimentation of the American economy and people, and that optimum preparedness is both an expensive illusion and a dangerous one.

A detailed Industrial Mobilization Plan was developed following the First World War which the War and Navy Departments tried hard, but in vain, to induce Congress to adopt before the Second World War occurred. Even without this, the coming of the war in 1941 found the United States equipped with an unrivaled industrial plant, a reservoir of natural resorces, a transportation and communication system second to none, a reserve of trained scientists and well-equipped laboratories, armed services capable of reasonably prompt expansion, and millions of trained workers.

Since the war no master plan for mobilization has been approved by Congress, but various defense agencies have made preparations for meeting emergencies. The agency most responsible for this task at present is the Office of Defense Mobilization. It is involved in stockpiling essential materials and supplies; safeguarding vital resources; drafting detailed plans for meeting military and civilian manpower needs, for rationing, and for price, wage, and rent control. It is also involved in planning with representatives of industry, agriculture, and labor for prompt expansion of productive facilities; anticipating housing, health, and educational needs; and taking leadership to ensure adequate transport and telecommunications in the event of war.

Civilian Defense. While defense of the homeland is primarily the function of the armed forces, state militias, and local police, modern wars require civilian participation. Recognizing this, the Office of Civilian Defense was established in May, 1941. This agency worked through state and local defense councils composed largely of volunteers.

Through this machinery an elaborate air-raid defense system was established which in certain regions entailed constant surveillance of the air by volunteer watchers, practice air raids, and blackouts. Emergency first-aid and fire-fighting training were also given in hundreds of communities. The defense councils also provided a medium for bringing information to the public on matters pertaining to health, hygiene, dietetics, conservation, and other community needs. At home, these plans were never seriously put to the test, while abroad even the best that could be devised could not prevent serious suffering and losses among civilians. The Office of Civilian Defense was abolished in 1945.

Alarmed over developments in Korea, Congress passed the Federal Civil Defense Act of 1950, which among other things authorized the establishment of the Federal Civil Defense Administration. With the help of an advisory board and committees, this Administration attempts to alert the American people to danger and prepare them for war. More particularly, this involves conducting studies, preparing plans, sponsoring educational programs, providing a nationwide warning system, storing emergency supplies and equipment, training leaders, making financial contributions to states and local governments for programs and projects, and assisting states to negotiate interstate compacts for mutual assistance.

While much money and effort has been spent on civil defense, results have been disappointing. It is difficult to arouse and sustain public interest in the absence of an acute emergency; the character of modern weapons leads many to feel that civil-defense planning is futile; many believe effective planning requires dispersal of population and industry, but this is costly, disruptive, and unpopular; and opinion varies over the appropriate division of responsibility and cost between the Federal government, the states, and the local governments. Although these difficulties continue, Federal, state, and local governments (especially in large cities) have made extensive preparations for civil defense.

MILITARY COMMITMENTS ABROAD

As noted in Chap. 22, the United States has abandoned isolation for collective and regional security. This development has involved military commitments in practically all parts of the world, the total of which reach startling proportions. Some obligations arose from the necessity of governing areas conquered during the war; some arose from pledges made by joining the United Nations; others have sprung from efforts to "contain" communism.

Government of Occupied Areas. When enemy territory is occupied, law and order must be maintained, usually by conquering military forces. Military government at its best is arbitrary and often ruthless, but it is limited by national and international law. Congress has enacted general and special statutes which provide the basis for governing areas occupied by American forces. Supplementing these are orders issued from time to time by the President acting as Commander in Chief.

Within an occupied area the military commander, sometimes called "governor" or "civil affairs administrator," bears full responsibility. Within limits of military law he has supreme legislative, executive, and judicial authority, although much of this is delegated to subordinates. Military law and orders are enforced through courts-martial. Local sovereignty is suspended, and governments formerly in control exist and function at the discretion of the commander. Control is as strict and extensive as is deemed necessary to achieve the objectives of the occupying power. Generally speaking, the Bill of Rights does not extend to the inhabitants of occupied territory.

Military government operated in North Africa for many months after invasion in 1942–1943. Later Italy became the most important theater; still later, Austria, parts of Germany, Japan and some of her former island possessions, and South Korea. While commitments to assist these areas continue, by military force if necessary, occupation forces have been completely withdrawn or severely reduced in most of them.

United Nations Obligations. As noted in Chap. 22, the United Nations Charter makes provision for having armed forces in readiness at all times. It also pledges every member to cooperate to the fullest extent. Thus far the United Nations has been unable to agree sufficiently to provide the international police force contemplated. A small corps of guards, with distinctive uniforms and insignia, has been established, but that is all.

If and when the Charter provisions are put into effect, the world police force would consist of "contingents" of soldiers, naval vessels, and air forces which the respective nations had agreed in advance to keep in readiness for immediate use when asked for by the Security Council. How many each would contribute is to be worked out by the Security Council with the advice of a Military Staff Committee, which would also direct whatever military operations might be undertaken. Thus far, none of the great powers has shown much disposition to see the United Nations adequately equipped with military forces. A committee appointed to work on the matter has been in stalemate almost from the start. In the meantime, the General Assembly has undertaken the task of planning to meet aggression with collective measures which it has authority to recommend but not to order.

Even though it has not been possible to implement Charter provisions fully, the United States has a continuing obligation to support the United Nations with military strength if ordered or requested to do so. That this can be a major undertaking was attested by the experience in Korea.

"Containment." When the war ended American forces and installations were based at strategic spots around the world. Some bases were abandoned but many were not. The Soviet Union viewed with alarm those which remained and as East-West tension mounted their number and importance increased. The United States considered them essential for "containing" communism in general and the Soviet Union in particular. Much was said about needing them to deter aggression by threatening "massive retaliation" with atomic and hydrogen weapons if necessary. Wherever they are, American bases are under military rule. Details surrounding the location, maintenance, and operation of bases on foreign soil are set forth in agreements negotiated with governments concerned. Needless to say, building, maintaining, and manning the bases is a major operation.

Meanwhile, the United States has entered into regional pacts mentioned in Chap. 22. These do not specifically commit this country to armed intervention in the event of conflict, since to do so would encroach on the congressional prerogative of declaring war. But the obligation to consult and assist is clear and requires preparations for military intervention if this should be decided upon.

The policy of "containment" has had still another military phase—one of providing aid to friendly powers. Greece, Turkey, Spain, Pakistan, Yugoslavia—indeed practically all "free nations"—have been recipients. Sometimes the aid takes the form of technical advice on military matters, sometimes supplies and equipment are furnished, often grants and loans are provided, again steps are taken to improve economic and social life as a means of improving military potential. In all its forms the effort and cost of the "containment" policy has been great, with far-reaching implications for American defense agencies and personnel.

ATOMIC ENERGY CONTROL AND DISARMAMENT

While maintaining a large military establishment the United States has nevertheless spent much time and effort on behalf of universal disarmament. The objective has been an international agreement in which all nations agree to outlaw weapons of mass destruction and reduce other armaments and armed forces to agreed-upon levels required for domestic policing and fulfillment of international obligations. The United Nations has been the scene of most postwar efforts, but American studies and policies have been shaped in the Department of State in cooperation with other agencies, especially the Atomic Energy Commission and the Department of Defense. In 1955 the President appointed Mr. Harold Stassen as Special Assistant on Disarmament to spearhead studies, recommend policies, and help keep the public informed on this important subject.

Disarmament Commissions. The United Nations Charter authorized the General Assembly to establish principles of disarmament while the Security Council was empowered to develop concrete plans. With these authorizations, an Atomic Energy Commission was established in 1946 and a Commission for Conventional Armaments was created a year later. In January, 1952, these were merged into a new Disarmament Commission composed of the eleven members of the Security Council plus Canada.

Plans and Counter Plans. Shortly after the Atomic Energy Commission was established, the United States introduced what became known as the "Baruch Plan." This was prepared under the direction of Dean G. Acheson, David E. Lilienthal, and Bernard Baruch, then American representative on the Atomic Energy Commission. The plan called for: (1) setting up a TVA-like International Development Authority and giving it a monopoly of the world's dangerous atomic resources and facilities; (2) banning atomic and other weapons of mass destruction and empowering the world authority to license use of nondangerous atomic energy for peaceful purposes only; (3) impartial inspection on a permanent and continuing basis, meaning that the international authority, as manager of the world's dangerous facilities and resources, would account for all its holdings and also send inspectors anywhere at any time in search of clandestine activity; (4) the control organ to operate within the framework of the Security Council, but the permanent members to waive their right to veto collective measures against an offender of the atomic control plan; (5) the disarmament plan to go into effect by a series of "stages," or step by step, proceeding from disclosure and verification of the least secret data to the most secret and finally, when the control organ had demonstrated its ability to function as intended, the use, possession, and manufacture of atomic weapons would be banned. Meanwhile, in the Commission for Conventional Armaments, the United States had proposed plans calling for a world census of armaments and verification which would then be followed by a series of steps looking toward progressive and balanced reduction.

The Soviet Union objected to many features of the plans sketched above and proposed instead (1) an immediate and unconditional ban on atomic and other weapons of mass destruction; (2) establishment of a control organ within the framework of the Security Council; (3) national ownership of permitted atomic facilities and resources under strict regulation by the control organ; (4) waiver of the veto in the control organ but not in the Security Council; (5) impartial inspection of reported facilities periodically and clandestine activity whenever suspected. As for conventional armaments, the Soviets proposed a flat one-third reduction of all types within one year.

Continuing Disagreements. A majority of the United Nations approved American proposals for the control of atomic weapons substantially as presented, but this could have little meaning until a plan acceptable to all big powers could be devised. The deadlock continues in the Disarmament Commission, although in the meantime both blocs have modified their proposals in significant respects. Western powers have dropped their insistence upon international ownership in favor of national ownership under strict control. They have also modified their proposals with regard to stages and dropped insistence on waiver of the veto in the Security Council. Meanwhile, the Soviet Union has moved closer to the Western proposals for inspection and stages. While the area of disagreement has been narrowed, difficult problems remain.

With respect to conventional weapons the area of disagreement has also been narrowed. For years Western powers have insisted that these weapons should be reduced progressively and in a balanced manner. Under this plan criteria are required for calculating maximums and quotas. The United States has suggested that Russia, China, and the United States reduce armed forces to between 1 million and 1½ million, France to 800,000, Britain to 700,000, and other nations to 1 per cent or less of population. American spokesmen have also suggested that expenditures for military purposes be cut to 5 per cent of gross national product with maximums to equalize expenditures of big powers. For years the Soviet Union rejected the principle underlying these proposals and insisted on a flat one-third reduction within 1 year. In 1955, however, the Soviet Union agreed to the principle set forth by Western powers, although there remain differences over details.

Atomic Pool for Peaceful Purposes. Emphasis upon the frightful military potential of atomic energy has obscured possible peaceful uses to which the energy might be put. Nevertheless, peaceful uses were envisaged from the start and have steadily, albeit slowly, expanded in all nations that have plumbed the mystery of the atom. Within the United States small amounts of uranium have been put to work in medicine, science, and industry.

In 1953 President Eisenhower proposed, in a dramatic appearance before the General Assembly of the United Nations, that a plan be launched to put atomic energy to work for peaceful purposes in all parts of the world. Specifically, he proposed that all nations involved in the atomic arms race give part of their atomic stockpiles to an international pool from which any nation might draw for peaceful uses. The Soviet Union at first rejected the plan, insisting that the unconditional prohibition of atomic weapons was an indispensable prerequisite. Nevertheless, a majority of the General Assembly endorsed the President's proposal in 1954 and the Soviet Union has since indicated willingness to cooperate. First steps have been taken to establish the pool but many details have still to be agreed upon.

Domestic Control of Atomic Energy. With the success of wartime experimentation demonstrated, attention quickly turned to domestic legislation for controlling atomic energy. During debates in Congress a major issue was over whether atomic energy should be placed under military or civilian control. The Atomic Energy Act of 1946, while a compromise, was considered a triumph for those who advocated civilian control.

The act created the Atomic Energy Commission of five members to be appointed by the President with senatorial approval for terms of 5 years. A general manager was provided to handle administration. Several divisions were created with the stipulation that the chief of the Division of Military Application should be a member of the armed forces. This superstructure was to operate under the constant scrutiny of three committees: a general advisory committee of nine members appointed by the President for 6-year terms; a military-liaison committee; and a joint committee of Congress composed of nine from each house. The legislation then gave the United States government a monopoly of fissionable material and gave the Commission broad authority over research, production, and utilization. The Commission was given authority to keep certain data secret and prosecute those who disclosed it.

So far as international aspects were concerned,

the law anticipated control by saying that its provisions were to be superseded by conflicting treaties or agreements which might be entered into. It further stated, however, that American secrets were not to be made known to the rest of the world until "effective and enforceable international safeguards against the use of atomic energy for destructive purposes have been established." Some distrust of the President was evinced by provisions stating that only Congress was to determine when it was safe to relinquish unilateral knowledge and control.

Changes made by the Atomic Energy Act of 1954 grant the Atomic Energy Commission greater latitude in sharing atomic energy and information with friendly powers; permit the Commission to allow, through licensing, more participation by private enterprise in research and development; and allow the Commission greater freedom to declassify secret information and thereby share it with a greater number of people.

The Commission maintains operating offices, research, and production facilities at places scattered over the nation. Much of its work is carried on through contractual arrangements with industrial firms, colleges and universities, and government agencies.

FOR FURTHER READING

Ageton, Arthur A.: *The Naval Officer's Guide* (McGraw-Hill, 4th ed., 1951).

American Friends Service Committee: *Toward Security through Disarmament* (Philadelphia: The Committee, 1952).

Baldwin, Hanson W.: *The Price of Power* (Harper, 1947).

——: *Navy at War* (Morrow, 1943).

Blackett, Patrick M. S.: *Fear, War, and the Atom Bomb: Military and Political Consequences of Atomic Energy* (McGraw-Hill, 1949).

Boutwell, William D., et al.: *America Prepares for Tomorrow: The Story of Our Total Defense Effort* (Harper, 1941).

Bush, Vannevar: *Modern Arms and Free Men* (Simon and Schuster, 1949).

Cornell, Julien: *The Conscientious Objector and the Law* (John Day, 1942).

Corwin, Edward S.: *The President: Office and Powers* (New York University Press, 1940).

Dahl, Robert A., and Ralph S. Brown, Jr.: *Domestic Control of Atomic Energy* (New York: Social Science Research Council, pamphlet no. 8, 1951).

Eliot, George Fielding: *The Strength We Need: A Military Program for America Pending Peace* (Viking, 1946).

Fitzpatrick, Edward A.: *Universal Military Training* (McGraw-Hill, 1945).

French, Paul C.: *We Won't Murder* (Hastings House, 1940).

Ganoe, William A.: *A History of the United States Army* (Appleton-Century-Crofts, rev. ed., 1942).

Glenn, Garrard, and Arthur A. Schiller: *The Army and the Law* (Columbia University Press, 1943).

Huzar, Elias: *The Purse and the Sword: Control of the Army by Congress through Military Appropriations, 1933–1950* (Cornell University Press, 1950).

Kerwin, Jerome G.: *Civil-Military Relationships in American Life* (University of Chicago Press, 1948).

Lasswell, Harold D.: *National Security and Individual Freedom* (McGraw-Hill, 1950).

Leach, Jack Franklin: *Conscription in the United States* (Charles E. Tuttle Co., 1952).

Leighton, Alexander H.: *Governing of Men: General Principles and Recommendations Based on Experiences at a Japanese Relocation Camp* (Princeton University Press, 1945).

Leonard, L. Larry: *International Organization* (McGraw-Hill, 1951).

Military Service Publishing Co.: *The Officer's Guide* (Harrisburg, Pa.: The Telegraph Press, 10th ed., 1944).

Mock, James R., and Evangeline W. Thurber: *Report on Demobilization* (University of Oklahoma Press, 1944).

Nelson, Donald M.: *Arsenal of Democracy—The Story of American War Production* (Harcourt, Brace, 1946).

Newman, James R., and Byron S. Miller: *The Control of Atomic Energy: A Study of Its Social, Economic, and Political Implications* (McGraw-Hill, 1948).

Palmer, John M.: *America in Arms: The Experience of the United States with Military Organization* (Yale University Press, 1941).

Rankin, Robert S.: *When Civil Law Fails* (Duke University Press, 1939).

Rich, Bennett M.: *The Presidents and Civil Disorder* (Brookings, 1941).

Rosebury, Theodore: *Peace or Pestilence* (McGraw-Hill, 1949).

Rossiter, Clinton L.: *The Supreme Court and Commander in Chief* (Cornell University Press, 1951).

——: *Constitutional Dictatorship: Crisis Government in the Modern Democracies* (Princeton University Press, 1948).

Smith, Louis: *American Democracy and Military Power* (University of Chicago Press, 1951).

Tate, Merze: *The United States and Armaments* (Harvard University Press, 1948).

Thomas, Norman M.: *The Conscientious Objector in America* (Viking, 1923).

Tobin, Harold J., and Percy W. Bidwell: *Mobilizing Civilian America* (Council on Foreign Relations, 2d printing, 1940).

U.S. Commission on Organization of the Executive Branch of the Government (first Hoover Commission): *The National Security Organization* (1949).

——: *Task Force Report on National Security Organization* (1949).

U.S. National Security Training Commission: *Universal Military Training, Foundation of Enduring National Strength* (1951).

U.S. Secretary of State's Committee on Atomic Energy: *A Report on the International Control of Atomic Energy* (1946). This is the famous Acheson-Lilienthal report.

U.S. Senate, Committee on Armed Forces: *Report of the Rockefeller Committee on Department of Defense Organization*, 83d Cong., 1st Sess. (1953).

Wallace, Donald H.: *Economic Controls and Defense* (Twentieth Century Fund, 1953).

REVIEW QUESTIONS

1. What "war powers" does the Constitution give to Congress? To the President?

2. What constitutional problems were involved in (*a*) the wartime treatment of Japanese-Americans along the West coast; (*b*) martial law in Hawaii; (*c*) conscription of manpower and property in peace and war?

3. What limits are there to the war powers?

4. What defense powers and responsibilities remain with the states?

5. Compare the national defense establishment before and after unification.

6. Defend and criticize unification of the armed forces.

7. What functions are performed by each of the military Departments?

8. Explain to a prospective draftee how the Selective Service System works.

9. Defend and criticize universal military training proposals.

10. Trace disarmament discussions since 1946, and indicate present points of agreement and disagreement.

11. Explain the provisions of the present program for creating a reserve of trained manpower. What changes should be made in these provisions?

12. Explain the powers and functions of the United States Atomic Energy Commission.

CHAPTER 25

The Commerce Power and Aids to General Business

> But, alas, men are drowning themselves, economically, in the flood of the very abundance they are creating. The world's markets are choked with products that do not move out to fill half-empty stomachs and cover backs that are practically bare. Widespread destitution exists in the sight of plenty. . . . Plainly, invention in the socio-economic field is far—very far—behind invention in the field of production. — O. W. Willcox [1]

The first part of this chapter deals with the commerce power at some length because it has been the one most consciously used by the Federal government to aid and regulate economic affairs. The remainder of the chapter introduces several other grants of power briefly and some of the many federal programs carried on to assist the economy in general and "general business" in particular. The term "general business" refers to ordinary competitive private enterprises with which all are familiar. Federal relationships with businesses of special types are discussed in chapters which follow.

THE COMMERCE POWER

The Constitutional Provision. One of the most serious defects of the Articles of Confederation, it will be recalled, was the inability of Congress to regulate interstate and foreign commerce. Accordingly, after conflicting views had been compromised, the Constitutional Convention, meeting in Philadelphia in 1787, approved the following clause without a dissenting vote: "Congress shall have power . . . to regulate Commerce with foreign Nations, among the several States, and with the Indian Tribes."

The words "regulate" and "commerce" were

chosen with great care. The authors desired a clause that would grant to the Federal government unquestioned authority to control all forms of intercourse affecting two or more states, foreign nations, and the Indian tribes, while at the same time leaving to the states authority over the multiplicity of affairs that concern only localities.

Importance of the Commerce Power. Next to the power to tax, the commerce clause has become one of the most important grants of authority contained in the Constitution. Turning to the *United States Code,*[2] which contains the acts of Congress presently effective, one finds innumerable statutes based upon the commerce power.

One discovers, for example, statutes enacting tariffs and embargoes; admitting and excluding immigrants; regulating the marketing of agricultural products, the buying and selling of articles for export and shipment among the states, canals, rivers, harbors, ships at sea, railroads, airways, radio broadcasting, busses, trucks, bridges and ferries, pipe lines, transmission of electric energy, telephone, telegraph, monopolies, unfair trade practices; regulating the inter-

---

[1] *Can Industry Govern Itself?* (Norton, 1936), p. x.

[2] *United States Code Annotated,* Title 15, Secs. 1011–1012.

state transportation of foods and drugs, firearms, women for immoral purposes, stolen automobiles, kidnaped persons, intoxicating beverages; regulating minimum wages and maximum hours; guaranteeing the right of employees to join unions and bargain collectively, and a host of others.

Indeed, the commerce power is authority for most of the distinctly regulatory activities of the Federal government. It, more than any other power, has been the means whereby the national government has assumed ever-increasing authority over matters affecting the daily lives of the American people.

Distinction between Intrastate and Interstate Commerce. Before the Civil War when society was predominantly rural and businesses were small, the line of demarcation between intrastate and interstate commerce could be drawn with comparative ease. Today the situation is different. The transformation from a simple agrarian society to a gigantic industrial nation has caused all economic activity to become commingled. As the ripples of a pool radiate to the farthest extremity, so every business transaction may affect the economic life of the nation to some degree. Economically, then, no clear-cut division can be made between commerce that is interstate and that which is local.

Nevertheless, the Constitution requires that a distinction be made. While permitting a broad interpretation, the Supreme Court has recently said that federal authority may not be pushed to such an extent as to destroy the distinction that the commerce clause establishes between commerce among the states and the internal concerns of the state. Where the line shall be drawn cannot be determined in advance but must await specific situations.

The review which follows suggests that the pendulum has swung from a broad to a narrow construction and has now swung back to a broader interpretation than was hitherto imaginable. Chief Justice Waite spoke prophetically when he said the commerce power is "not confined to the instrumentalities . . . known or in use when the Constitution was adopted," but "keeps pace with the progress of the country"

and adapts itself "to the new developments of time and circumstances." [3]

The Original Package Doctrine. As early as 1827 [4] the Supreme Court evolved a formula which has helped determine where interstate commerce starts and ends. According to that formula, known since as the "original package doctrine," interstate commerce begins as soon as the original package has been delivered to, and accepted by, a carrier for shipment across one or more state lines or to a foreign country. Interstate commerce continues as long as the article shipped remains in the original package unopened, unused, or unsold. State jurisdiction begins when the original package is opened and the article becomes mingled in the general mass of property within the state.

Businesses Which Are Intrastate. All businesses are intrastate in the sense that they, or parts of them, are situated within one of the states. Some of them, like the peanut vender, the bakery, barbershop, and hardware store, are probably very small; others, like the Ford Motor Company, are very large; while still others range somewhere in between. In this field it is harder than in almost any other to draw the line between intra- and interstate commerce. Since the National Industrial Recovery Act, enacted in 1933, went further in regulating businesses, both large and small, than any law previously or subsequently enacted, reference to the Supreme Court decision in which its constitutionality was considered may help to illustrate the line of demarcation.

NIRA and Local Business. Among other things, the NIRA authorized the formation of codes of fair competition, several hundred of which were put into effect. The groups that formed the codes wrote into them regulations governing wages, hours, fair trade practices, prices, etc. Among the businesses affected were barbershops, local retail stores, small mines and factories, and many other businesses heretofore understood to be engaged in local commerce, hence not subject to federal control.

[3] Pensacola Telegraph Co. *v.* Western Union Telegraph Co., 96 U.S. 1, 9 (1877).

[4] Brown *v.* Maryland, 12 Wheat. 419 (U.S. 1827).

After several months of operation the law was challenged by the Schechter Brothers,[5] who operated slaughterhouses in New York City for the purpose of killing poultry purchased from near-by New Jersey and Pennsylvania and sold to retail poultry dealers and butchers within New York City, who, in turn, sold directly to consumers. Though nearly all the poultry handled by the Schechter Brothers originated outside the State of New York, they sold all of it within the state; hence there was no flow from one state through New York and thence into another. The Supreme Court was unanimous in saying that the Schechter Brothers, and inferentially many others governed by the codes, were not engaged in interstate commerce. Their business, the Court said, had only an indirect effect upon interstate commerce, hence could not be regulated by Congress.

Local Business Today. Although, as will be seen, the Supreme Court has greatly expanded the commerce clause since the demise of NIRA, some commerce is still considered so local as to fall exclusively within state jurisdiction. This includes very small businesses like locally owned restaurants, hotels, barbershops, retail stores, and bakeries. Agricultural production (but not marketing), very small mines, factories, and utilities are also still generally considered to be intrastate commerce. The hunting and fishing of game is still considered local in character.[6] Professionals like doctors, dentists, lawyers, accountants, and architects are still engaged in local commerce, although when they unite in national or regional associations their conduct may come under federal control.[7] Commercialized amusements like circuses, boxing, baseball, and football have long been considered local exhibitions,[8] although recent decisions of the Supreme Court

upholding the conviction of a professional boxing syndicate and a legitimate theater [9] for violating the Sherman Antitrust Act suggests that when amusements operate on a national scale they may forfeit local status.

State Authority over Interstate Commerce. In asserting powers that are legitimately theirs the states often impose controls on commerce which is interstate, and the propriety of their conduct is questioned. From a welter of decisions three conclusions emerge: First, if Congress has already legislated on the subject, the states may not enact conflicting measures. Second, if Congress has not acted, silence does not authorize states to intervene where the subject requires uniform national control. Third, if Congress has not acted and the subject does not require national uniform control, the states may regulate provided their laws are reasonable and do not discriminate against commerce that is interstate.

Illustrations of Invalid State Laws. In the early days of the republic, Congress legislated permitting vessels with federal licenses to operate on navigable waters. Later, the state of New York granted monopoly rights to Robert Fulton to operate steamboats on waters within the state. This, the Court held, conflicted with federal law and was therefore invalid.[10] Congress has required the enrollment and licensing of vessels; hence a state law requiring ships leaving a port within the state to file a statement at the office of the probate judge of the county setting forth the name of the vessel, name of the owners, etc., was an invalid interference with interstate and foreign commerce.[11]

Recently, the Supreme Court had before it an interesting case [12] illustrating federal-state limits. This involved the Wisconsin Public Utility Anti-Strike Law, which made it a misdemeanor for any group of public-utility employees to en-

---

[5] Schechter Poultry Corp. *v.* United States, 295 U.S. 495 (1935).

[6] The leading case is Geer *v.* Connecticut, 161 U.S. 519 (1896).

[7] American Medical Association *v.* United States, 317 U.S. 519 (1942).

[8] Federal Baseball Club of Baltimore *v.* National Baseball League, 259 U.S. 200 (1922); Toolson *v.* New York Yankees, 346 U.S. 356 (1953).

[9] The boxing case was United States *v.* International Boxing Club of New York, 348 U.S. 236 (1954); for the theater case see United States *v.* Lee Shubert *et al.,* 348 U.S. 222 (1954).

[10] Gibbons *v.* Ogden, 9 Wheat. 1 (U.S. 1824).

[11] Sinnot *v.* Davenport, 22 How. 287 (U.S. 1859).

[12] Bus Employees *v.* Wisconsin Employment Relations Board, 340 U.S. 383 (1950).

gage in a strike which would cause interruption of an essential public service. Employees of a Milwaukee gas and transit company walked out, an injunction ordering them to return to work was not obeyed, the employees were convicted of contempt of court and fined. The conviction was later upheld by the Wisconsin Supreme Court. But Congress had already prescribed methods in the National Labor Relations and Taft-Hartley Acts for settling disputes affecting interstate and foreign commerce. On appeal to the United States Supreme Court, the decision was that the local utility was a business affecting interstate commerce, Congress had already legislated, the state law was in conflict, and therefore the state law had to give way.

In the instances just mentioned, Congress had already acted. In the following, Congress had not legislated but the subject required uniform control; hence state laws were invalid. New York and other states imposed taxes upon immigrants entering their ports, but when challenged, the Supreme Court held that immigration required uniform control; hence the state laws were unconstitutional.[13]

Prior to 1886 the states imposed numerous regulations upon all railroads within their borders, but in the year mentioned the Court ruled that railroads that had become interstate required uniform control; hence state laws were invalid.[14] This forced Congress into action, which resulted in creation of the Interstate Commerce Commission. A similar situation arose around 1920 with respect to control of rates for interstate shipments of natural gas. Because uniformity was required, state laws were invalid.[15]

Most numerous of all cases are those in which Congress has not acted but the states have passed laws discriminating against commerce of other states. Thus, during the depression California made it illegal to bring an indigent person into the state. Many states have tried to prevent the importation of oleomargarine by taxing it heavily. Mississippi placed a privilege tax on persons soliciting business for a laundry not licensed in the state. Minnesota went so far as to prohibit the sale of meat products that were not produced within 100 miles of the place sold. A state law required trains to slow down or stop at all railroad crossings, thus seriously impeding their speed. Many Southern states required interstate busses and trains to practice "Jim Crow" segregation in seating and bedding passengers. In all these instances, and many more, Federal courts have held that interstate commerce had been unduly burdened.

Illustrations of Permissible State Regulation. As indicated above, states may enact local laws affecting interstate commerce where they do not conflict with federal enactments, the subject does not require uniform control, and the legislation is not unreasonable or unduly burdensome. Thus, in the interest of safety, states may prescribe rules governing railroad crossings even to the extent of requiring an interstate railroad to eliminate one or more of them. States may penalize operation of freight trains that are manned by fewer than three brakemen, or a "full crew." Limits may be placed upon the width and weight of trucks operating on state highways. Motion-picture films have been censored even though produced in other states. States may prohibit tobacco advertising on billboards and placards by resident and nonresident companies; and they may regulate the retail (but not wholesale) price of out-of-state products such as natural gas, electricity, and milk.

Definition of Interstate Commerce. Because the term "interstate commerce" is nowhere defined in the Constitution, its meaning must be sought elsewhere, especially in court decisions. The famous Steamboat Case[16] was the first in which the Court had occasion to construe the power. The New York legislature had given Robert R. Livingston and Robert Fulton an exclusive right to navigate steamboats on the waters of the state. Ogden secured a license for steamboat navigation from Fulton and Living-

[13] Smith *v.* Turner (The Passenger Cases), 7 How. 283 (U.S. 1849).

[14] Wabash, St. L. & P. R. Co. *v.* Illinois, 118 U.S. 557 (1886).

[15] Public Utility Commission *v.* Landon, 249 U.S. 236 (1919); Missouri *v.* Kansas Gas Co., 265 U.S. 298 (1923).

[16] Gibbons *v.* Ogden, 9 Wheat. 1 (U.S. 1824).

ston. Gibbons, who had originally been a partner with Ogden but was now his rival, was operating steamboats between New York and New Jersey by authority of a license obtained from the Federal government. Ogden, wishing to eliminate his competitor, brought suit in the courts of New York and obtained a ruling enjoining Gibbons from further operations. Whereupon, Gibbons appealed to the United States Supreme Court.

In one of his most celebrated opinions, Chief Justice Marshall, speaking for the Court, ruled in favor of Gibbons. Navigation upon navigable rivers, said he, is interstate commerce. Congress had legislated with respect to such navigation; hence all state laws in conflict with federal must give way. The case was of the utmost importance at the time, eliminating as it did the merciless commercial rivalry between the states, but its future significance derives from the broad definition of commerce contained in the words: "Commerce, undoubtedly, is traffic, but it is something more; it is intercourse. It describes the commercial intercourse between nations, and parts of nations, in all its branches, and is regulated by prescribing rules for carrying on that intercourse."

Transportation. Transportation of persons and goods across state lines is the clearest form of interstate and foreign commerce. The method of conveyance is immaterial, whether it be people walking, cattle leisurely grazing first in one state and then in another, or travel by ship, train, canoe, airplane, pipe line, motorcar, or bicycle, it is still interstate commerce. Even logs floated down a navigable stream are interstate commerce. Though a carrier begins and ends its journey within a single state, it is, nevertheless, subject to federal control if it carries passengers or goods destined for points outside the state or if it competes substantially with interstate carriers. Though a vehicle begins its journey in one state, leaves the state for a considerable distance en route, and returns to the state of origin, it is engaged in interstate commerce.

Communications. At various times the contention has been put forth that only the interstate transportation of tangible things, like persons and property, constituted interstate commerce. But this idea was rejected long ago. Soon after their invention federal regulation of interstate transmission of messages by telephone and telegraph was upheld.[17] In the first case just cited, Mr. Justice Waite said:

The powers thus granted are not confined to the instrumentalities of Commerce or the postal service known or in use when the Constitution was adopted, but they keep pace with the progress of the country, and adapt themselves to the new developments of time and circumstances. They extend from the horse with its rider to the stagecoach, from the sailing vessel to the steamboat, from the coach and the steamboat to the railroad, and from the railroad to the telegraph as these new agencies are successively brought into use to meet the demands of increasing population and wealth.

More recently, regulation of radio broadcasting and the transmission of news by wire or wireless have been held to be within the scope of the commerce power.[18]

Buying and Selling. Buying and selling of goods intended for shipment or use in other states is interstate commerce. Accordingly, Congress has made illegal all sorts of contracts that monopolize interstate commerce; it has outlawed price discrimination between buyers; it has legalized contracts whereby manufacturers may force retailers to maintain resale prices of nationally advertised products; it has regulated the buying and selling of livestock, agricultural products, and stocks and bonds; and it has outlawed unfair trade practices that may injure buyers and sellers.

Moreover, Congress has fixed the rates that sellers may charge and buyers pay for interstate carriers, electric power, natural gas, and bitumi-

---

[17] One of the earliest cases involving telegraph was Pensacola Telegraph Co. *v.* Western Union Telegraph Co., 96 U.S. 1 (1878), while early cases involving telephone were Delaware and Atlantic Telegraph and Telephone Co. *v.* Delaware, 50 Fed. 677 (1892), and Muskegee Nat. Tel. Co. *v.* Hall, 118 Fed. 382 (1902).

[18] Fisher's Blend Station, Inc. *v.* State Tax Commission, 297 U.S. 650 (1936); Associated Press *v.* National Labor Relations Board, 301 U.S. 103 (1937).

nous coal. A corollary of this, as was explained more fully above, is that states cannot impose burdens upon the buying and selling of interstate products. This explains why salesmen for out-of-state concerns, such as the Fuller Brush Company and the Real Silk Hosiery Mills, who merely take and subsequently deliver orders, cannot be compelled to pay local license fees for doing business within a state.

Production and Commerce. Transportation, buying and selling, and transmission of electricity or messages imply movement or conveyance from somewhere within one state into another. But what of the actual manufacture of a product or its extraction from the earth? Because it is ultimately bought and sold or transported across state lines, is its production a part of interstate commerce? The question became important toward the end of the last century when businesses were rapidly becoming national in size.

The Old Doctrine. A leading case was that of United States *v*. E. C. Knight.[19] The American Sugar Refining Company had acquired control of 98 per cent of all sugar refining in the United States. Suit was brought by the Department of Justice charging the company with monopolizing interstate commerce in violation of the Sherman Act. Acknowledging that the company was of enormous size and in control of virtually all sugar refining in the country, the Court nevertheless dismissed the suit saying that the company was not engaged in interstate commerce, hence was beyond the scope of federal regulation.

The Court distinguished between production and commerce, saying that the former involved merely a change in *form* while commerce involved change of *place*. The refining of sugar was antecedent to commerce but not a part of it. In other words, no matter how large a production unit became, its effect upon economic affairs in other states was so indirect and remote as to cause it to be beyond federal control under the commerce power. Subsequently, by similar reasoning, Congress was prevented from regulating not only manufacturing but also the production

of oil and natural gas, mining, quarrying, and electric power.

The Present Doctrine. This doctrine was followed until 1937, since which time the courts have greatly expanded the scope of the commerce power. The entering wedge was driven in a case involving the constitutionality of the National Labor Relations Act.[20] The Jones and Laughlin Steel Corporation was accused of violating the act by discharging several employees for union activities in production units at its plant at Aliquippa, Pa.

The company admitted the charges but denied that the Federal government could do anything about them because the men were engaged in manufacture which was not interstate commerce. The company was the fourth largest producer of steel in the country. Though incorporated under the laws of Pennsylvania, it had nineteen subsidiaries which comprised an integrated empire. It owned or leased mines, ships, railroads, stores, mills, plants, factories, pipe lines, and refineries in several states and maintained sales offices in twenty cities and one in Canada. Approximately 75 per cent of its products were shipped out of Pennsylvania.

Admitting that the dismissed men were engaged in production, the Supreme Court went on to say that the labor practices of the employer had such an immediate and direct effect upon interstate commerce as to come within the scope of federal power. Writing for the majority, Chief Justice Hughes observed:

In view of respondent's far-flung activities it is idle to say that the effect would be indirect or remote. It is obvious that it would be immediate and might be catastrophic. . . . When industries organize themselves on a national scale, making their relation to interstate commerce the dominant factor in their activities, how can it be maintained that their industrial labor relations constitute a forbidden field into which Congress may not enter when it is necessary to protect interstate commerce from paralyzing consequences of industrial war?

[19] 156 U.S. 1 (1895).

[20] National Labor Relations Board *v*. Jones and Laughlin Steel Corp., 301 U.S. 1 (1937).

This meant that manufacturing, or any other form of productive enterprise, was interstate commerce if organized on a national scale and carried on in two or more states. This is a wide departure from the doctrine enunciated in the Knight case and subsequently followed.

Recent Trends. Since the historic reversal of 1937 the commerce power has been applied to productive activities of various sorts. Though agricultural production itself remains local, considerable federal restraint has been approved through control of quantities that may be marketed.[21] In 1939 federal legislation fixing prices for bituminous coal was approved.[22] In the following year the Court upheld federal regulation of wages, hours, child labor, and working conditions for businesses engaged in the manufacture of lumber products,[23] and incidentally mines and other types of enterprises considered beyond the reach of federal power prior to 1937. During the same year, comprehensive federal regulation of natural gas companies was approved,[24] and still more recently long-standing decisions have been overruled, bringing insurance within the scope of the commerce clause.[25] Though the trend has been in the direction of applying the commerce power broadly, there is still a huge volume of economic activities that remain intrastate.

AIDS TO GENERAL BUSINESS

Department of Commerce. The Department of Commerce is to businessmen what the Department of Agriculture is to farmers and the Department of Labor is to workingmen. Cre-

[21] Currin *v.* Wallace, 306 U.S. 1 (1939); Mulford *v.* Smith, 307 U.S. 38 (1938); Wickard *v.* Filburn, 317 U.S. 111 (1942).

[22] Sunshine Anthracite Coal Co. *v.* Adkins, 310 U.S. 381 (1940).

[23] United States *v.* Darby Lumber Co., 312 U.S. 100 (1941).

[24] Federal Power Commission *v.* National Gas Pipeline Co., 315 U.S. 590 (1941). See also Federal Power Commission *v.* Hope Natural Gas Co., 320 U.S. 591 (1943).

[25] United States *v.* South-Eastern Underwriters Association *et al.,* 322 U.S. 533 (1944). The case overruled was Paul *v.* Virginia, 8 Wall. 168 (U.S. 1869).

ated in 1903, it was known as the Department of Commerce and Labor until Labor was set off in a separate Department in 1913. The Department occupies one of the largest buildings in Washington, a structure built during the Coolidge and Hoover administrations when business interests tended to predominate in national politics.

At the head of the Department is a Secretary who is also a member of the President's cabinet. This officer is nearly always someone who has supported the President's party and usually reflects the attitude of the Administration toward business. Principal assistants and internal organization of the Department are shown on the chart on page 479.

The first Hoover Commission proposed several important changes.[26] In addition to its general recommendations for improving administration, the Commission suggested the Department's focus should be on (1) nonregulatory transportation activities, and (2) industrial and commercial services. To the first should be added the nonregulatory functions then performed by such agencies as the Interstate Commerce Commission, Maritime Commission, and Civil Aeronautics Board. Also to be added were the services of the Customs Bureau relating to marine transport, the Public Roads Administration, and the Coast Guard. To industrial and commercial services should be added the commercial-fisheries activities then centered in the Fish and Wildlife Service, Department of Interior.

In response to these suggestions, functions of the Maritime Commission and Public Roads Administration were transferred to the Department. Another suggestion made by the first Hoover Commission, *viz.,* that the Inland Waterways Corporation be sold to private enterprise, was accomplished in 1953-1954.

Economic Planning. Various agencies of the Federal government have long been concerned with long-term planning. Not until the great depression, however, was there much official recognition of the need for over-all planning of the national economy.

Federal economic planning was first begun in 1934 by an agency ultimately known as the

[26] *Department of Commerce* (1949), pp. 1-7.

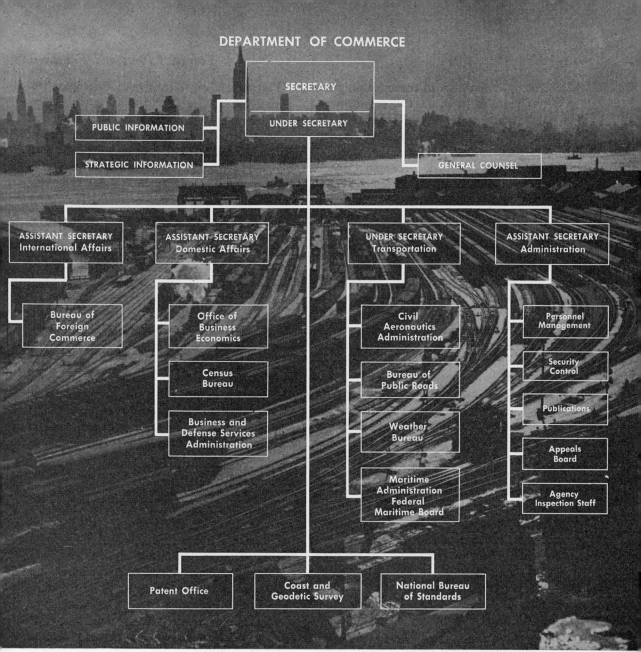

DEPARTMENT OF COMMERCE

- SECRETARY
- UNDER SECRETARY
- PUBLIC INFORMATION
- STRATEGIC INFORMATION
- GENERAL COUNSEL

ASSISTANT SECRETARY International Affairs
- Bureau of Foreign Commerce

ASSISTANT SECRETARY Domestic Affairs
- Office of Business Economics
- Census Bureau
- Business and Defense Services Administration

UNDER SECRETARY Transportation
- Civil Aeronautics Administration
- Bureau of Public Roads
- Weather Bureau
- Maritime Administration Federal Maritime Board

ASSISTANT SECRETARY Administration
- Personnel Management
- Security Control
- Publications
- Appeals Board
- Agency Inspection Staff

- Patent Office
- Coast and Geodetic Survey
- National Bureau of Standards

Standard Oil Co. (N.J.) photograph

National Resources Planning Board. It was given the task of inventorying national resources and suggesting their wise use, studying economic trends and recommending ways to avoid booms and busts, and planning public works in cooperation with state and local governments. The Board was abolished in 1943, but it established the concept of planning, stimulated the establishment of state and local planning bodies, and left behind a number of useful studies.

The demise of the National Resources Planning Board and the threat of postwar unemployment caused much agitation for new legislation, which culminated in the Employment Act of 1946.[27] In its original form the legislation would have pledged the government to plan and

[27] For an excellent review of the legislative history of this measure, see Stephen K. Bailey, *Congress Makes a Law: The Story behind the Employment Act of 1946* (Columbia University Press, 1949).

place into operation a broad economic program whenever required to ensure full employment. As finally passed, after heated argument, the measure was a greatly "watered-down" version of the original bill.

The legislation created a three-man Council of Economic Advisers in the Executive Office of the President. The Council, aided by a staff of economists and statisticians, prepares comprehensive economic reports for the President dealing with current conditions and trends. The President later submits these to Congress with his own recommendations. To facilitate consideration of them Congress has created a Joint Committee on the Economic Report comprised of seven members from each house.

Public Works Planning. Public works consist of those activities that entail construction by, or on behalf of, governmental agencies. While a large volume of construction cannot be postponed, some of it can be put off until prices are favorable or the economy lags. The omnipresent threat of depression makes it imperative that governments and private concerns maintain portfolios of carefully planned projects, the construction of which can be timed to economic conditions. Recognition of this truth has led to the expenditure of much time, energy, and money, especially in recent years.

The General Services Administration has been the focal point of public-works planning, although it must be remembered that each agency does most of its project planning itself. Most current nondefense planning activities center around federal buildings, national parks and monuments, public roads, housing, public works in some of the territories, and public health. Most public-works planning is done in close cooperation with the states.

Legislation in 1949 established a plan whereby interest-free loans could be made to the states and their subdivisions for public-works planning, other than housing, but new advances were discontinued as of June 30, 1951. An ambitious program of cooperative federal-state highway expansion was proposed in 1955 and 1956.[28]

[28] See p. 90.

Protective Tariffs. Tariffs are levies upon imported goods. The Constitution, it will be remembered, gives Congress the power to lay and collect "duties" and "imposts," meaning tariffs. Every American tariff law, including the first adopted in 1789, has had two purposes: one, to raise revenue; the other, to "protect" domestic industries, at least certain of them. The intent of a "protective" tariff is to keep foreign products out in order to give American-made products a competitive advantage in the home market. The advantage results from the fact that by restricting foreign selling, competition is eased, causing domestic prices to remain higher than they otherwise would. By this process a tax is levied upon American consumers, the proceeds of which are paid as a subsidy to the makers of American goods.

Whether this is a wise or an unwise policy cannot concern us here. Whether for good or ill, many American businesses ("infant industries") have been built behind tariff walls and, without such assistance, probably would never have been "born" or would have fallen by the wayside. Tariffs not only play a large role in deciding what kind of goods shall enter the country, but they also determine, to a considerable extent, the volume of exports, since countries will not readily buy here unless they can also sell. Indeed, tariffs affect the entire economy and an unwise tariff policy may have devastating effects not only upon the United States but upon the entire world. The intense interest of businessmen in tariff policy accounts for the fact that tariff making has provided more controversy in Congress than almost any other issue.

Tariff Schedules. Tariff laws include many schedules, or classifications of commodities, wherein each product is listed together with the amount of the tax, if any. Tariffs are either "specific," *i.e.,* so much per unit, or ad valorem, *i.e.,* a stated percentage of the value of the commodity. Before goods leave foreign ports for the United States invoices must be certified by American consular officers, and upon arrival they must be appraised by officers attached to the Customs Bureau of the Treasury Department. Decisions of the customs officers may be reviewed by the United States Customs Court, and further appeal may be taken on questions of law to the Court of Customs and Patent Appeals.

Unless revised frequently, tariff schedules and accompanying rules and regulations which must be followed by customs officers tend to become archaic and often ridiculous. Concern over the extent to which the "dead hand of the past" restricted and hampered trade caused Congress to pass the Customs Simplifications Acts of 1953 and 1954.

The Tariff Commission. Making tariffs is an exceedingly complicated and technical task for which Congressional committees seldom have either the time or training. Hence, in 1916, a bipartisan Commission was created with twelve members appointed by the President with the advice and consent of the Senate. In 1930 the membership was reduced to six, who serve for terms of 6 years. The Commission is not a quasi-legislative or quasi-judicial body, nor does it exercise administrative powers. It is an investigational and advisory agent whose primary duty is that of conducting research and furnishing information to Congress and the President on matters relating to American and foreign tariffs.

"Flexible" Tariffs. Formerly when Congress fixed tariff rates, they remained unalterable until changed by Congress. Not only did this produce rigidity, but it invited incessant agitation and lobbying on the part of special interests to secure favorable changes. The McKinley Tariff of 1890 empowered the President to levy special rates upon certain imports in retaliation for "unjust and unreasonable" charges levied by foreign nations upon American products. Since 1922 tariff rates have been based upon the cost-of-production theory, *i.e.,* the duty fixed is supposed to be determined by the difference between the cost of production at home and abroad. When the Tariff Commission finds a difference between foreign and American costs, a report is made to the President, who may raise or lower the tariff to the advantage of the American producer. Maximum and minimum rates are stated in the law, and the President is forbidden to raise or

lower any existing tariff by more than 50 per cent. Articles covered by a reciprocal tariff agreement, described below, are exempt from these provisions.

Reciprocal Tariffs. Still greater flexibility was provided in the Reciprocal Tariff Act of 1934. This sought to regain vanishing American export markets by authorizing the President to negotiate tariff agreements with countries willing to make satisfactory concessions. Negotiations are conducted under direction of an Interdepartmental Committee on Trade Agreements, while hearings for interested domestic producers are conducted by an Interdepartmental Committee for Reciprocity Information.

Although trade agreements resemble treaties, they are not considered to be such, and they do not require Senate approval. Being executive agreements, they are more flexible than treaties, and the disgraceful performances which inevitably accompany tariff making by statute are avoided.

Present legislation runs until June, 1958. It permits the President to negotiate agreements but adds safeguards. These include the following: (1) no rates may be raised or lowered by more than 50 per cent; (2) articles on the dutiable list may not be transferred to the free list, or vice versa; (3) no agreement to reduce the indebtedness of a foreign government may be made; and (4) "peril-point" and "escape-clause" provisions must be respected.

Peril-point provisions are borrowed from the 1948 version of the act. These require the President to notify the Tariff Commission of his intention to negotiate a trade agreement and also to submit a list of items under consideration. The Tariff Commission then has 120 days to hold hearings and report. Among other things, the Commission is to indicate a peril point for each item, *i.e.,* it must state the tariff rate below which imports would, or might, come in sufficient quantity to seriously injure, or threaten to injure, the domestic producer. The Commission must report to the President and also to Congress if the President fixes a rate, or fails to adjust a rate, at or above the peril point. The President is also instructed to report to Congress justi-fying his action if rates are fixed below the peril point. The assumption behind this procedure is that, with reports from both the Tariff Commis-sion and the President, Congress would be in a position to investigate and air opposition views.

Escape-clause provisions require that tariff rates stated in the agreements be adjusted when-ever investigation discloses they injure, or threaten injury to, domestic producers. Emer-gency investigation and action is authorized for perishable agricultural products.

The legislation has had 3- or 2-year time limits; hence it comes up for periodic congres-sional review. The discussions are always heated, if not acrimonious. Principal critics are usually high-tariff advocates, industries that think they have been injured or fear they might be, and those who claim that they are opposed in prin-ciple to the broad grant of discretion given to the President. Most of these refrain from advo-cating outright repeal but urge the use of peril points, escape clauses, and some sort of congres-sional review before agreements go into effect.

On the whole, the agreements have generally, but not drastically, lowered tariffs and stimu-lated trade. Foreign nations have urged lower tariffs as a means of helping them pay debts owed to the United States and getting credits needed to buy goods in this country. Many of them would prefer to be aided in this way rather than continue to partake of bountiful grants and loans for recovery and rearmament.

ITO, GATT, and OTC. In recent years much attention has been given by nations of the world to collective measures designed to reduce trade barriers. A charter to establish an International Trade Organization (ITO) was negotiated at Havana, Cuba, by delegates from 56 countries during the winter of 1947–1948, which had two purposes: (1) to establish rules of conduct for governing international economic relations; (2) to provide information and technical assistance, interpret and administer the charter, and settle disputes. The charter has not been implemented chiefly because of the failure of the American government to ratify.

Meanwhile, since 1948, a General Agreement on Tariffs and Trade (GATT) has been opera-tive. This is an agreement between 34 nations to promote trade by reducing such restrictions as tariffs, quotas, and discriminatory taxes. A basic principle is the "most-favored nation" rule under which each GATT country agrees to give all other members, immediately and uncondition-ally, any trade advantage, favor. privilege, or immunity it grants to any other country. This rule was welcomed by the United States, since it had been a feature of American commercial policy since 1923 and it greatly facilitated the trade agreement program.

Unlike the proposed ITO charter, this agree-ment provides for no formal administrative body. Rather, GATT provides for periodic ses-sions of member nations at which matters of mutual concern are discussed. At these meetings members can also interpret the agreement and decide whether a member nation has lived up to its commitments. They can also release nations from their commitments if circumstances war-rant. But aside from asserting moral force, GATT cannot compel a country to do anything against its will.

Several years of experience with GATT con-vinced members of the need for an administra-tive body. Accordingly, they proposed creation of an Organization for Trade Cooperation (OTC). This would have a General Assembly, an Executive Committee, and a Secretariat. The new organization would administer GATT but it would have no supranational powers. President Eisenhower first made the proposal to Congress early in 1955; the reception has been cool.

Subsidies. In addition to tariffs, the list of di-rect and indirect subsidies made to business groups is a long one. Only a few will be sug-gested here. Generous land grants were made to railroads during the last century. Federal grants for rivers and harbors have been a boon to many localities, businessmen, and shippers. Appropria-tions for public roads have been an important direct and indirect subsidy to the construction industry, the makers of automobiles, carriers by bus and truck, as well as an invaluable service to the general public. Generous payments have been made to rail, water, and air carriers for carrying the mail; while mail has been carried for below-cost rates, or free of charge, for the benefit of special groups as well as the public. The construction of airlines and airports has been an important stimulus to the aircraft industry. Several federally owned utilities, like the former Inland Waterways Corporation and the Alaskan Railroad, have subsidized certain groups and areas by below-cost operations. Shipbuilders and the Merchant Marine have been generously assisted. During the depression the Federal government deliberately spent huge sums to stimulate business activity; while throughout the war federal funds were lavishly spent to encourage the production of war materials and hold prices in line. Although other groups in the country—farmers, workmen, unemployed, veterans, consumers, etc.—have also received financial assistance on innumerable occasions, the business community has without doubt done well by itself.

Promotion of Foreign Trade. Foreign trade has always been important to the United States, and it has become more so. Not only do Americans have billions of dollars invested abroad and trade interests in all parts of the world, but the dwarfed world, the growing awareness that our prosperity and welfare is tied to that of other nations, UN and regional security commitments, and the insatiable demands of modern war have made world trade of direct and vital importance to all. Although many agencies of the Federal government are involved, only the Bureau of Foreign Commerce and the Export-Import Bank of Washington will be noted here.

Bureau of Foreign Commerce. This bureau, a part of the Department of Commerce, has the difficult task of promoting trade in a badly disorganized and divided world. While it works for a "balanced growth of international trade" it must also issue licenses for the control of exports, cope with monetary limitations and restrictions, contend with tariffs and quotas, help to boycott communist nations, and collaborate with other federal agencies, the United Nations and its specialized bodies, and private businesses and organizations. Flowing through this office is a constant stream of economic data from all parts

of the world that is made available to all who ask or read its bulletins.

The Export-Import Bank of Washington. This corporation dates back to 1934. After being a part of several agencies it is now a permanent independent establishment. It is organized under the laws of the District of Columbia, and its capital stock is owned entirely by the Federal government. The bank was originally intended to help finance trade with Russia; it later proved more helpful in the Latin-American theater; and it is now aiding trade with American territories and friendly nations.

The bank has two primary functions: one to lend money to exporters and importers who cannot obtain desired funds from private sources to help them take advantage of foreign business opportunities; the other, to make loans to foreign governments to help them develop their resources, stabilize their economies, market products in an orderly manner, and recover from war.

Fixing Standards. The Constitution gives Congress the power to "fix the standards of weights and measures," but the power is a concurrent one in the sense that the states may legislate until the time Congress does and afterwards they may do whatever is not inconsistent with federal law.

Prior to 1838 the country operated under state standards inherited from the Colonial period, but in the year mentioned Congress legalized the English system (foot, inch, gallon, quart, pound, ounce, etc.), with which everyone is familiar. In 1866 the metric system (meter, liter, gram, etc.) commonly used in Europe was also legalized. Today Congress has fixed standards of a wide variety but leaves the enforcement of most of them to the states. The National Bureau of Standards, a part of the Department of Commerce, is the principal agency working in this field.

Census Taking. A federal census was required, if for no other reason than to provide the data for apportioning members of the House of Representatives and direct taxes. The constitutional mandate reads: "The actual enumeration [of people] shall be made within three years after the first meeting of the Congress . . . and within every subsequent term of ten years, in such manner as they shall by law direct." The seventeenth census was taken in 1950. The Bureau of the Census, in the Department of Commerce, is the administering agent. The Bureau does more than take censuses; it has become the principal statistical agency of the Federal government. It is concerned not only with gathering and compiling statistics but also with improving statistical methods.

Census data record much more than a population count. They include occupations, unemployment, housing, agriculture, irrigation, manufactures, mineral industries, and the like. In addition to the decennial census, special ones are taken from time to time. Here is a mine of information which is widely used by businesses of all sorts.

Weather Forecasting. The Weather Bureau was transferred from the Department of Agriculture to that of Commerce in 1940. Weather observations are made at thousands of places throughout the country. Its airway stations make observations and telegraph reports at scheduled times throughout the day, while others make observations daily and report as required. Summary reports are exchanged with meteorological centers of other nations. Observations comprise all surface weather conditions, river and flood stages, and upper-air conditions. In addition, the Bureau sponsors a number of research projects seeking fuller knowledge of meteorology. Its results provide the basis for weather maps and reports which appear in the daily press and which are broadcast over radio and television. Special warnings are given of storms, hurricanes, cold waves, frosts, forest fires, and floods, while specialized daily forecasts are issued for aeronautics, agriculture, engineering, and navigation. Here is a basic and invaluable service to businessmen and the general public.

Coastal Surveys. Shortly after the new nation was established, Congress authorized a survey of the coast and set up an agency for this purpose which is known today as the Coast and Geodetic Survey. A part of the Department of Commerce, this agency has several tasks. It continues to survey and chart the coasts of the United States and its territories; surveys inland waters; determines elevations along the coast and in the interior of the country; studies tides and currents; compiles aeronautical charts; observes the earth's magnetism; makes seismological and astronomical observations; and attempts to improve methods of surveying and mapping.

The agency's surveys, charts, maps, and reports are of special value to those interested in navigation, fishing, engineering, aeronautics, building, and radio. While its work is basic to the American nation and its economy, it is seldom dramatized. The average citizen hears of it only at times of earthquakes.

Patents and Copyrights. Borrowing from English experience, the Constitution provides that "Congress shall have Power . . . to promote the Progress of Science and useful Arts by securing for limited Times to Authors and Inventors the exclusive Right to their respective Writings and Discoveries." This power is one granted exclusively to Congress.

The phrase "to promote the progress of science and useful arts" does not convey power to do whatever Congress wishes in order to advance science and the arts. Rather, the phrase merely states the purpose for which patents and copyrights may be issued. Note also that patents and copyrights can be granted for "limited times" only. This prevents monopolies in perpetuity; although it does not prevent renewals for limited times.

Patents must be issued to "inventors" and copyrights to "authors"—not to anyone else, other than bona fide heirs and assigns. Furthermore, patents can be issued only for "discoveries" and copyrights for "writings." To be the former, it must be a new and useful creation or contrivance discovered by intellectual labor. This definition precludes obtaining a patent for merely an ingenious readjustment of existing devices; nor could one patent something found, stolen, or given to him.

To be a "writing" the production must be an original, meritorious work of literature or art created by intellectual labor and published for public use. This would include books, newspapers, paintings, motion-picture films, songs, and even private letters; but it would not include prints, labels, trade-marks, ideas expressed in a copyrighted book, titles of books and songs, the news itself, or the mere publication of statutes of a state or ordinances of a city.

Patent Legislation. Patent laws of the United States were revised and codified in 1952. They are administered by the Patent Office, a unit of the Department of Commerce. When applications are filed they are carefully studied; if rejected twice an appeal may be taken to a three-man Board of Patent Appeals. From there appeals may be taken to the United States Court of Customs and Patent Appeals, or civil action may be taken against the Commissioner of Patents in the district court for the District of Columbia. While the Patent Office tries to avoid issuing patents that infringe upon those granted to others, it does not guarantee this result. Accordingly, if infringement is detected, an inventor who wishes to protect his interest must bring suit in a Federal district court.

Patents may be issued to the following: (1) anyone who invents or discovers any new and useful process, machine, manufacture, or composition of matter, or any new and useful improvement thereof; (2) anyone who invents or discovers and asexually reproduces any distinct and new variety of plant, other than a tuber-propagated plant; and (3) anyone who invents any new, original, and ornamental design for an article of manufacture.

When patents are issued, they convey the exclusive right to make, use, refrain from using, and vend the invention throughout the United States and its territories. Patent rights run for 17 years, except for designs, which continue for 3½, 7, or 14 years as elected by the applicant.

Copyrights. Responsibility for handling copyrights rests with the Copyright Office, in the Library of Congress. Copyrights may be obtained only *after* writings are published. To secure them two copies must be sent to the Copyright Office with an appropriate fee. When received, the work is registered and the author is duly notified. Henceforth he enjoys the exclusive right to "print, reprint, publish, copy and vend" the work. The privilege extends for a period of 28 years and is renewable for a second, but not a third, period of the same duration. Notice of copyright must be printed somewhere near the front of the publication; if it is not, others may copy or reproduce the work in any way they please. As compared with the issuance of patents, the procedure is simple and brief. As in the case of patents, the Copyright Office does not guarantee the originality of the writing, nor will it protect the author from infringement. Such protection must be obtained by resort to the United States district court.

At present one may copyright the following:

1. Books, including composite and encyclopedic work directories, gazetteers, and other compilations
2. Periodicals, including newspapers
3. Lectures, sermons, addresses (prepared for oral delivery)
4. Dramatic and dramatico-musical compositions
5. Musical compositions
6. Maps
7. Works of art, models or designs for works of art
8. Reproductions of a work of art
9. Drawings or plastic works of a scientific or technical character
10. Photographs
11. Prints and pictorial illustrations
12. Motion-picture photoplays
13. Motion pictures other than photoplays

There is a fundamental difference between patents and copyrights. The former protects the subject matter for which patents are granted even against a bona fide inventor who may independently make the same invention. A copyright, on the other hand, protects only against actual copying. One may write a book, for example, describing Niagara Falls, and secure a copyright thereon; this does not prevent someone else from writing a book on the same subject, as long as he does not copy from the former. One may take a photograph and have it copyrighted, but this would not prevent someone else from taking a picture of the same scene. Several authors may write textbooks about the same subject; their books will necessarily be similar, but their copyrights will not be infringed unless one actually copies from another.

Trade-marks. Trade-marks are governed by Congress under its power to regulate interstate and foreign commerce. The latest legislation is the Lanham Trade-mark Act of 1946—a measure long striven for by interested parties. This law generally codifies, revises, and simplifies common and federal statutory law on the subject.

Under the new legislation not only trademarks may be registered but also service marks, collective marks, and certification marks. A trade-mark is a word, name, symbol, or device, or any combination of them, which identifies and distinguishes goods. Examples are "Kodak" for cameras and "Philco" for radios. A service mark is one which identifies and distinguishes a service, for example "Greyhound" for bus transportation and "Amos 'n' Andy" for entertainment.

A collective mark is one used by a group or association to identify or distinguish goods or services of members, for example "Indian River" for oranges, "Mohawk Valley" for apples, the pine tree for Rochdale cooperatives, and the Boy Scout emblem. A certification mark is one used for goods and services of any person other than owners to certify regional origin, quality, accuracy, mode of manufacture, and the like. Examples are various seals, like the "Good Housekeeping Seal of Approval" and the labor union symbol used to indicate that work was done by organized labor under collective bargaining.

Marks of all types are registered with the Patent Office. The procedure is much the same as that explained above for patents. Among marks not to be registered are those showing a flag or symbol of any American or foreign government; those that are immoral, deceptive, or scandalous; those which may suggest a connection with or likeness to persons living or dead, institutions, beliefs, or national symbols; or those that closely resemble marks already registered.

Marks of all types are good for 20 years provided that after 5 years registrants file affidavits showing that their marks are still in use or that nonuse is due to special circumstances. After the first 20 years registrations may be renewed for subsequent periods of similar length. As in the case of patents and copyrights, registrants must protect their own rights by resort, if need be, to the courts.

Bankruptcy. The Constitution grants Congress the power to establish "uniform Laws on the subject of Bankruptcies throughout the United States." The clause clearly implies that the power is a concurrent one. Like other powers of this type, the states may continue their laws until such time as Congress decides to bring about uniformity. When Congress does legislate, state laws that are in conflict are suspended, but those not in conflict remain in effect. If Congress should repeal its provisions, as it did on three occasions during the nineteenth century, then the state laws could once more be enforced without reenactment. Federal law is now so complete and comprehensive that it leaves little room for state matters, although there are important instances where state insolvency laws still apply.

Except for three brief periods, all of which followed major or minor depressions, Congress left the handling of bankruptcies entirely to the states prior to the enactment of the Nelson Act of 1898. Numerous bankruptcy frauds and widespread criticism of the Nelson Act led President Hoover, in 1931, to initiate a nation-wide survey of the results of the law. The disclosures, coupled with hardships growing out of the depression, led to a number of amendments. In 1938 the Chandler Act was passed, which, while retaining the framework of the Nelson Act, embodied many changes and codified existing law on the subject.

No agency of the executive branch has been set up to administer laws relative to insolvent businesses. The Administrative Office of the United States Courts acts as a clearing house for matters pertaining to bankruptcies, but proceedings themselves originate as civil actions before United States district courts.

With a few exceptions, proceedings may be started either by the debtor himself or by his creditors. After a debtor has been declared a bankrupt, settlement of the estate usually takes place under the supervision of a referee appointed by the court and one or more trustees chosen by the creditors. Appeal may be taken to the United States Courts of Appeals or the Supreme Court.

Housing. While housing has always been a necessity, "adequate" housing has only recently

over a generation, but it was not until recently that the public became sufficiently aroused to support vigorous action by the Federal government.

Except for the building done in Washington and other critical areas during the First World War, federal housing activities stemmed from

THE HOUSING SITUATION

THE TREND OF HOME BUILDING

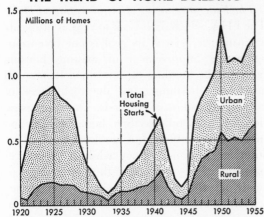

THE EQUIPMENT IN OUR HOMES

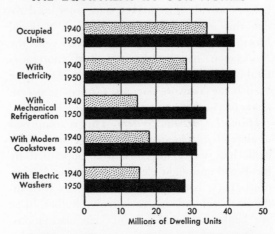

THE CONDITION OF OUR HOMES

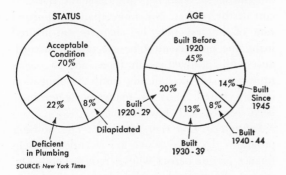

SOURCE: *New York Times*

THE SHIFT TO HOME OWNERSHIP

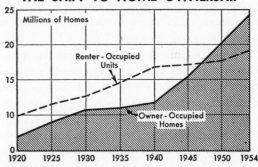

become so, and even yet millions still live in dwellings that are scarcely fit for human occupancy. All important cities have their "slums" or "blighted areas," and many rural sections are covered with dwellings that are equally bad, if not worse. Not only are there many substandard dwellings, but there is also an over-all shortage of houses, as anyone who has tried moving during recent years can attest. Social workers and others have called attention to this situation for

the great depression. An act creating a system of Federal Home Loan Banks in 1932 was the first venture. Then followed other legislation aimed at helping distressed mortgagees refinance their obligations, making credit more easily available for home renovation and building, clearing slums and providing low-cost housing for low-income groups, and, later, providing housing in critical areas for defense and war workers, returning veterans, and others. Since

1947 Federal housing activities have been centered in the Housing and Home Finance Agency, an independent establishment.

Buying and Selling Mortgages. Funds for new homes or for mortgages are usually provided by banks, building and loan associations, insurance companies, and similar institutions. But these companies often sell their mortgages to provide cash or find better investments. This buying and selling is commonly described as a "secondary mortgage market." The Federal government has helped provide this market since 1935, and today this is the task of the Federal National Mortgage Association. During postwar years the Association has bought and sold mortgages totaling billions of dollars. Most of these have been home loans to veterans, farmers, and residents of Alaska.

Home Loan Bank System. This is comprised of eleven banks located in principal cities.[29] Each bank has twelve directors, four appointed by the Board and eight elected by member institutions. These banks do not deal directly with individuals who desire to borrow. Rather, they are banks for building and loan associations, savings and loan associations, cooperative banks, homestead associations, insurance companies, or savings banks which in turn lend directly to borrowing home builders.

The great bulk of member institutions are of the savings and loan type. Loans are made to member, and nonmember institutions in some instances, primarily on the basis of first-mortgage collateral. By so doing they supply funds with which member institutions can meet the home-financing needs of their communities and the withdrawal demands of savers and investors.

Savings and Loan Associations. Rather than deposit their savings in the local bank many people prefer to place them with savings and loan associations either as an investment or with the expectation of later financing a home. These were all organized under state laws until 1933 but since then they may be established under

federal auspices. These can be organized anywhere in the United States or its territories upon the application of a responsible group of citizens to the nearest Federal Home Loan Bank. When approved and established, each one automatically becomes a member of the Federal Home Loan Bank System and must insure its deposits with a federal corporation[30] provided for the purpose. The principal function of the associations is one of financing home building within the vicinity of their home offices.

The Federal Housing Administration (FHA). The FHA, which dates back to 1934, is primarily an insurance agency. Its goal is one of encouraging the improvement of existing housing facilities, the building of new small homes and apartment dwellings, and the manfacture of housing by industrial methods. The administration does not lend directly to home builders and manufacturers. Instead, it lets local financial institutions lend the money while it guarantees payment of the mortgage, thus removing virtually all risk of nonpayment to the money lender. A premium is charged the financial institution for this service, the income from which is expected to pay the cost of operation. The amount of the loan depends upon the size and cost of the project. Not more than a stipulated rate of interest may be charged on insured loans, the projects must be executed in accordance with approved specifications, and payments must be made periodically until the obligation is fully retired. Thus far, many mortgages have been insured with few defaults.

Subsidized Low-rent Housing. The housing programs described above are intended to help finance private parties whose credit is good. The role of the Federal Public Housing Authority (FPHA) is very different. Here is a government corporation whose primary purpose is to clear slums and provide low-rent housing. It does not do so directly, however. Rather, it enters into contracts with municipal, county, and state authorities, where state laws permit, to get the job

---

[29] Boston, New York, Pittsburgh, Greensboro, N.C., Cincinnati, Indianapolis, Chicago, Des Moines, Little Rock, Topeka, and San Francisco.

[30] This is the Federal Savings and Loan Insurance Corporation. Its plan is similar to that conducted by the Federal Deposit Insurance Corporation for ordinary commercial banks.

done. The procedure is for a local authority to frame plans for slum clearance and new construction, then submit them to FPHA for approval. If the plans are approved, a contract is entered into whereby the federal agency agrees (1) to lend a large part of the cost of the project at prevailing rates of interest plus a small charge for administrative costs, the principal to be repaid over a long period of years; and (2) to make annual contributions over a period of years as a subsidy for low rents.

Thereupon, the federal agency may make grants and loans for clearing and preparing the area for new construction, make long-term loans to local authorities which will be repaid out of rentals, and make annual contributions over a period of years as a subsidy for low rents. Tenants must be citizens and in the low-income category; none may be admitted whose aggregate income exceeds fixed amounts. If, after occupancy, the size of the family or income increases beyond what the regulations permit, different quarters must be found.[31] Under the stimulus of this program the landscapes of many large American cities have changed from slums to large low-rent dwellings.

[31] An interesting story of one of the municipal housing authorities is told by Dr. M. Nelson McGeary in *The Pittsburgh Housing Authority* (The Pennsylvania State University, 1943).

FOR FURTHER READING

Bailey, Stephen K.: *Congress Makes a Law: The Story behind the Employment Act of 1946* (Columbia University Press, 1949).

Beckett, Grace L.: *Reciprocal Trade Agreements Program* (Columbia University Press, 1941).

Berle, Adolph A., and Gardner C. Means: *The Modern Corporation and Private Property* (Macmillan, 1933).

Blinken, Donald M.: *Wool Tariffs and American Policy* (Washington, D.C.: Public Affairs Press, 1948).

Corwin, Edward S.: *The Commerce Power v. States Rights* (Princeton University Press, 1936).

Currie, Brainerd (ed.): "The Patent System," *Law and Contemporary Problems,* vol. 12, no. 4 (Duke University School of Law, 1947).

Fischer, Louis A.: *History of the Standard Weights and Measures of the United States,* Bureau of Standards Publication M 64, 1905 (1905).

Gavit, Bernard C.: *The Commerce Clause of the United States Constitution* (Bloomington, Ind.: Principia Press, 1932).

Gordon, Robert A.: *Business Leadership in the Large Corporation* (Brookings, 1945).

Hamilton, Walton H., and Douglass Adair: *The Power to Govern* (Norton, 1937).

Kallenbach, Joseph E.: *Federal Cooperation with the States under the Commerce Clause* (University of Michigan Press, 1942).

Kobbe, Herman: *Housing and Regional Planning* (Dutton, 1941).

Kreps, Clifton H., Jr., and J. M. Kreps (eds.): *Aid, Trade and Tariffs* (H. W. Wilson, 1953).

Larkin, John D.: *The President's Control over the Tariff* (Harvard University Press, 1936).

Letiche, John M.: *Reciprocal Trade Agreements in the World Economy* (Houghton Mifflin, 1941).

Lynch, David: *The Concentration of Economic Power* (Columbia University Press, 1946).

McGeary, M. Nelson: *The Pittsburgh Housing Authority* (The Pennsylvania State University, 1943).

Moulton, Harold G.: *Controlling Factors in Economic Development* (Brookings, 1949).

Ribble, Frederick D. G.: *State and National Power over Commerce* (Columbia University Press, 1937).

Ruml, Beardsley: *Government, Business, and Values* (Harper, 1943).

Schapp, Adelbert: *Patent Fundamentals* (The Industrial Press, 1939).

Schattschneider, Elmer E.: *Politics, Pressures and the Tariff* (Farrar, Straus, 1942).

Toulmin, Harry A.: *Patents and the Public Interest* (Harper, 1939).

Twentieth Century Fund: *American Housing* (Twentieth Century Fund, 1944).

——: *Big Business: Its Growth and Place* (Twentieth Century Fund, 1937).

U.S. Board of Investigation and Research: *Public Aids to Domestic Transportation,* H. Doc. 159, 79th Cong., 1st Sess. (1945).

U.S. Commission on Organization of the Executive Branch of the Government (first Hoover Commission): *Department of Commerce* (1949).

——: *Federal Business Enterprises* (1949).

——: *Task Force Report on Public Works* (1949).

——: *Task Force Report on Regulatory Commissions* (1949).

U.S. Congress, Temporary National Economic Committee: *Investigation of Concentration of Economic Power,* Monograph 24, "Consumer Standards"; 31, "Patents and Free Enterprise"; 18, "Trade Associations"; and various other monographs and volumes containing hearings (1939–1941).

U.S. Council of Economic Advisers: *The Economic Report of the President* (annual).

U.S. Federal Trade Commission: *Report of . . . on the Concentration of Productive Facilities, 1947* (1949).

——: *Report of . . . on the Merger Movement* (1948).

U.S. National Resources Committee: *The Structure of the American Economy* (1939).

Warren, Charles: *The Making of the Constitution* (Little, Brown, 1937).

——: *Bankruptcy in United States History* (Harvard University Press, 1935).

Weinstein, Jacob I.: *The Bankruptcy Law of 1938 . . .* (New York: National Association of Credit Men, 1938).

Willoughby, Westel W.: *The Constitutional Law of the United States* (New York: Baker, Voorhis, 2d ed., 3 vols., 1929).

REVIEW QUESTIONS

1. What considerations caused the commerce clause to be written as it was?

2. Compare recent interpretations of the commerce power with earlier decisions relating to fish and game, insurance, manufacturing, and amusements.

3. Give illustrations of business activities that are intrastate.

4. What practical difference does it make whether a businessman is engaged in interstate or intrastate commerce?

5. Under what circumstances may a state regulate interstate and foreign commerce?

6. List as many important aids or services as you can think of which the Federal government provides primarily for the benefit of general business.

7. Explain the organization and principal functions of the Department of Commerce.

8. Give illustrations of some of the planning activities of the Federal government.

9. Defend and criticize reciprocal tariff legislation and agreements.

10. Defend and criticize greater American participation in organizations like GATT for the purpose of eliminating barriers to international trade.

11. Summarize provisions of our patent, copyright, trade-mark, and bankruptcy legislation. What changes would you recommend?

12. What federal housing programs would you expand? What would you contract or eliminate altogether?

CHAPTER 26

General Business Regulation

For two generations American political and economic life has been moving swiftly toward "bigness," toward monolithic organization. We live by, in, and among bigger and bigger governments. On all sides individual freedom and responsibility have shrunk. Absorbed into organizations bigger than himself, the American tends to be overpowered by these organizations, whether of industry, labor or agriculture. And whatever his orientation, he must operate in and under an over-expanding multilateral network of occupational and governmental regulation. — Alpheus T. Mason [1]

With all its virtues and achievements, American business has come to require a large amount of government regulation as well as the services reviewed in the previous chapter. Contrary to popular assumption, regulation is seldom undertaken merely because politicians and bureaucrats crave power; rather, its primary causation appears to be the failure of the economy as a whole or particular business groups to measure up to community expectations. Thus, when some businessmen exploit investors, clamor goes up for remedial measures. Or when competition is eliminated, antimonopoly legislation is demanded. Or when consumers expect purer foods and drugs they turn to government for protection and assistance.

THE GROWTH OF BIG BUSINESS

Changing Character of Ownership. Small, individually owned businesses are still the most numerous in the United States, but they are dwarfed by corporations in assets, income, volume of business, numbers of employees, economic and political power. The corporation accounts for half of the national income, with sole proprietorships and partnerships running a poor second and government enterprises a poor third.[2] The corporate form is found in practically all walks of economic life. Indeed, in some fields it accounts for almost the entire income. It has even invaded agriculture, and the trend seems likely to continue.

Predominance of the corporate form has had, and continues to have, a profound effect upon economic life and upon social and political as well. Among other things, it has changed the once intimate personal relationships among owners, managers, employees, and the public. It has encouraged the movement to cities. It has made possible the concentration of business on an unprecedented scale. It makes possible the control of business by a comparatively few managers, financiers, and investors. It has helped change concepts of property, rights, and democracy. It has helped make the world more inter-

[1] "American Individualism: Fact and Fiction," *American Political Science Review,* vol. 46 (March, 1952), p. 1.

[2] A. D. H. Kaplan, *Big Enterprise in a Competitive Economy* (Brookings, 1954), pp. 118–119.

dependent. It has changed the character of competition. It emits a constant and pervasive stream of influence seeking to mold attitudes and public policies favorable to its existence and welfare. Big business invites big government, big labor, and big agriculture, and it encourages consumers to organize.

All this in turn paves the way, with the help of wars and depressions, for the "welfare state"

serious problems of public policy; it also accounts in large part for the many controls imposed upon business enterprise, some of which are discussed below.

REGULATION OF SECURITIES AND EXCHANGES

When corporations organize, their securities—stocks, bonds, debentures, certificates, etc.—are

DISTRIBUTION OF FIRMS BY LEGAL FORM OF ORGANIZATION FOR EACH EMPLOYEE-SIZE CLASS

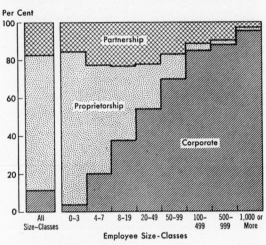

SOURCE: U. S. Department of Commerce

PROPRIETORSHIPS WITH LESS THAN FOUR EMPLOYEES COMPRISE THREE-FIFTHS OF ALL BUSINESS CONCERNS

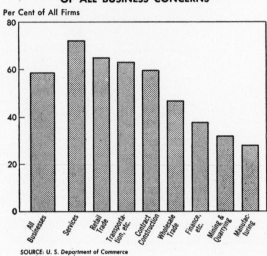

SOURCE: U. S. Department of Commerce

of which we are a part. While doing all this, the corporation has helped work scientific, productive, and distributive miracles that have made possible the relatively high standard of living to which Americans have grown accustomed.

Concentration of Control. Not only do corporations predominate over other types of economic enterprise, but a few of them have acquired a commanding position in many lines of business. This was illustrated by figures released in 1949 by the Federal Trade Commission, some of which are shown on page 493. This tendency for a few large companies to lead the field is popularly referred to as "oligopoly."

Some corporations have grown large by natural growth and prosperity. Others have grown through mergers, trusts, holding companies, and similar arrangements. The trend has presented

sold to the public, generally through "stock markets" or "security exchanges." Corporate securities are owned by millions of persons, many of whom own only a few shares. Without governmental regulation, poorly informed investors may easily be misled, even by reliable brokers, while many will fall prey to unscrupulous promoters.

The states have attempted to protect the investing public by "blue-sky laws" aimed primarily at fraudulent sales, and by statutes requiring the registration of securities with some state agency. While of value, these provided inadequate protection and the states hesitated to enact drastic laws fearing exchanges would move to some more accommodating state. Moreover, the interstate character of corporate financing made effective state control virtually impossible.

Securities and Exchange Legislation. The stock-market crash of 1929 and subsequent disclosures clearly revealed the necessity for federal control. Congress responded by enacting the Federal Securities Act in 1933 and the Securities Exchange Act in 1934. These laws are adminis-

More specifically, the basic requirement is that corporations issuing securities to the public, security exchanges, and persons dealing in securities outside the exchanges ("over-the-counter" sales) must register with the Securities and Exchange Commission.

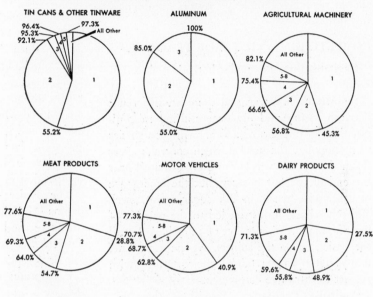

CONCENTRATION OF PRODUCTIVE FACILITIES
Cumulative Percentages of Net Capital Assets Owned by Largest Corporations, 1947

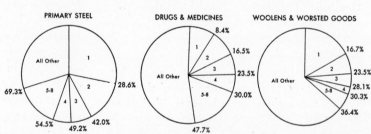

A high degree of concentration in basic industries is indicated by these charts. In both tin and aluminum over 50 per cent of net capital assets were held by a single company. Adapted from: U.S. Federal Trade Commission, *Report . . . on the Concentration of Productive Facilities, 1947* (1950).

tered by a Securities and Exchange Commission, created in 1934 and composed of five members appointed for terms of 5 years.

The Federal Securities Act seeks to provide the public with accurate information about corporate securities, while the Securities Exchange Act provides for the regulation of buying and selling of stocks and bonds on security exchanges throughout the country. Their purpose is not to guarantee the investments of individuals but to provide them with essential information by which to judge the securities they buy, and to protect them from misrepresentation.

Before offering securities for sale, corporations must file with the commission a statement containing essential information about the business upon which the value of their securities depends. Exchanges, brokers, and dealers are required to keep accounts in accordance with methods prescribed by the commission, and make periodic reports. In addition, the law makes illegal certain unfair competitive practices such as "washed sales" and "matched orders." [3] As a means of

[3] The former is an arrangement whereby one speculator agrees to sell at a point higher than that commanded by a security on the market at a given time

further controlling speculative booms, the Federal Reserve Board is empowered to fix "margins," *i.e.,* fix the amount of credit that may be extended to those who buy securities.

It is now generally agreed that legislation such as this was long overdue and will be retained regardless of which party is in office, although there are some who believe the regulations should be relaxed to help "restore confidence" in business.

COMPETITION AND TRADE PRACTICES

Capitalist theory assumes that private business should and will compete freely. Experience demonstrates, however, that there is a difference between theory and practice resulting in combinations of one sort or another with tendencies to monopolize the market. Such control as was deemed necessary was left to the states until near the end of the last century, but the emergence of large-scale trusts in oil, sugar, meat, steel, and other basic industries led to the passage of the Sherman Antitrust Act of 1890. This is still the basic law on the subject. At the same time many states have retained their statutes with respect to intrastate commerce.

Antitrust Legislation. Provisions that proscribe monopolies and monopolistic practices in general businesses engaged in interstate and foreign commerce are found in three principal statutes—the Sherman Act of 1890, the Clayton Act of 1914, and the Federal Trade Commission Act of 1914—and various amendments added from time to time.

The Sherman Act forbids the following:

Every contract, combination, in the form of trust or otherwise, or conspiracy in the restraint of trade or commerce among the several states, or with foreign nations. . . .

It says further:

Every person who shall monopolize, or attempt to monopolize, or combine or conspire with any

and another agrees to buy for the purpose of creating the impression that the security is commanding buyers. "Matched orders" are those in which a party hires two brokers unknown to each other, one to offer for sale

person or persons, to monopolize any part of the trade or commerce among the several states, or with foreign nations, shall be deemed guilty of a misdemeanor. . . .

The Clayton Act supplements these provisions by outlawing three specific evils: (1) price discrimination, (2) exclusive agreements, and (3) interlocking directorates and purchases of stock among competitors. As amended by the Robinson-Patman Act, the law also made illegal transactions through which chain stores and other large purchasers received discounts, rebates, and other concessions that did not always correctly reflect all legitimate costs. Now such concessions are banned where the effect is to diminish competition and injure competitors. As amended in 1950, the law also forbids the acquisition of *assets* where the effect is to substantially lessen competition or tend to create a monopoly.

The Federal Trade Commission Act condemns "unfair methods of competition" in interstate and foreign commerce while the Wheeler-Lea amendment of 1938 forbids "unfair or deceptive acts or practices."

Exemptions from Antitrust Laws. Although the law is broadly stated, there are many exemptions from its provisions. After a long and bitter contest, labor organizations are finally immune, except possibly where they combine with nonlabor forces in activities that restrain trade. The Webb-Pomerene Act of 1918 permits cooperative arrangements among those engaged in export trade as long as their agreements are registered with the Federal Trade Commission. The Transportation Act of 1920 permits railroad consolidations that are approved by the Interstate Commerce Commission. The Agricultural Exemption Act of 1922 and later amendments permit farmers, planters, dairymen, and others engaged in agriculture to form associations for the more effective marketing of products.

The National Industrial Recovery Act, now invalid, and later the Guffey Coal Acts, now expired, exempted codified industries from the antitrust laws under the theory that the public

and the other to buy, in order to create the impression of an active market to attract buyers.

was sufficiently protected by code and public authorities. The Merchant Marine Act of 1936 permits agreements among shipping lines if approved by the Maritime Board, while mergers and combinations are permitted among gas and electric holding companies, interstate motor carriers, interstate electric-power and natural-gas companies, and to a limited extent telephone, telegraph, and cable companies if approved by the regulatory commissions having jurisdiction over them.

mits common carriers of particular classes to agree among themselves on rates and charges provided approval of the ICC is first obtained.

The Rule of Reason. Note that the provisions quoted above from the Sherman Act appear to ban "every" contract, combination, etc., and to

TYPES OF BUSINESS ACQUISITIONS

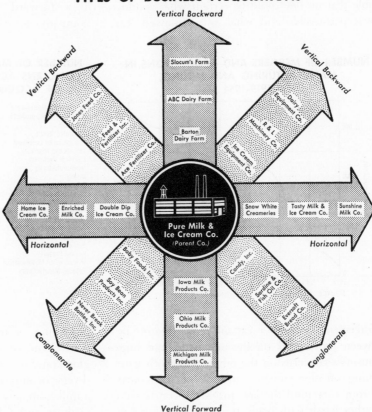

This hypothetical milk and ice cream company has grown big by acquiring a variety of enterprises. American businesses have adopted many variations of this pattern. For illustrations of what has been happening in particular companies and industries, see: U.S. Federal Trade Commission, *Report of . . . on the Merger Movements* (1948).

The Miller-Tydings Act of 1937 legalized resale-price-maintenance agreements between manufacturers and distributors in those states where such agreements are not illegal so far as local commerce is concerned. The McGuire Act of 1952 made resale-price agreements enforceable on both nonsigners and signers of the contracts. The Reed-Bulwinkle Act of 1948 per-

apply to "every" person. A literal interpretation was followed at first, but the courts later shifted their position. The break came in the famous oil and tobacco decisions of 1911.[4]

While the government was upheld in both cases, Chief Justice White announced the court had followed the common-law rule of reason in reaching its decisions. Not every contract leading to monopoly was forbidden, said he, but only those which were "unreasonably restrictive

[4] United States *v.* Standard Oil Co. of New Jersey, 221 U.S. 1 (1911); United States *v.* American Tobacco Company, 221 U.S. 106 (1911).

of competitive conditions." This approach, said the Chief Justice, made it necessary to look into the character of the agreement under suspicion, consider surrounding circumstances, and investigate the intent of those forming the agreement.

A storm of protest followed this announcement, but the new rule stuck. Henceforth, the standards to be applied were so vague and variable that no one could be certain what conduct was permissible and what was outlawed. En-

acquires one or more others. Vertical combinations are either "backward" or "forward."

In the former, a parent company acquires sources of raw materials or products and services helpful to the production of its goods or services. An example would be a case in which a steel mill acquired coal mines and power plants for supplying its productive operations. In a "forward" vertical combination, the parent company acquires businesses for fabricating,

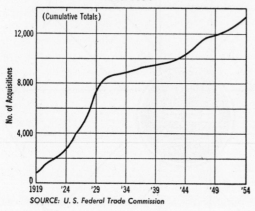

NUMBER OF MERGERS AND ACQUISITIONS IN MANUFACTURING AND MINING, 1919-1954

SOURCE: U. S. Federal Trade Commission

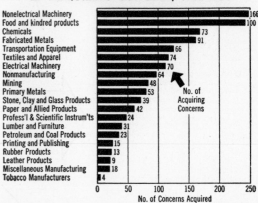

NUMBER OF MANUFACTURING AND MINING CONCERNS ACQUIRED BY INDUSTRY GROUP OF ACQUIRING CONCERN, 1948-1954

forcement became a cat-and-mouse game between prosecutors on the one hand and huge business concerns on the other, with both gambling on the probable attitude of the courts. From 1911 until the late 1930's the courts were rather harsh with pools, trade-association activities, labor unions, and other loose arrangements, but, paradoxically, they were lenient with close combinations like those which prompted the Sherman Act. In recent years the courts have taken a stiffer attitude toward agreements and combinations of all sorts, except labor unions which they held to be largely immune in 1941.

The Problem of Mergers. Business mergers were generally looked upon as being reasonable combinations even though competitors were "gobbled up." Some mergers are of the horizontal type where one company acquires others engaged in identical or similar lines of endeavor, as when a grocery store, steel mill, or coal mine

processing, or merchandising its primary products. Some combinations are known as "conglomerate," *i.e.,* they include businesses of highly diverse or unrelated types, as, for example, when a milk company acquires a factory for producing sardines and fish oil and another one for producing pharmaceuticals. The various types of mergers are illustrated on the chart on page 495.

The Clayton Act struck at interlocking directorates and intercompany acquisitions of stock, but it said nothing which would prevent companies from buying or otherwise acquiring assets other than share capital. One consequence was oligopoly, or a circumstance where a few giant corporations dominated the industry. The Federal Trade Commission and other investigators repeatedly urged that this loophole be plugged, but Congress was slow to act. Now, most utilities engaged in interstate and foreign commerce must submit proposed combinations to appropriate federal commissions for approval, and since 1950 intercompany acquisition of assets is brought under control.

The new legislation amends the Clayton Act to read:

No corporation engaged in commerce shall acquire, directly or indirectly, the whole or part of the stock or other share capital and no corporation subject to the jurisdiction of the Federal Trade Commission shall acquire in whole or any part of the assets of another corporation engaged also in commerce, where in any line of commerce in any section of the country, the effect of such acquisition may be substantially to lessen competition, or tend to create a monopoly.

Note that not all intercompany acquisitions are banned but only those that substantially lessen competition and tend to create a monopoly. The law is not retroactive. The purchase of stocks for investment is not forbidden where competition is not diminished thereby. Nor are subsidiaries forbidden where they carry on their lawful business and competition is not substantially lessened.

Controversy over Basing Points. Other types of agreements looked upon by the courts as being reasonable were those establishing basing points.[5] If a single-basing-point system was established, all competitors agreed to sell anywhere for a base price plus transportation from some particular point. Thus, in the case of steel, Pittsburgh was made the basing point and all steel companies, regardless of location, agreed to charge all purchasers of steel a base price plus rail transportation from Pittsburgh.

For example, if a steel mill at Gary, Indiana, sold steel to a firm located in Wheeling, West Virginia, it might charge a base price of $40 a ton plus $10 for transportation, or a total of $50. The $10 for transportation might not actu-

ally be the cost of shipping from Gary but, rather, it would be the cost of shipping from the basing point at Pittsburgh. In this case, the Gary firm would have to absorb the difference between what was actually paid for freight and the cheaper cost of shipping from Pittsburgh.

By doing so, and taking a smaller net return, both the Gary firm and Pittsburgh firms would sell in West Virginia at identical prices. In some industries, multiple basing points were used. These differed chiefly in that instead of using one city, like Pittsburgh in the illustration given above, two or more were used for purposes of setting identical prices by competitors.

This system has been strongly defended by those who use it. While conceding that the system diminishes price competition, defenders insist that both the industry and nation benefit from price stabilization, and nonprice competition is actually increased. Buyers of steel near Pittsburgh, for example, would normally buy in that area, but if they can buy Gary steel for the same delivered price they might choose to do so. This, it was contended, would increase rather than decrease competition for markets even though price would not be a factor.

Critics contend that this is not in fact the result and that besides the system leads to much economic waste. The Federal Trade Commission ordered the steel industry to discontinue its "Pittsburgh plus" system in 1924, whereupon the industry substituted the multiple-basing-point system. Finally, in 1945, the Supreme Court agreed with the Trade Commission that single-basing-point systems were illegal,[6] and in the famous Cement Institute case decided in 1948 the Supreme Court declared multiple basing points illegal also.[7] In the meantime powerful pressures have developed to get Congress to legalize these price-fixing schemes.

Controversy over Resale-price Maintenance. If left to their own devices many producers of nationally advertised brand-name products pre-

---

[5] For excellent discussions of this subject see Earl Latham, *The Group Basis of Politics: A Study of Basing Point Legislation* (Cornell University Press, 1952), and George W. Stocking, *Basing Point Pricing and Regional Development: A Case Study of the Iron and Steel Industry* (The University of North Carolina Press, 1954).

[6] Corn Products Co. *v.* Federal Trade Commission, 324 U.S. 726 (1945); Federal Trade Commission *v.* Staley Co., 324 U.S. 746 (1945).

[7] Federal Trade Commission *v.* Cement Institute *et al.,* 333 U.S. 683 (1947).

fer to dictate prices at which retail dealers are to sell their products. One method is to require dealers to sign contracts wherein they promise to maintain dictated prices and make themselves liable for damage suits if they fail to live up to their agreements. But for producers to require written contracts of all dealers is bothersome, costly, and often provocative of ill will. To make the matter simpler, business groups have prevailed upon nearly all states to pass Fair Trade Acts. These legalize resale-price maintenance, and most of them say that when one or a few contracts have gone into effect within a particular state they become binding upon all dealers handling the products, including both signers and nonsigners. The Supreme Court upheld their application to nonsigners in 1937.[8]

But state laws could validate resale-price-maintenance contracts only for intrastate commerce, and the Supreme Court had outlawed them so far as interstate commerce was concerned as early as 1911.[9] Encouraged by their success with state legislatures, and by the fact that resale-price maintenance had in fact been legalized in interstate commerce for the short period when the NIRA codes were in effect, business groups turned pressure on Congress to amend the Sherman Act.

These efforts succeeded in 1937 with passage of the Miller-Tydings amendment as a rider to the District of Columbia Appropriations Act. President Roosevelt signed the bill but not without castigating those who had resorted to the rider tactic to legalize price fixing. The amendment provides that resale-price-maintenance agreements are legal so far as interstate commerce is concerned where states have given similar approval for commerce that is intrastate.

The Miller-Tydings amendment said nothing about nonsigners. As suggested above, the Supreme Court had upheld the constitutionality of nonsigner provisions in state laws, but doubt remained over whether these were enforceable as applied to interstate commerce. The issue

reached the Supreme Court in 1950.[10] In this case, Louisiana had a Fair Trade Act applying to both signers and nonsigners of contracts. Calvert Corporation sold liquor in Louisiana and had succeeded in getting over a hundred dealers to sign price-maintenance agreements. Schwegmann Brothers, retailers in New Orleans, refused to sign and proceeded to sell Calvert's products at cut-rate prices. Thereupon, since interstate commerce was involved, Calvert invoked the Miller-Tydings amendment and brought suit to compel cooperation. The Supreme Court, however, ruled against the corporation, saying, among other things, that Congress had not intended the federal amendment to require compliance of nonsigners.

Pandemonium immediately broke loose all over the country, with Macy's of New York taking the lead. The Court had not ruled all price fixing through contracts illegal; it had merely said nonsigners engaged in interstate commerce could not be compelled to comply under existing federal law. Pressure groups again trained their guns on Congress trying to get legislation passed legalizing coercion of nonsigners. The desired measure (the McGuire Act) passed Congress in June, 1952, with the result that if state laws permit the coercion of signers and nonsigners, federal law is the same for interstate commerce within those states.

Enforcement of Antitrust Laws. Alleged violations are dealt with in three ways: by criminal prosecutions, by civil actions initiated by either the government or injured competitors, and by administrative adjudication by the Federal Trade Commission. Over the years, few, if any, offenders have gone to prison, almost no property has been confiscated, and total fines paid (at the rate of not more than $5,000 for each offense until 1955; $50,000 since) have been puny compared with the profits made through illegal conduct.

The threat of prosecution has, however, doubtless had deterrence value. Civil proceedings brought by the government have produced injunctions, consent decrees wherein offenders

---

[8] Old Dearborn Distributing Co. *v.* Seagrams-Distillers Corp., 229 U.S. 183 (1937).

[9] Dr. Miles Medical Co. *v.* Parks and Songs, 220 U.S. 373 (1911).

[10] Schwegmann Bros. *et al. v.* Calvert Corp., 341 U.S. 384 (1950).

admit their guilt and agree to mend their ways, and business dissolutions. Injured competitors have won a few damage suits, while the Trade Commission has stopped certain practices by stipulations and by cease and desist orders, as is noted more fully below. Government cases are handled in the courts by the Department of Justice, which has created a special Antitrust Division for the purpose, with the Trade Commission helping make investigations.

Enforcement has been one of the most difficult assignments imaginable. In the Cement Institute case, referred to above, 10 years elapsed between the date of the complaint and the Supreme Court decision. Seventy-four corporations were involved in the complaint; it took a trial examiner 3 years to hear the evidence consisting of 49,000 pages of oral testimony and 50,000 pages of exhibits; findings and conclusions of the Trade Commission covered 176 pages; and legal briefs with appendixes contained more than 4,000 pages.

Investigations like these require a large staff with ample funds, a clear legal mandate, and a reservoir of determination that is too often dissipated by time and political processes. A combination of all these has seldom if ever existed. In spite of the difficulties, recent years (excepting the war period) have been characterized by growing concern over mounting bigness and declining competition accompanied by more vigorous enforcement of the antitrust laws.

Proposed Remedies. Countless public and private studies of the antitrust laws have been made. One of the most notable was done by the Temporary National Economic Commission and reported in 1941.[11] A more recent and legalistic one was made by the Attorney General's National Committee to Study the Antitrust Laws and reported in 1955.[12] Both recommended

changes too numerous and technical to recite and analyze here.

A few of the changes most frequently suggested include: (1) provide enforcement agencies with funds and personnel adequate for the task; (2) clarify what is legal and what is not; (3) stiffen criminal penalties for violations; (4) outlaw basing points by statute; (5) repeal laws permitting resale price maintenance; (6) restrict the scope of patent monopolies; (7) proscribe more activities of trade unions; (8) require trade associations to register; and (9) permit greater use of trade-practice conferences by the Federal Trade Commission to establish rules of business conduct.

Proposed Alternatives. Numerous alternatives have also been proposed. Some suggest that corporations be licensed by the Federal government and required to conform to a stated code of conduct as a condition for obtaining and keeping the license. It has also been suggested that basic industries like steel, automobile manufacturing, and aluminum be declared public utilities and brought under continuous regulation by a federal commission. Also proposed is a pattern whereby the government and basic industries would undertake joint ownership and control. Some advocate outright government ownership and operation either of all industries or of certain basic industries like steel, oil, coal, etc., somewhat along lines followed in Britain and Scandinavian countries.

There are still some who suggest return to a system of codes, like those followed in NIRA days. Others suggest expanded use of cooperatives. And one occasionally hears it suggested that Congress establish a national economic council composed of representatives of business, labor, and consumers for the purpose of devising whatever controls may be needed. Where these have been used in other countries they have usually been advisory to parliaments although ways might be devised whereby they could participate directly in making public law. There are still many, of course, who profess a yearning for *laissez faire* with little or no attempt being made to restrain business processes by antitrust laws or other governmental action.

[11] A brief summary is contained in U.S. Congress, Temporary National Economic Committee, *Investigation of Concentration of Economic Power, Final Report and Recommendations*, S. Doc. 35, 77th Cong., 1st Sess. (1941).

[12] This was published under title of *Report of the Attorney General's National Committee to Study the Antitrust Laws* (1955).

Unfair Methods of Competition. Among other duties, the Federal Trade Commission is charged with responsibility for preventing "unfair methods of competition" and "unfair or deceptive acts or practices" on the part of those engaged in interstate and foreign commerce. Unfair methods are all attempts to achieve business gains through wrongdoing or undue restraints that injure competitors or the public.

The list of methods declared to be illegal, unfair, and deceptive is long, but it falls into two classes: unfair methods that are opposed to good morals; and unfair methods that tend unduly to hinder competition and effect trade restraints and monopoly. Only a few illustrations can be mentioned.

Methods Inconsistent with Good Morals. Some which fall in this class are:

1. The use of false or misleading advertising concerning, and the misbranding of, commodities.

2. Representing products to have been made in the United States when the mechanism or movements, in whole or in important part, are of foreign origin.

3. Selling rebuilt, secondhand, renovated, or old products by representing them as new or failing to indicate that they are not made of new materials.

4. Using merchandising schemes based on lot or chance, or on a pretended contest of skill.

5. Schemes to create the impression that the customer is being offered an opportunity to make purchases under unusually favorable conditions when such is not the case (as the use of the "free goods" or service device to create the impression that something is actually being thrown in without charge, when it is fully covered by the amount exacted in the transaction as a whole, or by services to be rendered by the recipient).

6. Using deceptive containers.

7. Giving products misleading names so as to give them a value that they would not otherwise possess (*e.g.,* saying a coat made of rabbit fur is made of "Baltic fox" or "beaver"; or falsely suggesting that a product has been approved by some well-known medical, dental, or other professional organization).

8. Simulation of competitors' trade names, labels, dress of goods, counter-display, or catalogues (*e.g.,* using such words as "Importing," "Manufacturing Co." or "Foundry" when the firms involved were merely processors or dealers; using the name "Westinghouse Union Company" in simulation of "Westinghouse Electric Co.," or using the title *Who's Who and Why* in competition with the well-known *Who's Who in America*).

Methods Tending to Restraints and Monopoly. A few of these are:

1. Conspiring to maintain uniform selling prices, terms, and conditions of sale through the use of a patent-licensing system.

2. Trade boycotts or combinations of traders to prevent certain wholesale and retail dealers from procuring goods at the same terms accorded to the boycotters or conspirators.

3. Buying up supplies for the purpose of hampering competitors and stifling or eliminating competition.

4. Using concealed subsidiaries, ostensibly independent, to obtain competitive business otherwise unavailable.

5. Combinations or agreements of competitors to fix, enhance, or depress prices, maintain prices, bring about substantial uniformity in prices, or divide territory or business, to cut off or interfere with competitors' source of supply, or to close markets to competitors.

6. Intimidation or coercion of a producer or distributor to cause him to organize, join, or contribute to, or to prevent him from organizing, joining, or contributing to, a producers' cooperative association, or other association, advertising agency, or publisher.

7. Harassing competitors (*e.g.,* by bribing or hiring their employees, by threatening needless and vexatious lawsuits, and by making false and misleading statements about competitors and their products).

8. Selling below cost or giving products without charge, with the intent of hindering or suppressing competition.

9. Coercing and forcing uneconomic and monopolistic reciprocal dealing.

False and Misleading Advertising. Prior to 1938 the Federal Trade Commission had no specific authorization to deal with advertising affecting commerce but had to proceed on the basis that false and misleading advertising was an unfair and deceptive trade practice. This is still the basis for action with respect to most commodities, but an amendment in 1938 grants specific authority to suppress false and misleading advertising of foods, drugs, devices, and cosmetics.[13] The amendment also grants authority for the Commission to intercede not merely when competitors are injured but when the public is also.

Reports of the Trade Commission are filled with illustrations of false and misleading advertising, of which only a few can be mentioned. A firm in Los Angeles was stopped from advertising that its fingernail polish "Nailife" provided a "perfect nail food" which "will transform irregular broken nails into well formed symmetrical ones" and "make your nails strong and healthy." A physical culture firm was ordered to discontinue advertising that its course of study would "make muscles grow like magic" or "start new inches of massive power pushing out your chest" or "put regular mountains of muscles under your biceps" or "banish constipation, poor digestion, pimples, skin blotches, and similar conditions that rob you of the good things of life." Another firm was stopped from advertising coffee under the trade name "Rico Café" when it was not a coffee grown in Puerto Rico or even a blend thereof.

Federal Trade Commission Procedure. The Trade Commission has evolved a procedure for handling violations that has received wide acclaim and provided a model for several regulatory agencies more recently established. First, it should be noted that the function of the Commission is primarily remedial, not punitive. Although it has power to impose penalties, its principal object is to protect the public, not to punish the offender.

Violations are suspected either as a result of complaints that reach the Commission or through investigations conducted by the Commission's own accountants, economists, and attorneys. When a questionable practice is being followed by several in the same trade, a trade-practice conference is called at which codes of fair competition may be agreed upon wherein members of the trade agree to discontinue the obnoxious practice. Where particular individuals are involved, a thorough investigation is made, following which the case may be dismissed for lack of merit or the suspected party may enter into what is known as a "stipulation," whereby the charges are admitted and the respondent stipulates that he will mend his ways.

Unless the charges are withdrawn or a stipulation is issued, the Commission makes a formal complaint. Thereupon, a hearing is held before a trial examiner, testimony is taken, and a report is made to the Commission by the examiner. If the Commission finds the respondent guilty, it issues a "cease and desist" order. Appeals may be taken to the United States Courts of Appeals but the Commission's findings of facts, if supported by sufficient evidence, are final. Prior to 1938 the Commission lacked power to impose penalties but was required to rely upon the courts for enforcement. In the year mentioned, however, it was authorized to impose penalties of not more than $5,000 for disobedience to final orders.

LIQUOR, NARCOTICS, FOOD, AND DRUGS

Legal Results of Repeal. From a legal point of view, the much-controverted Eighteenth (prohibition) Amendment was due in part to court decisions which made it difficult if not impossible for dry states to control the interstate aspects of the liquor traffic. The Eighteenth Amendment abolished both interstate and intrastate manufacture, transportation, and sale of alcoholic

---

[13] This work of the Federal Trade Commission should not be confused with that of the Food and Drug Administration which is discussed on p. 503. The Trade Commission polices trade practices and advertising, while the Food and Drug Administration checks the misbranding and adulteration of foods, drugs, devices, and cosmetics.

beverages and gave the Federal and state governments concurrent jurisdiction to enforce these provisions. Although the Twenty-first Amendment completely repealed the Eighteenth, it did not return legal matters entirely to where they were before prohibition. Rather, the Twenty-first contains this significant sentence: "The transportation or importation into any State, Territory, or possession of the United States for delivery or use therein of intoxicating liquors, in violation of the laws thereof, is hereby prohibited."

Thus federal law completely surrounds a dry state, helping with enforcement. Note that this does not prevent the transportation of liquors *across* dry states; it simply forbids transportation or importation *for delivery* or *use* therein.

Methods of State Control. Control of the traffic in liquor and its use has long been a concern of governments everywhere. The states have primary responsibility since the problem so intimately affects the health, safety, and morals of the community.

The states follow a variety of plans. Two states (Mississippi and Oklahoma) have retained prohibition. Twenty-nine states and the District of Columbia depend upon a licensing system whereby all activities incident to the manufacture, distribution, and sale of liquor are handled by individuals licensed by the states. In Wyoming state stores monopolize all wholesale transactions, while sixteen states monopolize retail outlets. In both situations other aspects of the industry are controlled through licensing.

Federal Regulation. In addition to aiding dry states, federal legislation has had three objectives: The first has been to protect American producers from foreign competition. The second has been to obtain revenue. The third has been to apply controls with respect to competition, unfair trade practices, adulteration, misbranding, advertising, wages, hours, and working conditions similar to those applied to other industries. The latter was first done under NRA codes, but when these were declared unconstitutional similar provisions were reenacted which have since remained in effect. As a means to this end,

federal permits are required of all importers, distillers, rectifiers, and wholesalers, but not brewers and retail distributors.

Much to the consternation of those who feel strongly about the evils of the liquor traffic, the Federal government, like most of the states, has not sponsored temperance instruction nor has it deliberately sought to diminish consumption by other means. Except for the fact that alcoholic beverages are luxury items and as such are heavily taxed, the Federal government has considered the liquor industry to be legitimate and entitled to the same rights as other businesses.

Tariffs are collected by the Customs Bureau; excise taxes by the Bureau of Internal Revenue. Criminal violations of revenue provisions and laws aimed at protecting the states are enforced by the Department of Justice. Labor provisions are handled by agencies dealing with those matters for other businesses. Under the NRA, the Federal Alcohol Control Administration administered the code, but upon its demise, a long struggle, still unended, ensued over whether a separate independent agency should be established or whether regulation should become the permanent responsibility of the Treasury Department.

The proponents of Treasury administration won at first with the creation of the Federal Alcohol Administration in 1935 as a division. A year later the FAA was separated from the Treasury and made an independent establishment, governed by a three-man board. In April, 1940, an executive order sent the FAA back into the Treasury Department where its functions were consolidated with the Bureau of Internal Revenue. Today, therefore, the Bureau of Internal Revenue is responsible for both tax collection and economic regulation of the interstate and foreign aspects of the liquor industry.

Control of Narcotics. Effective control of narcotics is an international, national, and local problem. The United States is a large user of narcotics for medicinal purposes and it has its share of addicts in both the states and territories. The United States is signatory to the Hague Convention of 1912 wherein a number of nations agree upon certain control measures. The League of Nations tried valiantly to get world cooperation and, although not a member of the League, this country participated in some of its conferences looking toward more effective control.

However, when it came to signing the Geneva Treaty of 1925, which was a great advance over the Hague Convention, the American government refused. In spite of many efforts, international control has been neither comprehensive nor effective. Within the country, all the states have legislation designed to control narcotic drugs and deal with addiction, but without federal assistance they are powerless to protect themselves from traffic originating outside their borders. Although the Federal government has intervened, there remains a large volume of illicit traffic within the nation. Effective control, therefore, remains an unsolved problem.

Federal legislation is contained in three principal acts: the Harrison Act of 1914; the Jones-Miller Act of 1922; and the Marihuana Tax Act of 1937. Among other things, these require licenses of all those who produce (grow, in the case of marihuana and poppies), transport, sell, or dispense opium, marihuana, and certain other narcotic drugs. Evidence of these provisions may be seen in any drugstore or physician's office. Exports and imports are regulated by permits, and imports are further restricted by a system of quotas and allocations designed to secure proper distribution for medical needs.

Penalties include fine, imprisonment, and confiscation of both the products and vehicles wherein they are transported. Administration and enforcement are done by the Bureau of Narcotics (a unit of the Treasury Department), Department of Justice, and the Public Health Service. There is always a considerable volume of business.

Food and Drug Regulation. Federal intervention to protect consumers from impure foods and drugs began in 1906 as a result of a wave of public indignation following publication of Upton Sinclair's sensational novel, *The Jungle,* dramatizing the unspeakable circumstances under which meats were handled in Chicago packing plants. Today three federal agencies concern themselves with the subject: the Food and Drug Administration (Department of Health, Education, and Welfare), the Federal Trade Commission, and the Bureau of Animal Industry (Department of Agriculture).

The Food and Drug Administration prevents the misbranding or adulteration of foods, drugs, devices, and cosmetics entering interstate and foreign commerce; the Federal Trade Commission is responsible for preventing the false and misleading advertising of the same products; while the Bureau of Animal Industry enforces laws relating to the inspection and purity of meats. The contest for powers adequate to deal with clever and powerful food and drug interests has been a long and difficult one.

In general, foods are adulterated if they contain poisonous, deleterious, filthy, putrid, or decomposed substances, if they are produced under unsanitary conditions, if they are produced from diseased animals, if their containers are composed of substances injurious to health, or if any substance has been mixed or packed with them so as to reduce their quality or strength. Similar standards exist for drugs, cosmetics, and devices although there are variations due to differences in products.

Misbranding is also carefully defined, but in general labeling, packaging, etc., in such a manner as to inform and not deceive the buyer is required. False and misleading advertising, also forbidden, includes practices of all sorts intended to create impressions of products that are untruthful. New drugs must be filed and accepted before going on the interstate market. Coal-tar colors and certain antibiotic drugs must be tested and certified to ensure harmlessness and purity in advance of distribution.

To prevent adulteration and misbranding, standards must be established. This is a lengthy process which requires consultations and hearings with scientific and business interests, for the results may cause drastic changes in methods and costs of production and distribution. A 1952 order, for example, setting standards for bread, ruled out a number of ingredients, including chemical softeners, blackstrap molasses, extracts of raisins and prunes, peanut flour, and rolled oats. Orders like these have far-reaching economic repercussions.

The Food and Drug Administration and the Bureau of Animal Industry have agents in all parts of the country who inspect places of manufacture and storage and examine countless articles in transit. Violators may be fined or imprisoned, and substandard products may be seized and later sold or destroyed. Violations are detected constantly.

The second Hoover Commission reported that the Food and Drug Administration was carry-

ing on activities that were "not worth the time, effort, and money." [14] The Commission strongly urged that the pretesting of antibiotic drugs be discontinued, except as new ones are discovered and offered to the public.

The Commission also recommended more funds and inspectors. They made the further suggestion that a study be made to discover ways of eliminating overlapping with the Federal Trade Commission and Department of Agriculture. The task force added that in its opinion better enforcement would result from more education and fewer threats of punishment.

[14] *Federal Medical Services* (1955), p. 55. See also the task-force report on the same subject.

FOR FURTHER READING

Adams, James T.: *Big Business in a Democracy* (Scribner, 1946).

Arnold, Thurman: *The Bottlenecks of Business* (Reynal & Hitchcock, 1940).

Berle, Adolph A., and Gardner C. Means: *The Modern Corporation and Private Property* (Macmillan, 1933).

Clark, John M.: *Alternative to Serfdom* (Knopf, 1947).

Copeland, Douglas B.: *The Road to High Employment: Administrative Controls in a Free Society* (Harvard University Press, 1945).

Graham, George A., and Henry Reining, Jr.: *Regulatory Administration* (Wiley, 1943).

Harris, Seymour E.: *Saving American Capitalism: A Liberal Economic Program* (Knopf, 1948).

———: *Price and Related Controls in the United States* (McGraw-Hill, 1945).

Harrison, Leonard V., and Elizabeth Laine: *After Repeal: A Study of Liquor Control Administration* (Harper, 1936).

Kaplan, A. D. H.: *Big Enterprise in a Competitive System* (Brookings, 1954).

Lamb, Ruth De F.: *American Chamber of Horrors: The Truth about Food and Drugs* (Grosset & Dunlap, 1938).

Latham, Earl: *The Group Basis of Politics: A Study of Basing-point Legislation* (Cornell University Press, 1952).

Norwood, John W.: *Trade Practice and Price Law—Federal* (New York: Commerce Clearing House, Inc., 1938).

Pearce, Charles A.: *NRA Trade Practice Programs* (Columbia University Press, 1939).

Pegrum, Dudley F.: *Regulation of Industry* (Irwin, 1949).

Simons, Henry C.: *Economic Policy for a Free Society* (University of Chicago Press, 1947).

Stein, Emanuel: *Government and the Investor* (Rinehart, 1941).

Stocking, George W., and Myron W. Watkins: *Monopoly and Free Enterprise* (Twentieth Century Fund, 1951).

———: *Cartels or Competition?* (Twentieth Century Fund, 1948).

Toulmin, Harry A.: *Treatise on the Law of Food, Drugs, and Cosmetics* (Cincinnati, Ohio: Anderson, 1942).

U.S. Attorney General: *Report of the . . . National Committee to Study the Antitrust Laws* (1955).

U.S. Commission on Organization of the Executive Branch of Government (second Hoover Commission): *Federal Medical Services* (1955).

——: *Task Force Report on Federal Medical Services* (1955).

U.S. Congress, Temporary National Economic Committee: *Investigation of Concentration of Economic Power, Final Report and Recommendations,* S. Doc. 35, 77th Cong., 1st Sess., pursuant to Pub. Res. 113 (1941). The *Hearings* were published in 31 parts; there were 43 monographs.

U.S. Federal Trade Commission: *Report of . . . on Interlocking Directorates* (1951).

——: *Report of . . . on the Concentration of Productive Facilities, 1947* (1949).

——: *Report of . . . on the Merger Movement* (1948).

——: *Report of . . . on Resale Price Maintenance* (1945).

Wilson, Stephen: *Food and Drug Regulation* (American Council on Public Affairs, 1942).

REVIEW QUESTIONS

1. What conditions or factors led the Federal government to become involved in business regulation as outlined in this chapter?

2. Review the manner and extent to which the Federal and state governments regulate securities and exchanges.

3. Identify: (*a*) basing point; (*b*) resale-price maintenance; (*c*) interlocking directorate; (*d*) merger; (*e*) oligopoly.

4. Summarize provisions of the major antitrust laws enacted by the Federal government.

5. What difficulties have hampered enforcement of the antitrust laws?

6. Explain the procedure by which the Federal Trade Commission handles a complaint charging that an unfair trade practice has been committed.

7. Review the controversy over basing points, and indicate the present status of these under federal law.

8. Review the controversy over resale-price-maintenance agreements, and indicate the present status of these under federal and state laws.

9. Summarize proposals for strengthening federal regulation of monopoly.

10. Indicate the division of responsibility between the Federal government and the states for the control of alcoholic beverages.

11. Which of the various state plans for controlling liquor do you think is best?

12. Summarize provisions of federal laws regulating the purity of foods, drugs, and cosmetics.

CHAPTER 27

Utility Regulation and Federal Enterprises

The New Deal . . . does not wish to run or manage any part of the economic machine which private enterprise can run and keep running. That should be left to individuals, to corporations, to any other form of private management, with profit for those who manage well. But when an abuse interferes with the ability of private enterprise to keep the national conveyor belt moving, government has a responsibility to eliminate that abuse. — Franklin D. Roosevelt [1]

Even if the government conduct of business could give us the maximum of efficiency instead of least efficiency, it would be purchased at the cost of freedom. — Herbert Hoover [2]

Whether primitive or highly complex, societies have always subjected some types of business to more public control than others. The vitality of particular businesses varies from time to time and from community to community, while from experience and need appropriate controls are established. Some communities prefer private ownership of vital businesses and subject their owners and managers to extensive regulation; others prefer outright public ownership and management by government. In either case serious problems arise that call for careful study. This chapter reviews how Americans regulate some vital businesses owned and managed by private parties and how they manage others through public authorities.

UTILITY REGULATION: GENERAL CONSIDERATIONS

Public Utility Defined. A public utility is a private business that renders an indispensable service to the community under circumstances that require continuous public regulation. Examples are railways, waterways, ferries and bridges, busses, wharves, grain elevators, gas, water, telephone, and electricity. Such businesses are sufficiently clothed with public interest to warrant regulation that would be considered unconstitutional if applied to businesses of the usual, competitive type. Whether an enterprise may be classified as a public utility depends upon a number of factors, including whether monopoly is present, geographic location, character of service, immediacy of patrons' needs, the amount of capital invested, the scale of operations, and whether it has been considered a public enterprise in times past. Congress and state legislatures make the classification subject to court approval.

While the list of businesses that may be considered utilities tends to become longer, the Supreme Court has ruled that ice plants,[3] theater-

[1] *The Public Papers and Addresses of Franklin D. Roosevelt* (Random House, Inc.), 1938 vol., p. 588.

[2] *The Challenge to Liberty* (Charles Scribner's Sons, 1934), p. 203.

[3] New State Ice Co. *v.* Liebmann, 285 U.S. 262 (1932).

ticket brokerages,[4] gasoline stations,[5] and meat-packing industries[6] may not be classed and regulated as utilities. Milk and coal productive and distributive agencies lack some of the essentials usually possessed by utilities, yet they are sufficiently affected with a public interest to permit at least fixing their prices.[7]

Types of Carriers. Running through discussions of public utilities are references to three types of carriers: common, contract, and self-servers. Common carriers are those that hold out their facilities and service for "common" or general use to all comers. Contract carriers are those that perform services only under terms of specific contracts entered into with customers. A bus, for example, that operates regularly over a given route, stopping for all who wish to ride, would be a common carrier; but a bus that had to be chartered every time an individual or group wished to use it would be a contract carrier. Then there are self-servers—those that provide service for themselves. A large industry, for example, may own its own railroad for carrying its own products, or its own power plant, water system, or busses. In framing legislation, provisions must be varied to account for differences between these three types of carriers.

Federal and State Spheres of Operation. Most utilities are local enterprises, hence remain under control of state and local governments. Public-utility commissions exist in the District of Columbia and all the states. Deciding where their jurisdiction begins and leaves off is not easy. Federal and state activities touch and overlap at innumerable points, requiring constant collaboration and cooperation between the officials involved.

In general, business activities that are primarily of local concern, like the location of grade crossings, the laying of water pipes under city streets,

taxi service, and retail sales to the ultimate consumers, are left to the states, but even matters like these may occasionally become of national concern.

The Regulatory Agencies. The Interstate Commerce Commission, established in 1887, is the oldest of the federal bodies. Its membership of eleven is also the largest. Data concerning this and other agencies are given in the accompanying table. Organizationally, all are much alike except for the two newest ones. Older agencies are outside departmental structure, and by recent action the chairmen were made responsible for administrative matters in several of the commissions. The Civil Aeronautics Authority and the new maritime agencies are within the Department of Commerce. The former is made up of a semiautonomous Civil Aeronautics Board, which handles economic regulation, and a Civil Aeronautics Administration that deals with nonregulative matters. Similarly, the Maritime Board handles regulatory matters, while the Maritime Administration deals with administrative and promotional activities relating to the Merchant Marine.

Members are appointed by the President with Senate approval; terms are staggered; most of the agencies are bipartisan. Unlike the state utility commissions, each of which usually regulates a wide variety of utilities, each federal commission devotes its attention to some particular functional group.

The Scope of Regulation. Because utilities are businesses affected with a public interest, they are subject to public regulation provided property rights guaranteed by the Constitution are not violated. The tendency has been to impose more and more controls and even to displace private ownership entirely, either for temporary emergencies or permanently. Besides general laws applicable to all corporations dealing with such things as incorporation, registration of securities, safety, collective bargaining, wages and hours, social security, and taxation, utilities may be subject to special legislation like that governing compulsory settlement of labor disputes. Moreover, they are subject to continuous regulation by commissions.

[4] Ribnick *v.* McBride, 277 U.S. 350 (1928).

[5] Williams *v.* Standard Oil Co. of Louisiana, 278 U.S. 235 (1929).

[6] Wolff Packing Co. *v.* Court of Industrial Relations of Kansas, 262 U.S. 522 (1923).

[7] Nebbia *v.* New York, 291 U.S. 502 (1934); Sunshine Anthracite Coal Co. *v.* Adkins, 310 U.S. 381 (1940).

Federal Utility Regulatory Commissions

Agency	Date established	Number of members	Terms, years	Utility jurisdiction
Interstate Commerce Commission	1887	11	7	Railroads; motor carriers; shipping by coastwise, intercoastal, and inland waters; pipe lines (except natural gas and water); express companies; carriers using rail-and-water routes; sleeping-car companies
Federal Power Commission	1920	5	5	Water-power sites, electric power, natural-gas sales and transportation
Securities and Exchange Commission	1934	5	5	Electric and natural-gas holding companies
Federal Communications Commission	1934	7	7	Radio, telephone, telegraph, cables
Civil Aeronautics Authority	1938	Board, 5; administration, 1	6	Air lines, airways, and airports
Federal Maritime Board	1950	3	4	Shipping in foreign commerce

The approval of the utility commission is required before a new service can be started. Accordingly a company wishing to establish a new bus line or other utility must file an application. The regulatory body may follow a policy of allowing an unlimited number of competitors to enter the field, but more often than not it follows a policy of allowing limited monopoly.

Thus, in the case of a railroad application the Interstate Commerce Commission would probably forbid a competitor to enter the business unless it could be clearly demonstrated that another railroad was necessary to serve the public interest. Authorizations usually take the form of "certificates of public convenience and necessity," licenses, or permits.

Regulation also usually involves control over security issues and intercorporate relationships. Once operations have started, utilities are generally required to submit budgets, reports, and proposed rate schedules. In doing so they are required to follow a uniform system of accounts to ensure that each entry has the same meaning to all concerned. The regulatory body may approve the schedule of rates proposed or, after investigation and hearing, insist upon changes. Rate control involves property valuations to determine the value of the service rendered, and this, in turn, usually involves extensive engineering surveys of the total plant.

As all this is being done, the regulatory body must hear and adjust complaints, see that proper safety practices are followed, and otherwise make sure the law and regulations are obeyed. Finally, if utilities wish to extend their facilities or services, go out of business, or sell or abandon some of their facilities, approval must be obtained.

The Problem of Rate Making. Rate fixing is the most difficult and controversial aspect of utility regulation. As a rule the law requires that rates be fixed high enough to earn a "fair return" on the property used and useful in rendering a public service. What is a "fair return" is usually not hard to determine; the law is generally satisfied if it is in the vicinity of 5 to 8 per cent.

Far more difficult is the task of ascertaining the value of the property, or of finding the "rate base." If the figure is set too low investors will lose money, in which case the matter will probably be taken to court, where it could be held that property had been taken without due process of law. If, on the other hand, it is set too high, the public will be gouged.

Theories of Valuation. The crux of effective utility-rate control boils down to the theories and methods followed in determining the "rate base." Several methods may be followed: one might take the original cost (sometimes referred to as "historical cost") and subtract depreciation; or one might settle for reproduction cost new, less depreciation; or one might take the value of outstanding securities; or, finally, one might follow the prudent-investment theory, whereby an attempt is made to ascertain what a prudent investor would have invested in the enterprise. The latter method places great weight upon prudent original cost. There are difficulties with each of these methods. The economic difficulties are little short of appalling, and they have been aggravated by court decisions.

Smyth v. Ames. The basic case on the subject of valuations was for many years Smyth *v.* Ames, decided in 1898.[8] There the Supreme Court had before it a case arising from rates fixed for a number of railroads by the Board of Transportation for the state of Nebraska. The state board had based its rates chiefly upon the reproduction-cost-new-less-depreciation theory, but the railroads involved had been constructed in a period of high prices, hence contended for a valuation based upon original cost less depreciation.

The Court, however, refused to accept either theory to the exclusion of the other. Instead, it said that in determining fair value, consideration must be given to a number of factors including

The original cost of construction, the amount expended in permanent improvements, the amount and market value of its bonds and stocks, the present as compared with the original cost of construction, the probable earning capacity of the property under particular rates prescribed by statutes, and the sum required to meet operating expenses. . . .

The difficulty with this is not only that the procedure entails extensive investigation, with

[8] 169 U.S. 466 (1898).

resultant costly delays, but also that the Court said nothing about how much weight should be given to each of the factors mentioned. It sometimes happens that an original-cost estimate differs from one of the same company based upon the reproduction-cost-new-less-depreciation estimate by millions of dollars. In such an event, what figure represents "fair value"?

Faced with this situation, regulatory bodies follow their personal predilections, meanwhile trying to guess what the courts might have to say and finally ending with a compromise favorable to the utilities. In 1939 Justice Frankfurter, with the concurrence of Justice Black, summed up the argument over Smyth *v.* Ames by saying it had been "widely rejected by the great weight of economic opinion, by authoritative legislative investigations, by utility commissions throughout the country, and by impressive judicial dissents."[9] Nevertheless, the Supreme Court refused to open the issue in the case cited.

More recently, however, the Court has not only reopened the matter but has seriously modified its historic position. This occurred in a series of cases dealing with the fixing of "just and reasonable" rates under the Natural Gas Act.[10] As matters now stand, regulatory commissions are not bound to follow any single formula (like reproduction cost new) or combination of formulas (like that required by Smyth *v.* Ames) in determining rates. Rather, prudent investment is the guiding rule, with emphasis on original cost. Beyond this the approach is a pragmatic one.

If rates established by a commission enable a company to operate successfully, to attract capital, and to compensate investors for the risks assumed, the courts may now sustain them regardless of the theory or formula followed by the regulatory body. Needless to say, this gives those responsible for regulation a freer hand in deter-

[9] Driscoll *v.* Edison Light and Power Co., 307 U.S. 104 (1939). One of the best analyses of the valuation controversy is found in Irston R. Barnes, *The Economics of Public Utility Regulation* (Appleton-Century-Crofts, 1942).

[10] See especially Federal Power Commission *et al. v.* Hope Natural Gas Co., 320 U.S. 591 (1943).

mining value and fixing rates than in the past. A number of states have modified their utility laws to permit their commissions to follow the new rule, but several of them continue to prescribe the old fair-value formula.

REGULATION OF TRANSPORTATION

Transport Policy. Practically all forms of commercial transport engaged in interstate and foreign commerce are now regulated by federal agencies. In general, Congress has declared national policy to be the development of a varied, integrated, and coordinated transport system, under private ownership but subject to continuous regulation, that will be adequate to meet the needs of peace and war. The word "varied" suggests that transportation by rail, water, motor, and air all have a place. By "integrated" is meant that mergers and other consolidations of existing facilities are permitted, while entry of new enterprises into service is restricted so that one or a comparatively few companies perform each type of service in particular areas. In New England, for example, service is restricted to a comparatively few rail, motor, and air carriers with each operating trunk and feeder lines. The word "coordinated" means that an attempt is being made to interconnect transport facilities to promote travel and shipment and provide the greatest flexibility. The bulk of American transport is privately owned, the chief exceptions occurring among city-owned subway and surface railways and busses, and the Merchant Marine.

As already intimated, the tendency has been to reduce overlapping and duplication as much as possible. Further evidence of the tendency to reduce competition among carriers of each type is contained in the Reed-Bulwinkle Act of 1948. This permits common carriers of each type of transport to consult and agree among themselves on rates and charges, provided the Interstate Commerce Commission gives approval of proposed changes. This means that railroads may consult and agree while water, motor, and air carriers each may do likewise. But this type of collaboration is not permitted between the various types of transport. Water and rail carriers, for example, are not authorized to agree on rates and charges.

Railroads. Railroads are subject to statutes, rules, and regulations, many of which date back to the 1880's. For purposes of regulation, railroads are divided into three classes on the basis of total operating revenues. Class I roads, which include those whose annual operating revenues exceed 1 billion dollars, do the bulk of the business. The Interstate Commerce Commission also divides railroads geographically into districts and subsidiary regions for various purposes. The commission is constantly engaged in applying the utility controls described above with respect to rates, accounts, security issues, etc. It also considers questions of basic policy and makes recommendations to the President and Congress.

Moreover, the Interstate Commerce Commission applies and enforces many special laws and regulations. Among other provisions, these forbid railroads to transport products made by enterprises in which they own or control an interest; forbid railroads to own or control any competing water carrier unless the ICC finds that it is in the public interest to do so and will not reduce competition; prevent charging more for short than long hauls over the same route; require the installation and use of safety devices; require the use of uniform bills of lading; forbid price discrimination and other unauthorized practices; and prescribe methods of transporting explosives and other dangerous articles.

The ICC must also investigate railway accidents, inspect locomotives, check and limit the hours of service for employees, and determine fair and reasonable rates for mail transportation by rail and by urban and interurban electric carriers. Legislation concerning labor-management relations and dispute settlement is not the responsibility of the ICC but of other agencies.

Motor Carriers. State regulation of motor carriers began in Pennsylvania in 1914. Other states soon followed and had the field to themselves until 1935 when, after a long and bitter fight, the Motor Carrier Act was adopted.

Motor carriers, like others, group themselves into common, contract, and private carriers. In addition to the carriers themselves, transportation brokers and forwarders are of considerable importance to the industry. Brokers are intermediaries who undertake to bring users and carriers together, while forwarders are persons, other than carriers, who offer to serve the public by assembling or consolidating property with a view to reshipment by rail, water, or other carriers. The ICC was given authority to regulate all these, with numerous exceptions, in about the same manner as railroads.

Water Carriers. Water carriers may be divided into four groups: inland, coastal, intercoastal, and foreign. Inland carriers include those operating on inland rivers, canals, connecting channels, and lakes. Coastal, or coastwise, carriers are those that operate along the various coasts of the United States but not through the Panama Canal. Intercoastal are those operating through the Panama Canal between Atlantic and Pacific ports. Foreign carriers are those engaged in commerce with foreign ports. Licensing vessels is the responsibility of the Customs Bureau (Treasury), while safety regulations are enforced by the Coast Guard (Treasury). The ICC regulates the economic aspects of inland, coastal, and intercoastal carriers. The Maritime Board is responsible for foreign shipping, while the Maritime Administration builds and manages government-owned merchant vessels and administers the subsidy program.

Water navigation is an ancient industry that has been of vital concern to the American people since they first sailed to these shores. Billions of dollars have been spent on river and harbor improvement, dredging canals, and subsidizing shipping lines and ship construction. Meanwhile, state and local governments have imposed regulations. In consequence, laws and rules cover practically every phase of water commerce.

Foreign commerce is freer of controls than other types. The Maritime Board does not have control over entry into service, except for ships that are owned or subsidized by the United States. This being the case, the door is wide open for extensive competition, and for the most part jungle law prevails. Nor does the Board have authority to regulate security issues and intercorporate relationships. Its authority over rates is limited to seeing that tariffs are filed and that they are not discriminatory, although in the case of charges for wharfage and dockage it may prescribe minimums. The Board does have authority to designate and approve routes; to hear and adjust complaints; to handle matters pertaining to wages, hours, and working conditions of seamen; and to prescribe accounts and require reports.

An interesting feature of foreign shipping regulation is the degree of cooperation permitted among shipping companies. Those who wish to may join a "conference," which resembles a domestic trade association, for the purpose of pooling information and entering into agreements regarding such matters as rates, allotment of traffic, pooling of earnings, and methods to be employed in meeting competition from nonconference members. If filed with the Maritime Board and approved, these agreements are immune from antitrust laws.

Air Commerce. Practically all aircraft are engaged in, or affect, interstate and foreign commerce. In consequence, federal law is comprehensive and there has been little economic regulation by the states. The latter have been chiefly concerned with safety, liability, and airports. Basic federal legislation was adopted in 1938. As indicated above, administration is the responsibility of the Civil Aeronautics Authority, although this body performs no functions itself. Instead, the Authority is divided into a Civil Aeronautics Board and a Civil Aeronautics Administration.

The Board is a quasi-legislative and judicial body concerned primarily with fact finding, rule making, and the adjudication of disputes; while the Administration is in charge of the administration and enforcement of rules and regulations. In addition to regulating air carriers to about the same extent as railways and other common carriers, much time, money, and effort have gone into making flights safer, building an up-to-date airway system, building federally owned airports and cooperating with the states and local governments in developing others, and promoting foreign air commerce.

Pipe Lines. Pipe lines are used for the transportation of various liquids and gases, but their predominating use in the United States is for the transportation of crude petroleum, gasoline, and natural gas. In rich petroleum centers the earth may be honeycombed with pipes. In the Pittsburgh area, for example, there is literally one pipe on top of another and they crisscross and parallel each other in a most confusing manner. The recent war saw rapid expansion and renovation of pipes lines for the transportation of petroleum. The most important and dramatic project was the construction of the "Big Inch"— a 24-inch line from east Texas to Philadelphia and New York, the longest and largest pipe line ever installed for transporting petroleum. The job was done by the Federal government; oil began moving through it in February, 1943; and by August of the same year through connections had been made to the East coast. After the war, the line was sold to private enterprise.

Federal control of interstate pipe lines began in 1906 in response to the fact that the lines were few in number and controlled by one company, Standard Oil. At the time, the ICC was given jurisdiction over all except those for transporting water and manufactured or natural gas. The last was brought under control in 1938, along with other aspects of the industry, but responsibility for administration was placed in the Federal Power Commission. As is noted below, the Holding Company Act of 1935 applied to natural-gas companies, many of whom own or control interstate pipe lines.

Thus, as matters stand, the ICC regulates pipe lines transporting crude oil, gasoline, and miscellaneous products; the Federal Power Commission deals with those conveying natural gas; while the Securities and Exchange Commission is engaged in reorganizing the holding-company structures for companies engaged in the production, transportation, and wholesale distribution of natural gas. The pipe-line companies are all declared to be common carriers and are regulated to about the same extent as electric power.

REGULATION OF ELECTRIC POWER, GAS, AND COMMUNICATIONS

Electric Power. Advent of the power age brought with it recognition that if the public interest was to be protected federal legislation was needed to supplement state control. A desire to conserve resources, threatened by the quest on the part of electric-power companies for sites along rivers and lakes, occasioned the first federal legislation in 1920.

The Water Power Act of that year created the Federal Power Commission for the primary purpose of surveying the water resources of the nation and passing on applications to establish hydroelectric projects along navigable waters and on public lands. Since then the powers of the commission over the interstate operations of electric utilities have been extended, and in 1938 it was given jurisdiction over the interstate transportation of natural gas.

Electric service divides itself naturally into three parts: generation, transmission, and distribution. Generation involves the manufacture of electric energy; transmission, its transportation from the generating station to the locality where it is consumed; and distribution, the retail sale and delivery of energy to the customers. Generation is usually highly localized, and the same is true of distribution. In most instances they are, therefore, controlled by state and local agencies. The Federal government interests itself with generation only at the point of approving water-power sites along navigable rivers and on public lands; and it is directly concerned with distribution only at the point of regulating the wholesale prices charged distributors who purchase electricity shipped from out of state. It is with transmission that the Federal government is primarily concerned, because this is frequently not localized and may be interstate in character.

As indicated above, the commission must approve all hydroelectric power projects on navigable waters and public lands. Licenses run for as long as 50 years, although the law expressly reserves the right for either the Federal or state government to reacquire the site at any time.

The commission lacks authority to require a showing of public necessity and convenience before electric companies extend their lines across state boundaries (this would be a matter reserved to the states), but it can encourage voluntary interconnections to be made under certain circumstances. To help accomplish this purpose, the commission has divided the country into regional districts. When it comes to transmission of electric energy to points outside the United States, however, the commission must approve every instance.

The commission also has complete jurisdiction over long-term security issues made by electric utilities under its jurisdiction. So far as short-term issues are concerned, it may scrutinize only those issued by companies organized and operating in states that do not provide for the regulation of security issues. Service must be adequate, although in obtaining such the commission must cooperate with state agencies. Rates (always wholesale, otherwise state utility commissions have jurisdiction) must be just, reasonable, and nonpreferential. Uniform accounts must be kept and reports filed. Interlocking relationships must also be approved.

Natural Gas. Very little *manufactured* gas is transported across state lines; hence its regulation is left to the states. With *natural* gas the situation is different. Most of this originates in the wells of a few states and is transported, principally by pipe lines, to others. Several states attempted regulation, but in a series of decisions [11] the Supreme Court ruled that neither the state in which the gas was produced nor the one in which it was distributed to the ultimate consumer could regulate the interstate rate. These decisions, together with the disclosures made in the Federal Trade Commission's survey of holding-company structures and practices, led Congress to pass the Natural Gas Act of 1938.

The controls given the Federal Power Commission over natural gas are much the same as for interstate electric utilities. Much controversy

has arisen in recent years over whether the commission had authority to regulate "gatherers" of natural gas, *i.e.,* those who assemble gas after it has been extracted from the earth for shipment in foreign and interstate commerce, usually through pipe lines. The commission began regulating these in 1942, and its action was upheld by the Supreme Court.[12] Early in 1956 a law freeing the industry from federal regulation was passed but met with Presidential veto.

There has also been controversy over Federal Power Commission regulation of the *distribution* and *sale* of gas shipped in foreign and interstate commerce. Congress amended the Natural Gas Act in 1954 to provide that a company engaged in distributing gas shall not be subject to federal regulation when the company receives gas at or within a state boundary, for use solely within a state. Federal regulation continues up to the state boundary. The new provision applies only in states having commissions which regulate the sales and service of natural-gas companies.

Electric and Gas Holding Companies. A holding company is one organized to "hold" securities of operating companies, supposedly for the purpose of profiting from their reinvestment. Illegal at common law, they were legalized by state statutes, beginning with New Jersey in 1888. By this device, securities of competing companies were brought together under single management, often with monopolistic results.

This was especially true in the electric-power field. By 1932, thirteen large holding companies controlled 75 per cent of the entire privately owned electric-utility industry, with more than 40 per cent concentrated in the hands of the three largest groups—United Corporation, Electric Bond and Share Company, and Insull. Even these three systems were not totally independent.

[11] For a review of this history with appropriate citations, see Federal Power Commission *et al. v.* Hope Natural Gas Co., 320 U.S. 591 (1943).

[12] *Ibid.* For a general review of this subject see Ralph K. Huitt, "Federal Regulation of the Uses of Natural Gas," *American Political Science Review,* vol. 46 (June, 1952), p. 468. See also a symposium entitled "The Regulation of Natural Gas," *Law and Contemporary Problems* (Duke University School of Law, Summer, 1954).

A report made in January, 1935, by the Federal Trade Commission disclosed a maze of unsound financial structures, widespread lobbying and propaganda activities intended to disparage government regulation and ownership, and extensive intercompany dealings which saddled operating companies, and ultimately consumers, with exorbitant expenditures.

The Holding Company Act. After one of the most sensational legislative contests in recent years, the Holding Company Act relating to electric and gas utility holding companies was approved on Aug. 26, 1935. Some of its provisions are:

1. Electric and gas holding companies register with the Securities and Exchange Commission.

2. Commission approval is necessary before new securities are issued or an interest is acquired in any other utility.

3. All holding companies above the second must be abolished, unless excepted by the commission, and their operations confined to integrated regional systems.

4. Intercompany loans and interlocking directorates with banking institutions were made illegal.

5. Holding companies might not, without commission approval, sell goods, perform services, or undertake construction work for any associated utility.

6. Holding companies might not contribute to political parties or candidates for public office, nor lobby without disclosing the object sought and expenditures.

7. Holding companies must use uniform accounts, make reports to the commission, and otherwise follow rules and regulations established by the commission.

Results of the "Death Sentence." During the legislative battle over the Holding Company Act, much was heard about the so-called "death sentence" provisions contained in Section 11 and referred to under No. 3 in the above list. This section makes it the duty of the Securities and Exchange Commission to simplify holding-company structures by confining them to integrated regional systems and eliminating all beyond the second degree.

Thus the holding companies that were pyramided several stories high and spread all over continental United States had to be completely revamped. They can exist only up to and including the second degree; which means that there may be an operating company, a holding company controlling the operating company, and a holding company controlling the first holding company—but no more. Moreover, the properties must be regrouped and confined to regional systems.

A large number of separate electric, gas, and nonutility properties have been removed from the control of registered holding companies; while many of the complicated holding-company structures have been dissolved or liquidated. Reorganization is virtually complete, and contrary to the dire predictions of those who opposed the law, the industry appears to be in a healthier condition than ever before.[13]

Communications. Prior to 1934, radio and wire communications were partially regulated by several agencies, chiefly the ICC, the Postmaster General, and the Federal Radio Commission. The laws were consolidated and broadened in the Communications Act of 1934. At the same time, their administration was placed in the hands of one agency, the Federal Communications Commission. Its jurisdiction extends to all radio, television, telephone, telegraph, and cable service, stations, and operators affecting interstate and foreign commerce.

Congress charged the commission with ensuring "a rapid, efficient, nation-wide and world-wide wire and radio communication service with adequate facilities at reasonable charges." So far as wire communications are concerned, ownership and control rest largely in the hands of three companies: the Bell Telephone Company, Western Union, and International Telephone and Telegraph Corporation. Until recently, competition aided in regulating telegraph service, but with the merger of Western Union

[13] For a review of achievements so far as natural-gas companies are concerned see Ralph K. Huitt, "Natural Gas Regulation under the Holding Company Act," *Law and Contemporary Problems* (Duke University School of Law, Summer, 1954), p. 455.

and Postal Telegraph in 1943, a single company dominates the field.

Controls are about the same as for other common carriers. However, the FCC has no jurisdiction over the issuance of securities; it can investigate but not control transactions between operating and affiliated companies (an area where such scandalous abuses were discovered among electric and gas holding companies); and it lacks authority to control fully consolidations and combinations.

Radio and Television. Radio and television broadcasting are regulated exclusively by the Federal government. The first legislation on the subject was in 1910 when Congress enacted a statute requiring steam vessels to have radio equipment for emergency use. A second act was passed in 1912 wherein the Secretary of Commerce was authorized to require and issue licenses for radio transmission, but it failed to make clear whether he had authority to determine the frequency, station, power, or the hours of transmission.

In 1926 a Chicago station "jumped" its frequency bands and broadcast at hours not permitted by its license. When the station was prosecuted, a United States district court [14] held that the Secretary was without power to enforce his order. Anarchy reigned on the ether, compelling Congress to provide more effective control. The Federal Radio Act of 1927 was the result. By this the Federal Radio Commission was created and the basic rules by which radio is regulated were laid down. The Radio Commission was abolished in 1934 and its functions were transferred to the newly created Federal Communications Commission.

Whoever broadcasts by radio and television from any point in the United States must obtain a license in order to operate legally. Among other things, this assigns the band and frequencies of operation. Licenses for standard broadcasts may be issued for a period not to exceed 3 years, while those for broadcasts of other types may run for 5 years. Issuing these is an exceedingly difficult task, because there are many applicants and relatively few frequencies to be divided among them.

The criteria established in the law for the guidance of the commission in issuing licenses are very general. The principal ones are: licenses may not be issued to aliens, foreign governments, or foreign interests; the commission must be convinced that the public interest, convenience, and necessity will be served; and licenses must be distributed among the states in such a way as to "provide a fair, efficient, and equitable distribution" of service.

The power of the commission to grant or deny licenses is one of the most powerful weapons possessed by any regulatory agency. Before 1939, when licenses had to be renewed every 6 months, broadcasting companies were kept in constant uncertainty over their prospects of obtaining renewals. While this doubtless had a potent corrective influence upon the industry, it led to charges of abuse and favoritism. Adoption of a longer period during which licenses are valid has diminished criticism but the possibility of abuse remains. Indeed, it is certain to remain as long as there is commission control of a privately owned industry like this.

The Communications Act expressly states that broadcasting stations are not common carriers. Accordingly, the commission lacks direct authority to regulate rates charged of advertisers, services, discrimination, security issues, and intercorporate relationships. Nor does it have the power of censorship. Such control as it has over these and other matters stems largely from its power to grant, renew, and revoke licenses.

The rules of the commission require all standard stations to keep daily logs of programs and incidents. No profanity or obscenity is permitted. All legally qualified candidates for particular political offices must be given equal opportunity to present their views, and to this end a record must be kept of all requests for political broadcasts. Typical of other regulations are those requiring that schedules of tariffs and charges be filed with the commission; that extensions be approved; that stations be tested and inspected; and that stations clearly identify themselves and the sponsors of broadcasts.

[14] United States *v.* Zenith Radio Co., 12 F.2d 614 (1926).

FEDERAL ENTERPRISES: GENERAL CONSIDERATIONS

The Problem of Government Ownership.
Whether government should become the owner and operator of business-type enterprises is one of the most controverted questions. The individualist would keep the number of government enterprises at an absolute minimum; the socialist seeks public ownership and operation of the major instruments of production and distribution. Most Americans occupy a middle ground, which to political theorists is known as "empirical collectivism." [15]

Little moved by abstract concepts, Americans have taken the pragmatic approach and devised practical solutions for immediate and concrete problems. The result, as Prof. Currin Shields has pointed out, is a parallel tradition of individualism and collectivism. One often finds, for example, that communities of rock-ribbed conservatives stanchly defend their municipally owned waterworks, electric systems, and other utilities, many of which have been owned for decades or, in the case of waterworks, for more than a century. While private ownership dominates most fields of business, public ownership has steadily increased in many.

Critics usually assert that government ownership is unfair because its enterprises are tax-free and otherwise subsidized by taxpayers.[16] It is also alleged that government ownership involves an excessive amount of bureaucracy and red tape. It is also argued that, because of the absence of personal risk, competitive factors, and the lure of profit, government-owned enterprises are lacking in incentive, imagination, and initiative. The issue is finally disposed of by asserting that a little bit of socialism leads to more and that this inevitably results in dictatorship. Critics find illustrations to prove one or all these assertions;

but, like most extremists, they try to prove too much.

Fortunately, the subject is no longer academic. There has been enough experience with government-owned corporations, both in this country and abroad, to suggest that they are probably here to stay, that they can be made to operate satisfactorily, that they often can meet public and social needs when private enterprise cannot or will not, that public and private ownership can coexist, and that resort to public ownership does not necessarily lead to the totalitarian state and loss of personal liberty.

This is not to advocate the wholesale extension of government ownership; it is merely to suggest that a wise person will try to understand the forces that have led to public ownership and bring to the solution of problems as they arise an awareness of the advantages, disadvantages, and pitfalls of both private and public ownership.

As the following discussion develops, it will be noted that some government-owned enterprises aim at operating within a framework of costs and prices that will provide a net profit to the public treasury. This is true of the electric-power aspects of the Tennessee Valley Authority, Hoover Dam, and the Bonneville Administration. Other enterprises are less concerned with costs, prices, and profit than with providing an essential service. This is the case with the Postal Service, reclamation projects, the Panama Canal, the Maritime Administration, the Alaskan Railroad, and others.

Whether the following examples of federal ownership are "profitable," therefore, depends upon the criteria used in making a judgment. If the enterprise is set up for the sole purpose of providing a service at a profit, it may be done with costs and prices that compare favorably with those of competing private enterprises. When, however, the government-owned agency is set up, as most of them are, for the purpose not only of providing a service but also of conserving natural resources, of meeting a defense need, or of providing a direct or indirect subsidy to some of the users, or something else, one cannot look merely at costs, prices, profits, or

---

[15] For an excellent recent development of this theme, see Currin V. Shields, "The American Tradition of Empirical Collectivism," *American Political Science Review,* vol. 46, no. 1 (March, 1952), p. 104.

[16] For a recent critical report see second Hoover Commission, *Business Enterprises* (1955), and *Water Resources and Power* (1955).

losses and conclude that government ownership is necessarily less "efficient" than private.

Whether under private or governmental operation, the important thing from the point of view of the public is not monetary profit or loss but whether high-quality service has been provided at a minimum cost as measured both in terms of money and the utilization of material and human resources.

The Proprietary Power. The Federal government (and states too) is a proprietor in the sense that it may acquire, hold, and dispose of property, enter into contracts, hire, manage, and discharge employees, and in general conduct its affairs. Though ample authority for the exercise of functions like these is contained in the implied clause, additional authorization is conveyed in the words "Congress shall have Power to dispose of and make all needful Rules and Regulations respecting Territory or other Property belonging to the United States. . . ." [17] In addition to its use for general functions, Congress has recently used this power for the attainment of purposes of a highly controversial nature.

In 1936 the Supreme Court relied on this power, together with the commerce and war powers, to justify the Tennessee Valley Authority.[18] In this instance the authority of TVA to dispose of surplus electric power in competition with existing utilities was at issue. The Court said that since surplus power was "property belonging to the United States" Congress was at liberty to "dispose of and make all needful rules" concerning it, even though competitors were hurt in the process.

In the same year the Court also justified the Walsh-Healy Act by this power.[19] At issue there was the authority of the Federal government to fix wages, hours, and working conditions in businesses bidding on government contracts involving $10,000 or more. As a proprietor, the Court said, the government could dictate the terms under which it would do business. This decision was of special importance because it permitted regulation of many large businesses at a time when the Supreme Court was still saying the commerce clause could not be used to regulate the internal operations of large-scale productive enterprises.

The proprietary power also provides one of the bases for loyalty review and dismissal of undesirable employees in the government service. Some federal enterprises, notably the postal system, stem from special grants of power; others are based on the commerce and war powers; but in every instance the proprietary power is an important factor.

Variety of Federal Undertakings. A list of business undertakings in which the Federal government is engaged is surprisingly large. These include the production of motion pictures for educational and propaganda purposes; operation of farms by federal penal, correctional, educational, and experimental agencies; manufacture of mailbags and locks; shipbuilding by the Maritime Administration and the Navy; manufacture of guns, ammunition, binoculars, rope, varnish, paint, furniture, mattresses, and other supplies for national defense; manufacture of clothing for the Army and Navy; manufacture of ink, stamps, gum for stamps and envelopes; providing musical concerts by military bands; operating pipe lines, railroads, air and shipping lines; printing and binding; manufacturing and selling electric power and fertilizers.[20] Space prevents a discussion of all governmental undertakings; hence consideration will be given to only a few of the more controversial.

[17] Art. IV, Sec. 3.

[18] Ashwander *v.* Tennessee Valley Authority *et al.,* 297 U.S. 288 (1936).

[19] Perkins *v.* Lukens Steel Company, 310 U.S. 113 (1936).

[20] For others, together with discussion, see U.S. House of Representatives, Special Committee to Investigate Government Competition with Private Enterprise, *Government Competition with Private Enterprise, Report.* . . . House Rep. 1985, 72d Cong., 2d Sess. (1933). See also first Hoover Commission, *Federal Business Enterprises* (1949) and *Task Force Report on Revolving Funds and Business Enterprises of the Government* (1949). See also second Hoover Commission, *Business Enterprises* (1955).

THE POSTAL SERVICE

The Postal Power. A colonial-wide postal service having been inherited from the period of British rule, few at the Constitutional Convention doubted the desirability of continuing something similar. Accordingly, the Constitution provided that "Congress shall have power . . . to establish Post Offices and Post Roads." The power is granted exclusively to Congress and the states have never sought to compete. Like other powers granted, this one may also be used for purposes that are, on their face at least, incidental to their primary purpose. Accordingly, Congress has passed many laws regulating the use of mails and excluding objectionable materials.

These, it is frequently contended, amount to usurpation of state powers in violation of the Tenth Amendment, but the courts have held otherwise. The power to establish a postal service, said the courts, also conveys authority to determine what mail would be carried and how. Accordingly, Congress excludes such things as poisons of all kinds, including poisonous animals, insects, and reptiles; explosives; inflammable materials; infernal machines; disease germs and scabs; obscene literature, including that calculated to inform people about contraception and abortion; lotteries; writings calculated to produce sedition or to incite to murder or arson; and fraudulent materials of various sorts.

During the depression Congress went further than ever before in using the postal power, partly because of the narrow construction the courts then placed on the commerce power. The Securities Act of 1933, the Securities and Exchange Act of 1934, and the Public Utility Holding Company Act of 1935 were all based in part on the postal power. The first two forbid the use of the mails for selling or dealing in the securities of large corporations unless the securities are first registered with the Securities and Exchange Commission. The third forbids electric and natural-gas holding companies from using the mails except when they have registered and are conducting their affairs according to the act. These are far-reaching and drastic measures, imposing a type of restraint which many supposed lay within the scope of reserved powers of the states. But their constitutionality has been upheld.[21]

Much controversy has also arisen over the manner in which postal regulations affect personal rights. As with other powers, this one must be reconciled with the Bill of Rights. Especially bothersome, from the standpoint of post-office officials, is the guaranty against unreasonable searches and seizures. One's mail is among the "papers" and "effects" that may not be unreasonably searched and seized. Accordingly, unless the sender gives consent, no letter, publication, or package sent through the mail can be opened without a search warrant.

This is not done by local postal employees. Instead, postmasters forward suspected mail to the dead-letter office where some authorized employee goes before a United States Commissioner or district judge, describes the mail to be searched and seized, and presents evidence to justify his suspicion. If the warrant is issued, the matter is turned over to the post-office inspectors for further investigation and appropriate action.

The Post Office Department. The head of the department, unlike most chiefs of executive departments who are called "Secretaries," is called Postmaster General. Though one of the earliest officers to be appointed in the young republic, he was not accorded cabinet status until Jackson's time, in 1829, and his office was not given departmental status until 1872. During all that time his office was considered a unit within the Treasury Department, although the Postmaster General himself was directly responsible to the President. In times past the Postmaster General was nearly always a politician. Indeed, it was long customary for him to be none other than the chairman of the President's political party. Associated with him is the usual staff and administrative personnel.

[21] There have been a number of cases. See, for example, Electric Bond and Share Co. *v.* Securities and Exchange Commission, 303 U.S. 419 (1938), and Jones *v.* Securities and Exchange Commission, 298 U.S. 1 (1936).

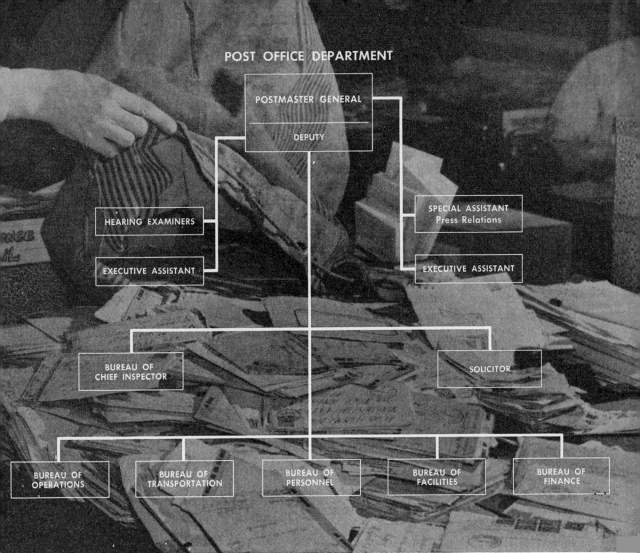

POST OFFICE DEPARTMENT

- POSTMASTER GENERAL / DEPUTY
  - HEARING EXAMINERS
  - EXECUTIVE ASSISTANT
  - SPECIAL ASSISTANT Press Relations
  - EXECUTIVE ASSISTANT
  - BUREAU OF CHIEF INSPECTOR
  - SOLICITOR
  - BUREAU OF OPERATIONS
  - BUREAU OF TRANSPORTATION
  - BUREAU OF PERSONNEL
  - BUREAU OF FACILITIES
  - BUREAU OF FINANCE

United Press photograph

Auxiliary Services. Besides handling the mail, the Post Office Department operates a parcel-post service; a system of registry and insurance for mail; a money-order system; a postal-savings business for small depositors; a cash-on-delivery collection service; and a special-delivery service. Moreover, it handles the sale of small-denomination government bonds and stamps and collects several types of taxes. In addition, it provides local headquarters for a number of federal agencies, especially the Civil Service Commission, Department of Justice, and Internal Revenue Service. Incidentally, through its far-flung activities, offices in almost every city and hamlet, and rural carriers, it has been the principal post through which the administration in power has observed current trends and sentiment. It has also been an important instrument for influencing local opinion and elections by the handling of federal patronage. The Post Office Department owns some of its nearly 41,000 post offices, but leases most of them. It operates shops for manufacturing and repairing mailbags, locks, etc., but purchases a huge quantity of its equipment and materials from other agencies, both governmental and private. While contracting with railway and other carriers for transporting huge quantities of mail and parcels, the department also owns and operates a fleet of trucks for this purpose.

Postal Profits and Losses. For the first quarter of a century, the postal service was operated along lines followed by private business and a profit was shown practically every year. After 1814, especially during and after the presidency of Andrew Jackson, three factors influenced the course of management: one, the spoils system; another, legislation providing for the extension of the postal service to all parts of the country, especially the developing West, even though uneconomic; and the third, legislation granting subsidies to special groups either in the form of higher prices paid to the railways and other carriers for mail transportation, free postage, or reduced rates. It is obvious that the terms "profits" and "losses" lose their usual meaning when considerations such as these must be reckoned with.

The situation today is somewhat the same, albeit on the road to improvement, one may at least hope. Among postal personnel are many political appointees, with the result that management is less efficient than it otherwise might be. Uneconomic expansion is a factor of diminishing importance, since the service now pretty well covers the country. It is still true that rates paid to water, motor, and air carriers for transporting mail carry hidden subsidies and are therefore higher than need be. Mail may be sent free by many, including congressmen, the blind, widows of former Presidents, agricultural colleges and experiment stations (for farm bulletins and reports), and publishers may send newspapers and other second-class mail free to subscribers within the county of publication. It is clear that rates for mail of all classes, except the first, have been too low to pay expenses assignable to them. Rates were readjusted and some of them raised in 1952 but not enough to meet the costs of operation, and a large subsidy paid out of taxes will still be required.

The first Hoover Commission was particularly critical of the Post Office Department. In line with its suggestions, President Truman appointed as Postmaster General a department career man. President Eisenhower, however, reverted to the practice of appointing a prominent party worker to this high post. Rates have been readjusted and the performance budget introduced. President Truman made an attempt in 1952 to place all postmasters under the merit system, but Congress objected.

Other recommendations which have not been adopted include the following: (1) decentralization of the postal service into fifteen regions under regional directors and district superintendents; (2) appointment of an unpaid advisory board of laymen representative of different elements of the public; (3) requirement that auditing be done by the Comptroller General; (4) simplification of departmental organization to provide greater flexibility; and (5) payment of transportation subsidies (for example, to airlines), where Congress thinks these necessary, from tax funds rather than from postal revenues. Until changes like these are made, one must assume that the public is less concerned with financial "profit" and efficiency than with the services and other values it is buying.

The second Hoover Commission recommended disposal of the postal-savings system, raising parcel-post rates to cover all operating costs and thereby diminish competition with private express companies, and transferring mailbag and lock manufacture and repair to Federal Prisons Industries, Inc.[22]

FEDERAL POWER PROJECTS

Power in the Valleys. Federal electric-power operations have reached gigantic proportions. The first Hoover Commission [23] reported that as of June 30, 1947, forty-seven hydroelectric and ten steam-power plants had been built or purchased, thirty-seven additional plants were under construction, and seventy-nine more had been authorized by Congress. This, according to the commission, would give the nation by about 1960 a total of 172 plants with a capacity of about 20,233,637 kilowatts. This trend has provoked intense controversy. In its current phase champions of public power resist strenuously intrusions by private utilities encouraged by the election of a Republican President in 1952.

Two general plans of development and administration have been followed. The valley-authority plan, illustrated by the TVA, em-

[22] *Op. cit.,* pp. 51–63.
[23] *Federal Business Enterprises* (1949), pp. 51–129.

powers a single, independent, federal corporation to operate within a region. Under this arrangement, a valley authority, headed by a small board, is responsible for planning, building, and operating public works for the conservation and utilization of the water resources of the valley, subject to the statutes defining its

sponsibility, permits unified planning and operation, and eliminates duplication, overlapping, and rivalry among the agencies; it should also lessen the possibility of extravagance and waste. For these reasons many have urged a Missouri Valley Authority, Columbia Valley Authority, Southwestern Authority, and perhaps others.

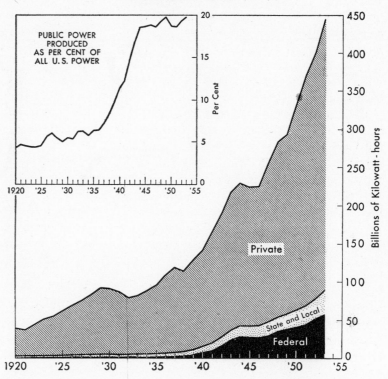

ELECTRIC POWER PRODUCTION
UNITED STATES, 1920-1953

PUBLIC POWER PRODUCED AS PER CENT OF ALL U.S. POWER

Electric power production has increased rapidly in recent years. Although four-fifths was produced by private facilities in 1953, public power's share is rising. Courtesy of National Industrial Conference Board.

authority and to a continuing control by the President and Congress. Its budget must be approved annually. Other federal agencies continue to operate within the valley, but their programs are affected by the studies and plans of the valley authority. The construction and operation of dams, hydro power plants, and reservoirs become the responsibility of the valley authority. The other plan, illustrated by Missouri Valley activities, calls for coordinated action on the part of several federal agencies including the Corps of Engineers, the Bureau of Reclamation, Soil Conservation Service, and others.

The valley-authority plan clearly focuses re-

Critics are numerous. The rivaling agencies insist that they are more competent and efficient than a newly established authority would be. Electric power utilities fear that a valley authority, following the example of the TVA, may drive down power rates and promote public ownership. Many state officials, and even some congressmen, profess to fear a single authority of such enormous power. A single authority is likely to do much of its own construction and otherwise lessen opportunities for contractors, realtors, and other private interests. These, and other reasons, evoke sympathy from States' rights advocates, champions of free enterprise, and opponents of such federal projects generally. Thus far, opposition has been strong enough to keep valley authorities to one, the TVA, but what the future holds cannot be foretold. The first Hoover Commission, while strongly condemning present interagency jealousy and overlapping, opposed the establishment of additional

would recommend broad policies and "devise methods of coordination of plans and actions of the agencies both at the Washington level and in the field." [25]

Another problem is whether river-valley projects should be developed and administered separately and independently of one another or be

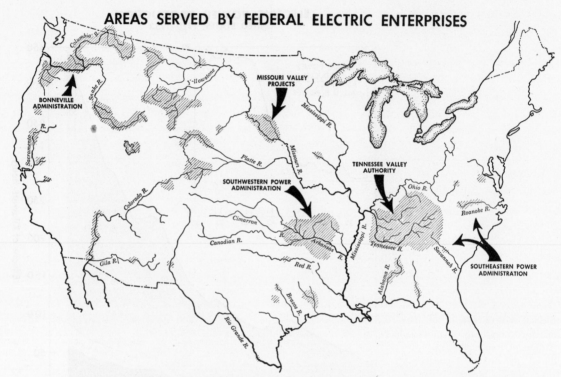

AREAS SERVED BY FEDERAL ELECTRIC ENTERPRISES

The national government has heavy responsibilities in power development along our river systems. Note the concentration of projects in the Far West, Mountain states, Southwest, and South, and the paucity of projects in the Middle West, North Atlantic, and New England states.

valley authorities.[24] Instead, it expressed preference for agency consolidation, with direct lines of responsibility running from central headquarters in Washington to the various river valley projects.

The second Hoover Commission also found lack of central planning, coordination, and cooperation among conservation agencies. The solution proposed, however, was limited to recommending a Water Resources Board located in the Executive Office of the President. The Board

[24] *Department of Interior* (1949). See also the task-force report entitled *Natural Resources,* pp. 16–39.

brought together under a single agency. A single agency, it is contended, would be better able to plan, coordinate, and utilize technical services, manpower, and equipment. It would be able to standardize accounting, personnel, and other administrative policies. Furthermore, it would give the President and Congress one agency to look to for reports and recommendations instead of the many that exist under present trends. The first Hoover Commission gave considerable thought to this problem and recommended that except for the TVA, valley developments should

[25] *Water Resources and Power,* vol. I, p. 38.

take place under a single agency, to be called the "Water Development and Use Service," to be located in a greatly changed Department of Interior.[26]

Department of Interior Projects. Power developments dot the nation. The Army Corps of Engineers has designed and built most of them and continues to operate a few of the hydroelectric plants. But most of the projects, outside the TVA region, are the responsibility of the Bureau of Reclamation (Interior). Most of these are scattered and small, with emphasis on irrigation rather than electric power. But those in the Colorado, Columbia, Arkansas, and Missouri River basins have assumed huge proportions. These are integrated, multiple-purpose, regional projects combining irrigation, electric power, conservation, flood control, and sometimes navigation features. Besides the Army Corps of Engineers and the Bureau of Reclamation, numerous other federal and state agencies are involved.

On the Colorado, the power plants at Hoover and Grand Valley dams are leased for operation to the City of Los Angeles and the Southern California Edison Company. In the Columbia basin, power generated at Bonneville, Grand Coulee, and other dams is marketed by the Bonneville Administration, a subsidiary of the Bureau of Reclamation. In the Arkansas basin, power generated at Dennison, Norfolk, and other dams is marketed by the Southwestern Power Administration, while the Southeastern Power Administration performs a similar function for the Southeastern states outside TVA territory.

In the Missouri Valley, where developments have proceeded slowly because of interagency rivalry, time-consuming consultations with representatives of the various states, and shortages of materials and appropriations, power is marketed by Bureau of Reclamation representatives. The Bureau sells most of its power at wholesale, giving preference to federal, state, and municipal bodies and farm cooperatives. On the whole, electric rates have been promotional, *i.e.,* low enough to encourage high consumption. Unlike the TVA, the Bureau lacks authority to dictate to its purchasers resale prices and accounting practices.

The Tennessee Valley Authority (TVA). The TVA stems from operations begun during the First World War. At that time the government started building Wilson Dam at Muscle Shoals, Ala., for the purpose of providing power with which to transform into munitions rich deposits of nitrate found there. The war ended before plans were completed, leaving the government with a large investment on its hands. Strong sentiment developed in favor of selling to private bidders, chief of whom was Henry Ford. These attempts were blocked by a small group of "insurgent" Senators led by the late Senator George W. Norris, of Nebraska, who later became popularly known as the "father of TVA" and for whom one of the largest dams and the near-by community of Norris, Tenn., is named. Senator Norris and others envisaged a large-scale regional program designed to bring about coordinated development and utilization of natural resources in the entire Tennessee River Valley.

The Authority is directed by a three-man board appointed by the President with Senate concurrence for 9-year terms,[27] while a general manager supervises administration. Its chief office is at Knoxville, Tenn., but activities are carried on in parts of seven states.

Status of the TVA. The TVA is organized as a government corporation outside the executive departments. It is not, however, in the same category as some of the regulatory agencies such as the Interstate Commerce Commission and Federal Trade Commission, chiefly because it does not perform quasi-legislative and judicial functions. Speaking of its administrative status in a case arising from the dismissal by President Roosevelt of the former chairman of the Authority, Dr. Arthur E. Morgan, on grounds of contumacy, the district court said[28]

It requires little to demonstrate that the Tennessee Valley Authority exercises predominantly an

[26] *Department of Interior* (1949), p. 14.

[27] The term was 5 years for those first appointed.

[28] Morgan *v.* Tennessee Valley Authority, 115 F.2d 990 (1940).

executive and administrative function. To it has been entrusted the carrying out of the dictates of the statute to construct dams, generate electricity, manage and develop government property. Many of these activities, prior to the setting up of the

Although independent of the executive departments, the Authority is subject to presidential direction, including a larger measure of control than the Chief Executive has over most of the "independent establishments."

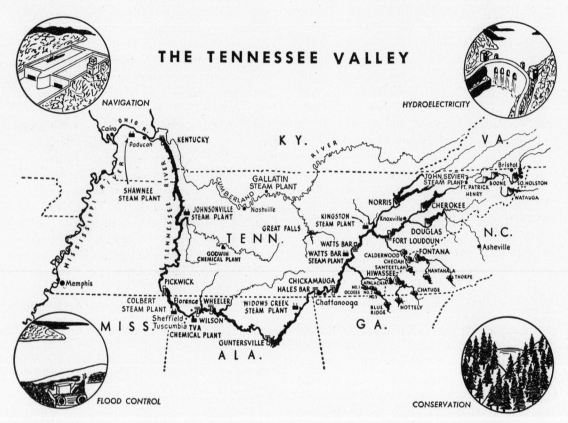

No federal developmental project in this century has aroused more interest abroad and more controversy at home than the TVA. Its main installations and multipurpose nature are shown here. Adapted from material supplied by TVA.

T.V.A. have rested with the several divisions of the executive branch of the government. . . . The Board does not sit in judgment upon private controversies, or controversies between private citizens and the government, and there is no judicial review of its decision, except as it may sue or be sued. . . . It is not to be aligned with the Federal Trade Commission, the Interstate Commerce Commission, or other administrative bodies mainly exercising clearly quasi-legislative or quasi-judicial functions—it is predominantly an administrative arm of the executive department. . . .

Purposes and Functions. The primary purpose of TVA is that of fostering the "orderly and proper physical, economic, and social development" of the area. Its first concern must be navigation and flood control. Beyond that it is directed to produce nitrate and phosphate products for use as fertilizers in peacetime and munitions in time of war, operate electric plants for its own use and sale of the surplus, foster afforestation, soil conservation, and diversification of industry. A valuable by-product of its activities is improved recreational opportunities which include some of the best fishing, camp-ing, swimming, and boating to be found.

Ranging up and down the Tennessee River and its tributaries are numerous dams. Behind these are impounded enormous lakes of water forming a total water line longer than the salt-water boundary of the entire continental United States.[29] Each of the main river dams has a spillway section, a navigation lock, and a power-house. The series of dams on the main river provides a navigation channel of 9-foot mini-mum depth for the entire 650-mile length of the Tennessee River. Tributary dams are essentially storage dams; none has a navigation lock, but most have, or will have when completed, hydro-electric generating plants.

The Authority also directs the operation of Aluminum Company of America dams on tribu-taries of the Tennessee, thereby assuring more efficient control and utilization of water power. In addition to its hydroelectric plants, the Au-thority has a number of plants at which power is generated by fuel instead of water. It main-tains a network of transmission lines, a switch-yard at each hydro or steam plant to put the power on the lines, and substations throughout the power-service area for taking power from the lines. The Authority also owns and operates chemical plants for manufacturing nitrate and phosphate products.

Electric Power Operations. Most controversy has centered around the sale by the Authority of surplus electric power. The act of 1933 per-mits the sale either at the generating stations or elsewhere. It also requires that in selecting cus-tomers preference be given to cooperative asso-ciations and municipalities. It has contracts for sale of power with municipalities, cooperatives, a number of privately owned utility companies, government plants, and large industrial con-cerns, the largest being the Aluminum Company of America.

All contracts with municipalities and coopera-tives stipulate not only the rates to be paid TVA but also the rates at which the energy will be resold. In the beginning those rates were from

[29] David E. Lilienthal, *TVA: Democracy on the March* (Harper, 2d ed., 1944), p. 13.

40 to 60 per cent lower than those previously charged by private utilities in the area, although now most private utilities in the area have low-ered rates to nearer the TVA level.[30] The statis-tics in the accompanying map show compar-isons.

Opposition and Criticism. Opposition to TVA came chiefly from private utilities, coal and

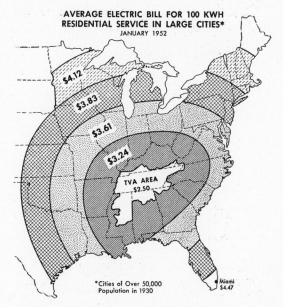

AVERAGE ELECTRIC BILL FOR 100 KWH
RESIDENTIAL SERVICE IN LARGE CITIES*
JANUARY 1952

$4.12
$3.83
$3.61
$3.24
TVA AREA
$2.50

*Cities of Over 50,000
Population in 1930

Miami
$4.47

Low TVA rates appear to have a substantial impact on electric rates in surrounding areas. Source: The Ten-nessee Valley Authority.

railway interests, local groups who feared their land would be taken or other interests adversely affected, banking and financial groups, States' rights advocates, manufacturers of fertilizers, and others opposed to the principle of govern-ment ownership or increased federal control. The entire controversy cannot be reviewed here;

[30] Basic TVA prescribed residential rates are as fol-lows: first 50 kilowatt-hours per month, 3 cents per kilowatt-hour; next 150 kilowatt-hours per month, 2 cents per kilowatt-hour; next 200 kilowatt-hours per month, 1 cent per kilowatt-hour; next 1,000 kilowatt-hours per month, 0.4 cent per kilowatt-hour; excess over 1,400 kilowatt-hours per month, 0.75 cent per kilo-watt-hour. While these are basic rates, a few munici-palities charge less.

all that can be done is to consider the question of fairness of the rate policies of TVA and mention a few general conclusions.

Two criticisms have been made of the rate policies of the Authority: first, that its wholesale rates do not accurately reflect all the cost of generating power; second, that the retail rates charged by cooperatives and municipalities, but dictated by TVA, do not reflect all proper costs. If either allegation is correct, clearly the users of TVA electricity enjoy a subsidy from the taxpayers of the entire country. At the same time, if either is true, TVA rates are an improper measurement ("yardstick") of what it should cost private utilities to render the same service.

Findings of Investigating Bodies. The nearest to an early impartial study available is the report of an investigation made by a joint committee of Congress in 1939,[31] but even this is not entirely convincing because members of the committee were divided sharply along political lines. In general, a majority of the committee approved the Authority's allocation of costs and rate policies.

The first Hoover Commission paid considerable attention to the TVA but ended by making no judgment about merits of the rate controversy. Its task force did, however, make the following observations:[32] (1) It noted, without confirmation or disapproval, that the General Accounting Office in 1949 had concluded that the TVA had allocated to power an insufficient share of the cost of multiple-use facilities. (2) On the basis of this allocation, "power revenues are well in excess of those required to repay over 50-year periods the cost of facilities allocated to power, even when construction interest is charged at 3 per cent on the unpaid debt balance." (3) TVA made payments to states and counties in lieu of taxes at rates gradually decreasing from 10 per cent to 5 per cent (beginning July 1, 1948) of gross revenue from power sales. By comparison, Class A and B electric

utilities paid in taxes for 1946 an average of 19 per cent of gross revenues.[33] (4) TVA annual reports were found to be comprehensive and to present clearly the financial condition of the Authority and the results of operation. The task force noted, again without comment, that the General Accounting Office had said in 1945 of TVA accounts that they "generally were well conceived, supervised, and maintained, and the Authority is to be commended as one of the foremost Government corporations in the use of accounting management, comparing quite favorably in this respect with well-managed private corporations."

The second Hoover Commission, and especially its task force,[34] was sharply critical of TVA and federal power enterprises generally, although there was vigorous dissent. The majority's chief complaints were that federal power policies were unfair to private utilities, subsidized particular sections of the country at the expense of taxpayers of the entire nation, and sapped state and local governments of their authority.

More particularly, the majority claimed TVA paid less than a fair share of taxes, paid too little interest on capital investment, duplicated private transmission lines, and injured private utilities by giving preference when making sales to cooperatives and public bodies. The majority also objected to further TVA expansion, especially the building of steam plants.

General Observations. Regardless of the merits of the rate issue, several things about the Authority and its operations are clear. All informed

[31] U.S. Congress, Joint Committee to Investigate the TVA, *Investigation of the Tennessee Valley Authority, Report . . .* S. Doc. 56, 76th Cong., 1st Sess. (1939).

[32] *Revolving Funds and Business Enterprises of the Government* (1949), pp. 88–97.

[33] This comparison may be unfair to the TVA, as one member of the first Hoover Commission pointed out (*ibid.,* pp. 116–117). Private utilities paid in taxes 19 per cent of gross revenues derived from all phases of their electric activities, including generation, transmission, and distribution. TVA activities, however, are confined largely to generation, transmission, and disposal at wholesale. If taxes paid by distributors of TVA power and value of free services be added to payments made by TVA in lieu of taxes, the comparison is decidedly favorable to the TVA.

[34] *Water Resources and Power* (2 vols., 1955); *Task Force Report on Water Resources and Power* (3 vols., 1955).

neutral observers agree that the corporation has been well run from an administrative point of view; it has been ruthlessly correct in abstention from political favoritism; from an engineering point of view dams and other structures were soundly and beautifully built; public ownership has been encouraged in the area; electric rates

developing the St. Lawrence River. Numerous studies were made and projects proposed,[35] in consequence of which a series of canals has been constructed enabling ships to sail from interior Great Lakes ports to Ogdensburg, N.Y., and Prescott, Ont. Unfortunately, from the points mentioned to Montreal on the Atlantic, a dis-

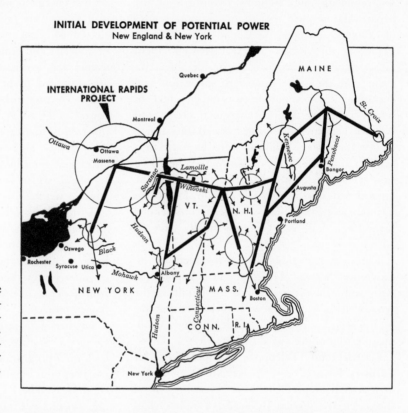

INITIAL DEVELOPMENT OF POTENTIAL POWER
New England & New York

Power developments in the Northeast area have been retarded both by the long controversy over the Great Lakes–St. Lawrence project and by federal-state disagreements over New England river development.

have been lowered generally throughout the area; low rates have greatly increased the use of electric energy, tended to stabilize population, diversify industry, and attract new capital; great strides have been made in controlling flood waters, conserving soil, and improving navigation; manufacture of nitrates and phosphates has helped to lower fertilizer prices and otherwise encourage its use; and the Authority has been unusually considerate in its handling of personnel and the social and cultural problems, of which there are many.

The St. Lawrence Waterway and Power Project. Both the United States and Canada have long been interested in the feasibility of

tance of 119 miles, the St. Lawrence channel is obstructed. Removal of the obstructions would open an uninterrupted course for ocean-going vessels to travel from as far interior as Duluth, Minn., to the Atlantic and thence to coastal and world ports. The St. Lawrence project contemplates removal of the impediments; construction of dams and locks; dredging canals; and the building of hydroelectric facilities at a dam to be erected on the International Rapids near Massena, N.Y.

All Presidents since Woodrow Wilson advocated completion of the project, and both major

[35] See especially, U.S. Department of Commerce, *The St. Lawrence Survey* (7 parts, 1941).

parties recorded approval. Canada indicated willingness and completed the Welland Canal, an essential feature in the project. A treaty embodying the proposal was submitted to the Senate but rejected in 1934. In 1941 the proposal was embodied in an executive agreement between Canada and the United States which, though not requiring ratification by two-thirds of the Senate, did require the assent of both houses of Congress as well as the Canadian parliament. Handling the matter by executive agreement rather than by treaty evoked considerable criticism.[36] At the same time stiff opposition was encountered from numerous sources, chief of which were rail, power, and coal interests, and Atlantic seaboard cities which feared diminished use of their ports. Matters were brought to a head in 1952 after Canada announced her decision to proceed with the project alone if the United States refused to take action. Presidents Truman and Eisenhower strongly recommended favorable action, and Congress finally gave its approval in 1954.

The new law establishes a five-member St. Lawrence Seaway Development Corporation, with authority to issue bonds for handling the American share. The New York Power Authority has been licensed by the Federal Power Commission to produce and distribute electric power.

Electric and Telephone Cooperatives for Farmers. In 1935 only 754,954 American farms, or less than 11 per cent, were receiving central station electric service. By 1949 this number had increased to 4,582,954, or over 78 per cent of all farms reported in the latest farm census. More than half of the increase in electrified farms was due to the Rural Electrification Administration (REA), established by executive order in 1935 and by statute the following year. The REA is a Department of Agriculture agency with funds and authority for aiding farmers who are not served by existing central station facilities.

The plan is simple. When enough farmers

with sufficient income and stability are willing to proceed, a cooperative is formed. The REA supplies advice, consults on legal and engineering matters, and may lend up to 100 per cent of installation cost. The cooperative may install generating facilities or merely a transmission and distribution system for the purpose of conveying energy bought at wholesale from other utilities, private or public. A board of officers, elected by participating farmers, handles business affairs and employs whatever technical personnel may be required. Rates charged farmers are supposed to be fixed high enough to pay operating costs and amortize indebtedness over a period of 25 to 35 years. The REA is also authorized to finance the wiring of farmsteads and the purchase and installation of electrical appliances and plumbing. These loans are made to suppliers, not to consumers, and are usually repayable within 5 years.

Although bitterly fought by private utilities and hampered by restrictive state legislation and utility commission rulings, the REA appears to have weathered the storm. It has been aided considerably by the availability of electric power from federal, and in some instances state, public power projects.

Satisfied with results in the field of electricity, Congress, in 1948, authorized the REA to embark on a program of expanding telephone (but not telegraph or radio broadcasting) facilities in rural areas. The REA may lend money to existing cooperatives, nonprofit, limited-dividend, or mutual associations, and in the future it may help finance new ones. Under this legislation, a rural area includes most places with fewer than 1,500 people.

The Alaskan Railroad. The Alaskan Railroad is a federally owned corporation under the direction of the Division of Territories and Island Possessions of the Department of the Interior. Federal ownership was authorized in 1914 after private companies had proved unprofitable and had been unable to extend service into the interior of the territory. Commercial operations began in 1923 and now extend over 500 miles, reaching from Seward to Fairbanks. In addition, the company owns and operates telephone

---

[36] For one of the best debates in print on this subject, see the testimony of Green H. Hackworth and Dr. Edwin Borchard in U.S. Senate, Committee on Commerce, *Hearings on Great Lakes—St. Lawrence Basin,* 78th Cong., 2d Sess. (1945).

and terminal facilities along the line, river boats on the Yukon, and some auxiliary ocean-going and coastwise vessels; promotes Alaskan agricultural and industrial development; investigates minerals and other resources; operates hotels at Curry and Mt. McKinley Park; and maintains a hospital and medical staff. Operations are under the direction of a business manager appointed by the Secretary of the Interior.

Here is another federally owned multiple-purpose agency whose success cannot be measured solely in terms of monetary profits. From a strictly economic point of view, the railroad has usually operated at a loss; nor has it been conspicuously successful in stimulating the economic development of the country. It is possible that as a result of new interest in the territory caused by the war, the Alaska Highway, and the development of air commerce the future picture will be brighter.

In spite of these shortcomings, there is little disposition to abandon the enterprise. Private capital might be interested in acquiring the lucrative parts of the program though probably not all; but to sell those would leave the government holding the most unprofitable segments, thus incurring even larger deficits. It is likely, therefore, that the American taxpayers will continue helping to subsidize transportation for the area if for no other reason than to promote the economic, social, and cultural development of the territory.

The second Hoover Commission recommended that rail rates be raised to make the road more nearly self-supporting. It also suggested that other commercial activities be leased or closed down whenever it would not interfere with operations of the railroad. A further suggestion was that the railroad be incorporated and made subject to the Government Corporation Control Act.[37]

The Merchant Marine. The American Merchant Marine consists of all merchant ships plying under the registry of the United States. There appears to be something gratifying to patriotic impulses for nations to have ships plying the seas and stopping at the world's ports.

At the same time, shipping interests the world over have enjoyed either natural economic advantages or governmental subsidies, making it difficult for American shippers and shipbuilders to compete successfully. This has led to the formation of powerful lobbies and incessant agitation by American interests for preferred treatment, which Congress has given in abundance.

No complete reckoning of the number and value of direct and indirect governmental aids to the Merchant Marine is possible. Needless to say, they are many. To be reminded of how solicitous the public and Congress have been for the welfare of the American Merchant Marine, one need only recall federal, state, and local assistance in improving rivers and harbors; dredging canals; operating lighthouses and other auxiliary services; profitable contracts for carrying the mail; legislation excluding foreign ships from coastal and intercoastal commerce; and others.

Although federal law has long dealt preferentially with American shipping interests, the floodgates were opened during the First World War. Since then the Federal government has followed two courses: first, it has operated shipping lines of its own; and secondly, it has built, bought, and sold ships and heavily subsidized both private shipping lines and shipbuilding industries.

Shipbuilding, Operation, and Sale. During the First World War the Shipping Board built many ships and placed them on the seas. Most of these were later scrapped or sold under generous terms to private shipping lines, but a few remained under Shipping Board operation. In 1936 the Maritime Commission displaced the Shipping Board and launched an expanded program. It built and subsidized many ships, but by 1940 most of these had been sold. When war began the Federal government took over all private lines and in the meantime stepped up its construction program. After the war, lines were restored to former owners, the building program was curtailed, and government-owned ships were sold whenever possible. Today, the Maritime Administration builds, reconditions, and re-

[37] *Op. cit.*, p. 68.

models ships for sale or charter to private lines; it charters war-built ships to private operators; it maintains a reserve of ships essential to national defense; and it maintains four stand-by, but inactive, shipyards for emergency use.

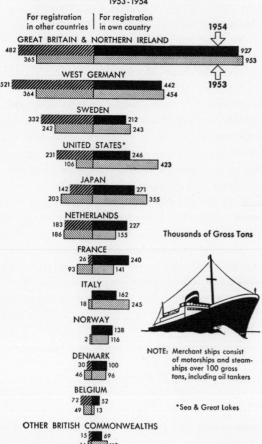

MERCHANT SHIPS LAUNCHED
1953-1954

| For registration in other countries | For registration in own country | 1954 |

GREAT BRITAIN & NORTHERN IRELAND
482 / 927
365 / 953

WEST GERMANY
521 / 442   1953
364 / 454

SWEDEN
332 / 212
242 / 243

UNITED STATES*
231 / 246
106 / 423

JAPAN
142 / 271
203 / 355

NETHERLANDS
183 / 227
186 / 155   **Thousands of Gross Tons**

FRANCE
26 / 240
93 / 141

ITALY
162
18 / 245

NORWAY
138
2 / 116

DENMARK
30 / 100
46 / 96

BELGIUM
72 / 52
49 / 13

OTHER BRITISH COMMONWEALTHS
15 / 69
16 / 110

NOTE: Merchant ships consist of motorships and steamships over 100 gross tons, including oil tankers

*Sea & Great Lakes

After making a phenomenal record in shipbuilding during the Second World War, the United States has dropped off to a poor fourth among the nations. Nevertheless, the United States still had the world's largest merchant fleet. Courtesy of National Industrial Conference Board.

Subsidies to Shippers and Shipbuilders. Since 1936, the Federal government has offered two principal types of subsidies: one to shipbuilders, called a "construction differential," and the other to ship operators, called an "operating differential." The first works this way: At the request of a private citizen wishing to engage in foreign shipping, the Maritime Administration may contract to have a vessel built in an American shipyard, pay the construction cost, and then sell the vessel to the applicant for an amount equal to the estimated cost of constructing the vessel if it had been built in a foreign shipyard. In no case may the differential be more than 50 per cent of the cost of making the vessel. The applicant is required to post a bond to ensure good faith pending completion of the vessel and is required to pay part of the purchase price in cash and the remainder plus interest over a period of years.

The operating differential works similarly. When a citizen operating a vessel used in an essential service, route, or line in foreign commerce (but not inland, coastal, or intercoastal) finds in his operating expense items that place him at a competitive disadvantage with foreign operators, the Maritime Administration will pay him a differential high enough to equalize the cost of operation.

The Administration may also aid citizens in the construction of new vessels to be operated in the foreign, coastal, or intercoastal trade when no construction differential is granted. Here the Administration will pay the cost of approved national-defense features and lend a large part of the cost of the vessel which is repayable, with interest, over a period of years. If the operator makes more than a 10 per cent profit over a 10-year period, the government may recapture half of the excess, up to the full amount of the subsidy paid.

From an economic point of view, federal operation of shipping lines as described has never been profitable, but rather it has been extremely expensive. The same must be said of most of the aids and subsidies. What the nation has paid for is not economical transportation but national defense, international prestige, gratification of patriotic impulses, and assistance to important industries. Whether results justify the expenditures must remain a matter of opinion. Few will doubt, however, that ships and shipyards are essential for national defense.

FOR
FURTHER
READING

Barnes, Irston R.: *Public Utility Regulation* (Appleton-Century-Crofts, 1938).

Bauer, John: *Transforming Public Utility Regulation: A Definite Administrative Program* (Harper, 1950).

——: *Public Organization of Electric Power: Conditions, Policies, and Programs* (Harper, 1949).

Baum, Robert D.: *Federal Power Commission and State Utility Regulation* (American Council on Public Affairs, 1943).

Beard, William: *Regulation of Pipe Lines as Common Carriers* (Columbia University Press, 1941).

Bonbright, James C.: *Public Utilities and the National Power Policies* (Columbia University Press, 1940).

Cushman, Robert E.: *The Independent Regulatory Commission* (Oxford, 1941).

Dearing, Charles L., and Wilfred Owen: *National Transportation Policy* (Brookings, 1949).

Dimock, Marshall E.: *Government-operated Enterprises in the Panama Canal Zone* (University of Chicago Press, 1934).

Eldridge, Seba, and Associates: *Development of Collective Enterprise* (University of Kansas Press, 1943).

Elsbree, Hugh L.: *Interstate Transmission of Electric Power* (Harvard University Press, 1931).

Goodman, Gilbert: *Government Policy toward Commercial Aviation: Competition and the Regulation of Rates* (New York: King's Crown Press, 1944).

Hall, Ford P.: *Concept of a Business Affected with a Public Interest* (Bloomington, Ind.: Principia Press, 1940).

Lewis, Ben W.: *British Planning and Nationalization* (Twentieth Century Fund, 1952).

McDiarmid, John: *Government Corporations and Federal Funds* (University of Chicago Press, 1938).

Merritt, LeRoy C.: *United States Government as Publisher* (University of Chicago Press, 1943).

Padelford, Norman J.: *The Panama Canal in Peace and War* (Macmillan, 1942).

Prichett, C. Herman: *The Tennessee Valley Authority: A Study in Public Administration* (The University of North Carolina Press, 1943).

Pusey, Merlo J.: *Big Government: Can We Control It?* (Harper, 1945).

Ruggles, Charles O.: *Aspects of the Organization, Functions and Financing of State Public Utility Commissions* (Harvard University Press, 1937).

Selznick, Philip: *TVA and the Grass Roots* (University of California Press, 1949).

Sharfman, Isaiah L.: *The Interstate Commerce Commission* (Commonwealth Fund, 5 vols., 1931–1937).

U.S. Board of Investigation and Research: *Public Aids to Domestic Transportation*, H. Doc. 159 (1945).

U.S. Commission on Organization of the Executive Branch of the Government (second Hoover Commission): *Business Enterprises* (1955).

——: *Task Force Report on Business Enterprises* (1955).

——: *Transportation* (1955), and subcommittee report by the same title (1955).

U.S. Commission on Organization of the Executive Branch of the Government (first Hoover Commission): See especially *Federal Business Enterprises; Task Force Re-*

port on Revolving Funds and Business Enterprises of the Government; Task Force Report on Natural Resources; Regulatory Commissions; Department of Interior (all 1949).

U.S. Congress, Joint Committee on the Investigation of TVA: *Investigation of the Tennessee Valley Authority Report . . .* S. Doc. 56, 76th Cong., 1st Sess., pursuant to Pub. Res. 83 (1939).

U.S. Federal Trade Commission: *Economic, Corporate, and Financial Phases of the Natural-gas-producing, Pipeline and Utility Industries,* S. Doc. 92, part 73A, 70th Cong., 1st Sess. (1936).

——: *Economic, Financial and Corporate Phases of Holding and Operating Companies of Electric and Gas Utilities,* S. Doc. 92, part 72B, 70th Cong., 1st Sess. (1936).

U.S. House of Representatives, Special Committee to Investigate Government Competition with Private Enterprise: *Government Competition with Private Enterprise, Report . . . ,* H. Rep. 1985, 72d Cong., 2d Sess. (1933).

U.S. National Resources Planning Board: *Transportation and National Policy* (1942).

U.S. President's Water Resources Policy Commission: *The Report of . . . , 1950.* Vol. 1, *A Water Policy for the American People;* vol. 2, *Ten Rivers in America's Future;* vol. 3, *Water Resources Law* (1950).

Van Zandt, John P.: *Civil Aviation and Peace* (Brookings, 1944).

Zeiss, Paul M.: *American Shipping Policy* (Princeton University Press, 1938).

REVIEW QUESTIONS

1. What is a public utility? How do public utilities differ from businesses of other types?

2. How is responsibility for utility regulation divided between the Federal and state governments?

3. How has substantive due process of law affected utility regulation in the United States?

4. As a practical matter, what difference does it make whether prudent investment or fair value is the formula upon which utility valuations are based?

5. Summarize the manner and extent to which the Federal government regulates (*a*) transportation; (*b*) electric power; (*c*) natural gas; (*d*) communications.

6. Defend and criticize federal ownership and operation of proprietary enterprises of the types mentioned in this chapter.

7. What justification is there for continuing federal ownership and operation of each of the enterprises discussed in this chapter?

8. Compare TVA and its operations with developments in other major river valleys.

9. Comparing the various river-valley developments, state the advantages and disadvantages of the TVA approach.

10. Describe the Post Office Department and its principal functions.

11. Summarize the work and accomplishments of the Rural Electrification Administration.

12. What changes were recommended by the first and second Hoover Commissions with respect to the development and administration of water and power resources?

CHAPTER 28

Labor

Everyone has the right to work, to free choice of employment, to just and favorable conditions of work and to protection against unemployment.

Everyone, without any discrimination, has the right to equal pay for equal work.

Everyone who works has the right to just and favorable remuneration insuring for himself and his family an existence worthy of human dignity, and supplemented, if necessary, by other means of social protection.

Everyone has the right to form and to join trade unions for the protection of his interests.—Universal Declaration of Human Rights [1]

While American society was chiefly agrarian there was little need for laws relating to wages, hours, industrial accidents, housing, old-age pensions, and the like. To be sure, there were the destitute, insane, and indigent aged, but they were left either to shift for themselves or to be provided for by relatives or by religious and philanthropic agencies. Local governments lent assistance through poor boards, poor houses, asylums, while relations between capital and labor were governed by public opinion and the common law.

The industrial revolution divorced millions from the land, made them dependent upon machines, urbanized more than half the population, and set in motion the forces that necessitated governmental intervention in increasing amounts. Little labor and social legislation was enacted prior to the Civil War and the bulk of it has come in this country since 1910. The substance of it is discussed in this and the following chapter.

The Labor Department. A Bureau of Labor was first established in 1884, under the Interior Department. Soon thereafter the Bureau was made independent as a Department of Labor, but without executive rank, and in 1903 it became a bureau in the Department of Commerce and Labor. Ten years later it was organized as a separate department with rank equal to that of the nine other departments. At its head is a Secretary who, like others of similar rank, is a member of the President's cabinet and directly responsible to him. This office has the distinction of being the first one in the cabinet ever held by a woman.[2] Normally the Secretary is a member of the President's party who is closely identified with the ranks of organized labor. Associated with the Secretary are the usual administrative assistants and clerical staff.

Reflecting the antagonism between management and workers, the Department of Labor has often been a storm center. Congressional critics have thought the Department too pro-

[1] Adopted by the United Nations General Assembly in December, 1948.

[2] Frances Perkins, of New York State, held the office from Mar. 4, 1933, until early in 1945.

533

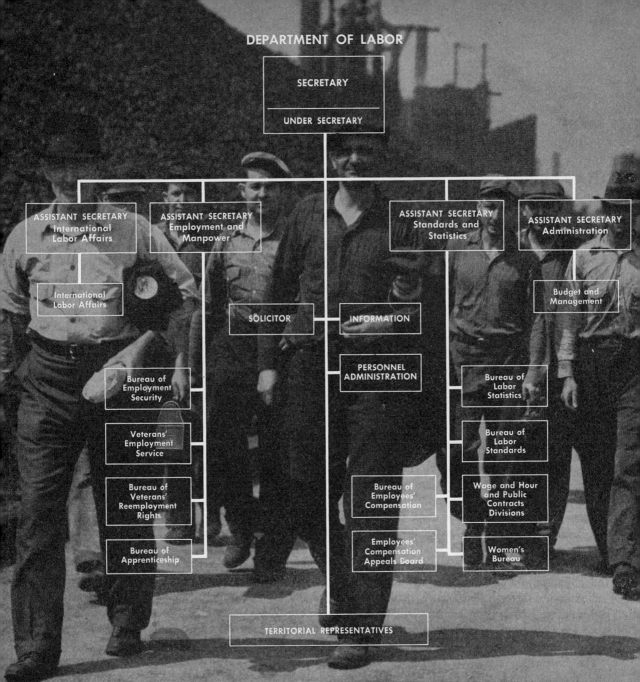

DEPARTMENT OF LABOR

- SECRETARY
- UNDER SECRETARY
  - ASSISTANT SECRETARY International Labor Affairs
    - International Labor Affairs
    - Bureau of Employment Security
    - Veterans' Employment Service
    - Bureau of Veterans' Reemployment Rights
    - Bureau of Apprenticeship
  - ASSISTANT SECRETARY Employment and Manpower
    - SOLICITOR
    - PERSONNEL ADMINISTRATION
    - Bureau of Employees' Compensation
    - Employees' Compensation Appeals Board
  - ASSISTANT SECRETARY Standards and Statistics
    - INFORMATION
    - Bureau of Labor Statistics
    - Bureau of Labor Standards
    - Wage and Hour and Public Contracts Divisions
    - Women's Bureau
  - ASSISTANT SECRETARY Administration
    - Budget and Management
- TERRITORIAL REPRESENTATIVES

Black Star photograph

labor and have at times given to other agencies certain functions to which it was properly entitled. The Eightieth Congress (January, 1947–January, 1949), the first controlled by the Republicans after 1932, was especially severe on the Department, transferring the Children's Bureau (except for its labor functions), the United States Conciliation Service, and the United States Employment Service to other departments.

The first Hoover Commission deplored this dispersion of labor activities,[3] saying that the Department "is now overmanned at the top levels for the functions which remain. The Department has lost much of its significance. It should be given more essential work to do if it is to maintain a significance comparable to the

[3] In *Department of Labor* (1949).

other great executive departments." Since this recommendation was made, the Department has been strengthened chiefly by the transfer to it of the Bureau of Employment Security, the Bureau of Employees' Compensation, and the Employees' Compensation Appeals Board. The Bureau of Employment Security handles employment services and unemployment insurance; the other two agencies handle workmen's compensation for employees of the Federal government and others covered by federal law.

CONCILIATION, MEDIATION, AND ARBITRATION

In a free society disputes between capital and management on one hand and labor on the other are inevitable. Other countries have tried various schemes for resolving such disputes, even to the extent of abolishing either the capitalists, as in Russia, or labor unions, as in prewar Germany and Italy. In this country, however, governmental efforts normally have been directed toward providing machinery by which voluntary settlement can be made.

Conciliation and mediation are synonymous terms used to refer to methods employed by neutral parties to bring about a more conciliatory attitude on the part of disputants for the purpose of effecting compromise settlements. Arbitration refers to a situation where both parties have agreed upon a third party to whom they are willing to submit the dispute with the understanding that he will judge the issues fairly and the disputants will abide by his decision. Compulsory arbitration has been advocated from time to time. It is now required in railroad disputes involving interpretation of existing contracts and by several states in public-utility enterprises.[4] And considerable compulsion was used during the last war, especially where wages and hours were at issue. There has been grave doubt about the constitutionality of measures like these,[5] but it is safe to say that the courts would now approve the principle, at least so far as utilities and defense industries are concerned. The basic legal issue involved in such proposals is whether life, liberty, and property are taken without due process of law.

The Mediation and Conciliation Service. Normally federal law provides only for voluntary conciliation, mediation, and arbitration. The principal agencies involved are the Federal Mediation and Conciliation Service and the National Mediation Board, although employees of other labor agencies, especially the National Labor Relations Board, effect a great many compromises in controversies that might otherwise flare into major disputes.

As already indicated, the Federal Mediation and Conciliation Service was transferred from the Department of Labor and made an independent establishment in 1947. The motive alleged for this action was the desire for greater objectivity on the part of the Service. Whether this treatment was deserved or wise from an administrative point of view is highly controverted.

The Service attempts to prevent disputes from arising by trying to improve human relations in industrial life. It also seeks to create an atmosphere congenial to collective bargaining and use of its personnel. In doing these things it works closely with state conciliation agencies. The Taft-Hartley Act of 1947 requires employers and unions to file with the Service notice of every dispute affecting commerce not settled within 30 days after one or the other party to a collective agreement gives notice of intention to terminate or modify an existing contract. When given this information, the Service proffers its assistance.

The procedure followed by the Conciliation Service varies somewhat depending upon the nature of the case. The Service keeps constantly informed about industrial conditions and special situations affecting interstate and foreign commerce which might become disturbed. If major disputes arise, the Secretary of Labor or someone in the Conciliation Service may take the ini-

[4] For an interesting evaluation of some of these, see Robert R. France and Richard A. Lester, *Compulsory Arbitration of Utility Disputes in New Jersey and Pennsylvania* (Industrial Relations Section, Princeton University, 1951).

[5] The leading case is Wolff Packing Co. *v.* Court of Industrial Relations, 262 U.S. 522 (1923).

tiative and propose that its services be used to mediate; or parties to the dispute may indicate that assistance is desired. Where both parties are willing, commissioners of conciliation intervene seeking to provide data pertinent to the argument and ascertain, in confidence, the most that one party will give and the least that the other will take without starting a lockout or a strike. While many agreements are effected in this way, agents of the Conciliation Service are powerless if either party is unwilling to cooperate or accept proffered proposals.

Occasionally both parties display enough confidence in a particular agent or panel of neutrals to submit the dispute to them for arbitration, but even where this is done there are no criminal penalties that can be imposed upon the parties if they should refuse to abide by the award.[6]

National Railroad Adjustment Board. By the Railway Labor Act of 1926, as amended, a National Railroad Adjustment Board of thirty-six members was established for the purpose of settling minor grievances arising from interpretation of agreements respecting wages, hours, and working conditions. The Board has no jurisdiction over major disputes of the type that usually arise at the time contracts are being negotiated, but once a contract is agreed upon, then disputes about how it should be interpreted and applied may come before the Board for decision.

Headquarters of the Board are in Chicago. It operates in four divisions, in each of which labor and management are equally represented. A division's finding of facts is final. In the event of deadlock, the National Mediation Board may appoint a referee to break the tie. Awards are enforceable in the Federal courts. Here is an instance of compulsory settlement of a particular type of dispute in a major public utility. As the name implies, the Board deals only with railway disputes.

National Mediation Board. Railway disputes unrelated to interpretation of existing agreements and commercial-air-line labor disputes are handled by the National Mediation Board, established in 1934. This agency is an independent establishment headed by three members who are appointed by the President with Senate approval. The Board is assisted by a staff of conciliators as well as the usual administrative and clerical employees.

When a dispute occurs, neither management may lock out nor labor strike until steps prescribed by law are taken. The National Mediation Board first attempts to mediate and, this failing, tries to induce the disputants to submit the matter to arbitration. If unsuccessful, compulsory investigation may follow. In this event, terms of the working agreement may not be changed for 60 days except by mutual consent while the President appoints an emergency fact-finding board that investigates and reports with recommendations. The recommendations may be rejected by either side; a majority of workers may vote to strike or management may lock out. If either occurs, and war powers given to the President by Congress are operative because of national emergency, the President may seize the carriers and continue their operation under governmental auspices.

Professor Robert D. Dishman has pointed out that in the 25 years after 1926 more than a hundred relatively minor disputes were referred to emergency boards for investigation and in only fourteen instances were their recommendations rejected.[7] Professor Dishman has also observed that in the early years "it was railway management which was most likely to be difficult," while in the last decade or so "it has been the brotherhoods which have been most inclined to flout the letter and spirit of the law."[8] Failure of the parties to accept recommended settlements led to a paralyzing nation-wide strike lasting for 48 hours in 1946 and threats of others

---

[6] There may be penalties provided for, however, in the basic agreement to arbitrate which would be enforceable in civil suits under state laws governing contracts.

[7] "The Public Interest in Emergency Labor Disputes," *American Political Science Review,* vol. 45 (December, 1951), p. 1109.

[8] *Ibid.*

nearly as serious in 1948 and 1950. In each instance, government seizure followed.

Fact-finding Boards for Other Industries. Experience with railway legislation led President Truman to propose, during December, 1945, adoption of similar measures for other businesses engaged in interstate and foreign commerce. The recommendation asked for a law requiring a 30-day "cooling-off" period before commencing a lockout or strike, during which time a fact-finding board might be appointed by the President with power to investigate and make recommendations.

The proposal did not provide for compulsory arbitration; *i.e.,* it was not suggested that the law should try to compel disputants to accept recommendations made by the fact-finding boards. Rather, it contemplated that after the "cooling-off" period management would be free to lock out and labor to strike. The expectation was that by full disclosures of facts, the government, supported by public opinion, would be better able to effect adjustments without serious work stoppages. The President's proposal encountered such strenuous opposition from both management and labor as to result in its defeat.

In the meantime, however, the President appointed several boards to investigate and report on important disputes, chief of which was one between General Motors Corporation and the United Automobile Workers and one between the steel companies and their employees (1949). Boards like these operate under the handicap of being unable to compel the appearance of witnesses and the submission of evidence. Moreover, since legislation is needed to keep industries operating during a "cooling-off" period, they often find it necessary to function after work stoppages have commenced. Nevertheless, the disclosures and recommendations of the boards do help to clear the atmosphere and frequently establish bases for settlements.

A modified version of President Truman's fact-finding board proposal was included in the Taft-Hartley Act for work stoppages involving "national emergencies." According to these provisions the President may, when a national-emergency work stoppage is threatened, appoint a board of inquiry with power to compel attendance of witnesses and production of pertinent materials. The board's report, the law states, is to set forth the facts and contentions "but shall not contain any recommendations."

When the report is received, the President is required to file a copy with the Mediation and Conciliation Service and make its contents public. Thereupon, the President may direct the Attorney General to go to court for an 80-day injunction restraining the threatened stoppage. During the 80-day "cooling-off" period the Service is required to do its best, and the board of inquiry is to be reconvened for study and to make a report that includes the employer's "best offer." This report is to be made public, and the National Labor Relations Board is directed to hold an election to determine whether a majority of workers wishes to accept or reject the best offer.

If at the expiration of 80 days the dispute remains unsettled, the injunction terminates, the President reports to Congress, and the work stoppage may take place unless Congress by that time decides upon more drastic action. Although this procedure has been used a few times, authorities are divided over its success and wisdom. That it has not prevented all serious strikes is obvious. Because of the antilabor flavor of the Taft-Hartley law, and the fact that labor usually has more to lose than management by "freezing" *status quo* by the use of injunctions, labor leaders are especially hostile to the use of these procedures.

Other critics point out that the time limits prescribed in the law force emergency boards to hurry their studies, that the ban contained in the act on board recommendations prevents public opinion from rallying around impartial proposals, and that during the 80-day "cooling-off" period the penalties and incentives for reaching agreement by collective bargaining are likely to be such as to merely postpone the date of a showdown. Instead of having government "take sides" or weaken collective bargaining, critics suggest remedies that will ensure impartiality and strengthen the process of collective bargaining.

The Problem of Seizures. Forced with the urgency of "doing something" when work stoppages occur in vital industries, the device was invented during the First World War of having government seize industry. If you can conscript men, the appeal went, why not draft business as well? Seizure was again authorized in the Second World War. Limited seizure authority was contained in the Selective Service and Training Act of 1948 and the Defense Production Act of 1950. The former authorized seizure of any plant that failed to perform a government order, or where a steel producer failed to allocate steel as directed for defense purposes. The Defense Production Act authorized the requisition of equipment and condemnation of real property needed without delay in the defense effort.

When the Taft-Hartley Act was under consideration, a seizure provision was considered but rejected in favor of having the President report to Congress after 80 days if national emergency disputes had not been settled. As has been discussed elsewhere,[9] President Truman assumed he had inherent power to seize the steel industry, and he did so in April, 1952, but was rebuffed by the courts. Apparently, therefore, without a specific delegation of authority by Congress, seizures are not authorized where work stoppages occur as a result of labor-management disputes.

After seizure, legal title rests with the government, supervisory responsibility is assigned to one or more federal agencies, property owners continue to receive profits at "stabilized" levels, management continues as normally, labor cannot strike and must work at "stabilized" wages. Both profits and wages may be higher or lower than might be obtainable without governmental intervention, depending upon the results of bargaining between the new owner, management and labor.

While this process has usually gotten results in terms of production, it is usually strongly resisted by both management and labor. If the administration in power is thought to be pro-labor, union leaders may prefer seizure to bargaining and negotiate accordingly; if the administration is considered promanagement, the opposite may occur. Both sides may decide that they will come out ahead under government ownership and therefore stall for seizure. This weakens collective bargaining, it may result in one side or the other using government to gain an advantage, it leads, at least temporarily, to sacrifice of traditional freedoms, and the public grows accustomed to greater governmental intervention in economic processes. What the alternatives are may be imagined more easily than put into effect. Some suggest compulsory arbitration; others, improved collective bargaining; others, seizure under terms that would prevent either labor or management from gaining economic advantages while negotiations continued; others, outright socialism.

PROTECTING RIGHTS OF EMPLOYERS AND EMPLOYEES

The Right to Organize and Bargain Collectively. At common law all combinations, whether of entrepreneurs or workmen, were long considered illegal conspiracies in restraint of trade. Early in the nineteenth century, merchants and other capitalists were granted the legal right to combine for business purposes, but it was not until later that combinations of workingmen were looked upon with favor by the courts. The turning point came when the Supreme Court of Massachusetts [10] recognized the legality of labor unions. The right is now recognized by all the states and the national government, but the conspiracy doctrine continues to influence the courts when they have to consider the legality of strikes, boycotts, and certain other union activities.

The primary purpose of labor organization is to enhance the bargaining ability of employees by enabling them to do it collectively. The desire for joint action grows out of the fact that in an unorganized market labor is extremely competitive, with those having labor for sale in a

---

[9] Pp. 290–291.

[10] Commonwealth *v.* Hunt, 45 Mass. 111 (1842).

much weaker bargaining position than employers. The situation was well explained by the United States Supreme Court in 1921: [11]

> They [labor unions] were organized out of the necessity of the situation. A single employee was helpless in dealing with an employer. He was dependent ordinarily on his daily wage for the main-

sometimes strong-arm methods. Moreover, employers were at liberty to fire or discriminate against employees who dared to participate in union activities.

Labor and Antitrust Laws. Whether Congress intended or not, the courts ruled that the Sherman Antitrust Act of 1890 applied to labor unions as well as to other groups. In conse-

GROWTH OF LABOR UNIONS IN U.S.

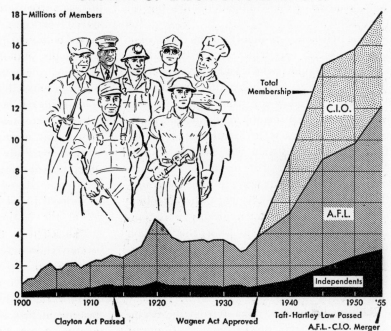

Organized labors' spectacular growth since the 1930's accounts in part for expanding governmental services, especially those in the fields of health, education, and welfare.

tenance of himself and family. If the employer refused to pay him the wages that he thought fair, he was nevertheless unable to leave the employ and to resist arbitrary and unfair treatment. Union was essential to give laborers opportunity to deal on equality with their employer.

While the legal right to organize and bargain collectively has been recognized for over a century, employers were free to use economic weapons to prevent labor from doing so. For years many employers tried to suppress unionization by the use of industrial spies, black lists, "yellow-dog" contracts, lockouts, company unions, and

[11] American Steel Foundries Co. *v.* Tri-city Central Trades Council, 257 U.S. 184 (1921).

quence, labor organizations were hauled before the courts so frequently as seriously to discourage unionization and the development of collective bargaining. The Clayton Act of 1914 brought some relief, but less than appeared on first sight. Among other things it declared that the labor of human beings was not a commodity or article of commerce and that nothing contained in the antitrust laws should be construed to forbid the existence and operation of labor, agricultural, or horticultural organizations instituted for the purpose of mutual help and not having capital stock or conducted for profit, or to forbid or restrain individual members of such organizations from lawfully carrying out their legitimate objects. It further provided that such organizations and their members should not be considered illegal combinations or conspiracies in restraint of trade. It also restricted the granting of injunctive relief in general and in labor disputes in particular. The courts soon ruled that the language used did not completely remove labor unions and their activities from provisions of the Sherman Act, but did so only insofar as they were "lawfully carrying out their legitimate objects." As a result, labor unions were involved in more litigation after the act than before.

Some relief was brought by the Norris-LaGuardia Act of 1932 which clearly defined the circumstances under which Federal courts might restrain union activity and entirely forbade enforcement of "yellow-dog" contracts. But it was not until 1941 that the apparent intent of previous acts of Congress to exempt labor unions from antitrust legislation was endorsed by the Supreme Court. In that decision[12] the high court ruled that unions were immune from antitrust laws except possibly when they combine or conspire with nonunion groups to restrain trade. Although a boon to labor, this decision was of less importance than the positive guaranties of the right to organize and bargain collectively that were given in legislation adopted during the depression.

Railway Labor Act. Almost from the beginning of federal regulation of railroads, Congress has legislated to encourage settlement of management-labor disputes by conciliation and arbitration. Moreover, from an early date Congress has recognized the need for restraining some of the worst forms of employer interference with the rights of employees to form unions and bargain collectively. Its first step in this direction was a provision in the Erdman Act of 1898 prohibiting "yellow-dog" contracts, but this provision was later declared an unconstitutional

abridgment of the right of contract.[13] The following years brought trials and errors which culminated in the Railway Labor Act of 1926 and subsequent amendments.

In addition to providing the conciliation and arbitration machinery described above, the Railway Labor Act guaranteed the right to organize and bargain collectively through unions of workers' choice, authorized the National Mediation Board to hold elections to determine appropriate bargaining units when unions disagreed over which represented a majority, required both management and labor to bargain in good faith, and outlawed certain unfair labor practices, including "yellow-dog" contracts, when committed by employers. Unlike legislation discussed below, however, unfair labor practices were made enjoinable by courts rather than by an administrative board. These provisions of the Railway Labor Act apply to interstate railroads and airways. This legislation has been declared constitutional.[14]

National Labor Relations Act of 1935. Section 7A of the National Industrial Recovery Act guaranteed the right of labor to organize and bargain collectively, free from employer interference, and also authorized the establishment of administrative machinery for the protection of those rights. Following the collapse of this measure in 1935, similar provisions were incorporated in the National Labor Relations Act. This measure was administered by a National Labor Relations Board composed of three men appointed by the President with Senate concurrence for terms of 5 years. The board had jurisdiction over all nongovernmental employees and employers engaged in interstate and foreign commerce except those in the railway and airway industries, which were handled by the National Mediation Board.

The board had two principal functions: one, to ascertain by conducting elections which union represented a majority within a plant or in-

[12] United States *v.* Hutcheson, 312 U.S. 219 (1940). For a later instance in which a labor union was declared guilty of violating the antitrust laws because of conspiracy with business organizations, see United States *v.* Employing Plasterers' Association *et al.,* 347 U.S. 186 (1953).

[13] Adair *v.* United States, 208 U.S. 161 (1908).
[14] Virginian Railway Co. *v.* System Federation No. 40 *et al.,* 300 U.S. 515 (1937); Texas & New Orleans R.R. *v.* Brotherhood of Ry. Clerks, 218 U.S. 548 (1930).

dustry;[15] the other, to prevent employers from committing certain unfair labor practices. The law stated that it was an unfair labor practice for an employer to (1) interfere with, restrain, or coerce employees in the exercise of their right to organize, participate in union activity, and bargain collectively through representatives of their own choosing; (2) dominate or interfere with the formation or administration of any labor organization or contribute financial or other support to it; (3) discriminate in regard to hire or tenure of employment or any term or condition of employment as a method of encouraging or discouraging membership in labor unions; (4) discharge or otherwise discriminate against an employee because he has filed charges or given testimony under the act; and (5) refuse to bargain collectively with representatives of his employees.

The National Labor Relations Act of 1935 was "one-sided" in that it restrained employers from interfering with the formation of unions or engaging in discriminatory practices against union members, but placed no restraints on unfair practices by labor unions against employers. The reason given for this was that employers, being stronger, were able to look after themselves; the evil to be cured was employer interference with the rights of economically and socially weaker workers.

This legislation was a boon to organized labor, and to them it became the most essential of federal statutes. Employers, understandably, vehemently objected and relentlessly fought its enforcement. Objection was made to its assumptions, purposes, controls, and methods of administration. Aided by postwar inflation and a series of nation-wide strikes, sufficient sentiment developed to elect a Congress that would tackle revision of the act. In 1947 Congress adopted, over the President's veto, the Labor Management Act of 1947, better known as the Taft-Hartley Act. This, in turn, incurred the uncompromising opposition of organized labor, and the feud continues.

[15] During the war it was also required to conduct elections before strikes could be called in war plants.

The Taft-Hartley Act. This act was in the form of an amendment to the National Labor Relations Act. It first changed membership of the board from three to five and circumscribed its role. Reflecting accusations that the board had been rule maker, prosecutor, judge, and jury, the board was given responsibility for general administration and adjudication, but the office of General Counsel was established to investigate charges, issue complaints, and prosecute. To this end, the General Counsel was empowered to supervise all board attorneys (except trial examiners and legal assistants to board members) and other officers and employees in regional offices.

Other provisions were numerous; only a few can be mentioned here. Union officers, but not employers, were required to file non-Communist affidavits or be denied board facilities and other benefits of the law. The closed shop was outlawed, but the union shop was permitted if approved by at least 70 per cent of the employees.[16] (A closed shop employs only union members, while a union shop may employ persons who are not union members, provided they join within a specified time.) Supervisors, including foremen, were denied benefits of the law. Employers were granted greater freedom of speech about plant and contract matters. The "check-off" was permitted but only for employees who gave advance consent in writing. Employer contributions to union health and welfare funds were permitted under certain conditions, one of which was that employers and employees be equally represented in the administration of the fund. Hiring through union halls was forbidden. Excessive and discriminatory union initiation fees were outlawed. Union and company contributions to political campaigns were forbidden. Thirty-day notice was required of inten-

[16] This has been changed, because union shops were approved by overwhelming majorities in nearly all elections and therefore the elections placed an unnecessary burden upon the National Labor Relations Board and the taxpayer. Now union shop is permitted unless disapproved in an election held upon petition of 30 per cent of the employees.

tion to modify or terminate contracts. Suits by employers and unions were authorized for alleged violations of collective-bargaining contracts. The board, but not employers, was authorized to obtain injunctions to prevent certain union conduct.

Unions were forbidden to commit unfair labor practices including: refusal to bargain collectively with an employer, restraint or coercion of other employees in the exercise of their rights, discrimination against employees, engaging in secondary boycotts and jurisdictional strikes, charging excessive or discriminatory initiation fees, and forcing employers to pay or deliver things of value for services not performed or to be performed. Finally, "national emergency" strikes were forbidden except under the circumstances noted above.

As matters stand, the NLRB and its agents have three principal functions: the first requires them to file materials required by the law, such as non-Communist affidavits and union financial reports; the second involves stopping by injunction or orders unfair labor practices when committed by employers or unions; the third requires the holding of elections to determine union shop authorizations and appropriate bargaining units when unions disagree over which one of them commands a majority. Most complaint cases, *i.e.,* those in which unfair labor practices are alleged, are settled informally, but a few go through a formal process resembling a trial without jury on criminal charges. In such cases, the board lacks authority to enforce its own decisions but may appeal to United States Courts of Appeals to do so.

Although the law was enacted in 1947 and strenuously opposed by President Truman and organized labor, only a few minor changes have occurred. The Democratic party has been pledged to seek its repeal, while the Republican party concedes that it needs slight amendment.

CHILD-LABOR LEGISLATION

Legal Contest over Child-labor Legislation. Since children are looked upon as special wards of the state, there has never been any question about the constitutionality of state laws regulating, or even prohibiting, their employment in industry. About the middle of the last century the movement began to forbid the employment of children, but states, fearing competition with other states, were reluctant to act. Ultimately it became clear that only by a uniform national law could the problem be met.

Accordingly, in 1916, Congress enacted the Keating-Owen Act forbidding the transportation in interstate commerce of products made in factories in which children under fourteen were employed, or in which children between fourteen and sixteen had worked more than 8 hours a day or 6 days a week, or at night. Similar prohibitions applied to products of mines in which children under sixteen were employed. Two years later this legislation was declared unconstitutional because it applied to productive facilities like factories or mines, which province the Supreme Court then considered reserved to the states.[17]

Undismayed, Congress turned to the power to tax to provide for the general welfare and included within the general Revenue Act of Feb. 24, 1919, a tax of 10 per cent upon the annual net profits of concerns violating certain standards, chief of which was the employment of children under fourteen. This also was declared an unconstitutional invasion of state powers.[18]

Following these two unsuccessful attempts, Congress mustered enough votes to propose a constitutional amendment giving the Federal government the desired authority.[19] To date the proposal has been ratified by twenty-eight states —eight fewer than the required number of thirty-six.

While the amendment was before the states, Congress again tried to abolish child labor by statute; this time by means of the National Industrial Recovery Act of 1933. All the NRA codes stipulated that the employment of children under sixteen was illegal and these pro-

[17] Hammer *v.* Dagenhart, 247 U.S. 251 (1918).
[18] Bailey *v.* Drexel Furniture Co., 259 U.S. 20 (1922).
[19] The full text of the proposed amendment is given on p. 725.

visions were generally obeyed until the act was declared unconstitutional in May, 1935.[20]

Still undeterred, Congress incorporated a provision in the Public Contracts Act of 1936, better known as the Walsh-Healy Act, prohibiting persons awarded government contracts involving sums in excess of $10,000 from employing male persons under sixteen and female persons under eighteen. This was an exercise of the proprietary power and doubtless constitutional, but it applied to only a comparatively few employers.

Finally, resorting to the commerce power again, more sweeping provisions were incorporated in the Fair Labor Standards Act of 1938. These received Supreme Court approval in 1941,[21] a decision that expressly reversed Hammer *v.* Dagenhart decided 23 years earlier. While this law applies only to interstate and foreign commerce, hence does not have the coverage which would be possible if the proposed child-labor amendment were finally ratified, it does cover the major industries and probably puts an end to attempts to get additional states to ratify the amendment.

Existing Child-labor Legislation. Child labor is now, therefore, governed by two federal statutes: the Public Contracts Act of 1936 and the Fair Labor Standards Act of 1938. Enforcement is handled by the Wage and Hour and Public Contracts Division, Department of Labor, in cooperation with the Children's Bureau, in the Department of Health, Education, and Welfare.

In cooperation with state governments, certificates of age are issued to minors fourteen through nineteen years of age who wish to be employed in controlled occupations. The Public Contracts Act forbids those working on government contracts involving more than $10,000 from employing anyone under nineteen without a certificate. It then prohibits employment of boys under sixteen and girls under eighteen. Exceptions may be granted by the Secretary of Labor.

[20] Schechter Poultry Corp. *v.* United States, 295 U.S. 495 (1935).

[21] United States *v.* Darby Lumber Co., 312 U.S. 100 (1941).

The Fair Labor Standards Act is more flexible. Under it, employments are divided into three categories: those that are completely exempt; those that are nonpermissible for fourteen- and fifteen-year-olds; and those that are too hazardous for those between sixteen and eighteen years old. Those that are completely exempt include retailing, personal service, street trades, motion pictures, children employed in agriculture at a time when they are not required to attend school, and children working for their parents, except in manufacturing and mining.

The list of nonpermissible employments for children of fourteen and fifteen excludes most school children from interstate mining, manufacturing, processing occupations that take them into rooms where manufacturing is going on, work on power-driven machinery and hoisting apparatus, operation of motor vehicles or service as helpers, and public messenger service. The third category, which includes hazardous occupations forbidden to those between sixteen and eighteen years old, prevents youths of the ages mentioned from working in explosive plants, as motor-vehicle driver and helper, coal mines, logging and sawmilling, operating metalworking and woodworking machines, and occupations involving exposure to radioactive substances.

Inspections are made by employees of the Wage and Hour and Public Contracts Division as they get around over the country checking up on other labor standards. Violations are also frequently reported by state officials, especially by state departments of labor and education. Legal responsibility for obeying the law rests with the employer rather than with youths or their parents. Each year sees a number of violations and the number increased greatly during the war. Many of the minors are very young; some are as young as eight years. The canning and packing industry is a conspicuous offender.

REGULATION OF HOURS AND WAGES

Legislation regulating hours and wages is filled with distinctions between children, women, and men. There has never been much question about whether states and the Federal government, within their respective jurisdictions, might regulate the employment of children. For women there was more doubt, and for men still more.

Constitutionality of Hour Laws. The basic constitutional question has been whether hour laws deprived liberty and property without due process of law. Because of woman's nature and the vital role she plays in society, the courts finally, albeit reluctantly, admitted that states might reasonably limit hours as a means of promoting the health, safety, and morals of the community.[22] Now nearly all states have such laws which, while they vary, tend in the direction of an 8-hour day and 44-hour week with special restrictions upon night work and employment in certain types of business, such as barrooms and restaurants.

Men were considered by the courts to be more rugged and less in need of legislative protection. At first state laws were declared unconstitutional; then legislation limiting employment in hazardous occupations was approved.[23] and finally, the courts permitted hour laws for men in general occupations.[24] Now most states have such laws, but the coverage is less general than for women. The same doubts have enshrouded federal hour laws but all these disappeared in 1941 when the Supreme Court upheld the Fair Labor Standards Act.[25]

Constitutionality of Wage Laws. The courts have been even more unwilling to uphold state and federal fixation of minimum wages. Massachusetts enacted the first minimum-wage law for women in 1912 and other states followed. Constitutionality was challenged promptly but the outcome remained doubtful until 1923 when a federal wage law for women in the District of Columbia came before the Supreme Court. In

that case [26] the law was declared an unconstitutional deprivation of liberty and property. During the next few years the states tried to devise laws that would circumvent the ruling of the court.

Formerly the statutes based minimum wages upon the cost of living of an entirely self-supporting woman; after the Adkins decision, they tried to base them upon the value of services rendered. One of these, that of New York State, came before the Supreme Court in 1935, but a majority of five of the Court's membership refused to see any essential difference between this and the legislation declared unconstitutional in Adkins v. Children's Hospital.[27] A year later, however, the Court reversed itself in another five-to-four decision, this time upholding a statute of the state of Washington.[28] This decision opened the door not only for state but also for federal minimum-wage legislation for women. An entering wedge having been driven, it was only a short time until the Supreme Court upheld federal, and incidentally state, wage control for men also.[29]

Fair Labor Standards Act. Federal wage and hour laws relate first of all to the government's own employees, whose wages are, of course, prescribed and whose hours are normally restricted to an 8-hour day and 40-hour week. Separate statutes limit the hours of seamen and longshoremen, employees of railway, motor, and air carriers. The first federal wage and hour legislation providing coverage for general occupations was the National Industrial Recovery Act, but this was short-lived. Then followed the Public Contracts Act of 1936 regulating hours and minimum wages for employees working on gov-

---

[22] See especially John R. Commons and John B. Andrews, *Principles of Labor Legislation* (Harper, 1936 ed.), pp. 113–116. The two early leading Supreme Court decisions upholding state hour laws for women are Holden v. Hardy, 169 U.S. 366 (1898), and Muller v. Oregon, 208 U.S. 412 (1908).

[23] Holden v. Hardy, 169 U.S. 366 (1898).

[24] Bunting v. Oregon, 243 U.S. 246 (1917).

[25] United States v. Darby Lumber Co., 312 U.S. 100 (1941).

[26] Adkins v. Children's Hospital, 261 U.S. 525 (1923).

[27] Morehead v. New York ex rel. Tipaldo, 298 U.S. 587 (1936).

[28] West Coast Hotel Co. v. Parrish, 300 U.S. 379 (1937). Within the year the Court's membership had not changed, but Justice Owen J. Roberts had changed his mind. By his doing so, legislation became valid which for 14 years had been considered unconstitutional.

[29] United States v. Darby Lumber Co., 312 U.S. 100 (1941).

ernment contracts, and finally the Fair Labor Standards Act in 1938 and subsequent amendments.

The wage-and-hour provisions of this legislation apply to all employees, including both men and women, in nonexempt businesses engaged in interstate commerce or in the production of goods for interstate commerce.[30] If even a small part of the goods he works on is moved in interstate commerce an employee is covered if the employer has reason to believe, at the time of production, that the goods will move in interstate commerce or will become a part of such goods (*e.g.,* putting buttons on shirts). Employees within the District of Columbia, territories, and possessions are also included.

A number of groups are exempt, however. Among these are executives, administrative and professional workers, outside salesmen, and persons engaged in local retail selling; employees of retail or service establishments, the greater part of whose business is intrastate; employees of air lines, railways,[31] and local transportation agencies; switchboard operators of small telephone exchanges; employees of small weekly or semiweekly county newspapers; fishermen, seamen, and agricultural workers, and those engaged in processing agricultural products within the area of production.

The act provided two ways by which minimum wages were to be fixed. First, the statute itself placed a "floor" under wages, saying that until Oct. 24, 1945, the minimum would be 30 cents an hour and after that date 40 cents. After much agitation and discussion Congress finally, in 1949, raised the minimum to 75 cents and in

[30] For an excellent review of the employments covered by the act, see John J. George and Richard E. Lambert, "Wage-Hour Coverage of the Fair Labor Standards Act," *Minnesota Law Review* (April, 1952), p. 454.

[31] So far as employees of interstate motor carriers are concerned, they are all subject to the wage provisions, but drivers, drivers' helpers, mechanics, and loaders are exempt from the hour provisions. Hours for these employees are governed by the Motor Carrier Act and regulated by the Interstate Commerce Commission.

1955 to $1. Second, minimum wages were fixed by administrative order. As a means of raising the general minimum to 40 cents by October, 1945, the administrator was authorized to appoint industry committees composed of equal representation of employers, employees, and the public. Upon their recommendation, the administrator might fix the minimum anywhere between 30 and 40 cents. By July, 1944, seventy

The minimum wage allowed in covered employment under the Fair Labor Standards Act has been raised repeatedly, reaching $1 in 1955.

industry committees had been appointed, many of whose recommendations were put into effect, thus making the transition to 40 cents easier than otherwise would have been the case.

The act provides no absolute limitation upon the number of hours that employees might work. It merely requires that time and a half be paid for all time worked beyond 40 hours a week. Nor does the law place any limitation on the number of hours that may be worked in any one day.

These wage and hour provisions are administered and enforced by the Wage and Hour and Public Contracts Division of the Department of Labor. Violators may be fined up to $10,000 or, in the case of a second conviction, imprisonment up to 6 months, or both. In addition, workers may collect in court double the back wages due them plus attorneys' fees and court costs. Inspections are made by a large force of officers working in and out of field offices located in principal cities.

EMPLOYMENT OFFICES

Employers who need workmen and men who need jobs must get together somehow. The usual method is for the employer to hang out a "Help Wanted" sign or advertise in newspapers, while the employee walks the streets, dropping in where there are signs, or answering advertisements. The procedure is haphazard, inefficient, and destructive of morale. Numerous fee-charging private employment agencies came into existence to help meet the need and as time has gone on philanthropic organizations and local, state, and federal governments have entered the scene.

Regulation of Private Employment Agencies. An employee in need of a job is peculiarly susceptible to exploitation and many fee-charging agencies have taken advantage of their opportunity. Various states have attempted regulation, but it is the almost unanimous testimony of investigators and public officials that state regulation has not succeeded in stamping out the abuses.[32] This experience led to attempts on the part of the states to outlaw private fee-charging agencies. This was stopped by the United States Supreme Court which ruled that such legislation was denial of liberty and property without due process of law and a denial of the equal protection under the law required by the Fourteenth Amendment.[33] Later, New Jersey declared employment services businesses affected with a public interest and provided for regulation similar to that applied to public utilities, including limitations upon fees. This, too, was disapproved by the Supreme Court for similar reasons.[34] Finally, in 1941, the Supreme Court reversed its precedents by upholding comprehensive state regulation[35] and inferentially federal.

[32] Commons and Andrews, *op. cit.,* p. 9.
[33] Adams *v.* Tanner, 244 U.S. 590 (1917).
[34] Ribnik *v.* McBride, 279 U.S. 350 (1928).
[35] Olsen *v.* Nebraska, 313 U.S. 236 (1941).

Public Employment Services. The Federal government has not yet undertaken to regulate private employment offices, but it has taken the lead in providing a nation-wide, coordinated system of public employment offices. This was done in the Wagner-Peyser Act of 1933, which established the United States Employment Service as a bureau in the Department of Labor. Since then the Service has had a stormy career. In 1939 its functions were consolidated with those pertaining to unemployment compensation and transferred to the Federal Security Agency. In 1942 employment services were transferred to the War Manpower Commission. They were returned to Labor in 1945, given back to the Federal Security Agency in 1948, and in 1949 returned to Labor.

The original plan called for federal grants to states on a matching basis, with the understanding that the states would administer their own programs but in accordance with federal standards. In January, 1942, as an aid to the war effort, all state services were taken over by the Federal government. Immediately after the war, sentiment arose demanding return to the states. This was authorized by Congress in 1946 over strong protest from President Truman, labor groups, and others who prefer an integrated national system to forty-eight federated plans. While the services are under state rule, some federal funds are granted on condition that uniform standards, including adherence to the merit system in appointing personnel, are maintained.

Whether under direct federal operation or as originally conceived, the employment services provide a ready source of assistance to both employers and employees. Offices exist in the principal towns of every state, and in smaller places representatives call at regular intervals to receive applications for jobs and to put employers in touch with suitable workers. Because they are coordinated, the offices maintain a nation-wide clearance system, so that workers who cannot be placed at home can be referred to jobs in other areas. These offices are also integral parts of the social-security system; all payments for unemployment compensation are made through them.

**FOR
FURTHER
READING**

American Association for Labor Legislation: *American Labor Legislation Review* (quarterly).

Berman, Edward: *Labor Disputes and the President of the United States* (Columbia University Press, 1924).

——: *Labor and the Sherman Act* (Harper, 1930).

Bernstein, Irving: *The New Deal Collective Bargaining Policy* (University of California Press, 1950).

Bowman, Dean O.: *Public Control of Labor Relations: A Study of the National Labor Relations Board* (Macmillan, 1942).

Breen, Vincent I.: *United States Conciliation Service* (The Catholic University of America Press, 1943).

Brooks, Robert R. R.: *Unions of Their Own Choosing: An Account of the National Labor Relations Board and Its Work* (Yale University Press, 1939).

——: *When Labor Organizes* (Yale University Press, 1937).

Bureau of National Affairs: *Wartime Wage Control and Dispute Settlement* (Washington, D.C.: The Bureau, 1945).

Commons, John R., and John B. Andrews: *Principles of Labor Legislation* (Harper, 4th ed., 1936).

Dunlop, John T., and Arthur D. Hill: *The Wage Adjustment Board* (Harvard University Press, 1950).

Eby, Herbert O.: *Labor Relations Acts in the Courts* . . . (Harper, 1943).

France, Robert R., and Richard A. Lester: *Compulsory Arbitration of Utility Disputes in New Jersey and Pennsylvania* (Industrial Relations Section, Princeton University, 1951).

Frankfurter, Felix, and Nathan Greene: *The Labor Injunction* (Macmillan, 1930).

Gregory, Charles O.: *Labor and the Law* (Norton, rev. and enl. ed., 1949).

Haber, William, and Others (eds.): *Manpower in the United States: Problems and Policies* (Harper, 1954).

Keller, Frances: *American Arbitration* (Harper, 1948).

Killingsworth, Charles C.: *State Labor Relations Acts: A Study in Public Policy* (University of Chicago Press, 1948).

Lombardi, John: *Labor's Voice in the Cabinet: A History of the Development of the Department of Labor from Its Origin to 1921* (Columbia University Press, 1942).

Lyon, Leverett S., and Others: *Government and Economic Life* (Brookings, 2 vols., 1940).

Mariano, John H.: *Wartime Labor Relations* (New York: National Public and Labor Relations Service, 1944).

Mason, Alpheus T.: *Organized Labor and the Law, with Special Reference to the Sherman and Clayton Acts* (Duke University Press, 1925).

Mathews, Robert E. (ed.): *Labor Relations and the Law* (Little, Brown, 1953).

McNaughton, Wayne L., and Joseph Lazar: *Industrial Relations and the Government* (McGraw-Hill, 1954).

Metz, Harold W.: *Labor Policy of the Federal Government* (Brookings, 1945).

National Manpower Council: *Policy for Skilled Manpower* (Columbia University Press, 1954).

Reede, Arthur H.: *Adequacy of Workmen's Compensation* (Harvard University Press, 1947).

Schlotterbeck, Karl T.: *Postwar Re-employment: The Magnitude of the Problem* (Brookings, 1943).

Seidman, Joel I.: *American Labor from Defense to Reconversion* (University of Chicago Press, 1953).

——: *The Yellow-dog Contract* (Johns Hopkins Press, 1932).

Somers, Herman Miles, and Anne Ramsay Somers: *Workmen's Compensation: Prevention, Insurance, and Rehabilitation of Occupational Disability* (Wiley, 1954).

Taft, Philip: *The Structure and Government of Labor Unions* (Harvard University Press, 1954).

U.S. Commission on Organization of the Executive Branch of the Government (first Hoover Commission): *Department of Labor* (1949).

Woytinsky, Wladimir S., and Others: *Employment and Wages in the United States* (Twentieth Century Fund, 1953).

REVIEW QUESTIONS

1. How do you explain the fact that the bulk of federal and state labor and welfare legislation is of comparatively recent date?

2. Describe the organization and principal functions of the Department of Labor.

3. Summarize provisions of the major federal laws discussed in this chapter.

4. What constitutional issues were involved in legislation dealing with child labor, wages and hours, the right to organize and bargain collectively, "yellow-dog" contracts?

5. Defend and criticize the National Labor Relations Act before and after Taft-Hartley amendments.

6. Make a list of the aids or services rendered by the Federal government primarily for the benefit of labor.

7. Distinguish between mediation and arbitration.

8. Trace the steps by which the National Labor Relations Board handles a complaint that an unfair labor practice has been committed.

9. Trace the steps by which a national-emergency dispute may be handled under the Taft-Hartley Act.

10. Compare federal laws pertaining to railway labor with those that apply to employees engaged in other forms of interstate and foreign commerce.

11. To what extent do federal antitrust laws now apply to the activities of trade-unions?

12. Defend and criticize compulsory arbitration of labor disputes.

13. Which is preferable: federal or state operation of employment offices?

CHAPTER 29

Welfare and Social Insurance

We can never insure one hundred percent of the population against one hundred percent of the hazards and vicissitudes of life, but we have tried to frame a law which will give some measure of protection to the average citizen and to his family against the loss of a job and against poverty-ridden old age. — Franklin D. Roosevelt [1]

The term "general welfare" appears twice in the Constitution: once in the preamble and again in the tax clause. As noted earlier, neither of these is a grant of power to Congress for doing whatever it thinks necessary to promote the general welfare. Rather, the first is merely a declaration of purpose, while the second states one of the objectives for which Congress might tax and spend. Nevertheless, through the latter provision and other grants of power from which Congress has implied authority, much legislation has been enacted intended to enhance the welfare of particular groups or of the populace as a whole.

Department of Health, Education, and Welfare. Federal welfare and educational programs traditionally have been scattered among several agencies. Consolidation under a new Department was recommended by the first Hoover Commission and by previous studies extending over three decades. President Roosevelt moved in this direction by establishing the Federal Security Agency in 1939 but departmental status was not achieved until 1953.

As its name implies, the Department embraces

three main services and three principal agencies: the Public Health Service, the Office of Education, and the Social Security Administration. Lesser units are the Food and Drug Administration, the Office of Vocational Rehabilitation, and some federally operated and aided institutions. From its first day of existence the new Department was one of the largest in terms of employees and appropriations; its services reach almost every family in the nation in direct or indirect form.

FEDERAL AIDS TO EDUCATION

Who teaches the youth of the country, what and how they are taught, are among the most vital of public issues. Generally speaking, the American people have viewed with alarm proposals looking toward diminution of local control, with the result that today primary responsibility rests in more than 125,000 local popularly elected school boards and numerous private institutions scattered throughout the land. Centralizing influences have been at work, however, in this field as in most others. First the county, then the state, and finally the Federal government have taken an interest, although hostility to federal intervention has been so strong as to limit its role severely.

[1] Statement upon signing the Social Security Act, Aug. 14, 1935, in *The Public Papers and Addresses of Franklin D. Roosevelt* (Random House, 1938), vol. 4, p. 324.

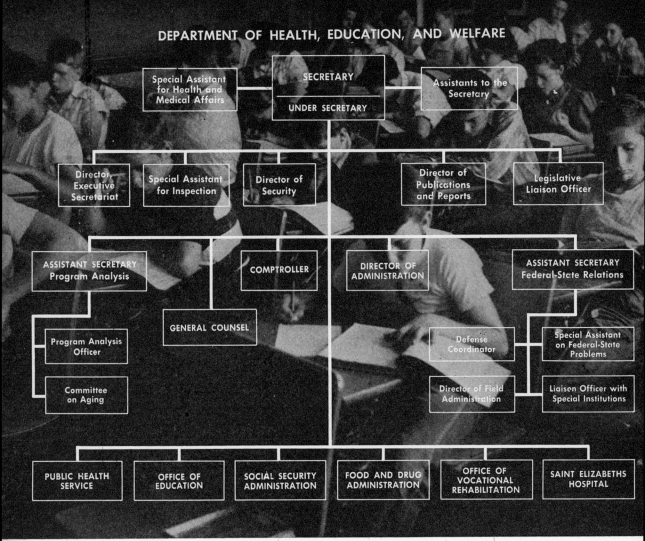

DEPARTMENT OF HEALTH, EDUCATION, AND WELFARE

- Special Assistant for Health and Medical Affairs
- SECRETARY / UNDER SECRETARY
- Assistants to the Secretary
- Director, Executive Secretariat
- Special Assistant for Inspection
- Director of Security
- Director of Publications and Reports
- Legislative Liaison Officer
- ASSISTANT SECRETARY Program Analysis
- COMPTROLLER
- DIRECTOR OF ADMINISTRATION
- ASSISTANT SECRETARY Federal-State Relations
- GENERAL COUNSEL
- Program Analysis Officer
- Committee on Aging
- Defense Coordinator
- Director of Field Administration
- Special Assistant on Federal-State Problems
- Liaison Officer with Special Institutions
- PUBLIC HEALTH SERVICE
- OFFICE OF EDUCATION
- SOCIAL SECURITY ADMINISTRATION
- FOOD AND DRUG ADMINISTRATION
- OFFICE OF VOCATIONAL REHABILITATION
- SAINT ELIZABETHS HOSPITAL

Black Star photograph

Nevertheless, an inventory of federal educational activities is long.[2] Merely to mention schools for Indians, the GI Bill of Rights, military and naval academies, the Foreign Service Institute, UNESCO, land-grant colleges, the Library of Congress, low postal rates for books and periodicals, student and faculty exchange with foreign nations, agricultural extension services, Bureau of Standards and Atomic Energy Commission scholarships, and school lunches is to suggest the wide scope of federal interest. On the whole, however, federal aid has been for special purposes stipulated in statutes rather than for general education.

[2] For a rather complete list, see first Hoover Commission, *Task Force Report on Public Welfare* (1949), p. 553.

United States Office of Education. Most federal activities in aid of education are centered in the Office of Education, which dates back to 1867. It was created "for the purpose of collecting such statistics and facts as shall show the condition and progress of education in the several States and Territories, and of diffusing such information respecting the organization and management of schools and school systems, and methods of teaching, as shall aid the people of the United States in the establishment and maintenance of efficient school systems, and otherwise promote the cause of education throughout the country." At its head is a commissioner who is appointed by the President with Senate approval.

The office is one of the smaller agencies. Among its duties are those related to research;

consultation with federal, state, and United Nations officials also concerned with education; the development of national policies designed to expand and improve educational opportunities and facilities; and the administration of certain action programs like those relating to vocational education, the blind, and vocational rehabilitation discussed below.

Land-grant Colleges. Passage of the Morrill Act in 1862 marks the beginning of federal grants-in-aid of education. That measure and supplementary legislation donated 11,367,832 acres of land to the states with the stipulation that it, or the proceeds from the sale thereof, be used for educational purposes. The "leading object," says the act, is "without excluding other scientific and classical studies, and including military tactics, to teach such branches of learning as are related to agriculture and the mechanic arts, . . . in order to promote the liberal and practical education of the industrial classes in the several pursuits and professions of life."

This legislation provides the basis for land-grant colleges which exist in the forty-eight states and three territories—Hawaii, Alaska, and Puerto Rico. Massachusetts has two institutions [3] and a number of states have divided their income between schools for whites and Negroes. In some states, *e.g.,* Illinois, Wisconsin, and Pennsylvania, schools of agriculture and mechanical arts are divisions of state universities; in one state—New York—the grants are given to a privately controlled institution (Cornell); in others, *e.g.,* Iowa, Michigan, and Indiana, separate colleges exist which include in their curriculums a wide variety of both technical and cultural courses.

In addition to offering resident instruction, each land-grant college maintains an experiment station and extension service which takes instruction directly to farms, homes, and communities within the states. Most of them offer courses in military science, but whether these will be compulsory or elective is left to each college to decide. Annual reports must be made to the United States Office of Education where they are scrutinized to make certain that the conditions have been met upon which federal grants are made.

Vocational Education. The First World War, like the Second, emphasized the need for vocational training and led Congress to enact the Smith-Hughes Act of 1917. The act provided that grants of money might be made to states and localities that would match federal funds for the purpose of providing training in agriculture and home economics. Since this beginning, the program has been greatly expanded, with the Federal government becoming ever more generous. Appropriations are still made under the Smith-Hughes Act, but the scope of the instruction and the basis of state and local participation have been altered. This was done by the George-Dean Act of 1936. By this measure vocational instruction became available not only to students interested in agriculture and home economics but also to those interested in trade and industry. Funds were also made available for the training of teachers anl supervisors in the new lines authorized. Virtually all the states are participating and sharing the costs on a matching basis with the Federal government. The program is administered by the Office of Education in cooperation with state boards, departments, and school officials.

Howard University. Howard University, located in the District of Columbia, was originally chartered by Congress in 1867 for the purpose of providing higher education for Negro students. Most of its funds come from the Federal government, and it is governed by a self-perpetuating twenty-four-member board of trustees of whom approximately half are colored and half white. Its students come from every state in the Union, a goodly number come from the Caribbean area, and occasionally students come from Africa and other parts of the world. Although intended primarily for Negroes, whites may attend and a few do. The faculty includes Negroes and whites. Howard University is doubtless the leading educational institution for Negroes in the world.

Schools for Indians. Most Indians in the United States live on reservations. Some of their children attend near-by public schools, others at-

---

[3] University of Massachusetts and Massachusetts Institute of Technology.

tend mission schools; but for others the Bureau of Indian Affairs (Department of the Interior) maintains a system of elementary and secondary schools. These are similar to ordinary public schools except that many of them are boarding schools. No special facilities are provided for college or professional study, although federal loans are available. Those who are interested and able must seek enrollment in the same colleges and universities as other Americans.

Schools for Indians are taught by teachers selected by the Bureau of Indian Affairs in accordance with civil service regulations. In addi-

MONTHLY AID TO THE PERMANENTLY AND TOTALLY DISABLED*
MARCH 1955

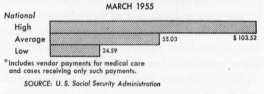

National
High
Average   55.03 $ 103.52
Low   24.59

*Includes vendor payments for medical care and cases receiving only such payments.

SOURCE: U. S. Social Security Administration

tion to the usual subjects, emphasis is placed upon instruction in agriculture, home economics, mechanical arts, the values inherent in native culture, arts, and crafts. Considerable attention is also given to adult education. Commendable as this program is, educational opportunities are admittedly inadequate and inferior to those for white children.

Vocational Rehabilitation. In an industrial society there are always numbers of individuals who have been so injured that they need help in retraining and rehabilitating themselves. Unless governmental assistance is given, many of these will be a heavy burden upon their relatives and ultimately may find themselves begging on public streets or inhabiting penal, mental, or other public institutions. Not only is it considered humane for assistance to be provided at opportune moments, but it is also generally considered sound public policy, even from a financial point of view.

Federal assistance was first provided by the Vocational Rehabilitation Act of 1920 but has been expanded since, especially by amendments adopted in 1943 and 1954. The federal program is administered by the Office of Vocational Re-

habilitation under the guidance of a National Advisory Council on Vocational Rehabilitation.

"Vocational rehabilitation" and "vocational rehabilitation services" are defined as any services necessary to render a disabled individual fit to engage in a remunerative occupation. Funds are granted to the states on the basis of needs and their ability to match federal funds, although certain costs are borne entirely by the Federal government.

In addition to training and guidance, federal grants may be used for extension and improvement of state services, research, physical restoration services, necessary hospitalization, transportation, occupational licenses, and tools, equipment, and prosthetic devices. More physical defects are of the orthopedic nature than any other, but many result from poliomyelitis, hernia, tuberculosis, defective vision and hearing, and mental illness. How extensive the program is may be imagined from the fact that as many as 60,000 persons were rehabilitated in a recent year.

A good many injured persons can never be rehabilitated. Congress had these in mind when amending the Social Security Act in 1950. As amended, the law provides that the Federal government will match state funds spent in aid of those who are totally and permanently injured. This inducement led many states to enact improved plans, with the result that general relief rolls dropped and the disabled got better care than formerly. With average monthly payments in the neighborhood of $55, the assistance is still inadequate, especially during periods of inflated prices. As a long-range plan, the Federal Security Administrator recommends a federal law requiring that employees be insured against disability arising from employment.

The National Science Foundation. The role played by science during the war, coupled with an awareness that the next conflict would be still more "scientific," led to the suggestion that the Federal government should assume more responsibility for leadership and direction in that field than it had in times past. After much discussion, and a presidential veto of one plan that passed Congress, a National Science Foundation was authorized in 1950 as an independent agency. It has a board of twenty-four members appointed by the President with senatorial approval from persons who have distinguished themselves in the basic sciences, medical science, engineering, agriculture, education, and public affairs. The board chooses a nine-member executive committee from its membership, while administration is centered in a director appointed by the President, also with senatorial approval.

The law establishing the Foundation requires that it concentrate on the physical sciences. More particularly, this involves initiating and supporting basic research, much of which is defense-related, appraising the impact of research upon industrial development and the general welfare, reviewing scientific research programs and activities of other federal agencies, awarding graduate scholarships and fellowships, maintaining a roster of scientific personnel, and encouraging the interchange of scientific information among scientists at home and abroad.

Some observers think the greatest need is not in the physical sciences but in the social sciences and the humanities, where men must learn how to live together peacefully and create a richer culture. Attempts to get support for research in these fields were made but failed when the bill was under discussion.

Proposals for the Extension of Federal Aid to Education. Surveys of state educational systems indicate that there are many areas where educational facilities are entirely lacking or woefully inadequate. This may be due to a number of factors, one of which frequently is the lack of sufficient wealth from which to obtain needed funds. A number of the states have tried to equalize opportunities within their limits by subsidizing poor areas more heavily than others, and while this helps it provides no solution for entire states whose resources are comparatively poorer than those of other areas.

To meet this situation many strenuously urge the enactment of federal legislation that will subsidize public-school education, especially in poorer states. Stimulus was given to this proposal by the White House Conference on Education held in late 1955. After the Conference gave strong endorsement, President Eisenhower recommended a plan providing aid to states for school buildings under terms that would not cause state and local governments to diminish their efforts or forfeit control.

Opponents stress the danger of federal domination. If federal funds are taken, they argue, sooner or later federal control will result. This, they insist, is likely to lead to thought control by the national government and diminution of a sense of responsibility at state and local levels. State and local governments can meet the need, opponents continue, if and when they realize the importance of the task. To meet these objections, bills in Congress usually specifically state that federal assistance must be confined to the granting of money, with only such accounting and reporting as will ensure honest use of funds for educational purposes. Still, many critics remain dubious.

Particularly thorny is the problem of what to do about private schools, many of which are church related. Everyone recognizes their great contribution to American education and also the fact they are doing a job that would otherwise need to be done and paid for by taxpayers. To grant federal aid to public schools and not to private ones adds an additional burden on those who prefer the latter and perhaps also makes it more difficult for private schools to compete for students and faculty. But to give them aid, it is contended, is contrary to the American doctrine of separation of church and state.

Many spokesmen for private schools do not want federal aid either for themselves or public schools; others do not mind federal aid for public schools but want none of it for themselves; still others, especially spokesmen for the Catholic Church, want federal aid for all, with assistance for private schools confined to things like buildings, textbooks, transportation, and school lunches. Such assistance is now given by a number of states without running afoul of Supreme Court interpretations of the appropriate role of church and state.

Proposed Workers' Education. Another proposal seriously advocated by responsible groups is federal participation in a state-operated plan of adult and workers' education along lines similar to those followed by the extension services of the land-grant colleges and the vocational educational plans described above. Proponents stress the need for an alert and well-informed citizenry in a democracy and point out that in spite of our vaunted educational system the educational level remains astonishingly low. They also stress the need for constant stimulation, discussion, and refresher training in a technological era when citizens are supposed to keep informed on a multiplicity of important issues. They also ask why educational services should be provided at federal expense for farmers, rural folk generally, and certain occupational groups, but not for industrial workers and other adults.

Here, again, opposition stems largely from fear of federal intrusion. There has been less public discussion of this proposal than the one mentioned in the previous paragraphs; hence opinions have not crystallized so firmly. The chief backers of the plan are prolabor forces and the land-grant colleges.

Federal Scholarships. Still another proposal currently under discussion is the suggestion whereby the Federal government would grant scholarships to worthy, and needy, college and graduate students. A number of scholarships are now granted by the Atomic Energy Commission, the National Science Foundation, the Public Health Service, the Bureau of Standards, and under the various exchange and military programs, but these are limited in number and for very specialized purposes.

The proposal is that worthy and needy students, chosen by highly selective and competitive means, would be given financial aid in the form of grants or loans to permit them to study whatever they wished. The closest parallels are the National Youth Administration program of the depression period and educational benefits contained in the GI Bill of Rights.

Getting an acceptable plan through Congress poses formidable obstacles. With resources being drained for military purposes, economy-minded congressmen are reluctant to add to federal outlays for education. Then, the old fear of federal domination of education rears its head. Whether

the plan should be handled exclusively by the Federal government or through federal grants-in-aid to the states is also a matter of dispute. These difficulties are compounded by wrangling over such matters as whether aid should accrue to the benefit of private and church-related colleges, whether the law should contain a provision forbidding the use of scholarships in states practicing racial segregation, and whether federal scholarships would not be further evidence of "creeping socialism." In view of these difficulties, early enactment does not seem likely.

SOCIAL INSURANCE

Individual insurance against hazards to life and property has long been common in the United States, but social insurance is something relatively new. Borrowing heavily from European ideas and experience, American states haltingly began experiments around 1900 that have since flourished. The Federal government soon began to reflect growing demand, but it took the depression of the 1930's to provide the impetus required to set in operation the large-scale programs of today.

Even with this expansion, social insurance still lags in the United States behind what it is in most European states. The central idea behind all types of social insurance is that the community should share the risks. By doing so risks and costs are spread while minimal standards of well-being are maintained for those covered by insurance plans, and the community is protected from the failure of its citizens to provide adequately for themselves. To spread the risks and costs as widely as possible, compulsory participation is usually a feature.

Workmen's Compensation. Until recent years employers generally assumed that they had no responsibility toward workmen injured during the course of employment. At common law, an injured workman's only recourse was a civil suit for damages, which he usually could ill afford. Besides being expensive and long drawn out, it was almost impossible for a workman to win because he was required to prove (1) that the employer had been negligent; (2) that negligence on his (the worker's) part in no way contributed to the accident; (3) that the accident was not due to the negligence of a fellow workman; and (4) that the accident was not the result of a risk he had assumed by consenting to work in the occupation.

Since 1902 all states have enacted statutes designed to give greater protection to workmen, and the Federal government has done likewise for certain types of workmen within its jurisdiction. Such legislation is based upon the theory that compensation for industrial accidents should be included in the cost of production and borne partially by the producers and the general public rather than entirely by injured workmen and their families.

Insurance for Government Employees. Most employees of the Federal government are insured against injuries received during the course of employment. For this purpose no insurance fund is established but, rather, Congress appropriates funds annually for direct payments to injured workmen. The amount paid is usually proportionate to seriousness of the injury and the amount of time lost from work. After a brief waiting period, and within minimums and maximums, payments are made for partial, permanent partial, and total disability. Payments may also be made for medical, surgical, and hospital service, death, and even burial in the case of death from accident received during the course of employment.

Administration involves considerable investigation, hearings, etc., which are handled by the Bureau of Employees' Compensation. Since 1946, appeals may be taken to a three-man Employees' Compensation Appeals Board and to Federal courts if constitutional issues are involved.

Insurance for District of Columbia, Longshoremen, and Harbor Workers. Federal law also compels private employers in the District of Columbia and employers of longshoremen and harbor workers to insure against accidents. Employers may either set up their own insurance funds or insure with a private company approved by the Federal Security Administrator. A schedule of benefits is provided for various types of disability and death while payments are also prescribed for medical, surgical, hospi-

tal, and burial service. The cost of insurance is borne by employers but administrative costs are paid by the Federal government.

These provisions are administered by the Bureau of Employees' Compensation which functions with the aid of regional districts, in charge of deputy commissioners, set up chiefly for the convenience of longshoremen and harbor workers. Appeals are not heard by an administrative board but by Federal district courts.

Provisions for Railway Workers and Seamen. Because these employees are engaged in interstate and foreign commerce, they are immune from state workmen's compensation laws. Nor has the Federal government made provision for them, although this has often been proposed. For their protection, therefore, injured workmen must resort to civil suits in state or Federal courts. Their lot is not so unfortunate as might appear, however, because federal laws have modified the common-law assumptions referred to above. This occurred for railway employees by the Employers' Liability Act of 1908, and for seamen by the Jones Act of 1920.

The changes made by these acts were first, the fellow-servant rule was eliminated, placing the entire responsibility for negligence either upon the employer or the employee; second, the contributory-negligence rule was modified to permit recovery of damages even though an employee may have been partly to blame, with the provision that a jury might reduce the amount of damages in proportion to the amount of the employee's negligence, and with the further provision that an employee was absolved from all negligence if the carrier had violated a safety statute; third, the rule of assumption of risks was eliminated.

As a result of these changes, an injured workman can always collect damages if an employer violated a safety statute or if the accident occurred because of negligence on the part of an employer. Even though both the company and he were negligent, he can also collect although a jury might reduce the amount of damages in proportion to the employee's share of the blame. While this legislation is of considerable help, it still involves an injured employee in more litigation, expense, uncertainty, and insecurity than if he were covered by compensation insurance statutes.

Unemployment Compensation under the Social Security Act. Unemployment is without doubt one of the most serious domestic problems facing modern nations. There is always a certain amount of unemployment among willing workers, even in so-called "normal" times, and the volume rises sharply during depressions. The large and prolonged unemployment which followed the collapse of 1929 hastened enactment of a plan that would provide an income to workmen during periods of unemployment.

WEEKLY UNEMPLOYMENT INSURANCE BENEFIT PAYMENTS
MARCH 1955

National	
High	$ 30.39
Average	24.96
Low	16.33

Source: U.S. Department of Health, Education, and Welfare.

This system is provided for in the Social Security Act of 1935 and administered by the Department of Labor, through its Bureau of Employment Security, in cooperation with the states. As amended, the act requires employers of four or more employees to pay a tax of 3 per cent of their payrolls, exclusive of amounts in excess of $3,000 paid to one employee in 1 year. It goes on to stipulate that a credit of 90 per cent of the amount collected will be allowed those employers situated in states that enact laws fitting the federal pattern.

This was such a heavy penalty upon employers in noncooperating states that it forced early enactment of state plans. Now all the states, and most of the territories, have unemployment insurance systems and 1954 amendments extended coverage to most civilian employees of the Federal government. The state laws vary considerably, but they must meet federal standards or else see their employers lose the 90 per cent tax credit and also forfeit the right to certain financial grants made in payment of the costs of administration.

All the states impose a payroll tax upon employers, and a few levy a similar tax upon employees. The money is deposited in an Unemployment Compensation Fund maintained by the United States Treasury. From this each state pays benefits to workmen as they become unemployed and make application at near-by employment offices. The amount paid varies among the states.

A typical plan provides that after a required waiting period of 2 weeks, during which time the employee must be physically able and available for work, he will receive weekly payments for a period of about 13 weeks of an amount which is determined by average earnings over a base period. The average weekly payment for the whole country during 1955 was about $25.

Unemployment Compensation for Railway Workers. Although railway employees are exempt from unemployment-insurance provisions of the Social Security Act, they are covered by separate legislation enacted in 1938.

The plan is administered by the Railroad Retirement Board. It is financed by a payroll tax paid by employers. In other respects the plan operates much like the general one explained above, with the exception that the states do not participate in administration.

Old-age and Survivors' Insurance (OASI). The Social Security Act also inaugurated a nation-wide plan of insurance intended to guarantee a minimum income to most wage earners and low-salaried workers after they reach the age of sixty-five and cease working. This program has grown to enormous proportions. Amendments added in 1950 and 1954 extended coverage to over 20 million additional employees, including many who are self-employed (farmers, business proprietors, architects, and the like).

At first, participation was made compulsory for covered employees, but later amendments permitted some groups to participate on an optional basis. Among the latter are employees of local and state governments, religious, charitable, educational, and other nonprofit organizations. As a result of federal provisions and state plans, most of the nation's paid workers, and many of its self-employed, are covered by some public retirement program.

Employers covered by the act must pay a tax on payrolls, and employees must pay an identical amount on their income, the total being collected from the employer. The amount each pays is 2 per cent on the first $4,200 of annual income. The rate is supposed to go up ½ of 1 per cent every 5 years until 1970, when it becomes 4 per cent.

The money is deposited in an Old-age and Survivors' Trust Fund in the United States Treasury, where it is invested in interest-bearing obligations of the Federal government or securities whose interest and principal are guaranteed by the national government.

Self-employed persons must pay 1½ times (3 per cent until 1960) the employee rate on net income up to $4,200, while those who enter on an optional basis pay equivalent amounts.

Annuities are paid monthly by those who retire at age sixty-five and earn less than $1,200 a year (until age seventy-two when there are no limits on earnings). Upon death, before or after retirement, benefits accrue to survivors. The amount received is based upon average monthly earnings over a lifetime in covered occupations. The maximum monthly benefit for a family is $200, or 80 per cent of average monthly wage, whichever is less. The minimum for most employees is $30 a month.

WELFARE PROGRAMS

Aids to Veterans. Nearly one-third of the population consists of veterans, their dependents, and their beneficiaries. These linger long after the war in which the veteran fought has been forgotten. Indeed, until a few years ago benefits were still being paid to survivors of a veteran of the War of 1812!

Although various governmental agencies administer laws affecting veterans, the principal one is the Veterans' Administration created in 1930. This is an independent establishment headed by an Administrator and the usual staff. Two special boards exist: a Board of Veterans' Appeals, which reviews veterans' claims, and the Veterans' Education Appeals Board, which reviews decisions of the Administrator affecting payments to educational institutions for tuition, fees, and similar items. In addition to the central office in Washington, the Administration maintains a number of regional, insular, and area offices.

The first Hoover Commission recommended merging the Veterans' Administration and other important agencies concerned with health and hospitalization, but veterans' groups have resisted so strongly that Congress has not approved the plan. Critics fear the Veterans' Administration would be less influential and effective on

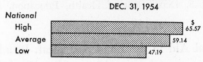

MONTHLY OLD AGE BENEFIT PAYMENTS
DEC. 31, 1954

National High $65.57
Average   59.14
Low   47.19

Source: U.S. Department of Health, Education, and Welfare.

behalf of veterans' interests if it lost independent status and became subordinate to a larger organization.

Services and benefits provided for veterans are too numerous to be explained in detail. Some veterans of the First World War receive bonuses representing the difference between what they earned while in service and what they might have earned had they remained at home. Many are hospitalized or receive outpatient medical and dental care. Thousands go to school under the GI Bill of Rights. Many borrow for homes, farms, and business with guaranteed loans. Large numbers receive compensation, popularly known as "pensions," for service-connected disability. Many retain life insurance provided during active service. Some receive allowances during periods of unemployment after release from service. Special housing and automobiles are provided for a few who are seriously disabled.

The second Hoover Commission took a close look at veterans' benefits and recommended changes that they estimated would save the taxpayers millions of dollars.[4] Among other things

[4] *Task Force Report on Federal Medical Services* (1955) and *Federal Medical Services* (1955).

they urged consolidation of the laws, rules, and regulations; closing some unneeded hospitals; tightening rules and administration to check abuse of benefits; more emphasis on preventive health and rehabilitation for aged veterans; and better coordination of veterans' health and medical programs with those of other agencies of the Federal government.

MONTHLY AID TO THE BLIND*
MARCH 1955

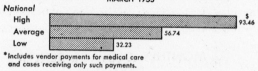

National
High — $93.46
Average — 56.74
Low — 32.23

*Includes vendor payments for medical care and cases receiving only such payments.

Source: U.S. Department of Health, Education, and Welfare.

Federal Aid to the Blind and Deaf. In addition to participation in the vocational training and rehabilitation programs mentioned above, the blind are beneficiaries of other federal legislation. In an earlier chapter mention was made of the fact that Braille reading materials may be sent through the mails postage free. Moreover, for many years the Federal government has appropriated funds to the American Print-

MONTHLY OLD AGE ASSISTANCE PAYMENTS*
MARCH 1955

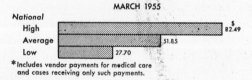

National
High — $82.49
Average — 51.85
Low — 27.70

*Includes vendor payments for medical care and cases receiving only such payments.

Source: U.S. Department of Health, Education, and Welfare.

ing House for the Blind, Inc., a privately owned and operated institution in Louisville, Ky., whose primary purpose is the production of Braille reading materials for state schools for the blind. Established in 1858, this is the oldest national institution for the blind in the United States and the largest printing house of its kind in the world.

Further assistance was provided by the Randolph-Sheppard Act of 1936 whereby the blind

were permitted to operate stands in federal buildings and the Office of Education was authorized to conduct surveys and otherwise try to find jobs for the blind.

Direct financial assistance was provided by the Social Security Act of 1935. This permits the Social Security Administration to help finance approved state plans for providing old-age pensions for the needy blind. Under this arrangement the Federal government will match state funds up to a total federal-state monthly grant of $50 for eligible blind persons sixty-five years of age or more who are not in public institutions and not receiving old-age assistance.

Deaf people may participate in the vocational rehabilitation programs. In addition, since 1857, the Federal government has operated the Columbia Institution of the Deaf, located in the District of Columbia, for the instruction of the deaf and dumb. The advanced department, known as Gallaudet College, offers the only advanced course especially for the deaf given anywhere in the world. A number of scholarships are available for those interested in attending this department.

Old-age Assistance. Both unemployment compensation and old-age and survivors' insurance require contributions on the part of employers or beneficiaries. Other sections of the Social Security Act, however, provide simply for assistance to certain important groups and functions. Among these are provisions for old-age assistance, dependent children, the blind, those who are permanently disabled, and public-health services.

Old-age assistance must not be confused with old-age and survivors' insurance. The latter is an insurance plan for employed workers, premiums for which are paid through taxes assessed upon both employers and employees; old-age assistance is given to aged people who are unemployed and in need. Old-age and survivors' insurance is administered solely by the Federal government, while old-age assistance is provided by a joint federal-state arrangement.

Under this plan the Federal government pays three-fourths of the first $20 a month per recipient plus one-half of the balance of all payments up to a maximum of $50 per recipient. Thus, if a state were willing to help pay the maximum of $50, the Federal government would pay $15 (three-fourths of the first $20) plus $17.50 (one-half of the balance), or a total of $32.50 per recipient. Payments averaged about $52 monthly in 1955.

To be eligible for a "pension," as grants are popularly known, an individual must be at least sixty-five, not an inmate of a public institution, a resident of the state for certain periods of time, a citizen (in most states), and in need. What constitutes need is a ticklish subject. Most states require applicants for aid to disclose their resources, assets, and income (if any), after which grants may be made that are sufficient, at least in the eyes of the administrators, to meet a minimum budget. Most states allow payments to more than one eligible person in a family if need warrants.

On the whole, the states have taken a defensive, miserly attitude in setting up their plans, with the result that complaints are widespread. The most frequent criticisms are that the grants are too low to provide security, that in many instances the states require applicants to be or become destitute before granting assistance, and that administration permits too much opportunity for snooping into personal and family affairs. These complaints partially explain the sustained support given by many to more extreme proposals like the Townsend and "Ham and Eggs" plans which are well known, especially along the West coast.

Aid to Dependent Children. The Social Security Administration also helps finance approved state plans aiding dependent children. A dependent child is defined as a needy person under the age of sixteen, or eighteen if regularly attending school, who has been deprived of parental support or care by reason of the death, continued absence from home, or physical or mental incapacity of a parent, and who is living and making his home with his father, mother, grandfather, or other near relative. The Federal government will pay monthly three-fourths of the first $12 per child plus one-half of the balance of all payments up to a maximum

of $27 for the first child and $18 for each additional child in the family. Seldom is the maximum grant paid, and the amounts vary considerably among the states. In 1955 payments per family averaged about $85.

State General Assistance. The Federal government is not engaged in providing general assistance, or what used to be called "direct relief," to those in need. Rather, this is a state responsibility.

Programs now operating in all states, and most of the territories, are usually administered through state and county welfare departments.

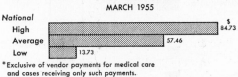

MONTHLY GENERAL ASSISTANCE PAYMENTS*
MARCH 1955

National	
High	$84.73
Average	57.46
Low	13.73

*Exclusive of vendor payments for medical care and cases receiving only such payments.

Source: U.S. Department of Health, Education, and Welfare.

The number of cases varies greatly among the states and in response to economic conditions. There is also variation in the size of the grants, the national average for March, 1955, being about $57.50. The Commissioner for Social Security for years recommended federal participation to equalize the burden and payments, but his advice has gone unheeded.

AIDS TO HEALTH

Federal medical services have grown to large proportions. The second Hoover Commission [5] pointed out that these programs entailed the annual expenditure of over two billion dollars; employed 10 per cent of the nation's doctors, 9 per cent of the dentists, 6 per cent of the graduate nurses; and controlled 13 per cent of the nation's hospital beds.

The Commission also reported that 26 federal departments and agencies had health responsibilities, although three of them—Departments of Defense and Health, Education, and

[5] In *Federal Medical Services* (1955).

Welfare and Veterans' Administration—accounted for 90 per cent of the services. Deploring the lack of central direction and coordination, the Commission strongly recommended the establishment of a Federal Advisory Council of Health to be located in the Executive Office of the President.

Federal aids to public health have been greatly stepped up in recent years, and the trend is

Research. For research purposes Institutes of Health exist to study cancer, heart, mental, dental and neurological diseases, blindness, and microbiology. The facilities of these institutes are available to research scientists generally, and much research is done in cooperation with other federal agencies and private parties.

Hospitals. Workmen's compensation laws impose a duty upon the Federal government to

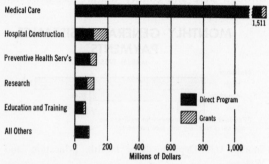

FEDERAL EXPENSE FOR HEALTH
BY FUNCTION, 1954

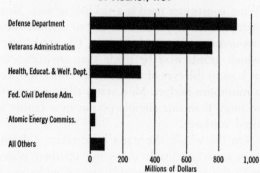

FEDERAL EXPENSE FOR HEALTH
BY AGENCY, 1954

SOURCE: Second Hoover Commission, *Task Force Report on Federal Medical Services* (1955).

The second Hoover Commission task force declared: "Federal medical service is big business. It entails the annual expenditure of over $2 billion; employs about 10 percent of the Nation's physicians, 9 percent of the dentists, and 6 percent of the graduate nurses; controls 13 percent of the hospital beds; and provides medical service to some millions of people." Source: *Task Force Report on Federal Medical Services* (1955).

likely to continue. Aside from what it does for veterans and for those for whom it has legal responsibility, federal efforts are concentrated on research, business regulation, inspection, and aid to the states.

Public Health Service. More health services for civilians are centered in the Public Health Service than in any other agency. The Service dates back to 1798 and is headed by a surgeon general who is appointed by the President with Senate approval. If not one already, the surgeon general is made a commissioned officer with the same rank as the Surgeon General of the Army. Principal assistants and administrative officers are also commissioned officers. Many Health Service employees are assigned to other federal agencies, particularly the Coast Guard, Immigration and Naturalization Service, and Departments of Army, Navy, and Air Force.

provide medical treatment and care for many civilians. The most numerous of these are members of the Coast Guard, longshoremen and harbor workers, and government employees. For these the Health Service operates a number of hospitals, outpatient clinics, and offices.

The Department of Health, Education, and Welfare operates other hospitals, but only one of them (Freedmen's) is under the Health Service. Freedmen's is a general hospital for Negroes located in the District of Columbia. St. Elizabeths, also in the District, serves mental patients. Hospitals for drug addicts are located at Fort Worth, Tex., and Lexington, Ky., and one for lepers is at Carville, La.

Regulation and Inspections. The Department of Health, Education, and Welfare is also involved in business regulation and inspection. Most of this work is centered in the Food and

Drug Administration and the Health Service. Activities of the former are discussed elsewhere. The Health Service must license the manufacture and interstate sale of serums, toxins, vaccines, and similar products. In doing so it must set standards and make investigations and tests. Attention was dramatically focused on this assignment by events surrounding the manufacture of polio vaccine which occurred in 1955.

tion-wide system of public-health services. The Federal government leads and assists chiefly through grants, most of which are of the matching type, to the states. All states are cooperating in one or more of the programs, although the number and quality of public-health services is far from uniform over the nation.

Current programs are numerous and varied. Grants for hospital surveys and construction

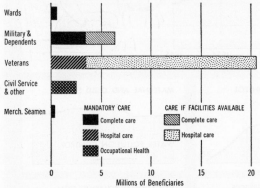

THE NUMBER OF PEOPLE POTENTIALLY ELIGIBLE FOR FEDERAL MEDICAL SERVICE, 1953

SOURCE: Second Hoover Commission, Task Force Report on Federal Medical Services (1955)

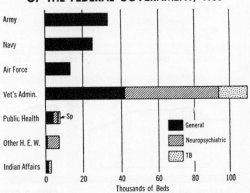

HOSPITAL FACILITIES OF THE FEDERAL GOVERNMENT, 1953

SOURCE: Second Hoover Commission, Task Force Report on Federal Medical Services (1955)

About 30 million Americans, according to the second Hoover Commission, are eligible to receive all or part of their medical care from federal agencies.

Both Hoover Commissions found much evidence of waste in hospital facilities, particularly among the armed services. Occupancy rate is often low, new construction excessive, and cross-servicing rare.

Since bugs and germs do not respect geographic boundaries, an elaborate quarantine system is operated by the Federal government in cooperation with the states. A special responsibility of the Health Service is the examination of immigrants, passengers, crews, vessels, and airplanes entering the country. Inspection stations surround the United States and its territories for this purpose.

Cooperation with the States. Federal-state cooperation on matters pertaining to health is of the utmost importance. The law requires the surgeon general to call an annual conference of state health authorities. It also stipulates that upon request of five or more states, the surgeon general must call special conferences of all state and territorial authorities joining in the request. At such conferences each state has one vote.

Ambitious programs have been launched in recent years looking toward a coordinated na-

were begun in 1946 and extended in 1954 to chronic-disease hospitals, diagnostic and treatment centers, nursing homes, and rehabilitation facilities. Grants have also been made for general health services, research, prevention, and control of particular diseases (tuberculosis, venereal, mental, cancer, heart). Grants have also been made for maternal and child health, crippled children's services, medical care for disabled but potentially employable persons, and for the indigent aged.

Although grants for the purposes indicated remain substantial, they have been reduced considerably in the past few years for reasons of economy and because many disapprove of too much federal intervention in a field historically reserved to the states, local governments, and private agencies. While the pendulum swings, federal assistance can be expected to continue

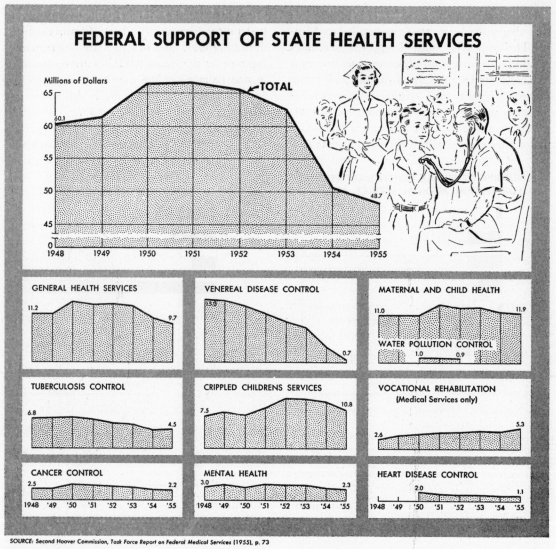

FEDERAL SUPPORT OF STATE HEALTH SERVICES

SOURCE: Second Hoover Commission, Task Force Report on Federal Medical Services (1955), p. 73

The task force criticized the abrupt reduction of federal aid for state health services, and called for restoration of the 1948–1953 average level.

as long as demand persists for more and better health services.

Proposed Compulsory National Health Insurance. The proposal to launch a national health-insurance plan immediately ran into a storm of controversy. Briefly, the proposal calls for a federal-state plan under which insured workers and their families would be entitled to receive medical service from doctors of their own choice, the cost to be borne by a fund derived from a tax on payrolls and incomes.

For the plan, it is argued that the state of the nation's health demands a bold attack; that millions cannot now afford adequate medical care; that national coverage will reduce the per capita cost; that present facilities are inadequate and cannot be sufficiently improved by voluntary efforts; and that the proposed plan is not revolutionary, modeled as it is after present social-security programs.

The chief spokesman for the opposition is the American Medical Association, backed by "conservative" interests generally. These contend that the nation's health is generally good and steadily improving; that the present voluntary medical insurance systems provide superior medical practitioners and service; that additional low-cost medical care can better be obtained through individual and voluntary cooperative efforts; that national insurance will result in a huge government administrative bureaucracy; that medical practitioners will inevitably shift from their present status to employees of Federal and state governments; that patients will lose their freedom to choose doctors of preference; and that similar plans abroad have failed or are unworthy of emulation.

The issue is joined as it has been at times past in many other parts of the world. In Britain and most other Western nations, the proponents of "socialized" medicine have won. In the United States, bills have been introduced in Congress and state legislatures, hearings have been held, lobbyists have been at work, and people are taking sides. The issue merits wide study and calm consideration. It is certain to be a lively one for a considerable period of time.

Regardless of merits of the argument, the debate has helped to stimulate interest in the nation's health. If advocates of the plan win, government will be given a new responsibility of immense proportions. This, in turn, will call for the best administrative minds and techniques the nation is capable of producing.

Health Reinsurance. Critical of proposals for compulsory health insurance, President Eisenhower proposed, in 1954, a much more modest plan of "health reinsurance." This would establish a federal fund for underwriting abnormal losses experienced by private groups which provide insurance for hospitalization, surgery, medical and dental care.

With insurance like this, it was assumed, private plans would expand to include greater numbers, many of whom are poor health risks. Abnormal losses would be guaranteed up to 75 per cent. Private groups would pay premiums and thereby make the federal plan self-financing after 5 years.

Critics pointed out that private groups felt no great need for such reinsurance. They also insisted the proposal would benefit few people with low incomes or poor health. Some critics saw in the President's proposal the entering wedge for socialized medicine.

Rebuffed by Congress, the President renewed his suggestion the following year. This time he asked Congress to include provisions that would provide special incentives for private insurance groups to extend coverage to people suffering from prolonged illness, living in rural areas, and with low incomes. He added the suggestion that Congress pass legislation authorizing grants to the states for improving medical care for those on public assistance, the permanently disabled, the blind, and dependent children.

FOR FURTHER READING

Adams, Grace K.: *Workers on Relief* (Yale University Press, 1939).

Becker, Joseph M.: *Problems of Abuse in Unemployment Benefits* (Columbia University Press, 1953).

Brown, Josephine Chapin: *Public Relief 1929–1939* (Holt, 1940).

Burns, Eveline M.: *Toward Social Security: An Explanation of the Social Security Act and a Survey of Larger Issues* (McGraw-Hill, 1936).

Chase, Stuart: *Goals for America* (Twentieth Century Fund, 1942).

Commons, John R., and John B. Andrews: *Principles of Labor Legislation* (Harper, 4th ed., 1943).

Douglas, Paul H.: *Social Security in the United States: An Analysis and Appraisal of the Social Security Act* (Random House, 1936).

Epstein, Abraham: *Insecurity—A Challenge to America: A Study of Social Insurance in the United States and Abroad* (Random House, 1936).

Ewing, Oscar R.: *The Nation's Health: A Ten Year Program* (Government Printing Office, 1948).

Falk, Isador S.: *Security against Sickness: A Study of Health Insurance* (Doubleday, 1936).

Federal Works Agency: *Final Statistical Report of the Federal Emergency Relief Administration* (1942).

Howard, Donald S.: *WPA and Federal Relief Policy* (Russell Sage Foundation, 1943).

Kramer, Victor H.: *National Institute of Health: A Study in Public Administration* (Washington: S. P. Kramer, 1937).

Macmahon, Arthur W., and Others: *Administration of Federal Work Relief* (Chicago: Public Administration Service, 1941).

Millis, Harry A., and Royal E. Montgomery: *Labor's Risks and Social Insurance* (McGraw-Hill, 1939).

Mustard, Harry S.: *Government in Public Health* (Commonwealth Fund, 1945).

Reed, Louis S.: *Health Insurance: The Next Step in Social Security* (Harper, 1937).

Rubinow, Isaac M.: *The Quest for Security* (Holt, 1934).

Smillie, Wilson G.: *Public Health Administration in the United States* (Macmillan, 1935).

Tobey, James A.: *Public Health Law* (Commonwealth Fund, 1939).

U.S. Advisory Committee on Education: *Report of the Committee* (1938).

U.S. Commission on Intergovernmental Relations: *Federal Aid to Public Health* (1955).

——: *Federal Aid to Welfare* (1955).

——: *Federal Responsibility in the Field of Education* (1955).

——: *Unemployment Compensation and Employment Service* (1955).

U.S. Commission on Organization of the Executive Branch of the Government (second Hoover Commission): *Federal Medical Services* (1955).

——: *Task Force Report on Medical Services* (1955).

U.S. Commission on Organization of the Executive Branch of the Government (first Hoover Commission): *Medical Activities* (1949).

——: *Social Security, Education, Indian Affairs* (1949).

——: *Task Force Report on Public Welfare* (1949).

REVIEW QUESTIONS

1. Describe the organization and functions of the Department of Health, Education, and Welfare. How do you explain the reluctance of Congress to establish this department?

2. Summarize federal legislation dealing with (*a*) social insurance; (*b*) health; (*c*) education; (*d*) aid to veterans; (*e*) vocational rehabilitation; (*f*) aid to crippled and dependent children; (*g*) old-age assistance; (*h*) aid to the blind.

3. Do you think the states are unduly coerced by conditional grants-in-aid for the functions mentioned in this chapter?

4. Defend and criticize federal aid to education.

5. Would it be advisable to eliminate states from participation in unemployment compensation in favor of a uniform federally administered program?

6. What were the common-law presumptions which made it difficult for injured workmen to collect damages before the advent of workmen's compensation?

7. Summarize recommendations made by the first and second Hoover Commissions on the subjects discussed in this chapter.

8. Defend and criticize proposals for (*a*) compulsory nation-wide prepaid medical, surgical, and hospital insurance; (*b*) reinsurance of voluntary health insurance plans.

9. What changes would you recommend in present provisions for old-age and survivors' insurance and old-age assistance?

10. How adequate are present federal health, education, and welfare provisions for Indians?

11. What more should the Federal government do to improve the nation's health?

12. What is the constitutional basis of federal intervention in the health, education, and welfare fields?

CHAPTER 30

Agriculture

Our thoughts may ordinarily be concentrated upon the cities and the hives of industry . . . but it is from the quiet interspaces of the open valleys and the free hillsides that we draw the sources of life and prosperity, from the farm and the ranch, from the forest and the mine. Without these every street would be silent, every office deserted, every factory fallen into disrepair. — President Woodrow Wilson [1]

Agriculture is America's basic industry, producing the foods and fibers and raw materials upon which our population is dependent, and on which much of our manufacturing relies. Farming has undergone a great transformation in recent years. Farm population has decreased strikingly, yet farm production has increased manifold. Forty years ago, one person gainfully employed in agriculture produced enough for himself and six others; in the 1950's one produced sufficient for seventeen. Agriculture's share of the national income decreased markedly too; in 1850, it has been estimated, agriculture contributed 34 per cent, but by 1953 this had declined to less than 6 per cent.

THE FARM PROBLEM IN PERSPECTIVE

American agriculture has many problems, but "the farm problem" that surpasses and overshadows all others concerns the adjustment of the supply of farm commodities to the demand for them. A manufacturer is alert to market conditions, is able to predict the production vol-

ume of his competitors, and can cut down or stop production when oversupply threatens the market. Farm producers number in the millions; they grow crops under conditions ever made uncertain by weather and insects; many of their commodities must be sold in the world market. Under the circumstances, it is not surprising that agriculture should have called upon government for help in stabilizing this chaotic sector of the economy.

Farm Programs of the Past. Between the mid-1920's and the mid-1950's the search for solutions led to proposals for export subsidies, government purchase and storage, production control, price supports, acreage allotments and marketing quotas, and a number of other devices. The major proposals, some of which were adopted and some rejected, will be considered in chronological order. Programs currently in operation are covered in subsequent sections.

The famed McNary-Haugen bill, passed by Congress and vetoed by President Coolidge in both 1927 and 1928, provided export subsidies, financed by fees on domestic sales, but no production control.

During the Hoover Administration, hope was placed in the Agricultural Marketing Act of

[1] First Annual Address, delivered Dec. 2, 1913, in James D. Richardson (ed.), *Messages and Papers of the Presidents* (New York: Bureau of National Literature, 20 vols., 1897–1916), vol. 18, p. 7908.

1929, which emphasized loans to cooperatives, and the purchase and holding of commodities by the Federal Farm Board during critical periods. Prices continued to fall, however, and the government was left with a large accumulation of wheat and cotton.

The Agricultural Adjustment Act of 1933 [2] was the first of a number of far-reaching farm-aid laws enacted during the Roosevelt Adminis-

The AAA of 1933 was declared unconstitutional in January, 1936.[3] Constitutional issues that were involved have been dealt with in an earlier chapter. Briefly restated, the Supreme Court ruled in a 6-to-3 decision that the Congress had exceeded its power in controlling production, and that the processing tax with earmarked revenues was discriminatory and invalid.

WHY RUSSIANS WANT TO STUDY U.S. FARMS

One U.S. farmer provides an abundant diet for **18** people—himself and **17** others

One Russian farmer provides a scanty diet for **3** people—himself and **2** others

The exchange visits of American and Russian farmers served to emphasize the enormous productivity of American agriculture. Reprinted from *U.S. News & World Report,* an independent weekly news magazine published at Washington. Copyright, 1955, United States News Publishing Corporation. Issue of July 15, 1955.

tration. Production control was introduced for the first time as the major method to bring supply and demand into adjustment. Contracts were offered to farmers willing to reduce production, to whom the government paid cash benefits. Funds were raised for the purpose through a tax collected at the processing stage. The tax rate was set at the estimated difference between market price and "parity," which was defined as the price necessary to give farmers purchasing power equal to that existing in 1909–1914. Some commodity loans were made to encourage withholding from the market; a penalty tax was imposed on excess production of cotton and tobacco.

[2] 48 Stat. 31.

In a transitional period that followed, the Soil Conservation and Domestic Allotment Act of 1936 [4] provided a statutory basis for an interim program in place of the invalidated features of the AAA. Farmers were induced to plant soil-conserving crops in place of soil-depleting ones by offering them "soil conservation payments," financed from the general funds of the Treasury up to 500 million dollars annually.

The Agricultural Adjustment Act of 1938 [5] restored much of the voided program of 1933, but employed methods that would not run afoul of the Court. First, farmers who cooperated by

[3] United States *v.* Butler, 297 U.S. 1 (1936).
[4] 49 Stat. 1148.
[5] 52 Stat. 31.

reducing acreage of soil-depleting crops were paid for "soil conservation" and for "parity." Second, producers of cotton, corn, wheat, rice, tobacco, and peanuts might, by securing a two-thirds majority vote in a referendum, establish acreage allotments and marketing quotas. Third, loans were made to farmers on many commodities in order to keep crops off the market in years of overproduction and low prices. Most of the 1938 program is still in operation.

During the Second World War and in the immediate postwar period the Steagall amendment set the basic pattern of farm-price support. For the duration of the war plus 2 years, price supports were made mandatory on the basic commodities at 90 per cent of parity. Other commodities could be included if an increase in production was required; eventually twenty commodities so qualified. Prices of most commodities were well above parity, but the guaranty served to provide the confidence that induced expanded production. Wartime price-support legislation expired in 1948.

Instead of allowing a full resumption of the 1938 act, Congress enacted the Agricultural Act of 1948, authored by Senator Aiken, which provided for flexible supports, largely ranging from 60 to 90 per cent of parity, on some nineteen commodities. Prices would be supported on a sliding scale, depending on the supply of a particular commodity. If the supply were abnormally large, support would be set at 60 per cent; if normal, at 75; if below normal, at 90. The 1948 legislation, enacted by the Republican Eightieth Congress, appears not to have satisfied key elements in the farm population. In the presidential election that followed, Mr. Truman, who advocated rigid 90 per cent support prices and a more favorable parity base, swept state after state in the Middle West.

Among the proposals before the Congress in 1949 was the Brannan plan, sponsored by the then Secretary of Agriculture. It would have permitted farm prices to find their "natural" levels through the operation of supply and demand. The consumer would enjoy the benefits of any fall in the price level. The farmer would be assisted and protected by direct subsidy payment of an amount representing the deficiency between price received and the parity price. Congress declined to permit even a trial run of the Brannan plan.

Congress then enacted the Agricultural Act of 1949, known as the Gore bill, which extended something like the wartime arrangement, including a fixed 90 per cent support program for commodities that are under production control and marketing quotas. The rigid supports were extended in 1952 to the crops of 1953 and 1954.

Agricultural Issues of the Present. The coming to office of the Eisenhower Administration, and the appointment of Ezra T. Benson as Secretary of Agriculture, changed the direction of support activities—at least temporarily. The new Secretary strongly opposed the mandatory and rigid features of the 1949 law. The Agricultural Act of 1954 represents some reappraisal of the impact of high support prices. The law reestablished flexible supports for five basic commodities. It was applicable for the first time to the 1955 crop.

Even before the new law went into effect, however, forces were at work to replace it and to restore rigid supports. The Democratic victory in the congressional elections of 1954 was interpreted in part as a mark of farmer hostility toward Benson policies and the 1954 law. The new Congress proceeded to consider bills to reestablish mandatory price supports at 90 per cent of parity.

The case for *flexible* supports is that high rigid supports stimulate overproduction, saddle the taxpayer with excessive burdens, and pile up huge quantities of commodities.

The case for *rigid* supports is that they are necessary in order to assure adequate production, to provide the farmer with a fair return, and to stabilize the rural economy.

As this is written, it appears that the Congress may permit the 1954 act and the flexible support arrangement to operate 2 or more years. But the political pressures for the rigid formula are very great. If the recession in agriculture should deepen, the demand for higher and more rigid price supports surely will grow, perhaps even to the extent that a presidential veto can be overridden.

The Parity Issue. Parity means securing for the farmer a price for his crop sufficient to give him purchasing power equal to that he enjoyed during an earlier "base period." The most common period used has been 1910–1914. As a farmer once explained it, parity means that if

of the support level. During the ten years after Pearl Harbor, supports were largely at 90 per cent, but prices averaged 108 per cent.

Continuing the rigid support levels after wartime scarcity had ceased, contributed to the overproduction of several farm commodities. The government's stocks of wheat and cotton were in 1955 enough for a full year of domestic use. The limit on Commodity Credit Corpora-

FARMERS' PRICES

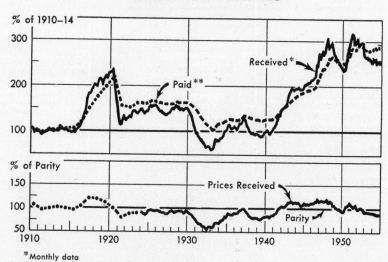

The relationship of prices a farmer receives for his products and what he pays for his needs is shown here. Farmers fear a long period, like that of the 1920's and 1930's, of below parity returns.

* Monthly data

** Includes interest, taxes, and wage rates. Annual av. data, 1910–23; By quarters, 1924–36; By months, 1937 to date

SOURCE: U. S. Department of Agriculture

in 1912 he could take a bushel of wheat to town and buy a shirt, he ought to be able to do the same thing now. Of course the formula takes into account a large number of things that a farmer purchases, such as food, clothing, machinery, fuel, and fertilizer.

Actual parity prices for a growing season are worked out by the Department of Agriculture. The price for a particular commodity takes into account fluctuations in prices of the goods and services the farmer must buy. A rise of the price level on things the farmer buys will be reflected in an increased parity price; a decline would lead to a reduction.

Parity prices provide a floor, not a ceiling. In times of scarcity, farm prices may soar far ahead

tion borrowing authority, 10 billion dollars in 1955, has been raised repeatedly to cover mandatory commitments under the law.

Disposal of these surpluses is an extremely troublesome problem. Losses are inevitable unless production decreases sharply or demand rises. For the year 1954 price support losses were 603 million dollars. It has been estimated that storage costs alone run about 1 million dollars per day. Reduction of inventory by selling on the domestic market normally would drive prices down and further burden the price-support program with purchases of current crop. Sales in the foreign markets may demoralize them and cause harm to friendly countries that produce the same commodities. Ways must and

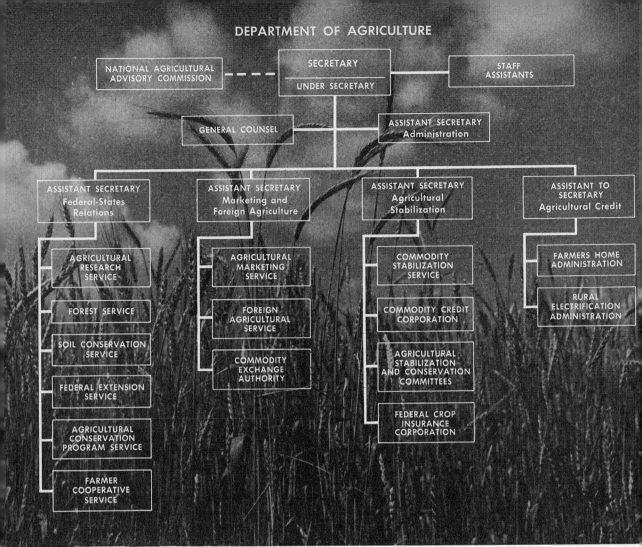

DEPARTMENT OF AGRICULTURE

NATIONAL AGRICULTURAL ADVISORY COMMISSION — SECRETARY / UNDER SECRETARY — STAFF ASSISTANTS

GENERAL COUNSEL — ASSISTANT SECRETARY Administration

ASSISTANT SECRETARY Federal-States Relations
- AGRICULTURAL RESEARCH SERVICE
- FOREST SERVICE
- SOIL CONSERVATION SERVICE
- FEDERAL EXTENSION SERVICE
- AGRICULTURAL CONSERVATION PROGRAM SERVICE
- FARMER COOPERATIVE SERVICE

ASSISTANT SECRETARY Marketing and Foreign Agriculture
- AGRICULTURAL MARKETING SERVICE
- FOREIGN AGRICULTURAL SERVICE
- COMMODITY EXCHANGE AUTHORITY

ASSISTANT SECRETARY Agricultural Stabilization
- COMMODITY STABILIZATION SERVICE
- COMMODITY CREDIT CORPORATION
- AGRICULTURAL STABILIZATION AND CONSERVATION COMMITTEES
- FEDERAL CROP INSURANCE CORPORATION

ASSISTANT TO SECRETARY Agricultural Credit
- FARMERS HOME ADMINISTRATION
- RURAL ELECTRIFICATION ADMINISTRATION

Charlton photograph from Black Star

are being found to increase consumption and improve nutritional standards, both at home and abroad. Subsidized consumption is often recommended as a means, through projects such as school-lunch program and the revival of a food-stamp plan for getting surplus commodities to low-income groups.

The Department of Agriculture. In many ways the Department of Agriculture constitutes a model in departmental organization. Frequently reorganized to improve its services to the American farmer, the Department has placed great stress on management and personnel techniques. Its vast organization has long been admirably administered by first-rate personnel with high morale. The administrative organiza-

tion prevailing in 1955 grouped the several operating services, administrations, and corporations as shown on the accompanying chart.

Most of the staff-type offices report to the Administrative Assistant Secretary; these include budget and finance, hearing examiners, information, library, personnel, and plant and operations. The Farm Credit Administration, made an independent agency in 1953, also plays a vital role in serving agriculture.

AGRICULTURAL STABILIZATION PROGRAMS

Efforts to stabilize American agriculture have occupied an important share of congressional time and interest for 30 years. The question for which an answer is sought here is: What programs to secure stabilization of agriculture are in force, and how do they operate?

Machinery of Price Supports. The Commodity Credit Corporation is the principal instrumentality through which the Federal government finances its price-support program to achieve "parity." The Corporation was created in 1933 as an agency of the United States, but incorporated in Delaware. In 1939 it was brought into the Department of Agriculture, and in 1948 was reincorporated under federal law. The board of CCC consists of the Secretary of Agriculture, who is ex officio chairman, and six members appointed by the President. An advisory board reviews general policy from time to time. In addition to its capitalization of 100 million dollars, the CCC has statutory authority to borrow, from the Treasury or from private sources, up to 10 billion dollars.

Price support is carried out through agreements to purchase, outright purchase, and conditional purchase of commodities. The latter is most widely used, and takes the form of a loan. If the stored commodity goes down in price, the producer may choose to turn it over to the CCC and keep the money advanced to him. If it goes up, he may pay off the loan, plus interest, and redeem his stored crop. Most CCC loans

are made through private lending agencies, but the producer may, if he chooses, deal directly with CCC.

Price support is mandatory, under present legislation, on eleven commodities, and permissive on others. The mandatory crops are wheat, corn, rice, tobacco, cotton, peanuts, wool, mohair, tung nuts, honey, and butterfat milk.

The CCC also has a farm storage-facilities program, under which it seeks to expand capacity either through itself buying granaries or loaning (or guaranteeing private loans) to producers for storage facilities.

Extensive procurement responsibilities are vested in the CCC, which buys farm products for some federal agencies, some foreign governments, and international relief agencies. It is authorized to exchange surplus farm products for strategic materials produced abroad. It may export commodities that are not in short supply in the United States.

Commodity Stabilization. Closely related to CCC is the Commodity Stabilization Service, which was established in 1953. It carried out the nonfiscal aspects of many of the functions assigned to CCC. Personnel and facilities are used interchangeably by the two agencies.

The Commodity Stabilization Service operates in Washington through an administrator,

After several years of operation under high and rigid price supports, the Federal government owned billions of dollars' worth of surplus commodities in storage, and had loans outstanding on additional quantities. Figures from Commodity Credit Corporation.

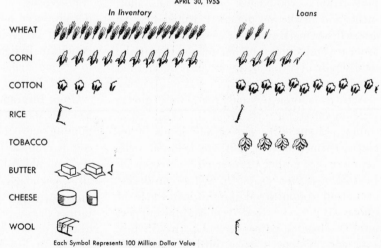

MAJOR COMMODITIES STATUS OF CCC PRICE SUPPORT OPERATIONS
APRIL 30, 1955

In Inventory   Loans

WHEAT

CORN

COTTON

RICE

TOBACCO

BUTTER

CHEESE

WOOL

Each Symbol Represents 100 Million Dollar Value

an associate administrator, and two deputy administrators—one for price support and one for adjustment. There are six commodity divisions, and a number of other staff and functional divisions. In the field, the programs are carried to farmer level through the county committees, which are farmer-elected.

First among the tasks of CSS is the adjustment of supply, when out of line with demand,

quotas. If they rejected the acreage allotments proposed by the Secretary, the support price would have been 50 per cent of parity; acceptance led to a 1955 price of 82.5 per cent of parity, and a 1956 price of 76 per cent. Should a farmer fail to comply with acreage allotment, he is not eligible for price support. Marketing quotas may not be used unless approved by a two-thirds vote of producers.

FORM MQ-5-WHEAT (1956)
(4-14-55)

Initials of committeeman issuing ballot _____

UNITED STATES DEPARTMENT OF AGRICULTURE
COMMODITY STABILIZATION SERVICE

WHEAT MARKETING QUOTA REFERENDUM BALLOT

Are you in favor of marketing quotas for wheat for the 1956 crop?

SAMPLE

If **FOR** quotas, put
"X" in this box

If **AGAINST** quotas, put
"X" in this box

☆ U. S. GOVERNMENT PRINTING OFFICE: 1955   O—340818

The ballot voted by wheat farmers in 1955 to adopt quotas for the 1956 crop.

for a number of farm products. Acreage allotments and marketing quotas are administered through agricultural stabilization and conservation committees on the county level. Under the Agricultural Act of 1949 eligibility for price support requires compliance with acreage allotments and marketing quotas. Penalties may be assessed for marketing in excess of quotas. Allotments and quotas are mandatory when the total supply of a commodity exceeds the normal supply by 20 per cent.

Acreage allotments and marketing quotas were in effect for 1955 crops of wheat, corn, cotton, peanuts, rice, and various kinds of tobacco. Farmer referendums are held on marketing quotas for one or more crop years ahead. In 1954–1955, for example, 346,542 producers of upland cotton voted on the acceptance of quotas; 92 per cent voted "yes," and the support level was fixed at 90 per cent of parity. In July 1954 and in June 1955 a third of a million wheat farmers went to the polls to vote on

Among the price support activities of the service is the reduction of the mountains of surplus commodities accumulated under support programs. Under the 1949 act commodities likely to spoil or deteriorate can be exchanged by federal agencies for goods needed from abroad and not produced here. In the last resort, commodities may be given to the school-lunch program, American Indians and other needy people, and to private welfare groups for use within or outside the United States.

Crop Insurance. Insurance of crops against loss was started by the Federal government, beginning with the wheat crop of 1939 and the cotton crop of 1942. It was authorized by the Agricultural Adjustment Act of 1938 and covers all unavoidable hazards such as hail, flood, drought, wind, disease, and insect damage. The farmer pays a premium computed from the loss history of the farm and other pertinent facts; in case of loss he receives from 50 to 75 per cent of the average yield, payments being made in commodities and not in cash. The program is carried out by the Federal Crop Insurance Corporation, which is within the Department of Agriculture. Crop insurance appears a practical and essential step toward building a security for the farmer roughly comparable to that provided by unemployment insurance for the wage earner. Crop insurance under existing legislation may cover wheat, cotton, flax, corn, tobacco, and other commodities in about one-third of the agricultural counties of the country. The second Hoover Commission concluded that the premiums charged for crop insurance were not sufficient to cover losses, administrative costs, and to provide desirable reserves.[6]

MARKETING SERVICES

From its beginning the United States Department of Agriculture concerned itself with the problems of increasing agricultural productivity. By the time of the First World War it was apparent that the American farmer no longer commanded European markets without serious competition. During the war new marginal areas were brought into production, adding to the complexities of postwar farm readjustments. Overproduction reached a serious level, and farmers sought aid in marketing and in planning for future crops. At first reliable information on markets was demanded and obtained. Later special devices for handling surpluses were explored. During the last two decades both marketing and production control have been resorted to in attempting to secure a measure of prosperity for the American farmer.

Agricultural Marketing Service. Since 1953 the marketing and distributive functions of the Department have been concentrated largely in the Agricultural Marketing Service. Much of the Department's economic and statistical work is done in the service. So is the administration of the national school-lunch program and the distribution of surplus foods acquired under various support programs. The marketing service carries out its programs, including inducement to greater consumption, new uses, and

[6] Second Hoover Commission, *Lending Agencies* (1955), p. 70.

new markets through seven commodity divisions: cotton, dairy, fruit and vegetables, grain, livestock, poultry, and tobacco. It also has sub-agencies for food distribution, freight rates, and warehouses.

One essential in deciding what to plant is data on what has been produced in the past and is likely to be produced in the future. Estimates are made of acreage, yields, sales, prices, and other facts concerning the various crops. Regular market-news service is maintained by the federal Department, giving farmers the benefit of the latest information on prices, demand, and market conditions generally.

The creation of distinct standards and grades for farm products is of benefit to both farmer and consumer. If adequate standards are defined and enforced, the farmer is assured a price based upon actual quality of his product. The consumer, if he is alert and informed, may rely upon the uniform grade as assurance of actual quality of the product being bought. The standards so established are nation-wide, but their application is largely voluntary. The consumer has a particularly great stake in pressing Congress to make grading and labeling of foods, both processed and unprocessed, compulsory. Standardization of containers has been accomplished through use of the federal power over weights and measures. Mandatory grading of products according to quality probably must rely upon federal power over interstate and foreign commerce.

Commodity Exchanges. Farmers also have a great concern in future transactions involving farm products. Traders and speculators have long been wont to buy and sell agricultural commodities long in advance of their availability. It is argued that such futures trading serves a useful purpose by establishing a price level on a given commodity at a date sufficiently in advance to create a measure of stability in the market. The first attempt of Congress to regulate futures transactions came in 1921 and was based on the taxing power; this was declared invalid by the Supreme Court. A modest grain-futures act was enacted in 1922; subsequent additions have brought the list of commodities under control to include wheat, cotton, corn, oats, rye, barley, flaxseed, grain sorghums, millfeeds, rice, butter, eggs, Irish potatoes, wool tops, fats and oils, cottonseed meal, cottonseed, peanuts, soybeans, and soybean meal.

Regulation is carried out by the Commodity Exchange Authority, which has power to designate which exchanges may engage in futures

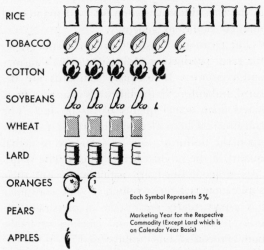

MANY U. S. FARMERS HAVE A STAKE IN EXPORT MARKET
AGRIC. EXPORTS AS A PERCENTAGE OF PRODUCTION, 1953

RICE

TOBACCO

COTTON

SOYBEANS

WHEAT

LARD

ORANGES

PEARS

APPLES

Each Symbol Represents 5%

Marketing Year for the Respective Commodity (Except Lard which is on Calendar Year Basis)

Although the home market is the principal one for the American farmer, producers in several commodity groups rely heavily upon export. The American Assembly, *United States Agriculture* (1955), p. 82.

trading, to register commission merchants and brokers, to limit the size of transactions, and to forbid manipulative and fraudulent practices.

Surplus Marketing. In the depth of the depression the existence of large surpluses of farm products, as well as millions of unemployed and hungry people, led to efforts to correct this situation. In 1933 an agency was created to remove surpluses from the market by purchasing them and then diverting them to needy families, school lunches, by-product uses, and export. Distribution to families was handled through regular retail outlets by the use of food stamps which could be presented as payment for surplus commodities.

The postwar diversion program places heavi-

est emphasis on the national school-lunch program, which was placed on a regular basis by legislation in 1946. Schools that cooperate receive both federal funds and surplus commodities. During fiscal 1953 nearly ten million children participated in the lunch program. Some surplus foods still go to charitable institutions and to families on relief.

Marketing Agreements. The "orderly marketing" of farm products is encouraged further by agreements between growers and handlers and the Secretary of Agriculture governing the marketing program of a particular commodity. Such agreements were first authorized in 1933, but the law has been amended several times since. Usually the request for such an agreement comes from the producers and handlers. After being petitioned for an agreement, the Department of Agriculture conducts a hearing. An agreement may then be drawn up for the commodity. It becomes effective when signed by handlers of one-half the commodity by volume; if an order is involved, a two-thirds vote of producers on referendum is required.

The usual agreement order involving fruits or vegetables covers both quantity and quality control; the volume of the product flowing on the market is regulated, as is the size or grade. Milk marketing agreements, in 1939 found constitutional,[7] govern minimum prices to producers and modes of payment. Milk marketing orders were effective in 1954 in fifty-three areas.

Thirty-five other agreements and orders covered a variety of citrus and other fruits, vegetables, potatoes, tree nuts, tobacco, and even hog-cholera serum! Under the terms of the act the agreement or order must cover the smallest practicable regional production area; for example, south Florida had an avocado program, but five New England states (excluding Maine) joined in a potato program. Programs, for commodities other than milk, are administered by a committee of growers, or handlers, or both.

Foreign Agriculture. The Foreign Agricultural Service was created in the general departmental reorganization of 1953. It has a variety

[7] U.S. *v.* Royal Rock Cooperative, 307 U.S. 533 (1939).

of responsibilities in the area of external relationship of American agriculture. The possibility of regaining foreign markets for our products is studied. Data on agriculture abroad is compiled. The Service represents the Department in foreign relations and technical assistance matters.

One of its most knotty tasks is to find ways of disposing of surplus farm products in overseas markets without disrupting foreign producers and demoralizing world markets. Although once a leading exporter of farm commodities, the United States by the Second World War was no longer so deeply involved in world trade. Domestic costs of production grew higher than foreign costs in many product fields. Other countries enacted tariffs, import and export controls, and placed other restrictions on the free movement of trade. We, of course, stimulated such action by adopting a high tariff law in 1930.

During the Second World War, America again became one of the great granaries of the world—producing not only for itself, but for much of the allied cause as well. After the war there was an immediate world-wide shortage of food, and the American farmer was able to sell much of his huge production abroad. A good deal of the purchasing from abroad was financed, however, through American grants and loans. In the early 1950's it became apparent that foreign markets for farm commodities were shrinking, as foreign aid declined and farm production in other countries was restored to normal. With American farm production costs at a high level, the outlook for export trade was not encouraging.

RESEARCH AND EXTENSION

Research services, designed to help farmers increase production, were among the earliest services performed by the national government for American agriculture. This work has continued, although its prominence has been surpassed in recent years by the emergence of colossal problems of production control, marketing, and stabilization. The results of research, symbolized by the lighted torch of scientific agriculture, are carried to the farmer through bulletins, extension services, and demonstrations. It may appear contradictory for the government on one hand to show farmers how to increase production through improved seed or stock, disease control, or fertilization, and on the other hand to encourage them to reduce production. Pending the time when some long-range solution is found, the country can scarcely afford to have either inefficient agricultural production or widespread bankruptcy in the farm sector of the economy.

Research. Most of the federal farm-research program is carried out under the Agricultural Research Service, which was created in 1953 by bringing together various agencies and activities already at work in the field. Both basic and applied research are included; among the areas touched are field crops, management, livestock, nutrition and home economics, and farm product utilization. Actually, there is a considerable amount of law enforcement or regulatory work intermingled with, or operating side by side with the research function.

This situation is found both in plant and animal programs. Not only do Department entomologists study insects, seeking methods to control harmful ones and ways to propagate helpful ones, but plant quarantine inspectors check plant life entering the United States, cooperate with the states in controlling insects and diseases attacking plants, and control interstate shipments of plants. On the animal front, extensive investigations are carried out in feeding and breeding, diseases and utilization of farm animals and poultry. Law-enforcement activities involving livestock include meat inspection, supervision of interstate transportation of animals, and quarantine enforcement on diseased animals.

Field and horticultural crops are studied by units of the Department with a view to improving yield, raising quality, reducing costs, and solving other problems. Soil, water, agricultural engineering, and production economic problems are the focus of interest of other branches of the Department. Both human nutrition and home economics have long been subjects of federal research.

The Federal government has not sought to monopolize research services, or even to compete directly with the states. A large share of national moneys spent for farm research is subvented to state experiment stations, for work on projects mutually deemed of importance. Many of the top-rank research projects in agriculture are co-operative federal-state ones, jointly conducted by the Department of Agriculture and one or more experiment stations.

Extension. The channels of information through which the story of research results flows to the farmer are many. The federal Department itself disseminates the results of research through its own information office, which handles publications, and arranges for radio, television, and press releases. The federal Extension Service supervises the national government's participation in the cooperative extension program operated jointly with the land-grant colleges of the states and county governments.

Under the program, agricultural, home-demonstration, and 4-H Club agents are located in most of the counties of America. These "county agents" are federal-state-county missionaries of better agriculture, who establish contact with the farmer and provide direct advice, group demonstrations, exhibits, and various organizational contacts. In important agricultural counties there often are several county agents with different specialties, such as livestock, field crops, and horticulture. They bridge the gap between research and action by bringing to the attention of the farmer the latest developments from laboratory or experimental farm, and by putting him in touch with the state college or federal staff member most likely to be able to help with a given problem.

AGRICULTURAL CREDIT

Another front on which American farmers needed help was credit; to buy land and to equip a farm it becomes necessary for the average agriculturist to go into debt. If the farmer is to succeed, this credit must be available at low interest rates and be repayable over a long period of time. Private capital is available for farm financing in most sections of the country, but where the risk is great the interest charges tend to be high. A small-town bank with heavy investments in farm mortgages may be wiped out by a series of bad crop years. After crop failures the farmers who owe the bank lose their farms through foreclosures.

Under these conditions, it is not surprising that pressure should have been exerted upon the government to assume responsibilities for farm financing.

Farm Credit Administration. The federal agency that coordinates most of the diverse agricultural loan activities is the Farm Credit Administration, which since 1953 has been an independent agency. The Federal Farm Credit Board is the policy-determining body of FCA; it also selects the governor, who exercises the administrative functions of FCA. The Board itself is composed of members appointed by the President for 6-year terms from each of the twelve farm-credit districts, and a thirteenth appointed by the Secretary of Agriculture. A deputy governor heads each of the credit services under FCA: cooperative bank, land bank, production credit, and intermediate credit bank. In addition to the credit services, FCA has a number of central divisions that perform housekeeping and examining functions for the whole farm-credit system. These include finance and accounts, personnel, information and extension, economic and credit analysis, and examination. The FCA is not itself a lending agency; it supervises and regulates the agencies which over the years have been created to provide credit facilities for those who seek to borrow for farm purposes.

Early Farm Loans. In order to understand the complicated farm-credit structure, it is well to see how it all began. The first step was taken in 1916, when Congress created a farm-loan board. The country was divided into twelve districts, in each of which a federal land bank was established to raise money through bond issues, and to lend through farm-loan associations. Short-term credit needs of farmers were provided for in 1923 by the creation of intermediate credit banks in the same districts. In 1933 additional short-term loan facilities were made available through the formation of production-credit corporations. In the same year the credit needs of agricultural cooperatives were met by the establishment of banks for cooperatives.

General Features. One of the outstanding characteristics of the farm-credit system is the extent of mutualization, or sharing of ownership and control by participating institutions and individuals. The twelve federal land banks, source of funds for long-term loans, were mutualized in 1947 when federal capital was replaced by funds of the affiliated farm-loan associations. The second Hoover Commission reported that 355 of the 498 local production-credit associations had their stock wholly owned by farmer members. Further mutualization was recommended in the second Hoover report, both in production-credit associations and in intermediate credit banks.[8]

Some of the farm-credit agencies in effect secure a hidden subsidy by holding government bonds and receiving interest on them, while at the same time using large sums of initial federal investment interest-free. The Hoover report of 1955 urged that such holdings of government bonds be exchanged for non-interest-bearing credits, or repayment of federal moneys invested.

A federal franchise tax of 25 per cent of net earnings was levied under the Farm Credit Act of 1953. By this means Congress sought to ensure some repayment of investment. It appears possible to avoid the tax, however, by keeping the earnings down.

The whole system is greatly decentralized in operation. Farmers secure their loans from local associations in which they are participants. The local associations are mutual or cooperative in nature, and involve a large measure of self-government. Therefore it is appropriate that the actual lending process be considered primarily from the standpoint of the individual farmer who requires credit facilities.

The principal agencies of the Farm Credit Administration are incorporated, and therefore are subject to the provisions of the Government Corporation Control Act.

Long-term Farm Loans. Federal land-bank loans are made through one of the 1,200 national

farm-loan associations. They are long-term borrowings secured by first mortgages upon farms. Interest rates are low, currently ranging from 4 to 5 per cent. While these loans primarily are for the purchase of farm land, the money is available also for improvements of mortgaged farms. If young John Perkins, just home from agricultural college, wants to settle down as a farmer near Sioux City, he first locates a piece of land that is suitable and for sale. He goes to the offices of the Woodbury County National Farm Loan Association and files application for a loan. If he is judged a good risk and the farm a good buy, the association will advance him up to 65 per cent of the value of the land, taking a first mortgage as security. In this case, the loan amounts to $13,000. Perkins must agree to repay in 20 to 30 years by annual or semiannual installments, and must buy some shares of stock in the land bank or local association. When the loan is paid off, the stock is redeemed.

Short-term Farm Credit. In order to finance the operations of producing, harvesting, and marketing of crops, farmers need loans for short periods. Credit is obtained for buying seed, feed, machinery, livestock, and many other purposes. The length of time of a short-term loan may be as long as 1 year. These loans are available from one of the 500 local production-credit associations, which, like the local farm-loan associations, are cooperative organizations of farmers. The local association obtains the money it lends largely from the Federal Intermediate Credit Bank of the farm-loan district, and from the regional production-credit corporations. The overhead financing operations are even more complicated than those connected with long-term farm loans. Farmer Sam Barnard, who needs cash for sugar-beet seed and other production costs in order to plant his next crop, travels to near-by Lamar, Col., and applies to the Prowers County Production Credit Association for a $1,500 loan for 6 months' duration. If the loan is made, Barnard is required to acquire a share in the association; he becomes thereby a voting member of the cooperative.

Credit for Farm Cooperatives. Special provision is made for financing farmers' coopera-

[8] Second Hoover Commission, *op. cit.,* pp. 53–56.

tives. Since 1933 cooperative credit needs have been served by the Central Bank for Cooperatives and the twelve district banks for cooperatives in the farm-credit districts. Farmers' cooperatives are organized for marketing of products, purchasing agricultural supplies, or for

service, and research assistance for agricultural cooperatives. Three program divisions—marketing, purchasing, and management—carry out the main work of the service. Among American farmers, 60 per cent are estimated to belong to cooperatives.

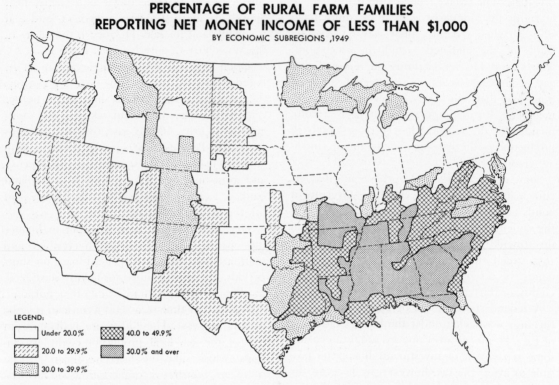

PERCENTAGE OF RURAL FARM FAMILIES
REPORTING NET MONEY INCOME OF LESS THAN $1,000
BY ECONOMIC SUBREGIONS ,1949

LEGEND:

- Under 20.0%
- 20.0 to 29.9%
- 30.0 to 39.9%
- 40.0 to 49.9%
- 50.0% and over

Rural poverty is widely distributed among the several states, but is most heavily concentrated in the South and border states. The American Assembly, *United States Agriculture* (1955), p. 92.

other purposes. The loans are of three types: Commodity loans, for which the interest rate is lowest, are used to finance the handling or processing of farm products. Operating capital loans, at middle interest, provide funds to supplement a cooperative's own capital during peak activities. Facility loans, bearing the highest interest, are used to finance land, buildings, and equipment needed for the cooperative. The cooperatives that borrow are required to buy 5 per cent of their loan in bank-for-cooperatives stock.

The Farmer Cooperative Service of the Department of Agriculture performs educational,

Farmers Home Administration. For small farmers unable to secure credit elsewhere at reasonable rates and terms, the Farmers Home Administration offers assistance and loans. The varied programs of the other lending agencies still do not reach some of the most deserving operators or potential operators of family-sized farms. The Farmers Home Administration also carries out educational and other activities through local offices in about one-half of the counties of the country. Aimed to help the marginal farmer, the program is bound to duplicate many of the services provided by other lending agencies, federal-state extension, and other bodies.

The loans available fall into the following categories:

Operating loans are for purchase of seed or feed, livestock, or fertilizer; they may be used for family living needs; some are made for joint purchase of farm machinery by two or more farmers.

Farm-ownership loans may be used to purchase a farm and to improve it, or to recondition and improve an existing family farm. If the farm is bought by borrowing from a private lending agency, the mortgage may be insured by the Farmers Home Administration.

Water-facility loans are available in the western states both to individuals and to water associations.

Emergency loans may be made, in designated areas, to help farmers who suffer from flood, drought, or other calamity. Special livestock loans have been authorized since 1953.

Veteran assistance is provided for ex-servicemen with agricultural experience, who are made eligible for the various types of loans granted by this agency.

The second Hoover Commission criticized the costliness of Farmers Home Administration programs. It urged that applicants for loans be screened more carefully, that charges on loans made be increased to cover costs, and that more adequate margins between value of property and amount of mortgage be required. Duplication with the Veterans' Administration and county-agent system were subjects of adverse comment by the Commission. The second Hoover task force showed little appreciation for the special problems of rural poverty when it recommended that the lending and insurance functions of the agency be discontinued.

President Eisenhower, on the other hand, recommended a broad program of expanded services to low-income farmers. In transmitting a report to Congress in April, 1955, he declared: "In this wealthiest of nations, where per capita income is the highest in the world, more than one-fourth of the families who live on American farms still have cash incomes of less than $1,000 per year." [9]

Rural Electrification Administration. Created by executive order in 1935, the REA subsequently received statutory authorization, and has operated in the Department of Agriculture since 1939. Initially its purpose was to provide loans to bring electric service to rural people; from 1949 it has been providing financing for rural telephone services as well. The agency does not loan directly to consumers, but to farmers cooperatives and to public and private enterprises providing utility services. In 20 years, REA-financed systems brought electric power to over four million farm homes.

The second Hoover Commission pointed out the considerable taxpayer subsidy involved when the REA borrows from the Treasury at 2 per cent money for which the government must pay 3 per cent to bondholders. Administrative costs also add to the burden on the general public, as do tax exemptions on cooperatives and certain other concessions. The Commission recommended that REA be made self-supporting, secure its financing from private sources, and be made subject to the Government Corporation Control Act.

[9] *Congressional Record,* vol. 101, Apr. 27, 1955, p. 4379. H. Doc. 149.

FOR FURTHER READING

Ackerman, Joseph, and Marshall Harris (eds.): *Family Farm Policy* (University of Chicago Press, 1947).

American Assembly: *United States Agriculture: Perspectives and Prospects* (Columbia University Press, 1955).

Baker, Gladys: *The County Agent* (University of Chicago Press, 1939).

Ball, Carleton R.: *Federal, State, and Local Interrelationships in Agriculture* (University of California Press, 2 vols., 1938).

Benedict, Murray R.: *Farm Policies of the United States, 1790–1950* (Twentieth Century Fund, 1953).

Black, John D.: *Parity, Parity, Parity* (Harvard University Press, 1942).

———: *Agricultural Reform in the United States* (McGraw-Hill, 1929).

Blaisdell, Donald C., Jr.: *Government and Agriculture* (Rinehart, 1940).

Clark, William H.: *Farms and Farmers: The Story of American Agriculture* (Page, 1945).

Davis, Joseph S.: *On Agricultural Policy* (New York: Food Research Institute, 1939).

Deering, Ferdie: *USDA, Manager of American Agriculture* (University of Oklahoma Press, 1945).

Fainsod, Merle, and Lincoln Gordon: *Government and the American Economy* (Norton, 1941).

Gaus, John M., and Leon O. Wolcott: *Public Administration and the United States Department of Agriculture* (Chicago: Public Administration Service, 1940).

Halcrow, Harold G.: *Agricultural Policy of the United States* (Prentice-Hall, 1953).

Hardin, Charles M.: *The Politics of Agriculture* (Glencoe, Ill.: Free Press, 1952).

McConnell, Grant: *The Decline of Agrarian Democracy* (University of California Press, 1953).

Rightmire, George W.: *Federal Aid and Regulation of Agriculture and Private Industrial Enterprise in the United States* (The Ohio State University Press, 1944).

Schickele, Rainer: *Agricultural Policy* (McGraw-Hill, 1954).

Shepherd, Geoffrey S.: *Agricultural Price Income Policy* (Iowa State College Press, 3rd ed., 1952).

Sparks, Earl S.: *History and Theory of Agricultural Credit in the United States* (Crowell, 1932).

Taylor, Paul S.: *Adrift on the Land,* Public Affairs Pamphlet No. 42 (New York: Public Affairs Committee, 1940).

Truman, David B.: *Administrative Decentralization: A Study of the Chicago Field Office of the United States Department of Agriculture* (University of Chicago Press, 1940).

U.S. Commission on Organization of the Executive Branch of the Government (second Hoover Commission): *Lending Agencies* (1955).

———: *Task Force Report on Lending Agencies* (1955).

U.S. Commission on Organization of the Executive Branch of the Government (first Hoover Commission): *Department of Agriculture* (1949).

———: *Task Force Report on Agriculture Activities* (1949).

U.S. Department of Agriculture: *Yearbook* (annual).

Wilcox, Walter W.: *Alternative Policies for American Agriculture,* Public Affairs Bulletin 67 (Library of Congress, 1949).

———: *The Farmer in the Second World War* (Iowa State College Press, 1947).

REVIEW QUESTIONS

1. Is there a bona fide contradiction involved when the government on one hand shows farmers how to produce more and on the other helps farmers to restrict the quantities of farm goods flowing onto the market? Discuss.

2. Describe research activities of the Department of Agriculture and the ways that have been used to get results of research to the farmers.

3. What kinds of credit has the Federal government provided for farmers and for what purposes?

4. Indicate the extent of federal services in the field of marketing farm products.

5. Trace the history of government attempts at farm-production control, with special reference to: McNary-Haugen Bill, AAA of 1933, Soil Conservation and Domestic Allotment, AAA of 1938, etc.

6. Explain the differences in farm-price supports contained in the following: Steagall amendment (wartime), Aiken Act of 1948, Gore-Anderson bills of 1949, and the Agricultural Act of 1954.

7. What was the Brannan plan?

8. How can the government dispose of huge supplies of farm commodities without disrupting home or foreign markets?

9. Give some indication of how widespread rural poverty is in the United States. What extra services or special approaches are needed to help low-income farmers?

CHAPTER 31

Natural Resources

Conservation means the wise use of the earth and its resources for the lasting good of men. Conservation is the foresighted utilization, preservation, and/or renewal of forests, waters, lands, and minerals, for the greatest good of the greatest number for the longest time. — Gifford Pinchot [1]

Nature provided America bounteously with great riches, living and inanimate. The story of man's use of them and of what he has done to preserve them for posterity is of greatest importance. The natural wealth of the United States makes possible a high standard of living if these resources are used wisely. But if our forests, soil, waters, minerals, fish, animals, and birds are exploited and wasted, future generations may be condemned to live in barren poverty.

THE CONSERVATION MOVEMENT

Nature's Balance and After. One of the first observations made by the student of nature is that a sort of balance exists. In the primeval forest a delicate adjustment developed naturally. Trees and grasses held and enriched the soil, and provided food and protection for birds and animals. Waters irrigated vegetation and harbored fish and fowl. Each animal appeared to have its natural enemy or rival, and one form of life rarely triumphed completely and permanently over another. The Indian disturbed the way of

nature but little. He fished and hunted and tilled the soil, but always in moderation. The fine balance of nature remained until the coming of the white man.

The Spoilers. The white man took what he wanted of nature's gifts. He chopped down trees for his houses, he cleared land for his fields, he killed off animals for food and for sport. For 300 years the North American continent was exploited with little consideration for the morrow. After the coming of industrialization the waste became even more obvious. Mineral deposits were tapped and exhausted, and the surface was littered with ugly debris. Mechanical tractors were used to plough up the prairie grasses that sustained life and held down the soil. Industrial plants and cities poured out their waste, polluting streams and rendering their waters unable to sustain fish and impossible for human consumption. Forests were ground up into pulp to feed the mills for paper, rayon, and a hundred other uses. Fabulous wealth was made from petroleum—black gold—but the American people have suffered the depletion of their oil resources and the loss of natural gases burned as waste.

The white man has not yet fully reformed; the spoiler is still around. But increasingly citi-

[1] *Breaking New Ground* (Harcourt, Brace, 1947), p. 505. Elsewhere in the same book, Pinchot credits Mr. W. J. McGee with originating the "greatest good of the greatest number for the longest time."

zens have recognized that the balance of nature must be restored, that the power of the government must be utilized to save what is left and to rebuild the resources that have been exploited. Those who have taken part in this work are called "conservationists," and the total program is called the "conservation movement."

An Inventory. The fact is that the natural resources of the United States already have been devastated and severed to a serious extent. Experts estimate that one-third of the nation's farm land has been ruined or impoverished by soil erosion. The inroads of wind and water are made because our people have overgrazed the grasslands, have farmed land that never should have been ploughed, have cleared land that should have remained in forest. After man removed the protective covering of trees, shrubs, and grasses, erosion began to take away the fertile topsoil, leaving waste lands. The removal of vegetation, together with the added numbers of hunters and fishers, brought death and destruction to wildlife as well.

Below the surface men tap mineral resources to serve a growing population. An obvious ugliness often accompanies severance of subsoil deposits. Even more serious, however, is the likelihood of exhaustion of essential mineral resources like oil, copper, zinc, and lead. At the present rate of severance, these deposits may soon be gone, and this will necessitate vast changes in the economic life of the country.

The Road Back. The original white American conservationist has not been found. Perhaps he was a pilgrim farmer who alternated his crops, or the frontiersman who was careful with his fire and who killed only such game as he could eat, or perhaps it was William Penn, who in 1681 required that one acre out of every five should not be cleared but left in trees. In any case, not all our forefathers were wasters: many recognized that a devastated farm was no heritage for their sons, and therefore did what they could to preserve the land and forests and waters.

Much more is known about the beginnings of organized attempts to save natural resources in the second half of the nineteenth century. One of the first organizations to commence

work in this field was the American Forestry Association, which was launched in 1875.[2] Soon Congress authorized a forestry agent in the Department of Agriculture and established the first national forest reserve in 1891. Attention was given even earlier to protection of fisheries; the post of Federal Commissioner of Fish and Fisheries was created in 1871. Two aspects of conservation developed from sections of the Geological Survey: An irrigation division was established in 1888 and it began federal reclamation work; the attention given to mining in the survey led to the development of the many services of the Bureau of Mines.

Roosevelt and Pinchot. Great impetus was given to the conservation movement during the Theodore Roosevelt Administration (1901–1909). The national forests, previously under the Department of the Interior, were transferred in 1905 to the Department of Agriculture. Roosevelt withdrew millions of acres from the public domain and placed them in national forests. In 1908 President Roosevelt assembled a distinguished company of federal officials, governors of states, and conservationists for a "White House Conference" on conservation. He followed this with the appointment of a National Conservation Commission, which was headed by Chief Forester Gifford Pinchot of Pennsylvania. Its task was to inventory natural resources of the country and to report on the possibility of their exhaustion. By the close of Roosevelt's full term great progress had been made toward saving the public lands and their resources from selfish exploitation, and an auspicious beginning had been made in the modern conservation movement.

Today's Challenge. By mid-century the conservation movement sparked by Theodore Roosevelt had run its course. Great champions like Roosevelt and Pinchot were gone, and public interest in natural resources waned. The public agencies that had been created, the citizens' associations that had been formed, the policies

[2] Wallace W. Atwood, "The Conservation Movement in America," in Almon E. Parkins and Joe R. Whitaker (eds.), *Our Natural Resources and Their Conservation* (Wiley, 2d ed., 1939), p. 3.

that had been written on the statute books—all these might hold the line against those who would overexploit resources *if* the people took an intelligent interest. Much evidence exists to indicate that the spoilers again constitute an acute threat to the nation's natural heritage. Only rarely is the issue black versus white, good against bad. Cattle and sheep graze on public lands under permits issued by federal agencies. Admittedly the livestock industry produces valuable foodstuffs for the American consumer. When, however, the stockman's urge to produce more leads him to overgraze the range, the results may be floods, erosion, destruction of wildlife, and ruin to grasslands.

The attack on conservation is made on many fronts. The Forest Service may be rendered less effective by reducing its appropriations below the level necessary for efficient operation. The public lands may be sold to private interests and thereby taken out of strict regulation. The housing shortage can be used as justification for relaxed standards in logging and reforestation rules. A high tariff can be used to exclude foreign petroleum, thus stimulating the further depletion of domestic reserves. Reclamation laws may be amended to allow big interests to swallow up small ones. So far the line has been held on most fronts. It remains to be seen whether leadership can be found again to stimulate public interest in conservation as did Roosevelt and Pinchot just after the turn of the century.[3]

Federal Conservation Agencies. The federal agencies primarily concerned with conservation of natural resources are located in the Departments of the Interior and Agriculture. The organization of Agriculture is described in Chap. 31. Interior is a vast department that spreads out like a great tent over diverse services. The major operating agencies of the Department which are concerned directly with natural resources are the Bureau of Land Management, Bureau of Reclamation, Fish and Wildlife Service, National Park Service, and Geological Survey. Indirect or less direct work in conservation is done by the

Bureau of Indian Affairs, Oil and Gas Division, and the Bureau of Mines.

In the Department of Agriculture, both the Soil Conservation Service and the Forest Service have jurisdiction over important conservation activities. The Agricultural Conservation Program Service carries out soil- and water-conserving practices on a cost-sharing basis.

A Natural Resources Department? Both the task force of the first Hoover Commission and a minority of the Commission itself recommended the transformation of Interior into a Department of Natural Resources. They proposed that it should consist mainly of existing Interior agencies, plus the water-development functions of the Army Corps of Engineers and the Federal Power Commission, and a few minor activities of other departments. A strong case was made for grouping together the conservation, development, and use of public resources. The Commission majority, however, proposed instead a reorganized Department of the Interior. It proposed to transfer out land management (to Agriculture), commercial fisheries (to Commerce), and Indian affairs (to a new department of social security and education). It recommended that the flood control, rivers, and harbors functions of Army Engineers be brought into Interior; also that a number of other works-type projects be transferred in. Congress failed to follow the recommendations of either majority or minority.

The Department of the Interior. Consequently the Department has continued with rather little change. As organized in 1955, under the general direction of the Secretary were one undersecretary, three assistant secretaries, and one administrative assistant secretary. The staff services such as budget and finance, management research, personnel, property, and security are divisions under the administrative assistant secretary. The solicitor's office and information office are directly under the Secretary.

Most of the operating agencies of the Department are grouped under one of the three assistant secretaries. The assistant secretary for mineral resources supervises the Bureau of Mines, Geological Survey, Division of Oil and Gas, and

---

[3] An able exponent of the conservation revival was the late Bernard DeVoto, who wrote the "Easy Chair" for *Harper's Magazine*.

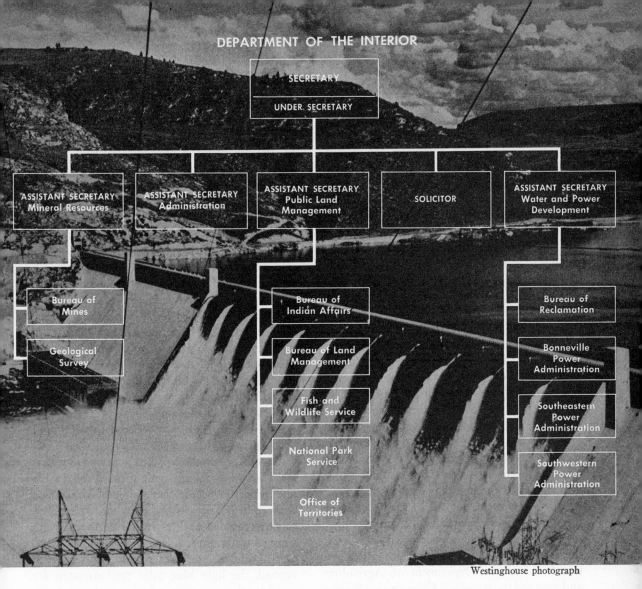

DEPARTMENT OF THE INTERIOR

```
                    SECRETARY
                  UNDER SECRETARY
```

ASSISTANT SECRETARY Mineral Resources	ASSISTANT SECRETARY Administration	ASSISTANT SECRETARY Public Land Management	SOLICITOR	ASSISTANT SECRETARY Water and Power Development
Bureau of Mines		Bureau of Indian Affairs		Bureau of Reclamation
Geological Survey		Bureau of Land Management		Bonneville Power Administration
		Fish and Wildlife Service		Southeastern Power Administration
		National Park Service		Southwestern Power Administration
		Office of Territories		

Westinghouse photograph

others. The assistant secretary for public-land management oversees the Bureau of Land Management, Fish and Wildlife Service, National Park Service, Bureau of Indian Affairs, and Office of Territories. The assistant secretary for water and power development looks after the Bureau of Reclamation and the regional power administrations.

SOIL AND WATER

Soil Conservation. The soil is the No. 1 natural resource. Waste of it has been spread over such a long period, however, that one has difficulty dramatizing the need for its conservation. When lands on the Eastern seaboard declined in fertility, settlers moved on west to new lands. So

long as new lands were still available in the West, farmers were able to avoid the consequences of wasteful cropping. After all good lands were taken up, the problem of proper care of the soil could no longer be avoided. Much more than restoring fertility to the soil was involved. The problem is one of restoring nature's balance or something akin to it.

In the first place, the early settlers removed the natural cover from the ground. The grasses, shrubs, and trees protected the soil from wind and water, conditioned it by adding humus—which made it porous, and restored minerals used in plant growth. Man ploughed and planted, and reaped the harvest. The most obvious destruction that followed came through water erosion. Hilly lands, stripped of the binding power of roots of natural vegetation, gullied and the soil washed down to the lowlands, perhaps to the sea. In many areas the whole layer of topsoil washed away. Moreover, the capacity of the soil to retain moisture was impaired seriously; for few farmers made provision for restoring vegetable matter to the land. The burning strawstack after the harvest often was a symbol of wastefulness and ignorance. After the water erosion came wind erosion: sweeping over cultivated land in the Middle West, winds have been known to carry great quantities of earth for a thousand miles and more across half a continent. Dust storms steal the nation's soil.

The first approach of the American governments to soil conservation was to encourage farmers to adopt soil-saving practices through educational work. The Department of Agriculture has long carried out investigations in soil building, and so have the experiment stations maintained by each of the states. The information is sent to farmers through publications, demonstrations, and the field work of farm-adviser or county-agent extension services. Among practices advocated through the years have been crop rotation, contour ploughing, check dams, reforestation, cover cropping, and the like.

In 1933 a soil-erosion service was established in the Department of the Interior; in 1935 it was transferred to the Department of Agriculture and assigned the name Soil Conservation Service. The service seeks to spread the use of soil-erosion-control practices through (1) demonstrations in selected areas, and (2) assistance of soil-conservation districts organized under state laws. By 1955 there were over 2,500 soil-conservation districts, embracing more than 4½ million farms. The service aids these farmer-managed districts with technical advice, materials, and equipment.

Agricultural Conservation Program. Combining soil and water conservation with stabilization activities, the ACP provides government assistance for farmers carrying out approved practices. The program is administered by the Agricultural Conservation Program Service of the Department of Agriculture. Heavy reliance is placed on the Soil Conservation Service for technical assistance.

Farmers make application to local stabilization and conservation committees for assistance in soil or water conserving practices. Many aspects of the program aim at soil conservation through conversion of tilled-crop land to grassland. Vegetative cover cuts down on erosion by wind and water. Other parts of the program are concerned with saving water resources by such practices as developing dams, wells, springs, and seeps.

In general the extent of government participation is one-half or less; the balance in cash or labor is provided by the cooperating farmer. The program has been subjected to much criticism from time to time: some argue that farmers need not be paid to carry out good husbandry practices; others maintain that the availability of aid induces producers to engage in unnecessary projects. Under the Eisenhower Administration the program was reduced in volume of spending.

Water Conservation. When angry flood waters swirl seaward, taking with them a toll in life and property, people may think of water as a demon. In ordinary times, however, water properly is regarded as life-giver. Enormous quantities of water are required to support plant and animal life. If you take a globe and whirl it around, the light blue color predominates; for roughly three-quarters of the surface of the earth is covered with water. Nature's process, of course, involves the taking up of moisture through evaporation, and returning it to the earth's surface through rain, snow, or other precipitation. Man has not interfered with this cycle seriously, but he has altered the power of the soil to hold moisture and the flow and purity of streams.

When settling in a new section of the country, one of the first considerations of the pioneer was to secure an adequate supply of water. If springs or lakes or streams were not available or were inadequate, wells were dug to tap subsurface waters. As consumption increased, water levels fell and deeper wells were required. Large cities in semiarid districts bring water great distances;

Los Angeles is served from behind the Sierra Nevada Mountains and from the Colorado River, distances of 170 and 270 miles, respectively. Great areas of the West have rich land but insufficient rainfall to support agriculture; vast reclamation projects of the Federal government have made the irrigated deserts bloom.

Government has played a major role in getting water to the people and to the land. Domestic water supply is furnished over much of the country by municipally owned projects. Water for irrigation often is supplied through public irrigation districts.

Reclamation. Although mentioned in connection with the development of hydroelectric power in Chap. 27, the Bureau of Reclamation was created and still functions mainly to bring water to arid and semiarid lands. In constructing irrigation works the Bureau incidentally provides, when possible, for the generation of electricity, the sale of which helps to repay the government for the cost of the development. Also included in the incidental purposes of the agency are flood control, drainage, stream regulation and silt control, provision of recreational facilities, protection of wildlife, and provision of some urban water supply.

The Bureau has constructed dams and other facilities to bring under irrigation over 7 million acres of land. The various laws governing reclamation projects require preference to public and cooperative agencies in power sales, "probable" ultimate repayment of cost of each project through charges and sales, and a 160-acre limitation on size of farm eligible to receive Bureau irrigation water. These restrictions explain in part why members of Congress and would-be users of water or power often prefer to place a given project under the Army Corps of Engineers rather than under the Bureau. Even when the Army constructs and controls a project, however, the marketing of power is assigned to the Bureau of Reclamation.

A sample of one year's work will give a picture of the far-reaching activities of the Bureau. During fiscal 1954, it spent 148 million dollars for new facilities, including dams, power and pumping plants, irrigation canals and laterals, and electric transmission lines. Construction completed during the year added 2.2 million acre-feet of water-storage capacity, nearly 300,000 kilowatts of electric generating capacity, 700 miles of canals and water lines, and more than 100 miles of major electric transmission lines. The water facilities were adequate to provide irrigation for over 320,000 acres of land. Approximately 125,000 irrigated farms received water from Bureau installations; crops valued at over 750 million dollars were harvested during the year. New farms were provided for 389 farm families, totaling 34,126 acres; there were 71 applicants for each farm unit opened for sale or homesteading.

Bureau vs. Corps. The conflict of jurisdiction among federal agencies dealing with water problems was the subject of much adverse comment by the first Hoover Commission. Since the Flood Control Act of 1936 the primary responsibility for flood protection on main streams has rested with the Corps of Engineers, and in the upper reaches with the Department of Agriculture. The Bureau of Reclamation, working on the same streams with irrigation and ancillary objectives, inevitably was in competition. As the task force said: ". . . the one agency working upstream met the other coming down."[4] The two openly contended for projects in the same river basins, including the Missouri, the Columbia, and the Central Valley of California. The first Hoover Commission recommended that the rivers, harbors, and flood-control work of the Army Engineers be transferred to the Department of the Interior,[5] but Congress has not approved and competition continues.

The distinguished task force also commented on friction between the Bureau of Reclamation and the Department of Agriculture over irrigation projects. It proposed that a report from the Department of Agriculture precede the authorization of a new project.

Other Water Problems. Protection of the flow and purity of streams has been approached from

[4] First Hoover Commission, *Task Force Report on Natural Resources* (1949), p. 23.
[5] First Hoover Commission, *Department of the Interior* (1949), p. 35.

several angles. Dams constructed for power, flood control, or domestic and irrigation purposes may serve also to regularize stream flow, which in turn permits fish propagation and recreational uses. Pollution is controlled primarily by state law, prohibiting dumping of industrial waste or raw sewage into rivers. Where a stream flows through several states, interstate action may prove necessary. Such is the case with the Delaware River, which is controlled by the Interstate Commission on the Delaware River Basin (Incodel), an agency of Delaware, New Jersey, New York, and Pennsylvania. Since 1936 this commission has provided the machinery through which joint state action can be planned for the orderly development of the basin and the correction of pollution.

In 1950 the Federal government published an important report on water policy [6] which stressed that the nation's water resources are limited and urged their careful management, conservation, and use. An aggressive program of water-resource development was recommended.

FORESTS AND WILDLIFE

Forest Conservation. In its virgin state, at the beginning of white settlement in North America, the land area that is now the United States was about 42 per cent forested.[7] These forests have been seriously depleted: some of the timber has been used for construction, fuel, and industry; the remainder has been wasted and destroyed. The many uses of wood in modern life are well known: of the total forest cut, 43 per cent is used for lumber and miscellaneous industrial products; 22 per cent for fuel; and 35 per cent is wasted.

It has already been shown that forests provide a natural cover for soil and for animal and bird life. When forests are cleared, soil is exposed to erosion, game is left without protective cover, and streams are filled with silt. Trees also act as

windbreaks, reducing wind erosion of the soil. It also appears that forests have a moderating influence on climate, reducing heat in summer, protecting against cold winds in winter, providing moisture for crops and comfort. The recreational value of forests has been recognized by national, state, and local governments in the parks, forests, and resorts that have been provided for public use and enjoyment.

All this is not to be taken as argument against any severance of the timber in American forests. The usual way of life could scarcely continue without utilization of timber resources. The point is that our remaining forest resources should be used wisely, in order that future generations may have an adequate supply for use and enjoyment. In evaluating the prospects for forest conservation, the ownership pattern of forest lands looms of great importance.

Ownership Pattern. The nation, excluding the territories, has about 622 million acres of forest land, of which 460 million are capable of producing timber on a commercial basis and 162 million are noncommercial. The commercial acreage is held 75 per cent under private ownership and 25 per cent under public.

Privately owned forest lands are about 40 per cent in the hands of farmers, another 35 per cent in small nonfarm holdings, and 25 per cent in large holdings by lumber companies and others.

Since governments hold their forests for purposes other than profit, they can be trusted to resist exploitation of their holdings. In general, logging operations are permitted only on a selective basis, with public foresters marking the trees that may be felled and enforcing rigid specifications for protection of young growth. Farm wood-lot trees are relatively safe from wholesale devastation, for the farmer commonly regards trees as a crop and recognizes the necessity of replanting.

The great problem is regulating the industrial owner of commercial forest lands. He is in the business of cutting and marketing timber products, and his primary motivation often is immediate profit. Mechanized logging operations take not only mature trees but destroy young

[6] U.S. President's Water Resources Policy Commission, *A Water Policy for the American People* (3 vols., 1950). See also p. 522.

[7] U.S. Department of Agriculture, Forest Service, *Our Forest Resources,* Agriculture Information Bulletin 131 (1954), p. 8.

growth and leave debris that constitutes a serious fire hazard. The more progressive lumbering concerns have cooperated with the Forest Service in fire prevention and reforestation work, but some have devastated the forests with little thought of the morrow. Governments can encourage wise use of timber by a tax policy that does not penalize the owner for keeping growing trees to full maturity; some states have done this by exempting forests from ordinary real-property taxes, and collecting instead a severance tax at the time the trees are felled. States can do more than they have to require reforestation by laws, based on the state police power, forcing a replanting program upon concerns or individuals who engage in lumbering operations.

Forest Regions. The geographical distribution of forest lands is worthy of attention. The South has nearly one-third of all forest acreage, but the Pacific coast has by far the greatest quantity of saw timber, capable of use as lumber. An important development in the South during recent years has been the establishment of pulp mills to utilize southern pine. Most of the publicly owned forest lands are in the West; one-half or more of commercial forest areas of the Rocky Mountain and Pacific coast regions are owned by governments. The ownership pattern in all other sections is predominantly private, with all the attendant problems of control. No one can estimate when our forest resources will be exhausted; trees are growing constantly and demand for lumber is inconstant. Virgin forests of large and slow-growing trees are likely to be exhausted rather soon, for their severance exceeds the rate of growth. By constant care and wise management, it is altogether possible that an adequate supply of forest products will be available for generations.

The Forest Service. The Forest Service, Department of Agriculture, is by far the most influential of government agencies working in the field of forest conservation. Custody of the 150 national forests is entrusted to the service. It provides fire protection, disease control, recreational facilities, and regulation of grazing and timber harvesting. In addition, the Forest Service conducts an extensive research program on every aspect of forest management and utilization. The service cooperates with the states in the development of state forests and works with private forest interests in conservation.

Forest Service control, including Alaskan and Puerto Rican forests, extends to 188 million acres, of which 180 million are in national forests. The Federal government began withdrawing forest lands from the public domain in 1891, but it was not until 1911 that the purchase of lands was authorized by law. Most of the national forest lands are remote and inaccessible, a fact that has handicapped the Forest Service in administering them. Many of the federally owned areas are poorly consolidated, being fragmentized by plots under private ownership. Until the Second World War, the Forest Service held most of the national forest timber on a stand-by basis, for use after private holdings were exploited. Despite heavy drains on national forests during and after the war, however, by 1948 they contained one-third of the nation's saw-timber resources. Receipts from timber sales, grazing fees, and other operations pay the expenses of the Forest Service and yield a modest profit.

The general principles that guide the management of the national forests were stated succinctly by the Forest Service as follows:[8] (1) to serve the greatest public good in the long run; (2) to build up and perpetuate forests through wise care and use; (3) to provide maximum public benefits through multiple use; and (4) to work closely with state, local, and regional agencies and to adapt to local conditions.

Other Public Forests. In addition to the vast holdings of the Forest Service, other federal agencies have jurisdiction over nearly 55 million acres of forest lands, of which over 12 million are commercial. The greatest block of this is under the Bureau of Land Management, Department of the Interior, which controls grazing lands, public domain, and certain other lands rich in timber resources. The Bureau of Indian Affairs, Department of the Interior, also manages a vast area of forest lands. The National Park Service

[8] U.S. Department of Agriculture, Forest Service, *Forests and National Prosperity,* Miscellaneous Publication 668 (1948), p. 88.

and other agencies account for the balance of federally owned forest lands.

The extent of state and local ownership of forest lands is approximately 38 million acres, the largest share of which is located in Northern states.

In recent years there has been much controversy over the continuation and expansion of publicly owned lands. Private grazing, lumbering, and other interests complain over the alleged severity of restrictions imposed upon users of federal lands. State and local governments are concerned over the large amounts of tax-exempt land within their territorial jurisdictions. The Forest Service lists six categories for which it regards public ownership of forest lands as best: (1) where soil, climate, species, or other factors make for slow growth or poor quality; (2) where large investment and long waiting will be required because of depletion of timber-growing stock; (3) where private management is inadequate and a threat to stable supplies and dependent communities; (4) where public ownership is vital to control the use of water; (5) where area has high value for recreation, wildlife propagation, and the like; and (6) where lands are so intermingled with public forests that they hamper proper management of the public portion.[9]

Applying such principles as these, and given fair dealing with affected private interests and generous payments in lieu of taxation to other governments, ways can be found to manage public forests and other lands to serve "the greatest good for the longest time."

The National Park Service. Our national park system, containing some of the great natural wonders of the world, is administered by the National Park Service, Department of the Interior. These beautiful park areas are preserved, maintained, and developed for the enjoyment of the people. The brash commercialization that has spoiled some Eastern works of nature is prevented from entering Yellowstone, Yosemite, Sequoia, Grand Canyon, Smoky Mountain, and the other national parks. The primary purpose of the service is to preserve and to develop natural

beauty spots and historical monuments for the recreation and enjoyment of the people. In the 1950's nearly 50 million visitors each year frequented the national parks, which provide a guaranty that the wonders included in them will never be despoiled by man.

Fish and Wildlife Conservation. Since 1940 the fish and wildlife conservation work of the Federal government has been performed by a consolidated Fish and Wildlife Service, Department of the Interior. Previously, two agencies—the Bureau of Fisheries and the Bureau of Biological Survey, both of the Department of the Interior—performed the work in their separate fields. The states have extensive fish and game functions, and much of the primary work of conservation in this field is done through state and local agencies and laws.

Fish represents an important food for man. Many thousands of people have an economic stake in the fishing industry, as fishermen, handlers, or canners. Many more are sportsmen, who fish for recreation and enjoyment. The last factor, especially, has given much impetus to the fish-conservation movement; some of the commercial fishing interests have shown intelligent interest in protecting the supply of fish.

The research investigations that disclose the principles upon which a fish-conservation program shall be based are conducted both by the Federal Fish and Wildlife Service and by the state fish and game agencies. Both levels of government operate hatcheries for the propagation of fishes; the young stock is then planted in suitable waters. State and federal agencies assist and regulate commercial fishermen; state authority is most extensive, but federal jurisdiction extends to the highly important Alaskan seal and salmon industry and permits patrol activities on the high seas under some treaty arrangements. Basic protection is obtained for the fish supply through the enforcement of seasonal limits and quantitative restrictions, mostly imposed by state law. Although at one time certain species of fish almost wholly disappeared, careful management and propagation have restored them.

Native animals and birds provided an important part of the foodstuffs consumed by the

[9] *Ibid.,* p. 91.

pioneers of this country. They are less important today as food but remain valuable for their furs, service to agriculture, and recreational incentive. Many types of wildlife have been reduced to extinction or near extinction. The buffalo, once numbering perhaps 60 million in North America, is now only a few thousand. The beautiful passenger pigeon is fully extinct; wild ducks and geese have been depleted to a fraction of their former numbers; antelope, elk, and moose have become rare. Wildlife has been decimated by excessive hunting and trapping, the destruction of natural haunts, lack of food, and other reasons. Some reduction of wildlife would have seemed inevitable as settlement spread across the country: predatory animals were killed off for good reason; fenced farms reduced the feeding areas of animals.

The Federal Fish and Wildlife Service forms the spearhead of the nation's bird and animal conservation work. It conducts research both of its own and in cooperation with state agencies. The service administers federal grants to states for wildlife restoration. One of its most important duties is to protect migratory birds covered by treaty; it licenses hunters and limits their kill of protected birds. Some 200 wildlife refuges have been created and maintained by the service. In the states well-developed fish and game agencies enforce the game laws, license hunters, and provide refuges and propagation facilities.

MINERALS AND LAND

Mineral Resources. After the Japanese invasion of Malaya and the Netherlands East Indies in 1942, great interest was shown in the loss to this country of its principal source of tin. The needs of modern war for aluminum emphasized our deficiencies in another mineral. The war brought out as nothing ever has the importance of having an adequate supply of the essential mineral resources. The United States was blessed by nature with a greater abundance of mineral deposits than those found in any other country. The chief deficiencies of this country in metals are in chromite, manganese, nickel and tin.[10] Our iron

supply comes primarily from the deposits around Lake Superior; while these may be exhausted in the next generation, adequate quantities of lower grade ore are available for posterity. Copper comes largely from the Western states; while the United States appears to have about one-third of the copper deposits of the world, it is using them at a fairly rapid rate and may someday suffer. Bauxite, the mineral from which aluminum is extracted, is found in Arkansas, but great quantities are imported also from British and Netherlands Guiana. Lead is a major product of Missouri, but the deposits are being mined so rapidly that a serious shortage may result. Zinc is highly important for galvanizing iron to prevent rust; American deposits are mainly in Oklahoma and New Jersey and are sufficiently limited to cause concern over future supply. Gold and silver are found in considerable quantities in the United States. The country is short on both chromium and manganese, which are so essential in steel production. Nickel and high-grade iron ore are available in Canada.

Prof. H. Ries has pointed out several methods by which mineral resources may be conserved: (1) Improved mining methods can reduce waste; (2) better processes of mineral separation to avoid loss; (3) more economical use of finished products; (4) extensive use of scrap materials; (5) federal and state measures of conservation to promote saving.[11] The Federal and state governments are working on each of the fronts suggested. The Bureau of Mines, Department of the Interior, carries on research programs touching upon the first four points mentioned above. It carries out a safety program directed toward saving life and property from loss in mining accidents. It produces helium gas for use by the Army and Navy. The bureau has extensive responsibilities for carrying out investigations of strategic minerals.

Still broader is the work of the Geological Survey, Department of the Interior, which in-

[10] See Charles K. Leith and D. M. Liddell, *The Mineral Resources of the United States and Its Capac-*

ity for Production (1936). A National Resources Board study.

[11] Heinrich Ries, "Conservation of Mineral Resources," in A. F. Gustafson and Others, *Conservation in the United States* (Comstock, 1939), p. 354.

vestigates mineral and water resources, classifies public lands, prepares topographic maps. The Survey is in a commanding position over government lands, in its role of supervisor of oil, gas, and mining operations under leases. It also investigates water supplies. During the war it was given crucial tasks in finding new sources of strategic minerals.

Coal Conservation. Coal is one of the most valuable nonmetal mineral resources. It is plenti-

SOURCES OF ENERGY
Quadrillions of British Thermal Units

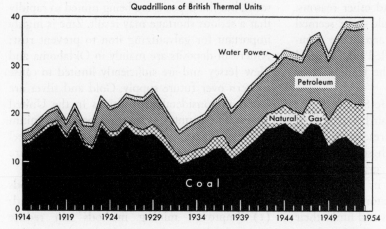

The United States is consuming ever larger amounts of energy, but the share of coal is declining and the roles of natural gas, petroleum, and water power are increasing. Courtesy of National Industrial Conference Board.

ful in the United States, with reserves adequate to care almost indefinitely for the needs of a great population. The distribution over the country is rather well known. Anthracite, or hard coal, is found only in the eastern half of Pennsylvania. Bituminous, soft coal, is found in a belt stretching from Pennsylvania to Alabama, on both sides of the Mississippi River, and in the southern Rocky Mountains. The lower grades of coal, lignite and subbituminous, are scattered through the South and West. New England and the Pacific coast are almost wholly without usable coal deposits.

The Bureau of Mines devotes much attention to coal production and utilization. Because the demand for coal slumped after the First World War, especially in the 1930's, special arrangements were made to care for the sick industry. The first remedial legislation was the Bituminous Coal Conservation Act of 1935, known as the Guffey Act, declared unconstitutional in Carter

v. Carter Coal Co.[12] In 1937 Congress enacted the more modest Bituminous Coal Act, which finally expired in 1943. The conservation aspects of its work were meager, for it existed primarily to enforce a code that covered fair trade practices, minimum prices, and the like. State governments and universities provide many services to coal miners and coal users.

Federal Land Policy. The greater portion of the country's land has, at one time or another, belonged to the Federal government. Had the government kept title to these lands, the tasks of planning and conservation might be much simpler today. On the other hand, the inducement of lands in the West drove men to seek their fortunes on the frontier. Of the total public lands most were turned over to state and private owners. These included homesteads, sales, grants to states, and grants to railroads. The acreage remaining under federal title included national forests and parks, grazing districts, Indian reservations, and other lands withdrawn from entry.

The Bureau of Land Management, Department of the Interior, is the agency with general custody of public lands. It handles the survey, management, and disposition of the public domain. Virtually all government lands suitable for agriculture have long since been granted or sold. The Bureau issues permits and leases for

[12] 298 U.S. 238 (1936).

grazing, mining, and other uses of the lands under its jurisdiction.

Grazing Problems. Among the most troublesome problems connected with public lands is the issuance and administration of grazing per-

privileges on a competitive-bid basis. Except on Indian lands, there is considerable pressure exerted by cattle and sheep raisers to secure allocations, for the fees charged are generally lower than the value of the forage available.

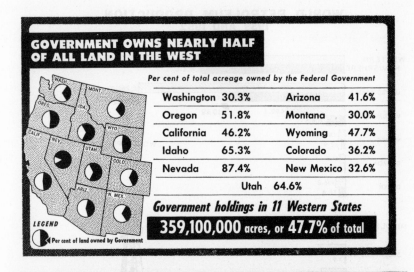

GOVERNMENT OWNS NEARLY HALF OF ALL LAND IN THE WEST

Per cent of total acreage owned by the Federal Government

Washington	30.3%	Arizona	41.6%
Oregon	51.8%	Montana	30.0%
California	46.2%	Wyoming	47.7%
Idaho	65.3%	Colorado	36.2%
Nevada	87.4%	New Mexico	32.6%
	Utah	64.6%	

Government holdings in 11 Western States
359,100,000 acres, or 47.7% of total

LEGEND — Per cent of land owned by Government

WHAT FEDERAL LANDS ARE USED FOR

Principal use	Number of acres	Principal use	Number of acres
Forests and wildlife	186.3 million	Reclamation and irrigation	8.8 million
Grazing	169.6 million	Flood control and navigation	3.2 million
Military (except airfields)	15.2 million	Industrial uses, including atomic energy	1.8 million
Airfields	2.0 million	Power development	1.5 million
Parks and historic sites	15.0 million	Sites for hospitals, offices, storage, housing, other purposes	1.7 million

TOTAL LAND OWNED BY THE GOVERNMENT IN THE U.S. — **405.1 million acres**
OR **21.3% of entire country**

Government ownership of such a large proportion of Western land area poses acute problems of financing local governmental services. Reprinted from *U.S. News & World Report,* an independent weekly news magazine published at Washington. Copyright, 1955, United States News Publishing Corporation. Issue of Apr. 29, 1955.

mits. An abundant source of difficulty is the different bases for fixing grazing fees that are employed by the several government agencies concerned. The Forest Service formula includes the value of the forage and fluctuations in livestock prices. Rather flat, inflexible fees are charged by the Bureau of Land Management. The Bureau of Indian Affairs awards grazing

Some idea of the extent of the problem can be gained from the statistics on permits issued and livestock grazed. In the 1950's, the Forest Service was issuing annual permits to around 25,000 stockmen, for approximately 1 million cattle and 3 million sheep. The Bureau of Land Management had outstanding, within its established grazing districts, about 20,000 permits, covering about 2½ million cattle and 6½ million sheep; nearly 10,000 additional stockmen had grazing leases. Indians grazed their livestock free on more than 75 per cent of Indian range land, but over 10 million acres was used by non-

Indian Affairs. An aspect of conservation and of social welfare that is frequently neglected, concerns the first American—the Indian. Unfortunately public policy on Indian problems has been inconsistent, and government has at

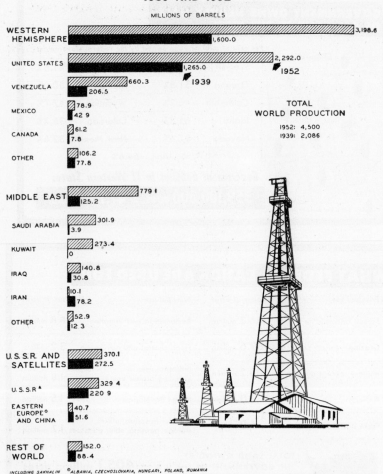

WORLD PETROLEUM PRODUCTION
1939 AND 1952

MILLIONS OF BARRELS

WESTERN HEMISPHERE — 3,198.6 / 1,600.0

UNITED STATES — 2,292.0 / 1,265.0 — 1952 — 1939

VENEZUELA — 660.3 / 206.5

MEXICO — 78.9 / 42.9

CANADA — 61.2 / 7.8

OTHER — 106.2 / 77.8

TOTAL WORLD PRODUCTION
1952: 4,500
1939: 2,086

MIDDLE EAST — 779.1 / 125.2

SAUDI ARABIA — 301.9 / 3.9

KUWAIT — 273.4 / 0

IRAQ — 140.8 / 30.8

IRAN — 10.1 / 78.2

OTHER — 52.9 / 12.3

U.S.S.R. AND SATELLITES — 370.1 / 272.5

U.S.S.R.ᵃ — 329.4 / 220.9

EASTERN EUROPE° AND CHINA — 40.7 / 51.6

REST OF WORLD — 152.0 / 88.4

INCLUDING SAKHALIN   °ALBANIA, CZECHOSLOVAKIA, HUNGARY, POLAND, RUMANIA

World petroleum output in 1952 was more than double pre-war levels. Although our reserves are limited, the United States is in a relatively strong position. Courtesy of National Industrial Conference Board.

Indians under cash permits. Most of the permits issued by the three agencies are for summer grazing, often at high elevations.

Although their methods differ, the objectives and many of the problems of the agencies are similar. The stock-carrying capacity is limited, and overgrazing leads to the destruction of protective vegetation and erosion. The job is to manage the limited resources to assure their regeneration.

times neglected our aboriginals, and at others has been overpaternalistic toward them. It has been estimated that the Indian population in 1492 was close to 850,000; in 1865 was under 300,000; the 1950 census showed 343,410 Indians in the 48 states and the District of Columbia. Our national history is blotted with episodes of land seizure, massacre, and treaty violation that has reduced the Indian to a pitiful condition.

Federal responsibilities have been in two areas:

The government is trustee for Indian lands and moneys; and it provides welfare, health, educational, and other services not otherwise available.

The lands held for Indian tribes and individuals total more than 54 million acres. Under the Indian Reorganization Act of 1934, Indian societies were recognized and given added power to govern themselves and their property. The Eisenhower Administration pushed termination of federal trusteeship, and the disposition of Indian property. Until full termination, however, Indian lands require much help in soil and water conservation, mineral development, and forest management. And few states with large Indian populations (Oklahoma, Arizona, New Mexico, have the largest) can or will soon offer Indians the full range of public services available to other citizens.

Critics of quick termination fear that it will intensify the poverty, ill-health, and ignorance that are so widespread among the Indian population. Legislation in 1953 permitted states, at their discretion, to extend their civil and criminal jurisdiction to Indian communities within their borders. The way appears to have been opened to violation of historic Indian rights and privileges, and perhaps interference with tribal self-government. Something approaching chaos may result from the pattern of termination set up for the Klamath Indian reservation over a 4–7 year period. Members of the tribe wishing to withdraw their shares are paid off by selling some tribal property; in view of the valuable timber lands of the Klamath, these individual shares may average more than $20,000; few are expected to make good use of the capital sum; some are likely to sustain complete loss.

The first Hoover Commission dealt with Indian affairs.[13] Its organizational recommendation was that the Bureau of Indian Affairs be transferred to the new department of social security and education. Its chief substantive recommendation was that the best solution of the "Indian problem" was integration of Indians into the rest of the population. Pending integration, it held that social programs for Indians should be

[13] *Social Security and Education, Indian Affairs* (1949), pp. 34–80.

transferred to the states. Leading commissioners dissented.

The Continental Shelf. Although the Congress by law in 1953 gave the states jurisdiction over the natural resources of their offshore territorial waters, the same act claimed for the Federal government the "continental shelf" beyond. The ex-

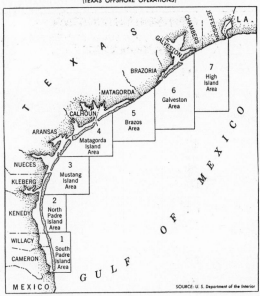

OUTER CONTINENTAL SHELF LEASING MAPS
(TEXAS OFFSHORE OPERATIONS)

SOURCE: U. S. Department of the Interior

The Submerged Lands Act of 1953 stipulated that Texas should have control of the coastal area three leagues (about 10.5 miles) into the Gulf of Mexico. Auctioning of leases off the Texas shore began in 1955 without serious incident.

tent of state jurisdiction, under the Submerged Lands Act, was to be the seaward limits as they were at the time the state was admitted to the union. In no case, however, were states to reach more than 3 miles into the Atlantic or Pacific, or 3 marine leagues (about 10½ miles) into the Gulf of Mexico. Not long after the legislation went into effect, the Federal government found itself in conflict with the maritime states over proper definition of seaward boundaries.

Petroleum resources of immense value are at stake, particularly in the Gulf area. Texas and Florida entered the union with their historic boundaries of 3 leagues into the sea, set by Spanish usage. Louisiana has claimed submerged lands as far out into the Gulf as 27 miles; Department of the Interior offers to lease for oil drilling the area beyond 3 miles come into direct conflict with Louisiana claims. The dispute will require a court decision before it is settled. California lays claim to as far as 30 miles offshore, the location of an outer chain of islands.

boundaries of the United States extend as far as the continental shelf, but that its jurisdiction over resources does.

The Outer Continental Shelf Lands Act of 1953 [14] authorizes the exploration and development of natural resources on submerged lands. It has been estimated that the "quitclaim" leg-

OUTER CONTINENTAL SHELF LEASING MAPS
(LOUISIANA OFFSHORE OPERATIONS)

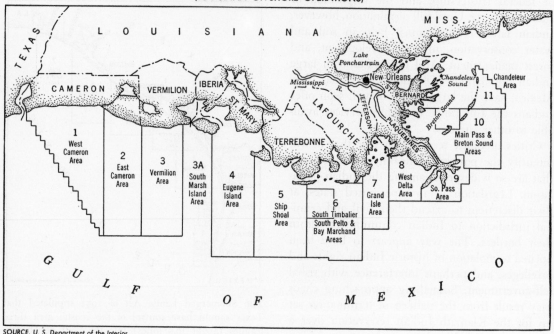

SOURCE. U. S. Department of the Interior

The 1953 act failed to recognize Louisiana's claims of jurisdiction beyond the customary three-mile limit. The United States brought suit against Louisiana to determine the state's historic boundary.

The 3-mile limit is the most widely recognized under international law, and the United States traditionally has supported this definition of territorial waters in the interests of the freedom of the seas. The claim of the "continental shelf," however, conflicts sharply with the concept of a 3-mile limit. Under contemporary interpretations, the shelf is conceived to be the shallow waters, usually under 600 feet, adjacent to territorial waters. In the Atlantic this definition could mean federal claim to submerged lands stretching up to 250 miles offshore; in the Gulf the shelf extends as much as 140 miles. The government has been careful not to claim that the

islation of 1953, giving the states jurisdiction over resources in and under territorial waters, allocated to the states only about 10 per cent of submerged lands. The 90 per cent claimed by the Federal government in the continental shelf included some proven oil producers and a great deal of promising area for exploration. In the Gulf area, despite the hazards of stormy weather, oil drilling has been carried on successfully from platforms resting on piles driven into submerged land through considerable water depths. Leasing maps have been prepared by the Department

[14] 67 Stat. 462.

of the Interior, but the conflict with the states on the extent of state jurisdiction must be settled before much progress can be made. The larger problem, which may ultimately be resolved in an international tribunal, concerns the power of an individual nation to make exclusive claims over the resources of an adjacent continental shelf.

FOR FURTHER READING

American Forestry Association: *American Forests* (Washington: The Association, monthly)

Bartley, Ernest R.: *The Tidelands Oil Controversy* (University of Texas Press, 1953).

Bateman, Allan M.: *Economic Mineral Deposits* (Wiley, 1942).

Bennett, Hugh Hammond: *Soil Conservation* (McGraw-Hill, 1939).

Chase, Stuart: *Rich Land, Poor Land* (McGraw-Hill, 1936).

Ciriacy-Wantrup, S. von: *Resource Conservation: Economics and Policies* (University of California Press, 1952).

Clawson, Marion: *Uncle Sam's Acres* (Dodd, Mead, 1951).

De Roos, Robert W.: *The Thirsty Land: The Story of the Central Valley Project* (Stanford University Press, 1948).

Dewhurst, J. Frederic, and Others: *America's Needs and Resources* (Twentieth Century Fund, 1947).

Du Puy, William A.: *The Nation's Forests* (Macmillan, 1938).

Finch, V. C., and Others: *The Earth and Its Resources* (McGraw-Hill, 2d ed., 1948).

Flynn, Harry E., and Floyd E. Perkins: *Conservation of the Nation's Resources* (Macmillan, 1941).

Gabrielson, Ira: *Wildlife Conservation* (Macmillan, 1941).

Glover, Katherine: *America Begins Again* (McGraw-Hill, 1939).

Gulick, Luther H.: *American Forest Policy* (Duell, Sloan & Pearce, 1951).

Gustafson, Axel F., and Others: *Conservation in the United States* (Comstock, 2d ed., 1944).

Holbrook, Stewart H.: *Burning an Empire: The Story of American Forest Fires* (Macmillan, 1943).

Ise, John: *United States Oil Policy* (Yale University Press, 1926).

Jacks, Graham V., and R. O. White: *Vanishing Lands* (Doubleday, 1939).

Leith, Charles K.: *World Minerals and World Peace* (Brookings, 1943).

National Parks Association: *Natonal Parks Magazine* (quarterly).

Neuberger, Richard L.: *Our Promised Land* (Macmillan, 1949).

Ordway, S. H.: *Resources and the American Dream* (Ronald Press, 1953).

Parkins, Almon E., and Joe R. Whitaker (eds.): *Our National Resources and Their Conservation* (Wiley, 2d ed., 1939).

Parks, W. R.: *Soil Conservation Districts in Action* (Iowa State College Press, 1952).

Pinchot, Gifford: *Breaking New Ground* (Harcourt, Brace, 1947).

Raushenbush, Stephen (ed.): "The Future of Our Natural Resources," *Annals of the American Academy,* vol. 281 (May, 1952).

Renner, George T.: *Conservation of Natural Resources: An Educational Approach to the Problem* (Wiley, 1942).

Robbins, Roy M.: *Our Landed Heritage, the Public Domain, 1776–1936* (Princeton University Press, 1942).

Royal Institute of International Affairs: *World Production of Raw Materials,* Information Department Papers, No. 18B (London: Oxford, 1941).

Schulz, W. F.: *Conservation Law and Administration* (Ronald Press, 1953).

Smith, Guy-Harold (ed.): *Conservation of Natural Resources* (Wiley, 1950).

U.S. Commission on Organization of the Executive Branch of the Government (first Hoover Commission): *Reorganization of the Department of the Interior* (1949).

——: *Task Force Report on Natural Resources* (1949).

U.S. Department of Agriculture, Forest Service: *Forests and National Prosperity*, Misc. Publication 668 (1948).

——: *A National Plan for American Forestry*, S. Doc. 12, 74th Cong., 1st Sess. (2 vols., 1933).

U.S. Department of the Interior, Bureau of Reclamation: *The Reclamation Era* (monthly).

U.S. Department of the Interior, Fish and Wildlife Service: *Fishery Resources of the United States*, H. Doc. 51, 78th Cong., 1st Sess. (1945).

Watkins, Myron W.: *Oil: Stabilization or Conservation?* (Harper, 1937).

REVIEW QUESTIONS

1. What is the conservation movement? What work remains for it to do?

2. Describe the problem of soil conservation. What has the Federal government done to help with the problem?

3. Why are forest resources so important to the nation? What is the role of the Forest Service in preserving them for posterity?

4. Which minerals of strategic importance are deficient in the United States? Which others are seriously being depleted?

5. Why should this country spend money for fish and wildlife conservation?

6. What agencies of the Federal government have roles in the conservation of water? To what extent is their jurisdiction overlapping?

7. Where has federal legislation drawn the line of demarcation between state and federal control over offshore natural resources? Discuss some of the problems that have arisen in granting petroleum leases.

8. What did the second Hoover Commission recommend concerning further federal water projects?

9. What is the purpose of the national park system?

10. Describe the functions of the Bureau of Land Management of the Department of the Interior.

11. What recent changes have been made in Indian policy?

12. Does the Federal government own too much land in the western states? Why or why not?

ON THE FACING PAGE: Pennsylvania Turnpike. (*Standard Oil Co. (N.J.)*)

State and Local Governments

Public Works Magazine →

Colorado Municipalities ↑

Government at the local level is responsible for operating many services encountered daily. At the top of the opposite page is shown a Texas town council in session. Services of local government in-

Florida Municipal Record ↓

↑ *Library of Congress photo*   *Western City* →

clude disposal of garbage, operation of health clinics, maintenance of bridges, and protection by a well-organized fire department.

Seattle's Ross Dam and powerhouse, shown at the left, is one of the great municipal power projects in the Northwest. Below at the left is Cincinnati's new sewage-treatment plant, and at the right is a new high school in Aiken County, South Carolina.

↑ *Seattle City Light*

← *Westinghouse*

Architectural Record, Joseph W. Molitor, photographer ↑

CHAPTER 32

State Constitutions and Powers·

> Some States are still entangled in outworn constitutions written to restrain rather than to facilitate governmental actions; to maintain status quo rather than to adjust to new conditions and requirements. — Leonard D. White [1]

The basic principles of state and local government in the United States are set forth in the constitutions of the forty-eight states. The state constitution with which most people are familiar is the written constitution, but there are principles and rules of great importance that may not be recorded in the formal document at all. As with the Federal government, they become part and parcel of the fundamental law through custom and usage, judicial interpretation, statutory elaboration, and other means. Most of this chapter will be devoted to a consideration of the written constitutions, as construed by the courts.

CONSTITUTIONS PAST AND PRESENT

Study of state constitutions, and indeed of state governments generally, is difficult because of their diversity in form and content. One's natural interest is in the constitution of the state in which he lives. Why, then, should one take the trouble to examine the institutions of other states? The answer is that some comparative study is necessary in order to see a single state government in perspective. Through the experience of other states, one may learn the wisdom or pitfalls involved in a certain course of action or inaction. Moreover, this is one nation, and

it is no longer possible for a person to fulfill his civic responsibilities by being merely a good Vermonter or Texan or Oregonian or Minnesotan. Moreover, migration from state to state is an old American custom, recently revived in intensified form. A general view of American state institutions can provide orientation for closer study of a particular state.

Early State Constitutions. The general situation regarding colonial and early state governments has been traced already in Chap. 2, entitled Colonization, Independence, and Confederation. Most of the colonial "constitutions" were such in the British sense of basic principles rather than the later American sense of formal documents. The charter and proprietary types of colonies had fairly definite written limitations; the royal colonies had restrictions placed upon them through instructions to governors and by other means. Walter F. Dodd found three principles emerging from colonial experience and thought: (1) written instruments of government, (2) constitutions paramount over statute law, and (3) the theory of social contract.[2]

These principles and theories led the states during the Revolutionary War either to adopt

[1] *The States and the Nation* (Louisiana State University Press, 1953), p. 56.

[2] Walter F. Dodd, *The Revision and Amendment of State Constitutions* (Johns Hopkins Press, 1910), pp. 2–3.

wholly new constitutions or to revise existing charters, as did Rhode Island and Connecticut. There was no standard pattern by which new constitutions were framed and adopted. The methods used in drafting and ratifying the new constitutions finally adopted are shown in the table below.

The legislative bodies that played a key role in framing the new constitutions were variously known as provincial congresses, houses of representatives, general courts, provincial conventions, and assemblies. They were urged to act by the Continental Congress on three occasions during 1775 and 1776. Although drafted in haste by revolutionary bodies amid war and turmoil, the constitutions framed contained principles and provisions that have been in continuous use since that time. In one instance, that of Massachusetts, much of the original constitution is still in force.

In content these early state constitutions are of considerable interest to present-day students of government. Bills of rights were included in the constitutions of Virginia, Pennsylvania, Massachusetts, and others, but such instruments did not become a uniform feature of state fundamental laws until considerably after the Revolutionary War. The legislature was made the strongest branch of government. A bicameral body, except in Pennsylvania (until 1790), Georgia (until 1789), and Vermont (until 1836), the legislature was provided with a second chamber through the transformation of the governor's council into the state senate. Senators usually were elected directly for short terms, as were members of the lower house in most states.

Governors were made elective in four of the states and were selected by the legislature in the others. In the beginning only Massachusetts permitted the governor to veto legislation. Most of the original constitutions made many actions of

Framing and Adopting State Constitutions, 1776–1783 *

A. Drafting

Framed by	Authority	States
Legislative bodies	No express power	Virginia, New Jersey
Legislative bodies	Power expressly given	Delaware, Georgia, Maryland, New York, North Carolina, Pennsylvania, South Carolina, Vermont
Constitutional conventions	Chosen for purpose	Massachusetts, New Hampshire

B. Ratifying

Ratification	States
No ratification; proclaimed in effect	Delaware, Georgia, New Jersey, New York, Vermont, Virginia
Informal ratification through circulation among people, or advance instructions from people	Maryland, Pennsylvania, North Carolina, South Carolina
Popular ratification by vote of people	Massachusetts, New Hamsphire

* For a fuller account see Walter F. Dodd, *The Revision and Amendment of State Constitutions* (Johns Hopkins Press, 1910), pp. 3–29, and James Q. Dealey, *Growth of American State Constitutions* (Ginn, 1915), pp. 24–31. Rhode Island and Connecticut merely adapted their written charters.

the governors subject to approval by an executive council, which was selected by popular or legislative vote.

The judicial systems of Colonial days were carried over to the period of statehood with few changes. In most of the states, high court judges were either elected by the legislatures or appointed by the governors, often with senate or executive council approval.

The amending process was ill provided for in the original constitutions. In four states there was no provision for amendment at all; three permitted final action by the legislature; two provided for a council of censors that had power to call a constitutional convention; others used combinations and variations of the above methods.

Form and Content of State Constitutions. A review of state constitutions of today[3] reveals a general pattern with detailed variations. Just as human beings are long and short, plump and thin, yet possess similar limbs and organs, so the documents of state fundamental law vary in size and arrangement but have the same basic features. The typical state constitution includes the following features: (1) a bill of rights, guaranteeing civil liberties and rights; (2) an outline of the framework of government, providing for legislative, executive, and judicial branches; (3) enumeration of state powers and responsibilities; (4) provision for local government; (5) an amending clause, indicating the methods of formal constitutional change.

Preamble. The opening clauses of state constitutions uniformly are statements of aspirations and purposes. These preambles are similar to that in the Federal Constitution, except that the state clauses lean heavily upon divine guidance. The assertion of popular sovereignty is almost invariably found in the enacting clause. Most states use "We, the people . . . do ordain and establish . . ."

Bills of Rights. All state constitutions include bills of rights, although a majority call the article

"Declaration of Rights." Many existing state constitutions were adopted before the Fourteenth Amendment, which protects individual rights against the encroachment of state governments, was added to the Federal Constitution. Therefore, good reasons existed for a rather full statement of civil liberties, and some of these reasons are valid today. For example, state guaranties in respect to suffrage, judicial trials, and certain other fields are clearly in the area of state competence and are worth retaining.

On the other hand, there are several categories of obsolete and redundant guaranties contained in state bills of rights. Little good purpose is served by the expressions of the social-contract theory, drawn from eighteenth-century philosophers, or the elaborate statements of popular sovereignty, so dear to the hearts of phrasemakers. Some of the assertions of property rights are positively harmful, for they add to the already adequate guaranties of the federal Fourteenth Amendment and thus plague state legislatures in seeking solutions to acute social and economic problems. The model state constitution of the National Municipal League confines the bill of rights to twelve brief sections, yet appears to overlook no guaranty of importance. Now that much of the Federal Bill of Rights has been applied to states, perhaps two-thirds of the provisions of bills of rights could be eliminated without loss.

Structure of Government. The principal branches of state government generally are provided for in this order: legislative, executive, and judicial. About one-half the state constitutions specifically provide for the separation of powers through a "distribution of powers" clause; in the other states separation is presumed, as in the Federal Constitution, from the clauses creating the three branches of government. In respect to the legislature, many constitutions include requirements that become impossible of fulfillment, such as the common provision that bills must be read aloud three times; if this were honored in states where the volume of legislation is great the work of the legislature would indeed never be done. The better constitutions provide only a basic framework for the three

[3] A good compilation is New York State Constitutional Convention Committee, *Constitutions of the States and United States* (Albany: The Committee, 1938).

branches of government and leave details to be filled in subsequently by legislation.

Functions of Government. Most state constitutions specify in some detail what the state's activities may be. Powers over taxation and finance often are restricted. Education is made a state function. The responsibility of the state for

Proposal by Constitutional Convention. The constitutional convention is the recognized device for effecting a general revision of a state constitution. Provision for calling a convention is found in the fundamental laws of thirty-seven states. The methods by which a convention is called may be classified as follows: [4]

Methods of Calling a State Constitutional Convention

Legislature, majority	Alabama, Arizona, New York, Oklahoma, Oregon, Rhode Island, Tennessee, Virginia, West Virginia, Wisconsin. (Kentucky requires a majority in two successive sessions)
Legislature, two-thirds	California, Colorado, Delaware, Florida, Georgia, Idaho, Illinois, Kansas, Maine, Minnesota, Montana, Nevada, New Mexico, North Carolina, Ohio, South Carolina, South Dakota, Utah, Washington, Wyoming
Legislature, three-fifths	Nebraska
Question of calling mandatory in a given period (years indicated opposite state)	Iowa (10), Maryland (20), Michigan (16), Missouri (20), New Hampshire (7), New York (20), Ohio (20), Oklahoma (20)

regulating various business enterprises is established.

Local Government. A majority of the state constitutions contain provisions regarding the structure and powers of local authorities. In the home-rule states, the cities (some include counties) may, under certain circumstances, frame their own charters and conduct their local affairs without state interference.

Amending Clause. Three modes of proposing amendments are found in state constitutions: (1) by constitutional conventions, (2) by legislatures, and (3) by the people through initiative. Ratification is by popular referendum in nearly all states. A fuller discussion of the amending process appears in the next section.

CONSTITUTIONAL AMENDMENT

Although state constitutions, like the Federal, are constantly subject to change through alterations in usage, legislative action, judicial decisions, and other means, this section is devoted to formal amendments only.

In thirty-five of the states having definite provision for constitutional conventions, the question of calling a convention is placed before the people in the form of a referendum proposition. In all cases a majority vote is required to call the convention; in some cases this is a majority of those voting on the proposition and in others a majority of those participating in the election. Even in some states which have no provision for calling a convention, the courts have held the legislature possesses such power.

In structure, the constitutional convention is unicameral. In basis of representation, most delegates are elected by state legislative or congressional districts, but some occasionally are chosen on an at-large basis. New York's convention of 1938 had 168 delegates, of whom 153 were elected from state senate and assembly districts and 15 at large. Missouri's convention of 1943–

---

[4] These data are adapted from *The Book of the States, 1954–1955,* pp. 68–73. Hawaii's newly framed constitution makes the question of calling a convention mandatory every 10 years.

1944, which framed the first wholly new constitution adopted in an American state in 35 years, had 83 delegates, of whom 68 were elected by state senatorial districts and 15 at large.

In procedure, conventions usually have a free hand. They elect their own officers and make their own rules. Sometimes a legislature places limitations on a convention's powers, but normally that body is left free to propose whatever constitutional changes—complete or partial—it desires. Of necessity, conventions operate through committees so that they can give detailed consideration to particular problems. Approximately one-half the states which authorize constitutional conventions require that the proposals of the convention be placed before the people in a referendum; the legislatures in the remaining states often require a popular referendum on proposed changes when the law creating the convention is passed. Unless forbidden in constitution or law, a convention could proclaim a new constitution in effect without ratification, as was done in Virginia in 1902 and in Louisiana in 1921. Constitutional changes proposed by the constitutional convention may be in the form of (1) a whole new constitution, (2) a series of amendments, or (3) some alternative propositions. Except in Georgia, Missouri, and New Jersey, no complete revision has been adopted since 1909. Therefore, conventions have been inclined to propose piecemeal constitutional reform often relegating controversial matters into a series of alternative propositions.

Proposal by Legislatures. By far the most prolific source of proposals to amend constitutions is the state legislature. All states except one authorize the proposal of constitutional changes by the legislature; New Hampshire alone makes no provision. It is common to require more than an ordinary majority vote in the legislature to pass a constitutional amendment for submission to a referendum vote of the people. Eighteen states require a two-thirds vote in the legislature; eight require three-fifths; [5] three others require passage by more than a simple majority at two successive sessions. Nine states require a majority vote in the legislature for two successive sessions. Only in nine states does a simple majority in a single session suffice.

The legislature is in a good position to initiate constitutional amendments. It is in session regularly. Its work is of such a nature as to reveal needs for constitutional change. On the other hand, sole responsibility for initiating amendments ought not to be vested in the legislature, for, with the aid of a rotten-borough system of representation, it might hold out against public opinion.

Proposal by Constitutional Initiative. Twelve states permit the people to originate constitutional amendments directly. The constitutional initiative involves drafting a proposal and circulating it in the form of a petition. If a sufficient number of voters sign, the proposition is placed on the ballot at the next election. The constitutional initiative was adopted by the states between 1902 and 1918. [6] The states now possessing the device are: Arizona, Arkansas, California, Colorado, Massachusetts, Michigan, Missouri, Nebraska, North Dakota, Oklahoma, Ohio, and Oregon.

The number of signatures required to qualify an initiative constitutional amendment for a place on the ballot usually is stated in terms of percentage of the vote for a certain office, such as governor or justice of the supreme court, at the last general election. The range, among those states actually using the device, is from 8 to 15 per cent; both median and average are 10 per cent.

Although used in only one-fourth of the states, the constitutional initiative is an important device of direct democracy. It makes possible the proposal of amendments despite the opposition of a controlled legislature. It is a "safety valve" through which the electorate can act if sufficiently aroused. As with the initiative and the referendum on ordinary legislation, however, some disillusionment has occurred because signatures can be procured for nearly any proposition for which

---

[5] New Jersey is counted in this category; it also has an alternative arrangement of a majority in each house in two successive sessions.

[6] Winston W. Crouch, "The Constitutional Initiative in Operation," *American Political Science Review*, vol. 33 (August, 1939), pp. 634–645.

a sponsor is willing to pay "professional" petition circulators.

Ratification of Constitutional Amendments. In all states except Delaware, provision is made for ratifying amendments by popular vote. Thirty-five states require only a simple majority of those voting on the amendment. Seven require a majority of those participating in the election or voting for candidates for a certain office. The remaining states have special variations. Connecticut ratifies through a majority of voters in town meeting. New Hampshire, which can propose only through constitutional convention, ratifies by a two-thirds vote in town meetings. Illinois ratifies either by majority voting in election or by two-thirds vote on the amendment. Rhode Island requires a three-fifths vote on the amendment.

The method of ratifying constitutional changes is a decisive factor in the number of amendments. Except where the mode of proposing amendments is unduly restrictive, each of the thirty-five states requiring only a simple majority of those voting on the proposition can adapt its constitution to changing times rather readily. The states with more difficult ratification procedures adopt relatively few amendments.

The requirement of popular ratification of amendments places a large burden on the electorate. In a typical biennial election, two-thirds to three-fourths of the states vote on constitutional amendments. Louisiana, which now has the longest constitution, has *adopted* an average of close to nineteen amendments each biennium since its fundamental law went into effect in 1921. California has amended its constitution of 1879 an average of about ten times each 2 years.

APPRAISAL AND PROPOSALS

No governmental institution is perfect, but state constitutions are among the most imperfect. Depending upon the amending process, some constitutions are too rigid and difficult to change, and some are so easily amended that large quantities of statutory matter have gotten into them. General constitutional reform is very difficult to achieve because of the tendency of

Americans to glorify their constitutions and to revere what is ancient in government (at the same time embracing every new product of technology). Some of the more acute problems concerning constitutions require further consideration and analysis.

Excessive Length. Early state constitutions were relatively brief statements of basic principles. At that time the distinction between fundamental and statutory law had not been made fully, yet the drafters of those revolutionary state documents understood perhaps better than later constitutional craftsmen that details ought to be left to legislative bodies. The extent to which minute details have been written into state constitutions may be indicated in comparative terms. In 1800 the longest constitution, that of Massachusetts, contained about 12,000 words; the shortest, New Jersey's, about 2,500 words.[7] Now Louisiana and California compete for long-windedness with documents exceeding 70,000 words; Vermont and Rhode Island, with 5,700 and 6,500, respectively, have the shortest constitutions.[8]

There are many disadvantages to a constitution full of details. If a state is to keep up to date and meet the needs produced by changed situations, then it is necessary to amend the law from time to time. If statutory matter is written into the constitution, the extraordinary procedures required for constitutional amendments must be followed in order to secure the desired changes. This burdens the electorate with the necessity of passing judgment on numerous propositions on the ballot and it greatly diminishes the possibility of securing the reforms thought necessary.

The reasons for the expansion of state constitutions are several: First, people distrust the legislature and seek to write into the fundamental law provisions that cannot easily be altered. Second, judicial decisions are overridden effectively by constitutional amendment. Third, pressure groups attempt to consolidate their gains in permanent fashion by writing them into the

[7] James Q. Dealey, *Growth of American State Constitutions* (Ginn, 1915), p. 39.

[8] *The Book of the States, 1954–1955,* pp. 68–73.

constitution. Fourth, state and local functions have expanded, with a consequent necessity for new authorizations and agencies. Finally, the adoption by one-fourth of the states of the constitutional initiative has given the electorate a chance to propose constitutional change, and they have done so.

Excessive Age. Thomas Jefferson maintained that the social contract should be preserved through revolution and through periodical renewals of agreement. Given political democracy and freedom from barriers that might obstruct the achievement of majority rule, rebellion is not likely to occur in the United States. The idea of periodical renewals of agreement, however, has influenced state constitutional development considerably. Jefferson argued that each generation should establish its own organic law, for in a dynamic society men and conditions change, and therefore governments should change. The modern manifestation of this sentiment is found in constitutional requirements in eight states making mandatory the submission to the people periodically of the question: Should a constitutional convention be called?

Despite the reasonableness of the idea of periodical renewal, the plain fact is that the forces standing against change are nearly always able to prevent general reform. Most of them, motivated by some vested interest in the constitution as it stands, prefer to have things remain as they are rather than risk any change. Not only the utility corporations and others commonly identified with vested interests are involved, but local governments, school districts, civil servants, and many others may be numbered among the opponents of constitutional change. When a convention is proposed, they appeal to the natural conservatism of the people to oppose any general revision of the constitution.

As a result, most state constitutions have continued through many years without general revision. The oldest are those of Massachusetts, originally adopted in 1780; New Hampshire, which dates from 1784; and Vermont, which was framed in 1793. By way of contrast, the only fully revised constitutions adopted since 1910 are those of New Jersey (1947), Missouri (1945),

Georgia (1945), and Louisiana (1921). In 1955 the average state constitution had been in force over 76 years.

It is true, of course, that most of the old constitutions have been amended many times, but the amendments, as often as not, have added to the disorganization of the documents, making them increasingly worse in form and often contradictory. Until the adoption of the 1945 constitution, Missouri's organic law contained provisions governing the St. Louis World's Fair in 1904.

Model State Constitution. In an effort to induce states to modernize their constitutions, the National Municipal League in 1921 first issued its model state constitution, which was drafted by a committee of distinguished authorities on government.[9] The model constitution's great assets are its conciseness, its clarity, and its modernity. It is not a short document, but its present 11,000 words exceed the constitutions of only a few states. It is written in clear and simple language. It provides for the features of state and local government that are regarded by authorities as most essential: the single-house legislature, the concentration of executive power in the governor, a legislative council to plan and carry on research, the initiative and referendum, and county and city home rule.

No state has adopted the model constitution *in toto,* or even considerable parts of it. Progress in a field like this is likely to be slow and piecemeal. Some of the improvements of the Missouri constitution may have been inspired by the model. The rapid spread of the legislative council idea can be traced in part to the same source. Perhaps it has provided some incentive in the state executive reorganizations of the past twenty-five years. The important thing is to have people understand that governmental institutions and instruments can be improved.

[9] The original committee was composed of Charles A. Beard, Arthur E. Buck, Richard S. Childs, Walter F. Dodd, Harold W. Dodds, John A. Fairlie, A. R. Hatton, Arthur N. Holcombe, Raymond V. Ingersoll, Isidor Loeb, Lindsay Rogers, and Clinton Rogers Woodruff. There have been three revisions: in 1928, 1933, and 1941. The current edition is that of 1948.

In its latest form, the model constitution contains 116 sections which are grouped into thirteen articles, concerned with

Bill of rights	Local government
Suffrage and elections	Civil service
Legislature	Public welfare
Initiative and referendum	Intergovernmental relations
Executive	Constitutional revision
Judiciary	Schedule
Finance	

Missouri's New Constitution. Because Missouri has fully revised its constitution in the present generation, examination of its charter may give an insight into the kind of constitutional change that may be expected in other states. The first impression that one gets is the reduction of bulk; the constitution was reduced to 11,000 words, or about one-third its former length; the number of articles was reduced from fifteen to twelve. Major changes were also made in content. The bill of rights was extended to include guaranties of the right of labor to organize and bargain collectively, of freedom of speech for the press, radio, and other channels of communication, and of the eligibility of women for jury duty. The bicameral legislature was not changed but a number of procedural improvements were instituted, including a requirement of record votes in legislative committees and of a permanent committee on legislative research. The changes in the executive branch were most sweeping; the governor was given authority to group scattered agencies into departments; revenue and taxation matters were concentrated into a department of finance; and the merit system was extended, but not to all state functions. The lower judicial system was reorganized, replacing justices of the peace with salaried magistrates.

Local home rule, in which Missouri originally pioneered, was extended to cities of 10,000 and to counties of 85,000 population or over. City and county cooperation and functional consolidation, as well as cooperation or consolidation of two or more counties, were authorized. Improvements were made in the field of taxation; espe-

cially notable was the provision that the intangible personal property taxes be levied and collected by the state, but the proceeds returned to local governments.

POWERS OF THE STATES

As this book has stressed many times, the Federal government has only delegated powers; all remaining powers of government are left to the states. A closer examination, however, indicates that the Federal government holds a number of powers concurrently with the states. Among these are the power to tax, to borrow, and to maintain defense forces. In addition, the failure of the Federal government to utilize its powers fully has left to the states certain aspects of the regulation of interstate commerce, bankruptcy, weights and measures, and other matters. On the other hand, it is well known that state authority has been reduced considerably in the last few decades by the expansion of the laws and interpretations of federal powers—such as taxing, commerce, treaty, and monetary.

State Police Power. The police power of a state is its authority to provide for the health, morals, safety, and welfare of the people. It is not to be confused with the police function carried out by police departments. Under its general police power, which is not based on any specific provision of the state constitution but is a residual power, a state may, for example, set automobile speed limits, compel smallpox vaccinations, ban Sunday movies, defer mortgage foreclosures, or regulate the milk industry. To be sure, such legislation must come within the framework set by constitutions, both Federal and state. State regulations must not interfere unreasonably with the rights of liberty and property guaranteed under the Fourteenth Amendment. State laws may not violate any of the express prohibitions on state action listed in the Federal Constitution.[10] So long as they avoid the pitfalls of conflict with the Federal Constitution and laws properly enacted under it, and abide by the provisions of the state constitution, legislatures may proceed to legislate in the interests of the general welfare.

[10] See pp. 75–77.

Applications of the state police power will be examined in two fields: (1) legislation to promote social welfare, and (2) legislation to promote economic interests.

Social-welfare Laws. State efforts to protect the public health through restricting minors to an 8-hour day and women laundry workers to a 10-hour day have been upheld in the United States Supreme Court as reasonable exercises of the police power.[11] On the other hand, a New York law limiting bakery workers to 10 hours a day was found an unreasonable violation of freedom of contract.[12] After repeatedly reversing itself, the Court finally decided that the states might regulate the wages and hours of women workers.[13] A state statute forbidding the advertising of tobacco on billboards, alleged to be an interference with interstate commerce, was upheld as valid.[14] A Massachusetts compulsory vaccination law was declared not to be an unreasonable invasion of liberty guaranteed by the due process clause.[15]

Economic Legislation. Beginning in 1877, the United States Supreme Court conceded that states could regulate the rates and services of "businesses affected with public interest."[16] Regulation of meat packing, theater-ticket sales, private employment services, gasoline vending, and ice distribution were all held unconstitutional because they were not sufficiently affected with public interest.[17] In Nebbia *v.* New York, the court accepted as constitutional a state milk-control law that involved price fixing and rejected claims that freedom of contract was unreasonably interfered with or due process denied.[18] The same year the Court held valid the Minnesota moratorium law, which postponed foreclosure sales and extended the redemption period, as a valid exercise of the state police power which did not impair the obligation of contract.[19] In 1941 the Court clearly reversed an earlier decision when it found valid a Nebraska law setting the maximum fees that might be charged by a private employment agency.[20]

Power over Political Subdivisions. States inherently possess authority to create and control units of local government, subject, of course, to any limitations imposed by state constitutions and to the requirement that they qualify under the republican form of government clause. Counties, cities, and other subdivisions of the state are creatures of the state. So vigilant was the Supreme Court to see that this aspect of a state's sovereignty is not impaired that it declared void a mild bankruptcy law enacted by Congress which would have permitted local public bodies to adjust their debt burden with state approval.[21]

Power over Suffrage and Elections. The Federal government possesses no election machinery of its own but must rely upon the states to provide electoral services. Originally, definition of who might vote was left entirely to the states, but the adoption of the Fifteenth and Nineteenth Amendments prohibits discrimination on account of race and sex. Except for these limitations, each state may prescribe qualifications for voting, subject to the original limitation that the electorate for federal elections must be the same as that for the most numerous branch of the state legislature. Recent court decisions indicate, however, added federal authority over nominations and elections of federal officers.[22]

[11] Holden *v.* Hardy, 169 U.S. 366 (1898), and Muller *v.* Oregon, 208 U.S. 412 (1908).

[12] Lochner *v.* New York, 198 U.S. 45 (1905).

[13] West Coast Hotel Co. *v.* Parrish, 300 U.S. 379 (1937).

[14] Packer Corporation *v.* Utah, 285 U.S. 105 (1932).

[15] Jacobson *v.* Massachusetts, 197 U.S. 11 (1905).

[16] Munn *v.* Illinois, 94 U.S. 113 (1877).

[17] The cases were Wolff Packing Co. *v.* Industrial Court, 262 U.S. 522 (1923); Tyson Bros. *v.* Banton, 273 U.S. 418 (1927); Ribnik *v.* McBride, 277 U.S. 350 (1928); Williams *v.* Standard Oil Co., 278 U.S. 235 (1929); and New State Ice Co. *v.* Liebmann, 285 U.S. 262 (1932).

[18] 291 U.S. 502 (1934).

[19] Home Building and Loan Association *v.* Blaisdell, 290 U.S. 398 (1934).

[20] Olsen *v.* Nebraska, 313 U.S. 236 (1941).

[21] Ashton *v.* Cameron County Water Improvement District, 298 U.S. 513 (1937). Congress revised the law subsequently and many municipalities have taken advantage of its provisions.

[22] In United States *v.* Classic, 313 U.S. 299 (1941), the conviction of an election commissioner for mis-

Other Powers. Beyond those specifically mentioned, state powers are exceedingly difficult to classify. So long as it does not violate a limita-

counting ballots in a congressional primary election was upheld. Smith *v.* Allwright, 321 U.S. 649 (1944), held that Negroes cannot be denied the right to par-

tion placed upon it by the Federal Constitution, a state may tax, create and regulate private corporations, enact criminal and civil laws, and provide a wide range of services.

ticipate in Texas Democratic primaries, reversing earlier decisions.

FOR FURTHER READING

Baisden, Richard N.: *Charter for New Jersey: the New Jersey Constitutional Convention of 1947* (Trenton, N.J.: State Department of Education, 1952).

Bates, Frank G., and Others: *State Government* (Harper, 3d ed., 1949).

Callender, Clarence, and Others (eds.): "The State Constitution of the Future," *Annals of the American Academy of Political and Social Science,* vol. 181 (September, 1935), pp. 1–187.

Council of State Governments: *The Book of the States* (Chicago: The Council, biennial).

Dealey, James Q.: *Growth of American State Constitutions* (Ginn, 1915).

Dodd, Walter F.: *The Revision and Amendment of State Constitutions* (Johns Hopkins Press, 1910).

Faust, Martin L.: *Five Years Under the New Missouri Constitution* (Jefferson City, Mo.: Public Expenditures Survey, 1950).

Faust, Martin L. (ed.): *Organization Manual for the Missouri Constitutional Convention . . .* (Columbia, 1943). Missouri Constitutional Convention of 1943, no. 1.

Freund, Ernst: *The Police Power, Public Policy and Constitutional Rights* (Chicago: Callaghan, 1904).

Graves, W. Brooke: *American State Government* (Heath, 4th ed., 1953).

Hoar, Roger S.: *Constitutional Conventions, Their Nature, Powers, and Limitations* (Little, Brown, 1917).

Keith, John P.: *Methods of Constitutional Revision* (University of Texas, Bureau of Municipal Research, 1949).

McCarthy, Mary B.: *The Widening Scope of American Constitutions* (The Catholic University of America Press, 1928).

McClure, Wallace: *State Constitution-making* (Nashville: Marshall and Bruce, 1916).

National Municipal League: *Model State Constitution* (New York: National Municipal League, 1948).

New York State Constitutional Convention Committee: *Constitutions of the States and the United States* (Albany: The Committee, 1938).

O'Rourke, Vernon, and Douglas W. Campbell: *Constitution-making in a Democracy, Theory and Practice in New York State* (Johns Hopkins Press, 1943).

Selsam, J. Paul: *Pennsylvania's Constitution of 1776: A Study of Revolutionary Democracy* (University of Pennsylvania Press, 1935).

Steinbicker, Paul G., and Martin L. Faust: *Manual on Amending Procedure and the Initiative and Referendum . . .* (Columbia, 1943). Missouri Constitutional Convention of 1943, no. 8.

Sturm, Albert L.: *Methods of State Constitutional Reform* (University of Michigan Press, 1954).

Uhl, Raymond and Others: *Constitutional Conventions* (University of South Carolina, Bureau of Public Administration, 1951).

University of Hawaii, Legislative Reference Bureau: *Manual on State Constitutional Provisions* (1950).

REVIEW
QUESTIONS
1. Is there a contradiction involved when we embrace the newest in technological developments yet revere the old in constitutions and political institutions?

2. Discuss the transition of state constitutions from the end of the Colonial period to 1800.

3. What is the reasoning behind the provision made in a number of state constitutions for a mandatory submission to the voters at given intervals of the question of calling a constitutional convention?

4. Describe the several methods currently in use for proposing and ratifying amendments to state constitutions.

5. Describe the institution of the state constitutional convention, the methods of calling one, and the way in which one does its work.

6. Why not have a long constitution?

7. Why have so few states been able to renovate their constitutions during the last half century?

8. Compare the powers of state governments with those of the Federal government.

CHAPTER 33

Legislatures and Legislation

Hence the quality of a legislature, the integrity and capacity of its members, the efficiency of the methods by which it passes laws and supervises the conduct of the Executive, must continue to be of significance to a nation's welfare. — James Bryce [1]

The first branch of government mentioned in most state constitutions is the legislative. There is good historical justification for this arrangement, because the early state constitutions vested by far the largest share of governmental power in the hands of the legislatures. Since that time, however, the legislature has lost in power, prestige, and importance. As in the Federal government, the chief executive increasingly has been looked upon by the people as their champion and leader, even in legislative matters. Excessive localism, obsolete machinery, diffusion of responsibility—all these have undermined public confidence in legislatures. Adoption of the initiative and referendum by more than one-third of the states has reduced further the autonomy once possessed by legislatures.

On the other hand, the hopes of man for truly responsible government rest more upon reform of the legislature than upon any other proposed improvement. In 1946 Congress took a significant step toward bringing up to date its archaic machinery, but by and large state legislatures have changed little in the last hundred years. Action on that front must be placed high on the agenda of democracy.

[1] *Modern Democracies* (Macmillan, 1921), vol. II, p. 357. Used by permission of the publishers.

LEGISLATIVE STRUCTURE

The state legislature's most striking structural feature is bicameralism. Like so many American institutions, the two-house idea originated in England and was transplanted to this continent during the Colonial period. The steps in the evolution of American legislative bodies have been traced in the first of the chapters on Congress.

The Two-house System. With four exceptions, the American states have adhered to the bicameral plan. Early in the nation's history, single-house legislatures existed in Pennsylvania (1776–1790), Georgia (1777–1789), and Vermont (1777–1836). Nebraska put its unicameral plan into operation in 1937.[2]

The reasons for the original adoption of the two-house plan are numerous. It followed the bicameral pattern, which was widely used in the Colonial era. It provided a small second chamber which, in some states, could provide "advice and consent" to the state governors. It erected another barrier and check to the exercise of gov-

[2] The experience of Vermont is recorded in Daniel B. Carroll, *The Unicameral Legislature of Vermont* (University of Vermont, 1933); background for the Nebraska adoption is found in John P. Senning, *The One-house Legislature* (McGraw-Hill, 1937).

ernmental power, in keeping with the idea of limited government. De Tocqueville viewed the two-house plan with admiration, declaring

Time and experience, however, have convinced the Americans that, even if these are its only advantages, the division of legislative power is still a principle of the greatest necessity. . . . This theory, nearly unknown to the republics of antiquity, first introduced into the world almost by accident, like so many other great truths, and misunderstood by several great modern nations, has at length become an axiom in the political science of the present age.[3]

This enthusiasm for the checks of the double-chamber plan is little shared by many contemporary political scientists, who regard other checks as more adequate and effective and who place emphasis in clearing out obstructions to legislative progress.

Two additional arguments for bicameralism appeared subsequently. After the Federal Constitution was adopted, the desire to conform to the "federal plan" became strong; this consideration was a major factor in the abandonment of unicameralism by both Pennsylvania and Georgia. Second, as the states increased in population and diversity of economic endeavors, the two houses in many instances were placed on different bases of representation; many states today apportion one house by population and the other by units of local government.

In evaluating the bicameral principle, proponents urge the importance of the second chamber as a check on the actions of the first house, and as a vehicle for providing two bases of representation. Critics argue that other and more effective checks exist. The standing committee of the first house to consider a particular bill is the most apt to cull it out; eliminations at this stage run over 50 per cent of the total bills introduced. Through the veto power, the governor checks the legislature's work. In many states, an additional check is possessed by the people, acting directly through the referendum. Finally, the laws enacted must run the gamut of the courts, which may test the

[3] Alexis de Tocqueville, *Democracy in America* (Knopf, rev. ed., 2 vols., 1945), vol. I, p. 84.

constitutionality of legislation when cases are properly brought before them.

There is much to be said for having two bases of representation, especially in the more heterogeneous states with their urban-rural and other sectional divisions. The idea has merit but its use need not be confined to the bicameral system. It can be employed in a single-house scheme by providing, for example, that some of the legislators shall be elected by population districts and some according to area, but all shall convene together.

Unicameral Proposals. In the widespread debates and discussions of the single-house legislature during the 1930's, two principal arguments for the reform were advanced. First, the one-house plan would fix definitely responsibility for action. The bicameral plan makes "passing the buck" easy and fixing the blame difficult. The late Senator Norris once declared that special interests desiring to kill proposed legislation find it twice as easy when it is necessary to control only one of two houses. The conference committee, an inevitable institution under bicameralism, actually constitutes a sort of third house that sometimes operates in a most irresponsible fashion. Elimination of one house would simplify the legislative process by about 50 per cent and might serve to reduce the army of lobbyists who thrive on procedural complications that baffle the common man.

Second, reduction to one house should make possible some additional prestige and compensation for legislators. Most one-house plans call for a relatively small-sized legislature. Because the single house would have added responsibilities, legislators ought to be paid more and might well be expected to give more nearly full-time service in the larger states.

Features of unicameral plans are apt to vary considerably. Nebraska has forty-three members elected each two years on a nonpartisan basis from districts apportioned according to population. The model state constitution is silent on the number of members but would have them elected by proportional representation every two years. In other states that have seriously considered this reform, the number of members proposed has ranged up to eighty, often with 4-year terms and with salaries at $5,000 or more.

The Two-house Plan in Operation. While it is interesting to weigh the relative merits of the two plans, the plain fact is that nearly all the American states have bicameralism and are likely to retain it for a long time to come. Therefore this section is devoted to the existing structure of state legislatures.

The legislative branch is officially known as "legislature" in one-half the states; nineteen use "general assembly"; Massachusetts and New Hampshire retain "general court." Upper houses invariably are known as "senates." Lower houses most commonly are called "house of representatives"; four states use "assembly"; three retain "house of delegates"; New Jersey alone prefers "general assembly."

In all bicameral states the senate is a smaller body than the house, averaging in the forty-seven states one-third the house membership. The range in size of state senates is from seventeen in Nevada to sixty-seven in Minnesota, with the average number of senators per state at thirty-seven.

The other house ranges from thirty-five in Delaware to a maximum of 400 under New Hampshire's recently revised apportionment. The average number of members of the lower house is just short of 120.

In powers, the two houses are everywhere substantially coordinate in matters of legislation. The lower house traditionally is given the privilege of originating financial bills, but the senate usually may amend such bills freely. State senates customarily are assigned the task of passing upon certain classes of appointments by the governors. The function of impeachment, judicial in nature, usually involves both houses, the lower house instituting proceedings and the senate sitting as a court and rendering judgment.

LEGISLATORS

Basis of Representation. American states use two principal bases of representation in their legislative bodies: population and units of government. The usual procedure for apportioning legislative seats involves action by the legislature following a decennial census. In order to avoid the deadlock occasionally encountered in reapportionment controversies, several states have created special boards or commissions for the purpose of apportioning. Such bodies are provided for in Arkansas, Missouri, and Ohio; if the legislature fails to act in California or South Dakota, ex officio commissions may act; Maryland allows the governor to reapportion its house.

While there are many instances in which population is the sole criterion for apportionment and a few in which units of government are the only factors considered, an even larger number use some combination of the two methods. For example, it is common for a state to provide that the basis of apportionment shall be population but that each county shall have at least one member. On the whole, the legislative districts that emerge from the diverse methods of apportioning in the several states are not unreasonable. In most states that have metropolitan areas there is a tendency to underrepresent urban communities and overrepresent rural areas. This has reached a ridiculous extreme in California, which allows one state senator for over 5 million people in Los Angeles County and one for about 13,000 in three rural counties.

As with congressional districts, legislative districts may be drawn for personal or partisan advantage. Occasional requirements in state constitutions that districts must be composed of compact and contiguous territory have not been sufficient to prevent gerrymandering.

Legislative constituencies are normally single-member districts. This plan often magnifies the strength of the strongest group. For over half a century, however, Illinois has used a system which provides minority representation. The state is divided into senatorial districts only. Each district elects one senator and three representatives. In voting for representatives, the voter may cast all three votes for one candidate, or he may divide them. The highest three are declared elected.[4]

[4] George S. Blair, "Cumulative Voting: an Effective Electoral Device in Illinois Politics," *Southwestern Social Science Quarterly*, vol. 34 (March, 1954), pp. 3–18.

Proportional representation, explained in an earlier chapter,[5] has not yet been applied to the election of any state legislative body. Although PR, with the Hare plan of a single transferable vote, is technically a good device for securing a majority choice, the difficulty in understanding it, the slowness in counting ballots, and the charge that it aggravates factionalization are all formidable barriers to its adoption by states.

Sessions. Most of the state legislatures convene in regular sessions every two years; a growing number of states, including Arizona, California, Colorado, Maryland, Massachusetts, Michigan, New Jersey, New York, Rhode Island, and South Carolina, have annual sessions. In addition, legislators may be called together in special session at the discretion of the governor in most states. In the biennial-session states it is most common for the legislatures to meet in January of the odd-numbered years, but a few meet in even years or in other months. It is normal practice to limit, directly or indirectly, the number of days a legislature may be in session. Over one-half the legislatures have their regular sessions limited to a given number of days, ranging from 40 to 120. Other states in effect limit the length of sessions by arranging legislators' pay so that it expires after a stated period. These limitations are motivated in part through a desire to save money, especially in states that pay legislators by the day, and in part by suspicions that having a legislature in session too long is unsettling and "bad for business."

A few states have experimented with a split-session arrangement, the so-called "bifurcated" session. It involves convening the legislature for a limited period, usually not more than a month, at which bills are introduced, the houses are organized, and urgent measures passed. Then the legislature recesses for a month or so to confer with constituents and to study pending legislation. After the recess the legislature devotes its time to the passage of bills introduced in the earlier period. The privilege of introducing new measures is restricted rigidly in the second portion of the session. The bifurcated session was

[5] Chap. 11.

intended in part as a remedy for the rush that attends the end of a session, and in part to ensure time for full public consideration of proposed measures. While it has not ended the closing rush, it performs a real service in requiring that important measures be kept before the public for a longer period.

Terms and Compensation. Senators generally are given longer terms of office than are members of the lower house. The most common pattern is 4 years for the senate and 2 for the house, but sixteen state senates have only 2-year terms and four lower houses have 4-year terms.

Compensation of state legislators varies widely. Less than one-third of the states still compensate on a per diem basis, which ranges from $5 in Kansas to $25 in Kentucky. In the others, pay is stated in terms of so much a period. California leads with $6,000 per year; New Hampshire, with its host of legislators, manages to pay each one $200 for the 2-year term. In most states legislators are underpaid. In the larger states many of them put in a great part of their time on state work, but it is rare that one can live on the meager salary paid. The voters tend to look upon proposals for pay increases as "salary grabs," but substantial increments have been made. Most of the states have raised the salaries of their legislators since the end of the Second World War, and many have also provided per diem expense allowance during the sessions. The legislator cannot even live in the capital on the low per diem allowed by many states, much less support a family at home and put aside something to finance campaign for reelection.

Legislative Personnel. What sort of person serves in state legislatures? A number of factors condition the answer to that question. Legislators, as has been shown, are paid rather small amounts. They must serve actively for erratic periods, full time for a few months, and at odd times for the remainder of their terms. Occupationally, lawyers and farmers predominate, comprising more than two-fifths of all state legislators; businessmen follow third; the occupations of the remainder scatter over a wide field. A high rate of turnover prevails among legislators, who appear to tire quickly of the low pay, indefinite working period, and frequent election campaigns. In a tabulation made in 1950, only about 50 per cent of the state legislators were found to have served one or more previous terms in legislative office.[6]

It is alleged frequently that the level of competence among state legislators is low. While this is often overstressed, improvement might be accomplished by reducing the number, add-

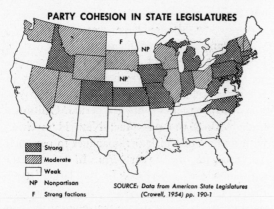

PARTY COHESION IN STATE LEGISLATURES

Strong
Moderate
Weak
NP   Nonpartisan
F   Strong factions

SOURCE: Data from *American State Legislatures*
(Crowell, 1954) pp. 190-1

The role of party in state legislatures varies widely. Classification of the states is made on the basis of information supplied by competent observers, but there is ample room for differences of opinion.

ing to prestige and responsibility, increasing the salary, and making available considerably more research, technical, and clerical assistance.

LEADERSHIP AND POLITICS

Legislative Officers. The standard pattern concerning presiding officers is for the popularly elected lieutenant governor to preside over the senate and for the house to elect a speaker from among its own members. Since ten states make no provision for lieutenant governors, their senates are chaired by presidents elected by the body. Powers of these presiding officers are much the same the country over. All speakers are empowered to appoint committees. Most of the senates allow their presiding officers to do likewise, but some permit a committee on rules or

committees to choose, or vest power of appointment in the president pro tempore, who is elected by the senate.

The presiding officers also have the prerogatives commonly assigned to chairmen of legislative bodies. In presiding they have a considerable amount of discretion in controlling the business of the house. In most states they decide to which committee a bill shall be referred, play a major role in the selection of bills for consideration on the floor of their legislative bodies, enforce the rules of the house and decide points of order, and control who speaks in debates through the power of recognition. Beyond these formal powers, the speaker of the house is often a political leader in his own right and is able to influence the course of legislation by throwing his weight to one side or the other. Therefore he has a high place in party and factional councils and may be cultivated carefully by the governor, who seeks the maximum support for his legislative program. The lieutenant governor, an officer of the people's choosing rather than the senate's, normally is much less powerful than the speaker.

In addition to the presiding officers, state legislative bodies have a number of attachés and employees—clerks, secretaries, chaplains, sergeants-at-arms, page boys, stenographers, and others. Usually they are selected by each house on the basis of personal or partisan sponsorship and patronage.

Legislative Politics. Most, but not all, American state legislatures are organized on partisan lines.[7] The usual division is Republicans *vs.* Democrats, and legislative procedure is dovetailed into party rivalry. The caucus is a feature of nearly every state legislative body. Party members meet to discuss matters affecting their party on the legislative front. In order to plumb

[6] American Political Science Association, Committee on American Legislatures, *American State Legislatures* (Crowell, 1954), pp. 65-70.

[7] Recent studies of state legislative politics include W. J. Keefe, "Parties, Partisanship and Public Policy in the Pennsylvania Legislature," *American Political Science Review,* vol. XLVIII (June, 1954), pp. 450-464; W. D. Lockard, "Legislative Politics in Connecticut," *ibid.,* vol. XLVIII (March, 1954), pp. 166-173; Duncan Macrae, Jr., "The Relation between Roll Call Votes and Constituencies in the Massachusetts House of Representatives," *ibid.,* vol. XLVI (December, 1952), pp. 1046-1055.

the inner springs of the legislative process in the Eastern and North Central states, much emphasis must be given to the formal party caucus. In these states party discipline tends to be relatively great, and the party serves to unify the directions of the legislative and executive branches. Only Minnesota and Nebraska have formally abolished party designations in their legislatures; in the former, party lines have reemerged despite their removal from the ballot.

In the politics of many states of the West and South there is no Democratic-Republican conflict of importance. On the contrary, the battle may be between different factions of the predominant party or among outstanding leaders and their followers. In every state there are great economic interests that strive for political ascendancy and legislative influence. Where party cleavage is strong, these interests are less obvious; where party lines are weak, pressure groups often come to the fore and play a major part in the alignment of the legislative body. The great importance of the relationship of state legislator to business corporation, labor union, farm group, and other interest often is overlooked. This is not merely a question of lobbying but involves the whole matter of representation. The representation system cannot represent all interests perfectly. Most lobbyists perform valuable services to the legislature. Suppression of group representation would serve no useful purpose, but no valid objections can be made to requiring lobbyists to register and file statements about their employers and the money they spend to influence legislation, as is now required of those who represent groups before Congress.

The Legislative Council Idea. As state legislative work has become increasingly heavier and more complex, means have been sought to provide the legislature with the leadership and planning facilities so sorely needed. The legislative council idea is the major method actually being tried for keeping the legislature abreast of its work. The council is a sort of master interim committee of the legislature, available to study state problems and to plan a legislative program. The legislative council has proven an admirable agency for taking charge of a research program,

and some of the most notable achievements of existing councils have been in the field of fact finding. The states that have adopted and still retain the plan, with the years of adoption, are as follows: Kansas (1933), Kentucky (1936), Virginia (1936), Connecticut (1937), Illinois (1937), Nebraska, (1937), Pennsylvania (1937), Maryland (1939), Oklahoma (1939), Maine (1939), Missouri (1943), Indiana (1945), Alabama (1945), Nevada (1945), North Dakota (1945), Arkansas (1947), Minnesota (1947),

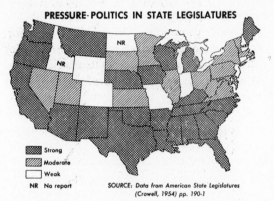

PRESSURE-POLITICS IN STATE LEGISLATURES

▓ Strong
▨ Moderate
☐ Weak
NR No report

SOURCE: *Data from American State Legislatures (Crowell, 1954) pp. 190-1*

Note the frequency with which the states with weak parties in legislatures have strong pressure groups.

Ohio (1947), Utah (1947), Washington (1947), Wisconsin (1947), Florida (1949), South Carolina (1949), Texas (1949), New Hampshire (1951), New Mexico (1951), South Dakota (1951), Wyoming (1951), Louisiana (1952), Arizona (1953), Colorado (1953), Montana (1953), Tennessee (1953), and Massachusetts (1954).

The legislative councils range in size from three members in South Carolina to the whole membership of the legislature in Nebraska, Oklahoma, and South Dakota. The usual plan is to have the entire membership of the council selected from the two houses, most commonly on an equal basis. Arkansas and Utah provide for representatives of the administration. In some of the states members of the council are selected by the presiding officers of the two houses; party affiliation is a factor in the choice in most of the states.

The arguments usually advanced against the

council idea are that legislative power might become concentrated and that legislators might be tempted to meddle unduly in administrative affairs. Such fears have not been justified from the experience of the states that have used the council plan for a period of time. The spread of the council idea is one of the most encouraging signs in the state legislative field.[8]

LEGISLATIVE PROCEDURE

Legislative Committees. Whether standing committees are appointed by the speaker of the house or the president of the senate, or chosen by a senate committee, considerations of seniority and political influence are apt to be major factors in determining committee assignments. As in Congress, state legislatures do the bulk of their work through standing committees. Therefore, rivalry for good committee assignments is very great. In most states seniority is not as potent a factor as in Congress. The speaker of the house may use committee appointments to repay political debts incurred in his campaign for the speakership. Pressure groups frequently exert themselves to see that the committees with which they are particularly concerned are loaded with legislators favorable to their cause.

The number of standing committees varies from state to state and from house to house, but the over-all average is thirty-two in the lower houses and twenty-five in the senates. Like congressional committees, state legislative committees have great power over the bills referred to them. The more important bills are deemed to justify public hearings. After committee discussion is completed, a vote is taken on the bill. If the committee is favorable, the bill is reported out to the floor of the legislative body with the recommendation that it be passed. If the committee is unfavorable, the bill may be tabled or pigeonholed. The burying of bills in committee is not as decisive in the states as in Congress, because nearly one-half the states require that all bills must be reported out; in both these and

other states bills may be withdrawn from committee through a discharge procedure, usually by a majority vote of the whole house.

One simple but highly desirable reform in committee procedure is the joint committee plan. Of course, every bicameral legislature must have some joint committees to deal with common problems of administering the legislative establishment. This proposal, however, involves the merger of similar standing committees of the two houses into joint committees. This would reduce the necessary hearings on a particular bill to one thus ending the needless duplication of time, testimony, and travel that takes place under the dual system. The plan has been used successfully by Maine, Connecticut, and Massachusetts. It is a mild reform that could be instituted in most states by a mere alteration of legislative rules.

Special or select committees usually are selected by the presiding officers. Such bodies are established for a specific purpose, such as investigation of a problem that is outside of or cuts across normal committee jurisdiction. Sometimes these are joint committees, including members of both houses. In some states they may be ad interim committees, empowered to work between sessions of the legislature. However, such bodies have been declared void in several states.

Procedure on the Floor. The legislative process in the American states follows rather closely the pattern set by Congress. Bills are introduced by any member, who merely sends the proposed measure to the "hopper" or basket on the clerk's desk. They are read the first time, often inaudibly and by title only, and referred to committee. The committee considers, rejects most of them, and recommends passage of some. The house in which the measure was introduced, on second and third reading, debates and amends, then adopts or rejects.

There is great variation in the method by which roll call is taken and in the conditions under which it is necessary. A few states make a record roll call mandatory for the passage of all bills. Others require that a record vote be taken if demanded by a relatively small number of legislators, ranging from one in some states to one-

[8] See Harold W. Davey, "The Legislative Council Movement in the United States, 1933–1953," *American Political Science Review,* vol. 42 (September, 1953), pp. 785–797.

fifth in others. Illinois and Utah make a roll-call vote mandatory only when demanded by a majority of members. If securing a record vote is made too difficult there is danger that legislators will hide behind the screen of anonymity when controversial matters arise. Constituents have a right to know how their representatives vote on final passage of every measure. Oral roll calls take time, but this factor is no longer a good excuse for not taking a record vote. Twenty-one states have now installed, in one or both houses, electric roll-call devices. The usual electric system provides each legislator with two push buttons at his desk, one marked "yes" and one marked "no." At the front of the chamber is a scoreboard on which appear the names of all members. When the presiding officer calls for a vote, the members push the button appropriate to their sentiments on the proposition at hand; the board lights up and opposite each legislator's name his vote is shown by a green light for "yes" and a red light for "no." An electrical machine punches the roll call on printed sheets, which may then be distributed to the press representatives and go into permanent records of the house.

Final passage having been achieved in the first house, a bill is sent to the second. There the process is repeated, beginning with reference to committee and ending with a vote on final passage. If different versions of the same bill are passed by the two houses and neither house is willing to recede, the differences are compromised in a conference committee, in which each house is represented by an equal number of its members. After the conference committee completes its work, the compromise version of the bill is voted upon in each house; if accepted it goes to the governor for signature.

State legislatures are bound by more constitutional and legal restrictions than is the Federal Congress. For example, nearly all states require that bills be read three times and nearly one-fourth of them require the three readings in full. Because this is a physical impossibility in the larger states, various dodges have developed, such as interpreting the printing of the bill as a reading, or accepting the mumbling of the title as oral reading. Generally the states have been stricter than has Congress about requiring that bills relate to a single subject and that amendments be germane or appropriate to the original bill; most state procedures would not tolerate riders of the sort so commonly added to bills in the United States Congress. Nearly all states have by constitution, statute, or rule set a time limit on the introduction of bills, requiring that bills be introduced early enough in a session to permit adequate time for consideration. The limits vary from a deadline set on the fifteenth day of a session to the last three days of a session. A deadline well in advance of halfway through the session is advisable in order to provide interested persons with an opportunity to examine proposed legislation and to testify on it in committee if desired. Without an adequate deadline, a bill may be introduced and passed in the closing rush without the knowledge of the public.

Governors and Legislation. Governors, in nearly all states, have the power to recommend legislation, call special sessions, and veto bills passed by the legislature. Only the veto power requires much discussion. Governors are given the veto power in every state except North Carolina. It normally extends to ordinary bills but not to constitutional amendments nor to initiative measures. In view of the great volume of legislation that reaches the governor's desk in the closing weeks of a session, the time allowed for consideration by the executive scarcely appears adequate. In all states with a gubernatorial veto, a bill becomes law after a stated number of days even if the governor does not sign, provided the legislature has not finally adjourned. The governor is given only 3 days in several states; the maximum allowed anywhere is 30 days; the median in the forty-eight states is 5 days.

If, however, the legislature has adjourned *sine die,* an entirely different situation prevails. About two-thirds of the states provide that a bill goes into effect if the governor does not sign within the specified time, which ranges from 5 to 45 days. Most of the other one-third deem the bill dead ("pocket vetoed") if the governor does not approve in the stated period, which varies from 3 to 30 days. Of course the latter states give the greatest power over legislation to the chief executive. In case the legislature is still in session when the governor vetoes, it has an opportunity to pass the negatived measure over his veto. Most of the states require a two-thirds vote of those present or elected in order to override a veto; five require a three-fifths vote; seven permit passage of bills over a veto by a simple majority.

It is the item veto over appropriation bills that might constitute a desirable reform for the Federal government. Thirty-eight states have vested in their governors power to eliminate particular items of appropriation bills. This is appropriate recognition of the governor's primary responsibility for budgetary matters. It has been successful in keeping state expenditures under control and constitutes a proper companion authority to the more recent power granted in many states, that of framing and submitting an executive budget.

Legislative Aids. All but five of the legislatures have provided themselves with or availed themselves of bill-drafting agencies. These services are uneven in quality, however, varying all the way from a single handy man who takes part time from other duties, to the modern legislative counsel bureau with its full-time staff of expert attorneys. A good bill-drafting agency not only earns its keep through avoiding loopholes in the law and future trouble in the courts, but it also frees the legislature to some extent from undue dependence upon executive-prepared legislation. A sensible use of legal talent from a drafting agency during the periods between legislative sessions is in the preparation of codifications or revisions of state laws.

Informational services are needed also, and most of the legislatures have some assistance in this field. Often it is provided through a division of the state library or a bureau of the state university. Although good reports do emerge from these sources, the most purposeful research work is done by the legislature's own agencies. Sometimes it comes from fact-finding personnel attached to legislative committees, standing and special, and at other times from research divisions of legislative councils. The important difference between research produced for the legis-

lature by an external agency and that done by the legislature through its own agency is that the latter is more apt to be closely related to legislative needs and more likely to gain legislative confidence.

DIRECT LEGISLATION

The Initiative. The initiative is an electoral device through which an individual or group may propose legislation by securing the signature of the requisite number of qualified voters. The proposition is then placed before the electorate for adoption or rejection.

The initiative is called "direct" when filing the petition is followed by the submission of the proposition to the voters. It is "indirect" when submission is first to the legislature. Then, if that body does not approve, it goes before the voters.

The nineteen states which have adopted the statutory initiative are as follows: Arizona, Arkansas, California, Colorado, Idaho, Maine, Massachusetts, Michigan, Missouri, Montana, Nebraska, Nevada, North Dakota, Ohio, Oklahoma, Oregon, South Dakota, Utah, and Washington. If this list is compared with that of the states using the constitutional initiative, it will be found that six additional states, Idaho, Maine, Montana, South Dakota, Utah, and Washington, have adopted the statutory initiative. The drafting of such measures normally is done by interested groups or their attorneys. The official title and the brief summary that appear on the ballot are the work of the attorney general or some other officer designated for the purpose. The number of signatures required to qualify a proposition for a place on the ballot is set in the state constitution or laws, in terms of a percentage of voters or a flat number. The percentage of voters required to initiate a statute ranges from 3 to 15 per cent.[9] Some states require that there be a minimum geographic distribution among those who sign. If a majority of voters vote in favor of an initiated measure, it becomes law; frequently statutes so adopted have a privileged status and may not be repealed by the legislature.

[9] Either of registered voters in the state or of those voting for a particular office in a recent election.

The Referendum. The referendum is a scheme through which voters may, by petition, force submission to the whole electorate of a bill passed by the legislature. The number or proportion of signatures required is usually less than for the initiative. Emergency measures commonly are excluded from referendum action. If the voters disapprove of the act as passed by the legislature, it becomes null and void. A law is postponed from going into effect by the filing of a valid and adequate referendum petition. Twenty-one states have adopted the referendum, including all those using the initiative, plus Maryland and New Mexico. The number of signatures required ranges from 1½ to 25 per cent of the voters, but most of the states require from 5 to 10 per cent. Some states base the signature requirement on the vote for the governor in the last election.

There are several variations of these two instruments of direct legislation, but most controversy on the matter centers around the general principles outlined above. The people of the states that saw fit to adopt one or both of these devices were probably influenced by the arguments that they would provide a check on corrupt and inert legislatures and provide a useful instrument for the education of the citizenry. The opponents of direct legislation usually assert that it places an additional load on the already overburdened electorate, and it modifies representative government by destroying legislative responsibility.

In addition to the state-wide use of the initiative and referendum, hundreds of cities and counties in the United States make extensive use of direct legislation.

FOR FURTHER READING

American Assembly: *The Forty-eight States: Their Tasks as Policy Makers and Administrators* (Columbia University, 1955).

American Political Science Association, Committee on American Legislatures (ed. by Belle Zeller): *American State Legislatures* (Crowell, 1954).

Bartley, Ernest R.: *The Legislative Process of Florida* (University of Florida, Public Administration Clearing Service, 1950).

Buck, Arthur E.: *Modernizing Our State Legislatures* (Philadelphia: American Academy of Political and Social Science, 1936).

Chamberlain, Joseph P.: *Legislative Processes, National and State* (Appleton-Century-Crofts, 1938).

Council of State Governments: *American Legislatures: Structure and Procedures* (Chicago: The Council, 1954).

Culver, Dorothy C.: *Legislative Reorganization,* Bureau of Public Administration, 1941 Legislative Problems, no. 4 (University of California Press, 1941).

Farmer, Hallie: *The Legislative Process in Alabama* (University of Alabama, Bureau of Public Administration, 1949).

Faust, Martin L.: *Manual on the Legislative Article . . .* (Columbia, 1943). Missouri Constitutional Convention of 1943, no. 6.

Gove, S. K., and Steiner, G. Y.: *The Illinois Legislative Process* (University of Illinois, Institute of Government and Public Affairs, 1954).

Graves, W. Brooke (ed.): "Our State Legislators," *Annals of the American Academy of Political and Social Science,* vol. 195 (January, 1938).

Hounshell, Charles D.: *The Legislative Process in Virginia* (University of Virginia, Extension Division, 1951).

Key, Vladimir O., and Winston W. Crouch: *The Initiative and Referendum in California* (University of California Press, 1939). Also Publication of the University of California at Los Angeles in Social Sciences, vol. 6, no. 4.

New York State Constitutional Convention Committee: *Problems Relating to Legislative Organization* (Albany: The Committee, 1938).

Page, Thomas: *Legislative Apportionment in Kansas* (University of Kansas, Bureau of Governmental Research, 1952).

Pollock, James K.: *The Initiative and Referendum in Michigan* (University of Michigan Press, 1940). Michigan Governmental Studies, no. 6.

Underwood, C. H.: *Legislative Process in West Virginia* (University of West Virginia, Bureau for Governmental Research, 1953).

Walker, Harvey: *Law Making in the United States* (Ronald, 1934).

Webster, Donald H., and Others: *The Legislature and Legislative Process in the State of Washington* (University of Washington Press, 1948).

Willoughby, William F.: *Principles of Legislative Organization and Administration* (Brookings, 1934).

Winslow, Clinton I.: *State Legislative Committees: A Study in Procedure* (Johns Hopkins Press, 1931). Also Johns Hopkins University Studies in History and Political Science, vol. 49, pp. 150–291.

Young, Clement C. (ed.): *The Legislature of California: Its Membership, Procedure, and Work* (San Francisco: Commonwealth Club, 1943).

REVIEW QUESTIONS

1. To what extent do the "real blemishes" Bryce found in "the composition or conduct of the legislatures" still exist? Discuss.

2. Do you regard bicameralism, as did de Tocqueville, as "an axiom of the political science of the present age"? Discuss.

3. What are the principal arguments for unicameralism? Why have states, except Nebraska, been unwilling to adopt it?

4. Discuss the major problems involved in finding a proper basis of representation in state legislatures.

5. Prepare a list of arguments for or against banning political parties from state legislative politics.

6. What is the legislative council idea? Where and in what form has it been put into effect?

7. Describe the legislative committee system found in American states. How could it be improved?

8. Trace normal state legislative procedure from introduction of a bill through gubernatorial action on it.

9. Explain the initiative and referendum as used in the states.

CHAPTER 34

The Governor and Administration

> A permanent service recruited on the basis of merit and fitness and so far as practicable through competitive examination; the grouping of administrative powers, with the necessary divisions or departments, under a chief administrative head; the enforcement of responsibility of the administrative head through an election upon which the attention of the people can be centered and with respect to the importance of which they are fully convinced,—in these, I believe, will be found important securities of efficient administration.
> — Charles Evans Hughes [1]

The experience of the American colonists with arbitrary royal and proprietary governors led to a deep-seated distrust of executive power. Therefore it was natural that early state constitutions, while providing for the office of governor, minimized executive authority. In many states, governors were elected by legislatures and were checked by executive councils.

EVOLUTION OF THE STATE EXECUTIVE

Colonial Governors. The office of governor existed in each of the thirteen colonies. In the royal colonies the governor was a sort of viceroy, sent out from London and representing the British government. Proprietary governors were appointees of the proprietors and carried out their wishes. Only in Massachusetts (before 1684), Connecticut, and Rhode Island did charters permit the colonists to choose their own executives. After the Massachusetts Company

moved to the continent, John Winthrop was chosen governor by the body of freemen, but it proved difficult to assemble them, with the result that legislative authority and gubernatorial selection were vested in the general court. The governors of Connecticut and Rhode Island were chosen by the voters, but they were not endowed with any of the coercive powers possessed by royal and proprietary governors or by state governors of today.

In both royal and proprietary colonies the governor was a powerful officer. On the executive side he possessed the power of appointment and was commander in chief of the military. On the judicial front, he was head of the colonial high court and dispenser of pardons and reprieves. For the legislative branch, he appointed the members of the upper house, recommended legislation, exercised the veto power, and dissolved the legislature at his own discretion. The governor's powers were limited, on the other hand, by the legislative assemblies which assumed control of the purse strings. The popularly elected chamber of the legislature insisted upon and received generally the financial prerog-

[1] An address on "Administrative Efficiency" at Yale University, 1910, while he was governor of New York. Quoted in A. E. Buck, *The Reorganization of State Governments in the United States* (Columbia University Press, 1938), p. 7.

atives that had been won by the British House of Commons.

First State Governors. Constitutions framed and adopted by the states in the revolutionary and confederation era invariably included the office of governor but subordinated it to the legislature. Most of the states vested power to select the governor in the legislature; only Massachusetts, New Hampshire, and New York provided for popular election. The gubernatorial veto, today used in all but one state, was granted originally only in Massachusetts; New York had a modified veto power vested in governor and council. The majority of the original states further held the executive accountable to the legislature or the voters by limiting his term to 1 year.

Development of the Governorship, 1800–1900. During the first half of the nineteenth century, the governors were gradually made elective by the people, and executive councils were abandoned in many states. But the process of making the governor a strong executive was not yet completed. A mania for popular election spread to other state executive offices. Attorneys general, auditors, controllers, treasurers, secretaries of state, and other officers were given their own constitutional pedestals and made elective by the people. Although substantial gubernatorial independence of the legislature was at last achieved, executive power was diffused by popular election of other executive officers and boards. This might be called "the era of the plural executive," and it continues down to date in several states.

Toward the latter half of the last century, the powers of the governors were strengthened somewhat. The veto power was gradually granted in nearly all states. The power to veto items of appropriation bills had been granted in about one-third of the states by the turn of the century. Executive councils were abolished in most states. Often referred to as "chief executive," the governor continued to wield only a part of the executive authority. Woodrow Wilson, near the end of the period under review, contrasted the offices of federal and state executives:

Of state officials associated with the governor it may, on the other hand, be said that both in law and in fact they are colleagues of the governor, in no sense his agents, or even his subordinates, except in formal rank in precedence. They, like himself, are elected by the people; he is in no way concerned in their choice. Nor do they serve him after election. They are not given him as advisers; they are, on the contrary, coordinated with him.[2]

Through the years, governors were given added independence through lengthening the term of office to 2 or 4 years in nearly all states. Growing prestige of the office was indicated by the more generous salaries provided.

Trends in the Twentieth Century. Since 1900 earlier tendencies to make the governor a weak executive have been reversed in a majority of the states. Beginning in the first decade of the century, states began to reexamine their administrative establishments and to propose reforms. During the second and third decades state after state put into effect reorganization plans. With few exceptions, the changes introduced centered around the expansion of gubernatorial powers over administration. The normal pattern was to abolish dozens of boards and commissions and to transfer their functions to regular departments, the heads of which were appointed by and responsible to the governor. Only in a few states, however, was the number of elective executive officers reduced. Elsewhere the reorganizations related mainly to agencies over which the legislature had control. Departmentalization of most state activities greatly expanded the authority of the governor.

Hand in hand with administrative consolidation went the creation of the executive budget system. The usual pattern in the reorganized states was to make the governor responsible for the preparation of a financial plan, including both revenues and expenditures, and its submission to the legislature. The chief executive's authority over the administration also was increased greatly by the vesting of fiscal controls

[2] Woodrow Wilson, *The State: Elements of Historical and Practical Politics* (Heath, 1898), p. 499.

in his hands or in those of a director of finance or other officer responsible to him. Among these controls are expenditure control, central purchasing, and others that will be discussed later.

Although many states have strengthened their chief executives' role, several have not. In the latter the governorship remains weak, the executive authority being shared with a large number of other elective administrative officers and with boards and commissions.

SELECTION PROCESS

Qualifications, Terms, and Pay. The governor and the lieutenant governor, if there is one, usually have identical formal qualifications for office. These are, almost always, that a person must be thirty years or more of age, a citizen of the United States, and a resident of the state for a minimum period of time. It is perhaps unnecessary to specify such matters, because it is unlikely that the electorate would offend any of these rules even if they were left out of the constitution.

The governor's term of office is 4 years in twenty-nine states and 2 years in nineteen states. There has been a tendency to make the term longer; the average of more than 3 years prevailing today may be contrasted with the average of slightly more than 1 year at the time of the adoption of the Federal Constitution. Two-fifths of the states, including Pennsylvania, New Jersey, and Indiana, forbid governors to serve more than one, two, or three successive terms, but this device has not led, as it has in some Latin-American countries, to *coups d'état* to keep the incumbent in by violence. The rest of the states have been content to keep their executives available for reelection in case the electorate so desires.

Salaries of state executives are on the upgrade. The larger are those of New York ($50,000), California ($40,000), New Jersey ($30,000), Pennsylvania ($25,000), and Michigan ($22,500). The lowest is that of Nevada ($7,600); the median is now $15,000. Even in the agricultural states of the West and South, the type of man chosen governor usually could make more

by staying on the farm or in professional practice. It is certainly poor policy to pay public servants so much less than the businessmen and other people with whom they deal. In most states, governors also have the use of a mansion and receive an allowance for entertaining.

Election. Everywhere governors are elected under party designations. They are nominated for office, in most states, by the direct primary. Even in primary states, however, there has been a recent tendency, led by New York and Indiana, to exempt the governorship from the primary and to nominate through party conventions. The return to the convention system of nominating candidates for the post of chief executive has added much interest to party organizational matters, has reduced expenditures of aspirants greatly, and may have improved the quality of the candidates chosen. The great majority of the states continue to use the primary plan; in order to assure a majority choice, a few states conduct a runoff primary.

Most states hold gubernatorial elections in even-numbered years, combined with congressional elections. A few, including many of the Southern states, have chosen odd-numbered years for state elections. Virtually all states elect governors on the highest vote cast, whether plurality or majority, but a few insist upon a majority and throw the election to the legislature if none is obtained. The popular-vote, at-large system of voting for governor is commonly assumed to be in universal use, but in Mississippi an electoral-vote scheme is still in effect. In Georgia the "county-block" plan, which has been used in party primaries, recently was proposed for general elections as well. In the 1946 Democratic primary, the Georgia scheme resulted in the nomination of Gene Talmadge for governor despite the fact that one of his rivals polled more popular votes than he did.

The governorship regularly attracts a considerable number of aspirants and candidates. Those who are successful generally have had some experience in the legislature; a term or two as county prosecutor also is common. The office commands respect and the powers make it a post to be desired. Governors frequently vault to United States senatorships and occasionally to the presidency. With such stakes, it is not surprising that competition for the office is keen.

Removal. The governor can be removed from office by impeachment. Indictment is by the lower house, and trial by the upper. The chief justice of the supreme court in many states presides when a governor is under impeachment trial. This method of removal has not been used to any great extent. New York, Texas, and Oklahoma each removed governors by impeachment in the period 1913–1923. The mere existence of the power may be a deterrent upon some governors. The fact that the legislature is in session for only limited periods in most of the states restricts the possibility of impeachment proceedings. Since the governor usually has the sole power to call special sessions and may even specify what the legislature can do in such sessions, there is little chance of impeaching him except at regular sessions.

Eleven states have provision for removal by recall. This device, explained in an earlier chapter,[3] permits voters, by signing petitions, to require a special election to determine whether or not an official should be superseded before his term expires. It has been used to remove a governor on only one occasion, in the state of North Dakota. When adequate safeguards are provided to ensure that it is not abused, the recall offers a weapon by which an officer can be dismissed whenever a sufficiently large proportion of the electorate judges such action desirable.

Whether the office of governor is vacated through impeachment, recall, death, or resignation, a successor is provided for in the constitution. In most cases this is the lieutenant governor; but when there is no such officer, usually the president of the senate or the speaker of the lower house succeeds to the governorship.

POWERS OF THE GOVERNOR

Appointment and Removal. One of the most decisive powers of the executive is that of appointment and removal. Through his power to

appoint, the governor may surround himself with fellow administrators who share his views and will carry out his policies. The governor also may secure, through his use of this power, the support of legislators. Although greatly reduced in volume since the adoption of merit systems in many states, gubernatorial appointments still loom large because of the increasing integration of authority in the major department heads and bureau chiefs.

The scope of the appointing power is limited by the persistence of constitutional offices, filled by popular election. Normally subject to confirmation, mostly senatorial, governors appoint secretaries of state in seven states, attorneys general in five, controllers in four, auditors in three, treasurers in three, and superintendents of public instruction in six.[4] These offices, in all other states in which they exist, are elective, in most cases by the people but occasionally by the legislature.

The mode of selection used for other department heads varies likewise. Taken as a whole, the most common pattern is to vest appointment in the governor, with or without senatorial confirmation, but a surprisingly large number of major state administrators are chosen by some means other than gubernatorial appointment. Almost inevitably this leads to some measure of irresponsibility, for neither the electorate nor the legislature is able to coordinate the functions or even judge the stewardship of a large number of semi-independent officials.

Legislative Powers. The role of the governor in legislative procedure was touched in the previous chapter. The governor's major legislative powers are (1) to call special sessions, (2) to recommend policies and legislation, and (3) to veto bills.

Power to convene extraordinary sessions of the legislature is universally vested in the governor. In most cases, the governor's power is an exclusive one, unshared with the legislature. New Hampshire alone permits the legislature to call itself into special session, but the power has not been exercised. In a few states, the governor is

---

[3] See p. 205.

[4] These figures are from *The Book of the States, 1954–1955*, p. 159.

required to convene the legislature if requested by a fixed proportion of the legislators.[5] It appears that about one-half the states further empower the governor to specify what matters may be taken up by the legislature in the special session.

Depending greatly on the political situation prevailing in a state and on the personal qualities of a governor, the power to recommend legislation can be one of the most influential possessed by the chief executive. Assembling not long after its election (usually in January after a November election), the legislature almost inevitably looks to the governor to propose a positive legislative program. If the governor produces a well-conceived plan and has the ability to sell it to the legislators, the program of the administration is likely to become the principal focus of attention during the session. On the other hand, if the legislature is hostile to the governor, or if he is weak, it may proceed to devise a program of its own. Happily, the former situation prevails most commonly, and the governor is able to exert positive leadership. Principal messages to the legislature often are delivered in person, with radio and television broadcasting facilities carrying his address throughout the state.

The veto power, described already in some detail, is not as negative as it might appear at first impression. It arms the governor with a weapon he can use to defend his positive program, to protect the financial position of the state, to curb excessive localism, and to ferret out ill-drafted and unconstitutional measures. Often the threat of veto is enough to keep the legislature off a course of action opposed by the governor. In recent years, governors of many states have held public hearings on major bills in order to permit proponents and opponents an opportunity to air their views. Because of the great volume of legislation passed in the closing rush, the governor's veto is often absolute; after the legislature has adjourned finally, it is im-

possible for him to return a disapproved bill to the house of origin, so his action is final. The power to pocket veto and to veto items of appropriation bills adds greatly to the sum total of gubernatorial authority in the states permitting those practices.

Military Powers. Early state constitutions placed great stress on the governor's role as commander in chief of the armed forces of the state. After the adoption of the Federal Constitution and the assumption by the Federal government of paramount authority in military matters, this aspect of the governor's power diminished greatly in importance. The enactment of National Guard legislation at the close of the First World War emphasized even more the supremacy of federal control over the former state militias. In time of national emergency and war, the various state units of the National Guard are called into active duty and operate as integral parts of the Army.

The governor has retained, however, a great deal of control over state armed forces. Except when in federal service, National Guard units are under gubernatorial command. Subject to the provisions of state constitution and law, the governor commissions officers and calls out the militia to suppress insurrections or deal with emergencies. During the last two decades, for example, governors have used state troops to restore order in strikes, quell outbreaks in state penitentiaries, do rescue and police work in flood and earthquake disasters, and perform several other services.

In practice, governors do not place great importance upon their functions as commanders in chief. Military matters are delegated to an adjutant general and his staff. Some governors pervert their power to commission officers to political purposes and honor untrained citizens with high rank. When this rank is purely honorary, no great harm is done, but when National Guard units are loaded with officers selected on a political basis, the effectiveness of that force in wartime may be undermined.

Financial Powers. As the reorganization of the administrative branches of state governments has proceeded, governors have been given more

[5] New York State Constitutional Convention Committee, *Problems Relating to Legislative Organization and Powers* (Albany: The Committee, 1938), pp 402–405.

and more authority over finances. Originally, the governor had control only over the expenditures of that portion of the administrative establishment that was placed under his direct jurisdiction. The spread of the veto power to state after state gave the chief executive at least a negative authority over proposed expenditures. The item veto expanded his measure of control very greatly.

It was the twentieth-century reorganizations that gave governors the most potent of their controls over money matters. Centering in the budget, they were (1) the power to formulate the financial plan, and (2) the power to execute it. The executive budget is a comprehensive financial plan, usually containing estimates of revenues, recommendations of new revenues (if any), and proposals of amounts of expenditures for each purpose and agency. In most reorganized states, the responsibility for formulating this budget is placed squarely on the shoulders of the governor. After the budget is authorized, the governor usually possesses powers which may be used to control the pattern of expenditures by executive agencies. The most effective of these controls affect purchases, construction, limitation of expenditures over particular financial periods (months or quarters), and the imposition of compulsory savings.

The Pardoning Power. The governor's power to grant pardons and reprieves is judicial in nature and is derived from the role of the royal colonial governor as chancellor. It exists to provide a remedy for mistakes that are made in the trial and conviction of alleged criminals and to release offenders who are deemed to have reformed. In the early days while populations were small and other duties of office not too heavy, governors could give applications for executive clemency their personal attention. The busy state executive of today rarely can find time to examine more than the most spectacular cases.

A tabulation made for the New York Constitutional Convention of 1938 [6] revealed that twenty states refrain from placing the sole au-

thority for pardoning in the governor. Of these states that have modified gubernatorial responsibility for pardons, sixteen have pardon boards, which may or may not include the governor, and four require ratification of executive action by either council or senate. Even in the states that have retained the pardoning power solely in the hands of the governor, nineteen states have established advisory pardon boards to investigate and recommend to the governor.

Few governors relish this aspect of their work. Applications for pardons and commutation of sentence consume great amounts of time and nervous energy, and are among the most distasteful tasks a state executive has. The present trend is to place primary emphasis on the decision or recommendation of a full-time board or staff, preferably trained in the field of penology.

Chief Administrator. State constitutions commonly refer to the governor as "chief executive" and assign him the task of seeing that laws are faithfully executed. Some even follow the Federal Constitution in giving him power to require department heads to render reports to him in writing. Although not always stated in so many words, the governor is usually expected to head the executive branch of state government and to use such powers as are delegated to him to get some order out of the chaos created by constitutional provisions written to fit another age and inspired by a political philosophy that is outmoded today. In addition, he is expected by public opinion, in nearly every state, to serve as chief legislator, despite constitutional provisions, express or implied, that the doctrine of separation of powers must prevail. Thus the modern governor is faced with the often difficult task of asserting himself as a real leader by utilizing such powers as he is given or can assume.

That it has been possible for the governor to emerge from figurehead to leader, as Leslie Lipson aptly puts it,[7] has been due less to formal powers vested by legal sanction than to the position of the chief executive as party leader and representative of all the people. At the head of

[6] New York State Constitutional Convention Committee, *Problems Relating to Executive Administration and Powers*, pp. 68–79.

[7] *The American Governor from Figurehead to Leader* (University of Chicago Press, 1939).

the state ticket of his party, the gubernatorial candidate commands a special position in party councils and frequently is the outstanding leader of his party. Like the President in the national field, the governor is selected by a process involving the whole electorate and therefore with some justice can claim to be their spokesman and leader.[8]

STATE ADMINISTRATION

Constitutional Officers. In addition to the governor, a number of state officials are popularly elected.

The *lieutenant governor* succeeds to the governorship in case of vacancy and is usually the presiding officer over the state senate. Sometimes he also has minor administrative assignments, such as serving on boards and commissions.

The *secretary of state* is the official custodian of records, keeper of the seal, issuer of corporate charters, and supervisor of election administration. His work is largely routine in nature.

The *attorney general* is the chief legal officer, who performs many types of legal services for the state including prosecution, the overseeing of local law-enforcement officials, defense of the state, and the furnishing of legal advice to state agencies.

The *treasurer* is custodian of the state purse; sometimes he collects taxes as well; and he disburses money when payments are authorized by appropriate authority.

The *auditor, controller,* or *comptroller* usually possesses power to authorize payments that are provided for by law; in most states such an officer also audits state financial accounts.

The *superintendent of public instruction* directs the state school system through his supervisory and financial powers over elementary, secondary, and teacher training schools.

Most of these officers, with the exceptions noted earlier, are elected by the people and therefore are independent of direct gubernatorial control. In cases in which such officers are the heads of executive departments, the departments have similar independence.

Departments. A department is an instrument into which related functions are grouped for convenience and efficient operation. Before the administrative reorganizations carried out in many states during the past thirty years, it was common to have up to a hundred or more uncoordinated agencies—bureaus, commissions, boards, offices, and the like—either directly responsible to the governor or independent of gubernatorial control. Since reorganization, most states have tended to set up departments presided over by single heads, called "directors" or "secretaries," but several states have retained boards or commissions in control of departments. In some fields, notably education and public welfare, there is a strong tendency to utilize boards, with or without an executive officer.

Because states vary considerably in the nomenclature employed and the duties assigned to departments, it is possible here to present no more than a list of the departments most commonly found in the American states:

Budget and/or finance	Justice
Revenue and/or taxation	Highways
Public instruction	Mental hygiene
Military	Insurance
Agriculture	Labor
Conservation	Public works
Health	Welfare

The typical department is subdivided further into bureaus, divisions, offices, or agencies, each with its chief who is responsible to the department head. In some states bureau chiefs are made appointive by the governor; in others they are under civil service.

Independent Agencies. In the states that have not yet reorganized, and in many that have, there remains a confused array of scattered agencies, boards, commissions, and officials. These independent agencies are administered in a variety of ways. Some have single heads chosen by the governor, functioning much like bureaus but reporting directly to the governor rather than through a department. Others have full-

[8] For a good recent case study, see *Gladys M. Kammerer,* "The Governor as Chief Administrator in Kentucky," *Journal of Politics,* vol. 16 (May, 1954), pp. 236–256.

or part-time boards, which may either divide administrative responsibilities among themselves or choose a full-time administrator to do the job. The use of the board or commission

The remainder of the states have merit systems covering employees only in certain functions or departments. The latter are mainly the result of a requirement imposed by Social Security Act

CALIFORNIA STATE GOVERNMENT ORGANIZATION

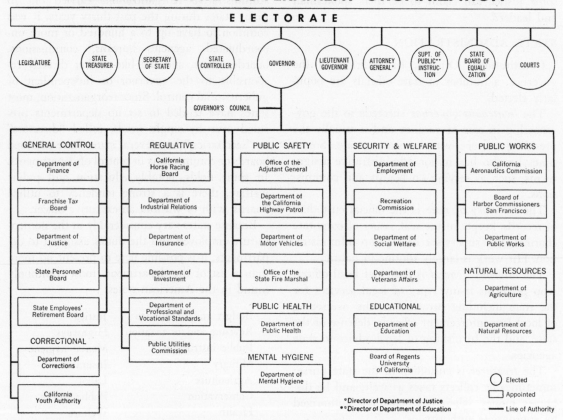

Although California took part in the administrative reorganization movement in the 1910–1930 era, its organization now illustrates many of the faults common among American states. The electorate chooses too many public officials, an excessive number of agencies report directly to the governor, and numerous boards and commissions blur responsibility. Moreover, some of the departments in California are "paper" departments, consisting of rather autonomous agencies with related functions.

has often been justified when a new function is being undertaken, or when the work to be done involves a combination of administrative, legislative, and judicial functions.

State Merit Systems. As recorded in an earlier chapter, some twenty-five states have adopted general civil-service systems on the merit basis.[9]

[9] See p. 331.

amendments in 1939, which made it mandatory for states receiving federal social security aid to use the merit system in the agencies concerned with its administration. The usual state agencies covered are those having to do with social welfare, public health, unemployment compensation, and employment services.

Most of the state-wide civil-service systems are directed by an agency called either "civil-service commission" or "personnel board," although a few have experimented with single-headed bodies. The agency classifies positions by the kind of work involved and by the relative degree of skill or responsibility required. The appropriate compensation is fixed for each job and a complete salary standardization plan drawn up.

The trend toward comprehensive state merit systems has been strong during the last decade. If it continues at the same rate in the future, nearly all states will have state-wide plans within another 20 years. State civil-service reform is opposed by many practicing politicians on the ground that those who work in campaigns must be rewarded. There is a good argument for making all policy-forming offices appointive by the governor, since he is entitled to have major officers around him who share his views and enjoy his full confidence. For the great bulk of state jobs, however, there is little rational defense for the old-fashioned spoils methods that belong to a bygone age.

The Administrative Reorganization Movement. As the American states acquired new population and new problems, the functions of state government multiplied. Lacking an overall plan or even a philosophy of administrative organization, legislatures created new agencies with little thought of their relationship to existing agencies. The result was like that achieved by a farmer who began with a small shed, which was quite adequate to shelter himself and the team of horses he possessed. Later the farmer chose a wife, and in due time they acquired several children. In the meantime, farming operations having multiplied several times over, the farmer required barns for hay, cover for animals and farm machinery, eventually even a garage. Each expansion brought new demands for buildings, and the Topsy-like growth of farm structures—here a room, there a lean-to, over yonder an outhouse, a new porch on the front, and new storeroom on the rear—was very similar to that of state governments.

The time came, around 1910, when public officials and students of government recognized that the scattered agencies of government often were inefficient and sometimes worked at cross-purposes with other agencies. Studies of the need for reorganization were made in several states before the first definite reforms were adopted by Illinois in 1917. There more than one hundred agencies, boards, and commissions were abolished and their functions regrouped into nine departments, which were headed by directors appointed by the governor. An executive budget system was created, which concentrated a great deal of authority in the newly created department of finance.

Most of the thirty-odd states that have instituted some degree of administrative reorganization have followed the Illinois model. A few, notably Virginia and New York, went further than Illinois and reduced the number of elective constitutional officers. On the other hand, Wisconsin and Michigan reorganized their agencies but avoided increasing the power of the governor by placing responsibility for coordination in the hands of agencies beyond his direct control.

The pattern of modern state administrative organization, then, is to concentrate most agencies and functions into a limited number of executive departments. These departments, headed by appointees of the governor, consist of appropriate bureaus and other subdivisions. Great emphasis is placed upon the establishment of the executive budget and the concentration of fiscal control powers in a department of finance or similar agency. Many of the states that have reorganized also have created central purchasing agencies and have installed uniform accounting systems. Another feature of many a reformed administration is the organization of department heads into a cabinet, presided over by the governor.

Following the creation of the first Commission on Organization of the Executive Branch of Government by Congress in 1947, two-thirds of the states set up bodies to survey their administrative problems. These "little Hoover" groups, as they were popularly called, studied a variety of problems in the several states, but the central focus of most was administrative organization. A common theme in most of the reports was that the governor should be placed in command of most of or all the administrative agencies, and that he should discharge his responsibility through departments headed by individuals rather than boards and commissions. Many of the reports stressed the desirability of strengthening financial controls in the hands of governors and legislatures.

In an evaluation written after the initial impact of state "little Hoover" reports, Karl A. Bosworth [10] found only two states—New Hampshire and New Jersey—in which legislatures

[10] "The Politics of Management Improvement in the States," *American Political Science Review,* vol. 47 (March, 1953), pp. 84–99.

moved positively and fully to put recommendations into effect. Some of the states did nothing or practically nothing. Perhaps one-half or more acted favorably on some of their "little Hoover" recommendations.[11]

[11] For case studies of particular states, see F. M. Landers and H. D. Hamilton, "State Administrative Reorganization in Michigan: The Legislative Approach," *Public Administration Review,* vol. 14 (Spring, 1954), pp. 99–111; S. K. Gove, "Reorganization in Illinois," *National Municipal Review,* vol. 42 (November, 1953), pp. 502–506; R. H. Weir, "Reorganization—1954 Style," *State Government,* vol. 27 (April, 1954), pp. 72–74; Bennett M. Rich, "Administrative Reorganization in New Jersey," *Public Administration Review,* vol. 12 (Autumn, 1952), pp. 251–257.

FOR FURTHER READING

Buck, Arthur E.: *The Reorganization of State Government in the United States* (Columbia University Press, 1938).

——: *Administrative Consolidation in State Governments* (New York: National Municipal League, rev. ed., 1930).

Carleton, Roderick L., and Staff: *The Reorganization and Consolidation of State Administration in Louisiana* (Louisiana State University Press, 1937).

Cheek, Roma S.: *The Pardoning Power of the Governor of North Carolina* (Duke University Press, 1932).

Council of State Governments: *Reorganizing State Government* (Chicago: The Council, 1950).

Faust, Martin L.: *Manual on the Executive Article . . .* (Columbia, 1943). Missouri Constitutional Convention of 1943, no. 4.

Governors' Conference: *Proceedings of the . . .* (Chicago: Council of State Governments, annual).

Jensen, Christen: *The Pardoning Power in the American States* (University of Chicago Press, 1922).

Lipson, Leslie: *The American Governor from Figurehead to Leader* (University of Chicago Press, 1939). Studies in Public Administration, vol. IX.

New York State Constitutional Convention Committee: *Problems Relating to Executive Administration and Powers* (Albany: The Committee, 1938).

Ransone, Coleman B.: *The Office of Governor in the South* (University of Alabama, Bureau of Public Administration, 1951).

Rohr, Charles J.: *The Governor of Maryland: A Constitutional Study* (Johns Hopkins Press, 1932). Also Johns Hopkins University Studies in Historical and Political Science, series L, pp. 303–475.

Scace, Homer E.: *The Organization of the Executive Office of the Governor* (New York: Institute of Public Administration, 1950).

1. Trace the evolution of the office of the governor and indicate the problems involved in developing a strong state executive.

2. To what extent is executive authority in the American states divided between elective constitutional officers and departments under gubernatorial control?

3. What are the principal powers of the American governor?

4. Explain the administrative reorganization movement in the states, and indicate how far it has proceeded.

5. Describe the appointive power of the governor. How extensively have the states adopted the merit system?

6. What are the ways by which a governor can influence lawmaking?

7. Would you strengthen or weaken the office of governor? What specific changes would you advocate?

8. Compare the office of governor with that of the President of the United States.

9. Outline a plan for making the administrative branch of the government of your state the best possible.

CHAPTER 35

The State Judiciary

> We are told in the Federalist that the judiciary is least able to hold its own in a competition of the three departments of government. . . . The legislature and the executive are aggressive in their will to power. The judiciary can do little more than obstruct when the departments of government come into conflict. There is nothing to be feared from making it efficient. — Roscoe Pound [1]

Alongside the federal machinery, discussed earlier, but with no organic relationship to it, stand forty-eight state judicial and law-enforcement systems that are completely independent of one another. Authorized by state constitutions, each is different, each operates solely within a single state, and each is concerned chiefly with the application, interpretation, and enforcement of state and local laws. Although often less publicized than Federal courts and agents, it is on this level that the bulk of controversies arising in the counties, towns, and cities throughout the nation are tried. The machinery and procedures are, therefore, of great importance.

GENERAL CONSIDERATIONS

State Law. While state and local governments must respect the Federal Constitution and laws, they are not under obligation to enforce them. Separate federal instrumentalities have been provided for that purpose. Instead, state law consists of state constitutions, statutes, and orders of the legislatures, executives, and administrative officers, charters and ordinances of units of local governments, and common law (except in Louisiana where the Napoleonic Civil Code prevails). Common law usually prevails in the absence of legislation dealing with a matter in controversy.

State Jurisdiction. The legal authority of states stops at their boundaries. If one state wishes to reach beyond its territorial limits, it can do so only through the Federal government or by the cooperation and approval of other states. Within state boundaries responsibility must, of course, be shared with the Federal government.

The jurisdiction of state courts extends to all cases and controversies at common law; those arising from state constitutions, statutes, and orders; those arising from charters and ordinances of local governments; and those arising between a state and its citizens or between a state and citizens of other states.[2] In addition, according to acts of Congress, state courts have exclusive jurisdiction over civil suits between parties with diverse citizenship involving less than $3,000, and concurrent jurisdiction in cases of diverse citizenship where larger sums are involved. Federal legislation also gives state courts exclusive jurisdiction over civil suits arising from federal laws where less than $3,000 is in-

[1] *Organization of Courts* (Little, Brown, 1940), p. 293.

[2] See the Eleventh Amendment.

volved and concurrent jurisdiction with Federal courts where sums are greater. Where concurrent jurisdiction exists the parties in dispute usually choose between launching the suit in a state or Federal court. Acts of Congress also permit state courts to share in the administration of a few matters such as naturalization, applications for passports, and bankruptcies.

Types of Cases. When the Federal courts were explained, disputes coming before them for decision were divided into the following types: criminal, civil, equity, and those arising under international law. Virtually all international law disputes come before Federal courts; hence, state judiciaries seldom encounter them. The bulk of cases coming before state courts are, therefore, criminal, civil, and equity. Criminal cases, it will be recalled, are those in which the state attempts to prove someone guilty of violating state laws. Civil are those arising between private parties who are seeking settlements, usually in the form of monetary payments. Cases in equity are those in which parties seek judicial determination of matters for which there are no readily available remedies "at law." Illustrations have been given in Chap. 16.

JUDICIAL ORGANIZATION

State Systems Decentralized. Under the federal judicial system considerable centralized direction stems from the Department of Justice, the Annual Judicial Conference of Senior Circuit Judges, the Administrative Office of the United States Courts, and the fact that judges and other personnel are appointive. But state judicial systems, organized as they are on a district or county basis with elective judges, have been characterized by extreme decentralization. Under these systems, each court acts as a nearly autonomous unit except as it is obliged to operate within limits laid down by the legislature and rules of procedures established, perhaps, by the state supreme court, or as it may be influenced by review of its proceedings in appellate courts. While most states have effected a degree of uniformity as far as procedure is concerned, in the field of judicial administration each court

proceeds about as it sees fit. Indeed, decentralization exists to such an extent that courts even lack the power to appoint and direct minor court personnel. "Even the pettiest agency," says Roscoe Pound, "has much more control than the average state court." [3]

The desirability of greater unification has been the subject of discussion for years. The American Judicature Society has pleaded for this end since its foundation in 1913,[4] the National Municipal League has constantly urged the reform and embodied its suggestion in the model state constitution,[5] and many others have joined in urging the reform. Some interest has been aroused and progress made in scattered places. Missouri, when changing her constitution in 1946, gave her Supreme Court broad rule-making authority and limited power of transferring judges. North Carolina made similar changes in 1950, and several other states have followed suit. But none has gone as far as New Jersey did in 1947 when it approximated a unified and flexible system.

Judicial Councils and Administrative Offices. Decentralized as their judicial systems are, states had until recently no central source of information or leadership on matters pertaining to the administration of justice. When data were desired the usual method of getting them was through unsystematized inquiries by the governor, attorney general, or chief justice, special investigations, or advisory committees set up by the bar associations. Experience demonstrated the need for continuous systematic study and review, to provide which judicial councils have been established. Ohio took the lead in 1923, Massachusetts and Oregon followed the next year. At present, councils are authorized by the laws of over thirty states.[6] A very recent trend

[3] *Op. cit.,* p. 286.

[4] See its *Journal* published bimonthly.

[5] The League's views also have been set forth in its monthly publication entitled *National Municipal Review.*

[6] A list of these states with pertinent data concerning their councils may be found in Council of State Governments, *The Book of the States, 1948–1949,* p. 506. Wisconsin was added to the list in 1951 and Florida in 1953.

is for the states to establish an agency resembling the Administrative Office of the United States Courts, discussed in Chap. 16. Idaho, in 1949, established an Office of Coordinator of the Courts, while North Carolina, in 1951, authorized the Chief Justice to appoint an admin-

by executive officers, legislatures, courts, and members of the bar. Although hampered by the lack of funds and personnel, councils have filled a recognized need and must now be considered established institutions. Progress has been discouragingly slow but the councils have,

NEW JERSEY'S COURT SYSTEM UNDER NEW CONSTITUTION

SUPREME COURT

Chief Justice & 6 Associates

with broad powers of administration over all courts in the state. Jurisdiction—Final appeals in all important cases. First term—7 years, tenure on re-appointment, retirement at 70.

SUPERIOR COURT

Minimum of 24 judges; term, tenure, and retirement same as Supreme Court.

LAW DIVISION	APPELLATE DIVISION	CHANCERY DIVISION
	Decides appeals from Law Division, Chacery Division, County Courts and as may be provided by law	

COUNTY COURT

Minimum of 1 County Judge in each county. Jurisdiction same as that of 5 old County Courts with equity powers when required for complete determination of a case. Jurisdiction subject to change by law.

INFERIOR COURTS

Not abolished by revision but may be established, altered or abolished by appeals therefrom as provided by law.

County Traffic Courts	District Courts	Police Recorder & Family Courts	Juvenile & Domestic Relations Courts	Surrogate Courts	Criminal Judicial District Courts	Small Cause Courts	Justice of Peace Courts

All judges appointed by governor with approval of senate, except municipal judges and surrogates.

Adapted from *Journal of the American Judicature Society,* vol. 31 (February, 1948), p. 143.

istrative assistant to perform a similar function. Similar measures are under consideration elsewhere.

Councils usually employ full- or part-time executive secretaries and a small staff. Functions are generally confined to compiling statistics, conducting research, and making recommendations. In no instance have they been given authority to direct or supervise the courts. The data assembled become the basis for recommendations by the councils in anticipation of action

without doubt, helped focus attention upon some of the most needed changes in judicial procedure and administration.

Supreme Courts. Standing at the pinnacle of the judicial structure of every state is a supreme tribunal, usually, although not always, called a "supreme court." The great majority of states have either five or seven judges on their highest court, although a few have only three. Judges are usually elected. Except for the issuance of writs their work is confined almost exclusively to hearing cases brought on appeal from the lower courts. They never "try" cases; nor do they permit the introduction of new evidence. Rather, they merely review the law and record and either sustain, reverse, or modify decisions made by lower courts. If more testimony seems necessary or retrial appears appropriate, the case is remanded to trial courts. Decisions are writ-

has several known as district courts of appeals; while in Oklahoma there is a court having jurisdiction in criminal cases only, known as criminal court of appeals.[7] Courts like these consist of from three to nine judges, who are usually elected. Their organization and procedure are in other ways much like that of supreme tribunals.

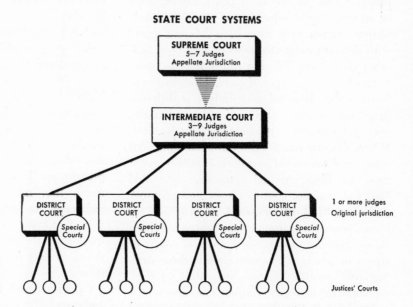

STATE COURT SYSTEMS

SUPREME COURT
5–7 Judges
Appellate Jurisdiction

INTERMEDIATE COURT
3–9 Judges
Appellate Jurisdiction

DISTRICT COURT — Special Courts

1 or more judges
Original jurisdiction

Justices' Courts

Except for the addition of intermediate and special courts, state judicial systems have changed little since Colonial days.

ten and published in volumes generally known as "state supreme court reports." Supreme courts are the ultimate interpreters of state constitutions and laws except where appeals may be taken to the Federal courts because of alleged conflicts between state and Federal constitutions and laws. In a few states they have been authorized to render advisory opinions upon important questions of law when requested by the governor or legislature.

Intermediate Courts. The more populous states have established one or more intermediate courts immediately below the highest court for the purpose of reviewing cases that need not necessarily demand the time of already overburdened supreme tribunals. These are also appellate courts. Their names are varied: Tennessee has one intermediate court called the court of appeals; Pennsylvania and New Jersey each has one called the superior court; California

District or County Courts. Beneath the courts of appeals stand the trial courts that handle the great majority of cases litigated throughout the country. It is these that most likely will try the home-town case of murder, burglary, assault and battery, rape, and suit for damages. These courts function within districts outlined by state legislatures in such a way as always to include at least one county, and frequently more in sparsely settled regions. California, for example, has fifty-eight districts—one for each county; New York has nine; Illinois has seventeen; and Pennsylvania has fifty-eight—nine fewer than the number of counties.

The names of courts like these vary. In Pennsylvania they are known as district courts; in California, superior courts; elsewhere, county

[7] Clarence N. Callender, *American Courts: Their Organization and Procedure* (McGraw-Hill, 1927), p. 27; *The Book of the States, 1945–1946*, p. 443.

or circuit courts or something else. Some cases reach them on appeal from summary courts, like those of justice of the peace, in which case it is customary to ignore the trial that took place before the summary court and rehear it from beginning to end. Most cases, however, originate here. Most end here, also, because there are comparatively few appeals. Sometimes the same judges sitting in the same court handle cases of all types but at separate and distinct periods of time. Again, some states have different courts with different judges for cases of each type. Still other states have different courts but the same judges for various types of cases. Thus, in Pennsylvania the same judge or judges at different times preside over courts of quarter session, oyer and terminer, orphans, and common pleas. Where separate courts exist, those handling civil cases are often called courts of common pleas; those handling criminal cases may be called courts of sessions, courts of oyer and terminer and general jail delivery, or, for less serious offenses, courts of quarter session; those handling equity cases are commonly known as courts of equity or courts of chancery; while those dealing with probate matters are called probate, orphans', or surrogate courts. The number of judges in each district varies from one to several and in most states judges are chosen by popular election.

Minor Courts. At the base of state judicial systems are numerous courts for handling minor disputes with little formality. In rural areas and small municipalities these are justices' courts presided over by justices of the peace. In larger places similar courts may be manned by magistrates, or occasionally aldermen. Usually two are chosen within each town, township, ward, or district for terms varying from 2 to 6 years. Officers like these usually need not be lawyers, nor for that matter possess any special qualifications other than the ability to get nominated and elected. Justices come from all walks of life. A recent study made in Pennsylvania disclosed that of 3,225 justices and aldermen, 61 per cent listed their occupations as being that of justice of the peace, farmer, laborer and unskilled worker, and skilled laborer. The study

even disclosed 50 housewives filling the office.[8] Justices usually hold other jobs; their compensation for official services ordinarily comes from fees, although a few states have put justices on a salary basis.

The duties of justices are extremely varied. Besides performing marriage ceremonies and notarial duties, they handle both civil and criminal cases. Civil suits, like those involving breaches of contract, trespass, action on notes, and bill collection, ordinarily involve sums of less than $300. Where sums of less than $100 are involved the justices' decisions are usually final; otherwise an appeal may be taken to a higher court. Often justices' courts exercise a concurrent jurisdiction with district courts, parties having the option of starting their suit in either place. In criminal matters where serious offenses are involved they may hold only preliminary hearings, but where offenses are minor they may try the case and pronounce judgment. Records of proceedings need not be kept, hence the term "courts not of record." In most cases the trial is without jury. Invariably decisions may be appealed to district or county courts.

Criticisms and Proposed Reforms of Minor Judiciary. The minor judiciary has been widely criticized in recent years with the result that it has been subjected to extensive study. Critics insist that there are far too many justices for modern times; that justices lack desirable training; that many justices are uninterested in their work, so much so that it is many times impossible to find anyone to run for office; that the nature of the office leads to dispersion of responsibility, inefficiency, and excessive costs; that the fee system often leads to undesirable solicitation of business and to petty extortion; that justices in large places have become integral parts of corrupt machines; and that justices do not render impartial justice but too often decide in fa-

[8] Committee on Minor Judiciary of the Pennsylvania Bar Association, *Survey of the Minor Judiciary of Pennsylvania* (State College, Pa.: The Pennsylvania Municipal Publications Service, 1942), pp. 27–28. For a good general discussion of the office, see George Warren, *Traffic Courts* (Little, Brown, 1942), pp. 186–234.

vor of the plaintiff because it is easier, more popular, or more profitable to do so—hence the accusation that the initials "J.P." mean "justice for the plaintiff."

The case in favor of reform is convincing. In England, home of the justices' court, their use has steadily declined in favor of appointive, full-time, legally trained "stipendiary magistrates." One should also remember that the Federal courts have functioned for years with United States Commissioners who are not elective lay justices as are those in the states. The remedy most commonly advocated is abolition of the justices' courts and transfer of their functions to district or county courts in rural areas and metropolitan courts in urban. A possible adaptation is to retain the justice of the peace but only as an assistant to the judge of the county court.[9] The least that might be done would be to consolidate jurisdictional areas, establish higher qualifications, provide for a larger measure of supervision by district courts, and abolish the fee system. A significant sign of the times is the fact that in Missouri's new constitution of 1945, justices' courts were replaced by a system of magistrate courts to be presided over only by persons with legal training. At the same time the fee system was abolished. New Jersey made similar changes in 1947. California in the early 1950's fully reorganized its inferior-court system.

Special Courts. The courts described above provide the warp and woof of state judiciaries. To these must be added a wide variety of special courts found particularly in metropolitan centers. Most common are municipal courts set up for handling problems peculiar to congested areas. These are usually headed by several elective judges, each of whom presides over one or more divisions specializing in criminal, civil, traffic, domestic relations, or juvenile cases. In addition to handling disputes arising from mu-

nicipal law, these nearly always have concurrent jurisdiction with the usual district or county courts. This means that for violating a city ordinance one would be prosecuted in the municipal court but for a state offense committed within the city's limits one might be tried in either the municipal court, a justice's court, or a county (or district) court. Needless to say, this is often quite confusing, especially where cities have spread out to include an entire county or more. Other special courts frequently found include those for handling small monetary claims, domestic relations, traffic, and juvenile cases.

COURT OFFICIALS

Judges. The principal court officers are, of course, the judges. As indicated above, there may be one or several for each court. Where there are several they may sit *en banc* (as a body) or one or more may preside over divisions into which the court has been divided. Except for justices of the peace and their counterparts, all but nine states require that judges be "learned in the law." A few states specify that a judge must be of "good character," while North Carolina requires that he "believe in God."[10] Methods of selection and appointment are discussed below. Terms vary from 2 years in Vermont to life in Massachusetts. The usual method of removal is by impeachment, but several states permit removal by the governor upon the address of two-thirds of both houses of the legislature; several states provide for popular recall; a few permit removal by the state supreme court; others follow variations of one or more of these methods.

Appointment vs. Election of Judges. During the Colonial period, it will be recalled, judges were appointive. After the Revolution, appointment by state legislatures became the rule. Mississippi broke with tradition in 1832 by providing for popular election. Other states were quick to follow with the result that by the time of the Civil War election became most common. Today, although as many as seven different methods are used, three predominate: (1) popu-

---

[9] For these and other suggestions, see especially William F. Willoughby, *Principles of Judicial Administration* (Brookings, 1929), pp. 302–306; State of New York, *Report of the Commission on the Administration of Justice in New York State* (Albany: The Commission, 1934), pp. 557–591; and Committee on Minor Judiciary of the Pennsylvania Bar Association, *op. cit.,* pp. 108–114.

[10] Qualifications and other data may be found in *The Book of the States* for various years.

lar election; (2) appointment by governors; and (3) selection by legislatures. The first is by far the most common, appointment by governors or legislatures being confined to about a dozen states, nearly all of them located along the Atlantic seaboard.

The adoption of popular election reflected a suspicion of aristocracy and control by financial and corporate interests. It also reflected a feeling that the best place to obtain judicial responsibility was at the ballot box. These views are still dominant throughout most of the country. Additional reasons advanced in defense of the practice are the following: the elective method has produced judges as competent as those chosen by other methods; evils attributable to state jurisprudence are due to other causes than the manner of selecting judges; with all their faults, elected judges render decisions more in keeping with popular desires and interests; and election prevents governors, or the dominant party in the legislature, from building powerful machines by rewarding partisans with judgeships.

Against popular election it is argued that political bosses and machines dictate and control nominations and elections; elective judges must of necessity be politically conscious and usually strongly partisan; voters are unlikely to give sufficient consideration to candidates' judicial temperament and legal expertness; ably qualified men, to whom "playing politics" and campaigning may be distasteful, are deterred from seeking office; elective judges decide cases with an eye to reelection rather than on merits; and election produces a highly decentralized judiciary without uniform standards and practices and one that defies effective administration.

In spite of the popular favor in which election is held, most professional students of government prefer selection by other methods. It is their conclusion that of the methods used executive appointment has worked best, legislative appointment worst, with other methods in between.[11] However, in view of the entrenched position of the elective procedure, many critics question the advisability of concentrating reform efforts on complete abandonment of the method. Instead, compromises are often suggested, one of which is contained in the model state constitution proposed by the National Municipal League. This suggests election of a chief justice every eight years who would be authorized to appoint all other state judges from a list of eligibles presented by the judicial council. Terms would run for 12 years, except that after 4 years every judge would be required to stand for approval or rejection at the polls. A modified version of this plan was adopted by California in 1934.[12] Missouri continued an interesting variation of the plan in its 1946 constitution.

There the judges are nominated by an impartial commission comprised of lawyers, laymen, and jurists. The governor appoints from this list with the proviso that after a short term incumbent judges will present themselves to the people for approval or rejection before serving a longer term. New Jersey's 1947 constitution contains still another variation. There the governor appoints judges for the higher courts, with senate approval, for 7-year terms. After 7 years the incumbent must run for popular approval before beginning tenure that lasts during good behavior or until the age of seventy. Lower-court judges are appointed by the governor with senate approval for 5-year terms. Meanwhile, other states continue using older methods, often attempting to mitigate evils by providing for election on nonpartisan or independent ballots, coupling election with rather long terms (as in Pennsylvania where elected district judges serve for 10 years and the Supreme Court judges for 21), recall of judges or even judicial decisions, and other devices.

The Clerk of Court. Next to the judge the principal court officer is the clerk, who is sometimes called "prothonotary." This officer handles the large volume of administrative work arising

[11] Cf. Walter F. Dodd, *State Government* (Appleton-Century-Crofts, 1924), pp. 330–335; W. Brooke Graves, *American State Government* (Heath, 1941), pp. 601–608; William S. Carpenter, *Judicial Tenure in the United States* (Yale University Press, 1918), p. 212; Willoughby, *op. cit.*, pp. 361–383.

[12] Winston W. Crouch and Dean E. McHenry, *California Government* (University of California Press, 2d ed., 1949), pp. 175–176.

from the judicial process. Among his duties are the issuing of writs and court processes, keeping the court's financial records, arranging dockets, collecting court costs, fees, and fines, recording, indexing, and filing the court's decisions and awards. In spite of the close relationship to the court and the fact that the work performed is entirely administrative, the clerk is seldom directly responsible to the court but, rather, he is usually popularly elected. Careful students are unanimous in saying that the substitution of appointment for election would result in greater responsibility, efficiency, and economy both in time and money.[13] They are also unanimous in urging that the clerk be paid on a salary rather than on a fee basis.

[13] See, for example, Pound, *op. cit.*, pp. 285–287; Willoughby, *op. cit.*, pp. 340–342.

FOR FURTHER READING

Callender, Clarence N.: *American Courts* (McGraw-Hill, 1927).

Carpenter, William S.: *Judicial Tenure in the United States* (Yale University Press, 1918).

Council of State Governments: *The Book of the States* (Chicago: The Council, biennial).

———: *Trial Courts of General Jurisdiction in the Forty-eight States* (Chicago, 1951).

———: *Courts of Last Resort in the Forty-eight States* (Chicago, 1950).

Dodd, Walter F.: *State Government* (Appleton-Century-Crofts, 1924).

Fairlie, John A., and Charles M. Kneier: *County Government and Administration* (Appleton-Century-Crofts, 1930).

Fosdick, Raymond, and Others: *Criminal Justice in Cleveland* (Cleveland: The Cleveland Foundation, 1922).

Frank, Jerome: *Courts on Trial* (Princeton University Press, 1949).

Gavit, Bernard C.: *Procedure in State Courts* (Practicing Law Institute, 1946).

Hart, Henry M., and Herbert Wechsler (eds.): *Federal Courts and the Federal System* (Foundation Press, 1953).

Lancaster, Lane W.: *Government in Rural America* (Van Nostrand, rev. ed., 1952).

Pound, Roscoe: *Organization of Courts* (Little, Brown, 1940).

Robinson, William M.: *Justice in Grey* (Harvard University Press, 1941).

Sunderland, Edson R.: *Judicial Administration* (Chicago: Callaghan, 2d ed., 1948).

Warren, George: *Traffic Courts* (Little, Brown, 1942).

Willoughby, William F.: *Principles of Judicial Administration* (Brookings, 1929).

REVIEW QUESTIONS

1. Distinguish between the types of cases which come before state courts and those that are tried by Federal courts.

2. How does the court system of a typical state differ from what it was during the Colonial period? The Revolutionary period?

3. Compare the judicial system of a typical state with the Federal court system.

4. What is meant when it is said that state judicial systems are decentralized?

5. Which is preferable, the appointment or election of judges? Which method is most widely used among American states? What method is recommended in the model state constitution?

6. Suggest changes that should be made in state courts and their procedures.

7. What is a judicial council? What factors have encouraged their adoption in a number of states?

8. What is the role of each of the principal state judicial officers mentioned in this chapter? How is each usually chosen?

CHAPTER 36

Cities and Their Government

> The city comes into being, vegetates or flourishes, survives or dies, juridically at the whim and wish of the State legislature. — U.S. National Resources Committee on Urbanism [1]

Scattered throughout the United States are thousands of urban communities, usually organized under state law for purposes of local self-government into "municipalities." In the several states such communities are designated by varying titles as cities, boroughs, villages, and towns. The Census Bureau reported 16,778 of these existing in 1952 and revealed that this was an increase of 3.4 per cent over 1942.[2]

The discussion here will be confined to larger municipalities commonly known as "cities," leaving consideration of the smaller units until the next chapter.

In Chap. 8, the fact was noted that since 1789 the United States has been transformed from a sparsely populated rural nation to one in which nearly two-thirds of the people now live in urban centers, many of them gigantic metropolitan areas. Some of the implications of this change for the political scientist were also commented upon.

STATE-MUNICIPAL RELATIONS

Municipalities Created by States. Municipalities owe their existence to the state and are creatures of the state. True, people may live wherever they choose without permission from the

state, but a muncipality is a corporation, a legal person, that can legally exist only by act of the legislature. Formerly, whenever a group wished to incorporate for self-government, it was necessary to petition the legislature for a special act incorporating a particular place. Special legislation of this kind led to extreme diversity; it also led to excessive meddling by the legislature with municipal affairs; and it was often accompanied by unconscionable lobbying and graft on the part of those desirous of seeing that the laws included provisions favorable to their particular interests. To correct this, most states inserted provisions in their constitutions prohibiting special legislation. This, in turn, led to classification of municipalities and the enactment of codes for each class. Although legislatures continue to devise methods of circumventing the ban on special legislation, the worst abuses have been eliminated. Today, then, municipalities are usually classified, codes exist for each class, and municipalities obtain charters in accordance with these general provisions. Charters are usually granted by some state agency upon receipt of petitions signed by either duly constituted authorities or a certain number of residents, or both.

Nature of Municipal Corporations. As suggested above, a municipality is a legal entity. The charter is a very formal and precise document stating the purposes, powers, functions, rights,

[1] *Urban Government* (1939), p. 19.

[2] *Governments in the United States in 1952* (1953), p. 1.

privileges, and form of government. The powers granted usually vary with the class into which a municipality falls but generally include authority to sue, tax, borrow money, promote and protect health, safety, and morals, exercise the power of eminent domain for certain purposes, operate certain utilities, and enforce the law.

Although municipalities may have considerable home rule they are, nevertheless, agents of the states. Accordingly, they possess the immunity from suit usually enjoyed by states. This means, among other things, that when municipalities engage in strictly "governmental" affairs, as distinguished from "proprietary" or "nongovernmental," they cannot be sued except by permission of state law. Thus, if city police use unnecessary violence the city cannot be sued, although the policemen as individuals may be. If a traffic accident results from negligently maintained and operated traffic signals the city is not liable. Or if a city fire engine en route to a fire crashes into private property, the city cannot be forced to pay damages. It is only when municipalities engage in "proprietary" or "nongovernmental" activities such as operating markets, street railways, waterworks, liquor stores, and toll bridges that they can be held responsible. This gives rise to the paradoxical situation that if one were run over by a police car the city would not be liable, but if one were hit by a truck operated by a municipal electric department damages could be collected.[3]

Being state agents, municipalities also enjoy the same immunity from federal interference as do states. This means, for example, that the Federal government does not tax their bonds, nor their revenues, nor purchases of supplies for "governmental" functions, nor payrolls for social security unless the municipality elects to participate. Nor can the Federal government otherwise burden municipalities. Here again immunity generally does not apply to "nongovernmental" functions.

Classification of Cities. Classification systems followed by the states are extremely varied and confusing.[4] In 1945, fourteen states had no statutory classification of "cities" by population and some did not even set a minimum population requirement for incorporation. Sixteen states had three or more classes of "cities." Ten states distinguished between cities, towns, and villages, but cities themselves were not classified. Eight states had only two classes of cities.

A closer look at Pennsylvania is suggestive of how states may classify. There the smallest municipalities are called "boroughs," for which no minimum and maximum populations have been fixed by law. Next in order of size are cities of the third class with minimum populations of 10,000 and maximums of 135,000. Then come second-class A cities[5] with populations between 135,000 and 500,000. Then come second-class cities[6] with populations ranging from 500,000 to 1 million. And finally there are first-class cities[7] with populations of over 1 million. Separate codes exist for each class with widely differing provisions. Boroughs, for example, may have the council-manager form, but third-class cities may not. On the other hand, third-class cities must use the commission form of government while the other classes cannot. To illustrate further, third-class cities may use the referendum whereas others cannot.

Overlapping Jurisdictions within Cities. As matters stand, five levels of government are usually at work simultaneously within municipal limits: school districts, the city government itself, the county, the state, and the Federal government. Not infrequently there are more in the form of special districts or authorities. The nature and extent of these operations and interrelationships are so varied as to defy simple description.

All employ and direct personnel. Nearly all tax and borrow money. All spend money, maintain buildings, and execute functions. Most of them participate in the detection and prosecu-

---

[3] For an interesting treatment of this subject, see Austin F. MacDonald, *American City Government and Administration* (Crowell, 4th ed., 1946), pp. 92–98.

[4] For a table showing state systems, see *The Municipal Year Book, 1945* (Chicago: International City Managers' Association, 1945), p. 91.

[5] Only one, Scranton.

[6] Only one, Pittsburgh.

[7] Philadelphia is the only one in this class.

tion of law violators. Counties and states usually handle elections, although cities often participate and even the Federal government has a measure of interest and responsibility. All but school and special districts have some responsibility for roads and highways. Cities and states exercise control over local businesses while the Federal government steps in where taxes and interstate commerce are involved. Cities, states, and the Federal government frequently cooperate in planning, promoting public health, and providing better housing, public works, relief and welfare programs, and national defense.

Functions Especially Controlled by the State. In addition to state controls imposed by charters, a number of municipal functions are especially supervised by the state. Municipal tax-assessment methods are usually prescribed. Sources of municipal revenue are usually limited by state law. Borrowing limits are commonly fixed either by the state constitution or by statutes, and frequently cities are required to report their indebtedness to state administrative agencies. The exercise of eminent domain is usually circumscribed. Often financial budgets, accounts, and reports are prescribed and required to be filed with a state agency where they are subject to scrutiny. The acquisition, construction, and operation of municipal utilities are usually subject to regulation by public-utility commissions. The establishment of municipal courts and their methods of operation are governed by state law. Municipal penal, correctional, and welfare institutions are commonly subject to some state supervision. The laying out and construction of streets, highways, bridges, tunnels, traffic lights, airports, etc., are often state supervised; the source and purity of the public water supply and other matters likely to affect public health are also of state concern. In view of the overlapping described above and this lengthy list, which is by no means all-inclusive, it is little wonder that the citizen may have difficulty in knowing where responsibility lies. Nor is it surprising that municipal officials themselves are often confused and not infrequently irritated by the limits that surround them.

Home Rule. The problem of properly dividing powers between a central government and subordinate ones is not confined to federal-state relationships. Equally heated and persistent controversy surrounds state-local relations. People of the entire state obviously have a legitimate interest in what happens within its municipalities, and yet this interest is seldom as direct, intimate, and compelling as that of persons who live in them. The state legislature, often composed of a majority of representatives from rural parts of the state, may deny legislation sought by the cities. Time and again cities have pleaded with state legislatures for charter amendments desired by overwhelming majorities, only to be rebuffed. State administrators, too, often appear unnecessarily meddlesome to local officials.

The persistence of the problem has led to many attempted solutions. The home-rule movement started in 1875 when a Missouri constitutional amendment gave the city of St. Louis extensive powers of self-government. Today, about half of the states have provisions in their constitutions permitting legislatures to grant varying amounts of home rule. This trend also brought with it many strictures upon state executive and administrative officers.

In spite of its apparent success, the home-rule movement is waning, because of several factors. One has been the unwillingness of state legislatures to implement home-rule provisions inserted in their constitutions. In Pennsylvania, for example, a home-rule amendment was adopted in 1922 but, except for Philadelphia in 1949, the provision has never been put into effect. Again, Utah and Nevada adopted home-rule amendments in 1925 but in neither state is there a "self-governing" city. Meanwhile, legal ambiguities and narrow construction by the courts have deprived municipalities of gains they thought had been won. Another factor has been the general centralization trend apparent in business, industry, labor, social life, and government. Another is that often municipalities were slow, inefficient, and corrupt. Still another has been the depression and war, during which municipalities were faced with problems that caused them to look to the states, and especially the Federal government, for financial assistance and leadership.

FORMS OF GOVERNMENT

Strong Mayor-Council Form. This form, which prevails usually in large cities, is patterned after the state and Federal governments. It assumes the desirability of separating executive and legislative powers and forcing each to vary considerably in size. A few have only two members; Chicago with fifty members has the largest. Philadelphia has seventeen; Los Angeles, fifteen; St. Louis, Mo., thirty; Cleveland, thirty-three; New York City has seventeen on the council and eight on the Board of Estimate; and until recently Newport, R.I., had as many as one hundred ninety-five. In over two-thirds of the larger cities, however, the membership is fixed at five or nine.

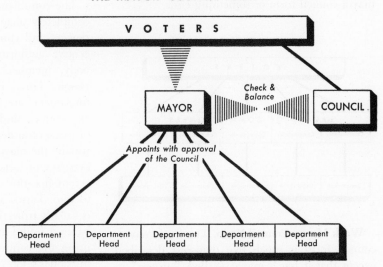

THE MAYOR—COUNCIL FORM

The mayor-council form favored by large cities is based on the separation of powers principle.

operate within the framework of checks and balances.

Soon after the Revolution, American cities abandoned one-house legislatures for bicameral, and the latter remained typical until after the Civil War. The tide then turned, sweeping aside bicameral councils, until today they exist in only Atlanta, Ga., New York City, and a few New England communities.[8] Present-day councils

[8] *The Municipal Yearbook* gives current figures about forms of city government. New York City has a peculiar arrangement where in addition to a council there exists a Board of Estimate consisting of the mayor, the elected comptroller, the president of the council, and the five borough presidents, each of whom has weighted voting power. This board shares responsibility with the council for certain financial legislation.

Nearly everywhere councilmen are elected. Election remains on the ward basis in a considerable number of places, with a strong trend toward substitution of election at large. The partisan ballot is still most common in mayor-council cities, but nonpartisan elections have become increasingly popular. Councilmen's terms vary from 1 to 6 years, with 2 or 4 the most common. Salaries vary from nothing to $13,000 in Washington, D.C., although in most of the smaller places the median is $500 or less.

In the strong mayor-council form, the mayor is usually not a member of the council but is nominated and elected to serve especially as chief executive. His term is usually 2 or 4 years and he generally is paid a salary. Although ordinarily not a member of the council, he may rec-

ommend legislation, maneuver to obtain coun-
cilmanic approval of his proposals, usually vote
to break a tie, and veto. The mayor is said to be
"strong" if he is given control over budgets, possesses power to appoint, remove, and direct department heads, has responsibility for administration, and has authority to veto items or total
bills.

The form is found in most American cities
with over 500,000 people. It is also found in a
number of medium-sized cities, but seldom in
smaller places, which usually prefer the weak
mayor-council form or something else.

THE COMMISSION FORM

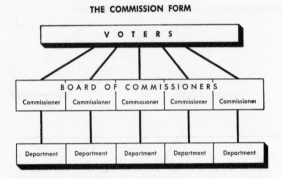

Weak Mayor-Council Form. The weak mayor-
council form is much like that just described
except that it has a mayor (called "burgess" in
boroughs) with fewer and less potent powers.
It results in the mayor's having little effective
control over either the council or administration.
The mayor may suggest legislation but unless he
is unusually popular and influential the council
does not look to him for leadership. He may veto
but his action is likely to be overridden. The
council usually appoints and removes officers
and supervises administration, often through
committees. Why, then, have a mayor or burgess
at all? He usually convenes newly elected councils, he sometimes may vote to break a tie, he is
often the chief police officer and justice of the
peace, and he attends to certain ceremonial matters. These are not impressive powers and duties,
but the form remains the one most widely used
in the United States.

The Commission Form. A third form is the
commission type. Although previously used, it

was popularized by adoption in Galveston, Tex.,
in 1901, after a tidal wave had deluged the city
and precipitated a crisis that the old regime was
too incompetent and corrupt to handle. The
"Galveston plan" was long afterward the re-
former's goal, but its popularity has since waned.
Although losing ground, in 1954 it was found in
14 per cent of all cities,[9] most of which were of
medium size. Some cities using the commission
form are Washington, D.C., Jersey City, N.J.,
Memphis, Tenn., Birmingham, Ala., Omaha,
Nebr., Portland, Ore., and St. Paul, Minn.

The commission plan is really very simple. It
completely abandons the idea of separation of
powers and concentrates all legislative and executive authority in a single small governing
body, members of which are elected by the
people. Three, five, or seven men called "commissioners" are elected to serve collectively as a
city council and individually as administrators
of the several departments. One commissioner is
usually the mayor who, in addition to heading a
department, acts as chairman, performs certain
ceremonial duties, and sometimes has the power
to veto. Terms are usually 2 or 4 years; election
is usually from the city at large. The nonpartisan
ballot is found in over three-fourths of the places
using the commission form. Because the commissioner's job combines that of both legislator
and department chief, it usually is full time and
better paid than that of councilman under other
forms.

Variations of the original commission form
have often been made. In its early days the principal objections were its lack of the usual checks
and balances and its failure to deal with the
spoils system. To correct these, the "Des Moines
plan," devised in 1907, has become especially
well known. In this, the people of Des Moines
merely superimposed several features upon the
Galveston charter. Among these were the merit
system, nonpartisan primary and election, initiative, referendum, and recall. The addition of
these features added confidence in the voters
and hastened spread of the commission form.
Des Moines abandoned the commission plan in
1949, New Orleans in 1952.

[9] *The Municipal Yearbook, 1955,* p. 57.

The Council-Manager Form. Still another form widely used in municipalities is the council-manager. First used in Staunton, Va., in 1908, the plan was popularized when introduced four years later in Dayton, Ohio, following a devastating flood. The plan has spread until in 1952 it was used in 30.3 per cent of all cities with population of over five thousand. Among the largest were Cincinnati, Ohio, Dallas, Tex., Fort Worth, Tex., and Kansas City, Mo.

Both the mayor and the council may be retained, although where the mayor has strong powers installation of the manager plan makes it necessary to shear his office of major administrative responsibilities. Like the commission form, the manager plan unifies powers in the council. Its essence, then, is a strong council and a weak mayor, with responsibility for administration placed in the hands of a trained, professional manager elected by the council for an indefinite term and responsible to the council at all times. This arrangement leaves policy formation where it belongs, with politically minded councilmen and mayors, but places administration in the hands of a professional, nonpartisan expert. A variation of this plan is retention of a strong mayor with an expert manager serving as his assistant.

Other reforms sometimes urged as indispensable to the success of the manager plan include the short ballot, nonpartisan ballot, election at large, proportional representation, and the initiative, referendum, and recall. While these are commendable, and sweeping reforms may be required in some places to guarantee any improvement at all, success or failure of the manager plan does not necessarily depend upon the adoption of any one or all of them. Rather, the manager plan can be adopted, where state law permits, whenever the council, the mayor, and the public sense the value of separating politics from administration sufficiently to employ a competent manager and give him free rein.

Advantages and Disadvantages of Various Forms. Fear and distrust of public officials and their exercise of power underlie the separation of powers found in the mayor-council form. Besides providing checks and balances, the plan sometimes attracts and produces colorful leaders, like La Guardia of New York, Hoan of Milwaukee, and Burton of Cleveland—men who are able to dramatize public issues and force their adoption. Moreover, its defenders insist that it keeps government closer to the people, keeps expenditures, taxes, and debts low, and still gets essential tasks done.

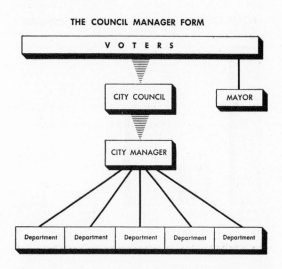

THE COUNCIL MANAGER FORM

Critics insist that at the municipal level powers can be effectively checked by other means than by separating them. They also contend that, although the form may occasionally attract colorful and able leaders, it actually has produced comparatively few and instead has probably produced many more bosses and henchmen. Separating powers, critics continue, so dissipates responsibility that the public is at a loss to know whom to praise or censure. This situation, it is argued, invites behind-the-scenes domination by bosses, political machines, and vested interests. Moreover, politics and administration become so inextricably mingled that competence and efficiency are rarely possible, with resultant inconvenience, expense, and contempt on the part of the public. Large American municipalities have been, on the whole, so badly managed and even today are so often feudal preserves of bosses and machines, as to force the conclusion that the mayor-council form has fundamental defects.

The case for the commission form is that it

corrects one of the fundamental weaknesses of the mayor-council form by focusing responsibility upon a few commissioners; it shortens the ballot; it changes election by wards to choice at large; it diminishes corruption and behind-the-scene domination; and it sometimes leads to improved services at lower cost to the public.

Professional students of government concede that many of the claims made for the commission

FORM OF GOVERNMENT IN 2527 CITIES OVER 5,000 POPULATION

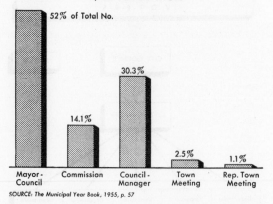

SOURCE: *The Municipal Year Book, 1955, p. 57*

Although the mayor-council plan still predominates, the council-manager plan is on the rise and seems likely to displace mayor-council as the most widely used form of municipal government.

form are valid. They are agreed, however, that it contains inherent defects. Chief of these is that because commissioners are at once politicians, lawmakers, and department heads, politics and policy formation cannot be separated from administration. Accordingly, partisanship tempers administration, with resulting loss in efficiency, economy, and public confidence. Moreover, because the exact number of commissioners is fixed and each must head a department, an inflexible administrative situation prevails. Furthermore, department heads who are elected are rarely qualified administrators, and the possibility exists that they will be of a different persuasion, or even hostile to one another, making unified direction of administration impossible. Fundamental differences of opinion are desirable in a legislative body, but the best administration is obtained from a unified command.

The council-manager plan has the unqualified endorsement of professional students of government. It focuses responsibility for policy formation in the hands of a comparatively few elected representatives of the people. Thus, the voters can, if they wish, watch what happens and place praise or blame where it belongs. At the same time it makes possible the separation of politics and administration, unifies the direction of city management, and, by placing a professional manager at the helm, introduces expert leadership, indifference toward political considerations, and devotion to the best principles of the manager's profession. Only a few cities, of which Cleveland is the largest, having once introduced the manager form, have later abandoned it.

INTERNAL ADMINISTRATIVE STRUCTURE

Municipal Officials. In addition to councils, mayors, and managers, many other officials are required. The office of treasurer is the most widely found, the clerk next, then assessor, auditor, and attorney. Election is the rule in more than half of the cities. This fact makes for a long ballot and seriously fragments responsibility. Election of the officers mentioned is often the rule regardless of the form used, though adoption of the commission form, and especially the council-manager form, has discouraged election in favor of appointment.

Municipal Boards and Departments. Formerly it was customary to center administrative responsibility in bipartisan boards, with the result that almost every city had its board of health, police board, water board, poor-relief board, school board, and others. Boards of this type are still widely used, although they are usually nonpartisan except where they deal with matters like elections and civil service. Accompanying this trend has been a shift to single-headed administrative departments, especially in cities using the commission or manager form.

In a large city one finds a bewildering array of boards, commissions, and departments. Where so many exist it is obviously difficult, if not impossible, for the mayor or manager to direct and supervise city administration. This fact has led to numerous reorganizations during which the agencies have been consolidated within as few as five or six principal departments. Those that serve the people directly, like departments of health, safety, education, and welfare, are commonly known as "line" agencies; while others that service and coordinate the primary agencies but serve the public only indirectly are called "staff" or "auxiliary" agencies. Included in the latter are those handling finance, accounting, law, personnel, central purchasing, and planning.

METROPOLITAN AREAS

Definition and Growth. According to the Census Bureau, a standard metropolitan area is one with a city of 50,000 population or more as a nucleus. When two cities of this size are within 20 miles of one another they ordinarily are included in the same area. Metropolitan areas numbered 168 in 1950, of which several touched more than one state. In addition to these, the Census Bureau lists 157 somewhat smaller urban areas. Living in these 325 areas is well over half the total population. First in population is the New York–Newark–Jersey City metropolitan area; then follow Chicago, Los Angeles, Philadelphia, and Detroit in the order mentioned. Like huge magnets, these centers draw people from the small town, village, farm, and foreign shore. At what point the tide will turn no one can tell. It was accelerated by the depression, the war, and the postwar crises. Even though the international situation should stabilize, the changing character of American industry is almost certain to cause population concentration to continue.

Jurisdictional Confusion. People who flock to cities in search of jobs and housing give little thought to whether they live in the city itself or in an adjacent borough, town, or township. Convenience, comfort, and economy are primary; political and governmental matters are comparatively unimportant. Population changes occur constantly, often quickly, but governmental systems seldom keep pace. These facts partially explain the continued existence of numerous units of government in metropolitan districts.

The metropolitan district itself is not a governmental unit but a conglomeration of them.

In 1952 a total of 1,071 local governments were reported for the New York area and 960 for the Chicago area. Annexations and consolidations have occurred, but the process has been slow. In consequence, some baffling problems exist.

Problems of Metropolitan Areas.[10] Overlapping is one of the most serious problems. A city police department, for example, must have a real concern over what happens in the city's environs. At the same time, sheriffs, constables,

MUNICIPAL ELECTIVE OFFICES OTHER THAN MAYOR AND COUNCIL IN CITIES OVER 5,000 POPULATION

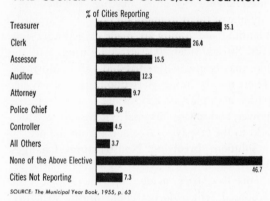

% of Cities Reporting

Treasurer	35.1
Clerk	26.4
Assessor	15.5
Auditor	12.3
Attorney	9.7
Police Chief	4.8
Controller	4.5
All Others	3.7
None of the Above Elective	46.7
Cities Not Reporting	7.3

SOURCE: *The Municipal Year Book*, 1955, p. 63

Many cities with the mayor-council plan continue to elect several other officers, thus diffusing executive power and making responsibility more difficult to fix.

and town police serving outlying areas cannot ignore the city. A vacuum, or no-man's zone, may result. Or friction may arise from mutual jealousies, or there may be wide disparity between the protection offered in the respective units of government. One of the worst features of this situation is that criminals and shady operators often make the city's periphery a base of operations. A unification or integration of services might well result in better protection at a

[10] The pioneer study of metropolitan areas and the problems presented was by Paul Studenski *et al., The Government of Metropolitan Areas in the United States* (New York: National Municipal League, 1930). Later studies are Victor Jones, *Metropolitan Government* (University of Chicago Press, 1942); Don J. Bogue, *The Structure of the Metropolitan Community* (University of Michigan Press, 1949); and Betty Tableman, *Governmental Organization in Metropolitan Areas* (University of Michigan Press, 1951).

lower per capita cost. The same is true of fire, street, health, transportation, and other municipal services.

Disparity between assessments and taxes is also a problem. With several hundred units, each having its own assessor and tax schedule, intercommunity differences and often multiple taxation are inevitable. In addition to confusion and unfairness, property owners within the central city may be lured by lower taxes to suburban communities, thereby adding to the financial worries of the city. Business regulations may differ among the units, making it difficult for any one of them to maintain effective standards. Planning and zoning are made exceedingly difficult. Streets, sidewalks, street lighting, and the like may be uncoordinated and lack uniformity. There may be unnecessary duplication of schools, parks and playgrounds, water supply, electric power, and sewage-disposal systems, all of which add to the taxpayer's cost and inconvenience.

Solutions Involving Nonstructural Changes. Under the spur of necessity a number of arrangements have been made, and others have been proposed, which do not entail drastic structural changes in existing governmental patterns. The simplest of these is a sort of informal cooperation where municipal officers confer with one another, borrow equipment, exchange information, and the like. A second arrangement is one in which one municipality, usually the central city, agrees to furnish services to other communities in the area. Interjurisdictional agreements such as these are numerous. Thus, it is quite common for suburban children to attend city schools, the tuition for the children being paid by their own governments. Cities often agree to provide fire protection, water, or electricity to near-by communities which pay for the service rendered.

A third arrangement is where two or more cities comprising a district agree to joint operation of a service such as a bridge or sewer system. An adaptation is for the states or governmental units concerned to superimpose a special corporation, called an "authority" or "district," upon an area, giving it authority to perform specified functions throughout the entire district. The Chicago Sanitary District is an example. It

has jurisdiction over the surrounding area and operates to keep Lake Michigan free from pollution. Another is the Boston Metropolitan District, whose authority extends over a number of cities and towns for the purpose of providing sewage disposal, water supply, recreational facilities, and planning. Still another example is the Port of New York Authority, jointly organized by New York and New Jersey, which now operates interstate bridges, parking facilities, airports, and tunnels.

A fourth possibility is for the state to give the central city extraterritorial powers. Thus cities may be authorized to build and maintain a water supply outside their borders, or lay sewers, establish parks, extend highways, or build bridges. Some cities may control contagious diseases within a radius of several miles, others may prohibit slaughterhouses, hog farms, and houses of prostitution in adjacent territory; while others may inspect milk in the entire milkshed. The principal difficulty is that occupants of outlying areas receive government without representation, hence are likely to be resentful and uncooperative.

A fifth possibility is for the county, with its board consisting of representatives of cities or towns within a county, to serve as the integrating unit. The difficulty of hitting upon a satisfactory apportionment of representatives, the fact that counties are seldom organized for effective and efficient administration, and the fact that metropolitan areas usually extend over more than one county render this solution of little promise.

Solutions Involving Structural Changes. The arrangements just mentioned provide only a partial solution. They do nothing to disturb the continued existence of the multiplicity of governmental units that obstruct district integration. Structural changes are extremely difficult to obtain; nevertheless, some have occurred and others have been seriously proposed.

The structural changes that have occurred oftenest are annexations and consolidations. Annexation takes place when one governmental unit merely acquires or absorbs additional unincorporated territory, but a consolidation takes place when two or more governmental units are merged. Virtually every city has grown by annexation or consolidation, but the process has been slow and presents almost insuperable problems where the metropolitan area straddles two or more states. Sometimes annexations and consolidations are voluntary, the people in all units giving consent. Sometimes they may be compulsory, in which case the state legislature usually makes the change with or without the consent of one or all the parties concerned.

Another proposal involving structural changes is that cities and counties separate entirely from one another, each remaining but without any concurrent jurisdiction. It has also been suggested that the various governmental units within a metropolitan area be combined to form a federated government. This would entail creation of a central government with delegated powers, leaving the participating units with authority over those matters that are distinctly local. A still more extreme proposal is that the largest cities be made city-states with direct relations with the Federal government.

Annexations and consolidations will doubtless continue, but in view of the increasing difficulties involved the rate is likely to be slow. There are also places where county-city merger, or even separation, might well take place, but since most metropolitan areas encompass more than one county and often two or more states, any intra-county changes can offer only a partial solution. The federated district arrangement appears promising, but the problems of apportionment and allocation of powers are formidable. Moreover, unless the federation could cut across state boundaries, many problems would remain. The city-state idea theoretically has much to commend it but it is probably unobtainable for political reasons, as well as because of the fact that the Federal Constitution forbids changing state boundaries without the consent of every state concerned. Unless annexations and consolidations can be expedited in some manner which is not now apparent, nonstructural solutions are likely to be the most practical, inadequate though they may be. The continued use of voluntary cooperative arrangements, and especially the authority or special district, appears at the moment to offer the greatest promise.

FOR FURTHER READING

Anderson, William: *The Units of Government in the United States: An Enumeration and Analysis* (Chicago: Public Administration Service, 1949).

Bogue, Don J.: *The Structure of the Metropolitan Community* (University of Michigan Press, 1949).

Bollens, John C.: *Appointed Executive Local Government* (Los Angeles: Haynes Foundation, 1952).

Carpenter, William S.: *Problems in Service Levels* (Princeton University Press, 1940).

Colean, Miles L.: *Renewing Our Cities* (Twentieth Century Fund, 1953).

Coleman, Woodbury: *The Future of Cities and Urban Redevelopment* (University of Chicago Press, 1953).

———: *Urban Redevelopment: Problems and Practices* (University of Chicago Press, 1953).

Council of State Governments: *The Book of the States* (Chicago: The Council, biennial).

Jones, Victor: *Metropolitan Government* (University of Chicago Press, 1942).

Kneir, Charles M.: *City Government in the United States* (Harper, rev. ed., 1947).

MacCorkle, Stuart A.: *American Municipal Government and Administration* (Heath, 1948).

MacDonald, Austin F.: *American City Government and Administration* (Crowell, 4th ed., 1946).

McKenzie, Roderick D.: *The Metropolitan Community* (McGraw-Hill, 1933).

Morlan, Robert L. (ed.): *Capitol, Courthouse and City Hall* (Houghton Mifflin, 1954).

National Municipal League: *Model City Charter* (New York: The League, 1941).

Pate, James E.: *Local Government and Administration: Principles and Problems* (American Book, 1954).

Reed, Thomas H.: *Municipal Management* (McGraw-Hill, 1941).

Ridley, Clarence E., and Orin F. Nolting (eds.): *The Municipal Yearbook* (Chicago: International City Managers' Association, annual).

Schulz, Ernst B.: *American City Government* (New York: Stackpole & Hecht, 1949).

Stone, Harold H., *et al.*: *City Manager Government in the United States* (Chicago: Public Administration Service, 1940).

Studenski, Paul, *et al.*: *The Government of Metropolitan Areas in the United States* (New York: National Municipal League, 1930).

Tableman, Betty: *Governmental Organization in the Metropolitan Areas* (University of Michigan Press, 1951).

U.S. Department of Commerce, Bureau of the Census: *Governments in the United States in 1952* (1953).

U.S. National Resources Committee on Urbanism: *Urban Government* (1939).

——: *Our Cities; Their Role in the National Economy* (1937).

REVIEW QUESTIONS

1. How are municipalities classified in a typical state?

2. Summarize the contents of a city charter.

3. How do functions of cities compare with those performed by counties and local governments of other types?

4. What are the advantages and disadvantages of each of the forms of municipal government mentioned in this chapter?

5. Defend and criticize greater "home rule" for American cities.

6. What is a "metropolitan area"? What problems of government do they present?

7. Distinguish between a "nonstructural" and "structural" solution for problems confronting metropolitan areas. Which of these offers greater promise of success?

8. Suggest changes required to improve municipal government in a typical state.

CHAPTER 37

Governments of Counties and Smaller Units

In over-all appraisal, the first half of the twentieth century must be considered as a period of progress, albeit slow and halting progress, in the field of county government. Functionally, the county is of greater importance today than a generation ago, and expansion of the services provided by its government appears likely to continue. As townships and other minor subdivisions continue to be deorganized or abolished, the county will be the logical heir to functions now performed by those units, and additions from these sources will further enhance the county's position. — Clyde F. Snider [1]

The transition from a predominantly rural nation to one that is urban has caused the Federal, state, and municipal governments to overshadow smaller political units. In consequence, the citizen is often woefully ill-informed about them and they have been the last to modernize. Those governments are still of great importance, nevertheless. They serve millions of people, employ large personnel, tax, borrow, spend large sums of money, and help shape attitudes toward government and politics.

GENERAL CONSIDERATIONS

Number and Distribution of Units of Government. The United States is blanketed with units of local government. The tabulation given elsewhere disclosed a total of 116,743. Some states and regions have more than others. Illinois has the largest total, while the West North Central region possesses proportionally more than others. Regardless of the considerations that might have led to their establishment, the number is too large for modern times. And yet to reduce the number is one of our hardest tasks.

Local Governments Agents of States. Like cities, other local governments owe their existence to state legislatures. Their powers, forms, and functions are defined for them. They are agents, or mere portions of the states, hence possess privileges and immunities similar to the states themselves. This means, among other things, that they cannot be sued for torts, except where state law permits, and they cannot be unreasonably burdened by the Federal government. Where breach of contract is involved, however, the immunity enjoyed by states has generally not been extended to counties, townships, school districts, and other local units, with the result that they usually can be sued for performance.

Constitutional Restrictions upon State Legislatures. Although state authority over local governments is broad, it is not unlimited. Constitutional provisions vary widely but can be reduced to four categories: [2] (1) Those of many states

[1] "American County Government: A Mid-century Review," *American Political Science Review,* vol. 46 (March, 1952), p. 78.

[2] Lane W. Lancaster, *Government in Rural America* (Van Nostrand, 1937), pp. 85-90; Kirk, H. Porter,

proscribe special legislation, with the result that all local governments of a particular type must be treated alike or they must be grouped into classes and general laws enacted for each class. (2) Some constitutions prohibit specific acts. Thus, to avoid legislative tampering with the number of counties, Oklahoma sets up its counties in the constitution itself. Some stipulate that boundaries can be changed only by following certain procedures, like obtaining a two-thirds vote. Some forbid boundary alterations that will move the line closer than a specified number of miles from the county seat. Others provide that new counties may not be created unless the proposed area has a certain assessed valuation. And it is sometimes stipulated that boundaries may not be changed until ratified by the voters concerned. (3) Most state constitutions forbid legislatures from moving county seats. (4) A number of constitutions deny legislatures the power to abolish local offices or to alter election by popular vote. Under such restrictions changes may be made only by constitutional amendment.

State-local Relations. In spite of constitutional restraints, the same centralizing trend noted elsewhere is conspicuous among all local governments. Everywhere, power and responsibility has shifted from smaller to large units, bringing with it the familiar conflict and demand for home rule. While a number of state constitutions and statutes accord home rule to counties and smaller places, the amount of state administrative control and supervision has increased. This is true of assessments, taxation and debts, of budgets and accounts, of schools, highways, roads, health, sanitation, police, courts, welfare, and nearly every other function. Where to draw the line is difficult indeed. It is safe to say that diminution of the trend toward centralization appears unlikely unless the tempo of technological change diminishes, or wars and depressions come less frequently. In any case, to justify public confidence, the multitude of units must be regrouped to conform more nearly with the facts of an industrial age and must be reor-

County and Township Government in the United States (Macmillan, 1922), pp. 77–87.

ganized to serve the public more competently than in the past.

COUNTIES

Origin and Development. When the American colonies were first settled, England was divided into shires, which, in turn, were subdivided into parishes, hundreds, manors, and boroughs. When transplanted to the colonies the term "shire" soon gave way to its synonym "county." First instituted in Virginia, the county later became the primary unit of local government and administration in the South. The middle states instituted both counties and townships, and while New England introduced both counties and towns, the former were relegated to a subordinate position. This general pattern remains along the Atlantic seaboard today. West of the original Southern states and the Rockies the county pattern was followed, but elsewhere the mixed county-township system was copied. As matters stand, counties exist in forty-six states. Rhode Island, because of its small size, has nothing comparable, while Louisiana designates similar units "parishes."

Number and Size of Counties. Counties number from three in Delaware to 254 in Texas, with an average of over sixty.[3] Each state has used its own criteria in determining the number and has drawn boundaries as it saw fit. The largest county is that of San Bernardino, Calif., with 20,131 square miles; the average is 961 square miles. Viewed from the standpoint of population, according to the 1950 census the most populous is Cook County, Ill., with over 4½ million, while one of the smallest is Loving County, Tex., with a population of 227. The average county has approximately 44,000 people.

Once in existence, a county is seldom abolished or merged with other counties, despite the fact that students of government are unanimous in saying that most states have too many counties. During the 1930's the number of county units declined by only three. Georgia consolidations reduced the number by two, while Louisiana lost

[3] For these and similar data consult U.S. Department of Commerce, Bureau of the Census, *Governments in the United States in 1952* (1953).

one by the absorption of New Orleans Parish into the city of New Orleans. During the 1940's the number of counties fell by only one.

Classification of Counties. Because counties vary in size, composition, and needs, it is seldom wise for them all to be treated alike by state legislation. And yet for state legislatures to deal separately with each of them is time-consuming; it leads to needless meddling, chaotic variation, and connivance for undesirable ends. The prohibitions against special legislation inserted in con-

rule charters or giving county residents a choice between two or more authorized forms.

Oddly enough, the separation of powers doctrine so entrenched elsewhere has had little acceptance at the county level. In consequence there is usually no county officer comparable with a city mayor, governor, or president. Instead, what executive functions are not delegated to elected officers are given to a body that performs also legislative and often judicial functions. That body is given various names: board

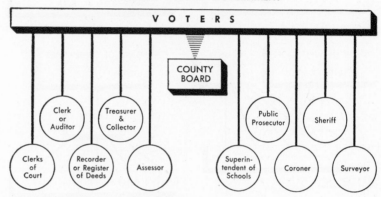

A TYPICAL COUNTY GOVERNMENT

County governments continue to disperse responsibility widely among elective officers.

stitutions about the turn of the century had the effect of stimulating classification, but the movement has not gone nearly as far as with cities.

Where counties are arranged in classes, the legislature can either legislate for all at once or only for counties falling within particular classes. Preferable as this undoubtedly is, legislatures often hit upon ingenious devices for dealing specifically with particular counties. Not infrequently the classifications are so devised as to leave only one or two counties in a class. Indeed, on one occasion California provided fifty-eight classes—one for each county.

County Boards. In organization, counties remain nearly the same today as they were during Colonial times. The classifications mentioned above are chiefly for legislative purposes rather than for structural organization. Some states require that all counties have exactly the same form of government. Others make the general pattern uniform but allow variation by permitting home-

of supervisors, board of county commissioners, county court, board of revenue, fiscal court, board of chosen freeholders, and police jury.

County boards are usually of two types. One is small and often referred to as the "commissioner form." A typical one consists of three members elected at large by county voters. The other is larger and known as the "supervisor form." It is comprised of representatives chosen from townships, cities, or districts within the county. Boards of the second type in rural areas have memberships varying between fifteen and twenty-five, while boards in counties with large cities may have as many as fifty or even a hundred. Some states, like Illinois, Nebraska, and New Jersey, permit the existence of both the small and large types. Where townships are non-existent, as in the South, the county is frequently subdivided into districts and each of these is represented on the county board. In this region justices of the peace, chosen from the districts, often constitute the county board. Large boards customarily meet quarterly or oftener, while small ones meet frequently. Meetings are held in the country courthouse and ordinarily are open to the public. Terms are usually 2 or 4 years. Compensation in a majority of states is on a per diem basis with allowance for mileage, although many small-board counties pay modest salaries.

Opinions differ as to which of the two types of boards is the better. Certainly the large one pro-

except by constitutional revision. This fact, more than almost any other, accounts for the slowness with which county governments modernize.

New Forms for Counties. Two alternative forms have some prospect of acceptance. One is adoption of a plan similar to the strong mayor-council form widely used in cities. Under this, the county board is retained but administrative officers, now elective, become appointive and responsible to the county mayor or president. This

ELECTIVE COUNTY EXECUTIVE FORM   APPOINTIVE COUNTY MANAGER FORM

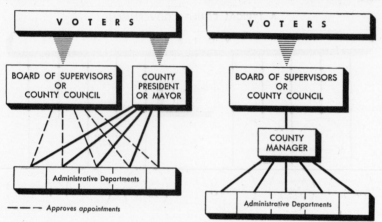

These charts reflect a preference in some areas for stronger executive leadership and management in county governments.

vides representation for more areas and this may increase both local interest and a sense of responsibility. For legislative purposes, therefore, it might well be superior. But a small body is without doubt the better for purposes of administration. This suggests the desirability of a compromise: a numerous body for purposes of policy formation, and a smaller one—or better still a manager—for administration.

Elective Officers. A typical county has a plethora of elected officers. Among others the list includes judges, sheriff, prosecuting attorney, county clerk or prothonotary, coroner, treasurer, auditor and comptroller, recorder of deeds, surveyor, jury commissioners, and superintendent of schools.

The existence of so many elective officers makes unified administration impossible and causes the ballot to be excessively long. Because these offices are often established by the state constitution, they cannot be altered or abolished

plan has several advantages: it separates legislative from executive functions, focuses administrative responsibility in the mayor or president, and shortens the ballot. A few counties, most of them urban, have adopted the plan. While this reform, if thorough, would be an improvement, it has all the weaknesses of the mayor-council form discussed in the previous chapter.

The second proposal is the county-manager plan modeled after the manager form so successful in cities. Under this the county board devotes itself to policy formation and legislation, leaving administration to a professional expert hired by and responsible to the board. Under ideal circumstances the manager appoints and directs, subject to board approval, all the other administrative officers of the county. This separates policy formation and administration, concentrates administrative responsibility in the manager, adds expertness to county management, and shortens the ballot. The plan has the endorsement of most professional students of government and has made some headway. Unhappily, the constitutionally entrenched position of elective county officers usually prevents unification of management to the same extent as cities. Fifteen counties in eight states have adopted the manager plan.[4] A few other counties have appointed executives somewhat analogous to managers, while a few states recently have amended their constitutions to make adoption of the manager plan possible.[5] By resolution of the county board, Los Angeles County has established a chief administrative officer, whose functions and authority are comparable to those of the county manager.[6]

VILLAGES, TOWNS, TOWNSHIPS, AND COUNTY DISTRICTS

Villages and Towns. In addition to counties and cities, most areas have smaller urban or semiurban units of government. The nomenclature varies extremely. In the South and West "town" is the term oftenest used, in the Northeastern and Middle Western states the term is "village," and in a few Eastern states the word "borough" is used. These units are more like cities than counties, and they should not be confused with the towns of New England or the townships of rural areas, discussed below.

Professor Anderson has stated the principal characteristics of villages and towns to be:[7] (1) Their areas are usually small, but vary from less than a square mile to several hundred square miles; (2) population within them is usually denser than in the surrounding countryside; (3)

the units remain a part of the county in which they are situated and yet they are set off by law as separate corporations for providing services required in urban places; (4) their corporate status is generally the same as larger municipal corporations; (5) many have special charters or are incorporated under general laws that are often referred to as the local charter; and (6) their functions are quite numerous and highly varied.

In form, the governments of villages and towns resemble those of cities. The weak mayor-council form is almost universally used. The chief executive, known as a "president," "mayor," or "burgess," is nearly always popularly elected. The legislative body, called "council" or "board of trustees," is usually made up of from three to nine members chosen at large by popular vote. Members are generally unsalaried. Other municipal officers, also commonly elected, are a clerk or secretary, treasurer, street commissioner, attorney or solicitor, and marshal. County and township functions may also be carried on within these units either by the municipality itself or by county and township officers. In either case, the officers most commonly found are an assessor, tax collector, justice of the peace, constables, and auditors.

Although much like cities, towns and villages differ in many ways. Their powers are fewer; their governmental structure is much simpler; their council is usually smaller and unpaid; the chief executive is usually much weaker, while administrative functions are dispersed widely among elected officers. Nevertheless, millions of citizens know simple governments like these better than any other and depend upon them for indispensable services.

New England Towns. The towns of New England date back to the earliest settlements on the "stern and rockbound coast." Several hundred of them exist, usually within irregular boundaries encompassing between 25 and 35 square miles. The entire area may be rural, in which case the town is virtually indistinguishable from townships that exist elsewhere. Or they may be partly rural but have within them one or more populous centers that have not in-

[4] *The Municipal Yearbook, 1955,* p. 279.

[5] For an excellent summary and evaluation, see Edward W. Weidner, "A Review of the Controversy over County Executives," *Public Administration Review,* vol. 8 (Winter, 1948), pp. 18–29. See also Snider, *op. cit,* p. 71.

[6] See Abraham Holtzman, *Los Angeles County Chief Administrative Office: Ten Years Experience,* Bureau of Governmental Research, Studies in Local Government, no. 10 (University of California Press, 1948).

[7] William Anderson, *The Units of Government in the United States* (Chicago: Public Administration Service, 1942), p. 16.

corporated for purposes of municipal government. Instead, and unlike the general practice elsewhere, they remain under the general town government. Thus the New England town is a combined township and municipality.

Political power in New England towns stems from town meetings. These are assemblies of qualified voters who gather annually or oftener to deliberate on matters of policy and choose officers for the ensuing year. During the interim between town meetings responsibility rests in a board of selectmen (usually three) and a number of elective officers, including a clerk, constable, school board, tax collector, treasurer, and often more. The town-manager plan, similar to the city-manager plan, may be and often is used.

The towns also serve as the units of representation in the state legislature. Because the towns are small and numerous the lower houses of the legislatures have large memberships—240 in Massachusetts, 279 in Connecticut, and 400 in New Hampshire.

In form, modern town governments have changed little since Colonial times. The town meeting itself, however, has lost most of its social value and much of its authority. Only a small proportion of a densely populated town will attend town meetings, but even though more did appear, their diversity of background and interests, coupled with the unwieldiness of large assemblies and the complexity of current issues and problems, would render them ineffective. Although town meetings are still important gatherings, the boards of selectmen have assumed more responsibility, while Federal, state, and municipal governments have absorbed a number of functions and injected an increasing amount of direction and control.

Townships. In sixteen states outside the New England area the township exists. Most of these lie in the area between New Jersey on the east and the Dakotas and Kansas on the west. Washington is the only Far Western state in which a few counties are organized into townships; none exists in the South. In New York, Pennsylvania, and New Jersey townships sprang up erratically, with the result that their boundaries are highly irregular. But from Ohio westward townships

were artificially plotted on the square, with regular boundaries usually enclosing 36 square miles. Where people cluster in these they are likely to incorporate into villages, towns, cities, or boroughs and thus, unlike those in New England towns, provide themselves with local governments separate from those of the townships. This is not always the case, however, for there are many populous communities, usually in the environs of cities, that prefer township status.

Half the states with townships provide for township meetings modeled after those held in New England towns. Whether primary assemblies like these are permissible or not, governmental machinery remains much alike. The principal governing body is an elective board known as a "board of trustees" or "board of supervisors." These are of two types: one is composed of members (usually three) specifically chosen for the position; the other is an ex officio board composed of such township officers as supervisor, clerk, treasurer, and justices of the peace. The former type is found in Indiana, Iowa, Minnesota, Missouri, the Dakotas, Ohio, Pennsylvania, and Wisconsin; the latter in other township states.

Whatever may have been the justification for townships originally, many students are of the opinion that they might well be dispensed with. The fact that more than half the states get along without them is proof that they are not indispensable. Many of them have already atrophied, while others have lost functions to larger units of government. While many townships, especially those in suburban areas, are still virile, the continuation of modern trends is likely to make their retention more difficult to justify. Certainly if the number of governmental units is to be materially reduced the township is a good place to begin.

County Districts.[8] In the South and the Far West, where neither town nor township exists, counties are usually divided into districts. These, lacking in corporate status, are merely county subdivisions for administrative and political purposes. Unlike towns and townships, which

[8] These are not to be confused with the special *ad hoc* districts discussed below.

have a general governmental responsibility, county districts usually perform only a few special functions.

Districts are known by several names. In Virginia and West Virginia they are called magisterial districts; in Tennessee, civil districts; in Georgia, militia districts; in Maryland, Florida, and Alabama, election districts or precincts; in Mississippi, supervisor's districts; in Delaware, the old English term "hundred" is still used. In Western states similar districts are commonly called "precincts," "townships," or "judicial townships." Whatever their name, they serve similar purposes. Most commonly they serve as electoral units for choosing members on the county board and other county officers. They also are convenient areas for handling elections, administering justice, law enforcement, tax assessment and collection, road, health, and school administration.

SPECIAL DISTRICTS

Number and Types. In addition to the hierarchy of governmental units described above, all states have a number of special, or *ad hoc,* districts. A variety of reasons account for their separate existence. Sometimes it was a desire to remove them from "politics." Often debt limitations on regular governments were too low to permit them to undertake additional functions. Again, agencies were desired that could operate more flexibly and freely across traditional boundaries. Sometimes it was thought unwise to saddle poorly paid and busy municipal officials with additional responsibilities. Often districts were created in order to permit the appointment of persons specially qualified for the tasks as directors of the new agency. Whatever the reasons, districts flourish, although the number has declined noticeably during the last two decades, chiefly because of the consolidation movement at work among school districts. The summary given elsewhere indicates that of a total 79,665 districts 67,346 were school and the remainder were organized for special purposes.

School Districts. Responsibility for school administration may rest in the county, city, town, or township, but for the most part school districts have been created for the purpose.[9] A comparatively few districts are county-wide; cities and other urban places usually have only one school district, whereas rural areas are generally divided into small districts for school purposes. Many of the latter are so small and sparsely populated as to have only a handful of students for the "little red schoolhouse," with correspondingly few resources for salaries, equipment, and supplies. Consolidations have improved the situation somewhat but rural instruction generally remains inferior. School districts are properly regarded as governmental units: they have the power to tax, borrow, and spend public funds for community purposes, and they are not liable for torts. This nonliability makes it impossible for them to be sued for injuries suffered by pupils, teachers, or laborers. They can, however, generally be sued for breach of contract.

With a few exceptions, school matters are the primary responsibility of nonsalaried boards elected by the voters. Urban school systems are usually supervised by a superintendent appointed by the school board, while rural schools are commonly given a measure of supervision by popularly elected county superintendents. At a higher level, most states have an elective or appointive superintendent of public instruction with responsibility for the enforcement and administration of state laws pertaining to public schools.

Other Districts. Districts for purposes other than school administration exist in all the states. These are specially incorporated units set up for operation independently of or in close cooperation with regular governments. Some have been given the power of taxation, others have not. Most of them may borrow money, and their legal status is generally like that of other small governmental units. The more than 12,000 districts follow no common pattern of organization or function, hence are difficult to classify and describe.

Roughly, however, they can be placed in three groups: general government, public service enterprise, and combined general government and public service enterprise. The first, or general-

[9] Statistical details may be found in U.S. Department of Commerce, Bureau of the Census, *loc. cit.*

government type, is dependent upon taxation or special assessments. It includes most of all non-school special districts. Among them are fire, highway, navigation, health and hospital, sewer, library, drainage, soil conservation, cemetery, and combinations of one or more of these and others. The second, or public-service-enterprise type, provides services for rates or charges just as do private corporations. Among them are water supply, power, light, gas, housing, and a number of multiple-purpose districts. The third, or combined general-government and public-service-enterprise type, accounts for only a very small per cent of the total. These collect both taxes and assessments, and set rates and charges. Chief among them are conservation, power, and a few miscellaneous districts.

Districts, or authorities like those just mentioned, have widely differing governmental organization. Perhaps the commonest is an elec-tive or appointive board that either divides administrative responsibility among its members or, what is more frequently the case, selects a director, supervisor, or manager to superintend operations. As noted in a previous chapter, resort is often had to bodies of this sort to conduct functions that transcend municipal boundaries, especially in metropolitan areas.

While the creation of special districts may be the only or the best practicable solution for particular situations, students of government look upon them with some skepticism. They add to the number of governmental units, thus further confusing the public, lengthening the ballot, and scattering responsibility. Moreover, their creation gives the appearance of solving problems and thus distracts attention from the basic need of consolidating and reorganizing governmental units in order to make them adequate for modern times.

FOR FURTHER READING

Anderson, William: *The Units of Government in the United States: An Enumeration and Analysis* (Chicago: Public Administration Service, 1949).

Council of State Governments: *The Book of the States* (Chicago: The Council, biennial).

Fairlie, John A., and Charles M. Kneier: *County Government and Administration* (Appleton-Century-Crofts, 1930).

Gilbertson, Henry S.: *The County: The "Dark Continent" of American Politics* (New York: The National Short Ballot Organization, 1917).

Jones, Victor: *Metropolitan Government* (University of Chicago Press, 1942).

Lancaster, Lane W.: *Government in Rural America* (Van Nostrand, rev. ed., 1952).

Muller, Helen M. (comp.): "County Manager Government," *The Reference Shelf*, vol. VI, no. 8 (H. W. Wilson, 1930).

Porter, Kirk H.: *County and Township Government in the United States* (Macmillan, 1922).

Ridley, Clarence E., and Orin F. Nolting (eds.): *The Municipal Yearbook* (Chicago: International City Managers' Association, annual).

Stein, Clarence: *Toward New Towns for America* (Chicago: Public Administration Service, 1951).

Studenski, Paul, *et al.*: *The Government of Metropolitan Areas in the United States* (New York: National Municipal League, 1930).

U.S. Department of Commerce, Bureau of the Census: *Governments in the United States in 1952* (1953).

Wager, Paul W. (ed.): *County Government across the Nation* (University of North Carolina Press, 1950).

Weidner, Edward W.: *The American County—Patchwork of Boards* (New York: National Municipal League, 1946).

Wells, Roger H.: *American Local Government* (McGraw-Hill, 1939).

REVIEW QUESTIONS

1. What is a county? How many are there in a typical state? What functions do they perform?

2. Describe the forms of county government found in the United States. Which form do you think is best?

3. What local governments exist in the United States in addition to municipalities and counties?

4. How are towns and townships governed? What functions do they perform?

5. With so many local governments already in existence how do you account for the growth of special districts or authorities in recent times?

6. Do you agree or disagree with those who say that the county is the dark continent of American politics?

7. Would you advocate more or less "home rule" to counties and smaller units of local government?

8. Why do students of government look with skepticism upon the creation of special districts and authorities?

9. Suggest changes which should be made in counties and smaller units of local government.

10. If the number of local governments is to be reduced, which would you eliminate? How could this be done?

CHAPTER 38

Finance: State and Local

The old theoretical ideal of having each unit of government raise the revenues necessary for the maintenance of the functions which it administers is naïve and outmoded, inasmuch as it clashes with the more modern concept that governmental functions should be assigned to those units which can most efficiently perform them, and that taxes should be levied by governmental units capable of assessing and collecting them effectively. — Seabury C. Mastick [1]

Public finance is a field of extraordinary importance to the whole economy. In these days, the average citizen is apt to think of it mainly in terms of taxation—who pays, how much, and on what. Subconsciously, of course, people may recognize that they get services of importance to them from governments, but their primary concern is usually concentrated on the point at which dollars and cents are separated from the individual by the tax collector. Governments have a big job to do in convincing the public that tax money is prudently spent for purposes that provide the greatest good for the greatest number. Beyond that, it is increasingly apparent that governmental revenue and expenditure patterns drastically affect the national economy. If the country is to enjoy full employment and rising living standards, governments must exert their influence to those ends mainly through their power to tax and power to spend.

REVENUES

A general picture of national revenues has been presented in Chap. 19. The purpose of this section is to examine in more detail the nature of revenue sources for state and local governments, to explore possible new sources, and to appraise from the state and local point of view some of the proposals for an intergovernmental tax program.

Existing Tax Sources. In 1953, state and local governments collected $20,757,000,000 in taxes, as compared with $65,188,000,000 for the Federal government. The state and local governments also had other revenues in the form of aid from other governments, proprietary earnings, and funds from miscellaneous sources. State taxes amounted to $10,542,000,000, while those of local governments totaled $10,215,000.[2]

In the same year, state tax revenue was derived chiefly from the following sources:

Source	Revenue (millions)
General sales	$2,433
Gasoline	2,017
Income	1,779
Motor vehicle	1,012
Alcoholic beverage	544
Tobacco	467

[1] *Tax Relations among Governmental Units* (Princeton, N.J.: Tax Institute, 1938).

[2] Tax collection figures have been drawn from various publications of the Bureau of the Census.

Three sources accounted for nearly all the revenue collected by local governments:

Source	Revenue (millions)
Property	$8,890
General sales	713
Licenses and permits	504

Sales and Gross Receipts Taxes. Emerging during the depression, sales taxes have become the most important single source of state revenue. Several types of sales taxes are employed by state and local governments. The most productive is the *retail sales tax,* which is levied on the sale of most commodities. More than one-half the states now use the general retail sales tax, the rates of which range from 1 to 3 per cent. Of course, the tax is never completely "general," for it is common to exempt food and some other commodities in order to reduce the regressiveness of the tax. As explained earlier, the burden of a general sales tax falls more heavily upon the low-income group than upon the high, for those with low earnings must spend a higher proportion of their income for commodities than do wealthy persons. This explains why the general retail sales tax has been fought so vigorously when it has been proposed in Congress. During the depression, however, this tax, with its steady flow, low collection cost, and enormous returns, rescued many a state from near insolvency.

A second type is the *selective sales tax,* which is levied on the sale of particular items, especially luxuries. Similar to the excise taxes of the Federal government are the state levies on motor fuels, alcoholic beverages, tobacco, and other commodities. Actually, gasoline is not regarded as a luxury item, but the tax is justified in terms of providing revenue for highways. It is now used by all states. Likewise, all states tax liquor, although some secure a much larger revenue through the operation of state liquor stores. Many other commodities are subject to selective sales taxes in the several states.

Third, there is the *gross receipts tax* or *gross tax.* It involves the collection of a small percentage of all receipts or income. Sometimes

grouped with it and sometimes in a separate category is the *turnover tax,* under which transactions are taxed. Gross income often bears little relation to net income. Thus a retail merchant might have $100,000 in gross receipts in a given year, yet suffer a net loss of $5,000 for the period. A professional man might gross $20,000 and net $10,000. Therefore, several different rates may

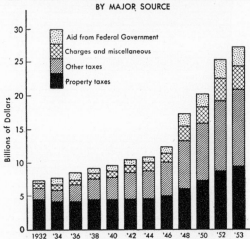

GENERAL REVENUE OF STATE AND LOCAL GOVERNMENTS BY MAJOR SOURCE

As state and local revenues have increased since depression days, the property tax has declined in relative importance; other taxes, especially sales taxes, and federal aid have shown the greatest relative increase. Adapted from U.S. Bureau of the Census, *Historical Statistics on State and Local Government Finances, 1902–1953* (1955), p. 12.

be necessitated if even a rough measure of justice is done. If the tax applies to all gross receipts or income, there is bound to be pyramiding, which is likely to increase the price of a commodity considerably, because each person or concern through which it has passed has been liable to a tax on its value. Perhaps the most successful of gross-receipts taxes have been those applied to companies that have a generally stable relationship between gross receipts and net returns, such as insurance and public utility corporations.

After sales taxes became a major source of state revenue, some cities and counties sought to share in this new and lucrative levy. Their boundaries are rarely arranged so that a sales tax is administratively feasible. New York City and a few other large municipalities have enjoyed modest success with a general retail sales tax but are plagued with exemptions for out-

to pay. Although retained, the sales tax may well in the next generation be supplemented to a greater extent by other taxes, such as personal and corporate income taxes, which adhere to the ability-to-pay principle.

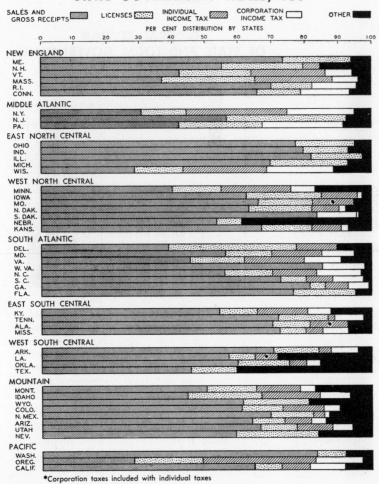

STATE GOVERNMENT TAXES, 1953

*Corporation taxes included with individual taxes

Sales and gross receipts taxes are the predominant source of tax revenue for the American states. Note the wide variation in individual-income tax revenues. The large "other" revenues of Texas, Oklahoma, and Louisiana are mainly from severance taxes on natural resources. Nebraska and a few other states raise significant amounts through the property tax. Courtesy of National Industrial Conference Board.

of-city sales. Sharing in sales-tax revenues by local governments is likely to come, if at all, through the willingness of the state to collect the tax for cities and counties and then to share the proceeds with them.

Regressive as it is, the sales tax is likely to remain indefinitely as a major state revenue producer. The incidence of the general retail sales tax, however, falls most heavily upon those least able to pay and least upon those most able

Property Taxes. Property taxes constitute the major source of revenue for American local governments, accounting for over 87 per cent of tax revenue in 1953. Until the events of crisis and war vastly increased federal income-tax and state sales-tax collections, the property tax was *the* major source of American governmental revenue. Despite the development of new forms of taxation during the depression, most states still make some use of property taxation. In 1953 only 2 per cent of state revenue was derived from the property tax.

Property taxes generally are thought to apply to real property only, but this is not always the case. Property is both tangible and intangible. A man who owns a farm has tangible property in the form of land, house, machinery, livestock, and the like. Another man may own very little real or personal property but own a million dollars' worth of bank deposits, stocks, and bonds, which are called "intangible property." The intangibles may or may not be taxed, depending upon the provisions of state law or local ordinance.

The first job in collecting the property tax is assessment. Taxing bodies set the rate of taxation at so much in dollars and cents for each one hundred dollars of assessed valuation. The local tax assessor is given the task of estimating the value of all kinds of property, and then he reduces it to an "assessed valuation," which is some given fraction of estimated true value. The job of an assessor is an almost impossible one. It is difficult enough to work out a proper formula for assessing real property, but it is next to impossible to make a fair assessment of intangibles.[3]

Another problem that plagues property-tax administrators is that of exemptions. Every state and community releases some property owners from liability for payment. It is common practice to exempt real property up to a certain maximum valuation if owned by a veteran. Similar exemptions often are extended to widows of veterans and the physically handicapped. Churches, schools, and charitable institutions usually are excepted. Several states have extended exemptions of farms and homes up to a set maximum if used as a "homestead" by the owner. Each exemption narrows the base on which the property tax is built and reduces the number of taxpayers but is defended by many on grounds of social justice.

[3] Authoritative works on assessment are *Assessment Principles* (Chicago: National Association of Assessing Officials, 1939), and J. D. Silverherz, *The Assessment of Real Property in the United States* (Albany: New York State Tax Commission, 1936).

Income Taxes. Nearly three-fourths of the states have some form of income taxes, personal or corporate. Unlike the inheritance or estates tax, the Federal government allows no offset or credit for state taxation. A sort of credit is given, however, in that a taxpayer may deduct from the income on which he pays a federal tax any amounts paid out in state income taxes. Therefore the existence of a state income tax means a reduction in the amount of federal revenue from this source. Personal income taxes in 1953 ranked first among federal revenues and fourth among state tax revenues; they were negligible sources for local governments because of the difficulty of collecting them at that level.

The question of levying a personal income tax has been controversial; thirty-one states have now adopted it in some form. The corporate income tax is used by thirty-three states.

State personal income-tax rates vary from 1 to 11 per cent, but most of them have a maximum of 5, 6, or 7 per cent. The high federal rates on large incomes have been a deterrent to higher state rates. State tax rates have also been held down by the fear of competition with other states which have little or no income tax. One of the arguments commonly given against a state personal income tax is that it can be evaded by those who command the best legal advice.

On the other hand, the progressive features of the personal income tax are admirably suited to offset the regressive features of sales and property taxes. The tax effectively reaches some persons who own no tangible property yet reap large incomes from intangibles. Its incidence is in little doubt; it falls directly upon the taxpayer and cannot be shifted to others.

Inheritance-estate Taxation. All states except Nevada have an inheritance or estate tax. Both are death duties; the estate tax is levied on a deceased person's estate; the inheritance tax is exacted from a beneficiary's share of the estate. As previously explained, federal law permits an offset or credit for state death duties up to 80 per cent of the 1926 estate-tax rate. The offset does not apply to later federal estate levies. Existence of the credit device was a powerful incentive for states to enact inheritance-tax laws, thus putting an end to the competition among states seeking to provide tax-free havens for rich and elderly people.

State inheritance taxes not only have progressive rates that increase with the size of a beneficiary's share, but they are also graduated according to the relationship of the beneficiary to the deceased. The largest exemption and lowest rates are usually allowed for a widow, followed by those for a widower and children. More distant relatives have a much smaller exemption and higher rates. Those who are not related at all have little or no exemption and the highest rates.

The inheritance and estate taxes have not been without their problems, but happily many of them have been solved, at least partially. In the beginning, gifts were used to avoid death taxes; both Federal and state governments plugged this loophole by enacting gift-tax laws, setting the rates nearly as high as the death duties. Next, states locked horns over jurisdictional matters, seeking to tax every estate over which they could establish any shred of jurisdiction. This situation was eased by reciprocity arrangements and later by Federal court decisions defining state jurisdiction. Death duties have great social significance, for they offer an opportunity to redistribute at least a portion of accumulated wealth. This function of the tax is more in the hands of the Federal than the state governments, for only the nation is in a position to apply the high rates necessary to accomplish this social purpose.

Business Taxation. Business taxes include corporation income taxes, license and privilege taxes, capital-stock taxes, and various levies on particular types of businesses. Taken together, they account for a good share of national, state, and local tax revenues.

The state corporate income tax, used by thirty-three states, poses many puzzling problems for the tax administrator. Here again the problem is one of jurisdiction. Business corporations that hold charters from one state often operate in many others. Which, then, can tax corporate net income? The question is not finally answered, but agreement is being reached. Using a stand-ard worked out by the National Tax Association, several states are now allocating corporate income among themselves for taxation purposes on the basis of business done in each state. The three criteria employed in making the allocation are location of tangible property, distribution of sales, and distribution of payrolls.

Corporations are also taxed through capital-stock taxes, which are levied against the assessed valuations of business-concern stocks. Formerly used in all states, more than one-third of the states have dropped the plan in favor of a corporate income tax. Some states use both. Some states also derive a considerable amount of revenue from the taxation of insurance companies, often a percentage of gross premiums in the state. This is usually justified on the basis that companies should pay something for the privilege of doing business in the state. State taxation of banks is complicated by the fact that most of the larger banks have national charters, and therefore the state power to tax these federal instrumentalities is restricted. Federal law does not permit state taxation of the personal property of national banks, nor does it permit levies on bank shares in excess of most other intangibles. One simple solution, to permit states to tax national banks on the same basis as they do state banks, appears reasonable but has not yet been accepted.

Motor-vehicle Taxes. All states levy taxes on motor vehicles, presumably for the privilege of operating them. They net the states an important share of revenue too, averaging about $700,000,-000 in recent years. Most Americans are familiar with this tax. It is usually graduated according to weight, type, and age of the vehicle, ranging from steep fees for trucks to insignificant ones for motorcycles. Collection is handled through the sale of license plates or tags, which makes compliance rather easy to secure. Like the gasoline tax, the proceeds of the motor-vehicle tax often are earmarked for use on the highways only. Nearly every state has been the scene of controversy between those who wish to use vehicle and fuel money for general purposes and those who demand retention for highway purposes.

Other Revenues. State and local governments also receive large amounts of revenue from nontax sources, especially from public enterprises operated by them. This category is relatively more important to municipal than to other levels of government.

State Nontax Revenues. The principal state enterprise is in the field of liquor. Seventeen states [4] have adopted the monopoly plan of liquor control, involving the operation of state stores. Although established primarily as a means of maintaining effective control over the sale of alcoholic beverages, the plan has produced large amounts of revenue for the states that have adopted it. In 1953, for example, sixteen state liquor authorities contributed $210,000,000 to the governments of their states.[5] In addition, these states received revenue from liquor taxes and fees. The licensing-plan states also secure revenue from liquor, but it comes via taxation and is relatively smaller in amount.

All other state enterprises net little profit. They are in diverse fields. California operates a short railway in San Francisco harbor, New York still runs vestiges of its once-great canal system. North Dakota is in the grain elevator business. Most of these enterprises have a heavy burden of debt and are able at best only to service that debt and pay operating expenses.

Local Nontax Revenues. Local governmental enterprises, mainly municipal, are sources of a good deal of nontax revenue, but usually have even greater expenditures. Cities commonly operate their own water-supply systems. Fewer municipalities run light and power systems. Other enterprises of American cities are transportation, gas, port, airport, and market. Some cities deliberately subsidize their transportation facilities as a service to the people.

County enterprises are few and far between.

[4] Alabama, Idaho, Iowa, Maine, Michigan, Montana, New Hampshire, North Carolina, Ohio, Oregon, Pennsylvania, Utah, Vermont, Virginia, Washington, West Virginia, and Wyoming. Wyoming's plan involves the operation of wholesale facilities only.

[5] U.S. Department of Commerce, Bureau of the Census, *Historical Statistics on State and Local Government Finances, 1902–1953* (1955), p. 19.

Thirty-three counties in North Carolina, Maryland, and Georgia were in 1943 operating liquor stores. They profit from their liquor enterprises by a comfortable margin. Other county enterprises are negligible.

Special districts often are created solely to provide utility services, such as water supply, light and power, and housing.

Although they handle rather large amounts of money, local enterprises as a whole show a net loss.

EXPENDITURES

Pattern of State Expenditures. The three functions for which nearly two-thirds of state expenditures are made are (1) education, (2) highways, and (3) public welfare. The remainder of state services—general government, public safety, conservation of natural resources, corrections, hospitals, recreation, debt service, and all the rest—are financed out of the remaining one-third.

Actually, a state legislature rarely if ever is in the position of being able to evaluate state functions anew and then make appropriations according to its appraisal of their worth to the state. To a great extent the appropriations for education, highways, public welfare, unemployment compensation, and debt service are beyond the control of the legislature. Most expenditures for education are in the form of grants-in-aid to local school districts, and it is common to have the basis for this allocation fixed in the state constitution. On highway appropriations the legislature is caught in a double squeeze; motor-vehicle and fuel taxes are usually earmarked for highway purposes, and the federal highway grants must be matched. A large portion of public-welfare expenditures is for assistance and other programs under the Social Security Act; state matching of federal funds is required, and a good deal of the money is spent through local governments with which the state may have a constitutional or contractual arrangement. Unemployment compensation is financed through payroll taxes, the proceeds of which are transferred to a trust fund; the function is so closely supervised by the Social Security Administration that there is little chance for state legislative discretion here. Interest and principal repayment on state debts constitute a top claim on the resources of a state and can be deferred or adjusted only with difficulty.

TOTAL EXPENDITURE OF STATE AND LOCAL GOVERNMENTS
BY FUNCTION

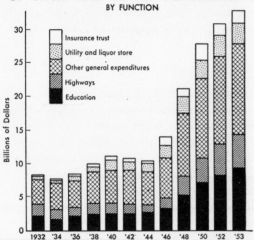

The trend in aggregate state and local expenditures shows no disproportionate increase for any function. *Historical Statistics on State and Local Government Finances, 1902–1953*, p. 13.

Local Governmental Expenditures. Counties made their largest expenditures in 1953 for the following functions (percentages of total county expenditures given):

	Per Cent
Highways	22.5
Public welfare	21.1
General control	10.7
Hospitals	9.9

Welfare is a traditional county function in most sections of the country, and states have inclined to keep counties involved in financing the expanded assistance program under the Social Security Act. General control includes charges for maintenance of the legislative, executive, and judicial branches, the conduct of elections, the operation of county buildings, and many other expenses; county expenditures in this category are higher than in any other level of government, probably because of the heavy burden imposed by election administration. Many highways are still under county control, but there is a significant tendency for states to assume more and more responsibility for maintenance and construction of secondary highways formerly under county control. The extent of health and hospital services provided by counties varies greatly from state to state; in few jurisdictions are services provided for the average citizen, since the emphasis is placed mainly on serving the underprivileged who cannot afford private facilities.

The largest expenditures of cities in 1953 were for

	Per Cent
Public safety	18.2
Schools	17.1
Streets and highways	11.3
Sanitation	10.4
Health and hospitals	8.0

In public safety, police costs more than fire protection, and the two together constitute the largest single expenditure of American urban municipalities. The large amount of city money spent for schools is rather surprising; this expenditure is greatest in the vast urban centers where, in some cases, school districts have been abolished and combined with city governments. The amount of welfare service varies greatly from city to city and state to state, depending in part on the program of city officeholders and in part on the extent and adequacy of county welfare services.

Townships may include wholly urban, wholly rural, or mixed areas. They spend the largest amount on

Schools
Roads and highways
Sanitation
Public safety
Public welfare

The diversity of this group is great, ranging from the New England mill town through the prairie-state rural township to the suburban township that provides high-class residential facilities for commuters from a great city.

School districts quite naturally spend most of

their resources for schools, but they have minor expenditures for overhead administration, health, and other services.

INTERGOVERNMENTAL FISCAL RELATIONS

State Grants to Local Governments. Just as federal grants to the states have become a fixed

based on the property tax, has proven inadequate to produce the new revenues required to provide desired services. Second, the states, aided and abetted by the Federal government, have sought to induce local governments to enter or expand functions deemed of social value.

The purposes for which local governments are given state grants are nearly always specified.

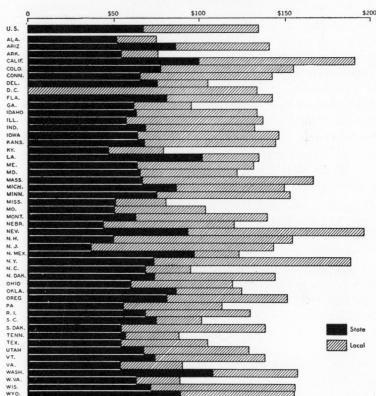

STATE & LOCAL TAX COLLECTIONS
PER CAPITA, FISCAL 1953

Per capita tax collections, state and local, show both the average aggregate tax burden in the several states and the relative burden borne in each state by state and local taxpayers. Courtesy of National Industrial Conference Board.

part of the fiscal system, so have state grants-in-aid to counties, cities, school districts, and other units of local government come to play a major role. Indeed, in amounts of money involved, state grants to localities exceed federal grants to states by nearly two to one. There is some duplication involved here; federal funds for public assistance, for example, are received by the states and often passed along to counties.

State grants to local governments have developed for two principal reasons: First, taxation,

In order of size of grant, the local functions aided by states in recent years have been schools, public assistance, and highways. Lesser amounts are granted for health and hospital services, libraries, and other functions. In 1952 schools accounted for $2,525,000,000, which was approximately one-half of all moneys granted by states to local governments. Public welfare and highways received sizable grants, with lesser amounts allocated to health and hospital services, libraries, and other functions.

Sources of state-aid moneys are specified only in a minority of cases. It is considered better practice to take moneys from the general fund, but many states allocate a portion of the proceeds of the gasoline tax to counties and cities, and several earmark other sources in whole or in part for aid to localities. The basis of allocation employed in state aid is sometimes the amount of collections of a certain tax, such as the gasoline tax, in each political subdivision; more often allocation is on a number-aided basis. In one sense this is fair, but in providing the same per-pupil state aid for a wealthy district as for an impoverished one, the important element of need is wholly overlooked.

State-administered Locally Shared Taxes. There has been a recent tendency for states to levy taxes and share a portion of all the proceeds with local governments. It is sometimes difficult to draw the line between a locally shared tax and a grant-in-aid. Take the gasoline tax, for example. The state levies the tax and earmarks a portion of its revenue for counties and cities, specifying that it must be used for streets, roads, and highways. Is it a grant-in-aid or a shared tax? It can be classed with either, but is considered here in the shared category.

The principal state-administered locally shared taxes are on gasoline, motor vehicles, alcoholic beverages, income, sales, and business. Gasoline taxes are shared with localities by about one-half of the states. Many require that the local share of this tax be spent on roads.

Several distinct methods of allocating are in use, including collections in the unit, equality among units, area, population, highway mileage, motor-car registration, assessed valuation, and statutory percentages. Motor-vehicle taxes are subject to similar controls.

Each of the other shared taxes is found in only a few states and the purposes for which it may be spent are less likely to be specified. In some cases, as in alcoholic beverages, there is a distinct local problem created by the commodity taxed, and it appears fair that tax money collected by the state should be handed over to aid in its solution. Naturally, local governmental officials and property taxpayers welcome the state's contributions and seek its expansion along other lines.

State Financial Controls over Local Units. During the last 30 years state controls over local finances have increased considerably. These restrictions have taken the form of debt and tax limitations and state administrative supervision. Debt limitations on local government may be stated in terms of relationship between debt and assessed valuation or may involve state review of proposals for bond issue. Although often deemed necessary to protect the credit of local taxing units, debt limitations are often honored more in the breach than in the observance. They have often been evaded through the creation of special districts, to which may be assigned expensive new functions of government, and by various other expedients.

Tax limitations are usually imposed in terms of either assessed valuation or restrictions on the amount of increase permitted in any given fiscal period. The first occasionally is avoided through an increase in the assessed valuation of property or the utilization of new sources of revenue. The latter is more restrictive. Indeed, its operation may greatly handicap a city or county in which there is a rapid increase in population and resulting necessity for expanded services.

The state administrative controls over local finance developed in Indiana in the 1920's attracted a great deal of attention. Its state tax board was given power to review local budgets and to disallow or reduce excessive ones. New York and some other states provide for state auditing of local accounts and installation of uniform accounting systems. Many variations in types of administrative controls are found in the several states.

FINANCIAL ADMINISTRATION

Both the budgetary process and financial administration were dealt with in a general way in an earlier chapter.[6] The object of the present section is to examine in more detail how state and local governments have developed their fiscal processes.

[6] See pp. 367–378.

State Agencies. Taxes are collected, in the various states, by officers, boards, commissions, departments, and other bodies. The diversity of nomenclature is so great that it is difficult to ascertain any pattern at first glance. Upon examination, however, states may be classified into three groups by types of tax-collecting agencies. First, some states have departments of revenue or finance. Second, others have tax commissions or boards. Third, still others have two, three, four, or five officers or agencies involved in tax collection. There has been a tendency, favorably regarded by students of public finance, to concentrate tax collection in the hands of a single officer, commission, or department.

The comprehensive financial plan called the "budget" is formulated from the estimates of needs and revenues submitted by the various agencies of government. In most states that have reorganized on a modern basis, the governor or some officer or agency directly responsible to him is placed in charge of preparing the budget for submission to the legislature. Most of the states require that all estimates be submitted in advance of a date fixed in one of the final months of the year. The budget document is then prepared and placed before the legislature on or before the appointed day, which is most commonly in January, February, or March.

In authorizing the budget, the legislatures of most states have unlimited power to increase, decrease, or eliminate items. The power to increase is denied to the Maryland and West Virginia legislatures, and restricted in the cases of Nebraska and Rhode Island. This represents an important departure from the traditional legislative supremacy over money matters. Actually, however, the same effect might be secured in many other states through the exercise of the item veto, but such action might be overridden by the legislature.

After the legislature passes the budget, the more advanced states place responsibility for administering it in the hands of a finance officer or agency who is almost always directly responsible to the governor. At this stage various controls may be imposed. It is common practice to set, either by statute or administrative rule, a maximum proportion of the annual or biennial budget that may be spent in a single month. If an agency wishes to deviate, it must secure permission from the finance authority. Controls also may be established over purchasing of supplies and employment of personnel. Discretionary power is often given a finance officer to reduce the amount of an agency's appropriation in order to effect savings.

When expenditures are proposed by an operating agency, the purchase order is checked against the appropriation or balance of account. This function is called "preaudit," and usually is vested in the finance officer but sometimes is retained by an elective comptroller. The payment is actually made by a treasurer, who is chief custodian of state funds. Finally the transaction is in many states postaudited by the auditor or comparable official, who usually is popularly elected or chosen by the legislature. Legislative choice increasingly is favored.

Local Agencies. The financial procedures and officers of counties, cities, towns and townships, school districts, and special districts are so diverse that a very general description is all that can be given. The budget ought to be formulated directly under the supervision of the chief executive authority, if one exists. It should be comprehensive, including all proposed expenditures and full statements concerning revenues and debt.

In some local governments there is a great need for a unified finance department. Financial functions are often widely distributed among many officers and agencies, making central control and direction virtually impossible of realization. Cities are apt to be better organized in this regard than counties, for in the former, whether the mayor-council plan exists or has been replaced by the council-manager form, there is a single executive in whom fiscal authority can be concentrated. Except where the county-manager plan has been installed, the typical plural executive of that level of government, like the cities under the commission plan, often leaves executive power so diffused that financial functions are brought together only with the greatest difficulty.

FOR FURTHER READING

Blakey, Roy G., and Gladys C. Blakey: *Sales Taxes and Other Excises* (Chicago: Public Administration Service, 1945).

Buck, Arthur E.: *The Budget in Governments of Today* (Macmillan, 1934).

——: *Budgeting for Small Cities* (New York: National Municipal League, 1931).

——: *Public Budgeting* (Harper, 1929).

——: *Municipal Finance* (Macmillan, 1926).

Durfee, Waite D., Jr.: *Intergovernmental Fiscal Relations* (University of Minnesota Press, 1950).

Federation of Tax Administrators: *Tax Administrators News* (Chicago: The Federation, monthly).

Haig, Robert M.: *The Sales Tax in the American States* (Columbia University Press, 1934).

Hansen, Alvin H., and Harvey S. Perloff: *State and Local Finance in the National Economy* (Norton, 1944).

Hillhouse, A. M., and Muriel Magelssen: *Where Cities Get Their Money* (Chicago: Municipal Finance Officers Association, 1945). Supplements have been issued in 1947 and 1949.

Hutchinson, Ruth G.: *State-administered Locally Shared Taxes* (Columbia University Press, 1934).

Kilpatrick, Wylie: *State Supervision of Local Finance* (Chicago: Public Administration Service, 1941).

MacMillan, T. E.: *State Supervision of Municipal Finance* (University of Texas, Institute of Public Affairs, 1953).

Municipal Finance Officers Association: *Municipal Finance* (Chicago: The Association, quarterly).

Ratchford, Benjamin U.: *American State Debts* (Duke University Press, 1941).

U.S. Department of Commerce, Bureau of the Census: *Compendium of City Government Finances* (annual).

——: *Governmental Finances in the United States* (annual).

REVIEW QUESTIONS

1. What are the principal sources of state tax revenue? Discuss.

2. What are the principal sources of local tax revenue? Discuss.

3. Discuss state grants to local governments.

4. What justifications are there for state-administered locally shared taxes? Mention the principal uses of this device.

5. Describe state financial controls over local governments.

6. What state agencies are charged with responsibility for financial administration?

CHAPTER 39

State and Local Law Enforcement

> But the unfortunate fact remains that all laws, however perfect, must in the end be administered by imperfect men. There is, alas! no such thing as a government of laws and not of men. You may have a government more of laws and less of men, or vice versa, but you cannot have an autoadministration of the Golden Rule. Sooner or later you come to a man—in the White House, or on a wool sack, or at a desk in an office, or in a blue coat and brass buttons—and then, to a considerable extent, the question of how far ours is a government of laws or men depends upon him. — Arthur Train [1]

In modern times major responsibility for the protection of life and property falls upon government. Until 1931 Pennsylvania permitted coal, iron, and other industrial concerns to have organized, uniformed police with authority to act not only as detectives and guards but also as public peace officers.[2] Some states now extend similar powers to railroad police, and it is quite common for sheriffs to deputize private police, guards, or detectives for special duty. Except for the Pennsylvania industrial police and present-day railroad police, however, no state has permitted the establishment of large, permanent, organized private police forces with powers concurrent with those of publicly paid peace officers.

Therefore unless specially commissioned by authority of statute or deputized by sheriffs, private police act in a purely private capacity without jurisdiction beyond the property of their employers. Instead, all three levels of government join in the task of protecting life and property. Primary responsibility falls upon state and local governments, which spend millions of dollars annually for this purpose. The principal instrumentalities, other than the courts, are discussed below.

STATE AND LOCAL POLICE

Detection and Arrest. Detection of crimes and offenders is preliminary to all else and requires great care. It is done by private individuals, administrative officers, federal agents who detect violations of state law during the course of their own activities, and especially by state and local police. When armed with sufficient evidence of suspected crime, criminal proceedings are started by making arrests. As noted elsewhere, arrests can sometimes be made without warrants, but not ordinarily. Warrants must be obtained from judicial officers who must first be convinced that

[1] *Courts and Criminals* (Scribner, 1926), p. 11.

[2] The famous, or perhaps notorious, Pennsylvania Coal and Iron Police, later called Industrial Police, was abolished in 1931. See Jeremiah P. Shalloo, *Private Police: With Special Reference to Pennsylvania* (Philadelphia: The American Academy of Political and Social Science, 1933). For an excellent discussion of the nature, extent, and cost of private police protection, see National Commission on Law Observation and Enforcement, *Report on the Cost of Crime* (12 reports, 1931), no. 12, pp. 351–358.

there is sufficient cause for action. After arrest follows preliminary hearing before a minor judicial officer, unconditional or conditional release on bail or on the offender's own recognizance, detention perhaps, investigation, grand-jury review, and trial. Following detection and apprehension the police officer's task is usually confined to that of acting as state's witness.

State Police. Governors have long been charged with the duty of seeing that state laws are faithfully executed, but until comparatively recent times they have had no forces constantly at their command with which to accomplish the task. Instead, they were dependent upon sheriffs, municipal police, constables, or, in emergencies, the militia. This situation often proved embarrassing. On one occasion the governor of Indiana, finding himself without power to compel locally elected sheriffs and constables to do his bidding, was forced to call out the militia to enforce a law prohibiting race-track gambling.[3] Former Governor Pennypacker of Pennsylvania emphasized the situation by saying:

In the year 1903, when I assumed the office of Chief Executive of the State I found myself thereby invested with supreme executive authority. I found that no power existed to interfere with me in my duty to enforce the laws of the State, and that, by the same token, no conditions could release me from my duty so to do. I then looked about to see what instruments I possessed wherewithal to accomplish this bounden obligation—what instruments on whose loyalty and obedience I could truly rely. I perceived three such instruments—my private secretary, a very small man, my woman stenographer, and the janitor, a Negro. So I made the State Police.[4]

Circumstances like these, coupled with the growth of cities, the arrival of trains and automobiles, and the continued breakdown of the sheriff-constable system, led to the establishment of state police systems. The Texas Rangers, or-

ganized for border patrol while Texas was still a republic, were the first. Massachusetts, in 1865, established a system of state constables; Arizona, in 1901, and New Mexico, in 1903, created border patrols modeled after the famed Texas Rangers; Connecticut established a small state force in 1903 and Pennsylvania its well-known motor police in 1905. Other states have followed until today thirty-five have police with general authority to enforce state laws, while the remaining thirteen have police with authority only over traffic violations. In addition to these basic police agencies a number of states have set up supplemental forces. Some are responsible for criminal investigation, others for special aspects of motor-vehicle law enforcement, and others for liquor law enforcement.

State police are usually directed by an agency in the state government called a department of public safety, highway patrol, or merely state police department. In addition to a central headquarters, state police are commonly based upon substations scattered throughout the state.

State Police Jurisdiction. Defining state police jurisdiction has been exceedingly difficult, due partly to public distrust of officers beyond local control and also to pride and jealousy on the part of local officials. As matters now stand, (1) thirty-five states have police forces with general criminal jurisdiction, which means that they are competent to act anywhere within state limits where state laws are violated; (2) upon the governor's request, state police are usually required to assist state administrative and regulatory agencies, like those concerned with public health, pure food and drugs, school attendance, etc.; (3) state police are universally prohibited from enforcing laws and ordinances of local governments except when invited to do so; (4) state forces usually refrain from operating within incorporated places, even for the enforcement of state laws, except where invited to do so, where necessary to continue pursuit started outside such places, or where they witness crimes committed; (5) legislation usually prohibits or carefully restricts the use of state police in industrial (labor) disputes; (6) state police are usually forbidden

[3] Bruce Smith, *Police Systems in the United States* (Harper, 1949), pp. 166–167.

[4] Katherine Mayo, *Justice to All* (Putnam, 1918), pp. 5–6. See also Smith, *loc. cit.*

to serve civil processes such as warrants, subpoenas, writs, and the like.[5]

Special Policing Agents. A trip to any state capital or city hall discloses a welter of administrative agencies, most of which are engaged in policing activities with or without the help of regular police. Most of them begin by registering or licensing buildings, restaurants, hotels, saloons, pool halls, drugstores, fishermen and hunters, automobiles and their drivers, public utilities, airports, hospitals, factories, mines, and many more. Then follow periodic or special inspection and perhaps the filing of reports. Offenders may be dealt with administratively by the revocation of licenses and permits or the payment of fines, or it may be necessary to haul them before courts. To catalogue the agencies involved is impractical. The ones employing the largest staffs are likely to be those charged with responsibility for enforcing laws relating to the use of motor vehicles, hunting and fishing, banking, school attendance, building location and design, health, sanitation, safety, food, drugs, narcotics, and liquor.

Sheriffs. The office of sheriff is one of the oldest in England and America. The sheriff is, at least in theory, the principal peace officer of the county. In Colonial days, sheriffs were generally appointed by the governor but the march of democracy during the early nineteenth century made them elective. Today, except in Rhode Island, where the legislature appoints the sheriffs, election by county voters is the rule. The terms of sheriffs are generally 2 years and often they are forbidden to succeed themselves. Their remuneration is usually derived from fees, mileage allowance, boarding prisoners in the county jail, and selling supplies to prisoners. Sheriffs are among the best-paid county officers, netting from $1,200 in small rural counties to $100,000 annually in some metropolitan centers. Their duties consist of detecting and apprehending criminals, summoning *posse comitatus* (groups of deputies) on rare occasions when made necessary by emergencies, caring for prisoners,[6] administering county jails, executing court orders and processes, making up jury rolls and summoning jurors, and in some places, assisting with tax collection and election administration. Many times sheriffs are assisted by deputies, constables, bailiffs, jailers, and others.

The office of sheriff, like so many others inherited from the rural past, is often under fire. Under modern conditions elective police are seldom qualified to detect and combat crime. The emergence of trained and well-equipped municipal, state, and federal police forces has caused sheriffs to slough their police role and confine themselves to the other duties mentioned above. Referring to this situation, a leading authority has said, "In a vast majority of American counties the sheriff system has already collapsed."[7] Some counties, however, have competently manned, well-organized, and modernly equipped sheriffs' offices.

Still, no state has moved to abolish the office, although a few have taken steps to abolish the fee system and prevent sheriffs from enriching themselves by collecting fixed prices for prisoners' meals but serving cheap and inadequate diets. Those who would abolish the office would turn what police functions remain over to state, municipal, or appointive county police. They would transfer the handling of prisoners and jails to state officers charged with responsibility for correctional institutions, and they would turn court duties over to some administrative officer responsible to the court.[8] The entrenched position of the office, written into

---

[5] This is a very general and brief summary. The student will do well to consult references dealing with the laws of his own state. The above summary is based chiefly upon Smith, *op. cit.; The Book of the States, 1954–1955;* and David G. Monroe, *State and Provincial Police* (Northwestern University Traffic Institute, 1941), Chap. II.

[6] Even federal prisoners when they are temporarily detained in county jails. See p. 305.

[7] Smith, *op. cit.,* p. 89.

[8] For these and other suggestions, see Arthur C. Millspaugh, *Local Democracy and Crime Control* (Brookings, 1936), pp. 231–234; Bruce Smith, *Rural Crime Control* (Institute of Public Administration, Columbia University, 1933), p. 73.

state constitutions and supported by local pride and resistance to change, makes abolition unlikely; meanwhile, milder reforms are long overdue.

Municipal Police. As cities grew, more protection was needed than could be provided by sheriffs and constables. At first a force of night watchmen to patrol the streets was thought sufficient; then followed shifts for day as well as night; finally, in 1853, New York established the first uniformed police force such as is common today. Early police forces were locally controlled, but because of mismanagement and collusion with corrupt political machines and the underworld, state control became the rule between 1860 and 1890. The cure proved worse than the disease. Too often it merely meant transferring responsibility from one corrupt setting to another. Today, local control has been restored in all the largest cities except Boston, Baltimore, and St. Louis, where the head of the police department is appointed by and removable by the governor. In smaller cities local direction is also the rule. Although locally controlled, municipal police are invariably responsible for the enforcement of state as well as municipal law within city limits.

The administration of municipal police, especially in large cities, presents a major problem.[9] Cities like New York, Chicago, and Los Angeles employ a police personnel of several thousand and spend huge sums for police protection. It is important, therefore, that the taxpayers get their money's worth—something which is most unlikely unless administration is divorced from politics, and sound principles of public management are followed. This entails a high degree of civic consciousness on the part of citizens, a clear line of authority untrammeled by partisan considerations, a modern civil service system which will ensure recruitment on the basis of merit, adequate pay scales, systematic promotion, security of tenure, provision for retirement, and

a highly trained personnel outfitted with the most modern equipment. While considerable improvement has taken place since the orgies of the past century, much remains to be done. Fortunately, many national and state agencies, associations of police officers themselves, and civic groups have come into existence to help with the problem.

Constables. Like so many local officers, that of constable was brought over from England and dates back to earliest Colonial days. The bailiwick of the constable has been the town, township, districts into which Southern counties are divided, and small incorporated places where he is often known as "town marshal." Constables are generally chosen by popular election for terms of 2 or 4 years and their compensation comes from fees. Although theoretically the local police officers chiefly responsible for maintaining the peace, they are almost invariably ill-qualified for crime control; hence their areas of operation are either poorly policed or municipal, county, and state police have taken over. The time now devoted to the job is spent almost entirely in serving warrants, summonses, subpoenas, and other processes of justices of the peace. Occasionally they help collect taxes and serve as poundkeepers.

The prestige of constables has steadily diminished until today it is often difficult to find candidates for the office. In England the office was swept away in 1856, while in this country it has either been abandoned or virtually ceased to function in most places employing full-time uniformed police. Those who advocate its complete abolition generally suggest that full-time police take over the small amount of criminal work remaining and that the assistance now given justices of the peace be performed either by police officers or, better still, by an administrative officer attached to a unified county court.

State Militias. All the states maintain militias to help with law enforcement and the maintenance of public peace. The Federal government, it will be recalled, may intervene within states where invasion, rebellion, or insurrection is involved, or where necessary to enforce federal law and protect federal property, or when in-

[9] The problem is treated fully in the International City Managers' Association, *Municipal Police Administration* (Chicago: The Association, 2d ed., 1943). See also O. W. Wilson, *Police Administration* (McGraw-Hill, 1950).

vited by state governments to assist. Federal intervention with military force is comparatively rare. The use of state forces is much more frequent, but county and local police are usually adequate.

State militias consist of two parts: the unorganized, which includes all able-bodied adult males, and the organized, which is better known as the National Guard. The unorganized militia is seldom called up either for training or duty but conceivably might be in the event of a serious emergency like a flood, fire, invasion, or widespread civil disorder. National Guard units, while financed largely by federal funds and trained in accordance with standards set by the United States Army, are nevertheless normally state bodies. When not mobilized for federal service, National Guard personnel is appointed by state governors and is responsible to them. Administrative supervision is commonly provided through a department of military affairs, the director of which is frequently called "adjutant general." Detailed work consists of coordinating the state's military activity with the federal, organizing, training, maintaining, disciplining, servicing, and equipping the National Guard, protecting federal military stores and properties, maintaining state arsenals, armories, camps, and reservations, administering state veterans' hospitals and state laws pertaining to ex-servicemen, and aiding with law enforcement upon command of the governor. Membership in the National Guard usually requires occasional training at some near-by armory followed by attendance at summer encampments. National Guard units were called into federal service during both world wars but were demobilized shortly after fighting ended. To fill the gap occasioned by their absence during the Second World War and the Korean conflict, most states organized special state or home guards.

PROSECUTION OF OFFENDERS

After detection and arrest, those suspected of crime are "arraigned" before appropriate judicial officers who may dismiss them, release them on their own recognizance or on bail, or put them in prison to await trial. In spite of impressive evidence to the contrary, those accused are presumed to be innocent until proved guilty. Responsibility for proof rests upon the state, which proceeds through the officers discussed below.

State Departments of Justice. All the states have an attorney general who generally presides over a department of justice. The attorney general is occasionally appointed but oftener he is elected, in which case he may be not only independent of the governor but actually hostile to him and his party. Terms for attorneys general vary from 2 to 8 years, and a majority of states restrict their participation in private practice during tenure. Regardless of how chosen, the attorney general seldom heads and directs a unified organization of public prosecutors throughout the state as does the United States Attorney General for the nation.

In Rhode Island and Delaware, both small states, the attorneys general conduct all criminal prosecutions. A direct line of responsibility and control also exists in New Jersey and Florida, where district attorneys are appointed by governors. In a number of states where district attorneys are elective, attorneys general may intervene, supersede, or even remove them either when ordered by the governor or invited by local authorities. Actually, however, this seldom occurs, with the result that in most counties over the nation elected prosecuting attorneys function with little or no direction or supervision from state central agencies. In consequence of this highly decentralized system, attorneys general confine their activities largely to giving legal advice to the governor and administrative officers and representing the state in civil cases in which it is a party. While these are important and difficult tasks, there is a large body of opinion favoring more centralized direction and supervision of law enforcement throughout the state.[10]

Prosecuting Attorneys. As suggested above, virtually all criminal prosecutions are handled by local officials. In rural areas the task is per-

[10] Millspaugh, *op. cit.,* pp. 44–48; William F. Willoughby, *Principles of Judicial Administration* (Brookings, 1929), pp. 105–126; National Commission on Law Observance and Enforcement, *Report on Prosecution* (12 reports, 1931), no. 4, pp. 6–38.

formed by "district" or "county" attorneys [11] who are usually elected for terms of 2 or 4 years. Thus, unlike their counterparts in England and the Federal government, the office is highly political. Indeed, it is the local office from which political careers are most likely to be launched. In urban areas prosecutions may be conducted either by the district attorneys just mentioned or by special solicitors or prosecutors appointed by municipal authorities.

Holders of this office do more than merely prosecute those accused of crime. By cooperation with police they can often carry on campaigns to uncover organized crime. They also must defend the state and county, or their officials, in actions brought against them within their territorial jurisdiction. They attend and participate in habeas corpus proceedings brought before county judges. They advise and represent the attorney general on many occasions. They must advise, without fee or reward, county officers and justices of the peace on questions of law. [12]

In spite of its frequent shabbiness, the office of prosecuting attorney is one of importance and power. By vigilance and tact the prosecuting attorney can greatly aid and stimulate local police and judicial officers. Upon him rests the decision of whether those who have been apprehended will or will not stand trial; indeed, his power to decide whether to prosecute or not is almost absolute. He has great influence over grand and petit juries. He can cause a case to drag or kill it by entering a plea of nolle prosequi. [13] His recommendation has great weight with the judge when fixing punishment. Indeed, from start to finish, he exercises a dominating

[11] See National Commission on Law Observance and Enforcement, *Report on Prosecution,* p. 10, for a list of titles used by the several states.

[12] Some take the latter function seriously enough to hold monthly meetings with justices in the county and furnish them with published handbooks and other materials.

[13] This is either a record entry that the prosecutor does not care to proceed further with a case or an entry showing that an agreement has been reached not to proceed further with a particular suit. This is often done, frequently under circumstances suggesting corrupt collusion with powerful criminals and their allies.

influence over prosecution. Whether crime will or will not flourish within the community depends to a large extent upon him.

The Coroner. Another local enforcement officer hoary with age is the coroner. Nearly always elected, his area of operation is the county. His compensation invariably comes from fees and his term varies from 2 to 6 years. His principal function is investigating and holding inquests in cases where death has occurred under violent or suspicious circumstances. Insofar as possible the coroner is supposed to fix the cause of death and name the party responsible. He may make his inquiries alone or he may impanel a jury, commonly of six persons. The report becomes the official basis for action in all subsequent affairs relating to the deceased.

If any office has outlived its usefulness it is this one. Although doctors, and not infrequently undertakers, often fill the post, the fact that it is political and poorly paid makes it unattractive to professional men of competence. In the Federal government the same function is performed by physicians employed at the instance of district attorneys, but a more practical solution for the states would be the plan followed in Massachusetts and New York. There the office of coroner has been abolished, his medical duties turned over to appointive medical examiners who are always physicians, and his judicial and legal duties given to judges, grand juries, and district attorneys.

The Grand Jury. Grand juries are used by the Federal government and by all the states. They are employed for two purposes: (1) to investigate the conduct of public affairs and officials; and (2) to decide whether available evidence is persuasive enough to justify bringing to trial someone accused of committing a crime. If general investigation suggests guilt, the grand jury returns a "presentment"; if hearings suggest that someone held for crime is guilty, the grand jury returns a "true bill" of "indictment." In both cases the charges listed become the basis for subsequent court proceedings. Federal grand juries must be comprised of the number required at common law—not fewer than sixteen nor more than twenty-three—but among the states they vary between six and twenty-three, with twelve common. After much controversy, women may serve unless prohibited by statute. A vote of a majority is usually sufficient to indict.[14]

Grand juries are usually appointed by district courts as often as thought desirable, although in

makes its decision in secret. If the evidence of guilt is unimpressive, "no bill" is recorded and the accused must be discharged; if persuasive, the accused is charged with specific crimes mentioned and described in the bill of indictment, then held for trial. One's life and limb are not in jeopardy in grand-jury proceedings; hence the

THE FLOW OF FELONIES THROUGH THE CRIMINAL PROCEDURE

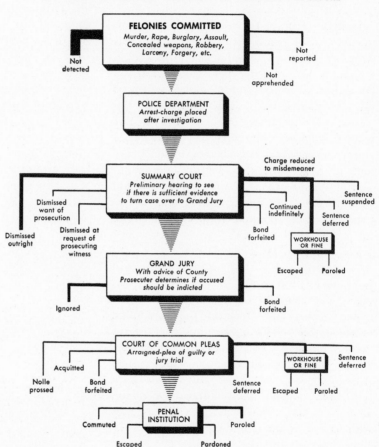

This is typical procedure, not that of a particular state or locality. Adapted from Cincinnati Bureau of Governmental Research.

some states the law compels the calling of one jury to serve for an entire year or for each term of court. In large cities they are often in continuous session. The accused may not appear as a matter of right—that is to say, proceedings are ex parte—but may occasionally be permitted to testify. The prosecuting attorney usually dominates proceedings although the jury always

[14] For statistical data concerning grand juries, see *The Book of the States, 1941–1942*, p. 157.

evidence may be reconsidered an indefinite number of times.

Today, the grand jury is frequently used to expose affairs of public concern such as ballot frauds, brutal treatment of mental hospital patients, and conspiracies to tamper with justice, but otherwise it steadily falls into desuetude. Federal authorities avoid using it whenever possible; twenty-five states permit the use of alternative methods; and a few states, notably Michigan, almost never use the grand jury. Since grand jurors are laymen picked at random, they are easily influenced by district attorneys. This being so, the trend is toward a simpler, more expeditious, more expert, and less expensive device.

The alternate oftenest used is the "information." Where this is permissible the district attorney appears before a judge with such evidence and witnesses as he deems necessary. The hearing is often perfunctory, as it also commonly is with grand juries, but at best it is thorough and even the accused is allowed to testify. If the judge is impressed he issues a document called an "information," which is much like and serves the same purpose as a bill of indictment.[15] After extensive use of this method, competent observers are agreed that it amply protects personal liberties while at the same time expediting the administration of justice. This trend is likely to continue, but it would be a mistake to dispense with the grand jury altogether, lest the community lose a potent device for probing public affairs.

The Petit Jury. The Federal Constitution guarantees the right of trial by jury "in all criminal prosecutions" and in all "suits at common law, where the value in controversy shall exceed twenty dollars," and similar provisions are found in a number of state constitutions. Petit, or "petty," juries sit throughout court trials to determine the guilt or innocence of accused parties. Although federal petit juries must consist of exactly twelve and the same number is common among the states, some states provide for juries with as few as three or even a number to be agreed upon by the parties in interest.[16] All but a few states permit the selection of an alternate juror who serves only when one of the regular number becomes incapacitated or disqualified. Unanimous verdicts are the rule where felony is charged, but in other suits several states permit

divided verdicts. Where unanimity is the rule, "hung juries" are frequent and usually necessitate retrial.

Juries are called into existence by order of trial courts. Prospective jurors are selected, usually by lot, from a list of citizens from which have been excluded the names of those whose occupations or personal affairs would suffer because of absence. As in federal law, state constitutions usually require that juries be "impartial" and because of this, counsel for all parties are permitted to challenge, while the judge must at all times be alert to avoid improper attempts to prejudice jurors. Jury service is one of the fundamental obligations of citizenship and may be compelled if necessary. A small per diem stipend and travel allowance are paid jurors for services rendered.

As with the grand jury, the trend has been away from the use of the petit jury. In England it is almost never used except in capital cases and often not then. Use by Federal courts has declined, and the same trend is seen in the states.[17] There cases involving misdemeanors are seldom tried by jury; in civil cases juries are dispensed with so often that some predict their abandonment; in an increasing number of states jury trial may be, and oftener than not is, waived in major cases. Where this ancient institution is dispensed with, courts of one or more judges render the verdict.

As the trend continues there are few who arise to disapprove, but many who insist that waiving jury trial makes the administration of justice cheaper, speedier, and fairer without jeopardizing personal liberty. While the right to trial by jury ought always to exist as an indispensable bulwark of human liberty, the states might well facilitate its waiver whenever agreeable to the parties concerned.

SENTENCE AND PUNISHMENT

Sentence. Shortly after the verdict is known, the judge pronounces sentence in criminal cases and announces the award in civil proceedings.

---

[15] It is important to note that, once drawn, an information can easily be amended but in order to change an indictment the entire grand jury must be reconvened.

[16] *The Book of the States, 1941–1942*, p. 158, gives jury statistics.

[17] Federal statistics can be found in annual reports of the Director of the Administrative Office of the United States Courts.

He is bound to follow the jury's determination of facts but not necessarily its recommendations, if it makes any. Where criminal offenses are involved the law may provide for "determinate" or "indeterminate" sentences. The former implies a definite sentence for a particular crime. This allows the judge little discretion; the exact punishment specified by statute must become the sentence.[18] When the term is up the offender must be released whether rehabilitated or not.

The indeterminate sentence is indefinite. It may be of the limited type where the law sets a minimum and maximum, like 5 to 10 years for larceny, leaving the exact amount of time to be served or fine to be paid up to the committing judge, the offender's conduct, and parole authorities. Or the indeterminate sentence may be of the absolute type that fixes no limits but allows the judge full discretion. A few states use only the determinate sentence for felonious cases; a few use only the indeterminate; most states use both —determinate for major crimes, indeterminate for minor offenses, especially those involving juveniles.[19]

There is considerable argument over which of the two types is the better. Modern criminologists tend to favor the indeterminate form because it provides greater incentives for offenders and makes parole easier. The Federal government, it should be noted, uses only the determinate sentence but there is strong sentiment in favor of change.[20]

Civil Awards. As with criminal offenses, the jury's task in civil cases is limited to finding the facts. When its verdict is known the judge makes an award. Inasmuch as civil cases are suits between private parties or between private individuals and governmental bodies, the settlement usually involves money, porperty, custody of children, and the like. The "judgment," as it is often called, becomes binding and enforceable in any state of the Union. While nonpayment of an obligation is not of itself punishable by fine or imprisonment, it may be that willful disobedience may become punishable as contempt of court.

The Problem of Capital Punishment. Putting persons to death for crimes is an old custom. The practice was most unrestrained during the medieval period and was transferred by the colonists to America. While its use has greatly diminished with the passing of time, it is still practiced by the Federal government and all but eight states.[21] Offenses punishable by death have been reduced until today they usually include only treason and willful homicide, although a few states continue the extreme penalty for rape. In 1954, 82 executions were reported for the states, the District of Columbia, and the Federal government.[22] Most state governments carry out executions in their own prisons and reformatories, but several leave the unpleasant task to local sheriffs. Electrocution is the method oftenest used; hanging is next; lethal gas is next; while Utah permits a choice between hanging or shooting.

Defenders of capital punishment, when not attempting to justify sheer revenge, usually begin with a concept of "justice" that assumes individuals to be free moral agents who must personally accept full responsibility for right and wrong choices. Such being the case, an individual must be prepared to pay with his life whenever his conduct becomes a threat to the community itself or to individual members thereof. It is also contended that the death sentence deters would-be criminals and that society ought not to be financially burdened by the

[18] The offender, however, may serve less than the term for which he was sentenced by satisfying parole requirements and earning credits for good behavior.

[19] Ronald H. Beattie and Leland L. Tolman, "State Sentencing Practices and Penal Systems," in *Report to the Judicial Conference of the Committee on Punishment for Crime* (Government Printing Office, 1942), pp. 81–126. For statistics related to the use of the two types of sentences, see U.S. Department of Justice, Bureau of Prisons, *National Prisoner Statistics, Prisoners Released from State and Federal Institutions 1951* (1955).

[20] See especially the *Report to the Judicial Conference of the Committee on Punishment for Crime*, cited above.

[21] Kansas, Maine, Michigan, Minnesota, North Dakota, Rhode Island, South Dakota, and Wisconsin.

[22] U.S. Department of Justice, Bureau of Prisons, *National Prisoner Statistics*, no. 12 (April, 1955).

necessity of keeping heinous criminals in prison for life or long terms.

Opponents often admit the fundamental moral and legal right of the community to execute human beings but insist that a policy of love and mercy represents a higher state of civilization and is more consistent with Christian ideals and ethics. Others believe that every human being is endowed with a spark of divinity which no one, not even society, ought to destroy. The testimony of sociologists is marshaled to show that men are not necessarily free moral agents but are conditioned by their heritage, the social climate in which they were born and raised, and their opportunities for guidance and growth. Modern psychologists are called in to deny that fear of consequences is an effective deterrent and they are supported by the fact that most capital crimes are unpremeditated and that statistics show either no correlation, or an adverse one, between the number of crimes and the severity of punishment. Other arguments are that with capital punishment there is always the risk of executing the innocent; the act of killing tends to cheapen human life and demoralize those who must carry out the ordeal; it causes unnecessary shame, grief, and often illness to relatives and friends; it makes the community think it is solving the problem of crime and by so doing causes indifference to social conditions that contribute to delinquency; in well-run prisons offenders more than pay their keep by work done in workshops, factories, and on farms; and, when the choice lies between freedom or death, juries often acquit those who should receive some punishment.

The arguments against capital punishment are persuasive. Fear of the consequences which might follow if the practice were dropped is doubtless the primary reason why states are slow to change. Still, writes a competent scholar:

Again and again in European and American states capital punishment has been abolished without any resulting increase in the homicide rate, and in many cases its revival has not resulted in the slightest diminution. Statistical evidence is uniformly negative. . . . Fear of capital punishment

is probably much less of a deterrent than fear of a less extreme but more certain punishment would be.[23]

Types of Prisons. The federal prison system has been noted elsewhere. Coexistent with this is a wide variety of state and local penal and correctional institutions known by such names as penitentiaries, prisons, reformatories, houses of correction, workhouses, jails, industrial and training schools, prison farms, and chain gangs. Some are for men, others for women, and still others are for juveniles. While states now directly operate some penal and correctional institutions, the great bulk are operated and maintained by counties, cities, and towns.[24] Prisons for long-term convicts are nearly all built on the old cell-block plan, the cell of which has been aptly described as "a diminutive box with an opening of some 15 inches square for inlet of light and air from the outside corridor."[25] Even in this day of "enlightenment" many prisons, including some of the largest, are still without any internal plumbing. Some progress has been made since 1930, when 21 per cent of the men's prisons in the country still used the bucket exclusively.[26]

Prison Administration. The administrative pattern varies so widely among the states as to defy simple classification. Most states operate some prisons and correctional institutions directly from the state capital. The chief exceptions are Georgia and South Carolina, where most offenders are turned over to county officials for control and supervision. In addition to direct operation, most states have reposed in some central agency a measure of responsibility for the maintenance and enforcement of standards in county and municipal penal and correctional in-

[23] George W. Kirchwey, *Encyclopedia of the Social Sciences,* vol. 3, p. 195.

[24] Perhaps the best treatment of the whole subject of prisons, probation, and parole is National Commission on Law Observance and Enforcement, *Report on Penal Institutions, Probation and Parole* (12 reports, 1931), no. 9.

[25] *Ibid.,* p. 10.

[26] *Ibid.*

stitutions. The same agencies are not infrequently charged with responsibility for state institutions such as mental hospitals.

In spite of the fact that the trend has been toward giving state bodies a measure of control, the administration of county and municipal institutions remains highly decentralized. As a rule, county penal and correctional institutions are controlled directly by the governing bodies themselves or by special boards of trustees appointed for each institution. Municipal institutions are controlled by councils, departments, general boards, or boards of trustees.

In general, prison and correctional administration in the forty-eight states is deplorable. As noted elsewhere, the inspections made by the federal Bureau of Prisons found comparatively few fit for the care of federal prisoners. Partisan considerations have dictated the selection and handling of personnel. Prison architecture and equipment are often archaic. Prison industries, which might well make many institutions self-supporting, are often so inefficiently run as to net huge financial losses. The emphasis generally is upon punishment rather than correction and rehabilitation. Willingness to profit by the discoveries of modern psychiatrists, criminologists, and others has been conspicuously lacking. Overcrowding is general. Poor diets, brutality, and riots are common. The conclusion reached in 1931 by the National Commission on Law Observance and Enforcement that our prisons had failed as business, educational, and disciplinary institutions [27] remains true today. While there are scattered instances of progressive features, rarely does one find a model institution. The problem involves extending the progressive features of particular institutions until a new general pattern is established.

PROBATION AND PAROLE

Probation. Instead of imprisoning all offenders, many states allow their judges to continue cases or suspend sentences while in the mean-

time placing guilty parties under the strict supervision of probation officers. Massachusetts, in 1836, was the first to give statutory authorization for the practice. At first only volunteer supervisors were used but later salaried probation officers were engaged. Creation of juvenile courts, first in Chicago in 1899 and then in a number of states, greatly encouraged the practice. By 1934 all the states except Wyoming had probation for children, and all but sixteen had probation for adults.[28] Today in some states as many as one-third of all persons tried and convicted are placed on probation, with the result that it is not unusual to find more at large under supervision than are incarcerated in prisons. Indeed, some see in the further development and use of probation and parole the eventual abolition of prisons except possibly for a few of the more hopeless offenders. While on probation, the offender carries with him constant awareness of his special status; he is supposed to make periodic reports to a probation officer; and he knows that a misstep is likely to result in imprisonment with little ceremony.

Parole. Parole refers to the practice of releasing prisoners before the expiration of terms as a reward for good behavior and with the expectation that they will "go straight." It is to be distinguished from probation, which also provides for freedom under supervision, by the fact that probation is granted before imprisonment, parole afterward. Parole is also to be distinguished from pardon. The latter, if unconditional, restores all civil rights and freedom under no supervision, without the possibility of reimprisonment. Parole is most effectively used with the indeterminate sentence. Nearly all prisoners are ultimately released, the bulk of them by parole. Most are released within two years.

Until after the Civil War, parole as we now know it was not used in the United States. Instead, release was obtained, if at all, by conditional pardon or by commutation laws adopted by legislatures. Ohio, in 1884, became the first state to make possible parole for inmates of state

---

[27] National Commission on Law Observation and Enforcement, *Report on Penal Institutions, Probation and Parole*, p. 41.

[28] Fred E. Haynes, *The American Prison System* (McGraw-Hill, 1939), p. 354.

prisons, while today all states use it for offenders of certain types. Although permitted in most states, its practice is not uniform and in some states parole is infrequent and difficult to obtain. In 1951, for example, South Carolina paroled only 4.3 per cent of its felon discharges, while the state of Washington paroled over 100 per cent of all felons leaving its prisons.[29] Generally, parole is less frequent in the South than elsewhere in the country.[30]

Probation and Parole Administration. Invariably it is up to the committing judges to decide whether offenders will or will not be placed on probation. In making the decision judges are often guided by recommendations made by probation officers, social workers, or friends of the parties concerned. Parole, however, is handled much differently. The decision to release is almost invariably made by a board known as parole board, board of pardons, court of pardons, or something similar. Usually such boards have state-wide jurisdiction, and it is only through them and/or the governor, who retains his pardoning power, that long-term offenders can be released from any penal institution in the state. How soon after incarceration a prisoner is eligible for parole is determined by statute and varies

accordingly; experience demonstrates that sentences are reduced from 10 to 20 per cent for sentences up to 3 years and from 30 to 40 per cent or more for longer sentences.[31]

In general, probation and parole administration is woefully inadequate. The decision to place on probation or parole is often made on an insufficient and unscientific basis, while after release the offender is frequently forgotten, with the result that often he again falls into evil company and ways and soon lands back in jail. A handful of states, and some counties and cities, have established central offices with sufficient trained personnel to make constant checks and provide friendly counsel, but all authorities agree that these are the exception. A number of states and local subdivisions merely attempt to keep in touch with released persons by correspondence. Some states not only have no salaried probation and parole officers but neither do they make use of sponsors, employers, or "first friends" to guarantee good conduct. The obvious answer to the problem is the creation of central offices equipped with sufficient trained field officers to provide constant supervision and counsel. Not only is this the humane thing to do but it can pay cash dividends by greatly reducing crime. Of course, merely to create offices for spoilsmen to plunder, as some jurisdictions have done, does not provide a solution.

[29] U.S. Department of Justice, Bureau of Prisons, *Prisoners in State and Federal Institutions 1950* (1954), pp. 17, 42–43.

[30] *Ibid.*

[31] Beattie and Tolman, *op. cit.,* p. 82.

FOR FURTHER READING

Beattie, Ronald H., and Leland L. Tolman: "State Sentencing Practices and Penal Systems," in *Report to the Judicial Conference of the Committee on Punishment for Crime* (Government Printing Office, 1942).

Council of State Governments: *The Book of the States* (Chicago: The Council, biennial).

Fosdick, Raymond: *Criminal Justice in Cleveland* (Cleveland: The Cleveland Foundation, 1922).

Frank, Jerome: *Courts on Trial* (Princeton University Press, 1949).

Haynes, Fred E.: *The American Prison System* (McGraw-Hill, 1939).

Mayo, Katherine: *Justice to All* (Putnam, 1918).

Millspaugh, Arthur C.: *Local Democracy and Crime Control* (Brookings, 1936).

National Commission on Law Observation and Enforcement: *Report on the Cost of Crime* (12 reports, 1931), no. 12.

———: *Report on Penal Institutions, Probation and Parole* (1931), no. 9.

Pigeon, Helen D.: *Probation and Parole in Theory and Practice* (New York: National Probation Association, 1942).

Shalloo, Jeremiah P.: *Private Police: With Reference to Pennsylvania* (Philadelphia: The American Academy of Political and Social Science, 1933).

Smith, Bruce: *Police Systems in the United States* (Harper, 1949).

———: *Rural Crime Control* (Institute of Public Administration, Columbia University, 1933).

———: *The State Police* (Macmillan, 1925).

Taft, Donald R.: *Criminology* (Macmillan, 1942).

U.S. Department of Justice, Bureau of Prisons: *National Prisoner Statistics, Prisoners Released from State and Federal Institutions 1951* (1955).

———: *National Prisoner Statistics, Prisoners in State and Federal Institutions 1950* (1954).

Weir, Eligius: *Criminology: A Scientific Study of the Modern Crime Problem* (Joliet, Ill.: Institute for the Scientific Study of Crime, 1941).

Willoughby, William F.: *Principles of Judicial Administration* (Brookings, 1929).

Wilson, O. W.: *Police Administration* (McGraw-Hill, 1950).

REVIEW QUESTIONS

1. Compare the police system of a state with that found in a city, county, and smaller unit of local government.

2. Which, if any, of the law-enforcement agencies and officers mentioned in this chapter should be discontinued?

3. How do you explain the fact that state police are of comparatively recent origin and usually have very limited jurisdiction?

4. How satisfactory is the office of district attorney? Attorney general? How can the work of these officers be improved?

5. Would you favor more or less use of grand and petit juries?

6. What is required to ensure competent municipal police systems?

7. Outline a plan for making the prison system of a typical state the best one possible.

8. Defend and criticize capital punishment.

9. What are the essentials of good probation and parole administration?

10. Trace the handling of a criminal case from detection to imprisonment.

CHAPTER 40

Functions: State and Local

The major task of state government—for the long pull—is to maintain, strengthen and vitalize our federal system while providing to the people the material services they need and demand. — Frank Bane [1]

Governments exist to provide services. Under our federal system, in spite of the impressive array of activities now performed by the central government, the greater portion of all governmental functions is left to the states. Because the states are unitary, their legislatures decide which tasks will be performed by the central state organization and which will be handled by subordinate local governments. In previous chapters numerous state activities have been mentioned and several general ones have been discussed in detail. Many others deserve extended consideration, but only a selected few of the most important will be discussed here.

Types of Functions. State and local functions may be divided into three broad classes. The first are general services provided for the public at large or for special groups. Among others, this includes such things as maintaining the public peace; protecting life and property; promoting health, safety, morals, and economic well-being; providing public roads and educational and recreational facilities; caring for special groups such as veterans, the aged, handicapped, and mentally ill; conducting elections; keeping vital statistics; and recording documents.

The second class includes those wherein em-

phasis is upon control or regulation of private economic enterprise. This includes such activities as regulating public utilities, supervising banking, controlling the issuance of stocks and bonds, fixing and maintaining prices, wages, and hours, preventing monopolistic practices, and the like. The third class includes governmental activities that are proprietary in character. These are governmentally owned and operated enterprises that either have been or might otherwise be carried on by private parties for profit. Illustrations are governmentally owned and operated water, light, power, and transportation companies, liquor monopolies, banks, and insurance plans.

SELECTED GENERAL FUNCTIONS

Health Service. At the state level each of the states has a health department, while counties, cities, and small units handle health matters through departments, boards, or committees. State health departments are headed by an official known as health officer, commissioner of health, director of health, or something else. In nearly all states there exist state boards of health, either with considerable authority or, as is oftener the case, with only advisory powers. Health officers are appointed by governors in a majority of states, and by boards of health

[1] "Progress and Opportunities of the States," *State Government,* vol. 27 (January, 1954), pp. 11–16.

in most of the others. While the core of state health activities centers in health departments, by no means all of them are concentrated there. According to a survey, in one state eighteen separate agencies had something to do with health, while in no state were fewer than six agencies employed. The median number was eleven per state.[2] This dispersion of responsibility is further emphasized by the discovery some years ago that for the nation as a whole only 18.5 per cent of funds spent for state health activities were expended through their departments of health, the remainder being spent by other departments, commissions, and boards.

Routine Health Services. State and local agencies are constantly engaged in routine activities for the protection and betterment of health. These may consist of setting standards for medical colleges, giving examinations and issuing licenses to doctors, dentists, veterinarians, nurses, druggists, and others. They may involve testing samples of drinking water, checking the purity of milk, inspecting restaurant kitchens and dishes, testing animals for diseases, checking water courses for evidence of stream pollution, inspecting hospitals, mines, factories, and workshops. They may also include the enforcement of child-labor laws, laws limiting the hours of work, pure food and drug, vaccination, sterilization, and quarantine laws.

Special Health Programs. The states also sponsor special health programs either by themselves or in cooperation with other states, the United States Public Health Service, or private institutions. States and municipally operated or supported clinics for inexpensive or free medical care are available in some areas, particularly the cities. Recent years have seen the inauguration in some states of frequent physical and dental examinations in public schools. Public-health nurses are becoming increasingly common. Some states provide free or inexpensive X-rays for detection of tuberculosis. Most states maintain mental hospitals, some operate general hospitals, and others provide hospitals or sanatoria for the care of special patients such as those

[2] Harry S. Mustard, *Government in Public Health* (Commonwealth Fund, 1945), pp. 95-97.

suffering from tuberculosis. Considerable attention to health matters results from state workmen's compensation laws, which require employers to insure against accident, injury, death, and occupational diseases. State programs for

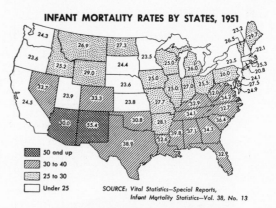

A clue to the effectiveness of public-health services can be gained by examining infant mortality rates.

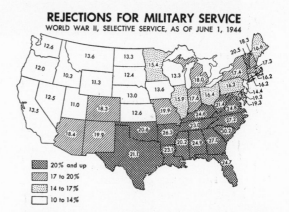

Another index to state health standards is the record of rejections under wartime Selective Service. Adapted from American Assembly, *United States Agriculture* (1955), p. 111.

veterans and general welfare also include certain health services.

The above paragraphs may give the impression that American governments are fully attentive to health needs, but such is not the case. General health laws have been common for some time, but not until recent years have governments undertaken positive programs. Increasingly, the Federal government has taken the lead, with the states following, but the situation still remains spotty.

Several of the state programs now in progress are partially subsidized with federal funds. Federal aid now extends to the control of tuberculosis, cancer, and heart diseases; general health

school compulsory to age sixteen or above, although in some states exceptions are numerous and laws are often indifferently enforced.

All states provide schools for elementary and secondary education, but in some rural sections these may be nonexistent, difficult of access, or

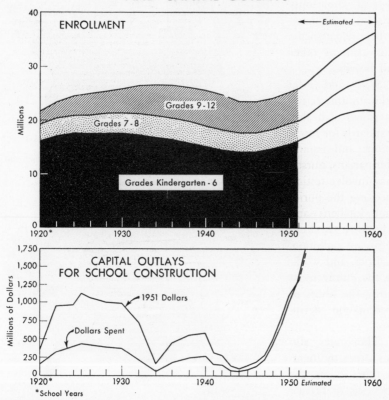

PUBLIC SCHOOL ENROLLMENT AND CAPITAL OUTLAYS

The high birth rate during and after the Second World War is now sending school enrollments soaring. School construction on a vast scale is needed to keep pace with enrollments. Courtesy of National Industrial Conference Board.

services and mental-health improvement; hospital surveys, planning, and construction; and studies for the control of water pollution. Grants are made on the basis of health needs, population, and the financial ability of the state and local governments. As noted elsewhere, all the states are now cooperating, although many of the counties still lack full-time health organizations.

Education. Public-school education, which began scarcely more than a century ago, is now the principal consumer of state and local tax funds. All states make attendance at public or private

available only through the generosity of churches or philanthropic societies. All the states maintain one or more institutions of higher learning, including teachers' colleges, and they often give financial support to private colleges and universities. In addition to instruction offered in the above-mentioned institutions, special facilities and guidance are often made available to the blind, the deaf, the retarded, and others who are handicapped. State-wide administration is almost invariably centered in a department of education presided over by a superintendent or commissioner, who is elected in some states, appointed in others. At other levels of government, control is usually in the hands of superintendents, school boards, or, in the case of institutions of higher learning, presidents and special boards of trustees.

In spite of all that has been done on behalf of education, there are still large areas of need. School buildings are often inadequate, teachers' salaries and other emoluments are pitifully low for the nation as a whole, special instruction for the gifted and handicapped is available in only a few schools, most of them in large cities, public-school health and recreational facilities leave much to be desired, and funds for visual aids, books, scholarships, laboratories, school lunches, busses, and the like are too small to permit maintenance of the highest standards.

While the amounts spent for public school education appear large, the total is small when compared with the number of people benefited or with expenditures for other purposes. In 1953 total funds expended (5.6 billion dollars) had to provide for more than thirty million children and youths enrolled in public elementary and secondary schools. The average expenditure per pupil was only $228.40. The range among the states is shown on the accompanying chart. Studies indicate that it is the farm and Negro children who have less educational opportunity than others. The fact that some states spend more than others may not be due to greater zeal but, rather, to more financial resources. There is impressive evidence suggesting that the poorer states at the bottom of the list spend a greater proportion of their income for education than the wealthier states at the top. It is because of this that many advocate federal assistance in aid of education to the states proportionate to their financial need.

Welfare Services. Society usually proceeds on the expectation that all men are capable of managing their affairs providently enough to take care of their needs throughout life. While this assumption is undoubtedly sound, experience demonstrates that at best large numbers will find themselves in dire straits for either brief or prolonged periods of time. Knowing this, governments of industrialized states provide many gratuitous services, and in recent times they have established several forms of social insurance to provide for rainy days. The former tendency for society to blame the individual and offer aid with pity or scorn is being rapidly replaced by one where society admits at least partial respon-

ESTIMATED EXPENSE PER PUPIL
(in average daily attendance)
PUBLIC ELEMENTARY & SECONDARY SCHOOLS—1952-53

N. Y.	$335
N. J.	329
Wyo.	320
Del.	315
Minn.	294
Oreg.	294
Colo.	285
Calif.	284
Mont.	284
Ill.	278
Md.	275
Ariz.	272
Mass.	260
Wash.	260
Wis.	260
Mich.	255
Nev.	254
R. I.	254
Conn.	251
Ind.	250
Kans.	250
Iowa	246
La.	235
N. Dak.	233
N. H.	230
N. Mex.	230
Average	228
S. Dak.	226
Mo.	217
Nebr.	217
Okla.	215
Ohio	207
Tex.	206
Pa.	204
Idaho	200
Me.	200
Fla.	198
Vt.	195
Utah	190
W. Va.	180
Ga.	162
Va.	158
Ky.	155
N. C.	154
Tenn.	135
S. C.	132
Ala.	127
Ark.	110
Miss.	97

SOURCE: *Book of the States, 1954-55, p.* 248

Although money is not the only factor in providing good schools, per-pupil expenditure figures provide one basis for comparing the several states.

sibility and offers assistance as a matter of respect or right.

Welfare services are provided by governments at all levels. At state capitals, there is usually a department of public welfare, although a few states use welfare boards. The principal administrative officer is called director, secretary, chairman, or something else. Although specialized departments exist, seldom are all welfare activities centered in them. Instead, one finds them scattered throughout several agencies, most commonly the departments of education, health, and labor. Large cities and some urban counties also usually have welfare departments, but other local governments are likely to operate through the governing bodies themselves, special boards, or committees.

Welfare services vary from boarding overnight guests in the town jail to administering billion-dollar insurance plans. A distinction is made between noninstitutional and those requiring institutional confinement and care. Another division may be made between those services provided free of charge to persons on the basis of need, and those available through insurance plans to which the recipient and others may have contributed over the years.

Among noninstitutional services are general relief for those eligible and unable to find suitable work; financial aid and guidance to widows with minor children; supervision for delinquent children on probation or parole; assistance for needy handicapped and crippled children in the homes of families or friends; finding foster homes for orphans; providing outpatient medical and dental care; and paying pensions to aged people who are in need. The institutions most commonly found are reformatories, orphans' homes, mental hospitals, schools for handicapped and mentally deficient children, and homes for old people.

Most of the services mentioned above are free to patients, or a small charge may be made of families able to pay. Others, usually of the insurance type, require contributions on the part of the recipient, his employer, or both. The most widely found welfare programs of the insurance type are those for paying benefits to employees injured on the job and unemployment compensation.[3]

Public Safety. Police systems, courts, and militias have been discussed elsewhere. In addition to their activities, state and local governments perform many other functions on behalf of safety. The administration of safety matters is probably more dispersed than others discussed in

this chapter. The departments of public safety, or police departments, that do exist in state capitals generally confine their activities largely to crime detection and highway patrol, leaving other safety matters to several agencies. At the city level there may be a single department, or safety matters may be divided among several.

Next to police, fire protection is without doubt the most important safety service. State governments usually confine their activities to enacting general laws and to protecting forests and public lands, although in a few states state police or inspectors check theaters, dry-cleaning establishments, and other especially hazardous places. Otherwise fire protection is left chiefly to municipal governments. Larger municipalities invariably employ full-time fire-fighting forces; smaller places may employ a full-time skeleton crew and supplement it with volunteers when necessary, or they may depend entirely upon volunteers. Where volunteer departments are found, they are usually partly subsidized with funds or supplies provided by local governments.

Other safety services are extremely varied. Usually standards are established by general laws; then inspections to ensure compliance follow. Inspection for safety normally extends to buildings, bridges, automobiles and other vehicles, elevators, mines, factories, and other hazardous places.

Highways, Roads, and Streets. All levels of government, from the state itself to the smallest town or township, have some responsibility for roads and streets. Laying them out, construction, and maintenance are all important tasks.

At the state level, administration is usually the responsibility of a highway department, commission, board, or department of public works, headed by a director, engineer, commissioner, or an officer bearing some other title. Elective road commissioners or supervisors are common among counties and townships, while in municipalities the work is usually made the responsibility of a department, committee of council, or engineer.

Aside from technical problems arising from planning and construction, two important questions constantly arise to complicate road admin-

[3] For a fuller discussion, see pp. 554–557. The old-age and survivors' insurance plan, it will be recalled, is operated entirely by the Federal government.

istration. One is how responsibility for construction and maintenance should be shared among the various levels of government. The second is concerned with the equitable division of costs.

In horse and buggy days, division of responsibility between county, town, and township was fairly easy. Now, automobiles, trucks, and busses speed through these places almost oblivious of their existence. The problem becomes more complicated as cities spread over county and even state lines. As a general proposition, albeit with many exceptions, the present plan in many states is for rural townships (where they exist) to retain responsibility for construction and maintenance of only minor rural roads; for cities to have jurisdiction over city streets, except where they are also interconnecting county roads or through state highways; for counties to build and maintain principal rural roads, except where they are also state highways; and for the state to accept responsibility for primary intercity and intercounty routes. Even though legislation attempts a precise solution, controversies inevitably arise. An almost universal tendency is for smaller units to yield jurisdiction to larger and higher levels of government.

The problem of assessing costs is equally difficult. The principal source of local tax revenues is the property tax. But why should city, county, or township property owners bear the full cost of providing arteries for a car, bus, or truck that speeds over their roads, often without stopping? Why shouldn't the car owner pay something for the privilege? Meanwhile, states (but seldom political subdivisions) collect gasoline taxes from all users of motor vehicles. Why should the state take revenues on gasoline expended while traveling on streets and roads paid for with local property holders' money?

One solution is for the larger political divisions, especially the state, to acquire full responsibility for more and more roads. While this has been happening, it might unfairly shift too much of the tax burden from property holders. A still more popular alternative now practiced in many states is for the state to return to the local governments a portion of the revenues derived from gasoline taxes. While this is undoubtedly fair in principle, it is difficult to make an equitable determination of the proportions that should be returned and kept.

SELECTED REGULATORY FUNCTIONS

In capitalist societies competition is the principal regulator. But it sometimes fails or is deliberately eliminated, in which event governmental regulation or ownership is usually instituted. Economic regulation, *i.e.,* the control of prices, wages, hours, and the like, is almost always done by the state government itself (except where the Federal government has jurisdiction), but on matters pertaining to health, safety, and morals, cities and other local governments may be permitted to undertake the job alone or to act in cooperation with other units or with the state. There may even be concurrent regulation by local, state, and the Federal government.

Regulation of Utilities. Public utilities, most of which are complete or partial monopolies, are among the most stringently regulated private economic enterprises. In all the states the task is assigned to a public-utility commission, which is usually, but not always, an independent establishment.[4] Commissions vary in size from one member in Rhode Island to seven in South Carolina, with three members nearly universal. In a majority of states commissioners are appointive, but in fifteen, most of them in the South, they are popularly elected. Terms vary from 10 years in two states (Pennsylvania and New York) to 2 years, with 6 years the most common.

While there is much variation, most states have given their commissions authority to regulate private companies of the following types: electric light and power, manufactured and natural gas, street railways, interurban railways, motor busses, taxicabs, water, telephone, telegraph, and oil and gas pipe lines. A number of commissions also regulate municipally owned

[4] For details concerning the various commissions, see Clyde O. Ruggles, *Aspects of the Organization, Functions, and Financing of State Public Utility Commissions* (Boston: Harvard Bureau of Business Research, 1937); *The Book of the States;* and *Moody's Manual of Investments, Public Utility Securities* (New York: Moody's Investors Service, annual).

and operated utilities, either in their entirety or when they serve customers living beyond their corporate limits.[5] Several states also authorize their commissions to regulate motor trucks even though these are not, strictly speaking, public utilities. Regulation usually involves control over entrance into service, extensions, reorganizations, abandonments, capital structures, rates, services, and accounts.

While commission control is now universal, it is viewed by many as inadequate, if not a near failure. This is due to many factors. Most important is the failure to place commission staffs under merit systems. Insistence by the courts upon excessive legal formulas, including an unworkable valuation basis, has favored the utilities and hampered commissions at nearly every turn. Meanwhile, utilities and their holding-company superstructures have become so closely related to interstate commerce that jurisdictional uncertainties and conflicts have arisen to obstruct effective regulation. More lenient judicial interpretation, increasing intervention by the Federal government, the increase of public ownership, and more effective criticism from labor and consumer groups have brought some improvement, but even so, commission regulation is still widely viewed with skepticism.

Regulation of Security Issues. Since passage of the Securities Act of 1933 and the Securities Exchange Act of 1934, the Federal government regulates the larger exchanges and most of the securities offered for sale through the mails and those for businesses engaged in interstate and foreign commerce. While this has greatly reduced the area of state activity, there is still much of a local or intrastate character for them to do. All the states but Nevada now have "blue sky" laws.[6] Either a single commissioner or a three-man body is usually in charge. Appointment of these officers is the rule often on a partisan political basis, while popular election is not uncommon.

State laws, like the federal, are not intended to guarantee buyers a profitable investment. Rather, they are aimed at preventing fraud and enforcing full disclosure of information. In general, the laws are of three types: (1) fraud laws, which do little more than provide for punishment of fraudulent issues and sales; (2) licensing laws, which seek to concentrate marketing in the hands of honest dealers; and (3) registration laws, which require securities to be registered along with information that will enable investors to decide whether or not they think them sound investments. Those of the first type are corrective in that they permit prosecution only after fraud has been perpetrated; the other types attempt to prevent fraud and other illegal practices before they reach their victims. The latter types are now found in a majority of states.

Enforcement involves issuing, revoking, and suspending licenses, examining the practices and financial status of dealers and issues, promulgating rules and regulations, and aiding with criminal prosecution where that becomes necessary. Before federal regulation, state laws were generally ineffective, due, in part, to the interstate character of many of the operations, to the many exemptions allowed by the laws, and to woefully inefficient administration. Suspected weaknesses became tragically apparent after the stock market crash of 1929. Today, state laws tend toward greater uniformity, while federal laws and operations of the Securities and Exchange Commission have tended to raise administrative standards. Nevertheless, state operations are still handicapped by the political character of their enforcement agencies and inadequate appropriations.

Regulation of Insurance. Insurance was long considered a field wholly under state jurisdiction. As the insurance business grew to gigantic proportions, all the states introduced regulation, although of diverse forms. Insurance companies

[5] For one of the best reviews of commission jurisdiction over municipally owned utilities, see Irston R. Barnes, *Public Utility Regulation* (Appleton-Century-Crofts, 1942), pp. 816–887.

[6] For a brief review, see Willard E. Atkins *et al.*, *The Regulation of the Security Markets* (Brookings, 1946). For details see current issues of *The Book of the States.*

must now contend with a formidable body of widely varying statutes, administrative rulings, and court interpretations. The universal pattern of administration is a single commissioner or superintendent, who may be placed in a department with banking and business regulation, or operate quite independently.

Although considered a business "affected with public interest," and subjected to close regulation, insurance is a field in which full competition is permitted. Regulation begins with incorporation, which requires that many standards be met. Licenses are issued to *domestic* companies (operating in the state of incorporation), *foreign* companies (incorporated in other states), and *alien* companies (incorporated in other countries). The insurance commissioner has power to issue or refuse, suspend or revoke, licenses of a company, broker, or agent. He may examine a company's books, approve or disapprove its investments, and enforce laws governing standard policy forms.

In 1944 the Supreme Court held[7] that insurance companies were covered by the federal commerce power and upheld a conviction of companies and individuals of antitrust law violation. Under the decision, Congress might at once have enacted federal legislation that would have superseded state regulation. It did not do so, however; rather, the states continue to play their ancient role with the Federal government insisting that insurance companies comply with federal antimonopoly laws. The insurance companies have made it very clear that they prefer to continue under state regulation.

Food and Drug Regulation. At least forty-three states have undertaken food and drug regulation, some of them even before the Federal government intervened in 1906. About half the states have enacted new statutes since 1938 patterned after the federal Food, Drug, and Cosmetic Act of that year, while the remainder have generally followed closely earlier federal laws. Where this has happened there exists a nearly uniform body of law applicable to both

interstate and intrastate commerce.[8] Administration is usually the primary responsibility of state agencies, chiefly departments of health and agriculture. The laws may be enforced throughout the state directly from state headquarters or field offices, or considerable reliance may be placed upon the officers of county and city governments. In California, for instance, the state board of health may appoint special agents but sheriffs are also enforcement agents, while responsibility for prosecution rests with the district attorneys of the districts in which violations occur. Where states have emulated recent federal laws, statutory provisions are generally looked upon as adequate, but enforcement often leaves much to be desired. Appointments for political reasons, inadequate inspectional and laboratory staffs, and inadequate appropriations are the principal handicaps at state and local levels.

Weights and Measures Regulation. The function of ensuring dependable weights and measures is of considerable importance to the consuming public. As noted elsewhere, the role of the Federal government is limited to "fixing" uniform standards, collaborating on a voluntary basis with private parties and state governments, and policing a few standards where interstate commerce is involved. This means that the states may legalize federal standards, as most have, or enact supplementary ones of their own. It also means that practically all supervision and enforcement of commercial standards are left to states and local governments.

Three plans of administration are in use among the states.[9] The simplest is that in which responsibility is centered in a state office of weights and measures. Under this plan state inspectors operate at large and there are no county or city officials performing similar functions. A second plan is a dual system in which both state

---

[7] United States *v.* South-Eastern Underwriters Association *et al.*, 322 U.S. 533 (1944). See also Chap. 18.

[8] For examples of state provisions, see Harry A. Toulmin, Jr., *A Treatise on the Law of Food, Drugs, and Cosmetics* (Cincinnati: W. H. Anderson Co., 1942), pp. 931–945, 1264*ff.*

[9] See Ralph W. Smith, *Weights and Measures Administration,* National Bureau of Standards Handbook H26 (1941), pp. 10–11.

and local governments engage in the task. This arrangement calls for a state office with inspectors operating at large and sealers of weights and measures in counties and cities. A third plan is for all inspectional and testing work to be left to local governments.

The first of the three plans outlined above provides the greatest uniformity. The second is most common. One of its advantages is that the presence of both state and local officers engaged in similar duties tends to check, balance, and stimulate activities. Another is that it permits regulation by local officers close to the scene. On the other hand, it makes for widely varying standards within a state, gives rise to jurisdictional disputes between local and state officers, and often permits considerable overlapping. Very little can be said in favor of the third plan.

The actual work may be divided into two divisions. The first, ordinarily referred to as "mechanical activities," involves inspection and testing of equipment varying in size from the smallest prescription weights to huge scales. This requires considerable expertness and exact standards. Licenses may be required as an evidence of approval. It is common practice to charge fees for inspections, although there is a growing opinion that the fee system should be discontinued. The second division, consisting of "supervisory activities," has to do with the way equipment is used. This involves such duties as check-weighing and check-measuring loads of coal, ice, wood, and packaged merchandise; investigating complaints; educating buyers and sellers to their rights under the weights and measures laws; assisting with prosecution; and the like.

Complaints are common over the fact that some state standards differ from those fixed by the Federal government, thus causing inconvenience and confusion. There is greater lament over the lackadaisical, if not downright incompetent, manner in which present laws are often administered and enforced. But there is greater cause for regret that some states have been so indifferent as to ignore the dangers inherent in providing little or no protection for the public.

These problems are being attacked through associations of weights and measures officials existing in several states and through annual conferences called by the United States Bureau of Standards, but more citizen interest and participation are required to hasten progress.

PROPRIETARY FUNCTIONS

State and local governments, like the Federal, often own and operate enterprises similar to those commonly under private ownership for profit. The motives leading to state and local ownership are much the same as those underlying federal enterprises, and the same general considerations must be kept in mind. For present purposes, proprietary enterprises may be divided into those created by and responsible to the state itself, and those created by and responsible to local governments. The former are fewer in number than the latter.

State Enterprises. *Liquor Monopolies.* The most lucrative state enterprises are the liquor monopolies mentioned elsewhere. One state (Wyoming), it will be recalled, monopolizes wholesale distribution, while sixteen states own and operate retail establishments. Administration is generally made the responsibility of a board or commission that functions with the aid of a central staff, field officers, and store personnel, although in a few of the monopoly states licensing and other administrative functions are shared with counties, municipalities, or both. The state board is generally given broad powers to regulate other handlers of alcoholic beverages, although a majority of states make prosecutions the responsibility of the office of attorney general or district attorneys.

Too little literature is available for making sound conclusions about the administrative competence of proprietary operations of this sort. That they are money-makers is obvious, but whether the net return is as great as it might be is not so clear. Only a few have placed personnel under merit systems. On grounds of public policy there is considerable justification for believing that monopoly states, like others, subordinate considerations of temperance and sobriety to those of maximum revenues.

Other State Enterprises. A complete list of other state projects would be long. All states own land from which proceeds are derived either from sales of the land itself or from rentals and sales of mineral and forest products. Extensive proprietary operations are carried on at state prisons, hospitals, and other institutions. Many of the states are heavily engaged in the insurance business, chiefly because of the passage of workmen's compensation, unemployment compensation, and civil-service retirement laws. Educational institutions, hospitals, research laboratories, and the like were once almost entirely provided by private enterprise, but all the states are now involved. Most of the states operate toll bridges and some of them ferries. A few maintain garages with mechanics for making automobile inspections. California owns a short railroad in San Francisco harbor. New York operates a barge system on its historic canal, a power authority for the development of the St. Lawrence project, including distribution of electric power, a health resort at Saratoga Springs at which mineral water is also bottled and sold, bridges and tunnels (in cooperation with New Jersey) through the Port of New York Authority. North Dakota is involved in an ambitious program involving the operation of mills, grain elevators, a state bank, insurance (fire, tornado, bonding, hail), and the financing of land sales. Alabama has for more than a score of years operated an elaborate system of docks, wharves, warehouses, and other terminal facilities at Mobile.

Generalizations about operations so divergent in character and scattered in location are dangerous. Doubtless some of them need to adopt more modern administrative policies and procedures, including merit systems. Some are heavily in debt, but even so, continued state operation may be justified on the grounds of public policy. With few exceptions, more studies are needed of each of the enterprises for the benefit of both those intimately concerned and students interested in the broader aspects of public administration and policy.

Local Enterprises. The list of proprietary projects under the management of local govern-

ments would duplicate many mentioned above. However, if public schools are eliminated, most of them fall under the heading of utilities and housing.

Public Utilities. Recent years have witnessed a considerable increase in the number of utilities owned and operated by local governments. In cities public ownership of water-supply and distribution systems is the rule rather than the exception. Sewage-treatment plants are next most numerous, followed by incinerators, electric

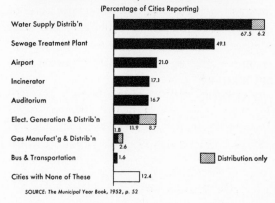

OWNERSHIP AND OPERATION OF UTILITIES IN CITIES OVER 5,000 POPULATION

(Percentage of Cities Reporting)

Water Supply Distrib'n	67.5 6.2
Sewage Treatment Plant	49.1
Airport	21.0
Incinerator	17.1
Auditorium	16.7
Elect. Generation & Distrib'n	11.9 8.7
Gas Manufact'g & Distrib'n	1.8 / 2.6
Bus & Transportation	1.6
Cities with None of These	12.4

▓ Distribution only

SOURCE: *The Municipal Year Book, 1952,* p. 52

generating and/or distribution systems, auditoriums, and airports.

Utilities are usually the responsibility of a committee of city council or the city manager, or a special board, authority, or district created for the purpose. The governing body usually appoints a utility superintendent or engineer for the purpose of overseeing operations. There has been endless controversy over private vs. public ownership of utilities, resulting in enough experience to suggest that while there are dangers involved, governmental ownership can prove highly advantageous where the public is willing and able to insist upon sound management.

Housing. California began subsidizing homes for veterans following the First World War, and New York enacted legislation in 1926 providing encouragement to limited-dividend housing corporations. It was not until depression years, however, that local governments stepped boldly

into the business of building and operating housing projects. The impetus came chiefly from the
United States Housing Act of 1937. This encouraged the states to enact legislation permitting local governments to establish housing authorities for the purpose of clearing slums and
building low-cost dwellings. A number of states
cooperated, with the result that several hundred
local units created authorities. These are locally
operated subject to state and federal laws, with
the Federal government granting subsidies to
aid in keeping rents low.

As a further aid a number of states have enacted urban redevelopment legislation authorizing and aiding private and municipal corporations at the point of assembling and clearing

sites for housing. When done by local governments, the acquisition of property and actual
work may be carried out by the governmental
bodies themselves, or by authorities created
especially for the purpose.

It is too early to assess the work of local governments in the housing field. Experience in
Europe and England, as well as in the United
States, suggests that private capital cannot or
will not fully meet the need; hence governments
are likely to become increasingly involved.[10]

[10] For a general study, see Miles L. Colean, *American
Housing Problems and Prospects* (Twentieth Century
Fund, 1944). For a special study, see M. Nelson
McGeary, *The Pittsburgh Housing Authority* (Penn-
sylvania State University, 1943).

FOR FURTHER READING

Barnes, Irston R.: *The Economics of Public Utility Regulation* (Appleton-Century-Crofts, 1942).

Colean, Miles L.: *American Housing, Problems and Prospects* (Twentieth Century Fund, 1944).

Council of State Governments: *The Book of the States* (Chicago: The Council, biennial).

Ferguson, John H., and Charles F. LeeDecker: *Municipally Owned Electric Plants in Pennsylvania* (Pennsylvania State University, Institute of Local Government, 1951).

—— and ——: *Municipally Owned Waterworks in Pennsylvania* (Pennsylvania State University, Institute of Local Government, 1948).

Ferrell, John A., and Pauline A. Mead: *History of County Health Organizations in the United States, 1908–1933* (Government Printing Office, Public Health Bulletin no. 222, 1936).

Marketing Laws Survey: *State Liquor Legislation* (Government Printing Office, 1941).

Mountin, Joseph W., and Others: *Distribution of Health Services in the Structure of State Government, 1950:* Part I, Administrative Provisions for State Health Services (Government Printing Office, 1952).

Municipal Fire Administration (Chicago: International City Managers' Association, 5th ed., 1950).

Municipal Police Administration (Chicago: International City Managers' Association, 4th ed., 1954).

Mustard, Harry S.: *Government in Public Health* (Commonwealth Fund, 1945).

New York State Constitutional Convention Committee: *State and Local Government in New York* (Albany: The Committee, 1938).

Patterson, Edwin W.: *Essentials of Insurance Law* (McGraw-Hill, 1935).

——: *The Insurance Commissioner in the United States* (Harvard University Press, 1927).

Ridley, Clarence E., and Orin F. Nolting (eds.): *The Municipal Yearbook* (Chicago: International City Managers' Association, annual).

Ruggles, Clyde O.: *Aspects of the Organization, Functions, and Financing of State Public Utility Commissions* (Boston: Harvard Bureau of Business Research, 1937).

Smillie, Wilson G.: *Public Health Administration in the United States* (Macmillan, rev. ed., 1947).

Smith, Ralph W.: *Weights and Measures Administration*, Bureau of Standards Handbook H26 (1941).

Toulmin, Harry A., Jr.: *A Treatise on the Law of Food, Drug, and Cosmetic Regulation* (Cincinnati: W. H. Anderson Co., 1942).

U.S. Congress, Subcommittees of the Committees on the Judiciary: *Hearings on Insurance,* 78th Cong., 1st Sess. (6 parts, 1943).

U.S. Department of Commerce, Bureau of the Census: *Governmental Finances in the United States* (annual).

U.S. President's Commission on Higher Education: *Higher Education for American Democracy* (6 vols., 1947).

Wyatt, Laurence: *Intergovernmental Relations in Public Health* (University of Minnesota Press, 1951).

White, R. Clyde: *Administration of Public Welfare* (American Book, 2d ed., 1950).

Wilson, O. W.: *Police Administration* (McGraw-Hill, 1950).

REVIEW QUESTIONS
1. Do you think present public-health services are adequate? How can these be improved?

2. Is the administrative structure of your state government properly organized for effective administration of the various services performed?

3. To what extent are the health, education, and welfare services of your state and local governments financed and controlled by the Federal government?

4. How do you explain the differences between expenditures for education in the various states? How can educational opportunity be equalized among the several states?

5. How effective is the regulation of public utilities in your state as compared with other states?

6. How do the laws of your state concerning the regulation of securities, insurance, food and drugs, and weights and measures compare with federal laws dealing with these subjects?

7. In what ways do Federal and state governments cooperate in regulating the matters mentioned in question 6?

8. What circumstances have led state and local governments to own and operate proprietary enterprises?

9. When proprietary businesses are owned and operated by governments, how can efficient management be ensured?

10. How can responsibility for highways, roads, and streets be most effectively apportioned among the various levels of government?

CHAPTER 41

Frontiers of Civic Responsibility

The states must, as the slang phrase goes, "put up or shut up"; either they must produce results or they must expect to continue to lose power and prestige. — W. Brooke Graves [1]

The challenge of our age is almost overpowering. This challenge can be successfully met only by uniting the intelligence of our people behind programs for responsible democratic political action. In the struggle for peace, prosperity, security and increasing freedom for all our people, no thoughtful citizen can remain on the sidelines. — Chester Bowles [2]

Men who think of themselves as Virginians or Rhode Islanders first and Americans second are about as rare as a surrey with a fringe on top in a present-day city street. After a century and three-quarters of nationhood, the old economic and cultural self-sufficiency that formerly characterized states, local communities, and even families, has been replaced by a complex interdependency. Economic progress has been rooted in division of labor and given great opportunity in a vast free-trade area which is tied together with efficient transport by land, water, and air. Interstate movement of people and ideas has contributed to a national culture. Foreign wars have stimulated national patriotism, caused men of different states to rub shoulders in training and combat, and taken those in the armed services far beyond the confines of their home states.

[1] *American State Government* (Heath, rev. ed., 1941), p. 871.
[2] "The Independent Voter Isn't Independent," *The New York Times Magazine*, Nov. 13, 1949.

STATE PROBLEMS AND PROSPECTS

Federalism Reappraised. With such unifying factors, it is not surprising that some problems that formerly were regarded as state or local matters should now concern the national government. Although federal centralization has proceeded a considerable distance, the states are not done. Their relative status has diminished since 1800, but their absolute importance has increased. While losing some functions to the national government, they have taken on new ones that nearly compensate for the loss. Indeed, the importance of the states to their people and to the Union has been increased as they have entered into federally induced functions like unemployment compensation and expanded public-assistance programs. Today, the states have larger budgets, perform a greater variety of services, and affect more intimately the lives of their people than ever before.

Meanwhile, states are learning to work together to an extent undreamed of a few decades ago. Through the Council of State Governments, the various associations of officials, compacts and agreements, public and private bureaus of research, and publications, common solutions are sought for common problems. Progress, while often discouragingly slow, appears to be sure. Purged of many of the responsibilities for which they were ill equipped, the states are now in a better position to win public confidence by doing well the functions that properly fall within their jurisdiction.

Constitutional Reform. For almost a whole generation it appeared that the American states had lost their capacity for full constitutional revision. From 1909 to 1945 no state succeeded in securing popular ratification for a fully revised constitution. Interest groups fought violently against any change that might deprive them of some special protection from a clause long since incorporated in the constitution. In many states frequent amendments added to the already great bulk of the organic law.

This deadlock was broken through in 1945. Missouri, through the method of constitutional convention and popular ratification, secured a new constitution that is concise, modern, and vastly improved. In Georgia a special commission drafted a full revision and in 1945 it was accepted by the voters. Although defeated in 1944, revision succeeded in New Jersey in 1947, giving that state one of the most up-to-date organic laws in the union. Tennessee in 1953 adopted eight amendments to its previously unamended 1870 constitution, as proposed by a limited constitutional convention. These victories for reform have encouraged other state movements for constitutional conventions. Proposals for conventions to revise fundamental law were before the legislatures of many states during recent sessions.

Many proponents of constitutional revision feel that the best way to accomplish it is through the ordinary amending process. But piecemeal amendment will not suffice in most states to accomplish the general revision that is long overdue. Experience has shown that the convention method is best for a general overhaul job.

Legislative Problems. The legislature remains the weakest link in the chain of state govern-ment. There have been some improvements since Bryce recorded that the "real blemishes" were in the legislative branch, but, on the whole, the composition and conduct of the legislature persist on an unsatisfactory basis.

Apportionment. The apportionment of representatives is arranged in such a fashion in most state legislatures that, in terms of population, rural areas are overrepresented in one or both houses, while cities are underrepresented. Most of the distortions of the democratic principle in state legislative representation arise from the use of units of government as a basis of representation. To justify the representing of counties or towns on a basis of equality or near equality, regardless of population, proponents of such schemes often cite the equal representation of states in the national Senate. But units of local government in no state play a role comparable to that of the states in the federal Union. Political subdivisions of a state are creatures of the state, neither historically nor constitutionally are they units from which the central whole was constructed. Town and county boundaries usually were determined by early transportation limits, historical accident, and other factors no longer operative.

The impact of the "rotten borough" on lawmaking may be seen readily in many states. Deadlock often results from the disagreement between the governor, who is elected by the people of the whole state and is reasonably representative of them, and the nonpopular house of the legislature. Conflict between popular and nonpopular houses also is a common source of legislative paralysis. Obviously, having a legislature of two houses with different bases of representation provides a "check" against hasty action; indeed it often constitutes a check against *any* action by handing to the representatives of a minority of the population a virtual veto power over the wishes of a majority. One might question also whether such a check is necessary in view of the others in existence: gubernatorial veto, judicial review of constitutionality, and, in one-third of the states, the referendum. Reform of nonpopular houses of the state legislatures would give impetus to the quest for solutions of the great social and economic problems that plague urban and industrial society.

Legislative Councils. The most conspicuous alteration in American state legislatures in the last generation has come through the establishment of legislative councils. Although they vary widely in composition and powers, the essential idea common to most of the councils is to provide a continuing body to study problems and plan a legislative program. State legislatures are large and noncontinuous assemblies, composed of quasi laymen who often are inexperienced and who meet for relatively short periods during their brief terms of office. Hemmed in by constitutional limits on the length of sessions and by the restricted compensation allowed, legislators function in a hectic atmosphere that is almost directly opposite to that of orderly deliberation. Since strong leadership has rarely come from within the legislatures, governors, with or without the whip of party, have emerged as chief legislators.

By vesting the power to study and plan in a council of its own choosing, many legislatures have restored to the legislative branch the ingredients prerequisite to exercise of the deliberative function. A few states, by including representatives of the governor on the council, have expanded the functions of that body to include legislative-executive collaboration. Instead of creating a committee that would become the legislature's master, as was feared by many critics of the idea, the legislative council has proved to be a useful instrument that has aided the quality of legislation through better fact finding and advance planning. Extension of the legislative council idea to the remaining one-half of the states that have not adopted it can strengthen democracy by assuring that the proper foundations are laid before legislative action is taken.

Some states secure the benefits of fact finding and informed recommendations in specific fields through the device of interim committees of the legislature. The constitutionality of such committees and the rules under which they must operate, if they may be used at all, vary greatly from state to state. In states that make generous financial provision for compensating legislators while they are on interim committee duty, the number of such committees is apt to be large.

Better results are obtained, as a general rule, when inquiries between legislative sessions are conducted by the standing committees (or their subcommittees) that would normally have jurisdiction over the subject matter in question. Interim committees that are not coordinated with the regular committee arrangement may produce solutions that are out of harmony with the thinking of those legislators who have the primary responsibility for scrutinizing proposals in that sector. Another danger is that the interim committee may be used for getting publicity for the chairman or making sensational disclosures on the basis of hearsay or quite inadequate evidence. Neither on the national nor on the state level has enough thought been given to devising standards of conduct for legislative investigative committees.

Legislative Reform. Bicameralism remains the chief structural feature of American state legislatures. Only Nebraska has yielded to the many logical arguments for unicameralism. After a decade of experience with a one-house legislature, Nebraska has shown that neither the proponents who heralded the millennium nor the opponents who predicted doom were right. Unicameralism has simplified Nebraska's legislative procedure and thereby has reduced public bewilderment over legislative matters. It has reduced "passing the buck" to a minimum; no longer can members of one house blame those of another for some legislative failure. The record has been one of modest achievement.

One of the great barriers to further expansion of the one-house idea is concern lest unicameralism mean the end of two different bases of representation in the legislature. If a state wished to adopt a single-house plan yet retain two apportionment bases, it could be done simply by providing that members of the former two houses meet together in a single chamber. Thus it would be possible to elect legislators on two or more bases, yet secure the advantages of a single tier of committees: fixed responsibility for the fate of legislation, public convenience from one hearing rather than two, reduced printing and attaché personnel costs, and a single debate that would be heard by all members of the legislature. Despite all these considerations, however, attachment to the old ways of doing things has kept all but one of the states on the bicameral stereotype.

Lesser reforms have proved more palatable. There is a commendable tendency to increase legislative salaries. Even in the states with the highest compensation, nevertheless, legislative service often involves financial sacrifice. Some of the largest state budgets now exceed the billion-per-year level; entrusting such a responsibility to underpaid, part-time legislators just does not make sense. Other improvements that are badly needed in the larger states are annual sessions of the legislature and annual budgets to provide for closer control over financial operations of the state.

The State Executive "New Look." The state administrative reorganization movement, which began nearly a half century ago, had pretty well run its course by the time the Second World War came. Renewed interest and some action has marked the period since 1945. Missouri, Georgia, and New Jersey, in their new constitutions, made substantial administrative improvements.

"Little Hoover Commissions." The example of the Hoover Commission and its broad study of federal administration led many states to launch inquiries of their own. Although the bodies that conducted these investigations varied widely in composition and in terms of reference, they were promptly referred to as "little Hoover Commissions." By 1955 committees or commissions in two-thirds of the states had been charged with studying state organization, which in some cases included constitutional revision and legislative reorganization as well as administrative reforms. Some of the probing bodies were executive-appointed; others were legislative committees; while a few were created in the image of the Hoover Commission, with some members designated by the chief executive and some by the legislative branch.

As this is written, some of the "little Hoover Commissions" are still in the stages of collecting information or publishing reports. On the executive side they often stress the desirability of applying some of the accepted principles of good administration. Such recommendations call for the grouping of virtually all state administrative agencies and services into a limited number of departments. The great debate is likely to center on the question of how much reduction there can be in the number of executive officers elected by the people. Can other states go the whole way, as did New Jersey under its 1947 constitution, and provide for the popular election of only the governor, with all other state administrative offices filled by appointment?

Another area of controversy is on the extent to which independent boards and commissions can be abolished. In welfare, utility regulation, personnel, and other fields sharp fights are being waged by these agencies and their supporters to retain their independence from gubernatorial control. Whether it is better to attempt to immunize a service from political influence by granting commissioners long, overlapping terms or to assure that it is administered in harmony with popular will as expressed through the election of a chief executive is being debated hotly. Those who believe in an independent "fight-the-spoilsmen" type of civil-service agency are to be pitted against advocates of a "modern" and "positive" personnel program with a single director of personnel responsible to the governor and with emphasis on getting the right man in the right job.

One might hope that the current renewal of interest in state administrative organization will lead to substantial improvement in the structure and procedure of government. Some of the states that have undertaken surveys have adopted the "Hoover Commission" method and set up investigating bodies that are deemed sufficiently financed and staffed to justify being classed as analogous to the federal commission.[3] The "outside" members, not holding governmental office, may bring to the survey fresh views and can

[3] John W. Lederle and Dorthee E. Strauss, "The Little Hoover Commissions," *Michigan Governmental Digest,* no. 4, Nov. 4, 1949.

add prestige to the recommendations. Not for a generation has so much intelligent attention been given to the problems of state management.

The Governorship. Opinion is divided over whether the governor should be continued as a real executive, or whether some other officer should play that role. The latter possibility has been considered in a few states in terms of a proposed state manager. If a manager, selected by the legislature, were to be given control over the administration, the office of governor would be reduced to presiding over ceremonies and perhaps over the legislature. Such an arrangement would have the merit of creating legislative supremacy and providing a responsible executive. On the other hand, it would hardly prove attractive to the people. As with the national presidency, the governorship is looked upon as an office that represents the whole people. American states need the unifying influence of political leadership. Government on the state level involves much more than administration. If the legislature could develop its own leadership, which might emerge in the form of a premier and his cabinet, that instrument might prove superior to gubernatorial leadership hobbled by the separation-of-powers doctrine. Should the American states turn to some form of the parliamentary system, they would probably do so by degrees and not adopt it outright. For our time, however, strengthening of the governorship appears most likely and desirable.

State Judicial and Legal Reforms. Less conspicuous, but equally important, are rumblings of discontent over judicial systems and legal procedures. Judicial councils—now used in nearly two-thirds of the states—are on the increase, with an expanding area of activity and public confidence. In 1949 there was formed a Conference of Chief Justices of the States to do for state jurisprudence what the annual conference of federal jurists has done over the years for federal. The most conspicuous achievements, however, are the changes made in the judicial systems of Missouri in 1946 and New Jersey in 1947. If these revisions are correct harbingers of the future, the end may be in sight for some

of the worst excesses of state and local jurisprudence.

Stirrings have been heard in other directions. Great strides have been made in modernizing, simplifying, unifying, and codifying the law. Some states are giving serious study to revision of rules of evidence. There are numerous indications that judges, bar associations, and law schools are becoming increasingly concerned over legal ethics, the training of future lawyers, restrictions upon admission to legal practice, and the high cost of justice for poor people.

Police-force training and professionalization have gone forward, especially at state and municipal levels. Prison facilities and care are still generally bad, but there is improvement in spots. Work programs suffer increasingly because of lobbying by "free enterprise" and drastic federal and state restrictions on the sale of prison-made products. The chain gang is gone except in a few Southern counties. Some improvement has been made in probation and parole practices and in supervision, but inadequate appropriations and the spoils system continue to plague these efforts. Traffic violations remain a serious problem, with various experiments under way. Several states have evolved traffic tickets that are supposed to be "fix-proof." Meanwhile, the National Committee on Traffic Law Enforcement has proposed standards toward which many state officials aspire. The jury system, seriously challenged by the 1949 trial of Communist leaders in New York and by chronic misuse in many parts of the country, especially the South, is being reexamined.

Considerable progress has been made in handling juvenile offenders. California, for example, led the way by establishing a Youth Authority. Similar programs have been adopted in New York and New Jersey. Minnesota has established a Youth Conservation Commission; Wisconsin, a Youth Service Division; and Massachusetts, a Youth Service Board. These agencies emphasize the importance of clinical analysis followed by varied practicable programs aimed at correcting and eliminating the causes of delinquency. Outdoor work is an integral part of most of the programs. In spite of encouraging signs like these, juvenile offenders in many states are dealt with by a heavy hand and often incarcerated with hardened criminals.

TOWARD LOCAL DEMOCRACY

Local government is bound to have a place in any conceivable political system. Although they may change individually and internally, the basic pattern of counties, cities, and other local units is apt to survive. Certain types of services are better performed under the direction of those who know the mood of the community. Local self-government allows a rather broad form of local option; acting through their elected representatives, the people decide what they want done and what they will spend to do it. One of the strongest arguments for retaining a large measure of discretion in the hands of local authorities is that it permits experimentation, the results of which may be of great value to other localities and to higher units of government. It also provides greater vitality in local government, which becomes the training ground for future members of state legislatures and of Congress.

State-Local Relations. Not only must the changing pattern of intergovernmental relationships be assessed in terms of the trend toward federal centralization, but also attention must be given to the shift of power and responsibility from local to state government. The problems involved in the latter sphere were examined in an outstanding report of the Council of State Governments in 1946. The report stressed four major problem areas: finances, functions, legal relationships, and multiplicity of local units.[4]

Finances. On the financial front, local governments have relied most heavily on the property tax, which is often badly assessed and unevenly collected, especially as regards intangibles. Frequently local governments find themselves without adequate revenues to perform the services legally required by the state or strongly demanded by the people. During the great depression hundreds of local governments went broke.

[4] Council of State Governments, *State-Local Relations, Report of the Committee on . . .* (Chicago: The Council, 1946).

Schools were closed, services were abandoned, and grass grew in the streets. Property taxpayers became delinquent in wholesale numbers. After some improvement in economic conditions, property-tax collections improved too, but the vulnerability of local government remained. Dependent almost completely on a single source of revenue, local governments run the same sort of risk as does a man with all his eggs in a single basket. Unable to finance ever-growing functions upon a rigid tax base, local governments ought, according to the Council report, to be given broader taxing powers rather than be aided by expanding state grants-in-aid or extending shared revenues. With the higher costs of city government since the end of the Second World War, and increased demands on cities, many of them have adopted new forms of taxes to broaden the tax base.

Functions. Each level of government should be assigned the functions it is capable of performing with both efficiency and maximum participation by those affected. The Council report stressed that maintaining local discretion is important to democracy and democratic procedures. Local government is an important fountainhead from which democracy flows. In the counties, cities, and other local units of this country, large numbers of men and women officeholders are getting experience in government and are at work interpreting its problems to people in their constituencies. Local home rule quickens the sense of civic responsibility in citizens by assuring that decisions on local matters shall be made locally.

Legal Relationship. In terms of legal relationships, local government remains everywhere the creature of the state. Most states impose detailed restrictions on local activities through constitutional and statutory provisions and through administrative supervision. One-third of the American states have granted constitutional home rule to some of their cities, involving the privilege of drawing up their own charters and governing so far as "municipal affairs" are concerned. Although home rule has been circumscribed, in some of the states that have adopted it, by restrictive judicial interpretations and constitutional and statutory amendments, it remains a principal approach to freeing local governments to find their own solutions to local problems and to relieve state legislatures of some of the mass of detailed legislation on local matters. States like Michigan and California have demonstrated that home rule, while not a panacea for all local ills, can enlarge the scope of self-government and sharpen civic alertness.

Even more important than the formal limitations on local powers, however, are the forces of modern life that make communities interdependent and make problems state-wide and nation-wide that formerly were local. The story of relief will serve to illustrate. Poor relief was a traditional function of English local government and as such it was transplanted to America. The burden of caring for the poor was borne by local units for over a century and a quarter after nationhood was achieved. Then the great depression, following the crash of 1929, struck with unprecedented violence. At first counties, cities, and townships struggled valiantly to take care of their unemployed. When their resources were exhausted, the states began to help out. Finally, in 1933, the Federal government assumed a large share of the obligation by providing work for the able-bodied unemployed. Under the Social Security program inaugurated in 1935, the Federal government began financing a share of state and local public-assistance programs, launched a federal system of old-age insurance, and induced the states to begin unemployment-compensation schemes.

Multiplicity of Units. Few, if any, governmental problems are more impervious to suggestions for change than that of the multiplicity of local units. Like the weather, everyone talks about it but no one does very much about it. Governmentally speaking, the United States is divided into nearly 120,000 units, of which over one-half are school districts. Nearly every state has too many counties and other general local units of government. The typical urban resident pays taxes to two or more taxing authorities, and is confused over which services from what level of government he receives in return. Most metropolitan areas have chronic problems arising from the common pattern of development. A central city is incorporated with boundaries that embrace the greater part of the urban population in the vicinity. As the city grows, population spills beyond the city limits. Annexation by the central city may operate for a time, but usually the satellite city emerges to play the role of dormitory for people who work in the city. Eventually as much as half or more of the population of a metropolitan area may be found outside the jurisdiction of the central city, not sharing directly in the solution of many of the problems that rightfully belong to the metropolitan area as a whole—health, transportation, delinquency, dependency, and poverty.

There is some possibility of consolidating counties, since they are creatures of the state and usually fairly subject to its will. But county pride is aroused by such proposals and a howl goes up that can be heard around the state. The number of counties has remained so static in most states that one might think they were defined in the Federal Constitution. Establishment of a county is likely to mean its eternal existence unless some new plan of inducing consolidations can be worked out. The states that allow their legislatures to determine county boundaries and jurisdictions are in a good position to merge smaller ones and otherwise recast outmoded arrangements on the county-government level.

One of the most needed consolidations is that of cities and counties. In metropolitan areas an instrument of government is required that will permit central administration of metropolitan district problems and local solutions for community ones. The separate existence of city and county governments in great urban centers usually involves duplication, waste, and confusion.

The greatest quantitative consolidation, however, is possible in school districts. The small rural district, operating only a single one-room school, rarely has the facilities and resources necessary to provide the best in educational services. District consolidation can be accomplished without consolidating schools. Retention of the one-room school or merger into a consolidated school is a question quite apart from the larger unit. The enlarged district can effect savings through purchase of supplies, maintenance of buildings, provision of nursing facilities, and in many other ways.

Most urgent of all is the incorporation of special districts into other local units. Many states have left the door for the formation of special districts so wide open that hundreds of these jurisdictions have been established. Some of them have important functions that are best performed by special units, but most of them ought to be assigned to a general local unit.

Local Organization. Generally speaking, local governments are ill organized to provide the services that the federal system and modern technology have thrust upon them. With few exceptions they have continued institutions the form of which was established generations ago to deal with problems vastly simpler than those of today and to serve relatively small populations. Of course, there have been changes. Bicameral city councils have been reduced to unicameral ones. Many city councils and a few county boards of supervisors have appointed managers.

Basically, however, the old forms still prevail. Except in counties and school and other districts, the line between the legislative and executive branches is too strictly drawn. Except where the manager plan is in use, the line between politics and administration rarely is drawn strongly enough. Separation of powers may prevent autocratic government, as its proponents allege, but it also often produces deadlock unless the breach is healed over under the binding sinews of party or the pressure of a strong executive. County government, once called "the dark continent of American politics," remains dusky except in a few advanced counties that have created executives. Council-manager cities constitute the only considerable number of local units that have developed an organizational form that meets modern demands for a responsible executive whose tenure depends upon the majority will of the legislative body.

There remain too many state and local officers elected by the people, making ballots so long that even moderately alert citizens can know little of the stewardship in office of their representatives. The urge to separate national, state, and local elections has produced so many election days that participation has been seriously diminished.

Need for Stronger Executives. Within local governments, the most pressing single need is for stronger and more responsible executives. Many local governments, especially counties and cities with the commission plan, have no real executive at all. Other cities have weak mayors whose executive powers are slight. An encouraging beginning has been made in the manager plan of cities and counties, and by the wise use of the school superintendent as the executive officer of boards of education. If local units are to be well governed, a responsible executive is a first essential. The local executive of the future may well be modeled on the office of the city manager, as developed in the municipalities making effective use of that form.

The manager plan is on the march. More than one-fourth of the incorporated municipalities of the United States have city managers. It appears entirely possible, as predicted by Charles Edison, when president of the National Municipal League, that by 1960 the manager plan will be used by a majority of American cities. Municipal progress in the next generation may well turn largely upon the soundness of the charters, statutes, and ordinances creating these managerships, and upon the training and professional integrity of those who are appointed as managers. In many ways the need for the manager plan is even more acute in counties than in cities, but its spread in the county sphere has been slow.

The Metropolitan Area. Not discounting the many forces and vested interests that support the *status quo,* one may say with some assurance that the development of metropolitan area governments will be an item of highest priority on the agenda of American democracy in the next generation. The great cities of today, in almost all cases, had their basic physical layouts determined before the development of the automobile. With few exceptions, the great metropolitan areas sprawl over many units of government— cities, counties, townships, school districts, special districts, and even states. Even where a bold consolidation is carried through, as in London in 1888 and in New York in 1898, the old problems of outgrown boundaries recur in another decade or two as the metropolis expands and improved transportation permits suburbanites to commute from greater and greater distances.

The outlines of metropolitan reform are far from clear. In the simplest and most drastic form, existing units of local government might be swept away and replaced by a centralized single government. Legitimate demands might be made for some subordinate units with limited powers, like the boroughs of New York or the metropolitan boroughs of London. Even more likely, however, is the possibility that order would be brought out of the existing metropolitan chaos in piecemeal fashion. Far from simple, this might result from a maze of contractual obligations among local units to provide each other with certain services, for which payment would be made. It is even possible that a considerable degree of functional consolidation might be achieved through the organization of metropolis-wide special districts. These later could be brought together into a single government.

Arousing Citizen Interest. In the America that De Tocqueville visited in the 1830's, as indeed in some rural communities of today, the level of citizen interest was high. Government belonged to the people. Participation in town affairs was expected of all New England freemen; they went to town meetings, and they accepted and discharged civic responsibilities. By way of contrast, De Tocqueville mentioned the civic sterility that existed in the communes of his native France. Because of centralization, he thought, people had no sense of belonging to the communes in which they lived, and they participated little in local affairs.

Today an overseas observer might get an entirely different impression of American local institutions. The typical American is more urban than rural. In the great metropolitan areas, he may not even know in which municipality he lives. He has little conception of governmental functions and is often unable to distinguish between state, county, municipal, and district services. The chances are that he votes occasionally in state elections but seldom in local elections. If he does vote, he is likely to support blindly the political party with which his parents were affiliated, or if no party labels are available, to vote as his daily newspaper or some friend recommends. Far from the active, participating freeman of the early days of the republic, today's average citizen is a drone, quite impotent in local affairs.

Once in a while, of course, he becomes aroused over something. It may be that his own toes get stepped on through a new ordinance, or a crime wave reaches his neighborhood, or local services break down. Sometimes he can become enthusiastic over the prospects of unseating a local boss or turning out a political machine.

American state and local government, traditionally the fountainhead of democracy, is not abreast of the needs and requirements of our urban-industrial civilization. Thrice in the last 40 years we have sent American soldiers forth to foreign battlefields, and each time the justifications for the enormous sacrifices were "free government," "freedom," and "democracy." We have been disappointed afterward, because democracy and freedom did not follow automatically in the countries defeated or liberated. If, in this period of postwar disillusionment, Americans would rededicate themselves wholeheartedly to the study and improvement of their institutions, perhaps some positive good would come from the investment of men and money in war.

Mind Your Own Business was the title of a book written by R. B. Suthers in 1905.[5] In it the author presented "the case for municipal housekeeping" in England, arguing convincingly for Britons to participate in local affairs. We in the United States need someone to inspire us to mind our own business. We need citizens in every county and city and town to agree to spend enough time on civic affairs to keep abreast of public business. President Eliot's famous bookshelf offered the equivalent of a college education through 15 minutes of reading a day. A quarter hour of intelligent attention ap-

[5] The latest revision (London: Fabian Society and G. Allen Unwin) was published in 1938.

plied daily to civic problems might transform a drone into a civic worker and lack of interest into informed opinion. A little more time and energy invested through participation in the political party of their choice and through non-partisan civic groups like the League of Women Voters will make leaders out of former indifferent citizens.

Startling international and national news focuses our attention upon the government at Washington. In a decade that has required the sacrifices of total war, it is both proper and inevitable that an alert citizen should devote time and attention to foreign affairs. In an era haunted by the nightmare of the great depression, we look to the national capital for the formulation of economic policies that will secure full employment and promote free enterprise. Preoccupation with national affairs, however, must not be carried so far that we neglect our state and locality, for there are the roots from which much of our political democracy stems.

FOR FURTHER READING

REFERENCES ON PARTICULAR STATES

Arkansas: Alexander, Henry M.: *Organization and Function of State and Local Government in Arkansas* (University of Arkansas, Bureau of Research, 1947).

California: Crouch, Winston W., and Dean E. McHenry: *California Government: Politics and Administration* (University of California Press, 2d ed., 1949).

Crouch, Winston W., and Others: *State and Local Government in California* (University of California Press, 1952).

Bollens, John C., and Stanley Scott: *Local Government in California* (University of California Press, 1951).

Delaware: Dolan, Paul: *The Organization of State Administration in Delaware* (Johns Hopkins Press, 1950).

Florida: Doyle, Wilson K., and Others: *The Government and Administration of Florida* (Crowell, 1954).

Georgia: Gosnell, Cullen B., and C. D. Anderson: *The Government and Administration of Georgia* (Crowell, 1955).

Illinois: Gore, S. K., and Others (eds.): *State and Local Government in Illinois* (University of Illinois, Institute of Government and Public Affairs, 1953).

Indiana: Sikes, Pressley S.: *Indiana State and Local Government* (Bloomington: Principia Press, rev. ed., 1951).

Iowa: Ross, Russell M.: *The Government and Administration of Iowa* (Crowell, 1955).

Mississippi: Highsaw, Robert B., and C. N. Fortenberry: *The Government and Administration of Mississippi* (Crowell, 1954).

Missouri: Karsch, Robert F.: *Essentials of Missouri Government* (Columbia, Mo.: Lucas Bros., 3d ed., 1953).

Montana: Renne, Roland R.: *The Government and Administration of Montana* (Crowell, 1955).

New Mexico: Donnelly, Thomas C.: *The Government of New Mexico* (University of New Mexico Press, 1947).

New York: Caldwell, Lynton K.: *The Government and Administration of New York* (Crowell, 1954).

Moscow, Warren: *Politics in the Empire State* (Knopf, 1948).

North Carolina: Wager, Paul W.: *North Carolina: The State and Its Government* (Oxford, 1947).

Rankin, Robert S.: *The Government and Administration of North Carolina* (Crowell, 1955).

Ohio: Walker, Harvey and F. R. Aumann: *The Government and Administration of Ohio* (Crowell, 1955).

Rose, Albert H.: *Ohio State and Local Government* (Dayton: University Book Store, 1948).

Pennsylvania: Tanger, Jacob, and Others: *Pennsylvania Government* (State College, Pa.: Penns Valley Press, 3d ed., 1950).

South Carolina: *Organization of the State Government of South Carolina* (Columbia: University of South Carolina, Bureau of Public Administration, 1952).

Tennessee: Combs, William H., and W. E. Cole: *Tennessee: A Political Study* (University of Tennessee Press, 1940).

Texas: MacCorkle, Stuart A., and Dick Smith: *Texas Government* (McGraw-Hill, 1949).

Patterson, Caleb P., and Others: *State and Local Government in Texas* (Macmillan, 2d ed., 1948).

Stewart, Frank M., and Joseph L. Clark: *The Constitution and Government of Texas* (Heath, 4th ed., 1949).

Washington: Webster, Donald H., and Others: *Washington State Government* (University of Washington Press, 1948).

Wyoming: Trachsel, Herman H., and Ralph M. Wade: *The Government and Administration of Wyoming* (Crowell, 1953).

REVIEW QUESTIONS

1. To what extent do you believe our economic prosperity rests upon the vastness of our free-trade area?

2. Is federalism "finished"? Discuss changes that have taken place. What do you expect in the future?

3. Has the deadlock on American state constitutional reform been broken by Missouri and New Jersey, or were those instances exceptions which prove the rule that general renovation is nearly impossible under present conditions?

4. What are the persistent problems that plague state legislatures with respect to apportionment, legislative councils, and general renovation and reform?

5. What are the prospects for state administrative reorganization?

6. Discuss some of the problems of state-local relations.

7. What structural and organizational improvements look promising in the field of local government?

8. What can be done to penetrate the inertia of the American people toward public affairs?

APPENDIX I

The Declaration of Independence

IN CONGRESS, JULY 4, 1776: THE UNANIMOUS DECLARATION OF THE
THIRTEEN UNITED STATES OF AMERICA

When in the Course of human events, it becomes necessary for one people to dissolve the political bands which have connected them with another, and to assume among the Powers of the earth, the separate and equal station to which the Laws of Nature and of Nature's God entitle them, a decent respect to the opinions of mankind requires that they should declare the causes which impel them to the separation.

We hold these truths to be self-evident, that all men are created equal, that they are endowed by their Creator with certain unalienable Rights, that among these are Life, Liberty and the pursuit of Happiness. That to secure these rights, Governments are instituted among Men, deriving their just powers from the consent of the governed, That whenever any Form of Government becomes destructive of these ends, it is the Right of the People to alter or to abolish it, and to institute new Government, laying its foundation on such principles and organizing its powers in such form, as to them shall seem most likely to effect their Safety and Happiness. Prudence, indeed, will dictate that Governments long established should not be changed for light and transient causes; and accordingly all experience hath shown, that mankind are more disposed to suffer, while evils are sufferable, than to right themselves by abolishing the forms to which they are accustomed. But when a long train of abuses and usurpations, pursuing in-variably the same Object evinces a design to reduce them under absolute Despotism, it is their right, it is their duty, to throw off such Government, and to provide new Guards for their future security.—Such has been the patient sufferance of these Colonies; and such is now the necessity which constrains them to alter their former Systems of Government. The history of the present King of Great Britain is a history of repeated injuries and usurpations, all having in direct object the establishment of an absolute Tyranny over these States. To prove this, let Facts be submitted to a candid world.

He has refused his Assent to Laws, the most wholesome and necessary for the public good.

He has forbidden his Governors to pass Laws of immediate and pressing importance, unless suspended in their operation till his Assent should be obtained; and when so suspended, he has utterly neglected to attend to them.

He has refused to pass other Laws for the accommodation of large districts of people, unless those people would relinquish the right of representation in the Legislature, a right inestimable to them and formidable to tyrants only.

He has called together legislative bodies at places unusual, uncomfortable, and distant from the depository of their Public Records, for the sole purpose of fatiguing them into compliance with his measures.

He has dissolved Representative Houses repeatedly, for opposing with manly firmness his invasions on the rights of the people.

He has refused for a long time, after such dissolutions, to cause others to be elected; whereby the Legislative Powers, incapable of Annihilation, have returned to the People at large for their exercise; the State remaining in the mean time exposed to all the dangers of invasion from without, and convulsions within.

He has endeavoured to prevent the population of these States; for that purpose obstructing the Laws of Naturalization of Foreigners; refusing to pass others to encourage their migration hither, and raising the conditions of new Appropriations of Lands.

He has obstructed the Administration of Justice, by refusing his Assent to Laws for establishing Judiciary Powers.

He has made Judges dependent on his Will alone, for the tenure of their offices, and the amount and payment of their salaries.

He has erected a multitude of New Offices, and sent hither swarms of Officers to harass our People, and eat out their substance.

He has kept among us, in times of peace, Standing Armies without the Consent of our legislature.

He has affected to render the Military independent of and superior to the Civil Power.

He has combined with others to subject us to a jurisdiction foreign to our constitution, and unacknowledged by our laws giving his Assent to their acts of pretended legislation:

For quartering large bodies of armed troops among us:

For protecting them, by a mock Trial, from Punishment for any Murders which they should commit on the Inhabitants of these States:

For cutting off our Trade with all parts of the world:

For imposing taxes on us without our Consent:

For depriving us in many cases, of the benefits of Trial by jury:

For transporting us beyond Seas to be tried for pretended offences:

For abolishing the free System of English Laws in a neighboring Province, establishing therein an Arbitrary government, and enlarging its Boundaries so as to render it at once an example and fit instrument for introducing the same absolute rule into these Colonies:

For taking away our Charters, abolishing our most valuable Laws, and altering fundamentally the Forms of our Governments:

For suspending our own legislature, and declaring themselves invested with Power to legislate for us in all cases whatsoever.

He has abdicated Government here, by declaring us out of his Protection and waging War against us.

He has plundered our seas, ravaged our Coasts. burnt our towns, and destroyed the lives of our people.

He is at this time transporting large armies of foreign mercenaries to compleat the works of death, desolation and tyranny, already begun with circumstances of Cruelty & perfidy scarcely paralleled in the most barbarous ages, and totally unworthy the Head of a civilized nation.

He has constrained our fellow Citizens taken Captive on the high Seas to bear Arms against their Country, to become the executioners of their friends and Brethren, or to fall themselves by their Hands.

He has excited domestic insurrections amongst us, and has endeavoured to bring on the inhabitants of our frontiers, the merciless Indian Savages, whose known rule of warfare, is an undistinguished destruction of all ages, sexes and conditions.

In every stage of these Oppressions We have Petitioned for Redress in the most humble terms: Our repeated Petitions have been answered only by repeated injury. A Prince, whose character is thus marked by every act which may define a Tyrant, is unfit to be the ruler of a free People.

Nor have We been wanting in attention to our British brethren. We have warned them from time to time of attempts by their legislature to extend an unwarrantable jurisdiction over us. We have reminded them of the circumstances of our emigration and settlement here. We have appealed to their native justice and magnanimity, and we have conjured them by the ties of our common kindred to disavow these usurpations, which would inevitably interrupt our connections and correspondence. They too have been deaf to the voice of justice and of consanguinity. We must, therefore, acquiesce in the necessity, which denounces our Separation, and hold them, as we hold the rest of mankind, Enemies in War, in Peace Friends.

We, therefore, the Representatives of the united States of America, in General Congress, Assembled, appealing to the Supreme Judge of the world for the rectitude of our intentions, do, in the Name, and by Authority of the good People of these Colonies, solemnly publish and declare, That these United Colonies are, and of Right ought to be Free and Independent States; that they are Absolved from all Allegiance to the British Crown, and that all political connection between them and the State of Great Britain, is and ought to be totally dissolved; and that as Free and Independent States, they have full Power to levy War, conclude Peace, contract Alliances, establish Commerce, and to do all other Acts and Things which Independent States may of right do. And for the support of this Declaration, with a firm reliance on the Protection of Divine Providence, we mutually pledge to each other our Lives, our Fortunes and our sacred Honor.

John Hancock [1]

[1] The remaining signatures are omitted.

Articles of Confederation

Articles of Confederation and perpetual Union between the States of Newhamshire, Massachusetts-bay, Rhodeisland and Providence Plantations, Connecticut, New-York, New-Jersey, Pennsylvania, Delaware, Maryland, Virginia, North-Carolina, South-Carolina and Georgia

Article I. The stile of this confederacy shall be "The United States of America."

Article II. Each State retains its sovereignty, freedom and independence, and every power, jurisdiction and right, which is not by this confederation expressly delegated to the United States, in Congress assembled.

Article III. The said States hereby severally enter into a firm league of friendship with each other, for their common defence, the security of their liberties, and their mutual and general welfare, binding themselves to assist each other, against all force offered to, or attacks made upon them, or any of them, on account of religion, sovereignty, trade, or any other pretence whatever.

Article IV. The better to secure and perpetuate mutual friendship and intercourse among the people of the different States in this Union, the free inhabitants of each of these States, paupers, vagabonds and fugitives from justice excepted, shall be entitled to all privileges and immunities of free citizens in the several States; and the people of each State shall have free ingress and regress to and from any other State, and shall enjoy therein all the privileges of trade and commerce, subject to the same duties, impositions and restrictions as the inhabitants thereof respectively, provided that such restrictions shall not extend so far as to prevent the removal of property imported into any State, to any other state of which the owner is an inhabitant; provided also that no imposition, duties, or restriction shall be laid by any State, on the property of the United States, or either of them.

If any Person guilty of, or charged with treason, felony, or other high misdemeanor in any State, shall flee from justice, and be found in any of the United States, he shall upon demand of the Governor or Executive power, of the State from which he fled, be delivered up and removed to the State having jurisdiction of his offence.

Full faith and credit shall be given in each of these States to the records, acts and judicial proceedings of the courts and magistrates of every other State.

Article V. For the more convenient management of the general interest of the United States, delegates shall be annually appointed in such manner as the legislature of each State shall direct, to meet in Congress on the first Monday in November, in every year, with a power reserved to each State, to recall its delegates, or any of them, at any time within the year, and to send others in their stead, for the remainder of the year.

No State shall be represented in Congress by less than two, nor by more than seven members; and no person shall be capable of being a delegate for more than three years in any term of six years; nor shall any person, being a delegate, be capable of holding any office under the United States, for which he, or another for his benefit receives any salary, fees or emolument of any kind.

Each State shall maintain its own delegates in a meeting of the States, and while they act as members of the committee of the States.

In determining questions in the United States, in Congress assembled, each State shall have one vote.

Freedom of speech and debate in Congress shall not be impeached or questioned in any court, or place out of Congress, and the members of Congress shall be protected in their persons from arrests and imprisonments, during the time of their going to and from, and attendance on Congress, except for treason, felony, or breach of the peace.

Article VI. No State without the consent of the United States in Congress assembled, shall send any embassy to, or receive any embassy from, or enter into any conference, agreement, alliance or treaty with any king, prince or state; nor shall any person holding any office of profit or trust under the United States, or any of them, accept of any present, emolument, office or title of any kind whatever from any king, prince, or foreign state; nor shall the United States in Congress assembled, or any of them, grant any title of nobility.

No two or more States shall enter into any treaty, confederation or alliance whatever between them, without the consent of the United States in Congress assembled, specifying accurately the purposes for which the same is to be entered into, and how long it shall continue.

No State shall lay any imposts or duties, which may interfere with any stipulations in treaties, entered into by the United States in Congress assembled, with any king, prince or state, in pursuance of any treaties already proposed by Congress, to the courts of France and Spain.

No vessels of war shall be kept up in time of peace by any State, except such number only, as shall be deemed necessary by the United States in Congress assembled, for the defence of such State, or its trade; nor shall any body of forces be kept up by any State, in time of peace, except such number only, as in the judgment of the United States,

in Congress assembled, shall be deemed requisite to garrison the forts necessary for the defence of such State; but every State shall always keep up a well regulated and disciplined militia, sufficiently armed and accoutered, and shall provide and constantly have ready for use, in public stores, a due number of field pieces and tents, and a proper quantity of arms, ammunition and camp equipage.

No State shall engage in any war without the consent of the United States in Congress assembled, unless such State be actually invaded by enemies, or shall have received certain advice of a resolution being formed by some nation of Indians to invade such State, and the danger is so imminent as not to admit of a delay, till the United States in Congress assembled can be consulted; nor shall any State grant commissions to any ships or vessels of war, nor letters of marque or reprisal, except it be after a declaration of war by the United States in Congress assembled, and then only against the kingdom or state and the subjects thereof, against which war has been so declared, and under such regulations as shall be established by the United States in Congress assembled, unless such State be infested by pirates, in which case vessels of war may be fitted out for that occasion, and kept so long as the danger shall continue, or until the United States in Congress assembled shall determine otherwise.

Article VII. When land-forces are raised by any State for the common defence, all officers of or under the rank of colonel, shall be appointed by the Legislature of each State respectively by whom such forces shall be raised, or in such manner as such State shall direct, and all vacancies shall be filled up by the State which first made the appointment.

Article VIII. All charges of war, and all other expenses that shall be incurred for the common defence or general welfare, and allowed by the United States in Congress assembled, shall be defrayed out of a common treasury, which shall be supplied by the several States, in proportion to the value of all land within each State, granted to or surveyed for any person, as such land and the buildings and improvements thereon shall be estimated according to such mode as the United States in Congress assembled, shall from time to time direct and appoint.

The taxes for paying that proportion shall be laid and levied by the authority and direction of the Legislatures of the several States within the time agreed upon by the United States in Congress assembled.

Article IX. The United States in Congress assembled, shall have the sole and exclusive right and power of determining on peace and war, except in the cases mentioned in the sixth article—of sending and receiving ambassadors—entering into treaties and alliances, provided that no treaty of commerce shall be made whereby the legislative power of the respective States shall be restrained from imposing such imposts and duties on foreigners, as their own people are subjected to, or from prohibiting the exportation or importation of any species of goods or commodities whatsoever— of establishing rules for deciding in all cases, what captures on land or water shall be legal, and in what manner prizes taken by land or naval forces in the service of the United States shall be divided or appropriated—of granting letters of marque and reprisal in times of peace—appointing courts for the trial of piracies and felonies committed on the high seas and establishing courts for receiving and determining finally appeals in all cases of captures, provided that no member of Congress shall be appointed a judge of any of the said courts.

The United States in Congress assembled shall also be the last resort on appeal in all disputes and differences now subsisting or that hereafter may arise between two or more States concerning boundary, jurisdiction or any other cause whatever; which authority shall always be exercised in the manner following. Whenever the legislative or executive authority or lawful agent of any State in controversy with another shall present a petition to Congress, stating the matter in question and praying for a hearing, notice thereof shall be given by order of Congress to the legislative or executive authority of the other State in controversy, and a day assigned for the appearance of the parties by their lawful agents, who shall then be directed to appoint by joint consent, commissioners, or judges to constitute a court for hearing and determining the matter in question: but if they cannot agree,

Congress shall name three persons out of each of the United States, and from the list of such persons each party shall alternately strike out one, the petitioners beginning, until the number shall be reduced to thirteen; and from that number not less than seven, nor more than nine names as Congress shall direct, shall in the presence of Congress be drawn out by lot, and the persons whose names shall be so drawn or any five of them, shall be commissioners or judges, to hear and finally determine the controversy, so always as a major part of the judges who shall hear the cause shall agree in the determination; and if either party shall neglect to attend at the day appointed, without showing reasons, which Congress shall judge sufficient, or being present shall refuse to strike, the Congress shall proceed to nominate three persons out of each State, and the Secretary of Congress shall strike in behalf of such party absent or refusing; and the judgment and sentence of the court to be appointed, in the manner before prescribed, shall be final and conclusive; and if any of the parties shall refuse to submit to the authority of such court, or to appear or defend their claim or cause, the court shall nevertheless proceed to pronounce sentence, or judgment, which shall in like manner be final and decisive, the judgment or sentence and other proceedings being in either case transmitted to Congress, and lodged among the acts of Congress for the security of the parties concerned: provided that every commissioner, before he sits in judgment, shall take an oath to be administered by one of the judges of the supreme or superior court of the State, where the cause shall be tried, "well and truly to hear and determine the matter in question, according to the best of his judgment, without favour, affection or hope of reward:" provided also that no State shall be deprived of territory for the benefit of the United States.

All controversies concerning the private right of soil claimed under different grants of two or more States, whose jurisdiction as they may respect such lands, and the States which passed such grants are adjusted; the said grants or either of them being at the same time claimed to have originated antecedent to such settlement of jurisdiction, shall on the petition of either party to the Congress of the

United States, be finally determined as near as may be in the same manner as is before prescribed for deciding disputes respecting territorial jurisdiction between different states.

The United States in Congress assembled shall also have the sole and exclusive right and power of regulating the alloy and value of coin struck by their own authority, or by that of the respective States—fixing the standard of weights and measures throughout the United States—regulating the trade and manageing all affairs with the Indians, not members of any of the States, provided that the legislative right of any State within its own limits be not infringed or violated—establishing and regulating post-offices from one State to another, throughout all the United States, and exacting such postage on the papers passing thro' the same as may be requisite to defray the expenses of the said office—appointing all officers of the land forces, in the service of the United States, excepting regimental officers—appointing all the officers of the naval forces, and commissioning all officers whatever in the service of the United States—making rules for the government and regulation of the said land and naval forces, and directing their operations.

The United States in Congress assembled shall have authority to appoint a committee, to sit in the recess of Congress, to be denominated "a Committee of the States," and to consist of one delegate from each State; and to appoint such other committees and civil officers as may be necessary for manageing the general affairs of the United States under their direction—to appoint one of their number to preside, provided that no person be allowed to serve in the office of president more than one year in any term of three years; to ascertain the necessary sums of money to be raised for the service of the United States, and to appropriate and apply the same for defraying the public expenses—to borrow money, or emit bills on the credit of the United States, transmitting every half year to the respective States an account of the sums of money so borrowed or emitted,—to build and equip a navy—to agree upon the number of land forces, and to make requisitions from each State for its quota, in proportion to the number of white inhabitants in such State; which requisition shall be binding, and there-

upon the Legislature of each State shall appoint the regimental officers, raise the men and cloath, arm and equip them in a soldier like manner, at the expense of the United States; and the officers and men so cloathed, armed and equipped shall march to the place appointed, and within the time agreed on by the United States in Congress assembled; but if the United States in Congress assembled shall, on consideration of circumstances judge proper that any State should not raise men, or should raise a smaller number than its quota, and that any other State should raise a greater number of men than the quota thereof, such extra number shall be raised, officered, cloathed, armed and equipped in the same manner as the quota of such State, unless the legislature of such State shall judge that such extra number cannot be safely spared out of the same, in which case they shall raise, officer, cloath, arm and equip as many of such extra number as they judge can be safely spared. And the officers and men so cloathed, armed and equipped, shall march to the place appointed, and within the time agreed on by the United States in Congress assembled.

The United States in Congress assembled shall never engage in a war, nor grant letters of marque and reprisal in time of peace, nor enter into any treaties or alliances, nor coin money, nor regulate the value thereof, nor ascertain the sums and expenses necessary for the defence and welfare of the United States, or any of them, nor emit bills, nor borrow money on the credit of the United States, nor appropriate money, nor agree upon the number of vessels of war, to be built or purchased, or the number of land or sea forces to be raised, nor appoint a commander in chief of the army or navy, unless nine States assent to the same: nor shall a question on any other point, except for adjourning from day to day be determined, unless by the votes of a majority of the United States in Congress assembled.

The Congress of the United States shall have power to adjourn to any time within the year, and to place within the United States, so that no period of adjournment be for a longer duration than the space of six months, and shall publish the journal of their proceedings monthly, except such parts thereof relating to treaties, alliances or military operations, as in their judgment require secresy; and the yeas and nays of the delegates of each State on any question shall be entered on the journal, when it is desired by any delegate; and the delegates of a State, or any of them, at his or their request shall be furnished with a transcript of the said journal, except such parts as are above excepted, to lay before the Legislatures of the several States.

Article X. The committee of the States, or any nine of them, shall be authorized to execute, in the recess of Congress, such of the powers of Congress as the United States in Congress assembled, by the consent of nine States, shall from time to time think expedient to vest with them; provided that no power be delegated to the said committee, for the exercise of which, by the articles of confederation, the voice of nine States in the Congress of the United States assembled is requisite.

Article XI. Canada acceding to this confederation, and joining in the measures of the United States, shall be admitted into, and entitled to all the advantages of this Union; but no other colony shall be admitted into the same, unless such admission be agreed to by nine States.

Article XII. All bills of credit emitted, monies borrowed and debts contracted by, or under the authority of Congress, before the assembling of the United States, in pursuance of the present confederation, shall be deemed and considered as a charge against the United States, for payment and satisfaction whereof the said United States, and the public faith are hereby solemnly pledged.

Article XIII. Every State shall abide by the determinations of the United States in Congress assembled, on all questions which by this confederation are submitted to them. And the articles of this confederation shall be inviolably observed by every State, and the Union shall be perpetual; nor shall any alteration at any time hereafter be made in any of them; unless such alteration be agreed to in a Congress of the United States, and be afterwards confirmed by the Legislatures of every State.

(handwritten: preamble
art I —)

APPENDIX III

Constitution of the United States of America

(handwritten: (Basis for popular sovereignty) ("State rights" right to revolt if sovereign))

We, the people of the United States, in order to form a more perfect union, establish justice, insure domestic tranquility, provide for the common defence, promote the general welfare, and secure the blessings of liberty to ourselves and our posterity, do ordain and establish this Constitution for the United States of America.

Article I *(handwritten: Legislature)*

Section 1. All legislative powers herein granted shall be vested in a Congress of the United States, which shall consist of a Senate and House of Representatives.

Section 2. (1) The House of Representatives shall be composed of members chosen every second year by the people of the several States, and the electors in each State shall have the qualifications requisite for electors of the most numerous branch of the State legislature.

(2) No person shall be a Representative who shall not have attained to the age of twenty-five years, and been seven years a citizen of the United States, and who shall not, when elected, be an inhabitant of that State in which he shall be chosen.

(3) Representatives and direct taxes shall be apportioned among the several States which may be included within this Union, according to their respective numbers, [which shall be determined by adding to the whole number of free persons,] [1] including those bound to service for a term of years, and excluding Indians not taxed, [three fifth for all other persons].[2] The actual enumeration shall be made within three years after the first meeting of the Congress of the United States, and

within every subsequent term of ten years, in such manner as they shall by law direct. The number of Representatives shall not exceed one for every thirty thousand, but each State shall have at least one Representative; [and until such enumeration shall be made, the State of New Hampshire shall be entitled to choose three, Massachusetts eight, Rhode Island and Providence Plantations one, Connecticut five, New York six, New Jersey four, Pennsylvania eight, Delaware one, Maryland six, Virginia ten, North Carolina five, South Carolina five, and Georgia three.] [3]

(4) When vacancies happen in the representation from any State, the executive authority thereof shall issue writs of election to fill such vacancies.

(5) The House of Representatives shall choose their Speaker and other officers; and shall have the sole power of impeachment.

Section 3. [(1) The Senate of the United States shall be composed of two Senators from each State, chosen by the legislature thereof, for six years; and each Senator shall have one vote.] [4]

(2) Immediately after they shall be assembled in consequence of the first election, they shall be divided as equally as may be into three classes. The seats of the Senators of the first class shall be va-

[1] Modified by Fourteenth Amendment.
[2] Superseded by Fourteenth Amendment.

[3] Temporary provision.
[4] Superseded by Seventeenth Amendment.

tues oct 28 — 11:AM.

cated at the expiration of the second year, of the second class at the expiration of the fourth year, and of the third class at the expiration of the sixth year, so that one third may be chosen every second year; [and if vacancies happen by resignation, or otherwise, during the recess of the legislature of any State, the executive thereof may make temporary appointments until the next meeting of the legislature, which shall then fill such vacancies.] [5]

(3) No person shall be a Senator who shall not have attained to the age of thirty years, and been nine years a citizen of the United States, and who shall not, when elected, be an inhabitant of that State for which he shall be chosen.

(4) The Vice President of the United States shall be president of the Senate, but shall have no vote, unless they be equally divided.

(5) The Senate shall choose their other officers, and also a president pro tempore, in the absence of the Vice President, or when he shall exercise the office of President of the United States.

(6) The Senate shall have the sole power to try all impeachments. When sitting for that purpose, they shall be on oath or affirmation. When the President of the United States is tried, the Chief Justice shall preside: and no person shall be convicted without the concurrence of two thirds of the members present.

(7) Judgment in cases of impeachment shall not extend further than to removal from office, and disqualification to hold and enjoy any office of honor, trust, or profit under the United States: but the party convicted shall nevertheless be liable and subject to indictment, trial, judgment, and punishment, according to law.

Section 4. (1) The times, places, and manner of holding elections for Senators and Representatives shall be prescribed in each State by the legislature thereof; but the Congress may at any time by law make or alter such regulations, except as to the places of choosing Senators.

[(2) The Congress shall assemble at least once in every year, and such meeting shall be on the first Monday in December, unless they shall by law appoint a different day.] [6]

[5] Modified by Seventeenth Amendment.
[6] Superseded by Twentieth Amendment.

Section 5. (1) Each House shall be the judge of the elections, returns, and qualifications of its own members, and a majority of each shall constitute a quorum to do business; but a smaller number may adjourn from day to day, and may be authorized to compel the attendance of absent members, in such manner, and under such penalties, as each House may provide.

(2) Each House may determine the rules of its proceedings, punish its members for disorderly behavior, and, with the concurrence of two thirds, expel a member.

(3) Each House shall keep a journal of its proceedings, and from time to time publish the same, excepting such parts as may in their judgment require secrecy; and the yeas and nays of the members of either House on any question shall, at the desire of one fifth of those present, be entered on the journal.

(4) Neither House, during the session of Congress, shall, without the consent of the other, adjourn for more than three days, nor to any other place than that in which the two Houses shall be sitting.

Section 6. (1) The Senators and Representatives shall receive a compensation for their services, to be ascertained by law, and paid out of the Treasury of the United States. They shall in all cases, except treason, felony, and breach of the peace, be privileged from arrest during their attendance at the session of their respective Houses, and in going to and returning from the same; and for any speech or debate in either House, they shall not be questioned in any other place.

(2) No Senator or Representative shall, during the time for which he was elected, be appointed to any civil office under the authority of the United States, which shall have been created, or the emoluments whereof shall have been increased, during such time; and no person holding any office under the United States shall be a member of either House during his continuance in office.

Section 7. (1) All bills for raising revenue shall originate in the House of Representatives; but the Senate may propose or concur with amendments as on other bills.

(2) Every bill which shall have passed the House of Representatives and the Senate, shall, before it

Balance of power proposed here

removal of office by senate

Little Federalism state here power of senator over time for election

become a law, be presented to the President of the United States; if he approve he shall sign it, but if not he shall return it, with his objections, to that House in which it shall have originated, who shall enter the objections at large on their journal, and proceed to reconsider it. If after such reconsideration two thirds of that House shall agree to pass the bill, it shall be sent, together with the objections, to the other House, by which it shall likewise be reconsidered, and if approved by two thirds of that House, it shall become a law. But in all such cases the votes of both Houses shall be determined by yeas and nays, and the names of the persons voting for and against the bill shall be entered on the journal of each House respectively. If any bill shall not be returned by the President within ten days (Sundays excepted) after it shall have been presented to him, the same shall be a law, in like manner as if he had signed it, unless the Congress by their adjournment prevent its return, in which case it shall not be a law.

(3) Every order, resolution, or vote to which the concurrence of the Senate and House of Representatives may be necessary (except on a question of adjournment) shall be presented to the President of the United States; and before the same shall take effect, shall be approved by him, or being disapproved by him, shall be repassed by two thirds of the Senate and House of Representatives, according to the rules and limitations prescribed in the case of a bill.

Section 8. (1) The Congress shall have power to lay and collect taxes, duties, imposts, and excises, to pay the debts and provide for the common defense and general welfare of the United States; but all duties, imposts, and excises shall be uniform throughout the United States;

(2) To borrow money on the credit of the United States;

(3) To regulate commerce with foreign nations, and among the several States, and with the Indian tribes;

(4) To establish a uniform rule of naturalization, and uniform laws on the subject of bankruptcies throughout the United States;

(5) To coin money, regulate the value thereof, and of foreign coin, and fix the standard of weights and measures;

(6) To provide for the punishment of counterfeiting the securities and current coin of the United States;

(7) To establish post offices and post roads;

(8) To promote the progress of science and useful arts, by securing for limited times to authors and inventors the exclusive right to their respective writings and discoveries;

(9) To constitute tribunals inferior to the Supreme Court;

(10) To define and punish piracies and felonies committed on the high seas, and offenses against the law of nations;

(11) To declare war, grant letters of marque and reprisal, and make rules concerning captures on land and water;

(12) To raise and support armies, but no appropriation of money to that use shall be for a longer term than two years;

(13) To provide and maintain a navy;

(14) To make rules for the government and regulation of the land and naval forces;

(15) To provide for calling forth the militia to execute the laws of the Union, suppress insurrections, and repel invasions;

(16) To provide for organizing, arming, and disciplining the militia, and for governing such part of them as may be employed in the service of the United States, reserving to the States respectively the appointment of the officers, and the authority of training the militia according to the discipline prescribed by Congress;

(17) To exercise exclusive legislation in all cases whatsoever, over such district (not exceeding ten miles square) as may, by cession of particular States, and the acceptance of Congress, become the seat of the government of the United States, and to exercise like authority over all places purchased by the consent of the legislature of the State in which the same shall be, for the erection of forts, magazines, arsenals, dock-yards, and other needful buildings; and

(18) To make all laws which shall be necessary and proper for carrying into execution the foregoing powers, and all other powers vested by this Constitution in the government of the United States, or in any department or officer thereof.

Section 9. [(1) The migration or importation of such persons as any of the States now existing shall think proper to admit, shall not be prohibited by the Congress prior to the year one thousand eight hundred and eight, but a tax or duty may be imposed on such importation, not exceeding ten dollars for each person.] [7]

(2) The privilege of the writ of habeas corpus shall not be suspended, unless when in cases of rebellion or invasion the public safety may require it.

(3) No bill of attainder or ex post facto law shall be passed.

[(4) No capitation, or other direct, tax shall be laid, unless in proportion to the census or enumeration hereinbefore directed to be taken.] [8]

(5) No tax or duty shall be laid on articles exported from any State.

(6) No preference shall be given by any regulation of commerce or revenue to the ports of one State over those of another: nor shall vessels bound to, or from, one State, be obliged to enter, clear, or pay duties in another.

(7) No money shall be drawn from the Treasury, but in consequence of appropriations made by law; and a regular statement and account of the receipts and expenditures of all public money shall be published from time to time.

(8) No title of nobility shall be granted by the United States: and no person holding any office of profit or trust under them, shall, without the consent of the Congress, accept of any present, emolument, office, or title, of any kind whatever, from any king, prince, or foreign State.

Section 10. (1) No State shall enter into any treaty, alliance, or confederation; grant letters of marque and reprisal; coin money; emit bills of credit; make anything but gold and silver coin a tender in payment of debts; pass any bill of attainder, ex post facto law, or law impairing the obligation of contracts, or grant any title of nobility.

(2) No State shall, without the consent of the Congress, lay any imposts or duties on imports or exports, except what may be absolutely necessary for executing its inspection laws: and the net produce of all duties and imposts, laid by any

[7] Temporary provision.

[8] Modified by Sixteenth Amendment.

State on imports or exports, shall be for the use of the treasury of the United States; and all such laws shall be subject to the revision and control of the Congress.

(3) No State shall, without the consent of Congress, lay any duty of tonnage, keep troops, or ships of war in time of peace, enter into any agreement or compact with another State, or with a foreign power, or engage in war, unless actually invaded, or in such imminent danger as will not admit of delay.

Article II

Section 1. (1) The executive power shall be vested in a President of the United States of America. He shall hold his office during the term of four years, and, together with the Vice President, chosen for the same term, be elected, as follows:

(2) Each State shall appoint, in such manner as the legislature thereof may direct, a number of electors, equal to the whole number of Senators and Representatives to which the State may be entitled in the Congress: but no Senator or Representative, or person holding an office of trust or profit under the United States, shall be appointed an elector.

[The electors shall meet in their respective States, and vote by ballot for two persons, of whom one at least shall not be an inhabitant of the same State with themselves. And they shall make a list of all the persons voted for, and of the number of votes for each; which list they shall sign and certify, and transmit sealed to the seat of the government of the United States, directed to the president of the Senate. The president of the Senate shall, in the presence of the Senate and House of Representatives, open all the certificates, and the votes shall then be counted. The person having the greatest number of votes shall be the President, if such number be a majority of the whole number of electors appointed; and if there be more than one who have such majority, and have an equal number of votes, then the House of Representatives shall immediately choose by ballot one of them for President; and if no person have a majority, then from the five highest on the list the said House shall in like manner choose the President. But in choosing the President, the votes shall be taken by States, the representation from each State having one vote;

[handwritten: Art I Legislature Art II Presidency Art III Judiciary]

a quorum for this purpose shall consist of a member or members from two thirds of the States, and a majority of all the States shall be necessary to a choice. In every case, after the choice of the President, the person having the greatest number of votes of the electors shall be the Vice President. But if there should remain two or more who have equal votes, the Senate shall choose from them by ballot the Vice President.] [9]

(3) The Congress may determine the time of choosing the electors, and the day on which they shall give their votes; which day shall be the same throughout the United States.

(4) No person except a natural-born citizen, or a citizen of the United States, at the time of the adoption of this Constitution, shall be eligible to the office of President; neither shall any person be eligible to that office who shall not have attained to the age of thirty-five years, and been fourteen years a resident within the United States.

(5) In case of the removal of the President from office, or of his death, resignation, or inability to discharge the powers and duties of the said office, the same shall devolve on the Vice President, and the Congress may by law provide for the case of removal, death, resignation, or inability, both of the President and Vice President, declaring what officer shall then act as President, and such officer shall act accordingly, until the disability be removed, or a President shall be elected.

(6) The President shall, at stated times, receive for his services a compensation, which shall neither be increased nor diminished during the period for which he shall have been elected, and he shall not receive within that period any other emolument from the United States, or any of them.

(7) Before he enter on the execution of his office, he shall take the following oath or affirmation: "I do solemnly swear (or affirm) that I will faithfully execute the office of President of the United States, and will, to the best of my ability, preserve, protect, and defend the Constitution of the United States."

Section 2. (1) The President shall be commander in chief of the army and navy of the United States,

[9] This paragraph superseded by Twelfth Amendment, which, in turn, is modified by the Twentieth Amendment.

and of the militia of the several States, when called into the actual service of the United States; he may require the opinion, in writing, of the principal officer in each of the executive departments, upon any subject relating to the duties of their respective offices, and he shall have power to grant reprieves and pardons for offenses against the United States, except in cases of impeachment.

(2) He shall have power, by and with the advice and consent of the Senate, to make treaties, provided two thirds of the Senators present concur; and he shall nominate, and by and with the advice and consent of the Senate, shall appoint ambassadors, other public ministers and consuls, judges of the Supreme Court, and all other officers of the *[handwritten: check.]* United States, whose appointments are not herein otherwise provided for, and which shall be established by law: but the Congress may by law vest the appointment of such inferior officers, as they think proper, in the President alone, in the courts of law, or in the heads of departments.

(3) The President shall have power to fill up all vacancies that may happen during the recess of the Senate, by granting commissions which shall expire at the end of their next session.

Section 3. He shall from time to time give to the Congress information of the state of the Union, and recommend to their consideration such measures as he shall judge necessary and expedient; he may, on extraordinary occasions, convene both Houses, or either of them, and in case of disagreement between them, with respect to the time of adjournment, he may adjourn them to such time as he shall think proper; he shall receive ambassadors and other public ministers; he shall take care that the laws be faithfully executed, and shall commission all the officers of the United States.

Section 4. The President, Vice President, and all civil officers of the United States, shall be removed from office on impeachment for, and conviction of, treason, bribery, or other high crimes and misdemeanors.

Article III *[handwritten: Judicial]*

Section 1. The judicial power of the United States shall be vested in one Supreme Court, and in such inferior courts as the Congress may from time to time ordain and establish. The judges, both of the

Supreme and inferior courts, shall hold their offices during good behavior, and shall, at stated times, receive for their services a compensation, which shall not be diminished during their continuance in office.

Section 2. (1) The judicial power shall extend to all cases, in law and equity, arising under this Constitution, the laws of the United States, and treaties made, or which shall be made, under their authority;—to all cases affecting ambassadors, other public ministers, and consuls;—to all cases of admiralty and maritime jurisdiction;—to controversies to which the United States shall be a party;—to controversies between two or more States; [—between a State and citizens of another State;] [10]—between citizens of different States;—between citizens of the same State claiming lands under grants of different States, and between a State, or the citizens thereof, and foreign States, citizens, or subjects.

(2) In all cases affecting ambassadors, other public ministers, and consuls, and those in which a State shall be party, the Supreme Court shall have original jurisdiction. In all the other cases before mentioned, the Supreme Court shall have appellate jurisdiction, both as to law and fact, with such exceptions, and under such regulations, as the Congress shall make.

(3) The trial of all crimes, except in cases of impeachment, shall be by jury; and such trial shall be held in the State where the said crimes shall have been committed; but when not committed within any State, the trial shall be at such place or places as the Congress may by law have directed.

Section 3. (1) Treason against the United States shall consist only in levying war against them, or in adhering to their enemies, giving them aid and comfort. No person shall be convicted of treason unless on the testimony of two witnesses to the same overt act, or on confession in open court.

(2) The Congress shall have power to declare the punishment of treason, but no attainder of treason shall work corruption of blood, or forfeiture except during the life of the person attainted.

Article IV

Section 1. Full faith and credit shall be given in each State to the public acts, records, and judicial

proceedings of every other State. And the Congress may by general laws prescribe the manner in which such acts, records, and proceedings shall be proved, and the effect thereof.

Section 2. (1) The citizens of each State shall be entitled to all privileges and immunities of citizens in the several States.

(2) A person charged in any State with treason, felony, or other crime, who shall flee from justice, and be found in another State, shall, on demand of the executive authority of the State from which he fled, be delivered up, to be removed to the State having jurisdiction of the crime.

[(3) No person held to service or labor in one State, under the laws thereof, escaping into another, shall, in consequence of any law or regulation therein, be discharged from such service or labor, but shall be delivered up on claim of the party to whom such service or labor may be due.] [11]

Section 3. (1) New States may be admitted by the Congress into this Union; but no new State shall be formed or erected within the jurisdiction of any other State; nor any State be formed by the junction of two or more States, or parts of States, without the consent of the legislatures of the States concerned as well as of the Congress.

(2) The Congress shall have power to dispose of and make all needful rules and regulations respecting the territory or other property belonging to the United States; and nothing in this Constitution shall be so construed as to prejudice any claims of the United States, or of any particular State.

Section 4. The United States shall guarantee to every State in this Union a republican form of government, and shall protect each of them against invasion; and, on application of the legislature, or of the executive (when the legislature cannot be convened), against domestic violence.

Article V

The Congress, whenever two thirds of both Houses shall deem it necessary, shall propose amendments to this Constitution, or, on the application of the legislatures of two thirds of the several States, shall call a convention for proposing amendments which, in either case, shall be valid

---

[10] Limited by Eleventh Amendment.

[11] Superseded by Thirteenth Amendment so far as it relates to slaves.

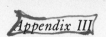

to all intents and purposes, as part of this Constitution, when ratified by the legislatures of three fourths of the several States, or by conventions in three fourths thereof, as the one or the other mode of ratification may be proposed by the Congress; provided [that no amendment which may be made prior to the year one thousand eight hundred and eight shall in any manner affect the first and fourth clauses in the ninth section of the first article; and] [12] that no State, without its consent, shall be deprived of its equal suffrage in the Senate.

Article VI

(1) All debts contracted and engagements entered into, before the adoption of this Constitution, shall be as valid against the United States under this Constitution, as under the Confederation.

(2) This Constitution, and the laws of the United States which shall be made in pursuance thereof; and all treaties made, or which shall be made, under the authority of the United States, shall be the supreme law of the land; and the judges in every State shall be bound thereby, anything in the constitution or laws of any State to the contrary notwithstanding.

(3) The Senators and Representatives before mentioned, and the members of the several State legislatures, and all executive and judicial officers, both of the United States and of the several States, shall be bound by oath or affirmation to support this Constitution; but no religious test shall ever be required as a qualification to any office or public trust under the United States.

Article VII

The ratification of the conventions of nine States shall be sufficient for the establishment of this Constitution between the States so ratifying the same.

Done in convention by the unanimous consent of the States present the seventeenth day of September in the year of our Lord one thousand seven hundred and eighty-seven, and of the independence of the United States of America the twelfth. In witness whereof, we have hereunto subscribed our names.

[12] Temporary provision.

AMENDMENTS

Article I

Congress shall make no law respecting an establishment of religion, or prohibiting the free exercise thereof; or abridging the freedom of speech, or of the press; or the right of the people peaceably to assemble, and to petition the government for a redress of grievances.

Article II

A well regulated militia, being necessary to the security of a free State, the right of the people to keep and bear arms shall not be infringed.

Article III

No soldier shall, in time of peace, be quartered in any house, without the consent of the owner, nor in time of war, but in a manner to be prescribed by law.

Article IV

The right of the people to be secure in their persons, houses, papers, and effects, against unreasonable searches and seizures, shall not be violated, and no warrants shall issue, but upon probable cause, supported by oath or affirmation, and particularly describing the place to be searched, and the persons or things to be seized.

Article V

No person shall be held to answer for a capital or otherwise infamous crime, unless on a presentment or indictment of a grand jury, except in cases arising in the land or naval forces, or in the militia, when in actual service in time of war or public danger; nor shall any person be subject for the same offence to be twice put in jeopardy of life or limb; nor shall be compelled in any criminal case to be a witness against himself, nor be deprived of life, liberty, or property, without due process of law; nor shall private property be taken for public use, without just compensation.

Article VI

In all criminal prosecutions the accused shall enjoy the right to a speedy and public trial, by an impartial jury of the State and district wherein the crime shall have been committed, which district shall have been previously ascertained by law, and to be informed of the nature and cause of the accusation; to be confronted with the witnesses against him; to have compulsory process for obtaining witnesses in his favor, and to have the assistance of counsel for his defense.

Article VII

In suits at common law, where the value in controversy shall exceed twenty dollars, the right of trial by jury shall be preserved, and no fact tried by a jury shall be otherwise re-examined in any court of the United States than according to the rules of the common law.

Article VIII

Excessive bail shall not be required, nor excessive fines imposed, nor cruel and unusual punishments inflicted.

Article IX

The enumeration in the Constitution of certain rights shall not be construed to deny or disparage others retained by the people.

Article X

The powers not delegated to the United States by the Constitution, nor prohibited by it to the States, are reserved to the States respectively, or to the people.[13]

Article XI [14]

The judicial power of the United States shall not be construed to extend to any suit in law or equity, commenced or prosecuted against one of the United States by citizens of another State, or by citizens or subjects of any foreign State.

Article XII [15]

The electors shall meet in their respective States, and vote by ballot for President and Vice President, one of whom, at least, shall not be an inhabitant of the same State with themselves; they shall name in their ballots the persons voted for as President, and

in distinct ballots the persons voted for as Vice President, and they shall make distinct lists of all persons voted for as President, and of all persons voted for as Vice President, and of the number of votes for each, which lists they shall sign and certify, and transmit sealed to the seat of the government of the United States, directed to the president of the Senate;—the president of the Senate shall, in the presence of the Senate and House of Representatives, open all the certificates, and the votes shall then be counted;—the person having the greatest number of votes for President, shall be the President, if such number be a majority of the whole number of electors appointed; and if no person have such majority, then from the persons having the highest numbers not exceeding three on the list of those voted for as President, the House of Representatives shall choose immediately, by ballot, the President. But in choosing the President, the votes shall be taken by States, the representation from each State having one vote; a quorum for this purpose shall consist of a member or members from two thirds of the States, and a majority of all the States shall be necessary to a choice. And if the House of Representatives shall not choose a President whenever the right of choice shall devolve upon them, before the fourth day of March next following, then the Vice President shall act as President, as in the case of the death or other constitutional disability of the President.—The person having the greatest number of votes as Vice President, shall be the Vice President, if such number be a majority of the whole number of electors appointed, and if no person have a majority, then from the two highest numbers on the list, the Senate shall choose the Vice President; a quorum for the purpose shall consist of two thirds of the whole number of Senators, and a majority of the whole number shall be necessary to a choice. But no person constitutionally ineligible to the office of President shall be eligible to that of Vice President of the United States.[16]

Article XIII [17]

Section 1. Neither slavery nor involuntary servitude, except as a punishment for crime whereof

---

[13] The first ten amendments appear to have been in force from Nov. 3, 1791.

[14] Proclaimed Jan. 8, 1798.

[15] Proclaimed Sept. 25, 1804.

[16] This amendment modified by the Twentieth.

[17] Proclaimed Dec. 18, 1865.

the party shall have been duly convicted, shall exist within the United States, or any place subject to their jurisdiction.

Section 2. Congress shall have power to enforce this article by appropriate legislation.

Article XIV [18]

Section 1. All persons born or naturalized in the United States, and subject to the jurisdiction thereof, are citizens of the United States and of the State wherein they reside. No State shall make or enforce any law which shall abridge the privileges or immunities of citizens of the United States; nor shall any State deprive any person of life, liberty, or property, without due process of law; nor deny to any person within its jurisdiction the equal protection of the laws.

Section 2. Representatives shall be apportioned among the several States according to their respective numbers, counting the whole number of persons in each State, excluding Indians not taxed. But when the right to vote at any election for the choice of electors for President and Vice President of the United States, Representatives in Congress, the executive and judicial officers of a State, or the members of the legislature thereof, is denied to any of the male inhabitants of such State, being twenty-one years of age, and citizens of the United States, or in any way abridged, except for participation in rebellion, or other crime, the basis of representation therein shall be reduced in the proportion which the number of such male citizens shall bear to the whole number of male citizens twenty-one years of age in such State.

Section 3. No person shall be a Senator or Representative in Congress, or elector of President and Vice President, or hold any office, civil or military, under the United States, or under any State, who, having previously taken an oath, as a member of Congress, or as an officer of the United States, or as a member of any State legislature, or as an executive or judicial officer of any State, to support the Constitution of the United States, shall have engaged in insurrection or rebellion against the same, or given aid or comfort to the enemies thereof. But Congress may by a vote of two thirds of each House, remove such disability.

[18] Proclaimed July 28, 1868.

Section 4. The validity of the public debt of the United States, authorized by law, including debts incurred for payment of pensions and bounties for services in suppressing insurrection or rebellion, shall not be questioned. But neither the United States nor any State shall assume or pay any debt or obligation incurred in aid of insurrection or rebellion against the United States, or any claim for the loss or emancipation of any slave; but all such debts, obligations, and claims shall be held illegal and void.

Section 5. The Congress shall have power to enforce, by appropriate legislation, the provisions of this article.

Article XV [19]

Section 1. The right of citizens of the United States to vote shall not be denied or abridged by the United States or by any State on account of race, color, or previous condition of servitude.

Section 2. The Congress shall have power to enforce this article by appropriate legislation.

Article XVI [20]

The Congress shall have power to lay and collect taxes on incomes, from whatever source derived, without apportionment among the several States, and without regard to any census or enumeration.

Article XVII [21]

The Senate of the United States shall be composed of two Senators from each State, elected by the people thereof, for six years; and each Senator shall have one vote. The electors in each State shall have the qualifications requisite for electors of the most numerous branch of the State legislature.

When vacancies happen in the representation of any State in the Senate, the executive authority of such State shall issue writs of election to fill such vacancies:

Provided, That the legislature of any State may empower the executive thereof to make temporary

[19] Proclaimed Mar. 30, 1870.

[20] Passed July, 1909, proclaimed Feb. 25, 1913.

[21] Passed May, 1912, in lieu of Article I, Section 3, Clause I, of the Constitution and so much of clause 2 of the same Section as relates to the filling of vacancies; proclaimed May 31, 1913.

appointments until the people fill the vacancies by election as the legislature may direct.

This amendment shall not be so construed as to affect the election or term of any Senator chosen before it becomes valid as part of the Constitution.

Article XVIII [22]

Section 1. After one year from the ratification of this article the manufacture, sale, or transportation of intoxicating liquors within, the importation thereof into, or the exportation thereof from the United States and all territory subject to the jurisdiction thereof for beverage purposes is hereby prohibited.

Section 2. The Congress and the several States shall have concurrent power to enforce this article by appropriate legislation.

Section 3. This article shall be inoperative unless it shall have been ratified as an amendment to the Constitution by the legislatures of the several States, as provided in the Constitution, within seven years from the date of the submission hereof to the States by the Congress.

Article XIX [23]

(1) The right of citizens of the United States to vote shall not be denied or abridged by the United States or by any State on account of sex.

(2) Congress shall have power, by appropriate legislation, to enforce the provisions of this article.

Article XX [24]

Section 1. The terms of the President and Vice President shall end at noon on the 20th day of January, and the terms of Senators and Representatives at noon on the 3rd day of January, of the years in which such terms would have ended if this article had not been ratified; and the terms of their successors shall then begin.

Section 2. The Congress shall assemble at least once in every year, and such meeting shall begin at noon on the 3rd day of January, unless they shall by law appoint a different day.

Section 3. If, at the time fixed for the beginning of the term of the President, the President elect shall have died, the Vice President elect shall become President. If a President shall not have been chosen before the time fixed for the beginning of his term, or if the President elect shall have failed to qualify, then the Vice President elect shall act as President until a President shall have qualified; and the Congress may by law provide for the case wherein neither a President elect nor a Vice President elect shall have qualified, declaring who shall then act as President, or the manner in which one who is to act shall be selected, and such person shall act accordingly until a President or Vice President shall have qualified.

Section 4. The Congress may by law provide for the case of the death of any of the persons from whom the House of Representatives may choose a President whenever the right of choice shall have devolved upon them, and for the case of the death of any of the persons from whom the Senate may choose a Vice President whenever the right of choice shall have devolved upon them.

Section 5. Sections 1 and 2 shall take effect on the 15th day of October following the ratification of this article.

Section 6. This article shall be inoperative unless it shall have been ratified as an amendment to the Constitution by the legislatures of three fourths of the several States within seven years from the date of its submission.

Article XXI [25]

Section 1. The eighteenth article of amendment to the Constitution of the United States is hereby repealed.

Section 2. The transportation or importation into any State, Territory, or possession of the United States for delivery or use therein of intoxicating liquors, in violation of the laws thereof, is hereby prohibited.

Section 3. This article shall be inoperative unless it shall have been ratified as an amendment to the Constitution by conventions in the several States, as provided in the Constitution, within seven years

[22] Passed Dec. 3, 1917; proclaimed Jan. 29, 1919. Repealed by the Twenty-first Amendment.

[23] Proclaimed Aug. 26, 1920.

[24] Proclaimed Feb. 6, 1933.

[25] Proclaimed Dec. 5, 1933. This amendment was ratified by state conventions.

from the date of submission hereof to the States by the Congress.

Article XXII [26]

Section 1. No person shall be elected to the office of the President more than twice, and no person who has held the office of President, or acted as President, for more than two years of a term to which some other person was elected President shall be elected to the office of the President more than once. But this Article shall not apply to any person holding the office of President when this Article was proposed by the Congress, and shall not prevent any person who may be holding the office of President, or acting as President, during the term within which this Article becomes operative from holding the office of President, or acting as President during the remainder of such term.

Section 2. This Article shall be inoperative unless it shall have been ratified as an amendment to the Constitution by the legislatures of three-fourths of the several States within seven years from the date of its submission to the States by the Congress.[27]

[26] Adopted Feb. 27, 1951.

[27] Five amendments have been proposed but not ratified. The first and second were proposed on Sept. 25, 1789, along with ten others which became the Bill of Rights. The first of these dealt with the apportionment of members of the House of Representatives. It was ratified by ten states, eleven being the necessary three-fourths. The second provided that "No law, varying the compensation for the services of the Senators and Representatives, shall take effect, until an election of Representatives shall have intervened." It was ratified by six states, eleven being necessary. A third was proposed on May 1, 1810, which would have abrogated the citizenship of any persons accepting foreign titles or honors. It was ratified by twelve states, fourteen being necessary. A fourth was proposed on Mar. 4, 1861, which prohibited the adoption of any amendment "to abolish or interfere, within any state, with the domestic institutions thereof, including that of persons held to labor or service by the laws of that state." This was approved by three states. The fifth, the proposed child-labor amendment, was proposed on June 2, 1924. It provides:

Section 1—The Congress shall have power to limit, regulate, and prohibit the labor of persons under eighteen years of age.

Section 2—The power of the several States is unimpaired by this article except that the operation of State laws shall be suspended to the extent necessary to give effect to legislation enacted by Congress.

This has been ratified by twenty-eight states and rejected in eleven. The approval of thirty-six states is necessary to complete ratification.

APPENDIX IV

Charter of the United Nations

We the peoples of the United Nations determined to save succeeding generations from the scourge of war, which twice in our lifetime has brought untold sorrow to mankind, and to reaffirm faith in fundamental human rights, in the dignity and worth of the human person, in the equal rights of men and women and of nations large and small, and to establish conditions under which justice and respect for the obligations arising from treaties and other sources of international law can be maintained, and to promote social progress and better standards of life in larger freedom, *and for these ends* to practice tolerance and live together in peace with one another as good neighbors, and to unite our strength to maintain international peace and security, and to ensure, by the acceptance of principles and the institution of methods, that armed force shall not be used, save in the common interest, and to employ international machinery for the promotion of the economic and social advancement of all peoples, *have resolved to combine our efforts to accomplish these aims.*

Accordingly, our respective Governments, through representatives assembled in the city of San Francisco, who have exhibited their full powers found to be in good and due form, have agreed to the present Charter of the United Nations and do hereby establish an international organization to be known as the United Nations.

CHAPTER I. Purposes and Principles

Article 1

The Purposes of the United Nations are:

1. To maintain international peace and security, and to that end: to take effective collective measures for the prevention and removal of threats to the peace, and for the suppression of acts of aggression or other breaches of the peace, and to bring about by peaceful means, and in conformity with the principles of justice and international law, adjustment or settlement of international disputes or situations which might lead to breach of the peace;

2. To develop friendly relations among nations based on respect for the principle of equal rights and self-determination of peoples, and to take other appropriate measures to strengthen universal peace;

3. To achieve international cooperation in solving international problems of an economic, social, cultural, or humanitarian character, and in promoting and encouraging respect for human rights and for fundamental freedoms for all without distinction as to race, sex, language, or religion; and

4. To be a center for harmonizing the actions of nations in the attainment of these common ends.

Article 2

The Organization and its Members, in pursuit of the Purposes stated in Article 1, shall act in accordance with the following Principles.

1. The Organization is based on the principle of the sovereign equality of all its Members.

2. All Members, in order to ensure to all of them the rights and benefits resulting from membership, shall fulfil in good faith the obligations assumed by them in accordance with the present Charter.

3. All Members shall settle their international disputes by peaceful means in such a manner that international peace and security, and justice, are not endangered.

4. All Members shall refrain in their international relations from the threat or use of force against the territorial integrity or political independence of any state, or in any other manner inconsistent with the Purposes of the United Nations.

5. All Members shall give the United Nations every assistance in any action it takes in accordance with the present Charter, and shall refrain from giving assistance to any state against which the United Nations is taking preventive or enforcement action.

6. The Organization shall ensure that states which are not Members of the United Nations act in accordance with these Principles so far as may be necessary for the maintenance of international peace and security.

7. Nothing contained in the present Charter shall authorize the United Nations to intervene in matters which are essentially within the domestic jurisdiction of any state or shall require the Members to submit such matters to settlement under the present Charter; but this principle shall not prejudice the application of enforcement measures under Chapter VII.

CHAPTER II. Membership

Article 3

The original Members of the United Nations shall be the states which, having participated in the United Nations Conference on International Organization at San Francisco, or having previously signed the Declaration by United Nations of January 1, 1942, sign the present Charter and ratify it in accordance with Article 110.

Article 4

1. Membership in the United Nations is open to all other peace-loving states which accept the obligations contained in the present Charter and, in the judgment of the Organization, are able and willing to carry out these obligations.

2. The admission of any such state to membership in the United Nations will be effected by a decision of the General Assembly upon the recommendation of the Security Council.

Article 5

A Member of the United Nations against which preventive or enforcement action has been taken by the Security Council may be suspended from the exercise of the rights and privileges of membership by the General Assembly upon the recommendation of the Security Council. The exercise of these rights and privileges may be restored by the Security Council.

Article 6

A Member of the United Nations which has persistently violated the Principles contained in the present Charter may be expelled from the Organization by the General Assembly upon the recommendation of the Security Council.

CHAPTER III. Organs

Article 7

1. There are established as the principal organs of the United Nations: a General Assembly, a Security Council, an Economic and Social Council, a Trusteeship Council, an International Court of Justice, and a Secretariat.

2. Such subsidiary organs as may be found necessary may be established in accordance with the present Charter.

Article 8

The United Nations shall place no restrictions on the eligibility of men and women to participate in any capacity and under conditions of equality in its principal and subsidiary organs.

CHAPTER IV. The General Assembly

COMPOSITION

Article 9

1. The General Assembly shall consist of all the Members of the United Nations.

2. Each Member shall have not more than five representatives in the General Assembly.

FUNCTIONS AND POWERS

Article 10

The General Assembly may discuss any questions or any matters within the scope of the present Charter or relating to the powers and functions of any organs provided for in the present Charter, and, except as provided in Article 12, may make recommendations to the Members of the United Nations or to the Security Council or to both on any such questions or matters.

Article 11

1. The General Assembly may consider the general principles of cooperation in the maintenance of international peace and security, including the principles governing disarmament and the regulation of armaments, and may make recommendations with regard to such principles to the Members or to the Security Council or to both.

2. The General Assembly may discuss any questions relating to the maintenance of international peace and security brought before it by any Member of the United Nations, or by the Security Council, or by a state which is not a Member of the United Nations in accordance with Article 35, paragraph 2, and, except as provided in Article 12, may make recommendations with regard to any such questions to the state or states concerned or to the Security Council or to both. Any such question on which action is necessary shall be referred to the Security Council by the General Assembly either before or after discussion.

3. The General Assembly may call the attention of the Security Council to situations which are likely to endanger international peace and security.

4. The powers of the General Assembly set forth in this Article shall not limit the general scope of Article 10.

Article 12

1. While the Security Council is exercising in respect of any dispute or situation the functions assigned to it in the present Charter, the General Assembly shall not make any recommendation with regard to that dispute or situation unless the Security Council so requests.

2. The Secretary-General, with the consent of the Security Council, shall notify the General Assembly at each session of any matters relative to the maintenance of international peace and security which are being dealt with by the Security Council and shall similarly notify the General Assembly, or the Members of the United Nations if the General Assembly is not in session, immediately the Security Council ceases to deal with such matters.

Article 13

1. The General Assembly shall initiate studies and make recommendations for the purpose of:

a. promoting international cooperation in the political field and encouraging the progressive development of international law and its codification;

b. promoting international cooperation in the economic, social, cultural, educational, and health fields, and assisting in the realization of human rights and fundamental freedoms for all without distinction as to race, sex, language, or religion.

2. The further responsibilities, functions, and powers of the General Assembly with respect to matters mentioned in paragraph 1 (b) above are set forth in Chapters IX and X.

Article 14

Subject to the provisions of Article 12, the General Assembly may recommend measures for the peaceful adjustment of any situation, regardless of origin, which it deems likely to impair the general welfare or friendly relations among nations, including situations resulting from a violation of the provisions of the present Charter setting forth the Purposes and Principles of the United Nations.

Article 15

1. The General Assembly shall receive and consider annual and special reports from the Security Council; these reports shall include an account of the measures that the Security Council has decided upon or taken to maintain international peace and security.

2. The General Assembly shall receive and consider reports from the other organs of the United Nations.

Article 16

The General Assembly shall perform such functions with respect to the international trusteeship system as are assigned to it under Chapters XII and XIII, including the approval of the trusteeship agreements for areas not designated as strategic.

Article 17

1. The General Assembly shall consider and approve the budget of the Organization.

2. The expenses of the Organization shall be borne by the Members as apportioned by the General Assembly.

3. The General Assembly shall consider and approve any financial and budgetary arrangements with specialized agencies referred to in Article 57 and shall examine the administrative budgets of such specialized agencies with a view to making recommendations to the agencies concerned.

VOTING

Article 18

1. Each member of the General Assembly shall have one vote.

2. Decisions of the General Assembly on important questions shall be made by a two-thirds majority of the members present and voting. These questions shall include: recommendations with respect to the maintenance of international peace and security, the election of the non-permanent members of the Security Council, the election of the members of the Economic and Social Council, the election of members of the Trusteeship Council in accordance with paragraph 1 (c) of Article 86, the admission of new Members to the United Nations, the suspension of the rights and privileges of membership, the expulsion of Members, questions relating to the operation of the trusteeship system, and budgetary questions.

3. Decisions on other questions, including the determination of additional categories of questions to be decided by a two-thirds majority, shall be made by a majority of the members present and voting.

Article 19

A Member of the United Nations which is in arrears in the payment of its financial contributions to the Organization shall have no vote in the General Assembly if the amount of its arrears equals or exceeds the amount of the contributions due from it for the preceding two full years. The General Assembly may, nevertheless, permit such a Member to vote if it is satisfied that the failure to pay is due to conditions beyond the control of the Member.

PROCEDURE

Article 20

The General Assembly shall meet in regular annual sessions and in such special sessions as occasion may require. Special sessions shall be convoked by the Secretary-General at the request of the Security Council or of a majority of the Members of the United Nations.

Article 21

The General Assembly shall adopt its own rules of procedure. It shall elect its President for each session.

Article 22

The General Assembly may establish such subsidiary organs as it deems necessary for the performance of its functions.

CHAPTER V. The Security Council

COMPOSITION

Article 23

1. The Security Council shall consist of eleven Members of the United Nations. The Republic of China, France, the Union of Soviet Socialist Republics, the United Kingdom of Great Britain and Northern Ireland, and the United States of America shall be permanent members of the Security Council. The General Assembly shall elect six other Members of the United Nations to be non-permanent members of the Security Council, due regard being specially paid, in the first instance to the contribution of Members of the United Nations to the maintenance of international peace and security and to the other purposes of the Organization, and also to equitable geographical distribution.

2. The non-permanent members of the Security

Council shall be elected for a term of two years. In the first election of the non-permanent members, however, three shall be chosen for a term of one year. A retiring member shall not be eligible for immediate re-election.

3. Each member of the Security Council shall have one representative.

FUNCTIONS AND POWERS

Article 24

1. In order to ensure prompt and effective action by the United Nations, its Members confer on the Security Council primary responsibility for the maintenance of international peace and security, and agree that in carrying out its duties under this responsibility the Security Council acts on their behalf.

2. In discharging these duties the Security Council shall act in accordance with the Purposes and Principles of the United Nations. The Specific powers granted to the Security Council for the discharge of these duties are laid down in Chapters VI, VII, VIII, and XII.

3. The Security Council shall submit annual and, when necessary, special reports to the General Assembly for its consideration.

Article 25

The Members of the United Nations agree to accept and carry out the decisions of the Security Council in accordance with the present Charter.

Article 26

In order to promote the establishment and maintenance of international peace and security with the least diversion for armaments of the world's human and economic resources, the Security Council shall be responsible for formulating, with the assistance of the Military Staff Committee referred to in Article 47, plans to be submitted to the Members of the United Nations for the establishment of a system for the regulation of armaments.

VOTING

Article 27

1. Each member of the Security Council shall have one vote.

2. Decisions of the Security Council on procedural matters shall be made by an affirmative vote of seven members.

3. Decisions of the Security Council on all other matters shall be made by an affirmative vote of seven members including the concurring votes of the permanent members; provided that, in decisions under Chapter VI, and under paragraph 3 of Article 52, a party to a dispute shall abstain from voting.

PROCEDURE

Article 28

1. The Security Council shall be so organized as to be able to function continuously. Each member of the Security Council shall for this purpose be represented at all times at the seat of the Organization.

2. The Security Council shall hold periodic meetings at which each of its members may, if it so desires, be represented by a member of the government or by some other specially designated representative.

3. The Security Council may hold meetings at such places other than the seat of the Organization as in its judgment will best facilitate its work.

Article 29

The Security Council may establish such subsidiary organs as it deems necessary for the performance of its functions.

Article 30

The Security Council shall adopt its own rules of procedure, including the method of selecting its President.

Article 31

Any Member of the United Nations which is not a member of the Security Council may participate, without vote, in the discussion of any question brought before the Security Council whenever the latter considers that the interests of that Member are specially affected.

Article 32

Any Member of the United Nations which is not a member of the Security Council or any state which is not a Member of the United Nations, if it is a party to a dispute under consideration by the Security Council, shall be invited to participate, without vote, in the discussion relating to the dispute. The Security Council shall lay down such conditions as it deems just for the participation of a state which is not a Member of the United Nations.

CHAPTER VI. Pacific Settlement of Disputes

Article 33

1. The parties to any dispute, the continuance of which is likely to endanger the maintenance of international peace and security, shall, first of all, seek a solution by negotiation, enquiry, mediation, conciliation, arbitration, judicial settlement, resort to regional agencies or arrangements, or other peaceful means of their own choice.

2. The Security Council shall, when it deems necessary, call upon the parties to settle their dispute by such means.

Article 34

The Security Council may investigate any dispute, or any situation which might lead to international friction or give rise to a dispute, in order to determine whether the continuance of the dispute or situation is likely to endanger the maintenance of international peace and security.

Article 35

1. Any Member of the United Nations may bring any dispute, or any situation of the nature referred to in Article 34, to the attention of the Security Council or of the General Assembly.

2. A state which is not a member of the United Nations may bring to the attention of the Security Council or of the General Assembly any dispute to which it is a party if it accepts in advance, for the purposes of the dispute, the obligations of pacific settlement provided in the present Charter.

3. The proceedings of the General Assembly in respect of matters brought to its attention under this Article will be subject to the provisions of Articles 11 and 12.

Article 36

1. The Security Council may, at any stage of a dispute of the nature referred to in Article 33 or of a situation of like nature, recommend appropriate procedures or methods of adjustment.

2. The Security Council should take into consideration any procedures for the settlement of the dispute which have already been adopted by the parties.

3. In making recommendations under this Article the Security Council should also take into consideration that legal disputes should as a general rule be referred by the parties to the International Court of Justice in accordance with the provisions of the Statute of the Court.

Article 37

1. Should the parties to a dispute of the nature referred to in Article 33 fail to settle it by the means indicated in that Article, they shall refer it to the Security Council.

2. If the Security Council deems that the continuance of the dispute is in fact likely to endanger the maintenance of international peace and security, it shall decide whether to take action under Article 36 or to recommend such terms of settlement as it may consider appropriate.

Article 38

Without prejudice to the provisions of Articles 33 to 37, the Security Council may, if all the parties to any dispute so request, make recommendations to the parties with a view to a pacific settlement of the dispute.

CHAPTER VII. Action with Respect to Threats to the Peace, Breaches of the Peace, and Acts of Aggression

Article 39

The Security Council shall determine the existence of any threat to the peace, breach of the peace, or act of aggression and shall make recommendations, or decide what measures shall be taken in accordance with Articles 41 and 42, to maintain or restore international peace and security.

Article 40

In order to prevent an aggravation of the situation, the Security Council may, before making the recommendations or deciding upon the measures provided for in Article 39, call upon the parties concerned to comply with such provisional measures as it deems necessary or desirable. Such provisional measures shall be without prejudice to the rights, claims, or position of the parties concerned. The Security Council shall duly take account of failure to comply with such provisional measures.

Article 41

The Security Council may decide what measures not involving the use of armed force are to be employed to give effect to its decisions, and it may call upon the Members of the United Nations to apply such measures. These may include complete or partial interruption of economic relations and of rail, sea, air, postal, telegraphic, radio, and other means of communication, and the severance of diplomatic relations.

Article 42

Should the Security Council consider that measures provided for in Article 41 would be inadequate or have proved to be inadequate, it may take such action by air, sea, or land forces as may be necessary to maintain or restore international peace and security. Such action may include demonstrations, blockade, and other operations by air, sea, or land forces of Members of the United Nations.

Article 43

1. All Members of the United Nations, in order to contribute to the maintenance of international peace and security, undertake to make available to the Security Council, on its call and in accordance with a special agreement or agreements, armed forces, assistance, and facilities, including rights of passage, necessary for the purpose of maintaining international peace and security.

2. Such agreement or agreements shall govern the numbers and types of forces, their degree of readiness and general location, and the nature of the facilities and assistance to be provided.

3. The agreement or agreements shall be negotiated as soon as possible on the initiative of the Security Council. They shall be concluded between the Security Council and Members or between the Security Council and groups of Members and shall be subject to ratification by the signatory states in accordance with their respective constitutional processes.

Article 44

When the Security Council has decided to use force it shall, before calling upon a Member not represented on it to provide armed forces in fulfillment of the obligations assumed under Article 43, invite that Member, if the Member so desires, to participate in the decisions of the Security Council concerning the employment of contingents of that Member's armed forces.

Article 45

In order to enable the United Nations to take urgent military measures, Members shall hold immediately available national air-force contingents for combined international enforcement action. The strength and degree of readiness of these contingents and plans for their combined action shall be determined, within the limits laid down in the special agreement or agreements referred to in Article 43, by the Security Council with the assistance of the Military Staff Committee.

Article 46

Plans for the application of armed force shall be made by the Security Council with the assistance of the Military Staff Committee.

Article 47

1. There shall be established a Military Staff Committee to advise and assist the Security Council on all questions relating to the Security Council's military requirements for the maintenance of international peace and security, the employment and command of forces placed at its disposal, the regulation of armaments, and possible disarmament.

2. The Military Staff Committee shall consist of the Chiefs of Staff of the permanent members of the Security Council or their representatives. Any Member of the United Nations not permanently represented on the Committee shall be invited by the Committee to be associated with it when the

efficient discharge of the Committee's responsibilities requires the participation of that Member in its work.

3. The Military Staff Committee shall be responsible under the Security Council for the strategic direction of any armed forces placed at the disposal of the Security Council. Questions relating to the command of such forces shall be worked out subsequently.

4. The Military Staff Committee, with the authorization of the Security Council and after consultation with appropriate regional agencies, may establish regional subcommittees.

Article 48

1. The action required to carry out the decisions of the Security Council for the maintenance of international peace and security shall be taken by all the Members of the United Nations or by some of them, as the Security Council may determine.

2. Such decisions shall be carried out by the Members of the United Nations directly and through their action in the appropriate international agencies of which they are members.

Article 49

The Members of the United Nations shall join in affording mutual assistance in carrying out the measures decided upon by the Security Council.

Article 50

If preventive or enforcement measures against any state are taken by the Security Council, any other state, whether a Member of the United Nations or not, which finds itself confronted with special economic problems arising from the carrying out of those measures shall have the right to consult the Security Council with regard to a solution of those problems.

Article 51

Nothing in the present Charter shall impair the inherent right of individual or collective self-defense if an armed attack occurs against a Member of the United Nations, until the Security Council has taken the measures necessary to maintain international peace and security. Measures taken by Members in the exercise of this right of self-defense shall be immediately reported to the Security Council and shall not in any way affect the authority and responsibility of the Security Council under the present Charter to take at any time such action as it deems necessary in order to maintain or restore international peace and security.

CHAPTER VIII. Regional Arrangements

Article 52

1. Nothing in the present Charter precludes the existence of regional arrangements or agencies for dealing with such matters relating to the maintenance of international peace and security as are appropriate for regional action, provided that such arrangements or agencies and their activities are consistent with the Purposes and Principles of the United Nations.

2. The Members of the United Nations entering into such arrangements or constituting such agencies shall make every effort to achieve pacific settlement of local disputes through such regional arrangements or by such regional agencies before referring them to the Security Council.

3. The Security Council shall encourage the development of pacific settlement of local disputes through such regional arrangements or by such regional agencies either on the initiative of the states concerned or by reference from the Security Council.

4. This Article in no way impairs the application of Articles 34 and 35.

Article 53

1. The Security Council shall, where appropriate, utilize such regional arrangements or agencies for enforcement action under its authority. But no enforcement action shall be taken under regional arrangements or by regional agencies without the authorization of the Security Council, with the exception of measures against any enemy state, as defined in paragraph 2 of this Article, provided for pursuant to Article 107 or in regional arrangements directed against renewal of aggressive policy on the part of any such state, until such time as the Organization may, on request of the Governments concerned, be charged with the responsibility for preventing further aggression by such a state.

2. The term enemy state as used in paragraph 1 of this Article applies to any state which during the Second World War has been an enemy of any signatory of the present Charter.

Article 54

The Security Council shall at all times be kept fully informed of activities undertaken or in contemplation under regional arrangements or by regional agencies for the maintenance of international peace and security.

CHAPTER IX. International Economic and Social Cooperation

Article 55

With a view to the creation of conditions of stability and well-being which are necessary for peaceful and friendly relations among nations based on respect for the principle of equal rights and self-determination of peoples, the United Nations shall promote:

a. higher standards of living, full employment, and conditions of economic and social progress and development;

b. solutions of international economic, social, health, and related problems; and international cultural and educational cooperation; and

c. universal respect for, and observance of, human rights and fundamental freedoms for all without distinction as to race, sex, language, or religion.

Article 56

All Members pledge themselves to take joint and separate action in cooperation with the Organization for the achievement of the purposes set forth in Article 55.

Article 57

1. The various specialized agencies, established by intergovernmental agreement and having wide international responsibilities, as defined in their basic instruments, in economic, social, cultural, educational, health, and related fields, shall be brought into relationship with the United Nations in accordance with the provisions of Article 63.

2. Such agencies thus brought into relationship with the United Nations are hereinafter referred to as specialized agencies.

Article 58

The Organization shall make recommendations for the coordination of the policies and activities of the specialized agencies.

Article 59

The Organization shall, where appropriate, initiate negotiations among the states concerned for the creation of any new specialized agencies required for the accomplishment of the purposes set forth in Article 55.

Article 60

Responsibility for the discharge of the functions of the Organization set forth in this Chapter shall be vested in the General Assembly and, under the authority of the General Assembly, in the Economic and Social Council, which shall have for this purpose the powers set forth in Chapter X.

CHAPTER X. The Economic and Social Council

COMPOSITION

Article 61

1. The Economic and Social Council shall consist of eighteen Members of the United Nations elected by the General Assembly.

2. Subject to the provisions of paragraph 3, six members of the Economic and Social Council shall be elected each year for a term of three years. A retiring member shall be eligible for immediate reelection.

3. At the first election, eighteen members of the Economic and Social Council shall be chosen. The term of office of six members so chosen shall expire at the end of one year, and of six other members at the end of two years, in accordance with arrangements made by the General Assembly.

4. Each member of the Economic and Social Council shall have one representative.

FUNCTIONS AND POWERS

Article 62

1. The Economic and Social Council may make or initiate studies and reports with respect to in-

ternational economic, social, cultural, educational, health, and related matters and may make recommendations with respect to any such matters to the General Assembly, to the Members of the United Nations, and to the specialized agencies concerned.

2. It may make recommendations for the purpose of promoting respect for, and observance of, human rights and fundamental freedoms for all.

3. It may prepare draft conventions for submission to the General Assembly, with respect to matters falling within its competence.

4. It may call, in accordance with the rules prescribed by the United Nations, international conferences on matters falling within its competence.

Article 63

1. The Economic and Social Council may enter into agreements with any of the agencies referred to in Article 57, defining the terms on which the agency concerned shall be brought into relationship with the United Nations. Such agreements shall be subject to approval by the General Assembly.

2. It may coordinate the activities of the specialized agencies through consultation with and recommendations to such agencies and through recommendations to the General Assembly and to the Members of the United Nations.

Article 64

1. The Economic and Social Council may take appropriate steps to obtain regular reports from the specialized agencies. It may make arrangements with the Members of the United Nations and with the specialized agencies to obtain reports on the steps taken to give effect to its own recommendations and to recommendations on matters falling within its competence made by the General Assembly.

2. It may communicate its observations on these reports to the General Assembly.

Article 65

The Economic and Social Council may furnish information to the Security Council and shall assist the Security Council upon its request.

Article 66

1. The Economic and Social Council shall perform such functions as fall within its competence

in connection with the carrying out of the recommendations of the General Assembly.

2. It may, with the approval of the General Assembly, perform services at the request of Members of the United Nations and at the request of specialized agencies.

3. It shall perform such other functions as are specified elsewhere in the present Charter or as may be assigned to it by the General Assembly.

VOTING

Article 67

1. Each member of the Economic and Social Council shall have one vote.

2. Decisions of the Economic and Social Council shall be made by a majority of the members present and voting.

PROCEDURE

Article 68

The Economic and Social Council shall set up commissions in economic and social fields and for the promotion of human rights, and such other commissions as may be required for the performance of its functions.

Article 69

The Economic and Social Council shall invite any Member of the United Nations to participate, without vote, in its deliberations on any matter of particular concern to that Member.

Article 70

The Economic and Social Council may make arrangements for representatives of the specialized agencies to participate, without vote, in its deliberations and in those of the commissions established by it, and for its representatives to participate in the deliberations of the specialized agencies.

Article 71

The Economic and Social Council may make suitable arrangements for consultation with non-governmental organizations which are concerned with matters within its competence. Such arrangements may be made with international organizations and, where appropriate, with national organizations after consultation with the Member of the United Nations concerned.

Article 72

1. The Economic and Social Council shall adopt its own rules of procedure, including the method of selecting its President.

2. The Economic and Social Council shall meet as required in accordance with its rules, which shall include provision for the convening of meetings on the request of a majority of its members.

CHAPTER XI. Declaration Regarding Non-Self-Governing Territories

Article 73

Members of the United Nations which have or assume responsibilities for the administration of territories whose peoples have not yet attained a full measure of self-government recognize the principle that the interests of the inhabitants of these territories are paramount, and accept as a sacred trust the obligation to promote to the utmost, within the system of international peace and security established by the present Charter, the well-being of the inhabitants of these territories, and, to this end:

a. to ensure, with due respect for the culture of the peoples concerned, their political, economic, social, and educational advancement, their just treatment, and their protection against abuses:

b. to develop self-government, to take due account of the political aspirations of the peoples, and to assist them in the progressive development of their free political institutions, according to the particular circumstances of each territory and its peoples and their varying stages of advancement;

c. to further international peace and security;

d. to promote constructive measures of development, to encourage research, and to cooperate with one another and, when and where appropriate, with specialized international bodies with a view to the practical achievement of the social, economic, and scientific purposes set forth in this Article; and

e. to transmit regularly to the Secretary-General for information purposes, subject to such limitation as security and constitutional considerations may require, statistical and other information of a tech-

nical nature relating to economic, social, and educational conditions in the territories for which they are respectively responsible other than those territories to which Chapters XII and XIII apply.

Article 74

Members of the United Nations also agree that their policy in respect of the territories to which this Chapter applies, no less than in respect of their metropolitan areas, must be based on the general principle of good-neighborliness, due account being taken of the interests and well-being of the rest of the world, in social, economic, and commercial matters.

CHAPTER XII. International Trusteeship System

Article 75

The United Nations shall establish under its authority an international trusteeship system for the administration and supervision of such territories as may be placed thereunder by subsequent individual agreements. These territories are hereinafter referred to as trust territories.

Article 76

The basic objectives of the trusteeship system, in accordance with the Purposes of the United Nations laid down in Article 1 of the present Charter, shall be:

a. to further international peace and security;

b. to promote the political, economic, social, and educational advancement of the inhabitants of the trust territories, and their progressive development towards self-government or independence as may be appropriate to the particular circumstances of each territory and its peoples and the freely expressed wishes of the peoples concerned, and as may be provided by the terms of each trusteeship agreement;

c. to encourage respect for human rights and for fundamental freedoms for all without distinction as to race, sex, language, or religion, and to encourage recognition of the interdependence of the peoples of the world; and

d. to ensure equal treatment in social, economic, and commercial matters for all Members of the

United Nations and their nationals, and also equal treatment for the latter in the administration of justice, without prejudice to the attainment of the foregoing objectives and subject to the provisions of Article 80.

Article 77

1. The trusteeship system shall apply to such territories in the following categories as may be placed thereunder by means of trusteeship agreements:

a. territories now held under mandate;

b. territories which may be detached from enemy states as a result of the Second World War; and

c. territories voluntarily placed under the system by states responsible for their administration.

2. It will be a matter for subsequent agreement as to which territories in the foregoing categories will be brought under the trusteeship system and upon what terms.

Article 78

The trusteeship system shall not apply to territories which have become Members of the United Nations, relationship among which shall be based on respect for the principle of sovereign equality.

Article 79

The terms of trusteeship for each territory to be placed under the trusteeship system, including any alteration or amendment, shall be agreed upon by the states directly concerned, including the mandatory power in the case of territories held under mandate by a Member of the United Nations, and and shall be approved as provided for in Articles 83 and 85.

Article 80

1. Except as may be agreed upon in individual trusteeship agreements, made under Articles 77, 79, and 81, placing each territory under the trusteeship system, and until such agreements have been concluded, nothing in this Chapter shall be construed in or of itself to alter in any manner the rights whatsoever of any states or any peoples or the terms of existing international instruments to which Members of the United Nations may respectively be parties.

2. Paragraph 1 of this Article shall not be interpreted as giving grounds for delay or postponement of the negotiation and conclusion of agreements for placing mandated and other territories under the trusteeship system as provided for in Article 77.

Article 81

The trusteeship agreement shall in each case include the terms under which the trust territory will be administered and designate the authority which will exercise the administration of the trust territory. Such authority, hereinafter called the administering authority, may be one or more states or the Organization itself.

Article 82

There may be designated, in any trusteeship agreement, a strategic area or areas which may inlude part or all of the trust territory to which the agreement applies, without prejudice to any special agreement or agreements made under Article 43.

Article 83

1. All functions of the United Nations relating to strategic areas, including the approval of the terms of the trusteeship agreements and of their alteration or amendment, shall be exercised by the Security Council.

2. The basic objectives set forth in Article 76 shall be applicable to the people of each strategic area.

3. The Security Council shall, subject to the provisions of the trusteeship agreements and without prejudice to security considerations, avail itself of the assistance of the Trusteeship Council to perform those functions of the United Nations under the trusteeship system relating to political, economic, social, and educational matters in the strategic areas.

Article 84

It shall be the duty of the administering authority to ensure that the trust territory shall play its part in the maintenance of international peace and security. To this end the administering authority may make use of volunteer forces, facilities, and assistance from the trust territory in carrying out the obligations towards the Security Council undertaken in this regard by the administering authority, as well as for local defense and the maintenance of law and order within the trust territory.

Article 85

1. The functions of the United Nations with regard to trusteeship agreements for all areas not designated as strategic, including the approval of the terms of the trusteeship agreements and of their alteration or amendment, shall be exercised by the General Assembly.

2. The Trusteeship Council, operating under the authority of the General Assembly, shall assist the General Assembly in carrying out these functions.

CHAPTER XIII. The Trusteeship Council

COMPOSITION

Article 86

1. The Trusteeship Council shall consist of the following Members of the United Nations:

a. those Members administering trust territories;

b. such of those Members mentioned by name in Article 23 as are not administering trust territories; and

c. as many other Members elected for three-year terms by the General Assembly as may be necessary to ensure that the total number of members of the Trusteeship Council is equally divided between those Members of the United Nations which administer trust territories and those which do not.

2. Each member of the Trusteeship Council shall designate one specially qualified person to represent it therein.

FUNCTIONS AND POWERS

Article 87

The General Assembly and, under its authority, the Trusteeship Council, in carrying out their functions, may:

a. consider reports submitted by the administering authority;

b. accept petitions and examine them in consultation with the administering authority;

c. provide for periodic visits to the respective trust territories at times agreed upon with the administering authority; and

d. take these and other actions in conformity with the terms of the trusteeship agreements.

Article 88

The Trusteeship Council shall formulate a questionnaire on the political, economic, social, and educational advancement of the inhabitants of each trust territory, and the administering authority for each trust territory within the competence of the General Assembly shall make an annual report to the General Assembly upon the basis of such questionnaire.

VOTING

Article 89

1. Each member of the Trusteeship Council shall have one vote.

2. Decisions of the Trusteeship Council shall be made by a majority of the members present and voting.

PROCEDURE

Article 90

1. The Trusteeship Council shall adopt its own rules of procedure, including the method of selecting its President.

2. The Trusteeship Council shall meet as required in accordance with its rules, which shall include provision for the convening of meetings on the request of a majority of its members.

Article 91

The Trusteeship Council shall, when appropriate, avail itself of the assistance of the Economic and Social Council and of the specialized agencies in regard to matters with which they are respectively concerned.

CHAPTER XIV. The International Court of Justice

Article 92

The International Court of Justice shall be the principal judicial organ of the United Nations. It shall function in accordance with the annexed Statute, which is based upon the Statute of the

Permanent Court of International Justice and forms an integral part of the present Charter.

Article 93

1. All Members of the United Nations are *ipso facto* parties to the Statute of the International Court of Justice.

2. A state which is not a Member of the United Nations may become a party to the Statute of the International Court of Justice on conditions to be determined in each case by the General Assembly upon the recommendation of the Security Council.

Article 94

1. Each Member of the United Nations undertakes to comply with the decision of the International Court of Justice in any case to which it is a party.

2. If any party to a case fails to perform the obligations incumbent upon it under a judgment rendered by the Court, the other party may have recourse to the Security Council, which may, if it deems necessary, make recommendations or decide upon measures to be taken to give effect to the judgment.

Article 95

Nothing in the present Charter shall prevent Members of the United Nations from entrusting the solution of their differences to other tribunals by virtue of agreements already in existence or which may be concluded in the future.

Article 96

1. The General Assembly or the Security Council may request the International Court of Justice to give an advisory opinion on any legal question.

2. Other organs of the United Nations and specialized agencies, which may at any time be so authorized by the General Assembly, may also request advisory opinions of the Court on legal questions arising within the scope of their activities.

CHAPTER XV. The Secretariat

Article 97

The Secretariat shall comprise a Secretary-General and such staff as the Organization may require.

The Secretary-General shall be appointed by the General Assembly upon the recommendation of the Security Council. He shall be the chief administrative officer of the Organization.

Article 98

The Secretary-General shall act in that capacity in all meetings of the General Assembly, of the Security Council, of the Economic and Social Council, and of the Trusteeship Council, and shall perform such other functions as are entrusted to him by these organs. The Secretary-General shall make an annual report to the General Assembly on the work of the Organization.

Article 99

The Secretary-General may bring to the attention of the Security Council any matter which in his opinion may threaten the maintenance of international peace and security.

Article 100

1. In the performance of their duties the Secretary-General and the staff shall not seek or receive instructions from any government or from any other authority external to the Organization. They shall refrain from any action which might reflect on their position as international officials responsible only to the Organization.

2. Each Member of the United Nations undertakes to respect the exclusively international character of the responsibilities of the Secretary-General and the staff and not to seek to influence them in the discharge of their responsibilities.

Article 101

1. The staff shall be appointed by the Secretary-General under regulations established by the General Assembly.

2. Appropriate staffs shall be permanently assigned to the Economic and Social Council, the Trusteeship Council, and, as required, to other organs of the United Nations. These staffs shall form a part of the Secretariat.

3. The paramount consideration in the employment of the staff and in the determination of the conditions of service shall be the necessity of secur-

ing the highest standards of efficiency, competence, and integrity. Due regard shall be paid to the importance of recruiting the staff on as wide a geographical basis as possible.

CHAPTER XVI. Miscellaneous Provisions

Article 102

1. Every treaty and every international agreement entered into by any Member of the United Nations after the present Charter comes into force shall as soon as possible be registered with the Secretariat and published by it.

2. No party to any such treaty or international agreement which has not been registered in accordance with the provisions of paragraph 1 of this Article may invoke that treaty or agreement before any organ of the United Nations.

Article 103

In the event of a conflict between the obligations of the Members of the United Nations under the present Charter and their obligations under any other international agreement, their obligations under the present Charter shall prevail.

Article 104

The Organization shall enjoy in the territory of each of its Members such legal capacity as may be necessary for the exercise of its functions and the fulfillment of its purposes.

Article 105

1. The Organization shall enjoy in the territory of each of its Members such privileges and immunities as are necessary for the fulfillment of its purposes.

2. Representatives of the Members of the United Nations and officials of the Organization shall similarly enjoy such privileges and immunities as are necessary for the independent exercise of their functions in connection with the Organization.

3. The General Assembly may make recommendations with a view to determining the details of the application of paragraphs 1 and 2 of this Article or may propose conventions to the Members of the United Nations for this purpose.

CHAPTER XVII. Transitional Security Arrangements

Article 106

Pending the coming into force of such special agreements referred to in Article 43 as in the opinion of the Security Council enable it to begin the exercise of its responsibilities under Article 42, the parties to the Four-Nation Declaration, signed at Moscow, October 30, 1943, and France, shall, in accordance with the provisions of paragraph 5 of that Declaration, consult with one another and as occasion requires with other Members of the United Nations with a view to such joint action on behalf of the Organization as may be necessary for the purpose of maintaining international peace and security.

Article 107

Nothing in the present Charter shall invalidate or preclude action, in relation to any state which during the Second World War has been an enemy of any signatory to the present Charter, taken or authorized as a result of that war by the Governments having responsibility for such action.

CHAPTER XVIII. Amendments

Article 108

Amendments to the present Charter shall come into force for all Members of the United Nations when they have been adopted by a vote of two thirds of the members of the General Assembly and ratified in accordance with their respective constitutional processes by two thirds of the Members of the United Nations, including all the permanent members of the Security Council.

Article 109

1. A General Conference of the Members of the United Nations for the purpose of reviewing the present Charter may be held at a date and place to be fixed by a two-thirds vote of the members of the General Assembly and by a vote of any seven members of the Security Council. Each Member of the United Nations shall have one vote in the conference.

2. Any alteration of the present Charter recom-

mended by a two-thirds vote of the conference shall take effect when ratified in accordance with their respective constitutional processes by two thirds of the Members of the United Nations including all the permanent members of the Security Council.

3. If such a conference has not been held before the tenth annual session of the General Assembly following the coming into force of the present Charter, the proposal to call such a conference shall be placed on the agenda of that session of the General Assembly, and the conference shall be held if so decided by a majority vote of the members of the General Assembly and by a vote of any seven members of the Security Council.

CHAPTER XIX. Ratification and Signature

Article 110

1. The present Charter shall be ratified by the signatory states in accordance with their respective constitutional processes.

2. The ratifications shall be deposited with the Government of the United States of America, which shall notify all the signatory states of each deposit as well as the Secretary-General of the Organization when he has been appointed.

3. The present Charter shall come into force upon the deposit of ratifications by the Republic of China, France, the Union of Soviet Socialist Republics, the United Kingdom of Great Britain and Northern Ireland, and the United States of America, and by a majority of the other signatory states. A protocol of the ratifications deposited shall thereupon be drawn up by the Government of the United States of America which shall communicate copies thereof to all the signatory states.

4. The states signatory to the present Charter which ratify it after it has come into force will become original Members of the United Nations on the date of the deposit of their respective ratifications.

Article III

The present Charter, of which the Chinese, French, Russian, English, and Spanish texts are equally authentic, shall remain deposited in the archives of the Government of the United States of America. Duly certified copies thereof shall be transmitted by that Government to the Governments of the other signatory states.

In faith whereof the representatives of the Governments of the United Nations have signed the present Charter.

Done at the city of San Francisco the twenty-sixth day of June, one thousand nine hundred and forty-five.

Index